Java™ for Programmers

Deitel® Developer Series

Deitel® Ser

How to Program Series

Java How to Program, 7/E

C++ How to Program, 6/E

Visual C++® 2008 How to Program, 2/E

C How to Program, 5/E

Internet & World Wide Web How to Program, 4/E

Visual Basic® 2008 How to Program

Visual C#® 2008 How to Program, 3/E

Small Java™ How to Program, 6/E

Small C++ How to Program, 5/E

Simply Series

Simply C++: An Application-Driven Tutorial Approach

Simply Java™ Programming: An Application-Driven Tutorial Approach

Simply C#: An Application-Driven Tutorial Approach

Simply Visual Basic® 2008, 3/E: An Application-Driven Tutorial Approach

SafariX Web Books

www.deitel.com/books/SafariX.html

C++ How to Program, 5/E & 6/E

Java How to Program, 6/E & 7/E

Simply C++: An Application-Driven Tutorial Approach

Simply Visual Basic 2008: An Application-Driven Tutorial Approach, 3/E

Small C++ How to Program, 5/E

Small Java How to Program, 6/E

Visual Basic 2008 How to Program

Visual C# 2008 How to Program, 3/E

ies Page

Deitel Developer Series

AJAX, Rich Internet Applications and
Web Development for Programmers

C++ for Programmers

C# 2008 for Programmers, 3/E

Java for Programmers

Javascript for Programmers

LiveLessons Video Learning Products

www.deitel.com/books/LiveLessons/

Java Fundamentals Parts 1 and 2

C# Fundamentals Parts 1 and 2

C++ Fundamentals Parts 1 and 2

JavaScript Fundamentals Parts 1 and 2

To follow the Deitel publishing program, please register for the free *Deitel® Buzz Online* e-mail newsletter at:

www.deitel.com/newsletter/subscribe.html

To communicate with the authors, send e-mail to:

deitel@deitel.com

For information on government and corporate *Dive-Into®* Series on-site seminars offered by Deitel & Associates, Inc. worldwide, visit:

www.deitel.com/training/

or write to

deitel@deitel.com

For continuing updates on Prentice Hall/Deitel publications visit:

www.deitel.com
www.prenhall.com/deitel

Check out our Resource Centers for valuable web resources that will help you master Visual C#, other important programming languages, software and Internet- and web-related topics:

www.deitel.com/ResourceCenters.html

The publisher offers excellent discounts on this book when ordered in quantity for bulk purchases or special sales, which may include electronic versions and/or custom covers and content particular to your business, training goals, marketing focus, and branding interests. For more information, please contact:

U. S. Corporate and Government Sales
(800) 382-3419
corpsales@pearsontechgroup.com

For sales outside the U. S., please contact:

International Sales
international@pearsoned.com

Visit us on the Web: informit.com/PH

Library of Congress Cataloging-in-Publication Data

On file

ISBN-10: 0-13-700129-0
ISBN-13: 978-0-13-700129-3

Text printed in the United States on recycled paper at R.R . Donnelley in Crawfordsville, Indiana.
2nd   Printing   January 2011

JAVA™ FOR PROGRAMMERS
DEITEL® DEVELOPER SERIES

Paul J. Deitel
Deitel & Associates, Inc.

Harvey M. Deitel
Deitel & Associates, Inc.

PRENTICE
HALL

Upper Saddle River, NJ • Boston • Indianapolis • San Francisco
New York • Toronto • Montreal • London • Munich • Paris • Madrid
Capetown • Sydney • Tokyo • Singapore • Mexico City

Trademarks

DEITEL, the double-thumbs-up bug and Dive Into are registered trademarks of Deitel and Associates, Inc.

Java and all Java-based marks are trademarks or registered trademarks of Sun Microsystems, Inc. in the United States and other countries. Pearson Education is independent of Sun Microsystems, Inc.

Microsoft, Internet Explorer and the Windows logo are either registered trademarks or trademarks of Microsoft Corporation in the United States and/or other countries.

UNIX is a registered trademark of The Open Group.

To Mark L. Taub,
  Editor-in-Chief of Prentice Hall Professional

  Thank you for being our friend and mentor in professional
  publishing. It's a privilege to work with someone who so loves
  the challenges of the leading edge.

  Paul and Harvey

Deitel Resource Centers

Our Resource Centers focus on the vast amounts of free content available online. Find resources, downloads, tutorials, documentation, books, e-books, journals, articles, blogs, RSS feeds and more on many of today's hottest programming and technology topics. For the most up-to-date list of our Resource Centers, visit:

www.deitel.com/ResourceCenters.html

Let us know what other Resource Centers you'd like to see! Also, please register for the free *Deitel®* *Buzz Online* e-mail newsletter at:

www.deitel.com/newsletter/subscribe.html

Computer Science
Functional Programming
Regular Expressions

Programming
ASP.NET 3.5
Adobe Flex
Ajax
Apex
ASP.NET Ajax
ASP.NET
C
C++
C++ Boost Libraries
C++ Game Programming
C#
Code Search Engines and Code Sites
Computer Game Programming
CSS 2.1
Dojo
Facebook Developer Platform
Flash 9
Functional Programming
Java
Java Certification and Assessment Testing
Java Design Patterns
Java EE 5
Java SE 6
Java SE 7 (Dolphin) Resource Center
JavaFX
JavaScript
JSON
Microsoft LINQ
Microsoft Popfly
.NET
.NET 3.0
.NET 3.5
OpenGL
Perl
PHP
Programming Projects
Python
Regular Expressions
Ruby
Ruby on Rails

Silverlight
Visual Basic
Visual C++
Visual Studio Team System
Web 3D Technologies
Web Services
Windows Presentation Foundation
XHTML
XML

Games and Game Programming
Computer Game Programming
Computer Games
Mobile Gaming
Sudoku

Internet Business
Affiliate Programs
Competitive Analysis
Facebook Social Ads
Google AdSense
Google Analytics
Google Services
Internet Advertising
Internet Business Initiative
Internet Public Relations
Link Building
Location-Based Services
Online Lead Generation
Podcasting
Search Engine Optimization
Selling Digital Content
Sitemaps
Web Analytics
Website Monetization
YouTube and AdSense

Java
Java
Java Certification and Assessment Testing
Java Design Patterns
Java EE 5
Java SE 6

Java SE 7 (Dolphin) Resource Center
JavaFX

Microsoft
ASP.NET
ASP.NET 3.5
ASP.NET Ajax
C#
DotNetNuke (DNN)
Internet Explorer 7 (IE7)
Microsoft LINQ
.NET
.NET 3.0
.NET 3.5
SharePoint
Silverlight
Visual Basic
Visual C++
Visual Studio Team System
Windows Presentation Foundation
Windows Vista
Microsoft Popfly

Open Source & LAMP Stack
Apache
DotNetNuke (DNN)
Eclipse
Firefox
Linux
MySQL
Open Source
Perl
PHP
Python
Ruby

Software
Apache
DotNetNuke (DNN)
Eclipse
Firefox
Internet Explorer 7 (IE7)
Linux
MySQL
Open Source
Search Engines

SharePoint
Skype
Web Servers
Wikis
Windows Vista

Web 2.0
Alert Services
Attention Economy
Blogging
Building Web Communities
Community Generated Content
Facebook Developer Platform
Facebook Social Ads
Google Base
Google Video
Google Web Toolkit (GWT)
Internet Video
Joost
Location-Based Services
Mashups
Microformats
Recommender Systems
RSS
Social Graph
Social Media
Social Networking
Software as a Service (SaaS)
Virtual Worlds
Web 2.0
Web 3.0
Widgets

Dive Into Web 2.0 eBook
Web 2 eBook

Other Topics
Computer Games
Computing Jobs
Gadgets and Gizmos
Ring Tones
Sudoku

Contents

Preface   xxiii

Before You Begin   xxxiii

1   Introduction   1
1.1   Introduction   2
1.2   The Internet and the World Wide Web   3
1.3   History of C and C++   3
1.4   History of Java   4
1.5   Java Class Libraries   4
1.6   Typical Java Development Environment   5
1.7   Notes about Java and Java for Programmers   8
1.8   Test-Driving a Java Application   9
1.9   Software Engineering Case Study: Introduction to Object Technology
        and the UML   13
1.10   Web 2.0   17
1.11   Software Technologies   18
1.12   Wrap-Up   19
1.13   Web Resources   20

2   Introduction to Java Applications   22
2.1   Introduction   23
2.2   A First Program in Java: Printing a Line of Text   23
2.3   Modifying Our First Java Program   29
2.4   Displaying Text with `printf`   32
2.5   Another Java Application: Adding Integers   33
2.6   Arithmetic   37
2.7   Decision Making: Equality and Relational Operators   39
2.8   (Optional) Software Engineering Case Study: Examining the
        Requirements Document   44
2.9   Wrap-Up   53

3   Introduction to Classes and Objects   54
3.1   Introduction   55

3.2	Classes, Objects, Methods and Instance Variables	55
3.3	Declaring a Class with a Method and Instantiating an Object of a Class	57
3.4	Declaring a Method with a Parameter	61
3.5	Instance Variables, *set* Methods and *get* Methods	64
3.6	Primitive Types vs. Reference Types	69
3.7	Initializing Objects with Constructors	70
3.8	Floating-Point Numbers and Type **double**	73
3.9	(Optional) Software Engineering Case Study: Identifying the Classes in a Requirements Document	78
3.10	Wrap-Up	86

4 Control Statements: Part 1   87

4.1	Introduction	88
4.2	Control Structures	88
4.3	**if** Single-Selection Statement	91
4.4	**if...else** Double-Selection Statement	91
4.5	**while** Repetition Statement	95
4.6	Counter-Controlled Repetition	96
4.7	Sentinel-Controlled Repetition	100
4.8	Nested Control Statements	106
4.9	Compound Assignment Operators	109
4.10	Increment and Decrement Operators	109
4.11	Primitive Types	112
4.12	(Optional) Software Engineering Case Study: Identifying Class Attributes	113
4.13	Wrap-Up	118

5 Control Statements: Part 2   119

5.1	Introduction	120
5.2	Essentials of Counter-Controlled Repetition	120
5.3	**for** Repetition Statement	122
5.4	Examples Using the **for** Statement	125
5.5	**do...while** Repetition Statement	130
5.6	**switch** Multiple-Selection Statement	132
5.7	**break** and **continue** Statements	139
5.8	Logical Operators	141
5.9	(Optional) Software Engineering Case Study: Identifying Objects' States and Activities	147
5.10	Wrap-Up	152

6 Methods: A Deeper Look   153

6.1	Introduction	154
6.2	Program Modules in Java	155
6.3	**static** Methods, **static** Fields and Class **Math**	155

6.4	Declaring Methods with Multiple Parameters	158
6.5	Notes on Declaring and Using Methods	162
6.6	Method-Call Stack and Activation Records	163
6.7	Argument Promotion and Casting	164
6.8	Java API Packages	165
6.9	Case Study: Random-Number Generation	167
6.9.1	Generalized Scaling and Shifting of Random Numbers	171
6.9.2	Random-Number Repeatability for Testing and Debugging	172
6.10	Case Study: A Game of Chance (Introducing Enumerations)	173
6.11	Scope of Declarations	177
6.12	Method Overloading	180
6.13	Introduction to Recursion	183
6.14	Recursion Concepts	184
6.15	Example Using Recursion: Factorials	184
6.16	Example Using Recursion: Fibonacci Series	187
6.17	Recursion and the Method-Call Stack	190
6.18	Recursion vs. Iteration	192
6.19	(Optional) Software Engineering Case Study: Identifying Class Operations	194
6.20	Wrap-Up	201

7   Arrays   202

7.1	Introduction	203
7.2	Arrays	203
7.3	Declaring and Creating Arrays	205
7.4	Examples Using Arrays	206
7.5	Case Study: Card Shuffling and Dealing Simulation	215
7.6	Enhanced **for** Statement	219
7.7	Passing Arrays to Methods	220
7.8	Case Study: Class **GradeBook** Using an Array to Store Grades	224
7.9	Multidimensional Arrays	229
7.10	Case Study: Class **GradeBook** Using a Two-Dimensional Array	233
7.11	Variable-Length Argument Lists	239
7.12	Using Command-Line Arguments	240
7.13	(Optional) Software Engineering Case Study: Collaboration Among Objects	242
7.14	Wrap-Up	249

8   Classes and Objects: A Deeper Look   251

8.1	Introduction	252
8.2	**Time** Class Case Study	253
8.3	Controlling Access to Members	256
8.4	Referring to the Current Object's Members with the **this** Reference	257
8.5	**Time** Class Case Study: Overloaded Constructors	259
8.6	Default and No-Argument Constructors	265

8.7	Notes on *Set* and *Get* Methods	266
8.8	Composition	267
8.9	Enumerations	270
8.10	Garbage Collection and Method **finalize**	273
8.11	**static** Class Members	274
8.12	**static** Import	278
8.13	**final** Instance Variables	279
8.14	Software Reusability	282
8.15	Data Abstraction and Encapsulation	283
8.16	**Time** Class Case Study: Creating Packages	284
8.17	Package Access	290
8.18	(Optional) Software Engineering Case Study: Starting to Program the Classes of the ATM System	291
8.19	Wrap-Up	297

9 Object-Oriented Programming: Inheritance 298

9.1	Introduction	299
9.2	Superclasses and Subclasses	300
9.3	**protected** Members	302
9.4	Relationship between Superclasses and Subclasses	303
	9.4.1 Creating and Using a CommissionEmployee Class	304
	9.4.2 Creating a BasePlusCommissionEmployee Class without Using Inheritance	308
	9.4.3 Creating a CommissionEmployee–BasePlusCommissionEmployee Inheritance Hierarchy	313
	9.4.4 CommissionEmployee–BasePlusCommissionEmployee Inheritance Hierarchy Using protected Instance Variables	316
	9.4.5 CommissionEmployee–BasePlusCommissionEmployee Inheritance Hierarchy Using private Instance Variables	322
9.5	Constructors in Subclasses	327
9.6	Software Engineering with Inheritance	333
9.7	**Object** Class	333
9.8	Wrap-Up	335

10 Object-Oriented Programming: Polymorphism 336

10.1	Introduction	337
10.2	Polymorphism Examples	339
10.3	Demonstrating Polymorphic Behavior	340
10.4	Abstract Classes and Methods	342
10.5	Case Study: Payroll System Using Polymorphism	345
	10.5.1 Creating Abstract Superclass Employee	346
	10.5.2 Creating Concrete Subclass SalariedEmployee	349
	10.5.3 Creating Concrete Subclass HourlyEmployee	350
	10.5.4 Creating Concrete Subclass CommissionEmployee	352

10.5.5   Creating Indirect Concrete Subclass `BasePlusCommissionEmployee`   353
10.5.6   Demonstrating Polymorphic Processing, Operator `instanceof` and Downcasting   355
10.5.7   Summary of the Allowed Assignments Between Superclass and Subclass Variables   359
10.6   `final` Methods and Classes   360
10.7   Case Study: Creating and Using Interfaces   361
10.7.1   Developing a `Payable` Hierarchy   362
10.7.2   Declaring Interface `Payable`   363
10.7.3   Creating Class `Invoice`   364
10.7.4   Modifying Class `Employee` to Implement Interface `Payable`   366
10.7.5   Modifying Class `SalariedEmployee` for Use in the `Payable` Hierarchy   368
10.7.6   Using Interface `Payable` to Process `Invoice`s and `Employee`s Polymorphically   370
10.7.7   Declaring Constants with Interfaces   371
10.7.8   Common Interfaces of the Java API   372
10.8   (Optional) Software Engineering Case Study: Incorporating Inheritance into the ATM System   373
10.9   Wrap-Up   380

11   GUI Components: Part I   381

11.1   Introduction   382
11.2   Simple GUI-Based Input/Output with `JOptionPane`   383
11.3   Overview of Swing Components   386
11.4   Displaying Text and Images in a Window   389
11.5   Text Fields and an Introduction to Event Handling with Nested Classes   393
11.6   Common GUI Event Types and Listener Interfaces   400
11.7   How Event Handling Works   401
11.8   `JButton`   404
11.9   Buttons That Maintain State   407
11.9.1   JCheckBox   407
11.9.2   JRadioButton   410
11.10   `JComboBox` and Using an Anonymous Inner Class for Event Handling   413
11.11   `JList`   417
11.12   Multiple-Selection Lists   420
11.13   Mouse Event Handling   422
11.14   Adapter Classes   427
11.15   `JPanel` Subclass for Drawing with the Mouse   430
11.16   Key-Event Handling   434
11.17   Layout Managers   438
11.17.1 FlowLayout   439
11.17.2 BorderLayout   442
11.17.3 GridLayout   445
11.18   Using Panels to Manage More Complex Layouts   447

11.19	**JTextArea**	449
11.20	Wrap-Up	452

12 **Graphics and Java 2D™**   **453**

12.1	Introduction	454
12.2	Graphics Contexts and Graphics Objects	456
12.3	Color Control	457
12.4	Font Control	464
12.5	Drawing Lines, Rectangles and Ovals	470
12.6	Drawing Arcs	474
12.7	Drawing Polygons and Polylines	476
12.8	Java 2D API	479
12.9	Wrap-Up	486

13 **Exception Handling**   **487**

13.1	Introduction	488
13.2	Exception-Handling Overview	489
13.3	Example: Divide by Zero without Exception Handling	490
13.4	Example: Handling **ArithmeticException**s and **InputMismatchExceptions**	492
13.5	When to Use Exception Handling	497
13.6	Java Exception Hierarchy	498
13.7	**finally** Block	500
13.8	Stack Unwinding	505
13.9	**printStackTrace**, **getStackTrace** and **getMessage**	506
13.10	Chained Exceptions	509
13.11	Declaring New Exception Types	511
13.12	Preconditions and Postconditions	512
13.13	Assertions	512
13.14	Wrap-Up	514

14 **Files and Streams**   **515**

14.1	Introduction	516
14.2	Data Hierarchy	517
14.3	Files and Streams	519
14.4	Class **File**	520
14.5	Sequential-Access Text Files	525
	14.5.1 Creating a Sequential-Access Text File	525
	14.5.2 Reading Data from a Sequential-Access Text File	532
	14.5.3 Case Study: A Credit-Inquiry Program	535
	14.5.4 Updating Sequential-Access Files	540
14.6	Object Serialization	540
	14.6.1 Creating a Sequential-Access File Using Object Serialization	541
	14.6.2 Reading and Deserializing Data from a Sequential-Access File	547

14.7	Additional **java.io** Classes	550
14.8	Opening Files with **JFileChooser**	552
14.9	Wrap-Up	555

15 Generics   **556**

15.1	Introduction	557
15.2	Motivation for Generic Methods	558
15.3	Generic Methods: Implementation and Compile-Time Translation	560
15.4	Additional Compile-Time Translation Issues: Methods That Use a Type Parameter as the Return Type	563
15.5	Overloading Generic Methods	566
15.6	Generic Classes	567
15.7	Raw Types	577
15.8	Wildcards in Methods That Accept Type Parameters	581
15.9	Generics and Inheritance: Notes	585
15.10	Wrap-Up	586
15.11	Internet and Web Resources	586

16 Collections   **587**

16.1	Introduction	588
16.2	Collections Overview	589
16.3	Class **Arrays**	590
16.4	Interface **Collection** and Class **Collections**	593
16.5	Lists	594
	16.5.1 ArrayList and Iterator	594
	16.5.2 LinkedList	597
	16.5.3 Vector	601
16.6	Collections Algorithms	605
	16.6.1 Algorithm sort	606
	16.6.2 Algorithm shuffle	610
	16.6.3 Algorithms reverse, fill, copy, max and min	613
	16.6.4 Algorithm binarySearch	615
	16.6.5 Algorithms addAll, frequency and disjoint	617
16.7	**Stack** Class of Package **java.util**	618
16.8	Class **PriorityQueue** and Interface **Queue**	621
16.9	Sets	622
16.10	Maps	625
16.11	**Properties** Class	629
16.12	Synchronized Collections	632
16.13	Unmodifiable Collections	633
16.14	Abstract Implementations	634
16.15	Wrap-Up	634

17 GUI Components: Part 2   635

17.1   Introduction   636
17.2   `JSlider`   636
17.3   Windows: Additional Notes   640
17.4   Using Menus with Frames   641
17.5   `JPopupMenu`   649
17.6   Pluggable Look-and-Feel   652
17.7   `JDesktopPane` and `JInternalFrame`   656
17.8   `JTabbedPane`   660
17.9   Layout Managers: `BoxLayout` and `GridBagLayout`   662
17.10 Wrap-Up   675

18 Multithreading   676

18.1   Introduction   677
18.2   Thread States: Life Cycle of a Thread   679
18.3   Thread Priorities and Thread Scheduling   681
18.4   Creating and Executing Threads   683
       18.4.1 Runnables and the `Thread` Class   683
       18.4.2 Thread Management with the `Executor` Framework   686
18.5   Thread Synchronization   687
       18.5.1 Unsynchronized Data Sharing   688
       18.5.2 Synchronized Data Sharing—Making Operations Atomic   693
18.6   Producer/Consumer Relationship without Synchronization   696
18.7   Producer/Consumer Relationship: `ArrayBlockingQueue`   703
18.8   Producer/Consumer Relationship with Synchronization   706
18.9   Producer/Consumer Relationship: Bounded Buffers   712
18.10 Producer/Consumer Relationship: The `Lock` and `Condition` Interfaces   720
18.11 Multithreading with GUI   726
       18.11.1 Performing Computations in a Worker Thread   728
       18.11.2 Processing Intermediate Results with `SwingWorker`   733
18.12 Other Classes and Interfaces in `java.util.concurrent`   741
18.13 Wrap-Up   741

19 Networking   743

19.1   Introduction   744
19.2   Manipulating URLs   745
19.3   Reading a File on a Web Server   750
19.4   Establishing a Simple Server Using Stream Sockets   753
19.5   Establishing a Simple Client Using Stream Sockets   755
19.6   Client/Server Interaction with Stream Socket Connections   756
19.7   Connectionless Client/Server Interaction with Datagrams   768
19.8   Client/Server Tic-Tac-Toe Using a Multithreaded Server   775
19.9   Security and the Network   790

19.10 [Web Bonus] Case Study: DeitelMessenger Server and Client   790
19.11 Wrap-Up   790

20 Accessing Databases with JDBC   79 I

20.1   Introduction   792
20.2   Relational Databases   793
20.3   Relational Database Overview: The **books** Database   794
20.4   SQL   797
    20.4.1   Basic SELECT Query   798
    20.4.2   WHERE Clause   799
    20.4.3   ORDER BY Clause   800
    20.4.4   Merging Data from Multiple Tables: INNER JOIN   802
    20.4.5   INSERT Statement   804
    20.4.6   UPDATE Statement   805
    20.4.7   DELETE Statement   805
20.5   Instructions for Installing MySQL and MySQL Connector/J   806
20.6   Instructions for Setting Up a MySQL User Account   807
20.7   Creating Database **books** in MySQL   808
20.8   Manipulating Databases with JDBC   809
    20.8.1   Connecting to and Querying a Database   809
    20.8.2   Querying the books Database   813
20.9   **RowSet** Interface   825
20.10 Java DB/Apache Derby   828
20.11 **PreparedStatement**s   829
20.12 Stored Procedures   844
20.13 Transaction Processing   845
20.14 Wrap-Up   846
20.15 Web Resources   846

21 JavaServer™ Faces Web Applications   847

21.1   Introduction   848
21.2   Simple HTTP Transactions   849
21.3   Multitier Application Architecture   852
21.4   Java Web Technologies   853
    21.4.1   Servlets   854
    21.4.2   JavaServer Pages   854
    21.4.3   JavaServer Faces   856
    21.4.4   Web Technologies in Netbeans   856
21.5   Creating and Running a Simple Application in Netbeans   857
    21.5.1   Examining a JSP Document   858
    21.5.2   Examining a Page Bean File   860
    21.5.3   Event-Processing Life Cycle   862
    21.5.4   Building a Web Application in Netbeans   862

21.6   JSF Components   870
    21.6.1   Text and Graphics Components   870
    21.6.2   Validation Using Validator Components and Custom Validators   874
21.7   Session Tracking   883
    21.7.1   Cookies   884
    21.7.2   Session Tracking with Session Beans   895
21.8   Wrap-Up   905

22   Ajax-Enabled JavaServer™ Faces Web Applications   906

22.1   Introduction   907
22.2   Accessing Databases in Web Applications   907
    22.2.1   Building a Web Application That Displays Data from a Database 908
    22.2.2   Modifying the Page Bean File for the AddressBook Application   917
22.3   Ajax-Enabled JSF Components   920
22.4   Creating an Autocomplete Text Field and Using Virtual Forms   922
    22.4.1   Configuring Virtual Forms   923
    22.4.2   JSP File with Virtual Forms and an Autocomplete Text Field   924
    22.4.3   Providing Suggestions for an Autocomplete Text Field   928
    22.4.4   Displaying the Contact's Information   931
22.5   Wrap-Up   932

23   JAX-WS Web Services   933

23.1   Introduction   934
23.2   Java Web Services Basics   936
23.3   Creating, Publishing, Testing and Describing a Web Service   936
    23.3.1   Creating a Web Application Project and Adding a Web
             Service Class in Netbeans   937
    23.3.2   Defining the HugeInteger Web Service in Netbeans   937
    23.3.3   Publishing the HugeInteger Web Service from Netbeans   942
    23.3.4   Testing the HugeInteger Web Service with GlassFish
             Application Server's Tester Web Page   943
    23.3.5   Describing a Web Service with the Web Service
             Description Language (WSDL)   945
23.4   Consuming a Web Service   946
    23.4.1   Creating a Client in Netbeans to Consume the HugeInteger
             Web Service   947
    23.4.2   Consuming the HugeInteger Web Service   949
23.5   SOAP   955
23.6   Session Tracking in Web Services   957
    23.6.1   Creating a Blackjack Web Service   957
    23.6.2   Consuming the Blackjack Web Service   962
23.7   Consuming a Database-Driven Web Service from a Web Application   973
    23.7.1   Creating the Reservation Database   974

23.7.2 Creating a Web Application to Interact with the Reservation
Web Service 977
23.8 Passing an Object of a User-Defined Type to a Web Service 982
23.9 Wrap-Up 992

24 Formatted Output 993

24.1 Introduction 994
24.2 Streams 994
24.3 Formatting Output with **printf** 994
24.4 Printing Integers 995
24.5 Printing Floating-Point Numbers 996
24.6 Printing Strings and Characters 998
24.7 Printing Dates and Times 999
24.8 Other Conversion Characters 1002
24.9 Printing with Field Widths and Precisions 1003
24.10 Using Flags in the **printf** Format String 1005
24.11 Printing with Argument Indices 1009
24.12 Printing Literals and Escape Sequences 1010
24.13 Formatting Output with Class **Formatter** 1010
24.14 Wrap-Up 1012

25 Strings, Characters and Regular Expressions 1013

25.1 Introduction 1014
25.2 Fundamentals of Characters and Strings 1014
25.3 Class **String** 1015
25.3.1 String Constructors 1015
25.3.2 String Methods length, charAt and getChars 1016
25.3.3 Comparing Strings 1018
25.3.4 Locating Characters and Substrings in Strings 1022
25.3.5 Extracting Substrings from Strings 1024
25.3.6 Concatenating Strings 1025
25.3.7 Miscellaneous String Methods 1025
25.3.8 String Method valueOf 1027
25.4 Class **StringBuilder** 1028
25.4.1 StringBuilder Constructors 1029
25.4.2 StringBuilder Methods length, capacity, setLength and
ensureCapacity 1029
25.4.3 StringBuilder Methods charAt, setCharAt, getChars
and reverse 1031
25.4.4 StringBuilder append Methods 1032
25.4.5 StringBuilder Insertion and Deletion Methods 1034
25.5 Class **Character** 1035
25.6 Class **StringTokenizer** 1039
25.7 Regular Expressions, Class **Pattern** and Class **Matcher** 1041
25.8 Wrap-Up 1049

Contents

A **Operator Precedence Chart** **1050**

A.1 Operator Precedence 1050

B **ASCII Character Set** **1052**

C **Keywords and Reserved Words** **1053**

D **Primitive Types** **1054**

E **GroupLayout** **1055**

E.1 Introduction 1055
E.2 GroupLayout Basics 1055
E.3 Building a **ColorChooser** 1056
E.4 GroupLayout Web Resources 1066

F **Java Desktop Integration Components (JDIC)** **1067**

F.1 Introduction 1067
F.2 Splash Screens 1067
F.3 **Desktop** Class 1069
F.4 Tray Icons 1072
F.5 JDIC Incubator Projects 1072
F.6 JDIC Demos 1072

G **Using the Java API Documentation** **1073**

G.1 Introduction 1073
G.2 Navigating the Java API 1074

H **ATM Case Study Code** **1082**

H.1 ATM Case Study Implementation 1082
H.2 Class **ATM** 1083
H.3 Class **Screen** 1088
H.4 Class **Keypad** 1089
H.5 Class **CashDispenser** 1090
H.6 Class **DepositSlot** 1091
H.7 Class **Account** 1092
H.8 Class **BankDatabase** 1094
H.9 Class **Transaction** 1097
H.10 Class **BalanceInquiry** 1098
H.11 Class **Withdrawal** 1098
H.12 Class **Deposit** 1103
H.13 Class **ATMCaseStudy** 1106
H.14 Wrap-Up 1106

I   UML 2: Additional Diagram Types   1107

I.1   Introduction   1107
I.2   Additional Diagram Types   1107

J   Using the Debugger   1109

J.1   Introduction   1110
J.2   Breakpoints and the **run**, **stop**, **cont** and **print** Commands   1110
J.3   The **print** and **set** Commands   1114
J.4   Controlling Execution Using the **step**, **step up** and **next** Commands   1116
J.5   The **watch** Command   1119
J.6   The **clear** Command   1121
J.7   Wrap-Up   1124

Index   1125

Preface

"Live in fragments no longer, only connect."

—Edgar Morgan Foster

Welcome to Java and *Java for Programmers*! At Deitel & Associates, we write programming language professional books and textbooks for Prentice Hall, deliver corporate training worldwide and develop Internet businesses. This book was a joy to create. It reflects recent changes to the Java language and to the preferred ways of teaching and learning programming.

Features

Here's some key features of *Java for Programmers*:

- The book uses Java Standard Edition 6; we carefully audited the manuscript against the *Java Language Specification*.

- The book is object-oriented throughout and the treatment of OOP is clear and accessible.

- The early classes and objects presentation features `Time`, `Employee` and `GradeBook` class case studies that weave their way through multiple sections and chapters, gradually introducing deeper OO concepts.

- The book contains a rich treatment of GUI and graphics.

- We tuned our object-oriented presentation to use the latest version of the *UML™ (Unified Modeling Language™)*—the *UML™ 2*—the industry-standard graphical language for modeling object-oriented systems.

- We include an optional OOD/UML 2 automated teller machine (ATM) case study in Chapters 1–8 and 10. An appendix contains the complete code implementation. Check out the back cover testimonials.

- We include several substantial object-oriented web programming case studies.

- Chapter 20, Accessing Databases with JDBC, includes JDBC 4 and uses the Java DB/Apache Derby and MySQL database management systems. The chapter features a database-driven address book case study that demonstrates prepared (precompiled) statements and JDBC 4's automatic driver discovery.

- Chapter 21, JavaServer Faces™ Web Applications, and Chapter 22, Ajax-Enabled JavaServer™ Faces Web Applications, introduce web application development with JavaServer Faces (JSF) technology and use it with the Netbeans IDE to build web applications quickly and easily. Chapter 21 includes examples on building web application GUIs, handling events, validating forms and session tracking.

Chapter 22 discusses developing Ajax-enabled web applications. The chapter features a database-driven multitier web address book application that allows users to add contacts and search for contacts. The application uses Ajax-enabled JSF components to suggest contact names while the user types a name to locate.

- Chapter 23, JAX-WS Web Services, uses a tools-based approach to creating and consuming web services—a signature Web 2.0 capability. Case studies include developing blackjack and airline reservation web services.

- We use a tools-based approach for rapid web applications development; all the tools are available free for download.

- We discuss key software engineering community concepts, such as Web 2.0, Ajax, SOA, web services, open source software, design patterns, refactoring, extreme programming, agile software development, rapid prototyping and more.

- Chapter 18, Multithreading, benefitted from the guidance of Brian Goetz and Joseph Bowbeer—co-authors of *Java Concurrency in Practice,* Addison-Wesley, 2006.

- We discuss the SwingWorker class for developing multithreaded user interfaces.

- We discuss the Java Desktop Integration Components (JDIC), such as splash screens and interactions with the system tray.

- We use the GroupLayout layout manager in the context of the GUI design tools provided by the NetBeans IDE to create portable GUIs that adhere to the underlying platform's GUI design guidelines.

- We present the JTable sorting and filtering capabilities which allow the user to re-sort the data in a JTable and filter it by regular expressions.

- We present an in-depth treatment of generics and generic collections.

- We discuss the StringBuilder class, which performs better than StringBuffer in non-threaded applications.

- We present annotations, which reduce the amount of code you have to write to build applications.

Other recent Java features discussed in Java for Programmers *include:*

- Obtaining formatted input with class Scanner
- Displaying formatted output with the System.out object's printf method
- Enhanced for statements to process array elements and collections
- Declaring methods with variable-length argument lists
- Using enum classes that declare sets of constants
- Importing the static members of one class for use in another
- Converting primitive-type values to type-wrapper objects and vice versa, using autoboxing and auto-unboxing, respectively
- Using generics to create general models of methods and classes that can be declared once, but used with many different data types

- Using the generics-enhanced data structures of the Collections API
- Using the Concurrency API to implement multithreaded applications
- Using JDBC RowSets to access data in a database

All of this has been carefully reviewed by distinguished industry developers and academics who worked with us on *Java How to Program, 6/e* and *Java How to Program, 7/e*—the book on which *Java for Programmers* is based.

As you read this book, if you have questions, send an e-mail to deitel@deitel.com; we'll respond promptly. For updates on this book and the status of all supporting Java software, and for the latest news on all Deitel publications and services, visit www.deitel.com. Sign up at www.deitel.com/newsletter/subscribe.html for the free *Deitel® Buzz Online* e-mail newsletter and check out www.deitel.com/resourcecenters.html for our growing list of Resource Centers on key Java and related topics.

Using the UML 2 to Develop an Object-Oriented Design of an ATM. UML 2 has become the preferred graphical modeling language for designing object-oriented systems. All the UML diagrams in the book comply with the UML 2 specification. We use UML activity diagrams to demonstrate the flow of control in each of Java's control statements, and we use UML class diagrams to visually represent classes and their inheritance relationships.

We include an optional (but highly recommended) case study on object-oriented design using the UML. The case study was reviewed by a distinguished team of OOD/UML industry professionals and academics, including leaders in the field from Rational (the creators of the UML) and the Object Management Group (responsible for evolving the UML). In the case study, we design and fully implement the software for a simple automated teller machine (ATM). The Software Engineering Case Study sections at the ends of Chapters 1–8 and 10 present a carefully paced introduction to object-oriented design using the UML. We introduce a concise, simplified subset of the UML 2, then guide you through a design experience. The case study is not an exercise—it's an end-to-end learning experience that concludes with a detailed walkthrough of the complete Java code. In the first of the case study sections at the end of Chapter 1, we introduce basic concepts and terminology of OOD. In the optional Software Engineering Case Study sections at the ends of Chapters 2–5, we consider more substantial issues, as we undertake a challenging problem with the techniques of OOD. We analyze a typical requirements document that specifies a system to be built, determine the objects needed to implement that system, determine the attributes these objects need to have, determine the behaviors these objects need to exhibit, and specify how the objects must interact with one another to meet the system requirements. In an appendix, we include a complete Java code implementation of the object-oriented system that we designed in the earlier chapters. We employ a carefully developed, incremental object-oriented design process to produce a UML 2 model for our ATM system. From this design, we produce a substantial working Java implementation using key object-oriented programming notions, including classes, objects, encapsulation, visibility, composition, inheritance and polymorphism.

Dependency Chart

The chart on the next page shows the dependencies among the chapters. Chapters 1–14 form an accessible introduction to object-oriented programming. Chapters 11, 12 and 17

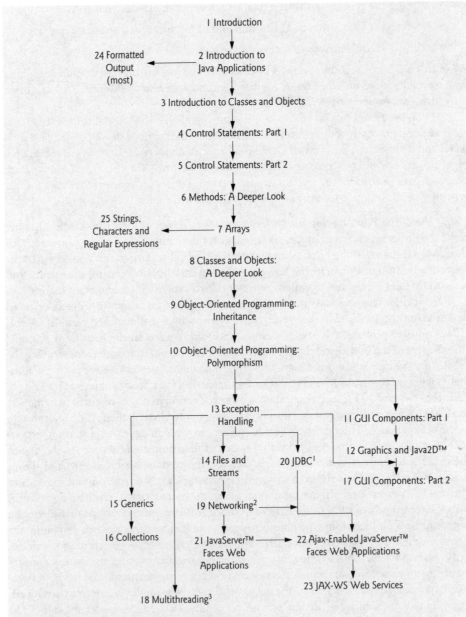

1. Chapter 20 is dependent on Chapter 11 for GUI used in one example.
2. The large case study at the end of Chapter 19 depends on Chapter 17 for GUI and Chapter 18 for multithreading.
3. Chapter 23 is dependent on Chapter 11 for GUI used in one example, and Chapters 15–16 for one example.

form a substantial GUI and graphics sequence. Chapters 20–23 form a clear database-intensive web development sequence.

Teaching Approach

Java for Programmers contains a rich collection of examples. The book concentrates on the principles of good software engineering and stresses program clarity. We teach by example. We are educators who teach leading-edge topics in government, industry, military and academic classrooms worldwide.

Live-Code Approach. Java for Programmers is loaded with "live-code" examples—by this we mean that each new concept is presented in the context of a complete working Java application that is immediately followed by one or more actual executions showing the program's inputs and outputs.

Syntax Shading. We syntax shade all the Java code, similar to the way Java integrated-development environments and code editors syntax color code. This improves code readability—an important goal, given that this book contains over 18,000 lines of code in complete, working Java programs. Our syntax-shading conventions are as follows:

```
comments appear in italic
keywords appear in bold italic
errors and ASP.NET script delimiters appear in bold black
constants and literal values appear in bold gray
all other code appears in plain black
```

Code Highlighting. We place white rectangles around each program's key code segments.

Using Fonts for Emphasis. We place the key terms and the index's page reference for each defining occurrence in *bold italic* text for easier reference. We emphasize on-screen components in the **bold Helvetica** font (e.g., the **File** menu) and emphasize Java program text in the Lucida font (for example, int x = 5).

Web Access. All of the source-code examples for *Java for Programmers* are available for download from:

www.deitel.com/books/javafp

Objectives. Each chapter begins with a statement of objectives.

Quotations. The learning objectives are followed by quotations. We hope that you enjoy relating these to the chapter material.

Illustrations/Figures. Abundant charts, tables, line drawings, programs and program output are included. We model the flow of control in control statements with UML activity diagrams. UML class diagrams model the fields, constructors and methods of classes. We make extensive use of six major UML diagram types in the optional OOD/UML 2 ATM case study.

Programming Tips. We include programming tips to help you focus on important aspects of program development. These tips and practices represent the best we've gleaned from a combined seven decades of programming and teaching experience.

 Good Programming Practice

The Good Programming Practices *call attention to techniques that will help you produce programs that are clearer, more understandable and more maintainable.*

Common Programming Error

Pointing out these Common Programming Errors *reduces the likelihood that you'll make the same mistakes.*

Error-Prevention Tip

These tips contain suggestions for exposing bugs and removing them from your programs; many describe aspects of Java that prevent bugs from getting into programs in the first place.

Performance Tip

These tips highlight opportunities for making your programs run faster or minimizing the amount of memory that they occupy.

Portability Tip

The Portability Tips *to help you write code that will run on a variety of platforms.*

Software Engineering Observation

The Software Engineering Observations *highlight architectural and design issues that affect the construction of software systems, especially large-scale systems.*

Look-and-Feel Observation

The Look-and-Feel Observations *highlight graphical-user-interface conventions. These observations help you design attractive, user-friendly graphical user interfaces that conform to industry norms.*

Wrap-Up Section. Each of the chapters ends with a "wrap-up" section that recaps the chapter content and transitions to the next chapter.

Thousands of Index Entries. We have included an extensive index which is especially useful when you use the book as a reference.

Software Used with *Java for Programmers*

Many Java development tools are available for purchase, but you do not need any of these to get started with Java. We wrote most of the examples in *Java for Programmers* using the free Java Standard Edition Development Kit (JDK) 6. The current JDK version (and separately its documentation) can be downloaded from Sun's Java website java.sun.com/javase/downloads/index.jsp. We also used the Netbeans IDE in several chapters. Netbeans is available as a bundle with the JDK from the preceding website or you can download it separately from www.netbeans.org. You can find additional resources and software downloads in our Java SE 6 Resource Center at:

www.deitel.com/JavaSE6Mustang/

Deitel® Buzz Online Free E-mail Newsletter

Each week, the *Deitel® Buzz Online* announces our latest Resource Center(s) and includes commentary on industry trends and developments, links to free articles and resources from our published books and upcoming publications, product-release schedules, errata, challenges, anecdotes, information on our corporate instructor-led training courses and more.

It's also a good way for you to keep posted about issues related to *Java for Programmers*. To subscribe, visit

    www.deitel.com/newsletter/subscribe.html

The Deitel Online Resource Centers

Our website www.deitel.com provides more than 100 Resource Centers on various topics including programming languages, software development, Web 2.0, Internet business and open-source projects—see the list of Resource Centers in the first few pages of this book or visit www.deitel.com/ResourceCenters.html. The Resource Centers evolve out of the research we do to support our books and business endeavors. We've found many exceptional resources online, including tutorials, documentation, software downloads, articles, blogs, podcasts, videos, code samples, books, e-books and more—most of them are free. Each week we announce our latest Resource Centers in our newsletter, the *Deitel® Buzz Online* (www.deitel.com/newsletter/subscribe.html). Some of the Resource Centers you might find helpful while studying this book are Java SE 6, Java, Java Assessment and Certification, Java Design Patterns, Java EE 5, Code Search Engines and Code Sites, Game programming, Programming Projects and many more.

Acknowledgments

It is a great pleasure to acknowledge the efforts of many people whose names may not appear on the cover, but whose hard work, cooperation, friendship and understanding were crucial to the production of the book. Many people at Deitel & Associates, Inc. devoted long hours to this project—thanks especially to Abbey Deitel and Barbara Deitel.

We'd also like to thank two participants of our Honors Internship program who contributed to this publication—Megan Schuster, a computer science major at Swarthmore College, and Henry Klementowicz, a computer science major at Columbia University.

We are fortunate to have worked on this project with the talented and dedicated team of publishing professionals at Prentice Hall. We appreciate the extraordinary efforts of Mark Taub, Editor-in-Chief of Prentice Hall Professional; John Fuller, Managing Editor of Prentice Hall Professional; and Marcia Horton, Editorial Director of Prentice Hall's Engineering and Computer Science Division. Sandra Schroeder did a wonderful job designing the book's cover. Scott Disanno and Robert Engelhardt did a marvelous job managing the book's production.

This book was adapted from our book *Java How to Program, 7/e*. We wish to acknowledge the efforts of our reviewers on that book. Adhering to a tight time schedule, they scrutinized the text and the programs, providing countless suggestions for improving the accuracy and completeness of the presentation.

Java How to Program, 7/e *Reviewers (including 6/e Post-Publication Reviewers)* **Sun Microsystems Reviewers:** Lance Andersen (JDBC/Rowset Specification Lead, Java SE Engineering), Ed Burns, Ludovic Champenois (Sun's Application Server for Java EE programmers with Sun Application Server and tools—NetBeans, Studio Enterprise and Studio Creator), James Davidson, Vadiraj Deshpande (Java Enterprise System Integration Group, Sun Microsystems India), Sanjay Dhamankar (Core Developer Platform Group), Jesse Glick (NetBeans Group), Brian Goetz (author of *Java Concurrency in Practice*, Addison-Wesley, 2006), Doug Kohlert (Web Technologies and Standards Group), Sandeep Konchady (Java Software Engineering Organization), John Morrison (Sun Java System Portal Server Product Group), Winston Prakash, Brandon Taylor (SysNet group within the Software Division), and Jayashri Visvanathan (Sun Microsystems Java Studio Creator Team). **Academic and Industry Reviewers:** Akram Al-Rawi (King Faisal University), Mark Biamonte (DataDirect), Ayad Boudiab (International School of Choueifat, Lebanon), Joe Bowbeer (Mobile App Consulting), Harlan Brewer (Select Engineering Services), Marita Ellixson (Eglin AFB, Indiana Wesleyan University, Lead Facilitator), John Goodson (DataDirect), Anne Horton (Lockheed Martin), Terrell Regis Hull (Logicalis Integration Solutions), Clark Richey (RABA Technologies, LLC, Java Sun Champion), Manfred Riem (Utah Interactive, LLC, Java Sun Champion), Karen Tegtmeyer (Model Technologies, Inc.), David Wolff (Pacific Lutheran University), and Hua Yan (Borough of Manhattan Community College, City University of New York). *Java How to Program, 6/e* **Post-Publication Reviewers:** Anne Horton (Lockheed Martin), William Martz (University of Colorado at Colorado Springs), Bill O'Farrell (IBM), Jeffry Babb (Virginia Commonwealth University), Jeffrey Six (University of Delaware, Adjunct Faculty), Jesse Glick (Sun Microsystems), Karen Tegtmeyer (Model Technologies, Inc.), Kyle Gabhart (L-3 Communications), Marita Ellixson (Eglin AFB, Indiana Wesleyan University, Lead Facilitator), and Sean Santry (Independent Consultant).

These reviewers scrutinized every aspect of the text and made countless suggestions for improving the accuracy and completeness of the presentation.

Well, there you have it! Java is a powerful programming language that will help you write programs quickly and effectively. It scales nicely into the realm of enterprise systems development to help organizations build their critical information systems. As you read the book, we would sincerely appreciate your comments, criticisms, corrections and suggestions for improving the text. Please address all correspondence to:

deitel@deitel.com

We'll respond promptly, and post corrections and clarifications on:

www.deitel.com/books/javafp/

We hope you find *Java for Programmers* helpful in your professional endeavors.

Paul J. Deitel
Dr. Harvey M. Deitel

About the Authors

Paul J. Deitel, CEO and Chief Technical Officer of Deitel & Associates, Inc., is a graduate of MIT's Sloan School of Management, where he studied Information Technology. He holds the Java Certified Programmer and Java Certified Developer certifications, and has been designated by Sun Microsystems as a Java Champion. Through Deitel & Associates, Inc., he has delivered Java, C, C++, C#, Visual Basic and Internet programming courses to industry clients, including Cisco, IBM, Sun Microsystems, Dell, Lucent Technologies, Fidelity, NASA at the Kennedy Space Center, the National Severe Storm Laboratory, White Sands Missile Range, Rogue Wave Software, Boeing, Stratus, Cambridge Technology Partners, Open Environment Corporation, One Wave, Hyperion Software, Adra Systems, Entergy, CableData Systems, Nortel Networks, Puma, iRobot, Invensys and many more. He has also lectured on Java and C++ for the Boston Chapter of the Association for Computing Machinery. He and his co-author, Dr. Harvey M. Deitel, are the world's best-selling programming language textbook authors.

Dr. Harvey M. Deitel, Chairman and Chief Strategy Officer of Deitel & Associates, Inc., has 47 years of academic and industry experience in the computer field. Dr. Deitel earned B.S. and M.S. degrees from the MIT and a Ph.D. from Boston University. He has 20 years of college teaching experience, including earning tenure and serving as the Chairman of the Computer Science Department at Boston College before founding Deitel & Associates, Inc., with his son, Paul J. Deitel. He and Paul are the co-authors of several dozen books and multimedia packages and they are writing many more. With translations published in Japanese, German, Russian, Spanish, Traditional Chinese, Simplified Chinese, Korean, French, Polish, Italian, Portuguese, Greek, Urdu and Turkish, the Deitels' texts have earned international recognition. Dr. Deitel has delivered hundreds of professional seminars to major corporations, academic institutions, government organizations and the military.

About Deitel & Associates, Inc.

Deitel & Associates, Inc., is an internationally recognized corporate training and authoring organization specializing in computer programming languages, Internet and web software technology, object-technology education and Internet business development through its Web 2.0 Internet Business Initiative. The company provides instructor-led courses on major programming languages and platforms, such as Java, C++, C, Visual C#, Visual Basic, Visual C++, XML, object technology, Internet and web programming, and a growing list of additional programming and software-development related courses. The founders of Deitel & Associates, Inc., are Paul J. Deitel and Dr. Harvey M. Deitel. The company's clients include many of the world's largest companies, government agencies, branches of the military, and academic institutions. Through its 33-year publishing partnership with Prentice Hall, Deitel & Associates, Inc., publishes leading-edge programming textbooks, professional books, interactive multimedia *Cyber Classrooms*, *LiveLessons* DVD-based and web-based video courses, and e-content for popular course-management systems. Deitel & Associates, Inc., and the authors can be reached via e-mail at:

    deitel@deitel.com

To learn more about Deitel & Associates, Inc., its publications and its worldwide *Dive Into*® *Series* Corporate Training curriculum, visit:

    www.deitel.com/training/

and subscribe to the free *Deitel*® *Buzz Online* e-mail newsletter at:

    www.deitel.com/newsletter/subscribe.html

Individuals wishing to purchase Deitel books, and *LiveLessons* DVD and web-based training courses can do so through www.deitel.com. Bulk orders by corporations, the government, the military and academic institutions should be placed directly with Prentice Hall. For more information, visit www.prenhall.com/mischtm/support.html#order.

Before You Begin

Please follow the instructions in this section to ensure that Java is installed properly on your computer before you begin using this book.

Font and Naming Conventions

We use fonts to distinguish between on-screen components (such as menu names and menu items) and Java code or commands. Our convention is to emphasize on-screen components in a sans-serif bold **Helvetica** font (for example, **File** menu) and to emphasize Java code and commands in a sans-serif Lucida font (for example, System.out.println()).

Java Standard Edition Development Kit (JDK) 6

Before you can run the applications in *Java for Programmers* or build your own applications, you must install the Java Standard Edition Development Kit (JDK) 6 or a Java development tool that supports Java SE 6. The system requirements for the Windows, Linux or Solaris platforms are located at java.sun.com/javase/6/webnotes/install/system-configurations.html.

You can download the latest version of JDK 6 and its documentation from

java.sun.com/javase/6/download.jsp

Click the » **DOWNLOAD** button for JDK 6. You must accept the license agreement before downloading. Once you accept the license agreement, click the link for your platform's installer. Save the installer on your hard disk and keep track of where you save it. Before installing, carefully read the JDK installation instructions for your platform, which are located at java.sun.com/javase/6/webnotes/install/index.html. If you are installing Java on Windows, please be sure to follow the instructions for setting the PATH environment variable. Visit developer.apple.com/java/ for information on using Java with Mac OS X.

Downloading the Code Examples

The examples for *Java for Programmers* are available for download at

www.deitel.com/books/javafp/

If you are not registered at our website, go to www.deitel.com and click the **Register** link below our logo in the upper-left corner of the page. Fill in your information. There is no charge to register, and we will not share your information with anyone. We send you only account-management e-mails unless you register separately for our free e-mail newsletter at www.deitel.com/newsletter/subscribe.html. After registering, you'll receive a confirmation e-mail with your verification code. You need this code to sign in at www.deitel.com for the first time.

Next, go to www.deitel.com and sign in using the **Login** link below our logo in the upper-left corner of the page. Go to www.deitel.com/books/javafp/. Click the **Examples** link to download the Examples.zip file to your computer. Write down the location where you choose to save the file on your computer.

We assume the examples are located at C:\Examples on a computer running Microsoft Windows; however, the examples should work on any platform that supports Java SE 6. Extract the contents of Examples.zip using a tool such as WinZip (www.winzip.com).

Setting the CLASSPATH Environment Variable

If you attempt to run a Java program then receive a message like

```
Exception in thread "main" java.lang.NoClassDefFoundError: YourClass
```

then your system has a CLASSPATH environment variable that must be modified. To fix this error, modify the CLASSPATH environment variable to include

```
.;
```

at the beginning of its value (with no spaces before or after these characters).

Introduction

Our life is frittered away by detail. ... Simplify, simplify.
—Henry David Thoreau

The chief merit of language is clearness.
—Galen

My object all sublime I shall achieve in time.
—W. S. Gilbert

He had a wonderful talent for packing thought close, and rendering it portable.
—Thomas B. Macaulay

"Egad, I think the interpreter is the hardest to be understood of the two!"
—Richard Brinsley Sheridan

Man is still the most extraordinary computer of all.
—John F. Kennedy

OBJECTIVES

In this chapter you'll learn:

- Basic object technology concepts, such as classes, objects, attributes, behaviors, encapsulation, inheritance and polymorphism.

- A typical Java program development environment.

- Java's role in developing distributed client/server applications for the Internet and the web.

- The history of UML—the industry-standard object-oriented design language, the UML.

- The history of the Internet and the web.

- To test-drive Java applications.

Outline

I.1 Introduction
I.2 The Internet and the World Wide Web
I.3 History of C and C++
I.4 History of Java
I.5 Java Class Libraries
I.6 Typical Java Development Environment
I.7 Notes about Java and Java for Programmers
I.8 Test-Driving a Java Application
I.9 Software Engineering Case Study: Introduction to Object Technology and the UML
I.10 Web 2.0
I.11 Software Technologies
I.12 Wrap-Up
I.13 Web Resources

I.1 Introduction

Welcome to Java! We have worked hard to create what we hope you'll find to be an informative, entertaining and challenging professional experience. Java is one of today's most popular and powerful software development languages and is appropriate for experienced programmers to use in building substantial information systems.

Pedagogy

The core of the book emphasizes achieving program *clarity* through the proven techniques of *object-oriented programming*. The presentation is clear, straightforward and abundantly illustrated. It includes hundreds of complete working Java programs and shows the outputs produced when those programs are run. We teach Java features in the context of complete working Java programs—we call this the *live-code approach*. The example programs can be downloaded from www.deitel.com/books/javafp/.

Fundamentals

The early chapters introduce the fundamentals of Java, providing a solid foundation for the deeper treatment in the later chapters. Experienced programmers tend to read the early chapters quickly and find the treatment of Java in the later chapters rigorous and challenging.

Java Standard Edition 6 (Java SE 6) and the Java Development Kit 6 (JDK 6)

This book is based on Sun's *Java Standard Edition 6 (Java SE 6)*. Sun provides a Java SE 6 implementation, called the *Java Development Kit (JDK)*, that includes the tools you need to write software in Java. We used JDK version 6 for the programs in this book. Sun updates the JDK on a regular basis to fix bugs. To download the most recent version of JDK 6, visit java.sun.com/javase/downloads/index.jsp.

Object-Oriented Programming

The book focuses on *object-oriented programming*. Object orientation is the key programming methodology used by programmers today. You'll create and work with many software objects in this text.

Language of Choice for Networked Applications

Java has become the language of choice for implementing Internet-based applications and software for devices that communicate over a network. Stereos and other devices in homes are now being networked together by Java technology. There are now billions of java-enabled computers, mobile phones and handheld devices! Java has evolved rapidly into the large-scale applications arena. It's the preferred language for meeting many organizations' enterprise programming needs.

Java has grown so large that it has two other editions. The *Java Enterprise Edition (Java EE)* is geared toward developing large-scale, distributed networking applications and web-based applications. The *Java Micro Edition (Java ME)* is geared toward developing applications for small, memory-constrained devices, such as cell phones, pagers and PDAs.

Staying in Touch with Us

If you would like to communicate with us, please send e-mail to deitel@deitel.com. We'll respond promptly. To keep up to date with Java developments at Deitel & Associates, please register for our free e-mail newsletter, the *Deitel® Buzz Online,* at

    www.deitel.com/newsletter/subscribe.html

For lots of additional Java material, visit our growing list of Java Resource centers at www.deitel.com/ResourceCenters.html.

1.2 The Internet and the World Wide Web

The *Internet* has its roots in the 1960s with funding supplied by the U.S. Department of Defense. Originally designed to connect the main computer systems of about a dozen universities and research organizations, the Internet is accessible by billions of computers and computer-controlled devices worldwide.

With the introduction of the *World Wide Web*—which allows computer users to locate and view multimedia-based documents on almost any subject over the Internet—the Internet has exploded into one of the world's premier communication mechanisms.

The Internet and the web are surely among humankind's most important and profound creations. In the past, most computer applications ran on computers that were not connected to one another. Today's applications can be written to communicate among the world's computers.

Java for Programmers presents programming techniques that allow Java applications to use the Internet and the web to interact with other applications. These capabilities and others allow Java programmers to develop the kind of enterprise-level distributed applications that are used in industry today. Java applications can be written to execute on every major type of computer, greatly reducing the time and cost of systems development. If you are interested in developing applications to run over the Internet and the web, learning Java may be the key to rewarding career opportunities for you.

1.3 History of C and C++

Java evolved from C++, which evolved from C, which evolved from BCPL and B. BCPL was developed in 1967 by Martin Richards as a language for writing operating systems software and compilers. Ken Thompson modeled many features in his B language after their counterparts in BCPL, using B to create early versions of the UNIX operating system at Bell Laboratories in 1970.

The C language was evolved from B by Dennis Ritchie at Bell Laboratories and was originally implemented in 1972. It initially became widely known as the development language of the UNIX operating system. Today, most of the code for general-purpose operating systems (e.g., those found in notebooks, desktops, workstations and small servers) is written in C or C++.

C++, an extension of C, was developed by Bjarne Stroustrup in the early 1980s at Bell Laboratories. C++ provides a number of features that "spruce up" the C language, but more important, it provides capabilities for *object-oriented programming* (discussed in more detail in Section 1.9 and throughout this book). C++ is a hybrid language—it is possible to program in either a C-like style, an object-oriented style or both.

Objects, or more precisely—as we'll see in Section 1.9—the classes objects come from, are essentially reusable software components. There are date objects, time objects, audio objects, automobile objects, people objects and so on. In fact, almost any noun can be represented as a software object in terms of *attributes* (e.g., name, color and size) and *behaviors* (e.g., calculating, moving and communicating). Software developers now know that using a modular, object-oriented design and implementation approach can make software-development groups much more productive than was possible with earlier popular programming techniques like structured programming. Object-oriented programs are often easier to understand, correct and modify. Java is the world's most widely used object-oriented programming language.

1.4 History of Java

Microprocessors are having a profound impact in intelligent consumer-electronic devices. Recognizing this, Sun Microsystems in 1991 funded an internal corporate research project code-named Green, which resulted in a C++-based language that its creator, James Gosling, called Oak after an oak tree outside his window at Sun. It was later discovered that there already was a computer language by that name. When a group of Sun people visited a local coffee shop, the name Java was suggested, and it stuck.

The Green project ran into some difficulties. The marketplace for intelligent consumer-electronic devices was not developing in the early 1990s as quickly as Sun had anticipated. The project was in danger of being canceled. By sheer good fortune, the World Wide Web exploded in popularity in 1993, and Sun people saw the immediate potential of using Java to add *dynamic content,* such as interactivity and animations, to web pages. This breathed new life into the project.

Sun formally announced Java at an industry conference in May 1995. Java garnered the attention of the business community because of the phenomenal interest in the web. Java is now used to develop large-scale enterprise applications, to enhance the functionality of web servers, to provide applications for consumer devices (e.g., cell phones, pagers and personal digital assistants) and for many other purposes.

1.5 Java Class Libraries

Java programs consist of pieces called *classes*. Classes include pieces called *methods* that perform tasks and return information when they complete them. Programmers can create each piece they need to form Java programs. However, most Java programmers take advantage of the rich collections of existing classes in the *Java class libraries*, which are also known as the *Java APIs (Application Programming Interfaces)*. Thus, there are really two aspects to learning the Java "world." The first is the Java language itself, so that you can program your own classes, and the second is the classes in the extensive Java class libraries. Throughout this book, we discuss many library classes. Class libraries are provided primarily by compiler vendors, but many are supplied by independent software vendors (ISVs).

Software Engineering Observation 1.1

Use a building-block approach to create programs. Avoid reinventing the wheel—use existing pieces wherever possible. This software reuse *is a key benefit of object-oriented programming.*

Software Engineering Observation 1.2

When programming in Java, you'll typically use the following building blocks: classes and methods from class libraries, classes and methods you create yourself and classes and methods that others create and make available to you.

The advantage of creating your own classes and methods is that you know exactly how they work and you can examine the Java code. The disadvantage is the time-consuming and potentially complex effort that is required.

Performance Tip 1.1

Using Java API classes and methods instead of writing your own versions can improve program performance, because they are carefully written to perform efficiently. This technique also shortens program development time.

Portability Tip 1.1

Using classes and methods from the Java API instead of writing your own improves program portability, because they are included in every Java implementation.

Software Engineering Observation 1.3

Extensive class libraries of reusable software components are available over the Internet, many at no charge.

You can view the Java API documentation online at java.sun.com/javase/6/docs/ or download the documentation from java.sun.com/javase/6/download.jsp.

1.6 Typical Java Development Environment

We now explain the commonly used steps in creating and executing a Java application using a Java development environment (illustrated in Fig. 1.1).

Java programs normally go through five phases—*edit, compile, load, verify* and *execute*. We discuss these phases in the context of the JDK 6.0 from Sun Microsystems, Inc., You can download the most up-to-date JDK and its documentation from java.sun.com/javase/downloads/index.jsp. *Carefully follow the installation instructions for the JDK provided in the* Before You Begin *section of this book (or at* java.sun.com/javase/6/webnotes/install/index.html*) to ensure that you set up your computer properly to compile and execute Java programs. [Note:* This website provides installation instructions for Win-

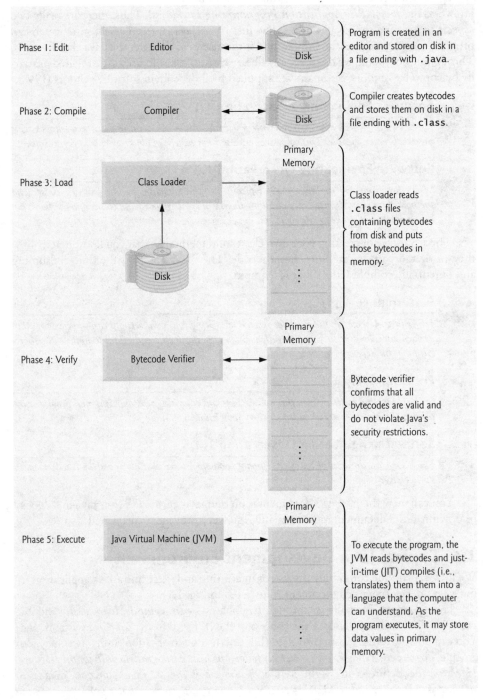

Fig. 1.1 | Typical Java development environment.

dows, Linux and Mac OS X. If you are not using one of these operating systems, refer to the manuals for your system's Java environment or ask your instructor how to accomplish these tasks based on your computer's operating system. In addition, please keep in mind that web links occasionally break as companies evolve their websites. If you encounter a problem with this link or any other links referenced in this book, please check www.deitel.com for errata and please notify us by e-mail at deitel@deitel.com. We'll respond promptly.]

Phase 1: Creating a Program

Phase 1 consists of editing a file with an editor. You type a Java source code program using the editor, make any necessary corrections and save the program. A file name ending with the .*java extension* indicates that the file contains Java source code.

Two editors widely used on Linux systems are vi and emacs. On Windows, a simple editing program like Windows Notepad will suffice. Many freeware and shareware editors are also available for download from the Internet on sites like www.download.com.

For developing substantial information systems, *integrated development environments (IDEs)* are available from many major software suppliers, including Sun Microsystems. IDEs provide tools that support the software development process, including editors for writing and editing programs and debuggers for locating logic errors. Popular IDEs and editors include Eclipse (www.eclipse.org), NetBeans (www.netbeans.org), JBuilder (www.borland.com), JCreator (www.jcreator.com), BlueJ (www.blueJ.org), jGRASP (www.jgrasp.org) and jEdit (www.jedit.org). [*Note:* Most of our example programs should operate properly with any Java integrated development environment that supports the JDK 6.]

Phase 2: Compiling a Java Program into Bytecodes

In Phase 2, the programmer uses the command *javac* (invoking, the *Java compiler*) to *compile* a program. For example, to compile a program called Welcome.java, you would type

```
javac Welcome.java
```

in the command window of your system (i.e., the MS-DOS prompt in Windows 95/98/ME, the Command Prompt in Windows NT/2000/XP, the shell prompt in Linux or the Terminal application in Mac OS X). If the program compiles, the compiler produces a .*class* file called Welcome.class that contains the compiled version of the program.

The Java compiler translates Java source code into *bytecodes* that represent the tasks to execute in the execution phase (Phase 5). Bytecodes are executed by the *Java Virtual Machine (JVM)*—a part of the JDK and the foundation of the Java platform. A *virtual machine (VM)* is a software application that simulates a computer, but hides the underlying operating system and hardware from the programs that interact with the VM. If the same VM is implemented on many computer platforms, applications that it executes can be used on all those platforms. The JVM is one of the most widely used virtual machines.

Unlike machine language, which is dependent on specific computer hardware, bytecodes are platform-independent instructions—they are not dependent on a particular hardware platform. So Java's bytecodes are *portable*—that is, the same bytecodes can execute on any platform containing a JVM that understands the version of Java in which the bytecodes were compiled. The JVM is invoked by the *java* command. For example, to execute a Java application called `Welcome`, you would type the command

```
java Welcome
```

in a command window to invoke the JVM, which would then initiate the steps necessary to execute the application. This begins Phase 3.

Phase 3: Loading a Program into Memory

In Phase 3, the program must be placed in memory before it can execute. The *class loader* takes the `.class` files containing the program's bytecodes and transfers them to primary memory. The class loader also loads any of the `.class` files provided by Java that your program uses. The `.class` files can be loaded from a disk on your system or over a network (e.g., your local college or company network, or the Internet).

Phase 4: Bytecode Verification

In Phase 4, as the classes are loaded, the *bytecode verifier* examines their bytecodes to ensure that they are valid and do not violate Java's security restrictions. Java enforces strong security, to make sure that Java programs arriving over the network do not damage your files or your system (as computer viruses and worms might).

Phase 5: Execution

In Phase 5, the JVM executes the program's bytecodes. In early Java versions, the JVM was simply an interpreter for Java bytecodes. This caused most Java programs to execute slowly because the JVM would interpret and execute one bytecode at a time. Today's JVMs typically execute bytecodes using a combination of interpretation and so-called *just-in-time (JIT) compilation*. In this process, The JVM analyzes the bytecodes as they are interpreted, searching for *hot spots*—parts of the bytecodes that execute frequently. For these parts, a *just-in-time (JIT) compiler*—known as the *Java HotSpot compiler*—translates the bytecodes into the underlying computer's machine language. When the JVM encounters these compiled parts again, the faster machine-language code executes. Thus Java programs actually go through two compilation phases—one in which source code is translated into bytecodes (for portability across JVMs on different computer platforms) and a second in which, during execution, the bytecodes are translated into machine language for the actual computer on which the program executes.

Problems That May Occur at Execution Time

Programs might not work on the first try. Each of the preceding phases can fail because of various errors that we'll discuss throughout this book. For example, an executing program might try to divide by zero (an illegal operation for whole-number arithmetic in Java). This would cause the Java program to display an error message. If this occurs, you would have to return to the edit phase, make the necessary corrections and proceed through the remaining phases again to determine that the corrections fix the problem(s).

1.7 Notes about Java and *Java for Programmers*

You have heard that Java is a portable language and that programs written in Java can run on many different computers. In general, *portability is an elusive goal.*

Portability Tip 1.2

Although it is easier to write portable programs in Java than in most other programming languages, differences between compilers, JVMs and computers can make portability difficult to achieve. Simply writing programs in Java does not guarantee portability.

Error-Prevention Tip 1.1

Always test your Java programs on all systems on which you intend to run them, to ensure that they will work correctly for their intended audiences.

We audited our presentation against Sun's Java documentation for completeness and accuracy. A web-based version of the Java API documentation can be found at java.sun.com/javase/6/docs/api/index.html or you can download this documentation to your own computer from java.sun.com/javase/6/download.jsp. For additional technical details on many aspects of Java development, visit java.sun.com/reference/docs/index.html.

1.8 Test-Driving a Java Application

In this section, you'll run and interact with your first Java application. You'll begin by running an ATM application that simulates the transactions that take place when using an ATM machine (e.g., withdrawing money, making deposits and checking account balances). You'll learn how to build this application in the optional, object-oriented case study included in Chapters 1–8 and 10. For the purpose of this section, we assume you're running Microsoft Windows.

In the following steps, you'll run the application and perform various transactions. The elements and functionality you see in this application are typical of what you'll learn to program in this book. [*Note:* We use fonts to distinguish between features you see on a screen (e.g., the **Command Prompt**) and elements that are not directly related to a screen. Our convention is to emphasize screen features like titles and menus (e.g., the **File** menu) in a semibold **sans-serif Helvetica** font and to emphasize non-screen elements, such as file names or input (e.g., ProgramName.java) in a sans-serif Lucida font. As you've already noticed, the defining occurrence of each key term is set in ***bold italic***. In the figures in this section, we highlight the user input required by each step and point out significant parts of the application with lines and text. To make these features more visible, we have modified the background color of the **Command Prompt** windows.]

1. ***Checking your setup.*** Read the Before You Begin section of the book to confirm that you have set up Java properly on your computer and that you have copied the book's examples to your hard drive.

2. ***Locating the completed application.*** Open a **Command Prompt** window. This can be done by selecting **Start > All Programs > Accessories > Command Prompt**. Change to the ATM application directory by typing cd C:\examples\ch01\ATM, then press *Enter* (Fig. 1.2). The command cd is used to change directories.

3. ***Running the ATM application.*** Type the command java ATMCaseStudy (Fig. 1.3) and press *Enter*. Recall that the java command, followed by the name of the application's .class file (in this case, ATMCaseStudy), executes the application. Specifying the .class extension when using the java command results in

Using the **cd** command to
change directories   File location of the ATM application

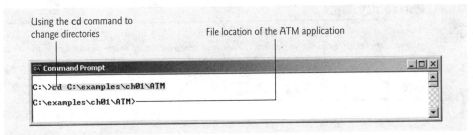

Fig. 1.2 | Opening a Windows XP **Command Prompt** and changing directories.

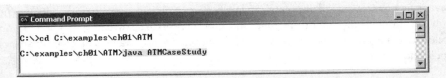

Fig. 1.3 | Using the java command to execute the ATM application.

an error. [*Note:* Java commands are case sensitive. It is important to type the name
of this application with a capital A, T and M in "ATM," a capital C in "Case"
and a capital S in "Study." Otherwise, the application will not execute.] If you
receive the error message, "Exception in thread "main" java.lang.NoClass-
DefFoundError: ATMCaseStudy," your system has a CLASSPATH problem. Please
refer to the *Before You Begin* section of the book for instructions to help you fix
this problem.

4. *Entering an account number.* When the application first executes, it displays a
"Welcome!" greeting and prompts you for an account number. Type 12345 at the
"Please enter your account number:" prompt (Fig. 1.4) and press *Enter.*

5. *Entering a PIN.* Once a valid account number is entered, the application displays
the prompt "Enter your PIN:". Type "54321" as your valid PIN (Personal Identification Number) and press *Enter.* The ATM main menu containing a list of
options will be displayed (Fig. 1.5).

6. *Viewing the account balance.* Select option 1, "View my balance", from the
ATM menu (Fig. 1.6). The application then displays two numbers—the Available balance ($1000.00) and the Total balance ($1,200.00). The available
balance is the maximum amount of money in your account which is available for

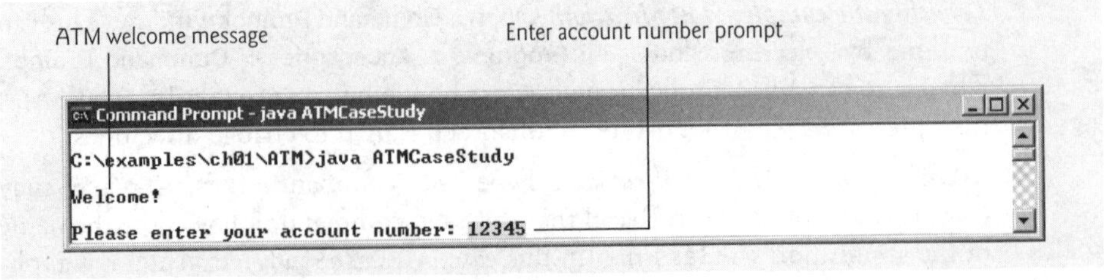

ATM welcome message   Enter account number prompt

C:\examples\ch01\ATM>java ATMCaseStudy
Welcome!
Please enter your account number: 12345

Fig. 1.4 | Prompting the user for an account number.

Enter valid PIN   ATM main menu

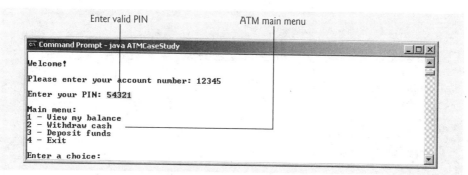

Fig. 1.5 | Entering a valid PIN number and displaying the ATM application's main menu.

Account balance information

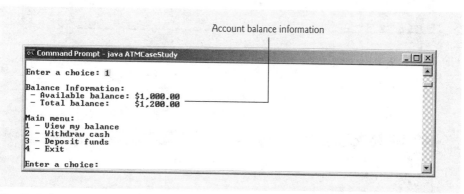

Fig. 1.6 | ATM application displaying user account balance information.

withdrawal at a given time. In some cases, certain funds, such as recent deposits, are not immediately available for the user to withdraw, so the available balance may be less than the total balance, as it is here. After the account balance information is shown, the application's main menu is displayed again.

7. *Withdrawing money from the account.* Select option 2, "Withdraw cash", from the application menu. You are then presented (Fig. 1.7) with a list of dollar amounts (e.g., 20, 40, 60, 100 and 200). You are also given the option to cancel the transaction and return to the main menu. Withdraw $100 by selecting option 4. The application displays "Please take your cash now." and returns to the main menu. [*Note:* Unfortunately, this application only *simulates* the behavior of a real ATM and thus does not actually dispense money.]

8. *Confirming that the account information has been updated.* From the main menu, select option 1 again to view your current account balance (Fig. 1.8). Note that both the available balance and the total balance have been updated to reflect your withdrawal transaction.

9. *Ending the transaction.* To end your current ATM session, select option 4, "Exit" from the main menu (Fig. 1.9). The ATM will exit the system and display a good-bye message to the user. The application will then return to its original prompt asking for the next user's account number.

ATM withdrawal menu

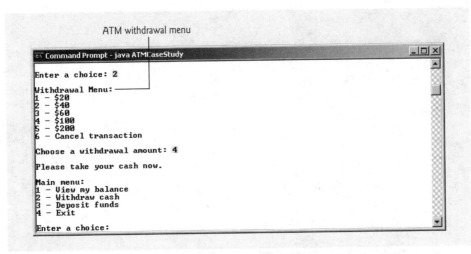

Fig. 1.7 | Withdrawing money from the account and returning to the main menu.

Confirming updated account balance
information after withdrawal transaction

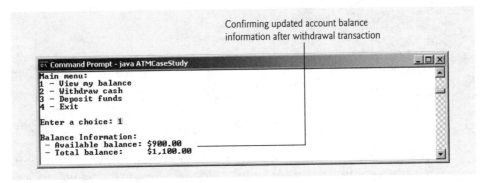

Fig. 1.8 | Checking the new balance.

ATM goodbye message   Account number prompt for next user

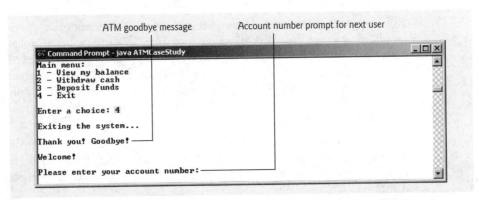

Fig. 1.9 | Ending an ATM transaction session.

10. *Exiting the ATM application and closing the* **Command Prompt** *window*. Most applications provide an option to exit and return to the **Command Prompt** direc-

tory from which the application was run. A real ATM does not provide a user with the option to turn off the ATM machine. Rather, when a user has completed all desired transactions and chooses the menu option to exit, the ATM resets itself and displays a prompt for the next user's account number. As Fig. 1.9 illustrates, the ATM application here behaves similarly. Choosing the menu option to exit ends only the current user's ATM session, not the entire ATM application. To actually exit the ATM application, click the close (**x**) button in the upper-right corner of the **Command Prompt** window. Closing the window causes the running application to terminate.

1.9 Software Engineering Case Study: Introduction to Object Technology and the UML

Now we begin our early introduction to object orientation, a natural way of thinking about the world and writing computer programs. Chapters 1–8 and 10 all end with a brief Software Engineering Case Study section in which we present a carefully paced introduction to object orientation. Our goal here is to help you develop an object-oriented way of thinking and to introduce you to the *Unified Modeling Language™ (UML™)*—a graphical language that allows people who design software systems to use an industry standard notation to represent them.

In this only required section, we introduce object-oriented concepts and terminology. The optional sections in Chapters 2–8 and 10 present an object-oriented design and implementation of the software for a simple automated teller machine (ATM). The Software Engineering Case Study sections at the ends of Chapters 2–7

- analyze a typical requirements document that describes a software system (the ATM) to be built
- determine the objects required to implement that system
- determine the attributes the objects will have
- determine the behaviors these objects will exhibit
- specify how the objects interact with one another to meet the system requirements.

The Software Engineering Case Study sections at the ends of Chapters 8 and 10 modify and enhance the design presented in Chapters 2–7. Appendix H contains a complete, working Java implementation of the object-oriented ATM system.

You'll experience a concise, yet solid introduction to object-oriented design with the UML. Also, you'll sharpen your code-reading skills by touring the complete, carefully written and well-documented Java implementation of the ATM in Appendix H.

Basic Object Technology Concepts
We begin our introduction to object orientation with some key terminology. Everywhere you look in the real world you see *objects*—people, animals, plants, cars, planes, buildings, computers and so on. Humans think in terms of objects. Telephones, houses, traffic lights, microwave ovens and water coolers are just a few more objects. Computer programs, such as the Java programs you'll read in this book and the ones you'll write, are composed of lots of interacting software objects.

We sometimes divide objects into two categories: animate and inanimate. Animate objects are "alive" in some sense—they move around and do things. Inanimate objects, on the other hand, do not move on their own. Objects of both types, however, have some things in common. They all have *attributes* (e.g., size, shape, color and weight), and they all exhibit *behaviors* (e.g., a ball rolls, bounces, inflates and deflates; a baby cries, sleeps, crawls, walks and blinks; a car accelerates, brakes and turns; a towel absorbs water). We'll study the kinds of attributes and behaviors that software objects have.

Humans learn about existing objects by studying their attributes and observing their behaviors. Different objects can have similar attributes and can exhibit similar behaviors. Comparisons can be made, for example, between babies and adults and between humans and chimpanzees.

Object-oriented design (OOD) models software in terms similar to those that people use to describe real-world objects. It takes advantage of *class* relationships, where objects of a certain class, such as a class of vehicles, have the same characteristics—cars, trucks, little red wagons and roller skates have much in common. OOD also takes advantage of *inheritance* relationships, where new classes of objects are derived by absorbing characteristics of existing classes and adding unique characteristics of their own. An object of class "convertible" certainly has the characteristics of the more general class "automobile," but more specifically, the roof goes up and down.

Object-oriented design provides a natural and intuitive way to view the software design process—namely, modeling objects by their attributes and behaviors just as we describe real-world objects. OOD also models communication between objects. Just as people send messages to one another (e.g., a sergeant commands a soldier to stand at attention), objects also communicate via messages. A bank account object may receive a message to decrease its balance by a certain amount because the customer has withdrawn that amount of money.

OOD *encapsulates* (i.e., wraps) attributes and *operations* (behaviors) into objects—an object's attributes and operations are intimately tied together. Objects have the property of *information hiding*. This means that objects may know how to communicate with one another across well-defined *interfaces*, but normally they are not allowed to know how other objects are implemented—implementation details are hidden within the objects themselves. We can drive a car effectively, for instance, without knowing the details of how engines, transmissions, brakes and exhaust systems work internally—as long as we know how to use the accelerator pedal, the brake pedal, the wheel and so on. Information hiding, as we'll see, is crucial to good software engineering.

Languages like Java are *object oriented*. Programming in such a language is called *object-oriented programming (OOP),* and it allows computer programmers to implement an object-oriented design as a working system. Languages like C, on the other hand, are *procedural,* so programming tends to be *action oriented.* In C, the unit of programming is the *function.* Groups of actions that perform some common task are formed into functions, and functions are grouped to form programs. In Java, the unit of programming is the class from which objects are eventually *instantiated* (created). Java classes contain *methods* (which implement operations and are similar to functions in C) as well as *fields* (which implement attributes).

Java programmers concentrate on creating classes. Each class contains fields, and the set of methods that manipulate the fields and provide services to *clients* (i.e., other classes that use the class). The programmer uses existing classes as the building blocks for constructing new classes.

Classes are to objects as blueprints are to houses. Just as we can build many houses from one blueprint, we can instantiate (create) many objects from one class. You cannot cook meals in the kitchen of a blueprint; you can cook meals in the kitchen of a house.

Classes can have relationships with other classes. For example, in an object-oriented design of a bank, the "bank teller" class needs to relate to the "customer" class, the "cash drawer" class, the "safe" class, and so on. These relationships are called *associations*.

Packaging software as classes makes it possible for future software systems to *reuse* the classes. Groups of related classes are often packaged as reusable *components*. Just as realtors often say that the three most important factors affecting the price of real estate are "location, location and location," people in the software community often say that the three most important factors affecting the future of software development are "reuse, reuse and reuse." Reuse of existing classes when building new classes and programs saves time and effort. Reuse also helps programmers build more reliable and effective systems, because existing classes and components often have gone through extensive testing, debugging and performance tuning.

Indeed, with object technology, you can build much of the software you'll need by combining classes, just as automobile manufacturers combine interchangeable parts. Each new class you create will have the potential to become a valuable software asset that you and other programmers can use to speed and enhance the quality of future software development efforts.

Introduction to Object-Oriented Analysis and Design (OOAD)

To create the best software, you should follow a detailed process for *analyzing* your project's *requirements* (i.e., determining *what* the system is supposed to do) and developing a *design* that satisfies them (i.e., deciding *how* the system should do it). Ideally, you would go through this process and carefully review the design (or have your design reviewed by other software professionals) before writing any code. If this process involves analyzing and designing your system from an object-oriented point of view, it is called an *object-oriented analysis and design (OOAD) process*.

Ideally, a group should agree on a strictly defined process for solving its problem and a uniform way of communicating the results of that process to one another. Although many different OOAD processes exist, a single graphical language for communicating the results of *any* OOAD process has come into wide use. This language, known as the Unified Modeling Language (UML), was developed in the mid-1990s under the initial direction of three software methodologists—Grady Booch, James Rumbaugh and Ivar Jacobson.

History of the UML

In the 1980s, increasing numbers of organizations began using OOP to build their applications, and a need developed for a standard OOAD process. Many methodologists—including Booch, Rumbaugh and Jacobson—individually produced and promoted separate processes to satisfy this need. Each process had its own notation, or "language" (in the form of graphical diagrams), to convey the results of analysis and design.

By the early 1990s, different organizations, and even divisions within the same organization, were using their own unique processes and notations. At the same time, these organizations also wanted to use software tools that would support their particular processes. Software vendors found it difficult to provide tools for so many processes. A standard notation and standard processes were needed.

In 1994, James Rumbaugh joined Grady Booch at Rational Software Corporation (now a division of IBM), and the two began working to unify their popular processes. They soon were joined by Ivar Jacobson. In 1996, the group released early versions of the UML to the software engineering community and requested feedback. Around the same time, an organization known as the *Object Management Group™ (OMG™)* invited submissions for a common modeling language. The OMG (www.omg.org) is a nonprofit organization that promotes the standardization of object-oriented technologies by issuing guidelines and specifications, such as the UML. Several corporations—among them HP, IBM, Microsoft, Oracle and Rational Software—had already recognized the need for a common modeling language. In response to the OMG's request for proposals, these companies formed *UML Partners*—the consortium that developed the UML version 1.1 and submitted it to the OMG. The OMG accepted the proposal and, in 1997, assumed responsibility for the continuing maintenance and revision of the UML. The UML version 2 now available marks the first major revision of the UML since the 1997 version 1.1 standard. We present UML 2 terminology and notation throughout this book.

What Is the UML?

The UML is now the most widely used graphical representation scheme for modeling object-oriented systems. It has indeed unified the various popular notational schemes. Those who design systems use the language (in the form of diagrams) to model their systems.

An attractive feature of the UML is its flexibility. The UML is *extensible* (i.e., capable of being enhanced with new features) and is independent of any particular OOAD process. UML modelers are free to use various processes in designing systems, but all developers can now express their designs with one standard set of graphical notations.

The UML is a complex, feature-rich graphical language. In our Software Engineering Case Study sections, we present a concise subset of these features. We then use this subset to guide you through an end-to-end design experience with the UML.

Web UML Resources

For more information about the UML, refer to the following websites:

www.uml.org
This UML resource page from the Object Management Group (OMG) provides specification documents for the UML and other object-oriented technologies.

www.ibm.com/software/rational/uml
This is the UML resource page for IBM Rational—the successor to the Rational Software Corporation (the company that created the UML).

en.wikipedia.org/wiki/Unified_Modeling_Language
Wikipedia's definition of the UML. This site also provides links to many additional UML resources.

Recommended Readings

The following books provide information about object-oriented design with the UML:

Ambler, S. *The Object Primer: Agile Model-Driven Development with UML 2.0, Third Edition*. New York: Cambridge University Press, 2005.

Arlow, J., and I. Neustadt. *UML and the Unified Process: Practical Object-Oriented Analysis and Design, Second Edition*. Boston: Addison-Wesley Professional, 2006.

Fowler, M. *UML Distilled, Third Edition: A Brief Guide to the Standard Object Modeling Language.* Boston: Addison-Wesley Professional, 2004.

Rumbaugh, J., I. Jacobson and G. Booch. *The Unified Modeling Language User Guide, Second Edition.* Boston: Addison-Wesley Professional, 2006.

Section 1.9 Self-Review Exercises

1.1   List three examples of real-world objects that we did not mention. For each object, list several attributes and behaviors.

1.2   Pseudocode is _____.
a) another term for OOAD
b) a programming language used to display UML diagrams
c) an informal means of expressing program logic
d) a graphical representation scheme for modeling object-oriented systems

1.3   The UML is used primarily to _____.
a) test object-oriented systems
b) design object-oriented systems
c) implement object-oriented systems
d) Both a and b

Answers to Section 1.9 Self-Review Exercises

1.1   [*Note:* Answers may vary.] a) A television's attributes include the size of the screen, the number of colors it can display, its current channel and its current volume. A television turns on and off, changes channels, displays video and plays sounds. b) A coffee maker's attributes include the maximum volume of water it can hold, the time required to brew a pot of coffee and the temperature of the heating plate under the coffee pot. A coffee maker turns on and off, brews coffee and heats coffee. c) A turtle's attributes include its age, the size of its shell and its weight. A turtle walks, retreats into its shell, emerges from its shell and eats vegetation.

1.2   c.

1.3   b.

1.10 Web 2.0

The web literally exploded in the mid-to-late 1990s, but hard times hit in the early 2000s due to the dot com economic bust. The resurgence that began in 2004 or so has been named Web 2.0. The first Web 2.0 Conference was held in 2004. A year into its life, the term "Web 2.0" garnered about 10 million hits on the *Google* search engine, growing to 60 million a year later. Google is widely regarded as the signature company of Web 2.0. Some others are Craigslist (free classified listings), Flickr (photo sharing), del.icio.us (social bookmarking), YouTube (video sharing), MySpace and FaceBook (social networking), Salesforce (business software offered as an online service), Second Life (a virtual world), Skype (Internet telephony) and Wikipedia (a free online encyclopedia).

At Deitel & Associates, we launched our Web 2.0-based *Internet Business Initiative* in 2005. We're researching the key technologies of Web 2.0 and using them to build Internet businesses. We're sharing our research in the form of Resource Centers at `www.deitel.com/resourcecenters.html`. Each week, we announce the latest Resource Centers in our newsletter, the *Deitel® Buzz Online* (`www.deitel.com/newsletter/subscribe.html`). Each lists many links to (mostly) free content and software on the Internet.

We include a substantial treatment of *web services* (Chapter 23). Web services are frequently used in the application development methodology of *mashups* in which you can rapidly develop powerful and intriguing applications by combining organizations' complementary web services and other forms of information feeds. A popular mashup is www.housingmaps.com which combines real estate listings of www.craigslist.org with the mapping capabilities of *Google Maps* to offer maps that show the locations of apartments for rent in a given area.

Ajax is one of the premier technologies of Web 2.0. Though the term's use exploded in 2005, it's just a term that names a group of technologies and programming techniques that have been in use since the late 1990s. Ajax helps Internet-based applications perform like desktop applications—a difficult task, given that such applications suffer transmission delays as data is shuttled back and forth between your computer and other computers on the Internet. Using Ajax techniques, applications like Google Maps have achieved excellent performance and the look and feel of desktop applications. Although we don't discuss "raw" Ajax programming (which is quite complex) in this text, we do show in Chapter 22 how to build Ajax-enabled applications using JavaServer Faces (JSF) Ajax-enabled components.

Blogs are websites (currently more than 100 million of them) that are like online diaries, with the most recent entries appearing first. Bloggers quickly post their opinions about news, product releases, politics, controversial issues, and just about everything else. The collection of all blogs and the blogging community is called the *blogosphere* and is becoming increasingly influential. *Technorati* is a leading blog search engine.

RSS feeds enable sites to push information to subscribers. A common use of RSS feeds is to deliver the latest blog postings to people who subscribe to blogs. The RSS information flows on the Internet are growing exponentially.

Web 3.0 is another name for the next generation of the web also called the *Semantic Web*. Web 1.0 was almost purely HTML-based. Web 2.0 is making increasing use of XML, especially in technologies like RSS feeds. Web 3.0 will make deep use of XML, creating a "web of meaning." If you're an entrepreneur looking for business opportunities, check out our Web 3.0 Resource Center.

To follow the latest developments in Web 2.0, read www.techcrunch.com and www.slashdot.org and check out the growing list of Web 2.0-related Resource Centers at www.deitel.com/resourcecenters.html.

1.11 Software Technologies

In this section, we discuss a number of software engineering buzzwords that you'll hear in the software development community. We've created Resource Centers on most of these topics, with more on the way.

Agile Software Development is a set of methodologies that try to get software implemented quickly with fewer resources then previous methodologies. Check out the Agile Alliance (www.agilealliance.org) and the Agile Manifesto (www.agilemanifesto.org).

Extreme programming (XP) is one of many agile development methodologies. It tries to develop software quickly. The software is released frequently in small increments to encourage rapid user feedback. XP recognizes that the users' requirements change often and that software must meet those new requirements quickly. Programmers work in pairs at one machine so code review is done immediately as the code is created.

Refactoring involves reworking code to make it clearer and easier to maintain while preserving its functionality. It's widely employed with agile development methodologies. Many refactoring tools are available to do major portions of the reworking automatically.

Design patterns are proven architectures for constructing flexible and maintainable object-oriented software. The field of design patterns tries to enumerate those recurring patterns, and encourage software designers to reuse them to develop better quality software with less time, money and effort.

Game programming. The computer game business is larger than the first-run movie business. Check out our Game Programming and Programming Projects Resource Centers.

Open source software is a style of developing software in contrast to proprietary development that dominated software's early years. With open source development, individuals and companies contribute their efforts in developing, maintaining and evolving software in exchange for the right to use that software for their own purposes, typically at no charge. Open source code generally gets scrutinized by a much larger audience than proprietary software, so bugs are often removed faster. Open source also encourages more innovation. Sun recently open sourced Java. Some organizations you'll hear a lot about in the open source community are the Eclipse Foundation (the Eclipse IDE is popular for Java software development), the Mozilla Foundation (creators of the Firefox browser), the Apache Software Foundation (creators of the Apache web server) and SourceForge (which provides the tools for managing open source projects and currently has over 150,000 open source projects under development).

Linux is an open source operating system and one of the greatest successes of the open source movement. *MySQL* is an open source database management system. *PHP* is a popular open source server-side Internet "scripting" language for developing Internet-based applications. *LAMP* is an acronym for the set of open source technologies that many developers used to build web applications—it stands for Linux, Apache, MySQL and PHP (or Perl or Python—two other languages used for similar purposes).

Ruby on Rails combines the scripting language Ruby with the Rails web application framework developed by the company 37Signals. Their book, *Getting Real*, is a must read for today's web application developers; read it free at gettingreal.37signals.com/toc.php. Many Ruby on Rails developers have reported significant productivity gains over using other languages when developing database-intensive web applications.

With *Software as a Service (SAAS)* the software, instead of being installed locally, runs on servers elsewhere on the Internet. When that server is updated, all clients worldwide see the new capabilities; no local installation is needed. You access the service through a browser—these are quite portable so you can run the same applications on different kinds of computers from anywhere is the world. Salesforce.com, Google, and Microsoft's Office Live and Windows Live all offer SAAS.

1.12 Wrap-Up

This chapter introduced basic object technology concepts, including classes, objects, attributes, behaviors, encapsulation, inheritance and polymorphism. You learned the steps for creating and executing a Java application using Sun's JDK 6. The chapter explored the history of the Internet and the World Wide Web, and Java's role in developing distributed client/server applications for the Internet and the web. You also learned about the history and purpose of the UML—the industry-standard graphical language for modeling software systems. Finally, you "test-drove" a sample Java application. In Chapter 2, you'll create your first Java applications.

1.13 Web Resources

This section provides many resources that will be useful to you as you learn Java. The sites include Java resources, Java development tools and our own websites where you can find downloads and resources associated with this book. We also provide a link where you can subscribe to our free *Deitel® Buzz Online* e-mail newsletter.

Deitel & Associates Websites

www.deitel.com
Contains updates, corrections and additional resources for all Deitel publications.

www.deitel.com/newsletter/subscribe.html
Subscribe to the free *Deitel® Buzz Online* e-mail newsletter to follow the Deitel & Associates publishing program, including updates and errata to this book.

www.deitel.com/books/javafp/
The Deitel & Associates home page for *Java for Programmers*. Here you'll find links to the book's examples (also included on the CD that accompanies the book) and other resources.

Deitel Java Resource Centers

www.deitel.com/Java/
Our Java Resource Center focuses on the enormous amount of Java free content available online. Start your search here for resources, downloads, tutorials, documentation, books, e-books, journals, articles, blogs and more that will help you develop Java applications.

www.deitel.com/JavaSE6Mustang/
Our Java SE 6 Resource Center is your guide to the latest release of Java. The site includes the best resources we found online to help you get started with Java SE 6 development.

www.deitel.com/JavaEE5/
Our Java Enterprise Edition 5 (Java EE 5) Resource Center.

www.deitel.com/JavaCertification/
Our Java Certification and Assessment Testing Resource Center.

www.deitel.com/JavaDesignPatterns/
Our Java Design Patterns Resource Center. In their book, *Design Patterns: Elements of Reusable Object-Oriented Software* (Boston: Addison-Wesley Professional, 1995), the "Gang of Four" (E. Gamma, R. Helm, R. Johnson, and J. Vlissides) describe 23 design patterns that provide proven architectures for building object-oriented software systems. In this resource center, you'll find discussions of many of these and other design patterns.

www.deitel.com/CodeSearchEngines/
Our Code Search Engines and Code Sites Resource Center includes resources developers use to find source code online.

Sun Microsystems Websites

java.sun.com/new2java/
The "New to Java Center" on the Sun Microsystems website features online training resources to help you get started with Java programming.

`java.sun.com/javase/downloads/index.jsp`
The download page for the Java Development Kit 6 (JDK 6) and its documentation. The JDK includes everything you need to compile and execute your Java SE 6 (Mustang) applications.

`java.sun.com/javase/6/webnotes/install/index.html`
Instructions for installing JDK 6 on Solaris, Windows and Linux platforms.

`java.sun.com/javase/6/docs/api/index.html`
The online site for the Java SE 6 API documentation.

`java.sun.com/javase`
The home page for the Java Standard Edition platform.

`java.sun.com`
Sun's Java technology home page provides downloads, references, forums, online tutorials and more.

`developers.sun.com`
Sun's home page for Java developers provides downloads, APIs, code samples, articles with technical advice and other resources on the best Java development practices.

Editors and Integrated Development Environments

`www.eclipse.org`
The Eclipse development environment can be used to develop code in any programming language. You can download the environment and several Java plug-ins to develop your Java programs.

`www.netbeans.org`
The NetBeans IDE. One of the most widely used, freely distributed Java development tools.

`www.codegear.com/products/jbuilder`
Codegear provides a free Turbo Edition version of its popular Java IDE JBuilder. The site also provides trial versions of the Enterprise and Professional editions.

`www.blueJ.org`
BlueJ—a free tool designed to help teach object-oriented Java to new programmers.

`www.jgrasp.org`
jGRASP downloads, documentation and tutorials. This tool displays visual representations of Java programs to aid comprehension.

`www.jedit.org`
jEdit—a text editor written in Java.

`developers.sun.com/prodtech/javatools/jsenterprise/index.jsp`
Sun Java Studio Enterprise IDE—the Sun Microsystems enhanced version of NetBeans.

`www.jcreator.com`
JCreator—a popular Java IDE. JCreator Lite Edition is available as a free download. A 30-day trial version of JCreator Pro Edition is also available.

`www.textpad.com`
TextPad—compile, edit and run your Java programs from this editor that provides syntax coloring and an easy-to-use interface.

2

Introduction to Java Applications

What's in a name?
That which we call a rose
By any other name
would smell as sweet.
—William Shakespeare

When faced with a decision,
I always ask, "What would
be the most fun?"
—Peggy Walker

"Take some more tea," the
March Hare said to Alice,
very earnestly. "I've had
nothing yet," Alice replied in
an offended tone: "so I can't
take more." "You mean you
can't take less," said the
Hatter: "it's very easy to take
more than nothing."
—Lewis Carroll

OBJECTIVES

In this chapter you'll learn:

- To write simple Java applications.
- Input and output statements.
- Java's primitive types.
- Arithmetic operators.
- The precedence of arithmetic operators.
- Decision-making statements.
- Relational and equality operators.

Outline

2.1 Introduction
2.2 A First Program in Java: Printing a Line of Text
2.3 Modifying Our First Java Program
2.4 Displaying Text with `printf`
2.5 Another Java Application: Adding Integers
2.6 Arithmetic
2.7 Decision Making: Equality and Relational Operators
2.8 (Optional) Software Engineering Case Study: Examining the Requirements Document
2.9 Wrap-Up

2.1 Introduction

We now introduce Java application programming. We begin with several examples that simply display messages on the screen. We then demonstrate a program that obtains two numbers from a user, calculates their sum and displays the result. You'll learn how to perform various arithmetic calculations and save their results for later use. The last example demonstrates decision-making fundamentals by showing you how to compare numbers, then display messages based on the comparison results.

2.2 A First Program in Java: Printing a Line of Text

A Java *application* is a program that executes when you use the `java` command to launch the Java Virtual Machine (JVM). Let us consider a simple application that displays a line of text. (Later in this section we'll discuss how to compile and run an application.) The program and its output are shown in Fig. 2.1. The output appears in the gray box at the end of the program. The program illustrates several important Java language features. For your convenience, each program we present in this book includes line numbers, which are not part of actual Java programs. We'll soon see that line 9 does the real work of the program—namely, displaying the phrase `Welcome to Java Programming!` on the screen. We now consider each line of the program in order.

```java
1   // Fig. 2.1: Welcome1.java
2   // Text-printing program.
3
4   public class Welcome1
5   {
6      // main method begins execution of Java application
7      public static void main( String args[] )
8      {
9         System.out.println( "Welcome to Java Programming!" );
10
11     } // end method main
12
13  } // end class Welcome1
```

Fig. 2.1 | Text-printing program. (Part 1 of 2.)

```
Welcome to Java Programming!
```

Fig. 2.1 | Text-printing program. (Part 2 of 2.)

Line 1

```
// Fig. 2.1: Welcome1.java
```

begins with //, indicating that the remainder of the line is a comment. The Java compiler ignores comments. By convention, we begin every program with a comment indicating the figure number and file name.

A comment that begins with // is called an *end-of-line* (or *single-line*) *comment*, because the comment terminates at the end of the line on which it appears. A // comment also can begin in the middle of a line and continue until the end of that line (as in lines 11 and 13).

Traditional comments (also called *multiple-line comments*), such as

```
/* This is a traditional
   comment. It can be
   split over many lines */
```

can be spread over several lines. This type of comment begins with the delimiter /* and ends with */. All text between the delimiters is ignored by the compiler. Java incorporated traditional comments and end-of-line comments from the C and C++ programming languages, respectively. In this book, we use end-of-line comments.

Java also provides *Javadoc comments* that are delimited by /** and */. As with traditional comments, all text between the Javadoc comment delimiters is ignored by the compiler. Javadoc comments enable programmers to embed program documentation directly in their programs. Such comments are the preferred Java documenting format in industry. The *javadoc* utility program (part of the Java SE Development Kit) reads Javadoc comments and uses them to prepare your program's documentation in HTML format. For more information on Javadoc comments and the javadoc utility, visit Sun's javadoc Tool Home Page at java.sun.com/javase/6/docs/technotes/guides/javadoc/index.html.

Common Programming Error 2.1

*Forgetting one of the delimiters of a traditional or Javadoc comment is a syntax error. The **syntax** of a programming language specifies the rules for creating a proper program in that language. A **syntax error** occurs when the compiler encounters code that violates Java's language rules (i.e., its syntax). In this case, the compiler issues an error message to help the programmer identify and fix the incorrect code. Syntax errors are also called **compiler errors**, **compile-time errors** or compilation errors, because the compiler detects them during the compilation phase. You'll be unable to execute your program until you correct all the syntax errors in it.*

Line 2

```
// Text-printing program.
```

is an end-of-line comment that describes the purpose of the program.

Good Programming Practice 2.1

Every program should begin with a comment that explains the purpose of the program, the author and the date and time the program was last modified. (We are not showing the author, date and time in this book's programs because this information would be redundant.)

Line 3 is a blank line. Together, blank lines, space characters and tab characters are known as ***white space***. (Space characters and tabs are known specifically as ***white-space characters***.) In this chapter and the next several chapters, we discuss conventions for using white space to enhance program readability.

Line 4

```
public class Welcome1
```

begins a ***class declaration*** for class Welcome1. Every program in Java consists of at least one class declaration that is defined by you—the programmer. These are known as ***programmer-defined classes*** or ***user-defined classes***. The **class keyword** introduces a class declaration in Java and is immediately followed by the ***class name*** (Welcome1). Keywords are reserved for use by Java and are always spelled with all lowercase letters. The complete list of Java keywords is shown in Appendix C.

By convention, all class names in Java begin with a capital letter and capitalize the first letter of each word they include (e.g., SampleClassName). A Java class name is an ***identifier***—a series of characters consisting of letters, digits, underscores (_) and dollar signs ($) that does not begin with a digit and does not contain spaces. Some valid identifiers are Welcome1, $value, _value, m_inputField1 and button7. The name 7button is not a valid identifier because it begins with a digit, and the name input field is not a valid identifier because it contains a space. Normally, an identifier that does not begin with a capital letter is not the name of a Java class. Java is ***case sensitive***—that is, uppercase and lowercase letters are distinct, so a1 and A1 are different (but both valid) identifiers.

Good Programming Practice 2.2

By convention, always begin a class name's identifier with a capital letter and start each subsequent word in the identifier with a capital letter. Java programmers know that such identifiers normally represent Java classes, so naming your classes in this manner makes your programs more readable.

Common Programming Error 2.2

Java is case sensitive. Not using the proper uppercase and lowercase letters for an identifier normally causes a compilation error.

In Chapters 2–7, every class we define begins with the **public** keyword. For now, we'll simply require this keyword. When you save your public class declaration in a file, the file name must be the class name followed by the **.java file-name extension**. For our application, the file name is Welcome1.java. You'll learn more about public and non-public classes in Chapter 8.

Common Programming Error 2.3

A public class must be placed in a file that has the same name as the class (in terms of both spelling and capitalization) plus the .java extension; otherwise, a compilation error occurs.

Common Programming Error 2.4

It is an error not to end a file name with the `.java` extension for a file containing a class declaration. The Java compiler compiles only files with the `.java` extension.

A *left brace* (at line 5 in this program), {, begins the *body* of every class declaration. A corresponding *right brace* (at line 13), }, must end each class declaration. Note that lines 6–11 are indented. This indentation is one of the spacing conventions mentioned earlier. We define each spacing convention as a Good Programming Practice.

Error-Prevention Tip 2.1

Whenever you type an opening left brace, {, in your program, immediately type the closing right brace, }, then reposition the cursor between the braces and indent to begin typing the body. This practice helps prevent errors due to missing braces.

Good Programming Practice 2.3

Indent the entire body of each class declaration one "level" of indentation between the left brace, {, and the right brace, }, that delimit the body of the class. This format emphasizes the class declaration's structure and makes it easier to read.

Common Programming Error 2.5

It is a syntax error if braces do not occur in matching pairs.

Line 6

```
// main method begins execution of Java application
```

is an end-of-line comment indicating the purpose of lines 7–11 of the program. Line 7

```
public static void main( String args[] )
```

is the starting point of every Java application. The *parentheses* after the identifier main indicate that it is a program building block called a *method*. Java class declarations normally contain one or more methods. For a Java application, exactly one of the methods must be called main and must be defined as shown in line 7; otherwise, the JVM will not execute the application. Methods are able to perform tasks and return information when they complete their tasks. Keyword *void* indicates that this method will perform a task but will not return any information when it completes its task. Later, we'll see that many methods return information when they complete their task. You'll learn more about methods in Chapters 3 and 6. For now, simply mimic main's first line in your Java applications. In line 7, the String args[] in parentheses is a required part of the method main's declaration. We discuss this in Chapter 7, Arrays.

The left brace, {, in line 8 begins the *body of the method declaration*. A corresponding right brace, }, must end the method declaration's body (line 11 of the program). Note that line 9 in the body of the method is indented between the braces.

Good Programming Practice 2.4

Indent the entire body of each method declaration one "level" of indentation between the left brace, {, and the right brace, }, that define the body of the method. This format makes the structure of the method stand out and makes the method declaration easier to read.

Line 9

```
System.out.println( "Welcome to Java Programming!" );
```

instructs the computer to ***perform an action***—namely, to print the ***string*** of characters contained between the double quotation marks (but not the quotation marks themselves). White-space characters in strings are not ignored by the compiler.

System.out is known as the ***standard output object***. System.out allows Java applications to display sets of characters in the ***command window*** from which the Java application executes. In Microsoft Windows 95/98/ME, the command window is the MS-DOS prompt. In more recent versions of Microsoft Windows, the command window is the Command Prompt. In UNIX/Linux/Mac OS X, the command window is called a terminal window or a shell. Many programmers refer to the command window simply as the ***command line***.

Method **System.out.println** displays (or prints) *a line* of text in the command window. The string in the parentheses in line 9 is the argument to the method. Method System.out.println performs its task by displaying (also called outputting) its argument in the command window. When System.out.println completes its task, it positions the output cursor (the location where the next character will be displayed) to the beginning of the next line in the command window.

The entire line 9, including System.out.println, the argument "Welcome to Java Programming!" in the parentheses and the ***semicolon*** (;), is called a ***statement***. Each statement ends with a semicolon. When the statement in line 9 of our program executes, it displays the message Welcome to Java Programming! in the command window. As we'll see in subsequent programs, a method is typically composed of one or more statements that perform the method's task.

 Common Programming Error 2.6

Omitting the semicolon at the end of a statement is a syntax error.

Some programmers find it difficult when reading or writing a program to match the left and right braces ({ and }) that delimit the body of a class declaration or a method declaration. For this reason, some programmers include an end-of-line comment after a closing right brace (}) that ends a method declaration and after a closing right brace that ends a class declaration. For example, line 11

```
} // end method main
```

specifies the closing right brace (}) of method main, and line 13

```
} // end class Welcome1
```

specifies the closing right brace (}) of class Welcome1. Each comment indicates the method or class that the right brace terminates.

 Good Programming Practice 2.5

Following the closing right brace (}) of a method body or class declaration with an end-of-line comment indicating the method or class declaration to which the brace belongs improves program readability.

Compiling and Executing Your First Java Application

We are now ready to compile and execute our program. For this purpose, we assume you are using the Sun Microsystems' Java SE Development Kit 6.0 (JDK 6.0). In our Java Resource Centers at `www.deitel.com/ResourceCenters.html`, we provide links to tutorials that help you get started with several popular Java development tools.

To prepare to compile the program, open a command window and change to the directory where the program is stored. Most operating systems use the command *cd* to *change directories*. For example,

```
cd c:\examples\ch02\fig02_01
```

changes to the `fig02_01` directory on Windows. The command

```
cd ~/examples/ch02/fig02_01
```

changes to the `fig02_01` directory on UNIX/Linux/Max OS X.

To compile the program, type

```
javac Welcome1.java
```

If the program contains no syntax errors, the preceding command creates a new file called `Welcome1.class` (known as the *class file* for `Welcome1`) containing the Java bytecodes that represent our application. When we use the `java` command to execute the application, these bytecodes will be executed by the JVM.

Error-Prevention Tip 2.2

When attempting to compile a program, if you receive a message such as "bad command or file-name," "javac: command not found" or "'javac' is not recognized as an internal or external command, operable program or batch file," then your Java software installation was not completed properly. If you are using the JDK, this indicates that the system's PATH environment variable was not set properly. Please review the installation instructions in the Before You Begin section of this book carefully. On some systems, after correcting the PATH, you may need to reboot your computer or open a new command window for these settings to take effect.

Error-Prevention Tip 2.3

The Java compiler generates syntax-error messages when the syntax of a program is incorrect. Each error message contains the file name and line number where the error occurred. For example, Welcome1.java:6 indicates that an error occurred in the file Welcome1.java at line 6. The remainder of the error message provides information about the syntax error.

Error-Prevention Tip 2.4

The compiler error message "Public class ClassName must be defined in a file called ClassName.java" indicates that the file name does not exactly match the name of the public class in the file or that you typed the class name incorrectly when compiling the class.

Figure 2.2 shows the program of Fig. 2.1 executing in a Microsoft® Windows® XP **Command Prompt** window. To execute the program, type `java Welcome1`. This launches the JVM, which loads the "`.class`" file for class `Welcome1`. Note that the "`.class`" file-name extension is omitted from the preceding command; otherwise, the JVM will not execute the program. The JVM calls method `main`. Next, the statement at line 9 of `main`

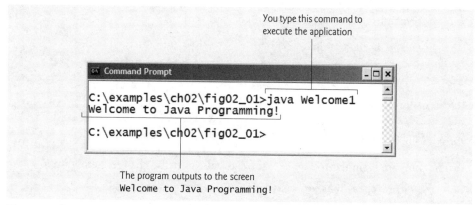

You type this command to
execute the application

The program outputs to the screen
`Welcome to Java Programming!`

Fig. 2.2 | Executing `Welcome1` in a Microsoft Windows XP **Command Prompt** window.

displays "`Welcome to Java Programming!`" [*Note:* Many environments show command prompts with black backgrounds and white text. We adjusted these settings in our environment to make our screen captures more readable.]

Error-Prevention Tip 2.5

When attempting to run a Java program, if you receive a message such as "Exception in thread "main" `java.lang.NoClassDefFoundError: Welcome1`," your CLASSPATH environment variable has not been set properly. Please review the installation instructions in the Before You Begin section of this book carefully. On some systems, you may need to reboot your computer or open a new command window after configuring the CLASSPATH.

2.3 Modifying Our First Java Program

This section continues our introduction to Java programming with two examples that modify the example in Fig. 2.1 to print text on one line by using multiple statements and to print text on several lines by using a single statement.

Displaying a Single Line of Text with Multiple Statements

`Welcome to Java Programming!` can be displayed several ways. Class `Welcome2`, shown in Fig. 2.3, uses two statements to produce the same output as that shown in Fig. 2.1. From this point forward, we highlight the new and key features in each code listing, as shown in lines 9–10 of this program.

```
1   // Fig. 2.3: Welcome2.java
2   // Printing a line of text with multiple statements.
3
4   public class Welcome2
5   {
6      // main method begins execution of Java application
7      public static void main( String args[] )
8      {
9         System.out.print( "Welcome to " );
```

Fig. 2.3 | Printing a line of text with multiple statements. (Part I of 2.)

```
10            System.out.println( "Java Programming!" );
11
12        } // end method main
13
14    } // end class Welcome2
```

```
Welcome to Java Programming!
```

Fig. 2.3 | Printing a line of text with multiple statements. (Part 2 of 2.)

The program is similar to Fig. 2.1, so we discuss only the changes here. Line 2

```
// Printing a line of text with multiple statements.
```

is an end-of-line comment stating the purpose of this program. Line 4 begins the Welcome2 class declaration.

Lines 9–10 of method main

```
System.out.print( "Welcome to " );
System.out.println( "Java Programming!" );
```

display one line of text in the command window. The first statement uses System.out's method print to display a string. Unlike println, after displaying its argument, print does not position the output cursor at the beginning of the next line in the command window—the next character the program displays will appear immediately after the last character that print displays. Thus, line 10 positions the first character in its argument (the letter "J") immediately after the last character that line 9 displays (the space character before the string's closing double-quote character). Each print or println statement resumes displaying characters from where the last print or println statement stopped displaying characters.

Displaying Multiple Lines of Text with a Single Statement

A single statement can display multiple lines by using *newline characters*, which indicate to System.out's print and println methods when they should position the output cursor at the beginning of the next line in the command window. Like blank lines, space characters and tab characters, newline characters are white-space characters. Figure 2.4 outputs four lines of text, using newline characters to determine when to begin each new line. Most of the program is identical to those in Fig. 2.1 and Fig. 2.3, so we discuss only the changes here.

Line 2

```
// Printing multiple lines of text with a single statement.
```

is a comment stating the program's purpose. Line 4 begins the Welcome3 class declaration.

Line 9

```
System.out.println( "Welcome\nto\nJava\nProgramming!" );
```

displays four separate lines of text in the command window. Normally, the characters in a string are displayed exactly as they appear in the double quotes. Note, however, that the two characters \ and n (repeated three times in the statement) do not appear on the screen. The *backslash* (\) is called an *escape character*. It indicates to System.out's print and

```
 1   // Fig. 2.4: Welcome3.java
 2   // Printing multiple lines of text with a single statement.
 3
 4   public class Welcome3
 5   {
 6      // main method begins execution of Java application
 7      public static void main( String args[] )
 8      {
 9         System.out.println( "Welcome\nto\nJava\nProgramming!" );
10
11      } // end method main
12
13   } // end class Welcome3
```

```
Welcome
to
Java
Programming!
```

Fig. 2.4 | Printing multiple lines of text with a single statement.

println methods that a "special character" is to be output. When a backslash appears in a string of characters, Java combines the next character with the backslash to form an *escape sequence*. The escape sequence \n represents the newline character. When a newline character appears in a string being output with System.out, the newline character causes the screen's output cursor to move to the beginning of the next line in the command window. Figure 2.5 lists several common escape sequences and describes how they affect the display of characters in the command window. For the complete list of escape sequences, visit java.sun.com/docs/books/jls/third_edition/html/lexical.html#3.10.6.

Escape sequence	Description
\n	Newline. Position the screen cursor at the beginning of the next line.
\t	Horizontal tab. Move the screen cursor to the next tab stop.
\r	Carriage return. Position the screen cursor at the beginning of the current line—do not advance to the next line. Any characters output after the carriage return overwrite the characters previously output on that line.
\\	Backslash. Used to print a backslash character.
\"	Double quote. Used to print a double-quote character. For example, `System.out.println( "\"in quotes\"" );` displays `"in quotes"`

Fig. 2.5 | Some common escape sequences.

2.4 Displaying Text with printf

Java SE 5.0 added the ***System.out.printf*** method for displaying formatted data—the f in the name printf stands for "formatted." Figure 2.6 outputs the strings "Welcome to" and "Java Programming!" with System.out.printf.

Lines 9–10

```
System.out.printf( "%s\n%s\n",
    "Welcome to", "Java Programming!" );
```

call method System.out.printf to display the program's output. The method call specifies three arguments. When a method requires multiple arguments, the arguments are separated with commas (,)—this is known as a ***comma-separated list***.

Good Programming Practice 2.6

Place a space after each comma (,) in an argument list to make programs more readable.

Remember that all statements in Java end with a semicolon (;). Therefore, lines 9–10 represent only one statement. Java allows large statements to be split over many lines. However, you cannot split a statement in the middle of an identifier or in the middle of a string.

Common Programming Error 2.7

Splitting a statement in the middle of an identifier or a string is a syntax error.

Method printf's first argument is a ***format string*** that may consist of ***fixed text*** and ***format specifiers***. Fixed text is output by printf just as it would be output by print or println. Each format specifier is a placeholder for a value and specifies the type of data to output. Format specifiers also may include optional formatting information.

Format specifiers begin with a percent sign (%) and are followed by a character that represents the data type. For example, the format specifier ***%s*** is a placeholder for a string.

```
 1   // Fig. 2.6: Welcome4.java
 2   // Printing multiple lines in a dialog box.
 3
 4   public class Welcome4
 5   {
 6      // main method begins execution of Java application
 7      public static void main( String args[] )
 8      {
 9         System.out.printf( "%s\n%s\n",
10            "Welcome to", "Java Programming!" );
11
12      } // end method main
13
14   } // end class Welcome4
```

```
Welcome to
Java Programming!
```

Fig. 2.6 | Displaying multiple lines with method System.out.printf.

The format string in line 9 specifies that `printf` should output two strings and that each string should be followed by a newline character. At the first format specifier's position, `printf` substitutes the value of the first argument after the format string. At each subsequent format specifier's position, `printf` substitutes the value of the next argument in the argument list. So this example substitutes "Welcome to" for the first `%s` and "Java Programming!" for the second `%s`. The output shows that two lines of text were displayed.

We introduce various formatting features as they are needed in our examples. Chapter 24 presents the details of formatting output with `printf`.

2.5 Another Java Application: Adding Integers

Our next application reads (or inputs) two *integers* (whole numbers, like –22, 7, 0 and 1024) typed by a user at the keyboard, computes the sum of the values and displays the result. This program must keep track of the numbers supplied by the user for the calculation later in the program. Programs remember numbers and other data in the computer's memory and access that data through program elements called *variables*. The program of Fig. 2.7 demonstrates these concepts. In the sample output, we use highlighting to differentiate between the user's input and the program's output.

```java
1   // Fig. 2.7: Addition.java
2   // Addition program that displays the sum of two numbers.
3   import java.util.Scanner; // program uses class Scanner
4
5   public class Addition
6   {
7      // main method begins execution of Java application
8      public static void main( String args[] )
9      {
10        // create Scanner to obtain input from command window
11        Scanner input = new Scanner( System.in );
12
13        int number1; // first number to add
14        int number2; // second number to add
15        int sum; // sum of number1 and number2
16
17        System.out.print( "Enter first integer: " ); // prompt
18        number1 = input.nextInt(); // read first number from user
19
20        System.out.print( "Enter second integer: " ); // prompt
21        number2 = input.nextInt(); // read second number from user
22
23        sum = number1 + number2; // add numbers
24
25        System.out.printf( "Sum is %d\n", sum ); // display sum
26
27     } // end method main
28
29  } // end class Addition
```

Fig. 2.7 | Addition program that displays the sum of two numbers. (Part 1 of 2.)

```
Enter first integer: 45
Enter second integer: 72
Sum is 117
```

Fig. 2.7 | Addition program that displays the sum of two numbers. (Part 2 of 2.)

Lines 1–2

```
// Fig. 2.7: Addition.java
// Addition program that displays the sum of two numbers.
```

state the figure number, file name and purpose of the program. Line 3

```
import java.util.Scanner; // program uses class Scanner
```

is an **import** *declaration* that helps the compiler locate a class that is used in this program. A great strength of Java is its rich set of predefined classes that you can reuse rather than "reinventing the wheel." These classes are grouped into *packages*—named collections of related classes—and are collectively referred to as the *Java class library*, or the *Java Application Programming Interface* (*Java API*). Programmers use import declarations to identify the predefined classes used in a Java program. The import declaration in line 3 indicates that this example uses Java's predefined Scanner class (discussed shortly) from package *java.util*. Then the compiler attempts to ensure that you use class Scanner correctly.

Common Programming Error 2.8

All import declarations must appear before the first class declaration in the file. Placing an import declaration inside a class declaration's body or after a class declaration is a syntax error.

Error-Prevention Tip 2.6

Forgetting to include an import declaration for a class used in your program typically results in a compilation error containing a message such as "cannot resolve symbol." When this occurs, check that you provided the proper import declarations and that the names in the import declarations are spelled correctly, including proper use of uppercase and lowercase letters.

Line 5

```
public class Addition
```

begins the declaration of class Addition. The file name for this public class must be Addition.java. Remember that the body of each class declaration starts with an opening left brace (line 6), {, and ends with a closing right brace (line 29), }.

The application begins execution with method main (lines 8–27). The left brace (line 9) marks the beginning of main's body, and the corresponding right brace (line 27) marks the end of main's body. Note that method main is indented one level in the body of class Addition and that the code in the body of main is indented another level for readability.

Line 11

```
Scanner input = new Scanner( System.in );
```

is a *variable declaration statement* (also called a *declaration*) that specifies the name (input) and type (Scanner) of a variable that is used in this program. A *variable* is a location in the computer's memory where a value can be stored for use later in a program. All variables must be declared with a *name* and a *type* before they can be used. A variable's name enables the program to access the value of the variable in memory. A variable's name can be any valid identifier. (See Section 2.2 for identifier naming requirements.) A variable's type specifies what kind of information is stored at that location in memory. Like other statements, declaration statements end with a semicolon (;).

The declaration in line 11 specifies that the variable named input is of type Scanner. A *Scanner* enables a program to read data (e.g., numbers) for use in a program. The data can come from many sources, such as a file on disk or the user at the keyboard. Before using a Scanner, the program must create it and specify the source of the data.

The equal sign (=) in line 11 indicates that Scanner variable input should be *initialized* (i.e., prepared for use in the program) in its declaration with the result of the expression *new Scanner(System.in)* to the right of the equal sign. This expression creates a Scanner object that reads data typed by the user at the keyboard. Recall that the standard output object, System.out, allows Java applications to display characters in the command window. Similarly, the *standard input object*, System.in, enables Java applications to read information typed by the user. So, line 11 creates a Scanner that enables the application to read information typed by the user at the keyboard.

The variable declaration statements at lines 13–15

```
int number1; // first number to add
int number2; // second number to add
int sum; // sum of number1 and number2
```

declare that variables number1, number2 and sum hold data of type *int*—these variables can hold *integer* values (whole numbers such as 7, –11, 0 and 31,914). These variables are not yet initialized. The range of values for an int is –2,147,483,648 to +2,147,483,647. We'll soon discuss types *float* and *double*, for holding real numbers, and type *char*, for holding character data. Real numbers are numbers that contain decimal points, such as 3.4, 0.0 and –11.19. Variables of type char represent individual characters, such as an uppercase letter (e.g., A), a digit (e.g., 7), a special character (e.g., * or %) or an escape sequence (e.g., the newline character, \n). Types such as int, float, double and char are called *primitive types* or *built-in types*. Primitive-type names are keywords and therefore must appear in all lowercase letters. Appendix D, summarizes the characteristics of the eight primitive types (boolean, byte, char, short, int, long, float and double).

Variable declaration statements can be split over several lines, with the variable names separated by commas (i.e., a comma-separated list of variable names). Several variables of the same type may be declared in one declaration or in multiple declarations. For example, lines 13–15 can also be written as a single statement as follows:

```
int number1, // first number to add
    number2, // second number to add
    sum; // sum of number1 and number2
```

Note that we used end-of-line comments in lines 13–15. This use of comments is a common programming practice for indicating the purpose of each variable in the program.

Good Programming Practice 2.7

Declare each variable on a separate line. This format allows a descriptive comment to be easily inserted next to each declaration.

Good Programming Practice 2.8

*Choosing meaningful variable names helps a program to be **self-documenting** (i.e., one can understand the program simply by reading it rather than by reading manuals or viewing an excessive number of comments).*

Good Programming Practice 2.9

By convention, variable-name identifiers begin with a lowercase letter, and every word in the name after the first word begins with a capital letter. For example, variable-name identifier firstNumber *has a capital* N *in its second word,* Number.

Line 17

```
System.out.print( "Enter first integer: " ); // prompt
```

uses System.out.print to display the message "Enter first integer: ". This message is called a *prompt* because it directs the user to take a specific action. Recall from Section 2.2 that identifiers starting with capital letters represent class names. So, System is a class. Class System is part of package *java.lang*. Notice that class System is not imported with an import declaration at the beginning of the program.

Software Engineering Observation 2.1

By default, package java.lang *is imported in every Java program; thus, classes in* java.lang *are the only ones in the Java API that do not require an* import *declaration.*

Line 18

```
number1 = input.nextInt(); // read first number from user
```

uses Scanner object input's nextInt method to obtain an integer from the user at the keyboard. At this point the program waits for the user to type the number and press the *Enter* key to submit the number to the program.

Technically, the user can type anything as the input value. Our program assumes that the user enters a valid integer value as requested. In this program, if the user types a noninteger value, a runtime logic error will occur and the program will terminate. Chapter 13, Exception Handling, discusses how to make your programs more robust by enabling them to handle such errors. This is also known as making your program *fault tolerant*.

In line 18, the result of the call to method nextInt (an int value) is placed in variable number1 by using the *assignment operator*, =. The statement is read as "number1 gets the value of input.nextInt()." Operator = is called a *binary operator* because it has two operands—number1 and the result of the method call input.nextInt(). Everything to the right of the assignment operator, =, is always evaluated before the assignment is performed.

Line 20

```
System.out.print( "Enter second integer: " ); // prompt
```

prompts the user to input the second integer.

Line 21

```
number2 = input.nextInt(); // read second number from user
```

reads the second integer and assigns it to variable number2.

Line 23

```
sum = number1 + number2; // add numbers
```

is an assignment statement that calculates the sum of the variables `number1` and `number2` and assigns the result to variable `sum` by using the assignment operator, =. The statement is read as "`sum` gets the value of `number1 + number2`." Most calculations are performed in assignment statements. When the program encounters the addition operation, it uses the values stored in the variables `number1` and `number2` to perform the calculation. In the preceding statement, the addition operator is a binary operator—its two operands are `number1` and `number2`. Portions of statements that contain calculations are called *expressions*. In fact, an expression is any portion of a statement that has a value associated with it. For example, the value of the expression `number1 + number2` is the sum of the numbers. Similarly, the value of the expression `input.nextInt()` is an integer typed by the user.

After the calculation has been performed, line 25

```
System.out.printf( "Sum is %d\n", sum ); // display sum
```

uses method `System.out.printf` to display the `sum`. The format specifier *%d* is a placeholder for an `int` value (in this case the value of `sum`)—the letter d stands for "decimal integer." Note that other than the `%d` format specifier, the remaining characters in the format string are all fixed text. So method `printf` displays "`Sum is `", followed by the value of `sum` (in the position of the `%d` format specifier) and a newline.

Note that calculations can also be performed inside `printf` statements. We could have combined the statements at lines 23 and 25 into the statement

```
System.out.printf( "Sum is %d\n", ( number1 + number2 ) );
```

The parentheses around the expression `number1 + number2` are not required—they are included to emphasize that the value of the expression is output in the position of the `%d` format specifier.

Java API Documentation
For each new Java API class we use, we indicate the package in which it is located. This package information is important because it helps you locate descriptions of each package and class in the *Java API documentation*. A web-based version of this documentation can be found at

```
java.sun.com/javase/6/docs/api/
```

Also, you can download this documentation to your own computer from

```
java.sun.com/javase/downloads/index.jsp
```

The download is approximately 53 megabytes (MB). Appendix G, describes how to use the Java API documentation.

2.6 Arithmetic

The *arithmetic operators* are summarized in Fig. 2.8. Note the use of various special symbols not used in algebra. The *asterisk* (*) indicates multiplication, and the *percent sign*

Java operation	Arithmetic operator	Algebraic expression	Java expression
Addition	+	$f + 7$	f + 7
Subtraction	–	$p - c$	p - c
Multiplication	*	bm	b * m
Division	/	x / y or $\dfrac{x}{y}$ or $x \div y$	x / y
Remainder	%	$r \bmod s$	r % s

Fig. 2.8 | Arithmetic operators.

(**%**) is the *remainder operator* (*called modulus* in some languages), which we'll discuss shortly. The arithmetic operators in Fig. 2.8 are binary operators because they each operate on two operands. For example, the expression f + 7 contains the binary operator + and the two operands f and 7.

Integer division yields an integer quotient—for example, the expression 7 / 4 evaluates to 1, and the expression 17 / 5 evaluates to 3. Any fractional part in integer division is simply discarded (i.e., truncated)—no rounding occurs. Java provides the remainder operator, %, which yields the remainder after division. The expression x % y yields the remainder after x is divided by y. Thus, 7 % 4 yields 3, and 17 % 5 yields 2. This operator is most commonly used with integer operands but can also be used with other arithmetic types.

Arithmetic Expressions in Straight-Line Form

Arithmetic expressions in Java must be written in *straight-line form* to facilitate entering programs into the computer. Thus, expressions such as "a divided by b" must be written as a / b, so that all constants, variables and operators appear in a straight line. The following algebraic notation is generally not acceptable to compilers:

$$\frac{a}{b}$$

Parentheses for Grouping Subexpressions

Parentheses are used to group terms in Java expressions in the same manner as in algebraic expressions. For example, to multiply a times the quantity b + c, we write

```
a * ( b + c )
```

If an expression contains *nested parentheses*, such as

```
( ( a + b ) * c )
```

the expression in the innermost set of parentheses (a + b in this case) is evaluated first. [*Note:* As in algebra, it is acceptable to place unnecessary parentheses in an expression to make the expression clearer. These are called *redundant parentheses*.]

Rules of Operator Precedence

Java applies the operators in arithmetic expressions in a precise sequence determined by the following *rules of operator precedence*, which are generally the same as those followed in algebra (Fig. 2.9):

1. Multiplication, division and remainder operations are applied first. If an expression contains several such operations, the operators are applied from left to right. Multiplication, division and remainder operators have the same level of precedence.

2. Addition and subtraction operations are applied next. If an expression contains several such operations, the operators are applied from left to right. Addition and subtraction operators have the same level of precedence.

These rules enable Java to apply operators in the correct order. When we say that operators are applied from left to right, we are referring to their *associativity*. You'll see that some operators associate from right to left. Figure 2.9 summarizes these rules of operator precedence. The table will be expanded as additional Java operators are introduced. A complete precedence chart is included in Appendix A.

Operator(s)	Operation(s)	Order of evaluation (precedence)
* / %	Multiplication Division Remainder	Evaluated first. If there are several operators of this type, they are evaluated from left to right.
+ –	Addition Subtraction	Evaluated next. If there are several operators of this type, they are evaluated from left to right.

Fig. 2.9 | Precedence of arithmetic operators.

2.7 Decision Making: Equality and Relational Operators

A *condition* is an expression that can be either *true* or *false*. This section introduces Java's *if statement* that allows a program to make a *decision* based on a condition's value. For example, the condition "grade is greater than or equal to 60" determines whether a student passed a test. If the condition in an if statement is true, the body of the if statement executes. If the condition is false, the body does not execute. We'll see an example shortly.

Conditions in if statements can be formed by using the *equality operators* (== and !=) and *relational operators* (>, <, >= and <=) summarized in Fig. 2.10. Both equality operators have the same level of precedence, which is lower than that of the relational operators. The equality operators associate from left to right. The relational operators all have the same level of precedence and also associate from left to right.

The application of Fig. 2.11 uses six if statements to compare two integers input by the user. If the condition in any of these if statements is true, the assignment statement associated with that if statement executes. The program uses a Scanner to input the two integers from the user and store them in variables number1 and number2. Then the program compares the numbers and displays the results of the comparisons that are true.

Standard algebraic equality or relational operator	Java equality or relational operator	Sample Java condition	Meaning of Java condition
Equality operators			
=	==	x == y	x is equal to y
≠	!=	x != y	x is not equal to y
Relational operators			
>	>	x > y	x is greater than y
<	<	x < y	x is less than y
≥	>=	x >= y	x is greater than or equal to y
≤	<=	x <= y	x is less than or equal to y

Fig. 2.10 | Equality and relational operators.

The declaration of class Comparison begins at line 6

```
public class Comparison
```

The class's main method (lines 9–41) begins the execution of the program. Line 12

```
Scanner input = new Scanner( System.in );
```

declares Scanner variable input and assigns it a Scanner that inputs data from the standard input (i.e., the keyboard).

```
1   // Fig. 2.11: Comparison.java
2   // Compare integers using if statements, relational operators
3   // and equality operators.
4   import java.util.Scanner; // program uses class Scanner
5
6   public class Comparison
7   {
8      // main method begins execution of Java application
9      public static void main( String args[] )
10     {
11        // create Scanner to obtain input from command window
12        Scanner input = new Scanner( System.in );
13
14        int number1; // first number to compare
15        int number2; // second number to compare
16
17        System.out.print( "Enter first integer: " ); // prompt
18        number1 = input.nextInt(); // read first number from user
```

Fig. 2.11 | Equality and relational operators. (Part 1 of 2.)

```
19
20          System.out.print( "Enter second integer: " ); // prompt
21          number2 = input.nextInt(); // read second number from user
22
23          if ( number1 == number2 )
24             System.out.printf( "%d == %d\n", number1, number2 );
25
26          if ( number1 != number2 )
27             System.out.printf( "%d != %d\n", number1, number2 );
28
29          if ( number1 < number2 )
30             System.out.printf( "%d < %d\n", number1, number2 );
31
32          if ( number1 > number2 )
33             System.out.printf( "%d > %d\n", number1, number2 );
34
35          if ( number1 <= number2 )
36             System.out.printf( "%d <= %d\n", number1, number2 );
37
38          if ( number1 >= number2 )
39             System.out.printf( "%d >= %d\n", number1, number2 );
40
41      } // end method main
42
43   } // end class Comparison
```

```
Enter first integer: 777
Enter second integer: 777
777 == 777
777 <= 777
777 >= 777
```

```
Enter first integer: 1000
Enter second integer: 2000
1000 != 2000
1000 < 2000
1000 <= 2000
```

```
Enter first integer: 2000
Enter second integer: 1000
2000 != 1000
2000 > 1000
2000 >= 1000
```

Fig. 2.11 | Equality and relational operators. (Part 2 of 2.)

Lines 14–15

```
int number1; // first number to compare
int number2; // second number to compare
```

declare the int variables used to store the values input from the user.

Lines 17–18

```
System.out.print( "Enter first integer: " ); // prompt
number1 = input.nextInt(); // read first number from user
```

prompt the user to enter the first integer and input the value, respectively. The input value is stored in variable number1.

Lines 20–21

```
System.out.print( "Enter second integer: " ); // prompt
number2 = input.nextInt(); // read second number from user
```

prompt the user to enter the second integer and input the value, respectively. The input value is stored in variable number2.

Lines 23–24

```
if ( number1 == number2 )
    System.out.printf( "%d == %d\n", number1, number2 );
```

declare an if statement that compares the values of the variables number1 and number2 to determine whether they are equal. An if statement always begins with keyword if, followed by a condition in parentheses. An if statement expects one statement in its body. The indentation of the body statement shown here is not required, but it improves the program's readability by emphasizing that the statement in line 24 is part of the if statement that begins at line 23. Line 24 executes only if the numbers stored in variables number1 and number2 are equal (i.e., the condition is true). The if statements at lines 26–27, 29–30, 32–33, 35–36 and 38–39 compare number1 and number2 with the operators !=, <, >, <= and >=, respectively. If the condition in any of the if statements is true, the corresponding body statement executes.

Common Programming Error 2.9

Forgetting the left and/or right parentheses for the condition in an if statement is a syntax error—the parentheses are required.

Common Programming Error 2.10

Confusing the equality operator, ==, with the assignment operator, =, can cause a logic error or a syntax error.

Good Programming Practice 2.10

Indent an if statement's body to make it stand out and to enhance program readability.

Note that there is no semicolon (;) at the end of the first line of each if statement. Such a semicolon would result in a logic error at execution time. For example,

```
if ( number1 == number2 ); // logic error
    System.out.printf( "%d == %d\n", number1, number2 );
```

would actually be interpreted by Java as

```
if ( number1 == number2 )
    ; // empty statement

System.out.printf( "%d == %d\n", number1, number2 );
```

where the semicolon on the line by itself—called the *empty statement*—is the statement to execute if the condition in the if statement is true. When the empty statement executes, no task is performed in the program. The program then continues with the output statement, which always executes, regardless of whether the condition is true or false, because the output statement is not part of the if statement.

Common Programming Error 2.11

Placing a semicolon immediately after the right parenthesis of the condition in an if statement is normally a logic error.

Note the use of white space in Fig. 2.11. Recall that white-space characters, such as tabs, newlines and spaces, are normally ignored by the compiler. So statements may be split over several lines and may be spaced according to the programmer's preferences without affecting the meaning of a program. It is incorrect to split identifiers and strings. Ideally, statements should be kept small, but this is not always possible.

Good Programming Practice 2.11

A lengthy statement can be spread over several lines. If a single statement must be split across lines, choose breaking points that make sense, such as after a comma in a comma-separated list, or after an operator in a lengthy expression. If a statement is split across two or more lines, indent all subsequent lines until the end of the statement.

Figure 2.12 shows the precedence of the operators introduced in this chapter. The operators are shown from top to bottom in decreasing order of precedence. All these operators, with the exception of the assignment operator, =, associate from left to right. Addition is left associative, so an expression like x + y + z is evaluated as if it had been written as (x + y) + z. The assignment operator, =, associates from right to left, so an expression like x = y = 0 is evaluated as if it had been written as x = (y = 0), which, as we'll soon see, first assigns the value 0 to variable y and then assigns the result of that assignment, 0, to x.

Error-Prevention Tip 2.7

Refer to the operator precedence chart (Appendix A) when writing expressions containing many operators. Confirm that the operations in the expression are performed in the order you expect. If you are uncertain about the order of evaluation in a complex expression, use parentheses to force the order, exactly as you would do in algebraic expressions.

Operators	Associativity	Type
* / %	left to right	multiplicative
+ -	left to right	additive
< <= > >=	left to right	relational
== !=	left to right	equality
=	right to left	assignment

Fig. 2.12 | Precedence and associativity of operations discussed.

2.8 (Optional) Software Engineering Case Study: Examining the Requirements Document

Now we begin our optional object-oriented design and implementation case study. The Software Engineering Case Study sections at the ends of this and the next several chapters will ease you into object orientation by examining an automated teller machine (ATM) case study. This case study will provide you with a concise, carefully paced, complete design and implementation experience. In Chapters 3–8 and 10, we'll perform the various steps of an object-oriented design (OOD) process using the UML while relating these steps to the object-oriented concepts discussed in the chapters. Appendix H implements the ATM using the techniques of object-oriented programming (OOP) in Java. We present the complete case-study solution. This is not an exercise; rather, it is an end-to-end learning experience that concludes with a detailed walkthrough of the Java code that implements our design.

We begin our design process by presenting a *requirements document* that specifies the overall purpose of the ATM system and *what* it must do. Throughout the case study, we refer to the requirements document to determine precisely what functionality the system must include.

Requirements Document

A local bank intends to install a new automated teller machine (ATM) to allow users (i.e., bank customers) to perform basic financial transactions (Fig. 2.13). Each user can have only one account at the bank. ATM users should be able to view their account balance, withdraw cash (i.e., take money out of an account) and deposit funds (i.e., place money

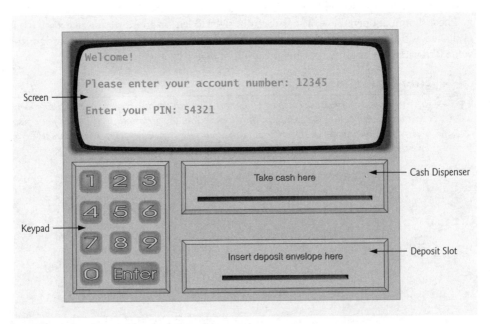

Fig. 2.13 | Automated teller machine user interface.

into an account). The user interface of the automated teller machine contains the following components:

- a screen that displays messages to the user
- a keypad that receives numeric input from the user
- a cash dispenser that dispenses cash to the user and
- a deposit slot that receives deposit envelopes from the user.

The cash dispenser begins each day loaded with 500 $20 bills. [*Note:* Due to the limited scope of this case study, certain elements of the ATM described here do not accurately mimic those of a real ATM. For example, a real ATM typically contains a device that reads a user's account number from an ATM card, whereas this ATM asks the user to type the account number on the keypad. A real ATM also usually prints a receipt at the end of a session, but all output from this ATM appears on the screen.]

The bank wants you to develop software to perform the financial transactions initiated by bank customers through the ATM. The bank will integrate the software with the ATM's hardware at a later time. The software should encapsulate the functionality of the hardware devices (e.g., cash dispenser, deposit slot) within software components, but it need not concern itself with how these devices perform their duties. The ATM hardware has not been developed yet, so instead of writing your software to run on the ATM, you should develop a first version of the software to run on a personal computer. This version should use the computer's monitor to simulate the ATM's screen, and the computer's keyboard to simulate the ATM's keypad.

An ATM session consists of authenticating a user (i.e., proving the user's identity) based on an account number and personal identification number (PIN), followed by creating and executing financial transactions. To authenticate a user and perform transactions, the ATM must interact with the bank's account information database (i.e., an organized collection of data stored on a computer). For each bank account, the database stores an account number, a PIN and a balance indicating the amount of money in the account. [*Note:* We assume that the bank plans to build only one ATM, so we do not need to worry about multiple ATMs accessing this database at the same time. Furthermore, we assume that the bank does not make any changes to the information in the database while a user is accessing the ATM. Also, any business system like an ATM faces reasonably complicated security issues that are beyond the scope of this book. We make the simplifying assumption, however, that the bank trusts the ATM to access and manipulate the information in the database without significant security measures.]

Upon first approaching the ATM (assuming no one is currently using it), the user should experience the following sequence of events (shown in Fig. 2.13):

1. The screen displays a welcome message and prompts the user to enter an account number.

2. The user enters a five-digit account number using the keypad.

3. The screen prompts the user to enter the PIN (personal identification number) associated with the specified account number.

4. The user enters a five-digit PIN using the keypad.

5. If the user enters a valid account number and the correct PIN for that account, the screen displays the main menu (Fig. 2.14). If the user enters an invalid account number or an incorrect PIN, the screen displays an appropriate message, then the ATM returns to *Step 1* to restart the authentication process.

After the ATM authenticates the user, the main menu (Fig. 2.14) should contain a numbered option for each of the three types of transactions: balance inquiry (option 1), withdrawal (option 2) and deposit (option 3). The main menu also should contain an option to allow the user to exit the system (option 4). The user then chooses either to perform a transaction (by entering 1, 2 or 3) or to exit the system (by entering 4).

If the user enters 1 to make a balance inquiry, the screen displays the user's account balance. To do so, the ATM must retrieve the balance from the bank's database.

The following steps describe the actions that occur when the user enters 2 to make a withdrawal:

1. The screen displays a menu (shown in Fig. 2.15) containing standard withdrawal amounts: $20 (option 1), $40 (option 2), $60 (option 3), $100 (option 4) and $200 (option 5). The menu also contains an option to allow the user to cancel the transaction (option 6).

2. The user enters a menu selection using the keypad.

3. If the withdrawal amount chosen is greater than the user's account balance, the screen displays a message stating this and telling the user to choose a smaller amount. The ATM then returns to *Step 1*. If the withdrawal amount chosen is less than or equal to the user's account balance (i.e., an acceptable amount), the ATM proceeds to *Step 4*. If the user chooses to cancel the transaction (option 6), the ATM displays the main menu and waits for user input.

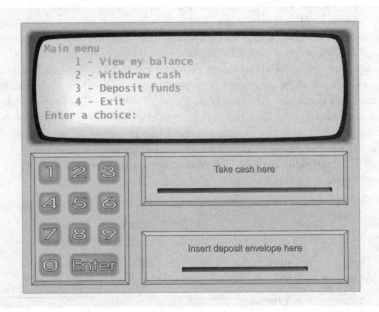

Fig. 2.14 | ATM main menu.

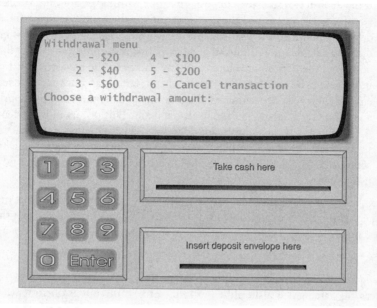

Fig. 2.15 | ATM withdrawal menu.

4. If the cash dispenser contains enough cash to satisfy the request, the ATM proceeds to *Step 5*. Otherwise, the screen displays a message indicating the problem and telling the user to choose a smaller withdrawal amount. The ATM then returns to *Step 1*.

5. The ATM debits the withdrawal amount from the user's account in the bank's database (i.e., subtracts the withdrawal amount from the user's account balance).

6. The cash dispenser dispenses the desired amount of money to the user.

7. The screen displays a message reminding the user to take the money.

The following steps describe the actions that occur when the user enters 3 to make a deposit:

1. The screen prompts the user to enter a deposit amount or type 0 (zero) to cancel the transaction.

2. The user enters a deposit amount or 0 using the keypad. [*Note:* The keypad does not contain a decimal point or a dollar sign, so the user cannot type a real dollar amount (e.g., $1.25). Instead, the user must enter a deposit amount as a number of cents (e.g., 125). The ATM then divides this number by 100 to obtain a number representing a dollar amount (e.g., $125 \div 100 = 1.25$).]

3. If the user specifies a deposit amount, the ATM proceeds to *Step 4*. If the user chooses to cancel the transaction (by entering 0), the ATM displays the main menu and waits for user input.

4. The screen displays a message telling the user to insert a deposit envelope into the deposit slot.

5. If the deposit slot receives a deposit envelope within two minutes, the ATM credits the deposit amount to the user's account in the bank's database (i.e., adds the deposit amount to the user's account balance). [*Note:* This money is not immediately available for withdrawal. The bank first must physically verify the amount of cash in the deposit envelope, and any checks in the envelope must clear (i.e., money must be transferred from the check writer's account to the check recipient's account). When either of these events occurs, the bank appropriately updates the user's balance stored in its database. This occurs independently of the ATM system.] If the deposit slot does not receive a deposit envelope within this time period, the screen displays a message that the system has canceled the transaction due to inactivity. The ATM then displays the main menu and waits for user input.

After the system successfully executes a transaction, it should return to the main menu so that the user can perform additional transactions. If the user chooses to exit the system, the screen should display a thank you message, then display the welcome message for the next user.

Analyzing the ATM System

The preceding statement is a simplified example of a requirements document. Typically, such a document is the result of a detailed process of *requirements gathering* that might include interviews with possible users of the system and specialists in fields related to the system. For example, a systems analyst who is hired to prepare a requirements document for banking software (e.g., the ATM system described here) might interview financial experts to gain a better understanding of what the software must do. The analyst would use the information gained to compile a list of *system requirements* to guide systems designers as they design the system.

The process of requirements gathering is a key task of the first stage of the software life cycle. The *software life cycle* specifies the stages through which software goes from the time it is first conceived to the time it is retired from use. These stages typically include: analysis, design, implementation, testing and debugging, deployment, maintenance and retirement. Several software life-cycle models exist, each with its own preferences and specifications for when and how often software engineers should perform each of these stages. *Waterfall models* perform each stage once in succession, whereas *iterative models* may repeat one or more stages several times throughout a product's life cycle.

The analysis stage of the software life cycle focuses on defining the problem to be solved. When designing any system, one must *solve the problem right*, but of equal importance, one must *solve the right problem*. Systems analysts collect the requirements that indicate the specific problem to solve. Our requirements document describes the requirements of our ATM system in sufficient detail that you do not need to go through an extensive analysis stage—it has been done for you.

To capture what a proposed system should do, developers often employ a technique known as *use case modeling*. This process identifies the *use cases* of the system, each of which represents a different capability that the system provides to its clients. For example, ATMs typically have several use cases, such as "View Account Balance," "Withdraw Cash," "Deposit Funds," "Transfer Funds Between Accounts" and "Buy Postage Stamps." The simplified ATM system we build in this case study allows only the first three use cases.

Each use case describes a typical scenario for which the user uses the system. You have already read descriptions of the ATM system's use cases in the requirements document; the lists of steps required to perform each transaction type (i.e., balance inquiry, withdrawal and deposit) actually described the three use cases of our ATM—"View Account Balance," "Withdraw Cash" and "Deposit Funds," respectively.

Use Case Diagrams

We now introduce the first of several UML diagrams in the case study. We create a *use case diagram* to model the interactions between a system's clients (in this case study, bank customers) and its use cases. The goal is to show the kinds of interactions users have with a system without providing the details—these are provided in other UML diagrams (which we present throughout this case study). Use case diagrams are often accompanied by informal text that describes the use cases in more detail—like the text that appears in the requirements document. Use case diagrams are produced during the analysis stage of the software life cycle. In larger systems, use case diagrams are indispensable tools that help system designers remain focused on satisfying the users' needs.

Figure 2.16 shows the use case diagram for our ATM system. The stick figure represents an *actor*, which defines the roles that an external entity—such as a person or another system—plays when interacting with the system. For our automated teller machine, the actor is a User who can view account balance, withdraw cash and deposit funds from the ATM. The User is not an actual person, but instead comprises the roles that a real person—when playing the part of a User—can play while interacting with the ATM. Note that a use case diagram can include multiple actors. For example, the use case diagram for a real bank's ATM system might also include an actor named Administrator who refills the cash dispenser each day.

Our requirements document supplies the actors—"ATM users should be able to view their account balance, withdraw cash and deposit funds." Therefore, the actor in each of the three use cases is the user who interacts with the ATM. An external entity—a real person—plays the part of the user to perform financial transactions. Figure 2.16 shows one actor, whose name, User, appears below the actor in the diagram. The UML models each use case as an oval connected to an actor with a solid line.

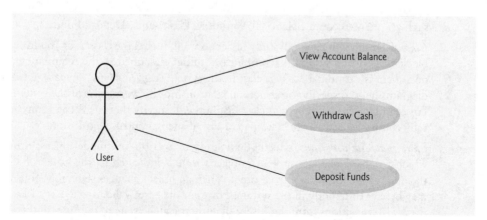

Fig. 2.16 | Use case diagram for the ATM system from the User's perspective.

Software engineers (more precisely, systems designers) must analyze the requirements document or a set of use cases and design the system before programmers implement it in a particular programming language. During the analysis stage, systems designers focus on understanding the requirements document to produce a high-level specification that describes *what* the system is supposed to do. The output of the design stage—a ***design specification***—should specify clearly *how* the system should be constructed to satisfy these requirements. In the next several Software Engineering Case Study sections, we perform the steps of a simple object-oriented design (OOD) process on the ATM system to produce a design specification containing a collection of UML diagrams and supporting text. The UML is designed for use with any OOD process. Many such processes exist, the most well-known of which is the Rational Unified Process™ (RUP) developed by Rational Software Corporation. RUP is a rich process intended for designing "industrial strength" applications. For this case study, we present our own simplified design process.

Designing the ATM System

We now begin the design stage of our ATM system. A ***system*** is a set of components that interact to solve a problem. For example, to perform the ATM system's designated tasks, our ATM system has a user interface (Fig. 2.13), contains software that executes financial transactions and interacts with a database of bank account information. ***System structure*** describes the system's objects and their interrelationships. ***System behavior*** describes how the system changes as its objects interact with one another. Every system has both structure and behavior—designers must specify both. There are several distinct types of system structures and behaviors. For example, the interactions among objects in the system differ from those between the user and the system, yet both constitute a portion of the system behavior.

The UML 2 standard specifies 13 diagram types for documenting the system models. Each models a distinct characteristic of a system's structure or behavior—six diagrams relate to system structure; the remaining seven relate to system behavior. We list here only the six types used in our case study—one of these (class diagrams) models system structure, whereas the remaining five model system behavior. We overview the remaining seven UML diagram types in y.

1. *Use case diagrams*, such as the one in Fig. 2.16, model the interactions between a system and its external entities (actors) in terms of use cases (system capabilities, such as "View Account Balance," "Withdraw Cash" and "Deposit Funds").

2. *Class diagrams*, which you'll study in Section 3.9, model the classes, or "building blocks," used in a system. Each noun or "thing" described in the requirements document is a candidate to be a class in the system (e.g., Account, Keypad). Class diagrams help us specify the structural relationships between parts of the system. For example, the ATM system class diagram will specify that the ATM is physically composed of a screen, a keypad, a cash dispenser and a deposit slot.

3. *State machine diagrams*, which you'll study in Section 5.9, model the ways in which an object changes state. An object's *state* is indicated by the values of all the object's attributes at a given time. When an object changes state, that object may behave differently in the system. For example, after validating a user's PIN, the ATM transitions from the "user not authenticated" state to the "user authenticated" state, at which point the ATM allows the user to perform financial transactions (e.g., view account balance, withdraw cash, deposit funds).

4. *Activity diagrams*, which you'll also study in Section 5.9, model an object's *activity*—the object's workflow (sequence of events) during program execution. An activity diagram models the actions the object performs and specifies the order in which the object performs these actions. For example, an activity diagram shows that the ATM must obtain the balance of the user's account (from the bank's account information database) before the screen can display the balance to the user.

5. *Communication diagrams* (called *collaboration diagrams* in earlier versions of the UML) model the interactions among objects in a system, with an emphasis on *what* interactions occur. You'll learn in Section 7.13 that these diagrams show which objects must interact to perform an ATM transaction. For example, the ATM must communicate with the bank's account information database to retrieve an account balance.

6. *Sequence diagrams* also model the interactions among the objects in a system, but unlike communication diagrams, they emphasize *when* interactions occur. You'll learn in Section 7.13 that these diagrams help show the order in which interactions occur in executing a financial transaction. For example, the screen prompts the user to enter a withdrawal amount before cash is dispensed.

In Section 3.9, we continue designing our ATM system by identifying the classes from the requirements document. We accomplish this by extracting key nouns and noun phrases from the requirements document. Using these classes, we develop our first draft of the class diagram that models the structure of our ATM system.

Internet and Web Resources

The following URLs provide information on object-oriented design with the UML.

`www-306.ibm.com/software/rational/offerings/design.html`
Provides information about IBM Rational software available for designing systems. Provides downloads of 30-day trial versions of several products, such as IBM Rational Application Developer.

`www.borland.com/us/products/together/index.html`
Provides a free 30-day license to download a trial version of Borland® Together® ControlCenter™—a software-development tool that supports the UML.

`argouml.tigris.org`
Contains information and downloads for ArgoUML, a free open-source UML tool written in Java.

`www.objectsbydesign.com/books/booklist.html`
Lists books on the UML and object-oriented design.

`www.objectsbydesign.com/tools/umltools_byCompany.html`
Lists software tools that use the UML, such as IBM Rational Rose, Embarcadero Describe, Sparx Systems Enterprise Architect, I-Logix Rhapsody and Gentleware Poseidon for UML.

`www.ootips.org/ood-principles.html`
Provides answers to the question, "What Makes a Good Object-Oriented Design?"

`parlezuml.com/tutorials/umlforjava.htm`
Provides a UML tutorial for Java developers that presents UML diagrams side by side with the Java code that implements them.

`www.cetus-links.org/oo_uml.html`
Introduces the UML and provides links to numerous UML resources.

`www.agilemodeling.com/essays/umlDiagrams.htm`
Provides in-depth descriptions and tutorials on each of the 13 UML-2 diagram types.

Recommended Readings

The following books provide information on object-oriented design with the UML.

Booch, G. *Object-Oriented Analysis and Design with Applications.* 3rd ed. Boston: Addison-Wesley, 2004.

Eriksson, H., et al. *UML 2 Toolkit.* Hoboken, NJ: John Wiley & Sons, 2003.

Fowler, M. *UML Distilled.* 3rd ed. Boston: Addison-Wesley Professional, 2004.

Kruchten, P. *The Rational Unified Process: An Introduction.* Boston: Addison-Wesley, 2004.

Larman, C. *Applying UML and Patterns: An Introduction to Object-Oriented Analysis and Design.* 2nd ed. Upper Saddle River, NJ: Prentice Hall, 2002.

Roques, P. *UML in Practice: The Art of Modeling Software Systems Demonstrated Through Worked Examples and Solutions.* Hoboken, NJ: John Wiley & Sons, 2004.

Rosenberg, D., and K. Scott. *Applying Use Case Driven Object Modeling with UML: An Annotated e-Commerce Example.* Reading, MA: Addison-Wesley, 2001.

Rumbaugh, J., I. Jacobson and G. Booch. *The Complete UML Training Course.* Upper Saddle River, NJ: Prentice Hall, 2000.

Rumbaugh, J., I. Jacobson and G. Booch. *The Unified Modeling Language Reference Manual.* Reading, MA: Addison-Wesley, 1999.

Rumbaugh, J., I. Jacobson and G. Booch. *The Unified Software Development Process.* Reading, MA: Addison-Wesley, 1999.

Schneider, G. and J. Winters. *Applying Use Cases: A Practical Guide.* 2nd ed. Boston: Addison-Wesley Professional, 2002.

Software Engineering Case Study Self-Review Exercises

2.1   Suppose we enabled a user of our ATM system to transfer money between two bank accounts. Modify the use case diagram of Fig. 2.16 to reflect this change.

2.2   _____ model the interactions among objects in a system with an emphasis on *when* these interactions occur.
   a) Class diagrams
   b) Sequence diagrams
   c) Communication diagrams
   d) Activity diagrams

2.3   Which of the following choices lists stages of a typical software life cycle in sequential order?
   a) design, analysis, implementation, testing
   b) design, analysis, testing, implementation
   c) analysis, design, testing, implementation
   d) analysis, design, implementation, testing

Answers to Software Engineering Case Study Self-Review Exercises

2.1   Figure 2.17 contains a use case diagram for a modified version of our ATM system that also allows users to transfer money between accounts.

2.2   b.

2.3   d.

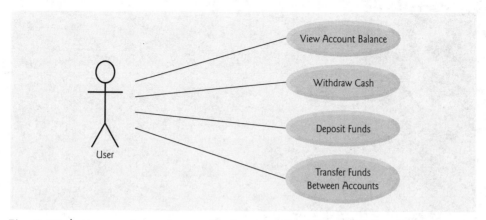

Fig. 2.17 | Use case diagram for a modified version of our ATM system that also allows users to transfer money between accounts.

2.9 Wrap-Up

You learned many important features of Java in this chapter, including displaying data on the screen in a Command Prompt, inputting data from the keyboard, performing calculations and making decisions. As you'll see in Chapter 3, Java applications typically contain just a few lines of code in method main—these statements normally create the objects that perform the work of the application. In Chapter 3, you'll see how to implement your own classes and use objects of those classes in applications.

3

Introduction to Classes and Objects

OBJECTIVES

In this chapter you'll learn:

- What classes, objects, methods and instance variables are.

- How to declare a class and use it to create an object.

- How to declare methods in a class to implement the class's behaviors.

- How to declare instance variables in a class to implement the class's attributes.

- How to call an object's methods to make those methods perform their tasks.

- The differences between instance variables of a class and local variables of a method.

- How to use a constructor to ensure that an object's data is initialized when the object is created.

- The differences between primitive and reference types.

You will see something new.
Two things. And I call them
Thing One and Thing Two.
—Dr. Theodor Seuss Geisel

Nothing can have value
without being an object of
utility.
—Karl Marx

Your public servants serve
you right.
—Adlai E. Stevenson

Knowing how to answer one
who speaks,
To reply to one who sends a
message.
—Amenemope

Outline

3.1 Introduction

3.2 Classes, Objects, Methods and Instance Variables

3.3 Declaring a Class with a Method and Instantiating an Object of a Class

3.4 Declaring a Method with a Parameter

3.5 Instance Variables, *set* Methods and *get* Methods

3.6 Primitive Types vs. Reference Types

3.7 Initializing Objects with Constructors

3.8 Floating-Point Numbers and Type `double`

3.9 (Optional) Software Engineering Case Study: Identifying the Classes in a Requirements Document

3.10 Wrap-Up

3.1 Introduction

We introduced the basic terminology and concepts of object-oriented programming in Section 1.9. In Chapter 2, you began to use those concepts to create simple applications that displayed messages to the user, obtained information from the user, performed calculations and made decisions. One common feature of every application in Chapter 2 was that all the statements that performed tasks were located in method `main`. Typically, the applications you develop in this book will consist of two or more classes, each containing one or more methods. If you become part of a development team in industry, you might work on applications that contain hundreds, or even thousands, of classes. In this chapter, we present a simple framework for organizing object-oriented applications in Java.

First, we motivate the notion of classes with a real-world example. Then we present five complete working applications to demonstrate creating and using your own classes. The first four of these examples begin our case study on developing a grade-book class that instructors can use to maintain student test scores. This case study is enhanced over the next several chapters, culminating with the version presented in Chapter 7, Arrays. The last example in the chapter introduces floating-point numbers—that is, numbers containing decimal points, such as 0.0345, −7.23 and 100.7—in the context of a bank account class that maintains a customer's balance.

3.2 Classes, Objects, Methods and Instance Variables

Let's begin with a simple analogy to help you understand classes and their contents. Suppose you want to drive a car and make it go faster by pressing down on its accelerator pedal. What must happen before you can do this? Well, before you can drive a car, someone has to design it. A car typically begins as engineering drawings, similar to the blueprints used to design a house. These engineering drawings include the design for an accelerator pedal to make the car go faster. The pedal "hides" from the driver the complex mechanisms that actually make the car go faster, just as the brake pedal "hides" the mechanisms that slow the car and the steering wheel "hides" the mechanisms that turn the car. This enables people with little or no knowledge of how engines work to drive a car easily.

Unfortunately, you cannot drive the engineering drawings of a car. Before you can drive a car, the car must be built from the engineering drawings that describe it. A completed car has an actual accelerator pedal to make the car go faster, but even that's not enough—the car won't accelerate on its own, so the driver must press the accelerator pedal.

Now let's use our car example to introduce the key programming concepts of this section. Performing a task in a program requires a method. The method describes the mechanisms that actually perform its tasks. The method hides from its user the complex tasks that it performs, just as the accelerator pedal of a car hides from the driver the complex mechanisms of making the car go faster. In Java, we begin by creating a program unit called a class to house a method, just as a car's engineering drawings house the design of an accelerator pedal. In a class, you provide one or more methods that are designed to perform the class's tasks. For example, a class that represents a bank account might contain one method to deposit money to an account, another to withdraw money from an account and a third to inquire what the current balance is.

Just as you cannot drive an engineering drawing of a car, you cannot "drive" a class. Just as someone has to build a car from its engineering drawings before you can actually drive a car, you must build an object of a class before you can get a program to perform the tasks the class describes how to do. That is one reason Java is known as an object-oriented programming language.

When you drive a car, pressing its gas pedal sends a message to the car to perform a task—that is, make the car go faster. Similarly, you send *messages* to an object—each message is known as a *method call* and tells a method of the object to perform its task.

Thus far, we've used the car analogy to introduce classes, objects and methods. In addition to a car's capabilities, a car also has many attributes, such as its color, the number of doors, the amount of gas in its tank, its current speed and its total miles driven (i.e., its odometer reading). Like the car's capabilities, these attributes are represented as part of a car's design in its engineering diagrams. As you drive a car, these attributes are always associated with the car. Every car maintains its own attributes. For example, each car knows how much gas is in its own gas tank, but not how much is in the tanks of other cars. Similarly, an object has attributes that are carried with the object as it is used in a program. These attributes are specified as part of the object's class. For example, a bank account object has a balance attribute that represents the amount of money in the account. Each bank account object knows the balance in the account it represents, but not the balances of the other accounts in the bank. Attributes are specified by the class's *instance variables*.

The remainder of this chapter presents examples that demonstrate the concepts we introduced in the context of the car analogy. The first four examples incrementally build a GradeBook class to demonstrate these concepts:

1. The first example presents a GradeBook class with one method that simply displays a welcome message when it is called. We then show how to create an object of that class and call the method so that it displays the welcome message.

2. The second example modifies the first by allowing the method to receive a course name as an argument and by displaying the name as part of the welcome message.

3. The third example shows how to store the course name in a GradeBook object. For this version of the class, we also show how to use methods to set the course name and obtain the course name.

4. The fourth example demonstrates how the data in a GradeBook object can be initialized when the object is created—the initialization is performed by the class's constructor.

The last example in the chapter presents an Account class that reinforces the concepts presented in the first four examples and introduces floating-point numbers. For this purpose, we present an Account class that represents a bank account and maintains its balance as a floating-point number. The class contains two methods—one that credits a deposit to the account, thus increasing the balance, and another that retrieves the balance. The class's constructor allows the balance of each Account object to be initialized as the object is created. We create two Account objects and make deposits into each to show that each object maintains its own balance. The example also demonstrates how to input and display floating-point numbers.

3.3 Declaring a Class with a Method and Instantiating an Object of a Class

We begin with an example that consists of classes GradeBook (Fig. 3.1) and GradeBookTest (Fig. 3.2). Class GradeBook (declared in file GradeBook.java) will be used to display a message on the screen (Fig. 3.2) welcoming the instructor to the grade-book application. Class GradeBookTest (declared in file GradeBookTest.java) is an application class in which the main method will use class GradeBook. Each class declaration that begins with keyword public must be stored in a file that has the same name as the class and ends with the .java file-name extension. Thus, classes GradeBook and GradeBookTest must be declared in separate files, because each class is declared public.

 Common Programming Error 3.1

Declaring more than one public class in the same file is a compilation error.

Class GradeBook
The GradeBook class declaration (Fig. 3.1) contains a displayMessage method (lines 7–10) that displays a message on the screen. Line 9 of the class performs the work of displaying the message. Recall that a class is like a blueprint—we'll need to make an object of this class and call its method to get line 9 to execute and display its message.

```
1   // Fig. 3.1: GradeBook.java
2   // Class declaration with one method.
3
4   public class GradeBook
5   {
6      // display a welcome message to the GradeBook user
7      public void displayMessage()
8      {
9         System.out.println( "Welcome to the Grade Book!" );
10     } // end method displayMessage
11
12  } // end class GradeBook
```

Fig. 3.1 | Class declaration with one method.

The class declaration begins in line 4. The keyword public is an *access modifier*. For now, we'll simply declare every class public. Every class declaration contains keyword class followed immediately by the class's name. Every class's body is enclosed in a pair of left and right braces ({ and }), as in lines 5 and 12 of class GradeBook.

In Chapter 2, each class we declared had one method named main. Class GradeBook also has one method—displayMessage (lines 7–10). Recall that main is a special method that is always called automatically by the Java Virtual Machine (JVM) when you execute an application. Most methods do not get called automatically. As you'll soon see, you must call method displayMessage to tell it to perform its task.

The method declaration begins with keyword public to indicate that the method is "available to the public"—that is, it can be called from outside the class declaration's body by methods of other classes. Keyword void indicates that this method will perform a task but will not return (i.e., give back) any information to its *calling method* when it completes its task. You have already used methods that return information—for example, in Chapter 2 you used Scanner method nextInt to input an integer typed by the user at the keyboard. When nextInt inputs a value, it returns that value for use in the program.

The name of the method, displayMessage, follows the return type. By convention, method names begin with a lowercase first letter and all subsequent words in the name begin with a capital letter. The parentheses after the method name indicate that this is a method. An empty set of parentheses, as shown in line 7, indicates that this method does not require additional information to perform its task. Line 7 is commonly referred to as the *method header*. Every method's body is delimited by left and right braces ({ and }), as in lines 8 and 10.

The body of a method contains statement(s) that perform the method's task. In this case, the method contains one statement (line 9) that displays the message "Welcome to the Grade Book!" followed by a newline in the command window. After this statement executes, the method has completed its task.

Next, we'd like to use class GradeBook in an application. As you learned in Chapter 2, method main begins the execution of every application. A class that contains method main is a Java application. Such a class is special because the JVM can use main as an entry point to begin execution. Class GradeBook is not an application because it does not contain main. Therefore, if you try to execute GradeBook by typing java GradeBook in the command window, you'll receive an error message like:

```
Exception in thread "main" java.lang.NoSuchMethodError: main
```

This was not a problem in Chapter 2, because every class you declared had a main method. To fix this problem for the GradeBook, we must either declare a separate class that contains a main method or place a main method in class GradeBook. To help you prepare for the larger programs you'll encounter later in this book and in industry, we use a separate class (GradeBookTest in this example) containing method main to test each new class we create in this chapter.

Class GradeBookTest

The GradeBookTest class declaration (Fig. 3.2) contains the main method that will control our application's execution. Any class that contains main declared as shown in line 7 can be used to execute an application. The GradeBookTest class declaration begins in line 4

```
1    // Fig. 3.2: GradeBookTest.java
2    // Create a GradeBook object and call its displayMessage method.
3
4    public class GradeBookTest
5    {
6       // main method begins program execution
7       public static void main( String args[] )
8       {
9          // create a GradeBook object and assign it to myGradeBook
10         GradeBook myGradeBook = new GradeBook();
11
12         // call myGradeBook's displayMessage method
13         myGradeBook.displayMessage();
14      } // end main
15
16   } // end class GradeBookTest
```

```
Welcome to the Grade Book!
```

Fig. 3.2 | Creating an object of class GradeBook and calling its displayMessage method.

and ends in line 16. The class contains only a main method, which is typical of many classes that begin an application's execution.

Lines 7–14 declare method main. Recall from Chapter 2 that the main header must appear as shown in line 7; otherwise, the application will not execute. A key part of enabling the JVM to locate and call method main to begin the application's execution is the static keyword (line 7), which indicates that main is a static method. A static method is special because it can be called without first creating an object of the class in which the method is declared. We thoroughly explain static methods in Chapter 6, Methods: A Deeper Look.

In this application, we'd like to call class GradeBook's displayMessage method to display the welcome message in the command window. Typically, you cannot call a method that belongs to another class until you create an object of that class, as shown in line 10. We begin by declaring variable myGradeBook. Note that the variable's type is GradeBook—the class we declared in Fig. 3.1. Each new class you create becomes a new type that can be used to declare variables and create objects. Programmers can declare new class types as needed; this is one reason why Java is known as an *extensible language*.

Variable myGradeBook is initialized with the result of the *class instance creation expression* new GradeBook(). Keyword new creates a new object of the class specified to the right of the keyword (i.e., GradeBook). The parentheses to the right of GradeBook are required. As you'll learn in Section 3.7, those parentheses in combination with a class name represent a call to a *constructor*, which is similar to a method, but is used only at the time an object is created to initialize the object's data. In that section you'll see that data can be placed in parentheses to specify initial values for the object's data. For now, we simply leave the parentheses empty.

Just as we can use object System.out to call methods print, printf and println, we can use object myGradeBook to call method displayMessage. Line 13 calls the method displayMessage (lines 7–10 of Fig. 3.1) using myGradeBook followed by a *dot separator*

(.), the method name displayMessage and an empty set of parentheses. This call causes the displayMessage method to perform its task. This method call differs from those in Chapter 2 that displayed information in a command window—each of those method calls provided arguments that specified the data to display. At the beginning of line 13, "myGradeBook." indicates that main should use the myGradeBook object that was created in line 10. Line 7 of Fig. 3.1 indicates that method displayMessage has an empty parameter list—that is, displayMessage does not require additional information to perform its task. For this reason, the method call (line 13 of Fig. 3.2) specifies an empty set of parentheses after the method name to indicate that no arguments are being passed to method displayMessage. When method displayMessage completes its task, method main continues executing in line 14. This is the end of method main, so the program terminates.

Compiling an Application with Multiple Classes

You must compile the classes in Fig. 3.1 and Fig. 3.2 before you can execute the application. First, change to the directory that contains the application's source-code files. Next, type the command

```
javac GradeBook.java GradeBookTest.java
```

to compile both classes at once. If the directory containing the application includes only this application's files, you can compile all the classes in the directory with the command

```
javac *.java
```

The asterisk (*) in *.java indicates that all files in the current directory that end with the file name extension ".java" should be compiled.

UML Class Diagram for Class GradeBook

Figure 3.3 presents a *UML class diagram* for class GradeBook of Fig. 3.1. Recall from Section 1.9 that the UML is a graphical language used by programmers to represent object-oriented systems in a standardized manner. In the UML, each class is modeled in a class diagram as a rectangle with three compartments. The top compartment contains the name of the class centered horizontally in boldface type. The middle compartment contains the class's attributes, which correspond to instance variables in Java. In Fig. 3.3, the middle compartment is empty because the version of class GradeBook in Fig. 3.1 does not have any attributes. The bottom compartment contains the class's operations, which correspond to methods in Java. The UML models operations by listing the operation name preceded by an access modifier and followed by a set of parentheses. Class GradeBook has one method, displayMessage, so the bottom compartment of Fig. 3.3 lists one operation with this name. Method displayMessage does not require additional information to per-

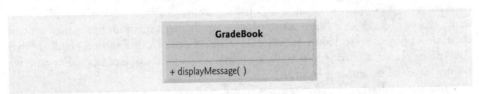

Fig. 3.3 | UML class diagram indicating that class GradeBook has a public displayMessage operation.

form its tasks, so the parentheses following the method name in the class diagram are empty, just as they were in the method's declaration in line 7 of Fig. 3.1. The plus sign (+) in front of the operation name indicates that displayMessage is a public operation in the UML (i.e., a public method in Java). We'll often use UML class diagrams to summarize a class's attributes and operations.

3.4 Declaring a Method with a Parameter

In our car analogy from Section 3.2, we discussed the fact that pressing a car's gas pedal sends a message to the car to perform a task—make the car go faster. But how fast should the car accelerate? As you know, the farther down you press the pedal, the faster the car accelerates. So the message to the car actually includes the task to perform and additional information that helps the car perform the task. This additional information is known as a *parameter*—the value of the parameter helps the car determine how fast to accelerate. Similarly, a method can require one or more parameters that represent additional information it needs to perform its task. A method call supplies values—called arguments—for each of the method's parameters. For example, the method System.out.println requires an argument that specifies the data to output in a command window. Similarly, to make a deposit into a bank account, a deposit method specifies a parameter that represents the deposit amount. When the deposit method is called, an argument value representing the deposit amount is assigned to the method's parameter. The method then makes a deposit of that amount.

Our next example declares class GradeBook (Fig. 3.4) with a displayMessage method that displays the course name as part of the welcome message. (See the sample execution in Fig. 3.5.) The new displayMessage method requires a parameter that represents the course name to output.

Before discussing the new features of class GradeBook, let's see how the new class is used from the main method of class GradeBookTest (Fig. 3.5). Line 12 creates a Scanner named input for reading the course name from the user. Line 15 creates an object of class GradeBook and assigns it to variable myGradeBook. Line 18 prompts the user to enter a course name. Line 19 reads the name from the user and assigns it to the nameOfCourse variable, using Scanner method nextLine to perform the input. The user types the course name and presses *Enter* to submit the course name to the program. Note that pressing *Enter*

```
1   // Fig. 3.4: GradeBook.java
2   // Class declaration with a method that has a parameter.
3
4   public class GradeBook
5   {
6      // display a welcome message to the GradeBook user
7      public void displayMessage( String courseName )
8      {
9         System.out.printf( "Welcome to the grade book for\n%s!\n",
10           courseName );
11      } // end method displayMessage
12
13   } // end class GradeBook
```

Fig. 3.4 | Class declaration with one method that has a parameter.

```
 1   // Fig. 3.5: GradeBookTest.java
 2   // Create GradeBook object and pass a String to
 3   // its displayMessage method.
 4   import java.util.Scanner; // program uses Scanner
 5
 6   public class GradeBookTest
 7   {
 8      // main method begins program execution
 9      public static void main( String args[] )
10      {
11         // create Scanner to obtain input from command window
12         Scanner input = new Scanner( System.in );
13
14         // create a GradeBook object and assign it to myGradeBook
15         GradeBook myGradeBook = new GradeBook();
16
17         // prompt for and input course name
18         System.out.println( "Please enter the course name:" );
19         String nameOfCourse = input.nextLine(); // read a line of text
20         System.out.println(); // outputs a blank line
21
22         // call myGradeBook's displayMessage method
23         // and pass nameOfCourse as an argument
24         myGradeBook.displayMessage( nameOfCourse );
25      } // end main
26
27   } // end class GradeBookTest
```

```
Please enter the course name:
CS101 Introduction to Java Programming

Welcome to the grade book for
CS101 Introduction to Java Programming!
```

Fig. 3.5 | Creating a GradeBook object and passing a String to its displayMessage method.

inserts a newline character at the end of the characters typed by the user. Method nextLine reads characters typed by the user until the newline character is encountered, then returns a String containing the characters up to, but not including, the newline. The newline character is discarded. Class Scanner also provides a similar method—next—that reads individual words. When the user presses *Enter* after typing input, method next reads characters until a white-space character (such as a space, tab or newline) is encountered, then returns a String containing the characters up to, but not including, the white-space character (which is discarded). All information after the first white-space character is not lost—it can be read by other statements that call the Scanner's methods later in the program.

Line 24 calls myGradeBooks's displayMessage method. The variable nameOfCourse in parentheses is the argument that is passed to method displayMessage so that the method can perform its task. The value of variable nameOfCourse in main becomes the value of method displayMessage's parameter courseName in line 7 of Fig. 3.4. When you execute this application, notice that method displayMessage outputs the name you type as part of the welcome message (Fig. 3.5).

Software Engineering Observation 3.1

Normally, objects are created with new. One exception is a string literal that is contained in quotes, such as "hello". String literals are references to String objects that are implicitly created by Java.

More on Arguments and Parameters

When you declare a method, you must specify whether the method requires data to perform its task. To do so, you place additional information in the method's *parameter list*, which is located in the parentheses that follow the method name. The parameter list may contain any number of parameters, including none at all. Empty parentheses following the method name (as in Fig. 3.1, line 7) indicate that a method does not require any parameters. In Fig. 3.4, displayMessage's parameter list (line 7) declares that the method requires one parameter. Each parameter must specify a type and an identifier. In this case, the type String and the identifier courseName indicate that method displayMessage requires a String to perform its task. At the time the method is called, the argument value in the call is assigned to the corresponding parameter (in this case, courseName) in the method header. Then, the method body uses the parameter courseName to access the value. Lines 9–10 of Fig. 3.4 display parameter courseName's value, using the %s format specifier in printf's format string. Note that the parameter variable's name (Fig. 3.4, line 7) can be the same or different from the argument variable's name (Fig. 3.5, line 24).

A method can specify multiple parameters by separating each parameter from the next with a comma (we'll see an example of this in Chapter 6). The number of arguments in a method call must match the number of parameters in the parameter list of the called method's declaration. Also, the argument types in the method call must be "consistent with" the types of the corresponding parameters in the method's declaration. (As you'll learn in subsequent chapters, an argument's type and its corresponding parameter's type are not always required to be identical.) In our example, the method call passes one argument of type String (nameOfCourse is declared as a String in line 19 of Fig. 3.5) and the method declaration specifies one parameter of type String (line 7 in Fig. 3.4). So in this example the type of the argument in the method call exactly matches the type of the parameter in the method header.

Common Programming Error 3.2

A compilation error occurs if the number of arguments in a method call does not match the number of parameters in the method declaration.

Common Programming Error 3.3

A compilation error occurs if the types of the arguments in a method call are not consistent with the types of the corresponding parameters in the method declaration.

Updated UML Class Diagram for Class GradeBook

The UML class diagram of Fig. 3.6 models class GradeBook of Fig. 3.4. Like Fig. 3.1, this GradeBook class contains public operation displayMessage. However, this version of displayMessage has a parameter. The UML models a parameter a bit differently from Java by listing the parameter name, followed by a colon and the parameter type in the parentheses following the operation name. The UML has its own data types similar to those of Java (but as you'll see, not all the UML data types have the same names as the corresponding Java

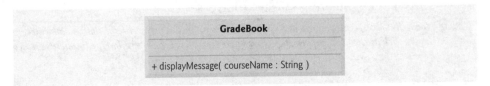

Fig. 3.6 | UML class diagram indicating that class `GradeBook` has a `displayMessage` operation with a `courseName` parameter of UML type `String`.

types). The UML type `String` does correspond to the Java type `String`. `GradeBook` method `displayMessage` (Fig. 3.4) has a `String` parameter named `courseName`, so Fig. 3.6 lists `courseName : String` between the parentheses following `displayMessage`.

Notes on import Declarations

Notice the `import` declaration in Fig. 3.5 (line 4). This indicates to the compiler that the program uses class `Scanner`. Why do we need to import class `Scanner`, but not classes `System`, `String` or `GradeBook`? Most classes you'll use in Java programs must be imported. Classes `System` and `String` are in package `java.lang`, which is implicitly imported into every Java program, so all programs can use package `java.lang`'s classes without explicitly importing them.

There is a special relationship between classes that are compiled in the same directory on disk, like classes `GradeBook` and `GradeBookTest`. By default, such classes are considered to be in the same package—known as the *default package*. Classes in the same package are implicitly imported into the source code files of other classes in the same package. Thus, an `import` declaration is not required when one class in a package uses another in the same package—such as when class `GradeBookTest` uses class `GradeBook`.

The `import` declaration in line 4 is not required if we always refer to class `Scanner` as `java.util.Scanner`, which includes the full package name and class name. This is known as the class's *fully qualified class name*. For example, line 12 could be written as

```
java.util.Scanner input = new java.util.Scanner( System.in );
```

> **Software Engineering Observation 3.2**
>
> *The Java compiler does not require import declarations in a Java source code file if the fully qualified class name is specified every time a class name is used in the source code. But most Java programmers consider using fully qualified names to be cumbersome, and instead prefer to use import declarations.*

3.5 Instance Variables, *set* Methods and *get* Methods

In Chapter 2, we declared all of an application's variables in the application's main method. Variables declared in the body of a particular method are known as *local variables* and can be used only in that method. When that method terminates, the values of its local variables are lost. Recall from Section 3.2 that an object has attributes that are carried with the object as it is used in a program. Such attributes exist before a method is called on an object and after the method completes execution.

A class normally consists of one or more methods that manipulate the attributes that belong to a particular object of the class. Attributes are represented as variables in a class declaration. Such variables are called *fields* and are declared inside a class declaration but outside the bodies of the class's method declarations. When each object of a class maintains its own copy of an attribute, the field that represents the attribute is also known as an instance variable—each object (instance) of the class has a separate instance of the variable in memory. The example in this section demonstrates a GradeBook class that contains a courseName instance variable to represent a particular GradeBook object's course name.

GradeBook Class with an Instance Variable, a set Method and a get Method

In our next application (Fig. 3.7–Fig. 3.8), class GradeBook (Fig. 3.7) maintains the course name as an instance variable so that it can be used or modified at any time during an application's execution. The class contains three methods—setCourseName, getCourseName and displayMessage. Method setCourseName stores a course name in a GradeBook. Method getCourseName obtains a GradeBook's course name. Method displayMessage, which now specifies no parameters, still displays a welcome message that includes the course name; as you'll see, the method now obtains the course name by calling another method in the same class—getCourseName.

```java
1   // Fig. 3.7: GradeBook.java
2   // GradeBook class that contains a courseName instance variable
3   // and methods to set and get its value.
4
5   public class GradeBook
6   {
7      private String courseName; // course name for this GradeBook
8
9      // method to set the course name
10     public void setCourseName( String name )
11     {
12        courseName = name; // store the course name
13     } // end method setCourseName
14
15     // method to retrieve the course name
16     public String getCourseName()
17     {
18        return courseName;
19     } // end method getCourseName
20
21     // display a welcome message to the GradeBook user
22     public void displayMessage()
23     {
24        // this statement calls getCourseName to get the
25        // name of the course this GradeBook represents
26        System.out.printf( "Welcome to the grade book for\n%s!\n",
27           getCourseName() );
28     } // end method displayMessage
29
30  } // end class GradeBook
```

Fig. 3.7 | GradeBook class that contains a courseName instance variable and methods to set and get its value.

A typical instructor teaches more than one course, each with its own course name. Line 7 declares that courseName is a variable of type String. Because the variable is declared in the body of the class but outside the bodies of the class's methods (lines 10–13, 16–19 and 22–28), line 7 is a declaration for an instance variable. Every instance (i.e., object) of class GradeBook contains one copy of each instance variable. For example, if there are two GradeBook objects, each object has its own copy of courseName (one per object). A benefit of making courseName an instance variable is that all the methods of the class (in this case, GradeBook) can manipulate any instance variables that appear in the class (in this case, courseName).

Access Modifiers public *and* private

Most instance variable declarations are preceded with the keyword private (as in line 7). Like public, keyword private is an access modifier. Variables or methods declared with access modifier private are accessible only to methods of the class in which they are declared. Thus, variable courseName can be used only in methods setCourseName, getCourseName and displayMessage of (every object of) class GradeBook.

Software Engineering Observation 3.3

Precede every field and method declaration with an access modifier. As a rule of thumb, instance variables should be declared private and methods should be declared public. (We'll see that it is appropriate to declare certain methods private, if they will be accessed only by other methods of the class.)

Good Programming Practice 3.1

We prefer to list the fields of a class first, so that, as you read the code, you see the names and types of the variables before you see them used in the methods of the class. It is possible to list the class's fields anywhere in the class outside its method declarations, but scattering them tends to lead to hard-to-read code.

Good Programming Practice 3.2

Place a blank line between method declarations to separate the methods and enhance program readability.

Declaring instance variables with access modifier private is known as *data hiding*. When a program creates (instantiates) an object of class GradeBook, variable courseName is encapsulated (hidden) in the object and can be accessed only by methods of the object's class. In class GradeBook, methods setCourseName and getCourseName manipulate the instance variable courseName.

Method setCourseName (lines 10–13) does not return any data when it completes its task, so its return type is void. The method receives one parameter—name—which represents the course name that will be passed to the method as an argument. Line 12 assigns name to instance variable courseName.

Method getCourseName (lines 16–19) returns a particular GradeBook object's courseName. The method has an empty parameter list, so it does not require additional information to perform its task. The method specifies that it returns a String—this is known as the method's *return type*. When a method that specifies a return type is called and completes its task, the method returns a result to its calling method. For example, when you go to an automated teller machine (ATM) and request your account balance, you expect the ATM to give you back a value that represents your balance. Similarly, when a statement calls method getCourseName on a GradeBook object, the statement expects to receive the GradeBook's course name (in this case, a String, as specified in the method declaration's return type). If you have a method square that returns the square of its argument, you would expect the statement

```
int result = square( 2 );
```

to return 4 from method square and assign 4 to the variable result. If you have a method maximum that returns the largest of three integer arguments, you would expect the following statement

```
int biggest = maximum( 27, 114, 51 );
```

to return 114 from method maximum and assign 114 to variable biggest.

Note that the statements in lines 12 and 18 each use courseName even though it was not declared in any of the methods. We can use courseName in the methods of class Grade-Book because courseName is a field of the class. Also note that the order in which methods are declared in a class does not determine when they are called at execution time. So method getCourseName could be declared before method setCourseName.

Method displayMessage (lines 22–28) does not return any data when it completes its task, so its return type is void. The method does not receive parameters, so the parameter list is empty. Lines 26–27 output a welcome message that includes the value of instance variable courseName. Once again, we need to create an object of class GradeBook and call its methods before the welcome message can be displayed.

GradeBookTest Class That Demonstrates Class GradeBook

Class GradeBookTest (Fig. 3.8) creates one object of class GradeBook and demonstrates its methods. Line 11 creates a Scanner that will be used to obtain a course name from the user. Line 14 creates a GradeBook object and assigns it to local variable myGradeBook of type GradeBook. Lines 17–18 display the initial course name calling the object's getCourseName method. Note that the first line of the output shows the name "null." Unlike local variables, which are not automatically initialized, every field has a *default initial value*—a value provided by Java when the programmer does not specify the field's initial value. Thus, fields are not required to be explicitly initialized before they are used in a program—unless they must be initialized to values other than their default values. The default value for a field of type String (like courseName in this example) is null, which we say more about in Section 3.6.

Line 21 prompts the user to enter a course name. Local String variable theName (declared in line 22) is initialized with the course name entered by the user, which is returned by the call to the nextLine method of the Scanner object input. Line 23 calls object myGradeBook's setCourseName method and supplies theName as the method's argument. When the method is called, the argument's value is assigned to parameter name (line 10, Fig. 3.7) of method setCourseName (lines 10–13, Fig. 3.7). Then the parameter's value is assigned to instance variable courseName (line 12, Fig. 3.7). Line 24 (Fig. 3.8) skips a line in the output, then line 27 calls object myGradeBook's displayMessage method to display the welcome message containing the course name.

```
1   // Fig. 3.8: GradeBookTest.java
2   // Create and manipulate a GradeBook object.
3   import java.util.Scanner; // program uses Scanner
4
5   public class GradeBookTest
6   {
7      // main method begins program execution
8      public static void main( String args[] )
9      {
10        // create Scanner to obtain input from command window
11        Scanner input = new Scanner( System.in );
12
13        // create a GradeBook object and assign it to myGradeBook
14        GradeBook myGradeBook = new GradeBook();
15
16        // display initial value of courseName
17        System.out.printf( "Initial course name is: %s\n\n",
18           myGradeBook.getCourseName() );
19
20        // prompt for and read course name
21        System.out.println( "Please enter the course name:" );
22        String theName = input.nextLine(); // read a line of text
23        myGradeBook.setCourseName( theName ); // set the course name
24        System.out.println(); // outputs a blank line
25
26        // display welcome message after specifying course name
27        myGradeBook.displayMessage();
28     } // end main
29
30  } // end class GradeBookTest
```

```
Initial course name is: null

Please enter the course name:
CS101 Introduction to Java Programming

Welcome to the grade book for
CS101 Introduction to Java Programming!
```

Fig. 3.8 | Creating and manipulating a GradeBook object.

set *and* get *Methods*

A class's private fields can be manipulated only by methods of that class. So a *client of an object*—that is, any class that calls the object's methods—calls the class's public methods to manipulate the private fields of an object of the class. This is why the statements in method main (Fig. 3.8) call the setCourseName, getCourseName and displayMessage methods on a GradeBook object. Classes often provide public methods to allow clients of the class to *set* (i.e., assign values to) or *get* (i.e., obtain the values of) private instance variables. The names of these methods need not begin with *set* or *get*, but this naming convention is highly recommended in Java and is required for special Java software components called JavaBeans that can simplify programming in many Java integrated development environments (IDEs). The method that *sets* instance variable courseName in this example is called setCourseName, and the method that *gets* the value of instance variable courseName is called getCourseName.

UML Class Diagram for class GradeBook with an Instance Variable and set *and* get *Methods*

Figure 3.9 contains an updated UML class diagram for the version of class GradeBook in Fig. 3.7. This diagram models class GradeBook's instance variable courseName as an attribute in the middle compartment of the class. The UML represents instance variables as attributes by listing the attribute name, followed by a colon and the attribute type. The UML type of attribute courseName is String. Instance variable courseName is private in Java, so the class diagram lists a minus sign (–) in front of the corresponding attribute's name. Class GradeBook contains three public methods, so the class diagram lists three operations in the third compartment. Recall that the plus (+) sign before each operation name indicates that the operation is public. Operation setCourseName has a String parameter called name. The UML indicates the return type of an operation by placing a colon and the return type after the parentheses following the operation name. Method getCourseName of class GradeBook (Fig. 3.7) has a String return type in Java, so the class diagram shows a String return type in the UML. Note that operations setCourseName and displayMessage do not return values (i.e., they return void in Java), so the UML class diagram does not specify a return type after the parentheses of these operations.

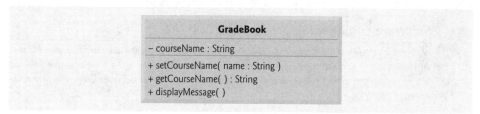

Fig. 3.9 | UML class diagram indicating that class GradeBook has a courseName attribute of UML type String and three operations—setCourseName (with a name parameter of UML type String), getCourseName (which returns UML type String) and displayMessage.

3.6 Primitive Types vs. Reference Types

Data types in Java are divided into two categories—primitive types and *reference types* (sometimes called *nonprimitive types*). The primitive types are boolean, byte, char, short, int, long, float and double. All nonprimitive types are reference types, so classes, which specify the types of objects, are reference types.

A primitive-type variable can store exactly one value of its declared type at a time. For example, an int variable can store one whole number (such as 7) at a time. When another value is assigned to that variable, its initial value is replaced. Primitive-type instance variables are initialized by default—variables of types byte, char, short, int, long, float and double are initialized to 0, and variables of type boolean are initialized to false. You can specify your own initial values for primitive-type variables. Recall that local variables are *not* initialized by default.

Error-Prevention Tip 3.1

Any attempt to use a local variable that has not been initialized results in a compilation error.

Programs use variables of reference types (normally called *references*) to store the locations of objects in the computer's memory. Such a variable is said to *refer to an object* in the program. Objects that are referenced may each contain many instance variables and methods. Line 14 of Fig. 3.8 creates an object of class GradeBook, and the variable myGradeBook contains a reference to that GradeBook object. Reference-type instance variables are initialized by default to the value null—a reserved word that represents a "reference to nothing." This is why the first call to getCourseName in line 18 of Fig. 3.8 returned null—the value of courseName had not been set, so the default initial value null was returned. The complete list of reserved words and keywords is listed in Appendix C, Keywords and Reserved Words.

A reference to an object is required to *invoke* (i.e., call) the object's methods. In the application of Fig. 3.8, the statements in method main use the variable myGradeBook to send messages to the GradeBook object. These messages are calls to methods (like setCourseName and getCourseName) that enable the program to interact with the GradeBook object. For example, the statement in line 23 uses myGradeBook to send the setCourseName message to the GradeBook object. The message includes the argument that setCourseName requires to perform its task. The GradeBook object uses this information to set the courseName instance variable. Note that primitive-type variables do not refer to objects, so such variables cannot be used to invoke methods.

Software Engineering Observation 3.4

A variable's declared type (e.g., int, double or GradeBook) indicates whether the variable is of a primitive or a reference type. If a variable's type is not one of the eight primitive types, then it is a reference type. For example, Account account1 indicates that account1 is a reference to an Account object).

3.7 Initializing Objects with Constructors

As mentioned in Section 3.5, when an object of class GradeBook (Fig. 3.7) is created, its instance variable courseName is initialized to null by default. What if you want to provide a course name when you create a GradeBook object? Each class you declare can provide a constructor that can be used to initialize an object of a class when the object is created. In fact, Java requires a constructor call for every object that is created. Keyword new calls the class's constructor to perform the initialization. The constructor call is indicated by the class name followed by parentheses—the constructor *must* have the same name as the class. For example, line 14 of Fig. 3.8 first uses new to create a GradeBook object. The empty parentheses after "new GradeBook" indicate a call to the class's constructor without arguments. By default, the compiler provides a *default constructor* with no parameters in any class that does not explicitly include a constructor. When a class has only the default constructor, its instance variables are initialized to their default values. Variables of types char, byte, short, int, long, float and double are initialized to 0, variables of type boolean are initialized to false, and reference-type variables are initialized to null.

When you declare a class, you can provide your own constructor to specify custom initialization for objects of your class. For example, you might want to specify a course name for a GradeBook object when the object is created, as in

```
GradeBook myGradeBook =
    new GradeBook( "CS101 Introduction to Java Programming" );
```

In this case, the argument "CS101 Introduction to Java Programming" is passed to the GradeBook object's constructor and used to initialize the courseName. The preceding statement requires that the class provide a constructor with a String parameter. Figure 3.10 contains a modified GradeBook class with such a constructor.

Lines 9–12 declare the constructor for class GradeBook. A constructor must have the same name as its class. Like a method, a constructor specifies in its parameter list the data it requires to perform its task. When you create a new object (as we'll do in Fig. 3.11), this

```java
 1   // Fig. 3.10: GradeBook.java
 2   // GradeBook class with a constructor to initialize the course name.
 3
 4   public class GradeBook
 5   {
 6      private String courseName; // course name for this GradeBook
 7
 8      // constructor initializes courseName with String supplied as argument
 9      public GradeBook( String name )
10      {
11         courseName = name; // initializes courseName
12      } // end constructor
13
14      // method to set the course name
15      public void setCourseName( String name )
16      {
17         courseName = name; // store the course name
18      } // end method setCourseName
19
20      // method to retrieve the course name
21      public String getCourseName()
22      {
23         return courseName;
24      } // end method getCourseName
25
26      // display a welcome message to the GradeBook user
27      public void displayMessage()
28      {
29         // this statement calls getCourseName to get the
30         // name of the course this GradeBook represents
31         System.out.printf( "Welcome to the grade book for\n%s!\n",
32            getCourseName() );
33      } // end method displayMessage
34
35   } // end class GradeBook
```

Fig. 3.10 | GradeBook class with a constructor to initialize the course name.

data is placed in the parentheses that follow the class name. Line 9 indicates that class GradeBook's constructor has a String parameter called name. The name passed to the constructor is assigned to instance variable courseName in line 11 of the constructor's body.

Figure 3.11 demonstrates initializing GradeBook objects using the constructor. Lines 11–12 create and initialize the GradeBook object gradeBook1. The constructor of class GradeBook is called with the argument "CS101 Introduction to Java Programming" to initialize the course name. The class instance creation expression to the right of the = in lines 11–12 returns a reference to the new object, which is assigned to the variable gradeBook1. Lines 13–14 repeat this process for another GradeBook object gradeBook2, this time passing the argument "CS102 Data Structures in Java" to initialize the course name for gradeBook2. Lines 17–20 use each object's getCourseName method to obtain the course names and show that they were indeed initialized when the objects were created. In the introduction to Section 3.5, you learned that each instance (i.e., object) of a class contains its own copy of the class's instance variables. The output confirms that each GradeBook maintains its own copy of instance variable courseName.

Like methods, constructors also can take arguments. However, an important difference between constructors and methods is that constructors cannot return values, so they cannot specify a return type (not even void). Normally, constructors are declared public. If a class does not include a constructor, the class's instance variables are initialized to their

```
1   // Fig. 3.11: GradeBookTest.java
2   // GradeBook constructor used to specify the course name at the
3   // time each GradeBook object is created.
4
5   public class GradeBookTest
6   {
7      // main method begins program execution
8      public static void main( String args[] )
9      {
10        // create GradeBook object
11        GradeBook gradeBook1 = new GradeBook(
12           "CS101 Introduction to Java Programming" );
13        GradeBook gradeBook2 = new GradeBook(
14           "CS102 Data Structures in Java" );
15
16        // display initial value of courseName for each GradeBook
17        System.out.printf( "gradeBook1 course name is: %s\n",
18           gradeBook1.getCourseName() );
19        System.out.printf( "gradeBook2 course name is: %s\n",
20           gradeBook2.getCourseName() );
21     } // end main
22
23  } // end class GradeBookTest
```

```
gradeBook1 course name is: CS101 Introduction to Java Programming
gradeBook2 course name is: CS102 Data Structures in Java
```

Fig. 3.11 | GradeBook constructor used to specify the course name at the time each GradeBook object is created.

default values. If a programmer declares any constructors for a class, the Java compiler will not create a default constructor for that class.

Error-Prevention Tip 3.2

Unless default initialization of your class's instance variables is acceptable, provide a constructor to ensure that your class's instance variables are properly initialized with meaningful values when each new object of your class is created.

Adding the Constructor to Class GradeBook's UML Class Diagram

The UML class diagram of Fig. 3.12 models class GradeBook of Fig. 3.10, which has a constructor that has a name parameter of type String. Like operations, the UML models constructors in the third compartment of a class in a class diagram. To distinguish a constructor from a class's operations, the UML requires that the word "constructor" be placed between guillemets (« and ») before the constructor's name. It is customary to list constructors before other operations in the third compartment.

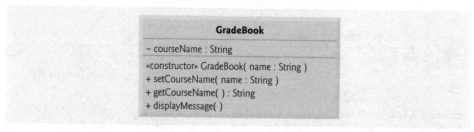

Fig. 3.12 │ UML class diagram indicating that class GradeBook has a constructor that has a name parameter of UML type String.

3.8 Floating-Point Numbers and Type double

In our next application, we depart temporarily from our GradeBook case study to declare a class called Account that maintains the balance of a bank account. Most account balances are not whole numbers (e.g., 0, –22 and 1024). For this reason, class Account represents the account balance as a *floating-point number* (i.e., a number with a decimal point, such as 7.33, 0.0975 or 1000.12345). Java provides two primitive types for storing floating-point numbers in memory—float and double. The primary difference between them is that double variables can store numbers with larger magnitude and finer detail (i.e., more digits to the right of the decimal point—also known as the number's *precision*) than float variables.

Floating-Point Number Precision and Memory Requirements

Variables of type float represent *single-precision floating-point numbers* and have seven significant digits. Variables of type double represent *double-precision floating-point numbers*. These require twice as much memory as float variables and provide 15 significant digits—approximately double the precision of float variables. For the range of values required by most programs, variables of type float should suffice, but you can use double to "play it safe." In some applications, even variables of type double will be inadequate—such applications are beyond the scope of this book. Most programmers represent floating-point numbers with type `double`. In fact, Java treats all floating-point numbers you type in a program's source code (such as 7.33 and 0.0975) as `double` values by default. Such values in the source code are known as *floating-point literals*. See Appendix D, Primitive Types, for the ranges of values for `float`s and `double`s.

Although floating-point numbers are not always 100% precise, they have numerous applications. For example, when we speak of a "normal" body temperature of 98.6, we do not need to be precise to a large number of digits. When we read the temperature on a thermometer as 98.6, it may actually be 98.5999473210643. Calling this number simply 98.6 is fine for most applications involving body temperatures. Due to the imprecise nature of floating-point numbers, type `double` is preferred over type `float` because `double` variables can represent floating-point numbers more accurately. For this reason, we use type `double` throughout the book.

Floating-point numbers also arise as a result of division. In conventional arithmetic, when we divide 10 by 3, the result is 3.3333333…, with the sequence of 3s repeating infinitely. The computer allocates only a fixed amount of space to hold such a value, so clearly the stored floating-point value can be only an approximation.

Common Programming Error 3.4

Using floating-point numbers in a manner that assumes they are represented precisely can lead to logic errors.

Account Class with an Instance Variable of Type `double`

Our next application (Figs. 3.13–3.14) contains a class named `Account` (Fig. 3.13) that maintains the balance of a bank account. A typical bank services many accounts, each with its own balance, so line 7 declares an instance variable named `balance` of type `double`. Variable `balance` is an instance variable because it is declared in the body of the class but outside the class's method declarations (lines 10–16, 19–22 and 25–28). Every instance (i.e., object) of class `Account` contains its own copy of `balance`.

```java
1   // Fig. 3.13: Account.java
2   // Account class with a constructor to
3   // initialize instance variable balance.
4
5   public class Account
6   {
7      private double balance; // instance variable that stores the balance
8
9      // constructor
10     public Account( double initialBalance )
11     {
12        // validate that initialBalance is greater than 0.0;
13        // if it is not, balance is initialized to the default value 0.0
14        if ( initialBalance > 0.0 )
15           balance = initialBalance;
16     } // end Account constructor
17
```

Fig. 3.13 | Account class with an instance variable of type `double`. (Part 1 of 2.)

```
18     // credit (add) an amount to the account
19     public void credit( double amount )
20     {
21        balance = balance + amount; // add amount to balance
22     } // end method credit
23
24     // return the account balance
25     public double getBalance()
26     {
27        return balance; // gives the value of balance to the calling method
28     } // end method getBalance
29
30  } // end class Account
```

Fig. 3.13 | Account class with an instance variable of type double. (Part 2 of 2.)

Class Account contains a constructor and two methods. Since it is common for someone opening an account to place money in the account immediately, the constructor (lines 10–16) receives a parameter initialBalance of type double that represents the account's starting balance. Lines 14–15 ensure that initialBalance is greater than 0.0. If so, initialBalance's value is assigned to instance variable balance. Otherwise, balance remains at 0.0—its default initial value.

Method credit (lines 19–22) does not return any data when it completes its task, so its return type is void. The method receives one parameter named amount—a double value that will be added to the balance. Line 21 adds amount to the current value of balance, then assigns the result to balance (thus replacing the prior balance amount).

Method getBalance (lines 25–28) allows clients of the class (i.e., other classes that use this class) to obtain the value of a particular Account object's balance. The method specifies return type double and an empty parameter list.

Once again, note that the statements in lines 15, 21 and 27 use instance variable balance even though it was not declared in any of the methods. We can use balance in these methods because it is an instance variable of the class.

AccountTest Class to Use Class Account

Class AccountTest (Fig. 3.14) creates two Account objects (lines 10–11) and initializes them with 50.00 and -7.53, respectively. Lines 14–17 output the balance in each Account by calling the Account's getBalance method. When method getBalance is called for account1 from line 15, the value of account1's balance is returned from line 27 of Fig. 3.13 and displayed by the System.out.printf statement (Fig. 3.14, lines 14–15). Similarly, when method getBalance is called for account2 from line 17, the value of the account2's balance is returned from line 27 of Fig. 3.13 and displayed by the System.out.printf statement (Fig. 3.14, lines 16–17). Note that the balance of account2 is 0.00 because the constructor ensured that the account could not begin with a negative balance. The value is output by printf with the format specifier %.2f. The format specifier %f is used to output values of type float or double. The .2 between % and f represents the number of decimal places (2) that should be output to the right of the decimal point in the floating-point number—also known as the number's *precision*. Any floating-point value output with %.2f will be rounded to the hundredths position—for example, 123.457 would be rounded to 123.46, and 27.333 would be rounded to 27.33.

```
1   // Fig. 3.14: AccountTest.java
2   // Inputting and outputting floating-point numbers with Account objects.
3   import java.util.Scanner;
4
5   public class AccountTest
6   {
7      // main method begins execution of Java application
8      public static void main( String args[] )
9      {
10        Account account1 = new Account( 50.00 ); // create Account object
11        Account account2 = new Account( -7.53 ); // create Account object
12
13        // display initial balance of each object
14        System.out.printf( "account1 balance: $%.2f\n",
15           account1.getBalance() );
16        System.out.printf( "account2 balance: $%.2f\n\n",
17           account2.getBalance() );
18
19        // create Scanner to obtain input from command window
20        Scanner input = new Scanner( System.in );
21        double depositAmount; // deposit amount read from user
22
23        System.out.print( "Enter deposit amount for account1: " ); // prompt
24        depositAmount = input.nextDouble(); // obtain user input
25        System.out.printf( "\nadding %.2f to account1 balance\n\n",
26           depositAmount );
27        account1.credit( depositAmount ); // add to account1 balance
28
29        // display balances
30        System.out.printf( "account1 balance: $%.2f\n",
31           account1.getBalance() );
32        System.out.printf( "account2 balance: $%.2f\n\n",
33           account2.getBalance() );
34
35        System.out.print( "Enter deposit amount for account2: " ); // prompt
36        depositAmount = input.nextDouble(); // obtain user input
37        System.out.printf( "\nadding %.2f to account2 balance\n\n",
38           depositAmount );
39        account2.credit( depositAmount ); // add to account2 balance
40
41        // display balances
42        System.out.printf( "account1 balance: $%.2f\n",
43           account1.getBalance() );
44        System.out.printf( "account2 balance: $%.2f\n",
45           account2.getBalance() );
46     } // end main
47
48  } // end class AccountTest
```

Fig. 3.14 | Inputting and outputting floating-point numbers with Account objects. (Part 1 of 2.)

```
account1 balance: $50.00
account2 balance: $0.00

Enter deposit amount for account1: 25.53

adding 25.53 to account1 balance

account1 balance: $75.53
account2 balance: $0.00

Enter deposit amount for account2: 123.45

adding 123.45 to account2 balance

account1 balance: $75.53
account2 balance: $123.45
```

Fig. 3.14 | Inputting and outputting floating-point numbers with `Account` objects. (Part 2 of 2.)

Line 20 creates a `Scanner` that will be used to obtain deposit amounts from a user. Line 21 declares local variable `depositAmount` to store each deposit amount entered by the user. Unlike the instance variable `balance` in class `Account`, local variable `depositAmount` in `main` is not initialized to 0.0 by default. However, this variable does not need to be initialized here because its value will be determined by the user's input.

Line 23 prompts the user to enter a deposit amount for `account1`. Line 24 obtains the input from the user by calling `Scanner` object `input`'s `nextDouble` method, which returns a `double` value entered by the user. Lines 25–26 display the deposit amount. Line 27 calls object `account1`'s `credit` method and supplies `depositAmount` as the method's argument. When the method is called, the argument's value is assigned to parameter `amount` (line 19 of Fig. 3.13) of method `credit` (lines 19–22 of Fig. 3.13), then method `credit` adds that value to the `balance` (line 21 of Fig. 3.13). Lines 30–33 (Fig. 3.14) output the balances of both `Account`s again to show that only `account1`'s balance changed.

Line 35 prompts the user to enter a deposit amount for `account2`. Line 36 obtains the input from the user by calling `Scanner` object `input`'s `nextDouble` method. Lines 37–38 display the deposit amount. Line 39 calls object `account2`'s `credit` method and supplies `depositAmount` as the method's argument, then method `credit` adds that value to the balance. Finally, lines 42–45 output the balances of both `Account`s again to show that only `account2`'s balance changed.

UML Class Diagram for Class `Account`
The UML class diagram in Fig. 3.15 models class `Account` of Fig. 3.13. The diagram models the `private` attribute `balance` with UML type `Double` to correspond to the class's instance variable `balance` of Java type `double`. The diagram models class `Account`'s constructor with a parameter `initialBalance` of UML type `Double` in the third compartment of the class. The class's two `public` methods are modeled as operations in the third compartment as well. The diagram models operation `credit` with an `amount` parameter of UML type `Double` (because the corresponding method has an `amount` parameter of Java type `double`) and operation `getBalance` with a return type of `Double` (because the corresponding Java method returns a `double` value).

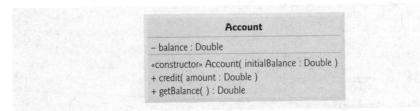

Fig. 3.15 | UML class diagram indicating that class `Account` has a `private balance` attribute of UML type `Double`, a constructor (with a parameter of UML type `Double`) and two `public` operations—`credit` (with an `amount` parameter of UML type `Double`) and `getBalance` (returns UML type `Double`).

3.9 (Optional) Software Engineering Case Study: Identifying the Classes in a Requirements Document

Now we begin designing the ATM system that we introduced in Chapter 2. In this section, we identify the classes that are needed to build the ATM system by analyzing the nouns and noun phrases that appear in the requirements document. We introduce UML class diagrams to model the relationships between these classes. This is an important first step in defining the structure of our system.

Identifying the Classes in a System

We begin our OOD process by identifying the classes required to build the ATM system. We'll eventually describe these classes using UML class diagrams and implement these classes in Java. First, we review the requirements document of Section 2.8 and identify key nouns and noun phrases to help us identify classes that comprise the ATM system. We may decide that some of these nouns and noun phrases are attributes of other classes in the system. We may also conclude that some of the nouns do not correspond to parts of the system and thus should not be modeled at all. Additional classes may become apparent to us as we proceed through the design process.

Figure 3.16 lists the nouns and noun phrases found in the requirements document of Section 2.8. We list them from left to right in the order in which we first encounter them in the requirements document. We list only the singular form of each noun or noun phrase.

Nouns and noun phrases in the ATM requirements document		
bank	money / funds	account number
ATM	screen	PIN
user	keypad	bank database
customer	cash dispenser	balance inquiry
transaction	$20 bill / cash	withdrawal
account	deposit slot	deposit
balance	deposit envelope	

Fig. 3.16 | Nouns and noun phrases in the ATM requirements document.

We create classes only for the nouns and noun phrases that have significance in the ATM system. We don't model "bank" as a class, because the bank is not a part of the ATM system—the bank simply wants us to build the ATM. "Customer" and "user" also represent outside entities—they are important because they interact with our ATM system, but we do not need to model them as classes in the ATM software. Recall that we modeled an ATM user (i.e., a bank customer) as the actor in the use case diagram of Fig. 2.16.

We do not model "$20 bill" or "deposit envelope" as classes. These are physical objects in the real world, but they are not part of what is being automated. We can adequately represent the presence of bills in the system using an attribute of the class that models the cash dispenser. (We assign attributes to the ATM system's classes in Section 4.12.) For example, the cash dispenser maintains a count of the number of bills it contains. The requirements document does not say anything about what the system should do with deposit envelopes after it receives them. We can assume that simply acknowledging the receipt of an envelope—an operation performed by the class that models the deposit slot—is sufficient to represent the presence of an envelope in the system. (We assign operations to the ATM system's classes in Section 6.19.)

In our simplified ATM system, representing various amounts of "money," including an account's "balance," as attributes of classes seems most appropriate. Likewise, the nouns "account number" and "PIN" represent significant pieces of information in the ATM system. They are important attributes of a bank account. They do not, however, exhibit behaviors. Thus, we can most appropriately model them as attributes of an account class.

Though the requirements document frequently describes a "transaction" in a general sense, we do not model the broad notion of a financial transaction at this time. Instead, we model the three types of transactions (i.e., "balance inquiry," "withdrawal" and "deposit") as individual classes. These classes possess specific attributes needed for executing the transactions they represent. For example, a withdrawal needs to know the amount of money the user wants to withdraw. A balance inquiry, however, does not require any additional data. Furthermore, the three transaction classes exhibit unique behaviors. A withdrawal includes dispensing cash to the user, whereas a deposit involves receiving deposit envelopes from the user. [*Note:* In Section 10.8, we "factor out" common features of all transactions into a general "transaction" class using the object-oriented concept of inheritance.]

We determine the classes for our system based on the remaining nouns and noun phrases from Fig. 3.16. Each of these refers to one or more of the following:

- ATM
- screen
- keypad
- cash dispenser
- deposit slot
- account
- bank database
- balance inquiry
- withdrawal
- deposit

The elements of this list are likely to be classes we'll need to implement our system.

We can now model the classes in our system based on the list we've created. We capitalize class names in the design process—a UML convention—as we'll do when we write the actual Java code that implements our design. If the name of a class contains more than one word, we run the words together and capitalize each word (e.g., `MultipleWordName`). Using this convention, we create classes `ATM`, `Screen`, `Keypad`, `CashDispenser`, `DepositSlot`, `Account`, `BankDatabase`, `BalanceInquiry`, `Withdrawal` and `Deposit`. We construct our system using these classes as building blocks. Before we begin building the system, however, we must gain a better understanding of how the classes relate to one another.

Modeling Classes

The UML enables us to model, via *class diagrams*, the classes in the ATM system and their interrelationships. Figure 3.17 represents class `ATM`. In the UML, each class is modeled as a rectangle with three compartments. The top compartment contains the name of the class centered horizontally in boldface. The middle compartment contains the class's attributes. (We discuss attributes in Section 4.12 and Section 5.9.) The bottom compartment contains the class's operations (discussed in Section 6.19). In Fig. 3.17, the middle and bottom compartments are empty because we have not yet determined this class's attributes and operations.

Class diagrams also show the relationships between the classes of the system. Figure 3.18 shows how our classes `ATM` and `Withdrawal` relate to one another. For the moment, we choose to model only this subset of classes for simplicity. We present a more complete class diagram later in this section. Notice that the rectangles representing classes in this diagram are not subdivided into compartments. The UML allows the suppression of class attributes and operations in this manner to create more readable diagrams, when appropriate. Such a diagram is said to be an *elided diagram*—one in which some information, such as the contents of the second and third compartments, is not modeled. We'll place information in these compartments in Section 4.12 and Section 6.19.

In Fig. 3.18, the solid line that connects the two classes represents an *association*—a relationship between classes. The numbers near each end of the line are *multiplicity* values, which indicate how many objects of each class participate in the association. In this case, following the line from one end to the other reveals that, at any given moment, one ATM object participates in an association with either zero or one `Withdrawal` objects—zero if the current user is not currently performing a transaction or has requested a different

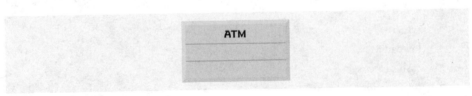

Fig. 3.17 | Representing a class in the UML using a class diagram.

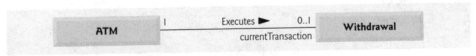

Fig. 3.18 | Class diagram showing an association among classes.

type of transaction, and one if the user has requested a withdrawal. The UML can model many types of multiplicity. Figure 3.19 lists and explains the multiplicity types.

An association can be named. For example, the word Executes above the line connecting classes ATM and Withdrawal in Fig. 3.18 indicates the name of that association. This part of the diagram reads "one object of class ATM executes zero or one objects of class Withdrawal." Note that association names are directional, as indicated by the filled arrowhead—so it would be improper, for example, to read the preceding association from right to left as "zero or one objects of class Withdrawal execute one object of class ATM."

The word currentTransaction at the Withdrawal end of the association line in Fig. 3.18 is a *role name*, which identifies the role the Withdrawal object plays in its relationship with the ATM. A role name adds meaning to an association between classes by identifying the role a class plays in the context of an association. A class can play several roles in the same system. For example, in a school personnel system, a person may play the role of "professor" when relating to students. The same person may take on the role of "colleague" when participating in an association with another professor, and "coach" when coaching student athletes. In Fig. 3.18, the role name currentTransaction indicates that the Withdrawal object participating in the Executes association with an object of class ATM represents the transaction currently being processed by the ATM. In other contexts, a Withdrawal object may take on other roles (e.g., the previous transaction). Notice that we do not specify a role name for the ATM end of the Executes association. Role names in class diagrams are often omitted when the meaning of an association is clear without them.

In addition to indicating simple relationships, associations can specify more complex relationships, such as objects of one class being composed of objects of other classes. Consider a real-world automated teller machine. What "pieces" does a manufacturer put together to build a working ATM? Our requirements document tells us that the ATM is composed of a screen, a keypad, a cash dispenser and a deposit slot.

In Fig. 3.20, the *solid diamonds* attached to the association lines of class ATM indicate that class ATM has a *composition* relationship with classes Screen, Keypad, CashDispenser and DepositSlot. Composition implies a whole/part relationship. The class that has the

Symbol	Meaning
0	None
1	One
m	An integer value
0..1	Zero or one
m, n	m or n
$m..n$	At least m, but not more than n
*	Any non-negative integer (zero or more)
0..*	Zero or more (identical to *)
1..*	One or more

Fig. 3.19 | Multiplicity types.

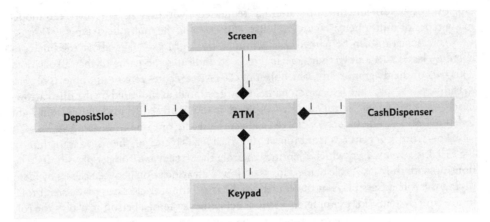

Fig. 3.20 | Class diagram showing composition relationships.

composition symbol (the solid diamond) on its end of the association line is the whole (in this case, ATM), and the classes on the other end of the association lines are the parts—in this case, classes Screen, Keypad, CashDispenser and DepositSlot. The compositions in Fig. 3.20 indicate that an object of class ATM is formed from one object of class Screen, one object of class CashDispenser, one object of class Keypad and one object of class DepositSlot. The ATM *has a* screen, a keypad, a cash dispenser and a deposit slot. The *has-a relationship* defines composition. (We'll see in the Software Engineering Case Study section in Chapter 10 that the *is-a* relationship defines inheritance.)

According to the UML specification (www.uml.org), composition relationships have the following properties:

1. Only one class in the relationship can represent the whole (i.e., the diamond can be placed on only one end of the association line). For example, either the screen is part of the ATM or the ATM is part of the screen, but the screen and the ATM cannot both represent the whole in the relationship.

2. The parts in the composition relationship exist only as long as the whole, and the whole is responsible for the creation and destruction of its parts. For example, the act of constructing an ATM includes manufacturing its parts. Also, if the ATM is destroyed, its screen, keypad, cash dispenser and deposit slot are also destroyed.

3. A part may belong to only one whole at a time, although the part may be removed and attached to another whole, which then assumes responsibility for the part.

The solid diamonds in our class diagrams indicate composition relationships that fulfill these three properties. If a *has-a* relationship does not satisfy one or more of these criteria, the UML specifies that hollow diamonds be attached to the ends of association lines to indicate *aggregation*—a weaker form of composition. For example, a personal computer and a computer monitor participate in an aggregation relationship—the computer *has a* monitor, but the two parts can exist independently, and the same monitor can be attached to multiple computers at once, thus violating the second and third properties of composition.

Figure 3.21 shows a class diagram for the ATM system. This diagram models most of the classes that we identified earlier in this section, as well as the associations between them that we can infer from the requirements document. [*Note:* Classes `BalanceInquiry` and `Deposit` participate in associations similar to those of class `Withdrawal`, so we have chosen to omit them from this diagram to keep the diagram simple. In Chapter 10, we expand our class diagram to include all the classes in the ATM system.]

Figure 3.21 presents a graphical model of the structure of the ATM system. This class diagram includes classes `BankDatabase` and `Account`, and several associations that were not present in either Fig. 3.18 or Fig. 3.20. The class diagram shows that class `ATM` has a *one-to-one relationship* with class `BankDatabase`—one `ATM` object authenticates users against one `BankDatabase` object. In Fig. 3.21, we also model the fact that the bank's database contains information about many accounts—one object of class `BankDatabase` participates in a composition relationship with zero or more objects of class `Account`. Recall from Fig. 3.19 that the multiplicity value 0..* at the `Account` end of the association between class `BankDatabase` and class `Account` indicates that zero or more objects of class `Account` take part in the association. Class `BankDatabase` has a *one-to-many relationship* with class `Account`—the `BankDatabase` stores many `Accounts`. Similarly, class `Account` has a *many-to-one relationship* with class `BankDatabase`—there can be many `Accounts` stored in the `BankDatabase`. [*Note:* Recall from Fig. 3.19 that the multiplicity value * is identical to 0..*. We include 0..* in our class diagrams for clarity.]

Figure 3.21 also indicates that if the user is performing a withdrawal, "one object of class `Withdrawal` accesses/modifies an account balance through one object of class `Bank-Database`." We could have created an association directly between class `Withdrawal` and

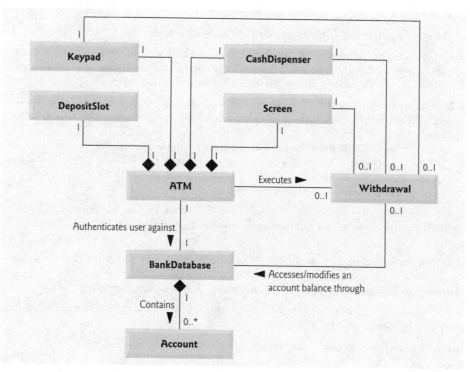

Fig. 3.21 | Class diagram for the ATM system model.

class Account. The requirements document, however, states that the "ATM must interact with the bank's account information database" to perform transactions. A bank account contains sensitive information, and systems engineers must always consider the security of personal data when designing a system. Thus, only the BankDatabase can access and manipulate an account directly. All other parts of the system must interact with the database to retrieve or update account information (e.g., an account balance).

The class diagram in Fig. 3.21 also models associations between class Withdrawal and classes Screen, CashDispenser and Keypad. A withdrawal transaction includes prompting the user to choose a withdrawal amount and receiving numeric input. These actions require the use of the screen and the keypad, respectively. Furthermore, dispensing cash to the user requires access to the cash dispenser.

Classes BalanceInquiry and Deposit, though not shown in Fig. 3.21, take part in several associations with the other classes of the ATM system. Like class Withdrawal, each of these classes associates with classes ATM and BankDatabase. An object of class BalanceInquiry also associates with an object of class Screen to display the balance of an account to the user. Class Deposit associates with classes Screen, Keypad and DepositSlot. Like withdrawals, deposit transactions require use of the screen and the keypad to display prompts and receive input, respectively. To receive deposit envelopes, an object of class Deposit accesses the deposit slot.

We have now identified the classes in our ATM system (although we may discover others as we proceed with the design and implementation). In Section 4.12, we determine the attributes for each of these classes, and in Section 5.9, we use these attributes to examine how the system changes over time.

Software Engineering Case Study Self-Review Exercises

3.1   Suppose we have a class Car that represents a car. Think of some of the different pieces that a manufacturer would put together to produce a whole car. Create a class diagram (similar to Fig. 3.20) that models some of the composition relationships of class Car.

3.2   Suppose we have a class File that represents an electronic document in a standalone, non-networked computer represented by class Computer. What sort of association exists between class Computer and class File?
  a) Class Computer has a one-to-one relationship with class File.
  b) Class Computer has a many-to-one relationship with class File.
  c) Class Computer has a one-to-many relationship with class File.
  d) Class Computer has a many-to-many relationship with class File.

3.3   State whether the following statement is *true* or *false*, and if *false*, explain why: A UML diagram in which a class's second and third compartments are not modeled is said to be an elided diagram.

3.4   Modify the class diagram of Fig. 3.21 to include class Deposit instead of class Withdrawal.

Answers to Software Engineering Case Study Self-Review Exercises

3.1   [*Note:* Answers may vary.] Figure 3.22 presents a class diagram that shows some of the composition relationships of a class Car.

3.2   c. [*Note:* In a computer network, this relationship could be many-to-many.]

3.3   True.

3.4   Figure 3.23 presents a class diagram for the ATM including class `Deposit` instead of class `Withdrawal` (as in Fig. 3.21). Note that `Deposit` does not access `CashDispenser`, but does access `DepositSlot`.

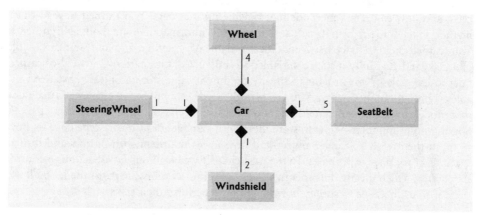

Fig. 3.22 | Class diagram showing composition relationships of a class `Car`.

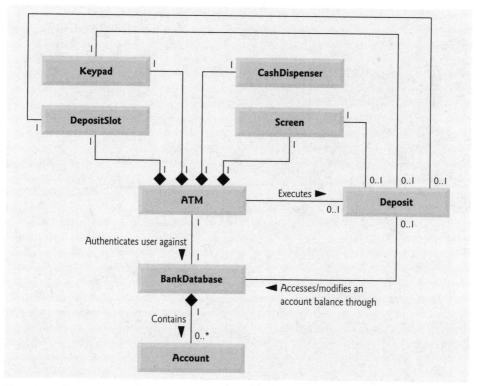

Fig. 3.23 | Class diagram for the ATM system model including class `Deposit`.

3.10 Wrap-Up

In this chapter, you learned the basic concepts of classes, objects, methods and instance variables—these will be used in most Java applications you create. In particular, you learned how to declare instance variables of a class to maintain data for each object of the class, and how to declare methods that operate on that data. You learned how to call a method to tell it to perform its task and how to pass information to methods as arguments. You learned the difference between a local variable of a method and an instance variable of a class and that only instance variables are initialized automatically. You also learned how to use a class's constructor to specify the initial values for an object's instance variables. Throughout the chapter, you saw how the UML can be used to create class diagrams that model the constructors, methods and attributes of classes. Finally, you learned about floating-point numbers—how to store them with variables of primitive type double, how to input them with a Scanner object and how to format them with printf and format specifier %f for display purposes. In the next chapter we begin our introduction to control statements, which specify the order in which a program's actions are performed. You'll use these in your methods to specify how they should perform their tasks.

4

Control Statements: Part 1

Let's all move one place on.
—Lewis Carroll

The wheel is come full circle.
—William Shakespeare

How many apples fell on Newton's head before he took the hint!
—Robert Frost

All the evolution we know of proceeds from the vague to the definite.
—Charles Sanders Peirce

OBJECTIVES

In this chapter you'll learn:

- To use the `if` and `if...else` selection statements to choose among alternative actions.

- To use the `while` repetition statement to execute statements in a program repeatedly.

- To use counter-controlled repetition and sentinel-controlled repetition.

- To use the compound assignment, increment and decrement operators.

- To use the primitive data types.

Outline

4.1 Introduction
4.2 Control Structures
4.3 `if` Single-Selection Statement
4.4 `if...else` Double-Selection Statement
4.5 `while` Repetition Statement
4.6 Counter-Controlled Repetition
4.7 Sentinel-Controlled Repetition
4.8 Nested Control Statements
4.9 Compound Assignment Operators
4.10 Increment and Decrement Operators
4.11 Primitive Types
4.12 (Optional) Software Engineering Case Study: Identifying Class Attributes
4.13 Wrap-Up

4.1 Introduction

In this chapter and in Chapter 5, Control Statements: Part 2, we present the theory and principles of structured programming. The concepts presented here are crucial in building classes and manipulating objects.

In this chapter, we introduce Java's `if...else` and `while` statements. We devote a portion of this chapter (and Chapters 5 and 7) to further developing the GradeBook class introduced in Chapter 3. In particular, we add a method to the GradeBook class that uses control statements to calculate the average of a set of student grades. Another example demonstrates additional ways to combine control statements to solve a similar problem. We introduce Java's compound assignment operators and explore Java's increment and decrement operators. These additional operators abbreviate and simplify many program statements. Finally, overview Java's primitive data types.

4.2 Control Structures

Normally, statements in a program are executed one after the other in the order in which they are written. This process is called *sequential execution*. Various Java statements, which we'll soon discuss, enable you to specify that the next statement to execute is not necessarily the next one in sequence. This is called *transfer of control.*

During the 1960s, it became clear that the indiscriminate use of transfers of control was the root of much difficulty experienced by software development groups. The blame was pointed at the *goto statement* (used in most programming languages of the time), which allows the programmer to specify a transfer of control to one of a very wide range of possible destinations in a program. The notion of so-called *structured programming* became almost synonymous with "goto elimination." [*Note:* Java does not have a goto statement; however, the word goto is reserved by Java and should not be used as an identifier in programs.]

Bohm and Jacopini's[1] work demonstrated that all programs could be written in terms of only three control structures—the *sequence structure*, the *selection structure* and the

---

1. Bohm, C., and G. Jacopini, "Flow Diagrams, Turing Machines, and Languages with Only Two Formation Rules," *Communications of the ACM*, Vol. 9, No. 5, May 1966, pp. 336–371.

repetition structure. The term "control structures" comes from the field of computer science—when we introduce Java's implementations of control structures, we'll refer to them in the terminology of the *Java Language Specification* as "control statements."

Sequence Structure in Java

The sequence structure is built into Java. Unless directed otherwise, Java statements execute one after the other in the order in which they are written—that is, in sequence. The *activity diagram* in Fig. 4.1 illustrates a typical sequence structure in which two calculations are performed in order. Java lets us have as many actions as we want in a sequence structure. As we'll soon see, anywhere a single action may be placed, we may place several actions in sequence.

Activity diagrams are part of the UML. An activity diagram models the *workflow* (also called the *activity*) of a portion of a software system. Such workflows may include a portion of an algorithm, such as the sequence structure in Fig. 4.1. Activity diagrams are composed of special-purpose symbols, such as *action-state symbols* (rectangles with their left and right sides replaced with arcs curving outward), *diamonds* and *small circles*. These symbols are connected by *transition arrows*, which represent the flow of the activity—that is, the order in which the actions should occur.

Activity diagrams help programmers develop and represent algorithms. Consider the activity diagram for the sequence structure in Fig. 4.1. It contains two *action states* that represent actions to perform. Each action state contains an *action expression*—for example, "add grade to total" or "add 1 to counter"—that specifies a particular action to perform. Other actions might include calculations or input/output operations. The arrows in the activity diagram represent *transitions*, which indicate the order in which the actions represented by the action states occur. The program that implements the activities illustrated by the diagram in Fig. 4.1 first adds grade to total, then adds 1 to counter.

The *solid circle* located at the top of the activity diagram represents the activity's *initial state*—the beginning of the workflow before the program performs the modeled actions. The *solid circle surrounded by a hollow circle* that appears at the bottom of the diagram represents the *final state*—the end of the workflow after the program performs its actions.

Figure 4.1 also includes rectangles with the upper-right corners folded over. These are UML *notes* (like comments in Java)—explanatory remarks that describe the purpose of

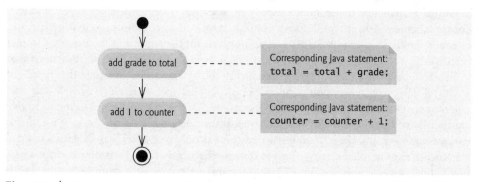

Fig. 4.1 | Sequence structure activity diagram.

symbols in the diagram. Figure 4.1 uses UML notes to show the Java code associated with each action state in the activity diagram. A *dotted line* connects each note with the element that the note describes. Activity diagrams normally do not show the Java code that implements the activity. We use notes for this purpose here to illustrate how the diagram relates to Java code. For more information on the UML, see our optional case study, which appears in the Software Engineering Case Study sections at the ends of Chapters 1–8 and 10, or visit www.uml.org.

Selection Statements in Java

Java has three types of *selection statements* (discussed in this chapter and Chapter 5). The if statement either performs (selects) an action, if a condition is true, or skips it, if the condition is false. The if...else statement performs an action if a condition is true and performs a different action if the condition is false. The switch statement (Chapter 5) performs one of many different actions, depending on the value of an expression.

The if statement is a *single-selection statement* because it selects or ignores a single action (or, as we'll soon see, a single group of actions). The if...else statement is called a *double-selection statement* because it selects between two different actions (or groups of actions). The switch statement is called a *multiple-selection statement* because it selects among many different actions (or groups of actions).

Repetition Statements in Java

Java provides three repetition statements that enable programs to perform statements repeatedly as long as a condition (called the *loop-continuation condition*) remains true. The repetition statements are the while, do...while and for statements. (Chapter 5 presents the do...while and for statements.) The while and for statements perform the action (or group of actions) in their bodies zero or more times—if the loop-continuation condition is initially false, the action (or group of actions) will not execute. The do...while statement performs the action (or group of actions) in its body one or more times.

The words if, else, switch, while, do and for are Java keywords. Keywords cannot be used as identifiers, such as variable names. A complete list of Java keywords appears in Appendix C.

Summary of Control Statements in Java

Java has only three kinds of control structures, which from this point forward we refer to as control statements: the sequence statement, selection statements (three types) and repetition statements (three types). Every program is formed by combining as many sequence, selection and repetition statements as is appropriate for the algorithm the program implements. As with the sequence statement in Fig. 4.1, we can model each control statement as an activity diagram. Each diagram contains an initial state and a final state that represent a control statement's entry point and exit point, respectively. *Single-entry/single-exit control statements* make it easy to build programs—we "attach" the control statements to one another by connecting the exit point of one to the entry point of the next. We call this *control-statement stacking*. We'll learn that there is only one other way in which control statements may be connected—*control-statement nesting*—in which one control statement appears inside another. Thus, Java programs are constructed from only three kinds of control statements, combined in only two ways. This is the essence of simplicity.

4.3 if **Single-Selection Statement**

Programs use selection statements to choose among alternative courses of action. For example, suppose that the passing grade on an exam is 60. The statement

```
if ( studentGrade >= 60 )
   System.out.println( "Passed" );
```

determines whether the condition "studentGrade >= 60" is true or false. If it is true, "Passed" is printed, and the next statement in order is "performed." If the condition is false, the println statement is ignored, and the next statement in order is performed.

Figure 4.2 illustrates the single-selection if statement. This figure contains what is perhaps the most important symbol in an activity diagram—the diamond, or *decision symbol*, which indicates that a decision is to be made. The workflow will continue along a path determined by the symbol's associated *guard conditions*, each of which can be true or false. Each transition arrow emerging from a decision symbol has a guard condition (specified in square brackets next to the transition arrow). If a guard condition is true, the workflow enters the action state to which the transition arrow points. In Fig. 4.2, if the grade is greater than or equal to 60, the program prints "Passed," then transitions to the final state of this activity. If the grade is less than 60, the program immediately transitions to the final state without displaying a message.

The if statement is a single-entry/single-exit control statement. We'll see that the activity diagrams for the remaining control statements also contain initial states, transition arrows, action states that indicate actions to perform, decision symbols (with associated guard conditions) that indicate decisions to be made and final states.

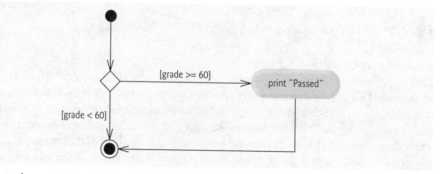

Fig. 4.2 | if single-selection statement UML activity diagram.

4.4 if...else **Double-Selection Statement**

The if single-selection statement performs an indicated action only when the condition is true; otherwise, the action is skipped. The if...else double-selection statement allows the programmer to specify an action to perform when the condition is true and a different action when the condition is false. For example, the statement

```
if ( grade >= 60 )
   System.out.println( "Passed" );
else
   System.out.println( "Failed" );
```

prints "Passed" if the student's grade is greater than or equal to 60, but prints "Failed" if it is less than 60. In either case, after printing occurs, the next pseudocode statement in sequence is "performed."

Note that the body of the else is also indented. Whatever indentation convention you choose should be applied consistently throughout your programs.

Figure 4.3 illustrates the flow of control in the if...else statement. Once again, the symbols in the UML activity diagram (besides the initial state, transition arrows and final state) represent action states and decisions. We continue to emphasize this action/decision model of computing. Imagine again a deep bin containing as many empty if...else statements as might be needed to build any Java program. Your job is to assemble these if...else statements (by stacking and nesting) with any other control statements required by the algorithm. You fill in the action states and decision symbols with action expressions and guard conditions appropriate to the algorithm you are developing.

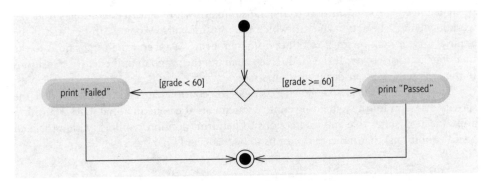

Fig. 4.3 | if...else double-selection statement UML activity diagram.

Conditional Operator (?:)

Java provides the *conditional operator* (?:) that can be used in place of an if...else statement. This is Java's only *ternary operator*—this means that it takes three operands. Together, the operands and the ?: symbol form a *conditional expression*. The first operand (to the left of the ?) is a *boolean* expression (i.e., a condition that evaluates to a boolean value—*true* or *false*), the second operand (between the ? and :) is the value of the conditional expression if the boolean expression is true and the third operand (to the right of the :) is the value of the conditional expression if the boolean expression evaluates to false. For example, the statement

```
System.out.println( studentGrade >= 60 ? "Passed" : "Failed" );
```

prints the value of println's conditional-expression argument. The conditional expression in this statement evaluates to the string "Passed" if the boolean expression studentGrade >= 60 is true and evaluates to the string "Failed" if the boolean expression is false. Thus, this statement with the conditional operator performs essentially the same function as the if...else statement shown earlier in this section. The precedence of the conditional operator is low, so the entire conditional expression is normally placed in parentheses. We'll see that conditional expressions can be used in some situations where if...else statements cannot.

Good Programming Practice 4.1

Conditional expressions are more difficult to read than if...else statements and should be used to replace only simple if...else statements that choose between two values.

Nested if...else Statements

A program can test multiple cases by placing if...else statements inside other if...else statements to create *nested if...else statements*. For example, the following nested if...else prints A for exam grades greater than or equal to 90, B for grades in the range 80 to 89, C for grades in the range 70 to 79, D for grades in the range 60 to 69 and F for all other grades:

```
if ( studentGrade >= 90 )
   System.out.println( "A" );
else
   if ( studentGrade >= 80 )
      System.out.println( "B" );
   else
      if ( studentGrade >= 70 )
         System.out.println( "C" );
      else
         if ( studentGrade >= 60 )
            System.out.println( "D" );
         else
            System.out.println( "F" );
```

If studentGrade is greater than or equal to 90, the first four conditions will be true, but only the statement in the if-part of the first if...else statement will execute. After that statement executes, the else-part of the "outermost" if...else statement is skipped. Most Java programmers prefer to write the preceding if...else statement as

```
if ( studentGrade >= 90 )
   System.out.println( "A" );
else if ( studentGrade >= 80 )
   System.out.println( "B" );
else if ( studentGrade >= 70 )
   System.out.println( "C" );
else if ( studentGrade >= 60 )
   System.out.println( "D" );
else
   System.out.println( "F" );
```

The two forms are identical except for the spacing and indentation, which the compiler ignores. The latter form is popular because it avoids deep indentation of the code to the right. Such indentation often leaves little room on a line of code, forcing lines to be split and decreasing program readability.

Dangling-else Problem

The Java compiler always associates an else with the immediately preceding if unless told to do otherwise by the placement of braces ({ and }). This behavior can lead to what is referred to as the *dangling-else problem*. For example,

```
if ( x > 5 )
   if ( y > 5 )
      System.out.println( "x and y are > 5" );
else
   System.out.println( "x is <= 5" );
```

appears to indicate that if x is greater than 5, the nested if statement determines whether y is also greater than 5. If so, the string "x and y are > 5" is output. Otherwise, it appears that if x is not greater than 5, the else part of the if...else outputs the string "x is <= 5".

Beware! This nested if...else statement does not execute as it appears. The compiler actually interprets the statement as

```
if ( x > 5 )
   if ( y > 5 )
      System.out.println( "x and y are > 5" );
   else
      System.out.println( "x is <= 5" );
```

in which the body of the first if is a nested if...else. The outer if statement tests whether x is greater than 5. If so, execution continues by testing whether y is also greater than 5. If the second condition is true, the proper string—"x and y are > 5"—is displayed. However, if the second condition is false, the string "x is <= 5" is displayed, even though we know that x is greater than 5. Equally bad, if the outer if statement's condition is false, the inner if...else is skipped and nothing is displayed.

To force the nested if...else statement to execute as it was originally intended, we must write it as follows:

```
if ( x > 5 )
{
   if ( y > 5 )
      System.out.println( "x and y are > 5" );
}
else
   System.out.println( "x is <= 5" );
```

The braces ({}) indicate to the compiler that the second if statement is in the body of the first if and that the else is associated with the *first* if.

Blocks

The if statement normally expects only one statement in its body. To include several statements in the body of an if (or the body of an else for an if...else statement), enclose the statements in braces ({ and }). A set of statements contained within a pair of braces is called a *block*. A block can be placed anywhere in a program that a single statement can be placed.

The following example includes a block in the else-part of an if...else statement:

```
if ( grade >= 60 )
   System.out.println( "Passed" );
else
{
   System.out.println( "Failed" );
   System.out.println( "You must take this course again." );
}
```

In this case, if grade is less than 60, the program executes both statements in the body of the else and prints

```
Failed.
You must take this course again.
```

Note the braces surrounding the two statements in the else clause. These braces are important. Without the braces, the statement

```
System.out.println( "You must take this course again." );
```

would be outside the body of the else-part of the if...else statement and would execute regardless of whether the grade was less than 60.

Common Programming Error 4.1

Forgetting one or both of the braces that delimit a block can lead to syntax errors or logic errors in a program.

Good Programming Practice 4.2

Always using braces in an if...else (or other) statement helps prevent their accidental omission, especially when adding statements to the if-part or the else-part at a later time. To avoid omitting one or both of the braces, some programmers type the beginning and ending braces of blocks before typing the individual statements within the braces.

Just as a block can be placed anywhere a single statement can be placed, it is also possible to have an empty statement. Recall from Section 2.7 that the empty statement is represented by placing a semicolon (;) where a statement would normally be.

Common Programming Error 4.2

Placing a semicolon after the condition in an if or if...else statement leads to a logic error in single-selection if statements and a syntax error in double-selection if...else statements (when the if-part contains an actual body statement).

4.5 while Repetition Statement

A *repetition statement* allows the programmer to specify that a program should repeat an action while some condition remains true. As an example of Java's *while* repetition statement, consider a program segment designed to find the first power of 3 larger than 100. Suppose that the int variable product is initialized to 3. When the following while statement finishes executing, product contains the result:

```
int product = 3;

while ( product <= 100 )
    product = 3 * product;
```

When this while statement begins execution, the value of variable product is 3. Each iteration of the while statement multiplies product by 3, so product takes on the values 9, 27, 81 and 243 successively. When variable product becomes 243, the while statement condition—product <= 100—becomes false. This terminates the repetition, so the final value of product is 243. At this point, program execution continues with the next statement after the while statement.

Common Programming Error 4.3

Not providing, in the body of a while statement, an action that eventually causes the condition in the while to become false normally results in an infinite loop.

The UML activity diagram in Fig. 4.4 illustrates the flow of control that corresponds to the preceding while statement. Once again, the symbols in the diagram (besides the initial state, transition arrows, a final state and three notes) represent an action state and a decision. This diagram also introduces the UML's *merge symbol*. The UML represents both the merge symbol and the decision symbol as diamonds. The merge symbol joins two flows of activity into one. In this diagram, the merge symbol joins the transitions from the initial state and from the action state, so they both flow into the decision that determines whether the loop should begin (or continue) executing. The decision and merge symbols can be distinguished by the number of "incoming" and "outgoing" transition arrows. A decision symbol has one transition arrow pointing to the diamond and two or more transition arrows pointing out from the diamond to indicate possible transitions from that point. In addition, each transition arrow pointing out of a decision symbol has a guard condition next to it. A merge symbol has two or more transition arrows pointing to the diamond and only one transition arrow pointing from the diamond, to indicate multiple activity flows merging to continue the activity. None of the transition arrows associated with a merge symbol has a guard condition.

Figure 4.4 clearly shows the repetition of the while statement discussed earlier in this section. The transition arrow emerging from the action state points back to the merge, from which program flow transitions back to the decision that is tested at the beginning of each iteration of the loop. The loop continues to execute until the guard condition product > 100 becomes true. Then the while statement exits (reaches its final state), and control passes to the next statement in sequence in the program.

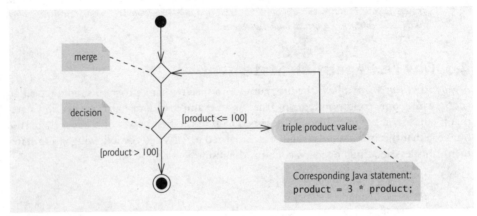

Fig. 4.4 | while repetition statement UML activity diagram.

4.6 Counter-Controlled Repetition

Consider the following problem statement:

A class of ten students took a quiz. The grades (integers in the range 0 to 100) for this quiz are available to you. Determine the class average on the quiz.

The class average is equal to the sum of the grades divided by the number of students. The program for solving this problem must input each grade, keep track of the total of all grades input, perform the averaging calculation and print the result.

Implementing Counter-Controlled Repetition in Class *GradeBook*

Class GradeBook (Fig. 4.5) contains a constructor (lines 11–14) that assigns a value to the class's instance variable courseName (declared in line 8). Lines 17–20, 23–26 and 29–34 declare methods setCourseName, getCourseName and displayMessage, respectively. Lines 37–66 declare method determineClassAverage, which implements the class-averaging algorithm.

```
 1   // Fig. 4.5: GradeBook.java
 2   // GradeBook class that solves class-average problem using
 3   // counter-controlled repetition.
 4   import java.util.Scanner; // program uses class Scanner
 5
 6   public class GradeBook
 7   {
 8      private String courseName; // name of course this GradeBook represents
 9
10      // constructor initializes courseName
11      public GradeBook( String name )
12      {
13         courseName = name; // initializes courseName
14      } // end constructor
15
16      // method to set the course name
17      public void setCourseName( String name )
18      {
19         courseName = name; // store the course name
20      } // end method setCourseName
21
22      // method to retrieve the course name
23      public String getCourseName()
24      {
25         return courseName;
26      } // end method getCourseName
27
28      // display a welcome message to the GradeBook user
29      public void displayMessage()
30      {
31         // getCourseName gets the name of the course
32         System.out.printf( "Welcome to the grade book for\n%s!\n\n",
33            getCourseName() );
34      } // end method displayMessage
35
36      // determine class average based on 10 grades entered by user
37      public void determineClassAverage()
38      {
39         // create Scanner to obtain input from command window
40         Scanner input = new Scanner( System.in );
```

Fig. 4.5 | Counter-controlled repetition: Class-average problem. (Part 1 of 2.)

```
41
42      int total; // sum of grades entered by user
43      int gradeCounter; // number of the grade to be entered next
44      int grade; // grade value entered by user
45      int average; // average of grades
46
47      // initialization phase
48      total = 0; // initialize total
49      gradeCounter = 1; // initialize loop counter
50
51      // processing phase
52      while ( gradeCounter <= 10 ) // loop 10 times
53      {
54          System.out.print( "Enter grade: " ); // prompt
55          grade = input.nextInt(); // input next grade
56          total = total + grade; // add grade to total
57          gradeCounter = gradeCounter + 1; // increment counter by 1
58      } // end while
59
60      // termination phase
61      average = total / 10; // integer division yields integer result
62
63      // display total and average of grades
64      System.out.printf( "\nTotal of all 10 grades is %d\n", total );
65      System.out.printf( "Class average is %d\n", average );
66  } // end method determineClassAverage
67
68  } // end class GradeBook
```

Fig. 4.5 | Counter-controlled repetition: Class-average problem. (Part 2 of 2.)

Line 40 declares and initializes Scanner variable input, which is used to read values entered by the user. Lines 42–45 declare local variables total, gradeCounter, grade and average to be of type int. Variable grade stores the user input.

Note that the declarations (in lines 42–45) appear in the body of method determine-ClassAverage. Recall that variables declared in a method body are local variables and can be used only from the line of their declaration in the method to the closing right brace (}) of the method declaration. A local variable's declaration must appear before the variable is used in that method and cannot be accessed outside the method in which it is declared.

In the versions of class GradeBook in this chapter, we simply read and process a set of grades. The averaging calculation is performed in method determineClassAverage using local variables—we do not preserve any information about student grades in instance variables of the class. In later versions of the class (in Chapter 7, Arrays), we maintain the grades in memory using an instance variable that refers to a data structure known as an array. This allows a GradeBook object to perform various calculations on the same set of grades without requiring the user to enter the grades multiple times.

The assignments (in lines 48–49) initialize total to 0 and gradeCounter to 1. Note that these initializations occur before the variables are used in calculations. Variables grade and average (for the user input and calculated average, respectively) need not be initialized here—their values will be assigned as they are input or calculated later in the method.

Common Programming Error 4.4

Reading the value of a local variable before it is initialized results in a compilation error. All local variables must be initialized before their values are read in expressions.

Line 52 indicates that the while statement should continue iterating as long as the value of gradeCounter is less than or equal to 10. While this condition remains true, the while statement repeatedly executes the statements between the braces that delimit its body (lines 54–57).

Line 54 displays the prompt "Enter grade: ". Line 55 reads the grade entered by the user and assigns it to variable grade. Then line 56 adds the new grade entered by the user to the total and assigns the result to total, which replaces its previous value.

Line 57 adds 1 to gradeCounter to indicate that the program has processed a grade and is ready to input the next grade from the user. Incrementing gradeCounter eventually causes gradeCounter to exceed 10. At that point the while loop terminates because its condition (line 52) becomes false.

When the loop terminates, line 61 performs the averaging calculation and assigns its result to the variable average. Line 64 uses System.out's printf method to display the text "Total of all 10 grades is " followed by variable total's value. Line 65 then uses printf to display the text "Class average is " followed by variable average's value. After reaching line 66, method determineClassAverage returns control to the calling method (i.e., main in GradeBookTest of Fig. 4.6).

Class GradeBookTest

Class GradeBookTest (Fig. 4.6) creates an object of class GradeBook (Fig. 4.5) and demonstrates its capabilities. Lines 10–11 of Fig. 4.6 create the GradeBook object and assign it to variable myGradeBook. The String in line 11 is passed to the GradeBook constructor (lines 11–14 of Fig. 4.5). Line 13 calls myGradeBook's displayMessage method to display a welcome message to the user. Line 14 then calls myGradeBook's determineClassAverage method to allow the user to enter 10 grades, then calculates and prints the average.

```java
1   // Fig. 4.6: GradeBookTest.java
2   // Create GradeBook object and invoke its determineClassAverage method.
3
4   public class GradeBookTest
5   {
6      public static void main( String args[] )
7      {
8         // create GradeBook object myGradeBook and
9         // pass course name to constructor
10        GradeBook myGradeBook = new GradeBook(
11           "CS101 Introduction to Java Programming" );
12
13        myGradeBook.displayMessage(); // display welcome message
14        myGradeBook.determineClassAverage(); // find average of 10 grades
15     } // end main
16
17  } // end class GradeBookTest
```

Fig. 4.6 | GradeBookTest class creates an object of class GradeBook (Fig. 4.5) and invokes its determineClassAverage method. (Part 1 of 2.)

```
Welcome to the grade book for
CS101 Introduction to Java Programming!

Enter grade: 67
Enter grade: 78
Enter grade: 89
Enter grade: 67
Enter grade: 87
Enter grade: 98
Enter grade: 93
Enter grade: 85
Enter grade: 82
Enter grade: 100

Total of all 10 grades is 846
Class average is 84
```

Fig. 4.6 | GradeBookTest class creates an object of class GradeBook (Fig. 4.5) and invokes its determineClassAverage method. (Part 2 of 2.)

Notes on Integer Division and Truncation

The averaging calculation performed by method determineClassAverage in response to the method call at line 14 in Fig. 4.6 produces an integer result. The program's output indicates that the sum of the grade values in the sample execution is 846, which, when divided by 10, should yield the floating-point number 84.6. However, the result of the calculation total / 10 (line 61 of Fig. 4.5) is the integer 84, because total and 10 are both integers. Dividing two integers results in integer division—any fractional part of the calculation is lost (i.e., truncated). We'll see how to obtain a floating-point result from the averaging calculation in the next section.

Common Programming Error 4.5

Assuming that integer division rounds (rather than truncates) can lead to incorrect results. For example, 7 ÷ 4, which yields 1.75 in conventional arithmetic, truncates to 1 in integer arithmetic, rather than rounding to 2.

4.7 Sentinel-Controlled Repetition

Let us generalize Section 4.6's class-average problem. Consider the following problem:

> *Develop a class-averaging program that processes grades for an arbitrary number of students each time it is run.*

In the previous class-average example, the problem statement specified the number of students, so the number of grades (10) was known in advance. In this example, no indication is given of how many grades the user will enter during the program's execution. The program must process an arbitrary number of grades. How can it determine when to stop the input of grades? How will it know when to calculate and print the class average?

One way to solve this problem is to use a special value called a *sentinel value* (also called a *signal value*, a *dummy value* or a *flag value*) to indicate "end of data entry." The user enters grades until all legitimate grades have been entered. The user then types the sentinel value to indicate that no more grades will be entered. Sentinel-controlled repetition is often called *indefinite repetition* because the number of repetitions is not known before the loop begins executing.

Clearly, a sentinel value must be chosen that cannot be confused with an acceptable input value. Grades on a quiz are nonnegative integers, so –1 is an acceptable sentinel value for this problem. Thus, a run of the class-average program might process a stream of inputs such as 95, 96, 75, 74, 89 and –1. The program would then compute and print the class average for the grades 95, 96, 75, 74 and 89; since –1 is the sentinel value, it should not enter into the averaging calculation.

Common Programming Error 4.6

Choosing a sentinel value that is also a legitimate data value is a logic error.

Implementing Sentinel-Controlled Repetition in Class *GradeBook*

Figure 4.7 shows the Java class GradeBook containing method determineClassAverage that implements the sentinel-controlled repetition solution to the calss averaging problem. Although each grade is an integer, the averaging calculation is likely to produce a number with a decimal point—in other words, a real (i.e., floating-point) number. The type int cannot represent such a number, so this class uses type double to do so.

```java
1   // Fig. 4.7: GradeBook.java
2   // GradeBook class that solves class-average program using
3   // sentinel-controlled repetition.
4   import java.util.Scanner; // program uses class Scanner
5
6   public class GradeBook
7   {
8      private String courseName; // name of course this GradeBook represents
9
10     // constructor initializes courseName
11     public GradeBook( String name )
12     {
13        courseName = name; // initializes courseName
14     } // end constructor
15
16     // method to set the course name
17     public void setCourseName( String name )
18     {
19        courseName = name; // store the course name
20     } // end method setCourseName
21
22     // method to retrieve the course name
23     public String getCourseName()
24     {
25        return courseName;
26     } // end method getCourseName
27
28     // display a welcome message to the GradeBook user
29     public void displayMessage()
30     {
```

Fig. 4.7 | Sentinel-controlled repetition: Class-average problem. (Part 1 of 2.)

```
31          // getCourseName gets the name of the course
32          System.out.printf( "Welcome to the grade book for\n%s!\n\n",
33             getCourseName() );
34       } // end method displayMessage
35
36       // determine the average of an arbitrary number of grades
37       public void determineClassAverage()
38       {
39          // create Scanner to obtain input from command window
40          Scanner input = new Scanner( System.in );
41
42          int total; // sum of grades
43          int gradeCounter; // number of grades entered
44          int grade; // grade value
45          double average; // number with decimal point for average
46
47          // initialization phase
48          total = 0; // initialize total
49          gradeCounter = 0; // initialize loop counter
50
51          // processing phase
52          // prompt for input and read grade from user
53          System.out.print( "Enter grade or -1 to quit: " );
54          grade = input.nextInt();
55
56          // loop until sentinel value read from user
57          while ( grade != -1 )
58          {
59             total = total + grade; // add grade to total
60             gradeCounter = gradeCounter + 1; // increment counter
61
62             // prompt for input and read next grade from user
63             System.out.print( "Enter grade or -1 to quit: " );
64             grade = input.nextInt();
65          } // end while
66
67          // termination phase
68          // if user entered at least one grade...
69          if ( gradeCounter != 0 )
70          {
71             // calculate average of all grades entered
72             average = (double) total / gradeCounter;
73
74             // display total and average (with two digits of precision)
75             System.out.printf( "\nTotal of the %d grades entered is %d\n",
76                gradeCounter, total );
77             System.out.printf( "Class average is %.2f\n", average );
78          } // end if
79          else // no grades were entered, so output appropriate message
80             System.out.println( "No grades were entered" );
81       } // end method determineClassAverage
82
83    } // end class GradeBook
```

Fig. 4.7 | Sentinel-controlled repetition: Class-average problem. (Part 2 of 2.)

In this example, we see that control statements may be stacked on top of one another (in sequence). The `while` statement (lines 57–65) is followed in sequence by an `if...else` statement (lines 69–80). Much of the code in this program is identical to that in Fig. 4.5, so we concentrate on the new concepts.

Line 45 declares `double` variable `average`, which allows us to store the calculated class average as a floating-point number. Line 49 initializes `gradeCounter` to 0, because no grades have been entered yet. Remember that this program uses sentinel-controlled repetition to input the grades from the user. To keep an accurate record of the number of grades entered, the program increments `gradeCounter` only when the user enters a valid grade value.x

Program Logic for Sentinel-Controlled Repetition vs. Counter-Controlled Repetition

Compare the program logic for sentinel-controlled repetition in this application with that for counter-controlled repetition in Fig. 4.5. In counter-controlled repetition, each iteration of the `while` statement (e.g., lines 52–58 of Fig. 4.5) reads a value from the user, for the specified number of iterations. In sentinel-controlled repetition, the program reads the first value (lines 53–54 of Fig. 4.7) before reaching the `while`. This value determines whether the program's flow of control should enter the body of the `while`. If the condition of the `while` is false, the user entered the sentinel value, so the body of the `while` does not execute (i.e., no grades were entered). If, on the other hand, the condition is true, the body begins execution, and the loop adds the `grade` value to the `total` (line 59). Then lines 63–64 in the loop body input the next value from the user. Next, program control reaches the closing right brace (}) of the loop body at line 65, so execution continues with the test of the `while`'s condition (line 57). The condition uses the most recent `grade` input by the user to determine whether the loop body should execute again. Note that the value of variable `grade` is always input from the user immediately before the program tests the `while` condition. This allows the program to determine whether the value just input is the sentinel value *before* the program processes that value (i.e., adds it to the `total`). If the sentinel value is input, the loop terminates, and the program does not add –1 to the `total`.

Good Programming Practice 4.3

In a sentinel-controlled loop, the prompts requesting data entry should explicitly remind the user of the sentinel value.

After the loop terminates, the `if...else` statement at lines 69–80 executes. The condition at line 69 determines whether any grades were input. If none were input, the `else` part (lines 79–80) of the `if...else` statement executes and displays the message "No grades were entered" and the method returns control to the calling method.

Error-Prevention Tip 4.1

When performing division by an expression whose value could be zero, explicitly test for this possibility and handle it appropriately in your program (e.g., by printing an error message) rather than allow the error to occur.

Notice the `while` statement's block in Fig. 4.7 (lines 58–65). Without the braces, the loop would consider its body to be only the first statement, which adds the `grade` to the `total`. The last three statements in the block would fall outside the loop body, causing the computer to interpret the code incorrectly as follows:

```
while ( grade != -1 )
   total = total + grade; // add grade to total
gradeCounter = gradeCounter + 1; // increment counter

// prompt for input and read next grade from user
System.out.print( "Enter grade or -1 to quit: " );
grade = input.nextInt();
```

The preceding code would cause an infinite loop in the program if the user did not input the sentinel -1 at line 54 (before the while statement).

Common Programming Error 4.7

Omitting the braces that delimit a block can lead to logic errors, such as infinite loops. To prevent this problem, some programmers enclose the body of every control statement in braces, even if the body contains only a single statement.

Explicitly and Implicitly Converting Between Primitive Types

If at least one grade was entered, line 72 of Fig. 4.7 calculates the average of the grades. Recall from Fig. 4.5 that integer division yields an integer result. Even though variable average is declared as a double (line 45), the calculation

```
average = total / gradeCounter;
```

loses the fractional part of the quotient before the result of the division is assigned to average. This occurs because total and gradeCounter are both integers, and integer division yields an integer result. To perform a floating-point calculation with integer values, we must temporarily treat these values as floating-point numbers for use in the calculation. Java provides the *unary cast operator* to accomplish this task. Line 72 uses the *(double)* cast operator—a unary operator—to create a *temporary* floating-point copy of its operand total (which appears to the right of the operator). Using a cast operator in this manner is called *explicit conversion*. The value stored in total is still an integer.

The calculation now consists of a floating-point value (the temporary double version of total) divided by the integer gradeCounter. Java knows how to evaluate only arithmetic expressions in which the operands' types are identical. To ensure that the operands are of the same type, Java performs an operation called *promotion* (or *implicit conversion*) on selected operands. For example, in an expression containing values of the types int and double, the int values are *promoted* to double values for use in the expression. In this example, the value of gradeCounter is promoted to type double, then the floating-point division is performed and the result of the calculation is assigned to average. As long as the (double) cast operator is applied to any variable in the calculation, the calculation will yield a double result. Later in this chapter, we discuss all the primitive types. You'll learn more about the promotion rules in Section 6.7.

Common Programming Error 4.8

The cast operator can be used to convert between primitive numeric types, such as int and double, and between related reference types (as we discuss in Chapter 10, Object-Oriented Programming: Polymorphism). Casting to the wrong type may cause compilation or runtime errors.

Cast operators are available for any type. The cast operator is formed by placing parentheses around the name of a type. The operator is a *unary operator* (i.e., an operator that takes only one operand). In Chapter 2, we studied the binary arithmetic operators. Java also supports unary versions of the plus (+) and minus (-) operators, so the programmer can write expressions like -7 or +5. Cast operators associate from right to left and have the same precedence as other unary operators, such as unary + and unary -. This precedence is one level higher than that of the *multiplicative operators* *, / and %. (See the operator precedence chart in Appendix A.) We indicate the cast operator with the notation (*type*) in our precedence charts, to indicate that any type name can be used to form a cast operator.

Line 77 outputs the class average using System.out's printf method. In this example, we display the class average rounded to the nearest hundredth. The format specifier %.2f in printf's format control string (line 77) indicates that variable average's value should be displayed with two digits of precision to the right of the decimal point—indicated by .2 in the format specifier. The three grades entered during the sample execution of class GradeBookTest (Fig. 4.8) total 257, which yields the average 85.666666.... Method printf uses the precision in the format specifier to round the value to the specified number of digits. In this program, the average is rounded to the hundredths position and the average is displayed as 85.67.

```
1    // Fig. 4.8: GradeBookTest.java
2    // Create GradeBook object and invoke its determineClassAverage method.
3
4    public class GradeBookTest
5    {
6       public static void main( String args[] )
7       {
8          // create GradeBook object myGradeBook and
9          // pass course name to constructor
10         GradeBook myGradeBook = new GradeBook(
11            "CS101 Introduction to Java Programming" );
12
13         myGradeBook.displayMessage(); // display welcome message
14         myGradeBook.determineClassAverage(); // find average of grades
15      } // end main
16
17   } // end class GradeBookTest
```

```
Welcome to the grade book for
CS101 Introduction to Java Programming!

Enter grade or -1 to quit: 97
Enter grade or -1 to quit: 88
Enter grade or -1 to quit: 72
Enter grade or -1 to quit: -1

Total of the 3 grades entered is 257
Class average is 85.67
```

Fig. 4.8 | GradeBookTest class creates an object of class GradeBook (Fig. 4.7) and invokes its determineClassAverage method.

4.8 Nested Control Statements

We have seen that control statements can be stacked on top of one another (in sequence). In this case study, we examine the only other structured way control statements can be connected, namely, by *nesting* one control statement within another.

Consider the following problem statement:

> *A college offers a course that prepares students for the state licensing exam for real estate brokers. Last year, ten of the students who completed this course took the exam. The college wants to know how well its students did on the exam. You have been asked to write a program to summarize the results. You have been given a list of these 10 students. Next to each name is written a 1 if the student passed the exam or a 2 if the student failed.*

> *Your program should analyze the results of the exam as follows:*

> 1. *Input each test result (i.e., a 1 or a 2). Display the message "Enter result" on the screen each time the program requests another test result.*

> 2. *Count the number of test results of each type.*

> 3. *Display a summary of the test results indicating the number of students who passed and the number who failed.*

> 4. *If more than eight students passed the exam, print the message "Raise tuition."*

After reading the problem statement carefully, we make the following observations:

1. The program must process test results for 10 students. A counter-controlled loop can be used because the number of test results is known in advance.

2. Each test result has a numeric value—either a 1 or a 2. Each time the program reads a test result, the program must determine whether the number is a 1 or a 2.

3. Two counters are used to keep track of the exam results—one to count the number of students who passed the exam and one to count the number of students who failed the exam.

4. After the program has processed all the results, it must decide whether more than eight students passed the exam.

The Java class that implements the preceding is shown in Fig. 4.9, and two sample executions appear in Fig. 4.10.

```
1   // Fig. 4.9: Analysis.java
2   // Analysis of examination results.
3   import java.util.Scanner; // class uses class Scanner
4
5   public class Analysis
6   {
7      public void processExamResults()
8      {
9         // create Scanner to obtain input from command window
10        Scanner input = new Scanner( System.in );
11
```

Fig. 4.9 | Nested control structures: Examination-results problem. (Part 1 of 2.)

```
12      // initializing variables in declarations
13      int passes = 0; // number of passes
14      int failures = 0; // number of failures
15      int studentCounter = 1; // student counter
16      int result; // one exam result (obtains value from user)
17
18      // process 10 students using counter-controlled loop
19      while ( studentCounter <= 10 )
20      {
21         // prompt user for input and obtain value from user
22         System.out.print( "Enter result (1 = pass, 2 = fail): " );
23         result = input.nextInt();
24
25         // if...else nested in while
26         if ( result == 1 )            // if result 1,
27            passes = passes + 1;       // increment passes;
28         else                          // else result is not 1, so
29            failures = failures + 1; // increment failures
30
31         // increment studentCounter so loop eventually terminates
32         studentCounter = studentCounter + 1;
33      } // end while
34
35      // termination phase; prepare and display results
36      System.out.printf( "Passed: %d\nFailed: %d\n", passes, failures );
37
38      // determine whether more than 8 students passed
39      if ( passes > 8 )
40         System.out.println( "Raise Tuition" );
41   } // end method processExamResults
42
43 } // end class Analysis
```

Fig. 4.9 | Nested control structures: Examination-results problem. (Part 2 of 2.)

Lines 13–16 of Fig. 4.9 declare the variables that method processExamResults of class Analysis uses to process the examination results. Several of these declarations use Java's ability to incorporate variable initialization into declarations (passes is assigned 0, failures is assigned 0 and studentCounter is assigned 1).

The while statement (lines 19–33) loops 10 times. During each iteration, the loop inputs and processes one exam result. Notice that the if...else statement (lines 26–29) for processing each result is nested in the while statement. If the result is 1, the if...else statement increments passes; otherwise, it assumes the result is 2 and increments failures. Line 32 increments studentCounter before the loop condition is tested again at line 19. After 10 values have been input, the loop terminates and line 36 displays the number of passes and failures. The if statement at lines 39–40 determines whether more than eight students passed the exam and, if so, outputs the message "Raise Tuition".

Error-Prevention Tip 4.2

Initializing local variables when they are declared helps the programmer avoid any compilation errors that might arise from attempts to use uninitialized data. While Java does not require that local variable initializations be incorporated into declarations, it does require that local variables be initialized before their values are used in an expression.

AnalysisTest *Class That Demonstrates Class* Analysis

Class AnalysisTest (Fig. 4.10) creates an Analysis object (line 8) and invokes the object's processExamResults method (line 9) to process a set of exam results entered by the user. Figure 4.10 shows the input and output from two sample executions of the program. During the first sample execution, the condition at line 39 of method processExamResults in Fig. 4.9 is true—more than eight students passed the exam, so the program outputs a message indicating that the tuition should be raised.

```java
1  // Fig. 4.10: AnalysisTest.java
2  // Test program for class Analysis.
3
4  public class AnalysisTest
5  {
6     public static void main( String args[] )
7     {
8        Analysis application = new Analysis(); // create Analysis object
9        application.processExamResults(); // call method to process results
10    } // end main
11
12 } // end class AnalysisTest
```

```
Enter result (1 = pass, 2 = fail): 1
Enter result (1 = pass, 2 = fail): 2
Enter result (1 = pass, 2 = fail): 1
Enter result (1 = pass, 2 = fail): 1
Enter result (1 = pass, 2 = fail): 1
Enter result (1 = pass, 2 = fail): 1
Enter result (1 = pass, 2 = fail): 1
Enter result (1 = pass, 2 = fail): 1
Enter result (1 = pass, 2 = fail): 1
Enter result (1 = pass, 2 = fail): 1
Passed: 9
Failed: 1
Raise Tuition
```

```
Enter result (1 = pass, 2 = fail): 1
Enter result (1 = pass, 2 = fail): 2
Enter result (1 = pass, 2 = fail): 1
Enter result (1 = pass, 2 = fail): 2
Enter result (1 = pass, 2 = fail): 1
Enter result (1 = pass, 2 = fail): 2
Enter result (1 = pass, 2 = fail): 2
Enter result (1 = pass, 2 = fail): 1
Enter result (1 = pass, 2 = fail): 1
Enter result (1 = pass, 2 = fail): 1
Passed: 6
Failed: 4
```

Fig. 4.10 | Test program for class Analysis (Fig. 4.9).

4.9 Compound Assignment Operators

Java provides several *compound assignment operators* for abbreviating assignment expressions. Any statement of the form

   variable = variable   operator   expression;

where *operator* is one of the binary operators +, -, *, / or % (or others we discuss later in the text) can be written in the form

   variable   operator= expression;

For example, you can abbreviate the statement

   c = c + 3;

with the *addition compound assignment operator*, +=, as

   c += 3;

The += operator adds the value of the expression on the right of the operator to the value of the variable on the left of the operator and stores the result in the variable on the left of the operator. Thus, the assignment expression c += 3 adds 3 to c. Figure 4.11 shows the arithmetic compound assignment operators, sample expressions using the operators and explanations of what the operators do.

Assignment operator	Sample expression	Explanation	Assigns
Assume: int c = 3, d = 5, e = 4, f = 6, g = 12;			
+=	c += 7	c = c + 7	10 to c
-=	d -= 4	d = d - 4	1 to d
*=	e *= 5	e = e * 5	20 to e
/=	f /= 3	f = f / 3	2 to f
%=	g %= 9	g = g % 9	3 to g

Fig. 4.11 | Arithmetic compound assignment operators.

4.10 Increment and Decrement Operators

Java provides two unary operators for adding 1 to or subtracting 1 from the value of a numeric variable. These are the unary *increment operator*, ++, and the unary *decrement operator*, --, which are summarized in Fig. 4.12. A program can increment by 1 the value of a variable called c using the increment operator, ++, rather than the expression c = c + 1 or c += 1. An increment or decrement operator that is prefixed to (placed before) a variable is referred to as the *prefix increment* or *prefix decrement operator*, respectively. An increment or decrement operator that is postfixed to (placed after) a variable is referred to as the *postfix increment* or *postfix decrement operator*, respectively.

Operator	Operator name	Sample expression	Explanation
++	prefix increment	++a	Increment a by 1, then use the new value of a in the expression in which a resides.
++	postfix increment	a++	Use the current value of a in the expression in which a resides, then increment a by 1.
--	prefix decrement	--b	Decrement b by 1, then use the new value of b in the expression in which b resides.
--	postfix decrement	b--	Use the current value of b in the expression in which b resides, then decrement b by 1.

Fig. 4.12 | Increment and decrement operators.

Using the prefix increment (or decrement) operator to add (or subtract) 1 from a variable is known as *preincrementing* (or *predecrementing*) the variable. Preincrementing (or predecrementing) a variable causes the variable to be incremented (decremented) by 1, and then the new value of the variable is used in the expression in which it appears. Using the postfix increment (or decrement) operator to add (or subtract) 1 from a variable is known as *postincrementing* (or *postdecrementing*) the variable. Postincrementing (or postdecrementing) the variable causes the current value of the variable to be used in the expression in which it appears, and then the variable's value is incremented (decremented) by 1.

 Good Programming Practice 4.4

Unlike binary operators, the unary increment and decrement operators should be placed next to their operands, with no intervening spaces.

Figure 4.13 demonstrates the difference between the prefix increment and postfix increment versions of the ++ increment operator. The decrement operator (--) works similarly. Note that this example contains only one class, with method main performing all the class's work. In this chapter and in Chapter 3, you have seen examples consisting of two classes—one class containing methods that perform useful tasks and one containing method main, which creates an object of the other class and calls its methods. In this example, we simply want to show the mechanics of the ++ operator, so we use only one class declaration containing method main. Occasionally, when it does not make sense to create a reusable class to demonstrate a simple concept, we'll use a "mechanical" example contained entirely within the main method of a single class.

Line 11 initializes the variable c to 5, and line 12 outputs c's initial value. Line 13 outputs the value of the expression c++. This expression postincrements the variable c, so c's original value (5) is output, then c's value is incremented (to 6). Thus, line 13 outputs c's initial value (5) again. Line 14 outputs c's new value (6) to prove that the variable's value was indeed incremented in line 13.

Line 19 resets c's value to 5, and line 20 outputs c's value. Line 21 outputs the value of the expression ++c. This expression preincrements c, so its value is incremented, then the new value (6) is output. Line 22 outputs c's value again to show that the value of c is still 6 after line 21 executes.

```
 1   // Fig. 4.13: Increment.java
 2   // Prefix increment and postfix increment operators.
 3
 4   public class Increment
 5   {
 6      public static void main( String args[] )
 7      {
 8         int c;
 9
10         // demonstrate postfix increment operator
11         c = 5; // assign 5 to c
12         System.out.println( c );    // prints 5
13         System.out.println( c++ ); // prints 5 then postincrements
14         System.out.println( c );    // prints 6
15
16         System.out.println(); // skip a line
17
18         // demonstrate prefix increment operator
19         c = 5; // assign 5 to c
20         System.out.println( c );    // prints 5
21         System.out.println( ++c ); // preincrements then prints 6
22         System.out.println( c );    // prints 6
23
24      } // end main
25
26   } // end class Increment
```

```
5
5
6

5
6
6
```

Fig. 4.13 | Preincrementing and postincrementing.

The arithmetic compound assignment operators and the increment and decrement operators can be used to simplify program statements. For example, the three assignment statements in Fig. 4.9 (lines 27, 29 and 32)

```
passes = passes + 1;
failures = failures + 1;
studentCounter = studentCounter + 1;
```

can be written more concisely with compound assignment operators as

```
passes += 1;
failures += 1;
studentCounter += 1;
```

with prefix increment operators as

```
++passes;
++failures;
++studentCounter;
```

or with postfix increment operators as

```
passes++;
failures++;
studentCounter++;
```

When incrementing or decrementing a variable in a statement by itself, the prefix increment and postfix increment forms have the same effect, and the prefix decrement and postfix decrement forms have the same effect. It is only when a variable appears in the context of a larger expression that preincrementing and postincrementing the variable have different effects (and similarly for predecrementing and postdecrementing).

Common Programming Error 4.9

Attempting to use the increment or decrement operator on an expression other than one to which a value can be assigned is a syntax error. For example, writing ++(x + 1) is a syntax error because (x + 1) is not a variable.

Figure 4.14 shows the precedence and associativity of the operators we have introduced to this point. The operators are shown from top to bottom in decreasing order of precedence. The second column describes the associativity of the operators at each level of precedence. The conditional operator (?:); the unary operators increment (++), decrement (--), plus (+) and minus (-); the cast operators and the assignment operators =, +=, -=, *=, /= and %= associate from right to left. All the other operators in the operator precedence chart in Fig. 4.14 associate from left to right. The third column lists the type of each group of operators.

Operators						Associativity	Type
++	--					right to left	unary postfix
++	--	+	-	(*type*)		right to left	unary prefix
*	/	%				left to right	multiplicative
+	-					left to right	additive
<	<=	>	>=			left to right	relational
==	!=					left to right	equality
?:						right to left	conditional
=	+=	-=	*=	/=	%=	right to left	assignment

Fig. 4.14 | Precedence and associativity of the operators discussed so far.

4.11 Primitive Types

The table in Appendix D, lists the eight primitive types in Java. Like its predecessor languages C and C++, Java requires all variables to have a type. For this reason, Java is referred to as a ***strongly typed language***.

In C and C++, programmers frequently have to write separate versions of programs to support different computer platforms, because the primitive types are not guaranteed to be identical from computer to computer. For example, an int value on one machine might be represented by 16 bits (2 bytes) of memory, and on another machine by 32 bits (4 bytes) of memory. In Java, int values are always 32 bits (4 bytes).

 Portability Tip 4.1

Unlike C and C++, the primitive types in Java are portable across all computer platforms that support Java.

Each type in Appendix D is listed with its size in bits (there are eight bits to a byte) and its range of values. Because the designers of Java want it to be maximally portable, they use internationally recognized standards for both character formats (Unicode; for more information, visit www.unicode.org) and floating-point numbers (IEEE 754; for more information, visit grouper.ieee.org/groups/754/).

Recall from Section 3.5 that variables of primitive types declared outside of a method as fields of a class are automatically assigned default values unless explicitly initialized. Instance variables of types char, byte, short, int, long, float and double are all given the value 0 by default. Instance variables of type boolean are given the value false by default. Reference-type instance variables are initialized by default to the value null.

4.12 (Optional) Software Engineering Case Study: Identifying Class Attributes

In Section 3.9, we began the first stage of an object-oriented design (OOD) for our ATM system—analyzing the requirements document and identifying the classes needed to implement the system. We listed the nouns and noun phrases in the requirements document and identified a separate class for each one that plays a significant role in the ATM system. We then modeled the classes and their relationships in a UML class diagram (Fig. 3.21). Classes have attributes (data) and operations (behaviors). Class attributes are implemented in Java programs as fields, and class operations are implemented as methods. In this section, we determine many of the attributes needed in the ATM system. In Chapter 5, we examine how these attributes represent an object's state. In Chapter 6, we determine class operations.

Identifying Attributes

Consider the attributes of some real-world objects: A person's attributes include height, weight and whether the person is left-handed, right-handed or ambidextrous. A radio's attributes include its station setting, its volume setting and its AM or FM setting. A car's attributes include its speedometer and odometer readings, the amount of gas in its tank and what gear it is in. A personal computer's attributes include its manufacturer (e.g., Dell, Sun, Apple or IBM), type of screen (e.g., LCD or CRT), main memory size and hard disk size.

We can identify many attributes of the classes in our system by looking for descriptive words and phrases in the requirements document. For each one we find that plays a significant role in the ATM system, we create an attribute and assign it to one or more of the classes identified in Section 3.9. We also create attributes to represent any additional data that a class may need, as such needs become clear throughout the design process.

Figure 4.15 lists the words or phrases from the requirements document that describe each class. We formed this list by reading the requirements document and identifying any words or phrases that refer to characteristics of the classes in the system. For example, the requirements document describes the steps taken to obtain a "withdrawal amount," so we list "amount" next to class Withdrawal.

Figure 4.15 leads us to create one attribute of class ATM. Class ATM maintains information about the state of the ATM. The phrase "user is authenticated" describes a state of the ATM (we introduce states in Section 5.9), so we include userAuthenticated as a ***Boolean attribute*** (i.e., an attribute that has a value of either true or false) in class ATM. Note that the Boolean attribute type in the UML is equivalent to the boolean type in Java. This attribute indicates whether the ATM has successfully authenticated the current user—userAuthenticated must be true for the system to allow the user to perform transactions and access account information. This attribute helps ensure the security of the data in the system.

Classes BalanceInquiry, Withdrawal and Deposit share one attribute. Each transaction involves an "account number" that corresponds to the account of the user making the transaction. We assign an integer attribute accountNumber to each transaction class to identify the account to which an object of the class applies.

Descriptive words and phrases in the requirements document also suggest some differences in the attributes required by each transaction class. The requirements document indicates that to withdraw cash or deposit funds, users must input a specific "amount" of money to be withdrawn or deposited, respectively. Thus, we assign to classes Withdrawal and Deposit an attribute amount to store the value supplied by the user. The amounts of

Class	Descriptive words and phrases
ATM	user is authenticated
BalanceInquiry	account number
Withdrawal	account number amount
Deposit	account number amount
BankDatabase	[no descriptive words or phrases]
Account	account number PIN balance
Screen	[no descriptive words or phrases]
Keypad	[no descriptive words or phrases]
CashDispenser	begins each day loaded with 500 $20 bills
DepositSlot	[no descriptive words or phrases]

Fig. 4.15 | Descriptive words and phrases from the ATM requirements.

money related to a withdrawal and a deposit are defining characteristics of these transactions that the system requires for these transactions to take place. Class BalanceInquiry, however, needs no additional data to perform its task—it requires only an account number to indicate the account whose balance should be retrieved.

Class Account has several attributes. The requirements document states that each bank account has an "account number" and "PIN," which the system uses for identifying accounts and authenticating users. We assign to class Account two integer attributes: accountNumber and pin. The requirements document also specifies that an account maintains a "balance" of the amount of money in the account and that money the user deposits does not become available for a withdrawal until the bank verifies the amount of cash in the deposit envelope, and any checks in the envelope clear. An account must still record the amount of money that a user deposits, however. Therefore, we decide that an account should represent a balance using two attributes: availableBalance and totalBalance. Attribute availableBalance tracks the amount of money that a user can withdraw from the account. Attribute totalBalance refers to the total amount of money that the user has "on deposit" (i.e., the amount of money available, plus the amount waiting to be verified or cleared). For example, suppose an ATM user deposits $50.00 into an empty account. The totalBalance attribute would increase to $50.00 to record the deposit, but the availableBalance would remain at $0. [*Note:* We assume that the bank updates the availableBalance attribute of an Account some length of time after the ATM transaction occurs, in response to confirming that $50 worth of cash or checks was found in the deposit envelope. We assume that this update occurs through a transaction that a bank employee performs using some piece of bank software other than the ATM. Thus, we do not discuss this transaction in our case study.]

Class CashDispenser has one attribute. The requirements document states that the cash dispenser "begins each day loaded with 500 $20 bills." The cash dispenser must keep track of the number of bills it contains to determine whether enough cash is on hand to satisfy withdrawal requests. We assign to class CashDispenser an integer attribute count, which is initially set to 500.

For real problems in industry, there is no guarantee that requirements documents will be rich enough and precise enough for the object-oriented systems designer to determine all the attributes or even all the classes. The need for additional classes, attributes and behaviors may become clear as the design process proceeds. As we progress through this case study, we too will continue to add, modify and delete information about the classes in our system.

Modeling Attributes

The class diagram in Fig. 4.16 lists some of the attributes for the classes in our system—the descriptive words and phrases in Fig. 4.15 lead us to identify these attributes. For simplicity, Fig. 4.16 does not show the associations among classes—we showed these in Fig. 3.21. This is a common practice of systems designers when designs are being developed. Recall from Section 3.9 that in the UML, a class's attributes are placed in the middle compartment of the class's rectangle. We list each attribute's name and type separated by a colon (:), followed in some cases by an equal sign (=) and an initial value.

Consider the userAuthenticated attribute of class ATM:

```
userAuthenticated : Boolean = false
```

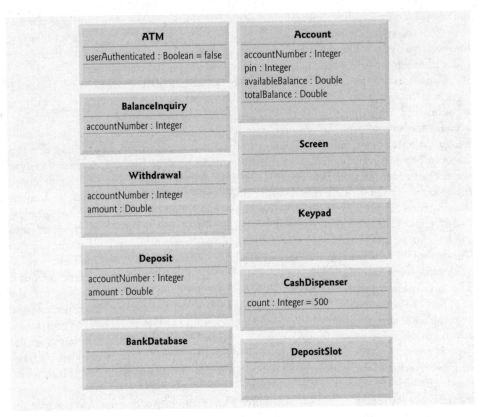

Fig. 4.16 | Classes with attributes.

This attribute declaration contains three pieces of information about the attribute. The *attribute name* is userAuthenticated. The *attribute type* is Boolean. In Java, an attribute can be represented by a primitive type, such as boolean, int or double, or a reference type like a class—as discussed in Chapter 3. We've chosen to model only primitive-type attributes in Fig. 4.16—we discuss the reasoning behind this decision shortly. [*Note:* The attribute types in Fig. 4.16 are in UML notation. We'll associate the types Boolean, Integer and Double in the UML diagram with the primitive types boolean, int and double in Java, respectively.]

We can also indicate an initial value for an attribute. The userAuthenticated attribute in class ATM has an initial value of false. This indicates that the system initially does not consider the user to be authenticated. If an attribute has no initial value specified, only its name and type (separated by a colon) are shown. For example, the accountNumber attribute of class BalanceInquiry is an integer. Here we show no initial value, because the value of this attribute is a number that we do not yet know. This number will be determined at execution time based on the account number entered by the current ATM user.

Figure 4.16 does not include any attributes for classes Screen, Keypad and DepositSlot. These are important components of our system, for which our design process simply has not yet revealed any attributes. We may still discover some, however, in the remaining phases of design or when we implement these classes in Java. This is perfectly normal.

Software Engineering Observation 4.1

At early stages in the design process, classes often lack attributes (and operations). Such classes should not be eliminated, however, because attributes (and operations) may become evident in the later phases of design and implementation.

Note that Fig. 4.16 also does not include attributes for class `BankDatabase`. Recall from Chapter 3 that in Java, attributes can be represented by either primitive types or reference types. We have chosen to include only primitive-type attributes in the class diagram in Fig. 4.16 (and in similar class diagrams throughout the case study). A reference-type attribute is modeled more clearly as an association (in particular, a composition) between the class holding the reference and the class of the object to which the reference points. For example, the class diagram in Fig. 3.21 indicates that class `BankDatabase` participates in a composition relationship with zero or more `Account` objects. From this composition, we can determine that when we implement the ATM system in Java, we'll be required to create an attribute of class `BankDatabase` to hold references to zero or more `Account` objects. Similarly, we can determine reference-type attributes of class `ATM` that correspond to its composition relationships with classes `Screen`, `Keypad`, `CashDispenser` and `DepositSlot`. These composition-based attributes would be redundant if modeled in Fig. 4.16, because the compositions modeled in Fig. 3.21 already convey the fact that the database contains information about zero or more accounts and that an ATM is composed of a screen, keypad, cash dispenser and deposit slot. Software developers typically model these whole/part relationships as compositions rather than as attributes required to implement the relationships.

The class diagram in Fig. 4.16 provides a solid basis for the structure of our model, but the diagram is not complete. In Section 5.9, we identify the states and activities of the objects in the model, and in Section 6.19 we identify the operations that the objects perform. As we present more of the UML and object-oriented design, we'll continue to strengthen the structure of our model.

Software Engineering Case Study Self-Review Exercises

4.1 We typically identify the attributes of the classes in our system by analyzing the _____ in the requirements document.
   a) nouns and noun phrases
   b) descriptive words and phrases
   c) verbs and verb phrases
   d) All of the above.

4.2 Which of the following is not an attribute of an airplane?
   a) length
   b) wingspan
   c) fly
   d) number of seats

4.3 Describe the meaning of the following attribute declaration of class `CashDispenser` in the class diagram in Fig. 4.16:

```
count : Integer = 500
```

Answers to Software Engineering Case Study Self-Review Exercises

4.1 b.

4.2 c. Fly is an operation or behavior of an airplane, not an attribute.

4.3 This indicates that count is an Integer with an initial value of 500. This attribute keeps track of the number of bills available in the CashDispenser at any given time.

4.13 Wrap-Up

Only three types of control structures—sequence, selection and repetition—are needed to develop any problem-solving algorithm. Specifically, this chapter demonstrated the if single-selection statement, the if...else double-selection statement and the while repetition statement. We used control-statement stacking to total and compute the average of a set of student grades with counter- and sentinel-controlled repetition, and we used control-statement nesting to analyze and make decisions based on a set of exam results. We introduced Java's compound assignment operators, and its increment and decrement operators. Finally, we discussed Java's primitive types. In Chapter 5, we continue our discussion of control statements, introducing the for, do...while and switch statements.

5

Control Statements: Part 2

OBJECTIVES

In this chapter you'll learn:

- To use the **for** and **do...while** repetition statements to execute statements in a program repeatedly.

- To understand multiple selection using the **switch** selection statement.

- To use the **break** and **continue** program control statements to alter the flow of control.

- To use the logical operators to form complex conditional expressions in control statements.

Outline

5.1 Introduction

5.2 Essentials of Counter-Controlled Repetition

5.3 for Repetition Statement

5.4 Examples Using the for Statement

5.5 do...while Repetition Statement

5.6 switch Multiple-Selection Statement

5.7 break and continue Statements

5.8 Logical Operators

5.9 (Optional) Software Engineering Case Study: Identifying Objects' States and Activities

5.10 Wrap-Up

5.1 Introduction

Chapter 4 began our introduction to the types of building blocks that are available for problem solving. This chapter introduces Java's remaining control statements. The control statements we study here and in Chapter 4 are helpful in building and manipulating objects.

In this chapter, we demonstrate Java's for, do...while and switch statements. Through a series of short examples using while and for, we explore the essentials of counter-controlled repetition. We devote a portion of the chapter (and Chapter 7) to expanding the GradeBook class presented in Chapters 3–4. In particular, we create a version of class GradeBook that uses a switch statement to count the number of A, B, C, D and F grade equivalents in a set of numeric grades entered by the user. We introduce the break and continue program control statements. We discuss Java's logical operators, which enable you to use more complex conditional expressions in control statements.

5.2 Essentials of Counter-Controlled Repetition

This section uses the while repetition statement introduced in Chapter 4 to formalize the elements required to perform counter-controlled repetition. Counter-controlled repetition requires

1. a *control variable* (or loop counter)

2. the *initial value* of the control variable

3. the *increment* (or *decrement*) by which the control variable is modified each time through the loop (also known as *each iteration of the loop*)

4. the *loop-continuation condition* that determines whether looping should continue.

To see these elements of counter-controlled repetition, consider the application of Fig. 5.1, which uses a loop to display the numbers from 1 through 10. Note that Fig. 5.1 contains only one method, main, which does all of the class's work. For most applications in Chapters 3–4 we have encouraged the use of two separate files—one that declares a reusable class (e.g., Account) and one that instantiates one or more objects of that class (e.g., AccountTest) and demonstrates its (their) functionality. Occasionally, however, it is more appropriate simply to create one class whose main method concisely illustrates a basic

```
 1   // Fig. 5.1: WhileCounter.java
 2   // Counter-controlled repetition with the while repetition statement.
 3
 4   public class WhileCounter
 5   {
 6      public static void main( String args[] )
 7      {
 8         int counter = 1; // declare and initialize control variable
 9
10         while ( counter <= 10 ) // loop-continuation condition
11         {
12            System.out.printf( "%d  ", counter );
13            ++counter; // increment control variable by 1
14         } // end while
15
16         System.out.println(); // output a newline
17      } // end main
18   } // end class WhileCounter
```

```
1  2  3  4  5  6  7  8  9  10
```

Fig. 5.1 | Counter-controlled repetition with the while repetition statement.

concept. Throughout this chapter, we use several one-class examples like Fig. 5.1 to demonstrate the mechanics of Java's control statements.

In Fig. 5.1, the elements of counter-controlled repetition are defined in lines 8, 10 and 13. Line 8 declares the control variable (counter) as an int, reserves space for it in memory and sets its initial value to 1. Variable counter could also have been declared and initialized with the following local-variable declaration and assignment statements:

```
int counter; // declare counter
counter = 1; // initialize counter to 1
```

Line 12 displays control variable counter's value during each iteration of the loop. Line 13 increments the control variable by 1 for each iteration of the loop. The loop-continuation condition in the while (line 10) tests whether the value of the control variable is less than or equal to 10 (the final value for which the condition is true). Note that the program performs the body of this while even when the control variable is 10. The loop terminates when the control variable exceeds 10 (i.e., counter becomes 11).

Common Programming Error 5.1

Because floating-point values may be approximate, controlling loops with floating-point variables may result in imprecise counter values and inaccurate termination tests.

Error-Prevention Tip 5.1

Control counting loops with integers.

Good Programming Practice 5.1

Place blank lines above and below repetition and selection control statements, and indent the statement bodies to enhance readability.

The program in Fig. 5.1 can be made more concise by initializing counter to 0 in line 8 and preincrementing counter in the while condition as follows:

```
while ( ++counter <= 10 ) // loop-continuation condition
    System.out.printf( "%d  ", counter );
```

This code saves a statement (and eliminates the need for braces around the loop's body), because the while condition performs the increment before testing the condition. (Recall from Section 4.10 that the precedence of ++ is higher than that of <=.) Coding in such a condensed fashion takes practice, might make code more difficult to read, debug, modify and maintain, and typically should be avoided.

5.3 for Repetition Statement

Section 5.2 presented the essentials of counter-controlled repetition. The while statement can be used to implement any counter-controlled loop. Java also provides the for repetition statement, which specifies the counter-controlled-repetition details in a single line of code. Figure 5.2 reimplements the application of Fig. 5.1 using for.

The application's main method operates as follows: When the for statement (lines 10–11) begins executing, the control variable counter is declared and initialized to 1. (Recall from Section 5.2 that the first two elements of counter-controlled repetition are the control variable and its initial value.) Next, the program checks the loop-continuation condition, counter <= 10, which is between the two required semicolons. Because the initial value of counter is 1, the condition initially is true. Therefore, the body statement (line 11) displays control variable counter's value, namely 1. After executing the loop's body, the program increments counter in the expression counter++, which appears to the right of the second semicolon. Then the loop-continuation test is performed again to determine whether the program should continue with the next iteration of the loop. At this point, the control variable value is 2, so the condition is still true (the final value is not exceeded)—thus, the program performs the body statement again (i.e., the next iteration

```
1   // Fig. 5.2: ForCounter.java
2   // Counter-controlled repetition with the for repetition statement.
3
4   public class ForCounter
5   {
6      public static void main( String args[] )
7      {
8         // for statement header includes initialization,
9         // loop-continuation condition and increment
10        for ( int counter = 1; counter <= 10; counter++ )
11           System.out.printf( "%d  ", counter );
12
13        System.out.println(); // output a newline
14     } // end main
15  } // end class ForCounter
```

```
1  2  3  4  5  6  7  8  9  10
```

Fig. 5.2 | Counter-controlled repetition with the for repetition statement.

of the loop). This process continues until the numbers 1 through 10 have been displayed and the counter's value becomes 11, causing the loop-continuation test to fail and repetition to terminate (after 10 repetitions of the loop body at line 11). Then the program performs the first statement after the for—in this case, line 13.

Note that Fig. 5.2 uses (in line 10) the loop-continuation condition counter <= 10. If you incorrectly specified counter < 10 as the condition, the loop would iterate only nine times. This mistake is a common logic error called an *off-by-one error*.

Figure 5.3 takes a closer look at the for statement in Fig. 5.2. The for's first line (including the keyword for and everything in parentheses after for)—line 10 in Fig. 5.2—is sometimes called the for statement header, or simply the for header. Note that the for header "does it all"—it specifies each item needed for counter-controlled repetition with a control variable. If there is more than one statement in the body of the for, braces ({ and }) are required to define the body of the loop.

The general format of the for statement is

> **for** (*initialization*; *loopContinuationCondition*; *increment*)
> *statement*

where the *initialization* expression names the loop's control variable and optionally provides its initial value, *loopContinuationCondition* is the condition that determines whether the loop should continue executing and *increment* modifies the control variable's value (possibly an increment or decrement), so that the loop-continuation condition eventually becomes false. The two semicolons in the for header are required.

Common Programming Error 5.2

Using commas instead of the two required semicolons in a for *header is a syntax error.*

In most cases, the for statement can be represented with an equivalent while statement as follows:

> *initialization*;
>
> **while** (*loopContinuationCondition*)
> {
>   *statement*
>   *increment*;
> }

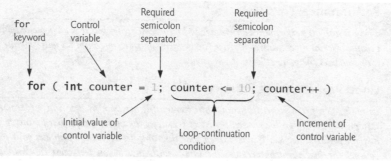

Fig. 5.3 | for statement header components.

In Section 5.7, we show a case in which a for statement cannot be represented with an equivalent while statement.

Typically, for statements are used for counter-controlled repetition and while statements for sentinel-controlled repetition. However, while and for can each be used for either repetition type.

If the *initialization* expression in the for header declares the control variable (i.e., the control variable's type is specified before the variable name, as in Fig. 5.2), the control variable can be used only in that for statement—it will not exist outside the for statement. This restricted use of the name of the control variable is known as the variable's *scope*. The scope of a variable defines where it can be used in a program. For example, a local variable can be used only in the method that declares the variable and only from the point of declaration through the end of the method. Scope is discussed in detail in Chapter 6, Methods: A Deeper Look.

Common Programming Error 5.3

When a for statement's control variable is declared in the initialization section of the for's header, using the control variable after the for's body is a compilation error.

All three expressions in a for header are optional. If the *loopContinuationCondition* is omitted, Java assumes that the loop-continuation condition is always true, thus creating an infinite loop. You might omit the *initialization* expression if the program initializes the control variable before the loop. You might omit the *increment* expression if the program calculates the increment with statements in the loop's body or if no increment is needed. The increment expression in a for acts as if it were a standalone statement at the end of the for's body. Therefore, the expressions

```
counter = counter + 1
counter += 1
++counter
counter++
```

are equivalent increment expressions in a for statement. Many programmers prefer counter++ because it is concise and because a for loop evaluates its increment expression after its body executes. Therefore, the postfix increment form seems more natural. In this case, the variable being incremented does not appear in a larger expression, so preincrementing and postincrementing actually have the same effect.

Performance Tip 5.1

There is a slight performance advantage to preincrementing, but if you choose to postincrement because it seems more natural (as in a for header), optimizing compilers will generate Java byte-code that uses the more efficient form anyway.

Good Programming Practice 5.2

In most cases, preincrementing and postincrementing are both used to add 1 to a variable in a statement by itself. In these cases, the effect is exactly the same, except that preincrementing has a slight performance advantage. Given that the compiler typically optimizes your code to help you get the best performance, use the idiom with which you feel most comfortable in these situations.

Common Programming Error 5.4

Placing a semicolon immediately to the right of the right parenthesis of a for header makes that for's body an empty statement. This is normally a logic error.

Error-Prevention Tip 5.2

Infinite loops occur when the loop-continuation condition in a repetition statement never becomes false. *To prevent this situation in a counter-controlled loop, ensure that the control variable is incremented (or decremented) during each iteration of the loop. In a sentinel-controlled loop, ensure that the sentinel value is eventually input.*

The initialization, loop-continuation condition and increment portions of a for statement can contain arithmetic expressions. For example, assume that x = 2 and y = 10. If x and y are not modified in the body of the loop, the statement

```
for ( int j = x; j <= 4 * x * y; j += y / x )
```

is equivalent to the statement

```
for ( int j = 2; j <= 80; j += 5 )
```

The increment of a for statement may also be negative, in which case it is really a decrement, and the loop counts downward.

If the loop-continuation condition is initially false, the program does not execute the for statement's body. Instead, execution proceeds with the statement following the for.

Programs frequently display the control variable value or use it in calculations in the loop body, but this use is not required. The control variable is commonly used to control repetition without mentioning the control variable in the body of the for.

Error-Prevention Tip 5.3

Although the value of the control variable can be changed in the body of a for loop, avoid doing so, because this practice can lead to subtle errors.

The for statement's UML activity diagram is similar to that of the while statement (Fig. 4.4). Figure 5.4 shows the activity diagram of the for statement in Fig. 5.2. The diagram makes it clear that initialization occurs once before the loop-continuation test is evaluated the first time, and that incrementing occurs each time through the loop after the body statement executes.

5.4 Examples Using the for Statement

The following examples show techniques for varying the control variable in a for statement. In each case, we write the appropriate for header. Note the change in the relational operator for loops that decrement the control variable.

a) Vary the control variable from 1 to 100 in increments of 1.

```
for ( int i = 1; i <= 100; i++ )
```

b) Vary the control variable from 100 to 1 in decrements of 1.

```
for ( int i = 100; i >= 1; i-- )
```

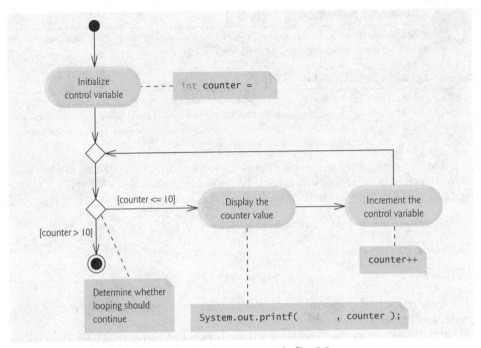

Fig. 5.4 | UML activity diagram for the `for` statement in Fig. 5.2.

c) Vary the control variable from 7 to 77 in increments of 7.

   for (***int*** i = 7; i <= 77; i += 7)

d) Vary the control variable from 20 to 2 in decrements of 2.

   for (***int*** i = 20; i >= 2; i -= 2)

e) Vary the control variable over the following sequence of values: 2, 5, 8, 11, 14, 17, 20.

   for (***int*** i = 2; i <= 20; i += 3)

f) Vary the control variable over the following sequence of values: 99, 88, 77, 66, 55, 44, 33, 22, 11, 0.

   for (***int*** i = 99; i >= 0; i -= 11)

 Common Programming Error 5.5

Not using the proper relational operator in the loop-continuation condition of a loop that counts downward (e.g., using i <= 1 *instead of* i >= 1 *in a loop counting down to 1) is usually a logic error.*

Application: Summing the Even Integers from 2 to 20

We now consider two sample applications that demonstrate simple uses of `for`. The application in Fig. 5.5 uses a `for` statement to sum the even integers from 2 to 20 and store the result in an `int` variable called `total`.

```
 1   // Fig. 5.5: Sum.java
 2   // Summing integers with the for statement.
 3
 4   public class Sum
 5   {
 6      public static void main( String args[] )
 7      {
 8         int total = 0; // initialize total
 9
10         // total even integers from 2 through 20
11         for ( int number = 2; number <= 20; number += 2 )
12            total += number;
13
14         System.out.printf( "Sum is %d\n", total ); // display results
15      } // end main
16   } // end class Sum
```

```
Sum is 110
```

Fig. 5.5 | Summing integers with the for statement.

The *initialization* and *increment* expressions can be comma-separated lists of expressions that enable you to use multiple initialization expressions or multiple increment expressions. For example, although this is discouraged, the body of the for statement in lines 11–12 of Fig. 5.5 could be merged into the increment portion of the for header by using a comma as follows:

```
for ( int number = 2; number <= 20; total += number, number += 2 )
   ; // empty statement
```

Good Programming Practice 5.3

Limit the size of control statement headers to a single line if possible.

Application: Compound-Interest Calculations

The next application uses the for statement to compute compound interest. Consider the following problem:

> A person invests $1000 in a savings account yielding 5% interest. Assuming that all the interest is left on deposit, calculate and print the amount of money in the account at the end of each year for 10 years. Use the following formula to determine the amounts:
>
> $$a = p (1 + r)^n$$
>
> *where*
>
> p is the original amount invested (i.e., the principal)
> r is the annual interest rate (e.g., use 0.05 for 5%)
> n is the number of years
> a is the amount on deposit at the end of the nth year.

This problem involves a loop that performs the indicated calculation for each of the 10 years the money remains on deposit. The solution is the application shown in Fig. 5.6.

```
1   // Fig. 5.6: Interest.java
2   // Compound-interest calculations with for.
3
4   public class Interest
5   {
6      public static void main( String args[] )
7      {
8         double amount; // amount on deposit at end of each year
9         double principal = 1000.0; // initial amount before interest
10        double rate = 0.05; // interest rate
11
12        // display headers
13        System.out.printf( "%s%20s\n", "Year", "Amount on deposit" );
14
15        // calculate amount on deposit for each of ten years
16        for ( int year = 1; year <= 10; year++ )
17        {
18           // calculate new amount for specified year
19           amount = principal * Math.pow( 1.0 + rate, year );
20
21           // display the year and the amount
22           System.out.printf( "%4d%,20.2f\n", year, amount );
23        } // end for
24     } // end main
25  } // end class Interest
```

```
Year    Amount on deposit
   1             1,050.00
   2             1,102.50
   3             1,157.63
   4             1,215.51
   5             1,276.28
   6             1,340.10
   7             1,407.10
   8             1,477.46
   9             1,551.33
  10             1,628.89
```

Fig. 5.6 | Compound-interest calculations with for.

Lines 8–10 in method main declare double variables amount, principal and rate, and initialize principal to 1000.0 and rate to 0.05. Java treats floating-point constants like 1000.0 and 0.05 as type double. Similarly, Java treats whole-number constants like 7 and -22 as type int.

Line 13 outputs the headers for this application's two columns of output. The first column displays the year, and the second column the amount on deposit at the end of that year. Note that we use the format specifier %20s to output the String "Amount on Deposit". The integer 20 between the % and the conversion character s indicates that the value output should be displayed with a *field width* of 20—that is, printf displays the value with at least 20 character positions. If the value to be output is less than 20 character positions wide (17 characters in this example), the value is *right justified* in the field by default. If the year value to be output were more than four character positions wide, the field width would be extended to the right to accommodate the entire value—this would push the amount field to the right, upsetting the neat columns of our tabular output. To indicate that values should be output *left justified*, simply precede the field width with the *minus sign (–) formatting flag*.

The for statement (lines 16–23) executes its body 10 times, varying control variable year from 1 to 10 in increments of 1. This loop terminates when control variable year becomes 11. (Note that year represents n in the problem statement.)

Classes provide methods that perform common tasks on objects. In fact, most methods must be called on a specific object. For example, to output text in Fig. 5.6, line 13 calls method printf on the System.out object. Many classes also provide methods that perform common tasks and do not require objects. Recall from Section 3.3 that these are called static methods. For example, Java does not include an exponentiation operator, so the designers of Java's Math class defined static method pow for raising a value to a power. You can call a static method by specifying the class name followed by a dot (.) and the method name, as in

> *ClassName*.*methodName*(*arguments*)

In Chapter 6, you'll learn how to implement static methods in your own classes.

We use static method pow of class Math to perform the compound-interest calculation in Fig. 5.6. Math.pow(x, y) calculates the value of x raised to the yth power. The method receives two double arguments and returns a double value. Line 19 performs the calculation $a = p (1 + r)^n$, where a is amount, p is principal, r is rate and n is year.

After each calculation, line 22 outputs the year and the amount on deposit at the end of that year. The year is output in a field width of four characters (as specified by %4d). The amount is output as a floating-point number with the format specifier %,20.2f. The *comma (,) formatting flag* indicates that the floating-point value should be output with a grouping separator. The actual separator used is specific to the user's locale (i.e., country). For example, in the United States, the number will be output using commas to separate every three digits and a decimal point to separate the fractional part of the number, as in 1,234.45. The number 20 in the format specification indicates that the value should be output right justified in a field width of 20 characters. The .2 specifies the formatted number's precision—in this case, the number is rounded to the nearest hundredth and output with two digits to the right of the decimal point.

We declared variables amount, principal and rate to be of type double in this example. We are dealing with fractional parts of dollars and thus need a type that allows decimal points in its values. Unfortunately, floating-point numbers can cause trouble. Here is a simple explanation of what can go wrong when using double (or float) to represent dollar amounts (assuming that dollar amounts are displayed with two digits to the right of the decimal point): Two double dollar amounts stored in the machine could be 14.234 (which would normally be rounded to 14.23 for display purposes) and 18.673 (which would normally be rounded to 18.67 for display purposes). When these amounts are added, they produce the internal sum 32.907, which would normally be rounded to 32.91 for display purposes. Thus, your output could appear as

```
  14.23
+ 18.67
-------
  32.91
```

but a person adding the individual numbers as displayed would expect the sum to be 32.90. You have been warned!

Good Programming Practice 5.4

Do not use variables of type double (or float) to perform precise monetary calculations. The imprecision of floating-point numbers can cause errors.

Note that some third-party vendors provide for-sale class libraries that perform precise monetary calculations. In addition, the Java API provides class java.math.BigDecimal for performing calculations with arbitrary precision floating-point values.

Note that the body of the for statement contains the calculation 1.0 + rate, which appears as an argument to the Math.pow method. In fact, this calculation produces the same result each time through the loop, so repeating the calculation every iteration of the loop is wasteful.

Performance Tip 5.2

In loops, avoid calculations for which the result never changes—such calculations should typically be placed before the loop. [Note: Optimizing compilers may place such calculations outside loops in the compiled code.]

5.5 do...while Repetition Statement

The do...while repetition statement is similar to the while statement. In the while, the program tests the loop-continuation condition at the beginning of the loop, before executing the loop's body; if the condition is false, the body never executes. The do...while statement tests the loop-continuation condition *after* executing the loop's body; therefore, the body always executes at least once. When a do...while statement terminates, execution continues with the next statement in sequence. Figure 5.7 uses a do...while (lines 10–14) to output the numbers 1–10.

```
1   // Fig. 5.7: DoWhileTest.java
2   // do...while repetition statement.
3
4   public class DoWhileTest
5   {
6      public static void main( String args[] )
7      {
8         int counter = 1; // initialize counter
9
10        do
11        {
12           System.out.printf( "%d  ", counter );
13           ++counter;
14        } while ( counter <= 10 ); // end do...while
15
16        System.out.println(); // outputs a newline
17     } // end main
18  } // end class DoWhileTest
```

Fig. 5.7 | do...while repetition statement. (Part 1 of 2.)

```
1  2  3  4  5  6  7  8  9  10
```

Fig. 5.7 | do...while repetition statement. (Part 2 of 2.)

Line 8 declares and initializes control variable counter. Upon entering the do...while statement, line 12 outputs counter's value and line 13 increments counter. Then the program evaluates the loop-continuation test at the bottom of the loop (line 14). If the condition is true, the loop continues from the first body statement in the do...while (line 12). If the condition is false, the loop terminates and the program continues with the next statement after the loop.

Figure 5.8 contains the UML activity diagram for the do...while statement. This diagram makes it clear that the loop-continuation condition is not evaluated until after the loop performs the action state at least once. Compare this activity diagram with that of the while statement (Fig. 4.4).

It is not necessary to use braces in the do...while repetition statement if there is only one statement in the body. However, most programmers include the braces, to avoid confusion between the while and do...while statements. For example,

> **while** (*condition*)

is normally the first line of a while statement. A do...while statement with no braces around a single-statement body appears as:

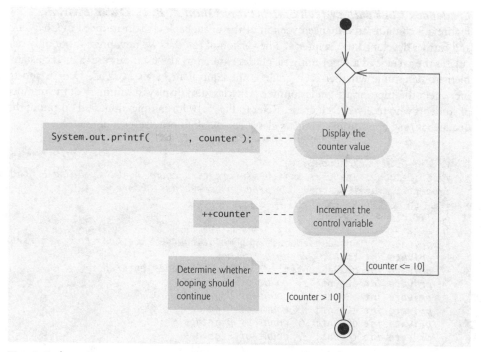

Fig. 5.8 | do...while repetition statement UML activity diagram.

```
do
    statement
while ( condition );
```

which can be confusing. A reader may misinterpret the last line—while(*condition*);—as a while statement containing an empty statement (the semicolon by itself). Thus, the do...while statement with one body statement is usually written as follows:

```
do
{
    statement
} while ( condition );
```

Good Programming Practice 5.5

Always include braces in a do...while statement, even if they are not necessary. This helps eliminate ambiguity between the while statement and a do...while statement.

5.6 switch Multiple-Selection Statement

We discussed the if single-selection statement and the if...else double-selection statement in Chapter 4. Java provides the switch multiple-selection statement to perform different actions based on the possible values of an integer variable or expression. Each action is associated with the value of a ***constant integral expression*** (i.e., a constant value of type byte, short, int or char, but not long) that the variable or expression on which the switch is based may assume.

GradeBook Class with switch Statement to Count A, B, C, D and F Grades

Figure 5.9 contains an enhanced version of the GradeBook class introduced in Chapter 3 and further developed in Chapter 4. The version of the class we now present not only calculates the average of a set of numeric grades entered by the user, but uses a switch statement to determine whether each grade is the equivalent of an A, B, C, D or F and to increment the appropriate grade counter. The class also displays a summary of the number of students who received each grade. Refer to Fig. 5.10 for sample input and output of the GradeBookTest application that uses class GradeBook to process a set of grades.

```
1   // Fig. 5.9: GradeBook.java
2   // GradeBook class uses switch statement to count A, B, C, D and F grades.
3   import java.util.Scanner; // program uses class Scanner
4
5   public class GradeBook
6   {
7       private String courseName; // name of course this GradeBook represents
8       private int total; // sum of grades
9       private int gradeCounter; // number of grades entered
10      private int aCount; // count of A grades
11      private int bCount; // count of B grades
12      private int cCount; // count of C grades
13      private int dCount; // count of D grades
14      private int fCount; // count of F grades
```

Fig. 5.9 | GradeBook class uses switch statement to count A, B, C, D and F grades. (Part 1 of 4.)

```
15
16      // constructor initializes courseName;
17      // int instance variables are initialized to 0 by default
18      public GradeBook( String name )
19      {
20         courseName = name; // initializes courseName
21      } // end constructor
22
23      // method to set the course name
24      public void setCourseName( String name )
25      {
26         courseName = name; // store the course name
27      } // end method setCourseName
28
29      // method to retrieve the course name
30      public String getCourseName()
31      {
32         return courseName;
33      } // end method getCourseName
34
35      // display a welcome message to the GradeBook user
36      public void displayMessage()
37      {
38         // getCourseName gets the name of the course
39         System.out.printf( "Welcome to the grade book for\n%s!\n\n",
40            getCourseName() );
41      } // end method displayMessage
42
43      // input arbitrary number of grades from user
44      public void inputGrades()
45      {
46         Scanner input = new Scanner( System.in );
47
48         int grade; // grade entered by user
49
50         System.out.printf( "%s\n%s\n   %s\n   %s\n",
51            "Enter the integer grades in the range 0-100.",
52            "Type the end-of-file indicator to terminate input:",
53            "On UNIX/Linux/Mac OS X type <ctrl> d then press Enter",
54            "On Windows type <ctrl> z then press Enter" );
55
56         // loop until user enters the end-of-file indicator
57         while ( input.hasNext() )
58         {
59            grade = input.nextInt(); // read grade
60            total += grade; // add grade to total
61            ++gradeCounter; // increment number of grades
62
63            // call method to increment appropriate counter
64            incrementLetterGradeCounter( grade );
65         } // end while
66      } // end method inputGrades
67
```

Fig. 5.9 | GradeBook class uses switch statement to count A, B, C, D and F grades. (Part 2 of 4.)

```
68        // add 1 to appropriate counter for specified grade
69        public void incrementLetterGradeCounter( int Grade )
70        {
71            // determine which grade was entered
72            switch ( grade / 10 )
73            {
74                case 9:  // grade was between 90
75                case 10: // and 100
76                    ++aCount; // increment aCount
77                    break; // necessary to exit switch
78
79                case 8: // grade was between 80 and 89
80                    ++bCount; // increment bCount
81                    break; // exit switch
82
83                case 7: // grade was between 70 and 79
84                    ++cCount; // increment cCount
85                    break; // exit switch
86
87                case 6: // grade was between 60 and 69
88                    ++dCount; // increment dCount
89                    break; // exit switch
90
91                default: // grade was less than 60
92                    ++fCount; // increment fCount
93                    break; // optional; will exit switch anyway
94            } // end switch
95        } // end method incrementLetterGradeCounter
96
97        // display a report based on the grades entered by user
98        public void displayGradeReport()
99        {
100            System.out.println( "\nGrade Report:" );
101
102            // if user entered at least one grade...
103            if ( gradeCounter != 0 )
104            {
105                // calculate average of all grades entered
106                double average = (double) total / gradeCounter;
107
108                // output summary of results
109                System.out.printf( "Total of the %d grades entered is %d\n",
110                    gradeCounter, total );
111                System.out.printf( "Class average is %.2f\n", average );
112                System.out.printf( "%s\n%s%d\n%s%d\n%s%d\n%s%d\n%s%d\n",
113                    "Number of students who received each grade:",
114                    "A: ", aCount,  // display number of A grades
115                    "B: ", bCount,  // display number of B grades
116                    "C: ", cCount,  // display number of C grades
117                    "D: ", dCount,  // display number of D grades
118                    "F: ", fCount ); // display number of F grades
119            } // end if
```

Fig. 5.9 | GradeBook class uses `switch` statement to count A, B, C, D and F grades. (Part 3 of 4.)

```
120            else // no grades were entered, so output appropriate message
121               System.out.println( "No grades were entered" );
122         } // end method displayGradeReport
123  } // end class GradeBook
```

Fig. 5.9 | GradeBook class uses switch statement to count A, B, C, D and F grades. (Part 4 of 4.)

Like earlier versions of the class, class GradeBook (Fig. 5.9) declares instance variable courseName (line 7) and contains methods setCourseName (lines 24–27), getCourseName (lines 30–33) and displayMessage (lines 36–41), which set the course name, store the course name and display a welcome message to the user, respectively. The class also contains a constructor (lines 18–21) that initializes the course name.

Class GradeBook also declares instance variables total (line 8) and gradeCounter (line 9), which keep track of the sum of the grades entered by the user and the number of grades entered, respectively. Lines 10–14 declare counter variables for each grade category. Class GradeBook maintains total, gradeCounter and the five letter-grade counters as instance variables so that these variables can be used or modified in any of the class's methods. Note that the class's constructor (lines 18–21) sets only the course name, because the remaining seven instance variables are ints and are initialized to 0 by default.

Class GradeBook (Fig. 5.9) contains three additional methods—inputGrades, incrementLetterGradeCounter and displayGradeReport. Method inputGrades (lines 44–66) reads an arbitrary number of integer grades from the user using sentinel-controlled repetition and updates instance variables total and gradeCounter. Method inputGrades calls method incrementLetterGradeCounter (lines 69–95) to update the appropriate letter-grade counter for each grade entered. Class GradeBook also contains method displayGradeReport (lines 98–122), which outputs a report containing the total of all grades entered, the average of the grades and the number of students who received each letter grade. Let's examine these methods in more detail.

Line 48 in method inputGrades declares variable grade, which will store the user's input. Lines 50–54 prompt the user to enter integer grades and to type the end-of-file indicator to terminate the input. The **end-of-file indicator** is a system-dependent keystroke combination which the user enters to indicate that there is no more data to input. In Chapter 14, Files and Streams, we'll see how the end-of-file indicator is used when a program reads its input from a file.

On UNIX/Linux/Mac OS X systems, end-of-file is entered by typing the sequence

   <Ctrl> d

on a line by itself. This notation means to simultaneously press both the *Ctrl* key and the *d* key. On Windows systems, end-of-file can be entered by typing

   <Ctrl> z

[*Note:* On some systems, you must press *Enter* after typing the end-of-file key sequence. Windows typically displays ^Z on the screen when the end-of-file indicator is typed.]

Portability Tip 5.1

The keystroke combinations for entering end-of-file are system dependent.

The while statement (lines 57–65) obtains the user input. The condition at line 57 calls Scanner method *hasNext* to determine whether there is more data to input. This method returns the boolean value true if there is more data; otherwise, it returns false. The returned value is then used as the value of the condition in the while statement. As long as the end-of-file indicator has not been typed, method hasNext will return true.

Line 59 inputs a grade value from the user. Line 60 uses the += operator to add grade to total. Line 61 increments gradeCounter. The class's displayGradeReport method uses these variables to compute the average of the grades. Line 64 calls the class's incrementLetterGradeCounter method (declared in lines 69–95) to increment the appropriate letter-grade counter based on the numeric grade entered.

Method incrementLetterGradeCounter contains a switch statement (lines 72–94) that determines which counter to increment. In this example, we assume that the user enters a valid grade in the range 0–100. A grade in the range 90–100 represents A, 80–89 represents B, 70–79 represents C, 60–69 represents D and 0–59 represents F. The switch statement consists of a block that contains a sequence of *case labels* and an optional *default case*. These are used in this example to determine which counter to increment based on the grade.

When the flow of control reaches the switch, the program evaluates the expression in the parentheses (grade / 10) following keyword switch. This is called the *controlling expression* of the switch. The program compares the value of the controlling expression (which must evaluate to an integral value of type byte, char, short or int) with each case label. The controlling expression in line 72 performs integer division, which truncates the fractional part of the result. Thus, when we divide any value for 0–100 by 10, the result is always a value from 0 to 10. We use several of these values in our case labels. For example, if the user enters the integer 85, the controlling expression evaluates to the int value 8. The switch compares 8 with each case label. If a match occurs (case 8: at line 79), the program executes the statements for that case. For the integer 8, line 80 increments bCount, because a grade in the 80s is a B. The break statement (line 81) causes program control to proceed with the first statement after the switch—in this program, we reach the end of method incrementLetterGradeCounter's body, so control returns to line 65 in method inputGrades (the first line after the call to incrementLetterGradeCounter). This line marks the end of the body of the while loop that inputs grades (lines 57–65), so control flows to the while's condition (line 57) to determine whether the loop should continue executing.

The cases in our switch explicitly test for the values 10, 9, 8, 7 and 6. Note the cases at lines 74–75 that test for the values 9 and 10 (both of which represent the grade A). Listing cases consecutively in this manner with no statements between them enables the cases to perform the same set of statements—when the controlling expression evaluates to 9 or 10, the statements in lines 76–77 will execute. The switch statement does not provide a mechanism for testing ranges of values, so every value that must be tested should be listed in a separate case label. Note that each case can have multiple statements. The switch statement differs from other control statements in that it does not require braces around multiple statements in a case.

Without break statements, each time a match occurs in the switch, the statements for that case and subsequent cases execute until a break statement or the end of the switch is encountered. This is often referred to as "falling through" to the statements in subsequent cases.

Common Programming Error 5.6

Forgetting a break statement when one is needed in a switch is a logic error.

If no match occurs between the controlling expression's value and a case label, the default case (lines 91–93) executes. We use the default case in this example to process all controlling-expression values that are less than 6—that is, all failing grades. If no match occurs and the switch does not contain a default case, program control simply continues with the first statement after the switch.

GradeBookTest Class That Demonstrates Class GradeBook

Class GradeBookTest (Fig. 5.10) creates a GradeBook object (lines 10–11). Line 13 invokes the object's displayMessage method to output a welcome message to the user. Line 14 invokes the object's inputGrades method to read a set of grades from the user and keep track of the sum of all the grades entered and the number of grades. Recall that method inputGrades also calls method incrementLetterGradeCounter to keep track of the number of students who received each letter grade. Line 15 invokes method displayGradeReport of class GradeBook, which outputs a report based on the grades entered (as in the input/output window in Fig. 5.10). Line 103 of class GradeBook (Fig. 5.9) determines whether the user entered at least one grade—this helps us avoid dividing by zero. If so, line 106 calculates the average of the grades. Lines 109–118 then output the total of all the grades, the class average and the number of students who received each letter grade. If no grades were entered, line 121 outputs an appropriate message. The output in Fig. 5.10 shows a sample grade report based on 10 grades.

Note that class GradeBookTest (Fig. 5.10) does not directly call GradeBook method incrementLetterGradeCounter (lines 69–95 of Fig. 5.9). This method is used exclusively by method inputGrades of class GradeBook to update the appropriate letter-grade counter as each new grade is entered by the user. Method incrementLetterGradeCounter exists solely to support the operations of class GradeBook's other methods and thus could be

```java
1   // Fig. 5.10: GradeBookTest.java
2   // Create GradeBook object, input grades and display grade report.
3
4   public class GradeBookTest
5   {
6      public static void main( String args[] )
7      {
8         // create GradeBook object myGradeBook and
9         // pass course name to constructor
10        GradeBook myGradeBook = new GradeBook(
11           "CS101 Introduction to Java Programming" );
12
13        myGradeBook.displayMessage(); // display welcome message
14        myGradeBook.inputGrades(); // read grades from user
15        myGradeBook.displayGradeReport(); // display report based on grades
16     } // end main
17  } // end class GradeBookTest
```

Fig. 5.10 | GradeBookTest creates a GradeBook object and invokes its methods. (Part 1 of 2.)

```
Welcome to the grade book for
CS101 Introduction to Java Programming!

Enter the integer grades in the range 0-100.
Type the end-of-file indicator to terminate input:
   On UNIX/Linux/Mac OS X type <ctrl> d then press Enter
   On Windows type <ctrl> z then press Enter
99
92
45
57
63
71
76
85
90
100
^Z

Grade Report:
Total of the 10 grades entered is 778
Class average is 77.80
Number of students who received each grade:
A: 4
B: 1
C: 2
D: 1
F: 2
```

Fig. 5.10 | GradeBookTest creates a GradeBook object and invokes its methods. (Part 2 of 2.)

declared private. Recall from Chapter 3 that methods declared with access modifier private can be called only by other methods of the class in which the private methods are declared. Such methods are commonly referred to as *utility methods* or *helper methods* because they can be called only by other methods of that class and are used to support the operation of those methods.

switch *Statement UML Activity Diagram*

Figure 5.11 shows the UML activity diagram for the general switch statement. Most switch statements use a break in each case to terminate the switch statement after processing the case. Figure 5.11 emphasizes this by including break statements in the activity diagram. The diagram makes it clear that the break statement at the end of a case causes control to exit the switch statement immediately.

The break statement is not required for the switch's last case (or the optional default case, when it appears last), because execution continues with the next statement after the switch.

Software Engineering Observation 5.1

Provide a default case in switch statements. Including a default case focuses you on the need to process exceptional conditions.

When using the switch statement, remember that the expression after each case must be a constant integral expression—that is, any combination of integer constants that eval-

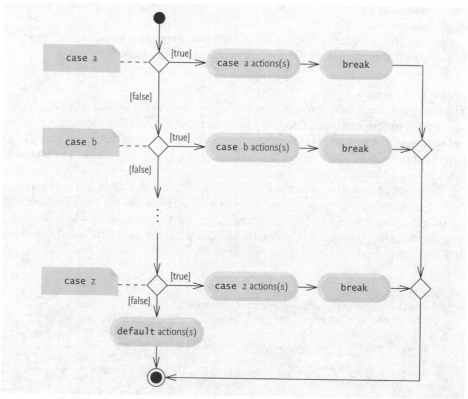

Fig. 5.11 | switch multiple-selection statement UML activity diagram with break statements.

uates to a constant integer value (e.g., –7, 0 or 221). An integer constant is simply an integer value. In addition, you can use *character constants*—specific characters in single quotes, such as 'A', '7' or '$'—which represent the integer values of characters. (Appendix B, shows the integer values of the characters in the ASCII character set, which is a subset of the Unicode character set used by Java.)

The expression in each case also can be a *constant variable*—a variable that contains a value which does not change for the entire program. Such a variable is declared with keyword final (discussed in Chapter 6, Methods: A Deeper Look). Java has a feature called enumerations, which we also present in Chapter 6. Enumeration constants can also be used in case labels. In Chapter 10, Object-Oriented Programming: Polymorphism, we present a more elegant way to implement switch logic—we use a technique called polymorphism to create programs that are often clearer, easier to maintain and easier to extend than programs using switch logic.

5.7 break and continue Statements

In addition to selection and repetition statements, Java provides statements break and continue to alter the flow of control. The preceding section showed how break can be used to terminate a switch statement's execution. This section discusses how to use break in repetition statements.

Java also provides the labeled break and continue statements for use in cases in which you need to conveniently alter the flow of control in nested control statements.

break *Statement*

The break statement, when executed in a while, for, do...while or switch, causes immediate exit from that statement. Execution continues with the first statement after the control statement. Common uses of the break statement are to escape early from a loop or to skip the remainder of a switch (as in Fig. 5.9). Figure 5.12 demonstrates a break statement exiting a for.

When the if statement nested at line 11 in the for statement (lines 9–15) detects that count is 5, the break statement at line 12 executes. This terminates the for statement, and the program proceeds to line 17 (immediately after the for statement), which displays a message indicating the value of the control variable when the loop terminated. The loop fully executes its body only four times instead of 10.

```java
1   // Fig. 5.12: BreakTest.java
2   // break statement exiting a for statement.
3   public class BreakTest
4   {
5      public static void main( String args[] )
6      {
7         int count; // control variable also used after loop terminates
8
9         for ( count = 1; count <= 10; count++ ) // loop 10 times
10        {
11           if ( count == 5 ) // if count is 5,
12              break;          // terminate loop
13
14           System.out.printf( "%d ", count );
15        } // end for
16
17        System.out.printf( "\nBroke out of loop at count = %d\n", count );
18     } // end main
19  } // end class BreakTest
```

```
1 2 3 4
Broke out of loop at count = 5
```

Fig. 5.12 | break statement exiting a for statement.

continue *Statement*

The continue statement, when executed in a while, for or do...while, skips the remaining statements in the loop body and proceeds with the next iteration of the loop. In while and do...while statements, the program evaluates the loop-continuation test immediately after the continue statement executes. In a for statement, the increment expression executes, then the program evaluates the loop-continuation test.

Figure 5.13 uses the `continue` statement in a `for` to skip the statement at line 12 when the nested `if` (line 9) determines that the value of `count` is 5. When the `continue` statement executes, program control continues with the increment of the control variable in the `for` statement (line 7).

In Section 5.3, we stated that `while` could be used in most cases in place of `for`. The one exception occurs when the increment expression in the `while` follows a `continue` statement. In this case, the increment does not execute before the program evaluates the repetition-continuation condition, so the `while` does not execute in the same manner as the `for`.

Software Engineering Observation 5.2

Some programmers feel that break *and* continue *violate structured programming. Since the same effects are achievable with structured programming techniques, these programmers do not use* break *or* continue.

Software Engineering Observation 5.3

There is a tension between achieving quality software engineering and achieving the best-performing software. Often, one of these goals is achieved at the expense of the other. For all but the most performance-intensive situations, apply the following rule of thumb: First, make your code simple and correct; then make it fast and small, but only if necessary.

```
1   // Fig. 5.13: ContinueTest.java
2   // continue statement terminating an iteration of a for statement.
3   public class ContinueTest
4   {
5      public static void main( String args[] )
6      {
7         for ( int count = 1; count <= 10; count++ ) // loop 10 times
8         {
9            if ( count == 5 ) // if count is 5,
10              continue; // skip remaining code in loop
11
12           System.out.printf( "%d ", count );
13        } // end for
14
15        System.out.println( "\nUsed continue to skip printing 5" );
16     } // end main
17  } // end class ContinueTest
```

```
1 2 3 4 6 7 8 9 10
Used continue to skip printing 5
```

Fig. 5.13 | `continue` statement terminating an iteration of a `for` statement.

5.8 Logical Operators

The `if`, `if...else`, `while`, `do...while` and `for` statements each require a condition to determine how to continue a program's flow of control. So far, we have studied only *simple conditions*, such as `count <= 10`, `number != sentinelValue` and `total > 1000`. Simple conditions are expressed in terms of the relational operators >, <, >= and <= and the equality operators == and !=, and each expression tests only one condition. To test multiple conditions in the process of making a decision, we performed these tests in separate statements or in nested if or if...else statements. Sometimes, control statements require more complex conditions to determine a program's flow of control.

Java provides *logical operators* to enable you to form more complex conditions by combining simple conditions. The logical operators are && (conditional AND), || (conditional OR), & (boolean logical AND), | (boolean logical inclusive OR), ∧ (boolean logical exclusive OR) and ! (logical NOT).

Conditional AND (&&) Operator

Suppose that we wish to ensure at some point in a program that two conditions are *both* true before we choose a certain path of execution. In this case, we can use the && (*conditional AND*) operator, as follows:

```
if ( gender == FEMALE && age >= 65 )
    ++seniorFemales;
```

This if statement contains two simple conditions. The condition gender == FEMALE compares variable gender to the constant FEMALE. This might be evaluated, for example, to determine whether a person is female. The condition age >= 65 might be evaluated to determine whether a person is a senior citizen. The if statement considers the combined condition

```
gender == FEMALE && age >= 65
```

which is true if and only if both simple conditions are true. If the combined condition is true, the if statement's body increments seniorFemales by 1. If either or both of the simple conditions are false, the program skips the increment. Some programmers find that the preceding combined condition is more readable when redundant parentheses are added, as in:

```
( gender == FEMALE ) && ( age >= 65 )
```

The table in Fig. 5.14 summarizes the && operator. The table shows all four possible combinations of false and true values for *expression1* and *expression2*. Such tables are called *truth tables*. Java evaluates to false or true all expressions that include relational operators, equality operators or logical operators.

expression1	expression2	expression1 && expression2
false	false	false
false	true	false
true	false	false
true	true	true

Fig. 5.14 | && (conditional AND) operator truth table.

Conditional OR (||) Operator

Now suppose that we wish to ensure that either *or* both of two conditions are true before we choose a certain path of execution. In this case, we use the **||** (*conditional OR*) operator, as in the following program segment:

```
if ( ( semesterAverage >= 90 ) || ( finalExam >= 90 ) )
    System.out.println ( "Student grade is A" );
```

This statement also contains two simple conditions. The condition semesterAverage >= 90 evaluates to determine whether the student deserves an A in the course because of a solid performance throughout the semester. The condition finalExam >= 90 evaluates to determine whether the student deserves an A in the course because of an outstanding performance on the final exam. The if statement then considers the combined condition

```
( semesterAverage >= 90 ) || ( finalExam >= 90 )
```

and awards the student an A if either or both of the simple conditions are true. The only time the message "Student grade is A" is *not* printed is when both of the simple conditions are false. Figure 5.15 is a truth table for operator conditional OR (||). Operator && has a higher precedence than operator ||. Both operators associate from left to right.

expression1	expression2	expression1 || expression2
false	false	false
false	true	true
true	false	true
true	true	true

Fig. 5.15 | || (conditional OR) operator truth table.

Short-Circuit Evaluation of Complex Conditions

The parts of an expression containing && or || operators are evaluated only until it is known whether the condition is true or false. Thus, evaluation of the expression

```
( gender == FEMALE ) && ( age >= 65 )
```

stops immediately if gender is not equal to FEMALE (i.e., the entire expression is false) and continues if gender *is* equal to FEMALE (i.e., the entire expression could still be true if the condition age >= 65 is true). This feature of conditional AND and conditional OR expressions is called *short-circuit evaluation*.

Common Programming Error 5.7

In expressions using operator &&, a condition—we'll call this the dependent condition—may require another condition to be true for the evaluation of the dependent condition to be meaningful. In this case, the dependent condition should be placed after the other condition, or an error might occur. For example, in the expression (i != 0) && (10 / i == 2), the second condition must appear after the first condition, or a divide-by-zero error might occur.

Boolean Logical AND (&) and Boolean Logical Inclusive OR (|) Operators
The *boolean logical AND (&)* and *boolean logical inclusive OR (|)* operators work identically to the && (conditional AND) and || (conditional OR) operators, with one exception: The boolean logical operators always evaluate both of their operands (i.e., they do not perform short-circuit evaluation). Therefore, the expression

```
( gender == 1 ) & ( age >= 65 )
```

evaluates age >= 65 regardless of whether gender is equal to 1. This is useful if the right operand of the boolean logical AND or boolean logical inclusive OR operator has a required *side effect*—a modification of a variable's value. For example, the expression

```
( birthday == true ) | ( ++age >= 65 )
```

guarantees that the condition ++age >= 65 will be evaluated. Thus, the variable age is incremented in the preceding expression, regardless of whether the overall expression is true or false.

Error-Prevention Tip 5.4

For clarity, avoid expressions with side effects in conditions. The side effects may look clever, but they can make it harder to understand code and can lead to subtle logic errors.

Boolean Logical Exclusive OR (^)
A simple condition containing the *boolean logical exclusive OR (^)* operator is true *if and only if one of its operands is true and the other is false*. If both operands are true or both are false, the entire condition is false. Figure 5.16 is a truth table for the boolean logical exclusive OR operator (^). This operator is also guaranteed to evaluate both of its operands.

expression1	expression2	expression1 ^ expression2
false	false	false
false	true	true
true	false	true
true	true	false

Fig. 5.16 | ^ (boolean logical exclusive OR) operator truth table.

Logical Negation (!) Operator
The *!* (*logical NOT*, also called *logical negation* or *logical complement*) operator "reverses" the meaning of a condition. Unlike the logical operators &&, ||, &, | and ^, which are binary operators that combine two conditions, the logical negation operator is a unary operator that has only a single condition as an operand. The logical negation operator is placed before a condition to choose a path of execution if the original condition (without the logical negation operator) is false, as in the program segment

```
if ( ! ( grade == sentinelValue ) )
    System.out.printf( "The next grade is %d\n", grade );
```

which executes the printf call only if grade is not equal to sentinelValue. The parentheses around the condition grade == sentinelValue are needed because the logical negation operator has a higher precedence than the equality operator.

In most cases, you can avoid using logical negation by expressing the condition differently with an appropriate relational or equality operator. For example, the previous statement may also be written as follows:

```
if ( grade != sentinelValue )
    System.out.printf( "The next grade is %d\n", grade );
```

This flexibility can help you express a condition in a more convenient manner. Figure 5.17 is a truth table for the logical negation operator.

expression	!expression
false	true
true	false

Fig. 5.17 | ! (logical negation, or logical NOT) operator truth table.

Logical Operators Example

Figure 5.18 demonstrates the logical operators and boolean logical operators by producing their truth tables. The output shows the expression that was evaluated and the boolean result of that expression. The values of the boolean expressions are displayed with printf using the **%b *format specifier***, which outputs the word "true" or the word "false" based on the expression's value. Lines 9–13 produce the truth table for &&. Lines 16–20 produce the truth table for ||. Lines 23–27 produce the truth table for &. Lines 30–35 produce the truth table for |. Lines 38–43 produce the truth table for ^. Lines 46–47 produce the truth table for !.

```
1   // Fig. 5.18: LogicalOperators.java
2   // Logical operators.
3
4   public class LogicalOperators
5   {
6      public static void main( String args[] )
7      {
8         // create truth table for && (conditional AND) operator
9         System.out.printf( "%s\n%s: %b\n%s: %b\n%s: %b\n%s: %b\n\n",
10           "Conditional AND (&&)", "false && false", ( false && false ),
11           "false && true", ( false && true ),
12           "true && false", ( true && false ),
13           "true && true", ( true && true ) );
14
```

Fig. 5.18 | Logical operators. (Part 1 of 3.)

```
15      // create truth table for || (conditional OR) operator
16      System.out.printf( "%s\n%s: %b\n%s: %b\n%s: %b\n%s: %b\n\n",
17         "Conditional OR (||)", "false || false", ( false || false ),
18         "false || true", ( false || true ),
19         "true || false", ( true || false ),
20         "true || true", ( true || true ) );
21
22      // create truth table for & (boolean logical AND) operator
23      System.out.printf( "%s\n%s: %b\n%s: %b\n%s: %b\n%s: %b\n\n",
24         "Boolean logical AND (&)", "false & false", ( false & false ),
25         "false & true", ( false & true ),
26         "true & false", ( true & false ),
27         "true & true", ( true & true ) );
28
29      // create truth table for | (boolean logical inclusive OR) operator
30.     System.out.printf( "%s\n%s: %b\n%s: %b\n%s: %b\n%s: %b\n\n",
31         "Boolean logical inclusive OR (|)",
32         "false | false", ( false | false ),
33         "false | true", ( false | true ),
34         "true | false", ( true | false ),
35         "true | true", ( true | true ) );
36
37      // create truth table for ^ (boolean logical exclusive OR) operator
38      System.out.printf( "%s\n%s: %b\n%s: %b\n%s: %b\n%s: %b\n\n",
39         "Boolean logical exclusive OR (^)",
40         "false ^ false", ( false ^ false ),
41         "false ^ true", ( false ^ true ),
42         "true ^ false", ( true ^ false ),
43         "true ^ true", ( true ^ true ) );
44
45      // create truth table for ! (logical negation) operator
46      System.out.printf( "%s\n%s: %b\n%s: %b\n", "Logical NOT (!)",
47         "!false", ( !false ), "!true", ( !true ) );
48   } // end main
49 } // end class LogicalOperators
```

```
Conditional AND (&&)
false && false: false
false && true: false
true && false: false
true && true: true

Conditional OR (||)
false || false: false
false || true: true
true || false: true
true || true: true

Boolean logical AND (&)
false & false: false
false & true: false
true & false: false
true & true: true
```

Fig. 5.18 | Logical operators. (Part 2 of 3.)

```
Boolean logical inclusive OR (|)
false | false: false
false | true: true
true | false: true
true | true: true

Boolean logical exclusive OR (^)
false ^ false: false
false ^ true: true
true ^ false: true
true ^ true: false

Logical NOT (!)
!false: true
!true: false
```

Fig. 5.18 | Logical operators. (Part 3 of 3.)

Figure 5.19 shows the precedence and associativity of the Java operators introduced so far. The operators are shown from top to bottom in decreasing order of precedence.

Operators	Associativity	Type
++ --	right to left	unary postfix
++ - + - ! (*type*)	right to left	unary prefix
* / %	left to right	multiplicative
+ -	left to right	additive
< <= > >=	left to right	relational
== !=	left to right	equality
&	left to right	boolean logical AND
^	left to right	boolean logical exclusive OR
|	left to right	boolean logical inclusive OR
&&	left to right	conditional AND
||	left to right	conditional OR
?:	right to left	conditional
= += -= *= /= %=	right to left	assignment

Fig. 5.19 | Precedence/associativity of the operators discussed so far.

5.9 (Optional) Software Engineering Case Study: Identifying Objects' States and Activities

In Section 4.12, we identified many of the class attributes needed to implement the ATM system and added them to the class diagram in Fig. 4.16. Next, we show how these attributes represent an object's state. We identify some key states that our objects may occupy and discuss how objects change state in response to events occurring in the system. We also discuss the workflow, or *activities*, that objects perform in the ATM system. We present the activities of BalanceInquiry and Withdrawal transaction objects in this section.

State Machine Diagrams

Each object in a system goes through a series of states. An object's current state is indicated by the values of the object's attributes at a given time. *State machine diagrams* (commonly called *state diagrams*) model several states of an object and show under what circumstances the object changes state. Unlike the class diagrams presented in earlier case study sections, which focused primarily on the structure of the system, state diagrams model some of the behavior of the system.

Figure 5.20 is a simple state diagram that models some of the states of an object of class ATM. The UML represents each state in a state diagram as a *rounded rectangle* with the name of the state placed inside it. A *solid circle* with an attached stick arrowhead designates the *initial state*. Recall that we modeled this state information as the Boolean attribute userAuthenticated in the class diagram of Fig. 4.16. This attribute is initialized to false, or the "User not authenticated" state, according to the state diagram.

The arrows with stick arrowheads indicate *transitions* between states. An object can transition from one state to another in response to various events that occur in the system. The name or description of the event that causes a transition is written near the line that corresponds to the transition. For example, the ATM object changes from the "User not authenticated" to the "User authenticated" state after the database authenticates the user. Recall from the requirements document that the database authenticates a user by comparing the account number and PIN entered by the user with those of an account in the database. If the database indicates that the user has entered a valid account number and the correct PIN, the ATM object transitions to the "User authenticated" state and changes its userAuthenticated attribute to a value of true. When the user exits the system by choosing the "exit" option from the main menu, the ATM object returns to the "User not authenticated" state.

Software Engineering Observation 5.4

Software designers do not generally create state diagrams showing every possible state and state transition for all attributes—there are simply too many of them. State diagrams typically show only key states and state transitions.

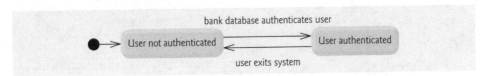

Fig. 5.20 | State diagram for the ATM object.

Activity Diagrams

Like a state diagram, an activity diagram models aspects of system behavior. Unlike a state diagram, an activity diagram models an object's *workflow* (sequence of events) during program execution. An activity diagram models the *actions* the object will perform and in what order. The activity diagram in Fig. 5.21 models the actions involved in executing a balance-inquiry transaction. We assume that a `BalanceInquiry` object has already been initialized and assigned a valid account number (that of the current user), so the object knows which balance to retrieve. The diagram includes the actions that occur after the user selects a balance inquiry from the main menu and before the ATM returns the user to the main menu—a `BalanceInquiry` object does not perform or initiate these actions, so we do not model them here. The diagram begins with retrieving the balance of the account from the database. Next, the `BalanceInquiry` displays the balance on the screen. This action completes the execution of the transaction. Recall that we have chosen to represent an account balance as both the `availableBalance` and `totalBalance` attributes of class `Account`, so the actions modeled in Fig. 5.21 refer to the retrieval and display of both balance attributes.

The UML represents an action in an activity diagram as an action state modeled by a rectangle with its left and right sides replaced by arcs curving outward. Each action state contains an action expression—for example, "get balance of account from database"—that specifies an action to be performed. An arrow with a stick arrowhead connects two action states, indicating the order in which the actions represented by the action states occur. The solid circle (at the top of Fig. 5.21) represents the activity's initial state—the beginning of the workflow before the object performs the modeled actions. In this case, the transaction first executes the "get balance of account from database" action expression. The transaction then displays both balances on the screen. The solid circle enclosed in an open circle (at the bottom of Fig. 5.21) represents the final state—the end of the workflow after the object performs the modeled actions. We used UML activity diagrams to illustrate the flow of control for the control statements presented in Chapters 4–5.

Figure 5.22 shows an activity diagram for a withdrawal transaction. We assume that a `Withdrawal` object has been assigned a valid account number. We do not model the user selecting a withdrawal from the main menu or the ATM returning the user to the main menu because these are not actions performed by a `Withdrawal` object. The transaction first displays a menu of standard withdrawal amounts (shown in Fig. 2.15) and an option to cancel the transaction. The transaction then receives a menu selection from the user. The activity flow now arrives at a decision (a fork indicated by the small diamond symbol). [*Note:* A decision was known as a branch in earlier versions of the UML.] This point determines the next action based on the associated guard condition (in square brackets next to

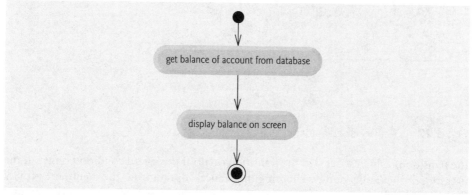

Fig. 5.21 | Activity diagram for a `BalanceInquiry` object.

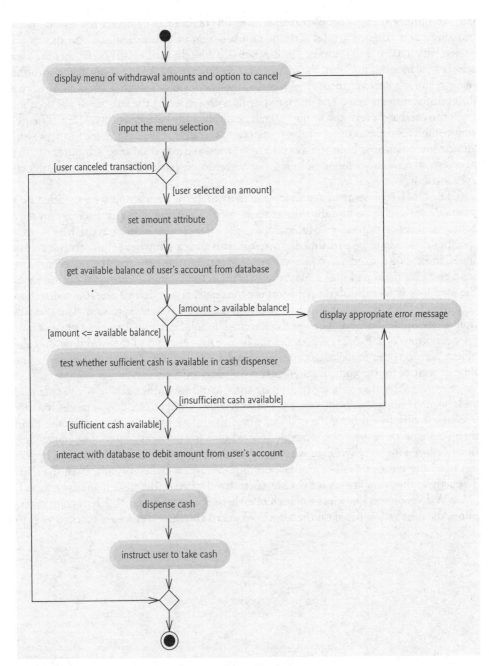

Fig. 5.22 | Activity diagram for a withdrawal transaction.

the transition), which states that the transition occurs if this guard condition is met. If the user cancels the transaction by choosing the "cancel" option from the menu, the activity flow immediately skips to the final state. Note the merge (indicated by the small diamond symbol) where the cancellation flow of activity joins the main flow of activity before reaching the activity's final state. If the user selects a withdrawal amount from the menu, Withdrawal sets amount (an attribute originally modeled in Fig. 4.16) to the value chosen by the user.

After setting the withdrawal amount, the transaction retrieves the available balance of the user's account (i.e., the availableBalance attribute of the user's Account object) from the database. The activity flow then arrives at another decision. If the requested withdrawal amount exceeds the user's available balance, the system displays an appropriate error message informing the user of the problem, then returns to the beginning of the activity diagram and prompts the user to input a new amount. If the requested withdrawal amount is less than or equal to the user's available balance, the transaction proceeds. The transaction next tests whether the cash dispenser has enough cash remaining to satisfy the withdrawal request. If it does not, the transaction displays an appropriate error message, then returns to the beginning of the activity diagram and prompts the user to choose a new amount. If sufficient cash is available, the transaction interacts with the database to debit the withdrawal amount from the user's account (i.e., subtract the amount from both the availableBalance and totalBalance attributes of the user's Account object). The transaction then dispenses the desired amount of cash and instructs the user to take the cash that is dispensed. Finally, the main flow of activity merges with the cancellation flow of activity before reaching the final state.

We've taken the first steps in modeling the ATM system's behavior and have shown how an object's attributes participate in performing the object's activities. In Section 6.19, we investigate the behaviors for all classes to give a more accurate interpretation of the system behavior by "filling in" the third compartments of the classes in our class diagram.

Software Engineering Case Study Self-Review Exercises

5.1 State whether the following statement is *true* or *false*, and if *false*, explain why: State diagrams model structural aspects of a system.

5.2 An activity diagram models the _____ that an object performs and the order in which it performs them.
 a) actions
 b) attributes
 c) states
 d) state transitions

5.3 Based on the requirements document, create an activity diagram for a deposit transaction.

Answers to Software Engineering Case Study Self-Review Exercises

5.1 False. State diagrams model some of the behavior of a system.

5.2 a.

5.3 Figure 5.23 presents an activity diagram for a deposit transaction. The diagram models the actions that occur after the user chooses the deposit option from the main menu and before the ATM returns the user to the main menu. Recall that part of receiving a deposit amount from the user involves converting an integer number of cents to a dollar amount. Also recall that crediting a deposit amount to an account involves increasing only the totalBalance attribute of the user's Account object. The bank updates the availableBalance attribute of the user's Account object only after confirming the amount of cash in the deposit envelope and after the enclosed checks clear—this occurs independently of the ATM system.

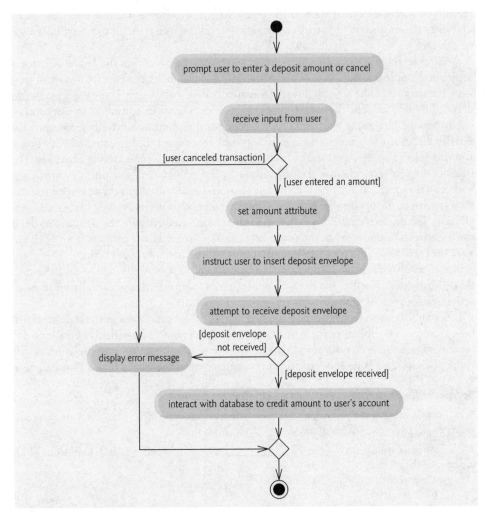

Fig. 5.23 | Activity diagram for a deposit transaction.

5.10 Wrap-Up

We've now completed our introduction to Java's control statements. Chapter 4 discussed the if, if...else and while statements. This chapter demonstrated the for, do...while and switch statements. We showed that any algorithm can be developed using combinations of the sequence structure, the three types of selection statements—if, if...else and switch—and the three types of repetition statements—while, do...while and for. This chapter also introduced Java's logical operators, which enable you to use more complex conditional expressions in control statements.

In Chapter 3, we introduced the basic concepts of objects, classes and methods. Chapter 4 and Chapter 5 introduced the types of control statements that you can use to specify program logic in methods. In Chapter 6, we examine methods in greater depth.

6

Methods:
A Deeper Look

The greatest invention of the nineteenth century was the invention of the method of invention.
—Alfred North Whitehead

Call me Ishmael.
—Herman Melville

When you call me that, smile!
—Owen Wister

Answer me in one word.
—William Shakespeare

O! call back yesterday, bid time return.
—William Shakespeare

There is a point at which methods devour themselves.
—Frantz Fanon

OBJECTIVES

In this chapter you'll learn:

- How `static` methods and fields are associated with an entire class rather than specific instances of the class.
- To use common `Math` methods available in the Java API.
- To understand the mechanisms for passing information between methods.
- How the method call/return mechanism is supported by the method-call stack and activation records.
- How packages group related classes.
- How to use random-number generation to implement game-playing applications.
- How the visibility of declarations is limited to specific regions of programs.
- What method overloading is and how to create overloaded methods.
- To write and use recursive functions, i.e., functions that call themselves.

Outline

6.1   Introduction
6.2   Program Modules in Java
6.3   `static` Methods, `static` Fields and Class `Math`
6.4   Declaring Methods with Multiple Parameters
6.5   Notes on Declaring and Using Methods
6.6   Method-Call Stack and Activation Records
6.7   Argument Promotion and Casting
6.8   Java API Packages
6.9   Case Study: Random-Number Generation
    6.9.1   Generalized Scaling and Shifting of Random Numbers
    6.9.2   Random-Number Repeatability for Testing and Debugging
6.10   Case Study: A Game of Chance (Introducing Enumerations)
6.11   Scope of Declarations
6.12   Method Overloading
6.13   Introduction to Recursion
6.14   Recursion Concepts
6.15   Example Using Recursion: Factorials
6.16   Example Using Recursion: Fibonacci Series
6.17   Recursion and the Method-Call Stack
6.18   Recursion vs. Iteration
6.19   (Optional) Software Engineering Case Study: Identifying Class Operations
6.20   Wrap-Up

6.1 Introduction

We introduced methods in Chapter 3. In this chapter, we study methods in more depth. We emphasize how to declare and use methods to facilitate the design, implementation, operation and maintenance of large programs.

You'll see that it is possible for `static` methods to be called without the need for an object of the class to exist. You'll learn how to declare a method with more than one parameter. You'll also learn how Java is able to keep track of which method is currently executing, how local variables of methods are maintained in memory and how a method knows where to return after it completes execution.

We'll take a brief diversion into simulation techniques with random-number generation and develop a version of the casino dice game called craps that uses most of the programming techniques you've used to this point in the book. In addition, you'll learn how to declare values that cannot change (i.e., constants) in your programs.

Many of the classes you'll use or create while developing applications will have more than one method of the same name. This technique, called overloading, is used to implement methods that perform similar tasks for arguments of different types or for different numbers of arguments. The chapter concludes with a discussion of functions that call themselves, either directly, or indirectly (through another function)—a topic called recursion.

6.2 Program Modules in Java

Three kinds of modules exist in Java—methods, classes and packages. Java programs are written by combining new methods and classes that you write with predefined methods and classes available in the ***Java Application Programming Interface*** (also referred to as the ***Java API*** or ***Java class library***) and in various other class libraries. Related classes are typically grouped into packages so that they can be imported into programs and reused. You'll see how to group your own classes into packages in Chapter 8. The Java API provides a rich collection of predefined classes that contain methods for performing common mathematical calculations, string manipulations, character manipulations, input/output operations, database operations, networking operations, file processing, error checking and many other useful operations.

Good Programming Practice 6.1

Familiarize yourself with the rich collection of classes and methods provided by the Java API (`java.sun.com/javase/6/docs/api/`). In Section 6.8, we present an overview of several common packages. In Appendix G, we explain how to navigate the Java API documentation.

Software Engineering Observation 6.1

Don't try to reinvent the wheel. When possible, reuse Java API classes and methods. This reduces program development time and avoids introducing programming errors.

One motivation for modularizing a program into methods is the divide-and-conquer approach, which makes program development more manageable by constructing programs from small, simple pieces. Another is ***software reusability***—using existing methods as building blocks to create new programs. Often, you can create programs mostly from standardized methods rather than by building customized code. For example, in earlier programs, we did not have to define how to read data values from the keyboard—Java provides these capabilities in class `Scanner`. A third motivation is to avoid repeating code. Dividing a program into meaningful methods makes the program easier to debug and maintain.

Software Engineering Observation 6.2

To promote software reusability, every method should be limited to performing a single, well-defined task, and the name of the method should express that task effectively. Such methods make programs easier to write, debug, maintain and modify.

Error-Prevention Tip 6.1

A small method that performs one task is easier to test and debug than a larger method that performs many tasks.

Software Engineering Observation 6.3

If you cannot choose a concise name that expresses a method's task, your method might be attempting to perform too many diverse tasks. It is often appropriate to break such a method into several smaller method declarations.

6.3 static Methods, static Fields and Class Math

As you know, every class provides methods that perform common tasks on objects of the class. For example, to input data from the keyboard, you have called methods on a Scanner object that was initialized in its constructor to obtain input from the standard input stream (System.in). As you'll learn in Chapter 14, Files and Streams, you can initialize a Scanner to obtain input from other sources, such as a file on disk. One program could have a Scanner object that inputs information from the standard input stream and a second Scanner that inputs information from a file. Each input method called on the standard input stream Scanner would obtain input from the keyboard, and each input method called on the file Scanner would obtain input from the specified file on disk.

Although most methods execute in response to method calls on specific objects, this is not always the case. Sometimes a method performs a task that does not depend on the contents of any object. Such a method applies to the class in which it is declared as a whole and is known as a static method or a *class method*. It is common for classes to contain convenient static methods to perform common tasks. For example, recall that we used static method pow of class Math to raise a value to a power in Fig. 5.6. To declare a method as static, place the keyword static before the return type in the method's declaration. You can call any static method by specifying the name of the class in which the method is declared, followed by a dot (.) and the method name, as in

ClassName.methodName(*arguments*)

We use various Math class methods here to present the concept of static methods. Class Math provides a collection of methods that enable you to perform common mathematical calculations. For example, you can calculate the square root of 900.0 with the static method call

```
Math.sqrt( 900.0 )
```

The preceding expression evaluates to 30.0. Method sqrt takes an argument of type double and returns a result of type double. To output the value of the preceding method call in the command window, you might write the statement

```
System.out.println( Math.sqrt( 900.0 ) );
```

In this statement, the value that sqrt returns becomes the argument to method println. Note that there was no need to create a Math object before calling method sqrt. Also note that *all* Math class methods are static—therefore, each is called by preceding the name of the method with the class name Math and the dot (.) separator.

Software Engineering Observation 6.4

Class Math is part of the java.lang package, which is implicitly imported by the compiler, so it is not necessary to import class Math to use its methods.

Method arguments may be constants, variables or expressions. If c = 13.0, d = 3.0 and f = 4.0, then the statement

```
System.out.println( Math.sqrt( c + d * f ) );
```

calculates and prints the square root of 13.0 + 3.0 * 4.0 = 25.0—namely, 5.0. Figure 6.1 summarizes several Math class methods. In the figure, x and y are of type double.

Math Class Constants PI and E
Class Math also declares two fields that represent commonly used mathematical constants: **Math.PI** and **Math.E**. The constant Math.PI (3.14159265358979323846) is the ratio of a

Method	Description	Example
abs(x)	absolute value of x	abs(23.7) is 23.7 abs(0.0) is 0.0 abs(-23.7) is 23.7
ceil(x)	rounds x to the smallest integer not less than x	ceil(9.2) is 10.0 ceil(-9.8) is -9.0
cos(x)	trigonometric cosine of x (x in radians)	cos(0.0) is 1.0
exp(x)	exponential method e^x	exp(1.0) is 2.71828 exp(2.0) is 7.38906
floor(x)	rounds x to the largest integer not greater than x	floor(9.2) is 9.0 floor(-9.8) is -10.0
log(x)	natural logarithm of x (base e)	log(Math.E) is 1.0 log(Math.E * Math.E) is 2.0
max(x, y)	larger value of x and y	max(2.3, 12.7) is 12.7 max(-2.3, -12.7) is -2.3
min(x, y)	smaller value of x and y	min(2.3, 12.7) is 2.3 min(-2.3, -12.7) is -12.7
pow(x, y)	x raised to the power y (i.e., x^y)	pow(2.0, 7.0) is 128.0 pow(9.0, 0.5) is 3.0
sin(x)	trigonometric sine of x (x in radians)	sin(0.0) is 0.0
sqrt(x)	square root of x	sqrt(900.0) is 30.0
tan(x)	trigonometric tangent of x (x in radians)	tan(0.0) is 0.0

Fig. 6.1 | Math class methods.

circle's circumference to its diameter. The constant Math.E (2.7182818284590452354) is the base value for natural logarithms (calculated with static Math method log). These fields are declared in class Math with the modifiers public, final and static. Making them public allows other programmers to use these fields in their own classes. Any field declared with keyword *final* is constant—its value cannot be changed after the field is initialized. Both PI and E are declared final because their values never change. Making these fields static allows them to be accessed via the class name Math and a dot (.) separator, just like class Math's methods. Recall from Section 3.5 that when each object of a class maintains its own copy of an attribute, the field that represents the attribute is also known as an instance variable—each object (instance) of the class has a separate instance of the variable in memory. There are fields for which each object of a class does not have a separate instance of the field. That is the case with static fields, which are also known as *class variables*. When objects of a class containing static fields are created, all the objects of that class share one copy of the class's static fields. Together the class variables (i.e., static variables) and instance variables represent the fields of a class. You'll learn more about static fields in Section 8.11.

Why Is Method main Declared static?

Why must main be declared static? When you execute the Java Virtual Machine (JVM) with the java command, the JVM attempts to invoke the main method of the class you specify—when no objects of the class have been created. Declaring main as static allows the JVM to invoke main without creating an instance of the class. Method main is declared with the header:

```
public static void main( String args[] )
```

When you execute your application, you specify its class name as an argument to the command java, as in

```
java ClassName argument1 argument2 ...
```

The JVM loads the class specified by *ClassName* and uses that class name to invoke method main. In the preceding command, *ClassName* is a **command-line argument** to the JVM that tells it which class to execute. Following the *ClassName*, you can also specify a list of Strings (separated by spaces) as command-line arguments that the JVM will pass to your application. Such arguments might be used to specify options (e.g., a file name) to run the application. As you'll learn in Chapter 7, Arrays, your application can access those command-line arguments and use them to customize the application.

Additional Comments about Method main

In earlier chapters, every application had one class that contained only main and possibly a second class that was used by main to create and manipulate objects. Actually, any class can contain a main method. In fact, each of our two-class examples could have been implemented as one class. For example, in the application in Fig. 5.9 and Fig. 5.10, method main (lines 6–16 of Fig. 5.10) could have been taken as is and placed in class GradeBook (Fig. 5.9). You would then execute the application by typing the command java Grade-Book in the command window—the application results would be identical to those of the two-class version. You can place a main method in every class you declare. The JVM invokes the main method only in the class used to execute the application. Some programmers take advantage of this to build a small test program into each class they declare.

6.4 Declaring Methods with Multiple Parameters

We now show how to write methods with multiple parameters. The application in Fig. 6.2 and Fig. 6.3 uses a programmer-declared method called maximum to determine and return the largest of three double values that are input by the user. When the application begins execution, class MaximumFinderTest's main method (lines 7–11 of Fig. 6.3) creates one object of class MaximumFinder (line 9) and calls the object's determineMaximum method (line 10) to produce the program's output. In class MaximumFinder (Fig. 6.2), lines 14–18 of method determineMaximum prompt the user to enter three double values, then read them from the user. Line 21 calls method maximum (declared in lines 28–41) to determine the largest of the three double values passed as arguments to the method. When method maximum returns the result to line 21, the program assigns maximum's return value to local variable result. Then line 24 outputs the maximum value. At the end of this section, we'll discuss the use of operator + in line 24.

```
 1    // Fig. 6.2: MaximumFinder.java
 2    // Programmer-declared method maximum.
 3    import java.util.Scanner;
 4
 5    public class MaximumFinder
 6    {
 7       // obtain three floating-point values and locate the maximum value
 8       public void determineMaximum()
 9       {
10          // create Scanner for input from command window
11          Scanner input = new Scanner( System.in );
12
13          // obtain user input
14          System.out.print(
15             "Enter three floating-point values separated by spaces: " );
16          double number1 = input.nextDouble(); // read first double
17          double number2 = input.nextDouble(); // read second double
18          double number3 = input.nextDouble(); // read third double
19
20          // determine the maximum value
21          double result = maximum( number1, number2, number3 );
22
23          // display maximum value
24          System.out.println( "Maximum is: " + result );
25       } // end method determineMaximum
26
27       // returns the maximum of its three double parameters
28       public double maximum( double x, double y, double z )
29       {
30          double maximumValue = x; // assume x is the largest to start
31
32          // determine whether y is greater than maximumValue
33          if ( y > maximumValue )
34             maximumValue = y;
35
36          // determine whether z is greater than maximumValue
37          if ( z > maximumValue )
38             maximumValue = z;
39
40          return maximumValue;
41       } // end method maximum
42    } // end class MaximumFinder
```

Fig. 6.2 | Programmer-declared method maximum that has three double parameters.

```
 1    // Fig. 6.3: MaximumFinderTest.java
 2    // Application to test class MaximumFinder.
 3
 4    public class MaximumFinderTest
 5    {
```

Fig. 6.3 | Application to test class MaximumFinder. (Part 1 of 2.)

```
 6       // application starting point
 7       public static void main( String args[] )
 8       {
 9          MaximumFinder maximumFinder = new MaximumFinder();
10          maximumFinder.determineMaximum();
11       } // end main
12    } // end class MaximumFinderTest
```

```
Enter three floating-point values separated by spaces: 9.35 2.74 5.1
Maximum is: 9.35
```

```
Enter three floating-point values separated by spaces: 5.8 12.45 8.32
Maximum is: 12.45
```

```
Enter three floating-point values separated by spaces: 6.46 4.12 10.54
Maximum is: 10.54
```

Fig. 6.3 | Application to test class `MaximumFinder`. (Part 2 of 2.)

Consider the declaration of method `maximum` (lines 28–41). Line 28 indicates that the method returns a `double` value, that the method's name is `maximum` and that the method requires three `double` parameters (x, y and z) to accomplish its task. When a method has more than one parameter, the parameters are specified as a comma-separated list. When maximum is called from line 21, the parameter x is initialized with the value of the argument `number1`, the parameter y is initialized with the value of the argument `number2` and the parameter z is initialized with the value of the argument `number3`. There must be one argument in the method call for each parameter (sometimes called a *formal parameter*) in the method declaration. Also, each argument must be consistent with the type of the corresponding parameter. For example, a parameter of type `double` can receive values like 7.35, 22 or –0.03456, but not `String`s like "hello" nor the `boolean` values `true` or `false`. Section 6.7 discusses the argument types that can be provided in a method call for each parameter of a primitive type.

To determine the maximum value, we begin with the assumption that parameter x contains the largest value, so line 30 declares local variable `maximumValue` and initializes it with the value of parameter x. Of course, it is possible that parameter y or z contains the actual largest value, so we must compare each of these values with `maximumValue`. The `if` statement at lines 33–34 determines whether y is greater than `maximumValue`. If so, line 34 assigns y to `maximumValue`. The `if` statement at lines 37–38 determines whether z is greater than `maximumValue`. If so, line 38 assigns z to `maximumValue`. At this point the largest of the three values resides in `maximumValue`, so line 40 returns that value to line 21. When program control returns to the point in the program where maximum was called, `maximum`'s parameters x, y and z no longer exist in memory. Note that methods can return at most one value, but the returned value could be a reference to an object that contains many values.

Note that `result` is a local variable in `determineMaximum` because it is declared in the block that represents the method's body. Variables should be declared as fields of a class only if they are required for use in more than one method of the class or if the program should save their values between calls to the class's methods.

Common Programming Error 6.1

Declaring method parameters of the same type as float x, y *instead of* float x, float y *is a syntax error—a type is required for each parameter in the parameter list.*

Software Engineering Observation 6.5

A method that has many parameters may be performing too many tasks. Consider dividing the method into smaller methods that perform the separate tasks. As a guideline, try to fit the method header on one line if possible.

Implementing Method maximum *by Reusing Method* Math.max

Recall from Fig. 6.1 that class Math has a max method that can determine the larger of two values. The entire body of our maximum method could also be implemented with two calls to Math.max, as follows:

```
return Math.max( x, Math.max( y, z ) );
```

The first call to Math.max specifies arguments x and Math.max(y, z). Before any method can be called, its arguments must be evaluated to determine their values. If an argument is a method call, the method call must be performed to determine its return value. So, in the preceding statement, Math.max(y, z) is evaluated first to determine the maximum of y and z. Then the result is passed as the second argument to the other call to Math.max, which returns the larger of its two arguments. This is a good example of software reuse— we find the largest of three values by reusing Math.max, which finds the largest of two values. Note how concise this code is compared to lines 30–40 of Fig. 6.2.

Assembling Strings with String Concatenation

Java allows String objects to be created by assembling smaller strings into larger strings using operator + (or the compound assignment operator +=). This is known as *string concatenation*. When both operands of operator + are String objects, operator + creates a new String object in which the characters of the right operand are placed at the end of those in the left operand. For example, the expression "hello " + "there" creates the String "hello there".

In line 24 of Fig. 6.2, the expression "Maximum is: " + result uses operator + with operands of types String and double. Every primitive value and object in Java has a String representation. When one of the + operator's operands is a String, the other is converted to a String, then the two are concatenated. In line 24, the double value is converted to its String representation and placed at the end of the String "Maximum is: ". If there are any trailing zeros in a double value, these will be discarded when the number is converted to a String. Thus, the number 9.3500 would be represented as 9.35 in the resulting String.

For primitive values used in string concatenation, the primitive values are converted to Strings. If a boolean is concatenated with a String, the boolean is converted to the String "true" or "false". All objects have a method named toString that returns a String representation of the object. When an object is concatenated with a String, the object's toString method is implicitly called to obtain the String representation of the object. You'll learn more about the method toString in Chapter 7.

When a large String literal is typed into a program's source code, programmers sometimes prefer to break that String into several smaller Strings and place them on multiple lines of code for readability. In this case, the Strings can be reassembled using concatenation. We discuss the details of Strings in Chapter 25, Strings, Characters and Regular Expressions.

Common Programming Error 6.2

It is a syntax error to break a String literal across multiple lines in a program. If a String does not fit on one line, split the String into several smaller Strings and use concatenation to form the desired String.

Common Programming Error 6.3

Confusing the + operator used for string concatenation with the + operator used for addition can lead to strange results. Java evaluates the operands of an operator from left to right. For example, if integer variable y has the value 5, the expression "y + 2 = " + y + 2 results in the string "y + 2 = 52", not "y + 2 = 7", because first the value of y (5) is concatenated with the string "y + 2 = ", then the value 2 is concatenated with the new larger string "y + 2 = 5". The expression "y + 2 = " + (y + 2) produces the desired result "y + 2 = 7".

6.5 Notes on Declaring and Using Methods

There are three ways to call a method:

1. Using a method name by itself to call another method of the same class—such as maximum(number1, number2, number3) in line 21 of Fig. 6.2.

2. Using a variable that contains a reference to an object, followed by a dot (.) and the method name to call a method of the referenced object—such as the method call in line 10 of Fig. 6.3, maximumFinder.determineMaximum(), which calls a method of class MaximumFinder from the main method of MaximumFinderTest.

3. Using the class name and a dot (.) to call a static method of a class—such as Math.sqrt(900.0) in Section 6.3.

Note that a static method can call only other static methods of the same class directly (i.e., using the method name by itself) and can manipulate only static fields in the same class directly. To access the class's non-static members, a static method must use a reference to an object of the class. Recall that static methods relate to a class as a whole, whereas non-static methods are associated with a specific instance (object) of the class and may manipulate the instance variables of that object. Many objects of a class, each with its own copies of the instance variables, may exist at the same time. Suppose a static method were to invoke a non-static method directly. How would the method know which object's instance variables to manipulate? What would happen if no objects of the class existed at the time the non-static method was invoked? Clearly, such a situation would be problematic. Thus, Java does not allow a static method to access non-static members of the same class directly.

There are three ways to return control to the statement that calls a method. If the method does not return a result, control returns when the program flow reaches the method-ending right brace or when the statement *return*;

is executed. If the method returns a result, the statement

     return expression;

evaluates the *expression*, then returns the result to the caller.

Common Programming Error 6.4
Declaring a method outside the body of a class declaration or inside the body of another method is a syntax error.

Common Programming Error 6.5
Omitting the return-value-type *in a method declaration is a syntax error.*

Common Programming Error 6.6
Placing a semicolon after the right parenthesis enclosing the parameter list of a method declaration is a syntax error.

Common Programming Error 6.7
Redeclaring a method parameter as a local variable in the method's body is a compilation error.

Common Programming Error 6.8
Forgetting to return a value from a method that should return a value is a compilation error. If a return-value-type *other than* void *is specified, the method must contain a* return *statement that returns a value consistent with the method's* return-value-type. *Returning a value from a method whose return type has been declared* void *is a compilation error.*

6.6 Method-Call Stack and Activation Records

To understand how Java performs method calls, we first need to consider a data structure (i.e., collection of related data items) known as a *stack*. Stacks are known as *last-in, first-out (LIFO) data structures*—the last item *pushed* (inserted) on the stack is the first item *popped* (removed) from the stack.

    When a program calls a method, the called method must know how to return to its caller, so the return address of the calling method is pushed onto the *program execution stack* (sometimes referred to as the *method-call stack*). If a series of method calls occurs, the successive return addresses are pushed onto the stack in last-in, first-out order so that each method can return to its caller.

    The program execution stack also contains the memory for the local variables used in each invocation of a method during a program's execution. This data, stored as a portion of the program execution stack, is known as the *activation record* or *stack frame* of the method call. When a method call is made, the activation record for that method call is pushed onto the program execution stack. When the method returns to its caller, the activation record for this method call is popped off the stack and those local variables are no longer known to the program. If a local variable holding a reference to an object is the only variable in the program with a reference to that object, when the activation record containing that local variable is popped off the stack, the object can no longer be accessed by the program and will eventually be deleted from memory by the JVM during "garbage collection." We'll discuss garbage collection in Section 8.10.

Of course, the amount of memory in a computer is finite, so only a certain amount of memory can be used to store activation records on the program execution stack. If more method calls occur than can have their activation records stored on the program execution stack, an error known as a *stack overflow* occurs.

6.7 Argument Promotion and Casting

Another important feature of method calls is *argument promotion*—converting an argument's value to the type that the method expects to receive in its corresponding parameter. For example, a program can call Math method sqrt with an integer argument even though the method expects to receive a double argument (but, as we'll soon see, not vice versa). The statement

```
System.out.println( Math.sqrt( 4 ) );
```

correctly evaluates Math.sqrt(4) and prints the value 2.0. The method declaration's parameter list causes Java to convert the int value 4 to the double value 4.0 before passing the value to sqrt. Attempting these conversions may lead to compilation errors if Java's *promotion rules* are not satisfied. The promotion rules specify which conversions are allowed—that is, which conversions can be performed without losing data. In the sqrt example above, an int is converted to a double without changing its value. However, converting a double to an int truncates the fractional part of the double value—thus, part of the value is lost. Converting large integer types to small integer types (e.g., long to int) may also result in changed values.

The promotion rules apply to expressions containing values of two or more primitive types and to primitive-type values passed as arguments to methods. Each value is promoted to the "highest" type in the expression. (Actually, the expression uses a temporary copy of each value—the types of the original values remain unchanged.) Figure 6.4 lists the primitive types and the types to which each can be promoted. Note that the valid promotions for a given type are always to a type higher in the table. For example, an int can be promoted to the higher types long, float and double.

Type	Valid promotions
double	None
float	double
long	float or double
int	long, float or double
char	int, long, float or double
short	int, long, float or double (but not char)
byte	short, int, long, float or double (but not char)
boolean	None (boolean values are not considered to be numbers in Java)

Fig. 6.4 | Promotions allowed for primitive types.

Converting values to types lower in the table of Fig. 6.4 will result in different values if the lower type cannot represent the value of the higher type (e.g., the int value 2000000 cannot be represented as a short, and any floating-point number with digits after its decimal point cannot be represented in an integer type such as long, int or short). Therefore, in cases where information may be lost due to conversion, the Java compiler requires you to use a cast operator (introduced in Section 4.7) to explicitly force the conversion to occur—otherwise a compilation error occurs. This enables you to "take control" from the compiler. You essentially say, "I know this conversion might cause loss of information, but for my purposes here, that's fine." Suppose method square calculates the square of an integer and thus requires an int argument. To call square with a double argument named doubleValue, we would be required to write the method call as

    square((*int*) doubleValue)

This method call explicitly casts (converts) the value of doubleValue to an integer for use in method square. Thus, if doubleValue's value is 4.5, the method receives the value 4 and returns 16, not 20.25.

Common Programming Error 6.9

Converting a primitive-type value to another primitive type may change the value if the new type is not a valid promotion. For example, converting a floating-point value to an integral value may introduce truncation errors (loss of the fractional part) into the result.

6.8 Java API Packages

As we have seen, Java contains many predefined classes that are grouped into categories of related classes called packages. Together, we refer to these packages as the Java Application Programming Interface (Java API), or the Java class library.

Throughout the text, import declarations specify the classes required to compile a Java program. For example, a program includes the declaration

    import java.util.Scanner;

to specify that the program uses class Scanner from the java.util package. This allows you to use the simple class name Scanner, rather than the fully qualified class name java.util.Scanner, in the code. A great strength of Java is the large number of classes in the packages of the Java API. Some key Java API packages are described in Fig. 6.5, which represents only a small portion of the reusable components in the Java API. When learning Java, spend a portion of your time browsing the packages and classes in the Java API documentation (java.sun.com/javase/6/docs/api/).

Package	Description
java.applet	The *Java Applet Package* contains a class and several interfaces required to create Java applets—programs that execute in web browsers. (Interfaces are discussed in Chapter 10, Object-Oriented Programming: Polymorphism.)

Fig. 6.5 | Java API packages (a subset). (Part 1 of 3.)

Package	Description
java.awt	The *Java Abstract Window Toolkit Package* contains the classes and interfaces required to create and manipulate GUIs in Java 1.0 and 1.1. In current versions of Java, the Swing GUI components of the javax.swing packages are often used instead. (Some elements of the java.awt package are discussed in Chapter 11, GUI Components: Part 1, Chapter 12, Graphics and Java 2D™, and Chapter 17, GUI Components: Part 2.)
java.awt.event	The *Java Abstract Window Toolkit Event Package* contains classes and interfaces that enable event handling for GUI components in both the java.awt and javax.swing packages. (You'll learn more about this package in Chapter 11, GUI Components: Part 1 and Chapter 17, GUI Components: Part 2.)
java.io	The *Java Input/Output Package* contains classes and interfaces that enable programs to input and output data. (You'll learn more about this package in Chapter 14, Files and Streams.)
java.lang	The *Java Language Package* contains classes and interfaces (discussed throughout this text) that are required by many Java programs. This package is imported by the compiler into all programs, so you do not need to do so.
java.net	The *Java Networking Package* contains classes and interfaces that enable programs to communicate via networks like the Internet. (You'll learn more about this in Chapter 19, Networking.)
java.text	The *Java Text Package* contains classes and interfaces that enable programs to manipulate numbers, dates, characters and strings. The package provides internationalization capabilities that enable a program to be customized to a specific locale (e.g., a program may display strings in different languages, based on the user's country).
java.util	The *Java Utilities Package* contains utility classes and interfaces that enable such actions as date and time manipulations, random-number processing (class Random), the storing and processing of large amounts of data and the breaking of strings into smaller pieces called tokens (class StringTokenizer). (You'll learn more about the features of this package in Chapter 16, Collections.)
javax.swing	The *Java Swing GUI Components Package* contains classes and interfaces for Java's Swing GUI components that provide support for portable GUIs. (You'll learn more about this package in Chapter 11, GUI Components: Part 1 and Chapter 17, GUI Components: Part 2.)

Fig. 6.5 | Java API packages (a subset). (Part 2 of 3.)

Package	Description
`javax.swing.event`	The *Java Swing Event Package* contains classes and interfaces that enable event handling (e.g., responding to button clicks) for GUI components in package `javax.swing`. (You'll learn more about this package in Chapter 11, GUI Components: Part 1 and Chapter 17, GUI Components: Part 2.)

Fig. 6.5 | Java API packages (a subset). (Part 3 of 3.)

The set of packages available in Java SE 6 is quite large. In addition to the packages summarized in Fig. 6.5, Java SE 6 includes packages for complex graphics, advanced graphical user interfaces, printing, advanced networking, security, database processing, multimedia, accessibility (for people with disabilities) and many other capabilities. For an overview of the packages in Java SE 6, visit

> `java.sun.com/javase/6/docs/api/overview-summary.html`

Many other packages are also available for download at `java.sun.com`.

You can locate additional information about a predefined Java class's methods in the Java API documentation at `java.sun.com/javase/6/docs/api/`. When you visit this site, click the **Index** link to see an alphabetical listing of Java API classes, interfaces and methods. Locate the class name and click its link to see the class's description. Click the **METHOD** link to see a table of the class's methods. Each `static` method is listed with the word "`static`" preceding the method's return type. For a more detailed overview of navigating the Java API documentation, see Appendix G.

Good Programming Practice 6.2

The online Java API documentation is easy to search and provides many details about each class. As you learn a class in this book, you should get in the habit of looking at the class in the online documentation for additional information.

6.9 Case Study: Random-Number Generation

We now take a brief and, hopefully, entertaining diversion into simulation and game playing. In this and the next section, we develop a nicely structured game-playing program with multiple methods. The program uses most of the control statements presented thus far in the book and introduces several new programming concepts.

There is something in the air of a casino that invigorates people—from the high rollers at the plush mahogany-and-felt craps tables to the quarter poppers at the one-armed bandits. It is the *element of chance*, the possibility that luck will convert a pocketful of money into a mountain of wealth. The element of chance can be introduced in a program via an object of class Random (package `java.util`) or via the `static` method random of class Math. Objects of class Random can produce random `boolean`, `byte`, `float`, `double`, `int`, `long` and Gaussian values, whereas Math method `random` can produce only `double` values in the range $0.0 \leq x < 1.0$, where x is the value returned by method `random`. In the next several examples, we use objects of class Random to produce random values.

A new random-number generator object can be created as follows:

```
Random randomNumbers = new Random();
```

The random-number generator object can then be used to generate random boolean, byte, float, double, int, long and Gaussian values—we discuss only random int values here. For more information on the Random class, see java.sun.com/javase/6/docs/api/ java/util/Random.html.

Consider the following statement:

```
int randomValue = randomNumbers.nextInt();
```

Method nextInt of class Random generates a random int value from –2,147,483,648 to +2,147,483,647. If the nextInt method truly produces values at random, then every value in that range should have an equal chance (or probability) of being chosen each time method nextInt is called. The values returned by nextInt are actually *pseudorandom numbers*—a sequence of values produced by a complex mathematical calculation. The calculation uses the current time of day (which, of course, changes constantly) to *seed* the random-number generator such that each execution of a program yields a different sequence of random values.

The range of values produced directly by method nextInt often differs from the range of values required in a particular Java application. For example, a program that simulates coin tossing might require only 0 for "heads" and 1 for "tails." A program that simulates the rolling of a six-sided die might require random integers in the range 1–6. A program that randomly predicts the next type of spaceship (out of four possibilities) that will fly across the horizon in a video game might require random integers in the range 1–4. For cases like these, class Random provides another version of method nextInt that receives an int argument and returns a value from 0 up to, but not including, the argument's value. For example, to simulate coin tossing, you might use the statement

```
int randomValue = randomNumbers.nextInt( 2 );
```

which returns 0 or 1.

Rolling a Six-Sided Die

To demonstrate random numbers, let us develop a program that simulates 20 rolls of a six-sided die and displays the value of each roll. We begin by using nextInt to produce random values in the range 0–5, as follows:

```
face = randomNumbers.nextInt( 6 );
```

The argument 6—called the *scaling factor*—represents the number of unique values that nextInt should produce (in this case six—0, 1, 2, 3, 4 and 5). This manipulation is called *scaling* the range of values produced by Random method nextInt.

A six-sided die has the numbers 1–6 on its faces, not 0–5. So we *shift* the range of numbers produced by adding a *shifting value*—in this case 1—to our previous result, as in

```
face = 1 + randomNumbers.nextInt( 6 );
```

The shifting value (1) specifies the first value in the desired set of random integers. The preceding statement assigns face a random integer in the range 1–6.

Figure 6.6 shows two sample outputs which confirm that the results of the preceding calculation are integers in the range 1–6, and that each run of the program can produce a different sequence of random numbers. Line 3 imports class Random from the java.util package. Line 9 creates the Random object randomNumbers to produce random values. Line 16 executes 20 times in a loop to roll the die. The if statement (lines 21–22) in the loop starts a new line of output after every five numbers.

```java
1  // Fig. 6.6: RandomIntegers.java
2  // Shifted and scaled random integers.
3  import java.util.Random; // program uses class Random
4
5  public class RandomIntegers
6  {
7     public static void main( String args[] )
8     {
9        Random randomNumbers = new Random(); // random number generator
10       int face; // stores each random integer generated
11
12       // loop 20 times
13       for ( int counter = 1; counter <= 20; counter++ )
14       {
15          // pick random integer from 1 to 6
16          face = 1 + randomNumbers.nextInt( 6 );
17
18          System.out.printf( "%d  ", face ); // display generated value
19
20          // if counter is divisible by 5, start a new line of output
21          if ( counter % 5 == 0 )
22             System.out.println();
23       } // end for
24    } // end main
25 } // end class RandomIntegers
```

```
1  5  3  6  2
5  2  6  5  2
4  4  4  2  6
3  1  6  2  2
```

```
6  5  4  2  6
1  2  5  1  3
6  3  2  2  1
6  4  2  6  4
```

Fig. 6.6 | Shifted and scaled random integers.

Rolling a Six-Sided Die 6000 Times

To show that the numbers produced by nextInt occur with approximately equal likelihood, let us simulate 6000 rolls of a die with the application in Fig. 6.7. Each integer from 1 to 6 should appear approximately 1000 times.

As the two sample outputs show, scaling and shifting the values produced by method nextInt enables the program to realistically simulate rolling a six-sided die. The application uses nested control statements (the switch is nested inside the for) to determine the number of times each side of the die occurred. The for statement (lines 21–47) iterates 6000 times. During each iteration, line 23 produces a random value from 1 to 6. That value is then used as the controlling expression (line 26) of the switch statement (lines 26–46). Based on the face value, the switch statement increments one of the six counter variables during each iteration of the loop. When we study arrays in Chapter 7, we'll show an elegant way to replace the entire switch statement in this program with a single statement! Note that the switch statement has no default case, because we have a case for every possible die value that the expression in line 23 could produce. Run the program several times, and observe the results. As you'll see, every time you execute this program, it produces different results.

```java
1   // Fig. 6.7: RollDie.java
2   // Roll a six-sided die 6000 times.
3   import java.util.Random;
4
5   public class RollDie
6   {
7      public static void main( String args[] )
8      {
9         Random randomNumbers = new Random(); // random number generator
10
11        int frequency1 = 0; // maintains count of 1s rolled
12        int frequency2 = 0; // count of 2s rolled
13        int frequency3 = 0; // count of 3s rolled
14        int frequency4 = 0; // count of 4s rolled
15        int frequency5 = 0; // count of 5s rolled
16        int frequency6 = 0; // count of 6s rolled
17
18        int face; // stores most recently rolled value
19
20        // summarize results of 6000 rolls of a die
21        for ( int roll = 1; roll <= 6000; roll++ )
22        {
23           face = 1 + randomNumbers.nextInt( 6 ); // number from 1 to 6
24
25           // determine roll value 1-6 and increment appropriate counter
26           switch ( face )
27           {
28              case 1:
29                 ++frequency1; // increment the 1s counter
30                 break;
31              case 2:
32                 ++frequency2; // increment the 2s counter
33                 break;
34              case 3:
35                 ++frequency3; // increment the 3s counter
36                 break;
37              case 4:
38                 ++frequency4; // increment the 4s counter
39                 break;
```

Fig. 6.7 | Rolling a six-sided die 6000 times. (Part 1 of 2.)

```
40              case 5:
41                  ++frequency5; // increment the 5s counter
42                  break;
43              case 6:
44                  ++frequency6; // increment the 6s counter
45                  break; // optional at end of switch
46          } // end switch
47      } // end for
48
49      System.out.println( "Face\tFrequency" ); // output headers
50      System.out.printf( "1\t%d\n2\t%d\n3\t%d\n4\t%d\n5\t%d\n6\t%d\n",
51          frequency1, frequency2, frequency3, frequency4,
52          frequency5, frequency6 );
53  } // end main
54 } // end class RollDie
```

Face	Frequency
1	982
2	1001
3	1015
4	1005
5	1009
6	988

Face	Frequency
1	1029
2	994
3	1017
4	1007
5	972
6	981

Fig. 6.7 | Rolling a six-sided die 6000 times. (Part 2 of 2.)

6.9.1 Generalized Scaling and Shifting of Random Numbers

Previously, we demonstrated the statement

```
face = 1 + randomNumbers.nextInt( 6 );
```

which simulates the rolling of a six-sided die. This statement always assigns to variable face an integer in the range $1 \le$ face ≤ 6. The width of this range (i.e., the number of consecutive integers in the range) is 6, and the starting number in the range is 1. Referring to the preceding statement, we see that the width of the range is determined by the number 6 that is passed as an argument to Random method nextInt, and the starting number of the range is the number 1 that is added to randomNumberGenerator.nextInt(6). We can generalize this result as

```
number = shiftingValue + randomNumbers.nextInt( scalingFactor );
```

where *shiftingValue* specifies the first number in the desired range of consecutive integers and *scalingFactor* specifies how many numbers are in the range.

It is also possible to choose integers at random from sets of values other than ranges of consecutive integers. For example, to obtain a random value from the sequence 2, 5, 8, 11 and 14, you could use the statement

```
number = 2 + 3 * randomNumbers.nextInt( 5 );
```

In this case, `randomNumberGenerator.nextInt( 5 )` produces values in the range 0–4. Each value produced is multiplied by 3 to produce a number in the sequence 0, 3, 6, 9 and 12. We then add 2 to that value to shift the range of values and obtain a value from the sequence 2, 5, 8, 11 and 14. We can generalize this result as

number = *shiftingValue* +
    differenceBetweenValues * `randomNumbers.nextInt(` *scalingFactor* `);`

where *shiftingValue* specifies the first number in the desired range of values, *difference-BetweenValues* represents the difference between consecutive numbers in the sequence and *scalingFactor* specifies how many numbers are in the range.

6.9.2 Random-Number Repeatability for Testing and Debugging

As we mentioned earlier in Section 6.9, the methods of class Random actually generate pseudorandom numbers based on complex mathematical calculations. Repeatedly calling any of Random's methods produces a sequence of numbers that appears to be random. The calculation that produces the pseudorandom numbers uses the time of day as a *seed value* to change the sequence's starting point. Each new Random object seeds itself with a value based on the computer system's clock at the time the object is created, enabling each execution of a program to produce a different sequence of random numbers.

When debugging an application, it is sometimes useful to repeat the exact same sequence of pseudorandom numbers during each execution of the program. This repeatability enables you to prove that your application is working for a specific sequence of random numbers before you test the program with different sequences of random numbers. When repeatability is important, you can create a Random object as follows:

```
Random randomNumbers = new Random( seedValue );
```

The `seedValue` argument (of type `long`) seeds the random-number calculation. If the same `seedValue` is used every time, the Random object produces the same sequence of random numbers. You can set a Random object's seed at any time during program execution by calling the object's `setSeed` method, as in

```
randomNumbers.setSeed( seedValue );
```

Error-Prevention Tip 6.2

While a program is under development, create the Random object with a specific seed value to produce a repeatable sequence of random numbers each time the program executes. If a logic error occurs, fix the error and test the program again with the same seed value—this allows you to reconstruct the same sequence of random numbers that caused the error. Once the logic errors have been removed, create the Random object without using a seed value, causing the Random object to generate a new sequence of random numbers each time the program executes.

6.10 Case Study: A Game of Chance (Introducing Enumerations)

A popular game of chance is a dice game known as craps, which is played in casinos and back alleys throughout the world. The rules of the game are straightforward:

> *You roll two dice. Each die has six faces, which contain one, two, three, four, five and six spots, respectively. After the dice have come to rest, the sum of the spots on the two upward faces is calculated. If the sum is 7 or 11 on the first throw, you win. If the sum is 2, 3 or 12 on the first throw (called "craps"), you lose (i.e., the "house" wins). If the sum is 4, 5, 6, 8, 9 or 10 on the first throw, that sum becomes your "point." To win, you must continue rolling the dice until you "make your point" (i.e., roll that same point value). You lose by rolling a 7 before making the point.*

The application in Fig. 6.8 and Fig. 6.9 simulates the game of craps, using methods to define the logic of the game. In the main method of class CrapsTest (Fig. 6.9), line 8 creates an object of class Craps (Fig. 6.8) and line 9 calls its play method to start the game. The play method (Fig. 6.8, lines 21–65) calls the rollDice method (Fig. 6.8, lines 68–81) as necessary to roll the two dice and compute their sum. Four sample outputs in Fig. 6.9 show winning on the first roll, losing on the first roll, winning on a subsequent roll and losing on a subsequent roll, respectively.

Let's discuss the declaration of class Craps in Fig. 6.8. In the rules of the game, the player must roll two dice on the first roll, and must do the same on all subsequent rolls. We declare method rollDice (lines 68–81) to roll the dice and compute and print their sum. Method rollDice is declared once, but it is called from two places (lines 26 and 50) in method play, which contains the logic for one complete game of craps. Method rollDice takes no arguments, so it has an empty parameter list. Each time it is called, rollDice returns the sum of the dice, so the return type int is indicated in the method header (line 68). Although lines 71 and 72 look the same (except for the die names), they do not necessarily produce the same result. Each of these statements produces a random value in the range 1–6. Note that randomNumbers (used in lines 71–72) is not declared in the method. Rather it is declared as a private instance variable of the class and initialized in line 8. This enables us to create one Random object that is reused in each call to rollDice.

```
1   // Fig. 6.8: Craps.java
2   // Craps class simulates the dice game craps.
3   import java.util.Random;
4
5   public class Craps
6   {
7       // create random number generator for use in method rollDice
8       private Random randomNumbers = new Random();
9
10      // enumeration with constants that represent the game status
11      private enum Status { CONTINUE, WON, LOST };
12
13      // constants that represent common rolls of the dice
14      private final static int SNAKE_EYES = 2;
15      private final static int TREY = 3;
```

Fig. 6.8 | Craps class simulates the dice game craps. (Part 1 of 3.)

```
16    private final static int SEVEN = 7;
17    private final static int YO_LEVEN = 11;
18    private final static int BOX_CARS = 12;
19
20    // plays one game of craps
21    public void play()
22    {
23       int myPoint = 0; // point if no win or loss on first roll
24       Status gameStatus; // can contain CONTINUE, WON or LOST
25
26       int sumOfDice = rollDice(); // first roll of the dice
27
28       // determine game status and point based on first roll
29       switch ( sumOfDice )
30       {
31          case SEVEN: // win with 7 on first roll
32          case YO_LEVEN: // win with 11 on first roll
33             gameStatus = Status.WON;
34             break;
35          case SNAKE_EYES: // lose with 2 on first roll
36          case TREY: // lose with 3 on first roll
37          case BOX_CARS: // lose with 12 on first roll
38             gameStatus = Status.LOST;
39             break;
40          default: // did not win or lose, so remember point
41             gameStatus = Status.CONTINUE; // game is not over
42             myPoint = sumOfDice; // remember the point
43             System.out.printf( "Point is %d\n", myPoint );
44             break; // optional at end of switch
45       } // end switch
46
47       // while game is not complete
48       while ( gameStatus == Status.CONTINUE ) // not WON or LOST
49       {
50          sumOfDice = rollDice(); // roll dice again
51
52          // determine game status
53          if ( sumOfDice == myPoint ) // win by making point
54             gameStatus = Status.WON;
55          else
56             if ( sumOfDice == SEVEN ) // lose by rolling 7 before point
57                gameStatus = Status.LOST;
58       } // end while
59
60       // display won or lost message
61       if ( gameStatus == Status.WON )
62          System.out.println( "Player wins" );
63       else
64          System.out.println( "Player loses" );
65    } // end method play
66
```

Fig. 6.8 | Craps class simulates the dice game craps. (Part 2 of 3.)

```
67        // roll dice, calculate sum and display results
68        public int rollDice()
69        {
70           // pick random die values
71           int die1 = 1 + randomNumbers.nextInt( 6 ); // first die roll
72           int die2 = 1 + randomNumbers.nextInt( 6 ); // second die roll
73
74           int sum = die1 + die2; // sum of die values
75
76           // display results of this roll
77           System.out.printf( "Player rolled %d + %d = %d\n",
78              die1, die2, sum );
79
80           return sum; // return sum of dice
81        } // end method rollDice
82     } // end class Craps
```

Fig. 6.8 | Craps class simulates the dice game craps. (Part 3 of 3.)

```
 1     // Fig. 6.9: CrapsTest.java
 2     // Application to test class Craps.
 3
 4     public class CrapsTest
 5     {
 6        public static void main( String args[] )
 7        {
 8           Craps game = new Craps();
 9           game.play(); // play one game of craps
10        } // end main
11     } // end class CrapsTest
```

```
Player rolled 5 + 6 = 11
Player wins
```

```
Player rolled 1 + 2 = 3
Player loses
```

```
Player rolled 5 + 4 = 9
Point is 9
Player rolled 2 + 2 = 4
Player rolled 2 + 6 = 8
Player rolled 4 + 2 = 6
Player rolled 3 + 6 = 9
Player wins
```

Fig. 6.9 | Application to test class Craps. (Part 1 of 2.)

```
Player rolled 2 + 6 = 8
Point is 8
Player rolled 5 + 1 = 6
Player rolled 2 + 1 = 3
Player rolled 1 + 6 = 7
Player loses
```

Fig. 6.9 | Application to test class Craps. (Part 2 of 2.)

The game is reasonably involved. The player may win or lose on the first roll, or may win or lose on any subsequent roll. Method play (lines 21–65 of Fig. 6.8) uses local variable myPoint (line 23) to store the "point" if the player does not win or lose on the first roll, local variable gameStatus (line 24) to keep track of the overall game status and local variable sumOfDice (line 26) to hold the sum of the dice for the most recent roll. Note that myPoint is initialized to 0 to ensure that the application will compile. If you do not initialize myPoint, the compiler issues an error, because myPoint is not assigned a value in every case of the switch statement, and thus the program could try to use myPoint before it is assigned a value. By contrast, gameStatus does not require initialization because it *is* assigned a value in every case of the switch statement—thus, it is guaranteed to be initialized before it is used.

Note that local variable gameStatus (line 24) is declared to be of a new type called Status, which we declared at line 11. Type Status is declared as a private member of class Craps, because Status will be used only in that class. Status is a programmer-declared type called an *enumeration*, which, in its simplest form, declares a set of constants represented by identifiers. An enumeration is a special kind of class that is introduced by the keyword enum and a type name (in this case, Status). As with any class, braces ({ and }) delimit the body of an enum declaration. Inside the braces is a comma-separated list of *enumeration constants*, each representing a unique value. The identifiers in an enum must be unique. (You'll learn more about enumerations in Chapter 8.)

Good Programming Practice 6.3

Use only uppercase letters in the names of enumeration constants. This makes the constants stand out and reminds you that enumeration constants are not variables.

Variables of type Status can be assigned only one of the three constants declared in the enumeration (line 11) or a compilation error will occur. When the game is won, the program sets local variable gameStatus to Status.WON (lines 33 and 54). When the game is lost, the program sets local variable gameStatus to Status.LOST (lines 38 and 57). Otherwise, the program sets local variable gameStatus to Status.CONTINUE (line 41) to indicate that the game is not over and the dice must be rolled again.

Good Programming Practice 6.4

Using enumeration constants (like Status.WON, Status.LOST and Status.CONTINUE) rather than literal integer values (such as 0, 1 and 2) can make programs easier to read and maintain.

Line 26 in method play calls rollDice, which picks two random values from 1 to 6, displays the value of the first die, the value of the second die and the sum of the dice, and returns the sum of the dice. Method play next enters the switch statement at lines 29–

45, which uses the sumOfDice value from line 26 to determine whether the game has been won or lost, or whether it should continue with another roll. The sums of the dice that would result in a win or loss on the first roll are declared as public final static int constants in lines 14–18. These are used in the cases of the switch statement. The identifier names use casino parlance for these sums. Note that these constants, like enum constants, are declared with all capital letters by convention, to make them stand out in the program. Lines 31–34 determine whether the player won on the first roll with SEVEN (7) or YO_LEVEN (11). Lines 35–39 determine whether the player lost on the first roll with SNAKE_EYES (2), TREY (3), or BOX_CARS (12). After the first roll, if the game is not over, the default case (lines 40–44) sets gameStatus to Status.CONTINUE, saves sumOfDice in myPoint and displays the point.

If we are still trying to "make our point" (i.e., the game is continuing from a prior roll), the loop in lines 48–58 executes. Line 50 rolls the dice again. In line 53, if sumOfDice matches myPoint, line 54 sets gameStatus to Status.WON, then the loop terminates because the game is complete. In line 56, if sumOfDice is equal to SEVEN (7), line 57 sets gameStatus to Status.LOST, and the loop terminates because the game is complete. When the game completes, lines 61–64 display a message indicating whether the player won or lost, and the program terminates.

Note the use of the various program-control mechanisms we have discussed. The Craps class in concert with class CrapsTest uses two methods—main, play (called from main) and rollDice (called twice from play)—and the switch, while, if...else and nested if control statements. Note also the use of multiple case labels in the switch statement to execute the same statements for sums of SEVEN and YO_LEVEN (lines 31–32) and for sums of SNAKE_EYES, TREY and BOX_CARS (lines 35–37).

You might be wondering why we declared the sums of the dice as public final static int constants rather than as enum constants. The answer lies in the fact that the program must compare the int variable sumOfDice (line 26) to these constants to determine the outcome of each roll. Suppose we were to declare enum Sum containing constants (e.g., Sum.SNAKE_EYES) representing the five sums used in the game, then use these constants in the cases of the switch statement (lines 29–45). Doing so would prevent us from using sumOfDice as the switch statement's controlling expression, because Java does not allow an int to be compared to an enumeration constant. To achieve the same functionality as the current program, we would have to use a variable currentSum of type Sum as the switch's controlling expression. Unfortunately, Java does not provide an easy way to convert an int value to a particular enum constant. Translating an int into an enum constant could be done with a separate switch statement. Clearly this would be cumbersome and not improve the readability of the program (thus defeating the purpose of using an enum).

6.11 Scope of Declarations

You have seen declarations of various Java entities, such as classes, methods, variables and parameters. Declarations introduce names that can be used to refer to such Java entities. The *scope* of a declaration is the portion of the program that can refer to the declared entity by its name. Such an entity is said to be "in scope" for that portion of the program. This section introduces several important scope issues. (For more scope information, see the *Java Language Specification, Section 6.3: Scope of a Declaration*, at java.sun.com/docs/ books/jls/second_edition/html/names.doc.html#103228.)

The basic scope rules are as follows:

1. The scope of a parameter declaration is the body of the method in which the declaration appears.

2. The scope of a local-variable declaration is from the point at which the declaration appears to the end of that block.

3. The scope of a local-variable declaration that appears in the initialization section of a `for` statement's header is the body of the `for` statement and the other expressions in the header.

4. The scope of a method or field of a class is the entire body of the class. This enables non-`static` methods of a class to use the class's fields and other methods.

Any block may contain variable declarations. If a local variable or parameter in a method has the same name as a field, the field is "hidden" until the block terminates execution—this is called **shadowing**. In Chapter 8, we discuss how to access shadowed fields.

Common Programming Error 6.10

A compilation error occurs when a local variable is declared more than once in a method.

Error-Prevention Tip 6.3

Use different names for fields and local variables to help prevent subtle logic errors that occur when a method is called and a local variable of the method shadows a field of the same name in the class.

The application in Fig. 6.10 and Fig. 6.11 demonstrates scoping issues with fields and local variables. When the application begins execution, class `ScopeTest`'s main method (Fig. 6.11, lines 7–11) creates an object of class `Scope` (line 9) and calls the object's `begin` method (line 10) to produce the program's output (shown in Fig. 6.11).

```
 1   // Fig. 6.10: Scope.java
 2   // Scope class demonstrates field and local variable scopes.
 3
 4   public class Scope
 5   {
 6      // field that is accessible to all methods of this class
 7      private int x = 1;
 8
 9      // method begin creates and initializes local variable x
10      // and calls methods useLocalVariable and useField
11      public void begin()
12      {
13         int x = 5; // method's local variable x shadows field x
14
15         System.out.printf( "local x in method begin is %d\n", x );
16
17         useLocalVariable(); // useLocalVariable has local x
18         useField(); // useField uses class Scope's field x
19         useLocalVariable(); // useLocalVariable reinitializes local x
```

Fig. 6.10 | Scope class demonstrating scopes of a field and local variables. (Part 1 of 2.)

```
20          useField(); // class Scope's field x retains its value
21
22          System.out.printf( "\nlocal x in method begin is %d\n", x );
23       } // end method begin
24
25       // create and initialize local variable x during each call
26       public void useLocalVariable()
27       {
28          int x = 25; // initialized each time useLocalVariable is called
29
30          System.out.printf(
31             "\nlocal x on entering method useLocalVariable is %d\n", x );
32          ++x; // modifies this method's local variable x
33          System.out.printf(
34             "local x before exiting method useLocalVariable is %d\n", x );
35       } // end method useLocalVariable
36
37       // modify class Scope's field x during each call
38       public void useField()
39       {
40          System.out.printf(
41             "\nfield x on entering method useField is %d\n", x );
42          x *= 10; // modifies class Scope's field x
43          System.out.printf(
44             "field x before exiting method useField is %d\n", x );
45       } // end method useField
46    } // end class Scope
```

Fig. 6.10 | Scope class demonstrating scopes of a field and local variables. (Part 2 of 2.)

```
1    // Fig. 6.11: ScopeTest.java
2    // Application to test class Scope.
3
4    public class ScopeTest
5    {
6       // application starting point
7       public static void main( String args[] )
8       {
9          Scope testScope = new Scope();
10          testScope.begin();
11       } // end main
12    } // end class ScopeTest
```

```
local x in method begin is 5

local x on entering method useLocalVariable is 25
local x before exiting method useLocalVariable is 26

field x on entering method useField is 1
field x before exiting method useField is 10
```

Fig. 6.11 | Application to test class Scope. (Part 1 of 2.)

```
local x on entering method useLocalVariable is 25
local x before exiting method useLocalVariable is 26

field x on entering method useField is 10
field x before exiting method useField is 100

local x in method begin is 5
```

Fig. 6.11 | Application to test class Scope. (Part 2 of 2.)

In class Scope, line 7 declares and initializes the field x to 1. This field is shadowed (hidden) in any block (or method) that declares a local variable named x. Method begin (lines 11–23) declares a local variable x (line 13) and initializes it to 5. This local variable's value is output to show that the field x (whose value is 1) is shadowed in method begin. The program declares two other methods—useLocalVariable (lines 26–35) and use-Field (lines 38–45)—that each take no arguments and do not return results. Method begin calls each method twice (lines 17–20). Method useLocalVariable declares local variable x (line 28). When useLocalVariable is first called (line 17), it creates local variable x and initializes it to 25 (line 28), outputs the value of x (lines 30–31), increments x (line 32) and outputs the value of x again (lines 33–34). When useLocalVariable is called a second time (line 19), it re-creates local variable x and re-initializes it to 25, so the output of each useLocalVariable call is identical.

Method useField does not declare any local variables. Therefore, when it refers to x, field x (line 7) of the class is used. When method useField is first called (line 18), it outputs the value (1) of field x (lines 40–41), multiplies the field x by 10 (line 42) and outputs the value (10) of field x again (lines 43–44) before returning. The next time method use-Field is called (line 20), the field has its modified value, 10, so the method outputs 10, then 100. Finally, in method begin, the program outputs the value of local variable x again (line 22) to show that none of the method calls modified begin's local variable x, because the methods all referred to variables named x in other scopes.

6.12 Method Overloading

Methods of the same name can be declared in the same class, as long as they have different sets of parameters (determined by the number, types and order of the parameters)—this is called *method overloading*. When an overloaded method is called, the Java compiler selects the appropriate method by examining the number, types and order of the arguments in the call. Method overloading is commonly used to create several methods with the same name that perform the same or similar tasks, but on different types or different numbers of arguments. For example, Math methods abs, min and max (summarized in Section 6.3) are overloaded with four versions each:

1. One with two double parameters.

2. One with two float parameters.

3. One with two int parameters.

4. One with two long parameters.

Our next example demonstrates declaring and invoking overloaded methods. We present examples of overloaded constructors in Chapter 8.

Declaring Overloaded Methods

In our class MethodOverload (Fig. 6.12), we include two overloaded versions of a method called square—one that calculates the square of an int (and returns an int) and one that calculates the square of a double (and returns a double). Although these methods have the same name and similar parameter lists and bodies, you can think of them simply as *different* methods. It may help to think of the method names as "square of int" and "square of double," respectively. When the application begins execution, class MethodOverload-Test's main method (Fig. 6.13, lines 6–10) creates an object of class MethodOverload (line 8) and calls the object's method testOverloadedMethods (line 9) to produce the program's output (Fig. 6.13).

```java
 1   // Fig. 6.12: MethodOverload.java
 2   // Overloaded method declarations.
 3
 4   public class MethodOverload
 5   {
 6      // test overloaded square methods
 7      public void testOverloadedMethods()
 8      {
 9         System.out.printf( "Square of integer 7 is %d\n", square( 7 ) );
10         System.out.printf( "Square of double 7.5 is %f\n", square( 7.5 ) );
11      } // end method testOverloadedMethods
12
13      // square method with int argument
14      public int square( int intValue )
15      {
16         System.out.printf( "\nCalled square with int argument: %d\n",
17            intValue );
18         return intValue * intValue;
19      } // end method square with int argument
20
21      // square method with double argument
22      public double square( double doubleValue )
23      {
24         System.out.printf( "\nCalled square with double argument: %f\n",
25            doubleValue );
26         return doubleValue * doubleValue;
27      } // end method square with double argument
28   } // end class MethodOverload
```

Fig. 6.12 | Overloaded method declarations.

```java
 1   // Fig. 6.13: MethodOverloadTest.java
 2   // Application to test class MethodOverload.
 3
```

Fig. 6.13 | Application to test class MethodOverload. (Part 1 of 2.)

```
 4    public class MethodOverloadTest
 5    {
 6       public static void main( String args[] )
 7       {
 8          MethodOverload methodOverload = new MethodOverload();
 9          methodOverload.testOverloadedMethods();
10       } // end main
11    } // end class MethodOverloadTest
```

```
Called square with int argument: 7
Square of integer 7 is 49

Called square with double argument: 7.500000
Square of double 7.5 is 56.250000
```

Fig. 6.13 | Application to test class `MethodOverload`. (Part 2 of 2.)

In Fig. 6.12, line 9 invokes method `square` with the argument 7. Literal integer values are treated as type `int`, so the method call in line 9 invokes the version of `square` at lines 14–19 that specifies an `int` parameter. Similarly, line 10 invokes method `square` with the argument 7.5. Literal floating-point values are treated as type `double`, so the method call in line 10 invokes the version of `square` at lines 22–27 that specifies a `double` parameter. Each method first outputs a line of text to prove that the proper method was called in each case. Note that the values in lines 10 and 24 are displayed with the format specifier `%f` and that we did not specify a precision in either case. By default, floating-point values are displayed with six digits of precision if the precision is not specified in the format specifier.

Distinguishing Between Overloaded Methods

The compiler distinguishes overloaded methods by their *signature*—a combination of the method's name and the number, types and order of its parameters. If the compiler looked only at method names during compilation, the code in Fig. 6.12 would be ambiguous— the compiler would not know how to distinguish between the two `square` methods (lines 14–19 and 22–27). Internally, the compiler uses longer method names that include the original method name, the types of each parameter and the exact order of the parameters to determine whether the methods in a class are unique in that class.

For example, in Fig. 6.12, the compiler might use the logical name "square of int" for the `square` method that specifies an `int` parameter and "square of double" for the `square` method that specifies a `double` parameter (the actual names the compiler uses are messier). If `method1`'s declaration begins as

> `void method1( int a, float b )`

then the compiler might use the logical name "method1 of int and float." If the parameters are specified as

> `void method1( float a, int b )`

then the compiler might use the logical name "method1 of float and int." Note that the order of the parameter types is important—the compiler considers the preceding two `method1` headers to be distinct.

Return Types of Overloaded Methods

In discussing the logical names of methods used by the compiler, we did not mention the return types of the methods. This is because method *calls* cannot be distinguished by return type. The program in Fig. 6.14 illustrates the compiler errors generated when two methods have the same signature and different return types. Overloaded methods can have different return types if the methods have different parameter lists. Also, overloaded methods need not have the same number of parameters.

 Common Programming Error 6.11

Declaring overloaded methods with identical parameter lists is a compilation error regardless of whether the return types are different.

```
1  // Fig. 6.14: MethodOverloadError.java
2  // Overloaded methods with identical signatures
3  // cause compilation errors, even if return types are different.
4
5  public class MethodOverloadError
6  {
7     // declaration of method square with int argument
8     public int square( int x )
9     {
10        return x * x;
11    }
12
13    // second declaration of method square with int argument
14    // causes compilation error even though return types are different
15    public double square( int y )
16    {
17       return y * y;
18    }
19 } // end class MethodOverloadError
```

```
MethodOverloadError.java:15: square(int) is already defined in
MethodOverloadError
   public double square( int y )
                 ^
1 error
```

Fig. 6.14 | Overloaded method declarations with identical signatures cause compilation errors, even if the return types are different.

6.13 Introduction to Recursion

The programs we've discussed so far are generally structured as methods that call one another in a disciplined, hierarchical manner. For some problems, however, it is useful to have a method call itself. Such a method is known as a ***recursive method***. A recursive method can be called either directly or indirectly through another method. We now consider recursion conceptually, then present several programs containing recursive methods.

6.14 Recursion Concepts

Recursive problem-solving approaches have a number of elements in common. When a recursive method is called to solve a problem, the method actually is capable of solving only the simplest case(s), or **base case(s)**. If the method is called with a base case, the method returns a result. If the method is called with a more complex problem, the method typically divides the problem into two conceptual pieces—a piece that the method knows how to do and a piece that it does not know how to do. To make recursion feasible, the latter piece must resemble the original problem, but be a slightly simpler or smaller version of it. Because this new problem looks like the original problem, the method calls a fresh copy of itself to work on the smaller problem—this is referred to as a **recursive call** and is also called the **recursion step**. The recursion step normally includes a `return` statement, because its result will be combined with the portion of the problem the method knew how to solve to form a result that will be passed back to the original caller. This concept of separating the problem into two smaller portions is a form of the divide-and-conquer approach introduced in Section 6.2.

The recursion step executes while the original call to the method is still active (i.e., while it has not finished executing). It can result in many more recursive calls as the method divides each new subproblem into two conceptual pieces. For the recursion to eventually terminate, each time the method calls itself with a simpler version of the original problem, the sequence of smaller and smaller problems must converge on a base case. At that point, the method recognizes the base case and returns a result to the previous copy of the method. A sequence of returns ensues until the original method call returns the final result to the caller.

A recursive method may call another method, which may in turn make a call back to the recursive method. Such a process is known as an **indirect recursive call** or **indirect recursion**. For example, method A calls method B, which makes a call back to method A. This is still considered recursion, because the second call to method A is made while the first call to method A is active—that is, the first call to method A has not yet finished executing (because it is waiting on method B to return a result to it) and has not returned to method A's original caller.

To better understand the concept of recursion, consider an example of recursion that is quite common to computer users—the recursive definition of a directory on a computer. A computer normally stores related files in a directory. A directory can be empty, can contain files and/or can contain other directories (usually referred to as subdirectories). Each of these subdirectories, in turn, may also contain both files and directories. If we want to list each file in a directory (including all the files in the directory's subdirectories), we need to create a method that first lists the initial directory's files, then makes recursive calls to list the files in each of that directory's subdirectories. The base case occurs when a directory is reached that does not contain any subdirectories. At this point, all the files in the original directory have been listed and no further recursion is necessary.

6.15 Example Using Recursion: Factorials

Let's write a recursive program to calculate the factorial of a positive integer n—written $n!$ (and pronounced "n factorial")—which is the product

$$n \cdot (n-1) \cdot (n-2) \cdot \ldots \cdot 1$$

with 1! equal to 1 and 0! defined to be 1. For example, 5! is the product $5 \cdot 4 \cdot 3 \cdot 2 \cdot 1$, which is equal to 120.

The factorial of integer number (where number ≥ 0) can be calculated *iteratively* (non-recursively) using a for statement as follows:

```
factorial = 1;

for ( int counter = number; counter >= 1; counter-- )
    factorial *= counter;
```

A recursive declaration of the factorial method is arrived at by observing the following relationship:

$$n! = n \cdot (n-1)!$$

For example, 5! is clearly equal to $5 \cdot 4!$, as is shown by the following equations:

$5! = 5 \cdot 4 \cdot 3 \cdot 2 \cdot 1$
$5! = 5 \cdot (4 \cdot 3 \cdot 2 \cdot 1)$
$5! = 5 \cdot (4!)$

The evaluation of 5! would proceed as shown in Fig. 6.15. Figure 6.15(a) shows how the succession of recursive calls proceeds until 1! (the base case) is evaluated to be 1, which terminates the recursion. Figure 6.15(b) shows the values returned from each recursive call to its caller until the final value is calculated and returned.

Figure 6.16 uses recursion to calculate and print the factorials of the integers from 0–10. The recursive method factorial (lines 7–13) first tests to determine whether a termi-

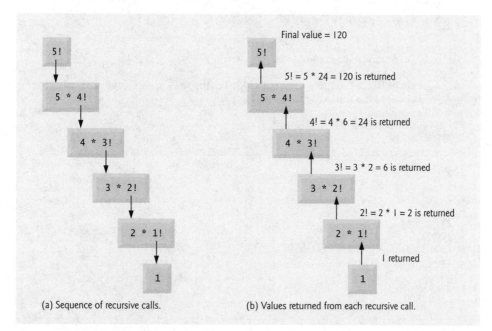

(a) Sequence of recursive calls.   (b) Values returned from each recursive call.

Fig. 6.15 | Recursive evaluation of 5!.

```
1   // Fig. 6.16: FactorialCalculator.java
2   // Recursive factorial method.
3
4   public class FactorialCalculator
5   {
6      // recursive method factorial
7      public long factorial( long number )
8      {
9         if ( number <= 1 ) // test for base case
10           return 1; // base cases: 0! = 1 and 1! = 1
11        else // recursion step
12           return number * factorial( number - 1 );
13     } // end method factorial
14
15     // output factorials for values 0-10
16     public void displayFactorials()
17     {
18        // calculate the factorials of 0 through 10
19        for ( int counter = 0; counter <= 10; counter++ )
20           System.out.printf( "%d! = %d\n", counter, factorial( counter ) );
21     } // end method displayFactorials
22  } // end class FactorialCalculator
```

Fig. 6.16 | Factorial calculations with a recursive method.

```
1   // Fig. 6.17: FactorialTest.java
2   // Testing the recursive factorial method.
3
4   public class FactorialTest
5   {
6      // calculate factorials of 0-10
7      public static void main( String args[] )
8      {
9         FactorialCalculator factorialCalculator = new FactorialCalculator();
10        factorialCalculator.displayFactorials();
11     } // end main
12  } // end class FactorialTest
```

```
0! = 1
1! = 1
2! = 2
3! = 6
4! = 24
5! = 120
6! = 720
7! = 5040
8! = 40320
9! = 362880
10! = 3628800
```

Fig. 6.17 | Testing the factorial method.

nating condition (line 9) is true. If number is less than or equal to 1 (the base case), factorial returns 1, no further recursion is necessary and the method returns. If number is greater than 1, line 12 expresses the problem as the product of number and a recursive call to factorial evaluating the factorial of number - 1, which is a slightly smaller problem than the original calculation, factorial(number).

Common Programming Error 6.12

*Either omitting the base case or writing the recursion step incorrectly so that it does not converge on the base case can cause a logic error known as **infinite recursion**, where recursive calls are continuously made until memory has been exhausted. This error is analogous to the problem of an infinite loop in an iterative (nonrecursive) solution.*

Method displayFactorials (lines 16–21) displays the factorials of 0–10. The call to method factorial occurs in line 20. Method factorial receives a parameter of type long and returns a result of type long. Figure 6.17 tests our factorial and displayFactorials methods by calling displayFactorials (line 10). The output of Fig. 6.17 shows that factorial values become large quickly. We use type long (which can represent relatively large integers) so the program can calculate factorials greater than 12!. Unfortunately, the factorial method produces large values so quickly that factorial values soon exceed the maximum value that can be stored even in a long variable.

Due to the limitations of integral types, float or double variables may ultimately be needed to calculate factorials of larger numbers. This points to a weakness in most programming languages—namely, that the languages are not easily extended to handle unique application requirements. Java is an extensible language that allows us to create arbitrarily large integers if we wish. In fact, package java.math provides classes BigInteger and Big-Decimal explicitly for arbitrary precision mathematical calculations that cannot be performed with primitive types. For more information on these classes visit, java.sun.com/javase/6/docs/api/java/math/BigInteger.html and java.sun.com/javase/6/docs/api/java/math/BigDecimal.html, respectively.

6.16 Example Using Recursion: Fibonacci Series

The *Fibonacci series,*

0, 1, 1, 2, 3, 5, 8, 13, 21, ...

begins with 0 and 1 and has the property that each subsequent Fibonacci number is the sum of the previous two Fibonacci numbers. This series occurs in nature and describes a form of spiral. The ratio of successive Fibonacci numbers converges on a constant value of 1.618..., a number that has been called the *golden ratio* or the *golden mean.* Humans tend to find the golden mean aesthetically pleasing. Architects often design windows, rooms and buildings whose length and width are in the ratio of the golden mean. Postcards are often designed with a golden-mean length-to-width ratio.

The Fibonacci series may be defined recursively as follows:

fibonacci(0) = 0
fibonacci(1) = 1
fibonacci(n) = fibonacci(n – 1) + fibonacci(n – 2)

Note that there are two base cases for the Fibonacci calculation: fibonacci(0) is defined to be 0, and fibonacci(1) is defined to be 1. The program in Fig. 6.18 calculates the *i*th Fibonacci number recursively, using method fibonacci (lines 7–13). Method display-Fibonacci (lines 15–20) tests fibonacci, displaying the Fibonacci values of 0–10. The variable counter created in the for header in line 17 indicates which Fibonacci number to calculate for each iteration of the for statement. Fibonacci numbers tend to become large quickly. Therefore, we use type long as the parameter type and the return type of method fibonacci. Line 9 of Fig. 6.19 calls method displayFibonacci (line 9) to calculate the Fibonacci values.

The call to method fibonacci (line 19 of Fig. 6.18) from displayFibonacci is not a recursive call, but all subsequent calls to fibonacci performed from the body of fibonacci (line 12 of Fig. 6.18) are recursive, because at that point the calls are initiated by method fibonacci itself. Each time fibonacci is called, it immediately tests for the base

```java
1   // Fig. 6.18: FibonacciCalculator.java
2   // Recursive fibonacci method.
3
4   public class FibonacciCalculator
5   {
6      // recursive declaration of method fibonacci
7      public long fibonacci( long number )
8      {
9         if ( ( number == 0 ) || ( number == 1 ) ) // base cases
10           return number;
11        else // recursion step
12           return fibonacci( number - 1 ) + fibonacci( number - 2 );
13     } // end method fibonacci
14
15     public void displayFibonacci()
16     {
17        for ( int counter = 0; counter <= 10; counter++ )
18           System.out.printf( "Fibonacci of %d is: %d\n", counter,
19              fibonacci( counter ) );
20     } // end method displayFibonacci
21  } // end class FibonacciCalculator
```

Fig. 6.18 | Fibonacci numbers generated with a recursive method.

```java
1   // Fig. 6.19: FibonacciTest.java
2   // Testing the recursive fibonacci method.
3
4   public class FibonacciTest
5   {
6      public static void main( String args[] )
7      {
8         FibonacciCalculator fibonacciCalculator = new FibonacciCalculator();
9         fibonacciCalculator.displayFibonacci();
10     } // end main
11  } // end class FibonacciTest
```

Fig. 6.19 | Testing the fibonacci method. (Part 1 of 2.)

```
Fibonacci of 0 is: 0
Fibonacci of 1 is: 1
Fibonacci of 2 is: 1
Fibonacci of 3 is: 2
Fibonacci of 4 is: 3
Fibonacci of 5 is: 5
Fibonacci of 6 is: 8
Fibonacci of 7 is: 13
Fibonacci of 8 is: 21
Fibonacci of 9 is: 34
Fibonacci of 10 is: 55
```

Fig. 6.19 | Testing the fibonacci method. (Part 2 of 2.)

cases—number equal to 0 or number equal to 1 (line 9). If this condition is true, fibonacci simply returns number because fibonacci(0) is 0, and fibonacci(1) is 1. Interestingly, if number is greater than 1, the recursion step generates *two* recursive calls (line 12), each for a slightly smaller problem than the original call to fibonacci.

Figure 6.20 shows how method fibonacci evaluates fibonacci(3). Note that at the bottom of the figure, we are left with the values 1, 0 and 1—the results of evaluating the base cases. The first two return values (from left to right), 1 and 0, are returned as the values for the calls fibonacci(1) and fibonacci(0). The sum 1 plus 0 is returned as the value of fibonacci(2). This is added to the result (1) of the call to fibonacci(1), producing the value 2. This final value is then returned as the value of fibonacci(3).

Figure 6.20 raises some interesting issues about the order in which Java compilers evaluate the operands of operators. This order is different from the order in which operators are applied to their operands—namely, the order dictated by the rules of operator precedence. From Figure 6.20, it appears that while fibonacci(3) is being evaluated, two recursive calls will be made—fibonacci(2) and fibonacci(1). But in what order will these calls be made? The Java language specifies that the order of evaluation of the oper-

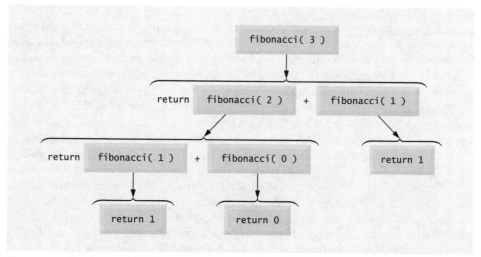

Fig. 6.20 | Set of recursive calls for fibonacci(3).

ands is from left to right. Thus, the call fibonacci(2) is made first and the call fibonacci(1) is made second.

A word of caution is in order about recursive programs like the one we use here to generate Fibonacci numbers. Each invocation of the fibonacci method that does not match one of the base cases (0 or 1) results in two more recursive calls to the fibonacci method. Hence, this set of recursive calls rapidly gets out of hand. Calculating the Fibonacci value of 20 with the program in Fig. 6.18 requires 21,891 calls to the fibonacci method; calculating the Fibonacci value of 30 requires 2,692,537 calls! As you try to calculate larger Fibonacci values, you'll notice that each consecutive Fibonacci number results in a substantial increase in calculation time and in the number of calls to the fibonacci method. For example, the Fibonacci value of 31 requires 4,356,617 calls, and the Fibonacci value of 32 requires 7,049,155 calls! As you can see, the number of calls to fibonacci increases quickly—1,664,080 additional calls between Fibonacci values of 30 and 31 and 2,692,538 additional calls between Fibonacci values of 31 and 32! The difference in the number of calls made between Fibonacci values of 31 and 32 is more than 1.5 times the difference in the number of calls for Fibonacci values between 30 and 31. Problems of this nature can humble even the world's most powerful computers. [*Note:* In the field of complexity theory, computer scientists study how hard algorithms work to complete their tasks.]

Performance Tip 6.1

Avoid Fibonacci-style recursive programs, because they result in an exponential "explosion" of method calls.

6.17 Recursion and the Method-Call Stack

In Section 6.6, the stack data structure was introduced in the context of understanding how Java performs method calls. We discussed both the method-call stack (also known as the program execution stack) and activation records. In this section, we'll use these concepts to demonstrate how the program execution stack handles recursive method calls.

Let's begin by returning to the Fibonacci example—specifically, calling method fibonacci with the value 3, as in Fig. 6.20. To show the order in which the method calls' activation records are placed on the stack, we have lettered the method calls in Fig. 6.21.

When the first method call (A) is made, an activation record is pushed onto the program execution stack which contains the value of the local variable number (3, in this case). The program execution stack, including the activation record for method call A, is illustrated in part (a) of Fig. 6.22. [*Note:* We use a simplified stack here. In an actual computer, the program execution stack and its activation records would be more complex than in Fig. 6.22, containing such information as where the method call is to return to when it has completed execution.]

Within method call A, method calls B and E are made. The original method call has not yet completed, so its activation record remains on the stack. The first method call to be made from within A is method call B, so the activation record for method call B is pushed onto the stack on top of the activation record for method call A. Method call B must execute and complete before method call E is made. Within method call B, method calls C and D will be made. Method call C is made first, and its activation record is pushed

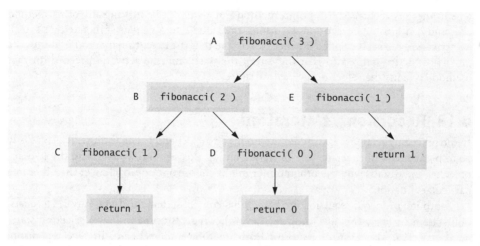

Fig. 6.21 | Method calls made within the call `fibonacci( 3 )`.

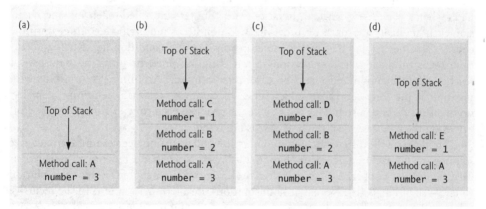

Fig. 6.22 | Method calls on the program execution stack.

onto the stack [part (b) of Fig. 6.22]. Method call B has not yet finished, and its activation record is still on the method-call stack. When method call C executes, it does not make any further method calls, but simply returns the value 1. When this method returns, its activation record is popped off the top of the stack. The method call at the top of the stack is now B, which continues to execute by performing method call D. The activation record for method call D is pushed onto the stack [part (c) of Fig. 6.22]. Method call D completes without making any more method calls, and returns the value 0. The activation record for this method call is then popped off the stack. Now, both method calls made from within method call B have returned. Method call B continues to execute, returning the value 1. Method call B completes and its activation record is popped off the stack. At this point, the activation record for method call A is at the top of the stack and the method continues its execution. This method makes method call E, whose activation record is now pushed onto the stack [part (d) of Fig. 6.22]. Method call E completes and returns the value 1. The activation record for this method call is popped off the stack, and once again method call

A continues to execute. At this point, method call A will not be making any other method calls and can finish its execution, returning the value 2 to A's caller (fibonacci(3) = 2). A's activation record is popped off the stack. Note that the executing method is always the one whose activation record is at the top of the stack, and the activation record for that method contains the values of its local variables.

6.18 Recursion vs. Iteration

In the preceding sections, we studied methods factorial and fibonacci, which can easily be implemented either recursively or iteratively. In this section, we compare the two approaches and discuss why the programmer might choose one approach over the other in a particular situation.

Both iteration and recursion are based on a control statement: Iteration uses a repetition statement (e.g., for, while or do...while), whereas recursion uses a selection statement (e.g., if, if...else or switch). Both iteration and recursion involve repetition: Iteration explicitly uses a repetition statement, whereas recursion achieves repetition through repeated method calls. Iteration and recursion each involve a termination test: Iteration terminates when the loop-continuation condition fails, whereas recursion terminates when a base case is reached. Iteration with counter-controlled repetition and recursion each gradually approach termination: Iteration keeps modifying a counter until the counter assumes a value that makes the loop-continuation condition fail, whereas recursion keeps producing smaller versions of the original problem until the base case is reached. Both iteration and recursion can occur infinitely: An infinite loop occurs with iteration if the loop-continuation test never becomes false, whereas infinite recursion occurs if the recursion step does not reduce the problem each time in a manner that converges on the base case, or if the base case is not tested.

To illustrate the differences between iteration and recursion, let's examine an iterative solution to the factorial problem (Figs. 6.23–6.24). Note that a repetition statement is used (lines 12–13 of Fig. 6.23) rather than the selection statement of the recursive solution (lines 9–12 of Fig. 6.16). Note that both solutions use a termination test. In the recursive solution, line 9 tests for the base case. In the iterative solution, line 12 tests the loop-continuation condition—if the test fails, the loop terminates. Finally, note that instead of producing smaller versions of the original problem, the iterative solution uses a counter that is modified until the loop-continuation condition becomes false.

```java
1   // Fig. 6.23: FactorialCalculator.java
2   // Iterative factorial method.
3
4   public class FactorialCalculator
5   {
6      // recursive declaration of method factorial
7      public long factorial( long number )
8      {
9         long result = 1;
10
```

Fig. 6.23 | Iterative factorial solution. (Part 1 of 2.)

```
11        // iterative declaration of method factorial
12        for ( long i = number; i >= 1; i-- )
13           result *= i;
14
15        return result;
16     } // end method factorial
17
18     // output factorials for values 0-10
19     public void displayFactorials()
20     {
21        // calculate the factorials of 0 through 10
22        for ( int counter = 0; counter <= 10; counter++ )
23           System.out.printf( "%d! = %d\n", counter, factorial( counter ) );
24     } // end method displayFactorials
25  } // end class FactorialCalculator
```

Fig. 6.23 | Iterative factorial solution. (Part 2 of 2.)

```
1   // Fig. 6.24: FactorialTest.java
2   // Testing the iterative factorial method.
3
4   public class FactorialTest
5   {
6      // calculate factorials of 0-10
7      public static void main( String args[] )
8      {
9         FactorialCalculator factorialCalculator = new FactorialCalculator();
10        factorialCalculator.displayFactorials();
11     } // end main
12  } // end class FactorialTest
```

```
0! = 1
1! = 1
2! = 2
3! = 6
4! = 24
5! = 120
6! = 720
7! = 5040
8! = 40320
9! = 362880
10! = 3628800
```

Fig. 6.24 | Testing the iterative factorial solution.

Recursion has many negatives. It repeatedly invokes the mechanism, and consequently the overhead, of method calls. This repetition can be expensive in terms of both processor time and memory space. Each recursive call causes another copy of the method (actually, only the method's variables, stored in the activation record) to be created—this set of copies can consume considerable memory space. Since iteration occurs within a method, repeated method calls and extra memory assignment are avoided. So why choose recursion?

Software Engineering Observation 6.6

Any problem that can be solved recursively can also be solved iteratively (nonrecursively). A recursive approach is normally preferred over an iterative approach when the recursive approach more naturally mirrors the problem and results in a program that is easier to understand and debug. A recursive approach can often be implemented with fewer lines of code. Another reason to choose a recursive approach is that an iterative one might not be apparent.

Performance Tip 6.2

Avoid using recursion in situations requiring high performance. Recursive calls take time and consume additional memory.

Common Programming Error 6.13

Accidentally having a nonrecursive method call itself either directly or indirectly through another method can cause infinite recursion.

6.19 (Optional) Software Engineering Case Study: Identifying Class Operations

In the Software Engineering Case Study sections at the ends of Chapters 3–5, we performed the first few steps in the object-oriented design of our ATM system. In Chapter 3, we identified the classes that we'll need to implement and created our first class diagram. In Chapter 4, we described some attributes of our classes. In Chapter 5, we examined objects' states and modeled objects' state transitions and activities. In this section, we determine some of the class operations (or behaviors) that are needed to implement the ATM system.

Identifying Operations

An operation is a service that objects of a class provide to clients (users) of the class. Consider the operations of some real-world objects. A radio's operations include setting its station and volume (typically invoked by a person adjusting the radio's controls). A car's operations include accelerating (invoked by the driver pressing the accelerator pedal), decelerating (invoked by the driver pressing the brake pedal or releasing the gas pedal), turning and shifting gears. Software objects can offer operations as well—for example, a software graphics object might offer operations for drawing a circle, drawing a line, drawing a square and the like. A spreadsheet software object might offer operations like printing the spreadsheet, totaling the elements in a row or column and graphing information in the spreadsheet as a bar chart or pie chart.

We can derive many of the operations of each class by examining the key verbs and verb phrases in the requirements document. We then relate each of these to particular classes in our system (Fig. 6.25). The verb phrases in Fig. 6.25 help us determine the operations of each class.

Modeling Operations

To identify operations, we examine the verb phrases listed for each class in Fig. 6.25. The "executes financial transactions" phrase associated with class ATM implies that class ATM instructs transactions to execute. Therefore, classes BalanceInquiry, Withdrawal and Deposit each need an operation to provide this service to the ATM. We place this opera-

Class	Verbs and verb phrases
ATM	executes financial transactions
BalanceInquiry	[none in the requirements document]
Withdrawal	[none in the requirements document]
Deposit	[none in the requirements document]
BankDatabase	authenticates a user, retrieves an account balance, credits a deposit amount to an account, debits a withdrawal amount from an account
Account	retrieves an account balance, credits a deposit amount to an account, debits a withdrawal amount from an account
Screen	displays a message to the user
Keypad	receives numeric input from the user
CashDispenser	dispenses cash, indicates whether it contains enough cash to satisfy a withdrawal request
DepositSlot	receives a deposit envelope

Fig. 6.25 | Verbs and verb phrases for each class in the ATM system.

tion (which we have named `execute`) in the third compartment of the three transaction classes in the updated class diagram of Fig. 6.26. During an ATM session, the `ATM` object will invoke these transaction operations as necessary.

The UML represents operations (which are implemented as methods in Java) by listing the operation name, followed by a comma-separated list of parameters in parentheses, a colon and the return type:

operationName(parameter1, parameter2, ..., parameterN) : return type

Each parameter in the comma-separated parameter list consists of a parameter name, followed by a colon and the parameter type:

parameterName : parameterType

For the moment, we do not list the parameters of our operations—we'll identify and model the parameters of some of the operations shortly. For some of the operations, we do not yet know the return types, so we also omit them from the diagram. These omissions are perfectly normal at this point. As our design and implementation proceed, we'll add the remaining return types.

Figure 6.25 lists the phrase "authenticates a user" next to class `BankDatabase`—the database is the object that contains the account information necessary to determine whether the account number and PIN entered by a user match those of an account held at the bank. Therefore, class `BankDatabase` needs an operation that provides an authentication service to the ATM. We place the operation `authenticateUser` in the third compartment of class `BankDatabase` (Fig. 6.26). However, an object of class `Account`, not class `BankDatabase`, stores the account number and PIN that must be accessed to authenticate

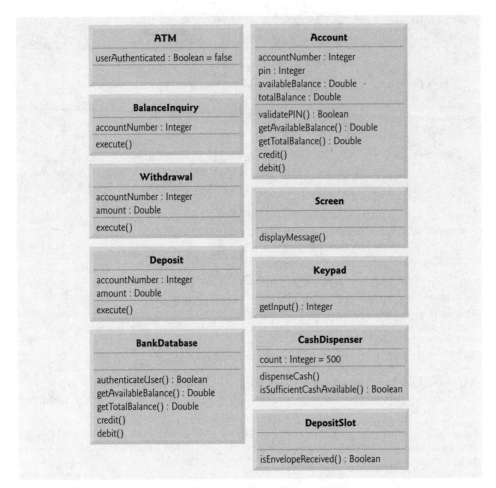

Fig. 6.26 | Classes in the ATM system with attributes and operations.

a user, so class Account must provide a service to validate a PIN obtained through user input against a PIN stored in an Account object. Therefore, we add a validatePIN operation to class Account. Note that we specify a return type of Boolean for the authenticateUser and validatePIN operations. Each operation returns a value indicating either that the operation was successful in performing its task (i.e., a return value of true) or that it was not (i.e., a return value of false).

Figure 6.25 lists several additional verb phrases for class BankDatabase: "retrieves an account balance," "credits a deposit amount to an account" and "debits a withdrawal amount from an account." Like "authenticates a user," these remaining phrases refer to services that the database must provide to the ATM, because the database holds all the account data used to authenticate a user and perform ATM transactions. However, objects of class Account actually perform the operations to which these phrases refer. Thus, we assign an operation to both class BankDatabase and class Account to correspond to each of these phrases. Recall from Section 3.9 that, because a bank account contains sensitive information, we do not allow the ATM to access accounts directly. The database acts as an intermediary between the ATM and the account data, thus preventing unauthorized access. As we'll see in Section 7.13, class ATM invokes the operations of class BankDatabase, each of which in turn invokes the operation with the same name in class Account.

The phrase "retrieves an account balance" suggests that classes BankDatabase and Account each need a getBalance operation. However, recall that we created two attributes in class Account to represent a balance—availableBalance and totalBalance. A balance inquiry requires access to both balance attributes so that it can display them to the user, but a withdrawal needs to check only the value of availableBalance. To allow objects in the system to obtain each balance attribute individually, we add operations getAvailableBalance and getTotalBalance to the third compartment of classes Bank-Database and Account (Fig. 6.26). We specify a return type of Double for these operations because the balance attributes which they retrieve are of type Double.

The phrases "credits a deposit amount to an account" and "debits a withdrawal amount from an account" indicate that classes BankDatabase and Account must perform operations to update an account during a deposit and withdrawal, respectively. We there-fore assign credit and debit operations to classes BankDatabase and Account. You may recall that crediting an account (as in a deposit) adds an amount only to the totalBalance attribute. Debiting an account (as in a withdrawal), on the other hand, subtracts the amount from both balance attributes. We hide these implementation details inside class Account. This is a good example of encapsulation and information hiding.

If this were a real ATM system, classes BankDatabase and Account would also provide a set of operations to allow another banking system to update a user's account balance after either confirming or rejecting all or part of a deposit. Operation confirmDepositAmount, for example, would add an amount to the availableBalance attribute, thus making deposited funds available for withdrawal. Operation rejectDepositAmount would sub-tract an amount from the totalBalance attribute to indicate that a specified amount, which had recently been deposited through the ATM and added to the totalBalance, was not found in the deposit envelope. The bank would invoke this operation after deter-mining either that the user failed to include the correct amount of cash or that any checks did not clear (i.e., they "bounced"). While adding these operations would make our system more complete, we do not include them in our class diagrams or our implementation because they are beyond the scope of the case study.

Class Screen "displays a message to the user" at various times in an ATM session. All visual output occurs through the screen of the ATM. The requirements document describes many types of messages (e.g., a welcome message, an error message, a thank you message) that the screen displays to the user. The requirements document also indicates that the screen displays prompts and menus to the user. However, a prompt is really just a message describing what the user should input next, and a menu is essentially a type of prompt consisting of a series of messages (i.e., menu options) displayed consecutively. Therefore, rather than assign class Screen an individual operation to display each type of message, prompt and menu, we simply create one operation that can display any message specified by a parameter. We place this operation (displayMessage) in the third compart-ment of class Screen in our class diagram (Fig. 6.26). Note that we do not worry about the parameter of this operation at this time—we model the parameter later in this section.

From the phrase "receives numeric input from the user" listed by class Keypad in Fig. 6.25, we conclude that class Keypad should perform a getInput operation. Because the ATM's keypad, unlike a computer keyboard, contains only the numbers 0–9, we specify that this operation returns an integer value. Recall from the requirements document that in different situations the user may be required to enter a different type of number (e.g., an account number, a PIN, the number of a menu option, a deposit amount as a number of cents). Class Keypad simply obtains a numeric value for a client of the class—it does not determine whether the value meets any specific criteria. Any class that uses this operation must verify that the user entered an appropriate number in a given situation, then respond accordingly (i.e., display an error message via class Screen). [*Note:* When we implement the system, we simulate the ATM's keypad with a computer keyboard, and for simplicity we assume that the user does not enter non-numeric input using keys on the computer keyboard that do not appear on the ATM's keypad.]

Figure 6.25 lists "dispenses cash" for class CashDispenser. Therefore, we create operation dispenseCash and list it under class CashDispenser in Fig. 6.26. Class CashDispenser also "indicates whether it contains enough cash to satisfy a withdrawal request." Thus, we include isSufficientCashAvailable, an operation that returns a value of UML type Boolean, in class CashDispenser. Figure 6.25 also lists "receives a deposit envelope" for class DepositSlot. The deposit slot must indicate whether it received an envelope, so we place an operation isEnvelopeReceived, which returns a Boolean value, in the third compartment of class DepositSlot. [*Note:* A real hardware deposit slot would most likely send the ATM a signal to indicate that an envelope was received. We simulate this behavior, however, with an operation in class DepositSlot that class ATM can invoke to find out whether the deposit slot received an envelope.]

We do not list any operations for class ATM at this time. We are not yet aware of any services that class ATM provides to other classes in the system. When we implement the system with Java code, however, operations of this class, and additional operations of the other classes in the system, may emerge.

Identifying and Modeling Operation Parameters

So far, we have not been concerned with the parameters of our operations—we have attempted to gain only a basic understanding of the operations of each class. Let's now take a closer look at some operation parameters. We identify an operation's parameters by examining what data the operation requires to perform its assigned task.

Consider the authenticateUser operation of class BankDatabase. To authenticate a user, this operation must know the account number and PIN supplied by the user. Thus we specify that operation authenticateUser takes integer parameters userAccountNumber and userPIN, which the operation must compare to the account number and PIN of an Account object in the database. We prefix these parameter names with "user" to avoid confusion between the operation's parameter names and the attribute names that belong to class Account. We list these parameters in the class diagram in Fig. 6.27 that models only class BankDatabase. [*Note:* It is perfectly normal to model only one class in a class diagram. In this case, we are most concerned with examining the parameters of this one class in particular, so we omit the other classes. In class diagrams later in the case study, in which parameters are no longer the focus of our attention, we omit these parameters to save space. Remember, however, that the operations listed in these diagrams still have parameters.]

Recall that the UML models each parameter in an operation's comma-separated parameter list by listing the parameter name, followed by a colon and the parameter type

BankDatabase
authenticateUser(userAccountNumber : Integer : userPIN : Integer) : Boolean getAvailableBalance(userAccountNumber : Integer) : Double getTotalBalance(userAccountNumber : Integer) : Double credit(userAccountNumber : Integer, amount : Double) debit(userAccountNumber : Integer, amount : Double)

Fig. 6.27 | Class BankDatabase with operation parameters.

(in UML notation). Figure 6.27 thus specifies that operation authenticateUser takes two parameters—userAccountNumber and userPIN, both of type Integer. When we implement the system in Java, we'll represent these parameters with int values.

Class BankDatabase operations getAvailableBalance, getTotalBalance, credit and debit also each require a userAccountNumber parameter to identify the account to which the database must apply the operations, so we include these parameters in the class diagram of Fig. 6.27. In addition, operations credit and debit each require a Double parameter amount to specify the amount of money to be credited or debited, respectively.

The class diagram in Fig. 6.28 models the parameters of class Account's operations. Operation validatePIN requires only a userPIN parameter, which contains the user-specified PIN to be compared with the PIN associated with the account. Like their counterparts in class BankDatabase, operations credit and debit in class Account each require a Double parameter amount that indicates the amount of money involved in the operation. Operations getAvailableBalance and getTotalBalance in class Account require no additional data to perform their tasks. Note that class Account's operations do not require an account number parameter to distinguish between Accounts, because these operations can be invoked only on a specific Account object.

Figure 6.29 models class Screen with a parameter specified for operation displayMessage. This operation requires only a String parameter message that indicates the text to be displayed. Recall that the parameter types listed in our class diagrams are in UML notation, so the String type listed in Fig. 6.29 refers to the UML type. When we implement the system in Java, we'll in fact use the Java class String to represent this parameter.

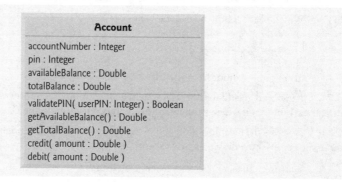

Account
accountNumber : Integer pin : Integer availableBalance : Double totalBalance : Double
validatePIN(userPIN: Integer) : Boolean getAvailableBalance() : Double getTotalBalance() : Double credit(amount : Double) debit(amount : Double)

Fig. 6.28 | Class Account with operation parameters.

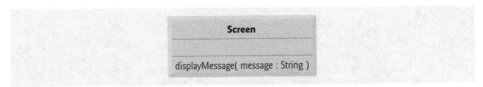

Fig. 6.29 | Class Screen with operation parameters.

The class diagram in Fig. 6.30 specifies that operation dispenseCash of class CashDispenser takes a Double parameter amount to indicate the amount of cash (in dollars) to be dispensed. Operation isSufficientCashAvailable also takes a Double parameter amount to indicate the amount of cash in question.

Note that we do not discuss parameters for operation execute of classes BalanceInquiry, Withdrawal and Deposit, operation getInput of class Keypad and operation isEnvelopeReceived of class DepositSlot. At this point in our design process, we cannot determine whether these operations require additional data to perform their tasks, so we leave their parameter lists empty. As we progress through the case study, we may decide to add parameters to these operations.

In this section, we have determined many of the operations performed by the classes in the ATM system. We have identified the parameters and return types of some of the operations. As we continue our design process, the number of operations belonging to each class may vary—we might find that new operations are needed or that some current operations are unnecessary—and we might determine that some of our class operations need additional parameters and different return types.

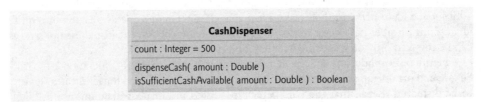

Fig. 6.30 | Class CashDispenser with operation parameters.

Software Engineering Case Study Self-Review Exercises

6.1 Which of the following is not a behavior?
  a) reading data from a file
  b) printing output
  c) text output
  d) obtaining input from the user

6.2 If you were to add to the ATM system an operation that returns the amount attribute of class Withdrawal, how and where would you specify this operation in the class diagram of Fig. 6.26?

6.3 Describe the meaning of the following operation listing that might appear in a class diagram for an object-oriented design of a calculator:

```
add( x : Integer, y : Integer ) : Integer
```

Answers to Software Engineering Case Study Self-Review Exercises

6.1   c.

6.2   To specify an operation that retrieves the amount attribute of class Withdrawal, the following operation listing would be placed in the operation (i.e., third) compartment of class Withdrawal:

```
getAmount( ) : Double
```

6.3   This operation listing indicates an operation named add that takes integers x and y as parameters and returns an integer value.

6.20 Wrap-Up

In this chapter, you learned more about the details of method declarations. You also learned the difference between non-static and static methods and how to call static methods by preceding the method name with the name of the class in which it appears and the dot (.) separator. You learned how to use operator + to perform string concatenations. You learned how to declare named constants using both enum types and public final static variables. You saw how to use class Random to generate sets of random numbers that can be used for simulations. You also learned about the scope of fields and local variables in a class. Finally, you learned that multiple methods in one class can be overloaded by providing methods with the same name and different signatures. Such methods can be used to perform the same or similar tasks using different types or different numbers of parameters.

In Chapter 7, you'll learn how to maintain lists and tables of data in arrays. You'll see a more elegant implementation of the application that rolls a die 6000 times and two enhanced versions of our GradeBook case study that you studied in Chapters 3–5. You'll also learn how to access an application's command-line arguments that are passed to method main when an application begins execution.

7

Arrays

OBJECTIVES

In this chapter you'll learn:

- To use arrays to store data in and retrieve data from lists and tables of values.

- To declare arrays, initialize arrays and refer to individual elements of arrays.

- To use the enhanced for statement to iterate through arrays.

- To pass arrays to methods.

- To declare and manipulate multidimensional arrays.

- To write methods that use variable-length argument lists.

- To read command-line arguments into a program.

Now go, write it before them in a table, and note it in a book.
—Isaiah 30:8

To go beyond is as wrong as to fall short.
—Confucius

Begin at the beginning, ... and go on till you come to the end: then stop.
—Lewis Carroll

Outline

7.1 Introduction

7.2 Arrays

7.3 Declaring and Creating Arrays

7.4 Examples Using Arrays

7.5 Case Study: Card Shuffling and Dealing Simulation

7.6 Enhanced `for` Statement

7.7 Passing Arrays to Methods

7.8 Case Study: Class `GradeBook` Using an Array to Store Grades

7.9 Multidimensional Arrays

7.10 Case Study: Class `GradeBook` Using a Two-Dimensional Array

7.11 Variable-Length Argument Lists

7.12 Using Command-Line Arguments

7.13 (Optional) Software Engineering Case Study: Collaboration Among Objects

7.14 Wrap-Up

7.1 Introduction

This chapter introduces *data structures*—collections of related data items. *Arrays* are data structures consisting of related data items of the same type. Arrays are fixed-length entities—they remain the same length once they are created, although an array variable may be reassigned such that it refers to a new array of a different length. We study several of the Java API's built-in data structures in Chapter 16.

After discussing how arrays are declared, created and initialized, we present a series of practical examples that demonstrate several common array manipulations. We also present a case study that examines how arrays can help simulate the shuffling and dealing of playing cards for use in an application that implements a card game. The chapter then introduces Java's enhanced `for` statement, which allows a program to access the data in an array more easily than does the counter-controlled `for` statement presented in Section 5.3. Two sections of the chapter enhance the case study of class `GradeBook` in Chapters 3–5. In particular, we use arrays to enable the class to maintain a set of grades in memory and analyze student grades from multiple exams in a semester—two capabilities that were absent from previous versions of the class. These and other chapter examples demonstrate the ways in which arrays allow programmers to organize and manipulate data.

7.2 Arrays

An array is a group of variables (called *elements* or *components*) containing values that all have the same type. Recall that types are divided into two categories—primitive types and reference types. Arrays are objects, so they are considered reference types. As you'll soon see, what we typically think of as an array is actually a reference to an array object in memory. The elements of an array can be either primitive types or reference types (including arrays, as we'll see in Section 7.9). To refer to a particular element in an array, we specify the name of the reference to the array and the position number of the element in the array. The position number of the element is called the element's *index* or *subscript*.

Figure 7.1 shows a logical representation of an integer array called c. This array contains 12 elements. A program refers to any one of these elements with an *array-access expression* that includes the name of the array followed by the index of the particular element in *square brackets* ([]). The first element in every array has *index zero* and is sometimes called the *zeroth element.* Thus, the elements of array c are c[0], c[1], c[2] and so on. The highest index in array c is 11, which is 1 less than 12—the number of elements in the array. Array names follow the same conventions as other variable names.

An index must be a nonnegative integer. A program can use an expression as an index. For example, if we assume that variable a is 5 and variable b is 6, then the statement

```
c[ a + b ] += 2;
```

adds 2 to array element c[11]. Note that an indexed array name is an array-access expression. Such expressions can be used on the left side of an assignment to place a new value into an array element.

Common Programming Error 7.1

Using a value of type long as an array index results in a compilation error. An index must be an int value or a value of a type that can be promoted to int—namely, byte, short or char, but not long.

Let us examine array c in Fig. 7.1 more closely. The *name* of the array is c. Every array object knows its own length and maintains this information in a length field. The expression c.length accesses array c's length field to determine the length of the array. Note that, even though the length member of an array is public, it cannot be changed because it is a final variable. This array's 12 elements are referred to as c[0], c[1], c[2], ..., c[11]. The value of c[0] is -45, the value of c[1] is 6, the value of c[2] is 0, the value of c[7] is 62 and the value of c[11] is 78. To calculate the sum of the values contained in the first three elements of array c and store the result in variable sum, we would write

```
sum = c[ 0 ] + c[ 1 ] + c[ 2 ];
```

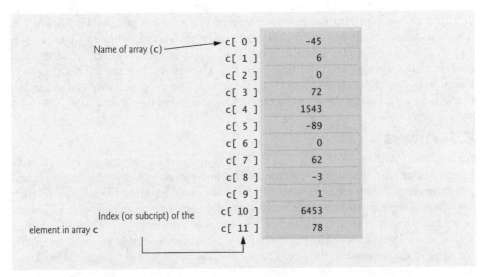

Fig. 7.1 | A 12-element array.

To divide the value of c[6] by 2 and assign the result to the variable x, we would write

```
x = c[ 6 ] / 2;
```

7.3 Declaring and Creating Arrays

Array objects occupy space in memory. Like other objects, arrays are created with keyword new. To create an array object, the programmer specifies the type of the array elements and the number of elements as part of an *array-creation expression* that uses keyword new. Such an expression returns a reference that can be stored in an array variable. The following declaration and array-creation expression create an array object containing 12 int elements and store the array's reference in variable c:

```
int c[] = new int[ 12 ];
```

This expression can be used to create the array shown in Fig. 7.1. This task also can be performed in two steps as follows:

```
int c[];            // declare the array variable
c = new int[ 12 ];  // create the array; assign to array variable
```

In the declaration, the square brackets following the variable name c indicate that c is a variable that will refer to an array (i.e., the variable will store an array reference). In the assignment statement, the array variable c receives the reference to a new array of 12 int elements. When an array is created, each element of the array receives a default value— zero for the numeric primitive-type elements, false for boolean elements and null for references (any nonprimitive type). As we'll soon see, we can provide specific, nondefault initial element values when we create an array.

Common Programming Error 7.2

In an array declaration, specifying the number of elements in the square brackets of the declaration (e.g., int c[12];) is a syntax error.

A program can create several arrays in a single declaration. The following String array declaration reserves 100 elements for b and 27 elements for x:

```
String b[] = new String[ 100 ], x[] = new String[ 27 ];
```

In this case, the class name String applies to each variable in the declaration. For readability, we prefer to declare only one variable per declaration, as in:

```
String b[] = new String[ 100 ]; // create array b
String x[] = new String[ 27 ];  // create array x
```

When an array is declared, the type of the array and the square brackets can be combined at the beginning of the declaration to indicate that all the identifiers in the declaration are array variables. For example, the declaration

```
double[] array1, array2;
```

indicates that array1 and array2 are each "array of double" variables. The preceding declaration is equivalent to:

```
double array1[];
double array2[];
```

or

```
double[] array1;
double[] array2;
```

The preceding pairs of declarations are equivalent—when only one variable is declared in each declaration, the square brackets can be placed either after the type or after the array variable name.

Common Programming Error 7.3

Declaring multiple array variables in a single declaration can lead to subtle errors. Consider the declaration int[] a, b, c;. If a, b and c should be declared as array variables, then this declaration is correct—placing square brackets directly following the type indicates that all the identifiers in the declaration are array variables. However, if only a is intended to be an array variable, and b and c are intended to be individual int variables, then this declaration is incorrect—the declaration int a[], b, c; would achieve the desired result.

A program can declare arrays of any type. Every element of a primitive-type array contains a value of the array's declared type. Similarly, in an array of a reference type, every element is a reference to an object of the array's declared type. For example, every element of an int array is an int value, and every element of a String array is a reference to a String object.

7.4 Examples Using Arrays

This section presents several examples that demonstrate declaring arrays, creating arrays, initializing arrays and manipulating array elements.

Creating and Initializing an Array

The application of Fig. 7.2 uses keyword new to create an array of 10 int elements, which are initially zero (the default for int variables). Line 8 declares array—a reference capable of referring to an array of int elements. Line 10 creates the array object and assigns its reference to variable array. Line 12 outputs the column headings. The first column contains the index (0–9) of each array element, and the second column contains the default value (0) of each array element.

The for statement in lines 15–16 outputs the index number (represented by counter) and the value of each array element (represented by array[counter]). Note that the loop control variable counter is initially 0—index values start at 0, so using zero-based counting allows the loop to access every element of the array. The for's loop-continuation condition uses the expression array.length (line 15) to determine the length of the array. In this example, the length of the array is 10, so the loop continues executing as long as the value of control variable counter is less than 10. The highest index value of a 10-element array is 9, so using the less-than operator in the loop-continuation condition guarantees that the loop does not attempt to access an element beyond the end of the array (i.e., during the final iteration of the loop, counter is 9). We'll soon see what Java does when it encounters such an out-of-range index at execution time.

```
 1   // Fig. 7.2: InitArray.java
 2   // Creating an array.
 3
 4   public class InitArray
 5   {
 6      public static void main( String args[] )
 7      {
 8         int array[]; // declare array named array
 9
10         array = new int[ 10 ]; // create the space for array
11
12         System.out.printf( "%s%8s\n", "Index", "Value" ); // column headings
13
14         // output each array element's value
15         for ( int counter = 0; counter < array.length; counter++ )
16            System.out.printf( "%5d%8d\n", counter, array[ counter ] );
17      } // end main
18   } // end class InitArray
```

```
Index    Value
    0        0
    1        0
    2        0
    3        0
    4        0
    5        0
    6        0
    7        0
    8        0
    9        0
```

Fig. 7.2 | Initializing the elements of an array to default values of zero.

Using an Array Initializer

A program can create an array and initialize its elements with an *array initializer*, which is a comma-separated list of expressions (called an *initializer list*) enclosed in braces ({ and }); the array length is determined by the number of elements in the initializer list. For example, the declaration

```
int n[] = { 10, 20, 30, 40, 50 };
```

creates a five-element array with index values 0, 1, 2, 3 and 4. Element n[0] is initialized to 10, n[1] is initialized to 20, and so on. This declaration does not require new to create the array object. When the compiler encounters an array declaration that includes an initializer list, it counts the number of initializers in the list to determine the size of the array, then sets up the appropriate new operation "behind the scenes."

The application in Fig. 7.3 initializes an integer array with 10 values (line 9) and displays the array in tabular format. The code for displaying the array elements (lines 14–15) is identical to that in Fig. 7.2 (lines 15–16).

```
1   // Fig. 7.3: InitArray.java
2   // Initializing the elements of an array with an array initializer.
3
4   public class InitArray
5   {
6      public static void main( String args[] )
7      {
8         // initializer list specifies the value for each element
9         int array[] = { 32, 27, 64, 18, 95, 14, 90, 70, 60, 37 };
10
11        System.out.printf( "%s%8s\n", "Index", "Value" ); // column headings
12
13        // output each array element's value
14        for ( int counter = 0; counter < array.length; counter++ )
15           System.out.printf( "%5d%8d\n", counter, array[ counter ] );
16     } // end main
17  } // end class InitArray
```

```
Index   Value
    0      32
    1      27
    2      64
    3      18
    4      95
    5      14
    6      90
    7      70
    8      60
    9      37
```

Fig. 7.3 | Initializing the elements of an array with an array initializer.

Calculating the Values to Store in an Array

The application in Fig. 7.4 creates a 10-element array and assigns to each element one of the even integers from 2 to 20 (2, 4, 6, ..., 20). Then the application displays the array in tabular format. The for statement at lines 12–13 calculates an array element's value by multiplying the current value of the control variable counter by 2, then adding 2.

```
1   // Fig. 7.4: InitArray.java
2   // Calculating values to be placed into elements of an array.
3
4   public class InitArray
5   {
6      public static void main( String args[] )
7      {
8         final int ARRAY_LENGTH = 10; // declare constant
9         int array[] = new int[ ARRAY_LENGTH ]; // create array
10
11        // calculate value for each array element
12        for ( int counter = 0; counter < array.length; counter++ )
13           array[ counter ] = 2 + 2 * counter;
```

Fig. 7.4 | Calculating the values to be placed into the elements of an array. (Part 1 of 2.)

```
14
15          System.out.printf( "%s%8s\n", "Index", "Value" ); // column headings
16
17          // output each array element's value
18          for ( int counter = 0; counter < array.length; counter++ )
19              System.out.printf( "%5d%8d\n", counter, array[ counter ] );
20      } // end main
21  } // end class InitArray
```

```
Index   Value
    0       2
    1       4
    2       6
    3       8
    4      10
    5      12
    6      14
    7      16
    8      18
    9      20
```

Fig. 7.4 | Calculating the values to be placed into the elements of an array. (Part 2 of 2.)

Line 8 uses the modifier final to declare the *constant variable* ARRAY_LENGTH with the value 10. Constant variables (also known as final variables) must be initialized before they are used and cannot be modified thereafter. If you attempt to modify a final variable after it is initialized in its declaration (as in line 8), the compiler issues the error message

> cannot assign a value to final variable *variableName*

If an attempt is made to access the value of a final variable before it is initialized, the compiler issues the error message

> variable *variableName* might not have been initialized

Good Programming Practice 7.1

*Constant variables also are called **named constants** or **read-only variables**. Such variables often make programs more readable than programs that use literal values (e.g., 10)—a named constant such as ARRAY_LENGTH clearly indicates its purpose, whereas a literal value could have different meanings based on the context in which it is used.*

Common Programming Error 7.4

Assigning a value to a constant after the variable has been initialized is a compilation error.

Common Programming Error 7.5

Attempting to use a constant before it is initialized is a compilation error.

Summing the Elements of an Array

Often, the elements of an array represent a series of values to be used in a calculation. For example, if the elements of an array represent exam grades, a professor may wish to total the elements of the array and use that sum to calculate the class average for the exam. The examples using class GradeBook later in the chapter, namely Fig. 7.14 and Fig. 7.18, use this technique.

The application in Fig. 7.5 sums the values contained in a 10-element integer array. The program declares, creates and initializes the array at line 8. The for statement performs the calculations. [*Note:* The values supplied as array initializers are often read into a program rather than specified in an initializer list. For example, an application could input the values from a user or from a file on disk (as discussed in Chapter 14, Files and Streams). Reading the data into a program makes the program more reusable, because it can be used with different sets of data.]

```
1   // Fig. 7.5: SumArray.java
2   // Computing the sum of the elements of an array.
3
4   public class SumArray
5   {
6      public static void main( String args[] )
7      {
8         int array[] = { 87, 68, 94, 100, 83, 78, 85, 91, 76, 87 };
9         int total = 0;
10
11         // add each element's value to total
12         for ( int counter = 0; counter < array.length; counter++ )
13            total += array[ counter ];
14
15         System.out.printf( "Total of array elements: %d\n", total );
16      } // end main
17   } // end class SumArray
```

```
Total of array elements: 849
```

Fig. 7.5 | Computing the sum of the elements of an array.

Using Bar Charts to Display Array Data Graphically

Many programs present data to users in a graphical manner. For example, numeric values are often displayed as bars in a bar chart. In such a chart, longer bars represent proportionally larger numeric values. One simple way to display numeric data graphically is with a bar chart that shows each numeric value as a bar of asterisks (*).

Professors often like to examine the distribution of grades on an exam. A professor might graph the number of grades in each of several categories to visualize the grade distribution. Suppose the grades on an exam were 87, 68, 94, 100, 83, 78, 85, 91, 76 and 87. Note that there was one grade of 100, two grades in the 90s, four grades in the 80s, two grades in the 70s, one grade in the 60s and no grades below 60. Our next application (Fig. 7.6) stores this grade distribution data in an array of 11 elements, each corresponding to a category of grades. For example, array[0] indicates the number of grades in the range 0–9, array[7] indicates the number of grades in the range 70–79 and array[10] indicates the number of 100 grades. The two versions of class GradeBook later in the chapter (Fig. 7.14 and Fig. 7.18) contain code that calculates these grade frequencies based on a set of grades. For now, we manually create the array by looking at the set of grades.

```
 1   // Fig. 7.6: BarChart.java
 2   // Bar chart printing program.
 3
 4   public class BarChart
 5   {
 6      public static void main( String args[] )
 7      {
 8         int array[] = { 0, 0, 0, 0, 0, 0, 1, 2, 4, 2, 1 };
 9
10         System.out.println( "Grade distribution:" );
11
12         // for each array element, output a bar of the chart
13         for ( int counter = 0; counter < array.length; counter++ )
14         {
15            // output bar label ( "00-09: ", ..., "90-99: ", "100: " )
16            if ( counter == 10 )
17               System.out.printf( "%5d: ", 100 );
18            else
19               System.out.printf( "%02d-%02d: ",
20                  counter * 10, counter * 10 + 9 );
21
22            // print bar of asterisks
23            for ( int stars = 0; stars < array[ counter ]; stars++ )
24               System.out.print( "*" );
25
26            System.out.println(); // start a new line of output
27         } // end outer for
28      } // end main
29   } // end class BarChart
```

```
Grade distribution:
00-09:
10-19:
20-29:
30-39:
40-49:
50-59:
60-69: *
70-79: **
80-89: ****
90-99: **
  100: *
```

Fig. 7.6 | Bar chart printing program.

The application reads the numbers from the array and graphs the information as a bar chart. The program displays each grade range followed by a bar of asterisks indicating the number of grades in that range. To label each bar, lines 16–20 output a grade range (e.g., "70-79: ") based on the current value of counter. When counter is 10, line 17 outputs 100 with a field width of 5, followed by a colon and a space, to align the label "100: " with the other bar labels. The nested for statement (lines 23–24) outputs the bars. Note the loop-continuation condition at line 23 (stars < array[counter]). Each time the program reaches the inner for, the loop counts from 0 up to array[counter], thus using a value in array to determine the number of asterisks to display. In this example, array[0]–array[5] contain zeroes because no students received a grade below 60. Thus, the program displays no asterisks next to the first six grade ranges. Note that line 19 uses the format specifier %02d to output the numbers in a grade range. This specifier indicates that an int value should be formatted as a field of two digits. The *0 flag* in the format specifier indicates that values with fewer digits than the field width (2) should begin with a leading 0.

Using the Elements of an Array as Counters

Sometimes, programs use counter variables to summarize data, such as the results of a survey. In Fig. 6.7, we used separate counters in our die-rolling program to track the number of occurrences of each side of a die as the program rolled the die 6000 times. An array version of the application in Fig. 6.7 is shown in Fig. 7.7.

Fig. 7.7 uses the array frequency (line 10) to count the occurrences of each side of the die. *The single statement in line 14 of this program replaces lines 23–46 of Fig. 6.7.* Line 14 uses the random value to determine which frequency element to increment during each iteration of the loop. The calculation in line 14 produces random numbers from 1 to 6, so the array frequency must be large enough to store six counters. However, we use a

```java
1   // Fig. 7.7: RollDie.java
2   // Roll a six-sided die 6000 times.
3   import java.util.Random;
4
5   public class RollDie
6   {
7      public static void main( String args[] )
8      {
9         Random randomNumbers = new Random(); // random number generator
10        int frequency[] = new int[ 7 ]; // array of frequency counters
11
12        // roll die 6000 times; use die value as frequency index
13        for ( int roll = 1; roll <= 6000; roll++ )
14           ++frequency[ 1 + randomNumbers.nextInt( 6 ) ];
15
16        System.out.printf( "%s%10s\n", "Face", "Frequency" );
17
18        // output each array element's value
19        for ( int face = 1; face < frequency.length; face++ )
20           System.out.printf( "%4d%10d\n", face, frequency[ face ] );
21     } // end main
22  } // end class RollDie
```

```
Face Frequency
   1       988
   2       963
   3      1018
   4      1041
   5       978
   6      1012
```

Fig. 7.7 | Die-rolling program using arrays instead of switch.

seven-element array in which we ignore frequency[0]—it is more logical to have the face value 1 increment frequency[1] than frequency[0]. Thus, each face value is used as an index for array frequency. We also replaced lines 50–52 from Fig. 6.7 by looping through array frequency to output the results (lines 19–20).

Using Arrays to Analyze Survey Results

Our next example uses arrays to summarize the results of data collected in a survey:

> Forty students were asked to rate the quality of the food in the student cafeteria on a scale of 1 to 10 (where 1 means awful and 10 means excellent). Place the 40 responses in an integer array, and summarize the results of the poll.

This is a typical array-processing application (see Fig. 7.8). We wish to summarize the number of responses of each type (i.e., 1 through 10). The array responses (lines 9–11) is a 40-element integer array of the students' responses to the survey. We use an 11-element array frequency (line 12) to count the number of occurrences of each response. Each element of the array is used as a counter for one of the survey responses and is initialized to zero by default. As in Fig. 7.7, we ignore frequency[0].

The for loop at lines 16–17 takes the responses one at a time from array responses and increments one of the 10 counters in the frequency array (frequency[1] to frequency[10]). The key statement in the loop is line 17, which increments the appropriate frequency counter, depending on the value of responses[answer].

```java
 1  // Fig. 7.8: StudentPoll.java
 2  // Poll analysis program.
 3
 4  public class StudentPoll
 5  {
 6     public static void main( String args[] )
 7     {
 8        // array of survey responses
 9        int responses[] = { 1, 2, 6, 4, 8, 5, 9, 7, 8, 10, 1, 6, 3, 8, 6,
10           10, 3, 8, 2, 7, 6, 5, 7, 6, 8, 6, 7, 5, 6, 6, 5, 6, 7, 5, 6,
11           4, 8, 6, 8, 10 };
12        int frequency[] = new int[ 11 ]; // array of frequency counters
13
14        // for each answer, select responses element and use that value
15        // as frequency index to determine element to increment
16        for ( int answer = 0; answer < responses.length; answer++ )
17           ++frequency[ responses[ answer ] ];
18
19        System.out.printf( "%s%10s", "Rating", "Frequency" );
20
21        // output each array element's value
22        for ( int rating = 1; rating < frequency.length; rating++ )
23           System.out.printf( "%d%10d", rating, frequency[ rating ] );
24     } // end main
25  } // end class StudentPoll
```

Fig. 7.8 | Poll analysis program. (Part 1 of 2.)

```
Rating Frequency
   1        2
   2        2
   3        2
   4        2
   5        5
   6       11
   7        5
   8        7
   9        1
  10        3
```

Fig. 7.8 | Poll analysis program. (Part 2 of 2.)

Let's consider several iterations of the for loop. When control variable answer is 0, the value of responses[answer] is the value of responses[0] (i.e., 1), so the program interprets ++frequency[responses[answer]] as

```
++frequency[ 1 ]
```

which increments the value in array element 1. To evaluate the expression, start with the value in the innermost set of square brackets (answer). Once you know answer's value (which is the value of the loop control variable in line 16), plug it into the expression and evaluate the next outer set of square brackets (i.e., responses[answer], which is a value selected from the responses array in lines 9–11). Then use the resulting value as the index for the frequency array to specify which counter to increment.

When answer is 1, responses[answer] is the value of responses[1] (2), so the program interprets ++frequency[responses[answer]] as

```
++frequency[ 2 ]
```

which increments array element 2.

When answer is 2, responses[answer] is the value of responses[2] (6), so the program interprets ++frequency[responses[answer]] as

```
++frequency[ 6 ]
```

which increments array element 6, and so on. Regardless of the number of responses processed in the survey, the program requires only an 11-element array (ignoring element zero) to summarize the results, because all the response values are between 1 and 10 and the index values for an 11-element array are 0 through 10.

If the data in the responses array had contained invalid values, such as 13, the program would have attempted to add 1 to frequency[13], which is outside the bounds of the array. Java disallows this. When a Java program executes, the JVM checks array indices to ensure that they are valid (i.e., they must be greater than or equal to 0 and less than the length of the array). If a program uses an invalid index, Java generates a so-called exception to indicate that an error occurred in the program at execution time. A control statement can be used to prevent such an "out-of-bounds" error from occurring. For example, the condition in a control statement could determine whether an index is valid before allowing it to be used in an array-access expression.

Error-Prevention Tip 7.1

An exception indicates that an error has occurred in a program. A programmer often can write code to recover from an exception and continue program execution, rather than abnormally terminating the program. When a program attempts to access an element outside the array bounds, an ArrayIndexOutOfBoundsException *occurs. Exception handling is discussed in Chapter 13.*

Error-Prevention Tip 7.2

When writing code to loop through an array, ensure that the array index is always greater than or equal to 0 and less than the length of the array. The loop-continuation condition should prevent the accessing of elements outside this range.

7.5 Case Study: Card Shuffling and Dealing Simulation

The examples in the chapter thus far have used arrays containing elements of primitive types. Recall from Section 7.2 that the elements of an array can be either primitive types or reference types. This section uses random number generation and an array of reference-type elements, namely objects representing playing cards, to develop a class that simulates card shuffling and dealing. This class can then be used to implement applications that play specific card games.

We first develop class Card (Fig. 7.9), which represents a playing card that has a face (e.g., "Ace", "Deuce", "Three", ..., "Jack", "Queen", "King") and a suit (e.g., "Hearts", "Diamonds", "Clubs", "Spades"). Next, we develop the DeckOfCards class (Fig. 7.10), which creates a deck of 52 playing cards in which each element is a Card object. We then build a test application (Fig. 7.11) that demonstrates class DeckOfCards's card shuffling and dealing capabilities.

Class Card

Class Card (Fig. 7.9) contains two String instance variables—face and suit—that are used to store references to the face name and suit name for a specific Card. The constructor for the class (lines 10–14) receives two Strings that it uses to initialize face and suit. Method toString (lines 17–20) creates a String consisting of the face of the card, the String " of " and the suit of the card. Recall from Chapter 6 that the + operator can be used to concatenate (i.e., combine) several Strings to form one larger String. Card's toString method can be invoked explicitly to obtain a string representation of a Card object (e.g., "Ace of Spades"). The toString method of an object is called implicitly when the object is used where a String is expected (e.g., when printf outputs the object as a String using the %s format specifier or when the object is concatenated to a String using the + operator). For this behavior to occur, toString must be declared with the header shown in Fig. 7.9.

```
1   // Fig. 7.9: Card.java
2   // Card class represents a playing card.
3
4   public class Card
5   {
```

Fig. 7.9 | Card class represents a playing card. (Part 1 of 2.)

```
 6        private String face; // face of card ("Ace", "Deuce", ...)
 7        private String suit; // suit of card ("Hearts", "Diamonds", ...)
 8
 9        // two-argument constructor initializes card's face and suit
10        public Card( String cardFace, String cardSuit )
11        {
12           face = cardFace; // initialize face of card
13           suit = cardSuit; // initialize suit of card
14        } // end two-argument Card constructor
15
16        // return String representation of Card
17        public String toString()
18        {
19           return face + " of " + suit;
20        } // end method toString
21     } // end class Card
```

Fig. 7.9 | Card class represents a playing card. (Part 2 of 2.)

Class DeckOfCards

Class DeckOfCards (Fig. 7.10) declares an instance variable array named deck of Card objects (line 7). Like primitive-type array declarations, the declaration of an array of objects includes the type of the elements in the array, followed by the name of the array variable and square brackets (e.g., Card deck[]). Class DeckOfCards also declares an integer instance variable currentCard (line 8) representing the next Card to be dealt from the deck array and a named constant NUMBER_OF_CARDS (line 9) indicating the number of Cards in the deck (52).

```
 1    // Fig. 7.10: DeckOfCards.java
 2    // DeckOfCards class represents a deck of playing cards.
 3    import java.util.Random;
 4
 5    public class DeckOfCards
 6    {
 7       private Card deck[]; // array of Card objects
 8       private int currentCard; // index of next Card to be dealt
 9       private final int NUMBER_OF_CARDS = 52; // constant number of Cards
10       private Random randomNumbers; // random number generator
11
12       // constructor fills deck of Cards
13       public DeckOfCards()
14       {
15          String faces[] = { "Ace", "Deuce", "Three", "Four", "Five", "Six",
16             "Seven", "Eight", "Nine", "Ten", "Jack", "Queen", "King" };
17          String suits[] = { "Hearts", "Diamonds", "Clubs", "Spades" };
18
19          deck = new Card[ NUMBER_OF_CARDS ]; // create array of Card objects
20          currentCard = 0; // set currentCard so first Card dealt is deck[ 0 ]
21          randomNumbers = new Random(); // create random number generator
```

Fig. 7.10 | DeckOfCards class represents a deck of playing cards that can be shuffled and dealt one at a time. (Part 1 of 2.)

```
22
23        // populate deck with Card objects
24        for ( int count = 0; count < deck.length; count++ )
25           deck[ count ] =
26              new Card( faces[ count % 13 ], suits[ count / 13 ] );
27     } // end DeckOfCards constructor
28
29     // shuffle deck of Cards with one-pass algorithm
30     public void shuffle()
31     {
32        // after shuffling, dealing should start at deck[ 0 ] again
33        currentCard = 0; // reinitialize currentCard
34
35        // for each Card, pick another random Card and swap them
36        for ( int first = 0; first < deck.length; first++ )
37        {
38           // select a random number between 0 and 51
39           int second =  randomNumbers.nextInt( NUMBER_OF_CARDS );
40
41           // swap current Card with randomly selected Card
42           Card temp = deck[ first ];
43           deck[ first ] = deck[ second ];
44           deck[ second ] = temp;
45        } // end for
46     } // end method shuffle
47
48     // deal one Card
49     public Card dealCard()
50     {
51        // determine whether Cards remain to be dealt
52        if ( currentCard < deck.length )
53           return deck[ currentCard++ ]; // return current Card in array
54        else
55           return null; // return null to indicate that all Cards were dealt
56     } // end method dealCard
57  } // end class DeckOfCards
```

Fig. 7.10 | DeckOfCards class represents a deck of playing cards that can be shuffled and dealt one at a time. (Part 2 of 2.)

The class's constructor instantiates the deck array (line 19) to be of size NUMBER_OF_CARDS. When first created, the elements of the deck array are null by default, so the constructor uses a for statement (lines 24–26) to fill the deck array with Cards. The for statement initializes control variable count to 0 and loops while count is less than deck.length, causing count to take on each integer value from 0 to 51 (the indices of the deck array). Each Card is instantiated and initialized with two Strings—one from the faces array (which contains the Strings "Ace" through "King") and one from the suits array (which contains the Strings "Hearts", "Diamonds", "Clubs" and "Spades"). The calculation count % 13 always results in a value from 0 to 12 (the 13 indices of the faces array in lines 15–16), and the calculation count / 13 always results in a value from 0 to 3 (the four indices of the suits array in line 17). When the deck array is initialized, it contains the Cards with faces "Ace" through "King" in order for each suit ("Hearts" then "Diamonds" then "Clubs" then "Spades").

Method shuffle (lines 30–46) shuffles the Cards in the deck. The method loops through all 52 Cards (array indices 0 to 51). For each Card, a number between 0 and 51 is picked randomly to select another Card. Next, the current Card object and the randomly selected Card object are swapped in the array. This exchange is performed by the three assignments in lines 42–44. The extra variable temp temporarily stores one of the two Card objects being swapped. The swap cannot be performed with only the two statements

```
deck[ first ] = deck[ second ];
deck[ second ] = deck[ first ];
```

If deck[first] is the "Ace" of "Spades" and deck[second] is the "Queen" of "Hearts", after the first assignment, both array elements contain the "Queen" of "Hearts" and the "Ace" of "Spades" is lost—hence, the extra variable temp is needed. After the for loop terminates, the Card objects are randomly ordered. A total of only 52 swaps are made in a single pass of the entire array, and the array of Card objects is shuffled!

Method dealCard (lines 49–56) deals one Card in the array. Recall that currentCard indicates the index of the next Card to be dealt (i.e., the Card at the top of the deck). Thus, line 52 compares currentCard to the length of the deck array. If the deck is not empty (i.e., currentCard is less than 52), line 53 returns the "top" Card and postincrements currentCard to prepare for the next call to dealCard—otherwise, null is returned. Recall from Chapter 3 that null represents a "reference to nothing."

Shuffling and Dealing Cards

The application of Fig. 7.11 demonstrates the card dealing and shuffling capabilities of class DeckOfCards (Fig. 7.10). Line 9 creates a DeckOfCards object named myDeckOf-Cards. Recall that the DeckOfCards constructor creates the deck with the 52 Card objects in order by suit and face. Line 10 invokes myDeckOfCards's shuffle method to rearrange the Card objects. The for statement in lines 13–19 deals all 52 Cards in the deck and prints them in four columns of 13 Cards each. Lines 16–18 deal and print four Card objects, each obtained by invoking myDeckOfCards's dealCard method. When printf outputs a Card with the %-20s format specifier, the Card's toString method (declared in lines 17–20 of Fig. 7.9) is implicitly invoked, and the result is output left justified in a field of width 20.

```
1   // Fig. 7.11: DeckOfCardsTest.java
2   // Card shuffling and dealing application.
3
4   public class DeckOfCardsTest
5   {
6      // execute application
7      public static void main( String args[] )
8      {
9         DeckOfCards myDeckOfCards = new DeckOfCards();
10        myDeckOfCards.shuffle(); // place Cards in random order
11
```

Fig. 7.11 | Card shuffling and dealing. (Part 1 of 2.)

```
12        // print all 52 Cards in the order in which they are dealt
13        for ( int i = 0; i < 13; i++ )
14        {
15            // deal and print 4 Cards
16            System.out.printf( "%-20s%-20s%-20s%-20s\n",
17                myDeckOfCards.dealCard(), myDeckOfCards.dealCard(),
18                myDeckOfCards.dealCard(), myDeckOfCards.dealCard() );
19        } // end for
20    } // end main
21 } // end class DeckOfCardsTest
```

Six of Spades	Eight of Spades	Six of Clubs	Nine of Hearts
Queen of Hearts	Seven of Clubs	Nine of Spades	King of Hearts
Three of Diamonds	Deuce of Clubs	Ace of Hearts	Ten of Spades
Four of Spades	Ace of Clubs	Seven of Diamonds	Four of Hearts
Three of Clubs	Deuce of Hearts	Five of Spades	Jack of Diamonds
King of Clubs	Ten of Hearts	Three of Hearts	Six of Diamonds
Queen of Clubs	Eight of Diamonds	Deuce of Diamonds	Ten of Diamonds
Three of Spades	King of Diamonds	Nine of Clubs	Six of Hearts
Ace of Spades	Four of Diamonds	Seven of Hearts	Eight of Clubs
Deuce of Spades	Eight of Hearts	Five of Hearts	Queen of Spades
Jack of Hearts	Seven of Spades	Four of Clubs	Nine of Diamonds
Ace of Diamonds	Queen of Diamonds	Five of Clubs	King of Spades
Five of Diamonds	Ten of Clubs	Jack of Spades	Jack of Clubs

Fig. 7.11 | Card shuffling and dealing. (Part 2 of 2.)

7.6 Enhanced for Statement

In previous examples, we demonstrated how to use counter-controlled for statements to iterate through the elements of an array. In this section, we introduce the *enhanced for statement*, which iterates through the elements of an array or a collection without using a counter (thus avoiding the possibility of "stepping outside" the array). This section discusses how to use the enhanced for statement to loop through an array. We show how to use the enhanced for statement with collections in Chapter 16. The syntax of an enhanced for statement is:

> **for** (*parameter* : *arrayName*)
>   *statement*

where *parameter* has two parts—a type and an identifier (e.g., int number)—and *arrayName* is the array through which to iterate. The type of the parameter must be consistent with the type of the elements in the array. As the next example illustrates, the identifier represents successive values in the array on successive iterations of the enhanced for statement.

Figure 7.12 uses the enhanced for statement (lines 12–13) to sum the integers in an array of student grades. The type specified in the parameter to the enhanced for is int, because array contains int values—the loop selects one int value from the array during each iteration. The enhanced for statement iterates through successive values in the array one by one. The enhanced for header can be read as "for each iteration, assign the next element of array to int variable number, then execute the following statement." Thus, for

```
 I   // Fig. 7.12: EnhancedForTest.java
 2   // Using enhanced for statement to total integers in an array.
 3
 4   public class EnhancedForTest
 5   {
 6      public static void main( String args[] )
 7      {
 8         int array[] = { 87, 68, 94, 100, 83, 78, 85, 91, 76, 87 };
 9         int total = 0;
10
11         // add each element's value to total
12         for ( int number : array )
13            total += number;
14
15         System.out.printf( "Total of array elements: %d\n", total );
16      } // end main
17   } // end class EnhancedForTest
```

```
Total of array elements: 849
```

Fig. 7.12 | Using the enhanced for statement to total integers in an array.

each iteration, identifier number represents an int value in array. Lines 12–13 are equivalent to the following counter-controlled repetition used in lines 12–13 of Fig. 7.5 to total the integers in array:

```
for ( int counter = 0; counter < array.length; counter++ )
   total += array[ counter ];
```

The enhanced for statement simplifies the code for iterating through an array. Note, however, that the enhanced for statement can be used only to obtain array elements—it cannot be used to modify elements. If your program needs to modify elements, use the traditional counter-controlled for statement.

The enhanced for statement can be used in place of the counter-controlled for statement whenever code looping through an array does not require access to the counter indicating the index of the current array element. For example, totaling the integers in an array requires access only to the element values—the index of each element is irrelevant. However, if a program must use a counter for some reason other than simply to loop through an array (e.g., to print an index number next to each array element value, as in the examples earlier in this chapter), use the counter-controlled for statement.

7.7 Passing Arrays to Methods

This section demonstrates how to pass arrays and individual array elements as arguments to methods. At the end of the section, we discuss how all types of arguments are passed to methods. To pass an array argument to a method, specify the name of the array without any brackets. For example, if array hourlyTemperatures is declared as

```
double hourlyTemperatures[] = new double[ 24 ];
```

then the method call

```
modifyArray( hourlyTemperatures );
```

passes the reference of array `hourlyTemperatures` to method `modifyArray`. Every array object "knows" its own length (via its `length` field). Thus, when we pass an array object's reference into a method, we need not pass the array length as an additional argument.

For a method to receive an array reference through a method call, the method's parameter list must specify an array parameter. For example, the method header for method `modifyArray` might be written as

```
void modifyArray( int b[] )
```

indicating that `modifyArray` receives the reference of an integer array in parameter b. The method call passes array `hourlyTemperature`'s reference, so when the called method uses the array variable b, it refers to the same array object as `hourlyTemperatures` in the caller.

When an argument to a method is an entire array or an individual array element of a reference type, the called method receives a copy of the reference. However, when an argument to a method is an individual array element of a primitive type, the called method receives a copy of the element's value. Such primitive values are called *scalars* or *scalar quantities*. To pass an individual array element to a method, use the indexed name of the array element as an argument in the method call.

Figure 7.13 demonstrates the difference between passing an entire array and passing a primitive-type array element to a method. The enhanced `for` statement at lines 16–17 outputs the five elements of array (an array of int values). Line 19 invokes method `modifyArray`, passing array as an argument. Method `modifyArray` (lines 36–40) receives a copy of array's reference and uses the reference to multiply each of array's elements by 2. To prove that array's elements were modified, the for statement at lines 23–24 outputs the five elements of array again. As the output shows, method `modifyArray` doubled the value of each element. Note that we could not use the enhanced for statement in lines 38–39 because we are modifying the array's elements.

```
 1   // Fig. 7.13: PassArray.java
 2   // Passing arrays and individual array elements to methods.
 3
 4   public class PassArray
 5   {
 6      // main creates array and calls modifyArray and modifyElement
 7      public static void main( String args[] )
 8      {
 9         int array[] = { 1, 2, 3, 4, 5 };
10
11         System.out.println(
12            "Effects of passing reference to entire array:\n" +
13            "The values of the original array are:" );
14
15         // output original array elements
16         for ( int value : array )
17            System.out.printf( "   %d", value );
18
```

Fig. 7.13 | Passing arrays and individual array elements to methods. (Part 1 of 2.)

```
19          modifyArray( array ); // pass array reference
20          System.out.println( "\n\nThe values of the modified array are:" );
21
22          // output modified array elements
23          for ( int value : array )
24              System.out.printf( "   %d", value );
25
26          System.out.printf(
27              "\n\nEffects of passing array element value:\n" +
28              "array[3] before modifyElement: %d\n", array[ 3 ] );
29
30          modifyElement( array[ 3 ] ); // attempt to modify array[ 3 ]
31          System.out.printf(
32              "array[3] after modifyElement: %d\n", array[ 3 ] );
33      } // end main
34
35      // multiply each element of an array by 2
36      public static void modifyArray( int array2[] )
37      {
38          for ( int counter = 0; counter < array2.length; counter++ )
39              array2[ counter ] *= 2;
40      } // end method modifyArray
41
42      // multiply argument by 2
43      public static void modifyElement( int element )
44      {
45          element *= 2;
46          System.out.printf(
47              "Value of element in modifyElement: %d\n", element );
48      } // end method modifyElement
49  } // end class PassArray
```

```
Effects of passing reference to entire array:
The values of the original array are:
   1   2   3   4   5

The values of the modified array are:
   2   4   6   8   10

Effects of passing array element value:
array[3] before modifyElement: 8
Value of element in modifyElement: 16
array[3] after modifyElement: 8
```

Fig. 7.13 | Passing arrays and individual array elements to methods. (Part 2 of 2.)

Figure 7.13 next demonstrates that when a copy of an individual primitive-type array element is passed to a method, modifying the copy in the called method does not affect the original value of that element in the calling method's array. Lines 26–28 output the value of array[3] (8) before invoking method modifyElement. Line 30 calls method modifyElement and passes array[3] as an argument. Remember that array[3] is actually one int value (8) in array. Therefore, the program passes a copy of the value of array[3]. Method modifyElement (lines 43–48) multiplies the value received as an argument by 2, stores the result in its parameter element, then outputs the value of element (16). Since method parameters, like local variables, cease to exist when the method in which they are declared completes execution, the method parameter element is destroyed when method modifyElement terminates. Thus, when the program returns control to main, lines 31–32 output the unmodified value of array[3] (i.e., 8).

Notes on Passing Arguments to Methods

The preceding example demonstrated the different ways that arrays and primitive-type array elements are passed as arguments to methods. We now take a closer look at how arguments in general are passed to methods. Two ways to pass arguments in method calls in many programming languages are *pass-by-value* and *pass-by-reference* (also called *call-by-value* and *call-by-reference*). When an argument is passed by value, a copy of the argument's value is passed to the called method. The called method works exclusively with the copy. Changes to the called method's copy do not affect the original variable's value in the caller.

When an argument is passed by reference, the called method can access the argument's value in the caller directly and modify that data, if necessary. Pass-by-reference improves performance by eliminating the need to copy possibly large amounts of data.

Unlike some other languages, Java does not allow programmers to choose pass-by-value or pass-by-reference—all arguments are passed by value. A method call can pass two types of values to a method—copies of primitive values (e.g., values of type int and double) and copies of references to objects (including references to arrays). Objects themselves cannot be passed to methods. When a method modifies a primitive-type parameter, changes to the parameter have no effect on the original argument value in the calling method. For example, when line 30 in main of Fig. 7.13 passes array[3] to method modifyElement, the statement in line 45 that doubles the value of parameter element has no effect on the value of array[3] in main. This is also true for reference-type parameters. If you modify a reference-type parameter by assigning it the reference of another object, the parameter refers to the new object, but the reference stored in the caller's variable still refers to the original object.

Although an object's reference is passed by value, a method can still interact with the referenced object by calling its public methods using the copy of the object's reference. Since the reference stored in the parameter is a copy of the reference that was passed as an argument, the parameter in the called method and the argument in the calling method refer to the same object in memory. For example, in Fig. 7.13, both parameter array2 in method modifyArray and variable array in main refer to the same array object in memory. Any changes made using the parameter array2 are carried out on the same object that is referenced by the variable that was passed as an argument in the calling method. In Fig. 7.13, the changes made in modifyArray using array2 affect the contents of the array object referenced by array in main. Thus, with a reference to an object, the called method can manipulate the caller's object directly.

Performance Tip 7.1

Passing arrays by reference makes sense for performance reasons. If arrays were passed by value, a copy of each element would be passed. For large, frequently passed arrays, this would waste time and consume considerable storage for the copies of the arrays.

7.8 Case Study: Class GradeBook Using an Array to Store Grades

This section further evolves class GradeBook, introduced in Chapter 3 and expanded in Chapters 4–5. Recall that this class represents a grade book used by a professor to store and analyze a set of student grades. Previous versions of the class process a set of grades entered by the user, but do not maintain the individual grade values in instance variables of the class. Thus, repeat calculations require the user to reenter the same grades. One way to solve this problem would be to store each grade entered in an individual instance of the class. For example, we could create instance variables grade1, grade2, ..., grade10 in class GradeBook to store 10 student grades. However, the code to total the grades and determine the class average would be cumbersome, and the class would not be able to process any more than 10 grades at a time. In this section, we solve this problem by storing grades in an array.

Storing Student Grades in an Array in Class GradeBook

The version of class GradeBook (Fig. 7.14) presented here uses an array of integers to store the grades of several students on a single exam. This eliminates the need to repeatedly input the same set of grades. Array grades is declared as an instance variable in line 7—therefore, each GradeBook object maintains its own set of grades. The class's constructor (lines 10–14) has two parameters—the name of the course and an array of grades. When an application (e.g., class GradeBookTest in Fig. 7.15) creates a GradeBook object, the application passes an existing int array to the constructor, which assigns the array's reference to instance variable grades (line 13). The size of the array grades is determined by the class that passes the array to the constructor. Thus, a GradeBook object can process a variable number of grades. The grade values in the passed array could have been input from a user or read from a file on disk (see Chapter 14). In our test application, we simply initialize an array with a set of grade values (Fig. 7.15, line 10). Once the grades are stored in instance variable grades of class GradeBook, all the class's methods can access the elements of grades as often as needed to perform various calculations.

```java
1   // Fig. 7.14: GradeBook.java
2   // Grade book using an array to store test grades.
3
4   public class GradeBook
5   {
6      private String courseName; // name of course this GradeBook represents
7      private int grades[]; // array of student grades
8
9      // two-argument constructor initializes courseName and grades array
10     public GradeBook( String name, int gradesArray[] )
11     {
12        courseName = name; // initialize courseName
13        grades = gradesArray; // store grades
14     } // end two-argument GradeBook constructor
15
```

Fig. 7.14 | GradeBook class using an array to store test grades. (Part 1 of 4.)

```
16    // method to set the course name
17    public void setCourseName( String name )
18    {
19       courseName = name; // store the course name
20    } // end method setCourseName
21
22    // method to retrieve the course name
23    public String getCourseName()
24    {
25       return courseName;
26    } // end method getCourseName
27
28    // display a welcome message to the GradeBook user
29    public void displayMessage()
30    {
31       // getCourseName gets the name of the course
32       System.out.printf( "Welcome to the grade book for\n%s!\n\n",
33          getCourseName() );
34    } // end method displayMessage
35
36    // perform various operations on the data
37    public void processGrades()
38    {
39       // output grades array
40       outputGrades();
41
42       // call method getAverage to calculate the average grade
43       System.out.printf( "\nClass average is %.2f\n", getAverage() );
44
45       // call methods getMinimum and getMaximum
46       System.out.printf( "Lowest grade is %d\nHighest grade is %d\n\n",
47          getMinimum(), getMaximum() );
48
49       // call outputBarChart to print grade distribution chart
50       outputBarChart();
51    } // end method processGrades
52
53    // find minimum grade
54    public int getMinimum()
55    {
56       int lowGrade = grades[ 0 ]; // assume grades[ 0 ] is smallest
57
58       // loop through grades array
59       for ( int grade : grades )
60       {
61          // if grade lower than lowGrade, assign it to lowGrade
62          if ( grade < lowGrade )
63             lowGrade = grade; // new lowest grade
64       } // end for
65
66       return lowGrade; // return lowest grade
67    } // end method getMinimum
```

Fig. 7.14 | GradeBook class using an array to store test grades. (Part 2 of 4.)

```
68
69      // find maximum grade
70      public int getMaximum()
71      {
72         int highGrade = grades[ 0 ]; // assume grades[ 0 ] is largest
73
74         // loop through grades array
75         for ( int grade : grades )
76         {
77            // if grade greater than highGrade, assign it to highGrade
78            if ( grade > highGrade )
79               highGrade = grade; // new highest grade
80         } // end for
81
82         return highGrade; // return highest grade
83      } // end method getMaximum
84
85      // determine average grade for test
86      public double getAverage()
87      {
88         int total = 0; // initialize total
89
90         // sum grades for one student
91         for ( int grade : grades )
92            total += grade;
93
94         // return average of grades
95         return (double) total / grades.length;
96      } // end method getAverage
97
98      // output bar chart displaying grade distribution
99      public void outputBarChart()
100     {
101        System.out.println( "Grade distribution:" );
102
103        // stores frequency of grades in each range of 10 grades
104        int frequency[] = new int[ 11 ];
105
106        // for each grade, increment the appropriate frequency
107        for ( int grade : grades )
108           ++frequency[ grade / 10 ];
109
110        // for each grade frequency, print bar in chart
111        for ( int count = 0; count < frequency.length; count++ )
112        {
113           // output bar label ( "00-09: ", ..., "90-99: ", "100: " )
114           if ( count == 10 )
115              System.out.printf( "%5d: ", 100 );
116           else
117              System.out.printf( "%02d-%02d: ",
118                 count * 10, count * 10 + 9 );
119
```

Fig. 7.14 | GradeBook class using an array to store test grades. (Part 3 of 4.)

```
120             // print bar of asterisks
121             for ( int stars = 0; stars < frequency[ count ]; stars++ )
122                System.out.print( "*" );
123
124             System.out.println(); // start a new line of output
125          } // end outer for
126       } // end method outputBarChart
127
128       // output the contents of the grades array
129       public void outputGrades()
130       {
131          System.out.println( "The grades are:\n" );
132
133          // output each student's grade
134          for ( int student = 0; student < grades.length; student++ )
135             System.out.printf( "Student %2d: %3d\n",
136                student + 1, grades[ student ] );
137       } // end method outputGrades
138    } // end class GradeBook
```

Fig. 7.14 | GradeBook class using an array to store test grades. (Part 4 of 4.)

Method processGrades (lines 37–51) contains a series of method calls that output a report summarizing the grades. Line 40 calls method outputGrades to print the contents of the array grades. Lines 134–136 in method outputGrades use a for statement to output the students' grades. A counter-controlled for must be used in this case, because lines 135–136 use counter variable student's value to output each grade next to a particular student number (see Fig. 7.15). Although array indices start at 0, a professor would typically number students starting at 1. Thus, lines 135–136 output student + 1 as the student number to produce grade labels "Student 1: ", "Student 2: ", and so on.

Method processGrades next calls method getAverage (line 43) to obtain the average of the grades in the array. Method getAverage (lines 86–96) uses an enhanced for statement to total the values in array grades before calculating the average. The parameter in the enhanced for's header (e.g., int grade) indicates that for each iteration, the int variable grade takes on a value in the array grades. Note that the averaging calculation in line 95 uses grades.length to determine the number of grades being averaged.

Lines 46–47 in method processGrades calls methods getMinimum and getMaximum to determine the lowest and highest grades of any student on the exam, respectively. Each of these methods uses an enhanced for statement to loop through array grades. Lines 59–64 in method getMinimum loop through the array. Lines 62–63 compare each grade to lowGrade; if a grade is less than lowGrade, lowGrade is set to that grade. When line 66 executes, lowGrade contains the lowest grade in the array. Method getMaximum (lines 70–83) works similarly to method getMinimum.

Finally, line 50 in method processGrades calls method outputBarChart to print a distribution chart of the grade data using a technique similar to that in Fig. 7.6. In that example, we manually calculated the number of grades in each category (i.e., 0–9, 10–19, …, 90–99 and 100) by simply looking at a set of grades. In this example, lines 107–108 use a technique similar to that in Fig. 7.7 and Fig. 7.8 to calculate the frequency of grades in each category. Line 104 declares and creates array frequency of 11 ints to store the frequency of grades in each grade category. For each grade in array grades, lines 107–108 increment the appropriate element of the frequency array. To determine which element to increment, line 108 divides the current grade by 10 using integer division. For example, if grade is 85, line 108 increments frequency[8] to update the count of grades in the range 80–89. Lines 111–125 next print the bar chart (see Fig. 7.15) based on the values in array frequency. Like lines 23–24 of Fig. 7.6, lines 121–122 of Fig. 7.14 use a value in array frequency to determine the number of asterisks to display in each bar.

Class GradeBookTest That Demonstrates Class GradeBook

The application of Fig. 7.15 creates an object of class GradeBook (Fig. 7.14) using the int array gradesArray (declared and initialized in line 10). Lines 12–13 pass a course name and gradesArray to the GradeBook constructor. Line 14 displays a welcome message, and line 15 invokes the GradeBook object's processGrades method. The output summarizes the 10 grades in myGradeBook.

```java
1   // Fig. 7.15: GradeBookTest.java
2   // Creates GradeBook object using an array of grades.
3
4   public class GradeBookTest
5   {
6      // main method begins program execution
7      public static void main( String args[] )
8      {
9         // array of student grades
10        int gradesArray[] = { 87, 68, 94, 100, 83, 78, 85, 91, 76, 87 };
11
12        GradeBook myGradeBook = new GradeBook(
13           "CS101 Introduction to Java Programming", gradesArray );
14        myGradeBook.displayMessage();
15        myGradeBook.processGrades();
16     } // end main
17  } // end class GradeBookTest
```

```
Welcome to the grade book for
CS101 Introduction to Java Programming!

The grades are:

Student  1:  87
Student  2:  68
Student  3:  94
Student  4: 100
Student  5:  83
Student  6:  78
Student  7:  85
Student  8:  91
Student  9:  76
Student 10:  87
```

Fig. 7.15 | GradeBookTest creates a GradeBook object using an array of grades, then invokes method processGrades to analyze them. (Part 1 of 2.)

```
Class average is 84.90
Lowest grade is 68
Highest grade is 100

Grade distribution:
00-09:
10-19:
20-29:
30-39:
40-49:
50-59:
60-69: *
70-79: **
80-89: ****
90-99: **
  100: *
```

Fig. 7.15 | GradeBookTest creates a GradeBook object using an array of grades, then invokes method processGrades to analyze them. (Part 2 of 2.)

Software Engineering Observation 7.1

A test harness (or test application) is responsible for creating an object of the class being tested and providing it with data. This data could come from any of several sources. Test data can be placed directly into an array with an array initializer, it can come from the user at the keyboard, it can come from a file (as you'll see in Chapter 14), or it can come from a network (as you'll see in Chapter 19). After passing this data to the class's constructor to instantiate the object, the test harness should call upon the object to test its methods and manipulate its data. Gathering data in the test harness like this allows the class to manipulate data from several sources.

7.9 Multidimensional Arrays

Multidimensional arrays with two dimensions are often used to represent *tables of values* consisting of information arranged in *rows* and *columns*. To identify a particular table element, we must specify two indices. By convention, the first identifies the element's row and the second its column. Arrays that require two indices to identify a particular element are called *two-dimensional arrays*. (Multidimensional arrays can have more than two dimensions.) Java does not support multidimensional arrays directly, but it does allow the programmer to specify one-dimensional arrays whose elements are also one-dimensional arrays, thus achieving the same effect. Figure 7.16 illustrates a two-dimensional array a that contains three rows and four columns (i.e., a three-by-four array). In general, an array with *m* rows and *n* columns is called an *m-by-n array*.

Every element in array a is identified in Fig. 7.16 by an array-access expression of the form a[row][column]; a is the name of the array, and row and column are the indices that uniquely identify each element in array a by row and column number. Note that the names of the elements in row 0 all have a first index of 0, and the names of the elements in column 3 all have a second index of 3.

Arrays of One-Dimensional Arrays

Like one-dimensional arrays, multidimensional arrays can be initialized in their declarations with array initializers. For example, a two-dimensional array named b with two rows

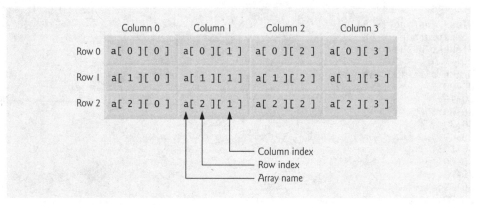

Fig. 7.16 | Two-dimensional array with three rows and four columns.

and two columns could be declared and initialized with *nested array initializers* as follows:

```
int b[][] = { { 1, 2 }, { 3, 4 } };
```

The initializer values are grouped by row in braces. So 1 and 2 initialize b[0][0] and b[0][1], respectively, and 3 and 4 initialize b[1][0] and b[1][1], respectively. The compiler counts the number of nested array initializers (represented by sets of braces within the outer braces) in the array declaration to determine the number of rows in array b. The compiler counts the initializer values in the nested array initializer for a row to determine the number of columns in that row. As we'll see momentarily, this means that rows can have different lengths.

Multidimensional arrays are maintained as arrays of one-dimensional arrays. Therefore array b in the preceding declaration is actually composed of two separate one-dimensional arrays—one containing the values in the first nested initializer list { 1, 2 } and one containing the values in the second nested initializer list { 3, 4 }. Thus, array b itself is an array of two elements, each a one-dimensional array of int values.

Two-Dimensional Arrays with Rows of Different Lengths
The manner in which multidimensional arrays are represented makes them quite flexible. In fact, the lengths of the rows in array b are not required to be the same. For example,

```
int b[][] = { { 1, 2 }, { 3, 4, 5 } };
```

creates integer array b with two elements (determined by the number of nested array initializers) that represent the rows of the two-dimensional array. Each element of b is a reference to a one-dimensional array of int variables. The int array for row 0 is a one-dimensional array with two elements (1 and 2), and the int array for row 1 is a one-dimensional array with three elements (3, 4 and 5).

Creating Two-Dimensional Arrays with Array-Creation Expressions
A multidimensional array with the same number of columns in every row can be created with an array-creation expression. For example, the following lines declare array b and assign it a reference to a three-by-four array:

```
int b[][] = new int[ 3 ][ 4 ];
```

In this case, we use the literal values 3 and 4 to specify the number of rows and number of columns, respectively, but this is not required. Programs can also use variables to specify array dimensions, because new creates arrays at execution time—not at compile time. As with one-dimensional arrays, the elements of a multidimensional array are initialized when the array object is created.

A multidimensional array in which each row has a different number of columns can be created as follows:

```
int b[][] = new int[ 2 ][ ];   // create 2 rows
b[ 0 ] = new int[ 5 ]; // create 5 columns for row 0
b[ 1 ] = new int[ 3 ]; // create 3 columns for row 1
```

The preceding statements create a two-dimensional array with two rows. Row 0 has five columns, and row 1 has three columns.

Two-Dimensional Array Example: Displaying Element Values

Figure 7.17 demonstrates initializing two-dimensional arrays with array initializers and using nested for loops to *traverse* the arrays (i.e., manipulate every element of each array).

Class InitArray's main declares two arrays. The declaration of array1 (line 9) uses nested array initializers to initialize the first row of the array to the values 1, 2 and 3, and the second row to the values 4, 5 and 6. The declaration of array2 (line 10) uses nested initializers of different lengths. In this case, the first row is initialized to have two elements with the values 1 and 2, respectively. The second row is initialized to have one element with the value 3. The third row is initialized to have three elements with the values 4, 5 and 6, respectively.

```
1   // Fig. 7.17: InitArray.java
2   // Initializing two-dimensional arrays.
3
4   public class InitArray
5   {
6      // create and output two-dimensional arrays
7      public static void main( String args[] )
8      {
9         int array1[][] = { { 1, 2, 3 }, { 4, 5, 6 } };
10        int array2[][] = { { 1, 2 }, { 3 }, { 4, 5, 6 } };
11
12        System.out.println( "Values in array1 by row are" );
13        outputArray( array1 ); // displays array1 by row
14
15        System.out.println( "\nValues in array2 by row are" );
16        outputArray( array2 ); // displays array2 by row
17     } // end main
18
19     // output rows and columns of a two-dimensional array
20     public static void outputArray( int array[][] )
21     {
22        // loop through array's rows
23        for ( int row = 0; row < array.length; row++ )
24        {
```

Fig. 7.17 | Initializing two-dimensional arrays. (Part 1 of 2.)

```
25              // loop through columns of current row
26              for ( int column = 0; column < array[ row ].length; column++ )
27                  System.out.printf( "%d  ", array[ row ][ column ] );
28
29              System.out.println(); // start new line of output
30          } // end outer for
31      } // end method outputArray
32  } // end class InitArray
```

```
Values in array1 by row are
1  2  3
4  5  6

Values in array2 by row are
1  2
3
4  5  6
```

Fig. 7.17 | Initializing two-dimensional arrays. (Part 2 of 2.)

Lines 13 and 16 call method outputArray (lines 20–31) to output the elements of array1 and array2, respectively. Method outputArray specifies the array parameter as int array[][] to indicate that the method receives a two-dimensional array. The for statement (lines 23–30) outputs the rows of a two-dimensional array. In the loop-continuation condition of the outer for statement, the expression array.length determines the number of rows in the array. In the inner for statement, the expression array[row].length determines the number of columns in the current row of the array. This condition enables the loop to determine the exact number of columns in each row.

Common Multidimensional-Array Manipulations Performed with for Statements
Many common array manipulations use for statements. As an example, the following for statement sets all the elements in row 2 of array a in Fig. 7.16 to zero:

```
for ( int column = 0; column < a[ 2 ].length; column++)
    a[ 2 ][ column ] = 0;
```

We specified row 2; therefore, we know that the first index is always 2 (0 is the first row, and 1 is the second row). This for loop varies only the second index (i.e., the column index). If row 2 of array a contains four elements, then the preceding for statement is equivalent to the assignment statements

```
a[ 2 ][ 0 ] = 0;
a[ 2 ][ 1 ] = 0;
a[ 2 ][ 2 ] = 0;
a[ 2 ][ 3 ] = 0;
```

The following nested for statement totals the values of all the elements in array a:

```
int total = 0;

for ( int row = 0; row < a.length; row++ )
{
    for ( int column = 0; column < a[ row ].length; column++ )
        total += a[ row ][ column ];
} // end outer for
```

This nested for statements total the array elements one row at a time. The outer for statement begins by setting the row index to 0 so that the first row's elements can be totaled by the inner for statement. The outer for then increments row to 1 so that the second row can be totaled. Then, the outer for increments row to 2 so that the third row can be totaled. The variable total can be displayed when the outer for statement terminates. In the next example, we show how to process a two-dimensional array in a similar manner using nested enhanced for statements.

7.10 Case Study: Class GradeBook Using a Two-Dimensional Array

In Section 7.8, we presented class GradeBook (Fig. 7.14), which used a one-dimensional array to store student grades on a single exam. In most semesters, students take several exams. Professors are likely to want to analyze grades across the entire semester, both for a single student and for the class as a whole.

Storing Student Grades in a Two-Dimensional Array in Class GradeBook

Figure 7.18 contains a version of class GradeBook that uses a two-dimensional array grades to store the grades of a number of students on multiple exams. Each row of the array represents a single student's grades for the entire course, and each column represents a grade on one of the exams the students took during the course. An application such as GradeBookTest (Fig. 7.19) passes the array as an argument to the GradeBook constructor. In this example, we use a ten-by-three array containing ten students' grades on three exams. Five methods perform array manipulations to process the grades. Each method is similar to its counterpart in the earlier one-dimensional array version of class GradeBook (Fig. 7.14). Method getMinimum (lines 52–70) determines the lowest grade of any student for the semester. Method getMaximum (lines 73–91) determines the highest grade of any student for the semester. Method getAverage (lines 94–104) determines a particular student's semester average. Method outputBarChart (lines 107–137) outputs a bar chart of the distribution of all student grades for the semester. Method outputGrades (lines 140–164) outputs the two-dimensional array in a tabular format, along with each student's semester average.

```
1   // Fig. 7.18: GradeBook.java
2   // Grade book using a two-dimensional array to store grades.
3
4   public class GradeBook
5   {
6      private String courseName; // name of course this grade book represents
7      private int grades[][]; // two-dimensional array of student grades
8
9      // two-argument constructor initializes courseName and grades array
10     public GradeBook( String name, int gradesArray[][] )
11     {
12        courseName = name; // initialize courseName
13        grades = gradesArray; // store grades
14     } // end two-argument GradeBook constructor
```

Fig. 7.18 | GradeBook class using a two-dimensional array to store grades. (Part 1 of 4.)

```
15
16      // method to set the course name
17      public void setCourseName( String name )
18      {
19         courseName = name; // store the course name
20      } // end method setCourseName
21
22      // method to retrieve the course name
23      public String getCourseName()
24      {
25         return courseName;
26      } // end method getCourseName
27
28      // display a welcome message to the GradeBook user
29      public void displayMessage()
30      {
31         // getCourseName gets the name of the course
32         System.out.printf( "Welcome to the grade book for\n%s!\n\n",
33            getCourseName() );
34      } // end method displayMessage
35
36      // perform various operations on the data
37      public void processGrades()
38      {
39         // output grades array
40         outputGrades();
41
42         // call methods getMinimum and getMaximum
43         System.out.printf( "\n%s %d\n%s %d\n\n",
44            "Lowest grade in the grade book is", getMinimum(),
45            "Highest grade in the grade book is", getMaximum() );
46
47         // output grade distribution chart of all grades on all tests
48         outputBarChart();
49      } // end method processGrades
50
51      // find minimum grade
52      public int getMinimum()
53      {
54         // assume first element of grades array is smallest
55         int lowGrade = grades[ 0 ][ 0 ];
56
57         // loop through rows of grades array
58         for ( int studentGrades[] : grades )
59         {
60            // loop through columns of current row
61            for ( int grade : studentGrades )
62            {
63               // if grade less than lowGrade, assign it to lowGrade
64               if ( grade < lowGrade )
65                  lowGrade = grade;
66            } // end inner for
67         } // end outer for
```

Fig. 7.18 | GradeBook class using a two-dimensional array to store grades. (Part 2 of 4.)

```
68
69        return lowGrade; // return lowest grade
70     } // end method getMinimum
71
72     // find maximum grade
73     public int getMaximum()
74     {
75        // assume first element of grades array is largest
76        int highGrade = grades[ 0 ][ 0 ];
77
78        // loop through rows of grades array
79        for ( int studentGrades[] : grades )
80        {
81           // loop through columns of current row
82           for ( int grade : studentGrades )
83           {
84              // if grade greater than highGrade, assign it to highGrade
85              if ( grade > highGrade )
86                 highGrade = grade;
87           } // end inner for
88        } // end outer for
89
90        return highGrade; // return highest grade
91     } // end method getMaximum
92
93     // determine average grade for particular set of grades
94     public double getAverage( int setOfGrades[] )
95     {
96        int total = 0; // initialize total
97
98        // sum grades for one student
99        for ( int grade : setOfGrades )
100           total += grade;
101
102        // return average of grades
103        return (double) total / setOfGrades.length;
104    } // end method getAverage
105
106    // output bar chart displaying overall grade distribution
107    public void outputBarChart()
108    {
109       System.out.println( "Overall grade distribution:" );
110
111       // stores frequency of grades in each range of 10 grades
112       int frequency[] = new int[ 11 ];
113
114       // for each grade in GradeBook, increment the appropriate frequency
115       for ( int studentGrades[] : grades )
116       {
117          for ( int grade : studentGrades )
118             ++frequency[ grade / 10 ];
119       } // end outer for
120
```

Fig. 7.18 | GradeBook class using a two-dimensional array to store grades. (Part 3 of 4.)

```
121         // for each grade frequency, print bar in chart
122         for ( int count = 0; count < frequency.length; count++ )
123         {
124            // output bar label ( "00-09: ", ..., "90-99: ", "100: " )
125            if ( count == 10 )
126               System.out.printf( "%5d: ", 100 );
127            else
128               System.out.printf( "%02d-%02d: ",
129                  count * 10, count * 10 + 9 );
130
131            // print bar of asterisks
132            for ( int stars = 0; stars < frequency[ count ]; stars++ )
133               System.out.print( "*" );
134
135            System.out.println(); // start a new line of output
136         } // end outer for
137      } // end method outputBarChart
138
139      // output the contents of the grades array
140      public void outputGrades()
141      {
142         System.out.println( "The grades are:\n" );
143         System.out.print( "            " ); // align column heads
144
145         // create a column heading for each of the tests
146         for ( int test = 0; test < grades[ 0 ].length; test++ )
147            System.out.printf( "Test %d  ", test + 1 );
148
149         System.out.println( "Average" ); // student average column heading
150
151         // create rows/columns of text representing array grades
152         for ( int student = 0; student < grades.length; student++ )
153         {
154            System.out.printf( "Student %2d", student + 1 );
155
156            for ( int test : grades[ student ] ) // output student's grades
157               System.out.printf( "%8d", test );
158
159            // call method getAverage to calculate student's average grade;
160            // pass row of grades as the argument to getAverage
161            double average = getAverage( grades[ student ] );
162            System.out.printf( "%9.2f\n", average );
163         } // end outer for
164      } // end method outputGrades
165   } // end class GradeBook
```

Fig. 7.18 | GradeBook class using a two-dimensional array to store grades. (Part 4 of 4.)

Methods getMinimum, getMaximum, outputBarChart and outputGrades each loop through array grades by using nested for statements—for example, the nested enhanced for statement from the declaration of method getMinimum (lines 58–67). The outer enhanced for statement iterates through the two-dimensional array grades, assigning successive rows to parameter studentGrades on successive iterations. The square brackets following the parameter name indicate that studentGrades refers to a one-dimensional int array—namely, a row in array grades containing one student's grades. To find the lowest overall grade, the inner for statement compares the elements of the current one-dimensional array studentGrades to variable lowGrade. For example, on the first iteration of the outer for, row 0 of grades is assigned to parameter studentGrades. The inner enhanced for statement then loops through studentGrades and compares each grade value with lowGrade. If a grade is less than lowGrade, lowGrade is set to that grade. On the second iteration of the outer enhanced for statement, row 1 of grades is assigned to student-Grades, and the elements of this row are compared with variable lowGrade. This repeats until all rows of grades have been traversed. When execution of the nested statement is complete, lowGrade contains the lowest grade in the two-dimensional array. Method get-Maximum works similarly to method getMinimum.

Method outputBarChart in Fig. 7.18 is nearly identical to the one in Fig. 7.14. However, to output the overall grade distribution for a whole semester, the method here uses a nested enhanced for statement (lines 115–119) to create the one-dimensional array frequency based on all the grades in the two-dimensional array. The rest of the code in each of the two outputBarChart methods that displays the chart is identical.

Method outputGrades (lines 140–164) also uses nested for statements to output values of the array grades and each student's semester average. The output in Fig. 7.19 shows the result, which resembles the tabular format of a professor's physical grade book. Lines 146–147 print the column headings for each test. We use a counter-controlled for statement here so that we can identify each test with a number. Similarly, the for statement in lines 152–163 first outputs a row label using a counter variable to identify each student (line 154). Although array indices start at 0, note that lines 147 and 154 output test + 1 and student + 1, respectively, to produce test and student numbers starting at 1 (see Fig. 7.19). The inner for statement in lines 156–157 uses the outer for statement's counter variable student to loop through a specific row of array grades and output each student's test grade. Note that an enhanced for statement can be nested in a counter-controlled for statement, and vice versa. Finally, line 161 obtains each student's semester average by passing the current row of grades (i.e., grades[student]) to method getAverage.

Method getAverage (lines 94–104) takes one argument—a one-dimensional array of test results for a particular student. When line 161 calls getAverage, the argument is grades[student], which specifies that a particular row of the two-dimensional array grades should be passed to getAverage. For example, based on the array created in Fig. 7.19, the argument grades[1] represents the three values (a one-dimensional array of grades) stored in row 1 of the two-dimensional array grades. Recall that a two-dimensional array is an array whose elements are one-dimensional arrays. Method getAverage calculates the sum of the array elements, divides the total by the number of test results and returns the floating-point result as a double value (line 103).

Class GradeBookTest That Demonstrates Class GradeBook

The application in Fig. 7.19 creates an object of class GradeBook (Fig. 7.18) using the two-dimensional array of ints named gradesArray (declared and initialized in lines 10–19). Lines 21–22 pass a course name and gradesArray to the GradeBook constructor. Lines 23–24 then invoke myGradeBook's displayMessage and processGrades methods to display a welcome message and obtain a report summarizing the students' grades for the semester, respectively.

```
1   // Fig. 7.19: GradeBookTest.java
2   // Creates GradeBook object using a two-dimensional array of grades.
3
4   public class GradeBookTest
5   {
6      // main method begins program execution
7      public static void main( String args[] )
8      {
9         // two-dimensional array of student grades
10        int gradesArray[][] = { { 87, 96, 70 },
11                                { 68, 87, 90 },
12                                { 94, 100, 90 },
13                                { 100, 81, 82 },
14                                { 83, 65, 85 },
15                                { 78, 87, 65 },
16                                { 85, 75, 83 },
17                                { 91, 94, 100 },
18                                { 76, 72, 84 },
19                                { 87, 93, 73 } };
20
21        GradeBook myGradeBook = new GradeBook(
22           "CS101 Introduction to Java Programming", gradesArray );
23        myGradeBook.displayMessage();
24        myGradeBook.processGrades();
25     } // end main
26  } // end class GradeBookTest
```

```
Welcome to the grade book for
CS101 Introduction to Java Programming!

The grades are:

            Test 1  Test 2  Test 3  Average
Student  1      87      96      70    84.33
Student  2      68      87      90    81.67
Student  3      94     100      90    94.67
Student  4     100      81      82    87.67
Student  5      83      65      85    77.67
Student  6      78      87      65    76.67
Student  7      85      75      83    81.00
Student  8      91      94     100    95.00
Student  9      76      72      84    77.33
Student 10      87      93      73    84.33

Lowest grade in the grade book is 65
Highest grade in the grade book is 100

Overall grade distribution:
00-09:
10-19:
20-29:
30-39:
```

Fig. 7.19 | Creates GradeBook object using a two-dimensional array of grades, then invokes method processGrades to analyze them. (Part 1 of 2.)

```
40-49:
50-59:
60-69: ***
70-79: ******
80-89: ***********
90-99: *******
  100: ***
```

Fig. 7.19 | Creates GradeBook object using a two-dimensional array of grades, then invokes method processGrades to analyze them. (Part 2 of 2.)

7.11 Variable-Length Argument Lists

With *variable-length argument lists*, you can create methods that receive an unspecified number of arguments. An argument type followed by an *ellipsis (...) in a method's parameter list* indicates that the method receives a variable number of arguments of that particular type. This use of the ellipsis can occur only once in a parameter list, and the ellipsis, together with its type, must be placed at the end of the parameter list. While programmers can use method overloading and array passing to accomplish much of what is accomplished with "varargs," or variable-length argument lists, using an ellipsis in a method's parameter list is more concise.

Figure 7.20 demonstrates method average (lines 7–16), which receives a variable-length sequence of doubles. Java treats the variable-length argument list as an array whose elements are all of the same type. Hence, the method body can manipulate the parameter numbers as an array of doubles. Lines 12–13 use the enhanced for loop to walk through the array and calculate the total of the doubles in the array. Line 15 accesses numbers.length to obtain the size of the numbers array for use in the averaging calculation. Lines 29, 31 and 33 in main call method average with two, three and four arguments, respectively. Method average has a variable-length argument list (line 7), so it can average as many double arguments as the caller passes. The output shows that each call to method average returns the correct value.

```
1   // Fig. 7.20: VarargsTest.java
2   // Using variable-length argument lists.
3
4   public class VarargsTest
5   {
6      // calculate average
7      public static double average( double... numbers )
8      {
9         double total = 0.0; // initialize total
10
11         // calculate total using the enhanced for statement
12         for ( double d : numbers )
13            total += d;
14
15         return total / numbers.length;
16      } // end method average
```

Fig. 7.20 | Using variable-length argument lists. (Part 1 of 2.)

```
17
18     public static void main( String args[] )
19     {
20        double d1 = 10.0;
21        double d2 = 20.0;
22        double d3 = 30.0;
23        double d4 = 40.0;
24
25        System.out.printf( "d1 = %.1f\nd2 = %.1f\nd3 = %.1f\nd4 = %.1f\n\n",
26           d1, d2, d3, d4 );
27
28        System.out.printf( "Average of d1 and d2 is %.1f\n",
29           average( d1, d2 ) );
30        System.out.printf( "Average of d1, d2 and d3 is %.1f\n",
31           average( d1, d2, d3 ) );
32        System.out.printf( "Average of d1, d2, d3 and d4 is %.1f\n",
33           average( d1, d2, d3, d4 ) );
34     } // end main
35  } // end class VarargsTest
```

```
d1 = 10.0
d2 = 20.0
d3 = 30.0
d4 = 40.0

Average of d1 and d2 is 15.0
Average of d1, d2 and d3 is 20.0
Average of d1, d2, d3 and d4 is 25.0
```

Fig. 7.20 | Using variable-length argument lists. (Part 2 of 2.)

Common Programming Error 7.6

Placing an ellipsis indicating a variable-length argument list in the middle of a method parameter list is a syntax error. An ellipsis may be placed only at the end of the parameter list.

7.12 Using Command-Line Arguments

On many systems it is possible to pass arguments from the command line (these are known as *command-line arguments*) to an application by including a parameter of type String[] (i.e., an array of Strings) in the parameter list of main, exactly as we have done in every application in the book. By convention, this parameter is named args. When an application is executed using the java command, Java passes the command-line arguments that appear after the class name in the java command to the application's main method as Strings in the array args. The number of arguments passed in from the command line is obtained by accessing the array's length attribute. For example, the command "java MyClass a b" passes two command-line arguments, a and b, to application MyClass. Note that command-line arguments are separated by white space, not commas. When this command executes, MyClass's main method receives the two-element array args (i.e., args.length is 2) in which args[0] contains the String "a" and args[1] contains the String "b". Common uses of command-line arguments include passing options and file names to applications.

Figure 7.21 uses three command-line arguments to initialize an array. When the program executes, if args.length is not 3, the program prints an error message and terminates (lines 9–12). Otherwise, lines 14–32 initialize and display the array based on the values of the command-line arguments.

```java
1   // Fig. 7.21: InitArray.java
2   // Using command-line arguments to initialize an array.
3
4   public class InitArray
5   {
6      public static void main( String args[] )
7      {
8         // check number of command-line arguments
9         if ( args.length != 3 )
10           System.out.println(
11              "Error: Please re-enter the entire command, including\n" +
12              "an array size, initial value and increment." );
13        else
14        {
15           // get array size from first command-line argument
16           int arrayLength = Integer.parseInt( args[ 0 ] );
17           int array[] = new int[ arrayLength ]; // create array
18
19           // get initial value and increment from command-line arguments
20           int initialValue = Integer.parseInt( args[ 1 ] );
21           int increment = Integer.parseInt( args[ 2 ] );
22
23           // calculate value for each array element
24           for ( int counter = 0; counter < array.length; counter++ )
25              array[ counter ] = initialValue + increment * counter;
26
27           System.out.printf( "%s%8s\n", "Index", "Value" );
28
29           // display array index and value
30           for ( int counter = 0; counter < array.length; counter++ )
31              System.out.printf( "%5d%8d\n", counter, array[ counter ] );
32        } // end else
33     } // end main
34  } // end class InitArray
```

```
java InitArray
Error: Please re-enter the entire command, including
an array size, initial value and increment.
```

```
java InitArray 5 0 4
Index    Value
    0        0
    1        4
    2        8
    3       12
    4       16
```

Fig. 7.21 | Initializing an array using command-line arguments. (Part 1 of 2.)

```
java InitArray 10 1 2
Index    Value
   0       1
   1       3
   2       5
   3       7
   4       9
   5      11
   6      13
   7      15
   8      17
   9      19
```

Fig. 7.21 | Initializing an array using command-line arguments. (Part 2 of 2.)

The command-line arguments become available to main as Strings in args. Line 16 gets args[0]—a String that specifies the array size—and converts it to an int value that the program uses to create the array in line 17. The static method parseInt of class Integer converts its String argument to an int.

Lines 20–21 convert the args[1] and args[2] command-line arguments to int values and store them in initialValue and increment, respectively. Lines 24–25 calculate the value for each array element.

The output of the first execution shows that the application received an insufficient number of command-line arguments. The second execution uses command-line arguments 5, 0 and 4 to specify the size of the array (5), the value of the first element (0) and the increment of each value in the array (4), respectively. The corresponding output shows that these values create an array containing the integers 0, 4, 8, 12 and 16. The output from the third execution shows that the command-line arguments 10, 1 and 2 produce an array whose 10 elements are the nonnegative odd integers from 1 to 19.

7.13 (Optional) Software Engineering Case Study: Collaboration Among Objects

In this section, we concentrate on the collaborations (interactions) among objects. When two objects communicate with each other to accomplish a task, they are said to *collaborate*—objects do this by invoking one another's operations. A *collaboration* consists of an object of one class sending a *message* to an object of another class. Messages are sent in Java via method calls.

In Section 6.19, we determined many of the operations of the classes in our system. In this section, we concentrate on the messages that invoke these operations. To identify the collaborations in the system, we return to the requirements document in Section 2.8. Recall that this document specifies the range of activities that occur during an ATM session (e.g., authenticating a user, performing transactions). The steps used to describe how the system must perform each of these tasks are our first indication of the collaborations in our system. As we proceed through this and the remaining Software Engineering Case Study sections, we may discover additional collaborations.

Identifying the Collaborations in a System

We identify the collaborations in the system by carefully reading the sections of the requirements document that specify what the ATM should do to authenticate a user and to perform each transaction type. For each action or step described in the requirements document, we decide which objects in our system must interact to achieve the desired result. We identify one object as the sending object and another as the receiving object. We then select one of the receiving object's operations (identified in Section 6.19) that must be invoked by the sending object to produce the proper behavior. For example, the ATM displays a welcome message when idle. We know that an object of class Screen displays a message to the user via its displayMessage operation. Thus, we decide that the system can display a welcome message by employing a collaboration between the ATM and the Screen in which the ATM sends a displayMessage message to the Screen by invoking the displayMessage operation of class Screen. [*Note:* To avoid repeating the phrase "an object of class...," we refer to an object by using its class name preceded by an article (e.g., "a," "an" or "the")—for example, "the ATM" refers to an object of class ATM.]

Figure 7.22 lists the collaborations that can be derived from the requirements document. For each sending object, we list the collaborations in the order in which they first occur during an ATM session (i.e., the order in which they are discussed in the requirements document). We list each collaboration involving a unique sender, message and recipient only once, even though the collaborations may occur at several different times throughout an ATM session. For example, the first row in Fig. 7.22 indicates that the ATM collaborates with the Screen whenever the ATM needs to display a message to the user.

Let's consider the collaborations in Fig. 7.22. Before allowing a user to perform any transactions, the ATM must prompt the user to enter an account number, then to enter a PIN. It accomplishes each of these tasks by sending a displayMessage message to the

An object of class...	sends the message...	to an object of class...
ATM	displayMessage	Screen
	getInput	Keypad
	authenticateUser	BankDatabase
	execute	BalanceInquiry
	execute	Withdrawal
	execute	Deposit
BalanceInquiry	getAvailableBalance	BankDatabase
	getTotalBalance	BankDatabase
	displayMessage	Screen
Withdrawal	displayMessage	Screen
	getInput	Keypad
	getAvailableBalance	BankDatabase
	isSufficientCashAvailable	CashDispenser
	debit	BankDatabase
	dispenseCash	CashDispenser

Fig. 7.22 | Collaborations in the ATM system. (Part 1 of 2.)

An object of class...	sends the message...	to an object of class...
Deposit	displayMessage	Screen
	getInput	Keypad
	isEnvelopeReceived	DepositSlot
	credit	BankDatabase
BankDatabase	validatePIN	Account
	getAvailableBalance	Account
	getTotalBalance	Account
	debit	Account
	credit	Account

Fig. 7.22 | Collaborations in the ATM system. (Part 2 of 2.)

Screen. Both of these actions refer to the same collaboration between the ATM and the Screen, which is already listed in Fig. 7.22. The ATM obtains input in response to a prompt by sending a getInput message to the Keypad. Next, the ATM must determine whether the user-specified account number and PIN match those of an account in the database. It does so by sending an authenticateUser message to the BankDatabase. Recall that the BankDatabase cannot authenticate a user directly—only the user's Account (i.e., the Account that contains the account number specified by the user) can access the user's PIN on record to authenticate the user. Figure 7.22 therefore lists a collaboration in which the BankDatabase sends a validatePIN message to an Account.

After the user is authenticated, the ATM displays the main menu by sending a series of displayMessage messages to the Screen and obtains input containing a menu selection by sending a getInput message to the Keypad. We have already accounted for these collaborations, so we do not add anything to Fig. 7.22. After the user chooses a type of transaction to perform, the ATM executes the transaction by sending an execute message to an object of the appropriate transaction class (i.e., a BalanceInquiry, a Withdrawal or a Deposit). For example, if the user chooses to perform a balance inquiry, the ATM sends an execute message to a BalanceInquiry.

Further examination of the requirements document reveals the collaborations involved in executing each transaction type. A BalanceInquiry retrieves the amount of money available in the user's account by sending a getAvailableBalance message to the BankDatabase, which responds by sending a getAvailableBalance message to the user's Account. Similarly, the BalanceInquiry retrieves the amount of money on deposit by sending a getTotalBalance message to the BankDatabase, which sends the same message to the user's Account. To display both measures of the user's balance at the same time, the BalanceInquiry sends a displayMessage message to the Screen.

A Withdrawal sends a series of displayMessage messages to the Screen to display a menu of standard withdrawal amounts (i.e., $20, $40, $60, $100, $200). The Withdrawal sends a getInput message to the Keypad to obtain the user's menu selection. Next, the Withdrawal determines whether the requested withdrawal amount is less than or equal to the user's account balance. The Withdrawal can obtain the amount of money available in the user's account by sending a getAvailableBalance message to the BankDatabase. The

Withdrawal then tests whether the cash dispenser contains enough cash by sending an isSufficientCashAvailable message to the CashDispenser. A Withdrawal sends a debit message to the BankDatabase to decrease the user's account balance. The BankDatabase in turn sends the same message to the appropriate Account. Recall that debiting funds from an Account decreases both the totalBalance and the availableBalance. To dispense the requested amount of cash, the Withdrawal sends a dispenseCash message to the CashDispenser. Finally, the Withdrawal sends a displayMessage message to the Screen, instructing the user to take the cash.

A Deposit responds to an execute message first by sending a displayMessage message to the Screen to prompt the user for a deposit amount. The Deposit sends a getInput message to the Keypad to obtain the user's input. The Deposit then sends a displayMessage message to the Screen to tell the user to insert a deposit envelope. To determine whether the deposit slot received an incoming deposit envelope, the Deposit sends an isEnvelopeReceived message to the DepositSlot. The Deposit updates the user's account by sending a credit message to the BankDatabase, which subsequently sends a credit message to the user's Account. Recall that crediting funds to an Account increases the totalBalance but not the availableBalance.

Interaction Diagrams

Now that we have identified a set of possible collaborations between the objects in our ATM system, let us graphically model these interactions using the UML. The UML provides several types of *interaction diagrams* that model the behavior of a system by modeling how objects interact. The *communication diagram* emphasizes *which objects* participate in collaborations. [*Note:* Communication diagrams were called *collaboration diagrams* in earlier versions of the UML.] Like the communication diagram, the *sequence diagram* shows collaborations among objects, but it emphasizes *when* messages are sent between objects *over time*.

Communication Diagrams

Figure 7.23 shows a communication diagram that models the ATM executing a BalanceInquiry. Objects are modeled in the UML as rectangles containing names in the form objectName : ClassName. In this example, which involves only one object of each type, we disregard the object name and list only a colon followed by the class name. [*Note:* Specifying the name of each object in a communication diagram is recommended when modeling multiple objects of the same type.] Communicating objects are connected with solid lines, and messages are passed between objects along these lines in the direction shown by arrows. The name of the message, which appears next to the arrow, is the name of an operation (i.e., a method in Java) belonging to the receiving object—think of the name as a "service" that the receiving object provides to sending objects (its "clients").

The solid filled arrow in Fig. 7.23 represents a message—or *synchronous call*—in the UML and a method call in Java. This arrow indicates that the flow of control is from the

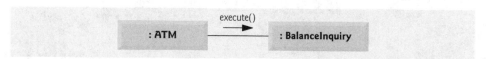

Fig. 7.23 | Communication diagram of the ATM executing a balance inquiry.

sending object (the ATM) to the receiving object (a BalanceInquiry). Since this is a synchronous call, the sending object may not send another message, or do anything at all, until the receiving object processes the message and returns control to the sending object. The sender just waits. For example, in Fig. 7.23, the ATM calls method execute of a BalanceInquiry and may not send another message until execute has finished and returns control to the ATM. [*Note:* If this were an ***asynchronous call***, represented by a stick arrowhead, the sending object would not have to wait for the receiving object to return control—it would continue sending additional messages immediately following the asynchronous call. Asynchronous calls are implemented in Java using a technique called multithreading, which is discussed in Chapter 18.]

Sequence of Messages in a Communication Diagram

Figure 7.24 shows a communication diagram that models the interactions among objects in the system when an object of class BalanceInquiry executes. We assume that the object's accountNumber attribute contains the account number of the current user. The collaborations in Fig. 7.24 begin after the ATM sends an execute message to a BalanceInquiry (i.e., the interaction modeled in Fig. 7.23). The number to the left of a message name indicates the order in which the message is passed. The ***sequence of messages*** in a communication diagram progresses in numerical order from least to greatest. In this diagram, the numbering starts with message 1 and ends with message 3. The BalanceInquiry first sends a getAvailableBalance message to the BankDatabase (message 1), then sends a getTotalBalance message to the BankDatabase (message 2). Within the parentheses following a message name, we can specify a comma-separated list of the names of the parameters sent with the message (i.e., arguments in a Java method call)—the BalanceInquiry passes attribute accountNumber with its messages to the BankDatabase to indicate which Account's balance information to retrieve. Recall from Fig. 6.27 that operations getAvailableBalance and getTotalBalance of class BankDatabase each

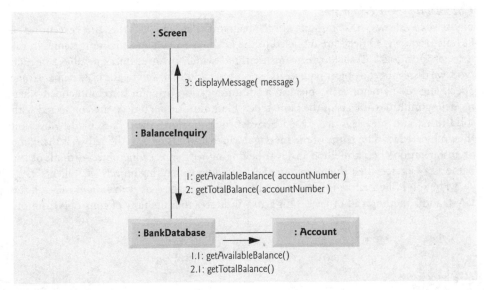

Fig. 7.24 | Communication diagram for executing a balance inquiry.

require a parameter to identify an account. The `BalanceInquiry` next displays the availableBalance and the `totalBalance` to the user by passing a `displayMessage` message to the `Screen` (message 3) that includes a parameter indicating the `message` to be displayed.

Note that Fig. 7.24 models two additional messages passing from the `BankDatabase` to an `Account` (message `1.1` and message `2.1`). To provide the `ATM` with the two balances of the user's `Account` (as requested by messages 1 and 2), the `BankDatabase` must pass a `getAvailableBalance` and a `getTotalBalance` message to the user's `Account`. Such messages passed within the handling of another message are called **nested messages**. The UML recommends using a decimal numbering scheme to indicate nested messages. For example, message `1.1` is the first message nested in message 1—the `BankDatabase` passes a `getAvailableBalance` message during `BankDatabase`'s processing of a message by the same name. [*Note:* If the `BankDatabase` needed to pass a second nested message while processing message 1, the second message would be numbered `1.2`.] A message may be passed only when all the nested messages from the previous message have been passed. For example, the `BalanceInquiry` passes message 3 only after messages 2 and `2.1` have been passed, in that order.

The nested numbering scheme used in communication diagrams helps clarify precisely when and in what context each message is passed. For example, if we numbered the messages in Fig. 7.24 using a flat numbering scheme (i.e., 1, 2, 3, 4, 5), someone looking at the diagram might not be able to determine that `BankDatabase` passes the `getAvailableBalance` message (message `1.1`) to an `Account` *during* the `BankDatabase`'s processing of message 1, as opposed to *after* completing the processing of message 1. The nested decimal numbers make it clear that the second `getAvailableBalance` message (message `1.1`) is passed to an `Account` within the handling of the first `getAvailableBalance` message (message 1) by the `BankDatabase`.

Sequence Diagrams

Communication diagrams emphasize the participants in collaborations, but model their timing a bit awkwardly. A sequence diagram helps model the timing of collaborations more clearly. Figure 7.25 shows a sequence diagram modeling the sequence of interactions that occur when a `Withdrawal` executes. The dotted line extending down from an object's rectangle is that object's **lifeline**, which represents the progression of time. Actions occur along an object's lifeline in chronological order from top to bottom—an action near the top happens before one near the bottom.

Message passing in sequence diagrams is similar to message passing in communication diagrams. A solid arrow with a filled arrowhead extending from the sending object to the receiving object represents a message between two objects. The arrowhead points to an activation on the receiving object's lifeline. An **activation**, shown as a thin vertical rectangle, indicates that an object is executing. When an object returns control, a return message, represented as a dashed line with a stick arrowhead, extends from the activation of the object returning control to the activation of the object that initially sent the message. To eliminate clutter, we omit the return-message arrows—the UML allows this practice to make diagrams more readable. Like communication diagrams, sequence diagrams can indicate message parameters between the parentheses following a message name.

The sequence of messages in Fig. 7.25 begins when a `Withdrawal` prompts the user to choose a withdrawal amount by sending a `displayMessage` message to the `Screen`. The `Withdrawal` then sends a `getInput` message to the `Keypad`, which obtains input from the

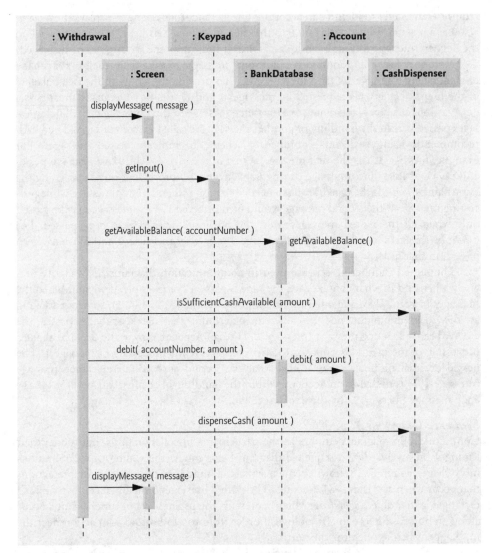

Fig. 7.25 | Sequence diagram that models a `Withdrawal` executing.

user. We have already modeled the control logic involved in a `Withdrawal` in the activity diagram of Fig. 5.22, so we do not show this logic in the sequence diagram of Fig. 7.25. Instead, we model the best-case scenario in which the balance of the user's account is greater than or equal to the chosen withdrawal amount, and the cash dispenser contains a sufficient amount of cash to satisfy the request. For information on how to model control logic in a sequence diagram, please refer to the web resources and recommended readings listed at the end of Section 2.8.

After obtaining a withdrawal amount, the `Withdrawal` sends a `getAvailableBalance` message to the `BankDatabase`, which in turn sends a `getAvailableBalance` message to the user's `Account`. Assuming that the user's account has enough money available to permit the transaction, the `Withdrawal` next sends an `isSufficientCashAvailable` message to the CashDispenser. Assuming that there is enough cash available, the Withdrawal decreases the balance of the user's account (i.e., both the totalBalance and the availableBalance) by sending a debit message to the BankDatabase. The BankDatabase responds by sending a debit message to the user's Account. Finally, the Withdrawal sends a dispenseCash message to the CashDispenser and a displayMessage message to the Screen, telling the user to remove the cash from the machine.

We have identified the collaborations among objects in the ATM system and modeled some of these collaborations using UML interaction diagrams—both communication diagrams and sequence diagrams. In the next Software Engineering Case Study section (Section 8.18), we enhance the structure of our model to complete a preliminary object-oriented design, then we begin implementing the ATM system in Java.

Software Engineering Case Study Self-Review Exercises

7.1   A(n) _____ consists of an object of one class sending a message to an object of another class.
   a) association
   b) aggregation
   c) collaboration
   d) composition

7.2   Which form of interaction diagram emphasizes *what* collaborations occur? Which form emphasizes *when* collaborations occur?

7.3   Create a sequence diagram that models the interactions among objects in the ATM system that occur when a Deposit executes successfully, and explain the sequence of messages modeled by the diagram.

Answers to Software Engineering Case Study Self-Review Exercises

7.1   c.

7.2   Communication diagrams emphasize *what* collaborations occur. Sequence diagrams emphasize *when* collaborations occur.

7.3   Figure 7.26 presents a sequence diagram that models the interactions between objects in the ATM system that occur when a Deposit executes successfully. Figure 7.26 indicates that a Deposit first sends a displayMessage message to the Screen to ask the user to enter a deposit amount. Next the Deposit sends a getInput message to the Keypad to receive input from the user. The Deposit then instructs the user to enter a deposit envelope by sending a displayMessage message to the Screen. The Deposit next sends an isEnvelopeReceived message to the DepositSlot to confirm that the deposit envelope has been received by the ATM. Finally, the Deposit increases the totalBalance attribute (but not the availableBalance attribute) of the user's Account by sending a credit message to the BankDatabase. The BankDatabase responds by sending the same message to the user's Account.

7.14 Wrap-Up

This chapter began our introduction to data structures, exploring the use of arrays to store data in and retrieve data from lists and tables of values. The chapter examples demonstrated how to declare an array, initialize an array and refer to individual elements of an array. The chapter introduced the enhanced for statement to iterate through arrays. We also illustrated how to pass arrays to methods and how to declare and manipulate multidimen-

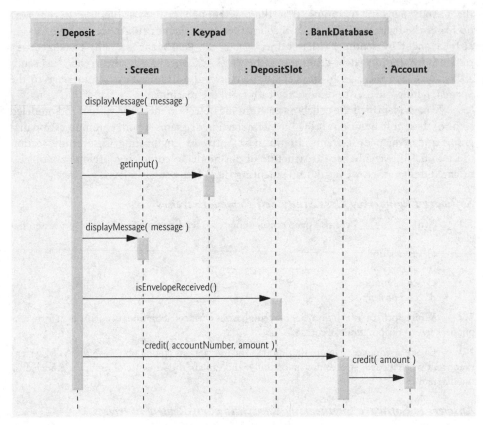

Fig. 7.26 | Sequence diagram that models a `Deposit` executing.

sional arrays. Finally, the chapter showed how to write methods that use variable-length argument lists and how to read arguments passed to a program from the command line.

We continue our coverage of data structures in Chapter 15 with generics, which provide the means to create general models of methods and classes that can be declared once, but used with many different data types. In Chapter 16, Collections, we introduce the Java Collections Framework, which uses generics to allow you to specify the exact types of objects that a particular data structure will store. Chapter 16 also introduces Java's predefined data structures, which you can use instead of building your own. Chapter 16 discusses many data structures classes, including `Vector` and `ArrayList`, which are array-like data structures that can grow and shrink in response to a program's changing storage requirements. The Collections API also provides class `Arrays`, which contains utility methods for array manipulation. Chapter 16 uses several `static` methods of class `Arrays` to perform such manipulations as sorting and searching the data in an array. You'll be able to use some of the `Arrays` methods discussed in Chapter 16 after reading the current chapter, but some of the `Arrays` methods require knowledge of concepts presented later in the book.

We have now introduced the basic concepts of classes, objects, control statements, methods and arrays. In Chapter 8, we take a deeper look at classes and objects.

8

Classes and Objects: A Deeper Look

OBJECTIVES

In this chapter you'll learn:

- Encapsulation and data hiding.

- The notions of data abstraction and abstract data types (ADTs).

- To use keyword `this`.

- To use `static` variables and methods.

- To import `static` members of a class.

- To use the `enum` type to create sets of constants with unique identifiers.

- To declare `enum` constants with parameters.

- To organize classes in packages to promote reuse.

Outline

8.1 Introduction

8.2 Time Class Case Study

8.3 Controlling Access to Members

8.4 Referring to the Current Object's Members with the `this` Reference

8.5 Time Class Case Study: Overloaded Constructors

8.6 Default and No-Argument Constructors

8.7 Notes on *Set* and *Get* Methods

8.8 Composition

8.9 Enumerations

8.10 Garbage Collection and Method `finalize`

8.11 `static` Class Members

8.12 `static` Import

8.13 `final` Instance Variables

8.14 Software Reusability

8.15 Data Abstraction and Encapsulation

8.16 Time Class Case Study: Creating Packages

8.17 Package Access

8.18 (Optional) Software Engineering Case Study: Starting to Program the Classes of the ATM System

8.19 Wrap-Up

8.1 Introduction

In our prior discussions of object-oriented programs, we introduced many basic concepts and terminology that relate to Java object-oriented programming (OOP). We also discussed our program development methodology: We selected appropriate variables and methods for each program and specified the manner in which an object of our class collaborated with objects of Java API classes to accomplish the program's overall goals.

In this chapter, we take a deeper look at building classes, controlling access to members of a class and creating constructors. We discuss composition—a capability that allows a class to have references to objects of other classes as members. We reexamine the use of *set* and *get* methods and further explore the class type enum that enables programmers to declare and manipulate sets of unique identifiers that represent constant values. In Section 6.10, we introduced the basic enum type, which appeared within another class and simply declared a set of constants. In this chapter, we discuss the relationship between enum types and classes, demonstrating that an enum, like a class, can be declared in its own file with constructors, methods and fields. The chapter also discusses static class members and final instance variables in detail. We investigate issues such as software reusability, data abstraction and encapsulation. Finally, we explain how to organize classes in packages to help manage large applications and promote reuse, then show a special relationship between classes in the same package.

Chapter 9, Object-Oriented Programming: Inheritance, and Chapter 10, Object-Oriented Programming: Polymorphism, introduce two additional key object-oriented programming technologies.

8.2 Time Class Case Study

Time1 Class Declaration

Our first example consists of two classes—Time1 (Fig. 8.1) and Time1Test (Fig. 8.2). Class Time1 represents the time of day. Class Time1Test is an application class in which the main method creates one object of class Time1 and invokes its methods. These classes must be declared in separate files because they are both public classes. The output of this program appears in Fig. 8.2.

Class Time1 contains three private instance variables of type int (Fig. 8.1, lines 6–8)—hour, minute and second—that represent the time in universal-time format (24-hour clock format in which hours are in the range 0–23). Class Time1 contains public methods setTime (lines 12–17), toUniversalString (lines 20–23) and toString (lines 26–31). These methods are also called the ***public services*** or the ***public interface*** that the class provides to its clients.

In this example, class Time1 does not declare a constructor, so the class has a default constructor that is supplied by the compiler. Each instance variable implicitly receives the

```java
 1   // Fig. 8.1: Time1.java
 2   // Time1 class declaration maintains the time in 24-hour format.
 3
 4   public class Time1
 5   {
 6      private int hour;    // 0 - 23
 7      private int minute;  // 0 - 59
 8      private int second;  // 0 - 59
 9
10      // set a new time value using universal time; ensure that
11      // the data remains consistent by setting invalid values to zero
12      public void setTime( int h, int m, int s )
13      {
14         hour = ( ( h >= 0 && h < 24 ) ? h : 0 );   // validate hour
15         minute = ( ( m >= 0 && m < 60 ) ? m : 0 ); // validate minute
16         second = ( ( s >= 0 && s < 60 ) ? s : 0 ); // validate second
17      } // end method setTime
18
19      // convert to String in universal-time format (HH:MM:SS)
20      public String toUniversalString()
21      {
22         return String.format( "%02d:%02d:%02d", hour, minute, second );
23      } // end method toUniversalString
24
25      // convert to String in standard-time format (H:MM:SS AM or PM)
26      public String toString()
27      {
28         return String.format( "%d:%02d:%02d %s",
29            ( ( hour == 0 || hour == 12 ) ? 12 : hour % 12 ),
30            minute, second, ( hour < 12 ? "AM" : "PM" ) );
31      } // end method toString
32   } // end class Time1
```

Fig. 8.1 | Time1 class declaration maintains the time in 24-hour format.

default value 0 for an int. Note that instance variables also can be initialized when they are declared in the class body using the same initialization syntax as with a local variable.

Method setTime (lines 12–17) is a public method that declares three int parameters and uses them to set the time. A conditional expression tests each argument to determine whether the value is in a specified range. For example, the hour value (line 14) must be greater than or equal to 0 and less than 24, because universal-time format represents hours as integers from 0 to 23 (e.g., 1 PM is hour 13 and 11 PM is hour 23; midnight is hour 0 and noon is hour 12). Similarly, both minute and second values (lines 15 and 16) must be greater than or equal to 0 and less than 60. Any values outside these ranges are set to zero to ensure that a Time1 object always contains *consistent data*—that is, the object's data values are always kept in range, even if the values provided as arguments to method setTime were *incorrect*. In this example, zero is a consistent value for hour, minute and second.

A value passed to setTime is a correct value if it is in the allowed range for the member it is initializing. So, any number in the range 0–23 would be a correct value for the hour. A correct value is always a consistent value. However, a consistent value is not necessarily a correct value. If setTime sets hour to 0 because the argument received was out of range, then setTime is taking an incorrect value and making it consistent, so the object remains in a consistent state at all times. The *correct* time of day could actually be 11 AM, but because the person may have accidentally entered an out-of-range (incorrect) time, we choose to set the hour to the consistent value of zero. In this case, you might want to indicate that the object is incorrect. In Chapter 13, Exception Handling, you'll learn elegant techniques that enable your classes to indicate when incorrect values are received.

Software Engineering Observation 8.1

Methods that modify the values of private variables should verify that the intended new values are proper. If they are not, the set methods should place the private variables into an appropriate consistent state.

Method toUniversalString (lines 20–23) takes no arguments and returns a String in universal-time format, consisting of six digits—two for the hour, two for the minute and two for the second. For example, if the time were 1:30:07 PM, method toUniversal-String would return 13:30:07. The return statement (line 22) uses static method *format* of class String to return a String containing the formatted hour, minute and second values, each with two digits and possibly a leading 0 (specified with the 0 flag). Method format is similar to method System.out.printf except that format returns a formatted String rather than displaying it in a command window. The formatted String is returned by method toUniversalString.

Method toString (lines 26–31) takes no arguments and returns a String in standard-time format, consisting of the hour, minute and second values separated by colons and followed by an AM or PM indicator (e.g., 1:27:06 PM). Like method toUniversal-String, method toString uses static String method format to format the minute and second as two-digit values with leading zeros if necessary. Line 29 uses a conditional operator (?:) to determine the value for hour in the string—if the hour is 0 or 12 (AM or PM), it appears as 12—otherwise, the hour appears as a value from 1 to 11. The conditional operator in line 30 determines whether AM or PM will be returned as part of the String.

Recall from Section 6.4 that all objects in Java have a toString method that returns a String representation of the object. We chose to return a String containing the time in standard-time format. Method toString can be called implicitly whenever a Time1 object appears in the code where a String is needed, such as the value to output with a %s format specifier in a call to System.out.printf.

Using Class Time1

As you learned in Chapter 3, each class you declare represents a new type in Java. Therefore, after declaring class Time1, we can use it as a type in declarations such as

```
Time1 sunset; // sunset can hold a reference to a Time1 object
```

The Time1Test application class (Fig. 8.2) uses class Time1. Line 9 declares and creates a Time1 object and assigns it to local variable time. Note that new implicitly invokes class Time1's default constructor, since Time1 does not declare any constructors. Lines 12–16 output the time first in universal-time format (by invoking time's toUniversalString method in line 13), then in standard-time format (by explicitly invoking time's toString method in line 15) to confirm that the Time1 object was initialized properly.

```java
 1   // Fig. 8.2: Time1Test.java
 2   // Time1 object used in an application.
 3
 4   public class Time1Test
 5   {
 6      public static void main( String args[] )
 7      {
 8         // create and initialize a Time1 object
 9         Time1 time = new Time1(); // invokes Time1 constructor
10
11         // output string representations of the time
12         System.out.print( "The initial universal time is: " );
13         System.out.println( time.toUniversalString() );
14         System.out.print( "The initial standard time is: " );
15         System.out.println( time.toString() );
16         System.out.println(); // output a blank line
17
18         // change time and output updated time
19         time.setTime( 13, 27, 6 );
20         System.out.print( "Universal time after setTime is: " );
21         System.out.println( time.toUniversalString() );
22         System.out.print( "Standard time after setTime is: " );
23         System.out.println( time.toString() );
24         System.out.println(); // output a blank line
25
26         // set time with invalid values; output updated time
27         time.setTime( 99, 99, 99 );
28         System.out.println( "After attempting invalid settings:" );
29         System.out.print( "Universal time: " );
30         System.out.println( time.toUniversalString() );
31         System.out.print( "Standard time: " );
32         System.out.println( time.toString() );
33      } // end main
34   } // end class Time1Test
```

Fig. 8.2 | Time1 object used in an application. (Part 1 of 2.)

```
The initial universal time is: 00:00:00
The initial standard time is: 12:00:00 AM

Universal time after setTime is: 13:27:06
Standard time after setTime is: 1:27:06 PM

After attempting invalid settings:
Universal time: 00:00:00
Standard time: 12:00:00 AM
```

Fig. 8.2 | `Time1` object used in an application. (Part 2 of 2.)

Line 19 invokes method `setTime` of the `time` object to change the time. Then lines 20–24 output the time again in both formats to confirm that the time was set correctly.

To illustrate that method `setTime` maintains the object in a consistent state, line 27 calls method `setTime` with arguments of 99 for the `hour`, `minute` and `second`. Lines 28–32 output the time again in both formats to confirm that `setTime` maintained the object's consistent state, then the program terminates. The last two lines of the application's output show that the time is reset to midnight—the initial value of a `Time1` object—after an attempt to set the time with three out-of-range values.

Notes on the *Time1* Class Declaration

Consider several issues of class design with respect to class `Time1`. The instance variables `hour`, `minute` and `second` are each declared `private`. The actual data representation used within the class is of no concern to the class's clients. For example, it would be perfectly reasonable for `Time1` to represent the time internally as the number of seconds since midnight or the number of minutes and seconds since midnight. Clients could use the same `public` methods and get the same results without being aware of this.

Software Engineering Observation 8.2

Classes simplify programming, because the client can use only the `public` *methods exposed by the class. Such methods are usually client oriented rather than implementation oriented. Clients are neither aware of, nor involved in, a class's implementation. Clients generally care about what the class does but not* how *the class does it.*

Software Engineering Observation 8.3

Interfaces change less frequently than implementations. When an implementation changes, implementation-dependent code must change accordingly. Hiding the implementation reduces the possibility that other program parts will become dependent on class implementation details.

8.3 Controlling Access to Members

The access modifiers `public` and `private` control access to a class's variables and methods. (In Chapter 9, we'll introduce the additional access modifier `protected`.) As we stated in Section 8.2, the primary purpose of `public` methods is to present to the class's clients a view of the services the class provides (the class's public interface). Clients of the class need not be concerned with how the class accomplishes its tasks. For this reason, the `private` variables and `private` methods of a class (i.e., the class's implementation details) are not directly accessible to the class's clients.

Figure 8.3 demonstrates that private class members are not directly accessible outside the class. Lines 9–11 attempt to access directly the private instance variables hour, minute and second of the Time1 object time. When this program is compiled, the compiler generates error messages stating that these private members are not accessible. [*Note:* This program assumes that the Time1 class from Fig. 8.1 is used.]

Common Programming Error 8.1

An attempt by a method that is not a member of a class to access a private member of that class is a compilation error.

```
1   // Fig. 8.3: MemberAccessTest.java
2   // Private members of class Time1 are not accessible.
3   public class MemberAccessTest
4   {
5      public static void main( String args[] )
6      {
7         Time1 time = new Time1(); // create and initialize Time1 object
8
9         time.hour = 7;    // error: hour has private access in Time1
10        time.minute = 15; // error: minute has private access in Time1
11        time.second = 30; // error: second has private access in Time1
12     } // end main
13  } // end class MemberAccessTest
```

```
MemberAccessTest.java:9: hour has private access in Time1
      time.hour = 7;    // error: hour has private access in Time1
          ^
MemberAccessTest.java:10: minute has private access in Time1
      time.minute = 15; // error: minute has private access in Time1
          ^
MemberAccessTest.java:11: second has private access in Time1
      time.second = 30; // error: second has private access in Time1
          ^
3 errors
```

Fig. 8.3 | Private members of class Time1 are not accessible.

8.4 Referring to the Current Object's Members with the this Reference

Every object can access a reference to itself with keyword ***this*** (sometimes called the ***this reference***). When a non-static method is called for a particular object, the method's body implicitly uses keyword this to refer to the object's instance variables and other methods. As you'll see in Fig. 8.4, you can also use keyword this explicitly in a non-static method's body. Section 8.5 shows another interesting use of keyword this. Section 8.11 explains why keyword this cannot be used in a static method.

We now demonstrate implicit and explicit use of the this reference to enable class ThisTest's main method to display the private data of a class SimpleTime object (Fig. 8.4). Note that this example is the first in which we declare two classes in one file—class ThisTest is declared in lines 4–11, and class SimpleTime is declared in lines 14–47.

```
1   // Fig. 8.4: ThisTest.java
2   // this used implicitly and explicitly to refer to members of an object.
3
4   public class ThisTest
5   {
6      public static void main( String args[] )
7      {
8         SimpleTime time = new SimpleTime( 15, 30, 19 );
9         System.out.println( time.buildString() );
10     } // end main
11  } // end class ThisTest
12
13  // class SimpleTime demonstrates the "this" reference
14  class SimpleTime
15  {
16     private int hour;   // 0-23
17     private int minute; // 0-59
18     private int second; // 0-59
19
20     // if the constructor uses parameter names identical to
21     // instance variable names the "this" reference is
22     // required to distinguish between names
23     public SimpleTime( int hour, int minute, int second )
24     {
25        this.hour = hour;      // set "this" object's hour
26        this.minute = minute;  // set "this" object's minute
27        this.second = second;  // set "this" object's second
28     } // end SimpleTime constructor
29
30     // use explicit and implicit "this" to call toUniversalString
31     public String buildString()
32     {
33        return String.format( "%24s: %s\n%24s: %s",
34           "this.toUniversalString()", this.toUniversalString(),
35           "toUniversalString()", toUniversalString() );
36     } // end method buildString
37
38     // convert to String in universal-time format (HH:MM:SS)
39     public String toUniversalString()
40     {
41        // "this" is not required here to access instance variables,
42        // because method does not have local variables with same
43        // names as instance variables
44        return String.format( "%02d:%02d:%02d",
45           this.hour, this.minute, this.second );
46     } // end method toUniversalString
47  } // end class SimpleTime
```

```
this.toUniversalString(): 15:30:19
   toUniversalString(): 15:30:19
```

Fig. 8.4 | this used implicitly and explicitly to refer to members of an object.

We did this to demonstrate that when you compile a `.java` file that contains more than one class, the compiler produces a separate class file with the `.class` extension for every compiled class. In this case two separate files are produced—`SimpleTime.class` and `ThisTest.class`. When one source-code (`.java`) file contains multiple class declarations, the class files for those classes are both placed in the same directory by the compiler. Also, note that only class `ThisTest` is declared `public` in Fig. 8.4. A source-code file can contain only one `public` class—otherwise, a compilation error occurs.

Class `SimpleTime` (lines 14–47) declares three `private` instance variables—hour, minute and second (lines 16–18). The constructor (lines 23–28) receives three `int` arguments to initialize a `SimpleTime` object. Note that we used parameter names for the constructor (line 23) that are identical to the class's instance variable names (lines 16–18). We don't recommend this practice, but we did it here to shadow (hide) the corresponding instance variables so that we could illustrate explicit use of the `this` reference. If a method contains a local variable with the same name as a field, that method will refer to the local variable rather than the field. In this case, the local variable shadows the field in the method's scope. However, the method can use the `this` reference to refer to the shadowed field explicitly, as shown in lines 25–27 for `SimpleTime`'s shadowed instance variables.

Method `buildString` (lines 31–36) returns a `String` created by a statement that uses the `this` reference explicitly and implicitly. Line 34 uses the `this` reference explicitly to call method `toUniversalString`. Line 35 uses the `this` reference implicitly to call the same method. Note that both lines perform the same task. Programmers typically do not use `this` explicitly to reference other methods within the current object. Also, note that line 45 in method `toUniversalString` explicitly uses the `this` reference to access each instance variable. This is not necessary here, because the method does not have any local variables that shadow the instance variables of the class.

Common Programming Error 8.2

It is often a logic error when a method contains a parameter or local variable that has the same name as a field of the class. In this case, use reference `this` if you wish to access the field of the class—otherwise, the method parameter or local variable will be referenced.

Error-Prevention Tip 8.1

Avoid method parameter names or local variable names that conflict with field names. This helps prevent subtle, hard-to-locate bugs.

Application class `ThisTest` (lines 4–11) demonstrates class `SimpleTime`. Line 8 creates an instance of class `SimpleTime` and invokes its constructor. Line 9 invokes the object's `buildString` method, then displays the results.

Performance Tip 8.1

Java conserves storage by maintaining only one copy of each method per class—this method is invoked by every object of the class. Each object, on the other hand, has its own copy of the class's instance variables (i.e., non-`static` fields). Each method of the class implicitly uses `this` to determine the specific object of the class to manipulate.

8.5 Time Class Case Study: Overloaded Constructors

As you know, you can declare your own constructor to specify how objects of a class should be initialized. Next, we demonstrate a class with several *overloaded constructors* that enable objects of that class to be initialized in different ways. To overload constructors, simply provide multiple constructor declarations with different signatures. Recall from Section 6.12 that the compiler differentiates signatures by the number of parameters, the types of the parameters and the order of the parameter types in each signature.

Class Time2 with Overloaded Constructors

The default constructor for class Time1 (Fig. 8.1) initialized hour, minute and second to their default 0 values (which is midnight in universal time). The default constructor does not enable the class's clients to initialize the time with specific nonzero values. Class Time2 (Fig. 8.5) contains five overloaded constructors that provide convenient ways to initialize objects of the new class Time2. Each constructor initializes the object to begin in a consistent state. In this program, four of the constructors invoke a fifth, which in turn calls method setTime to ensure that the value supplied for hour is in the range 0 to 23, and the values for minute and second are each in the range 0 to 59. If a value is out of range, it is set to zero by setTime (once again ensuring that each instance variable remains in a consistent state). The compiler invokes the appropriate constructor by matching the number, types and order of the types of the arguments specified in the constructor call with the number, types and order of the types of the parameters specified in each constructor declaration. Note that class Time2 also provides *set* and *get* methods for each instance variable.

```java
1   // Fig. 8.5: Time2.java
2   // Time2 class declaration with overloaded constructors.
3
4   public class Time2
5   {
6      private int hour;   // 0 - 23
7      private int minute; // 0 - 59
8      private int second; // 0 - 59
9
10     // Time2 no-argument constructor: initializes each instance variable
11     // to zero; ensures that Time2 objects start in a consistent state
12     public Time2()
13     {
14        this( 0, 0, 0 ); // invoke Time2 constructor with three arguments
15     } // end Time2 no-argument constructor
16
17     // Time2 constructor: hour supplied, minute and second defaulted to 0
18     public Time2( int h )
19     {
20        this( h, 0, 0 ); // invoke Time2 constructor with three arguments
21     } // end Time2 one-argument constructor
22
23     // Time2 constructor: hour and minute supplied, second defaulted to 0
24     public Time2( int h, int m )
25     {
26        this( h, m, 0 ); // invoke Time2 constructor with three arguments
27     } // end Time2 two-argument constructor
28
```

Fig. 8.5 | Time2 class with overloaded constructors. (Part 1 of 3.)

```
29    // Time2 constructor: hour, minute and second supplied
30    public Time2( int h, int m, int s )
31    {
32       setTime( h, m, s ); // invoke setTime to validate time
33    } // end Time2 three-argument constructor
34
35    // Time2 constructor: another Time2 object supplied
36    public Time2( Time2 time )
37    {
38       // invoke Time2 three-argument constructor
39       this( time.getHour(), time.getMinute(), time.getSecond() );
40    } // end Time2 constructor with a Time2 object argument
41
42    // Set Methods
43    // set a new time value using universal time; ensure that
44    // the data remains consistent by setting invalid values to zero
45    public void setTime( int h, int m, int s )
46    {
47       setHour( h );   // set the hour
48       setMinute( m ); // set the minute
49       setSecond( s ); // set the second
50    } // end method setTime
51
52    // validate and set hour
53    public void setHour( int h )
54    {
55       hour = ( ( h >= 0 && h < 24 ) ? h : 0 );
56    } // end method setHour
57
58    // validate and set minute
59    public void setMinute( int m )
60    {
61       minute = ( ( m >= 0 && m < 60 ) ? m : 0 );
62    } // end method setMinute
63
64    // validate and set second
65    public void setSecond( int s )
66    {
67       second = ( ( s >= 0 && s < 60 ) ? s : 0 );
68    } // end method setSecond
69
70    // Get Methods
71    // get hour value
72    public int getHour()
73    {
74       return hour;
75    } // end method getHour
76
77    // get minute value
78    public int getMinute()
79    {
80       return minute;
81    } // end method getMinute
```

Fig. 8.5 | Time2 class with overloaded constructors. (Part 2 of 3.)

```
82
83       // get second value
84       public int getSecond()
85       {
86          return second;
87       } // end method getSecond
88
89       // convert to String in universal-time format (HH:MM:SS)
90       public String toUniversalString()
91       {
92          return String.format(
93             "%02d:%02d:%02d", getHour(), getMinute(), getSecond() );
94       } // end method toUniversalString
95
96       // convert to String in standard-time format (H:MM:SS AM or PM)
97       public String toString()
98       {
99          return String.format( "%d:%02d:%02d %s",
100            ( (getHour() == 0 || getHour() == 12) ? 12 : getHour() % 12 ),
101            getMinute(), getSecond(), ( getHour() < 12 ? "AM" : "PM" ) );
102      } // end method toString
103   } // end class Time2
```

Fig. 8.5 | Time2 class with overloaded constructors. (Part 3 of 3.)

Class Time2's Constructors

Lines 12–15 declare a so-called *no-argument constructor*—that is, a constructor invoked without arguments. Such a constructor simply initializes the object as specified in the constructor's body. In the body, we introduce a use of the this reference that is allowed only as the first statement in a constructor's body. Line 14 uses this in method-call syntax to invoke the Time2 constructor that takes three arguments (lines 30–33). The no-argument constructor passes values of 0 for the hour, minute and second to the constructor with three parameters. Using the this reference as shown here is a popular way to reuse initialization code provided by another of the class's constructors rather than defining similar code in the no-argument constructor's body. We use this syntax in four of the five Time2 constructors to make the class easier to maintain and modify. If we need to change how objects of class Time2 are initialized, only the constructor that the class's other constructors call will need to be modified. In fact, even that constructor might not need modification in this example. That constructor simply calls the setTime method to perform the actual initialization, so it is possible that the changes the class might require would be localized to the *set* methods.

Common Programming Error 8.3

It is a syntax error when this is used in a constructor's body to call another constructor of the same class if that call is not the first statement in the constructor. It is also a syntax error when a method attempts to invoke a constructor directly via this.

Lines 18–21 declare a Time2 constructor with a single int parameter representing the hour, which is passed with 0 for the minute and second to the constructor at lines 30–33. Lines 24–27 declare a Time2 constructor that receives two int parameters representing the hour and minute, which are passed with 0 for the second to the constructor at lines 30–33. Like the no-argument constructor, each of these constructors invokes the constructor at lines 30–33 to minimize code duplication. Lines 30–33 declare the Time2 constructor that receives three int parameters representing the hour, minute and second. This constructor calls setTime to initialize the instance variables to consistent values.

Common Programming Error 8.4

A constructor can call methods of the class. Be aware that the instance variables might not yet be in a consistent state, because the constructor is in the process of initializing the object. Using instance variables before they have been initialized properly is a logic error.

Lines 36–40 declare a Time2 constructor that receives a Time2 reference to another Time2 object. In this case, the values from the Time2 argument are passed to the three-argument constructor at lines 30–33 to initialize the hour, minute and second. Note that line 39 could have directly accessed the hour, minute and second values of the constructor's argument time with the expressions time.hour, time.minute and time.second—even though hour, minute and second are declared as private variables of class Time2. This is due to a special relationship between objects of the same class. We'll see in a moment why it's preferable to use the *get* methods.

Software Engineering Observation 8.4

When one object of a class has a reference to another object of the same class, the first object can access all the second object's data and methods (including those that are private).

Notes Regarding Class Time2's Set and Get Methods and Constructors

Note that Time2's *set* and *get* methods are called throughout the body of the class. In particular, method setTime calls methods setHour, setMinute and setSecond in lines 47–49, and methods toUniversalString and toString call methods getHour, getMinute and getSecond in line 93 and lines 100–101, respectively. In each case, these methods could have accessed the class's private data directly without calling the *set* and *get* methods. However, consider changing the representation of the time from three int values (requiring 12 bytes of memory) to a single int value representing the total number of seconds that have elapsed since midnight (requiring only 4 bytes of memory). If we made such a change, only the bodies of the methods that access the private data directly would need to change—in particular, the individual *set* and *get* methods for the hour, minute and second. There would be no need to modify the bodies of methods setTime, toUniversalString or toString because they do not access the data directly. Designing the class in this manner reduces the likelihood of programming errors when altering the class's implementation.

Similarly, each Time2 constructor could be written to include a copy of the appropriate statements from methods setHour, setMinute and setSecond. Doing so may be slightly more efficient, because the extra constructor call and call to setTime are eliminated. However, duplicating statements in multiple methods or constructors makes changing the class's internal data representation more difficult. Having the Time2 constructors call the constructor with three arguments (or even call setTime directly) requires any changes to the implementation of setTime to be made only once.

Software Engineering Observation 8.5

When implementing a method of a class, use the class's set and get methods to access the class's private data. This simplifies code maintenance and reduces the likelihood of errors.

Using Class Time2's Overloaded Constructors

Class Time2Test (Fig. 8.6) creates six Time2 objects (lines 8–13) to invoke the overloaded Time2 constructors. Line 8 shows that the no-argument constructor (lines 12–15 of Fig. 8.5) is invoked by placing an empty set of parentheses after the class name when allocating a Time2 object with new. Lines 9–13 of the program demonstrate passing arguments to the other Time2 constructors. Line 9 invokes the constructor at lines 18–21 of Fig. 8.5. Line 10 invokes the constructor at lines 24–27 of Fig. 8.5. Lines 11–12 invoke the constructor at lines 30–33 of Fig. 8.5. Line 13 invokes the constructor at lines 36–40 of Fig. 8.5. The application displays the String representation of each initialized Time2 object to confirm that it was initialized properly.

```java
 1   // Fig. 8.6: Time2Test.java
 2   // Overloaded constructors used to initialize Time2 objects.
 3
 4   public class Time2Test
 5   {
 6      public static void main( String args[] )
 7      {
 8         Time2 t1 = new Time2();            // 00:00:00
 9         Time2 t2 = new Time2( 2 );         // 02:00:00
10         Time2 t3 = new Time2( 21, 34 );    // 21:34:00
11         Time2 t4 = new Time2( 12, 25, 42 ); // 12:25:42
12         Time2 t5 = new Time2( 27, 74, 99 ); // 00:00:00
13         Time2 t6 = new Time2( t4 );        // 12:25:42
14
15         System.out.println( "Constructed with:" );
16         System.out.println( "t1: all arguments defaulted" );
17         System.out.printf( "   %s\n", t1.toUniversalString() );
18         System.out.printf( "   %s\n", t1.toString() );
19
20         System.out.println(
21            "t2: hour specified; minute and second defaulted" );
22         System.out.printf( "   %s\n", t2.toUniversalString() );
23         System.out.printf( "   %s\n", t2.toString() );
24
25         System.out.println(
26            "t3: hour and minute specified; second defaulted" );
27         System.out.printf( "   %s\n", t3.toUniversalString() );
28         System.out.printf( "   %s\n", t3.toString() );
29
30         System.out.println( "t4: hour, minute and second specified" );
31         System.out.printf( "   %s\n", t4.toUniversalString() );
32         System.out.printf( "   %s\n", t4.toString() );
33
34         System.out.println( "t5: all invalid values specified" );
35         System.out.printf( "   %s\n", t5.toUniversalString() );
```

Fig. 8.6 | Overloaded constructors used to initialize Time2 objects. (Part 1 of 2.)

```
36            System.out.printf( "   %s\n", t5.toString() );
37
38            System.out.println( "t6: Time2 object t4 specified" );
39            System.out.printf( "   %s\n", t6.toUniversalString() );
40            System.out.printf( "   %s\n", t6.toString() );
41        } // end main
42    } // end class Time2Test
```

```
t1: all arguments defaulted
   00:00:00
   12:00:00 AM
t2: hour specified; minute and second defaulted
   02:00:00
   2:00:00 AM
t3: hour and minute specified; second defaulted
   21:34:00
   9:34:00 PM
t4: hour, minute and second specified
   12:25:42
   12:25:42 PM
t5: all invalid values specified
   00:00:00
   12:00:00 AM
t6: Time2 object t4 specified
   12:25:42
   12:25:42 PM
```

Fig. 8.6 | Overloaded constructors used to initialize Time2 objects. (Part 2 of 2.)

8.6 Default and No-Argument Constructors

Every class must have at least one constructor. Recall from Section 3.7, that if you do not provide any constructors in a class's declaration, the compiler creates a default constructor that takes no arguments when it is invoked. The default constructor initializes the instance variables to the initial values specified in their declarations or to their default values (zero for primitive numeric types, false for boolean values and null for references). In Section 9.4.1, you'll learn that the default constructor performs another task in addition to initializing each instance variable to its default value.

If your class declares constructors, the compiler will not create a default constructor. In this case, to specify the default initialization for objects of your class, you must declare a no-argument constructor—as in lines 12–15 of Fig. 8.5. Like a default constructor, a no-argument constructor is invoked with empty parentheses. Note that the Time2 no-argument constructor explicitly initializes a Time2 object by passing to the three-argument constructor 0 for each parameter. Since 0 is the default value for int instance variables, the no-argument constructor in this example could actually be declared with an empty body. In this case, each instance variable would receive its default value when the no-argument constructor was called. If we omit the no-argument constructor, clients of this class would not be able to create a Time2 object with the expression new Time2().

Common Programming Error 8.5

If a class has constructors, but none of the public constructors are no-argument constructors, and a program attempts to call a no-argument constructor to initialize an object of the class, a com-

pilation error occurs. A constructor can be called with no arguments only if the class does not have any constructors (in which case the default constructor is called) or if the class has a `public` no-argument constructor.

Software Engineering Observation 8.6

Java allows other methods of the class besides its constructors to have the same name as the class and to specify return types. Such methods are not constructors and will not be called when an object of the class is instantiated. Java determines which methods are constructors by locating the methods that have the same name as the class and do not specify a return type.

8.7 Notes on *Set* and *Get* Methods

As you know, a class's `private` fields can be manipulated only by methods of that class. A typical manipulation might be the adjustment of a customer's bank balance (e.g., a `private` instance variable of a class `BankAccount`) by a method `computeInterest`. Classes often provide `public` methods to allow clients of the class to *set* (i.e., assign values to) or *get* (i.e., obtain the values of) `private` instance variables.

As a naming example, a method that sets instance variable `interestRate` would typically be named `setInterestRate` and a method that gets the `interestRate` would typically be called `getInterestRate`. *Set* methods are also commonly called ***mutator methods***, because they typically change a value. *Get* methods are also commonly called ***accessor methods*** or ***query methods***.

Set *and* Get *Methods vs.* `public` *Data*

It would seem that providing *set* and *get* capabilities is essentially the same as making the instance variables `public`. This is a subtlety of Java that makes the language so desirable for software engineering. A `public` instance variable can be read or written by any method that has a reference to an object that contains the instance variable. If an instance variable is declared `private`, a `public` *get* method certainly allows other methods to access the variable, but the *get* method can control how the client can access the variable. For example, a *get* method might control the format of the data it returns and thus shield the client code from the actual data representation. A `public` *set* method can—and should—carefully scrutinize attempts to modify the variable's value to ensure that the new value is appropriate for that data item. For example, an attempt to *set* the day of the month to 37 would be rejected, an attempt to *set* a person's weight to a negative value would be rejected, and so on. Thus, although *set* and *get* methods provide access to `private` data, the access is restricted by the programmer's implementation of the methods. This helps promote good software engineering.

Validity Checking in Set Methods

The benefits of data integrity are not automatic simply because instance variables are declared `private`—the programmer must provide validity checking. Java enables programmers to design better programs in a convenient manner. A class's *set* methods can return values indicating that attempts were made to assign invalid data to objects of the class. A client of the class can test the return value of a *set* method to determine whether the client's attempt to modify the object was successful and to take appropriate action.

Software Engineering Observation 8.7

When necessary, provide `public` methods to change and retrieve the values of `private` instance variables. This architecture helps hide the implementation of a class from its clients, which improves program modifiability.

Software Engineering Observation 8.8

Class designers need not provide set or get methods for each `private` field. These capabilities should be provided only when it makes sense.

Predicate Methods

Another common use for accessor methods is to test whether a condition is true or false—such methods are often called *predicate methods*. An example would be an `isEmpty` method for a *container class*—a class capable of holding many objects, such as a linked list, a stack or a queue. (These data structures are discussed in Chapter 16.) A program might test `isEmpty` before attempting to read another item from a container object. A program might test `isFull` before attempting to insert another item into a container object.

Using Set and Get Methods to Create a Class That Is Easier to Debug and Maintain

If only one method performs a particular task, such as setting the hour in a `Time2` object, it is easier to debug and maintain the class. If the `hour` is not being set properly, the code that actually modifies instance variable `hour` is localized to one method's body—`setHour`. Thus, your debugging efforts can be focused on method `setHour`.

8.8 Composition

A class can have references to objects of other classes as members. Such a capability is called *composition* and is sometimes referred to as a *has-a relationship*. For example, an object of class `AlarmClock` needs to know the current time and the time when it is supposed to sound its alarm, so it is reasonable to include two references to `Time` objects as members of the `AlarmClock` object.

Software Engineering Observation 8.9

One form of software reuse is composition, in which a class has as members references to objects of other classes.

Our example of composition contains three classes—`Date` (Fig. 8.7), `Employee` (Fig. 8.8) and `EmployeeTest` (Fig. 8.9). Class `Date` (Fig. 8.7) declares instance variables month, day and year (lines 6–8) to represent a date. The constructor receives three `int` parameters. Line 14 invokes utility method `checkMonth` (lines 23–33) to validate the month—an out-of-range value is set to 1 to maintain a consistent state. Line 15 assumes that the value for year is correct and does not validate it. Line 16 invokes utility method `checkDay` (lines 36–52) to validate the value for day based on the current month and year. Lines 42–43 determine whether the day is correct based on the number of days in the particular month. If the day is not correct, lines 46–47 determine whether the month is February, the day is 29 and the year is a leap year. If lines 42–48 do not return a correct value for day, line 51 returns 1 to maintain the `Date` in a consistent state. Note that lines 18–19 in the constructor output the `this` reference as a `String`. Since `this` is a reference to the current Date object, the object's toString method (lines 55–58) is called implicitly to obtain the object's String representation.

```java
1   // Fig. 8.7: Date.java
2   // Date class declaration.
3
4   public class Date
5   {
6      private int month; // 1-12
7      private int day;   // 1-31 based on month
8      private int year;  // any year
9
10     // constructor: call checkMonth to confirm proper value for month;
11     // call checkDay to confirm proper value for day
12     public Date( int theMonth, int theDay, int theYear )
13     {
14        month = checkMonth( theMonth ); // validate month
15        year = theYear; // could validate year
16        day = checkDay( theDay ); // validate day
17
18        System.out.printf(
19           "Date object constructor for date %s\n", this );
20     } // end Date constructor
21
22     // utility method to confirm proper month value
23     private int checkMonth( int testMonth )
24     {
25        if ( testMonth > 0 && testMonth <= 12 ) // validate month
26           return testMonth;
27        else // month is invalid
28        {
29           System.out.printf(
30              "Invalid month (%d) set to 1.", testMonth );
31           return 1; // maintain object in consistent state
32        } // end else
33     } // end method checkMonth
34
35     // utility method to confirm proper day value based on month and year
36     private int checkDay( int testDay )
37     {
38        int daysPerMonth[] =
39           { 0, 31, 28, 31, 30, 31, 30, 31, 31, 30, 31, 30, 31 };
40
41        // check if day in range for month
42        if ( testDay > 0 && testDay <= daysPerMonth[ month ] )
43           return testDay;
44
45        // check for leap year
46        if ( month == 2 && testDay == 29 && ( year % 400 == 0 ||
47           ( year % 4 == 0 && year % 100 != 0 ) ) )
48           return testDay;
49
```

Fig. 8.7 | Date class declaration. (Part 1 of 2.)

```
50          System.out.printf( "Invalid day (%d) set to 1.", testDay );
51          return 1;   // maintain object in consistent state
52       } // end method checkDay
53
54       // return a String of the form month/day/year
55       public String toString()
56       {
57          return String.format( "%d/%d/%d", month, day, year );
58       } // end method toString
59    } // end class Date
```

Fig. 8.7 | Date class declaration. (Part 2 of 2.)

Class Employee (Fig. 8.8) has instance variables firstName, lastName, birthDate and
hireDate. Members birthDate and hireDate (lines 8–9) are references to Date objects.
This demonstrates that a class can have as instance variables references to objects of other
classes. The Employee constructor (lines 12–19) takes four parameters—first, last,
dateOfBirth and dateOfHire. The objects referenced by the parameters dateOfBirth and
dateOfHire are assigned to the Employee object's birthDate and hireDate instance variables, respectively. Note that when class Employee's toString method is called, it returns
a String containing the String representations of the two Date objects. Each of these
Strings is obtained with an implicit call to the Date class's toString method.

```
1    // Fig. 8.8: Employee.java
2    // Employee class with references to other objects.
3
4    public class Employee
5    {
6       private String firstName;
7       private String lastName;
8       private Date birthDate;
9       private Date hireDate;
10
11      // constructor to initialize name, birth date and hire date
12      public Employee( String first, String last, Date dateOfBirth,
13         Date dateOfHire )
14      {
15         firstName = first;
16         lastName = last;
17         birthDate = dateOfBirth;
18         hireDate = dateOfHire;
19      } // end Employee constructor
20
21      // convert Employee to String format
22      public String toString()
23      {
24         return String.format( "%s, %s  Hired: %s  Birthday: %s",
25            lastName, firstName, hireDate, birthDate );
26      } // end method toString
27   } // end class Employee
```

Fig. 8.8 | Employee class with references to other objects.

Class EmployeeTest (Fig. 8.9) creates two Date objects (lines 8–9) to represent an Employee's birthday and hire date, respectively. Line 10 creates an Employee and initializes its instance variables by passing to the constructor two Strings (representing the Employee's first and last names) and two Date objects (representing the birthday and hire date). Line 12 implicitly invokes the Employee's toString method to display the values of its instance variables and demonstrate that the object was initialized properly.

```
1   // Fig. 8.9: EmployeeTest.java
2   // Composition demonstration.
3
4   public class EmployeeTest
5   {
6      public static void main( String args[] )
7      {
8         Date birth = new Date( 7, 24, 1949 );
9         Date hire = new Date( 3, 12, 1988 );
10        Employee employee = new Employee( "Bob", "Blue", birth, hire );
11
12        System.out.println( employee );
13     } // end main
14  } // end class EmployeeTest
```

```
Date object constructor for date 7/24/1949
Date object constructor for date 3/12/1988
Blue, Bob  Hired: 3/12/1988  Birthday: 7/24/1949
```

Fig. 8.9 | Composition demonstration.

8.9 Enumerations

In Fig. 6.8 (Craps.java), we introduced the basic enum type which defines a set of constants that are represented as unique identifiers. In that program, the enum constants represented the game's status. In this section, we discuss the relationship between enum types and classes. Like classes, all enum types are reference types. An enum type is declared with an *enum declaration*, which is a comma-separated list of enum constants—the declaration may optionally include other components of traditional classes, such as constructors, fields and methods. Each enum declaration declares an enum class with the following restrictions:

1. enum types are implicitly final, because they declare constants that should not be modified.

2. enum constants are implicitly static.

3. Any attempt to create an object of an enum type with operator new results in a compilation error.

The enum constants can be used anywhere constants can be used, such as in the case labels of switch statements and to control enhanced for statements.

Figure 8.10 illustrates how to declare instance variables, a constructor and methods in an enum type. The enum declaration (lines 5–37) contains two parts—the enum constants and the other members of the enum type. The first part (lines 8–13) declares six enum constants. Each enum constant is optionally followed by arguments which are passed to the

```
 1   // Fig. 8.10: Book.java
 2   // Declaring an enum type with constructor and explicit instance fields
 3   // and accessors for these fields
 4
 5   public enum Book
 6   {
 7      // declare constants of enum type
 8      JHTP6( "Java How to Program 6e", "2005" ),
 9      CHTP4( "C How to Program 4e", "2004" ),
10      IW3HTP3( "Internet & World Wide Web How to Program 3e", "2004" ),
11      CPPHTP4( "C++ How to Program 4e", "2003" ),
12      VBHTP2( "Visual Basic .NET How to Program 2e", "2002" ),
13      CSHARPHTP( "C# How to Program", "2002" );
14
15      // instance fields
16      private final String title; // book title
17      private final String copyrightYear; // copyright year
18
19      // enum constructor
20      Book( String bookTitle, String year )
21      {
22         title = bookTitle;
23         copyrightYear = year;
24      } // end enum Book constructor
25
26      // accessor for field title
27      public String getTitle()
28      {
29         return title;
30      } // end method getTitle
31
32      // accessor for field copyrightYear
33      public String getCopyrightYear()
34      {
35         return copyrightYear;
36      } // end method getCopyrightYear
37   } // end enum Book
```

Fig. 8.10 | Declaring enum type with instance fields, constructor and methods.

enum constructor (lines 20–24). Like the constructors you have seen in classes, an enum constructor can specify any number of parameters and can be overloaded. In this example, the enum constructor has two String parameters, hence each enum constant is followed by parentheses containing two String arguments. The second part (lines 16–36) declares the other members of the enum type—two instance variables (lines 16–17), a constructor (lines 20–24) and two methods (lines 27–30 and 33–36).

Lines 16–17 declare the instance variables title and copyrightYear. Each enum constant in Book is actually an object of type Book that has its own copy of instance variables title and copyrightYear. The constructor (lines 20–24) takes two String parameters, one that specifies the book title and one that specifies the copyright year of the book. Lines 22–23 assign these parameters to the instance variables. Lines 27–36 declare two methods, which return the book title and copyright year, respectively.

Figure 8.11 tests the enum type declared in Fig. 8.10 and illustrates how to iterate through a range of enum constants. For every enum, the compiler generates the static method **values** (called in line 12) that returns an array of the enum's constants in the order they were declared. Recall from Section 7.6 that the enhanced for statement can be used to iterate through an array. Lines 12–14 use the enhanced for statement to display all the constants declared in the enum Book. Line 14 invokes the enum Book's getTitle and getCopyrightYear methods to get the title and copyright year associated with the constant. Note that when an enum constant is converted to a String (e.g., book in line 13), the constant's identifier is used as the String representation (e.g., JHTP6 for the first enum constant).

```java
1   // Fig. 8.11: EnumTest.java
2   // Testing enum type Book.
3   import java.util.EnumSet;
4
5   public class EnumTest
6   {
7      public static void main( String args[] )
8      {
9         System.out.println( "All books:\n" );
10
11         // print all books in enum Book
12         for ( Book book : Book.values() )
13            System.out.printf( "%-10s%-45s%s\n", book,
14               book.getTitle(), book.getCopyrightYear() );
15
16         System.out.println( "\nDisplay a range of enum constants:\n" );
17
18         // print first four books
19         for ( Book book : EnumSet.range( Book.JHTP6, Book.CPPHTP4 ) )
20            System.out.printf( "%-10s%-45s%s\n", book,
21               book.getTitle(), book.getCopyrightYear() );
22      } // end main
23   } // end class EnumTest
```

```
All books:

JHTP6      Java How to Program 6e                          2005
CHTP4      C How to Program 4e                             2004
IW3HTP3    Internet & World Wide Web How to Program 3e     2004
CPPHTP4    C++ How to Program 4e                           2003
VBHTP2     Visual Basic .NET How to Program 2e             2002
CSHARPHTP  C# How to Program                               2002

Display a range of enum constants:

JHTP6      Java How to Program 6e                          2005
CHTP4      C How to Program 4e                             2004
IW3HTP3    Internet & World Wide Web How to Program 3e     2004
CPPHTP4    C++ How to Program 4e                           2003
```

Fig. 8.11 | Testing an enum type.

Lines 19–21 use the static method *range* of class **EnumSet** (declared in package java.util) to display a range of the enum Book's constants. Method range takes two parameters—the first and the last enum constants in the range—and returns an EnumSet that contains all the constants between these two constants, inclusive. For example, the expression EnumSet.range(Book.JHTP6, Book.CPPHTP4) returns an EnumSet containing Book.JHTP6, Book.CHTP4, Book.IW3HTP3 and Book.CPPHTP4. The enhanced for statement can be used with an EnumSet just as it can with an array, so lines 19–21 use the enhanced for statement to display the title and copyright year of every book in the EnumSet. Class EnumSet provides several other static methods for creating sets of enum constants from the same enum type. For more details of class EnumSet, visit java.sun.com/javase/6/docs/api/java/util/EnumSet.html.

Common Programming Error 8.6

In an enum declaration, it is a syntax error to declare enum constants after the enum type's constructors, fields and methods in the enum declaration.

8.10 Garbage Collection and Method finalize

Every class in Java has the methods of class Object (package java.lang), one of which is the *finalize method*. This method is rarely used. In fact, we searched over 6500 source-code files for the Java API classes and found fewer than 50 declarations of the finalize method. Nevertheless, because finalize is part of every class, we discuss it here to help you understand its intended purpose in case you encounter it in your studies or in industry. The complete details of the finalize method are beyond the scope of this book, and most programmers should not use it—you'll soon see why. You'll learn more about class Object in Chapter 9, Object-Oriented Programming: Inheritance.

Every object you create uses various system resources, such as memory. To avoid "resource leaks," we need a disciplined way to give resources back to the system when they are no longer needed. The Java Virtual Machine (JVM) performs automatic *garbage collection* to reclaim the memory occupied by objects that are no longer in use. When there are no more references to an object, the object is *marked for garbage collection* by the JVM. The memory for such an object can be reclaimed when the JVM executes its *garbage collector*, which is responsible for retrieving the memory of objects that are no longer used so it can be used for other objects. Therefore, memory leaks that are common in other languages like C and C++ (because memory is not automatically reclaimed in those languages) are less likely in Java (but some can still happen in subtle ways). Other types of resource leaks can occur. For example, an application could open a file on disk to modify the file's contents. If the application does not close the file, no other application can use it until the application that opened the file completes.

The finalize method is called by the garbage collector to perform *termination housekeeping* on an object just before the garbage collector reclaims the object's memory. Method finalize does not take parameters and has return type void. A problem with method finalize is that the garbage collector is not guaranteed to execute at a specified time. In fact, the garbage collector may never execute before a program terminates. Thus, it is unclear if, or when, method finalize will be called. For this reason, most programmers should avoid method finalize. In Section 8.11, we demonstrate a situation in which method finalize is called by the garbage collector.

Software Engineering Observation 8.10

A class that uses system resources, such as files on disk, should provide a method to eventually release the resources. Many Java API classes provide close *or* dispose *methods for this purpose. For example, class* Scanner *(java.sun.com/javase/6/docs/api/java/util/Scanner.html) has a* close *method.*

8.11 static Class Members

Every object has its own copy of all the instance variables of the class. In certain cases, only one copy of a particular variable should be shared by all objects of a class. A **static field**—called a **class variable**—is used in such cases. A static variable represents **classwide information**—all objects of the class share the same piece of data. The declaration of a static variable begins with the keyword static.

Let's motivate static data with an example. Suppose that we have a video game with Martians and other space creatures. Each Martian tends to be brave and willing to attack other space creatures when the Martian is aware that at least four other Martians are present. If fewer than five Martians are present, each of them becomes cowardly. Thus each Martian needs to know the martianCount. We could endow class Martian with martianCount as an instance variable. If we do this, then every Martian will have a separate copy of the instance variable, and every time we create a new Martian, we'll have to update the instance variable martianCount in every Martian. This wastes space with the redundant copies, wastes time in updating the separate copies and is error prone. Instead, we declare martianCount to be static, making martianCount classwide data. Every Martian can see the martianCount as if it were an instance variable of class Martian, but only one copy of the static martianCount is maintained. This saves space. We save time by having the Martian constructor increment the static martianCount—there is only one copy, so we do not have to increment separate copies of martianCount for each Martian object.

Software Engineering Observation 8.11

Use a static *variable when all objects of a class must use the same copy of the variable.*

Static variables have class scope. A class's public static members can be accessed through a reference to any object of the class, or by qualifying the member name with the class name and a dot (.), as in Math.random(). A class's private static class members can be accessed only through methods of the class. Actually, static class members exist even when no objects of the class exist—they are available as soon as the class is loaded into memory at execution time. To access a public static member when no objects of the class exist (and even when they do), prefix the class name and a dot (.) to the static member, as in Math.PI. To access a private static member when no objects of the class exist, a public static method must be provided and the method must be called by qualifying its name with the class name and a dot.

Software Engineering Observation 8.12

Static class variables and methods exist, and can be used, even if no objects of that class have been instantiated.

Our next program declares two classes—Employee (Fig. 8.12) and EmployeeTest (Fig. 8.13). Class Employee declares private static variable count (Fig. 8.12, line 9), and public static method getCount (lines 46–49). The static variable count is initialized to zero in line 9. If a static variable is not initialized, the compiler assigns a default value to the variable—in this case 0, the default value for type int. Variable count maintains a count of the number of objects of class Employee that currently reside in memory. This includes objects that have already been marked for garbage collection by the JVM but have not yet been reclaimed by the garbage collector.

```java
1   // Fig. 8.12: Employee.java
2   // Static variable used to maintain a count of the number of
3   // Employee objects in memory.
4
5   public class Employee
6   {
7      private String firstName;
8      private String lastName;
9      private static int count = 0; // number of objects in memory
10
11     // initialize employee, add 1 to static count and
12     // output String indicating that constructor was called
13     public Employee( String first, String last )
14     {
15        firstName = first;
16        lastName = last;
17
18        count++;   // increment static count of employees
19        System.out.printf( "Employee constructor: %s %s; count = %d\n",
20           firstName, lastName, count );
21     } // end Employee constructor
22
23     // subtract 1 from static count when garbage
24     // collector calls finalize to clean up object;
25     // confirm that finalize was called
26     protected void finalize()
27     {
28        count--; // decrement static count of employees
29        System.out.printf( "Employee finalizer: %s %s; count = %d\n",
30           firstName, lastName, count );
31     } // end method finalize
32
33     // get first name
34     public String getFirstName()
35     {
36        return firstName;
37     } // end method getFirstName
38
39     // get last name
40     public String getLastName()
41     {
42        return lastName;
43     } // end method getLastName
```

Fig. 8.12 | static variable used to maintain a count of the number of Employee objects in memory. (Part I of 2.)

```
44
45      // static method to get static count value
46      public static int getCount()
47      {
48         return count;
49      } // end method getCount
50   } // end class Employee
```

Fig. 8.12 | static variable used to maintain a count of the number of Employee objects in memory. (Part 2 of 2.)

When Employee objects exist, member count can be used in any method of an Employee object—this example increments count in the constructor (line 18) and decrements it in the finalize method (line 28). When no objects of class Employee exist, member count can still be referenced, but only through a call to public static method getCount (lines 46–49), as in Employee.getCount(), which returns the number of Employee objects currently in memory. When objects exist, method getCount can also be called through any reference to an Employee object, as in the call e1.getCount().

Good Programming Practice 8.1

Invoke every static method by using the class name and a dot (.) to emphasize that the method being called is a static method.

Note that the Employee class has a finalize method (lines 26–31). This method is included only to show when the garbage collector executes in this program. Method finalize is normally declared protected, so it is not part of the public services of a class. We'll discuss the protected member access modifier in detail in Chapter 9.

EmployeeTest method main (Fig. 8.13) instantiates two Employee objects (lines 13–14). When each Employee object's constructor is invoked, lines 15–16 of Fig. 8.12 assign the Employee's first name and last name to instance variables firstName and lastName. Note that these two statements do not make copies of the original String arguments. Actually, String objects in Java are immutable—they cannot be modified after they are

```
1    // Fig. 8.13: EmployeeTest.java
2    // Static member demonstration.
3
4    public class EmployeeTest
5    {
6       public static void main( String args[] )
7       {
8          // show that count is 0 before creating Employees
9          System.out.printf( "Employees before instantiation: %d\n",
10            Employee.getCount() );
11
12          // create two Employees; count should be 2
13          Employee e1 = new Employee( "Susan", "Baker" );
14          Employee e2 = new Employee( "Bob", "Blue" );
15
```

Fig. 8.13 | static member demonstration. (Part 1 of 2.)

```
16         // show that count is 2 after creating two Employees
17         System.out.println( "\nEmployees after instantiation: " );
18         System.out.printf( "via e1.getCount(): %d\n", e1.getCount() );
19         System.out.printf( "via e2.getCount(): %d\n", e2.getCount() );
20         System.out.printf( "via Employee.getCount(): %d\n",
21            Employee.getCount() );
22
23         // get names of Employees
24         System.out.printf( "\nEmployee 1: %s %s\nEmployee 2: %s %s\n\n",
25            e1.getFirstName(), e1.getLastName(),
26            e2.getFirstName(), e2.getLastName() );
27
28         // in this example, there is only one reference to each Employee,
29         // so the following two statements cause the JVM to mark each
30         // Employee object for garbage collection
31         e1 = null;
32         e2 = null;
33
34         System.gc(); // ask for garbage collection to occur now
35
36         // show Employee count after calling garbage collector; count
37         // displayed may be 0, 1 or 2 based on whether garbage collector
38         // executes immediately and number of Employee objects collected
39         System.out.printf( "\nEmployees after System.gc(): %d\n",
40            Employee.getCount() );
41      } // end main
42 } // end class EmployeeTest
```

```
Employees before instantiation: 0
Employee constructor: Susan Baker; count = 1
Employee constructor: Bob Blue; count = 2

Employees after instantiation:
via e1.getCount(): 2
via e2.getCount(): 2
via Employee.getCount(): 2

Employee 1: Susan Baker
Employee 2: Bob Blue

Employee finalizer: Bob Blue; count = 1
Employee finalizer: Susan Baker; count = 0

Employees after System.gc(): 0
```

Fig. 8.13 | static member demonstration. (Part 2 of 2.)

created. Therefore, it is safe to have many references to one String object. This is not normally the case for objects of most other classes in Java. If String objects are immutable, you might wonder why are we able to use operators + and += to concatenate String objects. String concatenation operations actually result in a new Strings object containing the concatenated values. The original String objects are not modified.

When main has finished using the two Employee objects, the references e1 and e2 are set to null at lines 31–32. At this point, references e1 and e2 no longer refer to the objects that were instantiated in lines 13–14. This "marks the objects for garbage collection" because there are no more references to the objects in the program.

Eventually, the garbage collector might reclaim the memory for these objects (or the operating system surely will reclaim the memory when the program terminates). The JVM does not guarantee when the garbage collector will execute (or even whether it will execute), so this program explicitly calls the garbage collector in line 34 (Fig. 8.13) using static method gc of class System (package java.lang) to indicate that the garbage collector should make a best-effort attempt to reclaim objects that are eligible for garbage collection. This is just a best effort—it is possible that no objects or only a subset of the eligible objects will be collected. In Fig. 8.13's sample output, the garbage collector did execute before lines 39–40 displayed current Employee count. The last output line indicates that the number of Employee objects in memory is 0 after the call to System.gc(). The third- and second-to-last lines of the output show that the Employee object for Bob Blue was finalized before the Employee object for Susan Baker. The output on your system may differ, because the garbage collector is not guaranteed to execute when System.gc() is called, nor is it guaranteed to collect objects in a specific order.

[*Note:* A method declared static cannot access non-static class members, because a static method can be called even when no objects of the class have been instantiated. For the same reason, the this reference cannot be used in a static method—it must refer to a specific object of the class, and when a static method is called, there might not be any objects of its class in memory. The this reference is required to allow a method of a class to access other non-static members of the same class.]

Common Programming Error 8.7

A compilation error occurs if a static method calls an instance (non-static) method in the same class by using only the method name. Similarly, a compilation error occurs if a static method attempts to access an instance variable in the same class by using only the variable name.

Common Programming Error 8.8

Referring to this in a static method is a syntax error.

8.12 static Import

In Section 6.3, you learned about the static fields and methods of class Math. We invoked class Math's static fields and methods by preceding each with the class name Math and a dot (.). A static *import* declaration enables you to refer to imported static members as if they were declared in the class that uses them—the class name and a dot (.) are not required to use an imported static member.

A static import declaration has two forms—one that imports a particular static member (which is known as *single static import*) and one that imports all static members of a class (which is known as *static import on demand*). The following syntax imports a particular static member:

> **import static** *packageName.ClassName.staticMemberName*;

where *packageName* is the package of the class (e.g., java.lang), *ClassName* is the name of the class (e.g., Math) and *staticMemberName* is the name of the static field or method (e.g., PI or abs). The following syntax imports all static members of a class:

import static *packageName.ClassName.**;

where *packageName* is the package of the class (e.g., java.lang) and *ClassName* is the name of the class (e.g., Math). The asterisk (*) indicates that *all* static members of the specified class should be available for use in the class(es) declared in the file. Note that static import declarations import only static class members. Regular import statements should be used to specify the classes used in a program.

Figure 8.14 demonstrates a static import. Line 3 is a static import declaration, which imports all static fields and methods of class Math from package java.lang. Lines 9–12 access the Math class's static field E (line 11) and the static methods sqrt (line 9), ceil (line 10), log (line 11) and cos (line 12) without preceding the field name or method names with class name Math and a dot.

Common Programming Error 8.9

A compilation error occurs if a program attempts to import static methods that have the same signature or static fields that have the same name from two or more classes.

```
1  // Fig. 8.14: StaticImportTest.java
2  // Using static import to import static methods of class Math.
3  import static java.lang.Math.*;
4
5  public class StaticImportTest
6  {
7     public static void main( String args[] )
8     {
9        System.out.printf( "sqrt( 900.0 ) = %.1f\n", sqrt( 900.0 ) );
10       System.out.printf( "ceil( -9.8 ) = %.1f\n", ceil( -9.8 ) );
11       System.out.printf( "log( E ) = %.1f\n", log( E ) );
12       System.out.printf( "cos( 0.0 ) = %.1f\n", cos( 0.0 ) );
13    } // end main
14 } // end class StaticImportTest
```

```
sqrt( 900.0 ) = 30.0
ceil( -9.8 ) = -9.0
log( E ) = 1.0
cos( 0.0 ) = 1.0
```

Fig. 8.14 | Static import Math methods.

8.13 **final** Instance Variables

The *principle of least privilege* is fundamental to good software engineering. In the context of an application, the principle states that code should be granted only the amount of privilege and access that it needs to accomplish its designated task, but no more. Let us see how this principle applies to instance variables.

Some instance variables need to be modifiable and some do not. You can use the keyword final to specify that a variable is not modifiable (i.e., it is a constant) and that any attempt to modify it is an error. For example,

private final int INCREMENT;

declares a final (constant) instance variable INCREMENT of type int. Although constants can be initialized when they are declared, this is not required. Constants can be initialized by each of the class's constructors.

Software Engineering Observation 8.13

Declaring an instance variable as final *helps enforce the principle of least privilege. If an instance variable should not be modified, declare it to be* final *to prevent modification.*

Our next example contains two classes—class Increment (Fig. 8.15) and class IncrementTest (Fig. 8.16). Class Increment contains a final instance variable of type int named INCREMENT (Fig. 8.15, line 7). Note that the final variable is not initialized in its declaration, so it must be initialized by the class's constructor (lines 9–13). If the class provided multiple constructors, every constructor would be required to initialize the final variable. The constructor receives int parameter incrementValue and assigns its value to INCREMENT (line 12). A final variable cannot be modified by assignment after it is initialized. Application class IncrementTest creates an object of class Increment (Fig. 8.16, line 8) and provides as the argument to the constructor the value 5 to be assigned to the constant INCREMENT.

Common Programming Error 8.10

Attempting to modify a final *instance variable after it is initialized is a compilation error.*

```
1   // Fig. 8.15: Increment.java
2   // final instance variable in a class.
3
4   public class Increment
5   {
6      private int total = 0; // total of all increments
7      private final int INCREMENT; // constant variable (uninitialized)
8
9      // constructor initializes final instance variable INCREMENT
10     public Increment( int incrementValue )
11     {
12        INCREMENT = incrementValue; // initialize constant variable (once)
13     } // end Increment constructor
14
15     // add INCREMENT to total
16     public void addIncrementToTotal()
17     {
18        total += INCREMENT;
19     } // end method addIncrementToTotal
20
21     // return String representation of an Increment object's data
22     public String toString()
23     {
24        return String.format( "total = %d", total );
25     } // end method toIncrementString
26  } // end class Increment
```

Fig. 8.15 | final instance variable in a class.

```
1   // Fig. 8.16: IncrementTest.java
2   // final variable initialized with a constructor argument.
3
4   public class IncrementTest
5   {
6      public static void main( String args[] )
7      {
8         Increment value = new Increment( 5 );
9
10        System.out.printf( "Before incrementing: %s\n\n", value );
11
12        for ( int i = 1; i <= 3; i++ )
13        {
14           value.addIncrementToTotal();
15           System.out.printf( "After increment %d: %s\n", i, value );
16        } // end for
17     } // end main
18  } // end class IncrementTest
```

```
Before incrementing: total = 0

After increment 1: total = 5
After increment 2: total = 10
After increment 3: total = 15
```

Fig. 8.16 | final variable initialized with a constructor argument.

Error-Prevention Tip 8.2

Attempts to modify a final instance variable are caught at compilation time rather than causing execution-time errors. It is always preferable to get bugs out at compilation time, if possible, rather than allow them to slip through to execution time (where studies have found that repair is often many times more expensive).

Software Engineering Observation 8.14

A final field should also be declared static if it is initialized in its declaration. Once a final field is initialized in its declaration, its value can never change. Therefore, it is not necessary to have a separate copy of the field for every object of the class. Making the field static enables all objects of the class to share the final field.

If a final variable is not initialized, a compilation error occurs. To demonstrate this, we placed line 12 of Fig. 8.15 in a comment and recompiled the class. Figure 8.17 shows the error message produced by the compiler.

```
Increment.java:13: variable INCREMENT might not have been initialized
   } // end Increment constructor
   ^
1 error
```

Fig. 8.17 | final variable INCREMENT must be initialized.

Common Programming Error 8.11

Not initializing a final instance variable in its declaration or in every constructor of the class yields a compilation error indicating that the variable might not have been initialized. The same error occurs if the class initializes the variable in some, but not all, of the class's constructors.

8.14 Software Reusability

Java programmers concentrate on crafting new classes and reusing existing classes. Many class libraries exist, and others are being developed worldwide. Software is then constructed from existing, well-defined, carefully tested, well-documented, portable, widely available components. This kind of software reusability speeds the development of powerful, high-quality software. *Rapid application development (RAD)* is of great interest today.

There are thousands of classes in the Java API from which to choose to help you implement Java programs. Indeed, Java is not just a programming language. It is a framework in which Java developers can work to achieve true reusability and rapid application development. Java programmers can focus on the task at hand when developing their programs and leave the lower-level details to the classes of the Java API. For example, to write a program that draws graphics, a Java programmer does not require knowledge of graphics on every computer platform where the program will execute. Instead, the programmer can concentrate on learning Java's graphics capabilities (which are quite substantial and growing) and write a Java program that draws the graphics, using Java's API classes, such as Graphics. When the program executes on a given computer, it is the job of the JVM to translate Java commands into commands that the local computer can understand.

The Java API classes enable Java programmers to bring new applications to market faster by using preexisting, tested components. Not only does this reduce development time, it also improves the programmer's ability to debug and maintain applications. To take advantage of Java's many capabilities, it is essential that you familiarize yourself with the variety of packages and classes in the Java API. There are many web-based resources at java.sun.com to help you with this task. The primary resource for learning about the Java API is the Java API documentation, which can be found at

    java.sun.com/javase/6/docs/api/

We overview how to use the documentation in Appendix G. You can download the API documentation from

    java.sun.com/javase/downloads/ea.jsp

In addition, java.sun.com provides many other resources, including tutorials, articles and sites specific to individual Java topics.

Good Programming Practice 8.2

Avoid reinventing the wheel. Study the capabilities of the Java API. If the API contains a class that meets your program's requirements, use that class rather than create your own.

To realize the full potential of software reusability, we need to improve cataloging schemes, licensing schemes, protection mechanisms which ensure that master copies of classes are not corrupted, description schemes that system designers use to determine whether existing objects meet their needs, browsing mechanisms that determine what classes are available and how closely they meet software developer requirements, and the like. Many interesting research and development problems have been solved and many more need to be solved. These problems will likely be solved because the potential value of increased software reuse is enormous.

8.15 Data Abstraction and Encapsulation

Classes normally hide the details of their implementation from their clients. This is called *information hiding*. As an example, let us consider the *stack* data structure introduced in Section 6.6. Recall that a stack is a *last-in, first-out (LIFO)* data structure—the last item pushed (inserted) on the stack is the first item popped (removed) from the stack.

Stacks can be implemented with arrays and with other data structures, such as linked lists. A client of a stack class need not be concerned with the stack's implementation. The client knows only that when data items are placed in the stack, they will be recalled in last-in, first-out order. The client cares about what functionality a stack offers, not about how that functionality is implemented. This concept is referred to as *data abstraction*. Although programmers might know the details of a class's implementation, they should not write code that depends on these details. This enables a particular class (such as one that implements a stack and its operations, *push* and *pop*) to be replaced with another version without affecting the rest of the system. As long as the public services of the class do not change (i.e., every original method still has the same name, return type and parameter list in the new class declaration), the rest of the system is not affected.

Most programming languages emphasize actions. In these languages, data exists to support the actions that programs must take. Data is "less interesting" than actions. Data is "crude." Only a few primitive types exist, and it is difficult for programmers to create their own types. Java and the object-oriented style of programming elevate the importance of data. The primary activities of object-oriented programming in Java are the creation of types (e.g., classes) and the expression of the interactions among objects of those types. To create languages that emphasize data, the programming-languages community needed to formalize some notions about data. The formalization we consider here is the notion of *abstract data types (ADTs)*, which improve the program-development process.

Consider primitive type int, which most people would associate with an integer in mathematics. Rather, an int is an abstract representation of an integer. Unlike mathematical integers, computer ints are fixed in size. For example, type int in Java is limited to the range –2,147,483,648 to +2,147,483,647. If the result of a calculation falls outside this range, an error occurs, and the computer responds in some machine-dependent manner. It might, for example, "quietly" produce an incorrect result, such as a value too large to fit in an int variable (commonly called *arithmetic overflow*). Mathematical integers do not have this problem. Therefore, the notion of a computer int is only an approximation of the notion of a real-world integer. The same is true of float and other built-in types.

We have taken the notion of int for granted until this point, but we now consider it from a new perspective. Types like int, float, and char are all examples of abstract data types. They are representations of real-world notions to some satisfactory level of precision within a computer system.

An ADT actually captures two notions: a *data representation* and the *operations* that can be performed on that data. For example, in Java, an int contains an integer value (data) and provides addition, subtraction, multiplication, division and remainder operations—division by zero is undefined. Java programmers use classes to implement abstract data types.

> **Software Engineering Observation 8.15**
>
> *Programmers create types through the class mechanism. New types can be designed to be convenient to use as the built-in types. This marks Java as an extensible language. Although the language is easy to extend via new types, you cannot alter the base language itself.*

Another abstract data type we discuss is a ***queue***, which is similar to a "waiting line." Computer systems use many queues internally. A queue offers well-understood behavior to its clients: Clients place items in a queue one at a time via an *enqueue* operation, then get them back one at a time via a *dequeue* operation. A queue returns items in ***first-in, first-out (FIFO)*** order, which means that the first item inserted in a queue is the first item removed from the queue. Conceptually, a queue can become infinitely long, but real queues are finite.

The queue hides an internal data representation that keeps track of the items currently waiting in line, and it offers operations to its clients (*enqueue* and *dequeue*). The clients are not concerned about the implementation of the queue—they simply depend on the queue to operate "as advertised." When a client enqueues an item, the queue should accept that item and place it in some kind of internal FIFO data structure. Similarly, when the client wants the next item from the front of the queue, the queue should remove the item from its internal representation and deliver it in FIFO order (i.e., the item that has been in the queue the longest should be the next one returned by the next dequeue operation).

The queue ADT guarantees the integrity of its internal data structure. Clients cannot manipulate this data structure directly—only the queue ADT has access to its internal data. Clients are able to perform only allowable operations on the data representation—the ADT rejects operations that its public interface does not provide.

8.16 Time Class Case Study: Creating Packages

We have seen in almost every example in the text that classes from preexisting libraries, such as the Java API, can be imported into a Java program. Each class in the Java API belongs to a package that contains a group of related classes. As applications become more complex, packages help programmers manage the complexity of application components. Packages also facilitate software reuse by enabling programs to import classes from other packages (as we have done in most examples). Another benefit of packages is that they provide a convention for unique class names, which helps prevent class-name conflicts (discussed later in this section). This section introduces how to create your own packages.

Steps for Declaring a Reusable Class

Before a class can be imported into multiple applications, it must be placed in a package to make it reusable. Figure 8.18 shows how to specify the package in which a class should be placed. Figure 8.19 shows how to import our packaged class so that it can be used in an application. The steps for creating a reusable class are:

1. Declare a `public` class. If the class is not `public`, it can be used only by other classes in the same package.

2. Choose a unique package name and add a ***package*** *declaration* to the source-code file for the reusable class declaration. There can be only one package declaration in each Java source-code file, and it must precede all other declarations and statements in the file. Note that comments are not statements, so comments can be placed before a package statement in a file.

3. Compile the class so that it is placed in the appropriate package directory structure.

4. Import the reusable class into a program and use the class.

Steps 1 and 2: Creating a `public` Class and Adding the `package` Statement

For *Step 1*, we modify the `public` class `Time1` declared in Fig. 8.1. The new version is shown in Fig. 8.18. No modifications have been made to the implementation of the class, so we'll not discuss its implementation details again here.

For *Step 2*, we add a `package` declaration (line 3) that declares a `package` named `com.deitel.javafp.ch08`. Placing a package declaration at the beginning of a Java source

```
1   // Fig. 8.18: Time1.java
2   // Time1 class declaration maintains the time in 24-hour format.
3   package com.deitel.javafp.ch08;
4
5   public class Time1
6   {
7      private int hour;   // 0 - 23
8      private int minute; // 0 - 59
9      private int second; // 0 - 59
10
11     // set a new time value using universal time; perform
12     // validity checks on the data; set invalid values to zero
13     public void setTime( int h, int m, int s )
14     {
15        hour = ( ( h >= 0 && h < 24 ) ? h : 0 );   // validate hour
16        minute = ( ( m >= 0 && m < 60 ) ? m : 0 ); // validate minute
17        second = ( ( s >= 0 && s < 60 ) ? s : 0 ); // validate second
18     } // end method setTime
19
20     // convert to String in universal-time format (HH:MM:SS)
21     public String toUniversalString()
22     {
23        return String.format( "%02d:%02d:%02d", hour, minute, second );
24     } // end method toUniversalString
25
26     // convert to String in standard-time format (H:MM:SS AM or PM)
27     public String toString()
28     {
29        return String.format( "%d:%02d:%02d %s",
30           ( ( hour == 0 || hour == 12 ) ? 12 : hour % 12 ),
31           minute, second, ( hour < 12 ? "AM" : "PM" ) );
32     } // end method toString
33  } // end class Time1
```

Fig. 8.18 | Packaging class `Time1` for reuse.

file indicates that the class declared in the file is part of the specified package. Only package declarations, import declarations and comments can appear outside the braces of a class declaration. A Java source-code file must have the following order:

1. a package declaration (if any),

2. import declarations (if any), then

3. class declarations.

Only one of the class declarations in a particular file can be public. Other classes in the file are placed in the package and can be used only by the other classes in the package. Non-public classes are in a package to support the reusable classes in the package.

In an effort to provide unique names for every package, Sun Microsystems specifies a convention for package naming that all Java programmers should follow. Every package name should start with your Internet domain name in reverse order. For example, our domain name is deitel.com, so our package names begin with com.deitel. For the domain name *yourcollege*.edu, the package name should begin with edu.*yourcollege*. After the domain name is reversed, you can choose any other names you want for your package. If you are part of a company with many divisions or a university with many schools, you may want to use the name of your division or school as the next name in the package. We chose to use javafp as the next name in our package name to indicate that this class is from *Java for Programmers*. The last name in our package name specifies that this package is for Chapter 8 (ch08).

Step 3: Compiling the Packaged Class

Step 3 is to compile the class so that it is stored in the appropriate package. When a Java file containing a package declaration is compiled, the resulting class file is placed in the directory specified by the package declaration. The package declaration in Fig. 8.18 indicates that class Time1 should be placed in the directory

```
com
   deitel
      javafp
         ch08
```

The directory names in the package declaration specify the exact location of the classes in the package.

When compiling a class in a package, the javac command-line option **-d** causes the javac compiler to create appropriate directories based on the class's package declaration. The option also specifies where the directories should be stored. For example, in a command window, we used the compilation command

```
javac -d . Time1.java
```

to specify that the first directory in our package name should be placed in the current directory. The period (.) after -d in the preceding command represents the current directory on the Windows; UNIX and Linux operating systems (and several others as well). After executing the compilation command, the current directory contains a directory called com, com contains a directory called deitel, deitel contains a directory called javafp and javafp contains a directory called ch08. In the ch08 directory, you can find the file

Time1.class. [*Note:* If you do not use the -d option, then you must copy or move the class file to the appropriate package directory after compiling it.]

The package name is part of the fully qualified class name, so the name of class Time1 is actually com.deitel.javafp.ch08.Time1. You can use this fully qualified name in your programs, or you can import the class and use its *simple name* (the class name by itself—Time1) in the program. If another package also contains a Time1 class, the fully qualified class names can be used to distinguish between the classes in the program and prevent a *name conflict* (also called a *name collision*).

Step 4: Importing the Reusable Class

Once the class is compiled and stored in its package, the class can be imported into programs (*Step 4*). In the Time1PackageTest application of Fig. 8.19, line 3 specifies that class Time1 should be imported for use in class Time1PackageTest. Class Time1PackageTest is in the default package because the class's .java file does not contain a package declaration.

```java
 1   // Fig. 8.19: Time1PackageTest.java
 2   // Time1 object used in an application.
 3   import com.deitel.javafp.ch08.Time1; // import class Time1
 4
 5   public class Time1PackageTest
 6   {
 7      public static void main( String args[] )
 8      {
 9         // create and initialize a Time1 object
10         Time1 time = new Time1(); // calls Time1 constructor
11
12         // output string representations of the time
13         System.out.print( "The initial universal time is: " );
14         System.out.println( time.toUniversalString() );
15         System.out.print( "The initial standard time is: " );
16         System.out.println( time.toString() );
17         System.out.println(); // output a blank line
18
19         // change time and output updated time
20         time.setTime( 13, 27, 6 );
21         System.out.print( "Universal time after setTime is: " );
22         System.out.println( time.toUniversalString() );
23         System.out.print( "Standard time after setTime is: " );
24         System.out.println( time.toString() );
25         System.out.println(); // output a blank line
26
27         // set time with invalid values; output updated time
28         time.setTime( 99, 99, 99 );
29         System.out.println( "After attempting invalid settings:" );
30         System.out.print( "Universal time: " );
31         System.out.println( time.toUniversalString() );
32         System.out.print( "Standard time: " );
33         System.out.println( time.toString() );
34      } // end main
35   } // end class Time1PackageTest
```

Fig. 8.19 | Time1 object used in an application. (Part 1 of 2.)

```
The initial universal time is: 00:00:00
The initial standard time is: 12:00:00 AM

Universal time after setTime is: 13:27:06
Standard time after setTime is: 1:27:06 PM

After attempting invalid settings:
Universal time: 00:00:00
Standard time: 12:00:00 AM
```

Fig. 8.19 | Time1 object used in an application. (Part 2 of 2.)

Since the two classes are in different packages, the import at line 3 is required so that class Time1PackageTest can use class Time1.

Line 3 is known as a *single-type-import declaration*—that is, the import declaration specifies one class to import. When your program uses multiple classes from the same package, you can import those classes with a single import declaration. For example, the import declaration

> *import* java.util.*; // *import classes from package java.util*

uses an asterisk (*) at the end of the import declaration to inform the compiler that all classes from the java.util package are available for use in the program. This is known as a *type-import-on-demand declaration*. Only the classes from package java.util that are used in the program are loaded by the JVM. The preceding import allows you to use the simple name of any class from the java.util package in the program. Throughout this book, we use single-type-import declarations for clarity.

 Common Programming Error 8.12

Using the import *declaration* import java.*; *causes a compilation error. You must specify the exact name of the package from which you want to import classes.*

Specifying the Classpath During Compilation

When compiling Time1PackageTest, javac must locate the .class file for Time1 to ensure that class Time1PackageTest uses class Time1 correctly. The compiler uses a special object called a *class loader* to locate the classes it needs. The class loader begins by searching the standard Java classes that are bundled with the JDK. Then it searches for *optional packages*. Java provides an *extension mechanism* that enables new (optional) packages to be added to Java for development and execution purposes. [*Note:* The extension mechanism is beyond the scope of this book. For more information, visit java.sun.com/javase/6/docs/technotes/guides/extensions/.] If the class is not found in the standard Java classes or in the extension classes, the class loader searches the *classpath*, which contains a list of locations in which classes are stored. The classpath consists of a list of directories or *archive files*, each separated by a *directory separator*—a semicolon (;) on Windows or a colon (:) on UNIX/Linux/Mac OS X. Archive files are individual files that contain directories of other files, typically in a compressed format. For example, the standard classes used by your programs are contained in the archive file rt.jar, which is installed with the JDK. Archive files normally end with the .jar or .zip file-name extensions. The directories and archive files specified in the classpath contain the classes you wish to make available to the Java compiler and the JVM.

By default, the classpath consists only of the current directory. However, the classpath can be modified by

1. providing the *-classpath* option to the javac compiler or

2. setting the CLASSPATH environment variable (a special variable that you define and the operating system maintains so that applications can search for classes in the specified locations).

For more information on the classpath, visit java.sun.com/javase/6/docs/technotes/tools/index.html. The section entitled "General Information" contains information on setting the classpath for UNIX/Linux and Windows.

Common Programming Error 8.13

Specifying an explicit classpath eliminates the current directory from the classpath. This prevents classes in the current directory (including packages in the current directory) from loading properly. If classes must be loaded from the current directory, include a dot (.) in the classpath to specify the current directory.

Software Engineering Observation 8.16

In general, it is a better practice to use the -classpath option of the compiler, rather than the CLASSPATH environment variable, to specify the classpath for a program. This enables each application to have its own classpath.

Error-Prevention Tip 8.3

Specifying the classpath with the CLASSPATH environment variable can cause subtle and difficult-to-locate errors in programs that use different versions of the same package.

For the example of Fig. 8.18 and Fig. 8.19, we did not specify an explicit classpath. Thus, to locate the classes in the com.deitel.javafp.ch08 package from this example, the class loader looks in the current directory for the first name in the package—com. Next, the class loader navigates the directory structure. Directory com contains the subdirectory deitel. Directory deitel contains the subdirectory javafp. Finally, directory javafp contains subdirectory ch08. In the ch08 directory is the file Time1.class, which is loaded by the class loader to ensure that the class is used properly in our program.

Specifying the Classpath When Executing an Application

When you execute an application, the JVM must be able to locate the classes used in that application. Like the compiler, the java command uses a class loader that searches the standard classes and extension classes first, then searches the classpath (the current directory by default). The classpath for the JVM can be specified explicitly by using either of the techniques discussed for the compiler. As with the compiler, it is better to specify an individual program's classpath via command-line options to the JVM. You can specify the classpath in the java command via the -classpath or -cp command-line options, followed by a list of directories or archive files separated by semicolons (;) on Microsoft Windows or by colons (:) on UNIX/Linux/Mac OS X. Again, if classes must be loaded from the current directory, be sure to include a dot (.) in the classpath to specify the current directory.

8.17 Package Access

If no access modifier (public, protected or private—protected is discussed in Chapter 9) is specified for a method or variable when it is declared in a class, the method or variable is considered to have *package access*. In a program that consists of one class declaration, this has no specific effect. However, if a program uses multiple classes from the same package (i.e., a group of related classes), these classes can access each other's package-access members directly through references to objects of the appropriate classes.

The application in Fig. 8.20 demonstrates package access. The application contains two classes in one source-code file—the PackageDataTest application class (lines 5–21) and the PackageData class (lines 24–41). When you compile this program, the compiler produces two separate .class files—PackageDataTest.class and PackageData.class. The compiler places the two .class files in the same directory, so the classes are considered to be part of the same package. Since they are part of the same package, class PackageDataTest is allowed to modify the package-access data of PackageData objects.

In the PackageData class declaration, lines 26–27 declare the instance variables number and string with no access modifiers—therefore, these are package-access instance variables. The PackageDataTest application's main method creates an instance of the PackageData class (line 9) to demonstrate the ability to modify the PackageData instance variables directly (as shown in lines 15–16). The results of the modification can be seen in the output window.

```java
 1   // Fig. 8.20: PackageDataTest.java
 2   // Package-access members of a class are accessible by other classes
 3   // in the same package.
 4
 5   public class PackageDataTest
 6   {
 7      public static void main( String args[] )
 8      {
 9         PackageData packageData = new PackageData();
10
11         // output String representation of packageData
12         System.out.printf( "After instantiation:\n%s\n", packageData );
13
14         // change package access data in packageData object
15         packageData.number = 77;
16         packageData.string = "Goodbye";
17
18         // output String representation of packageData
19         System.out.printf( "\nAfter changing values:\n%s\n", packageData );
20      } // end main
21   } // end class PackageDataTest
22
23   // class with package access instance variables
24   class PackageData
25   {
```

Fig. 8.20 | Package-access members of a class are accessible by other classes in the same package. (Part 1 of 2.)

```
26      int number; // package-access instance variable
27      String string; // package-access instance variable
28
29      // constructor
30      public PackageData()
31      {
32         number = 0;
33         string = "Hello";
34      } // end PackageData constructor
35
36      // return PackageData object String representation
37      public String toString()
38      {
39         return String.format( "number: %d; string: %s", number, string );
40      } // end method toString
41   } // end class PackageData
```

```
After instantiation:
number: 0; string: Hello

After changing values:
number: 77; string: Goodbye
```

Fig. 8.20 | Package-access members of a class are accessible by other classes in the same package. (Part 2 of 2.)

8.18 (Optional) Software Engineering Case Study: Starting to Program the Classes of the ATM System

In the Software Engineering Case Study sections in Chapters 1–7, we introduced the fundamentals of object orientation and developed an object-oriented design for our ATM system. Earlier in this chapter, we discussed many of the details of programming with classes. We now begin implementing our object-oriented design in Java. At the end of this section, we show how to convert class diagrams to Java code. In the final Software Engineering Case Study section (Section 10.8), we modify the code to incorporate the object-oriented concept of inheritance. We present the full Java code implementation in Appendix H.

Visibility

We now apply access modifiers to the members of our classes. In Chapter 3, we introduced access modifiers public and private. Access modifiers determine the *visibility* or accessibility of an object's attributes and methods to other objects. Before we can begin implementing our design, we must consider which attributes and methods of our classes should be public and which should be private.

In Chapter 3, we observed that attributes normally should be private and that methods invoked by clients of a given class should be public. Methods that are called only by other methods of the class as "utility methods," however, normally should be private. The UML employs *visibility markers* for modeling the visibility of attributes and operations. Public visibility is indicated by placing a plus sign (+) before an operation or an attribute, whereas a minus sign (–) indicates private visibility. Figure 8.21 shows our updated

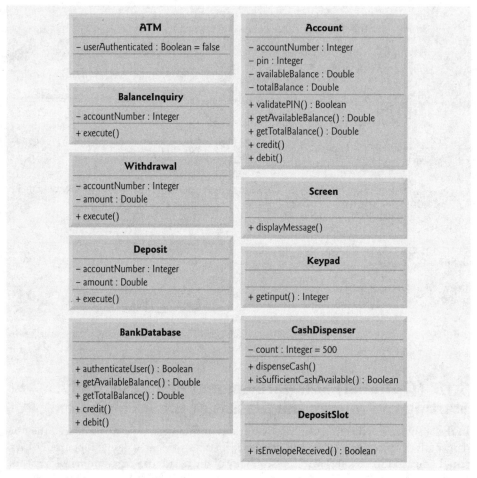

Fig. 8.21 | Class diagram with visibility markers.

class diagram with visibility markers included. [*Note:* We do not include any operation parameters in Fig. 8.21—this is perfectly normal. Adding visibility markers does not affect the parameters already modeled in the class diagrams of Figs. 6.27–6.30.]

Navigability

Before we begin implementing our design in Java, we introduce an additional UML notation. The class diagram in Fig. 8.22 further refines the relationships among classes in the ATM system by adding navigability arrows to the association lines. *Navigability arrows* (represented as arrows with stick arrowheads in the class diagram) indicate in which direction an association can be traversed. When implementing a system designed using the UML, programmers use navigability arrows to help determine which objects need references to other objects. For example, the navigability arrow pointing from class ATM to class BankDatabase indicates that we can navigate from the former to the latter, thereby enabling the ATM to invoke the BankDatabase's operations. However, since Fig. 8.22 does not contain a navigability arrow pointing from class BankDatabase to class ATM, the Bank-

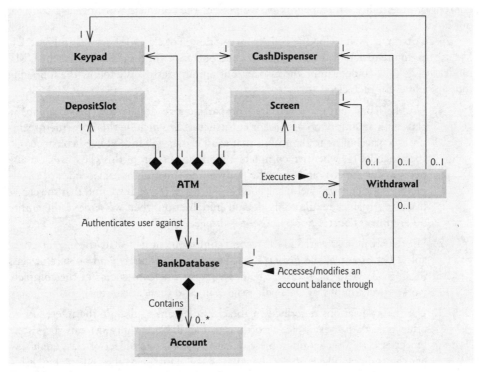

Fig. 8.22 | Class diagram with navigability arrows.

Database cannot access the ATM's operations. Note that associations in a class diagram that have navigability arrows at both ends or do not have navigability arrows at all indicate *bidirectional navigability*—navigation can proceed in either direction across the association.

Like the class diagram of Fig. 3.21, the class diagram of Fig. 8.22 omits classes BalanceInquiry and Deposit to keep the diagram simple. The navigability of the associations in which these classes participate closely parallels the navigability of class Withdrawal. Recall from Section 3.9 that BalanceInquiry has an association with class Screen. We can navigate from class BalanceInquiry to class Screen along this association, but we cannot navigate from class Screen to class BalanceInquiry. Thus, if we were to model class BalanceInquiry in Fig. 8.22, we would place a navigability arrow at class Screen's end of this association. Also recall that class Deposit associates with classes Screen, Keypad and DepositSlot. We can navigate from class Deposit to each of these classes, but not vice versa. We therefore would place navigability arrows at the Screen, Keypad and DepositSlot ends of these associations. [*Note:* We model these additional classes and associations in our final class diagram in Section 10.8, after we have simplified the structure of our system by incorporating the object-oriented concept of inheritance.]

Implementing the ATM System from Its UML Design
We are now ready to begin implementing the ATM system. We first convert the classes in the diagrams of Fig. 8.21 and Fig. 8.22 into Java code. The code will represent the "skeleton" of the system. In Chapter 10, we modify the code to incorporate the object-oriented

concept of inheritance. In Appendix H, we present the complete working Java code for our model.

As an example, we develop the code from our design of class Withdrawal in Fig. 8.21. We use this figure to determine the attributes and operations of the class. We use the UML model in Fig. 8.22 to determine the associations among classes. We follow the following four guidelines for each class:

1. Use the name located in the first compartment to declare the class as a public class with an empty no-argument constructor. We include this constructor simply as a placeholder to remind us that most classes will indeed need constructors. In Appendix H, when we complete a working version of this class, we add any necessary arguments and code the body of the constructor as needed. For example, class Withdrawal yields the code in Fig. 8.23. [*Note:* If we find that the class's instance variables require only default initialization, then we remove the empty no-argument constructor because it is unnecessary.]

2. Use the attributes located in the second compartment to declare the instance variables. For example, the private attributes accountNumber and amount of class Withdrawal yield the code in Fig. 8.24. [*Note:* The constructor of the complete working version of this class will assign values to these attributes.]

3. Use the associations described in the class diagram to declare the references to other objects. For example, according to Fig. 8.22, Withdrawal can access one object of class Screen, one object of class Keypad, one object of class CashDispenser and one object of class BankDatabase. This yields the code in Fig. 8.25.

```
1   // Class Withdrawal represents an ATM withdrawal transaction
2   public class Withdrawal
3   {
4      // no-argument constructor
5      public Withdrawal()
6      {
7      } // end no-argument Withdrawal constructor
8   } // end class Withdrawal
```

Fig. 8.23 | Java code for class Withdrawal based on Fig. 8.21 and Fig. 8.22.

```
1    // Class Withdrawal represents an ATM withdrawal transaction
2    public class Withdrawal
3    {
4       // attributes
5       private int accountNumber; // account to withdraw funds from
6       private double amount; // amount to withdraw
7
8       // no-argument constructor
9       public Withdrawal()
10      {
11      } // end no-argument Withdrawal constructor
12   } // end class Withdrawal
```

Fig. 8.24 | Java code for class Withdrawal based on Fig. 8.21 and Fig. 8.22.

```
1    // Class Withdrawal represents an ATM withdrawal transaction
2    public class Withdrawal
3    {
4       // attributes
5       private int accountNumber; // account to withdraw funds from
6       private double amount; // amount to withdraw
7
8       // references to associated objects
9       private Screen screen; // ATM's screen
10      private Keypad keypad; // ATM's keypad
11      private CashDispenser cashDispenser; // ATM's cash dispenser
12      private BankDatabase bankDatabase; // account info database
13
14      // no-argument constructor
15      public Withdrawal()
16      {
17      } // end no-argument Withdrawal constructor
18   } // end class Withdrawal
```

Fig. 8.25 | Java code for class Withdrawal based on Fig. 8.21 and Fig. 8.22.

[*Note:* The constructor of the complete working version of this class will initialize these instance variables with references to actual objects.]

4. Use the operations located in the third compartment of Fig. 8.21 to declare the shells of the methods. If we have not yet specified a return type for an operation, we declare the method with return type void. Refer to the class diagrams of Figs. 6.27–6.30 to declare any necessary parameters. For example, adding the public operation execute in class Withdrawal, which has an empty parameter list, yields the code in Fig. 8.26. [*Note:* We code the bodies of methods when we implement the complete system in Appendix H.]

```
1    // Class Withdrawal represents an ATM withdrawal transaction
2    public class Withdrawal
3    {
4       // attributes
5       private int accountNumber; // account to withdraw funds from
6       private double amount; // amount to withdraw
7
8       // references to associated objects
9       private Screen screen; // ATM's screen
10      private Keypad keypad; // ATM's keypad
11      private CashDispenser cashDispenser; // ATM's cash dispenser
12      private BankDatabase bankDatabase; // account info database
13
14      // no-argument constructor
15      public Withdrawal()
16      {
17      } // end no-argument Withdrawal constructor
18
```

Fig. 8.26 | Java code for class Withdrawal based on Fig. 8.21 and Fig. 8.22. (Part 1 of 2.)

```
19      // operations
20      public void execute()
21      {
22      } // end method execute
23  } // end class Withdrawal
```

Fig. 8.26 | Java code for class Withdrawal based on Fig. 8.21 and Fig. 8.22. (Part 2 of 2.)

This concludes our discussion of the basics of generating classes from UML diagrams.

Software Engineering Case Study Self-Review Exercises

8.1 State whether the following statement is *true* or *false*, and if *false*, explain why: If an attribute of a class is marked with a minus sign (-) in a class diagram, the attribute is not directly accessible outside of the class.

8.2 In Fig. 8.22, the association between the ATM and the Screen indicates that:
a) we can navigate from the Screen to the ATM
b) we can navigate from the ATM to the Screen
c) Both (a) and (b); the association is bidirectional
d) None of the above

8.3 Write Java code to begin implementing the design for class Keypad.

Answers to Software Engineering Case Study Self-Review Exercises

8.1 True. The minus sign (-) indicates private visibility.

8.2 b.

8.3 The design for class Keypad yields the code in Fig. 8.27. Recall that class Keypad has no attributes for the moment, but attributes may become apparent as we continue the implementation. Also note that if we were designing a real ATM, method getInput would need to interact with the ATM's keypad hardware. We'll actually do input from the keyboard of a personal computer when we write the complete Java code in Appendix H.

```
1   // Class Keypad represents an ATM's keypad
2   public class Keypad
3   {
4       // no attributes have been specified yet
5
6       // no-argument constructor
7       public Keypad()
8       {
9       } // end no-argument Keypad constructor
10
11      // operations
12      public int getInput()
13      {
14      } // end method getInput
15  } // end class Keypad
```

Fig. 8.27 | Java code for class Keypad based on Fig. 8.21 and Fig. 8.22.

8.19 Wrap-Up

In this chapter, we presented additional class concepts. The Time class case study presented a complete class declaration consisting of private data, overloaded public constructors for initialization flexibility, *set* and *get* methods for manipulating the class's data, and methods that returned String representations of a Time object in two different formats. You also learned that every class can declare a toString method that returns a String representation of an object of the class and that method toString can be called implicitly whenever an object of a class appears in the code where a String is expected.

You learned that the this reference is used implicitly in a class's non-static methods to access the class's instance variables and other non-static methods. You also saw explicit uses of the this reference to access the class's members (including shadowed fields) and how to use keyword this in a constructor to call another constructor of the class.

We discussed the differences between default constructors provided by the compiler and no-argument constructors provided by the programmer. You learned that a class can have references to objects of other classes as members—a concept known as composition. You saw the enum class type and learned how it can be used to create a set of constants for use in a program. You learned about Java's garbage collection capability and how it reclaims the memory of objects that are no longer used. The chapter explained the motivation for static fields in a class and demonstrated how to declare and use static fields and methods in your own classes. You also learned how to declare and initialize final variables.

You learned how to package your own classes for reuse and how to import those classes into an application. Finally, you learned that fields declared without an access modifier are given package access by default. You saw the relationship between classes in the same package that allows each class in a package to access the package-access members of other classes in the package.

In the next chapter, you'll learn about an important aspect of object-oriented programming in Java—inheritance. You'll see that all classes in Java are related directly or indirectly to the class called Object. You'll also begin to understand how the relationships between classes enable you to build more powerful applications.

9

Object-Oriented Programming: Inheritance

*Say not you know
another entirely,
till you have divided an
inheritance with him.*

—Johann Kasper Lavater

*This method is to define as
the number of a class the
class of all classes similar to
the given class.*

—Bertrand Russell

*Good as it is to inherit
a library, it is better to
collect one.*

—Augustine Birrell

*Save base authority from
others' books.*

—William Shakespeare

OBJECTIVES

In this chapter you'll learn:

- How inheritance promotes software reusability.

- The notions of superclasses and subclasses.

- To use keyword `extends` to create a class that inherits attributes and behaviors from another class.

- To use access modifier `protected` to give subclass methods access to superclass members.

- To access superclass members with `super`.

- How constructors are used in inheritance hierarchies.

- The methods of class `Object`, the direct or indirect superclass of all classes in Java.

Outline

9.1 Introduction

9.2 Superclasses and Subclasses

9.3 protected Members

9.4 Relationship between Superclasses and Subclasses

　9.4.1 Creating and Using a CommissionEmployee Class

　9.4.2 Creating a BasePlusCommissionEmployee Class without Using Inheritance

　9.4.3 Creating a CommissionEmployee–BasePlusCommissionEmployee Inheritance Hierarchy

　9.4.4 CommissionEmployee–BasePlusCommissionEmployee Inheritance Hierarchy Using protected Instance Variables

　9.4.5 CommissionEmployee–BasePlusCommissionEmployee Inheritance Hierarchy Using private Instance Variables

9.5 Constructors in Subclasses

9.6 Software Engineering with Inheritance

9.7 Object Class

9.8 Wrap-Up

9.1 Introduction

This chapter continues our discussion of object-oriented programming (OOP) by introducing one of its primary features—*inheritance*, which is a form of software reuse in which a new class is created by absorbing an existing class's members and embellishing them with new or modified capabilities. With inheritance, programmers save time during program development by reusing proven and debugged high-quality software. This also increases the likelihood that a system will be implemented effectively.

When creating a class, rather than declaring completely new members, you can designate that the new class should inherit the members of an existing class. The existing class is called the *superclass*, and the new class is the *subclass*. (The C++ programming language refers to the superclass as the *base class* and the subclass as the *derived class*.) Each subclass can become the superclass for future subclasses.

A subclass normally adds its own fields and methods. Therefore, a subclass is more specific than its superclass and represents a more specialized group of objects. Typically, the subclass exhibits the behaviors of its superclass and additional behaviors that are specific to the subclass. This is why inheritance is sometimes referred to as *specialization*.

The *direct superclass* is the superclass from which the subclass explicitly inherits. An *indirect superclass* is any class above the direct superclass in the *class hierarchy*, which defines the inheritance relationships between classes. In Java, the class hierarchy begins with class Object (in package java.lang), which *every* class in Java directly or indirectly *extends* (or "inherits from"). Section 9.7 lists the methods of class Object, which every other class inherits. In the case of *single inheritance,* a class is derived from one direct superclass. Java, unlike C++, does not support multiple inheritance (which occurs when a class is derived from more than one direct superclass). In Chapter 10, Object-Oriented Programming:

Polymorphism, we explain how Java programmers can use interfaces to realize many of the benefits of multiple inheritance while avoiding the associated problems.

Experience in building software systems indicates that significant amounts of code deal with closely related special cases. When you are preoccupied with special cases, the details can obscure the big picture. With object-oriented programming, you focus on the commonalities among objects in the system rather than on the special cases.

We distinguish between the *is-a relationship* and the *has-a relationship*. Is-a represents inheritance. In an *is-a* relationship, an object of a subclass can also be treated as an object of its superclass. For example, a car *is a* vehicle. By contrast, *has-a* represents composition (see Chapter 8). In a *has-a* relationship, an object contains as members references to other objects. For example, a car *has a* steering wheel (and a car object has a reference to a steering wheel object).

New classes can inherit from classes in *class libraries*. Organizations develop their own class libraries and can take advantage of others available worldwide. Some day, most new software likely will be constructed from *standardized reusable components*, just as automobiles and most computer hardware are constructed today. This will facilitate the development of more powerful, abundant and economical software.

9.2 Superclasses and Subclasses

Often, an object of one class *is an* object of another class as well. For example, in geometry, a rectangle *is a* quadrilateral (as are squares, parallelograms and trapezoids). Thus, in Java, class `Rectangle` can be said to inherit from class `Quadrilateral`. In this context, class `Quadrilateral` is a superclass and class `Rectangle` is a subclass. A rectangle *is a* specific type of quadrilateral, but it is incorrect to claim that every quadrilateral *is a* rectangle—the quadrilateral could be a parallelogram or some other shape. Figure 9.1 lists several simple examples of superclasses and subclasses—note that superclasses tend to be "more general" and subclasses "more specific."

Because every subclass object *is an* object of its superclass, and one superclass can have many subclasses, the set of objects represented by a superclass is typically larger than the set of objects represented by any of its subclasses. For example, the superclass `Vehicle` represents all vehicles, including cars, trucks, boats, bicycles and so on. By contrast, subclass `Car` represents a smaller, more specific subset of vehicles.

Superclass	Subclasses
Student	GraduateStudent, UndergraduateStudent
Shape	Circle, Triangle, Rectangle
Loan	CarLoan, HomeImprovementLoan, MortgageLoan
Employee	Faculty, Staff
BankAccount	CheckingAccount, SavingsAccount

Fig. 9.1 | Inheritance examples.

Inheritance relationships form tree-like hierarchical structures. A superclass exists in a hierarchical relationship with its subclasses. When classes participate in inheritance relationships, they become "affiliated" with other classes. A class becomes either a superclass, supplying members to other classes, or a subclass, inheriting its members from other classes. In some cases, a class is both a superclass and a subclass.

Let's develop a sample class hierarchy (Fig. 9.2), also called an *inheritance hierarchy*. A university community has thousands of members, including employees, students and alumni. Employees are either faculty or staff members. Faculty members are either administrators (e.g., deans and department chairpersons) or teachers. Note that the hierarchy could contain many other classes. For example, students can be graduate or undergraduate students. Undergraduate students can be freshmen, sophomores, juniors or seniors.

Each arrow in the hierarchy represents an *is-a* relationship. As we follow the arrows in this class hierarchy, we can state, for instance, that "an `Employee` *is a* `CommunityMember`" and "a `Teacher` *is a* `Faculty` member." `CommunityMember` is the direct superclass of `Employee`, `Student` and `Alumnus`, and is an indirect superclass of all the other classes in the diagram. Starting from the bottom of the diagram, the reader can follow the arrows and apply the *is-a* relationship up to the topmost superclass. For example, an `Administrator` *is a* `Faculty` member, *is an* `Employee` and *is a* `CommunityMember`.

Now consider the `Shape` inheritance hierarchy in Fig. 9.3. This hierarchy begins with superclass `Shape`, which is extended by subclasses `TwoDimensionalShape` and `ThreeDimensionalShape`—Shapes are either `TwoDimensionalShapes` or `ThreeDimensionalShapes`. The third level of this hierarchy contains some more specific types of `TwoDimensionalShapes` and `ThreeDimensionalShapes`. As in Fig. 9.2, we can follow the arrows from the bottom of the diagram to the topmost superclass in this class hierarchy to identify several *is-a* relationships. For instance, a `Triangle` *is a* `TwoDimensionalShape` and *is a* `Shape`, while a `Sphere` *is a* `ThreeDimensionalShape` and *is a* `Shape`. Note that this hierarchy could contain many other classes. For example, ellipses and trapezoids are `TwoDimensionalShapes`.

Not every class relationship is an inheritance relationship. In Chapter 8, we discussed the *has-a* relationship, in which classes have members that are references to objects of other classes. Such relationships create classes by composition of existing classes. For example,

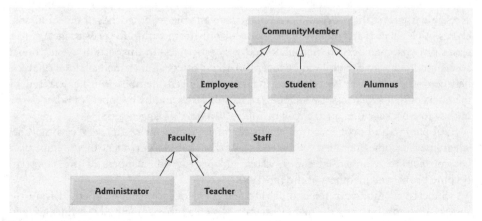

Fig. 9.2 | Inheritance hierarchy for university `CommunityMembers`.

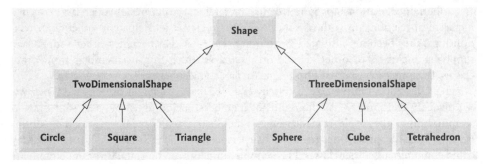

Fig. 9.3 | Inheritance hierarchy for Shapes.

given the classes Employee, BirthDate and TelephoneNumber, it is improper to say that an Employee *is a* BirthDate or that an Employee *is a* TelephoneNumber. However, an Employee *has a* BirthDate, and an Employee *has a* TelephoneNumber.

It is possible to treat superclass objects and subclass objects similarly—their commonalities are expressed in the members of the superclass. Objects of all classes that extend a common superclass can be treated as objects of that superclass (i.e., such objects have an *is a* relationship with the superclass). However, superclass objects cannot be treated as objects of their subclasses. For example, all cars are vehicles, but not all vehicles are cars (the other vehicles could be trucks, planes or bicycles, for example). Later in this chapter and in Chapter 10, Object-Oriented Programming: Polymorphism, we consider many examples that take advantage of the *is-a* relationship.

One problem with inheritance is that a subclass can inherit methods that it does not need or should not have. Even when a superclass method is appropriate for a subclass, that subclass often needs a customized version of the method. In such cases, the subclass can *override* (redefine) the superclass method with an appropriate implementation, as we'll see often in the chapter's code examples.

9.3 protected Members

Chapter 8 discussed access modifiers public and private. A class's public members are accessible wherever the program has a reference to an object of that class or one of its subclasses. A class's private members are accessible only from within the class itself. A superclass's private members are not inherited by its subclasses. In this section, we introduce access modifier protected. Using protected access offers an intermediate level of access between public and private. A superclass's protected members can be accessed by members of that superclass, by members of its subclasses and by members of other classes in the same package (i.e., protected members also have package access).

All public and protected superclass members retain their original access modifier when they become members of the subclass (i.e., public members of the superclass become public members of the subclass, and protected members of the superclass become protected members of the subclass).

Subclass methods can refer to public and protected members inherited from the superclass simply by using the member names. When a subclass method overrides a superclass method, the superclass method can be accessed from the subclass by preceding the superclass method name with keyword `super` and a dot (.) separator. We discuss accessing overridden members of the superclass in Section 9.4.

Software Engineering Observation 9.1

Methods of a subclass cannot directly access `private` members of their superclass. A subclass can change the state of `private` superclass instance variables only through non-private methods provided in the superclass and inherited by the subclass.

Software Engineering Observation 9.2

Declaring `private` instance variables helps programmers test, debug and correctly modify systems. If a subclass could access its superclass's `private` instance variables, classes that inherit from that subclass could access the instance variables as well. This would propagate access to what should be `private` instance variables, and the benefits of information hiding would be lost.

9.4 Relationship between Superclasses and Subclasses

In this section, we use an inheritance hierarchy containing types of employees in a company's payroll application to discuss the relationship between a superclass and its subclass. In this company, commission employees (who will be represented as objects of a superclass) are paid a percentage of their sales, while base-salaried commission employees (who will be represented as objects of a subclass) receive a base salary plus a percentage of their sales.

We divide our discussion of the relationship between commission employees and base-salaried commission employees into five examples. The first example declares class `CommissionEmployee`, which directly inherits from class `Object` and declares as `private` instance variables a first name, last name, social security number, commission rate and gross (i.e., total) sales amount.

The second example declares class `BasePlusCommissionEmployee`, which also directly inherits from class `Object` and declares as `private` instance variables a first name, last name, social security number, commission rate, gross sales amount and base salary. We create the latter class by writing every line of code the class requires—we'll soon see that it is much more efficient to create this class by inheriting from class `CommissionEmployee`.

The third example declares a separate `BasePlusCommissionEmployee2` class that extends class `CommissionEmployee` (i.e., a `BasePlusCommissionEmployee2` *is a* `CommissionEmployee` who also has a base salary) and attempts to access class `CommissionEmployee`'s `private` members—this results in compilation errors, because the subclass cannot access the superclass's `private` instance variables.

The fourth example shows that if `CommissionEmployee`'s instance variables are declared as `protected`, a `BasePlusCommissionEmployee3` class that extends class `CommissionEmployee2` can access that data directly. For this purpose, we declare class `CommissionEmployee2` with `protected` instance variables. Both of the `BasePlusCommissionEmployee` classes contain identical functionality, but we show how the class `BasePlusCommissionEmployee3` is easier to create and manage.

After we discuss the convenience of using `protected` instance variables, we create the fifth example, which sets the `CommissionEmployee` instance variables back to `private` in class `CommissionEmployee3` to enforce good software engineering. Then we show how a separate `BasePlusCommissionEmployee4` class, which extends class `CommissionEmployee3`, can use `CommissionEmployee3`'s `public` methods to manipulate `CommissionEmployee3`'s `private` instance variables.

9.4.1 Creating and Using a CommissionEmployee Class

We begin by declaring class CommissionEmployee (Fig. 9.4). Line 4 begins the class declaration and indicates that class CommissionEmployee *extends* (i.e., inherits from) class Object (from package java.lang). Java programmers use inheritance to create classes from existing classes. In fact, every class in Java (except Object) extends an existing class. Because class CommissionEmployee extends class Object, class CommissionEmployee inherits the methods of class Object—class Object does not have any fields. In fact, every Java class directly or indirectly inherits Object's methods. If a class does not specify that it extends another class, the new class implicitly extends Object. For this reason, programmers typically do not include "extends Object" in their code—we do so in this example only for demonstration purposes.

Software Engineering Observation 9.3

The Java compiler sets the superclass of a class to Object when the class declaration does not explicitly extend a superclass.

```
1   // Fig. 9.4: CommissionEmployee.java
2   // CommissionEmployee class represents a commission employee.
3
4   public class CommissionEmployee extends Object
5   {
6      private String firstName;
7      private String lastName;
8      private String socialSecurityNumber;
9      private double grossSales; // gross weekly sales
10     private double commissionRate; // commission percentage
11
12     // five-argument constructor
13     public CommissionEmployee( String first, String last, String ssn,
14        double sales, double rate )
15     {
16        // implicit call to Object constructor occurs here
17        firstName = first;
18        lastName = last;
19        socialSecurityNumber = ssn;
20        setGrossSales( sales ); // validate and store gross sales
21        setCommissionRate( rate ); // validate and store commission rate
22     } // end five-argument CommissionEmployee constructor
23
24     // set first name
25     public void setFirstName( String first )
26     {
27        firstName = first;
28     } // end method setFirstName
29
30     // return first name
31     public String getFirstName()
32     {
```

Fig. 9.4 | CommissionEmployee class represents an employee paid a percentage of gross sales. (Part 1 of 3.)

```
33        return firstName;
34     } // end method getFirstName
35
36     // set· last name
37     public void setLastName( String last )
38     {
39        lastName = last;
40     } // end method setLastName
41
42     // return last name
43     public String getLastName()
44     {
45        return lastName;
46     } // end method getLastName
47
48     // set social security number
49     public void setSocialSecurityNumber( String ssn )
50     {
51        socialSecurityNumber = ssn; // should validate
52     } // end method setSocialSecurityNumber
53
54     // return social security number
55     public String getSocialSecurityNumber()
56     {
57        return socialSecurityNumber;
58     } // end method getSocialSecurityNumber
59
60     // set gross sales amount
61     public void setGrossSales( double sales )
62     {
63        grossSales = ( sales < 0.0 ) ? 0.0 : sales;
64     } // end method setGrossSales
65
66     // return gross sales amount
67     public double getGrossSales()
68     {
69        return grossSales;
70     } // end method getGrossSales
71
72     // set commission rate
73     public void setCommissionRate( double rate )
74     {
75        commissionRate = ( rate > 0.0 && rate < 1.0 ) ? rate : 0.0;
76     } // end method setCommissionRate
77
78     // return commission rate
79     public double getCommissionRate()
80     {
81        return commissionRate;
82     } // end method getCommissionRate
83
```

Fig. 9.4 | CommissionEmployee class represents an employee paid a percentage of gross sales. (Part 2 of 3.)

```
84       // calculate earnings
85       public double earnings()
86       {
87          return commissionRate * grossSales;
88       } // end method earnings
89
90       // return String representation of CommissionEmployee object
91       public String toString()
92       {
93          return String.format( "%s: %s %s\n%s: %s\n%s: %.2f\n%s: %.2f",
94             "commission employee", firstName, lastName,
95             "social security number", socialSecurityNumber,
96             "gross sales", grossSales,
97             "commission rate", commissionRate );
98       } // end method toString
99    } // end class CommissionEmployee
```

Fig. 9.4 | CommissionEmployee class represents an employee paid a percentage of gross sales. (Part 3 of 3.)

The public services of class CommissionEmployee include a constructor (lines 13–22) and methods earnings (lines 85–88) and toString (lines 91–98). Lines 25–82 declare public *get* and *set* methods for manipulating the class's instance variables (declared in lines 6–10) firstName, lastName, socialSecurityNumber, grossSales and commissionRate. Class CommissionEmployee declares each of its instance variables as private, so objects of other classes cannot directly access these variables. Declaring instance variables as private and providing *get* and *set* methods to manipulate and validate the instance variables helps enforce good software engineering. Methods setGrossSales and setCommissionRate, for example, validate their arguments before assigning the values to instance variables gross-Sales and commissionRate, respectively.

Constructors are not inherited, so class CommissionEmployee does not inherit class Object's constructor. However, class CommissionEmployee's constructor calls class Object's constructor implicitly. In fact, the first task of any subclass constructor is to call its direct superclass's constructor, either explicitly or implicitly (if no constructor call is specified), to ensure that the instance variables inherited from the superclass are initialized properly. The syntax for calling a superclass constructor explicitly is discussed in Section 9.4.3. If the code does not include an explicit call to the superclass constructor, Java implicitly calls the superclass's default or no-argument constructor. The comment in line 16 of Fig. 9.4 indicates where the implicit call to the superclass Object's default constructor is made (the programmer does not write the code for this call). Object's default (empty) constructor does nothing. Note that even if a class does not have constructors, the default constructor that the compiler implicitly declares for the class will call the superclass's default or no-argument constructor.

After the implicit call to Object's constructor occurs, lines 17–21 of CommissionEmployee's constructor assign values to the class's instance variables. Note that we do not validate the values of arguments first, last and ssn before assigning them to the corresponding instance variables. We could validate the first and last names—perhaps by ensuring that they are of a reasonable length. Similarly, a social security number could be validated to ensure that it contains nine digits, with or without dashes (e.g., 123-45-6789 or 123456789).

Method earnings (lines 85–88) calculates a CommissionEmployee's earnings. Line 87 multiplies the commissionRate by the grossSales and returns the result.

Method toString (lines 91–98) is special—it is one of the methods that every class inherits directly or indirectly from class Object, which is the root of the Java class hierarchy. Section 9.7 summarizes class Object's methods. Method toString returns a String representing an object. This method is called implicitly by a program whenever an object must be converted to a string representation, such as when an object is output by printf or String method format using the %s format specifier. Class Object's toString method returns a String that includes the name of the object's class. It is primarily a placeholder that can be overridden by a subclass to specify an appropriate string representation of the data in a subclass object. Method toString of class CommissionEmployee overrides (redefines) class Object's toString method. When invoked, CommissionEmployee's toString method uses String method format to return a String containing information about the CommissionEmployee. To override a superclass method, a subclass must declare a method with the same signature (method name, number of parameters, parameter types and order of parameter types) as the superclass method—Object's toString method takes no parameters, so CommissionEmployee declares toString with no parameters.

Common Programming Error 9.1

It is a syntax error to override a method with a more restricted access modifier—a public method of the superclass cannot become a protected or private method in the subclass; a protected method of the superclass cannot become a private method in the subclass. Doing so would break the is-a relationship in which it is required that all subclass objects be able to respond to method calls that are made to public methods declared in the superclass. If a public method could be overridden as a protected or private method, the subclass objects would not be able to respond to the same method calls as superclass objects. Once a method is declared public in a superclass, the method remains public for all that class's direct and indirect subclasses.

Figure 9.5 tests class CommissionEmployee. Lines 9–10 instantiate a CommissionEmployee object and invoke CommissionEmployee's constructor (lines 13–22 of Fig. 9.4) to initialize it with "Sue" as the first name, "Jones" as the last name, "222-22-2222" as the social security number, 10000 as the gross sales amount and .06 as the commission rate. Lines 15–24 use CommissionEmployee's *get* methods to retrieve the object's instance vari-

```
 1  // Fig. 9.5: CommissionEmployeeTest.java
 2  // Testing class CommissionEmployee.
 3
 4  public class CommissionEmployeeTest
 5  {
 6     public static void main( String args[] )
 7     {
 8        // instantiate CommissionEmployee object
 9        CommissionEmployee employee = new CommissionEmployee(
10           "Sue", "Jones", "222-22-2222", 10000, .06 );
11
```

Fig. 9.5 | CommissionEmployee class test program. (Part 1 of 2.)

```
12        // get commission employee data
13        System.out.println(
14            "Employee information obtained by get methods: \n" );
15        System.out.printf( "%s %s\n", "First name is",
16            employee.getFirstName() );
17        System.out.printf( "%s %s\n", "Last name is",
18            employee.getLastName() );
19        System.out.printf( "%s %s\n", "Social security number is",
20            employee.getSocialSecurityNumber() );
21        System.out.printf( "%s %.2f\n", "Gross sales is",
22            employee.getGrossSales() );
23        System.out.printf( "%s %.2f\n", "Commission rate is",
24            employee.getCommissionRate() );
25
26        employee.setGrossSales( 500 ); // set gross sales
27        employee.setCommissionRate( .1 ); // set commission rate
28
29        System.out.printf( "\n%s:\n\n%s\n",
30            "Updated employee information obtained by toString", employee );
31    } // end main
32 } // end class CommissionEmployeeTest
```

```
Employee information obtained by get methods:

First name is Sue
Last name is Jones
Social security number is 222-22-2222
Gross sales is 10000.00
Commission rate is 0.06

Updated employee information obtained by toString:

commission employee: Sue Jones
social security number: 222-22-2222
gross sales: 500.00
commission rate: 0.10
```

Fig. 9.5 | CommissionEmployee class test program. (Part 2 of 2.)

able values for output. Lines 26–27 invoke the object's methods setGrossSales and set-CommissionRate to change the values of instance variables grossSales and commissionRate. Lines 29–30 output the string representation of the updated CommissionEmployee. Note that when an object is output using the %s format specifier, the object's toString method is invoked implicitly to obtain the object's string representation.

9.4.2 Creating a BasePlusCommissionEmployee Class without Using Inheritance

We now discuss the second part of our introduction to inheritance by declaring and testing (a completely new and independent) class BasePlusCommissionEmployee (Fig. 9.6), which contains a first name, last name, social security number, gross sales amount, commission rate and base salary. Class BasePlusCommissionEmployee's public services include a BasePlusCommissionEmployee constructor (lines 15–25) and methods earnings

```
1   // Fig. 9.6: BasePlusCommissionEmployee.java
2   // BasePlusCommissionEmployee class represents an employee that receives
3   // a base salary in addition to commission.
4
5   public class BasePlusCommissionEmployee
6   {
7      private String firstName;
8      private String lastName;
9      private String socialSecurityNumber;
10     private double grossSales; // gross weekly sales
11     private double commissionRate; // commission percentage
12     private double baseSalary; // base salary per week
13
14     // six-argument constructor
15     public BasePlusCommissionEmployee( String first, String last,
16        String ssn, double sales, double rate, double salary )
17     {
18        // implicit call to Object constructor occurs here
19        firstName = first;
20        lastName = last;
21        socialSecurityNumber = ssn;
22        setGrossSales( sales ); // validate and store gross sales
23        setCommissionRate( rate ); // validate and store commission rate
24        setBaseSalary( salary ); // validate and store base salary
25     } // end six-argument BasePlusCommissionEmployee constructor
26
27     // set first name
28     public void setFirstName( String first )
29     {
30        firstName = first;
31     } // end method setFirstName
32
33     // return first name
34     public String getFirstName()
35     {
36        return firstName;
37     } // end method getFirstName
38
39     // set last name
40     public void setLastName( String last )
41     {
42        lastName = last;
43     } // end method setLastName
44
45     // return last name
46     public String getLastName()
47     {
48        return lastName;
49     } // end method getLastName
50
```

Fig. 9.6 | BasePlusCommissionEmployee class represents an employee who receives a base salary in addition to a commission. (Part 1 of 3.)

```
51     // set social security number
52     public void setSocialSecurityNumber( String ssn )
53     {
54        socialSecurityNumber = ssn; // should validate
55     } // end method setSocialSecurityNumber
56
57     // return social security number
58     public String getSocialSecurityNumber()
59     {
60        return socialSecurityNumber;
61     } // end method getSocialSecurityNumber
62
63     // set gross sales amount
64     public void setGrossSales( double sales )
65     {
66        grossSales = ( sales < 0.0 ) ? 0.0 : sales;
67     } // end method setGrossSales
68
69     // return gross sales amount
70     public double getGrossSales()
71     {
72        return grossSales;
73     } // end method getGrossSales
74
75     // set commission rate
76     public void setCommissionRate( double rate )
77     {
78        commissionRate = ( rate > 0.0 && rate < 1.0 ) ? rate : 0.0;
79     } // end method setCommissionRate
80
81     // return commission rate
82     public double getCommissionRate()
83     {
84        return commissionRate;
85     } // end method getCommissionRate
86
87     // set base salary
88     public void setBaseSalary( double salary )
89     {
90        baseSalary = ( salary < 0.0 ) ? 0.0 : salary;
91     } // end method setBaseSalary
92
93     // return base salary
94     public double getBaseSalary()
95     {
96        return baseSalary;
97     } // end method getBaseSalary
98
99     // calculate earnings
100    public double earnings()
101    {
```

Fig. 9.6 | BasePlusCommissionEmployee class represents an employee who receives a base salary in addition to a commission. (Part 2 of 3.)

```
102             return baseSalary + ( commissionRate * grossSales );
103        } // end method earnings
104
105        // return String representation of BasePlusCommissionEmployee
106        public String toString()
107        {
108            return String.format(
109                "%s: %s %s\n%s: %s\n%s: %.2f\n%s: %.2f\n%s: %.2f",
110                "base-salaried commission employee", firstName, lastName,
111                "social security number", socialSecurityNumber,
112                "gross sales", grossSales, "commission rate", commissionRate,
113                "base salary", baseSalary );
114        } // end method toString
115 } // end class BasePlusCommissionEmployee
```

Fig. 9.6 | `BasePlusCommissionEmployee` class represents an employee who receives a base salary in addition to a commission. (Part 3 of 3.)

(lines 100–103) and `toString` (lines 106–114). Lines 28–97 declare public *get* and *set* methods for the class's private instance variables (declared in lines 7–12) `firstName`, `lastName`, `socialSecurityNumber`, `grossSales`, `commissionRate` and `baseSalary`. These variables and methods encapsulate all the necessary features of a base-salaried commission employee. Note the similarity between this class and class `CommissionEmployee` (Fig. 9.4)—in this example, we'll not yet exploit that similarity.

Note that class `BasePlusCommissionEmployee` does not specify "extends Object" in line 5, so the class implicitly extends `Object`. Also note that, like class `CommissionEmployee`'s constructor (lines 13–22 of Fig. 9.4), class `BasePlusCommissionEmployee`'s constructor invokes class `Object`'s default constructor implicitly, as noted in the comment in line 18.

Class `BasePlusCommissionEmployee`'s `earnings` method (lines 100–103) computes the earnings of a base-salaried commission employee. Line 102 returns the result of adding the employee's base salary to the product of the commission rate and the employee's gross sales.

Class `BasePlusCommissionEmployee` overrides `Object` method `toString` to return a `String` containing the `BasePlusCommissionEmployee`'s information. Once again, we use format specifier `%.2f` to format the gross sales, commission rate and base salary with two digits of precision to the right of the decimal point (line 109).

Figure 9.7 tests class `BasePlusCommissionEmployee`. Lines 9–11 instantiate a `BasePlusCommissionEmployee` object and pass "Bob", "Lewis", "333-33-3333", 5000, .04 and 300 to the constructor as the first name, last name, social security number, gross sales, commission rate and base salary, respectively. Lines 16–27 use `BasePlusCommissionEmployee`'s *get* methods to retrieve the values of the object's instance variables for output. Line 29 invokes the object's `setBaseSalary` method to change the base salary. Method `setBaseSalary` (Fig. 9.6, lines 88–91) ensures that instance variable `baseSalary` is not assigned a negative value, because an employee's base salary cannot be negative. Lines 31–33 of Fig. 9.7 invoke the object's `toString` method explicitly to get the object's string representation.

```java
 1   // Fig. 9.7: BasePlusCommissionEmployeeTest.java
 2   // Testing class BasePlusCommissionEmployee.
 3
 4   public class BasePlusCommissionEmployeeTest
 5   {
 6      public static void main( String args[] )
 7      {
 8         // instantiate BasePlusCommissionEmployee object
 9         BasePlusCommissionEmployee employee =
10            new BasePlusCommissionEmployee(
11            "Bob", "Lewis", "333-33-3333", 5000, .04, 300 );
12
13         // get base-salaried commission employee data
14         System.out.println(
15            "Employee information obtained by get methods: \n" );
16         System.out.printf( "%s %s\n", "First name is",
17            employee.getFirstName() );
18         System.out.printf( "%s %s\n", "Last name is",
19            employee.getLastName() );
20         System.out.printf( "%s %s\n", "Social security number is",
21            employee.getSocialSecurityNumber() );
22         System.out.printf( "%s %.2f\n", "Gross sales is",
23            employee.getGrossSales() );
24         System.out.printf( "%s %.2f\n", "Commission rate is",
25            employee.getCommissionRate() );
26         System.out.printf( "%s %.2f\n", "Base salary is",
27            employee.getBaseSalary() );
28
29         employee.setBaseSalary( 1000 ); // set base salary
30
31         System.out.printf( "\n%s:\n\n%s\n",
32            "Updated employee information obtained by toString",
33            employee.toString() );
34      } // end main
35   } // end class BasePlusCommissionEmployeeTest
```

```
Employee information obtained by get methods:

First name is Bob
Last name is Lewis
Social security number is 333-33-3333
Gross sales is 5000.00
Commission rate is 0.04
Base salary is 300.00

Updated employee information obtained by toString:

base-salaried commission employee: Bob Lewis
social security number: 333-33-3333
gross sales: 5000.00
commission rate: 0.04
base salary: 1000.00
```

Fig. 9.7 | BasePlusCommissionEmployee test program.

Much of class `BasePlusCommissionEmployee`'s code (Fig. 9.6) is similar, if not identical, to that of class `CommissionEmployee` (Fig. 9.4). For example, in class `BasePlusCommissionEmployee`, private instance variables `firstName` and `lastName` and methods `setFirstName`, `getFirstName`, `setLastName` and `getLastName` are identical to those of class `CommissionEmployee`. Classes `CommissionEmployee` and `BasePlusCommissionEmployee` also both contain private instance variables `socialSecurityNumber`, `commissionRate` and `grossSales`, as well as *get* and *set* methods to manipulate these variables. In addition, the `BasePlusCommissionEmployee` constructor is almost identical to that of class `CommissionEmployee`, except that `BasePlusCommissionEmployee`'s constructor also sets the `baseSalary`. The other additions to class `BasePlusCommissionEmployee` are private instance variable `baseSalary` and methods `setBaseSalary` and `getBaseSalary`. Class `BasePlusCommissionEmployee`'s `toString` method is nearly identical to that of class `CommissionEmployee` except that `BasePlusCommissionEmployee`'s `toString` also outputs instance variable `baseSalary` with two digits of precision to the right of the decimal point.

We literally copied code from class `CommissionEmployee` and pasted it into class `BasePlusCommissionEmployee`, then modified class `BasePlusCommissionEmployee` to include a base salary and methods that manipulate the base salary. This "copy-and-paste" approach is often error prone and time consuming. Worse yet, it can spread many physical copies of the same code throughout a system, creating a code-maintenance nightmare. Is there a way to "absorb" the instance variables and methods of one class in a way that makes them part of other classes without duplicating code? In the next several examples, we answer this question, using a more elegant approach to building classes that emphasizes the benefits of inheritance.

Software Engineering Observation 9.4

Copying and pasting code from one class to another can spread errors across multiple source-code files. To avoid duplicating code (and possibly errors), use inheritance or, in some cases, composition, rather than the "copy-and-paste" approach, in situations where you want one class to "absorb" the instance variables and methods of another class.

Software Engineering Observation 9.5

With inheritance, the common instance variables and methods of all the classes in the hierarchy are declared in a superclass. When changes are required for these common features, software developers need only to make the changes in the superclass—subclasses then inherit the changes. Without inheritance, changes would need to be made to all the source-code files that contain a copy of the code in question.

9.4.3 Creating a `CommissionEmployee`–`BasePlusCommissionEmployee` Inheritance Hierarchy

Now we declare class `BasePlusCommissionEmployee2` (Fig. 9.8), which extends class `CommissionEmployee` (Fig. 9.4). A `BasePlusCommissionEmployee2` object *is a* `CommissionEmployee` (because inheritance passes on the capabilities of class `CommissionEmployee`), but class `BasePlusCommissionEmployee2` also has instance variable `baseSalary` (Fig. 9.8, line 6). Keyword `extends` in line 4 of the class declaration indicates inheritance. As a subclass, `BasePlusCommissionEmployee2` inherits the `public` and `protected` instance variables and methods of class `CommissionEmployee`. The constructor of class `CommissionEmployee` is not inherited. Thus, the `public` services of `BasePlusCommissionEmployee2` include its constructor (lines 9–16), public methods inherited from class CommissionEmployee, method setBaseSalary (lines 19–22), method getBaseSalary (lines 25–28), method earnings (lines 31–35) and method toString (lines 38–47).

```java
1   // Fig. 9.8: BasePlusCommissionEmployee2.java
2   // BasePlusCommissionEmployee2 inherits from class CommissionEmployee.
3
4   public class BasePlusCommissionEmployee2 extends CommissionEmployee
5   {
6      private double baseSalary; // base salary per week
7
8      // six-argument constructor
9      public BasePlusCommissionEmployee2( String first, String last,
10        String ssn, double sales, double rate, double salary )
11     {
12        // explicit call to superclass CommissionEmployee constructor
13        super( first, last, ssn, sales, rate );
14
15        setBaseSalary( salary ); // validate and store base salary
16     } // end six-argument BasePlusCommissionEmployee2 constructor
17
18     // set base salary
19     public void setBaseSalary( double salary )
20     {
21        baseSalary = ( salary < 0.0 ) ? 0.0 : salary;
22     } // end method setBaseSalary
23
24     // return base salary
25     public double getBaseSalary()
26     {
27        return baseSalary;
28     } // end method getBaseSalary
29
30     // calculate earnings
31     public double earnings()
32     {
33        // not allowed: commissionRate and grossSales private in superclass
34        return baseSalary + ( commissionRate * grossSales );
35     } // end method earnings
36
37     // return String representation of BasePlusCommissionEmployee2
38     public String toString()
39     {
40        // not allowed: attempts to access private superclass members
41        return String.format(
42           "%s: %s %s\n%s: %s\n%s: %.2f\n%s: %.2f\n%s: %.2f",
43           "base-salaried commission employee", firstName, lastName,
44           "social security number", socialSecurityNumber,
45           "gross sales", grossSales, "commission rate", commissionRate,
46           "base salary", baseSalary );
47     } // end method toString
48  } // end class BasePlusCommissionEmployee2
```

Fig. 9.8 | private superclass members cannot be accessed in a subclass. (Part 1 of 2.)

```
BasePlusCommissionEmployee2.java:34: commissionRate has private access in
CommissionEmployee
      return baseSalary + ( commissionRate * grossSales );
                             ^
BasePlusCommissionEmployee2.java:34: grossSales has private access in
CommissionEmployee
      return baseSalary + ( commissionRate * grossSales );
                                              ^
BasePlusCommissionEmployee2.java:43: firstName has private access in
CommissionEmployee
         "base-salaried commission employee", firstName, lastName,
                                               ^
BasePlusCommissionEmployee2.java:43: lastName has private access in
CommissionEmployee
         "base-salaried commission employee", firstName, lastName,
                                                          ^
BasePlusCommissionEmployee2.java:44: socialSecurityNumber has private access
in CommissionEmployee
         "social security number", socialSecurityNumber,
                                   ^
BasePlusCommissionEmployee2.java:45: grossSales has private access in
CommissionEmployee
         "gross sales", grossSales, "commission rate", commissionRate,
                        ^
BasePlusCommissionEmployee2.java:45: commissionRate has private access in
CommissionEmployee
         "gross sales", grossSales, "commission rate", commissionRate,
                                                        ^
7 errors
```

Fig. 9.8 | `private` superclass members cannot be accessed in a subclass. (Part 2 of 2.)

Each subclass constructor must implicitly or explicitly call its superclass constructor to ensure that the instance variables inherited from the superclass are initialized properly. BasePlusCommissionEmployee2's six-argument constructor (lines 9–16) explicitly calls class CommissionEmployee's five-argument constructor to initialize the superclass portion of a BasePlusCommissionEmployee2 object (i.e., variables firstName, lastName, social-SecurityNumber, grossSales and commissionRate). Line 13 in BasePlusCommission-Employee2's six-argument constructor invokes the CommissionEmployee's five-argument constructor (declared at lines 13–22 of Fig. 9.4) by using the *superclass constructor call syntax*—keyword super, followed by a set of parentheses containing the superclass constructor arguments. The arguments first, last, ssn, sales and rate are used to initialize superclass members firstName, lastName, socialSecurityNumber, grossSales and commissionRate, respectively. If BasePlusCommissionEmployee2's constructor did not invoke CommissionEmployee's constructor explicitly, Java would attempt to invoke class CommissionEmployee's no-argument or default constructor—but the class does not have such a constructor, so the compiler would issue an error. The explicit superclass constructor call in line 13 of Fig. 9.8 must be the first statement in the subclass constructor's body. Also, when a superclass contains a no-argument constructor, you can use super() to call that constructor explicitly, but this is rarely done.

Common Programming Error 9.2

A compilation error occurs if a subclass constructor calls one of its superclass constructors with arguments that do not match exactly the number and types of parameters specified in one of the superclass constructor declarations.

The compiler generates errors for line 34 of Fig. 9.8 because superclass CommissionEmployee's instance variables commissionRate and grossSales are private—subclass BasePlusCommissionEmployee2's methods are not allowed to access superclass CommissionEmployee's private instance variables. Note that we used bold black text in Fig. 9.8 to indicate erroneous code. The compiler issues additional errors at lines 43–45 of BasePlusCommissionEmployee2's toString method for the same reason. The errors in BasePlusCommissionEmployee2 could have been prevented by using the *get* methods inherited from class CommissionEmployee. For example, line 34 could have used getCommissionRate and getGrossSales to access CommissionEmployee's private instance variables commissionRate and grossSales, respectively. Lines 43–45 also could have used appropriate *get* methods to retrieve the values of the superclass's instance variables.

9.4.4 CommissionEmployee–BasePlusCommissionEmployee Inheritance Hierarchy Using protected Instance Variables

To enable class BasePlusCommissionEmployee to directly access superclass instance variables firstName, lastName, socialSecurityNumber, grossSales and commissionRate, we can declare those members as protected in the superclass. As we discussed in Section 9.3, a superclass's protected members *are* inherited by all subclasses of that superclass. Class CommissionEmployee2 (Fig. 9.9) is a modification of class CommissionEmployee (Fig. 9.4) that declares instance variables firstName, lastName, socialSecurityNumber, grossSales and commissionRate as protected (Fig. 9.9, lines 6–10) rather than private. Other than the change in the class name (and thus the change in the constructor name) to CommissionEmployee2, the rest of the class declaration in Fig. 9.9 is identical to that of Fig. 9.4.

```
1   // Fig. 9.9: CommissionEmployee2.java
2   // CommissionEmployee2 class represents a commission employee.
3
4   public class CommissionEmployee2
5   {
6      protected String firstName;
7      protected String lastName;
8      protected String socialSecurityNumber;
9      protected double grossSales; // gross weekly sales
10     protected double commissionRate; // commission percentage
11
12     // five-argument constructor
13     public CommissionEmployee2( String first, String last, String ssn,
14        double sales, double rate )
15     {
16        // implicit call to Object constructor occurs here
17        firstName = first;
```

Fig. 9.9 | CommissionEmployee2 with protected instance variables. (Part 1 of 3.)

```
18          lastName = last;
19          socialSecurityNumber = ssn;
20          setGrossSales( sales ); // validate and store gross sales
21          setCommissionRate( rate ); // validate and store commission rate
22       } // end five-argument CommissionEmployee2 constructor
23
24       // set first name
25       public void setFirstName( String first )
26       {
27          firstName = first;
28       } // end method setFirstName
29
30       // return first name
31       public String getFirstName()
32       {
33          return firstName;
34       } // end method getFirstName
35
36       // set last name
37       public void setLastName( String last )
38       {
39          lastName = last;
40       } // end method setLastName
41
42       // return last name
43       public String getLastName()
44       {
45          return lastName;
46       } // end method getLastName
47
48       // set social security number
49       public void setSocialSecurityNumber( String ssn )
50       {
51          socialSecurityNumber = ssn; // should validate
52       } // end method setSocialSecurityNumber
53
54       // return social security number
55       public String getSocialSecurityNumber()
56       {
57          return socialSecurityNumber;
58       } // end method getSocialSecurityNumber
59
60       // set gross sales amount
61       public void setGrossSales( double sales )
62       {
63          grossSales = ( sales < 0.0 ) ? 0.0 : sales;
64       } // end method setGrossSales
65
66       // return gross sales amount
67       public double getGrossSales()
68       {
69          return grossSales;
70       } // end method getGrossSales
```

Fig. 9.9 | CommissionEmployee2 with protected instance variables. (Part 2 of 3.)

```
71
72      // set commission rate
73      public void setCommissionRate( double rate )
74      {
75         commissionRate = ( rate > 0.0 && rate < 1.0 ) ? rate : 0.0;
76      } // end method setCommissionRate
77
78      // return commission rate
79      public double getCommissionRate()
80      {
81         return commissionRate;
82      } // end method getCommissionRate
83
84      // calculate earnings
85      public double earnings()
86      {
87         return commissionRate * grossSales;
88      } // end method earnings
89
90      // return String representation of CommissionEmployee2 object
91      public String toString()
92      {
93         return String.format( "%s: %s %s\n%s: %s\n%s: %.2f\n%s: %.2f",
94            "commission employee", firstName, lastName,
95            "social security number", socialSecurityNumber,
96            "gross sales", grossSales,
97            "commission rate", commissionRate );
98      } // end method toString
99   } // end class CommissionEmployee2
```

Fig. 9.9 | CommissionEmployee2 with protected instance variables. (Part 3 of 3.)

We could have declared the superclass CommissionEmployee2's instance variables firstName, lastName, socialSecurityNumber, grossSales and commissionRate as public to enable subclass BasePlusCommissionEmployee2 to access the superclass instance variables. However, declaring public instance variables is poor software engineering because it allows unrestricted access to the instance variables, greatly increasing the chance of errors. With protected instance variables, the subclass gets access to the instance variables, but classes that are not subclasses and classes that are not in the same package cannot access these variables directly—recall that protected class members are also visible to other classes in the same package.

Class BasePlusCommissionEmployee3 (Fig. 9.10) is a modification of class Base-PlusCommissionEmployee2 (Fig. 9.8) that extends CommissionEmployee2 (line 5) rather than class CommissionEmployee. Objects of class BasePlusCommissionEmployee3 inherit CommissionEmployee2's protected instance variables firstName, lastName, socialSecurityNumber, grossSales and commissionRate—all these variables are now protected members of BasePlusCommissionEmployee3. As a result, the compiler does not generate errors when compiling line 32 of method earnings and lines 40–42 of method toString. If another class extends BasePlusCommissionEmployee3, the new subclass also inherits the protected members.

```
 1    // Fig. 9.10: BasePlusCommissionEmployee3.java
 2    // BasePlusCommissionEmployee3 inherits from CommissionEmployee2 and has
 3    // access to CommissionEmployee2's protected members.
 4
 5    public class BasePlusCommissionEmployee3 extends CommissionEmployee2
 6    {
 7       private double baseSalary; // base salary per week
 8
 9       // six-argument constructor
10       public BasePlusCommissionEmployee3( String first, String last,
11          String ssn, double sales, double rate, double salary )
12       {
13          super( first, last, ssn, sales, rate );
14          setBaseSalary( salary ); // validate and store base salary
15       } // end six-argument BasePlusCommissionEmployee3 constructor
16
17       // set base salary
18       public void setBaseSalary( double salary )
19       {
20          baseSalary = ( salary < 0.0 ) ? 0.0 : salary;
21       } // end method setBaseSalary
22
23       // return base salary
24       public double getBaseSalary()
25       {
26          return baseSalary;
27       } // end method getBaseSalary
28
29       // calculate earnings
30       public double earnings()
31       {
32          return baseSalary + ( commissionRate * grossSales );
33       } // end method earnings
34
35       // return String representation of BasePlusCommissionEmployee3
36       public String toString()
37       {
38          return String.format(
39             "%s: %s %s\n%s: %s\n%s: %.2f\n%s: %.2f\n%s: %.2f",
40             "base-salaried commission employee", firstName, lastName,
41             "social security number", socialSecurityNumber,
42             "gross sales", grossSales, "commission rate", commissionRate,
43             "base salary", baseSalary );
44       } // end method toString
45    } // end class BasePlusCommissionEmployee3
```

Fig. 9.10 | BasePlusCommissionEmployee3 inherits protected instance variables from CommissionEmployee2.

Class BasePlusCommissionEmployee3 does not inherit class CommissionEmployee2's constructor. However, class BasePlusCommissionEmployee3's six-argument constructor (lines 10–15) calls class CommissionEmployee2's five-argument constructor explicitly. BasePlusCommissionEmployee3's six-argument constructor must explicitly call the five-argument constructor of class CommissionEmployee2, because CommissionEmployee2 does not provide a no-argument constructor that could be invoked implicitly.

Figure 9.11 uses a BasePlusCommissionEmployee3 object to perform the same tasks that Fig. 9.7 performed on a BasePlusCommissionEmployee object (Fig. 9.6). Note that the outputs of the two programs are identical. Although we declared class BasePlusCommissionEmployee without using inheritance and declared class BasePlus-CommissionEmployee3 using inheritance, both classes provide the same functionality. The source code for class BasePlusCommissionEmployee3, which is 45 lines, is considerably shorter than that for class BasePlusCommissionEmployee, which is 115 lines, because class BasePlusCommissionEmployee3 inherits most of its functionality from Commission-Employee2, whereas class BasePlusCommissionEmployee inherits only class Object's functionality. Also, there is now only one copy of the commission employee functionality

```java
1   // Fig. 9.11: BasePlusCommissionEmployeeTest3.java
2   // Testing class BasePlusCommissionEmployee3.
3
4   public class BasePlusCommissionEmployeeTest3
5   {
6      public static void main( String args[] )
7      {
8         // instantiate BasePlusCommissionEmployee3 object
9         BasePlusCommissionEmployee3 employee =
10            new BasePlusCommissionEmployee3(
11            "Bob", "Lewis", "333-33-3333", 5000, .04, 300 );
12
13         // get base-salaried commission employee data
14         System.out.println(
15            "Employee information obtained by get methods: \n" );
16         System.out.printf( "%s %s\n", "First name is",
17            employee.getFirstName() );
18         System.out.printf( "%s %s\n", "Last name is",
19            employee.getLastName() );
20         System.out.printf( "%s %s\n", "Social security number is",
21            employee.getSocialSecurityNumber() );
22         System.out.printf( "%s %.2f\n", "Gross sales is",
23            employee.getGrossSales() );
24         System.out.printf( "%s %.2f\n", "Commission rate is",
25            employee.getCommissionRate() );
26         System.out.printf( "%s %.2f\n", "Base salary is",
27            employee.getBaseSalary() );
28
29         employee.setBaseSalary( 1000 ); // set base salary
30
31         System.out.printf( "\n%s:\n\n%s\n",
32            "Updated employee information obtained by toString",
33            employee.toString() );
34      } // end main
35   } // end class BasePlusCommissionEmployeeTest3
```

Fig. 9.11 | protected superclass members inherited into subclass BasePlusCommission-Employee3. (Part I of 2.)

```
Employee information obtained by get methods:

First name is Bob
Last name is Lewis
Social security number is 333-33-3333
Gross sales is 5000.00
Commission rate is 0.04
Base salary is 300.00

Updated employee information obtained by toString:

base-salaried commission employee: Bob Lewis
social security number: 333-33-3333
gross sales: 5000.00
commission rate: 0.04
base salary: 1000.00
```

Fig. 9.11 | protected superclass members inherited into subclass `BasePlusCommission-Employee3`. (Part 2 of 2.)

declared in class `CommissionEmployee2`. This makes the code easier to maintain, modify and debug, because the code related to a commission employee exists only in class `CommissionEmployee2`.

In this example, we declared superclass instance variables as `protected` so that subclasses could inherit them. Inheriting `protected` instance variables slightly increases performance, because we can directly access the variables in the subclass without incurring the overhead of a *set* or *get* method call. In most cases, however, it is better to use `private` instance variables to encourage proper software engineering, and leave code optimization issues to the compiler. Your code will be easier to maintain, modify and debug.

Using `protected` instance variables creates several potential problems. First, the subclass object can set an inherited variable's value directly without using a *set* method. Therefore, a subclass object can assign an invalid value to the variable, thus leaving the object in an inconsistent state. For example, if we were to declare `CommissionEmployee3`'s instance variable `grossSales` as `protected`, a subclass object (e.g., `BasePlusCommissionEmployee`) could then assign a negative value to `grossSales`. The second problem with using `protected` instance variables is that subclass methods are more likely to be written so that they depend on the superclass's data implementation. In practice, subclasses should depend only on the superclass services (i.e., non-`private` methods) and not on the superclass data implementation. With `protected` instance variables in the superclass, we may need to modify all the subclasses of the superclass if the superclass implementation changes. For example, if for some reason we were to change the names of instance variables `firstName` and `lastName` to `first` and `last`, then we would have to do so for all occurrences in which a subclass directly references superclass instance variables `firstName` and `lastName`. In such a case, the software is said to be *fragile* or *brittle*, because a small change in the superclass can "break" subclass implementation. The programmer should be able to change the superclass implementation while still providing the same services to the subclasses. (Of course, if the superclass services change, we must reimplement our subclasses.) A third problem is that a class's `protected` members are visible to all classes in the same package as the class containing the `protected` members—this is not always desirable.

Software Engineering Observation 9.6

Use the protected access modifier when a superclass should provide a method only to its subclasses and other classes in the same package, but not to other clients.

Software Engineering Observation 9.7

Declaring superclass instance variables private *(as opposed to* protected*) enables the superclass implementation of these instance variables to change without affecting subclass implementations.*

Error-Prevention Tip 9.1

When possible, do not include protected *instance variables in a superclass. Instead, include non-private methods that access* private *instance variables. This will ensure that objects of the class maintain consistent states.*

9.4.5 CommissionEmployee–BasePlusCommissionEmployee Inheritance Hierarchy Using private Instance Variables

We now reexamine our hierarchy once more, this time using the best software engineering practices. Class CommissionEmployee3 (Fig. 9.12) declares instance variables firstName, lastName, socialSecurityNumber, grossSales and commissionRate as private (lines 6–10) and provides public methods setFirstName, getFirstName, setLastName, getLast-Name, setSocialSecurityNumber, getSocialSecurityNumber, setGrossSales, get-GrossSales, setCommissionRate, getCommissionRate, earnings and toString for manipulating these values. Note that methods earnings (lines 85–88) and toString (lines 91–98) use the class's *get* methods to obtain the values of its instance variables. If we decide to change the instance variable names, the earnings and toString declarations will not require modification—only the bodies of the *get* and *set* methods that directly manipulate the instance variables will need to change. Note that these changes occur solely within the

```
1   // Fig. 9.12: CommissionEmployee3.java
2   // CommissionEmployee3 class represents a commission employee.
3
4   public class CommissionEmployee3
5   {
6      private String firstName;
7      private String lastName;
8      private String socialSecurityNumber;
9      private double grossSales; // gross weekly sales
10     private double commissionRate; // commission percentage
11
12     // five-argument constructor
13     public CommissionEmployee3( String first, String last, String ssn,
14        double sales, double rate )
15     {
16        // implicit call to Object constructor occurs here
17        firstName = first;
18        lastName = last;
19        socialSecurityNumber = ssn;
```

Fig. 9.12 | CommissionEmployee3 class uses methods to manipulate its private instance variables. (Part 1 of 3.)

```
20          setGrossSales( sales ); // validate and store gross sales
21          setCommissionRate( rate ); // validate and store commission rate
22       } // end five-argument CommissionEmployee3 constructor
23
24       // set first name
25       public void setFirstName( String first )
26       {
27          firstName = first;
28       } // end method setFirstName
29
30       // return first name
31       public String getFirstName()
32       {
33          return firstName;
34       } // end method getFirstName
35
36       // set last name
37       public void setLastName( String last )
38       {
39          lastName = last;
40       } // end method setLastName
41
42       // return last name
43       public String getLastName()
44       {
45          return lastName;
46       } // end method getLastName
47
48       // set social security number
49       public void setSocialSecurityNumber( String ssn )
50       {
51          socialSecurityNumber = ssn; // should validate
52       } // end method setSocialSecurityNumber
53
54       // return social security number
55       public String getSocialSecurityNumber()
56       {
57          return socialSecurityNumber;
58       } // end method getSocialSecurityNumber
59
60       // set gross sales amount
61       public void setGrossSales( double sales )
62       {
63          grossSales = ( sales < 0.0 ) ? 0.0 : sales;
64       } // end method setGrossSales
65
66       // return gross sales amount
67       public double getGrossSales()
68       {
69          return grossSales;
70       } // end method getGrossSales
```

Fig. 9.12 | CommissionEmployee3 class uses methods to manipulate its private instance variables. (Part 2 of 3.)

```
71
72      // set commission rate
73      public void setCommissionRate( double rate )
74      {
75         commissionRate = ( rate > 0.0 && rate < 1.0 ) ? rate : 0.0;
76      } // end method setCommissionRate
77
78      // return commission rate
79      public double getCommissionRate()
80      {
81         return commissionRate;
82      } // end method getCommissionRate
83
84      // calculate earnings
85      public double earnings()
86      {
87         return getCommissionRate() * getGrossSales();
88      } // end method earnings
89
90      // return String representation of CommissionEmployee3 object
91      public String toString()
92      {
93         return String.format( "%s: %s %s\n%s: %s\n%s: %.2f\n%s: %.2f",
94            "commission employee", getFirstName(), getLastName(),
95            "social security number", getSocialSecurityNumber(),
96            "gross sales", getGrossSales(),
97            "commission rate", getCommissionRate() );
98      } // end method toString
99   } // end class CommissionEmployee3
```

Fig. 9.12 | CommissionEmployee3 class uses methods to manipulate its private instance variables. (Part 3 of 3.)

superclass—no changes to the subclass are needed. Localizing the effects of changes like this is a good software engineering practice. Subclass BasePlusCommissionEmployee4 (Fig. 9.13) inherits CommissionEmployee3's non-private methods and can access the private superclass members via those methods.

Class BasePlusCommissionEmployee4 (Fig. 9.13) has several changes to its method implementations that distinguish it from class BasePlusCommissionEmployee3 (Fig. 9.10). Methods earnings (Fig. 9.13, lines 31–34) and toString (lines 37–41) each invoke method getBaseSalary to obtain the base salary value, rather than accessing baseSalary directly. If we decide to rename instance variable baseSalary, only the bodies of method setBaseSalary and getBaseSalary will need to change.

Class BasePlusCommissionEmployee4's earnings method (Fig. 9.13, lines 31–34) overrides class CommissionEmployee3's earnings method (Fig. 9.12, lines 85–88) to calculate the earnings of a base-salaried commission employee. The new version obtains the portion of the employee's earnings based on commission alone by calling CommissionEmployee3's earnings method with the expression super.earnings() (Fig. 9.13, line 33). BasePlusCommissionEmployee4's earnings method then adds the base salary to this value to calculate the total earnings of the employee. Note the syntax used to invoke an overridden superclass method from a subclass—place the keyword

```java
 1  // Fig. 9.13: BasePlusCommissionEmployee4.java
 2  // BasePlusCommissionEmployee4 class inherits from CommissionEmployee3 and
 3  // accesses CommissionEmployee3's private data via CommissionEmployee3's
 4  // public methods.
 5
 6  public class BasePlusCommissionEmployee4 extends CommissionEmployee3
 7  {
 8     private double baseSalary; // base salary per week
 9
10     // six-argument constructor
11     public BasePlusCommissionEmployee4( String first, String last,
12        String ssn, double sales, double rate, double salary )
13     {
14        super( first, last, ssn, sales, rate );
15        setBaseSalary( salary ); // validate and store base salary
16     } // end six-argument BasePlusCommissionEmployee4 constructor
17
18     // set base salary
19     public void setBaseSalary( double salary )
20     {
21        baseSalary = ( salary < 0.0 ) ? 0.0 : salary;
22     } // end method setBaseSalary
23
24     // return base salary
25     public double getBaseSalary()
26     {
27        return baseSalary;
28     } // end method getBaseSalary
29
30     // calculate earnings
31     public double earnings()
32     {
33        return getBaseSalary() + super.earnings();
34     } // end method earnings
35
36     // return String representation of BasePlusCommissionEmployee4
37     public String toString()
38     {
39        return String.format( "%s %s\n%s: %.2f", "base-salaried",
40           super.toString(), "base salary", getBaseSalary() );
41     } // end method toString
42  } // end class BasePlusCommissionEmployee4
```

Fig. 9.13 | BasePlusCommissionEmployee4 class extends CommissionEmployee3, which provides only private instance variables.

super and a dot (.) separator before the superclass method name. This method invocation is a good software engineering practice: Recall from *Software Engineering Observation 8.5* that if a method performs all or some of the actions needed by another method, call that method rather than duplicate its code. By having BasePlusCommissionEmployee4's earnings method invoke CommissionEmployee3's earnings method to calculate part of a BasePlusCommissionEmployee4 object's earnings, we avoid duplicating the code and reduce code-maintenance problems.

Common Programming Error 9.3

When a superclass method is overridden in a subclass, the subclass version often calls the super-class version to do a portion of the work. Failure to prefix the superclass method name with the keyword super and a dot (.) separator when referencing the superclass's method causes the sub-class method to call itself, potentially creating an error called infinite recursion.

Similarly, BasePlusCommissionEmployee4's toString method (Fig. 9.13, lines 37–41) overrides class CommissionEmployee3's toString method (Fig. 9.12, lines 91–98) to return a string representation that is appropriate for a base-salaried commission employee. The new version creates part of a BasePlusCommissionEmployee4 object's string representation (i.e., the string "commission employee" and the values of class Commission-Employee3's private instance variables) by calling CommissionEmployee3's toString method with the expression super.toString() (Fig. 9.13, line 40). BasePlus-CommissionEmployee4's toString method then outputs the remainder of a BasePlus-CommissionEmployee4 object's string representation (i.e., the value of class BasePlusCommissionEmployee4's base salary).

Figure 9.14 performs the same manipulations on a BasePlusCommissionEmployee4 object as did Fig. 9.7 and Fig. 9.11 on objects of classes BasePlusCommissionEmployee and BasePlusCommissionEmployee3, respectively. Although each "base-salaried commission employee" class behaves identically, class BasePlusCommissionEmployee4 is the best engineered. By using inheritance and by calling methods that hide the data and ensure consistency, we have efficiently and effectively constructed a well-engineered class.

```
 1   // Fig. 9.14: BasePlusCommissionEmployeeTest4.java
 2   // Testing class BasePlusCommissionEmployee4.
 3
 4   public class BasePlusCommissionEmployeeTest4
 5   {
 6      public static void main( String args[] )
 7      {
 8         // instantiate BasePlusCommissionEmployee4 object
 9         BasePlusCommissionEmployee4 employee =
10            new BasePlusCommissionEmployee4(
11            "Bob", "Lewis", "333-33-3333", 5000, .04, 300 );
12
13         // get base-salaried commission employee data
14         System.out.println(
15            "Employee information obtained by get methods: \n" );
16         System.out.printf( "%s %s\n", "First name is",
17            employee.getFirstName() );
18         System.out.printf( "%s %s\n", "Last name is",
19            employee.getLastName() );
20         System.out.printf( "%s %s\n", "Social security number is",
21            employee.getSocialSecurityNumber() );
22         System.out.printf( "%s %.2f\n", "Gross sales is",
23            employee.getGrossSales() );
```

Fig. 9.14 | Superclass private instance variables are accessible to a subclass via public or protected methods inherited by the subclass. (Part 1 of 2.)

```
24          System.out.printf( "%s %.2f\n", "Commission rate is",
25              employee.getCommissionRate() );
26          System.out.printf( "%s %.2f\n", "Base salary is",
27              employee.getBaseSalary() );
28
29          employee.setBaseSalary( 1000 ); // set base salary
30
31          System.out.printf( "\n%s:\n\n%s\n",
32              "Updated employee information obtained by toString",
33              employee.toString() );
34      } // end main
35  } // end class BasePlusCommissionEmployeeTest4
```

```
Employee information obtained by get methods:

First name is Bob
Last name is Lewis
Social security number is 333-33-3333
Gross sales is 5000.00
Commission rate is 0.04
Base salary is 300.00

Updated employee information obtained by toString:

base-salaried commission employee: Bob Lewis
social security number: 333-33-3333
gross sales: 5000.00
commission rate: 0.04
base salary: 1000.00
```

Fig. 9.14 | Superclass `private` instance variables are accessible to a subclass via `public` or `protected` methods inherited by the subclass. (Part 2 of 2.)

In this section, you saw an evolutionary set of examples that was designed to teach key capabilities for good software engineering with inheritance. You learned how to use the keyword `extends` to create a subclass using inheritance, how to use `protected` superclass members to enable a subclass to access inherited superclass instance variables and how to override superclass methods to provide versions that are more appropriate for subclass objects. In addition, you learned how to apply software engineering techniques from Chapter 8 and this chapter to create classes that are easy to maintain, modify and debug.

9.5 Constructors in Subclasses

As we explained in the preceding section, instantiating a subclass object begins a chain of constructor calls in which the subclass constructor, before performing its own tasks, invokes its direct superclass's constructor either explicitly (via the `super` reference) or implicitly (calling the superclass's default constructor or no-argument constructor). Similarly, if the superclass is derived from another class (as is, of course, every class except `Object`), the superclass constructor invokes the constructor of the next class up in the hierarchy, and so on. The last constructor called in the chain is always the constructor for class `Object`. The original subclass constructor's body finishes executing last. Each superclass's constructor manipulates the superclass instance variables that the subclass object inherits. For example, consider again the

CommissionEmployee3–BasePlusCommissionEmployee4 hierarchy from Fig. 9.12 and Fig. 9.13. When a program creates a BasePlusCommissionEmployee4 object, the BasePlus-CommissionEmployee4 constructor is called. That constructor calls CommissionEmployee3's constructor, which in turn calls Object's constructor. Class Object's constructor has an empty body, so it immediately returns control to CommissionEmployee3's constructor, which then initializes the private instance variables of CommissionEmployee3 that are part of the BasePlusCommissionEmployee4 object. When CommissionEmployee3's constructor completes execution, it returns control to BasePlusCommissionEmployee4's constructor, which initializes the BasePlusCommissionEmployee4 object's baseSalary.

Software Engineering Observation 9.8

When a program creates a subclass object, the subclass constructor immediately calls the superclass constructor (explicitly, via super, or implicitly). The superclass constructor's body executes to initialize the superclass's instance variables that are part of the subclass object, then the subclass constructor's body executes to initialize the subclass-only instance variables. Java ensures that even if a constructor does not assign a value to an instance variable, the variable is still initialized to its default value (e.g., 0 for primitive numeric types, false for booleans, null for references).

Our next example revisits the commission employee hierarchy by declaring a CommissionEmployee4 class (Fig. 9.15) and a BasePlusCommissionEmployee5 class (Fig. 9.16). Each class's constructor prints a message when invoked, enabling us to observe the order in which the constructors in the hierarchy execute.

```java
 1   // Fig. 9.15: CommissionEmployee4.java
 2   // CommissionEmployee4 class represents a commission employee.
 3
 4   public class CommissionEmployee4
 5   {
 6      private String firstName;
 7      private String lastName;
 8      private String socialSecurityNumber;
 9      private double grossSales; // gross weekly sales
10      private double commissionRate; // commission percentage
11
12      // five-argument constructor
13      public CommissionEmployee4( String first, String last, String ssn,
14         double sales, double rate )
15      {
16         // implicit call to Object constructor occurs here
17         firstName = first;
18         lastName = last;
19         socialSecurityNumber = ssn;
20         setGrossSales( sales ); // validate and store gross sales
21         setCommissionRate( rate ); // validate and store commission rate
22
23         System.out.printf(
24            "\nCommissionEmployee4 constructor:\n%s\n", this );
25      } // end five-argument CommissionEmployee4 constructor
26
```

Fig. 9.15 | CommissionEmployee4's constructor outputs text. (Part 1 of 3.)

```
27       // set first name
28       public void setFirstName( String first )
29       {
30          firstName = first;
31       } // end method setFirstName
32
33       // return first name
34       public String getFirstName()
35       {
36          return firstName;
37       } // end method getFirstName
38
39       // set last name
40       public void setLastName( String last )
41       {
42          lastName = last;
43       } // end method setLastName
44
45       // return last name
46       public String getLastName()
47       {
48          return lastName;
49       } // end method getLastName
50
51       // set social security number
52       public void setSocialSecurityNumber( String ssn )
53       {
54          socialSecurityNumber = ssn; // should validate
55       } // end method setSocialSecurityNumber
56
57       // return social security number
58       public String getSocialSecurityNumber()
59       {
60          return socialSecurityNumber;
61       } // end method getSocialSecurityNumber
62
63       // set gross sales amount
64       public void setGrossSales( double sales )
65       {
66          grossSales = ( sales < 0.0 ) ? 0.0 : sales;
67       } // end method setGrossSales
68
69       // return gross sales amount
70       public double getGrossSales()
71       {
72          return grossSales;
73       } // end method getGrossSales
74
75       // set commission rate
76       public void setCommissionRate( double rate )
77       {
78          commissionRate = ( rate > 0.0 && rate < 1.0 ) ? rate : 0.0;
79       } // end method setCommissionRate
```

Fig. 9.15 | CommissionEmployee4's constructor outputs text. (Part 2 of 3.)

```
80
81      // return commission rate
82      public double getCommissionRate()
83      {
84         return commissionRate;
85      } // end method getCommissionRate
86
87      // calculate earnings
88      public double earnings()
89      {
90         return getCommissionRate() * getGrossSales();
91      } // end method earnings
92
93      // return String representation of CommissionEmployee4 object
94      public String toString()
95      {
96         return String.format( "%s: %s %s\n%s: %s\n%s: %.2f\n%s: %.2f",
97            "commission employee", getFirstName(), getLastName(),
98            "social security number", getSocialSecurityNumber(),
99            "gross sales", getGrossSales(),
100           "commission rate", getCommissionRate() );
101     } // end method toString
102 } // end class CommissionEmployee4
```

Fig. 9.15 | CommissionEmployee4's constructor outputs text. (Part 3 of 3.)

Class CommissionEmployee4 (Fig. 9.15) contains the same features as the version of the class shown in Fig. 9.4. We modified the constructor (lines 13–25) to output text upon its invocation. Note that outputting this with the %s format specifier (lines 23–24) implicitly invokes the toString method of the object being constructed to obtain the object's string representation.

Class BasePlusCommissionEmployee5 (Fig. 9.16) is almost identical to BasePlus-CommissionEmployee4 (Fig. 9.13), except that BasePlusCommissionEmployee5's constructor also outputs text when invoked. As in CommissionEmployee4 (Fig. 9.15), we output this using the %s format specifier (line 16) to get the object's string representation.

```
1   // Fig. 9.16: BasePlusCommissionEmployee5.java
2   // BasePlusCommissionEmployee5 class declaration.
3
4   public class BasePlusCommissionEmployee5 extends CommissionEmployee4
5   {
6      private double baseSalary; // base salary per week
7
8      // six-argument constructor
9      public BasePlusCommissionEmployee5( String first, String last,
10        String ssn, double sales, double rate, double salary )
11     {
12        super( first, last, ssn, sales, rate );
13        setBaseSalary( salary ); // validate and store base salary
14
```

Fig. 9.16 | BasePlusCommissionEmployee5's constructor outputs text. (Part 1 of 2.)

```
15          System.out.printf(
16              "\nBasePlusCommissionEmployee5 constructor:\n%s\n", this );
17      } // end six-argument BasePlusCommissionEmployee5 constructor
18
19      // set base salary
20      public void setBaseSalary( double salary )
21      {
22          baseSalary = ( salary < 0.0 ) ? 0.0 : salary;
23      } // end method setBaseSalary
24
25      // return base salary
26      public double getBaseSalary()
27      {
28          return baseSalary;
29      } // end method getBaseSalary
30
31      // calculate earnings
32      public double earnings()
33      {
34          return getBaseSalary() + super.earnings();
35      } // end method earnings
36
37      // return String representation of BasePlusCommissionEmployee5
38      public String toString()
39      {
40          return String.format( "%s %s\n%s: %.2f", "base-salaried",
41              super.toString(), "base salary", getBaseSalary() );
42      } // end method toString
43  } // end class BasePlusCommissionEmployee5
```

Fig. 9.16 | BasePlusCommissionEmployee5's constructor outputs text. (Part 2 of 2.)

Figure 9.17 demonstrates the order in which constructors are called for objects of classes that are part of an inheritance hierarchy. Method main begins by instantiating CommissionEmployee4 object employee1 (lines 8–9). Next, lines 12–14 instantiate BasePlusCommissionEmployee5 object employee2. This invokes the CommissionEmployee4 constructor, which prints output with the values passed from the BasePlusCommissionEmployee5 constructor, then performs the output specified in the BasePlusCommissionEmployee5 constructor. Lines 17–19 then instantiate BasePlusCommissionEmployee5 object employee3. Again, the CommissionEmployee4 and BasePlusCommissionEmployee5 constructors are both called. In each case, the body of the CommissionEmployee4 constructor executes before the body of the BasePlusCommissionEmployee5 constructor executes. Note that employee2 is constructed completely before construction of employee3 begins.

```
1   // Fig. 9.17: ConstructorTest.java
2   // Display order in which superclass and subclass constructors are called.
3
```

Fig. 9.17 | Constructor call order. (Part 1 of 2.)

```
4   public class ConstructorTest
5   {
6      public static void main( String args[] )
7      {
8         CommissionEmployee4 employee1 = new CommissionEmployee4(
9            "Bob", "Lewis", "333-33-3333", 5000, .04 );
10
11         System.out.println();
12         BasePlusCommissionEmployee5 employee2 =
13            new BasePlusCommissionEmployee5(
14               "Lisa", "Jones", "555-55-5555", 2000, .06, 800 );
15
16         System.out.println();
17         BasePlusCommissionEmployee5 employee3 =
18            new BasePlusCommissionEmployee5(
19               "Mark", "Sands", "888-88-8888", 8000, .15, 2000 );
20      } // end main
21   } // end class ConstructorTest
```

```
CommissionEmployee4 constructor:
commission employee: Bob Lewis
social security number: 333-33-3333
gross sales: 5000.00
commission rate: 0.04


CommissionEmployee4 constructor:
base-salaried commission employee: Lisa Jones
social security number: 555-55-5555
gross sales: 2000.00
commission rate: 0.06
base salary: 0.00

BasePlusCommissionEmployee5 constructor:
base-salaried commission employee: Lisa Jones
social security number: 555-55-5555
gross sales: 2000.00
commission rate: 0.06
base salary: 800.00


CommissionEmployee4 constructor:
base-salaried commission employee: Mark Sands
social security number: 888-88-8888
gross sales: 8000.00
commission rate: 0.15
base salary: 0.00

BasePlusCommissionEmployee5 constructor:
base-salaried commission employee: Mark Sands
social security number: 888-88-8888
gross sales: 8000.00
commission rate: 0.15
base salary: 2000.00
```

Fig. 9.17 | Constructor call order. (Part 2 of 2.)

9.6 Software Engineering with Inheritance

When a new class extends an existing class, the new class inherits the non-`private` members of the existing class. We can customize the new class to meet our needs by including additional members and by overriding superclass members. Doing this does not require the subclass programmer to change the superclass's source code. Java simply requires access to the superclass's `.class` file so it can compile and execute any program that uses or extends the superclass. This powerful capability is attractive to independent software vendors (ISVs), who can develop proprietary classes for sale or license and make them available to users in bytecode format. Users then can derive new classes from these library classes rapidly and without accessing the ISVs' proprietary source code.

Software Engineering Observation 9.9

Although inheriting from a class does not require access to its source code, developers often insist on seeing the source code to understand the class's is implementation. Developers in industry want to ensure that they are extending a solid class that performs well and is implemented securely.

People experienced with large-scale software projects in industry say that effective software reuse improves the software-development process. Object-oriented programming facilitates software reuse, potentially shortening development time.

The availability of substantial and useful class libraries delivers the maximum benefits of software reuse through inheritance. Application designers build their applications with these libraries, and library designers are rewarded by having their libraries included with the applications. The standard Java class libraries that are shipped with Java SE 6 tend to be rather general purpose. Many special-purpose class libraries exist and more are being created.

Software Engineering Observation 9.10

In an object-oriented system, the designer often finds closely related classes, then "factors out" common instance variables and methods into a superclass. The designer uses inheritance to develop subclasses, specializing them with capabilities beyond those inherited from the superclass.

Software Engineering Observation 9.11

Declaring a subclass does not affect its superclass's source code. Inheritance preserves the integrity of the superclass.

Software Engineering Observation 9.12

Just as designers of non-object-oriented systems should avoid method proliferation, designers of object-oriented systems should avoid class proliferation. Such proliferation creates management problems and can hinder software reusability, because in a huge class library it becomes difficult for a client to locate the most appropriate classes. The alternative is to create fewer classes that provide more substantial functionality, but such classes might prove cumbersome.

Reading subclass declarations can be confusing, because inherited members are not declared explicitly in the subclasses, but are nevertheless present in them. A similar problem exists in documenting subclass members.

9.7 Object Class

All Java classes inherit directly or indirectly from class `Object` (package `java.lang`), so its 11 methods are inherited by all other classes. Figure 9.18 summarizes `Object`'s methods.

Method	Description
clone	This protected method, which takes no arguments and returns an Object reference, makes a copy of the object on which it is called. When cloning is required for objects of a class, the class should override method clone as a public method and should implement interface Cloneable (package java.lang). The default implementation of this method performs a so-called *shallow copy*—instance variable values in one object are copied into another object of the same type. For reference types, only the references are copied. A typical overridden clone method's implementation would perform a *deep copy* that creates a new object for each reference-type instance variable. There are many subtleties to overriding method clone. You can learn more about cloning in the following article: java.sun.com/developer/JDCTechTips/2001/tt0306.html
equals	This method compares two objects for equality and returns true if they are equal and false otherwise. The method takes any Object as an argument. When objects of a particular class must be compared for equality, the class should override method equals to compare the contents of the two objects. The method's implementation should meet the following requirements: • It should return false if the argument is null. • It should return true if an object is compared to itself, as in object1.equals(object1). • It should return true only if both object1.equals(object2) and object2.equals(object1) would return true. • For three objects, if object1.equals(object2) returns true and object2.equals(object3) returns true, then object1.equals(object3) should also return true. • If equals is called multiple times with the two objects and the objects do not change, the method should consistently return true if the objects are equal and false otherwise.
equals (continued)	A class that overrides equals should also override hashCode to ensure that equal objects have identical hashcodes. The default equals implementation uses operator == to determine whether two references *refer to the same object* in memory. Section 25.3.3 demonstrates class String's equals method and differentiates between comparing String objects with == and with equals.
finalize	This protected method (introduced in Section 8.10 and Section 8.11) is called by the garbage collector to perform termination housekeeping on an object just before the garbage collector reclaims the object's memory. It is not guaranteed that the garbage collector will reclaim an object, so it cannot be guaranteed that the object's finalize method will execute. The method must specify an empty parameter list and must return void. The default implementation of this method serves as a placeholder that does nothing.
getClass	Every object in Java knows its own type at execution time. Method getClass (used in Section 10.5) returns an object of class Class (package java.lang) that contains information about the object's type, such

Fig. 9.18 | Object methods that are inherited directly or indirectly by all classes. (Part 1 of 2.)

Method	Description
	as its class name (returned by Class method getName). You can learn more about class Class in the online API documentation at java.sun.com/javase/6/docs/api/java/lang/Class.html.
hashCode	A hashtable is a data structure (discussed in Section 16.10) that relates one object, called the key, to another object, called the value. When initially inserting a value into a hashtable, the key's hashCode method is called. The hashcode value returned is used by the hashtable to determine the location at which to insert the corresponding value. The key's hashcode is also used by the hashtable to locate the key's corresponding value.
notify, notifyAll, wait	Methods notify, notifyAll and the three overloaded versions of wait are related to multithreading, which is discussed in Chapter 18. In recent versions of Java, the multithreading model has changed substantially, but these features continue to be supported.
toString	This method (introduced in Section 9.4.1) returns a String representation of an object. The default implementation of this method returns the package name and class name of the object's class followed by a hexadecimal representation of the value returned by the object's hashCode method.

Fig. 9.18 | Object methods that are inherited directly or indirectly by all classes. (Part 2 of 2.)

You can learn more about Object's methods in the online API documentation and in *The Java Tutorial* at java.sun.com/javase/6/docs/api/java/lang/Object.html and java.sun.com/docs/books/tutorial/java/IandI/objectclass.html, respectively.

Recall from Chapter 7 that arrays are objects. As a result, an array inherits the members of class Object. Every array has an overridden clone method that copies the array, but if the array stores references to objects, the objects are not copied. You can learn more about the relationship between arrays and class Object in the *Java Language Specification, Chapter 10*, at java.sun.com/docs/books/jls/second_edition/html/arrays.doc.html.

9.8 Wrap-Up

This chapter introduced inheritance—the ability to create classes by absorbing an existing class's members and embellishing them with new capabilities. You learned the notions of superclasses and subclasses and used keyword extends to create a subclass that inherits members from a superclass. The chapter introduced the access modifier protected; subclass methods can access protected superclass members. You learned how to access superclass members with super. You also saw how constructors are used in inheritance hierarchies. Finally, you learned about the methods of class Object, the direct or indirect superclass of all classes in Java.

In Chapter 10, Object-Oriented Programming: Polymorphism, we build on our discussion of inheritance by introducing polymorphism—an object-oriented concept that enables us to write programs that conveniently handle, in a more general manner, objects of a wide variety of classes related by inheritance. After studying Chapter 10, you'll be familiar with classes, objects, encapsulation, inheritance and polymorphism—the key technologies of object-oriented programming.

10

Object-Oriented Programming: Polymorphism

OBJECTIVES

In this chapter you'll learn:

- The concept of polymorphism.

- To use overridden methods to effect polymorphism.

- To distinguish between abstract and concrete classes.

- To declare abstract methods to create abstract classes.

- How polymorphism makes systems extensible and maintainable.

- To determine an object's type at execution time.

- To declare and implement interfaces.

One Ring to rule them all,
One Ring to find them,
One Ring to bring them all
and in the darkness bind
them.
—**John Ronald Reuel Tolkien**

General propositions do not
decide concrete cases.
—Oliver Wendell Holmes

A philosopher of imposing
stature doesn't think in a
vacuum. Even his most
abstract ideas are, to some
extent, conditioned by
what is or is not known
in the time when he lives.
—Alfred North Whitehead

Why art thou cast down,
O my soul?
—Psalms 42:5

Outline

10.1 Introduction

10.2 Polymorphism Examples

10.3 Demonstrating Polymorphic Behavior

10.4 Abstract Classes and Methods

10.5 Case Study: Payroll System Using Polymorphism

    10.5.1 Creating Abstract Superclass `Employee`

    10.5.2 Creating Concrete Subclass `SalariedEmployee`

    10.5.3 Creating Concrete Subclass `HourlyEmployee`

    10.5.4 Creating Concrete Subclass `CommissionEmployee`

    10.5.5 Creating Indirect Concrete Subclass `BasePlusCommissionEmployee`

    10.5.6 Demonstrating Polymorphic Processing, Operator `instanceof` and Downcasting

    10.5.7 Summary of the Allowed Assignments Between Superclass and Subclass Variables

10.6 `final` Methods and Classes

10.7 Case Study: Creating and Using Interfaces

    10.7.1 Developing a `Payable` Hierarchy

    10.7.2 Declaring Interface `Payable`

    10.7.3 Creating Class `Invoice`

    10.7.4 Modifying Class `Employee` to Implement Interface `Payable`

    10.7.5 Modifying Class `SalariedEmployee` for Use in the `Payable` Hierarchy

    10.7.6 Using Interface `Payable` to Process `Invoice`s and `Employee`s Polymorphically

    10.7.7 Declaring Constants with Interfaces

    10.7.8 Common Interfaces of the Java API

10.8 (Optional) Software Engineering Case Study: Incorporating Inheritance into the ATM System

10.9 Wrap-Up

10.1 Introduction

We now continue our study of object-oriented programming by explaining and demonstrating *polymorphism* with inheritance hierarchies. Polymorphism enables us to "program in the general" rather than "program in the specific." In particular, polymorphism enables us to write programs that process objects that share the same superclass in a class hierarchy as if they are all objects of the superclass; this can simplify programming.

Consider the following example of polymorphism. Suppose we create a program that simulates the movement of several types of animals for a biological study. Classes Fish, Frog and Bird represent the three types of animals under investigation. Imagine that each of these classes extends superclass Animal, which contains a method move and maintains an animal's current location as *x-y* coordinates. Each subclass implements method move. Our program maintains an array of references to objects of the various Animal subclasses.

To simulate the animals' movements, the program sends each object the same message once per second—namely, move. However, each specific type of Animal responds to a move message in a unique way—a Fish might swim three feet, a Frog might jump five feet and a Bird might fly ten feet. The program issues the same message (i.e., move) to each animal object generically, but each object knows how to modify its *x-y* coordinates appropriately for its specific type of movement. Relying on each object to know how to "do the right thing" (i.e., do what is appropriate for that type of object) in response to the same method call is the key concept of polymorphism. The same message (in this case, move) sent to a variety of objects has "many forms" of results—hence the term polymorphism.

With polymorphism, we can design and implement systems that are easily extensible—new classes can be added with little or no modification to the general portions of the program, as long as the new classes are part of the inheritance hierarchy that the program processes generically. The only parts of a program that must be altered to accommodate new classes are those that require direct knowledge of the new classes that the programmer adds to the hierarchy. For example, if we extend class Animal to create class Tortoise (which might respond to a move message by crawling one inch), we need to write only the Tortoise class and the part of the simulation that instantiates a Tortoise object. The portions of the simulation that process each Animal generically can remain the same.

This chapter has several parts. First, we discuss common examples of polymorphism. We then provide an example demonstrating polymorphic behavior. We'll use superclass references to manipulate both superclass objects and subclass objects polymorphically.

We then present a case study that revisits the employee hierarchy of Section 9.4.5. We develop a simple payroll application that polymorphically calculates the weekly pay of several different types of employees using each employee's earnings method. Though the earnings of each type of employee are calculated in a specific way, polymorphism allows us to process the employees "in the general." In the case study, we enlarge the hierarchy to include two new classes—SalariedEmployee (for people paid a fixed weekly salary) and HourlyEmployee (for people paid an hourly salary and so-called time-and-a-half for overtime). We declare a common set of functionality for all the classes in the updated hierarchy in a so-called abstract class, Employee, from which classes SalariedEmployee, HourlyEmployee and CommissionEmployee inherit directly and class BasePlusCommission-Employee4 inherits indirectly. As you'll soon see, when we invoke each employee's earnings method off a superclass Employee reference, the correct earnings calculation is performed due to Java's polymorphic capabilities.

Occasionally, when performing polymorphic processing, we need to program "in the specific." Our Employee case study demonstrates that a program can determine the type of an object at execution time and act on that object accordingly. In the case study, we use these capabilities to determine whether a particular employee object *is a* BasePlus-CommissionEmployee. If so, we increase that employee's base salary by 10%.

Next, the chapter introduces interfaces. An interface describes methods that can be called on an object, but does not provide concrete method implementations. You can declare classes that *implement* (i.e., provide concrete implementations for the methods of) one or more interfaces. Each interface method must be declared in all the classes that implement the interface. Once a class implements an interface, all objects of that class have an *is-a* relationship with the interface type, and all objects of the class are guaranteed to provide the functionality described by the interface. This is true of all subclasses of that class as well.

Interfaces are particularly useful for assigning common functionality to possibly unrelated classes. This allows objects of unrelated classes to be processed polymorphically— objects of classes that implement the same interface can respond to the same method calls. To demonstrate creating and using interfaces, we modify our payroll application to create a general accounts payable application that can calculate payments due for company employees and invoice amounts to be billed for purchased goods. As you'll see, interfaces enable polymorphic capabilities similar to those possible with inheritance.

10.2 Polymorphism Examples

Let's consider several other examples of polymorphism. If class Rectangle is derived from class Quadrilateral, then a Rectangle object is a more specific version of a Quadrilateral object. Any operation (e.g., calculating the perimeter or the area) that can be performed on a Quadrilateral object can also be performed on a Rectangle object. These operations can also be performed on other Quadrilaterals, such as Squares, Parallelograms and Trapezoids. The polymorphism occurs when a program invokes a method through a superclass variable—at execution time, the correct subclass version of the method is called, based on the type of the reference stored in the superclass variable. You'll see a simple code example that illustrates this process in Section 10.3.

As another example, suppose we design a video game that manipulates objects of classes Martian, Venusian, Plutonian, SpaceShip and LaserBeam. Imagine that each class inherits from the common superclass called SpaceObject, which contains method draw. Each subclass implements this method. A screen-manager program maintains a collection (e.g., a SpaceObject array) of references to objects of the various classes. To refresh the screen, the screen manager periodically sends each object the same message—namely, draw. However, each object responds in a unique way. For example, a Martian object might draw itself in red with green eyes and the appropriate number of antennae. A SpaceShip object might draw itself as a bright silver flying saucer. A LaserBeam object might draw itself as a bright red beam across the screen. Again, the same message (in this case, draw) sent to a variety of objects has "many forms" of results.

A screen manager might use polymorphism to facilitate adding new classes to a system with minimal modifications to the system's code. Suppose that we want to add Mercurian objects to our video game. To do so, we must build a class Mercurian that extends SpaceObject and provides its own draw method implementation. When objects of class Mercurian appear in the SpaceObject collection, the screen manager code invokes method draw, exactly as it does for every other object in the collection, regardless of its type. So the new Mercurian objects simply "plug right in" without any modification of the screen manager code. Thus, without modifying the system (other than to build new classes and modify the code that creates new objects), programmers can use polymorphism to conveniently include additional types that were not envisioned when the system was created.

With polymorphism, the same method name and signature can be used to cause different actions to occur, depending on the type of object on which the method is invoked. This gives the programmer tremendous expressive capability.

Software Engineering Observation 10.1

Polymorphism enables programmers to deal in generalities and let the execution-time environment handle the specifics. Programmers can command objects to behave in manners appropriate to those objects, without knowing the types of the objects (as long as the objects belong to the same inheritance hierarchy).

Software Engineering Observation 10.2

Polymorphism promotes extensibility: Software that invokes polymorphic behavior is independent of the object types to which messages are sent. New object types that can respond to existing method calls can be incorporated into a system without requiring modification of the base system. Only client code that instantiates new objects must be modified to accommodate new types.

10.3 Demonstrating Polymorphic Behavior

Section 9.4 created a commission employee class hierarchy, in which class `BasePlusCommissionEmployee` inherited from class `CommissionEmployee`. The examples in that section manipulated `CommissionEmployee` and `BasePlusCommissionEmployee` objects by using references to them to invoke their methods—we aimed superclass references at superclass objects and subclass references at subclass objects. These assignments are natural and straightforward—superclass references are intended to refer to superclass objects, and subclass references are intended to refer to subclass objects. However, as you'll soon see, other assignments are possible.

In the next example, we aim a superclass reference at a subclass object. We then show how invoking a method on a subclass object via a superclass reference invokes the subclass functionality—the type of the *actual referenced object*, not the type of the *reference*, determines which method is called. This example demonstrates the key concept that an object of a subclass can be treated as an object of its superclass. This enables various interesting manipulations. A program can create an array of superclass references that refer to objects of many subclass types. This is allowed because each subclass object *is an* object of its superclass. For instance, we can assign the reference of a `BasePlusCommissionEmployee` object to a superclass `CommissionEmployee` variable because a `BasePlusCommissionEmployee` *is a* `CommissionEmployee`—we can treat a `BasePlusCommissionEmployee` as a `CommissionEmployee`.

As you'll learn later in the chapter, we cannot treat a superclass object as a subclass object because a superclass object is not an object of any of its subclasses. For example, we cannot assign the reference of a `CommissionEmployee` object to a subclass `BasePlusCommissionEmployee` variable because a `CommissionEmployee` is not a `BasePlusCommissionEmployee`—a `CommissionEmployee` does not have a `baseSalary` instance variable and does not have methods `setBaseSalary` and `getBaseSalary`. The *is-a* relationship applies only from a subclass to its direct (and indirect) superclasses, and not vice versa.

The Java compiler does allow the assignment of a superclass reference to a subclass variable if we explicitly cast the superclass reference to the subclass type—a technique we discuss in detail in Section 10.5. Why would we ever want to perform such an assignment? A superclass reference can be used to invoke only the methods declared in the superclass—attempting to invoke subclass-only methods through a superclass reference results in compilation errors. If a program needs to perform a subclass-specific operation on a subclass object referenced by a superclass variable, the program must first cast the superclass reference to a subclass reference through a technique known as ***downcasting***. This enables the program to invoke subclass methods that are not in the superclass. We show a concrete example of downcasting in Section 10.5.

The example in Fig. 10.1 demonstrates three ways to use superclass and subclass variables to store references to superclass and subclass objects. The first two are straightforward—as in Section 9.4, we assign a superclass reference to a superclass variable, and we assign a subclass reference to a subclass variable. Then we demonstrate the relationship between subclasses and superclasses (i.e., the *is-a* relationship) by assigning a subclass reference to a superclass variable. [*Note:* This program uses classes CommissionEmployee3 and BasePlusCommissionEmployee4 from Fig. 9.12 and Fig. 9.13, respectively.]

In Fig. 10.1, lines 10–11 create a CommissionEmployee3 object and assign its reference to a CommissionEmployee3 variable. Lines 14–16 create a BasePlusCommissionEmployee4 object and assign its reference to a BasePlusCommissionEmployee4 variable. These assignments are natural—for example, a CommissionEmployee3 variable's primary purpose is to hold a reference to a CommissionEmployee3 object. Lines 19–21 use reference

```java
 1   // Fig. 10.1: PolymorphismTest.java
 2   // Assigning superclass and subclass references to superclass and
 3   // subclass variables.
 4
 5   public class PolymorphismTest
 6   {
 7      public static void main( String args[] )
 8      {
 9         // assign superclass reference to superclass variable
10         CommissionEmployee3 commissionEmployee = new CommissionEmployee3(
11            "Sue", "Jones", "222-22-2222", 10000, .06 );
12
13         // assign subclass reference to subclass variable
14         BasePlusCommissionEmployee4 basePlusCommissionEmployee =
15            new BasePlusCommissionEmployee4(
16            "Bob", "Lewis", "333-33-3333", 5000, .04, 300 );
17
18         // invoke toString on superclass object using superclass variable
19         System.out.printf( "%s %s:\n\n%s\n\n",
20            "Call CommissionEmployee3's toString with superclass reference ",
21            "to superclass object", commissionEmployee.toString() );
22
23         // invoke toString on subclass object using subclass variable
24         System.out.printf( "%s %s:\n\n%s\n\n",
25            "Call BasePlusCommissionEmployee4's toString with subclass",
26            "reference to subclass object",
27            basePlusCommissionEmployee.toString() );
28
29         // invoke toString on subclass object using superclass variable
30         CommissionEmployee3 commissionEmployee2 =
31            basePlusCommissionEmployee;
32         System.out.printf( "%s %s:\n\n%s\n",
33            "Call BasePlusCommissionEmployee4's toString with superclass",
34            "reference to subclass object", commissionEmployee2.toString() );
35      } // end main
36   } // end class PolymorphismTest
```

Fig. 10.1 | Assigning superclass and subclass references to superclass and subclass variables. (Part 1 of 2.)

```
Call CommissionEmployee3's toString with superclass reference to superclass
object:

commission employee: Sue Jones
social security number: 222-22-2222
gross sales: 10000.00
commission rate: 0.06

Call BasePlusCommissionEmployee4's toString with subclass reference to
subclass object:

base-salaried commission employee: Bob Lewis
social security number: 333-33-3333
gross sales: 5000.00
commission rate: 0.04
base salary: 300.00

Call BasePlusCommissionEmployee4's toString with superclass reference to
subclass object:

base-salaried commission employee: Bob Lewis
social security number: 333-33-3333
gross sales: 5000.00
commission rate: 0.04
base salary: 300.00
```

Fig. 10.1 | Assigning superclass and subclass references to superclass and subclass variables. (Part 2 of 2.)

commissionEmployee to invoke toString explicitly. Because commissionEmployee refers to a CommissionEmployee3 object, superclass CommissionEmployee3's version of toString is called. Similarly, lines 24–27 use basePlusCommissionEmployee to invoke toString explicitly on the BasePlusCommissionEmployee4 object. This invokes subclass BasePlusCommissionEmployee4's version of toString.

Lines 30–31 then assign the reference to subclass object basePlusCommissionEmployee to a superclass CommissionEmployee3 variable, which lines 32–34 use to invoke method toString. When a superclass variable contains a reference to a subclass object, and that reference is used to call a method, the subclass version of the method is called. Hence, commissionEmployee2.toString() in line 34 actually calls class BasePlusCommissionEmployee4's toString method. The Java compiler allows this "crossover" because an object of a subclass *is an* object of its superclass (but not vice versa). When the compiler encounters a method call made through a variable, the compiler determines if the method can be called by checking the variable's class type. If that class contains the proper method declaration (or inherits one), the call is compiled. At execution time, the type of the object to which the variable refers determines the actual method to use.

10.4 Abstract Classes and Methods

When we think of a class type, we assume that programs will create objects of that type. In some cases, however, it is useful to declare classes for which the programmer never intends to instantiate objects. Such classes are called *abstract classes*. Because they are used only as superclasses in inheritance hierarchies, we refer to them as *abstract superclasses*. These classes cannot be used to instantiate objects, because, as we'll soon see, abstract classes are incomplete. Subclasses must declare the "missing pieces." We demonstrate abstract classes in Section 10.5.

An abstract class's purpose is to provide an appropriate superclass from which other classes can inherit and thus share a common design. In the Shape hierarchy of Fig. 9.3, for example, subclasses inherit the notion of what it means to be a Shape—common attributes such as location, color and borderThickness, and behaviors such as draw, move, resize and changeColor. Classes that can be used to instantiate objects are called *concrete classes*. Such classes provide implementations of every method they declare (some of the implementations can be inherited). For example, we could derive concrete classes Circle, Square and Triangle from abstract superclass TwoDimensionalShape. Similarly, we could derive concrete classes Sphere, Cube and Tetrahedron from abstract superclass ThreeDimensionalShape. Abstract superclasses are too general to create real objects—they specify only what is common among subclasses. We need to be more specific before we can create objects. For example, if you send the draw message to abstract class TwoDimensionalShape, it knows that two-dimensional shapes should be drawable, but it does not know what specific shape to draw, so it cannot implement a real draw method. Concrete classes provide the specifics that make it reasonable to instantiate objects.

Not all inheritance hierarchies contain abstract classes. However, programmers often write client code that uses only abstract superclass types to reduce client code's dependencies on a range of specific subclass types. For example, a programmer can write a method with a parameter of an abstract superclass type. When called, such a method can be passed an object of any concrete class that directly or indirectly extends the superclass specified as the parameter's type.

Abstract classes sometimes constitute several levels of the hierarchy. For example, the Shape hierarchy of Fig. 9.3 begins with abstract class Shape. On the next level of the hierarchy are two more abstract classes, TwoDimensionalShape and ThreeDimensionalShape. The next level of the hierarchy declares concrete classes for TwoDimensionalShapes (Circle, Square and Triangle) and for ThreeDimensionalShapes (Sphere, Cube and Tetrahedron).

You make a class abstract by declaring it with keyword *abstract*. An abstract class normally contains one or more *abstract methods*. An abstract method is one with keyword abstract in its declaration, as in

```
public abstract void draw(); // abstract method
```

Abstract methods do not provide implementations. A class that contains any abstract methods must be declared as an abstract class even if that class contains some concrete (nonabstract) methods. Each concrete subclass of an abstract superclass also must provide concrete implementations of each of the superclass's abstract methods. Constructors and static methods cannot be declared abstract. Constructors are not inherited, so an abstract constructor could never be implemented. Though static methods are inherited, they are not associated with particular objects of the classes that declare the static methods. Since abstract methods are meant to be overridden so they can process objects based on their types, it would not make sense to declare a static method as abstract.

Software Engineering Observation 10.3

An abstract class declares common attributes and behaviors of the various classes in a class hierarchy. An abstract class typically contains one or more abstract methods that subclasses must override if the subclasses are to be concrete. The instance variables and concrete methods of an abstract class are subject to the normal rules of inheritance.

Common Programming Error 10.1

Attempting to instantiate an object of an abstract class is a compilation error.

Common Programming Error 10.2

Failure to implement a superclass's abstract methods in a subclass is a compilation error unless the subclass is also declared abstract.

Although we cannot instantiate objects of abstract superclasses, you'll soon see that we *can* use abstract superclasses to declare variables that can hold references to objects of any concrete class derived from those abstract superclasses. Programs typically use such variables to manipulate subclass objects polymorphically. We also can use abstract superclass names to invoke static methods declared in those abstract superclasses.

Consider another application of polymorphism. A drawing program needs to display many shapes, including new shape types that the programmer will add to the system after writing the drawing program. The drawing program might need to display shapes, such as Circles, Triangles, Rectangles or others, that derive from abstract superclass Shape. The drawing program uses Shape variables to manage the objects that are displayed. To draw any object in this inheritance hierarchy, the drawing program uses a superclass Shape variable containing a reference to the subclass object to invoke the object's draw method. This method is declared abstract in superclass Shape, so each concrete subclass *must* implement method draw in a manner specific to that shape. Each object in the Shape inheritance hierarchy knows how to draw itself. The drawing program does not have to worry about the type of each object or whether the drawing program has ever encountered objects of that type.

Polymorphism is particularly effective for implementing so-called layered software systems. In operating systems, for example, each type of physical device could operate quite differently from the others. Even so, commands to read or write data from and to devices may have a certain uniformity. For each device, the operating system uses a piece of software called a device driver to control all communication between the system and the device. The write message sent to a device-driver object needs to be interpreted specifically in the context of that driver and how it manipulates devices of a specific type. However, the write call itself really is no different from the write to any other device in the system: Place some number of bytes from memory onto that device. An object-oriented operating system might use an abstract superclass to provide an "interface" appropriate for all device drivers. Then, through inheritance from that abstract superclass, subclasses are formed that all behave similarly. The device-driver methods are declared as abstract methods in the abstract superclass. The implementations of these abstract methods are provided in the subclasses that correspond to the specific types of device drivers. New devices are always being developed, and often long after the operating system has been released. When you buy a new device, it comes with a device driver provided by the device vendor. The device is immediately operational after you connect it to your computer and install the driver. This is another elegant example of how polymorphism makes systems extensible.

It is common in object-oriented programming to declare an *iterator class* that can traverse all the objects in a collection, such as an array (Chapter 7) or an ArrayList (Chapter 16, Collections). For example, a program can print an ArrayList of objects by creating an iterator object and using it to obtain the next list element each time the iterator is called. Iterators often are used in polymorphic programming to traverse a collection that contains references to objects from various levels of a hierarchy. (Chapter 16 presents a thorough treatment of ArrayList, iterators and "generics" capabilities.) An ArrayList of objects of class TwoDimensionalShape, for example, could contain objects from subclasses Square, Circle, Triangle and so on. Calling method draw for each TwoDimensionalShape object off a TwoDimensionalShape variable would polymorphically draw each object correctly on the screen.

10.5 Case Study: Payroll System Using Polymorphism

This section reexamines the CommissionEmployee-BasePlusCommissionEmployee hierarchy that we explored throughout Section 9.4. Now we use an abstract method and polymorphism to perform payroll calculations based on the type of employee. We create an enhanced employee hierarchy to solve the following problem:

> *A company pays its employees on a weekly basis. The employees are of four types: Salaried employees are paid a fixed weekly salary regardless of the number of hours worked, hourly employees are paid by the hour and receive overtime pay for all hours worked in excess of 40 hours, commission employees are paid a percentage of their sales and salaried-commission employees receive a base salary plus a percentage of their sales. For the current pay period, the company has decided to reward salaried-commission employees by adding 10% to their base salaries. The company wants to implement a Java application that performs its payroll calculations polymorphically.*

We use abstract class Employee to represent the general concept of an employee. The classes that extend Employee are SalariedEmployee, CommissionEmployee and HourlyEmployee. Class BasePlusCommissionEmployee—which extends CommissionEmployee—represents the last employee type. The UML class diagram in Fig. 10.2 shows the inheritance hierarchy for our polymorphic employee-payroll application. Note that abstract class Employee is italicized, as per the convention of the UML.

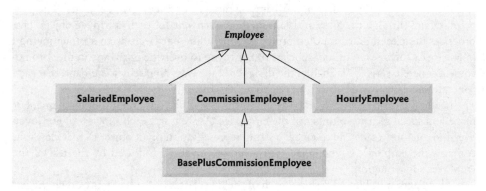

Fig. 10.2 | Employee hierarchy UML class diagram.

Abstract superclass `Employee` declares the "interface" to the hierarchy—that is, the set of methods that a program can invoke on all `Employee` objects. We use the term "interface" here in a general sense to refer to the various ways programs can communicate with objects of any `Employee` subclass. Be careful not to confuse the general notion of an "interface" to something with the formal notion of a Java interface, the subject of Section 10.7. Each employee, regardless of the way his or her earnings are calculated, has a first name, a last name and a social security number, so `private` instance variables `firstName`, `lastName` and `socialSecurityNumber` appear in abstract superclass `Employee`.

Software Engineering Observation 10.4

*A subclass can inherit "interface" or "implementation" from a superclass. Hierarchies designed for **implementation inheritance** tend to have their functionality high in the hierarchy—each new subclass inherits one or more methods that were implemented in a superclass, and the subclass uses the superclass implementations. Hierarchies designed for **interface inheritance** tend to have their functionality lower in the hierarchy—a superclass specifies one or more abstract methods that must be declared for each concrete class in the hierarchy, and the individual subclasses override these methods to provide subclass-specific implementations.*

The following sections implement the `Employee` class hierarchy. Each of the first four sections implements one of the concrete classes. The last section implements a test program that builds objects of all these classes and processes those objects polymorphically.

10.5.1 Creating Abstract Superclass Employee

Class `Employee` (Fig. 10.4) provides methods `earnings` and `toString`, in addition to the *get* and *set* methods that manipulate `Employee`'s instance variables. An `earnings` method certainly applies generically to all employees. But each earnings calculation depends on the employee's class. So we declare `earnings` as `abstract` in superclass `Employee` because a default implementation does not make sense for that method—there is not enough information to determine what amount `earnings` should return. Each subclass overrides `earnings` with an appropriate implementation. To calculate an employee's earnings, the program assigns a reference to the employee's object to a superclass `Employee` variable, then invokes the `earnings` method on that variable. We maintain an array of `Employee` variables, each of which holds a reference to an `Employee` object (of course, there cannot be `Employee` objects because `Employee` is an abstract class—because of inheritance, however, all objects of all subclasses of `Employee` may nevertheless be thought of as `Employee` objects). The program iterates through the array and calls method `earnings` for each `Employee` object. Java processes these method calls polymorphically. Including `earnings` as an abstract method in `Employee` forces every direct subclass of `Employee` to override `earnings` in order to become a concrete class. This enables the designer of the class hierarchy to demand that each concrete subclass provide an appropriate pay calculation.

Method `toString` in class `Employee` returns a `String` containing the first name, last name and social security number of the employee. As we'll see, each subclass of `Employee` overrides method `toString` to create a string representation of an object of that class that contains the employee's type (e.g., `"salaried employee:"`) followed by the rest of the employee's information.

The diagram in Fig. 10.3 shows each of the five classes in the hierarchy down the left side and methods `earnings` and `toString` across the top. For each class, the diagram

	earnings	toString
Employee	abstract	*firstName lastName* social security number: *SSN*
Salaried-Employee	weeklySalary	salaried employee: *firstName lastName* social security number: *SSN* weekly salary: *weeklysalary*

Hourly-Employee	if hours <= 40
	  wage * hours
	else if hours > 40
	  40 * wage +
	  (hours - 40) *
	  wage * 1.5
		hourly employee: *firstName lastName*
		social security number: *SSN*
		hourly wage: *wage*; hours worked: *hours*

Commission-Employee	commissionRate * grossSales	commission employee: *firstName lastName* social security number: *SSN* gross sales: *grossSales*; commission rate: *commissionRate*
BasePlus-Commission-Employee	(commissionRate * grossSales) + baseSalary	base salaried commission employee: *firstName lastName* social security number: *SSN* gross sales: *grossSales*; commission rate: *commissionRate*; base salary: *baseSalary*

Fig. 10.3 | Polymorphic interface for the Employee hierarchy classes.

shows the desired results of each method. [*Note:* We do not list superclass Employee's *get* and *set* methods because they are not overridden in any of the subclasses—each of these methods is inherited and used "as is" by each of the subclasses.]

Let us consider class Employee's declaration (Fig. 10.4). The class includes a constructor that takes the first name, last name and social security number as arguments (lines 11–16); *get* methods that return the first name, last name and social security number (lines 25–28, 37–40 and 49–52, respectively); *set* methods that set the first name, last name and social security number (lines 19–22, 31–34 and 43–46, respectively); method toString (lines 55–59), which returns the string representation of Employee; and abstract method earnings (line 62), which will be implemented by subclasses. Note that the Employee constructor does not validate the social security number in this example. Normally, such validation should be provided.

Why did we decide to declare earnings as an abstract method? It simply does not make sense to provide an implementation of this method in class Employee. We cannot calculate the earnings for a general Employee—we first must know the specific Employee type to determine the appropriate earnings calculation. By declaring this method abstract, we indicate that each concrete subclass *must* provide an appropriate earnings implementation and that a program will be able to use superclass Employee variables to invoke method earnings polymorphically for any type of Employee.

```java
1   // Fig. 10.4: Employee.java
2   // Employee abstract superclass.
3
4   public abstract class Employee
5   {
6      private String firstName;
7      private String lastName;
8      private String socialSecurityNumber;
9
10     // three-argument constructor
11     public Employee( String first, String last, String ssn )
12     {
13        firstName = first;
14        lastName = last;
15        socialSecurityNumber = ssn;
16     } // end three-argument Employee constructor
17
18     // set first name
19     public void setFirstName( String first )
20     {
21        firstName = first;
22     } // end method setFirstName
23
24     // return first name
25     public String getFirstName()
26     {
27        return firstName;
28     } // end method getFirstName
29
30     // set last name
31     public void setLastName( String last )
32     {
33        lastName = last;
34     } // end method setLastName
35
36     // return last name
37     public String getLastName()
38     {
39        return lastName;
40     } // end method getLastName
41
42     // set social security number
43     public void setSocialSecurityNumber( String ssn )
44     {
45        socialSecurityNumber = ssn; // should validate
46     } // end method setSocialSecurityNumber
47
48     // return social security number
49     public String getSocialSecurityNumber()
50     {
51        return socialSecurityNumber;
52     } // end method getSocialSecurityNumber
53
```

Fig. 10.4 | Employee abstract superclass. (Part 1 of 2.)

```
54        // return String representation of Employee object
55        public String toString()
56        {
57           return String.format( "%s %s\nsocial security number: %s",
58              getFirstName(), getLastName(), getSocialSecurityNumber() );
59        } // end method toString
60
61        // abstract method overridden by subclasses
62        public abstract double earnings(); // no implementation here
63     } // end abstract class Employee
```

Fig. 10.4 | Employee abstract superclass. (Part 2 of 2.)

10.5.2 Creating Concrete Subclass SalariedEmployee

Class SalariedEmployee (Fig. 10.5) extends class Employee (line 4) and overrides earnings (lines 29–32), which makes SalariedEmployee a concrete class. The class includes a constructor (lines 9–14) that takes a first name, a last name, a social security number and a weekly salary as arguments; a *set* method to assign a new nonnegative value to instance variable weeklySalary (lines 17–20); a *get* method to return weeklySalary's value (lines 23–26); a method earnings (lines 29–32) to calculate a SalariedEmployee's earnings; and a method toString (lines 35–39), which returns a String including the employee's type, namely, "salaried employee: " followed by employee-specific information produced by superclass Employee's toString method and SalariedEmployee's getWeeklySalary method. Class SalariedEmployee's constructor passes the first name, last name and social security number to the Employee constructor (line 12) to initialize the private instance variables not inherited from the superclass. Method earnings overrides abstract method earnings in Employee to provide a concrete implementation that returns the SalariedEmployee's weekly salary. If we do not implement earnings, class SalariedEmployee must be declared abstract—otherwise, a compilation error occurs (and, of course, we want SalariedEmployee here to be a concrete class).

```
 1    // Fig. 10.5: SalariedEmployee.java
 2    // SalariedEmployee class extends Employee.
 3
 4    public class SalariedEmployee extends Employee
 5    {
 6       private double weeklySalary;
 7
 8       // four-argument constructor
 9       public SalariedEmployee( String first, String last, String ssn,
10          double salary )
11       {
12          super( first, last, ssn ); // pass to Employee constructor
13          setWeeklySalary( salary ); // validate and store salary
14       } // end four-argument SalariedEmployee constructor
15
```

Fig. 10.5 | SalariedEmployee class derived from Employee. (Part 1 of 2.)

```
16          // set salary
17          public void setWeeklySalary( double salary )
18          {
19              weeklySalary = salary < 0.0 ? 0.0 : salary;
20          } // end method setWeeklySalary
21
22          // return salary
23          public double getWeeklySalary()
24          {
25              return weeklySalary;
26          } // end method getWeeklySalary
27
28          // calculate earnings; override abstract method earnings in Employee
29          public double earnings()
30          {
31              return getWeeklySalary();
32          } // end method earnings
33
34          // return String representation of SalariedEmployee object
35          public String toString()
36          {
37              return String.format( "salaried employee: %s\n%s: $%,.2f",
38                  super.toString(), "weekly salary", getWeeklySalary() );
39          } // end method toString
40      } // end class SalariedEmployee
```

Fig. 10.5 | SalariedEmployee class derived from Employee. (Part 2 of 2.)

Method toString (lines 35–39) of class SalariedEmployee overrides Employee method toString. If class SalariedEmployee did not override toString, SalariedEmployee would have inherited the Employee version of toString. In that case, SalariedEmployee's toString method would simply return the employee's full name and social security number, which does not adequately represent a SalariedEmployee. To produce a complete string representation of a SalariedEmployee, the subclass's toString method returns "salaried employee: " followed by the superclass Employee-specific information (i.e., first name, last name and social security number) obtained by invoking the superclass's toString method (line 38)—this is a nice example of code reuse. The string representation of a SalariedEmployee also contains the employee's weekly salary obtained by invoking the class's getWeeklySalary method.

10.5.3 Creating Concrete Subclass HourlyEmployee

Class HourlyEmployee (Fig. 10.6) also extends Employee (line 4). The class includes a constructor (lines 10–16) that takes as arguments a first name, a last name, a social security number, an hourly wage and the number of hours worked. Lines 19–22 and 31–35 declare *set* methods that assign new values to instance variables wage and hours, respectively. Method setWage (lines 19–22) ensures that wage is nonnegative, and method setHours (lines 31–35) ensures that hours is between 0 and 168 (the total number of hours in a week) inclusive. Class HourlyEmployee also includes *get* methods (lines 25–28 and 38–41) to return the values of wage and hours, respectively; a method earnings (lines 44–50) to calculate an HourlyEmployee's earnings; and a method toString (lines 53–58), which returns the employee's type, namely, "hourly employee: " and Employee-specific information. Note that the HourlyEmployee constructor, like the SalariedEmployee constructor, passes the first name, last name and social security number to the superclass Employee constructor (line 13) to initialize the private instance variables. In addition, method toString calls superclass method toString (line 56) to obtain the Employee-specific information (i.e., first name, last name and social security number)—this is another nice example of code reuse.

```java
1   // Fig. 10.6: HourlyEmployee.java
2   // HourlyEmployee class extends Employee.
3
4   public class HourlyEmployee extends Employee
5   {
6      private double wage; // wage per hour
7      private double hours; // hours worked for week
8
9      // five-argument constructor
10     public HourlyEmployee( String first, String last, String ssn,
11        double hourlyWage, double hoursWorked )
12     {
13        super( first, last, ssn );
14        setWage( hourlyWage ); // validate hourly wage
15        setHours( hoursWorked ); // validate hours worked
16     } // end five-argument HourlyEmployee constructor
17
18     // set wage
19     public void setWage( double hourlyWage )
20     {
21        wage = ( hourlyWage < 0.0 ) ? 0.0 : hourlyWage;
22     } // end method setWage
23
24     // return wage
25     public double getWage()
26     {
27        return wage;
28     } // end method getWage
29
30     // set hours worked
31     public void setHours( double hoursWorked )
32     {
33        hours = ( ( hoursWorked >= 0.0 ) && ( hoursWorked <= 168.0 ) ) ?
34           hoursWorked : 0.0;
35     } // end method setHours
36
37     // return hours worked
38     public double getHours()
39     {
40        return hours;
41     } // end method getHours
42
43     // calculate earnings; override abstract method earnings in Employee
44     public double earnings()
45     {
```

Fig. 10.6 | HourlyEmployee class derived from Employee. (Part I of 2.)

```
46          if ( getHours() <= 40 ) // no overtime
47              return getWage() * getHours();
48          else
49              return 40 * getWage() + ( gethours() - 40 ) * getWage() * 1.5;
50      } // end method earnings
51
52      // return String representation of HourlyEmployee object
53      public String toString()
54      {
55          return String.format( "hourly employee: %s\n%s: $%,.2f; %s: %,.2f",
56              super.toString(), "hourly wage", getWage(),
57              "hours worked", getHours() );
58      } // end method toString
59  } // end class HourlyEmployee
```

Fig. 10.6 | HourlyEmployee class derived from Employee. (Part 2 of 2.)

10.5.4 Creating Concrete Subclass CommissionEmployee

Class CommissionEmployee (Fig. 10.7) extends class Employee (line 4). The class includes a constructor (lines 10–16) that takes a first name, a last name, a social security number, a sales amount and a commission rate; *set* methods (lines 19–22 and 31–34) to assign new values to instance variables commissionRate and grossSales, respectively; *get* methods (lines 25–28 and 37–40) that retrieve the values of these instance variables; method earnings (lines 43–46) to calculate a CommissionEmployee's earnings; and method toString (lines 49–55), which returns the employee's type, namely, "commission employee: " and Employee-specific information. The constructor also passes the first name, last name and social security number to Employee's constructor (line 13) to initialize Employee's private instance variables. Method toString calls superclass method toString (line 52) to obtain the Employee-specific information (i.e., first name, last name and social security number).

```
1   // Fig. 10.7: CommissionEmployee.java
2   // CommissionEmployee class extends Employee.
3
4   public class CommissionEmployee extends Employee
5   {
6       private double grossSales; // gross weekly sales
7       private double commissionRate; // commission percentage
8
9       // five-argument constructor
10      public CommissionEmployee( String first, String last, String ssn,
11          double sales, double rate )
12      {
13          super( first, last, ssn );
14          setGrossSales( sales );
15          setCommissionRate( rate );
16      } // end five-argument CommissionEmployee constructor
17
```

Fig. 10.7 | CommissionEmployee class derived from Employee. (Part 1 of 2.)

```
18      // set commission rate
19      public void setCommissionRate( double rate )
20      {
21         commissionRate = ( rate > 0.0 && rate < 1.0 ) ? rate : 0.0;
22      } // end method setCommissionRate
23
24      // return commission rate
25      public double getCommissionRate()
26      {
27         return commissionRate;
28      } // end method getCommissionRate
29
30      // set gross sales amount
31      public void setGrossSales( double sales )
32      {
33         grossSales = ( sales < 0.0 ) ? 0.0 : sales;
34      } // end method setGrossSales
35
36      // return gross sales amount
37      public double getGrossSales()
38      {
39         return grossSales;
40      } // end method getGrossSales
41
42      // calculate earnings; override abstract method earnings in Employee
43      public double earnings()
44      {
45         return getCommissionRate() * getGrossSales();
46      } // end method earnings
47
48      // return String representation of CommissionEmployee object
49      public String toString()
50      {
51         return String.format( "%s: %s\n%s: $%,.2f; %s: %.2f",
52            "commission employee", super.toString(),
53            "gross sales", getGrossSales(),
54            "commission rate", getCommissionRate() );
55      } // end method toString
56   } // end class CommissionEmployee
```

Fig. 10.7 | CommissionEmployee class derived from Employee. (Part 2 of 2.)

10.5.5 Creating Indirect Concrete Subclass BasePlusCommissionEmployee

Class BasePlusCommissionEmployee (Fig. 10.8) extends class CommissionEmployee (line 4) and therefore is an indirect subclass of class Employee. Class BasePlusCommission-Employee has a constructor (lines 9–14) that takes as arguments a first name, a last name, a social security number, a sales amount, a commission rate and a base salary. It then passes the first name, last name, social security number, sales amount and commission rate to the CommissionEmployee constructor (line 12) to initialize the inherited members. Base-PlusCommissionEmployee also contains a *set* method (lines 17–20) to assign a new value to instance variable baseSalary and a *get* method (lines 23–26) to return baseSalary's value. Method earnings (lines 29–32) calculates a BasePlusCommissionEmployee's earnings. Note that line 31 in method earnings calls superclass CommissionEmployee's earnings method to calculate the commission-based portion of the employee's earnings. This is a nice example of code reuse. BasePlusCommissionEmployee's toString method (lines 35–40) creates a string representation of a BasePlusCommissionEmployee that contains "base-salaried", followed by the String obtained by invoking superclass CommissionEmployee's toString method (another example of code reuse), then the base salary. The result is a String beginning with "base-salaried commission employee" followed by the rest of the BasePlusCommissionEmployee's information. Recall that CommissionEmployee's toString obtains the employee's first name, last name and social security number by invoking the toString method of its superclass (i.e., Employee)—yet another example of code reuse. Note that BasePlusCommissionEmployee's toString initiates a chain of method calls that span all three levels of the Employee hierarchy.

```java
 1   // Fig. 10.8: BasePlusCommissionEmployee.java
 2   // BasePlusCommissionEmployee class extends CommissionEmployee.
 3
 4   public class BasePlusCommissionEmployee extends CommissionEmployee
 5   {
 6      private double baseSalary; // base salary per week
 7
 8      // six-argument constructor
 9      public BasePlusCommissionEmployee( String first, String last,
10         String ssn, double sales, double rate, double salary )
11      {
12         super( first, last, ssn, sales, rate );
13         setBaseSalary( salary ); // validate and store base salary
14      } // end six-argument BasePlusCommissionEmployee constructor
15
16      // set base salary
17      public void setBaseSalary( double salary )
18      {
19         baseSalary = ( salary < 0.0 ) ? 0.0 : salary; // non-negative
20      } // end method setBaseSalary
21
22      // return base salary
23      public double getBaseSalary()
24      {
25         return baseSalary;
26      } // end method getBaseSalary
27
28      // calculate earnings; override method earnings in CommissionEmployee
29      public double earnings()
30      {
31         return getBaseSalary() + super.earnings();
32      } // end method earnings
33
34      // return String representation of BasePlusCommissionEmployee object
35      public String toString()
36      {
```

Fig. 10.8 | BasePlusCommissionEmployee derives from CommissionEmployee. (Part 1 of 2.)

```
37              return String.format( "%s %s; %s: $%,.2f",
38                  "base-salaried", super.toString(),
39                  "base salary", getBaseSalary() );
40          } // end method toString
41      } // end class BasePlusCommissionEmployee
```

Fig. 10.8 | `BasePlusCommissionEmployee` derives from `CommissionEmployee`. (Part 2 of 2.)

10.5.6 Demonstrating Polymorphic Processing, Operator `instanceof` and Downcasting

To test our `Employee` hierarchy, the application in Fig. 10.9 creates an object of each of the four concrete classes `SalariedEmployee`, `HourlyEmployee`, `CommissionEmployee` and `BasePlusCommissionEmployee`. The program manipulates these objects, first via variables of each object's own type, then polymorphically, using an array of `Employee` variables. While processing the objects polymorphically, the program increases the base salary of each `BasePlusCommissionEmployee` by 10% (this, of course, requires determining the object's type at execution time). Finally, the program polymorphically determines and outputs the type of each object in the `Employee` array. Lines 9–18 create objects of each of the four concrete `Employee` subclasses. Lines 22–30 output the string representation and earnings of each of these objects. Note that each object's `toString` method is called implicitly by `printf` when the object is output as a `String` with the %s format specifier.

```
1   // Fig. 10.9: PayrollSystemTest.java
2   // Employee hierarchy test program.
3
4   public class PayrollSystemTest
5   {
6       public static void main( String args[] )
7       {
8           // create subclass objects
9           SalariedEmployee salariedEmployee =
10              new SalariedEmployee( "John", "Smith", "111-11-1111", 800.00 );
11          HourlyEmployee hourlyEmployee =
12              new HourlyEmployee( "Karen", "Price", "222-22-2222", 16.75, 40 );
13          CommissionEmployee commissionEmployee =
14              new CommissionEmployee(
15              "Sue", "Jones", "333-33-3333", 10000, .06 );
16          BasePlusCommissionEmployee basePlusCommissionEmployee =
17              new BasePlusCommissionEmployee(
18              "Bob", "Lewis", "444-44-4444", 5000, .04, 300 );
19
20          System.out.println( "Employees processed individually:\n" );
21
22          System.out.printf( "%s\n%s: $%,.2f\n\n",
23              salariedEmployee, "earned", salariedEmployee.earnings() );
24          System.out.printf( "%s\n%s: $%,.2f\n\n",
25              hourlyEmployee, "earned", hourlyEmployee.earnings() );
26          System.out.printf( "%s\n%s: $%,.2f\n\n",
27              commissionEmployee, "earned", commissionEmployee.earnings() );
```

Fig. 10.9 | `Employee` class hierarchy test program. (Part 1 of 3.)

```
28        System.out.printf( "%s\n%s: $%,.2f\n\n",
29           basePlusCommissionEmployee,
30           "earned", basePlusCommissionEmployee.earnings() );
31
32        // create four-element Employee array
33        Employee employees[] = new Employee[ 4 ];
34
35        // initialize array with Employees
36        employees[ 0 ] = salariedEmployee;
37        employees[ 1 ] = hourlyEmployee;
38        employees[ 2 ] = commissionEmployee;
39        employees[ 3 ] = basePlusCommissionEmployee;
40
41        System.out.println( "Employees processed polymorphically:\n" );
42
43        // generically process each element in array employees
44        for ( Employee currentEmployee : employees )
45        {
46           System.out.println( currentEmployee ); // invokes toString
47
48           // determine whether element is a BasePlusCommissionEmployee
49           if ( currentEmployee instanceof BasePlusCommissionEmployee )
50           {
51              // downcast Employee reference to
52              // BasePlusCommissionEmployee reference
53              BasePlusCommissionEmployee employee =
54                 ( BasePlusCommissionEmployee ) currentEmployee;
55
56              double oldBaseSalary = employee.getBaseSalary();
57              employee.setBaseSalary( 1.10 * oldBaseSalary );
58              System.out.printf(
59                 "new base salary with 10%% increase is: $%,.2f\n",
60                 employee.getBaseSalary() );
61           } // end if
62
63           System.out.printf(
64              "earned $%,.2f\n\n", currentEmployee.earnings() );
65        } // end for
66
67        // get type name of each object in employees array
68        for ( int j = 0; j < employees.length; j++ )
69           System.out.printf( "Employee %d is a %s\n", j,
70              employees[ j ].getClass().getName() );
71     } // end main
72  } // end class PayrollSystemTest
```

```
Employees processed individually:

salaried employee: John Smith
social security number: 111-11-1111
weekly salary: $800.00
earned: $800.00
```

Fig. 10.9 | Employee class hierarchy test program. (Part 2 of 3.)

```
hourly employee: Karen Price
social security number: 222-22-2222
hourly wage: $16.75; hours worked: 40.00
earned: $670.00

commission employee: Sue Jones
social security number: 333-33-3333
gross sales: $10,000.00; commission rate: 0.06
earned: $600.00

base-salaried commission employee: Bob Lewis
social security number: 444-44-4444
gross sales: $5,000.00; commission rate: 0.04; base salary: $300.00
earned: $500.00

Employees processed polymorphically:

salaried employee: John Smith
social security number: 111-11-1111
weekly salary: $800.00
earned $800.00

hourly employee: Karen Price
social security number: 222-22-2222
hourly wage: $16.75; hours worked: 40.00
earned $670.00

commission employee: Sue Jones
social security number: 333-33-3333
gross sales: $10,000.00; commission rate: 0.06
earned $600.00

base-salaried commission employee: Bob Lewis
social security number: 444-44-4444
gross sales: $5,000.00; commission rate: 0.04; base salary: $300.00
new base salary with 10% increase is: $330.00
earned $530.00

Employee 0 is a SalariedEmployee
Employee 1 is a HourlyEmployee
Employee 2 is a CommissionEmployee
Employee 3 is a BasePlusCommissionEmployee
```

Fig. 10.9 | Employee class hierarchy test program. (Part 3 of 3.)

Line 33 declares employees and assigns it an array of four Employee variables. Line 36 assigns the reference to a SalariedEmployee object to employees[0]. Line 37 assigns the reference to an HourlyEmployee object to employees[1]. Line 38 assigns the reference to a CommissionEmployee object to employees[2]. Line 39 assigns the reference to a BasePlusCommissionEmployee object to employee[3]. Each assignment is allowed, because a SalariedEmployee *is an* Employee, an HourlyEmployee *is an* Employee, a CommissionEmployee *is an* Employee and a BasePlusCommissionEmployee *is an* Employee. Therefore, we can assign the references of SalariedEmployee, HourlyEmployee, CommissionEmployee and BasePlusCommissionEmployee objects to superclass Employee variables, even though Employee is an abstract class.

Lines 44–65 iterate through array `employees` and invoke methods `toString` and `earnings` with `Employee` control variable `currentEmployee`. The output illustrates that the appropriate methods for each class are indeed invoked. All calls to method `toString` and `earnings` are resolved at execution time, based on the type of the object to which `currentEmployee` refers. This process is known as *dynamic binding* or *late binding*. For example, line 46 implicitly invokes method `toString` of the object to which `currentEmployee` refers. As a result of dynamic binding, Java decides which class's `toString` method to call at execution time rather than at compile time. Note that only the methods of class `Employee` can be called via an `Employee` variable (and `Employee`, of course, includes the methods of class `Object`). (Section 9.7 discusses the set of methods that all classes inherit from class `Object`.) A superclass reference can be used to invoke only methods of the superclass (and the superclass can invoke overridden versions of these in the subclass).

We perform special processing on `BasePlusCommissionEmployee` objects—as we encounter these objects, we increase their base salary by 10%. When processing objects polymorphically, we typically do not need to worry about the "specifics," but to adjust the base salary, we do have to determine the specific type of `Employee` object at execution time. Line 49 uses the ***instanceof*** operator to determine whether a particular `Employee` object's type is `BasePlusCommissionEmployee`. The condition in line 49 is true if the object referenced by `currentEmployee` *is a* `BasePlusCommissionEmployee`. This would also be true for any object of a `BasePlusCommissionEmployee` subclass because of the *is-a* relationship a subclass has with its superclass. Lines 53–54 downcast `currentEmployee` from type `Employee` to type `BasePlusCommissionEmployee`—this cast is allowed only if the object has an *is-a* relationship with `BasePlusCommissionEmployee`. The condition at line 49 ensures that this is the case. This cast is required if we are to invoke subclass `BasePlusCommissionEmployee` methods `getBaseSalary` and `setBaseSalary` on the current `Employee` object—as you'll see momentarily, attempting to invoke a subclass-only method directly on a superclass reference is a compilation error.

Common Programming Error 10.3

Assigning a superclass variable to a subclass variable (without an explicit cast) is a compilation error.

Software Engineering Observation 10.5

If at execution time the reference of a subclass object has been assigned to a variable of one of its direct or indirect superclasses, it is acceptable to cast the reference stored in that superclass variable back to a reference of the subclass type. Before performing such a cast, use the `instanceof` operator to ensure that the object is indeed an object of an appropriate subclass type.

Common Programming Error 10.4

When downcasting an object, a `ClassCastException` occurs if at execution time the object does not have an is-a *relationship with the type specified in the cast operator. An object can be cast only to its own type or to the type of one of its superclasses.*

If the `instanceof` expression in line 49 is `true`, the body of the `if` statement (lines 49–61) performs the special processing required for the `BasePlusCommissionEmployee` object. Using `BasePlusCommissionEmployee` variable `employee`, lines 56 and 57 invoke subclass-only methods `getBaseSalary` and `setBaseSalary` to retrieve and update the employee's base salary with the 10% raise.

Lines 63–64 invoke method `earnings` on `currentEmployee`, which calls the appropriate subclass object's `earnings` method polymorphically. As you can see, obtaining the earnings of the `SalariedEmployee`, `HourlyEmployee` and `CommissionEmployee` polymorphically in lines 63–64 produces the same result as obtaining these employees' earnings individually in lines 22–27. However, the earnings amount obtained for the `BasePlusCommissionEmployee` in lines 63–64 is higher than that obtained in lines 28–30, due to the 10% increase in its base salary.

Lines 68–70 display each employee's type as a string. Every object in Java knows its own class and can access this information through the **_getClass_** method, which all classes inherit from class `Object`. The `getClass` method returns an object of type **_Class_** (from package `java.lang`), which contains information about the object's type, including its class name. Line 70 invokes the `getClass` method on the object to get its runtime class (i.e., a `Class` object that represents the object's type). Then method **_getName_** is invoked on the object returned by `getClass` to get the class's name. To learn more about class `Class`, see its online documentation at `java.sun.com/javase/6/docs/api/java/lang/Class.html`.

In the previous example, we avoided several compilation errors by downcasting an `Employee` variable to a `BasePlusCommissionEmployee` variable in lines 53–54. If you remove the cast operator (`BasePlusCommissionEmployee`) from line 54 and attempt to assign `Employee` variable `currentEmployee` directly to `BasePlusCommissionEmployee` variable `employee`, you'll receive an "`incompatible types`" compilation error. This error indicates that the attempt to assign the reference of superclass object `commissionEmployee` to subclass variable `basePlusCommissionEmployee` is not allowed. The compiler prevents this assignment because a `CommissionEmployee` is not a `BasePlusCommissionEmployee`—the _is-a_ relationship applies only between the subclass and its superclasses, not vice versa.

Similarly, if lines 56, 57 and 60 used superclass variable `currentEmployee`, rather than subclass variable `employee`, to invoke subclass-only methods `getBaseSalary` and `setBaseSalary`, we would receive a "`cannot find symbol`" compilation error on each of these lines. Attempting to invoke subclass-only methods on a superclass reference is not allowed. While lines 56, 57 and 60 execute only if `instanceof` in line 49 returns `true` to indicate that `currentEmployee` has been assigned a reference to a `BasePlusCommission-Employee` object, we cannot attempt to invoke subclass `BasePlusCommissionEmployee` methods `getBaseSalary` and `setBaseSalary` on superclass `Employee` reference `currentEmployee`. The compiler would generate errors in lines 56, 57 and 60, because `getBaseSalary` and `setBaseSalary` are not superclass methods and cannot be invoked on a superclass variable. Although the actual method that is called depends on the object's type at execution time, a variable can be used to invoke only those methods that are members of that variable's type, which the compiler verifies. Using a superclass `Employee` variable, we can invoke only methods found in class `Employee`—`earnings`, `toString` and `Employee`'s _get_ and _set_ methods.

10.5.7 Summary of the Allowed Assignments Between Superclass and Subclass Variables

Now that you have seen a complete application that processes diverse subclass objects polymorphically, we summarize what you can and cannot do with superclass and subclass objects and variables. Although a subclass object also _is a_ superclass object, the two objects are nevertheless different. As discussed previously, subclass objects can be treated as if they are superclass objects. But because the subclass can have additional subclass-only members, assigning a superclass reference to a subclass variable is not allowed without an explicit cast—such an assignment would leave the subclass members undefined for the superclass object.

In the current section and in Section 10.3 and Chapter 9, we have discussed four ways to assign superclass and subclass references to variables of superclass and subclass types:

1. Assigning a superclass reference to a superclass variable is straightforward.

2. Assigning a subclass reference to a subclass variable is straightforward.

3. Assigning a subclass reference to a superclass variable is safe, because the subclass object *is an* object of its superclass. However, this reference can be used to refer only to superclass members. If this code refers to subclass-only members through the superclass variable, the compiler reports errors.

4. Attempting to assign a superclass reference to a subclass variable is a compilation error. To avoid this error, the superclass reference must be cast to a subclass type explicitly. At execution time, if the object to which the reference refers is not a subclass object, an exception will occur. (For more on exception handling, see Chapter 13.) The `instanceof` operator can be used to ensure that such a cast is performed only if the object is a subclass object.

10.6 `final` Methods and Classes

We saw in Section 6.10 that variables can be declared `final` to indicate that they cannot be modified after they are initialized—such variables represent constant values. It is also possible to declare methods, method parameters and classes with the `final` modifier.

A method that is declared `final` in a superclass cannot be overridden in a subclass. Methods that are declared `private` are implicitly `final`, because it is impossible to override them in a subclass. Methods that are declared `static` are also implicitly `final`. A `final` method's declaration can never change, so all subclasses use the same method implementation, and calls to `final` methods are resolved at compile time—this is known as *static binding*. Since the compiler knows that `final` methods cannot be overridden, it can optimize programs by removing calls to `final` methods and replacing them with the expanded code of their declarations at each method call location—a technique known as *inlining the code*.

> **Performance Tip 10.1**
>
> *The compiler can decide to inline a `final` method call and will do so for small, simple `final` methods. Inlining does not violate encapsulation or information hiding, but does improve performance because it eliminates the overhead of making a method call.*

A class that is declared `final` cannot be a superclass (i.e., a class cannot extend a `final` class). All methods in a `final` class are implicitly `final`. Class `String` is an example of a `final` class. This class cannot be extended, so programs that use `Strings` can rely on the functionality of `String` objects as specified in the Java API. Making the class `final` also prevents programmers from creating subclasses that might bypass security restrictions. For more information on `final` classes and methods, visit `java.sun.com/docs/books/tutorial/java/IandI/final.html`. This site contains additional insights into using `final` classes to improve the security of a system.

Common Programming Error 10.5

Attempting to declare a subclass of a final class is a compilation error.

Software Engineering Observation 10.6

In the Java API, the vast majority of classes are not declared final. This enables inheritance and polymorphism—the fundamental capabilities of object-oriented programming. However, in some cases, it is important to declare classes final—typically for security reasons.

10.7 Case Study: Creating and Using Interfaces

Our next example (Figs. 10.11–10.13) reexamines the payroll system of Section 10.5. Suppose that the company involved wishes to perform several accounting operations in a single accounts payable application—in addition to calculating the earnings that must be paid to each employee, the company must also calculate the payment due on each of several invoices (i.e., bills for goods purchased). Though applied to unrelated things (i.e., employees and invoices), both operations have to do with obtaining some kind of payment amount. For an employee, the payment refers to the employee's earnings. For an invoice, the payment refers to the total cost of the goods listed on the invoice. Can we calculate such different things as the payments due for employees and invoices in a single application polymorphically? Does Java offer a capability that requires that unrelated classes implement a set of common methods (e.g., a method that calculates a payment amount)? Java *interfaces* offer exactly this capability.

Interfaces define and standardize the ways in which things such as people and systems can interact with one another. For example, the controls on a radio serve as an interface between radio users and a radio's internal components. The controls allow users to perform only a limited set of operations (e.g., changing the station, adjusting the volume, choosing between AM and FM), and different radios may implement the controls in different ways (e.g., using push buttons, dials, voice commands). The interface specifies *what* operations a radio must permit users to perform but does not specify *how* the operations are performed. Similarly, the interface between a driver and a car with a manual transmission includes the steering wheel, the gear shift, the clutch pedal, the gas pedal and the brake pedal. This same interface is found in nearly all manual transmission cars, enabling someone who knows how to drive one particular manual transmission car to drive just about any manual transmission car. The components of each individual car may look different, but their general purpose is the same—to allow people to drive the car.

Software objects also communicate via interfaces. A Java interface describes a set of methods that can be called on an object, to tell the object to perform some task or return some piece of information, for example. The next example introduces an interface named Payable to describe the functionality of any object that must be capable of being paid and thus must offer a method to determine the proper payment amount due. An *interface declaration* begins with the keyword *interface* and contains only constants and abstract methods. Unlike classes, all interface members must be public, and interfaces may not specify any implementation details, such as concrete method declarations and instance variables. So all methods declared in an interface are implicitly public abstract methods and all fields are implicitly public, static and final.

Good Programming Practice 10.1

According to Chapter 9 of the Java Language Specification, *it is proper style to declare an interface's methods without keywords* public *and* abstract *because they are redundant in interface method declarations. Similarly, constants should be declared without keywords* public, static *and* final *because they, too, are redundant.*

To use an interface, a concrete class must specify that it *implements* the interface and must declare each method in the interface with the signature specified in the interface declaration. A class that does not implement all the methods of the interface is an abstract class and must be declared abstract. Implementing an interface is like signing a contract with the compiler that states, "I will declare all the methods specified by the interface or I will declare my class abstract."

Common Programming Error 10.6

Failing to implement any method of an interface in a concrete class that implements *the interface results in a compilation error indicating that the class must be declared* abstract.

An interface is typically used when disparate (i.e., unrelated) classes need to share common methods and constants. This allows objects of unrelated classes to be processed polymorphically—objects of classes that implement the same interface can respond to the same method calls. You can create an interface that describes the desired functionality, then implement this interface in any classes that require that functionality. For example, in the accounts payable application developed in this section, we implement interface Payable in any class that must be able to calculate a payment amount (e.g., Employee, Invoice).

An interface is often used in place of an abstract class when there is no default implementation to inherit—that is, no fields and no default method implementations. Interfaces are typically public types, so they are normally declared in files by themselves with the same name as the interface and the .java file-name extension.

10.7.1 Developing a Payable Hierarchy

To build an application that can determine payments for employees and invoices alike, we first create interface Payable, which contains method getPaymentAmount that returns a double amount that must be paid for an object of any class that implements the interface. Method getPaymentAmount is a general purpose version of method earnings of the Employee hierarchy—method earnings calculates a payment amount specifically for an Employee, while getPaymentAmount can be applied to a broad range of unrelated objects. After declaring interface Payable, we introduce class Invoice, which implements interface Payable. We then modify class Employee such that it also implements interface Payable. Finally, we update Employee subclass SalariedEmployee to "fit" into the Payable hierarchy (i.e., we rename SalariedEmployee method earnings as getPaymentAmount).

Good Programming Practice 10.2

When declaring a method in an interface, choose a method name that describes the method's purpose in a general manner, because the method may be implemented by many unrelated classes.

Classes Invoice and Employee both represent things for which the company must be able to calculate a payment amount. Both classes implement Payable, so a program can invoke method getPaymentAmount on Invoice objects and Employee objects alike. As we'll soon see, this enables the polymorphic processing of Invoices and Employees required for our company's accounts payable application.

The UML class diagram in Fig. 10.10 shows the hierarchy used in our accounts payable application. The hierarchy begins with interface Payable. The UML distinguishes an interface from other classes by placing the word "interface" in guillemets (« and ») above the interface name. The UML expresses the relationship between a class and an interface through a relationship known as a *realization*. A class is said to "realize," or implement, the methods of an interface. A class diagram models a realization as a dashed arrow with a hollow arrowhead pointing from the implementing class to the interface. The diagram in Fig. 10.10 indicates that classes Invoice and Employee each realize (i.e., implement) interface Payable. Note that, as in the class diagram of Fig. 10.2, class Employee appears in italics, indicating that it is an abstract class. Concrete class SalariedEmployee extends Employee and inherits its superclass's realization relationship with interface Payable.

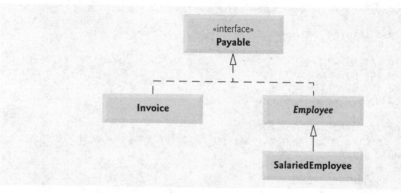

Fig. 10.10 | Payable interface hierarchy UML class diagram.

10.7.2 Declaring Interface Payable

The declaration of interface Payable begins in Fig. 10.11 at line 4. Interface Payable contains public abstract method getPaymentAmount (line 6). Note that the method is not explicitly declared public or abstract. Interface methods must be public and abstract, so they do not need to be declared as such. Interface Payable has only one method—interfaces can have any number of methods. (We'll see later in the book the notion of "tagging interfaces"—these actually have *no* methods. In fact, a tagging interface contains no constant values, either—it simply contains an empty interface declaration.) In addition, method getPaymentAmount has no parameters, but interface methods can have parameters.

```
1    // Fig. 10.11: Payable.java
2    // Payable interface declaration.
3
4    public interface Payable
5    {
6        double getPaymentAmount(); // calculate payment; no implementation
7    } // end interface Payable
```

Fig. 10.11 | Payable interface declaration.

10.7.3 Creating Class `Invoice`

We now create class `Invoice` (Fig. 10.12) to represent a simple invoice that contains billing information for only one kind of part. The class declares `private` instance variables `partNumber`, `partDescription`, `quantity` and `pricePerItem` (in lines 6–9) that indicate the part number, a description of the part, the quantity of the part ordered and the price per item. Class `Invoice` also contains a constructor (lines 12–19), *get* and *set* methods (lines 22–67) that manipulate the class's instance variables and a `toString` method (lines 70–75) that returns a string representation of an `Invoice` object. Note that methods `setQuantity` (lines 46–49) and `setPricePerItem` (lines 58–61) ensure that `quantity` and `pricePerItem` obtain only nonnegative values.

```
1    // Fig. 10.12: Invoice.java
2    // Invoice class implements Payable.
3
4    public class Invoice implements Payable
5    {
6       private String partNumber;
7       private String partDescription;
8       private int quantity;
9       private double pricePerItem;
10
11      // four-argument constructor
12      public Invoice( String part, String description, int count,
13         double price )
14      {
15         partNumber = part;
16         partDescription = description;
17         setQuantity( count ); // validate and store quantity
18         setPricePerItem( price ); // validate and store price per item
19      } // end four-argument Invoice constructor
20
21      // set part number
22      public void setPartNumber( String part )
23      {
24         partNumber = part;
25      } // end method setPartNumber
26
27      // get part number
28      public String getPartNumber()
29      {
30         return partNumber;
31      } // end method getPartNumber
32
33      // set description
34      public void setPartDescription( String description )
35      {
36         partDescription = description;
37      } // end method setPartDescription
38
```

Fig. 10.12 | `Invoice` class that implements `Payable`. (Part 1 of 2.)

```
39        // get description
40        public String getPartDescription()
41        {
42            return partDescription;
43        } // end method getPartDescription
44
45        // set quantity
46        public void setQuantity( int count )
47        {
48            quantity = ( count < 0 ) ? 0 : count; // quantity cannot be negative
49        } // end method setQuantity
50
51        // get quantity
52        public int getQuantity()
53        {
54            return quantity;
55        } // end method getQuantity
56
57        // set price per item
58        public void setPricePerItem( double price )
59        {
60            pricePerItem = ( price < 0.0 ) ? 0.0 : price; // validate price
61        } // end method setPricePerItem
62
63        // get price per item
64        public double getPricePerItem()
65        {
66            return pricePerItem;
67        } // end method getPricePerItem
68
69        // return String representation of Invoice object
70        public String toString()
71        {
72            return String.format( "%s: \n%s: %s (%s) \n%s: %d \n%s: $%,.2f",
73                "invoice", "part number", getPartNumber(), getPartDescription(),
74                "quantity", getQuantity(), "price per item", getPricePerItem() );
75        } // end method toString
76
77        // method required to carry out contract with interface Payable
78        public double getPaymentAmount()
79        {
80            return getQuantity() * getPricePerItem(); // calculate total cost
81        } // end method getPaymentAmount
82    } // end class Invoice
```

Fig. 10.12 | Invoice class that implements Payable. (Part 2 of 2.)

Line 4 of Fig. 10.12 indicates that class Invoice implements interface Payable. Like all classes, class Invoice also implicitly extends Object. Java does not allow subclasses to inherit from more than one superclass, but it does allow a class to inherit from a superclass and implement more than one interface. In fact, a class can implement as many interfaces as it needs, in addition to extending one other class. To implement more than one interface, use a comma-separated list of interface names after keyword `implements` in the class declaration, as in:

```
public class ClassName extends SuperclassName implements FirstInterface,
   SecondInterface, ...
```

All objects of a class that implement multiple interfaces have the *is-a* relationship with each implemented interface type.

Class `Invoice` implements the one method in interface `Payable`. Method `getPaymentAmount` is declared in lines 78–81. The method calculates the total payment required to pay the invoice. The method multiplies the values of `quantity` and `pricePer-Item` (obtained through the appropriate *get* methods) and returns the result (line 80). This method satisfies the implementation requirement for this method in interface `Payable`—we have fulfilled the interface contract with the compiler.

10.7.4 Modifying Class `Employee` to Implement Interface `Payable`

We now modify class `Employee` such that it implements interface `Payable`. Figure 10.13 contains the modified `Employee` class. This class declaration is identical to that of Fig. 10.4 with only two exceptions. First, line 4 of Fig. 10.13 indicates that class `Employee` now implements interface `Payable`. Second, since `Employee` now implements interface `Payable`, we must rename `earnings` to `getPaymentAmount` throughout the `Employee` hierarchy. As with method `earnings` in the version of class `Employee` in Fig. 10.4, however, it does not make sense to implement method `getPaymentAmount` in class `Employee` because we cannot calculate the earnings payment owed to a general `Employee`—first we must know the specific type of `Employee`. In Fig. 10.4, we declared method `earnings` as abstract for this reason, and as a result class `Employee` had to be declared abstract. This forced each Employee subclass to override `earnings` with a concrete implementation.

```java
1   // Fig. 10.13: Employee.java
2   // Employee abstract superclass implements Payable.
3
4   public abstract class Employee implements Payable
5   {
6      private String firstName;
7      private String lastName;
8      private String socialSecurityNumber;
9
10     // three-argument constructor
11     public Employee( String first, String last, String ssn )
12     {
13        firstName = first;
14        lastName = last;
15        socialSecurityNumber = ssn;
16     } // end three-argument Employee constructor
17
18     // set first name
19     public void setFirstName( String first )
20     {
```

Fig. 10.13 | `Employee` class that implements `Payable`. (Part 1 of 2.)

```
21          firstName = first;
22      } // end method setFirstName
23
24      // return first name
25      public String getFirstName()
26      {
27          return firstName;
28      } // end method getFirstName
29
30      // set last name
31      public void setLastName( String last )
32      {
33          lastName = last;
34      } // end method setLastName
35
36      // return last name
37      public String getLastName()
38      {
39          return lastName;
40      } // end method getLastName
41
42      // set social security number
43      public void setSocialSecurityNumber( String ssn )
44      {
45          socialSecurityNumber = ssn; // should validate
46      } // end method setSocialSecurityNumber
47
48      // return social security number
49      public String getSocialSecurityNumber()
50      {
51          return socialSecurityNumber;
52      } // end method getSocialSecurityNumber
53
54      // return String representation of Employee object
55      public String toString()
56      {
57          return String.format( "%s %s\nsocial security number: %s",
58              getFirstName(), getLastName(), getSocialSecurityNumber() );
59      } // end method toString
60
61      // Note: We do not implement Payable method getPaymentAmount here so
62      // this class must be declared abstract to avoid a compilation error.
63  } // end abstract class Employee
```

Fig. 10.13 | Employee class that implements Payable. (Part 2 of 2.)

In Fig. 10.13, we handle this situation differently. Recall that when a class implements an interface, the class makes a contract with the compiler stating either that the class will implement each of the methods in the interface or that the class will be declared abstract. If the latter option is chosen, we do not need to declare the interface methods as abstract in the abstract class—they are already implicitly declared as such in the interface. Any concrete subclass of the abstract class must implement the interface methods to fulfill the superclass's contract with the compiler. If the subclass does not do so, it too must be declared abstract. As indicated by the comments in lines 61–62, class Employee of Fig. 10.13 does not implement method getPaymentAmount, so the class is declared abstract. Each direct Employee subclass inherits the superclass's contract to implement method getPaymentAmount and thus must implement this method to become a concrete class for which objects can be instantiated. A class that extends one of Employee's concrete subclasses will inherit an implementation of getPaymentAmount and thus will also be a concrete class.

10.7.5 Modifying Class SalariedEmployee for Use in the Payable Hierarchy

Figure 10.14 contains a modified version of class SalariedEmployee that extends Employee and fulfills superclass Employee's contract to implement method getPaymentAmount of interface Payable. This version of SalariedEmployee is identical to that of Fig. 10.5 with the exception that the version here implements method getPaymentAmount (lines 30–33) instead of method earnings. The two methods contain the same functionality but have different names. Recall that the Payable version of the method has a more general name to be applicable to possibly disparate classes. The remaining Employee subclasses (e.g., HourlyEmployee, CommissionEmployee and BasePlusCommissionEmployee) also must be modified to contain method getPaymentAmount in place of earnings to reflect the fact that Employee now implements Payable. We leave these modifications as an exercise and use only SalariedEmployee in our test program in this section.

```java
1   // Fig. 10.14: SalariedEmployee.java
2   // SalariedEmployee class extends Employee, which implements Payable.
3
4   public class SalariedEmployee extends Employee
5   {
6      private double weeklySalary;
7
8      // four-argument constructor
9      public SalariedEmployee( String first, String last, String ssn,
10        double salary )
11     {
12        super( first, last, ssn ); // pass to Employee constructor
13        setWeeklySalary( salary ); // validate and store salary
14     } // end four-argument SalariedEmployee constructor
15
16     // set salary
17     public void setWeeklySalary( double salary )
18     {
19        weeklySalary = salary < 0.0 ? 0.0 : salary;
20     } // end method setWeeklySalary
21
22     // return salary
23     public double getWeeklySalary()
24     {
25        return weeklySalary;
26     } // end method getWeeklySalary
```

Fig. 10.14 | SalariedEmployee class that implements interface Payable method getPaymentAmount. (Part I of 2.)

```
27
28      // calculate earnings; implement interface Payable method that was
29      // abstract in superclass Employee
30      public double getPaymentAmount()
31      {
32         return getWeeklySalary();
33      } // end method getPaymentAmount
34
35      // return String representation of SalariedEmployee object
36      public String toString()
37      {
38         return String.format( "salaried employee: %s\n%s: $%,.2f",
39            super.toString(), "weekly salary", getWeeklySalary() );
40      } // end method toString
41   } // end class SalariedEmployee
```

Fig. 10.14 | SalariedEmployee class that implements interface Payable method getPaymentAmount. (Part 2 of 2.)

When a class implements an interface, the same *is-a* relationship provided by inheritance applies. For example, class Employee implements Payable, so we can say that an Employee *is a* Payable. In fact, objects of any classes that extend Employee are also Payable objects. SalariedEmployee objects, for instance, are Payable objects. As with inheritance relationships, an object of a class that implements an interface may be thought of as an object of the interface type. Objects of any subclasses of the class that implements the interface can also be thought of as objects of the interface type. Thus, just as we can assign the reference of a SalariedEmployee object to a superclass Employee variable, we can assign the reference of a SalariedEmployee object to an interface Payable variable. Invoice implements Payable, so an Invoice object also *is a* Payable object, and we can assign the reference of an Invoice object to a Payable variable.

Software Engineering Observation 10.7

Inheritance and interfaces are similar in their implementation of the is-a *relationship. An object of a class that implements an interface may be thought of as an object of that interface type. An object of any subclasses of a class that implements an interface also can be thought of as an object of the interface type.*

Software Engineering Observation 10.8

The is-a *relationship that exists between superclasses and subclasses, and between interfaces and the classes that implement them, holds when passing an object to a method. When a method parameter receives a variable of a superclass or interface type, the method processes the object received as an argument polymorphically.*

Software Engineering Observation 10.9

Using a superclass reference, we can polymorphically invoke any method specified in the superclass declaration (and in class Object). Using an interface reference, we can polymorphically invoke any method specified in the interface declaration (and in class Object— because a variable of an interface type must refer to an object to call methods, and all objects contain the methods of class Object).

10.7.6 Using Interface Payable to Process Invoices and Employees Polymorphically

PayableInterfaceTest (Fig. 10.15) illustrates that interface Payable can be used to process a set of Invoices and Employees polymorphically in a single application. Line 9 declares payableObjects and assigns it an array of four Payable variables. Lines 12–13 assign the references of Invoice objects to the first two elements of payableObjects. Lines 14–17 then assign the references of SalariedEmployee objects to the remaining two elements of payableObjects. These assignments are allowed because an Invoice *is a* Payable, a SalariedEmployee *is an* Employee and an Employee *is a* Payable. Lines 23–29 use the enhanced for statement to polymorphically process each Payable object in payableObjects, printing the object as a String, along with the payment amount due. Note that line 27 invokes method toString off a Payable interface reference, even though toString is not declared in interface Payable—all references (including those of interface types) refer to objects that extend Object and therefore have a toString method. (Note that toString also can be invoked implicitly here.) Line 28 invokes Payable method getPaymentAmount to obtain the payment amount for each object in payableObjects, regardless of the actual type of the object. The output reveals that the method calls in lines 27–28 invoke the appropriate class's implementation of methods toString and getPaymentAmount. For instance, when currentEmployee refers to an Invoice during the first iteration of the for loop, class Invoice's toString and getPaymentAmount execute.

> ### Software Engineering Observation 10.10
>
> *All methods of class Object can be called by using a reference of an interface type. A reference refers to an object, and all objects inherit the methods of class Object.*

```java
1   // Fig. 10.15: PayableInterfaceTest.java
2   // Tests interface Payable.
3
4   public class PayableInterfaceTest
5   {
6      public static void main( String args[] )
7      {
8         // create four-element Payable array
9         Payable payableObjects[] = new Payable[ 4 ];
10
11        // populate array with objects that implement Payable
12        payableObjects[ 0 ] = new Invoice( "01234", "seat", 2, 375.00 );
13        payableObjects[ 1 ] = new Invoice( "56789", "tire", 4, 79.95 );
14        payableObjects[ 2 ] =
15           new SalariedEmployee( "John", "Smith", "111-11-1111", 800.00 );
16        payableObjects[ 3 ] =
17           new SalariedEmployee( "Lisa", "Barnes", "888-88-8888", 1200.00 );
18
19        System.out.println(
20           "Invoices and Employees processed polymorphically:\n" );
21
```

Fig. 10.15 | Payable interface test program processing Invoices and Employees polymorphically. (Part 1 of 2.)

```
22          // generically process each element in array payableObjects
23          for ( Payable currentPayable : payableObjects )
24          {
25             // output currentPayable and its appropriate payment amount
26             System.out.printf( "%s \n%s: $%,.2f\n\n",
27                currentPayable.toString(),
28                "payment due", currentPayable.getPaymentAmount() );
29          } // end for
30       } // end main
31    } // end class PayableInterfaceTest
```

```
Invoices and Employees processed polymorphically:

invoice:
part number: 01234 (seat)
quantity: 2
price per item: $375.00
payment due: $750.00

invoice:
part number: 56789 (tire)
quantity: 4
price per item: $79.95
payment due: $319.80

salaried employee: John Smith
social security number: 111-11-1111
weekly salary: $800.00
payment due: $800.00

salaried employee: Lisa Barnes
social security number: 888-88-8888
weekly salary: $1,200.00
payment due: $1,200.00
```

Fig. 10.15 | Payable interface test program processing Invoices and Employees polymorphically. (Part 2 of 2.)

10.7.7 Declaring Constants with Interfaces

As we mentioned an interface can declare constants. The constants are implicitly public, static and final—again, these keywords are not required in the interface declaration. One popular use of an interface is to declare a set of constants that can be used in many class declarations. Consider interface Constants:

```
public interface Constants
{
    int ONE = 1;
    int TWO = 2;
    int THREE = 3;
}
```

A class can use these constants by importing the interface, then referring to each constant as Constants.ONE, Constants.TWO and Constants.THREE. Note that a class can refer to the imported constants with just their names (i.e., ONE, TWO and THREE) if it uses a static import declaration (presented in Section 8.12) to import the interface.

Software Engineering Observation 10.11

As of Java SE 5.0, it became a better programming practice to create sets of constants as enumerations with keyword enum. See Section 6.10 for an introduction to enum and Section 8.9 for additional enum details.

10.7.8 Common Interfaces of the Java API

In this section, we overview several common interfaces found in the Java API. The power and flexibility of interfaces is used frequently throughout the Java API. These interfaces are implemented and used in the same manner as the interfaces you create (e.g., interface Payable in Section 10.7.2). As you'll see throughout this book, the Java API's interfaces enable you to use your own classes within the frameworks provided by Java, such as comparing objects of your own types and creating tasks that can execute concurrently with other tasks in the same program. Figure 10.16 presents a brief overview of a few of the more popular interfaces of the Java API.

Interface	Description
Comparable	As you learned in Chapter 2, Java contains several comparison operators (e.g., <, <=, >, >=, ==, !=) that allow you to compare primitive values. However, these operators cannot be used to compare the contents of objects. Interface Comparable is used to allow objects of a class that implements the interface to be compared to one another. The interface contains one method, compareTo, that compares the object that calls the method to the object passed as an argument to the method. Classes must implement compareTo such that it returns a value indicating whether the object on which it is invoked is less than (negative integer return value), equal to (0 return value) or greater than (positive integer return value) the object passed as an argument, using any criteria specified by the programmer. For example, if class Employee implements Comparable, its compareTo method could compare Employee objects by their earnings amounts. Interface Comparable is commonly used for ordering objects in a collection such as an array. We use Comparable in Chapter 15, Generics, and Chapter 16, Collections.
Serializable	An interface used to identify classes whose objects can be written to (i.e., serialized) or read from (i.e., deserialized) some type of storage (e.g., file on disk, database field) or transmitted across a network. We use Serializable in Chapter 14, Files and Streams, and Chapter 19, Networking.
Runnable	Implemented by any class for which objects of that class should be able to execute in parallel using a technique called multithreading (discussed in Chapter 18, Multithreading). The interface contains one method, run, which describes the behavior of an object when executed.
GUI event-listener interfaces	You work with graphical user interfaces (GUIs) every day. For example, in your web browser, you might type in a text field the address of a website to visit, or you might click a button to return to the previous site you

Fig. 10.16 | Common interfaces of the Java API. (Part 1 of 2.)

Interface	Description
	visited. When you type a website address or click a button in the web browser, the browser must respond to your interaction and perform the desired task for you. Your interaction is known as an event, and the code that the browser uses to respond to an event is known as an event handler. In Chapter 11, GUI Components: Part 1, and Chapter 17, GUI Components: Part 2, you'll learn how to build Java GUIs and how to build event handlers to respond to user interactions. The event handlers are declared in classes that implement an appropriate event-listener interface. Each event-listener interface specifies one or more methods that must be implemented to respond to user interactions.
`SwingConstants`	Contains constants used in GUI programming to position GUI elements on the screen. We explore GUI programming in Chapters 11 and 17.

Fig. 10.16 | Common interfaces of the Java API. (Part 2 of 2.)

10.8 (Optional) Software Engineering Case Study: Incorporating Inheritance into the ATM System

We now revisit our ATM system design to see how it might benefit from inheritance. To apply inheritance, we first look for commonality among classes in the system. We create an inheritance hierarchy to model similar (yet not identical) classes in a more elegant and efficient manner. We then modify our class diagram to incorporate the new inheritance relationships. Finally, we demonstrate how our updated design is translated into Java code.

In Section 3.9, we encountered the problem of representing a financial transaction in the system. Rather than create one class to represent all transaction types, we decided to create three individual transaction classes—`BalanceInquiry`, `Withdrawal` and `Deposit`— to represent the transactions that the ATM system can perform. Figure 10.17 shows the attributes and operations of classes `BalanceInquiry`, `Withdrawal` and `Deposit`. Note that these classes have one attribute (`accountNumber`) and one operation (`execute`) in common. Each class requires attribute `accountNumber` to specify the account to which the

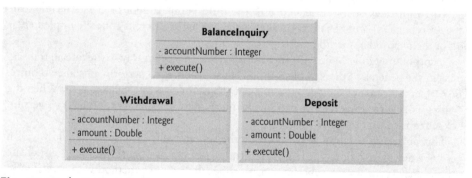

Fig. 10.17 | Attributes and operations of classes `BalanceInquiry`, `Withdrawal` and `Deposit`.

transaction applies. Each class contains operation execute, which the ATM invokes to perform the transaction. Clearly, BalanceInquiry, Withdrawal and Deposit represent *types of* transactions. Figure 10.17 reveals commonality among the transaction classes, so using inheritance to factor out the common features seems appropriate for designing classes BalanceInquiry, Withdrawal and Deposit. We place the common functionality in a superclass, Transaction, that classes BalanceInquiry, Withdrawal and Deposit extend.

The UML specifies a relationship called a *generalization* to model inheritance. Figure 10.18 is the class diagram that models the generalization of superclass Transaction and subclasses BalanceInquiry, Withdrawal and Deposit. The arrows with triangular hollow arrowheads indicate that classes BalanceInquiry, Withdrawal and Deposit extend class Transaction. Class Transaction is said to be a generalization of classes BalanceInquiry, Withdrawal and Deposit. Class BalanceInquiry, Withdrawal and Deposit are said to be *specializations* of class Transaction.

Classes BalanceInquiry, Withdrawal and Deposit share integer attribute accountNumber, so we factor out this common attribute and place it in superclass Transaction. We no longer list accountNumber in the second compartment of each subclass, because the three subclasses inherit this attribute from Transaction. Recall, however, that subclasses cannot access private attributes of a superclass. We therefore include public method getAccountNumber in class Transaction. Each subclass will inherit this method, enabling the subclass to access its accountNumber as needed to execute a transaction.

According to Fig. 10.17, classes BalanceInquiry, Withdrawal and Deposit also share operation execute, so we decided that superclass Transaction should contain public method execute. However, it does not make sense to implement execute in class Transaction, because the functionality that this method provides depends on the type of the actual transaction. We therefore declare method execute as abstract in superclass Transaction. Any class that contains at least one abstract method must also be declared abstract. This forces any subclass of Transaction that must be a concrete class (i.e., BalanceInquiry, Withdrawal and Deposit) to implement method execute. The UML requires that we place abstract class names (and abstract methods) in italics, so Transaction and its method execute appear in italics in Fig. 10.18. Note that method execute is not italicized in subclasses BalanceInquiry, Withdrawal and Deposit. Each subclass overrides superclass Transaction's execute method with a concrete implementation that performs the steps appropriate for completing that type of transaction. Note that Fig. 10.18 includes operation execute in the third compartment of classes BalanceInquiry, Withdrawal and Deposit, because each class has a different concrete implementation of the overridden method.

Incorporating inheritance provides the ATM with an elegant way to execute all transactions "in the general." For example, suppose a user chooses to perform a balance inquiry. The ATM sets a Transaction reference to a new object of class BalanceInquiry. When the ATM uses its Transaction reference to invoke method execute, BalanceInquiry's version of execute is called.

This polymorphic approach also makes the system easily extensible. Should we wish to create a new transaction type (e.g., funds transfer or bill payment), we would just create an additional Transaction subclass that overrides the execute method with a version of the method appropriate for executing the new transaction type. We would need to make only minimal changes to the system code to allow users to choose the new transaction type

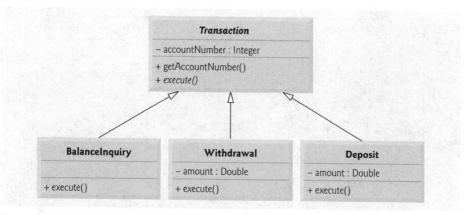

Fig. 10.18 | Class diagram modeling generalization of superclass `Transaction` and subclasses `BalanceInquiry`, `Withdrawal` and `Deposit`. Note that abstract class names (e.g., `Transaction`) and method names (e.g., `execute` in class `Transaction`) appear in italics.

from the main menu and for the ATM to instantiate and execute objects of the new subclass. The ATM could execute transactions of the new type using the current code, because it executes all transactions polymorphically using a general `Transaction` reference.

An abstract class like `Transaction` is one for which the programmer never intends to instantiate objects. An abstract class simply declares common attributes and behaviors of its subclasses in an inheritance hierarchy. Class `Transaction` defines the concept of what it means to be a transaction that has an account number and executes. You may wonder why we bother to include abstract method `execute` in class `Transaction` if it lacks a concrete implementation. Conceptually, we include this method because it corresponds to the defining behavior of all transactions—executing. Technically, we must include method `execute` in superclass `Transaction` so that the ATM (or any other class) can polymorphically invoke each subclass's overridden version of this method through a `Transaction` reference. Also, from a software engineering perspective, including an abstract method in a superclass forces the implementor of the subclasses to override that method with concrete implementations in the subclasses, or else the subclasses, too, will be abstract, preventing objects of those subclasses from being instantiated.

Subclasses `BalanceInquiry`, `Withdrawal` and `Deposit` inherit attribute account-Number from superclass `Transaction`, but classes `Withdrawal` and `Deposit` contain the additional attribute amount that distinguishes them from class `BalanceInquiry`. Classes `Withdrawal` and `Deposit` require this additional attribute to store the amount of money that the user wishes to withdraw or deposit. Class `BalanceInquiry` has no need for such an attribute and requires only an account number to execute. Even though two of the three `Transaction` subclasses share this attribute, we do not place it in superclass `Transaction`—we place only features common to all the subclasses in the superclass, otherwise subclasses could inherit attributes (and methods) that they do not need and should not have.

Figure 10.19 presents an updated class diagram of our model that incorporates inheritance and introduces class `Transaction`. We model an association between class ATM and class `Transaction` to show that the ATM, at any given moment is either executing a trans-

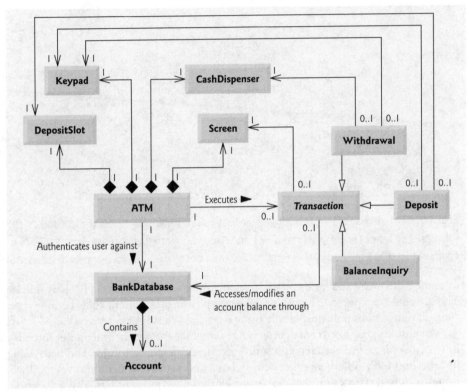

Fig. 10.19 | Class diagram of the ATM system (incorporating inheritance). Note that abstract class names (e.g., Transaction) appear in italics.

action or it is not (i.e., zero or one objects of type Transaction exist in the system at a time). Because a Withdrawal is a type of Transaction, we no longer draw an association line directly between class ATM and class Withdrawal. Subclass Withdrawal inherits superclass Transaction's association with class ATM. Subclasses BalanceInquiry and Deposit inherit this association, too, so the previously omitted associations between ATM and classes BalanceInquiry and Deposit no longer exist either.

We also add an association between class Transaction and the BankDatabase (Fig. 10.19). All Transactions require a reference to the BankDatabase so they can access and modify account information. Because each Transaction subclass inherits this reference, we no longer model the association between class Withdrawal and the BankDatabase. Similarly, the previously omitted associations between the BankDatabase and classes BalanceInquiry and Deposit no longer exist.

We show an association between class Transaction and the Screen. All Transactions display output to the user via the Screen. Thus, we no longer include the association previously modeled between Withdrawal and the Screen, although Withdrawal still participates in associations with the CashDispenser and the Keypad. Our class diagram incorporating inheritance also models Deposit and BalanceInquiry. We show associations between Deposit and both the DepositSlot and the Keypad. Note that class BalanceInquiry takes part in no associations other than those inherited from class Transaction—a BalanceInquiry needs to interact only with the BankDatabase and with the Screen.

The class diagram of Fig. 8.21 showed attributes and operations with visibility markers. Now we present a modified class diagram that incorporates inheritance in Fig. 10.20. This abbreviated diagram does not show inheritance relationships, but instead shows the attributes and methods after we have employed inheritance in our system. To save space, as we did in Fig. 4.16, we do not include those attributes shown by associations in Fig. 10.19—we do, however, include them in the Java implementation in Appendix H. We also omit all operation parameters, as we did in Fig. 8.21—incorporating inheritance does not affect the parameters already modeled in Figs. 6.27–6.30.

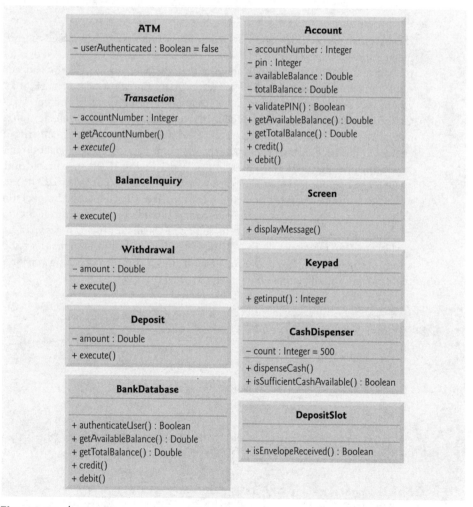

Fig. 10.20 | Class diagram with attributes and operations (incorporating inheritance). Note that abstract class names (e.g., Transaction) and method names (e.g., execute in class Transaction) appear in italics.

Software Engineering Observation 10.12

A complete class diagram shows all the associations among classes and all the attributes and operations for each class. When the number of class attributes, methods and associations is substantial, a good practice that promotes readability is to divide this information between two class diagrams—one focusing on associations and the other on attributes and methods.

Implementing the ATM System Design (Incorporating Inheritance)

In Section 8.18, we began implementing the ATM system design. We now modify our implementation to incorporate inheritance, using class Withdrawal as an example.

1. If a class A is a generalization of class B, then class B extends class A in the class declaration. For example, abstract superclass Transaction is a generalization of class Withdrawal. Figure 10.21 contains the shell of class Withdrawal containing the appropriate class declaration.

2. If class A is an abstract class and class B is a subclass of class A, then class B must implement the abstract methods of class A if class B is to be a concrete class. For example, class Transaction contains abstract method execute, so class Withdrawal must implement this method if we want to instantiate a Withdrawal object. Figure 10.22 is the Java code for class Withdrawal from Fig. 10.19 and Fig. 10.20. Class Withdrawal inherits field accountNumber from superclass Transaction, so Withdrawal does not need to declare this field. Class Withdrawal also inherits references to the Screen and the BankDatabase from its superclass Transaction, so we do not include these references in our code. Figure 10.20 specifies attribute amount and operation execute for class Withdrawal. Line 6 of Fig. 10.22 declares a field for attribute amount. Lines 16–18 declare the shell of a method for operation execute. Recall that subclass Withdrawal must provide a concrete implementation of the abstract method execute in superclass Transaction. The keypad and cashDispenser references (lines 7–8) are fields derived from Withdrawal's associations in Fig. 10.19. [*Note:* The constructor in the complete working version of this class will initialize these references to actual objects.]

```
1    // Class Withdrawal represents an ATM withdrawal transaction
2    public class Withdrawal extends Transaction
3    {
4    } // end class Withdrawal
```

Fig. 10.21 | Java code for shell of class Withdrawal.

```
1    // Withdrawal.java
2    // Generated using the class diagrams in Fig. 10.21 and Fig. 10.22
3    public class Withdrawal extends Transaction
4    {
5       // attributes
6       private double amount; // amount to withdraw
7       private Keypad keypad; // reference to keypad
8       private CashDispenser cashDispenser; // reference to cash dispenser
```

Fig. 10.22 | Java code for class Withdrawal based on Figs. 10.19 and 10.20. (Part 1 of 2.)

```
 9
10        // no-argument constructor
11        public Withdrawal()
12        {
13        } // end no-argument Withdrawal constructor
14
15        // method overriding execute
16        public void execute()
17        {
18        } // end method execute
19   } // end class Withdrawal
```

Fig. 10.22 | Java code for class `Withdrawal` based on Figs. 10.19 and 10.20. (Part 2 of 2.)

Software Engineering Observation 10.13

Several UML modeling tools convert UML-based designs into Java code and can speed the implementation process considerably. For more information on these tools, refer to the web resources listed at the end of Section 2.8.

Congratulations on completing the design portion of the case study! We completely implement the ATM system in 670 lines of Java code in Appendix H. We recommend that you carefully read the code and its description. The code is abundantly commented and precisely follows the design with which you are now familiar. The accompanying description is carefully written to guide your understanding of the implementation based on the UML design. Mastering this code is a wonderful culminating accomplishment after studying Chapters 1–8.

Software Engineering Case Study Self-Review Exercises

10.1 The UML uses an arrow with a _____ to indicate a generalization relationship.
a) solid filled arrowhead
b) triangular hollow arrowhead
c) diamond-shaped hollow arrowhead
d) stick arrowhead

10.2 State whether the following statement is *true* or *false*, and if *false*, explain why: The UML requires that we underline abstract class names and method names.

10.3 Write Java code to begin implementing the design for class `Transaction` specified in Figs. 10.19 and 10.20. Be sure to include `private` reference-type attributes based on class `Transaction`'s associations. Also be sure to include `public` *get* methods that provide access to any of these `private` attributes that the subclasses require to perform their tasks.

Answers to Software Engineering Case Study Self-Review Exercises

10.1 b.

10.2 False. The UML requires that we italicize abstract class names and method names.

10.3 The design for class `Transaction` yields the code in Fig. 10.23. The bodies of the class constructor and methods will be completed in Appendix H. When fully implemented, methods `getScreen` and `getBankDatabase` will return superclass `Transaction`'s `private` reference attributes `screen` and `bankDatabase`, respectively. These methods allow the `Transaction` subclasses to access the ATM's screen and interact with the bank's database.

```
1   // Abstract class Transaction represents an ATM transaction
2   public abstract class Transaction
3   {
4      // attributes
5      private int accountNumber; // indicates account involved
6      private Screen screen; // ATM's screen
7      private BankDatabase bankDatabase; // account info database
8
9      // no-argument constructor invoked by subclasses using super()
10     public Transaction()
11     {
12     } // end no-argument Transaction constructor
13
14     // return account number
15     public int getAccountNumber()
16     {
17     } // end method getAccountNumber
18
19     // return reference to screen
20     public Screen getScreen()
21     {
22     } // end method getScreen
23
24     // return reference to bank database
25     public BankDatabase getBankDatabase()
26     {
27     } // end method getBankDatabase
28
29     // abstract method overridden by subclasses
30     public abstract void execute();
31  } // end class Transaction
```

Fig. 10.23 | Java code for class `Transaction` based on Figs. 10.19 and 10.20.

10.9 Wrap-Up

This chapter introduced polymorphism—the ability to process objects that share the same superclass in a class hierarchy as if they are all objects of the superclass. The chapter discussed how polymorphism makes systems extensible and maintainable, then demonstrated how to use overridden methods to effect polymorphic behavior. We introduced abstract classes, which allow programmers to provide an appropriate superclass from which other classes can inherit. You learned that an abstract class can declare abstract methods that each subclass must implement to become a concrete class and that a program can use variables of an abstract class to invoke the subclasses' implementations of abstract methods polymorphically. You also learned how to determine an object's type at execution time. Finally, the chapter discussed declaring and implementing an interface as another way to achieve polymorphic behavior.

You should now be familiar with classes, objects, encapsulation, inheritance, interfaces and polymorphism—the most essential aspects of object-oriented programming. In the next chapter, we take a deeper look at graphical user interfaces (GUIs).

GUI
Components:
Part 1

OBJECTIVES

In this chapter you'll learn:

- The design principles of graphical user interfaces (GUIs).

- To build GUIs and handle events generated by user interactions with GUIs.

- To understand the packages containing GUI components, event-handling classes and interfaces.

- To create and manipulate buttons, labels, lists, text fields and panels.

- To handle mouse events and keyboard events.

- To use layout managers to arrange GUI components

Outline

11.1 Introduction

11.2 Simple GUI-Based Input/Output with `JOptionPane`

11.3 Overview of Swing Components

11.4 Displaying Text and Images in a Window

11.5 Text Fields and an Introduction to Event Handling with Nested Classes

11.6 Common GUI Event Types and Listener Interfaces

11.7 How Event Handling Works

11.8 `JButton`

11.9 Buttons That Maintain State

    11.9.1 `JCheckBox`

    11.9.2 `JRadioButton`

11.10 `JComboBox` and Using an Anonymous Inner Class for Event Handling

11.11 `JList`

11.12 Multiple-Selection Lists

11.13 Mouse Event Handling

11.14 Adapter Classes

11.15 `JPanel` Subclass for Drawing with the Mouse

11.16 Key Event Handling

11.17 Layout Managers

    11.17.1 `FlowLayout`

    11.17.2 `BorderLayout`

    11.17.3 `GridLayout`

11.18 Using Panels to Manage More Complex Layouts

11.19 `JTextArea`

11.20 Wrap-Up

11.1 Introduction

A *graphical user interface (GUI)* presents a user-friendly mechanism for interacting with an application. A GUI (pronounced "GOO-ee") gives an application a distinctive "look" and "feel." Providing different applications with consistent, intuitive user interface components allows users to be somewhat familiar with an application, so that they can learn it more quickly and use it more productively.

Look-and-Feel Observation 11.1

Consistent user interfaces enable a user to learn new applications faster.

As an example of a GUI, Fig. 11.1 contains an Internet Explorer web-browser window with some of its GUI components labeled. At the top is a *title bar* that contains the window's title. Below that is a *menu bar* containing *menus* (File, Edit, View, etc.). Below the menu bar is a set of *buttons* that the user can click to perform tasks in Internet Explorer. Below the buttons is a *combo box*; the user can type into it the name of a website

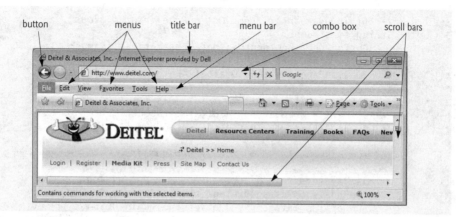

Fig. 11.1 | Window with GUI components.

to visit or can click the down arrow at the right side of the box to select from a list of sites previously visited. The menus, buttons and combo box are part of Internet Explorer's GUI. They enable you to interact with Internet Explorer.

GUIs are built from *GUI components*. These are sometimes called *controls* or *widgets*—short for *window gadgets*—in other languages. A GUI component is an object with which the user interacts via the mouse, the keyboard or another form of input, such as voice recognition. In this chapter and Chapter 17, GUI Components: Part 2, you'll learn about many of Java's GUI components.

11.2 Simple GUI-Based Input/Output with JOptionPane

The applications in Chapters 2–10 display text at the command window and obtain input from the command window. Most applications you use on a daily basis use windows or *dialog boxes* (also called *dialogs*) to interact with the user. For example, e-mail programs allow you to type and read messages in a window provided by the e-mail program. Typically, dialog boxes are windows in which programs display important messages to the user or obtain information from the user. Java's *JOptionPane* class (package javax.swing) provides prepackaged dialog boxes for both input and output. These dialogs are displayed by invoking static JOptionPane methods. Figure 11.2 presents a simple addition application that uses two *input dialogs* to obtain integers from the user and a *message dialog* to display the sum of the integers the user enters.

```java
1   // Fig. 11.2: Addition.java
2   // Addition program that uses JOptionPane for input and output.
3   import javax.swing.JOptionPane; // program uses JOptionPane
4
5   public class Addition
6   {
7      public static void main( String args[] )
8      {
```

Fig. 11.2 | Addition program that uses JOptionPane for input and output. (Part 1 of 2.)

```
 9      // obtain user input from JOptionPane input dialogs
10      String firstNumber =
11         JOptionPane.showInputDialog( "Enter first integer" );
12      String secondNumber =
13         JOptionPane.showInputDialog( "Enter second integer" );
14
15      // convert String inputs to int values for use in a calculation
16      int number1 = Integer.parseInt( firstNumber );
17      int number2 = Integer.parseInt( secondNumber );
18
19      int sum = number1 + number2; // add numbers
20
21      // display result in a JOptionPane message dialog
22      JOptionPane.showMessageDialog( null, "The sum is " + sum,
23         "Sum of Two Integers", JOptionPane.PLAIN_MESSAGE );
24   } // end method main
25 } // end class Addition
```

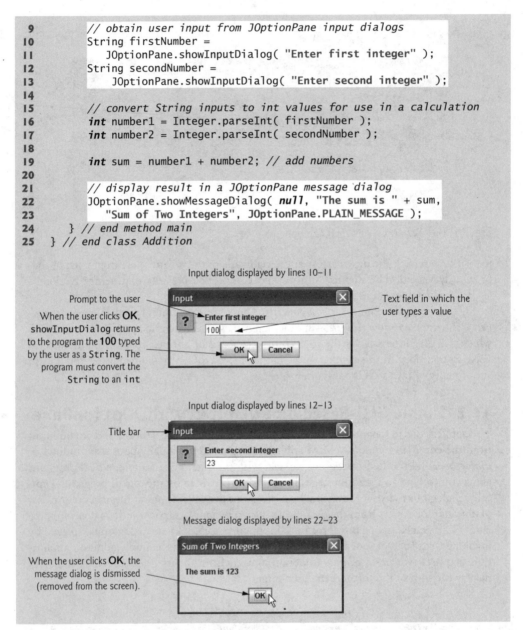

Fig. 11.2 | Addition program that uses JOptionPane for input and output. (Part 2 of 2.)

Input Dialogs

Line 3 imports class JOptionPane for use in this application. Lines 10–11 declare the local String variable firstNumber and assign it the result of the call to JOptionPane static method ***showInputDialog***. This method displays an input dialog (see the first screen capture in Fig. 11.2), using the method's String argument ("Enter first integer") as a prompt.

Look-and-Feel Observation 11.2

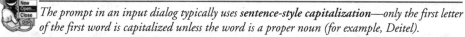

*The prompt in an input dialog typically uses **sentence-style capitalization**—only the first letter of the first word is capitalized unless the word is a proper noun (for example, Deitel).*

The user types characters in the text field, then clicks the **OK** button or presses the *Enter* key to submit the String to the program. Clicking **OK** also *dismisses* (*hides*) *the dialog*. [*Note:* If you type in the text field and nothing appears, activate the text field by clicking it with the mouse.] Unlike Scanner, which can be used to input values of several types from the user at the keyboard, an input dialog can input only input Strings. This is typical of most GUI components. Technically, the user can type anything in the input dialog's text field. Our program assumes that the user enters a valid integer value. If the user clicks the **Cancel** button, showInputDialog returns null. If the user either types a noninteger value or clicks the **Cancel** button in the input dialog, a runtime logic error will occur in this program and it will not operate correctly. Chapter 13, Exception Handling, discusses how to handle such errors. Lines 12–13 display another input dialog that prompts the user to enter the second integer.

Converting Strings to int Values

To perform the calculation in this application, we must convert the Strings that the user entered to int values. Recall from Section 7.12 that the Integer class's static method parseInt converts its String argument to an int value. Lines 16–17 assign the converted values to local variables number1 and number2. Then, line 19 sums these values and assigns the result to local variable sum.

Message Dialogs

Lines 22–23 use JOptionPane static method ***showMessageDialog*** to display a message dialog (the last screen capture of Fig. 11.2) containing the sum. The first argument helps the Java application determine where to position the dialog box. The value null indicates that the dialog should appear in the center of the computer screen. The first argument can also be used to specify that the dialog should appear centered over a particular window, which we'll demonstrate later in Section 11.8. The second argument is the message to display—in this case, the result of concatenating the String "The sum is " and the value of sum. The third argument—"Sum of Two Integers"—represents the string that should appear in the dialog's title bar at the top of the dialog. The fourth argument—***JOption-Pane.PLAIN_MESSAGE***—is the type of message dialog to display. A PLAIN_MESSAGE dialog does not display an icon to the left of the message. Class JOptionPane provides several overloaded versions of methods showInputDialog and showMessageDialog, as well as methods that display other dialog types. For complete information on class JOptionPane, visit java.sun.com/javase/6/docs/api/javax/swing/JOptionPane.html.

Look-and-Feel Observation 11.3

*The title bar of a window typically uses **book-title capitalization**—a style that capitalizes the first letter of each significant word in the text and does not end with any punctuation (for example, Capitalization in a Book Title).*

JOptionPane Message Dialog Constants

The constants that represent the message dialog types are shown in Fig. 11.3. All message dialog types except PLAIN_MESSAGE display an icon to the left of the message. These icons provide a visual indication of the message's importance to the user. Note that a QUESTION_MESSAGE icon is the default icon for an input dialog box (see Fig. 11.2).

Message dialog type	Icon	Description
ERROR_MESSAGE		A dialog that indicates an error to the user.
INFORMATION_MESSAGE		A dialog with an informational message to the user.
WARNING_MESSAGE		A dialog warning the user of a potential problem.
QUESTION_MESSAGE		A dialog that poses a question to the user. This dialog normally requires a response, such as clicking a **Yes** or a **No** button.
PLAIN_MESSAGE	no icon	A dialog that contains a message, but no icon.

Fig. 11.3 | JOptionPane static constants for message dialogs.

11.3 Overview of Swing Components

Though it is possible to perform input and output using the JOptionPane dialogs presented in Section 11.2, most GUI applications require more elaborate, customized user interfaces. The remainder of this chapter discusses many GUI components that enable application developers to create robust GUIs. Figure 11.4 lists several *Swing GUI components* from package *javax.swing* that are used to build Java GUIs. Most Swing components are *pure Java* components—they are written, manipulated and displayed completely in Java. They are part of the *Java Foundation Classes (JFC)*—Java's libraries for cross-platform GUI development. Visit java.sun.com/products/jfc for more information on JFC.

Component	Description
JLabel	Displays uneditable text or icons.
JTextField	Enables user to enter data from the keyboard. Can also be used to display editable or uneditable text.
JButton	Triggers an event when clicked with the mouse.
JCheckBox	Specifies an option that can be selected or not selected.
JComboBox	Provides a drop-down list of items from which the user can make a selection by clicking an item or possibly by typing into the box.
JList	Provides a list of items from which the user can make a selection by clicking on any item in the list. Multiple elements can be selected.
JPanel	Provides an area in which components can be placed and organized. Can also be used as a drawing area for graphics.

Fig. 11.4 | Some basic GUI components.

Swing vs. AWT

There are actually two sets of GUI components in Java. Before Swing was introduced in Java SE 1.2, Java GUIs were built with components from the *Abstract Window Toolkit (AWT)* in package **java.awt**. When a Java application with an AWT GUI executes on different Java platforms, the application's GUI components display differently on each platform. Consider an application that displays an object of type Button (package java.awt). On a computer running the Microsoft Windows operating system, the Button will have the same appearance as the buttons in other Windows applications. Similarly, on a computer running the Apple Mac OS X operating system, the Button will have the same look and feel as the buttons in other Macintosh applications. Sometimes, the manner in which a user can interact with a particular AWT component differs between platforms.

Together, the appearance and the way in which the user interacts with the application are known as that application's *look-and-feel*. Swing GUI components allow you to specify a uniform look-and-feel for your application across all platforms or to use each platform's custom look-and-feel. An application can even change the look-and-feel during execution to enable users to choose their own preferred look-and-feel.

Portability Tip 11.1

Swing components are implemented in Java, so they are more portable and flexible than the original Java GUI components from package java.awt, *which were based on the GUI components of the underlying platform. For this reason, Swing GUI components are generally preferred.*

Lightweight vs. Heavyweight GUI Components

Most Swing components are not tied to actual GUI components supported by the underlying platform on which an application executes. Such GUI components are known as *lightweight components*. AWT components (many of which parallel the Swing components) are tied to the local platform and are called *heavyweight components*, because they rely on the local platform's *windowing system* to determine their functionality and their look-and-feel.

Several Swing components are heavyweight components. Like AWT components, heavyweight Swing GUI components require direct interaction with the local windowing system, which may restrict their appearance and functionality, making them less flexible than lightweight components.

Look-and-Feel Observation 11.4

The look-and-feel of a GUI defined with heavyweight GUI components from package java.awt *may vary across platforms. Because heavyweight components are tied to the local-platform GUI, the look-and-feel varies from platform to platform.*

Superclasses of Swing's Lightweight GUI Components

The UML class diagram of Fig. 11.5 shows an inheritance hierarchy containing classes from which lightweight Swing components inherit their common attributes and behaviors. As discussed in Chapter 9, class Object is the superclass of the Java class hierarchy.

Software Engineering Observation 11.1

Study the attributes and behaviors of the classes in the class hierarchy of Fig. 11.5. These classes declare the features that are common to most Swing components.

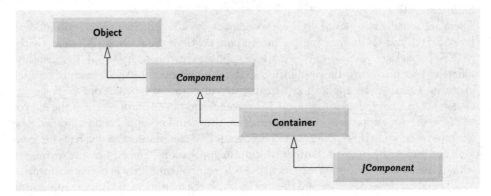

Fig. 11.5 | Common superclasses of many of the Swing components.

Class **Component** (package java.awt) is a subclass of Object that declares many of the attributes and behaviors common to the GUI components in packages java.awt and javax.swing. Most GUI components extend class Component directly or indirectly. Visit java.sun.com/javase/6/docs/api/java/awt/Component.html for a complete list of these common features.

Class **Container** (package java.awt) is a subclass of Component. As you'll soon see, Components are attached to Containers (such as windows) so the Components can be organized and displayed on the screen. Any object that *is a* Container can be used to organize other Components in a GUI. Because a Container *is a* Component, you can attach Containers to other Containers to help organize a GUI. Visit java.sun.com/javase/6/docs/api/java/awt/Container.html for a complete list of the Container features that are common to Swing lightweight components.

Class **JComponent** (package javax.swing) is a subclass of Container. JComponent is the superclass of all lightweight Swing components and declares their common attributes and behaviors. Because JComponent is a subclass of Container, all lightweight Swing components are also Containers. Some common lightweight component features supported by JComponent include:

1. A *pluggable look-and-feel* that can be used to customize the appearance of components (e.g., for use on particular platforms). You'll see an example of this in Section 17.6.

2. Shortcut keys (called *mnemonics*) for direct access to GUI components through the keyboard. You'll see an example of this in Section 17.4.

3. Common event-handling capabilities for cases where several GUI components initiate the same actions in an application.

4. Brief descriptions of a GUI component's purpose (called *tool tips*) that are displayed when the mouse cursor is positioned over the component for a short time. You'll see an example of this in the next section.

5. Support for assistive technologies, such as braille screen readers for the visually impaired.

6. Support for user-interface *localization*—that is, customizing the user interface to display in different languages and use local cultural conventions.

These are just some of the many features of the Swing components. Visit java.sun.com/
javase/6/docs/api/javax/swing/JComponent.html for more details of the common
lightweight component features.

11.4 Displaying Text and Images in a Window

Our next example introduces a framework for building GUI applications. This framework
uses several concepts that you'll see in many of our GUI applications. This is our first example in which the application appears in its own window. Most windows you'll create
are an instance of class JFrame or a subclass of JFrame. JFrame provides the basic attributes
and behaviors of a window—a title bar at the top of the window, and buttons to minimize,
maximize and close the window. Since an application's GUI is typically specific to the application, most of our examples will consist of two classes—a subclass of JFrame that helps
us demonstrate new GUI concepts and an application class in which main creates and displays the application's primary window.

Labeling GUI Components

A typical GUI consists of many components. In a large GUI, it can be difficult to identify
the purpose of every component unless the GUI designer provides text instructions or information stating the purpose of each component. Such text is known as a *label* and is created with class *JLabel*—a subclass of JComponent. A JLabel displays a single line of read-
only text, an image, or both text and an image. Applications rarely change a label's contents after creating it.

Look-and-Feel Observation 11.5

Text in a JLabel *normally uses sentence-style capitalization.*

    The application of Figs. 11.6–11.7 demonstrates several JLabel features and presents
the framework we use in most of our GUI examples. We did not highlight the code in this
example, since most of it is new. [*Note:* There are many more features for each GUI component than we can cover in our examples. To learn the complete details of each GUI
component, visit its page in the online documentation. For class JLabel, visit
java.sun.com/javase/6/docs/api/javax/swing/JLabel.html.]

    Class LabelFrame (Fig. 11.6) is a subclass of JFrame. We'll use an instance of class
LabelFrame to display a window containing three JLabels. Lines 3–8 import the classes
used in class LabelFrame. The class extends JFrame to inherit the features of a window.
Lines 12–14 declare the three JLabel instance variables, each of which is instantiated in
the LabelFrame constructor (lines 17–41). Typically, the JFrame subclass's constructor
builds the GUI that is displayed in the window when the application executes. Line 19
invokes superclass JFrame's constructor with the argument "Testing JLabel". JFrame's
constructor uses this String as the text in the window's title bar.

```
1   // Fig. 11.6: LabelFrame.java
2   // Demonstrating the JLabel class.
3   import java.awt.FlowLayout; // specifies how components are arranged
```

Fig. 11.6 | JLabels with text and icons. (Part 1 of 2.)

```
4    import javax.swing.JFrame; // provides basic window features
5    import javax.swing.JLabel; // displays text and images
6    import javax.swing.SwingConstants; // common constants used with Swing
7    import javax.swing.Icon; // interface used to manipulate images
8    import javax.swing.ImageIcon; // loads images
9
10   public class LabelFrame extends JFrame
11   {
12      private JLabel label1; // JLabel with just text
13      private JLabel label2; // JLabel constructed with text and icon
14      private JLabel label3; // JLabel with added text and icon
15
16      // LabelFrame constructor adds JLabels to JFrame
17      public LabelFrame()
18      {
19         super( "Testing JLabel" );
20         setLayout( new FlowLayout() ); // set frame layout
21
22         // JLabel constructor with a string argument
23         label1 = new JLabel( "Label with text" );
24         label1.setToolTipText( "This is label1" );
25         add( label1 ); // add label1 to JFrame
26
27         // JLabel constructor with string, Icon and alignment arguments
28         Icon bug = new ImageIcon( getClass().getResource( "bug1.gif" ) );
29         label2 = new JLabel( "Label with text and icon", bug,
30            SwingConstants.LEFT );
31         label2.setToolTipText( "This is label2" );
32         add( label2 ); // add label2 to JFrame
33
34         label3 = new JLabel(); // JLabel constructor no arguments
35         label3.setText( "Label with icon and text at bottom" );
36         label3.setIcon( bug ); // add icon to JLabel
37         label3.setHorizontalTextPosition( SwingConstants.CENTER );
38         label3.setVerticalTextPosition( SwingConstants.BOTTOM );
39         label3.setToolTipText( "This is label3" );
40         add( label3 ); // add label3 to JFrame
41      } // end LabelFrame constructor
42   } // end class LabelFrame
```

Fig. 11.6 | JLabels with text and icons. (Part 2 of 2.)

```
1    // Fig. 11.7: LabelTest.java
2    // Testing LabelFrame.
3    import javax.swing.JFrame;
4
5    public class LabelTest
6    {
7       public static void main( String args[] )
8       {
9          LabelFrame labelFrame = new LabelFrame(); // create LabelFrame
```

Fig. 11.7 | Test class for LabelFrame. (Part 1 of 2.)

```
10          labelFrame.setDefaultCloseOperation( JFrame.EXIT_ON_CLOSE );
11          labelFrame.setSize( 275, 180 ); // set frame size
12          labelFrame.setVisible( true ); // display frame
13       } // end main
14    } // end class LabelTest
```

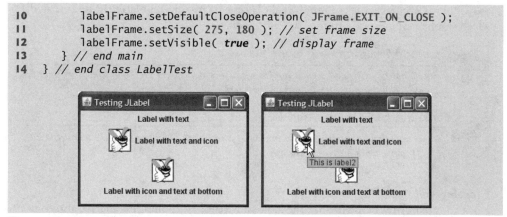

Fig. 11.7 | Test class for LabelFrame. (Part 2 of 2.)

Specifying the Layout

When building a GUI, each GUI component must be attached to a container, such as a window created with a JFrame. Also, you typically must decide where to position each GUI component. This is known as specifying the layout of the GUI components. As you'll learn at the end of this chapter and in Chapter 17, GUI Components: Part 2, Java provides several *layout managers* that can help you position components.

Many integrated development environments provide GUI design tools in which you can specify the exact size and location of a component in a visual manner by using the mouse, then the IDE will generate the GUI code for you. Though such IDEs can greatly simplify GUI creation, they are each different in capability.

To ensure that the code in this book can be used with any IDE, we did not use an IDE to create the GUI code in most of our examples. For this reason, we use Java's layout managers in our GUI examples. One such layout manager is *FlowLayout*, in which GUI components are placed on a container from left to right in the order in which the program attaches them to the container. When there is no more room to fit components left to right, components continue to display left to right on the next line. If the container is resized, a FlowLayout reflows (i.e., rearranges) the components to accommodate the new width of the container, possibly with fewer or more rows of GUI components. Line 20 specifies that the layout of the LabelFrame should be a FlowLayout. Method *setLayout* is inherited into class LabelFrame indirectly from class Container. The argument to the method must be an object of a class that implements the LayoutManager interface (e.g., FlowLayout). Line 20 creates a new FlowLayout object and pass its reference as the argument to setLayout.

Creating and Attaching label1

Now that we have specified the window's layout, we can begin creating and attaching GUI components to the window. Line 23 creates a JLabel object and passes "Label with text" to the constructor. The JLabel displays this text on the screen as part of the application's GUI. Line 24 uses method *setToolTipText* (inherited by JLabel from JComponent) to specify the tool tip that is displayed when the user positions the mouse cursor over the JLabel in the GUI. You can see a sample tool tip in the second screen capture of Fig. 11.7. When you execute this application, try positioning the mouse over each JLabel to see its tool tip. Line 25 attaches label1 to the LabelFrame by passing label1 to the **add** method, which is inherited indirectly from class Container.

Common Programming Error 11.1

If you do not explicitly add a GUI component to a container, the GUI component will not be displayed when the container appears on the screen.

Look-and-Feel Observation 11.6

Use tool tips to add descriptive text to your GUI components. This text helps the user determine the GUI component's purpose in the user interface.

Creating and Attaching label2

Icons are a popular way to enhance the look-and-feel of an application and are also commonly used to indicate functionality. For examples, most of today's VCRs and DVD players use the same icon to play a tape or DVD. Several Swing components can display images. An icon is normally specified with an **Icon** argument to a constructor or to the component's **setIcon** method. An Icon is an object of any class that implements interface Icon (package javax.swing). One such class is **ImageIcon** (package javax.swing), which supports several image formats, including *Graphics Interchange Format (GIF)*, *Portable Network Graphics (PNG)* and *Joint Photographic Experts Group (JPEG)*. File names for each of these types end with .gif, .png or .jpg (or .jpeg), respectively.

Line 28 declares an ImageIcon object. The file bug1.gif contains the image to load and store in the ImageIcon object. (This image is included in the directory for this example on the CD that accompanies this book.) The ImageIcon object is assigned to Icon reference bug. Remember, class ImageIcon implements interface Icon; an ImageIcon *is an* Icon.

In line 28, the expression getClass().getResource("bug1.gif") invokes method **getClass** (inherited from class Object) to retrieve a reference to the Class object that represents the LabelFrame class declaration. That reference is then used to invoke Class method **getResource**, which returns the location of the image as a URL. The ImageIcon constructor uses the URL to locate the image, then loads it into memory. As we discussed in Chapter 1, the JVM loads class declarations into memory, using a class loader. The class loader knows where each class it loads is located on disk. Method getResource uses the Class object's class loader to determine the location of a resource, such as an image file. In this example, the image file is stored in the same location as the LabelFrame.class file. The techniques described here enable an application to load image files from locations that are relative to LabelFrame's .class file on disk.

A JLabel can display an Icon. Lines 29–30 use another JLabel constructor to create a JLabel that displays the text "Label with text and icon" and the Icon bug created in line 28. The last constructor argument indicates that the label's contents are left justified, or *left aligned* (i.e., the icon and text are at the left side of the label's area on the screen). Interface **SwingConstants** (package javax.swing) declares a set of common integer constants (such as SwingConstants.LEFT) that are used with many Swing components. By default, the text appears to the right of the image when a label contains both text and an image. Note that the horizontal and vertical alignments of a JLabel can be set with methods **setHorizontalAlignment** and **setVerticalAlignment**, respectively. Line 31 specifies the tool-tip text for label2, and line 32 adds label2 to the JFrame.

Creating and Attaching label3

Class JLabel provides many methods to change a label's appearance after the label has been instantiated. Line 34 creates a JLabel and invokes its no-argument constructor. Such a label initially has no text or Icon. Line 35 uses JLabel method *setText* to set the text displayed on the label. The corresponding method *getText* retrieves the current text displayed on a label. Line 36 uses JLabel method *setIcon* to specify the Icon to display on the label. The corresponding method *getIcon* retrieves the current Icon displayed on a label. Lines 37–38 use JLabel methods *setHorizontalTextPosition* and *setVerticalTextPosition* to specify the text position in the label. In this case, the text will be centered horizontally and will appear at the bottom of the label. Thus, the Icon will appear above the text. The horizontal-position constants in SwingConstants are LEFT, CENTER and RIGHT (Fig. 11.8). The vertical-position constants in SwingConstants are TOP, CENTER and BOTTOM (Fig. 11.8). Line 39 sets the tool-tip text for label3. Line 40 adds label3 to the JFrame.

Constant	Description
Horizontal-position constants	
SwingConstants.LEFT	Place text on the left.
SwingConstants.CENTER	Place text in the center.
SwingConstants.RIGHT	Place text on the right.
Vertical-position constants	
SwingConstants.TOP	Place text at the top.
SwingConstants.CENTER	Place text in the center.
SwingConstants.BOTTOM	Place text at the bottom.

Fig. 11.8 | Some basic GUI components.

Creating and Displaying a LabelFrame Window

Class LabelTest (Fig. 11.7) creates an object of class LabelFrame (line 9), then specifies the default close operation for the window. By default, closing a window simply hides the window. However, when the user closes the LabelFrame window, we would like the application to terminate. Line 10 invokes LabelFrame's *setDefaultCloseOperation* method (inherited from class JFrame) with constant *JFrame.EXIT_ON_CLOSE* as the argument to indicate that the program should terminate when the window is closed by the user. This line is important. Without it the application will not terminate when the user closes the window. Next, line 11 invokes LabelFrame's *setSize* method to specify the width and height of the window. Finally, line 12 invokes LabelFrame's *setVisible* method with the argument true to display the window on the screen. Try resizing the window to see how the FlowLayout changes the JLabel positions as the window width changes.

11.5 Text Fields and an Introduction to Event Handling with Nested Classes

Normally, a user interacts with an application's GUI to indicate the tasks that the application should perform. For example, when you write an e-mail in an e-mail application, clicking the **Send** button tells the application to send the e-mail to the specified e-mail addresses. GUIs are *event driven*. When the user interacts with a GUI component, the interaction—known as an *event*—drives the program to perform a task. Some common events (user interactions) that might cause an application to perform a task include clicking a button, typing in a text field, selecting an item from a menu, closing a window and moving the mouse. The code that performs a task in response to an event is called an *event handler* and the overall process of responding to events is known as *event handling*.

In this section, we introduce two new GUI components that can generate events—*JTextFields* and *JPasswordFields* (package javax.swing). Class JTextField extends class *JTextComponent* (package javax.swing.text), which provides many features common to Swing's text-based components. Class JPasswordField extends JTextField and adds several methods that are specific to processing passwords. Each of these components is a single-line area in which the user can enter text via the keyboard. Applications can also display text in a JTextField (see the output of Fig. 11.10). A JPasswordField shows that characters are being typed as the user enters them, but hides the actual characters with an *echo character*, assuming that they represent a password that should remain known only to the user.

When the user types data into a JTextField or a JPasswordField, then presses *Enter*, an event occurs. Our next example demonstrates how a program can perform a task in response to that event. The techniques shown here are applicable to all GUI components that generate events.

The application of Figs. 11.9–11.10 uses classes JTextField and JPasswordField to create and manipulate four text fields. When the user types in one of the text fields, then presses *Enter*, the application displays a message dialog box containing the text the user typed. You can only type in the text field that is "in *focus*." A component receives the focus when the user clicks the component. This is important, because the text field with the focus is the one that generates an event when the user presses *Enter*. In this example, when the user presses *Enter* in the JPasswordField, the password is revealed. We begin by discussing the setup of the GUI, then discuss the event-handling code.

```
1   // Fig. 11.9: TextFieldFrame.java
2   // Demonstrating the JTextField class.
3   import java.awt.FlowLayout;
4   import java.awt.event.ActionListener;
5   import java.awt.event.ActionEvent;
6   import javax.swing.JFrame;
7   import javax.swing.JTextField;
8   import javax.swing.JPasswordField;
9   import javax.swing.JOptionPane;
10
11  public class TextFieldFrame extends JFrame
12  {
13     private JTextField textField1; // text field with set size
14     private JTextField textField2; // text field constructed with text
15     private JTextField textField3; // text field with text and size
16     private JPasswordField passwordField; // password field with text
17
```

Fig. 11.9 | JTextFields and JPasswordFields. (Part 1 of 3.)

```
18    // TextFieldFrame constructor adds JTextFields to JFrame
19    public TextFieldFrame()
20    {
21       super( "Testing JTextField and JPasswordField" );
22       setLayout( new FlowLayout() ); // set frame layout
23
24       // construct textfield with 10 columns
25       textField1 = new JTextField( 10 );
26       add( textField1 ); // add textField1 to JFrame
27
28       // construct textfield with default text
29       textField2 = new JTextField( "Enter text here" );
30       add( textField2 ); // add textField2 to JFrame
31
32       // construct textfield with default text and 21 columns
33       textField3 = new JTextField( "Uneditable text field", 21 );
34       textField3.setEditable( false ); // disable editing
35       add( textField3 ); // add textField3 to JFrame
36
37       // construct passwordfield with default text
38       passwordField = new JPasswordField( "Hidden text" );
39       add( passwordField ); // add passwordField to JFrame
40
41       // register event handlers
42       TextFieldHandler handler = new TextFieldHandler();
43       textField1.addActionListener( handler );
44       textField2.addActionListener( handler );
45       textField3.addActionListener( handler );
46       passwordField.addActionListener( handler );
47    } // end TextFieldFrame constructor
48
49    // private inner class for event handling
50    private class TextFieldHandler implements ActionListener
51    {
52       // process text field events
53       public void actionPerformed( ActionEvent event )
54       {
55          String string = ""; // declare string to display
56
57          // user pressed Enter in JTextField textField1
58          if ( event.getSource() == textField1 )
59             string = String.format( "textField1: %s",
60                event.getActionCommand() );
61
62          // user pressed Enter in JTextField textField2
63          else if ( event.getSource() == textField2 )
64             string = String.format( "textField2: %s",
65                event.getActionCommand() );
66
67          // user pressed Enter in JTextField textField3
68          else if ( event.getSource() == textField3 )
69             string = String.format( "textField3: %s",
70                event.getActionCommand() );
```

Fig. 11.9 | JTextFields and JPasswordFields. (Part 2 of 3.)

```
71
72              // user pressed Enter in JTextField passwordField
73              else if ( event.getSource() == passwordField )
74                  string = String.format( "passwordField: %s",
75                      new String( passwordField.getPassword() ) );
76
77              // display JTextField content
78              JOptionPane.showMessageDialog( null, string );
79          } // end method actionPerformed
80      } // end private inner class TextFieldHandler
81  } // end class TextFieldFrame
```

Fig. 11.9 | JTextFields and JPasswordFields. (Part 3 of 3.)

```
1   // Fig. 11.10: TextFieldTest.java
2   // Testing TextFieldFrame.
3   import javax.swing.JFrame;
4
5   public class TextFieldTest
6   {
7       public static void main( String args[] )
8       {
9           TextFieldFrame textFieldFrame = new TextFieldFrame();
10          textFieldFrame.setDefaultCloseOperation( JFrame.EXIT_ON_CLOSE );
11          textFieldFrame.setSize( 350, 100 ); // set frame size
12          textFieldFrame.setVisible( true ); // display frame
13      } // end main
14  } // end class TextFieldTest
```

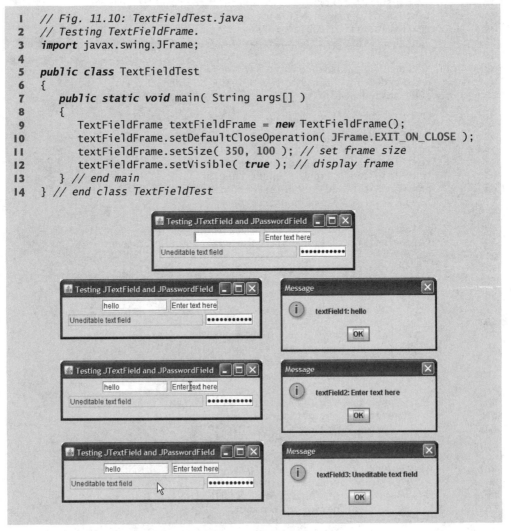

Fig. 11.10 | Test class for TextFieldFrame. (Part 1 of 2.)

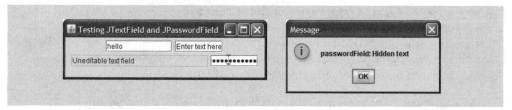

Fig. 11.10 | Test class for `TextFieldFrame`. (Part 2 of 2.)

Lines 3–9 import the classes and interfaces we use in this example. Class `TextField-Frame` extends `JFrame` and declares three `JTextField` variables and a `JPasswordField` variable (lines 13–16). Each of the corresponding text fields is instantiated and attached to the `TextFieldFrame` in the constructor (lines 19–47).

Creating the GUI

Line 22 sets the layout of the `TextFieldFrame` to `FlowLayout`. Line 25 creates `textField1` with 10 columns of text. The width of a text column is determined by the average width of a character in the text field's current font. When text is displayed in a text field and the text is wider than the text field itself, a portion of the text at the right side is not visible. If you are typing in a text field and the cursor reaches the right edge of the text field, the text at the left edge is pushed off the left side of the text field and will no longer be visible. Users can use the left and right arrow keys to move through the complete text even though the entire text will not be visible at one time. Line 26 adds `textField1` to the `JFrame`.

Line 29 creates `textField2` with the initial text `"Enter text here"` to display in the text field. The width of the text field is determined by the width of the default text specified in the constructor. Line 30 adds `textField2` to the `JFrame`.

Line 33 creates `textField3` and calls the `JTextField` constructor with two arguments—the default text `"Uneditable text field"` to display and the number of columns (21). The width of the text field is determined by the number of columns specified. Line 34 uses method ***setEditable*** (inherited by `JTextField` from class `JTextComponent`) to make the text field uneditable—i.e., the user cannot modify the text in the text field. Line 35 adds `textField3` to the `JFrame`.

Line 38 creates `passwordField` with the text `"Hidden text"` to display in the text field. The width of the text field is determined by the width of the default text. When you execute the application, notice that the text is displayed as a string of asterisks. Line 39 adds `passwordField` to the `JFrame`.

Steps Required to Set Up Event Handling for a GUI Component

This example should display a message dialog containing the text from a text field when the user presses *Enter* in that text field. Before an application can respond to an event for a particular GUI component, you must perform several coding steps:

1. Create a class that represents the event handler.

2. Implement an appropriate interface, known as an ***event-listener interface***, in the class from *Step 1*.

3. Indicate that an object of the class from *Steps 1* and *2* should be notified when the event occurs. This is known as ***registering the event handler***.

Using a Nested Class to Implement an Event Handler

All the classes discussed so far were so-called *top-level classes*—that is, the classes were not declared inside another class. Java allows you to declare classes inside other classes—these are called *nested classes*. Nested classes can be static or non-static. Non-static nested classes are called *inner classes* and are frequently used for event handling.

Software Engineering Observation 11.2

An inner class is allowed to directly access its top-level class's variables and methods, even if they are private.

Before an object of an inner class can be created, there must first be an object of the top-level class that contains the inner class. This is required because an inner-class object implicitly has a reference to an object of its top-level class. There is also a special relationship between these objects—the inner-class object is allowed to directly access all the instance variables and methods of the outer class. A nested class that is static does not require an object of its top-level class and does not implicitly have a reference to an object of the top-level class. As you'll see in Chapter 12, Graphics and Java 2D™, the Java 2D graphics API uses static nested classes extensively.

The event handling in this example is performed by an object of the private inner class TextFieldHandler (lines 50–80). This class is private because it will be used only to create event handlers for the text fields in top-level class TextFieldFrame. As with other members of a class, inner classes can be declared public, protected or private.

GUI components can generate a variety of events in response to user interactions. Each event is represented by a class and can be processed only by the appropriate type of event handler. In most cases, the events a GUI component supports are described in the Java API documentation for that component's class and its superclasses. When the user presses *Enter* in a JTextField or JPasswordField, the GUI component generates an **ActionEvent** (package java.awt.event). Such an event is processed by an object that implements the interface **ActionListener** (package java.awt.event). The information discussed here is available in the Java API documentation for classes JTextField and ActionEvent. Since JPasswordField is a subclass of JTextField, JPasswordField supports the same events.

To prepare to handle the events in this example, inner class TextFieldHandler implements interface ActionListener and declares the only method in that interface—actionPerformed (lines 53–79). This method specifies the tasks to perform when an ActionEvent occurs. So inner class TextFieldHandler satisfies *Steps 1* and *2* listed earlier in this section. We'll discuss the details of method actionPerformed shortly.

Registering the Event Handler for Each Text Field

In the TextFieldFrame constructor, line 42 creates a TextFieldHandler object and assigns it to variable handler. This object's actionPerformed method will be called automatically when the user presses *Enter* in any of the GUI's text fields. However, before this can occur, the program must register this object as the event handler for each text field. Lines 43–46 are the event-registration statements that specify handler as the event handler for the three JTextFields and the JPasswordField. The application calls JTextField method **addActionListener** to register the event handler for each component. This method receives as its argument an ActionListener object, which can be an object of any class that implements `ActionListener`. The object `handler` *is an* `ActionListener`, because class `TextFieldHandler` implements `ActionListener`. After lines 43–46 execute, the object `handler` *listens for events*. Now, when the user presses *Enter* in any of these four text fields, method `actionPerformed` (line 53–79) in class `TextFieldHandler` is called to handle the event. If an event handler is not registered for a particular text field, the event that occurs when the user presses *Enter* in that text field is *consumed*—i.e., it is simply ignored by the application.

Software Engineering Observation 11.3

The event listener for an event must implement the appropriate event-listener interface.

Common Programming Error 11.2

Forgetting to register an event-handler object for a particular GUI component's event type causes events of that type to be ignored.

Details of Class `TextFieldHandler`'s `actionPerformed` *Method*

In this example, we are using one event-handling object's `actionPerformed` method (lines 53–79) to handle the events generated by four text fields. Since we'd like to output the name of each text field's instance variable for demonstration purposes, we must determine which text field generated the event each time `actionPerformed` is called. The GUI component with which the user interacts is the *event source*. In this example, the event source is one of the text fields or the password field. When the user presses *Enter* while one of these GUI components has the focus, the system creates a unique `ActionEvent` object that contains information about the event that just occurred, such as the event source and the text in the text field. The system then passes this `ActionEvent` object in a method call to the event listener's `actionPerformed` method. In this example, we display some of that information in a message dialog. Line 55 declares the `String` that will be displayed. The variable is initialized with the *empty string*—a string containing no characters. The compiler requires this in case none of the branches of the nested `if` in lines 58–75 executes.

`ActionEvent` method `getSource` (called in lines 58, 63, 68 and 73) returns a reference to the event source. The condition in line 58 asks, "Is the *event source* `textField1`?" This condition compares the references on either side of the == operator to determine whether they refer to the same object. If they both refer to `textField1`, then the program knows that the user pressed *Enter* in `textField1`. In this case, lines 59–60 create a `String` containing the message that line 78 will display in a message dialog. Line 60 uses `ActionEvent` method ***getActionCommand*** to obtain the text the user typed in the text field that generated the event.

If the user interacted with the `JPasswordField`, lines 74–75 use `JPasswordField` method ***getPassword*** to obtain the password and create the `String` to display. This method returns the password as an array of type `char` that is used as an argument to a `String` constructor to create a string containing the characters in the array.

Class `TextFieldTest`

Class `TextFieldTest` (Fig. 11.10) contains the `main` method that executes this application and displays an object of class `TextFieldFrame`. When you execute the application, note that even the uneditable `JTextField` (`textField3`) can generate an `ActionEvent`. To test this, click the text field to give it the focus, then press *Enter*. Also note that the actual text of the password is displayed when you press *Enter* in the JPasswordField. Of course, you would normally not display the password!

This application used one TextFieldHandler object as the event listener for four text fields. Starting in Section 11.9, you'll see that it is possible to declare several event-listener objects of the same type and register each individual object for a separate GUI component's event. This technique enables us to eliminate the if...else logic used in this example's event handler by providing separate event handlers for each component's events.

11.6 Common GUI Event Types and Listener Interfaces

In Section 11.5, you learned that information about the event that occurs when the user presses *Enter* in a text field is stored in an ActionEvent object. Many different types of events can occur when the user interacts with a GUI. The information about any GUI event that occurs is stored in an object of a class that extends AWTEvent. Figure 11.11 illustrates a hierarchy containing many event classes from the package *java.awt.event*. Some of these are discussed in this chapter and Chapter 17. These event types are used

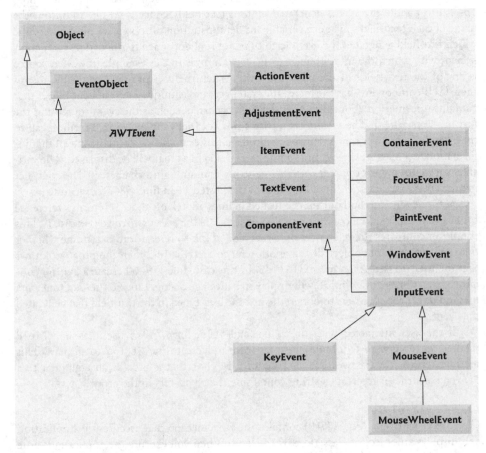

Fig. 11.11 | Some event classes of package java.awt.event.

with both AWT and Swing components. Additional event types that are specific to Swing GUI components are declared in package *javax.swing.event*.

Let's summarize the three parts to the event-handling mechanism that you saw in Section 11.5—the event source, the event object and the event listener. The event source is the particular GUI component with which the user interacts. The event object encapsulates information about the event that occurred, such as a reference to the event source and any event-specific information that may be required by the event listener for it to handle the event. The event listener is an object that is notified by the event source when an event occurs; in effect, it "listens" for an event, and one of its methods executes in response to the event. A method of the event listener receives an event object when the event listener is notified of the event. The event listener then uses the event object to respond to the event. The event-handling model described here is known as the *delegation event model*—an event's processing is delegated to a particular object (the event listener) in the application.

For each event-object type, there is typically a corresponding event-listener interface. An event listener for a GUI event is an object of a class that implements one or more of the event-listener interfaces from packages java.awt.event and javax.swing.event. Many of the event-listener types are common to both Swing and AWT components. Such types are declared in package java.awt.event, and some of them are shown in Fig. 11.12. Additional event-listener types that are specific to Swing components are declared in package javax.swing.event.

Each event-listener interface specifies one or more event-handling methods that must be declared in the class that implements the interface. Recall from Section 10.7 that any class which implements an interface must declare all the abstract methods of that interface; otherwise, the class is an abstract class and cannot be used to create objects.

When an event occurs, the GUI component with which the user interacted notifies its registered listeners by calling each listener's appropriate event-handling method. For example, when the user presses the *Enter* key in a JTextField, the registered listener's actionPerformed method is called. How did the event handler get registered? How does the GUI component know to call actionPerformed rather than another event-handling method? We answer these questions and diagram the interaction in the next section.

11.7 How Event Handling Works

Let us illustrate how the event-handling mechanism works, using textField1 from the example of Fig. 11.9. We have two remaining open questions from Section 11.5:

1. How did the event handler get registered?

2. How does the GUI component know to call actionPerformed rather than some other event-handling method?

The first question is answered by the event registration performed in lines 43–46 of the application. Figure 11.13 diagrams JTextField variable textField1, TextFieldHandler variable handler and the objects to which they refer.

Registering Events

Every JComponent has an instance variable called *listenerList* that refers to an object of class *EventListenerList* (package javax.swing.event). Each object of a JComponent

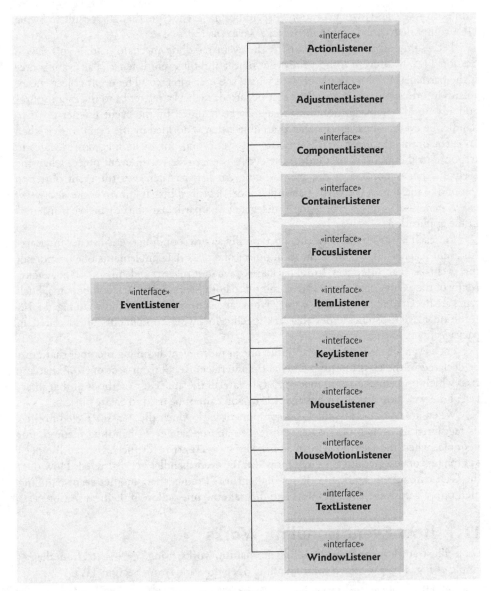

Fig. 11.12 | Some common event-listener interfaces of package `java.awt.event`.

subclass maintains a references to all its registered listeners in the `listenerList`. For simplicity, we have diagramed `listenerList` as an array below the `JTextField` object in Fig. 11.13.

When line 43 of Fig. 11.9

```
textField1.addActionListener( handler );
```

executes, a new entry containing a reference to the `TextFieldHandler` object is placed in `textField1`'s `listenerList`. Although not shown in the diagram, this new entry also in-

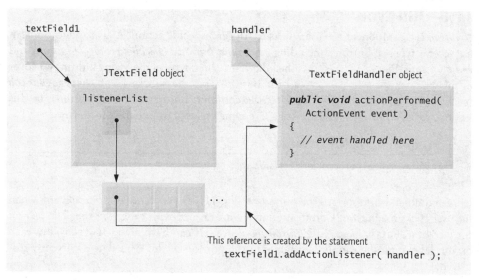

Fig. 11.13 | Event registration for JTextField textField1.

cludes the listener's type (in this case, ActionListener). Using this mechanism, each lightweight Swing GUI component maintains its own list of listeners that were registered to handle the component's events.

Event-Handler Invocation

The event-listener type is important in answering the second question: How does the GUI component know to call actionPerformed rather than another method? Every GUI component supports several event types—*mouse events*, *key events* and others. When an event occurs, the event is *dispatched* to only the event listeners of the appropriate type. Dispatching is the process by which the GUI component calls an event-handling method on each of its listeners that are registered for the particular event type that occurred.

Each event type has one or more corresponding event-listener interfaces. For example, ActionEvents are handled by ActionListeners, *MouseEvents* are handled by *MouseListeners* and *MouseMotionListeners*, and *KeyEvents* are handled by *KeyListeners*. When an event occurs, the GUI component receives (from the JVM) a unique *event ID* specifying the event type. The GUI component uses the event ID to decide the listener type to which the event should be dispatched and to decide which method to call on each listener object. For an ActionEvent, the event is dispatched to every registered ActionListener's actionPerformed method (the only method in interface ActionListener). For a MouseEvent, the event is dispatched to every registered MouseListener or MouseMotionListener, depending on the mouse event that occurs. The MouseEvent's event ID determines which of the several mouse event-handling methods are called. All these decisions are handled for you by the GUI components. All you need to do is register an event handler for the particular event type that your application requires, and the GUI component will ensure that the event handler's appropriate method gets called when the event occurs. [*Note:* We discuss other event types and event-listener interfaces as they are needed with each new component we introduce.]

11.8 JButton

A *button* is a component the user clicks to trigger a specific action. A Java application can use several types of buttons, including *command buttons*, *checkboxes*, *toggle buttons* and *radio buttons*. Figure 11.16 shows the inheritance hierarchy of the Swing buttons we cover in this chapter. As you can see, all the button types are subclasses of **AbstractButton** (package javax.swing), which declares the common features of Swing buttons. In this section, we concentrate on buttons that are typically used to initiate a command.

Look-and-Feel Observation 11.7

Buttons typically use book-title capitalization.

A command button (see the output of Fig. 11.14) generates an ActionEvent when the user clicks the button. Command buttons are created with class **JButton**. The text on the face of a JButton is called a *button label*. A GUI can have many JButtons, but each button label typically should be unique in the portion of the GUI that is currently displayed.

Look-and-Feel Observation 11.8

Having more than one JButton with the same label makes the JButtons ambiguous to the user. Provide a unique label for each button.

The application of Figs. 11.14 and 11.15 creates two JButtons and demonstrates that JButtons support the display of Icons. Event handling for the buttons is performed by a single instance of inner class ButtonHandler (lines 39–47).

```java
1   // Fig. 11.14: ButtonFrame.java
2   // Creating JButtons.
3   import java.awt.FlowLayout;
4   import java.awt.event.ActionListener;
5   import java.awt.event.ActionEvent;
6   import javax.swing.JFrame;
7   import javax.swing.JButton;
8   import javax.swing.Icon;
9   import javax.swing.ImageIcon;
10  import javax.swing.JOptionPane;
11
12  public class ButtonFrame extends JFrame
13  {
14      private JButton plainJButton; // button with just text
15      private JButton fancyJButton; // button with icons
16
17      // ButtonFrame adds JButtons to JFrame
18      public ButtonFrame()
19      {
20          super( "Testing Buttons" );
21          setLayout( new FlowLayout() ); // set frame layout
22
```

Fig. 11.14 | Command buttons and action events. (Part 1 of 2.)

```
23        plainJButton = new JButton( "Plain Button" ); // button with text
24        add( plainJButton ); // add plainJButton to JFrame
25
26        Icon bug1 = new ImageIcon( getClass().getResource( "bug1.gif" ) );
27        Icon bug2 = new ImageIcon( getClass().getResource( "bug2.gif" ) );
28        fancyJButton = new JButton( "Fancy Button", bug1 ); // set image
29        fancyJButton.setRolloverIcon( bug2 ); // set rollover image
30        add( fancyJButton ); // add fancyJButton to JFrame
31
32        // create new ButtonHandler for button event handling
33        ButtonHandler handler = new ButtonHandler();
34        fancyJButton.addActionListener( handler );
35        plainJButton.addActionListener( handler );
36     } // end ButtonFrame constructor
37
38     // inner class for button event handling
39     private class ButtonHandler implements ActionListener
40     {
41        // handle button event
42        public void actionPerformed( ActionEvent event )
43        {
44           JOptionPane.showMessageDialog( ButtonFrame.this, String.format(
45              "You pressed: %s", event.getActionCommand() ) );
46        } // end method actionPerformed
47     } // end private inner class ButtonHandler
48  } // end class ButtonFrame
```

Fig. 11.14 | Command buttons and action events. (Part 2 of 2.)

```
1   // Fig. 11.15: ButtonTest.java
2   // Testing ButtonFrame.
3   import javax.swing.JFrame;
4
5   public class ButtonTest
6   {
7      public static void main( String args[] )
8      {
9         ButtonFrame buttonFrame = new ButtonFrame(); // create ButtonFrame
10        buttonFrame.setDefaultCloseOperation( JFrame.EXIT_ON_CLOSE );
11        buttonFrame.setSize( 275, 110 ); // set frame size
12        buttonFrame.setVisible( true ); // display frame
13     } // end main
14  } // end class ButtonTest
```

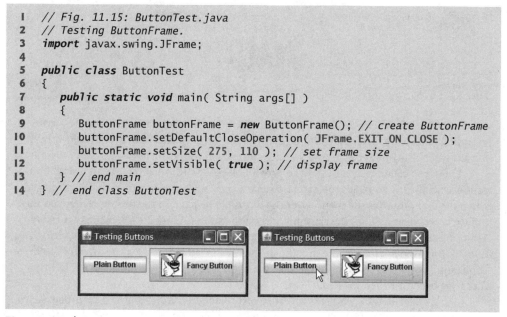

Fig. 11.15 | Test class for ButtonFrame. (Part 1 of 2.)

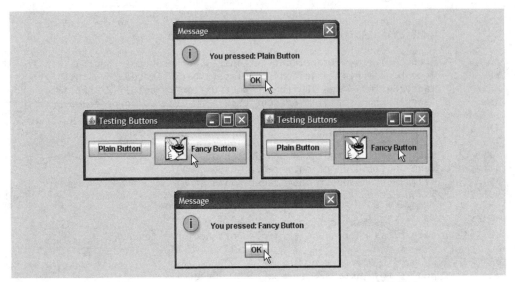

Fig. 11.15 | Test class for `ButtonFrame`. (Part 2 of 2.)

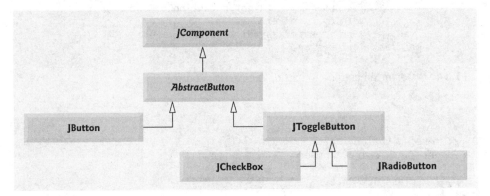

Fig. 11.16 | Swing button hierarchy.

Lines 14–15 declare `JButton` variables `plainButton` and `fancyButton`. The corresponding objects are instantiated in the constructor. Line 23 creates `plainButton` with the button label `"Plain Button"`. Line 24 adds the button to the `JFrame`.

A `JButton` can display an `Icon`. To provide the user with an extra level of visual interaction with the GUI, a `JButton` can also have a *rollover* `Icon`—an `Icon` that is displayed when the user positions the mouse over the button. The icon on the button changes as the mouse moves in and out of the button's area on the screen. Lines 26–27 create two `Image-Icon` objects that represent the default `Icon` and rollover `Icon` for the `JButton` created at line 28. Both statements assume that the image files are stored in the same directory as the application (which is commonly the case for applications that use images). These image files have been provided for you.

Line 28 creates `fancyButton` with the text `"Fancy Button"` and the icon `bug1`. By default, the text is displayed to the right of the icon. Line 29 uses ***setRolloverIcon*** (inherited from class `AbstractButton`) to specify the image displayed on the button when the user positions the mouse over it. Line 30 adds the button to the `JFrame`.

Look-and-Feel Observation 11.9

Because class `AbstractButton` supports displaying text and images on a button, all subclasses of `AbstractButton` also support displaying text and images.

Look-and-Feel Observation 11.10

Using rollover icons for `JButtons` provides users with visual feedback indicating that when they click the mouse while the cursor is positioned over the button, an action will occur.

`JButtons`, like `JTextFields`, generate `ActionEvents` that can be processed by any `ActionListener` object. Lines 33–35 create an object of private inner class `ButtonHandler` and register it as the event handler for each `JButton`. Class `ButtonHandler` (lines 39–47) declares `actionPerformed` to display a message dialog box containing the label for the button the user pressed. For a `JButton` event, `ActionEvent` method `getActionCommand` returns the label on the button.

Accessing the `this` Reference in an Object of a Top-Level Class From an Inner Class

When you execute this application and click one of its buttons, notice that the message dialog that appears is centered over the application's window. This occurs because the call to `JOptionPane` method `showMessageDialog` (lines 44–45 of Fig. 11.14) uses `Button-Frame.this` rather than `null` as the first argument. When this argument is not `null`, it represents the so-called parent GUI component of the message dialog (in this case the application window is the parent component) and enables the dialog to be centered over that component when the dialog is displayed. `ButtonFrame.this` represents the `this` reference of the object of top-level class `ButtonFrame`.

Software Engineering Observation 11.4

When used in an inner class, keyword `this` refers to the current inner-class object being manipulated. An inner-class method can use its outer-class object's `this` by preceding `this` with the outer-class name and a dot, as in `ButtonFrame.this`.

11.9 Buttons That Maintain State

The Swing GUI components contain three types of *state buttons*—*JToggleButton*, *JCheckBox* and *JRadioButton*—that have on/off or true/false values. Classes `JCheckBox` and `JRadioButton` are subclasses of `JToggleButton` (Fig. 11.16). A `JRadioButton` is different from a `JCheckBox` in that normally several `JRadioButtons` are grouped together, and are mutually exclusive—only one in the group can be selected at any time, just like the buttons on a car radio. We first discuss class `JCheckBox`. The next two subsections also demonstrate that an inner class can access the members of its top-level class.

11.9.1 JCheckBox

The application of Figs. 11.17–11.18 uses two `JCheckBox` objects to select the desired font style of the text displayed in a `JTextField`. When selected, one applies a bold style and the other an italic style. If both are selected, the style of the font is bold and italic. When the application initially executes, neither `JCheckBox` is checked (i.e., they are both `false`), so the font is plain. Class CheckBoxTest (Fig. 11.18) contains the main method that executes this application.

After the JTextField is created and initialized (Fig. 11.17, line 24), line 25 uses method **setFont** (inherited by JTextField indirectly from class Component) to set the font of the JTextField to a new object of class **Font** (package java.awt). The new Font is initialized with "Serif" (a generic font name representing a font such as Times and is supported on all Java platforms), Font.PLAIN style and 14-point size. Next, lines 28–29 create two JCheckBox objects. The string passed to the JCheckBox constructor is the *checkbox label* that appears to the right of the JCheckBox by default.

```
1   // Fig. 11.17: CheckBoxFrame.java
2   // Creating JCheckBox buttons.
3   import java.awt.FlowLayout;
4   import java.awt.Font;
5   import java.awt.event.ItemListener;
6   import java.awt.event.ItemEvent;
7   import javax.swing.JFrame;
8   import javax.swing.JTextField;
9   import javax.swing.JCheckBox;
10
11  public class CheckBoxFrame extends JFrame
12  {
13     private JTextField textField; // displays text in changing fonts
14     private JCheckBox boldJCheckBox; // to select/deselect bold
15     private JCheckBox italicJCheckBox; // to select/deselect italic
16
17     // CheckBoxFrame constructor adds JCheckBoxes to JFrame
18     public CheckBoxFrame()
19     {
20        super( "JCheckBox Test" );
21        setLayout( new FlowLayout() ); // set frame layout
22
23        // set up JTextField and set its font
24        textField = new JTextField( "Watch the font style change", 20 );
25        textField.setFont( new Font( "Serif", Font.PLAIN, 14 ) );
26        add( textField ); // add textField to JFrame
27
28        boldJCheckBox = new JCheckBox( "Bold" ); // create bold checkbox
29        italicJCheckBox = new JCheckBox( "Italic" ); // create italic
30        add( boldJCheckBox ); // add bold checkbox to JFrame
31        add( italicJCheckBox ); // add italic checkbox to JFrame
32
33        // register listeners for JCheckBoxes
34        CheckBoxHandler handler = new CheckBoxHandler();
35        boldJCheckBox.addItemListener( handler );
36        italicJCheckBox.addItemListener( handler );
37     } // end CheckBoxFrame constructor
38
39     // private inner class for ItemListener event handling
40     private class CheckBoxHandler implements ItemListener
41     {
```

Fig. 11.17 | JCheckBox buttons and item events. (Part 1 of 2.)

```
42          private int valBold = Font.PLAIN; // controls bold font style
43          private int valItalic = Font.PLAIN; // controls italic font style
44
45          // respond to checkbox events
46          public void itemStateChanged( ItemEvent event )
47          {
48             // process bold checkbox events
49             if ( event.getSource() == boldJCheckBox )
50                valBold =
51                   boldJCheckBox.isSelected() ? Font.BOLD : Font.PLAIN;
52
53             // process italic checkbox events
54             if ( event.getSource() == italicJCheckBox )
55                valItalic =
56                   italicJCheckBox.isSelected() ? Font.ITALIC : Font.PLAIN;
57
58             // set text field font
59             textField.setFont(
60                new Font( "Serif", valBold + valItalic, 14 ) );
61          } // end method itemStateChanged
62       } // end private inner class CheckBoxHandler
63    } // end class CheckBoxFrame
```

Fig. 11.17 | JCheckBox buttons and item events. (Part 2 of 2.)

```
1    // Fig. 11.18: CheckBoxTest.java
2    // Testing CheckBoxFrame.
3    import javax.swing.JFrame;
4
5    public class CheckBoxTest
6    {
7       public static void main( String args[] )
8       {
9          CheckBoxFrame checkBoxFrame = new CheckBoxFrame();
10         checkBoxFrame.setDefaultCloseOperation( JFrame.EXIT_ON_CLOSE );
11         checkBoxFrame.setSize( 275, 100 ); // set frame size
12         checkBoxFrame.setVisible( true ); // display frame
13      } // end main
14   } // end class CheckBoxTest
```

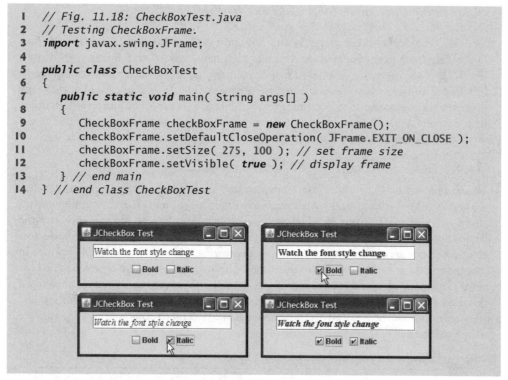

Fig. 11.18 | Test class for CheckBoxFrame.

When the user clicks a JCheckBox, an *ItemEvent* occurs. This event can be handled by an *ItemListener* object, which must implement method *itemStateChanged*. In this example, the event handling is performed by an instance of private inner class CheckBox-Handler (lines 40–62). Lines 34–36 create an instance of class CheckBoxHandler and register it with method *addItemListener* as the listener for both the JCheckBox objects.

Lines 42–43 declare instance variables for the inner class CheckBoxHandler. Together, these variables represent the font style for the text displayed in the JTextField. Initially both are Font.PLAIN to indicate that the font is not bold and is not italic. Method item-StateChanged (lines 46–61) is called when the user clicks the bold or the italic JCheckBox. The method uses event.getSource() to determine which JCheckBox the user clicked. If it was the boldJCheckBox, line 51 uses JCheckBox method *isSelected* to determine if the JCheckBox is selected (i.e., it is checked). If the checkbox is selected, local variable valBold is assigned Font.BOLD; otherwise, it is assigned Font.PLAIN. A similar statement executes if the user clicks the italicJCheckBox. If the italicJCheckBox is selected, local variable valItalic is assigned Font.ITALIC; otherwise, it is assigned Font.PLAIN. Lines 59–60 change the font of the JTextField, using the same font name and point size. The sum of valBold and valItalic represents the JTextField's new font style. Each of the Font constants represents a unique value. Font.PLAIN has the value 0, so if both valBold and valItalic are set to Font.PLAIN, the font will have the plain style. If one of the values is Font.BOLD or Font.ITALIC, the font will be bold or italic accordingly. If one is BOLD and the other is ITALIC, the font will be both bold and italic.

Relationship Between an Inner Class and Its Top-Level Class

Notice that class CheckBoxHandler used variables boldJCheckBox (Fig. 11.17, lines 49 and 51), italicJCheckBox (lines 54 and 56) and textField (line 59) even though they are not declared in the inner class. An inner class has a special relationship with its top-level class—the inner class is allowed to access directly all the instance variables and methods of the top-level class. Method itemStateChanged (line 46–61) of class CheckBoxHandler uses this relationship to determine which JCheckBox is the event source, to determine the state of a JCheckBox and to set the font on the JTextField. Notice that none of the code in inner class CheckBoxHandler requires a reference to the top-level class object.

11.9.2 JRadioButton

Radio buttons (declared with class *JRadioButton*) are similar to checkboxes in that they have two states—selected and not selected (also called deselected). However, radio buttons normally appear as a *group* in which only one button can be selected at a time (see the output of Fig. 11.20). Selecting a different radio button forces all others to be deselected. Radio buttons are used to represent *mutually exclusive* options (i.e., multiple options in the group cannot be selected at the same time). The logical relationship between radio buttons is maintained by a *ButtonGroup* object (package javax.swing), which itself is not a GUI component. A ButtonGroup object organizes a group of buttons and is not itself displayed in a user interface. Rather, the individual JRadioButton objects from the group are displayed in the GUI.

 Common Programming Error 11.3

Adding a ButtonGroup object (or an object of any other class that does not derive from Component) to a container results in a compilation error.

The application of Figs. 11.19–11.20 is similar to that of Figs. 11.17–11.18. The user can alter the font style of a JTextField's text. The application uses radio buttons that permit only a single font style in the group to be selected at a time. Class RadioButtonTest (Fig. 11.20) contains the main method that executes this application.

```java
1   // Fig. 11.19: RadioButtonFrame.java
2   // Creating radio buttons using ButtonGroup and JRadioButton.
3   import java.awt.FlowLayout;
4   import java.awt.Font;
5   import java.awt.event.ItemListener;
6   import java.awt.event.ItemEvent;
7   import javax.swing.JFrame;
8   import javax.swing.JTextField;
9   import javax.swing.JRadioButton;
10  import javax.swing.ButtonGroup;
11
12  public class RadioButtonFrame extends JFrame
13  {
14     private JTextField textField; // used to display font changes
15     private Font plainFont; // font for plain text
16     private Font boldFont; // font for bold text
17     private Font italicFont; // font for italic text
18     private Font boldItalicFont; // font for bold and italic text
19     private JRadioButton plainJRadioButton; // selects plain text
20     private JRadioButton boldJRadioButton; // selects bold text
21     private JRadioButton italicJRadioButton; // selects italic text
22     private JRadioButton boldItalicJRadioButton; // bold and italic
23     private ButtonGroup radioGroup; // buttongroup to hold radio buttons
24
25     // RadioButtonFrame constructor adds JRadioButtons to JFrame
26     public RadioButtonFrame()
27     {
28        super( "RadioButton Test" );
29        setLayout( new FlowLayout() ); // set frame layout
30
31        textField = new JTextField( "Watch the font style change", 25 );
32        add( textField ); // add textField to JFrame
33
34        // create radio buttons
35        plainJRadioButton = new JRadioButton( "Plain", true );
36        boldJRadioButton = new JRadioButton( "Bold", false );
37        italicJRadioButton = new JRadioButton( "Italic", false );
38        boldItalicJRadioButton = new JRadioButton( "Bold/Italic", false );
39        add( plainJRadioButton ); // add plain button to JFrame
40        add( boldJRadioButton ); // add bold button to JFrame
41        add( italicJRadioButton ); // add italic button to JFrame
42        add( boldItalicJRadioButton ); // add bold and italic button
43
44        // create logical relationship between JRadioButtons
45        radioGroup = new ButtonGroup(); // create ButtonGroup
46        radioGroup.add( plainJRadioButton ); // add plain to group
47        radioGroup.add( boldJRadioButton ); // add bold to group
```

Fig. 11.19 | JRadioButtons and ButtonGroups. (Part 1 of 2.)

```
48      radioGroup.add( italicJRadioButton ); // add italic to group
49      radioGroup.add( boldItalicJRadioButton ); // add bold and italic
50
51      // create font objects
52      plainFont = new Font( "Serif", Font.PLAIN, 14 );
53      boldFont = new Font( "Serif", Font.BOLD, 14 );
54      italicFont = new Font( "Serif", Font.ITALIC, 14 );
55      boldItalicFont = new Font( "Serif", Font.BOLD + Font.ITALIC, 14 );
56      textField.setFont( plainFont ); // set initial font to plain
57
58      // register events for JRadioButtons
59      plainJRadioButton.addItemListener(
60         new RadioButtonHandler( plainFont ) );
61      boldJRadioButton.addItemListener(
62         new RadioButtonHandler( boldFont ) );
63      italicJRadioButton.addItemListener(
64         new RadioButtonHandler( italicFont ) );
65      boldItalicJRadioButton.addItemListener(
66         new RadioButtonHandler( boldItalicFont ) );
67   } // end RadioButtonFrame constructor
68
69   // private inner class to handle radio button events
70   private class RadioButtonHandler implements ItemListener
71   {
72      private Font font; // font associated with this listener
73
74      public RadioButtonHandler( Font f )
75      {
76         font = f; // set the font of this listener
77      } // end constructor RadioButtonHandler
78
79      // handle radio button events
80      public void itemStateChanged( ItemEvent event )
81      {
82         textField.setFont( font ); // set font of textField
83      } // end method itemStateChanged
84   } // end private inner class RadioButtonHandler
85 } // end class RadioButtonFrame
```

Fig. 11.19 | JRadioButtons and ButtonGroups. (Part 2 of 2.)

```
1  // Fig. 11.20: RadioButtonTest.java
2  // Testing RadioButtonFrame.
3  import javax.swing.JFrame;
4
5  public class RadioButtonTest
6  {
7     public static void main( String args[] )
8     {
9        RadioButtonFrame radioButtonFrame = new RadioButtonFrame();
10       radioButtonFrame.setDefaultCloseOperation( JFrame.EXIT_ON_CLOSE );
```

Fig. 11.20 | Test class for RadioButtonFrame. (Part 1 of 2.)

```
11              radioButtonFrame.setSize( 300, 100 ); // set frame size
12              radioButtonFrame.setVisible( true ); // display frame
13         } // end main
14   } // end class RadioButtonTest
```

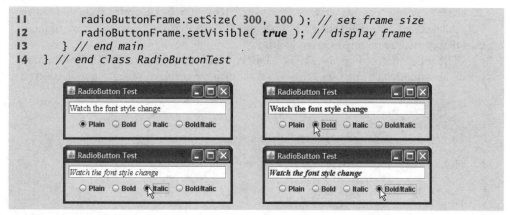

Fig. 11.20 | Test class for `RadioButtonFrame`. (Part 2 of 2.)

Lines 35–42 in the constructor (Fig. 11.19) create four `JRadioButton` objects and add them to the `JFrame`. Each `JRadioButton` is created with a constructor call like that in line 35. This constructor specifies the label that appears to the right of the `JRadioButton` by default and the initial state of the `JRadioButton`. A `true` second argument indicates that the `JRadioButton` should appear selected when it is displayed.

Line 45 instantiates `ButtonGroup` object `radioGroup`. This object is the "glue" that forms the logical relationship between the four `JRadioButton` objects and allows only one of the four to be selected at a time. It is possible that no `JRadioButtons` in a `ButtonGroup` are selected, but this can occur only if no preselected `JRadioButtons` are added to the But-tonGroup and the user has not selected a `JRadioButton` yet. Lines 46–49 use `ButtonGroup` method **add** to associate each of the `JRadioButtons` with `radioGroup`. If more than one selected `JRadioButton` object is added to the group, the selected one that was added first will be selected when the GUI is displayed.

`JRadioButtons`, like `JCheckBoxes`, generate `ItemEvents` when they are clicked. Lines 59–66 create four instances of inner class `RadioButtonHandler` (declared at lines 70–84). In this example, each event-listener object is registered to handle the `ItemEvent` generated when the user clicks a particular `JRadioButton`. Notice that each `RadioButtonHandler` object is initialized with a particular `Font` object (created in lines 52–55).

Class `RadioButtonHandler` (line 70–84) implements interface `ItemListener` so it can handle `ItemEvents` generated by the `JRadioButtons`. The constructor stores the `Font` object it receives as an argument in the event-listener object's instance variable `font` (declared at line 72). When the user clicks a `JRadioButton`, `radioGroup` turns off the pre-viously selected `JRadioButton` and method `itemStateChanged` (line 80–83) sets the font in the `JTextField` to the `Font` stored in the `JRadioButton`'s corresponding event-listener object. Notice that line 82 of inner class `RadioButtonHandler` uses the top-level class's `textField` instance variable to set the font.

11.10 JComboBox and Using an Anonymous Inner Class for Event Handling

A combo box (sometimes called a *drop-down list*) provides a list of items (Fig. 11.22) from which the user can make a single selection. Combo boxes are implemented with class

JComboBox, which extends class JComponent. JComboBoxes generate ItemEvents like
JCheckBoxes and JRadioButtons. This example also demonstrates a special form of inner
class that is used frequently in event handling.

The application of Figs. 11.21–11.22 uses a JComboBox to provide a list of four image
file names from which the user can select one image to display. When the user selects a

```
 1   // Fig. 11.21: ComboBoxFrame.java
 2   // Using a JComboBox to select an image to display.
 3   import java.awt.FlowLayout;
 4   import java.awt.event.ItemListener;
 5   import java.awt.event.ItemEvent;
 6   import javax.swing.JFrame;
 7   import javax.swing.JLabel;
 8   import javax.swing.JComboBox;
 9   import javax.swing.Icon;
10   import javax.swing.ImageIcon;
11
12   public class ComboBoxFrame extends JFrame
13   {
14      private JComboBox imagesJComboBox; // combobox to hold names of icons
15      private JLabel label; // label to display selected icon
16
17      private String names[] =
18         { "bug1.gif", "bug2.gif",  "travelbug.gif", "buganim.gif" };
19      private Icon icons[] = {
20         new ImageIcon( getClass().getResource( names[ 0 ] ) ),
21         new ImageIcon( getClass().getResource( names[ 1 ] ) ),
22         new ImageIcon( getClass().getResource( names[ 2 ] ) ),
23         new ImageIcon( getClass().getResource( names[ 3 ] ) ) };
24
25      // ComboBoxFrame constructor adds JComboBox to JFrame
26      public ComboBoxFrame()
27      {
28         super( "Testing JComboBox" );
29         setLayout( new FlowLayout() ); // set frame layout
30
31         imagesJComboBox = new JComboBox( names ); // set up JComboBox
32         imagesJComboBox.setMaximumRowCount( 3 ); // display three rows
33
34         imagesJComboBox.addItemListener(
35            new ItemListener() // anonymous inner class
36            {
37               // handle JComboBox event
38               public void itemStateChanged( ItemEvent event )
39               {
40                  // determine whether checkbox selected
41                  if ( event.getStateChange() == ItemEvent.SELECTED )
42                     label.setIcon( icons[
43                        imagesJComboBox.getSelectedIndex() ] );
44               } // end method itemStateChanged
45            } // end anonymous inner class
46         ); // end call to addItemListener
```

Fig. 11.21 | JComboBox that displays a list of image names. (Part 1 of 2.)

```
47
48              add( imagesJComboBox ); // add combobox to JFrame
49              label = new JLabel( icons[ 0 ] ); // display first icon
50              add( label ); // add label to JFrame
51         } // end ComboBoxFrame constructor
52    } // end class ComboBoxFrame
```

Fig. 11.21 | JComboBox that displays a list of image names. (Part 2 of 2.)

```
1     // Fig. 11.22: ComboBoxTest.java
2     // Testing ComboBoxFrame.
3     import javax.swing.JFrame;
4
5     public class ComboBoxTest
6     {
7         public static void main( String args[] )
8         {
9             ComboBoxFrame comboBoxFrame = new ComboBoxFrame();
10            comboBoxFrame.setDefaultCloseOperation( JFrame.EXIT_ON_CLOSE );
11            comboBoxFrame.setSize( 350, 150 ); // set frame size
12            comboBoxFrame.setVisible( true ); // display frame
13        } // end main
14    } // end class ComboBoxTest
```

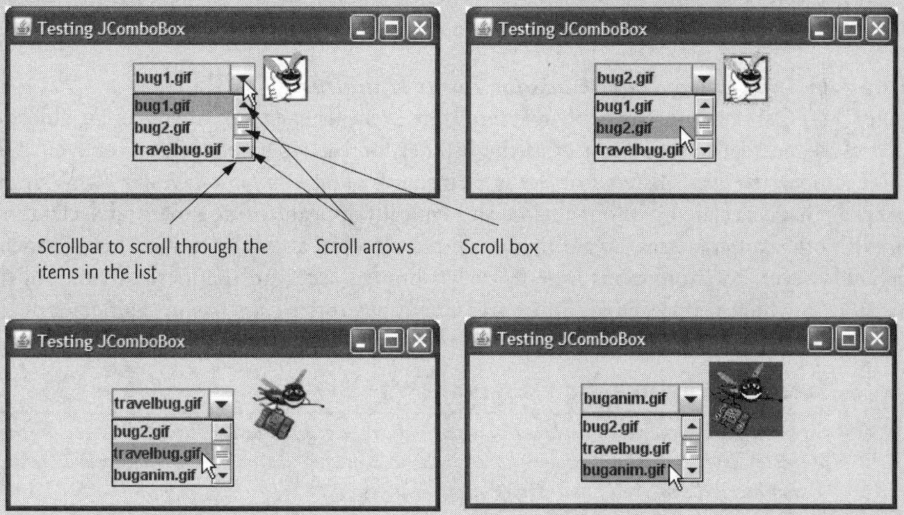

Scrollbar to scroll through the items in the list   Scroll arrows   Scroll box

Fig. 11.22 | Test class for ComboBoxFrame.

name, the application displays the corresponding image as an Icon on a JLabel. Class ComboBoxTest (Fig. 11.22) contains the main method that executes this application. The screen captures for this application show the JComboBox list after the selection was made to illustrate which image file name was selected.

Lines 19–23 (Fig. 11.21) declare and initialize array icons with four new ImageIcon objects. String array names (lines 17–18) contains the names of the four image files that are stored in the same directory as the application.

At line 31, the constructor creates a JComboBox object, using the Strings in array names as the elements in the list. Each item in the list has an **index**. The first item is added at index 0, the next at index 1 and so forth. The first item added to a JComboBox appears as the currently selected item when the JComboBox is displayed. Other items are selected by clicking the JComboBox, which expands into a list from which the user can make a selection.

Line 32 uses JComboBox method **setMaximumRowCount** to set the maximum number of elements that are displayed when the user clicks the JComboBox. If there are additional items, the JComboBox provides a **scrollbar** (see the first screen capture) that allows the user to scroll through all the elements in the list. The user can click the **scroll arrows** at the top and bottom of the scrollbar to move up and down through the list one element at a time, or else drag the **scroll box** in the middle of the scrollbar up and down. To drag the scroll box, position the mouse cursor on it, hold the mouse button down and move the mouse.

Look-and-Feel Observation 11.11

Set the maximum row count for a JComboBox to a number of rows that prevents the list from expanding outside the bounds of the window in which it is used. This configuration will ensure that the list displays correctly when it is expanded by the user.

Line 48 attaches the JComboBox to the ComboBoxFrame's FlowLayout (set in line 29). Line 49 creates the JLabel that displays ImageIcons and initializes it with the first ImageIcon in array icons. Line 50 attaches the JLabel to the ComboBoxFrame's FlowLayout.

Using an Anonymous Inner Class for Event Handling
Lines 34–46 are one statement that declares the event listener's class, creates an object of that class and registers that object as the listener for imagesJComboBox's ItemEvents. In this example, the event-listener object is an instance of an **anonymous inner class**—an inner class that is declared without a name and typically appears inside a method declaration. As with other inner classes, an anonymous inner class can access its top-level class's members. However, an anonymous inner class has limited access to the local variables of the method in which it is declared. Since an anonymous inner class has no name, an of the anonymous inner class must be created where the class is declared (starting at line 35).

Software Engineering Observation 11.5

An anonymous inner class declared in a method can access the instance variables and methods of the top-level class object that declared it, as well as the method's final local variables, but cannot access the method's non-final local variables.

Lines 34–46 are a call to imagesJComboBox's addItemListener method. The argument to this method must be an object that *is an* ItemListener (i.e., any object of a class that implements ItemListener). Lines 35–45 are a class-instance creation expression that declares an anonymous inner class and creates one object of that class. A reference to that object is then passed as the argument to addItemListener. The syntax ItemListener() after new begins the declaration of an anonymous inner class that implements interface ItemListener. This is similar to beginning a class declaration with

    public class MyHandler *implements* ItemListener

The parentheses after ItemListener indicate a call to the default constructor of the anonymous inner class.

The opening left brace ({) at 36 and the closing right brace (}) at line 45 delimit the body of the anonymous inner class. Lines 38–44 declare the ItemListener's itemState-Changed method. When the user makes a selection from imagesJComboBox, this method sets label's Icon. The Icon is selected from array icons by determining the index of the selected item in the JComboBox with method **getSelectedIndex** in line 43. Note that for each item selected from a JComboBox, another item is first deselected—so two ItemEvents occur when an item is selected. We wish to display only the icon for the item the user just selected. For this reason, line 41 determines whether ItemEvent method **getStateChange** returns ItemEvent.SELECTED. If so, lines 42–43 set label's icon.

> **Software Engineering Observation 11.6**
>
> *Like any other class, when an anonymous inner class implements an interface, the class must implement every method in the interface.*

The syntax shown in lines 35–45 for creating an event handler with an anonymous inner class is similar to the code that would be generated by a Java integrated development environment (IDE). Typically, an IDE enables the programmer to design a GUI visually, then the IDE generates code that implements the GUI. The programmer simply inserts statements in the event-handling methods that declare how to handle each event.

11.11 JList

A *list* displays a series of items from which the user may select one or more items (see the output of Fig. 11.23). Lists are created with class JList, which directly extends class JComponent. Class JList supports *single-selection lists* (which allow only one item to be selected at a time) and *multiple-selection lists* (which allow any number of items to be selected). In this section, we discuss single-selection lists.

The application of Figs. 11.23–11.24 creates a JList containing 13 color names. When a color name is clicked in the JList, a **ListSelectionEvent** occurs and the application changes the background color of the application window to the selected color. Class ListTest (Fig. 11.24) contains the main method that executes this application.

```
1    // Fig. 11.23: ListFrame.java
2    // Selecting colors from a JList.
3    import java.awt.FlowLayout;
4    import java.awt.Color;
5    import javax.swing.JFrame;
6    import javax.swing.JList;
7    import javax.swing.JScrollPane;
8    import javax.swing.event.ListSelectionListener;
9    import javax.swing.event.ListSelectionEvent;
10   import javax.swing.ListSelectionModel;
11
12   public class ListFrame extends JFrame
13   {
```

Fig. 11.23 | JList that displays a list of colors. (Part 1 of 2.)

```
14      private JList colorJList; // list to display colors
15      private final String colorNames[] = { "Black", "Blue", "Cyan",
16         "Dark Gray", "Gray", "Green", "Light Gray", "Magenta",
17         "Orange", "Pink", "Red", "White", "Yellow" };
18      private final Color colors[] = { Color.BLACK, Color.BLUE, Color.CYAN,
19         Color.DARK_GRAY, Color.GRAY, Color.GREEN, Color.LIGHT_GRAY,
20         Color.MAGENTA, Color.ORANGE, Color.PINK, Color.RED, Color.WHITE,
21         Color.YELLOW };
22
23      // ListFrame constructor add JScrollPane containing JList to JFrame
24      public ListFrame()
25      {
26         super( "List Test" );
27         setLayout( new FlowLayout() ); // set frame layout
28
29         colorJList = new JList( colorNames ); // create with colorNames
30         colorJList.setVisibleRowCount( 5 ); // display five rows at once
31
32         // do not allow multiple selections
33         colorJList.setSelectionMode( ListSelectionModel.SINGLE_SELECTION );
34
35         // add a JScrollPane containing JList to frame
36         add( new JScrollPane( colorJList ) );
37
38         colorJList.addListSelectionListener(
39            new ListSelectionListener() // anonymous inner class
40            {
41               // handle list selection events
42               public void valueChanged( ListSelectionEvent event )
43               {
44                  getContentPane().setBackground(
45                     colors[ colorJList.getSelectedIndex() ] );
46               } // end method valueChanged
47            } // end anonymous inner class
48         ); // end call to addListSelectionListener
49      } // end ListFrame constructor
50   } // end class ListFrame
```

Fig. 11.23 | JList that displays a list of colors. (Part 2 of 2.)

```
1    // Fig. 11.24: ListTest.java
2    // Selecting colors from a JList.
3    import javax.swing.JFrame;
4
5    public class ListTest
6    {
7       public static void main( String args[] )
8       {
9          ListFrame listFrame = new ListFrame(); // create ListFrame
10         listFrame.setDefaultCloseOperation( JFrame.EXIT_ON_CLOSE );
11         listFrame.setSize( 350, 150 ); // set frame size
```

Fig. 11.24 | Test class for ListFrame. (Part 1 of 2.)

```
12            listFrame.setVisible( true ); // display frame
13        } // end main
14    } // end class ListTest
```

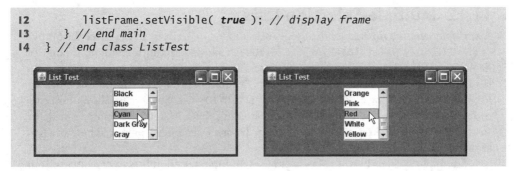

Fig. 11.24 | Test class for ListFrame. (Part 2 of 2.)

Line 29 (Fig. 11.23) creates JList object colorList. The JList constructor receives the array of Objects (in this case Strings) to display in the list. Line 30 uses JList method **setVisibleRowCount** to determine the number of items that are visible in the list.

Line 33 uses JList method **setSelectionMode** to specify the list's *selection mode*. Class **ListSelectionModel** (of package javax.swing) declares three constants that specify a JList's selection mode—**SINGLE_SELECTION** (which allows only one item to be selected at a time), **SINGLE_INTERVAL_SELECTION** (for a multiple-selection list that allows selection of several contiguous items) and **MULTIPLE_INTERVAL_SELECTION** (for a multiple-selection list that does not restrict the items that can be selected).

Unlike a JComboBox, a JList *does not* provide a scrollbar if there are more items in the list than the number of visible rows. In this case, a **JScrollPane** object is used to provide the scrolling capability. Line 36 adds a new instance of class JScrollPane to the JFrame. The JScrollPane constructor receives as its argument the JComponent that needs scrolling functionality (in this case, colorList). Notice in the screen captures that a scrollbar created by the JScrollPane appears at the right side of the JList. By default, the scrollbar appears only when the number of items in the JList exceeds the number of visible items.

Lines 38–48 use JList method **addListSelectionListener** to register an object that implements **ListSelectionListener** (package javax.swing.event) as the listener for the JList's selection events. Once again, we use an instance of an anonymous inner class (lines 39–47) as the listener. In this example, when the user makes a selection from colorList, method **valueChanged** (line 42–46) should change the background color of the List-Frame to the selected color. This is accomplished in lines 44–45. Note the use of JFrame method **getContentPane** in line 44. Each JFrame actually consists of three layers—the background, the content pane and the glass pane. The content pane appears in front of the background and is where the GUI components in the JFrame are displayed. The glass pane is used to display tool tips and other items that should appear in front of the GUI components on the screen. The content pane completely hides the background of the JFrame; thus, to change the background color behind the GUI components, you must change the content pane's background color. Method getContentPane returns a reference to the JFrame's content pane (an object of class Container). In line 44, we then use that reference to call method **setBackground**, which sets the content pane's background color to an element in the colors array. The color is selected from the array by using the selected item's index. JList method **getSelectedIndex** returns the selected item's index. As with arrays and JComboBoxes, JList indexing is zero based.

11.12 Multiple-Selection Lists

A *multiple-selection list* enables the user to select many items from a JList (see the output of Fig. 11.26). A SINGLE_INTERVAL_SELECTION list allows selecting a contiguous range of items. To do so, click the first item, then press and hold the *Shift* key while clicking the last item in the range. A MULTIPLE_INTERVAL_SELECTION list allows continuous range selection as described for a SINGLE_INTERVAL_SELECTION list. Such a list allows miscellaneous items to be selected by pressing and holding the *Ctrl* key (sometimes called the *Control* key) while clicking each item to select. To deselect an item, press and hold the *Ctrl* key while clicking the item a second time.

The application of Figs. 11.25–11.26 uses multiple-selection lists to copy items from one JList to another. One list is a MULTIPLE_INTERVAL_SELECTION list and the other is a SINGLE_INTERVAL_SELECTION list. When you execute the application, try using the selection techniques described previously to select items in both lists.

```java
 1   // Fig. 11.25: MultipleSelectionFrame.java
 2   // Copying items from one List to another.
 3   import java.awt.FlowLayout;
 4   import java.awt.event.ActionListener;
 5   import java.awt.event.ActionEvent;
 6   import javax.swing.JFrame;
 7   import javax.swing.JList;
 8   import javax.swing.JButton;
 9   import javax.swing.JScrollPane;
10   import javax.swing.ListSelectionModel;
11
12   public class MultipleSelectionFrame extends JFrame
13   {
14      private JList colorJList; // list to hold color names
15      private JList copyJList; // list to copy color names into
16      private JButton copyJButton; // button to copy selected names
17      private final String colorNames[] = { "Black", "Blue", "Cyan",
18         "Dark Gray", "Gray", "Green", "Light Gray", "Magenta", "Orange",
19         "Pink", "Red", "White", "Yellow" };
20
21      // MultipleSelectionFrame constructor
22      public MultipleSelectionFrame()
23      {
24         super( "Multiple Selection Lists" );
25         setLayout( new FlowLayout() ); // set frame layout
26
27         colorJList = new JList( colorNames ); // holds names of all colors
28         colorJList.setVisibleRowCount( 5 ); // show five rows
29         colorJList.setSelectionMode(
30            ListSelectionModel.MULTIPLE_INTERVAL_SELECTION );
31         add( new JScrollPane( colorJList ) ); // add list with scrollpane
32
33         copyJButton = new JButton( "Copy >>>" ); // create copy button
34         copyJButton.addActionListener(
35
```

Fig. 11.25 | JList that allows multiple selections. (Part 1 of 2.)

```
36              new ActionListener() // anonymous inner class
37              {
38                 // handle button event
39                 public void actionPerformed( ActionEvent event )
40                 {
41                    // place selected values in copyJList
42                    copyJList.setListData( colorJList.getSelectedValues() );
43                 } // end method actionPerformed
44              } // end anonymous inner class
45           ); // end call to addActionListener
46
47           add( copyJButton ); // add copy button to JFrame
48
49           copyJList = new JList(); // create list to hold copied color names
50           copyJList.setVisibleRowCount( 5 ); // show 5 rows
51           copyJList.setFixedCellWidth( 100 ); // set width
52           copyJList.setFixedCellHeight( 15 ); // set height
53           copyJList.setSelectionMode(
54              ListSelectionModel.SINGLE_INTERVAL_SELECTION );
55           add( new JScrollPane( copyJList ) ); // add list with scrollpane
56        } // end MultipleSelectionFrame constructor
57 } // end class MultipleSelectionFrame
```

Fig. 11.25 | JList that allows multiple selections. (Part 2 of 2.)

```
1  // Fig. 11.26: MultipleSelectionTest.java
2  // Testing MultipleSelectionFrame.
3  import javax.swing.JFrame;
4
5  public class MultipleSelectionTest
6  {
7     public static void main( String args[] )
8     {
9        MultipleSelectionFrame multipleSelectionFrame =
10          new MultipleSelectionFrame();
11       multipleSelectionFrame.setDefaultCloseOperation(
12          JFrame.EXIT_ON_CLOSE );
13       multipleSelectionFrame.setSize( 350, 140 ); // set frame size
14       multipleSelectionFrame.setVisible( true ); // display frame
15    } // end main
16 } // end class MultipleSelectionTest
```

Fig. 11.26 | Test class for MultipleSelectionFrame.

Line 27 of Fig. 11.25 creates JList colorJList and initializes it with the strings in the array colorNames. Line 28 sets the number of visible rows in colorJList to 5. Lines 29–30 specify that colorList is a MULTIPLE_INTERVAL_SELECTION list. Line 31 adds a new JScrollPane containing colorJList to the JFrame. Lines 49–55 perform similar tasks for copyJList, which is declared as a SINGLE_INTERVAL_SELECTION list. Line 51 uses JList method *setFixedCellWidth* to set copyJList's width to 100 pixels. Line 52 uses JList method *setFixedCellHeight* to set the height of each item in the JList to 15 pixels.

There are no events to indicate that a user has made multiple selections in a multiple-selection list. Normally, an event generated by another GUI component (known as an *external event*) specifies when the multiple selections in a JList should be processed. In this example, the user clicks the JButton called copyJButton to trigger the event that copies the selected items in colorJList to copyJList.

Lines 39–45 declare, create and register an ActionListener for the copyButton. When the user clicks copyJButton, method actionPerformed (lines 39–43) uses JList method *setListData* to set the items displayed in copyJList. Line 42 calls colorJList's method *getSelectedValues*, which returns an array of Objects representing the selected items in colorJList. In this example, the returned array is passed as the argument to copyJList's setListData method.

You might be wondering why copyJList can be used in line 42 even though the application does not create the object to which it refers until line 49. Remember that method actionPerformed (lines 39–43) does not execute until the user presses the copy-JButton, which cannot occur until after the constructor completes execution and the application displays the GUI. At that point in the application's execution, copyJList is already initialized with a new JList object.

11.13 Mouse Event Handling

This section presents the *MouseListener* and *MouseMotionListener* event-listener interfaces for handling *mouse events*. Mouse events can be trapped for any GUI component that derives from java.awt.Component. The methods of interfaces MouseListener and MouseMotionListener are summarized in Figure 11.27. Package javax.swing.event contains interface *MouseInputListener*, which extends interfaces MouseListener and MouseMotionListener to create a single interface containing all the MouseListener and MouseMotionListener methods. The MouseListener and MouseMotionListener meth-

MouseListener and MouseMotionListener interface methods
Methods of interface MouseListener
public void mousePressed(MouseEvent event)
Called when a mouse button is pressed while the mouse cursor is on a component.
public void mouseClicked(MouseEvent event)
Called when a mouse button is pressed and released while the mouse cursor remains stationary on a component. This event is always preceded by a call to mousePressed.

Fig. 11.27 | MouseListener and MouseMotionListener interface methods. (Part 1 of 2.)

MouseListener and MouseMotionListener interface methods
public void mouseReleased(MouseEvent event)
Called when a mouse button is released after being pressed. This event is always preceded by a call to mousePressed and one or more calls to mouseDragged.
public void mouseEntered(MouseEvent event)
Called when the mouse cursor enters the bounds of a component.
public void mouseExited(MouseEvent event)
Called when the mouse cursor leaves the bounds of a component.
Methods of interface MouseMotionListener
public void mouseDragged(MouseEvent event)
Called when the mouse button is pressed while the mouse cursor is on a component and the mouse is moved while the mouse button remains pressed. This event is always preceded by a call to mousePressed. All drag events are sent to the component on which the user began to drag the mouse.
public void mouseMoved(MouseEvent event)
Called when the mouse is moved when the mouse cursor is on a component. All move events are sent to the component over which the mouse is currently positioned.

Fig. 11.27 | MouseListener and MouseMotionListener interface methods. (Part 1 of 2.)

ods are called when the mouse interacts with a Component if appropriate event-listener objects are registered for that Component.

Each of the mouse event-handling methods takes a *MouseEvent* object as its argument. A MouseEvent object contains information about the mouse event that occurred, including the *x*- and *y*-coordinates of the location where the event occurred. These coordinates are measured from the upper-left corner of the GUI component on which the event occurred. The *x*-coordinates start at 0 and increase from left to right. The *y*-coordinates start at 0 and increase from top to bottom. In addition, the methods and constants of class *InputEvent* (MouseEvent's superclass) enable an application to determine which mouse button the user clicked.

Look-and-Feel Observation 11.12

Method calls to mouseDragged and mouseReleased are sent to the MouseMotionListener for the Component on which a mouse drag operation started. Similarly, the mouseReleased method call at the end of a drag operation is sent to the MouseListener for the Component on which the drag operation started.

Java also provides interface *MouseWheelListener* to enable applications to respond to the rotation of a mouse wheel. This interface declares method *mouseWheelMoved*, which receives a *MouseWheelEvent* as its argument. Class MouseWheelEvent (a subclass of Mouse-Event) contains methods that enable the event handler to obtain information about the amount of wheel rotation.

Tracking Mouse Events on a JPanel

The MouseTracker application (Figs. 11.28–11.29) demonstrates the MouseListener and MouseMotionListener interface methods. The application class implements both interfaces so it can listen for its own mouse events. Note that all seven methods from these two interfaces must be declared by the programmer when a class implements both interfaces. Each mouse event in this example displays a string in the JLabel called statusBar at the bottom of the window.

```java
1   // Fig. 11.28: MouseTrackerFrame.java
2   // Demonstrating mouse events.
3   import java.awt.Color;
4   import java.awt.BorderLayout;
5   import java.awt.event.MouseListener;
6   import java.awt.event.MouseMotionListener;
7   import java.awt.event.MouseEvent;
8   import javax.swing.JFrame;
9   import javax.swing.JLabel;
10  import javax.swing.JPanel;
11
12  public class MouseTrackerFrame extends JFrame
13  {
14     private JPanel mousePanel; // panel in which mouse events will occur
15     private JLabel statusBar; // label that displays event information
16
17     // MouseTrackerFrame constructor sets up GUI and
18     // registers mouse event handlers
19     public MouseTrackerFrame()
20     {
21        super( "Demonstrating Mouse Events" );
22
23        mousePanel = new JPanel(); // create panel
24        mousePanel.setBackground( Color.WHITE ); // set background color
25        add( mousePanel, BorderLayout.CENTER ); // add panel to JFrame
26
27        statusBar = new JLabel( "Mouse outside JPanel" );
28        add( statusBar, BorderLayout.SOUTH ); // add label to JFrame
29
30        // create and register listener for mouse and mouse motion events
31        MouseHandler handler = new MouseHandler();
32        mousePanel.addMouseListener( handler );
33        mousePanel.addMouseMotionListener( handler );
34     } // end MouseTrackerFrame constructor
35
36     private class MouseHandler implements MouseListener,
37        MouseMotionListener
38     {
39        // MouseListener event handlers
40        // handle event when mouse released immediately after press
41        public void mouseClicked( MouseEvent event )
42        {
```

Fig. 11.28 | Mouse event handling. (Part 1 of 2.)

```
43              statusBar.setText( String.format( "Clicked at [%d, %d]",
44                 event.getX(), event.getY() ) );
45          } // end method mouseClicked
46
47          // handle event when mouse pressed
48          public void mousePressed( MouseEvent event )
49          {
50              statusBar.setText( String.format( "Pressed at [%d, %d]",
51                 event.getX(), event.getY() ) );
52          } // end method mousePressed
53
54          // handle event when mouse released after dragging
55          public void mouseReleased( MouseEvent event )
56          {
57              statusBar.setText( String.format( "Released at [%d, %d]",
58                 event.getX(), event.getY() ) );
59          } // end method mouseReleased
60
61          // handle event when mouse enters area
62          public void mouseEntered( MouseEvent event )
63          {
64              statusBar.setText( String.format( "Mouse entered at [%d, %d]",
65                 event.getX(), event.getY() ) );
66              mousePanel.setBackground( Color.GREEN );
67          } // end method mouseEntered
68
69          // handle event when mouse exits area
70          public void mouseExited( MouseEvent event )
71          {
72              statusBar.setText( "Mouse outside JPanel" );
73              mousePanel.setBackground( Color.WHITE );
74          } // end method mouseExited
75
76          // MouseMotionListener event handlers
77          // handle event when user drags mouse with button pressed
78          public void mouseDragged( MouseEvent event )
79          {
80              statusBar.setText( String.format( "Dragged at [%d, %d]",
81                 event.getX(), event.getY() ) );
82          } // end method mouseDragged
83
84          // handle event when user moves mouse
85          public void mouseMoved( MouseEvent event )
86          {
87              statusBar.setText( String.format( "Moved at [%d, %d]",
88                 event.getX(), event.getY() ) );
89          } // end method mouseMoved
90      } // end inner class MouseHandler
91  } // end class MouseTrackerFrame
```

Fig. 11.28 | Mouse event handling. (Part 2 of 2.)

Line 23 in Fig. 11.28 creates JPanel mousePanel. This JPanel's mouse events will be tracked by the application. Line 24 sets mousePanel's background color to white. When

```
1   // Fig. 11.29: MouseTrackerFrame.java
2   // Testing MouseTrackerFrame.
3   import javax.swing.JFrame;
4
5   public class MouseTracker
6   {
7      public static void main( String args[] )
8      {
9         MouseTrackerFrame mouseTrackerFrame = new MouseTrackerFrame();
10        mouseTrackerFrame.setDefaultCloseOperation( JFrame.EXIT_ON_CLOSE );
11        mouseTrackerFrame.setSize( 300, 100 ); // set frame size
12        mouseTrackerFrame.setVisible( true ); // display frame
13     } // end main
14  } // end class MouseTracker
```

Fig. 11.29 | Test class for `MouseTrackerFrame`.

the user moves the mouse into the `mousePanel`, the application will change `mousePanel`'s background color to green. When the user moves the mouse out of the `mousePanel`, the application will change the background color back to white. Line 25 attaches `mousePanel` to the `JFrame`. As you learned in Section 11.4, you typically must specify the layout of the GUI components in a `JFrame`. In that section, we introduced the layout manager `FlowLayout`. Here we use the default layout of a `JFrame`'s content pane—***BorderLayout***. This layout manager arranges components into five regions: ***NORTH, SOUTH, EAST, WEST*** and ***CENTER***. NORTH corresponds to the top of the container. This example uses the CENTER and SOUTH regions. Line 25 uses a two-argument version of method `add` to place `mousePanel` in the CENTER region. The `BorderLayout` automatically sizes the component in the CENTER to use all the space in the `JFrame` that is not occupied by components in the other regions. Section 11.17.2 discusses `BorderLayout` in more detail.

Lines 27–28 in the constructor declare `JLabel statusBar` and attach it to the `JFrame`'s SOUTH region. This `JLabel` occupies the width of the `JFrame`. The region's height is determined by the `JLabel`.

Line 31 creates an instance of inner class `MouseHandler` (lines 36–90) called `handler` that responds to mouse events. Lines 32–33 register `handler` as the listener for mouse-

Panel's mouse events. Methods **addMouseListener** and **addMouseMotionListener** are inherited indirectly from class Component and can be used to register MouseListeners and MouseMotionListeners, respectively. A MouseHandler object is both a MouseListener and a MouseMotionListener because the class implements both interfaces. [*Note:* In this example, we chose to implement both interfaces to demonstrate a class that implements more than one interface. However, we also could have implemented interface MouseInputListener here.]

When the mouse enters and exits mousePanel's area, methods mouseEntered (lines 62–67) and mouseExited (lines 70–74) are called, respectively. Method mouseEntered displays a message in the statusBar indicating that the mouse entered the JPanel and changes the background color to green. Method mouseExited displays a message in the statusBar indicating that the mouse is outside the JPanel (see the first sample output window) and changes the background color to white.

When any of the other five events occurs, it displays a message in the statusBar that includes a string containing the event and the coordinates at which it occurred. MouseEvent methods **getX** and **getY** return the *x*- and *y*-coordinates, respectively, of the mouse at the time the event occurred.

11.14 Adapter Classes

Many event-listener interfaces, such as MouseListener and MouseMotionListener, contain multiple methods. It is not always desirable to declare every method in an event-listener interface. For instance, an application may need only the mouseClicked handler from MouseListener or the mouseDragged handler from MouseMotionListener. Interface WindowListener specifies seven window event-handling methods. For many of the listener interfaces that have multiple methods, packages java.awt.event and javax.swing.event provide event-listener adapter classes. An *adapter class* implements an interface and provides a default implementation (with an empty method body) of each method in the interface. Figure 11.30 shows several java.awt.event adapter classes and the interfaces they implement. You can extend an adapter class to inherit the default implementation of every method and subsequently override only the method(s) you need for event handling.

Event-adapter class in java.awt.event	Implements interface
ComponentAdapter	ComponentListener
ContainerAdapter	ContainerListener
FocusAdapter	FocusListener
KeyAdapter	KeyListener
MouseAdapter	MouseListener
MouseMotionAdapter	MouseMotionListener
WindowAdapter	WindowListener

Fig. 11.30 | Event-adapter classes and the interfaces they implement in package java.awt.event.

Software Engineering Observation 11.7

When a class implements an interface, the class has an is-a relationship with that interface. All direct and indirect subclasses of that class inherit this interface. Thus, an object of a class that extends an event-adapter class is an object of the corresponding event-listener type (e.g., an object of a subclass of MouseAdapter is a MouseListener).

Extending MouseAdapter

The application of Figs. 11.31–11.32 demonstrates how to determine the number of mouse clicks (i.e., the click count) and how to distinguish between the different mouse buttons. The event listener in this application is an object of inner class MouseClickHandler (lines 26–46) that extends MouseAdapter, so we can declare just the mouseClicked method we need in this example.

Common Programming Error 11.4

If you extend an adapter class and misspell the name of the method you are overriding, your method simply becomes another method in the class. This is a logic error that is difficult to detect, since the program will call the empty version of the method inherited from the adapter class.

```java
1  // Fig. 11.31: MouseDetailsFrame.java
2  // Demonstrating mouse clicks and distinguishing between mouse buttons.
3  import java.awt.BorderLayout;
4  import java.awt.Graphics;
5  import java.awt.event.MouseAdapter;
6  import java.awt.event.MouseEvent;
7  import javax.swing.JFrame;
8  import javax.swing.JLabel;
9
10 public class MouseDetailsFrame extends JFrame
11 {
12    private String details; // String representing
13    private JLabel statusBar; // JLabel that appears at bottom of window
14
15    // constructor sets title bar String and register mouse listener
16    public MouseDetailsFrame()
17    {
18       super( "Mouse clicks and buttons" );
19
20       statusBar = new JLabel( "Click the mouse" );
21       add( statusBar, BorderLayout.SOUTH );
22       addMouseListener( new MouseClickHandler() ); // add handler
23    } // end MouseDetailsFrame constructor
24
25    // inner class to handle mouse events
26    private class MouseClickHandler extends MouseAdapter
27    {
28       // handle mouse-click event and determine which button was pressed
29       public void mouseClicked( MouseEvent event )
30       {
31          int xPos = event.getX(); // get x-position of mouse
32          int yPos = event.getY(); // get y-position of mouse
```

Fig. 11.31 | Left, center and right mouse-button clicks. (Part 1 of 2.)

```
33
34          details = String.format( "Clicked %d time(s)",
35             event.getClickCount() );
36
37          if ( event.isMetaDown() ) // right mouse button
38             details += " with right mouse button";
39          else if ( event.isAltDown() ) // middle mouse button
40             details += " with center mouse button";
41          else // left mouse button
42             details += " with left mouse button";
43
44          statusBar.setText( details ); // display message in statusBar
45       } // end method mouseClicked
46    } // end private inner class MouseClickHandler
47 } // end class MouseDetailsFrame
```

Fig. 11.31 | Left, center and right mouse-button clicks. (Part 2 of 2.)

```
 1  // Fig. 11.32: MouseDetails.java
 2  // Testing MouseDetailsFrame.
 3  import javax.swing.JFrame;
 4
 5  public class MouseDetails
 6  {
 7     public static void main( String args[] )
 8     {
 9        MouseDetailsFrame mouseDetailsFrame = new MouseDetailsFrame();
10        mouseDetailsFrame.setDefaultCloseOperation( JFrame.EXIT_ON_CLOSE );
11        mouseDetailsFrame.setSize( 400, 150 ); // set frame size
12        mouseDetailsFrame.setVisible( true ); // display frame
13     } // end main
14  } // end class MouseDetails
```

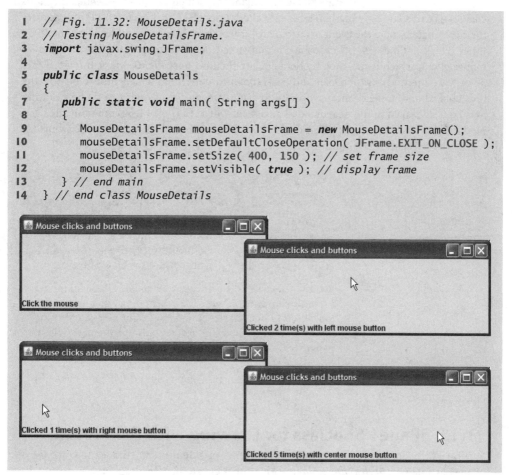

Fig. 11.32 | Test class for MouseDetailsFrame.

A user of a Java application may be on a system with a one-, two- or three-button mouse. Java provides a mechanism to distinguish among mouse buttons. Class Mouse-Event inherits several methods from class InputEvent that can distinguish among mouse buttons on a multi-button mouse or can mimic a multi-button mouse with a combined keystroke and mouse-button click. Figure 11.33 shows the InputEvent methods used to distinguish among mouse-button clicks. Java assumes that every mouse contains a left mouse button. Thus, it is simple to test for a left-mouse-button click. However, users with a one- or two-button mouse must use a combination of keystrokes and mouse-button clicks at the same time to simulate the missing buttons on the mouse. In the case of a one- or two-button mouse, a Java application assumes that the center mouse button is clicked if the user holds down the *Alt* key and clicks the left mouse button on a two-button mouse or the only mouse button on a one-button mouse. In the case of a one-button mouse, a Java application assumes that the right mouse button is clicked if the user holds down the *Meta* key and clicks the mouse button.

Line 22 of Fig. 11.31 registers a MouseListener for the MouseDetailsFrame. The event listener is an object of class MouseClickHandler, which extends MouseAdapter. This enables us to declare only method mouseClicked (lines 29–45). This method first captures the coordinates where the event occurred and stores them in local variables xPos and yPos (lines 31–32). Lines 34–35 create a String called details containing the number of mouse clicks, which is returned by MouseEvent method *getClickCount* at line 35. Lines 37–42 use methods *isMetaDown* and *isAltDown* to determine which mouse button the user clicked and append an appropriate String to details in each case. The resulting String is displayed in the statusBar. Class MouseDetails (Fig. 11.32) contains the main method that executes the application. Try clicking with each of your mouse's buttons repeatedly to see the click count increment.

InputEvent method	Description
isMetaDown()	Returns true when the user clicks the right mouse button on a mouse with two or three buttons. To simulate a right-mouse-button click on a one-button mouse, the user can hold down the *Meta* key on the keyboard and click the mouse button.
isAltDown()	Returns true when the user clicks the middle mouse button on a mouse with three buttons. To simulate a middle-mouse-button click on a one- or two-button mouse, the user can press the *Alt* key on the keyboard and click the only or left mouse button, respectively.

Fig. 11.33 | InputEvent methods that help distinguish among left-, center- and right-mouse-button clicks.

11.15 JPanel Subclass for Drawing with the Mouse

Section 11.13 showed how to track mouse events in a JPanel. In this section, we use a JPanel as a *dedicated drawing area* in which the user can draw by dragging the mouse. In addition, this section demonstrates an event listener that extends an adapter class.

Method *paintComponent*

Lightweight Swing components that extend class JComponent (such as JPanel) contain method *paintComponent*, which is called when a lightweight Swing component is displayed. By overriding this method, you can specify how to draw shapes using Java's graphics capabilities. When customizing a JPanel for use as a dedicated drawing area, the subclass should override method paintComponent and call the superclass version of paint-Component as the first statement in the body of the overridden method to ensure that the component displays correctly. The reason for this is that subclasses of JComponent support *transparency*. To display a component correctly, the program must determine whether the component is transparent. The code that determines this is in superclass JComponent's paintComponent implementation. When a component is transparent, paintComponent will not clear its background when the program displays the component. When a component is *opaque*, paintComponent clears the component's background before the component is displayed. If the superclass version of paintComponent is not called, an opaque GUI component typically will not display correctly on the user interface. Also, if the superclass version is called after performing the customized drawing statements, the results typically will be erased. The transparency of a Swing lightweight component can be set with method *setOpaque* (a false argument indicates that the component is transparent).

Look-and-Feel Observation 11.13

Most Swing GUI components can be transparent or opaque. If a Swing GUI component is opaque, its background will be cleared when its paintComponent method is called. Only opaque components can display a customized background color. JPanel objects are opaque by default.

Error-Prevention Tip 11.1

In a JComponent subclass's paintComponent method, the first statement should always call to the superclass's paintComponent method to ensure that an object of the subclass displays correctly.

Common Programming Error 11.5

If an overridden paintComponent method does not call the superclass's version, the subclass component may not display properly. If an overridden paintComponent method calls the superclass's version after other drawing is performed, the drawing will be erased.

Defining the Custom Drawing Area

The Painter application of Figs. 11.34–11.35 demonstrates a *customized subclass of JPanel* that is used to create a dedicated drawing area. The application uses the mouse-Dragged event handler to create a simple drawing application. The user can draw pictures by dragging the mouse on the JPanel. This example does not use method mouseMoved, so our event-listener class (the anonymous inner class at lines 22-34) extends Mouse-MotionAdapter. Since this class already declares both mouseMoved and mouseDragged, we can simply override mouseDragged to provide the event handling this application requires.

```
1   // Fig. 11.34: PaintPanel.java
2   // Using class MouseMotionAdapter.
3   import java.awt.Point;
```

Fig. 11.34 | Adapter classes used to implement event handlers. (Part 1 of 2.)

```java
4   import java.awt.Graphics;
5   import java.awt.event.MouseEvent;
6   import java.awt.event.MouseMotionAdapter;
7   import javax.swing.JPanel;
8
9   public class PaintPanel extends JPanel
10  {
11     private int pointCount = 0; // count number of points
12
13     // array of 10000 java.awt.Point references
14     private Point points[] = new Point[ 10000 ];
15
16     // set up GUI and register mouse event handler
17     public PaintPanel()
18     {
19        // handle frame mouse motion event
20        addMouseMotionListener(
21
22           new MouseMotionAdapter() // anonymous inner class
23           {
24              // store drag coordinates and repaint
25              public void mouseDragged( MouseEvent event )
26              {
27                 if ( pointCount < points.length )
28                 {
29                    points[ pointCount ] = event.getPoint(); // find point
30                    pointCount++; // increment number of points in array
31                    repaint(); // repaint JFrame
32                 } // end if
33              } // end method mouseDragged
34           } // end anonymous inner class
35        ); // end call to addMouseMotionListener
36     } // end PaintPanel constructor
37
38     // draw oval in a 4-by-4 bounding box at specified location on window
39     public void paintComponent( Graphics g )
40     {
41        super.paintComponent( g ); // clears drawing area
42
43        // draw all points in array
44        for ( int i = 0; i < pointCount; i++ )
45           g.fillOval( points[ i ].x, points[ i ].y, 4, 4 );
46     } // end method paintComponent
47  } // end class PaintPanel
```

Fig. 11.34 | Adapter classes used to implement event handlers. (Part 2 of 2.)

```java
1   // Fig. 11.35: Painter.java
2   // Testing PaintPanel.
3   import java.awt.BorderLayout;
4   import javax.swing.JFrame;
5   import javax.swing.JLabel;
```

Fig. 11.35 | Test class for PaintFrame. (Part 1 of 2.)

```
6
7   public class Painter
8   {
9      public static void main( String args[] )
10     {
11        // create JFrame
12        JFrame application = new JFrame( "A simple paint program" );
13
14        PaintPanel paintPanel = new PaintPanel(); // create paint panel
15        application.add( paintPanel, BorderLayout.CENTER ); // in center
16
17        // create a label and place it in SOUTH of BorderLayout
18        application.add( new JLabel( "Drag the mouse to draw" ),
19           BorderLayout.SOUTH );
20
21        application.setDefaultCloseOperation( JFrame.EXIT_ON_CLOSE );
22        application.setSize( 400, 200 ); // set frame size
23        application.setVisible( true ); // display frame
24     } // end main
25  } // end class Painter
```

Fig. 11.35 | Test class for PaintFrame. (Part 2 of 2.)

Class PaintPanel (Fig. 11.34) extends JPanel to create the dedicated drawing area. Lines 3–7 import the classes used in class PaintPanel. Class **Point** (package java.awt) represents an *x-y* coordinate. We use objects of this class to store the coordinates of each mouse drag event. Class **Graphics** is used to draw.

In this example, we use an array of 10,000 Points (line 14) to store the location at which each mouse-drag event occurs. As you'll see, method paintComponent uses these Points to draw. Instance variable pointCount (line 11) maintains the total number of Points captured from mouse drag events so far.

Lines 20–35 register a MouseMotionListener to listen for the PaintPanel's mouse-motion events. Lines 22–34 create an object of an anonymous inner class that extends the adapter class MouseMotionAdapter. Recall that MouseMotionAdapter implements Mouse-MotionListener, so the anonymous inner class object is a MouseMotionListener. The anonymous inner class inherits a default implementation of methods mouseMoved and mouseDragged, so it already satisfies the requirement that all methods of the interface must be implemented. However, the default methods do nothing when they are called. So, we override method mouseDragged at lines 25–33 to capture the coordinates of a mouse-dragged event and store them as a Point object. Line 27 ensures that we store the event's coordinates only if there are still empty elements in the array. If so, line 29 invokes the

MouseEvent's **getPoint** method to obtain the Point where the event occurred and stores it in the array at index pointCount. Line 30 increments the pointCount, and line 31 calls method **repaint** (inherited indirectly from class Component) to indicate that the Paint-Panel should be refreshed on the screen as soon as possible with a call to the PaintPanel's paintComponent method.

Method paintComponent (lines 39–46), which receives a Graphics parameter, is called automatically any time the PaintPanel needs to be displayed on the screen (such as when the GUI is first displayed) or refreshed on the screen (such as when method repaint is called or when the GUI component was hidden by another window on the screen and subsequently becomes visible again).

Look-and-Feel Observation 11.14

Calling repaint for a Swing GUI component indicates that the component should be refreshed on the screen as soon as possible. The background of the GUI component is cleared only if the component is opaque. JComponent method setOpaque can be passed a boolean argument indicating whether the component is opaque (true) or transparent (false).

Line 41 invokes the superclass version of paintComponent to clear the PaintPanel's background (JPanels are opaque by default). Lines 44–45 draw an oval at the location specified by each Point in the array (up to the pointCount). Graphics method **fillOval** draws a solid oval. The method's four parameters represent a rectangular area (called the *bounding box*) in which the oval is displayed. The first two parameters are the upper-left *x*-coordinate and the upper-left *y*-coordinate of the rectangular area. The last two coordinates represent the rectangular area's width and height. Method fillOval draws the oval so it touches the middle of each side of the rectangular area. In line 45, the first two arguments are specified by using class Point's two public instance variables—x and y. The loop terminates either when a null reference is encountered in the array or when the end of the array is reached. You'll learn more Graphics features in Chapter 12.

Look-and-Feel Observation 11.15

Drawing on any GUI component is performed with coordinates that are measured from the upper-left corner (0, 0) of that GUI component, not the upper-left corner of the screen.

Using the Custom JPanel in an Application
Class Painter (Fig. 11.35) contains the main method that executes this application. Line 14 creates a PaintPanel object on which the user can drag the mouse to draw. Line 15 attaches the PaintPanel to the JFrame.

11.16 Key Event Handling

This section presents the **KeyListener** interface for handling *key events*. Key events are generated when keys on the keyboard are pressed and released. A class that implements KeyListener must provide declarations for methods **keyPressed**, **keyReleased** and **keyTyped**, each of which receives a **KeyEvent** as its argument. Class KeyEvent is a subclass of InputEvent. Method keyPressed is called in response to pressing any key. Method keyTyped is called in response to pressing any key that is not an *action key*. (The action keys are any arrow key, *Home, End, Page Up, Page Down*, any function key, *Num Lock, Print*

Screen, Scroll Lock, Caps Lock and *Pause*.) Method keyReleased is called when the key is released after any keyPressed or keyTyped event.

The application of Figs. 11.36–11.37 demonstrates the KeyListener methods. Class KeyDemo implements the KeyListener interface, so all three methods are declared in the application.

```java
1   // Fig. 11.36: KeyDemoFrame.java
2   // Demonstrating keystroke events.
3   import java.awt.Color;
4   import java.awt.event.KeyListener;
5   import java.awt.event.KeyEvent;
6   import javax.swing.JFrame;
7   import javax.swing.JTextArea;
8
9   public class KeyDemoFrame extends JFrame implements KeyListener
10  {
11     private String line1 = ""; // first line of textarea
12     private String line2 = ""; // second line of textarea
13     private String line3 = ""; // third line of textarea
14     private JTextArea textArea; // textarea to display output
15
16     // KeyDemoFrame constructor
17     public KeyDemoFrame()
18     {
19        super( "Demonstrating Keystroke Events" );
20
21        textArea = new JTextArea( 10, 15 ); // set up JTextArea
22        textArea.setText( "Press any key on the keyboard..." );
23        textArea.setEnabled( false ); // disable textarea
24        textArea.setDisabledTextColor( Color.BLACK ); // set text color
25        add( textArea ); // add textarea to JFrame
26
27        addKeyListener( this ); // allow frame to process key events
28     } // end KeyDemoFrame constructor
29
30     // handle press of any key
31     public void keyPressed( KeyEvent event )
32     {
33        line1 = String.format( "Key pressed: %s",
34           event.getKeyText( event.getKeyCode() ) ); // output pressed key
35        setLines2and3( event ); // set output lines two and three
36     } // end method keyPressed
37
38     // handle release of any key
39     public void keyReleased( KeyEvent event )
40     {
41        line1 = String.format( "Key released: %s",
42           event.getKeyText( event.getKeyCode() ) ); // output released key
43        setLines2and3( event ); // set output lines two and three
44     } // end method keyReleased
45
```

Fig. 11.36 | Key event handling. (Part 1 of 2.)

```
46      // handle press of an action key
47      public void keyTyped( KeyEvent event )
48      {
49         line1 = String.format( "Key typed: %s", event.getKeyChar() );
50         setLines2and3( event ); // set output lines two and three
51      } // end method keyTyped
52
53      // set second and third lines of output
54      private void setLines2and3( KeyEvent event )
55      {
56         line2 = String.format( "This key is %san action key",
57            ( event.isActionKey() ? "" : "not " ) );
58
59         String temp = event.getKeyModifiersText( event.getModifiers() );
60
61         line3 = String.format( "Modifier keys pressed: %s",
62            ( temp.equals( "" ) ? "none" : temp ) ); // output modifiers
63
64         textArea.setText( String.format( "%s\n%s\n%s\n",
65            line1, line2, line3 ) ); // output three lines of text
66      } // end method setLines2and3
67   } // end class KeyDemoFrame
```

Fig. 11.36 | Key event handling. (Part 2 of 2.)

```
1    // Fig. 11.37: KeyDemo.java
2    // Testing KeyDemoFrame.
3    import javax.swing.JFrame;
4
5    public class KeyDemo
6    {
7       public static void main( String args[] )
8       {
9          KeyDemoFrame keyDemoFrame = new KeyDemoFrame();
10         keyDemoFrame.setDefaultCloseOperation( JFrame.EXIT_ON_CLOSE );
11         keyDemoFrame.setSize( 350, 100 ); // set frame size
12         keyDemoFrame.setVisible( true ); // display frame
13      } // end main
14   } // end class KeyDemo
```

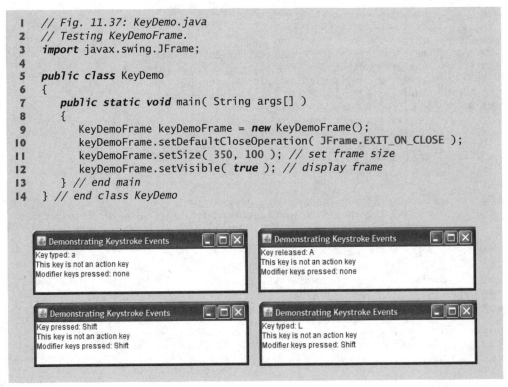

Fig. 11.37 | Test class for KeyDemoFrame. (Part 1 of 2.)

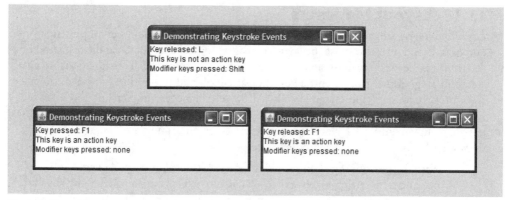

Fig. 11.37 | Test class for KeyDemoFrame. (Part 2 of 2.)

The constructor (Fig. 11.36, lines 17–28) registers the application to handle its own key events by using method **addKeyListener** at line 27. Method addKeyListener is declared in class Component, so every subclass of Component can notify KeyListener objects of key events for that Component.

At line 25, the constructor adds JTextArea textArea (where the application's output is displayed) to the JFrame. Notice in the screen captures that textArea occupies the entire window. This is due to the JFrame's default BorderLayout (discussed in Section 11.17.2 and demonstrated in Fig. 11.41). When a single Component is added to a BorderLayout, the Component occupies the entire Container. Note that line 24 uses method setDisabledTextColor to change the color of the text in the textarea to black.

Methods keyPressed (lines 31–36) and keyReleased (lines 39–44) use KeyEvent method **getKeyCode** to get the *virtual key code* of the key that was pressed. Class KeyEvent maintains a set of constants—the virtual key-code constants—that represents every key on the keyboard. These constants can be compared with the return value of getKeyCode to test for individual keys on the keyboard. The value returned by getKeyCode is passed to KeyEvent method **getKeyText**, which returns a string containing the name of the key that was pressed. For a complete list of virtual key constants, see the on-line documentation for class KeyEvent (package java.awt.event). Method keyTyped (lines 47–51) uses KeyEvent method **getKeyChar** to get the Unicode value of the character typed.

All three event-handling methods finish by calling method setLines2and3 (lines 54–66) and passing it the KeyEvent object. This method uses KeyEvent method **isActionKey** (line 57) to determine whether the key in the event was an action key. Also, InputEvent method **getModifiers** is called (line 59) to determine whether any modifier keys (such as *Shift*, *Alt* and *Ctrl*) were pressed when the key event occurred. The result of this method is passed to KeyEvent method **getKeyModifiersText**, which produces a string containing the names of the pressed modifier keys.

[*Note:* If you need to test for a specific key on the keyboard, class KeyEvent provides a *key constant* for every key on the keyboard. These constants can be used from the key event handlers to determine whether a particular key was pressed. Also, to determine whether the *Alt, Ctrl, Meta* and *Shift* keys are pressed individually, InputEvent methods isAltDown, **isControlDown**, isMetaDown and **isShiftDown** each return a boolean indicating if the particular key was pressed during the key event.]

11.17 Layout Managers

Layout managers are provided to arrange GUI components in a container for presentation purposes. Programmers can use the layout managers for basic layout capabilities instead of determining the exact position and size of every GUI component. This functionality enables the programmer to concentrate on the basic look-and-feel and lets the layout managers process most of the layout details. All layout managers implement the interface *LayoutManager* (in package java.awt). Class Container's setLayout method takes an object that implements the LayoutManager interface as an argument. There are basically three ways for you to arrange components in a GUI:

1. Absolute positioning: This provides the greatest level of control over a GUI's appearance. By setting a Container's layout to null, you can specify the absolute position of each GUI component with respect to the upper-left corner of the Container. If you do this, you also must specify each GUI component's size. Programming a GUI with absolute positioning can be tedious, unless you have an integrated development environment (IDE) that can generate the code for you.

2. Layout managers: Using layout managers to position elements can be simpler and faster than creating a GUI with absolute positioning, but you lose some control over the size and the precise positioning of GUI components.

3. Visual programming in an IDE: IDEs provide tools that make it easy to create GUIs. Each IDE typically provides a **GUI design tool** that allows you to drag and drop GUI components from a tool box onto a design area. You can then position, size and align GUI components as you like. The IDE generates the Java code that creates the GUI. In addition, you can typically add event-handling code for a particular component by double-clicking the component. Some design tools also allow you to use the layout managers described in this chapter and in Chapter 17.

Figure 11.38 summarizes the layout managers presented in this chapter. Other layout managers are discussed in Chapter 17.

Layout manager	Description
FlowLayout	Default for javax.swing.JPanel. Places components sequentially (left to right) in the order they were added. It is also possible to specify the order of the components by using the Container method add, which takes a Component and an integer index position as arguments.
BorderLayout	Default for JFrames (and other windows). Arranges the components into five areas: NORTH, SOUTH, EAST, WEST and CENTER.
GridLayout	Arranges the components into rows and columns.

Fig. 11.38 | Layout managers.

Look-and-Feel Observation 11.16

Most Java programming environments provide GUI design tools that help a programmer graphically design a GUI; the design tools then write the Java code to create the GUI. Such tools often provide greater control over the size, position and alignment of GUI components than do the built-in layout managers.

Look-and-Feel Observation 11.17

It is possible to set a Container's *layout to* null, *which indicates that no layout manager should be used. In a* Container *without a layout manager, the programmer must position and size the components in the given container and take care that, on resize events, all components are repositioned as necessary. A component's resize events can be processed by a* ComponentListener.

11.17.1 FlowLayout

FlowLayout is the simplest layout manager. GUI components are placed on a container from left to right in the order in which they are added to the container. When the edge of the container is reached, components continue to display on the next line. Class FlowLayout allows GUI components to be *left aligned*, *centered* (the default) and *right aligned*.

The application of Figs. 11.39–11.40 creates three JButton objects and adds them to the application, using a FlowLayout layout manager. The components are center aligned by default. When the user clicks **Left**, the alignment for the layout manager is changed to a left-aligned FlowLayout. When the user clicks **Right**, the alignment for the layout manager is changed to a right-aligned FlowLayout. When the user clicks **Center**, the alignment for the layout manager is changed to a center-aligned FlowLayout. Each button has its own event handler that is declared with an inner class that implements ActionListener. The sample output windows show each of the FlowLayout alignments. Also, the last sample output window shows the centered alignment after the window has been resized to a smaller width. Notice that the button **Right** flows onto a new line.

```
1   // Fig. 11.39: FlowLayoutFrame.java
2   // Demonstrating FlowLayout alignments.
3   import java.awt.FlowLayout;
4   import java.awt.Container;
5   import java.awt.event.ActionListener;
6   import java.awt.event.ActionEvent;
7   import javax.swing.JFrame;
8   import javax.swing.JButton;
9
10  public class FlowLayoutFrame extends JFrame
11  {
12     private JButton leftJButton; // button to set alignment left
13     private JButton centerJButton; // button to set alignment center
14     private JButton rightJButton; // button to set alignment right
15     private FlowLayout layout; // layout object
16     private Container container; // container to set layout
17
18     // set up GUI and register button listeners
19     public FlowLayoutFrame()
20     {
21        super( "FlowLayout Demo" );
22
23        layout = new FlowLayout(); // create FlowLayout
```

Fig. 11.39 | FlowLayout allows components to flow over multiple lines. (Part 1 of 3.)

```
24        container = getContentPane(); // get container to layout
25        setLayout( layout ); // set frame layout
26
27        // set up leftJButton and register listener
28        leftJButton = new JButton( "Left" ); // create Left button
29        add( leftJButton ); // add Left button to frame
30        leftJButton.addActionListener(
31
32           new ActionListener() // anonymous inner class
33           {
34              // process leftJButton event
35              public void actionPerformed( ActionEvent event )
36              {
37                 layout.setAlignment( FlowLayout.LEFT );
38
39                 // realign attached components
40                 layout.layoutContainer( container );
41              } // end method actionPerformed
42           } // end anonymous inner class
43        ); // end call to addActionListener
44
45        // set up centerJButton and register listener
46        centerJButton = new JButton( "Center" ); // create Center button
47        add( centerJButton ); // add Center button to frame
48        centerJButton.addActionListener(
49
50           new ActionListener() // anonymous inner class
51           {
52              // process centerJButton event
53              public void actionPerformed( ActionEvent event )
54              {
55                 layout.setAlignment( FlowLayout.CENTER );
56
57                 // realign attached components
58                 layout.layoutContainer( container );
59              } // end method actionPerformed
60           } // end anonymous inner class
61        ); // end call to addActionListener
62
63        // set up rightJButton and register listener
64        rightJButton = new JButton( "Right" ); // create Right button
65        add( rightJButton ); // add Right button to frame
66        rightJButton.addActionListener(
67
68           new ActionListener() // anonymous inner class
69           {
70              // process rightJButton event
71              public void actionPerformed( ActionEvent event )
72              {
73                 layout.setAlignment( FlowLayout.RIGHT );
74
```

Fig. 11.39 | FlowLayout allows components to flow over multiple lines. (Part 2 of 3.)

```
75                        // realign attached components
76                       layout.layoutContainer( container );
77                 } // end method actionPerformed
78             } // end anonymous inner class
79         ); // end call to addActionListener
80     } // end FlowLayoutFrame constructor
81 } // end class FlowLayoutFrame
```

Fig. 11.39 | FlowLayout allows components to flow over multiple lines. (Part 3 of 3.)

```
 1  // Fig. 11.40: FlowLayoutDemo.java
 2  // Testing FlowLayoutFrame.
 3  import javax.swing.JFrame;
 4
 5  public class FlowLayoutDemo
 6  {
 7      public static void main( String args[] )
 8      {
 9          FlowLayoutFrame flowLayoutFrame = new FlowLayoutFrame();
10          flowLayoutFrame.setDefaultCloseOperation( JFrame.EXIT_ON_CLOSE );
11          flowLayoutFrame.setSize( 300, 75 ); // set frame size
12          flowLayoutFrame.setVisible( true ); // display frame
13      } // end main
14  } // end class FlowLayoutDemo
```

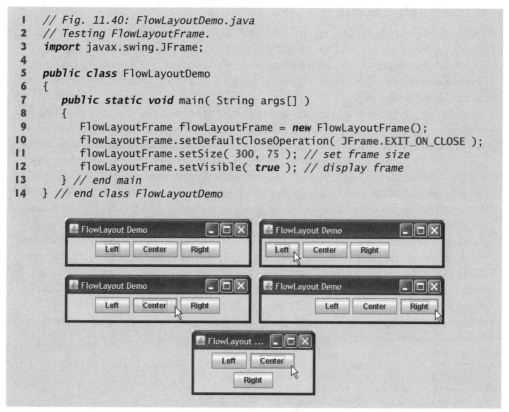

Fig. 11.40 | Test class for FlowLayoutFrame.

As seen previously, a container's layout is set with method setLayout of class Container. Line 25 sets the layout manager to the FlowLayout declared at line 23. Normally, the layout is set before any GUI components are added to a container.

Look-and-Feel Observation 11.18

Each container can have only one layout manager. Separate containers in the same application can use different layout managers.

Note in this example that each button's event handler is specified with a separate anonymous inner-class object (lines 30–43, 48–61 and 66–71, respectively). Each button's `actionPerformed` event handler executes two statements. For example, line 37 in method `actionPerformed` for button `left` uses `FlowLayout` method ***setAlignment*** to change the alignment for the `FlowLayout` to a left-aligned (***FlowLayout.LEFT***) Flow-Layout. Line 40 uses `LayoutManager` interface method ***layoutContainer*** (which is inherited by all layout managers) to specify that the `JFrame` should be rearranged based on the adjusted layout. According to which button was clicked, the `actionPerformed` method for each button sets the `FlowLayout`'s alignment to `FlowLayout.LEFT` (line 37), ***FlowLayout.CENTER*** (line 55) or ***FlowLayout.RIGHT*** (line 73).

11.17.2 BorderLayout

The `BorderLayout` layout manager (the default layout manager for a `JFrame`) arranges components into five regions: NORTH, SOUTH, EAST, WEST and CENTER. NORTH corresponds to the top of the container. Class `BorderLayout` extends `Object` and implements interface ***LayoutManager2*** (a subinterface of `LayoutManager` that adds several methods for enhanced layout processing).

A `BorderLayout` limits a `Container` to containing at most five components—one in each region. The component placed in each region can be a container to which other components are attached. The components placed in the NORTH and SOUTH regions extend horizontally to the sides of the container and are as tall as the components placed in those regions. The EAST and WEST regions expand vertically between the NORTH and SOUTH regions and are as wide as the components placed in those regions. The component placed in the CENTER region expands to fill all remaining space in the layout (which is the reason the `JTextArea` in Fig. 11.36 occupies the entire window). If all five regions are occupied, the entire container's space is covered by GUI components. If the NORTH or SOUTH region is not occupied, the GUI components in the EAST, CENTER and WEST regions expand vertically to fill the remaining space. If the EAST or WEST region is not occupied, the GUI component in the CENTER region expands horizontally to fill the remaining space. If the CENTER region is not occupied, the area is left empty—the other GUI components do not expand to fill the remaining space. The application of Figs. 11.41–11.42 demonstrates the BorderLayout layout manager by using five `JButton`s.

```
 1   // Fig. 11.41: BorderLayoutFrame.java
 2   // Demonstrating BorderLayout.
 3   import java.awt.BorderLayout;
 4   import java.awt.event.ActionListener;
 5   import java.awt.event.ActionEvent;
 6   import javax.swing.JFrame;
 7   import javax.swing.JButton;
 8
 9   public class BorderLayoutFrame extends JFrame implements ActionListener
10   {
11      private JButton buttons[]; // array of buttons to hide portions
12      private final String names[] = { "Hide North", "Hide South",
13         "Hide East", "Hide West", "Hide Center" };
14      private BorderLayout layout; // borderlayout object
15
```

Fig. 11.41 | BorderLayout containing five buttons. (Part 1 of 2.)

```
16      // set up GUI and event handling
17      public BorderLayoutFrame()
18      {
19         super( "BorderLayout Demo" );
20
21         layout = new BorderLayout( 5, 5 ); // 5 pixel gaps
22         setLayout( layout ); // set frame layout
23         buttons = new JButton[ names.length ]; // set size of array
24
25         // create JButtons and register listeners for them
26         for ( int count = 0; count < names.length; count++ )
27         {
28            buttons[ count ] = new JButton( names[ count ] );
29            buttons[ count ].addActionListener( this );
30         } // end for
31
32         add( buttons[ 0 ], BorderLayout.NORTH ); // add button to north
33         add( buttons[ 1 ], BorderLayout.SOUTH ); // add button to south
34         add( buttons[ 2 ], BorderLayout.EAST ); // add button to east
35         add( buttons[ 3 ], BorderLayout.WEST ); // add button to west
36         add( buttons[ 4 ], BorderLayout.CENTER ); // add button to center
37      } // end BorderLayoutFrame constructor
38
39      // handle button events
40      public void actionPerformed( ActionEvent event )
41      {
42         // check event source and lay out content pane correspondingly
43         for ( JButton button : buttons )
44         {
45            if ( event.getSource() == button )
46               button.setVisible( false ); // hide button clicked
47            else
48               button.setVisible( true ); // show other buttons
49         } // end for
50
51         layout.layoutContainer( getContentPane() ); // lay out content pane
52      } // end method actionPerformed
53   } // end class BorderLayoutFrame
```

Fig. 11.41 | BorderLayout containing five buttons. (Part 2 of 2.)

```
1    // Fig. 11.42: BorderLayoutDemo.java
2    // Testing BorderLayoutFrame.
3    import javax.swing.JFrame;
4
5    public class BorderLayoutDemo
6    {
7       public static void main( String args[] )
8       {
9          BorderLayoutFrame borderLayoutFrame = new BorderLayoutFrame();
10         borderLayoutFrame.setDefaultCloseOperation( JFrame.EXIT_ON_CLOSE );
11         borderLayoutFrame.setSize( 300, 200 ); // set frame size
```

Fig. 11.42 | Test class for BorderLayoutFrame. (Part 1 of 2.)

```
12          borderLayoutFrame.setVisible( true ); // display frame
13      } // end main
14  } // end class BorderLayoutDemo
```

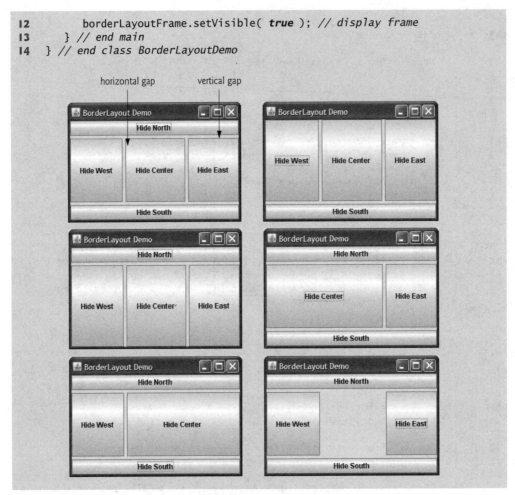

Fig. 11.42 | Test class for `BorderLayoutFrame`. (Part 2 of 2.)

Line 21 of Fig. 11.41 creates a `BorderLayout`. The constructor arguments specify the number of pixels between components that are arranged horizontally (*horizontal gap space*) and between components that are arranged vertically (*vertical gap space*), respectively. The default is one pixel of gap space horizontally and vertically. Line 22 uses method `setLayout` to set the content pane's layout to `layout`.

We add `Component`s to a `BorderLayout` with a version of `Container` method `add` that takes two arguments—the `Component` to add and the region in which it should appear. For example, line 32 specifies that `buttons[ 0 ]` should appear in the `NORTH` region. The components can be added in any order, but only one component should be added to each region.

Look-and-Feel Observation 11.19

If no region is specified when adding a `Component` to a `BorderLayout`, the layout manager assumes that the `Component` should be added to region `BorderLayout.CENTER`.

Common Programming Error 11.6

When more than one component is added to a region in a BorderLayout, only the last compo-nent added to that region will be displayed. There is no error that indicates this problem.

Note that class BorderLayoutFrame implements ActionListener directly in this example, so the BorderLayoutFrame will handle the events of the JButtons. For this reason, line 29 passes the this reference to the addActionListener method of each JButton. When the user clicks a particular JButton in the layout, method action-Performed (lines 40–52) executes. The enhanced for statement at lines 43–49 uses an if...else to hide the particular JButton that generated the event. Method *setVisible* (inherited into JButton from class Component) is called with a false argument (line 46) to hide the JButton. If the current JButton in the array is not the one that generated the event, method setVisible is called with a true argument (line 48) to ensure that the JButton is displayed on the screen. Line 51 uses LayoutManager method layoutCon-tainer to recalculate the layout of the content pane. Notice in the screen captures of Fig. 11.41 that certain regions in the BorderLayout change shape as JButtons are hidden and displayed in other regions. Try resizing the application window to see how the various regions resize based on the window's width and height. For more complex layouts, group components in JPanels, each with a separate layout manager. Place the JPanels on the JFrame using either the default BorderLayout or some other layout.

11.17.3 GridLayout

The *GridLayout* layout manager divides the container into a grid so that components can be placed in rows and columns. Class GridLayout inherits directly from class Object and implements interface LayoutManager. Every Component in a GridLayout has the same width and height. Components are added to a GridLayout starting at the top-left cell of the grid and proceeding left to right until the row is full. Then the process continues left to right on the next row of the grid, and so on. The application of Figs. 11.43–11.44 dem-onstrates the GridLayout layout manager by using six JButtons.

```java
 1   // Fig. 11.43: GridLayoutFrame.java
 2   // Demonstrating GridLayout.
 3   import java.awt.GridLayout;
 4   import java.awt.Container;
 5   import java.awt.event.ActionListener;
 6   import java.awt.event.ActionEvent;
 7   import javax.swing.JFrame;
 8   import javax.swing.JButton;
 9
10   public class GridLayoutFrame extends JFrame implements ActionListener
11   {
12      private JButton buttons[]; // array of buttons
13      private final String names[] =
14         { "one", "two", "three", "four", "five", "six" };
15      private boolean toggle = true; // toggle between two layouts
16      private Container container; // frame container
```

Fig. 11.43 | GridLayout containing six buttons. (Part 1 of 2.)

```
17    private GridLayout gridLayout1; // first gridlayout
18    private GridLayout gridLayout2; // second gridlayout
19
20    // no-argument constructor
21    public GridLayoutFrame()
22    {
23       super( "GridLayout Demo" );
24       gridLayout1 = new GridLayout( 2, 3, 5, 5 ); // 2 by 3; gaps of 5
25       gridLayout2 = new GridLayout( 3, 2 ); // 3 by 2; no gaps
26       container = getContentPane(); // get content pane
27       setLayout( gridLayout1 ); // set JFrame layout
28       buttons = new JButton[ names.length ]; // create array of JButtons
29
30       for ( int count = 0; count < names.length; count++ )
31       {
32          buttons[ count ] = new JButton( names[ count ] );
33          buttons[ count ].addActionListener( this ); // register listener
34          add( buttons[ count ] ); // add button to JFrame
35       } // end for
36    } // end GridLayoutFrame constructor
37
38    // handle button events by toggling between layouts
39    public void actionPerformed( ActionEvent event )
40    {
41       if ( toggle )
42          container.setLayout( gridLayout2 ); // set layout to second
43       else
44          container.setLayout( gridLayout1 ); // set layout to first
45
46       toggle = !toggle; // set toggle to opposite value
47       container.validate(); // re-lay out container
48    } // end method actionPerformed
49 } // end class GridLayoutFrame
```

Fig. 11.43 | GridLayout containing six buttons. (Part 2 of 2.)

```
1  // Fig. 11.44: GridLayoutDemo.java
2  // Testing GridLayoutFrame.
3  import javax.swing.JFrame;
4
5  public class GridLayoutDemo
6  {
7     public static void main( String args[] )
8     {
9        GridLayoutFrame gridLayoutFrame = new GridLayoutFrame();
10       gridLayoutFrame.setDefaultCloseOperation( JFrame.EXIT_ON_CLOSE );
11       gridLayoutFrame.setSize( 300, 200 ); // set frame size
12       gridLayoutFrame.setVisible( true ); // display frame
13    } // end main
14 } // end class GridLayoutDemo
```

Fig. 11.44 | Test class for GridLayoutFrame. (Part 1 of 2.)

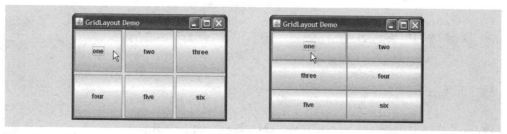

Fig. 11.44 | Test class for `GridLayoutFrame`. (Part 2 of 2.)

Lines 24–25 create two `GridLayout` objects. The `GridLayout` constructor used at line 24 specifies a `GridLayout` with 2 rows, 3 columns, 5 pixels of horizontal-gap space between Components in the grid and 5 pixels of vertical-gap space between Components in the grid. The `GridLayout` constructor used at line 25 specifies a `GridLayout` with 3 rows and 2 columns that uses the default gap space (1 pixel).

The `JButton` objects in this example initially are arranged using `gridLayout1` (set for the content pane at line 27 with method `setLayout`). The first component is added to the first column of the first row. The next component is added to the second column of the first row, and so on. When a `JButton` is pressed, method `actionPerformed` (lines 39–48) is called. Every call to `actionPerformed` toggles the layout between `gridLayout2` and `gridLayout1`, using `boolean` variable `toggle` to determine the next layout to set.

Line 47 shows another way to reformat a container for which the layout has changed. Container method *validate* recomputes the container's layout based on the current layout manager for the `Container` and the current set of displayed GUI components.

11.18 Using Panels to Manage More Complex Layouts

Complex GUIs (like Fig. 11.1) require that each component be placed in an exact location. They often consist of multiple panels, with each panel's components arranged in a specific layout. Class `JPanel` extends `JComponent` and `JComponent` extends class `Container`, so every `JPanel` is a `Container`. Thus, every `JPanel` may have components, including other panels, attached to it with `Container` method add. The application of Figs. 11.45–11.46 demonstrates how a `JPanel` can be used to create a more complex layout in which several `JButtons` are placed in the SOUTH region of a `BorderLayout`.

```
 1   // Fig. 11.45: PanelFrame.java
 2   // Using a JPanel to help lay out components.
 3   import java.awt.GridLayout;
 4   import java.awt.BorderLayout;
 5   import javax.swing.JFrame;
 6   import javax.swing.JPanel;
 7   import javax.swing.JButton;
 8
 9   public class PanelFrame extends JFrame
10   {
```

Fig. 11.45 | JPanel with five JButtons in a GridLayout attached to the SOUTH region of a BorderLayout. (Part 1 of 2.)

```
11        private JPanel buttonJPanel; // panel to hold buttons
12        private JButton buttons[]; // array of buttons
13
14        // no-argument constructor
15        public PanelFrame()
16        {
17           super( "Panel Demo" );
18           buttons = new JButton[ 5 ]; // create buttons array
19           buttonJPanel = new JPanel(); // set up panel
20           buttonJPanel.setLayout( new GridLayout( 1, buttons.length ) );
21
22           // create and add buttons
23           for ( int count = 0; count < buttons.length; count++ )
24           {
25              buttons[ count ] = new JButton( "Button " + ( count + 1 ) );
26              buttonJPanel.add( buttons[ count ] ); // add button to panel
27           } // end for
28
29           add( buttonJPanel, BorderLayout.SOUTH ); // add panel to JFrame
30        } // end PanelFrame constructor
31     } // end class PanelFrame
```

Fig. 11.45 | JPanel with five JButtons in a GridLayout attached to the SOUTH region of a BorderLayout. (Part 2 of 2.)

```
1     // Fig. 11.46: PanelDemo.java
2     // Testing PanelFrame.
3     import javax.swing.JFrame;
4
5     public class PanelDemo extends JFrame
6     {
7        public static void main( String args[] )
8        {
9           PanelFrame panelFrame = new PanelFrame();
10          panelFrame.setDefaultCloseOperation( JFrame.EXIT_ON_CLOSE );
11          panelFrame.setSize( 450, 200 ); // set frame size
12          panelFrame.setVisible( true ); // display frame
13       } // end main
14    } // end class PanelDemo
```

Fig. 11.46 | Test class for PanelFrame.

After JPanel buttonPanel is declared in line 11 and created at line 19, line 20 sets buttonPanel's layout to a GridLayout of one row and five columns (there are five JButtons in array buttons). Lines 23–27 add the five JButtons in array buttons to the JPanel in the loop. Line 26 adds the buttons directly to the JPanel—class JPanel does not have a content pane, unlike a JFrame. Line 29 uses the default BorderLayout to add buttonPanel to the SOUTH region. Note that the SOUTH region is as tall as the buttons on buttonPanel. A JPanel is sized to the components it contains. As more components are added, the JPanel grows (according to the restrictions of its layout manager) to accommodate the components. Resize the window to see how the layout manager affects the size of the JButtons.

11.19 JTextArea

A *JTextArea* provides an area for manipulating multiple lines of text. Like class JText-Field, JTextArea is a subclass of JTextComponent, which declares common methods for JTextFields, JTextAreas and several other text-based GUI components.

The application in Figs. 11.47–11.48 demonstrates JTextAreas. One JTextArea displays text that the user can select. The other JTextArea is uneditable and is used to display the text the user selected in the first JTextArea. Unlike JTextFields, JTextAreas do not have action events. As with multiple-selection JLists (Section 11.12), an external event from another GUI component indicates when to process the text in a JTextArea. For example, when typing an e-mail message, you normally click a **Send** button to send the text of the message to the recipient. Similarly, when editing a document in a word processor, you normally save the file by selecting a **Save** or **Save As...** menu item. In this program, the button **Copy >>>** generates the external event that copies the selected text in the left JTextArea and displays it in the right JTextArea.

```
1   // Fig. 11.47: TextAreaFrame.java
2   // Copying selected text from one textarea to another.
3   import java.awt.event.ActionListener;
4   import java.awt.event.ActionEvent;
5   import javax.swing.Box;
6   import javax.swing.JFrame;
7   import javax.swing.JTextArea;
8   import javax.swing.JButton;
9   import javax.swing.JScrollPane;
10
11  public class TextAreaFrame extends JFrame
12  {
13     private JTextArea textArea1; // displays demo string
14     private JTextArea textArea2; // highlighted text is copied here
15     private JButton copyJButton; // initiates copying of text
16
17     // no-argument constructor
18     public TextAreaFrame()
19     {
20        super( "TextArea Demo" );
21        Box box = Box.createHorizontalBox(); // create box
22        String demo = "This is a demo string to\n" +
23           "illustrate copying text\nfrom one textarea to \n" +
24           "another textarea using an\nexternal event\n";
```

Fig. 11.47 | Copying selected text from one JTextArea to another. (Part 1 of 2.)

```
25
26        textArea1 = new JTextArea( demo, 10, 15 ); // create textarea1
27        box.add( new JScrollPane( textArea1 ) ); // add scrollpane
28
29        copyJButton = new JButton( "Copy >>>" ); // create copy button
30        box.add( copyJButton ); // add copy button to box
31        copyJButton.addActionListener(
32
33           new ActionListener() // anonymous inner class
34           {
35              // set text in textArea2 to selected text from textArea1
36              public void actionPerformed( ActionEvent event )
37              {
38                 textArea2.setText( textArea1.getSelectedText() );
39              } // end method actionPerformed
40           } // end anonymous inner class
41        ); // end call to addActionListener
42
43        textArea2 = new JTextArea( 10, 15 ); // create second textarea
44        textArea2.setEditable( false ); // disable editing
45        box.add( new JScrollPane( textArea2 ) ); // add scrollpane
46
47        add( box ); // add box to frame
48     } // end TextAreaFrame constructor
49  } // end class TextAreaFrame
```

Fig. 11.47 | Copying selected text from one `JTextArea` to another. (Part 2 of 2.)

```
1   // Fig. 11.48: TextAreaDemo.java
2   // Copying selected text from one textarea to another.
3   import javax.swing.JFrame;
4
5   public class TextAreaDemo
6   {
7      public static void main( String args[] )
8      {
9         TextAreaFrame textAreaFrame = new TextAreaFrame();
10        textAreaFrame.setDefaultCloseOperation( JFrame.EXIT_ON_CLOSE );
11        textAreaFrame.setSize( 425, 200 ); // set frame size
12        textAreaFrame.setVisible( true ); // display frame
13     } // end main
14  } // end class TextAreaDemo
```

Fig. 11.48 | Test class for `TextAreaFrame`.

In the constructor (lines 18–48), line 21 creates a *Box* container (package javax.swing) to organize the GUI components. Box is a subclass of Container that uses a *BoxLayout* layout manager (discussed in detail in Section 17.9) to arrange the GUI components either horizontally or vertically. Box's static method *createHorizontalBox* creates a Box that arranges components from left to right in the order that they are attached.

Lines 26 and 43 create JTextAreas textArea1 and textArea2. Line 26 uses JTextArea's three-argument constructor, which takes a String representing the initial text and two ints specifying that the JTextArea has 10 rows and 15 columns. Line 43 uses JTextArea's two-argument constructor, specifying that the JTextArea has 10 rows and 15 columns. Line 26 specifies that demo should be displayed as the default JTextArea content. A JTextArea does not provide scrollbars if it cannot display its complete contents. So, line 27 creates a *JScrollPane* object, initializes it with textArea1 and attaches it to container box. By default, horizontal and vertical scrollbars will appear as necessary in a JScrollPane.

Lines 29–41 create JButton object copyButton with the label "Copy >>>", add copyButton to container box and register the event handler for copyButton's ActionEvent. This button provides the external event that determines when the program should copy the selected text in textArea1 to textArea2. When the user clicks copyButton, line 38 in actionPerformed indicates that method *getSelectedText* (inherited into JTextArea from JTextComponent) should return the selected text from textArea1. The user selects text by dragging the mouse over the desired text to highlight it. Method setText changes the text in textArea2 to the string returned by getSelectedText.

Lines 43–45 create textArea2, set its editable property to false and add it to container box. Line 47 adds box to the JFrame. Recall from Section 11.17 that the default layout of a JFrame is a BorderLayout and that the add method by default attaches its argument to the CENTER of the BorderLayout.

It is sometimes desirable, when text reaches the right side of a JTextArea, to have the text wrap to the next line. This is referred to as *line wrapping*. By default, JTextArea does not wrap lines.

Look-and-Feel Observation 11.20

*To provide line wrapping functionality for a JTextArea, invoke JTextArea method **setLineWrap** with a true argument.*

JScrollPane Scrollbar Policies

This example uses a JScrollPane to provide scrolling for a JTextArea. By default, JScrollPane displays scrollbars only if they are required. You can set the horizontal and vertical *scrollbar policies* of a JScrollPane when it is constructed. If a program has a reference to a JScrollPane, the program can use JScrollPane methods *setHorizontalScrollBarPolicy* and *setVerticalScrollBarPolicy* to change the scrollbar policies at any time. Class JScrollPane declares the constants

```
JScrollPane.VERTICAL_SCROLLBAR_ALWAYS
JScrollPane.HORIZONTAL_SCROLLBAR_ALWAYS
```

to indicate that a scrollbar should always appear, constants

```
JScrollPane.VERTICAL_SCROLLBAR_AS_NEEDED
JScrollPane.HORIZONTAL_SCROLLBAR_AS_NEEDED
```

to indicate that a scrollbar should appear only if necessary (the defaults) and constants

```
JScrollPane.VERTICAL_SCROLLBAR_NEVER
JScrollPane.HORIZONTAL_SCROLLBAR_NEVER
```

to indicate that a scrollbar should never appear. If the horizontal scrollbar policy is set to JScrollPane.HORIZONTAL_SCROLLBAR_NEVER, a JTextArea attached to the JScrollPane will automatically wrap lines.

11.20 Wrap-Up

In this chapter, you learned many GUI components and how to implement event handling. You also learned about nested classes, inner classes and anonymous inner classes. You saw the special relationship between an inner-class object and an object of its top-level class. You learned how to use JOptionPane dialogs to obtain text input from the user and how to display messages to the user. You also learned how to create applications that execute in their own windows. We discussed class JFrame and components that enable a user to interact with an application. We also showed you how to display text and images to the user. You learned how to customize JPanels to create custom drawing areas, which you'll use extensively in the next chapter. You saw how to organize components on a window using layout managers and how to creating more complex GUIs by using JPanels to organize components. Finally, you learned about the JTextArea component in which a user can enter text and an application can display text. In Chapter 17, GUI Components: Part 2, you'll learn about more advanced GUI components, such as sliders, menus and more complex layout managers. In the next chapter, you'll learn how to add graphics to your GUI application. Graphics allow you to draw shapes and text with colors and styles.

Graphics and Java 2D™

> *One picture is worth ten thousand words.*
> —Chinese proverb

> *Treat nature in terms of the cylinder, the sphere, the cone, all in perspective.*
> —Paul Cézanne

> *Colors, like features, follow the changes of the emotions.*
> —Pablo Picasso

> *Nothing ever becomes real till it is experienced—even a proverb is no proverb to you till your life has illustrated it.*
> —John Keats

OBJECTIVES

In this chapter you'll learn:

- To understand graphics contexts and graphics objects.
- To manipulate colors.
- To manipulate fonts.
- To use methods of class `Graphics` to draw lines, rectangles, rectangles with rounded corners, three-dimensional rectangles, ovals, arcs and polygons.
- To use methods of class `Graphics2D` from the `Java 2D` API to draw lines, rectangles, rectangles with rounded corners, ellipses, arcs and general paths.
- To specify `Paint` and `Stroke` characteristics of shapes displayed with `Graphics2D`.

Outline

12.1 Introduction

12.2 Graphics Contexts and Graphics Objects

12.3 Color Control

12.4 Font Control

12.5 Drawing Lines, Rectangles and Ovals

12.6 Drawing Arcs

12.7 Drawing Polygons and Polylines

12.8 Java 2D API

12.9 Wrap-Up

12.1 Introduction

In this chapter, we overview several of Java's capabilities for drawing two-dimensional shapes, controlling colors and controlling fonts. One of Java's initial appeals was its support for graphics that enabled programmers to visually enhance their applications. Java now contains many more sophisticated drawing capabilities as part of the Java 2D™ API. This chapter begins with an introduction to many of Java's original drawing capabilities. Next we present several of the more powerful Java 2D capabilities, such as controlling the style of lines used to draw shapes and the way shapes are filled with color and patterns.

Figure 12.1 shows a portion of the Java class hierarchy that includes several of the basic graphics classes and Java 2D API classes and interfaces covered in this chapter. Class ***Color*** contains methods and constants for manipulating colors. Class JComponent contains method paintComponent, which is used to draw graphics on a component. Class ***Font*** contains methods and constants for manipulating fonts. Class ***FontMetrics*** contains methods for obtaining font information. Class Graphics contains methods for drawing strings, lines, rectangles and other shapes. Class ***Graphics2D***, which extends class Graphics, is used for drawing with the Java 2D API. Class ***Polygon*** contains methods for creating polygons. The bottom half of the figure lists several classes and interfaces from the Java 2D API. Class ***BasicStroke*** helps specify the drawing characteristics of lines. Classes ***GradientPaint*** and ***TexturePaint*** help specify the characteristics for filling shapes with colors or patterns. Classes GeneralPath, Line2D, Arc2D, Ellipse2D, Rectangle2D and RoundRectangle2D represent several Java 2D shapes. [*Note:* We begin the chapter by discussing Java's original graphics capabilities, then move on to the Java 2D API. Now, the classes that were part of Java's original graphics capabilities are considered to be part of the Java 2D API.]

To begin drawing in Java, we must first understand Java's *coordinate system* (Fig. 12.2), which is a scheme for identifying every point on the screen. By default, the upper-left corner of a GUI component (e.g., a window) has the coordinates (0, 0). A coordinate pair is composed of an *x-coordinate* (the *horizontal coordinate*) and a *y-coordinate* (the *vertical coordinate*). The *x*-coordinate is the horizontal distance moving right from the left of the screen. The *y*-coordinate is the vertical distance moving down from the top of the screen. The *x-axis* describes every horizontal coordinate, and the *y-axis* every vertical coordinate. The coordinates are used to indicate where graphics should be displayed on a screen. Coordinate units are measured in *pixels* (which stands for "picture element"). A pixel is a display monitor's smallest unit of resolution.

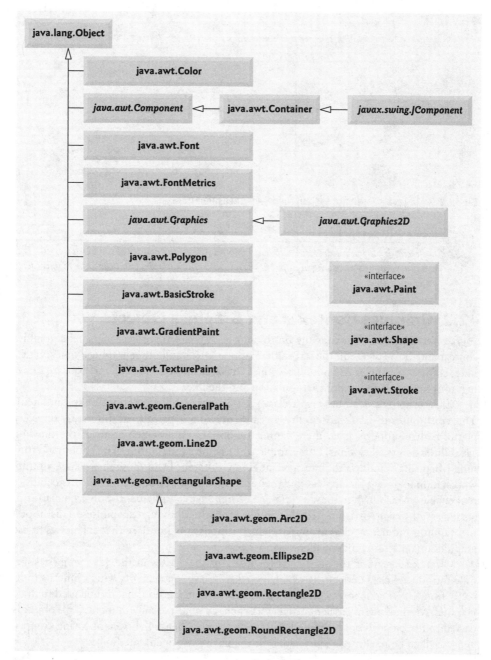

Fig. 12.1 | Classes and interfaces used in this chapter from Java's original graphics capabilities and from the Java 2D API. [*Note:* Class `Object` appears here because it is the superclass of the Java class hierarchy. Also, `abstract` classes appear in italics.]

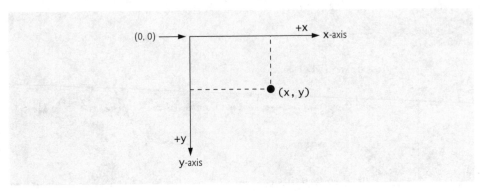

Fig. 12.2 | Java coordinate system. Units are measured in pixels.

 Portability Tip 12.1

Different display monitors have different resolutions (i.e., the density of the pixels varies). This can cause graphics to appear in different sizes on different monitors or on the same monitor with different settings.

12.2 Graphics Contexts and Graphics Objects

A *graphics context* enables drawing on the screen. A Graphics object manages a graphics context and draws pixels on the screen that represent text and other graphical objects (e.g., lines, ellipses, rectangles and other polygons). Graphics objects contain methods for drawing, font manipulation, color manipulation and the like.

Class Graphics is an abstract class (i.e., Graphics objects cannot be instantiated). This contributes to Java's portability. Because drawing is performed differently on every platform that supports Java, there cannot be only one implementation of the drawing capabilities across all systems. For example, the graphics capabilities that enable a PC running Microsoft Windows to draw a rectangle are different from those that enable a Linux workstation to draw a rectangle—and they are both different from the graphics capabilities that enable a Macintosh to draw a rectangle. When Java is implemented on each platform, a subclass of Graphics is created that implements the drawing capabilities. This implementation is hidden by class Graphics, which supplies the interface that enables us to use graphics in a platform-independent manner.

Class Component is the superclass for many of the classes in the java.awt package. (We introduced class Component in Chapter 11.) Class JComponent, which inherits indirectly from class Component, contains a paintComponent method that can be used to draw graphics. Method paintComponent takes a Graphics object as an argument. This object is passed to the paintComponent method by the system when a lightweight Swing component needs to be repainted. The header for the paintComponent method is

```
public void paintComponent( Graphics g )
```

Parameter g receives a reference to an instance of the system-specific subclass that Graphics extends. The preceding method header should look familiar to you—it is the same one we used in some of the applications in Chapter 11. Actually, class JComponent is a superclass of JPanel. Many capabilities of class JPanel are inherited from class JComponent.

Method `paintComponent` is seldom called directly by the programmer because drawing graphics is an event-driven process. When a GUI application executes, the application container calls method `paintComponent` for each lightweight component as the GUI is displayed. For `paintComponent` to be called again, an event must occur (such as covering and uncovering the component with another window).

If the programmer needs to have `paintComponent` execute (i.e., if the programmer wants to update the graphics drawn on the Swing component), a call is made to method *repaint*, which is inherited by all `JComponents` indirectly from class `Component` (package `java.awt`). Method `repaint` is frequently called to request a call to method `paintComponent`. The header for `repaint` is

  public void `repaint()`

12.3 Color Control

Class `Color` declares methods and constants for manipulating colors in a Java program. The predeclared color constants are summarized in Fig. 12.3, and several color methods and constructors are summarized in Fig. 12.4. Note that two of the methods in Fig. 12.4 are `Graphics` methods that are specific to colors.

Every color is created from a red, a green and a blue component. Together these components are called *RGB values*. All three RGB components can be integers in the range from 0 to 255, or they can be floating-point values in the range 0.0 to 1.0. The first RGB component specifies the amount of red, the second the amount of green and the third the amount of blue. The larger the RGB value, the greater the amount of that particular color. Java enables the programmer to choose from 256 × 256 × 256 (approximately 16.7

Color constant	RGB value
public final static Color RED	255, 0, 0
public final static Color GREEN	0, 255, 0
public final static Color BLUE	0, 0, 255
public final static Color ORANGE	255, 200, 0
public final static Color PINK	255, 175, 175
public final static Color CYAN	0, 255, 255
public final static Color MAGENTA	255, 0, 255
public final static Color YELLOW	255, 255, 0
public final static Color BLACK	0, 0, 0
public final static Color WHITE	255, 255, 255
public final static Color GRAY	128, 128, 128
public final static Color LIGHT_GRAY	192, 192, 192
public final static Color DARK_GRAY	64, 64, 64

Fig. 12.3 | Color constants and their RGB values.

Method	Description

Color constructors and methods

`public Color( int r, int g, int b )`

Creates a color based on red, green and blue components expressed as integers from 0 to 255.

`public Color( float r, float g, float b )`

Creates a color based on red, green and blue components expressed as floating-point values from 0.0 to 1.0.

`public int getRed()`

Returns a value between 0 and 255 representing the red content.

`public int getGreen()`

Returns a value between 0 and 255 representing the green content.

`public int getBlue()`

Returns a value between 0 and 255 representing the blue content.

Graphics methods for manipulating Colors

`public Color getColor()`

Returns `Color` object representing current color for the graphics context.

`public void setColor( Color c )`

Sets the current color for drawing with the graphics context.

Fig. 12.4 | `Color` methods and color-related `Graphics` methods .

million) colors. Not all computers are capable of displaying all these colors. The computer will display the closest color it can.

Two of class `Color`'s constructors are shown in Fig. 12.4—one that takes three `int` arguments and one that takes three `float` arguments, with each argument specifying the amount of red, green and blue. The `int` values must be in the range 0–255 and the `float` values must be in the range 0.0–1.0. The new `Color` object will have the specified amounts of red, green and blue. `Color` methods ***getRed***, ***getGreen*** and ***getBlue*** return integer values from 0 to 255 representing the amount of red, green and blue, respectively. `Graphics` method ***getColor*** returns a `Color` object representing the current drawing color. `Graphics` method ***setColor*** sets the current drawing color.

Figures 12.5–12.6 demonstrates several methods from Fig. 12.4 by drawing filled rectangles and strings in several different colors. When the application begins execution, class `ColorJPanel`'s `paintComponent` method (lines 10–37 of Fig. 12.5) is called to paint the window. Line 17 uses `Graphics` method `setColor` to set the drawing color. Method `setColor` receives a `Color` object. The expression `new Color( 255, 0, 0 )` creates a new `Color` object that represents red (red value 255, and 0 for the green and blue values). Line 18 uses `Graphics` method ***fillRect*** to draw a filled rectangle in the current color. Method `fillRect` draws a rectangle based on its four arguments. The first two integer values represent the upper-left *x*-coordinate and upper-left *y*-coordinate, where the `Graphics` object begins drawing the rectangle. The third and fourth arguments are nonnegative integers that represent the width and the height of the rectangle in pixels, respectively. A rectangle drawn using method fillRect is filled by the current color of the Graphics object.

```java
1   // Fig. 12.5: ColorJPanel.java
2   // Demonstrating Colors.
3   import java.awt.Graphics;
4   import java.awt.Color;
5   import javax.swing.JPanel;
6
7   public class ColorJPanel extends JPanel
8   {
9      // draw rectangles and Strings in different colors
10      public void paintComponent( Graphics g )
11      {
12         super.paintComponent( g ); // call superclass's paintComponent
13
14         this.setBackground( Color.WHITE );
15
16         // set new drawing color using integers
17         g.setColor( new Color( 255, 0, 0 ) );
18         g.fillRect( 15, 25, 100, 20 );
19         g.drawString( "Current RGB: " + g.getColor(), 130, 40 );
20
21         // set new drawing color using floats
22         g.setColor( new Color( 0.50f, 0.75f, 0.0f ) );
23         g.fillRect( 15, 50, 100, 20 );
24         g.drawString( "Current RGB: " + g.getColor(), 130, 65 );
25
26         // set new drawing color using static Color objects
27         g.setColor( Color.BLUE );
28         g.fillRect( 15, 75, 100, 20 );
29         g.drawString( "Current RGB: " + g.getColor(), 130, 90 );
30
31         // display individual RGB values
32         Color color = Color.MAGENTA;
33         g.setColor( color );
34         g.fillRect( 15, 100, 100, 20 );
35         g.drawString( "RGB values: " + color.getRed() + ", " +
36            color.getGreen() + ", " + color.getBlue(), 130, 115 );
37      } // end method paintComponent
38   } // end class ColorJPanel
```

Fig. 12.5 | Color changed for drawing.

```java
1   // Fig. 12.6: ShowColors.java
2   // Demonstrating Colors.
3   import javax.swing.JFrame;
4
5   public class ShowColors
6   {
```

Fig. 12.6 | Creating JFrame to display colors on JPanel. (Part 1 of 2.)

```
7      // execute application
8      public static void main( String args[] )
9      {
10        // create frame for ColorJPanel
11        JFrame frame = new JFrame( "Using colors" );
12        frame.setDefaultCloseOperation( JFrame.EXIT_ON_CLOSE );
13
14        ColorJPanel colorJPanel = new ColorJPanel(); // create ColorJPanel
15        frame.add( colorJPanel ); // add colorJPanel to frame
16        frame.setSize( 400, 180 ); // set frame size
17        frame.setVisible( true ); // display frame
18     } // end main
19  } // end class ShowColors
```

Fig. 12.6 | Creating JFrame to display colors on JPanel. (Part 2 of 2.)

Line 19 uses Graphics method **drawString** to draw a String in the current color. The expression g.getColor() retrieves the current color from the Graphics object. The returned Color object is concatenated with string "Current RGB: ", resulting in an implicit call to class Color's toString method. The String representation of a Color contains the class name and package (java.awt.Color), and the red, green and blue values.

Look-and-Feel Observation 12.1

Everyone perceives colors differently. Choose your colors carefully to ensure that your application is readable, both for people who can perceive color and for people who are color blind. Try to avoid using many different colors in close proximity.

Lines 22–24 and lines 27–29 perform the same tasks again. Line 22 uses the Color constructor with three float arguments to create a dark green color (0.50f for red, 0.75f for green and 0.0f for blue). Note the syntax of the values. The letter f appended to a floating-point literal indicates that the literal should be treated as type float. Recall that by default, floating-point literals are treated as type double.

Line 27 sets the current drawing color to one of the predeclared Color constants (Color.BLUE). The Color constants are static, so they are created when class Color is loaded into memory at execution time.

The statement in lines 35–36 makes calls to Color methods getRed, getGreen and getBlue on the predeclared Color.MAGENTA constant. Method main of class ShowColors (lines 8–18 of Fig. 12.6) creates the JFrame that will contain a ColorJPanel object where the colors will be displayed.

Software Engineering Observation 12.1

To change the color, you must create a new Color object (or use one of the predeclared Color constants). Like String objects, Color objects are immutable (not modifiable).

Package `javax.swing` provides class ***JColorChooser*** to enable application users to select colors. Figures 12.7–12.8 demonstrate a JColorChooser dialog. When you click the **Change Color** button, a JColorChooser dialog appears. When you select a color and press the dialog's **OK** button, the background color of the application window changes.

```java
1   // Fig. 12.7: ShowColors2JFrame.java
2   // Choosing colors with JColorChooser.
3   import java.awt.BorderLayout;
4   import java.awt.Color;
5   import java.awt.event.ActionEvent;
6   import java.awt.event.ActionListener;
7   import javax.swing.JButton;
8   import javax.swing.JFrame;
9   import javax.swing.JColorChooser;
10  import javax.swing.JPanel;
11
12  public class ShowColors2JFrame extends JFrame
13  {
14     private JButton changeColorJButton;
15     private Color color = Color.LIGHT_GRAY;
16     private JPanel colorJPanel;
17
18     // set up GUI
19     public ShowColors2JFrame()
20     {
21        super( "Using JColorChooser" );
22
23        // create JPanel for display color
24        colorJPanel = new JPanel();
25        colorJPanel.setBackground( color );
26
27        // set up changeColorJButton and register its event handler
28        changeColorJButton = new JButton( "Change Color" );
29        changeColorJButton.addActionListener(
30
31           new ActionListener() // anonymous inner class
32           {
33              // display JColorChooser when user clicks button
34              public void actionPerformed( ActionEvent event )
35              {
36                 color = JColorChooser.showDialog(
37                    ShowColors2JFrame.this, "Choose a color", color );
38
39                 // set default color, if no color is returned
40                 if ( color == null )
41                    color = Color.LIGHT_GRAY;
42
43                 // change content pane's background color
44                 colorJPanel.setBackground( color );
45              } // end method actionPerformed
46           } // end anonymous inner class
47        ); // end call to addActionListener
```

Fig. 12.7 | JColorChooser dialog. (Part 1 of 2.)

```
48
49          add( colorJPanel, BorderLayout.CENTER ); // add colorJPanel
50          add( changeColorJButton, BorderLayout.SOUTH ); // add button
51
52          setSize( 400, 130 ); // set frame size
53          setVisible( true ); // display frame
54       } // end ShowColor2JFrame constructor
55    } // end class ShowColors2JFrame
```

Fig. 12.7 | JColorChooser dialog. (Part 2 of 2.)

```
1    // Fig. 12.8: ShowColors2.java
2    // Choosing colors with JColorChooser.
3    import javax.swing.JFrame;
4
5    public class ShowColors2
6    {
7       // execute application
8       public static void main( String args[] )
9       {
10          ShowColors2JFrame application = new ShowColors2JFrame();
11          application.setDefaultCloseOperation( JFrame.EXIT_ON_CLOSE );
12       } // end main
13    } // end class ShowColors2
```

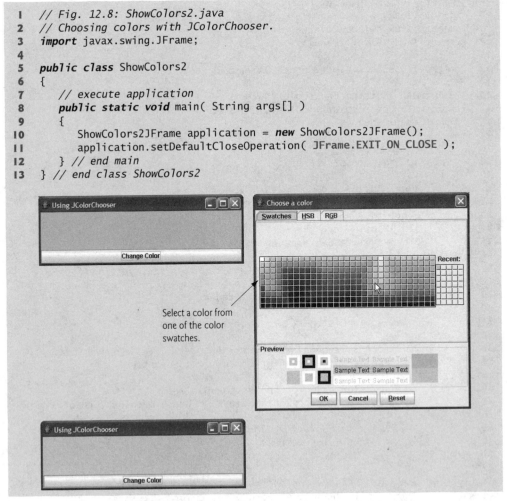

Select a color from
one of the color
swatches.

Fig. 12.8 | Choosing colors with JColorChooser.

Class JColorChooser provides static method ***showDialog***, which creates a JColor-Chooser object, attaches it to a dialog box and displays the dialog. Lines 36–37 of Fig. 12.7

invoke this method to display the color chooser dialog. Method showDialog returns the selected Color object, or null if the user presses **Cancel** or closes the dialog without pressing **OK**. The method takes three arguments—a reference to its parent Component, a String to display in the title bar of the dialog and the initial selected Color for the dialog. The parent component is a reference to the window from which the dialog is displayed (in this case the JFrame, with the reference name frame). The dialog will be centered on the parent. If the parent is null, the dialog is centered on the screen. While the color chooser dialog is on the screen, the user cannot interact with the parent component. This type of dialog is called a *modal dialog* (discussed in Chapter 17, GUI Components: Part 2).

After the user selects a color, lines 40–41 determine whether color is null, and, if so, set color to Color.LIGHT_GRAY. Line 44 invokes method setBackground to change the background color of the JPanel. Method setBackground is one of the many Component methods that can be used on most GUI components. Note that the user can continue to use the **Change Color** button to change the background color of the application. Figure 12.8 contains method main, which executes the program.

The second screen capture of Fig. 12.8 demonstrates the default JColorChooser dialog that allows the user to select a color from a variety of *color swatches*. Note that there are actually three tabs across the top of the dialog—**Swatches**, **HSB** and **RGB**. These represent three different ways to select a color. The **HSB** tab allows you to select a color based on *hue*, *saturation* and *brightness*—values that are used to define the amount of light in a color. We do not discuss HSB values. For more information on hue, saturation and brightness, visit whatis.techtarget.com/definition/0,,sid9_gci212262,00.html. The **RGB** tab allows you to select a color by using sliders to select the red, green and blue components. The **HSB** and **RGB** tabs are shown in Fig. 12.9.

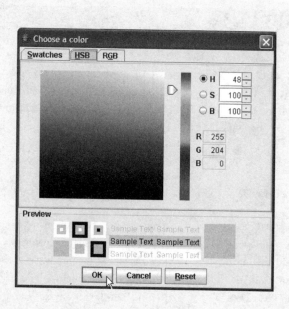

Fig. 12.9 | **HSB** and **RGB** tabs of the JColorChooser dialog. (Part 1 of 2.)

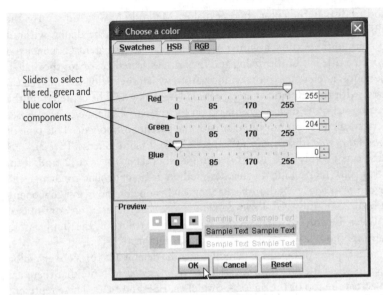

Sliders to select the red, green and blue color components

Fig. 12.9 | **HSB** and **RGB** tabs of the JColorChooser dialog. (Part 2 of 2.)

12.4 Font Control

This section introduces methods and constants for font control. Most font methods and font constants are part of class Font. Some methods of class Font and class Graphics are summarized in Fig. 12.10.

Method or constant	Description
Font constants, constructors and methods	
public final static int PLAIN	A constant representing a plain font style.
public final static int BOLD	A constant representing a bold font style.
public final static int ITALIC	A constant representing an italic font style.
public Font(String name, int style, int size)	Creates a Font object with the specified font name, style and size.
public int getStyle()	Returns an integer value indicating the current font style.
public int getSize()	Returns an integer value indicating the current font size.
public String getName()	Returns the current font name as a string.
public String getFamily()	Returns the font's family name as a string.
public boolean isPlain()	Returns true if the font is plain, else false.
public boolean isBold()	Returns true if the font is bold, else false.
public boolean isItalic()	Returns true if the font is italic, else false.

Fig. 12.10 | Font-related methods and constants. (Part 1 of 2.)

Method or constant	Description
Graphics methods for manipulating Fonts	
`public Font getFont()`	Returns a Font object reference representing the current font.
`public void setFont( Font f )`	Sets the current font to the font, style and size specified by the Font object reference f.

Fig. 12.10 | Font-related methods and constants. (Part 2 of 2.)

Class Font's constructor takes three arguments—the *font name, font style* and *font size*. The font name is any font currently supported by the system on which the program is running, such as standard Java fonts Monospaced, SansSerif and Serif. The font style is *Font.PLAIN*, *Font.ITALIC* or *Font.BOLD* (each is a static field of class Font). Font styles can be used in combination (e.g., Font.ITALIC + Font.BOLD). The font size is measured in points. A *point* is 1/72 of an inch. Graphics method *setFont* sets the current drawing font—the font in which text will be displayed—to its Font argument.

Portability Tip 12.2

The number of fonts varies greatly across systems. Java provides five font names—Serif, Monospaced, SansSerif, Dialog and DialogInput—that can be used on all Java platforms. The Java runtime environment (JRE) on each platform maps these logical font names to actual fonts installed on the platform. The actual fonts used may vary by platform.

The application of Figs. 12.11–12.12 displays text in four different fonts, with each font in a different size. Figure 12.11 uses the Font constructor to initialize Font objects (in lines 16, 20, 24 and 29) that are each passed to Graphics method setFont to change the drawing font. Each call to the Font constructor passes a font name (Serif, Monospaced or SansSerif) as a string, a font style (Font.PLAIN, Font.ITALIC or Font.BOLD) and a font size. Once Graphics method setFont is invoked, all text displayed following the call will appear in the new font until the font is changed. Each font's information is displayed in lines 17, 21, 25 and 30–31 using method drawString. Note that the coordinate passed to drawString corresponds to the lower-left corner of the baseline of the font. Line 28 changes the drawing color to red, so the next string displayed appears in red. Lines 30–31 display information about the final Font object. Method *getFont* of class Graphics returns a Font object representing the current font. Method *getName* returns the current font name as a string. Method *getSize* returns the font size in points.

```
1   // Fig. 12.11: FontJPanel.java
2   // Display strings in different fonts and colors.
3   import java.awt.Font;
4   import java.awt.Color;
5   import java.awt.Graphics;
6   import javax.swing.JPanel;
7
```

Fig. 12.11 | Graphics method setFont changes the drawing font. (Part 1 of 2.)

```
8   public class FontJPanel extends JPanel
9   {
10      // display Strings in different fonts and colors
11      public void paintComponent( Graphics g )
12      {
13          super.paintComponent( g ); // call superclass's paintComponent
14
15          // set font to Serif (Times), bold, 12pt and draw a string
16          g.setFont( new Font( "Serif", Font.BOLD, 12 ) );
17          g.drawString( "Serif 12 point bold.", 20, 50 );
18
19          // set font to Monospaced (Courier), italic, 24pt and draw a string
20          g.setFont( new Font( "Monospaced", Font.ITALIC, 24 ) );
21          g.drawString( "Monospaced 24 point italic.", 20, 70 );
22
23          // set font to SansSerif (Helvetica), plain, 14pt and draw a string
24          g.setFont( new Font( "SansSerif", Font.PLAIN, 14 ) );
25          g.drawString( "SansSerif 14 point plain.", 20, 90 );
26
27          // set font to Serif (Times), bold/italic, 18pt and draw a string
28          g.setColor( Color.RED );
29          g.setFont( new Font( "Serif", Font.BOLD + Font.ITALIC, 18 ) );
30          g.drawString( g.getFont().getName() + " " + g.getFont().getSize() +
31              " point bold italic.", 20, 110 );
32      } // end method paintComponent
33  } // end class FontJPanel
```

Fig. 12.11 | Graphics method setFont changes the drawing font. (Part 2 of 2.)

Figure 12.12 contains method main, which creates a JFrame. We add a FontJPanel object to this JFrame (line 15), which displays the graphics created in Fig. 12.11.

Software Engineering Observation 12.2

To change the font, you must create a new Font object. Font objects are immutable—class Font has no set methods to change the characteristics of the current font.

```
1   // Fig. 12.12: Fonts.java
2   // Using fonts.
3   import javax.swing.JFrame;
4
5   public class Fonts
6   {
7       // execute application
8       public static void main( String args[] )
9       {
10          // create frame for FontJPanel
11          JFrame frame = new JFrame( "Using fonts" );
12          frame.setDefaultCloseOperation( JFrame.EXIT_ON_CLOSE );
13
14          FontJPanel fontJPanel = new FontJPanel(); // create FontJPanel
```

Fig. 12.12 | Creating a JFrame to display fonts. (Part 1 of 2.)

```
15        frame.add( fontJPanel ); // add fontJPanel to frame
16        frame.setSize( 420, 170 ); // set frame size
17        frame.setVisible( true ); // display frame
18    } // end main
19 } // end class Fonts
```

> **Using fonts**
>
> **Serif 12 point bold.**
> *Monospaced 24 point italic.*
> SansSerif 14 point plain.
> ***Serif 18 point bold italic.***

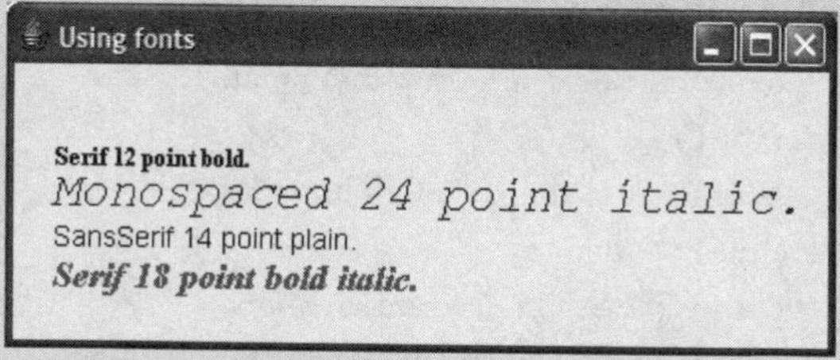

Fig. 12.12 | Creating a JFrame to display fonts. (Part 2 of 2.)

Font Metrics

Sometimes it is necessary to get information about the current drawing font, such as its name, style and size. Several Font methods used to get font information are summarized in Fig. 12.10. Method **getStyle** returns an integer value representing the current style. The integer value returned is either Font.PLAIN, Font.ITALIC, Font.BOLD or the combination of Font.ITALIC and Font.BOLD. Method **getFamily** returns the name of the font family to which the current font belongs. The name of the font family is platform specific. Font methods are also available to test the style of the current font, and these too are summarized in Fig. 12.10. Methods **isPlain**, **isBold** and **isItalic** return true if the current font style is plain, bold or italic, respectively.

Sometimes precise information about a font's metrics must be known—such as **height**, **descent** (the amount a character dips below the baseline), **ascent** (the amount a character rises above the baseline) and **leading** (the difference between the descent of one line of text and the ascent of the line of text below it—that is, the interline spacing). Figure 12.13 illustrates some of the common *font metrics*.

Class **FontMetrics** declares several methods for obtaining font metrics. These methods and Graphics method **getFontMetrics** are summarized in Fig. 12.14. The application of Figs. 12.15–12.16 uses the methods of Fig. 12.14 to obtain font metric information for two fonts.

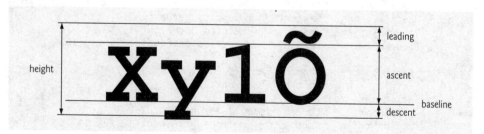

Fig. 12.13 | Font metrics.

Method	Description
FontMetrics methods	
public int getAscent()	
	Returns the ascent of a font in points.
public int getDescent()	
	Returns the descent of a font in points.
public int getLeading()	
	Returns the leading of a font in points.
public int getHeight()	
	Returns the height of a font in points.
Graphics methods for getting a Font's FontMetrics	
public FontMetrics getFontMetrics()	
	Returns the FontMetrics object for the current drawing Font.
public FontMetrics getFontMetrics(Font f)	
	Returns the FontMetrics object for the specified Font argument.

Fig. 12.14 | FontMetrics and Graphics methods for obtaining font metrics.

```
1   // Fig. 12.15: MetricsJPanel.java
2   // FontMetrics and Graphics methods useful for obtaining font metrics.
3   import java.awt.Font;
4   import java.awt.FontMetrics;
5   import java.awt.Graphics;
6   import javax.swing.JPanel;
7
8   public class MetricsJPanel extends JPanel
9   {
10     // display font metrics
11     public void paintComponent( Graphics g )
12     {
13        super.paintComponent( g ); // call superclass's paintComponent
14
15        g.setFont( new Font( "SansSerif", Font.BOLD, 12 ) );
16        FontMetrics metrics = g.getFontMetrics();
17        g.drawString( "Current font: " + g.getFont(), 10, 40 );
18        g.drawString( "Ascent: " + metrics.getAscent(), 10, 55 );
19        g.drawString( "Descent: " + metrics.getDescent(), 10, 70 );
20        g.drawString( "Height: " + metrics.getHeight(), 10, 85 );
21        g.drawString( "Leading: " + metrics.getLeading(), 10, 100 );
22
23        Font font = new Font( "Serif", Font.ITALIC, 14 );
24        metrics = g.getFontMetrics( font );
25        g.setFont( font );
26        g.drawString( "Current font: " + font, 10, 130 );
27        g.drawString( "Ascent: " + metrics.getAscent(), 10, 145 );
```

Fig. 12.15 | Font metrics. (Part 1 of 2.)

```
28              g.drawString( "Descent: " + metrics.getDescent(), 10, 160 );
29              g.drawString( "Height: " + metrics.getHeight(), 10, 175 );
30              g.drawString( "Leading: " + metrics.getLeading(), 10, 190 );
31          } // end method paintComponent
32      } // end class MetricsJPanel
```

Fig. 12.15 | Font metrics. (Part 2 of 2.)

```
1   // Fig. 12.16: Metrics.java
2   // Displaying font metrics.
3   import javax.swing.JFrame;
4
5   public class Metrics
6   {
7       // execute application
8       public static void main( String args[] )
9       {
10          // create frame for MetricsJPanel
11          JFrame frame = new JFrame( "Demonstrating FontMetrics" );
12          frame.setDefaultCloseOperation( JFrame.EXIT_ON_CLOSE );
13
14          MetricsJPanel metricsJPanel = new MetricsJPanel();
15          frame.add( metricsJPanel ); // add metricsJPanel to frame
16          frame.setSize( 510, 250 ); // set frame size
17          frame.setVisible( true ); // display frame
18      } // end main
19  } // end class Metrics
```

Fig. 12.16 | Creating JFrame to display font metric information.

Line 15 of Fig. 12.15 creates and sets the current drawing font to a SansSerif, bold, 12-point font. Line 16 uses Graphics method getFontMetrics to obtain the FontMetrics object for the current font. Line 17 outputs the String representation of the Font returned by g.getFont(). Lines 18–21 use FontMetric methods to obtain the ascent, descent, height and leading for the font.

Line 23 creates a new Serif, italic, 14-point font. Line 24 uses a second version of Graphics method getFontMetrics, which accepts a Font argument and returns a corresponding FontMetrics object. Lines 27–30 obtain the ascent, descent, height and leading for the font. Note that the font metrics are slightly different for the two fonts.

12.5 Drawing Lines, Rectangles and Ovals

This section presents Graphics methods for drawing lines, rectangles and ovals. The methods and their parameters are summarized in Fig. 12.17. For each drawing method that requires a width and height parameter, the width and height must be nonnegative values. Otherwise, the shape will not display.

Method	Description
`public void drawLine( int x1, int y1, int x2, int y2 )`	
	Draws a line between the point (x1, y1) and the point (x2, y2).
`public void drawRect( int x, int y, int width, int height )`	
	Draws a rectangle of the specified width and height. The top-left corner of the rectangle has the coordinates (x, y). Only the outline of the rectangle is drawn using the Graphics object's color—the body of the rectangle is not filled with this color.
`public void fillRect( int x, int y, int width, int height )`	
	Draws a filled rectangle with the specified width and height. The top-left corner of the rectangle has the coordinates (x, y). The rectangle is filled with the Graphics object's color.
`public void clearRect( int x, int y, int width, int height )`	
	Draws a filled rectangle with the specified width and height in the current background color. The top-left corner of the rectangle has the coordinates (x, y). This method is useful if the programmer wants to remove a portion of an image.
`public void drawRoundRect( int x, int y, int width, int height, int arcWidth, int arcHeight )`	
	Draws a rectangle with rounded corners in the current color with the specified width and height. The arcWidth and arcHeight determine the rounding of the corners (see Fig. 12.20). Only the outline of the shape is drawn.
`public void fillRoundRect( int x, int y, int width, int height, int arcWidth, int arcHeight )`	
	Draws a filled rectangle with rounded corners in the current color with the specified width and height. The arcWidth and arcHeight determine the rounding of the corners (see Fig. 12.20).
`public void draw3DRect( int x, int y, int width, int height, boolean b )`	
	Draws a three-dimensional rectangle in the current color with the specified width and height. The top-left corner of the rectangle has the coordinates (x, y). The rectangle appears raised when b is true and lowered when b is false. Only the outline of the shape is drawn.
`public void fill3DRect( int x, int y, int width, int height, boolean b )`	
	Draws a filled three-dimensional rectangle in the current color with the specified width and height. The top-left corner of the rectangle has the coordinates (x, y). The rectangle appears raised when b is true and lowered when b is false.

Fig. 12.17 | Graphics methods that draw lines, rectangles and ovals. (Part 1 of 2.)

Method	Description
public void drawOval(int x, int y, int width, int height)	
	Draws an oval in the current color with the specified width and height. The bounding rectangle's top-left corner is at the coordinates (x, y). The oval touches all four sides of the bounding rectangle at the center of each side (see Fig. 12.21). Only the outline of the shape is drawn.
public void fillOval(int x, int y, int width, int height)	
	Draws a filled oval in the current color with the specified width and height. The bounding rectangle's top-left corner is at the coordinates (x, y). The oval touches all four sides of the bounding rectangle at the center of each side (see Fig. 12.21).

Fig. 12.17 | Graphics methods that draw lines, rectangles and ovals. (Part 2 of 2.)

The application of Figs. 12.18–12.19 demonstrates drawing a variety of lines, rectangles, three-dimensional rectangles, rounded rectangles and ovals.

```
1   // Fig. 12.18: LinesRectsOvalsJPanel.java
2   // Drawing lines, rectangles and ovals.
3   import java.awt.Color;
4   import java.awt.Graphics;
5   import javax.swing.JPanel;
6
7   public class LinesRectsOvalsJPanel extends JPanel
8   {
9      // display various lines, rectangles and ovals
10     public void paintComponent( Graphics g )
11     {
12        super.paintComponent( g ); // call superclass's paint method
13
14        this.setBackground( Color.WHITE );
15
16        g.setColor( Color.RED );
17        g.drawLine( 5, 30, 380, 30 );
18
19        g.setColor( Color.BLUE );
20        g.drawRect( 5, 40, 90, 55 );
21        g.fillRect( 100, 40, 90, 55 );
22
23        g.setColor( Color.CYAN );
24        g.fillRoundRect( 195, 40, 90, 55, 50, 50 );
25        g.drawRoundRect( 290, 40, 90, 55, 20, 20 );
26
27        g.setColor( Color.YELLOW );
28        g.draw3DRect( 5, 100, 90, 55, true );
29        g.fill3DRect( 100, 100, 90, 55, false );
30
```

Fig. 12.18 | Drawing lines, rectangles and ovals. (Part 1 of 2.)

```
31         g.setColor( Color.MAGENTA );
32         g.drawOval( 195, 100, 90, 55 );
33         g.fillOval( 290, 100, 90, 55 );
34      } // end method paintComponent
35   } // end class LinesRectsOvalsJPanel
```

Fig. 12.18 | Drawing lines, rectangles and ovals. (Part 2 of 2.)

```
 1   // Fig. 12.19: LinesRectsOvals.java
 2   // Drawing lines, rectangles and ovals.
 3   import java.awt.Color;
 4   import javax.swing.JFrame;
 5
 6   public class LinesRectsOvals
 7   {
 8      // execute application
 9      public static void main( String args[] )
10      {
11         // create frame for LinesRectsOvalsJPanel
12         JFrame frame =
13            new JFrame( "Drawing lines, rectangles and ovals" );
14         frame.setDefaultCloseOperation( JFrame.EXIT_ON_CLOSE );
15
16         LinesRectsOvalsJPanel linesRectsOvalsJPanel =
17            new LinesRectsOvalsJPanel();
18         linesRectsOvalsJPanel.setBackground( Color.WHITE );
19         frame.add( linesRectsOvalsJPanel ); // add panel to frame
20         frame.setSize( 400, 210 ); // set frame size
21         frame.setVisible( true ); // display frame
22      } // end main
23   } // end class LinesRectsOvals
```

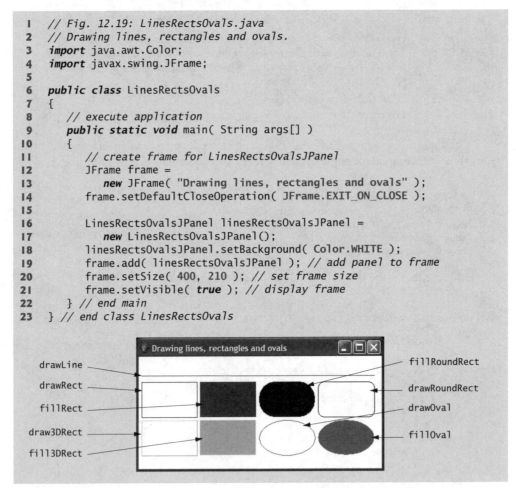

Fig. 12.19 | Creating JFrame to display lines, rectangles and ovals.

In Fig. 12.18, line 17 draws a red line, line 20 draws an empty blue rectangle and line 21 draws a filled blue rectangle. Methods **fillRoundRect** (line 24) and **drawRoundRect** (line 25) draw rectangles with rounded corners. Their first two arguments specify the coordinates of the upper-left corner of the *bounding rectangle*—the area in which the rounded rectangle will be drawn. Note that the upper-left corner coordinates are not the edge of the rounded rectangle, but the coordinates where the edge would be if the rectangle had square corners. The third and fourth arguments specify the width and height of the rectangle. The last two arguments determine the horizontal and vertical diameters of the arc (i.e., the arc width and arc height) used to represent the corners.

Figure 12.20 labels the arc width, arc height, width and height of a rounded rectangle. Using the same value for the arc width and arc height produces a quarter-circle at each corner. When the arc width, arc height, width and height have the same values, the result is a circle. If the values for width and height are the same and the values of arcWidth and arcHeight are 0, the result is a square.

Methods **draw3DRect** (line 28) and **fill3DRect** (line 29) take the same arguments. The first two arguments specify the top-left corner of the rectangle. The next two arguments specify the width and height of the rectangle, respectively. The last argument determines whether the rectangle is *raised* (true) or *lowered* (false). The three-dimensional effect of draw3DRect appears as two edges of the rectangle in the original color and two edges in a slightly darker color. The three-dimensional effect of fill3DRect appears as two edges of the rectangle in the original drawing color and the fill and other two edges in a slightly darker color. Raised rectangles have the original drawing color edges at the top and left of the rectangle. Lowered rectangles have the original drawing color edges at the bottom and right of the rectangle. The three-dimensional effect is difficult to see in some colors.

Methods **drawOval** and **fillOval** (lines 32–33) take the same four arguments. The first two arguments specify the top-left coordinate of the bounding rectangle that contains the oval. The last two arguments specify the width and height of the bounding rectangle, respectively. Figure 12.21 shows an oval bounded by a rectangle. Note that the oval touches the center of all four sides of the bounding rectangle. (The bounding rectangle is not displayed on the screen.)

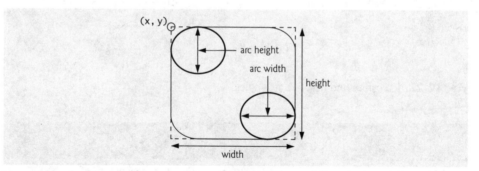

Fig. 12.20 | Arc width and arc height for rounded rectangles.

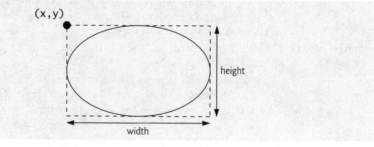

Fig. 12.21 | Oval bounded by a rectangle.

12.6 Drawing Arcs

An *arc* is drawn as a portion of an oval. Arc angles are measured in degrees. Arcs *sweep* (i.e., move along a curve) from a *starting angle* by the number of degrees specified by their *arc angle*. The starting angle indicates in degrees where the arc begins. The arc angle specifies the total number of degrees through which the arc sweeps. Figure 12.22 illustrates two arcs. The left set of axes shows an arc sweeping from zero degrees to approximately 110 degrees. Arcs that sweep in a counterclockwise direction are measured in *positive degrees*. The set of axes on the right shows an arc sweeping from zero degrees to approximately –110 degrees. Arcs that sweep in a clockwise direction are measured in *negative degrees*. Note the dashed boxes around the arcs in Fig. 12.22. When drawing an arc, we specify a bounding rectangle for an oval. The arc will sweep along part of the oval. Graphics methods *drawArc* and *fillArc* for drawing arcs are summarized in Fig. 12.23.

The application of Fig. 12.24–Fig. 12.25 demonstrates the arc methods of Fig. 12.23. The application draws six arcs (three unfilled and three filled). To illustrate the bounding rectangle that helps determine where the arc appears, the first three arcs are displayed inside a red rectangle that has the same x, y, width and height arguments as the arcs.

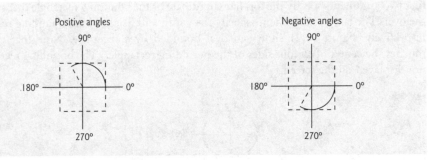

Fig. 12.22 | Positive and negative arc angles.

Method	Description
`public void drawArc( int x, int y, int width, int height,` `    int startAngle, int arcAngle )`	
	Draws an arc relative to the bounding rectangle's top-left x- and y-coordinates with the specified width and height. The arc segment is drawn starting at startAngle and sweeps arcAngle degrees.
`public void fillArc( int x, int y, int width, int height,` `    int startAngle, int arcAngle )`	
	Draws a filled arc (i.e., a sector) relative to the bounding rectangle's top-left x- and y-coordinates with the specified width and height. The arc segment is drawn starting at startAngle and sweeps arcAngle degrees.

Fig. 12.23 | Graphics methods for drawing arcs.

```
 1   // Fig. 12.24: ArcsJPanel.java
 2   // Drawing arcs.
 3   import java.awt.Color;
 4   import java.awt.Graphics;
 5   import javax.swing.JPanel;
 6
 7   public class ArcsJPanel extends JPanel
 8   {
 9      // draw rectangles and arcs
10      public void paintComponent( Graphics g )
11      {
12         super.paintComponent( g ); // call superclass's paintComponent
13
14         // start at 0 and sweep 360 degrees
15         g.setColor( Color.RED );
16         g.drawRect( 15, 35, 80, 80 );
17         g.setColor( Color.BLACK );
18         g.drawArc( 15, 35, 80, 80, 0, 360 );
19
20         // start at 0 and sweep 110 degrees
21         g.setColor( Color.RED );
22         g.drawRect( 100, 35, 80, 80 );
23         g.setColor( Color.BLACK );
24         g.drawArc( 100, 35, 80, 80, 0, 110 );
25
26         // start at 0 and sweep -270 degrees
27         g.setColor( Color.RED );
28         g.drawRect( 185, 35, 80, 80 );
29         g.setColor( Color.BLACK );
30         g.drawArc( 185, 35, 80, 80, 0, -270 );
31
32         // start at 0 and sweep 360 degrees
33         g.fillArc( 15, 120, 80, 40, 0, 360 );
34
35         // start at 270 and sweep -90 degrees
36         g.fillArc( 100, 120, 80, 40, 270, -90 );
37
38         // start at 0 and sweep -270 degrees
39         g.fillArc( 185, 120, 80, 40, 0, -270 );
40      } // end method paintComponent
41   } // end class ArcsJPanel
```

Fig. 12.24 | Arcs displayed with drawArc and fillArc.

```
 1   // Fig. 12.25: DrawArcs.java
 2   // Drawing arcs.
 3   import javax.swing.JFrame;
 4
 5   public class DrawArcs
 6   {
```

Fig. 12.25 | Creating JFrame to display arcs. (Part 1 of 2.)

```
7      // execute application
8      public static void main( String args[] )
9      {
10        // create frame for ArcsJPanel
11        JFrame frame = new JFrame( "Drawing Arcs" );
12        frame.setDefaultCloseOperation( JFrame.EXIT_ON_CLOSE );
13
14        ArcsJPanel arcsJPanel = new ArcsJPanel(); // create ArcsJPanel
15        frame.add( arcsJPanel ); // add arcsJPanel to frame
16        frame.setSize( 300, 210 ); // set frame size
17        frame.setVisible( true ); // display frame
18     } // end main
19  } // end class DrawArcs
```

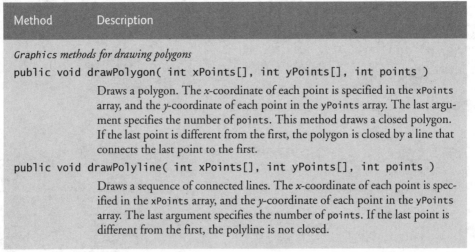

Fig. 12.25 | Creating `JFrame` to display arcs. (Part 2 of 2.)

12.7 Drawing Polygons and Polylines

Polygons are closed multisided shapes composed of straight-line segments. *Polylines* are sequences of connected points. Figure 12.26 discusses methods for drawing polygons and polylines. Note that some methods require a **Polygon** object (package java.awt). Class Polygon's constructors are also described in Fig. 12.26. The application of Figs. 12.27–12.28 draws polygons and polylines.

Method	Description
Graphics methods for drawing polygons	
public void drawPolygon(int xPoints[], int yPoints[], int points)	
	Draws a polygon. The *x*-coordinate of each point is specified in the xPoints array, and the *y*-coordinate of each point in the yPoints array. The last argument specifies the number of points. This method draws a closed polygon. If the last point is different from the first, the polygon is closed by a line that connects the last point to the first.
public void drawPolyline(int xPoints[], int yPoints[], int points)	
	Draws a sequence of connected lines. The *x*-coordinate of each point is specified in the xPoints array, and the *y*-coordinate of each point in the yPoints array. The last argument specifies the number of points. If the last point is different from the first, the polyline is not closed.

Fig. 12.26 | `Graphics` methods for polygons and class `Polygon` methods. (Part 1 of 2.)

Method	Description
`public void drawPolygon( Polygon p )`	
	Draws the specified polygon.
`public void fillPolygon( int xPoints[], int yPoints[], int points )`	
	Draws a filled polygon. The *x*-coordinate of each point is specified in the xPoints array, and the *y*-coordinate of each point in the yPoints array. The last argument specifies the number of points. This method draws a closed polygon. If the last point is different from the first, the polygon is closed by a line that connects the last point to the first.
`public void fillPolygon( Polygon p )`	
	Draws the specified filled polygon. The polygon is closed.
Polygon constructors and methods	
`public Polygon()`	
	Constructs a new polygon object. The polygon does not contain any points.
`public Polygon( int xValues[], int yValues[], int numberOfPoints )`	
	Constructs a new polygon object. The polygon has numberOfPoints sides, with each point consisting of an *x*-coordinate from xValues and a *y*-coordinate from yValues.
`public void addPoint( int x, int y )`	
	Adds pairs of *x*- and *y*-coordinates to the Polygon.

Fig. 12.26 | `Graphics` methods for polygons and class `Polygon` methods. (Part 2 of 2.)

```
 1   // Fig. 12.27: PolygonsJPanel.java
 2   // Drawing polygons.
 3   import java.awt.Graphics;
 4   import java.awt.Polygon;
 5   import javax.swing.JPanel;
 6
 7   public class PolygonsJPanel extends JPanel
 8   {
 9      // draw polygons and polylines
10      public void paintComponent( Graphics g )
11      {
12         super.paintComponent( g ); // call superclass's paintComponent
13
14         // draw polygon with Polygon object
15         int xValues[] = { 20, 40, 50, 30, 20, 15 };
16         int yValues[] = { 50, 50, 60, 80, 80, 60 };
17         Polygon polygon1 = new Polygon( xValues, yValues, 6 );
18         g.drawPolygon( polygon1 );
19
20         // draw polylines with two arrays
```

Fig. 12.27 | Polygons displayed with `drawPolygon` and `fillPolygon`. (Part 1 of 2.)

```
21            int xValues2[] = { 70, 90, 100, 80, 70, 65, 60 };
22            int yValues2[] = { 100, 100, 110, 110, 130, 110, 90 };
23            g.drawPolyline( xValues2, yValues2, 7 );
24
25            // fill polygon with two arrays
26            int xValues3[] = { 120, 140, 150, 190 };
27            int yValues3[] = { 40, 70, 80, 60 };
28            g.fillPolygon( xValues3, yValues3, 4 );
29
30            // draw filled polygon with Polygon object
31            Polygon polygon2 = new Polygon();
32            polygon2.addPoint( 165, 135 );
33            polygon2.addPoint( 175, 150 );
34            polygon2.addPoint( 270, 200 );
35            polygon2.addPoint( 200, 220 );
36            polygon2.addPoint( 130, 180 );
37            g.fillPolygon( polygon2 );
38         } // end method paintComponent
39    } // end class PolygonsJPanel
```

Fig. 12.27 | Polygons displayed with drawPolygon and fillPolygon. (Part 2 of 2.)

Lines 15–16 of Fig. 12.27 create two int arrays and use them to specify the points for Polygon polygon1. The Polygon constructor call in line 17 receives array xValues, which contains the *x*-coordinate of each point; array yValues, which contains the *y*-coordinate of each point and 6 (the number of points in the polygon). Line 18 displays polygon1 by passing it as an argument to Graphics method ***drawPolygon***.

Lines 21–22 create two int arrays and use them to specify the points for a series of connected lines. Array xValues2 contains the *x*-coordinate of each point and array yValues2 the *y*-coordinate of each point. Line 23 uses Graphics method ***drawPolyline*** to display the series of connected lines specified with the arguments xValues2, yValues2 and 7 (the number of points).

Lines 26–27 create two int arrays and use them to specify the points of a polygon. Array xValues3 contains the *x*-coordinate of each point and array yValues3 the *y*-coordinate of each point. Line 28 displays a polygon by passing to Graphics method ***fillPolygon*** the two arrays (xValues3 and yValues3) and the number of points to draw (4).

```
1    // Fig. 12.28: DrawPolygons.java
2    // Drawing polygons.
3    import javax.swing.JFrame;
4
5    public class DrawPolygons
6    {
7       // execute application
8       public static void main( String args[] )
9       {
10         // create frame for PolygonsJPanel
11         JFrame frame = new JFrame( "Drawing Polygons" );
```

Fig. 12.28 | Creating JFrame to display polygons. (Part 1 of 2.)

```
12          frame.setDefaultCloseOperation( JFrame.EXIT_ON_CLOSE );
13
14          PolygonsJPanel polygonsJPanel = new PolygonsJPanel();
15          frame.add( polygonsJPanel ); // add polygonsJPanel to frame
16          frame.setSize( 280, 270 ); // set frame size
17          frame.setVisible( true ); // display frame
18      } // end main
19  } // end class DrawPolygons
```

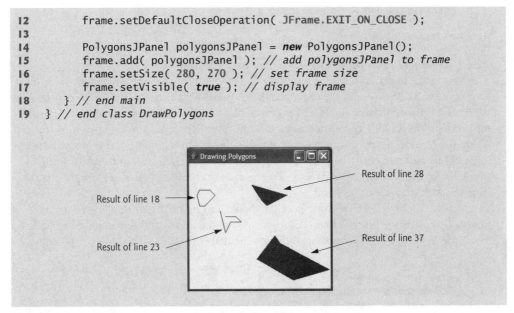

Fig. 12.28 | Creating JFrame to display polygons. (Part 2 of 2.)

 Common Programming Error 12.1

An ArrayIndexOutOfBoundsException is thrown if the number of points specified in the third argument to method drawPolygon or method fillPolygon is greater than the number of elements in the arrays of coordinates that specify the polygon to display.

Line 31 of Fig. 12.27 creates Polygon polygon2 with no points. Lines 32–36 use Polygon method ***addPoint*** to add pairs of *x*- and *y*-coordinates to the Polygon. Line 37 displays Polygon polygon2 by passing it to Graphics method fillPolygon.

12.8 Java 2D API

The *Java 2D API* provides advanced two-dimensional graphics capabilities for programmers who require detailed and complex graphical manipulations. The API includes features for processing line art, text and images in packages java.awt, java.awt.image, java.awt.color, java.awt.font, java.awt.geom, java.awt.print and java.awt.image.renderable. The capabilities of the API are far too broad to cover in this textbook. For an overview of the capabilities, see the Java 2D demo (located in your JDK's demo\jfc\Java2D directory) or visit the website java.sun.com/products/java-media/2D/index.html. In this section, we overview several Java 2D capabilities.

Drawing with the Java 2D API is accomplished with a ***Graphics2D*** reference (package java.awt). Graphics2D is an abstract subclass of class Graphics, so it has all the graphics capabilities demonstrated earlier in this chapter. In fact, the actual object used to draw in every paintComponent method is an instance of a subclass of Graphics2D that is passed to method paintComponent and accessed via the superclass Graphics. To access Graphics2D capabilities, we must cast the Graphics reference (g) passed to paintComponent into a Graphics2D reference with a statement such as

```
Graphics2D g2d = ( Graphics2D ) g;
```

The next two examples use this technique.

Lines, Rectangles, Round Rectangles, Arcs and Ellipses

The next example demonstrates several Java 2D shapes from package java.awt.geom, including *Line2D.Double*, *Rectangle2D.Double*, *RoundRectangle2D.Double*, *Arc2D.Double* and *Ellipse2D.Double*. Note the syntax of each class name. Each of these classes represents a shape with dimensions specified as double-precision floating-point values. There is a separate version of each represented with single-precision floating-point values (e.g., *Ellipse2D.Float*). In each case, Double is a static nested class of the class specified to the left of the dot (e.g., Ellipse2D). To use the static nested class, we simply qualify its name with the outer class name.

In Figs. 12.29–12.30, we draw Java 2D shapes and modify their drawing characteristics, such as changing line thickness, filling shapes with patterns and drawing dashed lines. These are just a few of the many capabilities provided by Java 2D.

```
 1   // Fig. 12.29: ShapesJPanel.java
 2   // Demonstrating some Java 2D shapes.
 3   import java.awt.Color;
 4   import java.awt.Graphics;
 5   import java.awt.BasicStroke;
 6   import java.awt.GradientPaint;
 7   import java.awt.TexturePaint;
 8   import java.awt.Rectangle;
 9   import java.awt.Graphics2D;
10   import java.awt.geom.Ellipse2D;
11   import java.awt.geom.Rectangle2D;
12   import java.awt.geom.RoundRectangle2D;
13   import java.awt.geom.Arc2D;
14   import java.awt.geom.Line2D;
15   import java.awt.image.BufferedImage;
16   import javax.swing.JPanel;
17
18   public class ShapesJPanel extends JPanel
19   {
20      // draw shapes with Java 2D API
21      public void paintComponent( Graphics g )
22      {
23         super.paintComponent( g ); // call superclass's paintComponent
24
25         Graphics2D g2d = ( Graphics2D ) g; // cast g to Graphics2D
26
27         // draw 2D ellipse filled with a blue-yellow gradient
28         g2d.setPaint( new GradientPaint( 5, 30, Color.BLUE, 35, 100,
29            Color.YELLOW, true ) );
30         g2d.fill( new Ellipse2D.Double( 5, 30, 65, 100 ) );
31
32         // draw 2D rectangle in red
33         g2d.setPaint( Color.RED );
```

Fig. 12.29 | Java 2D shapes. (Part 1 of 2.)

```
34          g2d.setStroke( new BasicStroke( 10.0f ) );
35          g2d.draw( new Rectangle2D.Double( 80, 30, 65, 100 ) );
36
37          // draw 2D rounded rectangle with a buffered background
38          BufferedImage buffImage = new BufferedImage( 10, 10,
39             BufferedImage.TYPE_INT_RGB );
40
41          // obtain Graphics2D from buffImage and draw on it
42          Graphics2D gg = buffImage.createGraphics();
43          gg.setColor( Color.YELLOW ); // draw in yellow
44          gg.fillRect( 0, 0, 10, 10 ); // draw a filled rectangle
45          gg.setColor( Color.BLACK );  // draw in black
46          gg.drawRect( 1, 1, 6, 6 ); // draw a rectangle
47          gg.setColor( Color.BLUE ); // draw in blue
48          gg.fillRect( 1, 1, 3, 3 ); // draw a filled rectangle
49          gg.setColor( Color.RED ); // draw in red
50          gg.fillRect( 4, 4, 3, 3 ); // draw a filled rectangle
51
52          // paint buffImage onto the JFrame
53          g2d.setPaint( new TexturePaint( buffImage,
54             new Rectangle( 10, 10 ) ) );
55          g2d.fill(
56             new RoundRectangle2D.Double( 155, 30, 75, 100, 50, 50 ) );
57
58          // draw 2D pie-shaped arc in white
59          g2d.setPaint( Color.WHITE );
60          g2d.setStroke( new BasicStroke( 6.0f ) );
61          g2d.draw(
62             new Arc2D.Double( 240, 30, 75, 100, 0, 270, Arc2D.PIE ) );
63
64          // draw 2D lines in green and yellow
65          g2d.setPaint( Color.GREEN );
66          g2d.draw( new Line2D.Double( 395, 30, 320, 150 ) );
67
68          // draw 2D line using stroke
69          float dashes[] = { 10 }; // specify dash pattern
70          g2d.setPaint( Color.YELLOW );
71          g2d.setStroke( new BasicStroke( 4, BasicStroke.CAP_ROUND,
72             BasicStroke.JOIN_ROUND, 10, dashes, 0 ) );
73          g2d.draw( new Line2D.Double( 320, 30, 395, 150 ) );
74       } // end method paintComponent
75    } // end class ShapesJPanel
```

Fig. 12.29 | Java 2D shapes. (Part 2 of 2.)

```
1    // Fig. 12.30: Shapes.java
2    // Demonstrating some Java 2D shapes.
3    import javax.swing.JFrame;
4
5    public class Shapes
6    {
```

Fig. 12.30 | Creating JFrame to display shapes. (Part 1 of 2.)

```
 7      // execute application
 8      public static void main( String args[] )
 9      {
10          // create frame for ShapesJPanel
11          JFrame frame = new JFrame( "Drawing 2D shapes" );
12          frame.setDefaultCloseOperation( JFrame.EXIT_ON_CLOSE );
13
14          // create ShapesJPanel
15          ShapesJPanel shapesJPanel = new ShapesJPanel();
16
17          frame.add( shapesJPanel ); // add shapesJPanel to frame
18          frame.setSize( 425, 200 ); // set frame size
19          frame.setVisible( true ); // display frame
20      } // end main
21  } // end class Shapes
```

Fig. 12.30 | Creating JFrame to display shapes. (Part 2 of 2.)

Line 25 of Fig. 12.29 casts the Graphics reference received by paintComponent to a Graphics2D reference and assigns it to g2d to allow access to the Java 2D features.

Ovals, Gradient Fills and Paint *Objects*

The first shape we draw is an oval filled with gradually changing colors. Lines 28–29 invoke Graphics2D method **setPaint** to set the **Paint** object that determines the color for the shape to display. A Paint object implements interface java.awt.Paint. It can be something as simple as one of the predeclared Color objects introduced in Section 12.3 (class Color implements Paint), or it can be an instance of the Java 2D API's Gradient-Paint, **SystemColor**, TexturePaint, LinearGradientPaint or RadialGradientPaint classes. In this case, we use a GradientPaint object.

Class GradientPaint helps draw a shape in gradually changing colors—called a *gradient*. The GradientPaint constructor used here requires seven arguments. The first two specify the starting coordinate for the gradient. The third specifies the starting Color for the gradient. The fourth and fifth specify the ending coordinate for the gradient. The sixth specifies the ending Color for the gradient. The last argument specifies whether the gradient is *cyclic* (true) or *acyclic* (false). The two sets of coordinates determine the direction of the gradient. Because the second coordinate (35, 100) is down and to the right of the first coordinate (5, 30), the gradient goes down and to the right at an angle. Because this gradient is cyclic (true), the color starts with blue, gradually becomes yellow, then gradually returns to blue. If the gradient is acyclic, the color transitions from the first color specified (e.g., blue) to the second color (e.g., yellow).

Line 30 uses `Graphics2D` method *fill* to draw a filled *Shape* object—an object that implements interface `Shape` (package `java.awt`). In this case, we display an `Ellipse2D.Double` object. The `Ellipse2D.Double` constructor receives four arguments specifying the bounding rectangle for the ellipse to display.

Rectangles, Strokes

Next we draw a red rectangle with a thick border. Line 33 invokes `setPaint` to set the `Paint` object to `Color.RED`. Line 34 uses `Graphics2D` method *setStroke* to set the characteristics of the rectangle's border (or the lines for any other shape). Method `setStroke` requires as its argument an object that implements interface *Stroke* (package `java.awt`). In this case, we use an instance of class `BasicStroke`. Class `BasicStroke` provides several constructors to specify the width of the line, how the line ends (called the *end caps*), how lines join together (called *line joins*) and the dash attributes of the line (if it is a dashed line). The constructor here specifies that the line should be 10 pixels wide.

Line 35 uses `Graphics2D` method *draw* to draw a `Shape` object—in this case, a `Rectangle2D.Double`. The `Rectangle2D.Double` constructor receives four arguments specifying the upper-left x-coordinate, upper-left y-coordinate, width and height of the rectangle.

Rounded Rectangles, BufferedImages and TexturePaint Objects

Next we draw a rounded rectangle filled with a pattern created in a *BufferedImage* (package `java.awt.image`) object. Lines 38–39 create the `BufferedImage` object. Class `BufferedImage` can be used to produce images in color and grayscale. This particular `BufferedImage` is 10 pixels wide and 10 pixels tall (as specified by the first two arguments of the constructor). The third argument *BufferedImage.TYPE_INT_RGB* indicates that the image is stored in color using the RGB color scheme.

To create the rounded rectangle's fill pattern, we must first draw into the `BufferedImage`. Line 42 creates a `Graphics2D` object (with a call to `BufferedImage` method *createGraphics*) that can be used to draw into the `BufferedImage`. Lines 43–50 use methods `setColor`, `fillRect` and `drawRect` (discussed earlier in this chapter) to create the pattern.

Lines 53–54 set the `Paint` object to a new `TexturePaint` (package `java.awt`) object. A `TexturePaint` object uses the image stored in its associated `BufferedImage` (the first constructor argument) as the fill texture for a filled-in shape. The second argument specifies the `Rectangle` area from the `BufferedImage` that will be replicated through the texture. In this case, the `Rectangle` is the same size as the `BufferedImage`. However, a smaller portion of the `BufferedImage` can be used.

Lines 55–56 use `Graphics2D` method `fill` to draw a filled `Shape` object—in this case, a `RoundRectangle2D.Double`. The constructor for class `RoundRectangle2D.Double` receives six arguments specifying the rectangle dimensions and the arc width and arc height used to determine the rounding of the corners.

Arcs

Next we draw a pie-shaped arc with a thick white line. Line 59 sets the `Paint` object to `Color.WHITE`. Line 60 sets the `Stroke` object to a new `BasicStroke` for a line 6 pixels wide. Lines 61–62 use `Graphics2D` method `draw` to draw a `Shape` object—in this case, an `Arc2D.Double`. The `Arc2D.Double` constructor's first four arguments specify the upper-left x-coordinate, upper-left y-coordinate, width and height of the bounding rectangle for the arc. The fifth argument specifies the start angle. The sixth argument specifies the arc angle. The last argument specifies how the arc is closed. Constant **Arc2D.PIE** indicates that the arc is closed by drawing two lines—one line from the arc's starting point to the center of the bounding rectangle and one line from the center of the bounding rectangle to the ending point. Class Arc2D provides two other static constants for specifying how the arc is closed. Constant **Arc2D.CHORD** draws a line from the starting point to the ending point. Constant **Arc2D.OPEN** specifies that the arc should not be closed.

Lines

Finally, we draw two lines using **Line2D** objects—one solid and one dashed. Line 65 sets the Paint object to Color.GREEN. Line 66 uses Graphics2D method draw to draw a Shape object—in this case, an instance of class Line2D.Double. The Line2D.Double constructor's arguments specify the starting coordinates and ending coordinates of the line.

Line 69 declares a one-element float array containing the value 10. This array will be used to describe the dashes in the dashed line. In this case, each dash will be 10 pixels long. To create dashes of different lengths in a pattern, simply provide the length of each dash as an element in the array. Line 70 sets the Paint object to Color.YELLOW. Lines 71–72 set the Stroke object to a new BasicStroke. The line will be 4 pixels wide and will have rounded ends (**BasicStroke.CAP_ROUND**). If lines join together (as in a rectangle at the corners), their joining will be rounded (**BasicStroke.JOIN_ROUND**). The dashes argument specifies the dash lengths for the line. The last argument indicates the starting index in the dashes array for the first dash in the pattern. Line 73 then draws a line with the current Stroke.

Creating Your Own Shapes with General Paths

Next we present a *general path*—a shape constructed from straight lines and complex curves. A general path is represented with an object of class **GeneralPath** (package java.awt.geom). The application of Figs. 12.31 and 12.32 demonstrates drawing a general path in the shape of a five-pointed star.

```
1   // Fig. 12.31: Shapes2JPanel.java
2   // Demonstrating a general path.
3   import java.awt.Color;
4   import java.awt.Graphics;
5   import java.awt.Graphics2D;
6   import java.awt.geom.GeneralPath;
7   import java.util.Random;
8   import javax.swing.JPanel;
9
10  public class Shapes2JPanel extends JPanel
11  {
12     // draw general paths
13     public void paintComponent( Graphics g )
14     {
15        super.paintComponent( g ); // call superclass's paintComponent
16        Random random = new Random(); // get random number generator
17
18        int xPoints[] = { 55, 67, 109, 73, 83, 55, 27, 37, 1, 43 };
19        int yPoints[] = { 0, 36, 36, 54, 96, 72, 96, 54, 36, 36 };
20
```

Fig. 12.31 | Java 2D general paths. (Part 1 of 2.)

```
21          Graphics2D g2d = ( Graphics2D ) g;
22          GeneralPath star = new GeneralPath(); // create GeneralPath object
23
24          // set the initial coordinate of the General Path
25          star.moveTo( xPoints[ 0 ], yPoints[ 0 ] );
26
27          // create the star--this does not draw the star
28          for ( int count = 1; count < xPoints.length; count++ )
29             star.lineTo( xPoints[ count ], yPoints[ count ] );
30
31          star.closePath(); // close the shape
32
33          g2d.translate( 200, 200 ); // translate the origin to (200, 200)
34
35          // rotate around origin and draw stars in random colors
36          for ( int count = 1; count <= 20; count++ )
37          {
38             g2d.rotate( Math.PI / 10.0 ); // rotate coordinate system
39
40             // set random drawing color
41             g2d.setColor( new Color( random.nextInt( 256 ),
42                random.nextInt( 256 ), random.nextInt( 256 ) ) );
43
44             g2d.fill( star ); // draw filled star
45          } // end for
46       } // end method paintComponent
47    } // end class Shapes2JPanel
```

Fig. 12.31 | Java 2D general paths. (Part 2 of 2.)

```
1     // Fig. 12.32: Shapes2.java
2     // Demonstrating a general path.
3     import java.awt.Color;
4     import javax.swing.JFrame;
5
6     public class Shapes2
7     {
8        // execute application
9        public static void main( String args[] )
10       {
11          // create frame for Shapes2JPanel
12          JFrame frame = new JFrame( "Drawing 2D Shapes" );
13          frame.setDefaultCloseOperation( JFrame.EXIT_ON_CLOSE );
14
15          Shapes2JPanel shapes2JPanel = new Shapes2JPanel();
16          frame.add( shapes2JPanel ); // add shapes2JPanel to frame
17          frame.setBackground( Color.WHITE ); // set frame background color
18          frame.setSize( 400, 400 ); // set frame size
19          frame.setVisible( true ); // display frame
20       } // end main
21    } // end class Shapes2
```

Fig. 12.32 | Creating JFrame to display stars. (Part 1 of 2.)

Fig. 12.32 | Creating JFrame to display stars. (Part 2 of 2.)

Lines 18–19 declare two int arrays representing the *x*- and *y*-coordinates of the points in the star. Line 22 creates GeneralPath object star. Line 25 uses GeneralPath method *moveTo* to specify the first point in the star. The for statement in lines 28–29 uses GeneralPath method *lineTo* to draw a line to the next point in the star. Each new call to lineTo draws a line from the previous point to the current point. Line 31 uses GeneralPath method *closePath* to draw a line from the last point to the point specified in the last call to moveTo. This completes the general path.

Line 33 uses Graphics2D method *translate* to move the drawing origin to location (200, 200). All drawing operations now use location (200, 200) as (0, 0).

The for statement in lines 36–45 draws the star 20 times by rotating it around the new origin point. Line 38 uses Graphics2D method *rotate* to rotate the next displayed shape. The argument specifies the rotation angle in radians (with 360° = 2π radians). Line 44 uses Graphics2D method fill to draw a filled version of the star.

12.9 Wrap-Up

In this chapter, you learned how to use Java's graphics capabilities to produce colorful drawings. You learned how to specify the location of an object using Java's coordinate system, and how to draw on a window using the paintComponent method. You were introduced to class Color, and learned how to use this class to specify different colors using their RGB components. You used the JColorChooser dialog to allow users to select colors in a program. You then learned how to work with fonts when drawing text on a window. You learned how to create a Font object from a font name, style and size, as well as how to access the metrics of a font. From there, you learned how to draw various shapes on a window, such as rectangles (regular, rounded and 3D), ovals and polygons, as well as lines and arcs. You then used the Java 2D API to create more complex shapes and to fill them with gradients or patterns. The chapter concluded with a discussion of general paths, used to construct shapes from straight lines and complex curves. In the next chapter, you'll learn about exceptions, useful for handling errors during a program's execution. Handling errors in this way provides for more robust programs.

13

Exception Handling

OBJECTIVES

In this chapter you'll learn:

- How exception and error handling works.

- To use `try`, `throw` and `catch` to detect, indicate and handle exceptions, respectively.

- To use the `finally` block to release resources.

- How stack unwinding enables exceptions not caught in one scope to be caught in another scope.

- How stack traces help in debugging.

- How exceptions are arranged in an exception-class hierarchy.

- To declare new exception classes.

- To create chained exceptions that maintain complete stack-trace information.

Outline

13.1 Introduction

13.2 Exception-Handling Overview

13.3 Example: Divide by Zero without Exception Handling

13.4 Example: Handling `ArithmeticException`s and `InputMismatchException`s

13.5 When to Use Exception Handling

13.6 Java Exception Hierarchy

13.7 `finally` Block

13.8 Stack Unwinding

13.9 `printStackTrace`, `getStackTrace` and `getMessage`

13.10 Chained Exceptions

13.11 Declaring New Exception Types

13.12 Preconditions and Postconditions

13.13 Assertions

13.14 Wrap-Up

13.1 Introduction

In this chapter, we introduce *exception handling*. An *exception* is an indication of a problem that occurs during a program's execution. The name "exception" implies that the problem occurs infrequently—if the "rule" is that a statement normally executes correctly, then the "exception to the rule" is that a problem occurs. Exception handling enables you to create applications that can resolve (or handle) exceptions. In many cases, handling an exception allows a program to continue executing as if no problem had been encountered. A more severe problem could prevent a program from continuing normal execution, instead requiring it to notify the user of the problem before terminating in a controlled manner. The features presented in this chapter enable programmers to write *robust* and *fault-tolerant programs* (i.e., programs that are able to deal with problems that may arise and continue executing). The style and details of Java exception handling are based in part on Andrew Koenig's and Bjarne Stroustrup's paper, "Exception Handling for C++ (revised)."[1]

Error-Prevention Tip 13.1

Exception handling helps improve a program's fault tolerance.

You have already been briefly introduced to exceptions in earlier chapters. In Chapter 7 you learned that an `ArrayIndexOutOfBoundsException` occurs when an attempt is made to access an element past the end of an array. Such a problem may occur if there is an "off-by-one" error in a `for` statement that manipulates an array. In Chapter 10, we introduced the `ClassCastException`, which occurs when an attempt is made to cast an object that does not have an *is-a* relationship with the type specified in the cast operator. Chapter 11 briefly mentioned the `NullPointerException`, which occurs whenever a `null` reference is used where an object is expected (for example, when an attempt is made to attach a GUI component to a `Container`, but the GUI component has not yet been created).

---

1.   Koenig, A., and B. Stroustrup. "Exception Handling for C++ (revised)," *Proceedings of the Usenix C++ Conference*, pp. 149–176, San Francisco, April 1990.

Throughout this text you have also used class Scanner—which, as you'll see in this chapter, also may cause exceptions.

We begin with an overview of exception-handling concepts, then demonstrate basic exception-handling techniques. We show these techniques in action by handling an exception that occurs when a method attempts to divide an integer by zero. Next, we introduce several classes at the top of Java's class hierarchy for exception handling. As you'll see, only classes that extend Throwable (package java.lang) directly or indirectly can be used with exception handling. We then discuss the chained exception feature that allows programmers to wrap information about an exception that occurred in another exception object to provide more detailed information about a problem in a program. Next, we discuss additional exception-handling issues, such as how to handle exceptions that occur in a constructor. We introduce preconditions and postconditions, which must be true when your methods are called and when those methods return, respectively. Finally, we present assertions, which programmers use at development time to help debug their code.

13.2 Exception-Handling Overview

Programs frequently test conditions to determine how program execution should proceed. Consider the following pseudocode:

> *Perform a task*
>
> *If the preceding task did not execute correctly*
>   *Perform error processing*
>
> *Perform next task*
>
> *If the preceding task did not execute correctly*
>   *Perform error processing*
>
> *...*

We begin by performing a task; then we test whether that task executed correctly. If not, we perform error processing; otherwise, we continue with the next task. Although this form of error handling works, intermixing program logic with error-handling logic can make programs difficult to read, modify, maintain and debug—especially in large applications.

Performance Tip 13.1

> *If the potential problems occur infrequently, intermixing program and error-handling logic can degrade a program's performance, because the program must perform (potentially frequent) tests to determine whether the task executed correctly and the next task can be performed.*

Exception handling enables programmers to remove error-handling code from the "main line" of the program's execution, improving program clarity and enhancing modifiability. You can decide to handle any exceptions you choose—all exceptions, all exceptions of a certain type or all exceptions of a group of related types (i.e., exception types that are related through an inheritance hierarchy). Such flexibility reduces the likelihood that errors will be overlooked, thus making programs more robust.

With programming languages that do not support exception handling, programmers often delay writing error-processing code or sometimes forget to include it. This results in less robust software products. Java enables programmers to deal with exception handling easily from the inception of a project.

13.3 Example: Divide by Zero without Exception Handling

First we demonstrate what happens when errors arise in an application that does not use exception handling. Figure 13.1 prompts the user for two integers and passes them to method quotient, which calculates the quotient and returns an int result. In this example, we'll see that exceptions are *thrown* (i.e., the exception occurs) when a method detects a problem and is unable to handle it.

```java
1   // Fig. 13.1: DivideByZeroNoExceptionHandling.java
2   // An application that attempts to divide by zero.
3   import java.util.Scanner;
4
5   public class DivideByZeroNoExceptionHandling
6   {
7      // demonstrates throwing an exception when a divide-by-zero occurs
8      public static int quotient( int numerator, int denominator )
9      {
10         return numerator / denominator; // possible division by zero
11      } // end method quotient
12
13      public static void main( String args[] )
14      {
15         Scanner scanner = new Scanner( System.in ); // scanner for input
16
17         System.out.print( "Please enter an integer numerator: " );
18         int numerator = scanner.nextInt();
19         System.out.print( "Please enter an integer denominator: " );
20         int denominator = scanner.nextInt();
21
22         int result = quotient( numerator, denominator );
23         System.out.printf(
24            "\nResult: %d / %d = %d\n", numerator, denominator, result );
25      } // end main
26   } // end class DivideByZeroNoExceptionHandling
```

```
Please enter an integer numerator: 100
Please enter an integer denominator: 7

Result: 100 / 7 = 14
```

```
Please enter an integer numerator: 100
Please enter an integer denominator: 0
Exception in thread "main" java.lang.ArithmeticException: / by zero
        at DivideByZeroNoExceptionHandling.quotient(
            DivideByZeroNoExceptionHandling.java:10)
        at DivideByZeroNoExceptionHandling.main(
            DivideByZeroNoExceptionHandling.java:22)
```

Fig. 13.1 | Integer division without exception handling. (Part 1 of 2.)

```
Please enter an integer numerator: 100
Please enter an integer denominator: hello
Exception in thread "main" java.util.InputMismatchException
        at java.util.Scanner.throwFor(Unknown Source)
        at java.util.Scanner.next(Unknown Source)
        at java.util.Scanner.nextInt(Unknown Source)
        at java.util.Scanner.nextInt(Unknown Source)
        at DivideByZeroNoExceptionHandling.main(
            DivideByZeroNoExceptionHandling.java:20)
```

Fig. 13.1 | Integer division without exception handling. (Part 2 of 2.)

The first of the three sample executions in Fig. 13.1 shows a successful division. In the second sample execution, the user enters the value 0 as the denominator. Notice that several lines of information are displayed in response to this invalid input. This information is known as the *stack trace*, which includes the name of the exception (java.lang.Arithmeticexception) in a descriptive message that indicates the problem that occurred and the complete method-call stack (i.e., the call chain) at the time the exception occurred. The stack trace includes the path of execution that led to the exception method by method. This information helps in debugging a program. The first line specifies that an ArithmeticException has occurred. The text after the name of the exception ("/ by zero") indicates that this exception occurred as a result of an attempt to divide by zero. Java does not allow division by zero in integer arithmetic. [*Note:* Java *does* allow division by zero with floating-point values. Such a calculation results in the value infinity, which is represented in Java as a floating-point value (but actually displays as the string Infinity).] When division by zero in integer arithmetic occurs, Java throws an *ArithmeticException*. ArithmeticExceptions can arise from a number of different problems in arithmetic, so the extra data ("/ by zero") gives us more information about this specific exception.

Starting from the last line of the stack trace, we see that the exception was detected in line 22 of method main. Each line of the stack trace contains the class name and method (DivideByZeroNoExceptionHandling.main) followed by the file name and line number (DivideByZeroNoExceptionHandling.java:22). Moving up the stack trace, we see that the exception occurs in line 10, in method quotient. The top row of the call chain indicates the *throw point*—the initial point at which the exception occurs. The throw point of this exception is in line 10 of method quotient.

In the third execution, the user enters "hello" as the denominator. This results in a stack trace informing us that an InputMismatchException (package java.util) has occurred. Our prior examples that read numeric values from the user assumed that the user would input a proper integer value. However, users sometimes make mistakes and input noninteger values. An *InputMismatchException* occurs when Scanner method nextInt receives a string that does not represent a valid integer. Starting from the end of the stack trace, we see that the exception was detected in line 20 of method main. Moving up the stack trace, we see that the exception occurs in method nextInt. Notice that in place of the file name and line number, we are provided with the text Unknown Source. This means that the JVM does not have access to the source code for where the exception occurred.

Notice that in the sample executions of Fig. 13.1 when exceptions occur and stack traces are displayed, the program also exits. This does not always occur in Java—sometimes a program may continue even though an exception has occurred and a stack trace has been printed. In such cases, the application may produce unexpected results. The next section demonstrates how to handle these exceptions and keep the program running successfully. In the next example, we'll see how to handle these exceptions to enable the program to run to normal completion.

13.4 Example: Handling ArithmeticExceptions and InputMismatchExceptions

The application in Fig. 13.2, which is based on Fig. 13.1, uses exception handling to process any ArithmeticExceptions and InputMismatchExceptions that arise. The application still prompts the user for two integers and passes them to method quotient, which calculates the quotient and returns an int result. This version of the application uses exception handling so that if the user makes a mistake, the program *catches* and *handles* (i.e., deals with) the exception—in this case, allowing the user to try to enter the input again.

```
1   // Fig. 13.2: DivideByZeroWithExceptionHandling.java
2   // An exception-handling example that checks for divide-by-zero.
3   import java.util.InputMismatchException;
4   import java.util.Scanner;
5
6   public class DivideByZeroWithExceptionHandling
7   {
8      // demonstrates throwing an exception when a divide-by-zero occurs
9      public static int quotient( int numerator, int denominator )
10        throws ArithmeticException
11     {
12        return numerator / denominator; // possible division by zero
13     } // end method quotient
14
15     public static void main( String args[] )
16     {
17        Scanner scanner = new Scanner( System.in ); // scanner for input
18        boolean continueLoop = true; // determines if more input is needed
19
20        do
21        {
22           try // read two numbers and calculate quotient
23           {
24              System.out.print( "Please enter an integer numerator: " );
25              int numerator = scanner.nextInt();
26              System.out.print( "Please enter an integer denominator: " );
27              int denominator = scanner.nextInt();
28
29              int result = quotient( numerator, denominator );
30              System.out.printf( "\nResult: %d / %d = %d\n", numerator,
31                 denominator, result );
32              continueLoop = false; // input successful; end looping
33           } // end try
```

Fig. 13.2 | Handling ArithmeticExceptions and InputMismatchExceptions. (Part 1 of 2.)

```
34          catch ( InputMismatchException inputMismatchException )
35          {
36             System.err.printf( "\nException: %s\n",
37                inputMismatchException );
38             scanner.nextLine(); // discard input so user can try again
39             System.out.println(
40                "You must enter integers. Please try again.\n" );
41          } // end catch
42          catch ( ArithmeticException arithmeticException )
43          {
44             System.err.printf( "\nException: %s\n", arithmeticException );
45             System.out.println(
46                "Zero is an invalid denominator. Please try again.\n" );
47          } // end catch
48       } while ( continueLoop ); // end do...while
49    } // end main
50 } // end class DivideByZeroWithExceptionHandling
```

```
Please enter an integer numerator: 100
Please enter an integer denominator: 7

Result: 100 / 7 = 14
```

```
Please enter an integer numerator: 100
Please enter an integer denominator: 0

Exception: java.lang.ArithmeticException: / by zero
Zero is an invalid denominator. Please try again.

Please enter an integer numerator: 100
Please enter an integer denominator: 7

Result: 100 / 7 = 14
```

```
Please enter an integer numerator: 100
Please enter an integer denominator: hello

Exception: java.util.InputMismatchException
You must enter integers. Please try again.

Please enter an integer numerator: 100
Please enter an integer denominator: 7

Result: 100 / 7 = 14
```

Fig. 13.2 | Handling ArithmeticExceptions and InputMismatchExceptions. (Part 2 of 2.)

The first sample execution in Fig. 13.2 shows a successful execution that does not encounter any problems. In the second execution, the user enters a zero denominator and an ArithmeticException exception occurs. In the third execution, the user enters the string "hello" as the denominator, and an InputMismatchException occurs. For each exception, the user is informed of the mistake and asked to try again, then is prompted for two new integers. In each sample execution, the program runs successfully to completion.

Class `InputMismatchException` is imported in line 3. Class `ArithmeticException` does not need to be imported because it is located in package `java.lang`. Method `main` (lines 15–49) creates a `Scanner` object at line 17. Line 18 creates the `boolean` variable continueLoop, which is true if the user has not yet entered valid input. Lines 20–48 repeatedly ask users for input until a valid input is received.

Enclosing Code in a try Block

Lines 22–33 contain a **try block**, which encloses the code that might `throw` an exception and the code that should not execute if an exception occurs (i.e., if an exception occurs, the remaining code in the `try` block will be skipped). A `try` block consists of the keyword `try` followed by a block of code enclosed in curly braces ({}). [*Note:* The term "`try` block" sometimes refers only to the block of code that follows the `try` keyword (not including the `try` keyword itself). For simplicity, we use the term "`try` block" to refer to the block of code that follows the `try` keyword, as well as the `try` keyword.] The statements that read the integers from the keyboard (lines 25 and 27) each use method `nextInt` to read an `int` value. Method `nextInt` throws an `InputMismatchException` if the value read in is not a valid integer.

The division that can cause an `ArithmeticException` is not performed in the `try` block. Rather, the call to method `quotient` (line 29) invokes the code that attempts the division (line 12); the JVM throws an `ArithmeticException` object when the denominator is zero.

Software Engineering Observation 13.1

Exceptions may surface through explicitly mentioned code in a try block, through calls to other methods, through deeply nested method calls initiated by code in a try block or from the Java Virtual Machine as it executes Java bytecodes.

Catching Exceptions

The `try` block in this example is followed by two `catch` blocks—one that handles an InputMismatchException (lines 34–41) and one that handles an `ArithmeticException` (lines 42–47). A **catch block** (also called a **catch clause** or *exception handler*) catches (i.e., receives) and handles an exception. A `catch` block begins with the keyword `catch` and is followed by a parameter in parentheses (called the exception parameter, discussed shortly) and a block of code enclosed in curly braces. [*Note:* The term "catch clause" is sometimes used to refer to the keyword `catch` followed by a block of code, where the term "catch block" refers to only the block of code following the `catch` keyword, but not including it. For simplicity, we use the term "catch block" to refer to the block of code following the catch keyword, as well as the keyword itself.]

At least one `catch` block or a **finally block** (discussed in Section 13.7) must immediately follow the `try` block. Each `catch` block specifies in parentheses an *exception parameter* that identifies the exception type the handler can process. When an exception occurs in a `try` block, the `catch` block that executes is the one whose type matches the type of the exception that occurred (i.e., the type in the `catch` block matches the thrown exception type exactly or is a superclass of it). The exception parameter's name enables the `catch` block to interact with a caught exception object—e.g., to implicitly invoke the caught exception's `toString` method (as in lines 37 and 44), which displays basic information about the exception. Line 38 of the first `catch` block calls `Scanner` method `nextLine`.

Because an InputMismatchException occurred, the call to method nextInt never successfully read in the user's data—so we read that input with a call to method nextLine. We do not do anything with the input at this point, because we know that it is invalid. Each catch block displays an error message and asks the user to try again. After either catch block terminates, the user is prompted for input. We'll soon take a deeper look at how this flow of control works in exception handling.

Common Programming Error 13.1

It is a syntax error to place code between a try block and its corresponding catch blocks.

Common Programming Error 13.2

Each catch block can have only a single parameter—specifying a comma-separated list of exception parameters is a syntax error.

An ***uncaught exception*** is an exception that occurs for which there are no matching catch blocks. You saw uncaught exceptions in the second and third outputs of Fig. 13.1. Recall that when exceptions occurred in that example, the application terminated early (after displaying the exception's stack trace). This does not always occur as a result of uncaught exceptions. As you'll learn in Chapter 18, Multithreading, Java uses a multithreaded model of program execution. Each ***thread*** is a parallel activity. One program can have many threads. If a program has only one thread, an uncaught exception will cause the program to terminate. If a program has multiple threads, an uncaught exception will terminate only the thread where the exception occurred. In such programs, however, certain threads may rely on others and if one thread terminates due to an uncaught exception, there may be adverse effects to the rest of the program.

Termination Model of Exception Handling

If an exception occurs in a try block (such as an InputMismatchException being thrown as a result of the code at line 25 of Fig. 13.2), the try block terminates immediately and program control transfers to the first of the following catch blocks in which the exception parameter's type matches the thrown exception's type. In Fig. 13.2, the first catch block catches InputMismatchExceptions (which occur if invalid input is entered) and the second catch block catches ArithmeticExceptions (which occur if an attempt is made to divide by zero). After the exception is handled, program control does not return to the throw point because the try block has expired (and its local variables have been lost). Rather, control resumes after the last catch block. This is known as the ***termination model of exception handling***. [*Note:* Some languages use the ***resumption model of exception handling***, in which, after an exception is handled, control resumes just after the throw point.]

Common Programming Error 13.3

Logic errors can occur if you assume that after an exception is handled, control will return to the first statement after the throw point.

Error-Prevention Tip 13.2

With exception handling, a program can continue executing (rather than terminating) after dealing with a problem. This helps ensure the kind of robust applications that contribute to what is called mission-critical computing or business-critical computing.

Notice that we name our exception parameters (`inputMismatchException` and `arithmeticException`) based on their type. Java programmers often simply use the letter e as the name of their exception parameters.

Good Programming Practice 13.1

Using an exception parameter name that reflects the parameter's type promotes clarity by reminding the programmer of the type of exception being handled.

After executing a `catch` block, this program's flow of control proceeds to the first statement after the last `catch` block (line 48 in this case). The condition in the do...while statement is `true` (variable `continueLoop` contains its initial value of `true`), so control returns to the beginning of the loop and the user is once again prompted for input. This control statement will loop until valid input is entered. At that point, program control reaches line 32, which assigns `false` to variable `continueLoop`. The `try` block then terminates. If no exceptions are thrown in the `try` block, the `catch` blocks are skipped and control continues with the first statement after the `catch` blocks (we'll learn about another possibility when we discuss the `finally` block in Section 13.7). Now the condition for the do...while loop is `false`, and method `main` ends.

The `try` block and its corresponding `catch` and/or `finally` blocks together form a *try statement*. Don't confuse the terms "try block" and "try statement"—the term "try block" refers to the keyword `try` followed by a block of code, while "try statement" includes the try block as well as the following `catch` blocks and/or `finally` block.

As with any other block of code, when a `try` block terminates, local variables declared in the block are destroyed. When a `catch` block terminates, local variables declared within the `catch` block (including the exception parameter of that `catch` block) also go out of scope and are destroyed. Any remaining `catch` blocks in the `try` statement are ignored, and execution resumes at the first line of code after the `try`...`catch` sequence—this will be a `finally` block, if one is present.

Using the throws Clause

Now let's examine method `quotient` (Fig. 13.2; lines 9–13). Line 10 incldues a *throws clause*, which specifies the exceptions the method throws. This clause appears after the method's parameter list and before the method's body. It contains a comma-separated list of the exceptions that the method might throw. Such exceptions may be thrown by statements in the method's body or by methods called from the body. A method can throw exceptions of the classes listed in its `throws` clause or of their subclasses. We've added the `throws` clause to indicate to the clients of method `quotient` that this method may throw an `ArithmeticException`. You'll learn more about the `throws` clause in Section 13.6.

Error-Prevention Tip 13.3

If you know that a method might throw an exception, include appropriate exception-handling code in your program to make it more robust.

Error-Prevention Tip 13.4

Read the online API documentation for a method before using that method in a program. The documentation specifies the exceptions thrown by the method (if any) and indicates reasons why such exceptions may occur. Then provide for handling those exceptions in your program.

Error-Prevention Tip 13.5

Read the online API documentation for an exception class before writing exception-handling code for that type of exception. The documentation for an exception class typically contains potential reasons that such exceptions occur during program execution.

When line 12 executes, if the denominator is zero, the JVM throws an Arithmet-icException object. This object will be caught by the catch block at lines 42–47, which displays basic information about the exception by implicitly invoking the exception's toString method, then asks the user to try again.

If the denominator is not zero, method quotient performs the division and returns the result to the point of invocation of method quotient in the try block (line 29). Lines 30–31 display the result of the calculation and line 32 sets continueLoop to false. In this case, the try block completes successfully, so the program skips the catch blocks and fails the condition at line 48, and method main completes execution normally.

Note that when quotient throws an ArithmeticException, quotient terminates and does not return a value, and quotient's local variables go out of scope (variables are destroyed). If quotient contained local variables that were references to objects and there were no other references to those objects, the objects would be marked for garbage collection. Also, when an exception occurs, the try block from which quotient was called terminates before lines 30–32 can execute. Here, too, if local variables were created in the try block prior to the exception being thrown, these variables would go out of scope.

If an InputMismatchException is generated by lines 25 or 27, the try block terminates and execution continues with the catch block at lines 34–41. In this case, method quotient is not called. Then method main continues after the last catch block (line 48).

13.5 When to Use Exception Handling

Exception handling is designed to process *synchronous errors*, which occur when a statement executes. Common examples we'll see throughout the book are out-of-range array indices, arithmetic overflow (i.e., a value outside the representable range of values), division by zero, invalid method parameters, thread interruption and unsuccessful memory allocation (due to lack of memory). Exception handling is not designed to process problems associated with *asynchronous events* (e.g., disk I/O completions, network message arrivals, mouse clicks and keystrokes), which occur in parallel with, and independent of, the program's flow of control.

Software Engineering Observation 13.2

Incorporate your exception-handling strategy into your system from the inception of the design process. Including effective exception handling after a system has been implemented can be difficult.

Software Engineering Observation 13.3

Exception handling provides a single, uniform technique for processing problems. This helps programmers working on large projects understand each other's error-processing code.

Software Engineering Observation 13.4

Avoid using exception handling as an alternate form of flow of control. These "additional" exceptions can "get in the way" of genuine error-type exceptions.

Software Engineering Observation 13.5

Exception handling simplifies combining software components and enables them to work together effectively by enabling predefined components to communicate problems to application-specific components, which can then process the problems in an application-specific manner.

13.6 Java Exception Hierarchy

All Java exception classes inherit, either directly or indirectly, from class **Exception**, forming an inheritance hierarchy. Programmers can extend this hierarchy to create their own exception classes.

Figure 13.3 shows a small portion of the inheritance hierarchy for class **Throwable** (a subclass of Object), which is the superclass of class Exception. Only Throwable objects can be used with the exception-handling mechanism. Class Throwable has two subclasses: Exception and Error. Class Exception and its subclasses—for instance, RuntimeException (package java.lang) and IOException (package java.io)—represent exceptional situations that can occur in a Java program and that can be caught by the application. Class **Error** and its subclasses (e.g., OutOfMemoryError) represent abnormal situations that could happen in the JVM. Errors happen infrequently and should not be caught by applications—it is usually not possible for applications to recover from Errors. [*Note:* The Java exception hierarchy contains hundreds of classes. Information about Java's exception classes can be found throughout the Java API. The documentation for class Throwable can be found at java.sun.com/javase/6/docs/api/java/lang/Throwable.html. From there, you can look at this class's subclasses to get more information about Java's Exceptions and Errors.]

Java distinguishes between two categories of exceptions: *checked exceptions* and *unchecked exceptions*. This distinction is important, because the Java compiler enforces

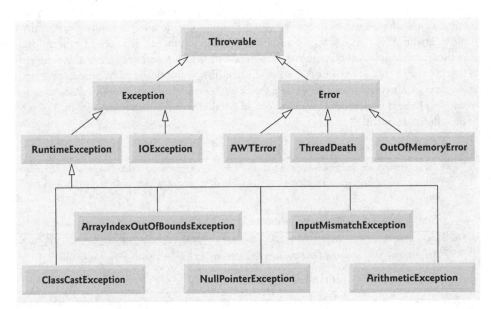

Fig. 13.3 | Portion of class Throwable's inheritance hierarchy.

a *catch-or-declare requirement* for checked exceptions. An exception's type determines whether the exception is checked or unchecked. All exception types that are direct or indirect subclasses of class ***RuntimeException*** (package `java.lang`) are unchecked exceptions. This includes exceptions you have seen already, such as `ArrayIndexOutOfBoundsExceptions` and `ArithmeticExceptions` (shown in Fig. 13.3). All classes that inherit from class `Exception` but not class `RuntimeException` are considered to be checked exceptions. Classes that inherit from class `Error` are considered to be unchecked. The compiler *checks* each method call and method declaration to determine whether the method throws checked exceptions. If so, the compiler ensures that the checked exception is caught or is declared in a `throws` clause. Recall from Section 13.4 that the `throws` clause specifies the exceptions a method throws. Such exceptions are not caught in the method's body. To satisfy the *catch* part of the catch-or-declare requirement, the code that generates the exception must be wrapped in a `try` block and must provide a `catch` handler for the checked-exception type (or one of its superclass types). To satisfy the *declare* part of the catch-or-declare requirement, the method containing the code that generates the exception must provide a `throws` clause containing the checked-exception type after its parameter list and before its method body. If the catch-or-declare requirement is not satisfied, the compiler will issue an error message indicating that the exception must be caught or declared. This forces programmers to think about the problems that may occur when a method that throws checked exceptions is called. Exception classes are defined to be checked when they are considered important enough to catch or declare.

Software Engineering Observation 13.6

Programmers are forced to deal with checked exceptions. This results in more robust code than would be created if programmers were able to simply ignore the exceptions.

Common Programming Error 13.4

A compilation error occurs if a method explicitly attempts to throw a checked exception (or calls another method that throws a checked exception) and that exception is not listed in that method's throws clause.

Common Programming Error 13.5

If a subclass method overrides a superclass method, it is an error for the subclass method to list more exceptions in its throws clause than the overridden superclass method does. However, a subclass's throws clause can contain a subset of a superclass's throws list.

Software Engineering Observation 13.7

If your method calls other methods that explicitly throw checked exceptions, those exceptions must be caught or declared in your method. If an exception can be handled meaningfully in a method, the method should catch the exception rather than declare it.

Unlike checked exceptions, the Java compiler does not check the code to determine whether an unchecked exception is caught or declared. Unchecked exceptions typically can be prevented by proper coding. For example, the unchecked `ArithmeticException` thrown by method `quotient` (lines 9–13) in Fig. 13.2 can be avoided if the method ensures that the denominator is not zero before attempting to perform the division. Unchecked exceptions are not required to be listed in a method's `throws` clause—even if they are, it is not required that such exceptions be caught by an application.

Software Engineering Observation 13.8

Although the compiler does not enforce the catch-or-declare requirement for unchecked exceptions, provide appropriate exception-handling code when it is known that such exceptions might occur. For example, a program should process the NumberFormatException *from* Integer *method* parseInt, *even though* NumberFormatException *(a subclass of* RuntimeException*) is an unchecked exception type. This makes your programs more robust.*

Exception classes can be derived from a common superclass. If a catch handler catches superclass-type exception objects, it can also catch all objects of that class's subclasses. This enables catch to handle related errors with a concise notation and allows for polymorphic processing of related exceptions. You can certainly catch each subclass type individually if those exceptions require different processing. Catching related exceptions in one catch block makes sense only if the handling behavior is the same for all subclasses.

If there are multiple catch blocks that match a particular exception type, only the first matching catch block executes when an exception of that type occurs. It is a compilation error to catch the exact same type in two different catch blocks associated with a particular try block. However, there may be several catch blocks that match an exception—i.e., several catch blocks whose types are the same as the exception type or a superclass of that type. For instance, we could follow a catch block for type ArithmeticException with a catch block for type Exception—both would match ArithmeticExceptions, but only the first matching catch block would execute.

Error-Prevention Tip 13.6

Catching subclass types individually is subject to error if you forget to test for one or more of the subclass types explicitly; catching the superclass guarantees that objects of all subclasses will be caught. Positioning a catch block for the superclass type after all other subclass catch blocks for subclasses of that superclass ensures that all subclass exceptions are eventually caught.

Common Programming Error 13.6

Placing a catch block for a superclass exception type before other catch blocks that catch subclass exception types prevents those catch blocks from executing, so a compilation error occurs.

13.7 finally Block

Programs that obtain certain types of resources must return them to the system explicitly to avoid so-called *resource leaks.* In programming languages such as C and C++, the most common kind of resource leak is a memory leak. Java performs automatic garbage collection of memory no longer used by programs, thus avoiding most memory leaks. However, other resource leaks can occur. For example, files, database connections and network connections that are not closed properly might not be available for use in other programs.

Error-Prevention Tip 13.7

A subtle issue is that Java does not entirely eliminate memory leaks. Java will not garbage-collect an object until there are no remaining references to it. Thus, if programmers erroneously keep references to unwanted objects, memory leaks can occur.

The finally block (which consists of the finally keyword, followed by code enclosed in curly braces) is optional, and is sometimes referred to as the *finally clause.* If it is present, it is placed after the last catch block, as in Fig. 13.4.

```
try
{
    statements
    resource-acquisition statements
} // end try
catch ( AKindOfException exception1 )
{
    exception-handling statements
} // end catch
 .
 .
 .
catch ( AnotherKindOfException exception2 )
{
    exception-handling statements
} // end catch
finally
{
    statements
    resource-release statements
} // end finally
```

Fig. 13.4 | A try statement with a finally block.

Java guarantees that a finally block (if one is present in a try statement) will execute whether or not an exception is thrown in the corresponding try block or any of its corresponding catch blocks. Java also guarantees that a finally block (if one is present) will execute if a try block exits by using a return, break or continue statement, or simply by reaching the try block's closing right brace. The finally block will *not* execute if the application exits early from a try block by calling method **System.exit**. This method, which we demonstrate in the next chapter, immediately terminates an application.

Because a finally block almost always executes, it typically contains resource-release code. Suppose a resource is allocated in a try block. If no exception occurs, the catch blocks are skipped and control proceeds to the finally block, which frees the resource. Control then proceeds to the first statement after the finally block. If an exception does occur in the try block, the program skips the rest of the try block. If the program catches the exception in one of the catch blocks, the program processes the exception, then the finally block releases the resource, and control proceeds to the first statement after the finally block.

Performance Tip 13.2

Always release each resource explicitly and at the earliest possible moment at which it is no longer needed. This makes resources immediately available to be reused by your program or other programs, thus improving resource utilization.

Error-Prevention Tip 13.8

Because the finally block is guaranteed to execute whether or not an exception occurs in the corresponding try block, this block is an ideal place to release resources acquired in a try block. This is also an effective way to eliminate resource leaks. For example, the finally block should close any files opened in the try block.

If an exception that occurs in a try block cannot be caught by one of that try block's catch handlers, the program skips the rest of the try block and control proceeds to the finally block. Then the program passes the exception to the next outer try block—normally in the calling method—where an associated catch block might catch it. This process can occur through many levels of try blocks. It is also possible that the exception could go uncaught.

If a catch block throws an exception, the finally block still executes. Then the exception is passed to the next outer try block—again, normally in the calling method.

Figure 13.5 demonstrates that the finally block executes even if an exception is not thrown in the corresponding try block. The program contains static methods main (lines 7–19), throwException (lines 22–45) and doesNotThrowException (lines 48–65). Methods throwException and doesNotThrowException are declared static, so main can call them directly without instantiating a UsingExceptions object.

Note the use of the **System.err** to output data (lines 15, 31–32, 40, 56 and 60–61). By default, System.err.println, like System.out.println, displays data to the command prompt.

```
1   // Fig. 13.5: UsingExceptions.java
2   // Demonstration of the try...catch...finally exception handling
3   // mechanism.
4
5   public class UsingExceptions
6   {
7      public static void main( String args[] )
8      {
9         try
10        {
11           throwException(); // call method throwException
12        } // end try
13        catch ( Exception exception ) // exception thrown by throwException
14        {
15           System.err.println( "Exception handled in main" );
16        } // end catch
17
18        doesNotThrowException();
19     } // end main
20
21     // demonstrate try...catch...finally
22     public static void throwException() throws Exception
23     {
24        try // throw an exception and immediately catch it
25        {
26           System.out.println( "Method throwException" );
27           throw new Exception(); // generate exception
28        } // end try
29        catch ( Exception exception ) // catch exception thrown in try
30        {
31           System.err.println(
32              "Exception handled in method throwException" );
```

Fig. 13.5 | try...catch...finally exception-handling mechanism. (Part 1 of 2.)

```
33              throw exception; // rethrow for further processing
34
35              // any code here would not be reached
36
37         } // end catch
38         finally // executes regardless of what occurs in try...catch
39         {
40              System.err.println( "Finally executed in throwException" );
41         } // end finally
42
43         // any code here would not be reached, exception rethrown in catch
44
45      } // end method throwException
46
47      // demonstrate finally when no exception occurs
48      public static void doesNotThrowException()
49      {
50         try // try block does not throw an exception
51         {
52              System.out.println( "Method doesNotThrowException" );
53         } // end try
54         catch ( Exception exception ) // does not execute
55         {
56              System.err.println( exception );
57         } // end catch
58         finally // executes regardless of what occurs in try...catch
59         {
60              System.err.println(
61                 "Finally executed in doesNotThrowException" );
62         } // end finally
63
64         System.out.println( "End of method doesNotThrowException" );
65      } // end method doesNotThrowException
66   } // end class UsingExceptions
```

```
Method throwException
Exception handled in method throwException
Finally executed in throwException
Exception handled in main
Method doesNotThrowException
Finally executed in doesNotThrowException
End of method doesNotThrowException
```

Fig. 13.5 | try...catch...finally exception-handling mechanism. (Part 2 of 2.)

Both System.out and System.err are *streams*—a sequence of bytes. While System.out (known as the *standard output stream*) is used to display a program's output, System.err (known as the *standard error stream*) is used to display a program's errors. Output from these streams can be redirected (i.e., sent somewhere other than the command prompt, such as to a file). Using two different streams enables the programmer to easily separate error messages from other output. For instance, data output from System.err could be sent to a log file, while data output from System.out can be displayed on the screen. For simplicity, this chapter will not redirect output from

System.err, but will display such messages to the command prompt. You'll learn more about streams in Chapter 14, Files and Streams.

Throwing Exceptions Using the throw Statement

Method main (Fig. 13.5) begins executing, enters its try block and immediately calls method throwException (line 11). Method throwException throws an Exception. The statement at line 27, known as a *throw statement*, indicates that an exception has occurred. So far, you've only caught exceptions thrown by called methods. You can throw exceptions with the throw statementto indicate to client applications that an error has occurred. A throw statement specifies an object to be thrown. The operand of a throw can be of any class derived from class Throwable.

Software Engineering Observation 13.9

When toString is invoked on any Throwable object, its resulting string includes the descriptive string that was supplied to the constructor, or simply the class name if no string was supplied.

Software Engineering Observation 13.10

An object can be thrown without containing information about the problem that occurred. In this case, simple knowledge that an exception of a particular type occurred may provide sufficient information for the handler to process the problem correctly.

Software Engineering Observation 13.11

Exceptions can be thrown from constructors. When an error is detected in a constructor, an exception should be thrown rather than creating an improperly formed object.

Rethrowing Exceptions

Line 33 of Fig. 13.5 *rethrows the exception*. Exceptions are rethrown when a catch block, upon receiving an exception, decides either that it cannot process that exception or that it can only partially process it. Rethrowing an exception defers the exception handling (or perhaps a portion of it) to another catch block associated with an outer try statement. An exception is rethrown by using the *throw keyword*, followed by a reference to the exception object that was just caught. Note that exceptions cannot be rethrown from a finally block, as the exception parameter from the catch block has expired.

When a rethrow occurs, the next enclosing try block detects the rethrown exception, and that try block's catch blocks attempt to handle the exception. In this case, the next enclosing try block is found at lines 9–12 in method main. Before the rethrown exception is handled, however, the finally block (lines 38–41) executes. Then method main detects the rethrown exception in the try block and handles it in the catch block (lines 13–16).

Next, main calls method doesNotThrowException (line 18). No exception is thrown in doesNotThrowException's try block (lines 50–53), so the program skips the catch block (lines 54–57), but the finally block (lines 58–62) nevertheless executes. Control proceeds to the statement after the finally block (line 64). Then control returns to main and the program terminates.

Common Programming Error 13.7

If an exception has not been caught when control enters a finally block and the finally block throws an exception that is not caught in the finally block, the first exception will be lost and the exception from the finally block will be returned to the calling method.

Error-Prevention Tip 13.9

Avoid placing code that can throw *an exception in a* finally *block. If such code is required, enclose the code in a* try...catch *within the* finally *block.*

Common Programming Error 13.8

Assuming that an exception thrown from a catch *block will be processed by that* catch *block or any other* catch *block associated with the same* try *statement can lead to logic errors.*

Good Programming Practice 13.2

Java's exception-handling mechanism is intended to remove error-processing code from the main line of a program's code to improve program clarity. Do not place try...catch...finally *around every statement that may throw an exception. This makes programs difficult to read. Rather, place one* try *block around a significant portion of your code, follow that* try *block with* catch *blocks that handle each possible exception and follow the* catch *blocks with a single* finally *block (if one is required).*

13.8 Stack Unwinding

When an exception is thrown but not caught in a particular scope, the method-call stack is "unwound," and an attempt is made to catch the exception in the next outer try block. This process is called *stack unwinding*. Unwinding the method-call stack means that the method in which the exception was not caught terminates, all local variables in that method are destroyed and control returns to the statement that originally invoked that method. If a try block encloses that statement, an attempt is made to catch the exception. If a try block does not enclose that statement, stack unwinding occurs again. If no catch block ever catches this exception and the exception is checked (as in the following example), compiling the program will result in an error. The program of Fig. 13.6 demonstrates stack unwinding.

When method main executes, line 10 in the try block calls method throwException (lines 19–35). In the try block of method throwException (lines 21–25), line 24 throws an Exception. This terminates the try block immediately, and control skips the catch

```
1   // Fig. 13.6: UsingExceptions.java
2   // Demonstration of stack unwinding.
3
4   public class UsingExceptions
5   {
6      public static void main( String args[] )
7      {
8         try // call throwException to demonstrate stack unwinding
9         {
10            throwException();
11         } // end try
12         catch ( Exception exception ) // exception thrown in throwException
13         {
14            System.err.println( "Exception handled in main" );
15         } // end catch
16      } // end main
```

Fig. 13.6 | Stack unwinding. (Part 1 of 2.)

```
17
18      // throwException throws exception that is not caught in this method
19      public static void throwException() throws Exception
20      {
21          try // throw an exception and catch it in main
22          {
23              System.out.println( "Method throwException" );
24              throw new Exception(); // generate exception
25          } // end try
26          catch ( RuntimeException runtimeException ) // catch incorrect type
27          {
28              System.err.println(
29                  "Exception handled in method throwException" );
30          } // end catch
31          finally // finally block always executes
32          {
33              System.err.println( "Finally is always executed" );
34          } // end finally
35      } // end method throwException
36  } // end class UsingExceptions
```

```
Method throwException
Finally is always executed
Exception handled in main
```

Fig. 13.6 | Stack unwinding. (Part 2 of 2.)

block at line 26, because the type being caught (RuntimeException) is not an exact match with the thrown type (Exception) and is not a superclass of it. Method throwException terminates (but not until its finally block executes) and returns control to line 10—the point from which it was called in the program. Line 10 is in an enclosing try block. The exception has not yet been handled, so the try block terminates and an attempt is made to catch the exception at line 12. The type being caught (Exception) does match the thrown type. Consequently, the catch block processes the exception, and the program terminates at the end of main. If there were no matching catch blocks, a compilation error would occur. Remember that this is not always the case—for unchecked exceptions, the application will compile, but will run with unexpected results.

13.9 printStackTrace, getStackTrace and getMessage

Recall from Section 13.6 that exceptions derive from class Throwable. Class Throwable offers a *printStackTrace* method that outputs to the standard error stream the stack trace (discussed in Section 13.3). Often, this is helpful in testing and debugging. Class Throwable also provides a *getStackTrace* method that retrieves stack-trace information that might be printed by printStackTrace. Class Throwable's *getMessage* method returns the descriptive string stored in an exception. The example in this section demonstrates these three methods.

Error-Prevention Tip 13.10

An exception that is not caught in an application causes Java's default exception handler to run. This displays the name of the exception, a descriptive message that indicates the problem that occurred and a complete execution stack trace. In an application with a single thread of execution, the application terminates. In an application with multiple threads, the thread that caused the exception terminates.

Error-Prevention Tip 13.11

Throwable method toString (inherited by all Throwable subclasses) returns a string containing the name of the exception's class and a descriptive message.

Figure 13.7 demonstrates getMessage, printStackTrace and getStackTrace. If we wanted to output the stack-trace information to streams other than the standard error stream, we could output the information returned from getStackTrace to another stream. Sending data to other streams is discussed in Chapter 14, Files and Streams.

In main, the try block (lines 8–11) calls method1 (declared at lines 35–38). Next, method1 calls method2 (declared at lines 41–44), which in turn calls method3 (declared at lines 47–50). Line 49 of method3 throws an Exception object—this is the throw point. Because the throw statement at line 49 is not enclosed in a try block, stack unwinding occurs—method3 terminates at line 49, then returns control to the statement in method2 that invoked method3 (i.e., line 43). Because no try block encloses line 43, stack unwinding occurs again—method2 terminates at line 43 and returns control to the statement in method1 that invoked method2 (i.e., line 37). Because no try block encloses line 37, stack unwinding occurs one more time—method1 terminates at line 37 and returns control to the statement in main that invoked method1 (i.e., line 10). The try block at lines 8–11 encloses this statement. The exception has not been handled, so the try block terminates and the first matching catch block (lines 12–31) catches and processes the exception.

```java
1   // Fig. 13.7: UsingExceptions.java
2   // Demonstrating getMessage and printStackTrace from class Exception.
3
4   public class UsingExceptions
5   {
6      public static void main( String args[] )
7      {
8         try
9         {
10            method1(); // call method1
11         } // end try
12         catch ( Exception exception ) // catch exception thrown in method1
13         {
14            System.err.printf( "%s\n\n", exception.getMessage() );
15            exception.printStackTrace(); // print exception stack trace
16
17            // obtain the stack-trace information
18            StackTraceElement[] traceElements = exception.getStackTrace();
19
```

Fig. 13.7 | Throwable methods getMessage, getStackTrace and printStackTrace. (Part 1 of 2.)

```
20          System.out.println( "\nStack trace from getStackTrace:" );
21          System.out.println( "Class\t\tFile\t\t\tLine\tMethod" );
22
23          // loop through traceElements to get exception description
24          for ( StackTraceElement element : traceElements )
25          {
26             System.out.printf( "%s\t", element.getClassName() );
27             System.out.printf( "%s\t", element.getFileName() );
28             System.out.printf( "%s\t", element.getLineNumber() );
29             System.out.printf( "%s\n", element.getMethodName() );
30          } // end for
31       } // end catch
32    } // end main
33
34    // call method2; throw exceptions back to main
35    public static void method1() throws Exception
36    {
37       method2();
38    } // end method method1
39
40    // call method3; throw exceptions back to method1
41    public static void method2() throws Exception
42    {
43       method3();
44    } // end method method2
45
46    // throw Exception back to method2
47    public static void method3() throws Exception
48    {
49       throw new Exception( "Exception thrown in method3" );
50    } // end method method3
51 } // end class UsingExceptions
```

```
Exception thrown in method3

java.lang.Exception: Exception thrown in method3
        at UsingExceptions.method3(UsingExceptions.java:49)
        at UsingExceptions.method2(UsingExceptions.java:43)
        at UsingExceptions.method1(UsingExceptions.java:37)
        at UsingExceptions.main(UsingExceptions.java:10)

Stack trace from getStackTrace:
Class           File                     Line    Method
UsingExceptions UsingExceptions.java     49      method3
UsingExceptions UsingExceptions.java     43      method2
UsingExceptions UsingExceptions.java     37      method1
UsingExceptions UsingExceptions.java     10      main
```

Fig. 13.7 | Throwable methods getMessage, getStackTrace and printStackTrace. (Part 2 of 2.)

Line 14 invokes the exception's getMessage method to get the exception description. Line 15 invokes the exception's printStackTrace method to output the stack trace that indicates where the exception occurred. Line 18 invokes the exception's getStackTrace method to obtain the stack-trace information as an array of ***StackTraceElement*** objects. Lines 24–30 get each StackTraceElement in the array and invoke its methods ***getClassName***, ***getFileName***, ***getLineNumber*** and ***getMethodName*** to get the class name, file name, line number and method name, respectively, for that StackTraceElement. Each StackTraceElement represents one method call on the method-call stack.

The output in Fig. 13.7 shows that the stack-trace information printed by printStackTrace follows the pattern: *className.methodName(fileName:lineNumber)*, where *className*, *methodName* and *fileName* indicate the names of the class, method and file in which the exception occurred, respectively, and the *lineNumber* indicates where in the file the exception occurred. You saw this in the output for Fig. 13.1. Method getStackTrace enables custom processing of the exception information. Compare the output of printStackTrace with the output created from the StackTraceElements to see that both contain the same stack-trace information.

Software Engineering Observation 13.12

Never ignore an exception you catch. At least use printStackTrace to output an error message. This will inform users that a problem exists, so that they can take appropriate actions.

13.10 Chained Exceptions

Sometimes a catch block catches one exception type, then throws a new exception of a different type to indicate that a program-specific exception occurred. In earlier Java versions, there was no mechanism to wrap the original exception information with the new exception's information to provide a complete stack trace showing where the original problem occurred in the program. This made debugging such problems particularly difficult. *Chained exceptions* enable an exception object to maintain the complete stack-trace information. Figure 13.8 demonstrates chained exceptions.

```
1  // Fig. 13.8: UsingChainedExceptions.java
2  // Demonstrating chained exceptions.
3
4  public class UsingChainedExceptions
5  {
6     public static void main( String args[] )
7     {
8        try
9        {
10          method1(); // call method1
11       } // end try
12       catch ( Exception exception ) // exceptions thrown from method1
13       {
14          exception.printStackTrace();
15       } // end catch
16    } // end main
17
18    // call method2; throw exceptions back to main
19    public static void method1() throws Exception
20    {
```

Fig. 13.8 | Chained exceptions. (Part 1 of 2.)

```
21          try
22          {
23              method2(); // call method2
24          } // end try
25          catch ( Exception exception ) // exception thrown from method2
26          {
27              throw new Exception( "Exception thrown in method1", exception );
28          } // end try
29      } // end method method1
30
31      // call method3; throw exceptions back to method1
32      public static void method2() throws Exception
33      {
34          try
35          {
36              method3(); // call method3
37          } // end try
38          catch ( Exception exception ) // exception thrown from method3
39          {
40              throw new Exception( "Exception thrown in method2", exception );
41          } // end catch
42      } // end method method2
43
44      // throw Exception back to method2
45      public static void method3() throws Exception
46      {
47          throw new Exception( "Exception thrown in method3" );
48      } // end method method3
49  } // end class UsingChainedExceptions
```

```
java.lang.Exception: Exception thrown in method1
        at UsingChainedExceptions.method1(UsingChainedExceptions.java:27)
        at UsingChainedExceptions.main(UsingChainedExceptions.java:10)
Caused by: java.lang.Exception: Exception thrown in method2
        at UsingChainedExceptions.method2(UsingChainedExceptions.java:40)
        at UsingChainedExceptions.method1(UsingChainedExceptions.java:23)
        ... 1 more
Caused by: java.lang.Exception: Exception thrown in method3
        at UsingChainedExceptions.method3(UsingChainedExceptions.java:47)
        at UsingChainedExceptions.method2(UsingChainedExceptions.java:36)
        ... 2 more
```

Fig. 13.8 | Chained exceptions. (Part 2 of 2.)

The program consists of four methods—main (lines 6–16), method1 (lines 19–29), method2 (lines 32–42) and method3 (lines 45–48). Line 10 in method main's try block calls method1. Line 23 in method1's try block calls method2. Line 36 in method2's try block calls method3. In method3, line 47 throws a new Exception. Because this statement is not in a try block, method3 terminates, and the exception is returned to the calling method (method2) at line 36. This statement *is* in a try block; therefore, the try block terminates and the exception is caught at lines 38–41. Line 40 in the catch block throws a new exception. In this case, the Exception constructor with two arguments is called. The second argument represents the exception that was the original cause of the problem. In this program, that exception occurred at line 47. Because an exception is thrown from the catch block, method2 terminates and returns the new exception to the calling method (method1) at line 23. Once again, this statement is in a try block, so the try block terminates and the exception is caught at lines 25–28. Line 27 in the catch block throws a new exception and uses the exception that was caught as the second argument to the Exception constructor. Because an exception is thrown from the catch block, method1 terminates and returns the new exception to the calling method (main) at line 10. The try block in main terminates, and the exception is caught at lines 12–15. Line 14 prints a stack trace.

Notice in the program output that the first three lines show the most recent exception that was thrown (i.e., the one from method1 at line 23). The next four lines indicate the exception that was thrown from method2 at line 40. Finally, the last four lines represent the exception that was thrown from method3 at line 47. Also notice that, as you read the output in reverse, it shows how many more chained exceptions remain.

13.11 Declaring New Exception Types

Most Java programmers use existing classes from the Java API, third-party vendors and freely available class libraries (usually downloadable from the Internet) to build Java applications. The methods of those classes typically are declared to throw appropriate exceptions when problems occur. Programmers write code that processes these existing exceptions to make programs more robust.

If you build classes that other programmers will use, you might find it useful to declare your own exception classes that are specific to the problems that can occur when another programmer uses your reusable classes.

Software Engineering Observation 13.13

If possible, indicate exceptions from your methods by using existing exception classes, rather than creating new exception classes. The Java API contains many exception classes that might be suitable for the type of problem your method needs to indicate.

A new exception class must extend an existing exception class to ensure that the class can be used with the exception-handling mechanism. Like any other class, an exception class can contains fields and methods. However, a typical new exception class contains only two constructors—one that takes no arguments and passes a default exception message to the superclass constructor, and one that receives a customized exception message as a string and passes it to the superclass constructor.

Good Programming Practice 13.3

Associating each type of serious execution-time malfunction with an appropriately named Exception class improves program clarity.

Software Engineering Observation 13.14

When defining your own exception type, study the existing exception classes in the Java API and try to extend a related exception class. For example, if you are creating a new class to represent when a method attempts a division by zero, you might extend class ArithmeticException because division by zero occurs during arithmetic. If the existing classes are not appropriate superclasses for your new exception class, decide whether your new class should be a checked or an unchecked exception class. The new exception class should be a checked exception (i.e., extend

Exception but not RuntimeException) *if possible clients should be required to handle the exception. The client application should be able to reasonably recover from such an exception. The new exception class should extend* RuntimeException *if the client code should be able to ignore the exception (i.e., the exception is an unchecked exception).*

Good Programming Practice 13.4

By convention, all exception-class names should end with the word Exception.

13.12 Preconditions and Postconditions

Programmers spend significant portions of their time maintaining and debugging code. To facilitate these tasks and to improve the overall design, they generally specify the expected states before and after a method's execution. These states are called preconditions and postconditions, respectively.

A *precondition* must be true when a method is invoked. Preconditions describe constraints on method parameters and any other expectations the method has about the current state of a program. If the preconditions are not met, then the method's behavior is undefined—it may throw an exception, proceed with an illegal value or attempt to recover from the error. However, you should never rely on or expect consistent behavior if the preconditions are not satisfied.

A *postcondition* is true after the method successfully returns. Postconditions describe constraints on the return value and any other side effects the method may have. When calling a method, you may assume that a method fulfills all of its postconditions. If you are writing your own method, you should document all postconditions so others know what to expect when they call your method, and you should make certain that your method honors all its postconditions if its preconditions are indeed met.

When their preconditions or postconditions are not met, methods typically throw exceptions. As an example, examine String method charAt, which has one int parameter—an index in the String. For a precondition, method charAt assumes that index is greater than or equal to zero and less than the length of the String. If the precondition is met, the postcondition states the method will return the character at the position in the String specified by the parameter index. Otherwise, the method throws an IndexOutOf-BoundsException. We trust that method charAt satisfies its postcondition, provided that we meet the precondition. We do not need to be concerned with the details of how the method actually retrieves the character at the index.

Some programmers state the preconditions and postconditions informally as part of the general method specification, while others prefer a more formal approach by explicitly defining them. When designing your own methods, you should state the preconditions and postconditions in a comment before the method declaration in whichever manner you prefer. Stating the preconditions and postconditions before writing a method will also help guide you as you implement the method.

13.13 Assertions

When implementing and debugging a class, it is sometimes useful to state conditions that should be true at a particular point in a method. These conditions, called *assertions*, help ensure a program's validity by catching potential bugs and identifying possible logic errors during development. Preconditions and postconditions are two types of assertions. Preconditions are assertions about a program's state when a method is invoked, and postconditions are assertions about a program's state after a method finishes.

While assertions can be stated as comments to guide the programmer during development, Java includes two versions of the **assert** statement for validating assertions programatically. The assert statement evaluates a boolean expression and determines whether it is true or false. The first form of the assert statement is

> **assert** *expression*;

This statement evaluates *expression* and throws an AssertionError if the expression is false. The second form is

> **assert** *expression1* : *expression2*;

This statement evaluates *expression1* and throws an AssertionError with *expression2* as the error message if *expression1* is false.

You can use assertions to programmatically implement preconditions and postconditions or to verify any other intermediate states that help you ensure your code is working correctly. The example in Fig. 13.9 demonstrates the functionality of the assert statement. Line 11 prompts the user to enter a number between 0 and 10, then line 12 reads the number from the command line. The assert statement at line 15 determines whether the user entered a number within the valid range. If the number is out of range, then the program reports an error; otherwise, the program proceeds normally.

```java
1   // Fig. 13.9: AssertTest.java
2   // Demonstrates the assert statement
3   import java.util.Scanner;
4
5   public class AssertTest
6   {
7      public static void main( String args[] )
8      {
9         Scanner input = new Scanner( System.in );
10
11         System.out.print( "Enter a number between 0 and 10: " );
12         int number = input.nextInt();
13
14         // assert that the absolute value is >= 0
15         assert ( number >= 0 && number <= 10 ) : "bad number: " + number;
16
17         System.out.printf( "You entered %d\n", number );
18      } // end main
19   } // end class AssertTest
```

```
Enter a number between 0 and 10: 5
You entered 5
```

Fig. 13.9 | Checking with assert that a value is within range. (Part 1 of 2.)

```
Enter a number between 0 and 10: 50
Exception in thread "main" java.lang.AssertionError: bad number: 50
        at AssertTest.main(AssertTest.java:15)
```

Fig. 13.9 | Checking with `assert` that a value is within range. (Part 2 of 2.)

Assertions are primarily used by the programmer for debugging and identifying logic errors in an application. By default, assertions are disabled when executing a program because they reduce performance and are unnecessary for the program's user. To enable assertions at runtime, use the java command's -ea command-line option. To execute the program in Fig. 13.9 with assertions enabled, type

```
java -ea AssertTest
```

You should not encounter any `AssertionError`s through normal execution of a properly written program. Such errors should only indicate bugs in the implementation. As a result, you should never catch an `AssertionError`. Rather, you should allow the program to terminate when the error occurs, so you can see the error message; then you should locate and fix the source of the problem. Since application users can choose not to enable assertions at runtime, you should not use the `assert` statement to indicate runtime problems in production code. Rather, you should use the exception mechanism for this purpose.

13.14 Wrap-Up

In this chapter, you learned how to use exception handling to deal with errors in an application. You learned that exception handling enables programmers to remove error-handling code from the "main line" of the program's execution. You saw exception handling in the context of a divide-by-zero example. You learned how to use `try` blocks to enclose code that may throw an exception, and how to use `catch` blocks to deal with exceptions that may arise. You learned about the termination model of exception handling, which dictates that after an exception is handled, program control does not return to the throw point. You learned the difference between checked and unchecked exceptions, and how to specify with the `throws` clause that specific exceptions occurring in a method will be thrown by that method to its caller. You learned how to use the `finally` block to release resources whether or not an exception occurs. You also learned how to throw and rethrow exceptions. You then learned how to obtain information about an exception using methods `printStackTrace`, `getStackTrace` and `getMessage`. The chapter continued with a discussion of chained exceptions, which allow programmers to wrap original exception information with new exception information. Next, we overviewed how to create your own exception classes. We then introduced preconditions and postconditions to help programmers using your methods understand conditions that must be true with the method is called and when it returns. When preconditions and postconditions are not met, methods typically throw exceptions. Finally, we discussed the `assert` statement and how it can be used to help you debug your programs. In particular, these can be used to ensure that preconditions and postconditions are met. In the next chapter, you'll learn about file processing, including how persistent data is stored and how to manipulate it.

14

Files and Streams

OBJECTIVES

In this chapter you'll learn:

- To create, read, write and update files.
- To use class `File` to retrieve information about files and directories.
- The Java input/output stream class hierarchy.
- The differences between text files and binary files.
- Sequential-access file processing.
- To use classes `Scanner` and `Formatter` to process text files.
- To use the `FileInputStream` and `FileOutputStream` classes.
- To use a `JFileChooser` dialog.
- To use the `ObjectInputStream` and `ObjectOutputStream` classes.

Outline

14.1 Introduction

14.2 Data Hierarchy

14.3 Files and Streams

14.4 Class `File`

14.5 Sequential-Access Text Files

    14.5.1 Creating a Sequential-Access Text File

    14.5.2 Reading Data from a Sequential-Access Text File

    14.5.3 Case Study: A Credit-Inquiry Program

    14.5.4 Updating Sequential-Access Files

14.6 Object Serialization

    14.6.1 Creating a Sequential-Access File Using Object Serialization

    14.6.2 Reading and Deserializing Data from a Sequential-Access File

14.7 Additional `java.io` Classes

14.8 Opening Files with `JFileChooser`

14.9 Wrap-Up

14.1 Introduction

Storage of data in variables and arrays is temporary—the data is lost when a local variable goes out of scope or when the program terminates. Computers use files for long-term retention of large amounts of data, even after the programs that created the data terminate. You use files every day for tasks such as writing an essay or creating a spreadsheet. We refer to data maintained in files as *persistent data* because it exists beyond the duration of program execution. Computers store files on *secondary storage devices* such as hard disks, optical disks and magnetic tapes. In this chapter, we explain how Java programs create, update and process files.

File processing is one of the most important capabilities a language must have to support commercial applications, which typically store and process massive amounts of persistent data. In this chapter, we discuss Java's powerful file-processing and stream input/output features. The term "stream" refers to ordered data that is read from or written to a file. We discuss streams in more detail in Section 14.3. File processing is a subset of Java's stream-processing capabilities, which enable a program to read and write data in memory, in files and over network connections. We have two goals in this chapter—to introduce file-processing concepts (making the reader more comfortable with using files programmatically) and to provide the reader with sufficient stream-processing capabilities to support the networking features introduced in Chapter 19, Networking. Java provides substantial stream-processing capabilities—far more than we can cover in one chapter. We discuss two forms of file processing here—text-file processing and object serialization.

We begin by discussing the hierarchy of data contained in files. We then cover Java's architecture for handling files programmatically by discussing several classes in package `java.io`. Next we explain that data can be stored in two different types of files—text files and binary files—and cover the differences between them. We demonstrate retrieving information about a file or directory using class `File` and then devote several sections to the different mechanisms for writing data to and reading data from files. First we demonstrate creating and manipulating sequential-access text files. Working with text files allows the reader to quickly and easily start manipulating files. As you'll learn, however, it is difficult to read data from text files back into object form. Fortunately, many object-oriented languages (including Java) provide ways to write objects to and read objects from files (known as object serialization and deserialization). To demonstrate this, we recreate some of the sequential-access programs that used text files, this time by storing objects in binary files.

14.2 Data Hierarchy

Ultimately, a computer processes all data items as combinations of zeros and ones, because it is simple and economical for engineers to build electronic devices that can assume two stable states—one representing 0 and the other representing 1. It is remarkable that the impressive functions performed by computers involve only the most fundamental manipulations of 0s and 1s.

The smallest data item in a computer can assume the values 0 or 1. Such a data item is called a *bit* (short for "binary digit"—a digit that can assume one of two values). Computer circuitry performs various simple bit manipulations, such as examining the value of a bit, setting the value of a bit and reversing the value of a bit (from 1 to 0 or from 0 to 1).

It is cumbersome for programmers to work with data in the low-level form of bits. Instead, they prefer to work with data in such forms as *decimal digits* (0–9), *letters* (A–Z and a–z), and *special symbols* (e.g., $, @, %, &, *, (,), –, +, ", :, ? and /). Digits, letters and special symbols are known as *characters.* The computer's *character set* is the set of all the characters used to write programs and represent data items. Computers process only 1s and 0s, so a computer's character set represents every character as a pattern of 1s and 0s. Characters in Java are *Unicode* characters composed of two *bytes*, each composed of eight bits. Java contains a data type, byte, that can be used to represent byte data. The Unicode character set contains characters for many of the world's languages. See Appendix B, ASCII Character Set, for more information on the *ASCII (American Standard Code for Information Interchange)* character set, a subset of the Unicode character set that represents uppercase and lowercase letters, digits and various common special characters.

Just as characters are composed of bits, *fields* are composed of characters or bytes. A field is a group of characters or bytes that conveys meaning. For example, a field consisting of uppercase and lowercase letters can be used to represent a person's name.

Data items processed by computers form a *data hierarchy* that becomes larger and more complex in structure as we progress from bits to characters to fields, and so on.

Typically, several fields compose a *record* (implemented as a class in Java). In a payroll system, for example, the record for an employee might consist of the following fields (possible types for these fields are shown in parentheses):

- Employee identification number (int)
- Name (String)
- Address (String)
- Hourly pay rate (double)
- Number of exemptions claimed (int)
- Year-to-date earnings (int or double)
- Amount of taxes withheld (int or double)

Thus, a record is a group of related fields. In the preceding example, all the fields belong to the same employee. Of course, a company might have many employees and thus have a payroll record for each employee. A *file* is a group of related records. [*Note:* More generally, a file contains arbitrary data in arbitrary formats. In some operating systems, a file is viewed as nothing more than a collection of bytes—any organization of the bytes in a file (e.g., organizing the data into records) is a view created by the applications programmer.] A company's payroll file normally contains one record for each employee. Thus, a payroll file for a small company might contain only 22 records, whereas one for a large company might contain 100,000 records. It is not unusual for a company to have many files, some containing billions, or even trillions, of characters of information. Figure 14.1 illustrates a portion of the data hierarchy.

To facilitate the retrieval of specific records from a file, at least one field in each record is chosen as a *record key*. A record key identifies a record as belonging to a particular person or entity and is unique to each record. This field typically is used to search and sort records. In the payroll record described previously, the employee identification number normally would be chosen as the record key.

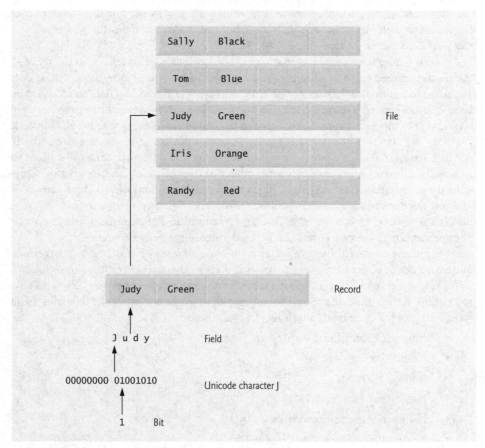

Fig. 14.1 | Data hierarchy.

There are many ways to organize records in a file. The most common is called a *sequential file*, in which records are stored in order by the record-key field. In a payroll file, records are placed in ascending order by employee identification number.

Most businesses store data in many different files. For example, companies might have payroll files, accounts receivable files (listing money due from clients), accounts payable files (listing money due to suppliers), inventory files (listing facts about all the items handled by the business) and many others. Often, a group of related files is called a *database*. A collection of programs designed to create and manage databases is called a *database management system* (DBMS). We discuss this topic in Chapter 20, Accessing Databases with JDBC.

14.3 Files and Streams

Java views each file as a sequential *stream* of bytes (Fig. 14.2). Every operating system provides a mechanism to determine the end of a file, such as an *end-of-file marker* or a count of the total bytes in the file that is recorded in a system-maintained administrative data structure. A Java program processing a stream of bytes simply receives an indication from the operating system when it reaches the end of the stream—the program does not need to know how the underlying platform represents files or streams. In some cases, the end-of-file indication occurs as an exception. In other cases, the indication is a return value from a method invoked on a stream-processing object.

File streams can be used to input and output data as either characters or bytes. Streams that input and output bytes to files are known as *byte-based streams*, storing data in its binary format. Streams that input and output characters to files are known as *character-based streams*, storing data as a sequence of characters. For instance, if the value 5 were being stored using a byte-based stream, it would be stored in the binary format of the numeric value 5, or 101. If the value 5 were being stored using a character-based stream, it would be stored in the binary format of the character 5, or 00000000 00110101 (this is the binary for the numeric value 53, which indicates the character 5 in the Unicode character set). The difference between the numeric value 5 and the character 5 is that the numeric value can be used as an integer in calculations, whereas the character 5 is simply a character that can be used in a string of text, as in "Sarah Miller is 15 years old". Files that are created using byte-based streams are referred to as *binary files*, while files created using character-based streams are referred to as *text files*. Text files can be read by text editors, while binary files are read by a program that converts the data to a human-readable format.

A Java program *opens* a file by creating an object and associating a stream of bytes or characters with it. The classes used to create these objects are discussed shortly. Java can also associate streams with different devices. In fact, Java creates three stream objects that are associated with devices when a Java program begins executing—System.in, System.out and System.err. Object System.in (the standard input stream object) normally enables a program to input bytes from the keyboard; object System.out (the stan-

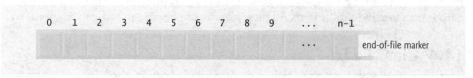

Fig. 14.2 | Java's view of a file of *n* bytes.

dard output stream object) normally enables a program to output data to the screen; and object System.err (the standard error stream object) normally enables a program to output error messages to the screen. Each of these streams can be *redirected*. For System.in, this capability enables the program to read bytes from a different source. For System.out and System.err, this capability enables the output to be sent to a different location, such as a file on disk. Class System provides methods setIn, setOut and setErr to redirect the standard input, output and error streams, respectively.

Java programs perform file processing by using classes from package java.io. This package includes definitions for stream classes, such as FileInputStream (for byte-based input from a file), FileOutputStream (for byte-based output to a file), FileReader (for character-based input from a file) and FileWriter (for character-based output to a file). Files are opened by creating objects of these stream classes, which inherit from classes InputStream, OutputStream, Reader and Writer, respectively (these classes will be discussed later in this chapter). Thus, the methods of these stream classes can all be applied to file streams as well.

Java contains classes that enable the programmer to perform input and output of objects or variables of primitive data types. The data will still be stored as bytes or characters behind the scenes, allowing the programmer to read or write data in the form of integers, strings, or other data types without having to worry about the details of converting such values to byte format. To perform such input and output, objects of classes ObjectInputStream and ObjectOutputStream can be used together with the byte-based file stream classes FileInputStream and FileOutputStream (these classes will be discussed in more detail shortly). The complete hierarchy of classes in package java.io can be viewed in the online documentation at

java.sun.com/javase/6/docs/api/java/io/package-tree.html

Each indentation level in the hierarchy indicates that the indented class extends the class under which it is indented. For example, class InputStream is a subclass of Object. Click a class's name in the hierarchy to view the details of the class.

As you can see in the hierarchy, Java offers many classes for performing input/output operations. We use several of these classes in this chapter to implement file-processing programs that create and manipulate sequential-access files. We also include a detailed example on class File, which is useful for obtaining information about files and directories. In Chapter 19, Networking, we use stream classes extensively to implement networking applications. Several other classes in the java.io package that we do not use in this chapter are discussed briefly in Section 14.7.

In addition to the classes in this package, character-based input and output can be performed with classes Scanner and Formatter. Class Scanner is used extensively to input data from the keyboard. As we'll see, this class can also read data from a file. Class Formatter enables formatted data to be output to the screen or to a file in a manner similar to System.out.printf. Chapter 24, Formatted Output, presents the details of formatted output with System.out.printf. All these features can be used to format text files as well.

14.4 Class File

This section presents class File, which is particularly useful for retrieving information about files or directories from disk. Objects of class File do not open files or provide any file-processing capabilities. However, File objects are used frequently with objects of other java.io classes to specify files or directories to manipulate.

Creating File Objects
Class File provides four constructors. The constructor

> **public** File(String name)

specifies the name of a file or directory to associate with the File object. The name can contain *path information* as well as a file or directory name. A file or directory's path specifies its location on disk. The path includes some or all of the directories leading to the file or directory. An *absolute path* contains all the directories, starting with the *root directory*, that lead to a specific file or directory. Every file or directory on a particular disk drive has the same root directory in its path. A *relative path* normally starts from the directory in which the application began executing, and is therefore a path that is "relative" to the current directory.

The constructor

> **public** File(String pathToName, String name)

uses argument pathToName (an absolute or relative path) to locate the file or directory specified by name.

The constructor

> **public** File(File directory, String name)

uses an existing File object directory (an absolute or relative path) to locate the file or directory specified by name. Figure 14.3 lists some common File methods. The complete list can be viewed at java.sun.com/javase/6/docs/api/java/io/File.html.

Method	Description
boolean canRead()	Returns true if a file is readable by the current application; false otherwise.
boolean canWrite()	Returns true if a file is writable by the current application; false otherwise.
boolean exists()	Returns true if the name specified as the argument to the File constructor is a file or directory in the specified path; false otherwise.
boolean isFile()	Returns true if the name specified as the argument to the File constructor is a file; false otherwise.
boolean isDirectory()	Returns true if the name specified as the argument to the File constructor is a directory; false otherwise.
boolean isAbsolute()	Returns true if the arguments specified to the File constructor indicate an absolute path to a file or directory; false otherwise.

Fig. 14.3 | File methods. (Part 1 of 2.)

Method	Description
`String getAbsolutePath()`	Returns a string with the absolute path of the file or directory.
`String getName()`	Returns a string with the name of the file or directory.
`String getPath()`	Returns a string with the path of the file or directory.
`String getParent()`	Returns a string with the parent directory of the file or directory (i.e., the directory in which the file or directory can be found).
`long length()`	Returns the length of the file, in bytes. If the `File` object represents a directory, 0 is returned.
`long lastModified()`	Returns a platform-dependent representation of the time at which the file or directory was last modified. The value returned is useful only for comparison with other values returned by this method.
`String[] list()`	Returns an array of strings representing the contents of a directory. Returns `null` if the `File` object does not represent a directory.

Fig. 14.3 | `File` methods. (Part 2 of 2.)

The constructor

```
public File( URI uri )
```

uses the given URI object to locate the file. A *Uniform Resource Identifier (URI)* is a more general form of the *Uniform Resource Locators (URLs)* that are used to locate websites. For example, `http://www.deitel.com/` is the URL for the Deitel & Associates' website. URIs for locating files vary across operating systems. On Windows platforms, the URI

```
file:/C:/data.txt
```

identifies the file `data.txt` stored in the root directory of the C: drive. On UNIX/Linux platforms, the URI

```
file:/home/student/data.txt
```

identifies the file `data.txt` stored in the home directory of the user `student`.

Error-Prevention Tip 14.1

*Use `File` method **isFile** to determine whether a `File` object represents a file (not a directory) before attempting to open the file.*

Demonstrating Class `File`

Figures 14.4–14.5 demonstrate class `File`. The application prompts the user to enter a file name or directory name, then outputs information about the file name or directory name input.

```
 1   // Fig. 14.4: FileDemonstration.java
 2   // Demonstrating the File class.
 3   import java.io.File;
 4
 5   public class FileDemonstration
 6   {
 7      // display information about file user specifies
 8      public void analyzePath( String path )
 9      {
10         // create File object based on user input
11         File name = new File( path );
12
13         if ( name.exists() ) // if name exists, output information about it
14         {
15            // display file (or directory) information
16            System.out.printf(
17               "%s%s\n%s\n%s\n%s\n%s%s\n%s%s\n%s%s\n%s%s\n%s%s",
18               name.getName(), " exists",
19               ( name.isFile() ? "is a file" : "is not a file" ),
20               ( name.isDirectory() ? "is a directory" :
21                  "is not a directory" ),
22               ( name.isAbsolute() ? "is absolute path" :
23                  "is not absolute path" ), "Last modified: ",
24               name.lastModified(), "Length: ", name.length(),
25               "Path: ", name.getPath(), "Absolute path: ",
26               name.getAbsolutePath(), "Parent: ", name.getParent() );
27
28            if ( name.isDirectory() ) // output directory listing
29            {
30               String directory[] = name.list();
31               System.out.println( "\n\nDirectory contents:\n" );
32
33               for ( String directoryName : directory )
34                  System.out.printf( "%s\n", directoryName );
35            } // end if
36         } // end outer if
37         else // not file or directory, output error message
38         {
39            System.out.printf( "%s %s", path, "does not exist." );
40         } // end else
41      } // end method analyzePath
42   } // end class FileDemonstration
```

Fig. 14.4 | File class used to obtain file and directory information.

```
 1   // Fig. 14.5: FileDemonstrationTest.java
 2   // Testing the FileDemonstration class.
 3   import java.util.Scanner;
 4
 5   public class FileDemonstrationTest
 6   {
```

Fig. 14.5 | Testing class FileDemonstration. (Part 1 of 2.)

```
7        public static void main( String args[] )
8        {
9           Scanner input = new Scanner( System.in );
10          FileDemonstration application = new FileDemonstration();
11
12          System.out.print( "Enter file or directory name here: " );
13          application.analyzePath( input.nextLine() );
14       } // end main
15    } // end class FileDemonstrationTest
```

```
Enter file or directory name here: C:\Program Files\Java\jdk1.6.0\demo\jfc
jfc exists
is not a file
is a directory
is absolute path
Last modified: 1162570370359
Length: 0
Path: C:\Program Files\Java\jdk1.6.0\demo\jfc
Absolute path: C:\Program Files\Java\jdk1.6.0\demo\jfc
Parent: C:\Program Files\Java\jdk1.6.0\demo

Directory contents:

CodePointIM
FileChooserDemo
Font2DTest
Java2D
Metalworks
Notepad
SampleTree
Stylepad
SwingApplet
SwingSet2
TableExample
```

```
Enter file or directory name here: C:\Program
Files\Java\jdk1.6.0\demo\jfc\Java2D\readme.txt
readme.txt exists
is a file
is not a directory
is absolute path
Last modified: 1162570365875
Length: 7518
Path: C:\Program Files\Java\jdk1.6.0\demo\jfc\Java2D\readme.txt
Absolute path: C:\Program Files\Java\jdk1.6.0\demo\jfc\Java2D\readme.txt
Parent: C:\Program Files\Java\jdk1.6.0\demo\jfc\Java2D
```

Fig. 14.5 | Testing class `FileDemonstration`. (Part 2 of 2.)

The program begins by prompting the user for a file or directory (line 12 of Fig. 14.5). Line 13 inputs the file name or directory name and passes it to method `analyzePath` (lines 8–41 of Fig. 14.4). The method creates a new `File` object (line 11) and assigns its reference to name. Line 13 invokes `File` method `exists` to determine whether the name input by the user exists (either as a file or as a directory) on the disk. If the name input by the user does not exist, control proceeds to lines 37–40 and displays a message to the screen containing the name the user typed, followed by "does not exist." Otherwise, the body of the if statement (lines 13–36) executes. The program outputs the name of the file or directory (line 18), followed by the results of testing the File object with isFile (line 19), isDirectory (line 20) and isAbsolute (line 22). Next, the program displays the values returned by lastModified (line 24), length (line 24), getPath (line 25), getAbsolute-Path (line 26) and getParent (line 26). If the File object represents a directory (line 28), the program obtains a list of the directory's contents as an array of Strings by using File method list (line 30) and displays the list on the screen.

The first output of this program demonstrates a File object associated with the jfc directory from the Java 2 Software Development Kit. The second output demonstrates a File object associated with the readme.txt file from the Java 2D example that comes with the Java 2 Software Development Kit. In both cases, we specified an absolute path on our personal computer.

A *separator character* is used to separate directories and files in the path. On a Windows computer, the separator character is a backslash (\) character. On a UNIX workstation, it is a forward slash (/) character. Java processes both characters identically in a path name. For example, if we were to use the path

```
c:\Program Files\Java\jdk1.6.0\demo/jfc
```

which employs each separator character, Java would still process the path properly. When building strings that represent path information, use File.separator to obtain the local computer's proper separator character rather than explicitly using / or \. This constant returns a String consisting of one character—the proper separator for the system.

Common Programming Error 14.1

Using \ as a directory separator rather than \\ in a string literal is a logic error. A single \ indicates that the \ followed by the next character represents an escape sequence. Use \\ to insert a \ in a string literal.

14.5 Sequential-Access Text Files

In this section, we create and manipulate sequential-access files. As mentioned earlier, these are files in which records are stored in order by the record-key field. We first demonstrate sequential-access files using text files, allowing the reader to quickly create and edit human-readable files. In the subsections of this chapter we discuss creating, writing data to, reading data from and updating sequential-access text files. We also include a credit-inquiry program that retrieves specific data from a file.

14.5.1 Creating a Sequential-Access Text File

Java imposes no structure on a file—notions such as a record do not exist as part of the Java language. Therefore, the programmer must structure files to meet the requirements of the intended application. In the following example, we see how to impose a record structure on a file.

The program in Figs. 14.6–14.7 and Fig. 14.9 creates a simple sequential-access file that might be used in an accounts receivable system to help keep track of the amounts owed to a company by its credit clients. For each client, the program obtains from the user an account number, the client's name and the client's balance (i.e., the amount the client owes the company for goods and services received). The data obtained for each client constitutes a "record" for that client. The account number is used as the record key in this application—the file will be created and maintained in account-number order. The program assumes that the user enters the records in account-number order. In a comprehensive accounts receivable system (based on sequential-access files), a sorting capability would be provided so that the user could enter the records in any order. The records would then be sorted and written to the file.

Class AccountRecord (Fig. 14.6) encapsulates the client record information (i.e., account, first name, and so on) used by the examples in this chapter. The class Account-Record is declared in package com.deitel.javafp.ch14 (line 3), so that it can be imported into several examples. Class AccountRecord contains private data members account, firstName, lastName and balance (lines 7–10). This class also provides public *set* and *get* methods for accessing the private fields.

```java
1   // Fig. 14.6: AccountRecord.java
2   // A class that represents one record of information.
3   package com.deitel.javafp.ch14; // packaged for reuse
4
5   public class AccountRecord
6   {
7      private int account;
8      private String firstName;
9      private String lastName;
10     private double balance;
11
12     // no-argument constructor calls other constructor with default values
13     public AccountRecord()
14     {
15        this( 0, "", "", 0.0 ); // call four-argument constructor
16     } // end no-argument AccountRecord constructor
17
18     // initialize a record
19     public AccountRecord( int acct, String first, String last, double bal )
20     {
21        setAccount( acct );
22        setFirstName( first );
23        setLastName( last );
24        setBalance( bal );
25     } // end four-argument AccountRecord constructor
26
27     // set account number
28     public void setAccount( int acct )
29     {
30        account = acct;
31     } // end method setAccount
32
33     // get account number
34     public int getAccount()
35     {
```

Fig. 14.6 | AccountRecord maintains information for one account. (Part 1 of 2.)

```
36          return account;
37     } // end method getAccount
38
39     // set first name
40     public void setFirstName( String first )
41     {
42        firstName = first;
43     } // end method setFirstName
44
45     // get first name
46     public String getFirstName()
47     {
48        return firstName;
49     } // end method getFirstName
50
51     // set last name
52     public void setLastName( String last )
53     {
54        lastName = last;
55     } // end method setLastName
56
57     // get last name
58     public String getLastName()
59     {
60        return lastName;
61     } // end method getLastName
62
63     // set balance
64     public void setBalance( double bal )
65     {
66        balance = bal;
67     } // end method setBalance
68
69     // get balance
70     public double getBalance()
71     {
72        return balance;
73     } // end method getBalance
74  } // end class AccountRecord
```

Fig. 14.6 | AccountRecord maintains information for one account. (Part 2 of 2.)

Compile class AccountRecord as follows:

```
javac -d c:\examples\ch14 com\deitel\javafp\ch14\AccountRecord.java
```

This places AccountRecord.class in its package directory structure and places the package in c:\examples\ch14. When you compile class AccountRecord (or any other classes that will be reused in this chapter), you should place them in a common directory (e.g., c:\examples\ch14). When you compile or execute classes that use AccountRecord (e.g., CreateTextFile in Fig. 14.7), you must specify the command-line argument -classpath to both javac and java, as in

```
javac -classpath .;c:\examples\ch14 CreateTextFile.java
java -classpath .;c:\examples\ch14 CreateTextFile
```

Note that the current directory (specified with .) is included in the classpath. This ensures that the compiler can locate other classes in the same directory as the class being compiled. The path separator used in the preceding commands should be the one that is appropriate for your platform—for example, a semicolon (;) on Windows and a colon (:) on UNIX/ Linux/Mac OS X.

Now let us examine class CreateTextFile (Fig. 14.7). Line 14 declares Formatter variable output. As discussed in Section 14.3, a Formatter object outputs formatted strings, using the same formatting capabilities as method System.out.printf. A Formatter object can output to various locations, such as the screen or a file, as is done here. The Formatter object is instantiated in line 21 in method openFile (lines 17–34). The constructor used in line 21 takes one argument—a String containing the name of the file, including its path. If a path is not specified, as is the case here, the JVM assumes that the files is in the directory from which the program was executed. For text files, we use the .txt file extension. If the file does not exist, it will be created. If an existing file is opened, its contents are *truncated*—all the data in the file is discarded. At this point the file is open for writing, and the resulting Formatter object can be used to write data to the file. Lines 23–28 handle the SecurityException, which occurs if the user does not have permission to write data to the file. Lines 29–33 handle the FileNotFoundException, which occurs if the file does not exist and a new file cannot be created. This exception may also occur if there is an error opening the file. Note that in both exception handlers, we call static method *System.exit*, and pass the value 1. This method terminates the application. An argument of 0 to method exit indicates successful program termination. A nonzero value, such as 1 in this example, normally indicates that an error has occurred. This value is passed to the command window that executed the program. The argument is useful if the program is executed from a *batch file* on Windows systems or a *shell script* on UNIX/ Linux/Mac OS X systems. Batch files and shell scripts offer a convenient way of executing several programs in sequence. When the first program ends, the next program begins execution. It is possible to use the argument to method exit in a batch file or shell script to determine whether other programs should execute. For more information on batch files or shell scripts, see your operating system's documentation.

```
1   // Fig. 14.7: CreateTextFile.java
2   // Writing data to a text file with class Formatter.
3   import java.io.FileNotFoundException;
4   import java.lang.SecurityException;
5   import java.util.Formatter;
6   import java.util.FormatterClosedException;
7   import java.util.NoSuchElementException;
8   import java.util.Scanner;
9
10  import com.deitel.javafp.ch14.AccountRecord
11
12  public class CreateTextFile
13  {
```

Fig. 14.7 | Creating a sequential text file. (Part 1 of 3.)

```java
14         private Formatter output; // object used to output text to file
15
16         // enable user to open file
17         public void openFile()
18         {
19            try
20            {
21               output = new Formatter( "clients.txt" );
22            } // end try
23            catch ( SecurityException securityException )
24            {
25               System.err.println(
26                  "You do not have write access to this file." );
27               System.exit( 1 );
28            } // end catch
29            catch ( FileNotFoundException filesNotFoundException )
30            {
31               System.err.println( "Error creating file." );
32               System.exit( 1 );
33            } // end catch
34         } // end method openFile
35
36         // add records to file
37         public void addRecords()
38         {
39            // object to be written to file
40            AccountRecord record = new AccountRecord();
41
42            Scanner input = new Scanner( System.in );
43
44            System.out.printf( "%s\n%s\n%s\n%s\n\n",
45               "To terminate input, type the end-of-file indicator ",
46               "when you are prompted to enter input.",
47               "On UNIX/Linux/Mac OS X type <ctrl> d then press Enter",
48               "On Windows type <ctrl> z then press Enter" );
49
50            System.out.printf( "%s\n%s",
51               "Enter account number (> 0), first name, last name and balance.",
52               "? " );
53
54            while ( input.hasNext() ) // loop until end-of-file indicator
55            {
56               try // output values to file
57               {
58                  // retrieve data to be output
59                  record.setAccount( input.nextInt() ); // read account number
60                  record.setFirstName( input.next() ); // read first name
61                  record.setLastName( input.next() ); // read last name
62                  record.setBalance( input.nextDouble() ); // read balance
63
64                  if ( record.getAccount() > 0 )
65                  {
```

Fig. 14.7 | Creating a sequential text file. (Part 2 of 3.)

```
66              // write new record
67              output.format( "%d %s %s %.2f\n", record.getAccount(),
68                 record.getFirstName(), record.getLastName(),
69                 record.getBalance() );
70           } // end if
71           else
72           {
73              System.out.println(
74                 "Account number must be greater than 0." );
75           } // end else
76        } // end try
77        catch ( FormatterClosedException formatterClosedException )
78        {
79           System.err.println( "Error writing to file." );
80           return;
81        } // end catch
82        catch ( NoSuchElementException elementException )
83        {
84           System.err.println( "Invalid input. Please try again." );
85           input.nextLine(); // discard input so user can try again
86        } // end catch
87
88        System.out.printf( "%s %s\n%s", "Enter account number (>0),",
89           "first name, last name and balance.", "? " );
90     } // end while
91  } // end method addRecords
92
93  // close file
94  public void closeFile()
95  {
96     if ( output != null )
97        output.close();
98  } // end method closeFile
99  } // end class CreateTextFile
```

Fig. 14.7 | Creating a sequential text file. (Part 3 of 3.)

Method addRecords (lines 37–91) prompts the user to enter the various fields for each record or to enter the end-of-file key sequence when data entry is complete. Figure 14.8 lists the key combinations for entering end-of-file for various computer systems.

Line 40 creates an AccountRecord object, which will be used to store the values of the current record entered by the user. Line 42 creates a Scanner object to read input from the user at the keyboard. Lines 44–48 and 50–52 prompt the user for input.

Operating system	Key combination
UNIX/Linux/Mac OS X	*<Enter> <Ctrl> d*
Windows	*<Ctrl> z*

Fig. 14.8 | End-of-file key combinations for various popular operating systems.

Line 54 uses Scanner method hasNext to determine whether the end-of-file key combination has been entered. The loop executes until hasNext encounters end-of-file.

Lines 59–62 read data from the user, storing the record information in the AccountRecord object. Each statement throws a NoSuchElementException (handled in lines 82–86) if the data is in the wrong format (e.g., a string when an int is expected) or if there is no more data to input. If the account number is greater than 0 (line 64), the record's information is written to clients.txt (lines 67–69) using method format. This method can perform identical formatting to the System.out.printf method used extensively in earlier chapters. This method outputs a formatted string to the output destination of the Formatter object, in this case the file clients.txt. The format string "%d %s %s %.2\n" indicates that the current record will be stored as an integer (the account number) followed by a string (the first name), another string (the last name) and a floating-point value (the balance). Each piece of information is separated from the next by a space, and the double value (the balance) is output with two digits to the right of the decimal point. The data in the text file can be viewed with a text editor, or retrieved later by a program designed to read the file (14.5.2). When lines 67–69 execute, if the Formatter object is closed, a FormatterClosedException will be thrown (handled in lines 77–81). [*Note:* You can also output data to a text file using class java.io.PrintWriter, which also provides method format for outputting formatted data.]

Lines 94–98 declare method closeFile, which closes the Formatter and the underlying output file. Line 97 closes the object by simply calling method *close*. If method close is not called explicitly, the operating system normally will close the file when program execution terminates—this is an example of operating system "housekeeping."

Figure 14.9 runs the program. Line 8 creates a CreateTextFile object, which is then used to open, add records to and close the file (lines 10–12). The sample data for this application is shown in Fig. 14.10. In the sample execution for this program, the user enters information for five accounts, then enters end-of-file to signal that data entry is complete. The sample execution does not show how the data records actually appear in the file. In the next section, to verify that the file has been created successfully, we present a program that reads the file and prints its contents. Because this is a text file, you can also verify the information by opening the file in a text editor.

```java
1   // Fig. 14.9: CreateTextFileTest.java
2   // Testing the CreateTextFile class.
3
4   public class CreateTextFileTest
5   {
6      public static void main( String args[] )
7      {
8         CreateTextFile application = new CreateTextFile();
9
10        application.openFile();
11        application.addRecords();
12        application.closeFile();
13     } // end main
14  } // end class CreateTextFileTest
```

Fig. 14.9 | Testing the CreateTextFile class. (Part 1 of 2.)

```
To terminate input, type the end-of-file indicator
when you are prompted to enter input.
On UNIX/Linux/Mac OS X type <ctrl> d then press Enter
On Windows type <ctrl> z then press Enter

Enter account number (> 0), first name, last name and balance.
? 100 Bob Jones 24.98
Enter account number (> 0), first name, last name and balance.
? 200 Steve Doe -345.67
Enter account number (> 0), first name, last name and balance.
? 300 Pam White 0.00
Enter account number (> 0), first name, last name and balance.
? 400 Sam Stone -42.16
Enter account number (> 0), first name, last name and balance.
? 500 Sue Rich 224.62
Enter account number (> 0), first name, last name and balance.
? ^Z
```

Fig. 14.9 | Testing the `CreateTextFile` class. (Part 2 of 2.)

Sample data			
100	Bob	Jones	24.98
200	Steve	Doe	-345.67
300	Pam	White	0.00
400	Sam	Stone	-42.16
500	Sue	Rich	224.62

Fig. 14.10 | Sample data for the program in Fig. 14.7.

14.5.2 Reading Data from a Sequential-Access Text File

Data is stored in files so that it may be retrieved for processing when needed. Section 14.5.1 demonstrated how to create a file for sequential access. This section shows how to read data sequentially from a text file. In this section, we demonstrate how class Scanner can be used to input data from a file rather than the keyboard.

The application in Figs. 14.11 and 14.12 reads records from the file "clients.txt" created by the application of Section 14.5.1 and displays the record contents. Line 13 of Fig. 14.11 declares a Scanner that will be used to retrieve input from the file.

```java
1   // Fig. 14.11: ReadTextFile.java
2   // This program reads a text file and displays each record.
3   import java.io.File;
4   import java.io.FileNotFoundException;
5   import java.lang.IllegalStateException;
6   import java.util.NoSuchElementException;
7   import java.util.Scanner;
```

Fig. 14.11 | Sequential file reading using a Scanner. (Part 1 of 3.)

```
 8
 9   import com.deitel.javafp.ch14.AccountRecord;
10
11   public class ReadTextFile
12   {
13      private Scanner input;
14
15      // enable user to open file
16      public void openFile()
17      {
18         try
19         {
20            input = new Scanner( new File( "clients.txt" ) );
21         } // end try
22         catch ( FileNotFoundException fileNotFoundException )
23         {
24            System.err.println( "Error opening file." );
25            System.exit( 1 );
26         } // end catch
27      } // end method openFile
28
29      // read record from file
30      public void readRecords()
31      {
32         // object to be written to screen
33         AccountRecord record = new AccountRecord();
34
35         System.out.printf( "%-10s%-12s%-12s%10s\n", "Account",
36            "First Name", "Last Name", "Balance" );
37
38         try // read records from file using Scanner object
39         {
40            while ( input.hasNext() )
41            {
42               record.setAccount( input.nextInt() ); // read account number
43               record.setFirstName( input.next() ); // read first name
44               record.setLastName( input.next() ); // read last name
45               record.setBalance( input.nextDouble() ); // read balance
46
47               // display record contents
48               System.out.printf( "%-10d%-12s%-12s%10.2f\n",
49                  record.getAccount(), record.getFirstName(),
50                  record.getLastName(), record.getBalance() );
51            } // end while
52         } // end try
53         catch ( NoSuchElementException elementException )
54         {
55            System.err.println( "File improperly formed." );
56            input.close();
57            System.exit( 1 );
58         } // end catch
59         catch ( IllegalStateException stateException )
60         {
```

Fig. 14.11 | Sequential file reading using a Scanner. (Part 2 of 3.)

```
61                System.err.println( "Error reading from file." );
62                System.exit( 1 );
63            } // end catch
64        } // end method readRecords
65
66        // close file and terminate application
67        public void closeFile()
68        {
69            if ( input != null )
70                input.close(); // close file
71        } // end method closeFile
72    } // end class ReadTextFile
```

Fig. 14.11 | Sequential file reading using a Scanner. (Part 3 of 3.)

```
 1    // Fig. 14.12: ReadTextFileTest.java
 2    // This program test class ReadTextFile.
 3
 4    public class ReadTextFileTest
 5    {
 6        public static void main( String args[] )
 7        {
 8            ReadTextFile application = new ReadTextFile();
 9
10            application.openFile();
11            application.readRecords();
12            application.closeFile();
13        } // end main
14    } // end class ReadTextFileTest
```

Account	First Name	Last Name	Balance
100	Bob	Jones	24.98
200	Steve	Doe	-345.67
300	Pam	White	0.00
400	Sam	Stone	-42.16
500	Sue	Rich	224.62

Fig. 14.12 | Testing the ReadTextFile class.

Method openFile (lines 16–27) opens the file for reading by instantiating a Scanner object in line 20. We pass a File object to the constructor, which specifies that the Scanner object will read from the file "clients.txt" located in the directory from which the application executes. If the file cannot be found, a FileNotFoundException occurs. The exception is handled in lines 22–26.

Method readRecords (lines 30–64) reads and displays records from the file. Line 33 creates AccountRecord object record to store the current record's information. Lines 35–36 display headers for the columns in the application's output. Lines 40–51 read data from the file until the end-of-file marker is reached (in which case, method hasNext will return false at line 40). Lines 42–45 use Scanner methods nextInt, next and nextDouble to input an integer (the account number), two strings (the first and last names) and a double value (the balance). Each record is one line of data in the file. The values are stored in object record. If the information in the file is not properly formed (e.g., there is a last name where there should be a balance), a NoSuchElementException occurs when the record is input. This exception is handled in lines 53–58. If the Scanner was closed before the data was input, an IllegalStateException occurs (handled in lines 59–63). If no exceptions occur, the record's information is displayed on the screen (lines 48–50). Note in the format string in line 48 that the account number, first name and last name are left justified, while the balance is right justified and output with two digits of precision. Each iteration of the loop inputs one line of text from the text file, which represents one record.

Lines 67–71 define method closeFile, which closes the Scanner. Method main is defined in Fig. 14.12, in lines 6–13. Line 8 creates a ReadTextFile object, which is then used to open, add records to and close the file (lines 10–12).

14.5.3 Case Study: A Credit-Inquiry Program

To retrieve data sequentially from a file, programs normally start reading from the beginning of the file and read all the data consecutively until the desired information is found. It might be necessary to process the file sequentially several times (from the beginning of the file) during the execution of a program. Class Scanner does not provide the ability to reposition to the beginning of the file. If it is necessary to read the file again, the program must close the file and reopen it.

The program in Figs. 14.13–14.15 allows a credit manager to obtain lists of customers with zero balances (i.e., customers who do not owe any money), customers with credit balances (i.e., customers to whom the company owes money) and customers with debit balances (i.e., customers who owe the company money for goods and services received). A credit balance is a negative amount, and a debit balance is a positive amount.

```
1   // Fig. 14.13: MenuOption.java
2   // Defines an enum type for the credit-inquiry program's options.
3
4   public enum MenuOption
5   {
6      // declare contents of enum type
7      ZERO_BALANCE( 1 ),
8      CREDIT_BALANCE( 2 ),
9      DEBIT_BALANCE( 3 ),
10     END( 4 );
11
12     private final int value; // current menu option
13
14     MenuOption( int valueOption )
15     {
16        value = valueOption;
17     } // end MenuOptions enum constructor
18
19     public int getValue()
20     {
21        return value;
22     } // end method getValue
23  } // end enum MenuOption
```

Fig. 14.13 | Enumeration for menu options.

```
 1    // Fig. 14.14: CreditInquiry.java
 2    // This program reads a file sequentially and displays the
 3    // contents based on the type of account the user requests
 4    // (credit balance, debit balance or zero balance).
 5    import java.io.File;
 6    import java.io.FileNotFoundException;
 7    import java.lang.IllegalStateException;
 8    import java.util.NoSuchElementException;
 9    import java.util.Scanner;
10
11    import com.deitel.javafp.ch14.AccountRecord;
12
13    public class CreditInquiry
14    {
15       private MenuOption accountType;
16       private Scanner input;
17       private MenuOption choices[] = { MenuOption.ZERO_BALANCE,
18          MenuOption.CREDIT_BALANCE, MenuOption.DEBIT_BALANCE,
19          MenuOption.END };
20
21       // read records from file and display only records of appropriate type
22       private void readRecords()
23       {
24          // object to be written to file
25          AccountRecord record = new AccountRecord();
26
27          try // read records
28          {
29             // open file to read from beginning
30             input = new Scanner( new File( "clients.txt" ) );
31
32             while ( input.hasNext() ) // input the values from the file
33             {
34                record.setAccount( input.nextInt() ); // read account number
35                record.setFirstName( input.next() ); // read first name
36                record.setLastName( input.next() ); // read last name
37                record.setBalance( input.nextDouble() ); // read balance
38
39                // if proper acount type, display record
40                if ( shouldDisplay( record.getBalance() ) )
41                   System.out.printf( "%-10d%-12s%-12s%10.2f\n",
42                      record.getAccount(), record.getFirstName(),
43                      record.getLastName(), record.getBalance() );
44             } // end while
45          } // end try
46          catch ( NoSuchElementException elementException )
47          {
48             System.err.println( "File improperly formed." );
49             input.close();
50             System.exit( 1 );
51          } // end catch
52          catch ( IllegalStateException stateException )
53          {
```

Fig. 14.14 | Credit-inquiry program. (Part 1 of 3.)

```
54                  System.err.println( "Error reading from file." );
55                  System.exit( 1 );
56              } // end catch
57              catch ( FileNotFoundException fileNotFoundException )
58              {
59                  System.err.println( "File cannot be found." );
60                  System.exit( 1 );
61              } // end catch
62              finally
63              {
64                  if ( input != null )
65                      input.close(); // close the Scanner and the file
66              } // end finally
67          } // end method readRecords
68
69          // use record type to determine if record should be displayed
70          private boolean shouldDisplay( double balance )
71          {
72              if ( ( accountType == MenuOption.CREDIT_BALANCE )
73                  && ( balance < 0 ) )
74                  return true;
75
76              else if ( ( accountType == MenuOption.DEBIT_BALANCE )
77                  && ( balance > 0 ) )
78                  return true;
79
80              else if ( ( accountType == MenuOption.ZERO_BALANCE )
81                  && ( balance == 0 ) )
82                  return true;
83
84              return false;
85          } // end method shouldDisplay
86
87          // obtain request from user
88          private MenuOption getRequest()
89          {
90              Scanner textIn = new Scanner( System.in );
91              int request = 1;
92
93              // display request options
94              System.out.printf( "\n%s\n%s\n%s\n%s\n%s\n",
95                  "Enter request", " 1 - List accounts with zero balances",
96                  " 2 - List accounts with credit balances",
97                  " 3 - List accounts with debit balances", " 4 - End of run" );
98
99              try // attempt to input menu choice
100             {
101                 do // input user request
102                 {
103                     System.out.print( "\n? " );
104                     request = textIn.nextInt();
105                 } while ( ( request < 1 ) || ( request > 4 ) );
106             } // end try
```

Fig. 14.14 | Credit-inquiry program. (Part 2 of 3.)

```
107        catch ( NoSuchElementException elementException )
108        {
109            System.err.println( "Invalid input." );
110            System.exit( 1 );
111        } // end catch
112
113        return choices[ request - 1 ]; // return enum value for option
114    } // end method getRequest
115
116    public void processRequests()
117    {
118        // get user's request (e.g., zero, credit or debit balance)
119        accountType = getRequest();
120
121        while ( accountType != MenuOption.END )
122        {
123            switch ( accountType )
124            {
125                case ZERO_BALANCE:
126                    System.out.println( "\nAccounts with zero balances:\n" );
127                    break;
128                case CREDIT_BALANCE:
129                    System.out.println( "\nAccounts with credit balances:\n" );
130                    break;
131                case DEBIT_BALANCE:
132                    System.out.println( "\nAccounts with debit balances:\n" );
133                    break;
134            } // end switch
135
136            readRecords();
137            accountType = getRequest();
138        } // end while
139    } // end method processRequests
140 } // end class CreditInquiry
```

Fig. 14.14 | Credit-inquiry program. (Part 3 of 3.)

```
1    // Fig. 14.15: CreditInquiryTest.java
2    // This program tests class CreditInquiry.
3
4    public class CreditInquiryTest
5    {
6        public static void main( String args[] )
7        {
8            CreditInquiry application = new CreditInquiry();
9            application.processRequests();
10        } // end main
11 } // end class CreditInquiryTest
```

Fig. 14.15 | Testing the CreditInquiry class.

We begin by creating an enum type (Fig. 14.13) to define the different menu options the user will have. The options and their values are listed in lines 7–10. Method getValue (lines 19–22) retrieves the value of a specific enum constant.

Figure 14.14 contains the functionality for the credit-inquiry program, and Fig. 14.15 contains the main method that executes the program. The program displays a text menu and allows the credit manager to enter one of three options to obtain credit information. Option 1 (ZERO_BALANCE) produces a list of accounts with zero balances. Option 2 (CREDIT_BALANCE) produces a list of accounts with credit balances. Option 3 (DEBIT_BALANCE) produces a list of accounts with debit balances. Option 4 (END) terminates program execution. A sample output is shown in Fig. 14.16.

The record information is collected by reading through the entire file and determining whether each record satisfies the criteria for the account type selected by the credit manager. Method processRequests (lines 116–139 of Fig. 14.14) calls method get-

```
Enter request
 1 - List accounts with zero balances
 2 - List accounts with credit balances
 3 - List accounts with debit balances
 4 - End of run

? 1

Accounts with zero balances:

300        Pam          White          0.00

Enter request
 1 - List accounts with zero balances
 2 - List accounts with credit balances
 3 - List accounts with debit balances
 4 - End of run

? 2

Accounts with credit balances:
200        Steve        Doe           -345.67
400        Sam          Stone          -42.16

Enter request
 1 - List accounts with zero balances
 2 - List accounts with credit balances
 3 - List accounts with debit balances
 4 - End of run

? 3

Accounts with debit balances:
100        Bob          Jones          24.98
500        Sue          Rich           224.62

? 4
```

Fig. 14.16 | Sample output of the credit-inquiry program in Fig. 14.15.

Request to display the menu options (line 119) and stores the result in MenuOption variable accountType. Note that getRequest translates the number typed by the user into a Menu-Option by using the number to select a MenuOption from array choices. Lines 121–138 loop until the user specifies that the program should terminate. The switch statement in lines 123–134 displays a header for the current set of records to be output to the screen. Line 136 calls method readRecords (lines 22–67), which loops through the file and reads every record.

Line 30 of method readRecords opens the file for reading with a Scanner. Note that the file will be opened for reading with a new Scanner object each time this method is called, so that we can again read from the beginning of the file. Lines 34–37 read a record. Line 40 calls method shouldDisplay (lines 70–85) to determine whether the current record satisfies the account type requested. If shouldDisplay returns true, the program displays the account information. When the end-of-file marker is reached, the loop terminates and line 65 calls the Scanner's close method to close the Scanner and the file. Notice that this occurs in a finally block, which will execute whether or not the file was successfully read. Once all the records have been read, control returns to method process-Requests and getRequest is again called (line 137) to retrieve the user's next menu option. Figure 14.15 contains method main, and calls method processRequests in line 9.

14.5.4 Updating Sequential-Access Files

The data in many sequential files cannot be modified without the risk of destroying other data in the file. For example, if the name "White" needed to be changed to "Worthington," the old name cannot simply be overwritten because the new name requires more space. The record for White was written to the file as

    300 Pam White 0.00

If the record is rewritten beginning at the same location in the file using the new name, the record will be

    300 Pam Worthington 0.00

The new record is larger (has more characters) than the original record. The characters beyond the second "o" in "Worthington" will overwrite the beginning of the next sequential record in the file. The problem here is that fields in a text file—and hence records—can vary in size. For example, 7, 14, –117, 2074 and 27383 are all ints stored in the same number of bytes (4) internally, but they are different-sized fields when displayed on the screen or written to a file as text.

Therefore, records in a sequential-access file are not usually updated in place. Instead, the entire file is usually rewritten. To make the preceding name change, the records before 300 Pam White 0.00 would be copied to a new file, the new record (which can be of a different size than the one it replaces) would be written and the records after 300 Pam White 0.00 would be copied to the new file. It is uneconomical to update just one record, but reasonable if a substantial portion of the records needs to be updated.

14.6 Object Serialization

In Section 14.5, we demonstrated how to write the individual fields of an AccountRecord object into a file as text, and how to read those fields from a file and place their values into an AccountRecord object in memory. In the examples, AccountRecord was used to aggregate the information for one record. When the instance variables for an AccountRecord were output to a disk file, certain information was lost, such as the type of each value. For instance, if the value "3" were read from a file, there is no way to tell whether the value came from an int, a String or a double. We have only data, not type information, on a disk. If the program that is going to read this data "knows" what object type the data corresponds to, then the data is simply read into objects of that type. For example, in Section 14.5.2, we know that we are inputting an int (the account number), followed by two Strings (the first and last name) and a double (the balance). We also know that these values are separated by spaces, with only one record on each line. Sometimes won't know exactly how the data is stored in a file. In such cases, we would like to read or write an entire object from a file. Java provides such a mechanism, called *object serialization*. A so-called *serialized object* is an object represented as a sequence of bytes that includes the object's data as well as information about the object's type and the types of data stored in the object. After a serialized object has been written into a file, it can be read from the file and *deserialized*—that is, the type information and bytes that represent the object and its data can be used to recreate the object in memory.

Classes ObjectInputStream and ObjectOutputStream, which respectively implement the ObjectInput and ObjectOutput interfaces, enable entire objects to be read from or written to a stream (possibly a file). To use serialization with files, we initialize Object-InputStream and ObjectOutputStream objects with stream objects that read from and write to files—objects of classes FileInputStream and FileOutputStream, respectively. Initializing stream objects with other stream objects in this manner is sometimes called *wrapping*—the new stream object being created wraps the stream object specified as a constructor argument. To wrap a FileInputStream in an ObjectInputStream, for instance, we pass the FileInputStream object to the ObjectInputStream's constructor.

The ObjectOutput interface contains method *writeObject*, which takes an Object that implements interface Serializable (discussed shortly) as an argument and writes its information to an OutputStream. Correspondingly, the ObjectInput interface contains method *readObject*, which reads and returns a reference to an Object from an Input-Stream. After an object has been read, its reference can be cast to the object's actual type. As you'll see in Chapter 19, Networking, applications that communicate via a network, such as the Internet, can also transmit entire objects across the network.

In this section, we create and manipulate sequential-access files using object serialization. Object serialization is performed with byte-based streams, so the sequential files created and manipulated will be binary files. Recall that binary files cannot be viewed in standard text editors. For this reason, we write a separate application that knows how to read and display serialized objects.

14.6.1 Creating a Sequential-Access File Using Object Serialization

We begin by creating and writing serialized objects to a sequential-access file. In this section, we reuse much of the code from Section 14.5, so we focus only on the new features.

Defining the AccountRecordSerializable Class

Let us begin by modifying our AccountRecord class so that objects of this class can be serialized. Class AccountRecordSerializable (Fig. 14.17) implements interface Serializable (line 7), which allows objects of AccountRecordSerializable to be serialized and deserialized with ObjectOutputStreams and ObjectInputStreams. Interface Serializable is a *tagging interface*. Such an interface does not contain methods. A class that implements Serializable is *tagged* as being a Serializable object. This is important because an ObjectOutputStream will not output an object unless it *is a* Serializable object, which is the case for any object of a class that implements Serializable.

```java
1   // Fig. 14.17: AccountRecordSerializable.java
2   // A class that represents one record of information.
3   package com.deitel.javafp.ch14; // packaged for reus
4
5   import java.io.Serializable;
6
7   public class AccountRecordSerializable implements Serializable
8   {
9      private int account;
10     private String firstName;
11     private String lastName;
12     private double balance;
13
14     // no-argument constructor calls other constructor with default values
15     public AccountRecordSerializable()
16     {
17        this( 0, "", "", 0.0 );
18     } // end no-argument AccountRecordSerializable constructor
19
20     // four-argument constructor initializes a record
21     public AccountRecordSerializable(
22        int acct, String first, String last, double bal )
23     {
24        setAccount( acct );
25        setFirstName( first );
26        setLastName( last );
27        setBalance( bal );
28     } // end four-argument AccountRecordSerializable constructor
29
30     // set account number
31     public void setAccount( int acct )
32     {
33        account = acct;
34     } // end method setAccount
35
36     // get account number
37     public int getAccount()
38     {
39        return account;
40     } // end method getAccount
41
42     // set first name
43     public void setFirstName( String first )
44     {
```

Fig. 14.17 | AccountRecordSerializable class for serializable objects. (Part 1 of 2.)

```
45          firstName = first;
46       } // end method setFirstName
47
48       // get first name
49       public String getFirstName()
50       {
51          return firstName;
52       } // end method getFirstName
53
54       // set last name
55       public void setLastName( String last )
56       {
57          lastName = last;
58       } // end method setLastName
59
60       // get last name
61       public String getLastName()
62       {
63          return lastName;
64       } // end method getLastName
65
66       // set balance
67       public void setBalance( double bal )
68       {
69          balance = bal;
70       } // end method setBalance
71
72       // get balance
73       public double getBalance()
74       {
75          return balance;
76       } // end method getBalance
77    } // end class AccountRecordSerializable
```

Fig. 14.17 | AccountRecordSerializable class for serializable objects. (Part 2 of 2.)

In a class that implements Serializable, the programmer must ensure that every instance variable of the class is a Serializable type. Any instance variable that is not serializable must be declared ***transient*** to indicate that it is not Serializable and should be ignored during the serialization process. By default, all primitive-type variables are serializable. For variables of reference types, you must check the definition of the class (and possibly its superclasses) to ensure that the type is Serializable. By default, array objects are serializable. However, if the array contains references to other objects, those objects may or may not be serializable.

Class AccountRecordSerializable contains private data members account, firstName, lastName and balance. This class also provides public *get* and *set* methods for accessing the private fields.

Now let's discuss the code that creates the sequential-access file (Figs. 14.18–14.19). We concentrate only on new concepts here. As stated in Section 14.3, a program can open a file by creating an object of stream class FileInputStream or FileOutputStream. In this example, the file is to be opened for output, so the program creates a FileOutputStream (line 21 of Fig. 14.18). The string argument that is passed to the FileOutputStream's constructor represents the name and path of the file to be opened. Existing files that are opened for output in this manner are truncated. Note that the .ser file extension is used—we use this file extension for binary files that contain serialized objects.

> **Common Programming Error 14.2**
>
> *It is a logic error to open an existing file for output when, in fact, the user wishes to preserve the file.*

```
1   // Fig. 14.18: CreateSequentialFile.java
2   // Writing objects sequentially to a file with class ObjectOutputStream.
3   import java.io.FileOutputStream;
4   import java.io.IOException;
5   import java.io.ObjectOutputStream;
6   import java.util.NoSuchElementException;
7   import java.util.Scanner;
8
9   import com.deitel.javafp.ch14.AccountRecordSerializable
10
11  public class CreateSequentialFile
12  {
13     private ObjectOutputStream output; // outputs data to file
14
15     // allow user to specify file name
16     public void openFile()
17     {
18        try // open file
19        {
20           output = new ObjectOutputStream(
21              new FileOutputStream( "clients.ser" ) );
22        } // end try
23        catch ( IOException ioException )
24        {
25           System.err.println( "Error opening file." );
26        } // end catch
27     } // end method openFile
28
29     // add records to file
30     public void addRecords()
31     {
32        AccountRecordSerializable record; // object to be written to file
33        int accountNumber = 0; // account number for record object
34        String firstName; // first name for record object
35        String lastName; // last name for record object
36        double balance; // balance for record object
37
38        Scanner input = new Scanner( System.in );
39
40        System.out.printf( "%s\n%s\n%s\n%s\n\n",
41           "To terminate input, type the end-of-file indicator ",
42           "when you are prompted to enter input.",
```

Fig. 14.18 | Sequential file created using ObjectOutputStream. (Part 1 of 3.)

```
43            "On UNIX/Linux/Mac OS X type <ctrl> d then press Enter",
44            "On Windows type <ctrl> z then press Enter" );
45
46       System.out.printf( "%s\n%s",
47          "Enter account number (> 0), first name, last name and balance.",
48          "? " );
49
50       while ( input.hasNext() ) // loop until end-of-file indicator
51       {
52          try // output values to file
53          {
54             accountNumber = input.nextInt(); // read account number
55             firstName = input.next(); // read first name
56             lastName = input.next(); // read last name
57             balance = input.nextDouble(); // read balance
58
59             if ( accountNumber > 0 )
60             {
61                // create new record
62                record = new AccountRecordSerializable( accountNumber,
63                   firstName, lastName, balance );
64                output.writeObject( record ); // output record
65             } // end if
66             else
67             {
68                System.out.println(
69                   "Account number must be greater than 0." );
70             } // end else
71          } // end try
72          catch ( IOException ioException )
73          {
74             System.err.println( "Error writing to file." );
75             return;
76          } // end catch
77          catch ( NoSuchElementException elementException )
78          {
79             System.err.println( "Invalid input. Please try again." );
80             input.nextLine(); // discard input so user can try again
81          } // end catch
82
83          System.out.printf( "%s %s\n%s", "Enter account number (>0),",
84             "first name, last name and balance.", "? " );
85       } // end while
86    } // end method addRecords
87
88    // close file and terminate application
89    public void closeFile()
90    {
91       try // close file
92       {
93          if ( output != null )
94             output.close();
95       } // end try
```

Fig. 14.18 | Sequential file created using `ObjectOutputStream`. (Part 2 of 3.)

```
96            catch ( IOException ioException )
97            {
98               System.err.println( "Error closing file." );
99               System.exit( 1 );
100           } // end catch
101        } // end method closeFile
102    } // end class CreateSequentialFile
```

Fig. 14.18 | Sequential file created using `ObjectOutputStream`. (Part 3 of 3.)

```
1    // Fig. 14.19: CreateSequentialFileTest.java
2    // Testing class CreateSequentialFile.
3
4    public class CreateSequentialFileTest
5    {
6       public static void main( String args[] )
7       {
8          CreateSequentialFile application = new CreateSequentialFile();
9
10         application.openFile();
11         application.addRecords();
12         application.closeFile();
13      } // end main
14   } // end class CreateSequentialFileTest
```

```
To terminate input, type the end-of-file indicator
when you are prompted to enter input.
On UNIX/Linux/Mac OS X type <ctrl> d then press Enter
On Windows type <ctrl> z then press Enter

Enter account number (> 0), first name, last name and balance.
? 100 Bob Jones 24.98
Enter account number (> 0), first name, last name and balance.
? 200 Steve Doe -345.67
Enter account number (> 0), first name, last name and balance.
? 300 Pam White 0.00
Enter account number (> 0), first name, last name and balance.
? 400 Sam Stone -42.16
Enter account number (> 0), first name, last name and balance.
? 500 Sue Rich 224.62
Enter account number (> 0), first name, last name and balance.
? ^Z
```

Fig. 14.19 | Testing class `CreateSequentialFile`.

Class `FileOutputStream` provides methods for writing byte arrays and individual bytes to a file. In this program we wish to write objects to a file—a capability not provided by `FileOutputStream`. For this reason, we wrap a `FileOutputStream` in an `ObjectOutputStream` by passing the new `FileOutputStream` object to the `ObjectOutputStream`'s constructor (lines 20–21). The `ObjectOutputStream` object uses the `FileOutputStream` object to write objects into the file. Lines 20–21 might throw an `IOException` if a problem occurs while opening the file (e.g., when a file is opened for writing on a drive with insufficient space or when a read-only file is opened for writing). If so, the program displays an error message (lines 23–26). If no exception occurs, the file is open and variable output can be used to write objects to the file.

This program assumes that data is input correctly and in the proper record-number order. Method addRecords (lines 30–86) performs the write operation. Lines 62–63 create an AccountRecordSerializable object from the data entered by the user. Line 64 calls ObjectOutputStream method writeObject to write the record object to the output file. Note that only one statement is required to write the entire object.

Method closeFile (lines 89–101) closes the file. Method closeFile calls ObjectOutputStream method *close* on output to close both the ObjectOutputStream and its underlying FileOutputStream (line 94). Note that the call to method close is contained in a try block. Method close throws an IOException if the file cannot be closed properly. In this case, it is important to notify the user that the information in the file might be corrupted. When using wrapped streams, closing the outermost stream also closes the underlying file.

In the sample execution for the program in Fig. 14.19, we entered information for five accounts—the same information shown in Fig. 14.10. The program does not show how the data records actually appear in the file. Remember that now we are using binary files, which are not humanly readable. To verify that the file has been created successfully, the next section presents a program to read the file's contents.

14.6.2 Reading and Deserializing Data from a Sequential-Access File

As discussed in Section 14.5.2, data is stored in files so that it may be retrieved for processing when needed. The preceding section showed how to create a file for sequential access using object serialization. In this section, we discuss how to read serialized data sequentially from a file.

The program in Figs. 14.20–14.21 reads records from a file created by the program in Section 14.6.1 and displays the contents. The program opens the file for input by creating a FileInputStream object (line 21). The name of the file to open is specified as an argument to the FileInputStream constructor. In Fig. 14.18, we wrote objects to the file, using an ObjectOutputStream object. Data must be read from the file in the same format in which it was written. Therefore, we use an ObjectInputStream wrapped around a FileInputStream in this program (lines 20–21). If no exceptions occur when opening the file, variable input can be used to read objects from the file.

```
1   // Fig. 14.20: ReadSequentialFile.java
2   // This program reads a file of objects sequentially
3   // and displays each record.
4   import java.io.EOFException;
5   import java.io.FileInputStream;
6   import java.io.IOException;
7   import java.io.ObjectInputStream;
8
9   import com.deitel.javafp.ch14.AccountRecordSerializable
```

Fig. 14.20 | Sequential file read using an ObjectInputStream. (Part 1 of 3.)

```
10
11   public class ReadSequentialFile
12   {
13      private ObjectInputStream input;
14
15      // enable user to select file to open
16      public void openFile()
17      {
18         try // open file
19         {
20            input = new ObjectInputStream(
21               new FileInputStream( "clients.ser" ) );
22         } // end try
23         catch ( IOException ioException )
24         {
25            System.err.println( "Error opening file." );
26         } // end catch
27      } // end method openFile
28
29      // read record from file
30      public void readRecords()
31      {
32         AccountRecordSerializable record;
33         System.out.printf( "%-10s%-12s%-12s%10s\n", "Account",
34            "First Name", "Last Name", "Balance" );
35
36         try // input the values from the file
37         {
38            while ( true )
39            {
40               record = ( AccountRecordSerializable ) input.readObject();
41
42               // display record contents
43               System.out.printf( "%-10d%-12s%-12s%10.2f\n",
44                  record.getAccount(), record.getFirstName(),
45                  record.getLastName(), record.getBalance() );
46            } // end while
47         } // end try
48         catch ( EOFException endOfFileException )
49         {
50            return; // end of file was reached
51         } // end catch
52         catch ( ClassNotFoundException classNotFoundException )
53         {
54            System.err.println( "Unable to create object." );
55         } // end catch
56         catch ( IOException ioException )
57         {
58            System.err.println( "Error during read from file." );
59         } // end catch
60      } // end method readRecords
61
```

Fig. 14.20 | Sequential file read using an ObjectInputStream. (Part 2 of 3.)

```
62        // close file and terminate application
63        public void closeFile()
64        {
65           try // close file and exit
66           {
67              if ( input != null )
68                 input.close();
69           } // end try
70           catch ( IOException ioException )
71           {
72              System.err.println( "Error closing file." );
73              System.exit( 1 );
74           } // end catch
75        } // end method closeFile
76     } // end class ReadSequentialFile
```

Fig. 14.20 | Sequential file read using an `ObjectInputStream`. (Part 3 of 3.)

```
1     // Fig. 14.21: ReadSequentialFileTest.java
2     // This program test class ReadSequentialFile.
3
4     public class ReadSequentialFileTest
5     {
6        public static void main( String args[] )
7        {
8           ReadSequentialFile application = new ReadSequentialFile();
9
10          application.openFile();
11          application.readRecords();
12          application.closeFile();
13       } // end main
14    } // end class ReadSequentialFileTest
```

Account	First Name	Last Name	Balance
100	Bob	Jones	24.98
200	Steve	Doe	-345.67
300	Pam	White	0.00
400	Sam	Stone	-42.16
500	Sue	Rich	224.62

Fig. 14.21 | Testing class `ReadSequentialFile`.

The program reads records from the file in method `readRecords` (lines 30–60). Line 40 calls `ObjectInputStream` method `readObject` to read an `Object` from the file. To use `AccountRecordSerializable`-specific methods, we downcast the returned `Object` to type `AccountRecordSerializable`. Method `readObject` throws an `EOFException` (processed at lines 48–51) if an attempt is made to read beyond the end of the file. Method `readObject` throws a `ClassNotFoundException` if the class for the object being read cannot be located. This might occur if the file is accessed on a computer that does not have the class. Figure 14.21 contains method `main` (lines 6–13), which opens the file, calls method `readRecords` and closes the file.

14.7 Additional java.io Classes

We now introduce you to other useful classes in the java.io package. We overview additional interfaces and classes for byte-based input and output streams and character-based input and output streams.

Interfaces and Classes for Byte-Based Input and Output

InputStream and OutputStream (subclasses of Object) are abstract classes that declare methods for performing byte-based input and output, respectively. We used concrete classes FileInputStream (a subclass of InputStream) and FileOutputStream (a subclass of OutputStream) to manipulate files in this chapter.

Pipes are synchronized communication channels between threads. We discuss threads in Chapter 18, Multithreading. Java provides PipedOutputStream (a subclass of Output-Stream) and PipedInputStream (a subclass of InputStream) to establish pipes between two threads in a program. One thread sends data to another by writing to a PipedOutput-Stream. The target thread reads information from the pipe via a PipedInputStream.

A FilterInputStream *filters* an InputStream, and a FilterOutputStream filters an OutputStream. Filtering means simply that the filter stream provides additional functionality, such as aggregating data bytes into meaningful primitive-type units. FilterInput-Stream and FilterOutputStream are abstract classes, so some of their filtering capabilities are provided by their concrete subclasses.

A PrintStream (a subclass of FilterOutputStream) performs text output to the specified stream. Actually, we have been using PrintStream output throughout the text to this point—System.out and System.err are PrintStream objects.

Reading data as raw bytes is fast, but crude. Usually, programs read data as aggregates of bytes that form ints, floats, doubles and so on. Java programs can use several classes to input and output data in aggregate form.

Interface DataInput describes methods for reading primitive types from an input stream. Classes DataInputStream and RandomAccessFile each implement this interface to read sets of bytes and view them as primitive-type values. Interface DataInput includes methods readLine (for byte arrays), readBoolean, readByte, readChar, readDouble, readFloat, readFully (for byte arrays), readInt, readLong, readShort, readUnsigned-Byte, readUnsignedShort, readUTF (for reading Unicode characters encoded by Java) and skipBytes.

Interface DataOutput describes a set of methods for writing primitive types to an output stream. Classes DataOutputStream (a subclass of FilterOutputStream) and Ran-domAccessFile each implement this interface to write primitive-type values as bytes. Interface DataOutput includes overloaded versions of method write (for a byte or for a byte array) and methods writeBoolean, writeByte, writeBytes, writeChar, writeChars (for Unicode Strings), writeDouble, writeFloat, writeInt, writeLong, writeShort and writeUTF (to output text modified for Unicode).

Buffering is an I/O-performance-enhancement technique. With a BufferedOutput-Stream (a subclass of class FilterOutputStream), each output statement does not necessarily result in an actual physical transfer of data to the output device (which is a slow operation compared to processor and main memory speeds). Rather, each output operation is directed to a region in memory called a *buffer* that is large enough to hold the data of many output operations. Then, actual transfer to the output device is performed in one large *physical output operation* each time the buffer fills. The output operations directed to the output buffer in memory are often called *logical output operations*. With a BufferedOutputStream, a partially filled buffer can be forced out to the device at any time by invoking the stream object's *flush* method.

Buffering can greatly increase an application's efficiency. Typical I/O operations are extremely slow compared to the speed of accessing computer memory. Buffering reduces the number of I/O operations by first combining smaller outputs together in memory. The number of actual physical I/O operations is small compared with the number of I/O requests issued by the program. Thus, the program that is using buffering is more efficient.

Performance Tip 14.1
Buffered I/O can yield significant performance improvements over unbuffered I/O.

With a BufferedInputStream (a subclass of class FilterInputStream), many "logical" chunks of data from a file are read as one large *physical input operation* into a memory buffer. As a program requests each new chunk of data, it is taken from the buffer. (This procedure is sometimes referred to as a *logical input operation*.) When the buffer is empty, the next actual physical input operation from the input device is performed to read in the next group of "logical" chunks of data. Thus, the number of actual physical input operations is small compared with the number of read requests issued by the program.

Java stream I/O includes capabilities for inputting from byte arrays in memory and outputting to byte arrays in memory. A ByteArrayInputStream (a subclass of Input-Stream) reads from a byte array in memory. A ByteArrayOutputStream (a subclass of OutputStream) outputs to a byte array in memory. One use of byte-array I/O is data validation. A program can input an entire line at a time from the input stream into a byte array. Then a validation routine can scrutinize the array's contents and correct the data if necessary. Finally, the program can proceed to input from the byte array, "knowing" that the input data is in the proper format. Outputting to a byte array is a nice way to take advantage of the powerful output-formatting capabilities of Java streams. For example, data can be stored in a byte array, using the same formatting that will be displayed at a later time, and the byte array can then be output to a disk file to preserve the screen image.

A SequenceInputStream (a subclass of InputStream) enables concatenation of several InputStreams, which means that the program sees the group as one continuous Input-Stream. When the program reaches the end of an input stream, that stream closes, and the next stream in the sequence opens.

Interfaces and Classes for Character-Based Input and Output

In addition to the byte-based streams, Java provides the Reader and Writer abstract classes, which are Unicode two-byte, character-based streams. Most of the byte-based streams have corresponding character-based concrete Reader or Writer classes.

Classes BufferedReader (a subclass of abstract class Reader) and BufferedWriter (a subclass of abstract class Writer) enable buffering for character-based streams. Remember that character-based streams use Unicode characters—such streams can process data in any language that the Unicode character set represents.

Classes CharArrayReader and CharArrayWriter read and write, respectively, a stream of characters to a character array. A LineNumberReader (a subclass of BufferedReader) is a buffered character stream that keeps track of the number of lines read (i.e., a newline, a return or a carriage-return–line-feed combination). Keeping track of line numbers can be useful if the program needs to inform the reader of an error on a specific line.

Class FileReader (a subclass of InputStreamReader) and class FileWriter (a subclass of OutputStreamWriter) read characters from and write characters to a file, respectively. Class PipedReader and class PipedWriter implement piped-character streams that can be used to transfer information between threads. Class StringReader and StringWriter read characters from and write characters to Strings, respectively. A PrintWriter writes characters to a stream.

14.8 Opening Files with JFileChooser

Class *JFileChooser* displays a dialog (known as the *JFileChooser dialog*) that enables the user to easily select files or directories. To demonstrate the JFileChooser dialog, we enhance the example in Section 14.4, as shown in Figs. 14.22–14.23. The example now contains a graphical user interface, but still displays the same data as before. The constructor calls method analyzePath in line 34. This method then calls method getFile in line 68 to retrieve the File object.

```java
1   // Fig. 14.22: FileDemonstration.java
2   // Demonstrating the File class.
3   import java.awt.BorderLayout;
4   import java.awt.event.ActionEvent;
5   import java.awt.event.ActionListener;
6   import java.io.File;
7   import javax.swing.JFileChooser;
8   import javax.swing.JFrame;
9   import javax.swing.JOptionPane;
10  import javax.swing.JScrollPane;
11  import javax.swing.JTextArea;
12  import javax.swing.JTextField;
13
14  public class FileDemonstration extends JFrame
15  {
16     private JTextArea outputArea; // used for output
17     private JScrollPane scrollPane; // used to provide scrolling to output
18
19     // set up GUI
20     public FileDemonstration()
21     {
22        super( "Testing class File" );
23
24        outputArea = new JTextArea();
25
26        // add outputArea to scrollPane
27        scrollPane = new JScrollPane( outputArea );
28
29        add( scrollPane, BorderLayout.CENTER ); // add scrollPane to GUI
30
31        setSize( 400, 400 ); // set GUI size
```

Fig. 14.22 | Demonstrating JFileChooser. (Part 1 of 3.)

```java
32        setVisible( true ); // display GUI
33
34        analyzePath(); // create and analyze File object
35     } // end FileDemonstration constructor
36
37     // allow user to specify file name
38     private File getFile()
39     {
40        // display file dialog, so user can choose file to open
41        JFileChooser fileChooser = new JFileChooser();
42        fileChooser.setFileSelectionMode(
43           JFileChooser.FILES_AND_DIRECTORIES );
44
45        int result = fileChooser.showOpenDialog( this );
46
47        // if user clicked Cancel button on dialog, return
48        if ( result == JFileChooser.CANCEL_OPTION )
49           System.exit( 1 );
50
51        File fileName = fileChooser.getSelectedFile(); // get selected file
52
53        // display error if invalid
54        if ( ( fileName == null ) || ( fileName.getName().equals( "" ) ) )
55        {
56           JOptionPane.showMessageDialog( this, "Invalid File Name",
57              "Invalid File Name", JOptionPane.ERROR_MESSAGE );
58           System.exit( 1 );
59        } // end if
60
61        return fileName;
62     } // end method getFile
63
64     // display information about file user specifies
65     public void analyzePath()
66     {
67        // create File object based on user input
68        File name = getFile();
69
70        if ( name.exists() ) // if name exists, output information about it
71        {
72           // display file (or directory) information
73           outputArea.setText( String.format(
74              "%s%s\n%s\n%s\n%s\n%s%s\n%s%s\n%s%s\n%s%s\n%s%s",
75              name.getName(), " exists",
76              ( name.isFile() ? "is a file" : "is not a file" ),
77              ( name.isDirectory() ? "is a directory" :
78                 "is not a directory" ),
79              ( name.isAbsolute() ? "is absolute path" :
80                 "is not absolute path" ), "Last modified: ",
81              name.lastModified(), "Length: ", name.length(),
82              "Path: ", name.getPath(), "Absolute path: ",
83              name.getAbsolutePath(), "Parent: ", name.getParent() ) );
84
```

Fig. 14.22 | Demonstrating JFileChooser. (Part 2 of 3.)

```
85            if ( name.isDirectory() ) // output directory listing
86            {
87               String directory[] = name.list();
88               outputArea.append( "\n\nDirectory contents:\n" );
89
90               for ( String directoryName : directory )
91                  outputArea.append( directoryName + "\n" );
92            } // end else
93         } // end outer if
94         else // not file or directory, output error message
95         {
96            JOptionPane.showMessageDialog( this, name +
97               " does not exist.", "ERROR", JOptionPane.ERROR_MESSAGE );
98         } // end else
99      } // end method analyzePath
100 } // end class FileDemonstration
```

Fig. 14.22 | Demonstrating `JFileChooser`. (Part 3 of 3.)

Method `getFile` is defined in lines 38–62 of Fig. 14.22. Line 41 creates a `JFile-Chooser` and assigns its reference to `fileChooser`. Lines 42–43 call method ***setFileSe-lectionMode*** to specify what the user can select from the `fileChooser`. We use

```
1   // Fig. 14.23: FileDemonstrationTest.java
2   // Testing the FileDmonstration class.
3   import javax.swing.JFrame;
4
5   public class FileDemonstrationTest
6   {
7      public static void main( String args[] )
8      {
9         FileDemonstration application = new FileDemonstration();
10        application.setDefaultCloseOperation( JFrame.EXIT_ON_CLOSE );
11     } // end main
12  } // end class FileDemonstrationTest
```

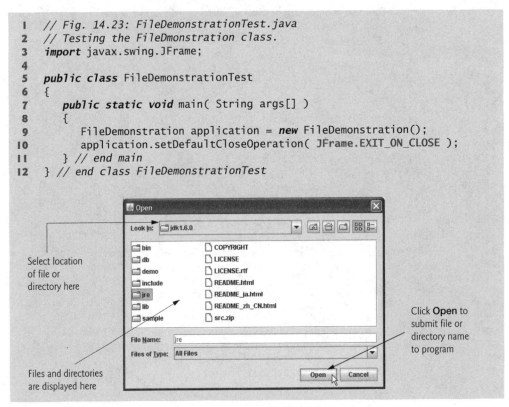

Fig. 14.23 | Testing class `FileDemonstration`. (Part 1 of 2.)

Fig. 14.23 | Testing class FileDemonstration. (Part 2 of 2.)

JFileChooser static constant **FILES_AND_DIRECTORIES** to indicate that files and directories can be selected. Other static constants include **FILES_ONLY** and **DIRECTORIES_ONLY**.

Line 45 calls method **showOpenDialog** to display the JFileChooser dialog titled **Open**. Argument this specifies the JFileChooser dialog's parent window, which determines the position of the dialog on the screen. If null is passed, the dialog is displayed in the center of the screen—otherwise, the dialog is centered over the application window (specified by the argument this). A JFileChooser dialog is a modal dialog that does not allow the user to interact with any other window in the program until the user closes the JFileChooser by clicking the **Open** or **Cancel** button. The user selects the drive, directory or file name, then clicks **Open**. Method showOpenDialog returns an integer specifying which button (**Open** or **Cancel**) the user clicked to close the dialog. Line 48 tests whether the user clicked **Cancel** by comparing the result with static constant **CANCEL_OPTION**. If they are equal, the program terminates. Line 51 retrieves the file the user selected by calling JFileChooser method **getSelectedFile**. The program then displays information about the selected file or directory.

14.9 Wrap-Up

In this chapter, you learned how to use file processing to manipulate persistent data. You learned that data is stored in computers as 0s and 1s, and that combinations of these values are used to form bytes, fields, records and eventually files. We compared character-based and byte-based streams, and introduced several file-processing classes provided by the java.io package. You used class File to retrieve information about a file or directory. You used sequential-access file processing to manipulate records that are stored in order by the record-key field. You learned the differences between text-file processing and object serialization, and used serialization to store and retrieve entire objects. The chapter concluded with an overview of other classes provided by the java.io package, and a small example of using a JFileChooser dialog to allow users to easily select files from a GUI. Chapter 15, Generics, presents a mechanism for declaring classes and methods without specific type information so that the classes and methods can be used with many different types. Generics are used extensively in Java's built-in set of data structures, known as the Collections API, which we discuss in Chapter 16.

15

Generics

OBJECTIVES

In this chapter you'll learn:

■ To create generic methods that perform identical tasks on arguments of different types.

■ To create a generic Stack class that can be used to store objects of any class or interface type.

■ To understand how to overload generic methods with non-generic methods or with other generic methods.

■ To understand raw types and how they help achieve backward compatibility.

■ To use wildcards when precise type information about a parameter is not required in the method body.

■ The relationship between generics and inheritance.

Every man of genius sees the world at a different angle from his fellows.
—Havelock Ellis

…our special individuality, as distinguished from our generic humanity.
—Oliver Wendell Holmes, Sr.

Born under one law, to another bound.
—Lord Brooke

You deal in the raw material of opinion, and, if my convictions have any validity, opinion ultimately governs the world.
—Woodrow Wilson

Outline

15.1 Introduction

15.2 Motivation for Generic Methods

15.3 Generic Methods: Implementation and Compile-Time Translation

15.4 Additional Compile-Time Translation Issues: Methods That Use a Type Parameter as the Return Type

15.5 Overloading Generic Methods

15.6 Generic Classes

15.7 Raw Types

15.8 Wildcards in Methods That Accept Type Parameters

15.9 Generics and Inheritance: Notes

15.10 Wrap-Up

15.11 Internet and Web Resources

15.1 Introduction

It would be nice if we could write a single sort method that could sort the elements in an Integer array, a String array or an array of any type that supports ordering (i.e., its elements can be compared). It would also be nice if we could write a single Stack class that could be used as a Stack of integers, a Stack of floating-point numbers, a Stack of Strings or a Stack of any other type. It would be even nicer if we could detect type mismatches at compile time—known as *compile-time type safety*. For example, if a Stack stores only integers, attempting to push a String on to that Stack should issue a compile-time error.

This chapter discusses *generics*, which provide the means to create the general models mentioned above. *Generic methods* and *generic classes* enable you to specify, with a single method declaration, a set of related methods or, with a single class declaration, a set of related types, respectively. Generics also provide compile-time type safety that allows invalid types to be caught at compile time.

We might write a generic method for sorting an array of objects, then invoke the generic method with Integer arrays, Double arrays, String arrays and so on, to sort the array elements. The compiler could perform type checking to ensure that the array passed to the sorting method contains the same type elements. We might write a single generic Stack class that manipulates a stack of objects, then instantiate Stack objects for a stack of Integers, a stack of Doubles, a stack of Strings and so on. The compiler could perform type checking to ensure that the Stack stores elements of the same type.

> **Software Engineering Observation 15.1**
>
> *Generic methods and classes are among Java's most powerful capabilities for software reuse with compile-time type safety.*

This chapter presents generic method and generic class examples. It also considers the relationships between generics and other Java features, such as overloading and inheritance. Chapter 16, Collections, presents an in-depth treatment of the Java Collections Framework's generic methods and classes. A collection is a data structure that maintains references to many objects. The Java Collections Framework uses generics to allow programmers to specify the exact types of objects that a particular collection will store in a program.

15.2 Motivation for Generic Methods

Overloaded methods are often used to perform similar operations on different types of data. To motivate generic methods, let's begin with an example (Fig. 15.1) that contains three overloaded printArray methods (lines 7–14, lines 17–24 and lines 27–34). These methods print the string representations of the elements of an Integer array, a Double array and a Character array, respectively. Note that we could have used arrays of primitive types int, double and char in this example. We chose to use arrays of type Integer, Double and Character to set up our generic method example, because only reference types can be used with generic methods and classes.

```java
1   // Fig. 15.1: OverloadedMethods.java
2   // Using overloaded methods to print arrays of different types.
3
4   public class OverloadedMethods
5   {
6      // method printArray to print Integer array
7      public static void printArray( Integer[] inputArray )
8      {
9         // display array elements
10        for ( Integer element : inputArray )
11           System.out.printf( "%s ", element );
12
13        System.out.println();
14     } // end method printArray
15
16     // method printArray to print Double array
17     public static void printArray( Double[] inputArray )
18     {
19        // display array elements
20        for ( Double element : inputArray )
21           System.out.printf( "%s ", element );
22
23        System.out.println();
24     } // end method printArray
25
26     // method printArray to print Character array
27     public static void printArray( Character[] inputArray )
28     {
29        // display array elements
30        for ( Character element : inputArray )
31           System.out.printf( "%s ", element );
32
33        System.out.println();
34     } // end method printArray
35
36     public static void main( String args[] )
37     {
38        // create arrays of Integer, Double and Character
39        Integer[] integerArray = { 1, 2, 3, 4, 5, 6 };
40        Double[] doubleArray = { 1.1, 2.2, 3.3, 4.4, 5.5, 6.6, 7.7 };
```

Fig. 15.1 | Printing array elements using overloaded methods. (Part 1 of 2.)

```
41          Character[] characterArray = { 'H', 'E', 'L', 'L', 'O' };
42
43          System.out.println( "Array integerArray contains:" );
44          printArray( integerArray ); // pass an Integer array
45          System.out.println( "\nArray doubleArray contains:" );
46          printArray( doubleArray ); // pass a Double array
47          System.out.println( "\nArray characterArray contains:" );
48          printArray( characterArray ); // pass a Character array
49      } // end main
50  } // end class OverloadedMethods
```

```
Array integerArray contains:
1 2 3 4 5 6

Array doubleArray contains:
1.1 2.2 3.3 4.4 5.5 6.6 7.7

Array characterArray contains:
H E L L O
```

Fig. 15.1 | Printing array elements using overloaded methods. (Part 2 of 2.)

The program begins by declaring and initializing three arrays—six-element Integer array integerArray (line 39), seven-element Double array doubleArray (line 40) and five-element Character array characterArray (line 41). Then, lines 43–48 output the arrays.

When the compiler encounters a method call, it always attempts to locate a method declaration that has the same method name and parameters that match the argument types in the method call. In this example, each printArray call exactly matches one of the printArray method declarations. For example, line 44 calls printArray with integerArray as its argument. At compile time, the compiler determines argument integerArray's type (i.e., Integer[]) and attempts to locate a method named printArray that specifies a single Integer[] parameter (lines 7–14) and sets up a call to that method. Similarly, when the compiler encounters the printArray call at line 46, it determines argument doubleArray's type (i.e., Double[]), then attempts to locate a method named printArray that specifies a single Double[] parameter (lines 17–24) and sets up a call to that method. Finally, when the compiler encounters the printArray call at line 48, it determines argument characterArray's type (i.e., Character[]), then attempts to locate a method named printArray that specifies a single Character[] parameter (lines 27–34) and sets up a call to that method.

Study each printArray method. Note that the array element type appears in two locations in each method—the method header (lines 7, 17 and 27) and the for statement header (lines 10, 20 and 30). If we were to replace the element types in each method with a generic name—by convention we'll use E to represent the "element" type—then all three methods would look like the one in Fig. 15.2. It appears that if we can replace the array element type in each of the three methods with a single generic type, then we should be able to declare one printArray method that can display the string representations of the elements of any array that contains objects. Note that the format specifier %s can be used to output any object's string representation—the object's toString method will be called implicitly. The method in Fig. 15.2 is similar to the generic printArray method declaration we discuss in Section 15.3.

```
1    public static void printArray( E[] inputArray )
2    {
3       // display array elements
4       for ( E element : inputArray )
5          System.out.printf( "%s ", element );
6
7       System.out.println();
8    } // end method printArray
```

Fig. 15.2 | printArray method in which actual type names are replaced by convention with the generic name E.

15.3 Generic Methods: Implementation and Compile-Time Translation

If the operations performed by several overloaded methods are identical for each argument type, the overloaded methods can be more compactly and conveniently coded using a generic method. You can write a single generic method declaration that can be called with arguments of different types. Based on the types of the arguments passed to the generic method, the compiler handles each method call appropriately.

Figure 15.3 reimplements the application of Fig. 15.1 using a generic printArray method (lines 7–14). Note that the printArray method calls in lines 24, 26 and 28 are identical to those of Fig. 15.1 (lines 44, 46 and 48) and that the outputs of the two applications are identical. This dramatically demonstrates the expressive power of generics.

```
1    // Fig. 15.3: GenericMethodTest.java
2    // Using generic methods to print arrays of different types.
3
4    public class GenericMethodTest
5    {
6       // generic method printArray
7       public static < E > void printArray( E[] inputArray )
8       {
9          // display array elements
10         for ( E element : inputArray )
11            System.out.printf( "%s ", element );
12
13         System.out.println();
14      } // end method printArray
15
16      public static void main( String args[] )
17      {
18         // create arrays of Integer, Double and Character
19         Integer[] intArray = { 1, 2, 3, 4, 5 };
20         Double[] doubleArray = { 1.1, 2.2, 3.3, 4.4, 5.5, 6.6, 7.7 };
21         Character[] charArray = { 'H', 'E', 'L', 'L', 'O' };
22
23         System.out.println( "Array integerArray contains:" );
24         printArray( integerArray ); // pass an Integer array
```

Fig. 15.3 | Printing array elements using generic method printArray. (Part 1 of 2.)

```
25        System.out.println( "\nArray doubleArray contains:" );
26        printArray( doubleArray ); // pass a Double array
27        System.out.println( "\nArray characterArray contains:" );
28        printArray( characterArray ); // pass a Character array
29     } // end main
30  } // end class GenericMethodTest
```

```
Array integerArray contains:
1 2 3 4 5 6

Array doubleArray contains:
1.1 2.2 3.3 4.4 5.5 6.6 7.7

Array characterArray contains:
H E L L O
```

Fig. 15.3 | Printing array elements using generic method `printArray`. (Part 2 of 2.)

Line 7 begins method `printArray`'s declaration. All generic method declarations have a *type parameter section* delimited by *angle brackets* (< and >) that precedes the method's return type (< E > in this example). Each type parameter section contains one or more *type parameters* (also called *formal type parameters*), separated by commas. A type parameter, also known as a *type variable*, is an identifier that specifies a generic type name. The type parameters can be used to declare the return type, parameter types and local variable types in a generic method declaration, and act as placeholders for the types of the arguments passed to the generic method, which are known as *actual type arguments*. A generic method's body is declared like that of any other method. Note that type parameters can represent only reference types—not primitive types (like `int`, `double` and `char`). Note, too, that the type parameter names throughout the method declaration must match those declared in the type parameter section. For example, line 10 declares `element` as type `E`, which matches the type parameter (`E`) declared in line 7. Also, a type parameter can be declared only once in the type parameter section but can appear more than once in the method's parameter list. For example, the type parameter name `E` appears twice in the following method's parameter list:

> **public static** < E > **void** printTwoArrays(E[] array1, E[] array2)

Type-parameter names need not be unique among different generic methods.

Common Programming Error 15.1

When declaring a generic method, failing to place a type parameter section before the return type of a method is a syntax error—the compiler will not understand the type parameter name when it is encountered in the method.

Method `printArray`'s type parameter section declares type parameter, `E`, as the placeholder for the array element type that `printArray` will output. Note that `E` appears in the parameter list as the array element type (line 7). The `for` statement header (line 10) also uses `E` as the element type. These are the same two locations where the overloaded `printArray` methods of Fig. 15.1 specified `Integer`, `Double` or `Character` as the array element type. The remainder of `printArray` is identical to the versions presented in Fig. 15.1.

Good Programming Practice 15.1

It is recommended that type parameters be specified as individual capital letters. Typically, a type parameter that represents an array element's type (or other collection) is named E for "element."

As in Fig. 15.1, the program begins by declaring and initializing six-element Integer array integerArray (line 19), seven-element Double array doubleArray (line 20) and five-element Character array characterArray (line 21). Then the program outputs each array by calling printArray (lines 24, 26 and 28)—once with argument integerArray, once with argument doubleArray and once with argument characterArray.

When the compiler encounters line 24, it first determines argument integerArray's type (i.e., Integer[]) and attempts to locate a method named printArray that specifies a single Integer[] parameter. There is no such method in this example. Next, the compiler determines whether there is a generic method named printArray that specifies a single array parameter and uses a type parameter to represent the array element type. The compiler determines that printArray (lines 7–14) is a match and sets up a call to the method. The same process is repeated for the calls to method printArray at lines 26 and 28.

Common Programming Error 15.2

If the compiler cannot match a method call to a non-generic or a generic method declaration, a compilation error occurs.

Common Programming Error 15.3

If the compiler does not find a method declaration that matches a method call exactly, but does find two or more generic methods that can satisfy the method call, a compilation error occurs.

In addition to setting up the method calls, the compiler also determines whether the operations in the method body can be applied to elements of the type stored in the array argument. The only operation performed on the array elements in this example is to output the string representation of the elements. Line 11 performs an implicit toString call on every element. To work with generics, every element of the array must be an object of a class or interface type. Since all objects have a toString method, the compiler is satisfied that line 11 performs a valid operation for any object in printArray's array argument. The toString methods of classes Integer, Double and Character return the string representation of the underlying int, double or char value, respectively.

When the compiler translates generic method printArray into Java bytecodes, it removes the type parameter section and replaces the type parameters with actual types. This process is known as *erasure*. By default all generic types are replaced with type Object. So the compiled version of method printArray appears as shown in Fig. 15.4—there is only one copy of this code which is used for all printArray calls in the example. This is quite different from other, similar mechanisms, such as C++'s templates, in which a separate copy of the source code is generated and compiled for every type passed as an argument to the method. As we'll discuss in Section 15.4, the translation and compilation of generics is a bit more involved than what we have discussed in this section.

By declaring printArray as a generic method in Fig. 15.3, we eliminated the need for the overloaded methods of Fig. 15.1, saving 20 lines of code and creating a reusable method that can output the string representations of the elements in any array that contains objects. However, this particular example could have simply declared the printArray method as shown in Fig. 15.4 using an Object array as the parameter. This would have

```
1   public static void printArray( Object[] inputArray )
2   {
3      // display array elements
4      for ( Object element : inputArray )
5         System.out.printf( "%s ", element );
6
7      System.out.println();
8   } // end method printArray
```

Fig. 15.4 | Generic method `printArray` after erasure is performed by the compiler.

yielded the same results, because any `Object` can be output as a `String`. In a generic method, the benefits become apparent when the method also uses a type parameter as the method's return type, as we demonstrate in the next section.

15.4 Additional Compile-Time Translation Issues: Methods That Use a Type Parameter as the Return Type

Let's consider a generic method example in which type parameters are used in the return type and in the parameter list (Fig. 15.5). The application uses a generic method `maximum` to determine and return the largest of its three arguments of the same type. Unfortunately, the relational operator > cannot be used with reference types. However, it is possible to compare two objects of the same class if that class implements the generic interface `Comparable< T >` (package `java.lang`). All the type-wrapper classes for primitive types implement this interface. Like generic classes, *generic interfaces* enable programmers to specify, with a single interface declaration, a set of related types. `Comparable< T >` objects have a `compareTo` method. For example, if we have two `Integer` objects, `integer1` and `integer2`, they can be compared with the expression:

```
integer1.compareTo( integer2 )
```

It is the responsibility of the programmer who declares a class that implements `Comparable< T >` to declare method `compareTo` such that it compares the contents of two objects of that class and returns the results of the comparison. The method must return 0 if the objects are equal, -1 if `object1` is less than `object2` or 1 if `object1` is greater than `object2`. For example, class `Integer`'s `compareTo` method compares the `int` values stored in two `Integer` objects. A benefit of implementing interface `Comparable< T >` is that `Comparable< T >` objects can be used with the sorting and searching methods of class `Collections` (package `java.util`). We discuss those methods in Chapter 16, Collections. In this example, we'll use method `compareTo` in method `maximum` to help determine the largest value.

Generic method `maximum` (lines 7–18) uses type parameter `T` as the return type of the method (line 7), as the type of method parameters x, y and z (line 7), and as the type of local variable max (line 9). The type parameter section specifies that `T` extends `Comparable< T >`—only objects of classes that implement interface `Comparable< T >` can be used with this method. In this case, `Comparable` is known as the ***upper bound*** of the type parameter. By default, `Object` is the upper bound. Note that type parameter declarations that ***bound*** the parameter always use keyword `extends` regardless of whether the type

```
1   // Fig. 15.5: MaximumTest.java
2   // Generic method maximum returns the largest of three objects.
3
4   public class MaximumTest
5   {
6      // determines the largest of three Comparable objects
7      public static < T extends Comparable< T > > T maximum( T x, T y, T z )
8      {
9         T max = x; // assume x is initially the largest
10
11        if ( y.compareTo( max ) > 0 )
12           max = y; // y is the largest so far
13
14        if ( z.compareTo( max ) > 0 )
15           max = z; // z is the largest
16
17        return max; // returns the largest object
18     } // end method maximum
19
20     public static void main( String args[] )
21     {
22        System.out.printf( "Maximum of %d, %d and %d is %d\n\n", 3, 4, 5,
23           maximum( 3, 4, 5 ) );
24        System.out.printf( "Maximum of %.1f, %.1f and %.1f is %.1f\n\n",
25           6.6, 8.8, 7.7, maximum( 6.6, 8.8, 7.7 ) );
26        System.out.printf( "Maximum of %s, %s and %s is %s\n", "pear",
27           "apple", "orange", maximum( "pear", "apple", "orange" ) );
28     } // end main
29  } // end class MaximumTest
```

```
Maximum of 3, 4 and 5 is 5

Maximum of 6.6, 8.8 and 7.7 is 8.8

Maximum of pear, apple and orange is pear
```

Fig. 15.5 | Generic method maximum with an upper bound on its type parameter.

parameter extends a class or implements an interface. This type parameter is more restrictive than the one specified for printArray in Fig. 15.3, which was able to output arrays containing any type of object. The restriction of using Comparable< T > objects is important, because not all objects can be compared. However, Comparable< T > objects are guaranteed to have a compareTo method.

Method maximum uses the same algorithm that we used in Section 6.4 to determine the largest of its three arguments. The method assumes that its first argument (x) is the largest and assigns it to local variable max (line 9). Next, the if statement at lines 11–12 determines whether y is greater than max. The condition invokes y's compareTo method with the expression y.compareTo(max), which returns -1, 0 or 1, to determine y's relationship to max. If the return value of the compareTo is greater than 0, then y is greater and is assigned to variable max. Similarly, the if statement at lines 14–15 determines whether z is greater than max. If so, line 15 assigns z to max. Then, line 17 returns max to the caller.

In main (lines 20–28), line 23 calls maximum with the integers 3, 4 and 5. When the compiler encounters this call, it first looks for a maximum method that takes three arguments of type int. There is no such method, so the compiler looks for a generic method that can be used and finds generic method maximum. However, recall that the arguments to a generic method must be of a reference type. So the compiler autoboxes the three int values as Integer objects and specifies that the three Integer objects will be passed to maximum. Note that class Integer (package java.lang) implements interface Comparable< Integer > such that method compareTo compares the int values in two Integer objects. Therefore, Integers are valid arguments to method maximum. When the Integer representing the maximum is returned, we attempt to output it with the %d format specifier, which outputs an int primitive type value. So maximum's return value is output as an int value.

A similar process occurs for the three double arguments passed to maximum in line 25. Each double is autoboxed as a Double object and passed to maximum. Again, this is allowed because class Double (package java.lang) implements the Comparable< Double > interface. The Double returned by maximum is output with the format specifier %.1f, which outputs a double primitive-type value. So maximum's return value is auto-unboxed and output as a double. The call to maximum in line 27 receives three Strings, which are also Comparable< String > objects. Note that we intentionally placed the largest value in a different position in each method call (lines 23, 25 and 27) to show that the generic method always finds the maximum value, regardless of its position in the argument list.

When the compiler translates generic method maximum into Java bytecodes, it uses erasure (introduced in Section 15.3) to replace the type parameters with actual types. In Fig. 15.3, all generic types were replaced with type Object. Actually, all type parameters are replaced with the upper bound of the type parameter—unless specified otherwise, Object is the default upper bound. The upper bound of a type parameter is specified in the type parameter section. To indicate the upper bound, follow the type parameter's name with the keyword extends and the class or interface name that represents the upper bound. In method maximum's type parameter section (Fig. 15.5), we specified the upper bound as type Comparable< T >. Thus, only Comparable< T > objects can be passed as arguments to maximum—anything that is not Comparable< T > will result in compilation errors. Figure 15.6 simulates the erasure of method maximum's types by showing the method's source code after the type parameter section is removed and type parameter T is

```
1   public static Comparable maximum(Comparable x, Comparable y, Comparable z)
2   {
3      Comparable max = x; // assume x is initially the largest
4
5      if ( y.compareTo( max ) > 0 )
6         max = y; // y is the largest so far
7
8      if ( z.compareTo( max ) > 0 )
9         max = z; // z is the largest
10
11     return max; // returns the largest object
12  } // end method maximum
```

Fig. 15.6 | Generic method maximum after erasure is performed by the compiler.

replaced with the upper bound, Comparable, throughout the method declaration. Note that the erasure of Comparable< T > is simply Comparable.

After erasure, the compiled version of method maximum specifies that it returns type Comparable. However, the calling method does not expect to receive a Comparable. Rather, the caller expects to receive an object of the same type that was passed to maximum as an argument—Integer, Double or String in this example. When the compiler replaces the type parameter information with the upper bound type in the method declaration, it also inserts explicit cast operations in front of each method call to ensure that the returned value is of the type expected by the caller. Thus, the call to maximum in line 23 (Fig. 15.5) is preceded by an Integer cast, as in

```
(Integer) maximum( 3, 4, 5 )
```

the call to maximum in line 25 is preceded by a Double cast, as in

```
(Double) maximum( 6.6, 8.8, 7.7 )
```

and the call to maximum in line 27 is preceded by a String cast, as in

```
(String) maximum( "pear", "apple", "orange" )
```

In each case, the type of the cast for the return value is inferred from the types of the method arguments in the particular method call, because, according to the method declaration, the return type and the argument types match.

In this example, you cannot use a method that accepts Objects, because class Object provides only an equality comparison. Also, without generics, you would be responsible for implementing the cast operation. Using generics ensures that the inserted cast will never throw a ClassCastException, assuming that generics are used throughout your code (i.e., you do not mix old code with new generics code).

15.5 Overloading Generic Methods

A generic method may be overloaded. A class can provide two or more generic methods that specify the same method name but different method parameters. For example, generic method printArray of Fig. 15.3 could be overloaded with another printArray generic method with the additional parameters lowSubscript and highSubscript to specify the portion of the array to output.

A generic method can also be overloaded by non-generic methods that have the same method name and number of parameters. When the compiler encounters a method call, it searches for the method declaration that most precisely matches the method name and the argument types specified in the call. For example, generic method printArray of Fig. 15.3 could be overloaded with a version that is specific to Strings, which outputs the Strings in neat, tabular format .

When the compiler encounters a method call, it performs a matching process to determine which method to invoke. The compiler tries to find and use a precise match in which the method names and argument types of the method call match those of a specific method declaration. If there is no such method, the compiler determines whether there is an inexact but applicable matching method.

15.6 Generic Classes

The concept of a data structure, such as a stack, can be understood independently of the element type it manipulates. Generic classes provide a means for describing the concept of a stack (or any other class) in a type-independent manner. We can then instantiate type-specific objects of the generic class. This capability provides a wonderful opportunity for software reusability.

Once you have a generic class, you can use a simple, concise notation to indicate the actual type(s) that should be used in place of the class's type parameter(s). At compilation time, the Java compiler ensures the type safety of your code and uses the erasure techniques described in Sections 15.3–15.4 to enable your client code to interact with the generic class.

One generic Stack class, for example, could be the basis for creating many logical Stack classes (e.g., "Stack of Double," "Stack of Integer," "Stack of Character," "Stack of Employee"). These classes are known as *parameterized classes* or *parameterized types* because they accept one or more parameters. Recall that type parameters represent only reference types, which means that the Stack generic class cannot be instantiated with primitive types. However, we can instantiate a Stack that stores objects of Java's type-wrapper classes and allow Java to use autoboxing to convert the primitive values into objects. Autoboxing occurs when a value of a primitive type (e.g., int) is pushed onto a Stack that contains wrapper-class objects (e.g., Integer). Auto-unboxing occurs when an object of the wrapper class is popped off the Stack and assigned to a primitive-type variable.

Figure 15.7 presents a generic Stack class declaration. A generic class declaration looks like a non-generic class declaration, except that the class name is followed by a type parameter section (line 4). In this case, type parameter E represents the element type the Stack will manipulate. As with generic methods, the type parameter section of a generic class can have one or more type parameters separated by commas. Type parameter E is used throughout the Stack class declaration to represent the element type. [*Note:* This example implements a Stack as an array.]

```
1   // Fig. 15.7: Stack.java
2   // Generic class Stack.
3
4   public class Stack< E >
5   {
6      private final int size; // number of elements in the stack
7      private int top; // location of the top element
8      private E[] elements; // array that stores stack elements
9
10     // no-argument constructor creates a stack of the default size
11     public Stack()
12     {
13        this( 10 ); // default stack size
14     } // end no-argument Stack constructor
15
```

Fig. 15.7 | Generic class Stack declaration. (Part 1 of 2.)

```
16      // constructor creates a stack of the specified number of elements
17      public Stack( int s )
18      {
19         size = s > 0 ? s : 10; // set size of Stack
20         top = -1; // Stack initially empty
21
22         elements = ( E[] ) new Object[ size ]; // create array
23      } // end Stack constructor
24
25      // push element onto stack; if successful, return true;
26      // otherwise, throw FullStackException
27      public void push( E pushValue )
28      {
29         if ( top == size - 1 ) // if stack is full
30            throw new FullStackException( String.format(
31               "Stack is full, cannot push %s", pushValue ) );
32
33         elements[ ++top ] = pushValue; // place pushValue on Stack
34      } // end method push
35
36      // return the top element if not empty; else throw EmptyStackException
37      public E pop()
38      {
39         if ( top == -1 ) // if stack is empty
40            throw new EmptyStackException( "Stack is empty, cannot pop" );
41
42         return elements[ top-- ]; // remove and return top element of Stack
43      } // end method pop
44   } // end class Stack< E >
```

Fig. 15.7 | Generic class Stack declaration. (Part 2 of 2.)

Class Stack declares variable elements as an array of type E (line 8). This array will store the Stack's elements. We would like to create an array of type E to store the elements. However, the generics mechanism does not allow type parameters in array-creation expressions because the type parameter (in this case, E) is not available at runtime. To create an array with the appropriate type, line 22 in the one-argument constructor creates the array as an array of type Object and casts the reference returned by new to type E[]. Any object could be stored in an Object array, but the compiler's type-checking mechanism ensures that only objects of the array variable's declared type can be assigned to the array via any array-access expression that uses variable elements. Yet when this class is compiled using the -Xlint:unchecked option, e.g.,

```
javac -Xlint:unchecked Stack.java
```

the compiler issues the following warning message about line 22:

```
Stack.java:22: warning: [unchecked] unchecked cast
found   : java.lang.Object[]
required: E[]
      elements = ( E[] ) new Object[ size ]; // create array
```

The reason for this message is that the compiler cannot ensure with 100% certainty that an array of type Object will never contain objects of types other than E. Assume that E represents type Integer, so that array elements should store Integer objects. It is possible to assign variable elements to a variable of type Object[], as in

```
Object[] objectArray = elements;
```

Then any object can be placed into the array with an assignment statement like

```
objectArray[ 0 ] = "hello";
```

This places a String in an array that should contain only Integers, which would lead to runtime problems when manipulating the Stack. As long as you do not perform statements like those shown here, your Stack will contain objects of only the correct element type.

Method push (lines 27–34) first determines whether an attempt is being made to push an element onto a full Stack. If so, lines 30–31 throw a FullStackException. Class FullStackException is declared in Fig. 15.8. If the Stack is not full, line 33 increments the top counter and places the argument in that location of array elements.

Method pop (lines 37–43) first determines whether an attempt is being made to pop an element from an empty Stack. If so, line 40 throws an EmptyStackException. Class EmptyStackException is declared in Fig. 15.9. Otherwise, line 42 returns the top element of the Stack, then postdecrements the top counter to indicate the position of the next top element.

Classes FullStackException (Fig. 15.8) and EmptyStackException (Fig. 15.9) each provide the conventional no-argument constructor and one-argument constructor of exception classes (as discussed in Section 13.11). The no-argument constructor sets the default error message, and the one-argument constructor sets a custom exception message.

As with generic methods, when a generic class is compiled, the compiler performs erasure on the class's type parameters and replaces them with their upper bounds. For class Stack (Fig. 15.7), no upper bound is specified, so the default upper bound, Object, is used. The scope of a generic class's type parameter is the entire class. However, type parameters cannot be used in a class's static declarations.

```
1   // Fig. 15.8: FullStackException.java
2   // Indicates a stack is full.
3   public class FullStackException extends RuntimeException
4   {
5      // no-argument constructor
6      public FullStackException()
7      {
8         this( "Stack is full" );
9      } // end no-argument FullStackException constructor
10
11     // one-argument constructor
12     public FullStackException( String exception )
13     {
14        super( exception );
15     } // end one-argument FullStackException constructor
16  } // end class FullStackException
```

Fig. 15.8 | FullStackException class declaration.

```
 I   // Fig. 15.9: EmptyStackException.java
 2   // Indicates a stack is full.
 3   public class EmptyStackException extends RuntimeException
 4   {
 5      // no-argument constructor
 6      public EmptyStackException()
 7      {
 8         this( "Stack is empty" );
 9      } // end no-argument EmptyStackException constructor
10
11      // one-argument constructor
12      public EmptyStackException( String exception )
13      {
14         super( exception );
15      } // end one-argument EmptyStackException constructor
16   } // end class EmptyStackException
```

Fig. 15.9 | EmptyStackException class declaration.

Now, let's consider the test application (Fig. 15.10) that uses the Stack generic class. Lines 9–10 declare variables of type Stack< Double > (pronounced "Stack of Double") and Stack< Integer > (pronounced "Stack of Integer"). The types Double and Integer are known as the Stack's *type arguments*. They are used by the compiler to replace the type parameters so that the compiler can perform type checking and insert cast operations as necessary. We'll discuss the cast operations in more detail shortly. Method testStack (called from main) instantiates objects doubleStack of size 5 (line 15) and integerStack of size 10 (line 16), then calls methods testPushDouble (lines 25–44), testPopDouble (lines 47–67), testPushInteger (lines 70–89) and testPopInteger (lines 92–112) to demonstrate the two Stacks in this example.

Method testPushDouble (lines 25–44) invokes method push to place the double values 1.1, 2.2, 3.3, 4.4 and 5.5 stored in array doubleElements onto doubleStack. The for loop terminates when the test program attempts to push a sixth value onto doubleStack (which is full, because doubleStack can store only five elements). In this case,

```
 I   // Fig. 15.10: StackTest.java
 2   // Stack generic class test program.
 3
 4   public class StackTest
 5   {
 6      private double[] doubleElements = { 1.1, 2.2, 3.3, 4.4, 5.5, 6.6 };
 7      private int[] integerElements = { 1, 2, 3, 4, 5, 6, 7, 8, 9, 10, 11 };
 8
 9      private Stack< Double > doubleStack; // stack stores Double objects
10      private Stack< Integer > integerStack; // stack stores Integer objects
11
12      // test Stack objects
13      public void testStacks()
14      {
15         doubleStack = new Stack< Double >( 5 ); // Stack of Doubles
```

Fig. 15.10 | Generic class Stack test program. (Part 1 of 4.)

```
16        integerStack = new Stack< Integer >( 10 ); // Stack of Integers
17
18        testPushDouble(); // push double onto doubleStack
19        testPopDouble(); // pop from doubleStack
20        testPushInteger(); // push int onto intStack
21        testPopInteger(); // pop from intStack
22     } // end method testStacks
23
24     // test push method with double stack
25     public void testPushDouble()
26     {
27        // push elements onto stack
28        try
29        {
30           System.out.println( "\nPushing elements onto doubleStack" );
31
32           // push elements to Stack
33           for ( double element : doubleElements )
34           {
35              System.out.printf( "%.1f ", element );
36              doubleStack.push( element ); // push onto doubleStack
37           } // end for
38        } // end try
39        catch ( FullStackException fullStackException )
40        {
41           System.err.println();
42           fullStackException.printStackTrace();
43        } // end catch FullStackException
44     } // end method testPushDouble
45
46     // test pop method with double stack
47     public void testPopDouble()
48     {
49        // pop elements from stack
50        try
51        {
52           System.out.println( "\nPopping elements from doubleStack" );
53           double popValue; // store element removed from stack
54
55           // remove all elements from Stack
56           while ( true )
57           {
58              popValue = doubleStack.pop(); // pop from doubleStack
59              System.out.printf( "%.1f ", popValue );
60           } // end while
61        } // end try
62        catch( EmptyStackException emptyStackException )
63        {
64           System.err.println();
65           emptyStackException.printStackTrace();
66        } // end catch EmptyStackException
67     } // end method testPopDouble
```

Fig. 15.10 | Generic class Stack test program. (Part 2 of 4.)

```
68
69      // test push method with integer stack
70      public void testPushInteger()
71      {
72         // push elements to stack
73         try
74         {
75            System.out.println( "\nPushing elements onto intStack" );
76
77            // push elements to Stack
78            for ( int element : integerElements )
79            {
80               System.out.printf( "%d ", element );
81               integerStack.push( element ); // push onto integerStack
82            } // end for
83         } // end try
84         catch ( FullStackException fullStackException )
85         {
86            System.err.println();
87            fullStackException.printStackTrace();
88         } // end catch FullStackException
89      } // end method testPushInteger
90
91      // test pop method with integer stack
92      public void testPopInteger()
93      {
94         // pop elements from stack
95         try
96         {
97            System.out.println( "\nPopping elements from intStack" );
98            int popValue; // store element removed from stack
99
100           // remove all elements from Stack
101           while ( true )
102           {
103              popValue = integerStack.pop(); // pop from intStack
104              System.out.printf( "%d ", popValue );
105           } // end while
106        } // end try
107        catch( EmptyStackException emptyStackException )
108        {
109           System.err.println();
110           emptyStackException.printStackTrace();
111        } // end catch EmptyStackException
112     } // end method testPopInteger
113
114     public static void main( String args[] )
115     {
116        StackTest application = new StackTest();
117        application.testStacks();
118     } // end main
119  } // end class StackTest
```

Fig. 15.10 | Generic class Stack test program. (Part 3 of 4.)

```
Pushing elements onto doubleStack
1.1 2.2 3.3 4.4 5.5 6.6
FullStackException: Stack is full, cannot push 6.6
        at Stack.push(Stack.java:30)
        at StackTest.testPushDouble(StackTest.java:36)
        at StackTest.testStacks(StackTest.java:18)
        at StackTest.main(StackTest.java:117)

Popping elements from doubleStack
5.5 4.4 3.3 2.2 1.1
EmptyStackException: Stack is empty, cannot pop
        at Stack.pop(Stack.java:40)
        at StackTest.testPopDouble(StackTest.java:58)
        at StackTest.testStacks(StackTest.java:19)
        at StackTest.main(StackTest.java:117)

Pushing elements onto integerStack
1 2 3 4 5 6 7 8 9 10 11
FullStackException: Stack is full, cannot push 11
        at Stack.push(Stack.java:30)
        at StackTest.testPushInteger(StackTest.java:81)
        at StackTest.testStacks(StackTest.java:20)
        at StackTest.main(StackTest.java:117)

Popping elements from integerStack
10 9 8 7 6 5 4 3 2 1
EmptyStackException: Stack is empty, cannot pop
        at Stack.pop(Stack.java:40)
        at StackTest.testPopInteger(StackTest.java:103)
        at StackTest.testStacks(StackTest.java:21)
        at StackTest.main(StackTest.java:117)
```

Fig. 15.10 | Generic class Stack test program. (Part 4 of 4.)

the method throws a FullStackException (Fig. 15.8) to indicate that the Stack is full. Lines 39–43 catch this exception and print the stack trace information. The stack trace indicates the exception that occurred and shows that Stack method push generated the exception at lines 30–31 of the file Stack.java (Fig. 15.7). The trace also shows that method push was called by StackTest method testPushDouble at line 36 of Stack-Test.java, that method testPushDouble was called from method testStacks at line 18 of StackTest.java and that method testStacks was called from method main at line 117 of StackTest.java. This information enables you to determine the methods that were on the method-call stack at the time that the exception occurred. Because the program catches the exception, the Java runtime environment considers the exception to have been handled and the program can continue executing. Note that autoboxing occurs in line 36 when the program tries to push a primitive double value onto the doubleStack, which stores only Double objects.

Method testPopDouble (lines 47–67) invokes Stack method pop in an infinite while loop to remove all the values from the stack. Note in the output that the values indeed pop off in last-in, first-out order (this, of course, is the defining characteristic of stacks). The while loop (lines 57–61) continues until the stack is empty (i.e., until an Empty-StackException occurs), which causes the program to proceed to the catch block (lines

62–66) and handle the exception, so the program can continue executing. When the test program attempts to pop a sixth value, the doubleStack is empty, so the pop throws an EmptyStackException. Auto-unboxing occurs in line 58 when the program assigns the Double object popped from the stack to a double primitive variable. Recall from Section 15.4 that the compiler inserts cast operations to ensure that the proper types are returned from generic methods. After erasure, Stack method pop returns type Object. However, the client code in method testPopDouble expects to receive a double when method pop returns. So the compiler inserts a Double cast, as in

```
popValue = ( Double ) doubleStack.pop();
```

to ensure that a reference of the appropriate type is returned, auto-unboxed and assigned to popValue.

Method testPushInteger (lines 70–89) invokes Stack method push to place values onto integerStack until it is full. Method testPopInteger (lines 92–112) invokes Stack method pop to remove values from integerStack until it is empty. Once again, note that the values pop off in last-in, first-out order. During the erasure process, the compiler recognizes that the client code in method testPopInteger expects to receive an int when method pop returns. So the compiler inserts an Integer cast, as in

```
popValue = ( Integer ) integerStack.pop();
```

to ensure that a reference of the appropriate type is returned, auto-unboxed and assigned to popValue.

Creating Generic Methods to Test Class Stack< E >

Note that the code in methods testPushDouble and testPushInteger is almost identical for pushing values onto a Stack< Double > or a Stack< Integer >, respectively, and the code in methods testPopDouble and testPopInteger is almost identical for popping values from a Stack< Double > or a Stack< Integer >, respectively. This presents another opportunity to use generic methods. Figure 15.11 declares generic method testPush (lines 26–46) to perform the same tasks as testPushDouble and testPushInteger in Fig. 15.10—that is, push values onto a Stack< T >. Similarly, generic method testPop (lines 49–69) performs the same tasks as testPopDouble and testPopInteger in Fig. 15.10—that is, pop values off a Stack< T >. Note that the output of Fig. 15.11 precisely matches the output of Fig. 15.10.

```
1   // Fig. 15.11: StackTest2.java
2   // Stack generic class test program.
3
4   public class StackTest2
5   {
6      private Double[] doubleElements = { 1.1, 2.2, 3.3, 4.4, 5.5, 6.6 };
7      private Integer[] integerElements =
8         { 1, 2, 3, 4, 5, 6, 7, 8, 9, 10, 11 };
9
10     private Stack< Double > doubleStack; // stack stores Double objects
11     private Stack< Integer > integerStack; // stack stores Integer objects
```

Fig. 15.11 | Passing a generic type Stack to a generic method. (Part 1 of 3.)

```
12
13      // test Stack objects
14      public void testStacks()
15      {
16         doubleStack = new Stack< Double >( 5 ); // Stack of Doubles
17         integerStack = new Stack< Integer >( 10 ); // Stack of Integers
18
19         testPush( "doubleStack", doubleStack, doubleElements );
20         testPop( "doubleStack", doubleStack );
21         testPush( "integerStack", integerStack, integerElements );
22         testPop( "integerStack", integerStack );
23      } // end method testStacks
24
25      // generic method testPush pushes elements onto a Stack
26      public < T > void testPush( String name, Stack< T > stack,
27         T[] elements )
28      {
29         // push elements onto stack
30         try
31         {
32            System.out.printf( "\nPushing elements onto %s\n", name );
33
34            // push elements onto Stack
35            for ( T element : elements )
36            {
37               System.out.printf( "%s ", element );
38               stack.push( element ); // push element onto stack
39            }
40         } // end try
41         catch ( FullStackException fullStackException )
42         {
43            System.out.println();
44            fullStackException.printStackTrace();
45         } // end catch FullStackException
46      } // end method testPush
47
48      // generic method testPop pops elements from a Stack
49      public < T > void testPop( String name, Stack< T > stack )
50      {
51         // pop elements from stack
52         try
53         {
54            System.out.printf( "\nPopping elements from %s\n", name );
55            T popValue; // store element removed from stack
56
57            // remove elements from Stack
58            while ( true )
59            {
60               popValue = stack.pop(); // pop from stack
61               System.out.printf( "%s ", popValue );
62            } // end while
63         } // end try
```

Fig. 15.11 | Passing a generic type Stack to a generic method. (Part 2 of 3.)

```
64          catch( EmptyStackException emptyStackException )
65          {
66             System.out.println();
67             emptyStackException.printStackTrace();
68          } // end catch EmptyStackException
69       } // end method testPop
70
71       public static void main( String args[] )
72       {
73          StackTest2 application = new StackTest2();
74          application.testStacks();
75       } // end main
76    } // end class StackTest2
```

```
Pushing elements onto doubleStack
1.1 2.2 3.3 4.4 5.5 6.6
FullStackException: Stack is full, cannot push 6.6
        at Stack.push(Stack.java:30)
        at StackTest2.testPush(StackTest2.java:38)
        at StackTest2.testStacks(StackTest2.java:19)
        at StackTest2.main(StackTest2.java:74)

Popping elements from doubleStack
5.5 4.4 3.3 2.2 1.1
EmptyStackException: Stack is empty, cannot pop
        at Stack.pop(Stack.java:40)
        at StackTest2.testPop(StackTest2.java:60)
        at StackTest2.testStacks(StackTest2.java:20)
        at StackTest2.main(StackTest2.java:74)

Pushing elements onto integerStack
1 2 3 4 5 6 7 8 9 10 11
FullStackException: Stack is full, cannot push 11
        at Stack.push(Stack.java:30)
        at StackTest2.testPush(StackTest2.java:38)
        at StackTest2.testStacks(StackTest2.java:21)
        at StackTest2.main(StackTest2.java:74)

Popping elements from integerStack
10 9 8 7 6 5 4 3 2 1
EmptyStackException: Stack is empty, cannot pop
        at Stack.pop(Stack.java:40)
        at StackTest2.testPop(StackTest2.java:60)
        at StackTest2.testStacks(StackTest2.java:22)
        at StackTest2.main(StackTest2.java:74)
```

Fig. 15.11 | Passing a generic type Stack to a generic method. (Part 3 of 3.)

The testStacks method (lines 14–23) creates the Stack< Double > (line 16) and Stack< Integer > (line 17) objects. Lines 19–22 invoke generic methods testPush and testPop to test the Stack objects. Recall that type parameters can represent only reference types. Therefore, to be able to pass arrays doubleElements and integerElements to generic method testPush, the arrays declared in lines 6–8 must be declared with the wrapper types Double and Integer. When these arrays are initialized with primitive values, the compiler autoboxes each primitive value.

Generic method `testPush` (lines 26–46) uses type parameter T (specified at line 26) to represent the data type stored in the Stack< T >. The generic method takes three arguments—a String that represents the name of the Stack< T > object for output purposes, a reference to an object of type Stack< T > and an array of type T—the type of elements that will be pushed onto Stack< T >. Note that the compiler enforces consistency between the type of the Stack and the elements that will be pushed onto the Stack when push is invoked, which is the real value of the generic method call. Generic method `testPop` (lines 49–69) takes two arguments—a String that represents the name of the Stack< T > object for output purposes and a reference to an object of type Stack< T >.

15.7 Raw Types

The test programs for generic class Stack in Section 15.6 instantiate Stacks with type arguments Double and Integer. It is also possible to instantiate generic class Stack without specifying a type argument, as follows:

```
Stack objectStack = new Stack( 5 ); // no type argument specified
```

In this case, the `objectStack` is said to have a *raw type*, which means that the compiler implicitly uses type Object throughout the generic class for each type argument. Thus the preceding statement creates a Stack that can store objects of any type. This is important for backward compatibility with prior versions of Java. For example, the data structures of the Java Collections Framework (see Chapter 16) all stored references to Objects, but are now implemented as generic types.

A raw type Stack variable can be assigned a Stack that specifies a type argument, such as a Stack< Double > object, as follows:

```
Stack rawTypeStack2 = new Stack< Double >( 5 );
```

because type Double is a subclass of Object. This assignment is allowed because the elements in a Stack< Double > (i.e., Double objects) are certainly objects—class Double is an indirect subclass of Object.

Similarly, a Stack variable that specifies a type argument in its declaration can be assigned a raw type Stack object, as in:

```
Stack< Integer > integerStack = new Stack( 10 );
```

Although this assignment is permitted, it is unsafe because a Stack of raw type might store types other than Integer. In this case, the compiler issues a warning message which indicates the unsafe assignment.

The test program of Fig. 15.12 uses the notion of raw type. Line 14 instantiates generic class Stack with raw type, which indicates that rawTypeStack1 can hold objects of any type. Line 17 assigns a Stack< Double > to variable rawTypeStack2, which is declared as a Stack of raw type. Line 20 assigns a Stack of raw type to Stack< Integer > variable, which is legal but causes the compiler to issue a warning message (Fig. 15.13) indicating a potentially unsafe assignment—again, this occurs because a Stack of raw type might store types other than Integer. Also, each of the calls to generic method testPush and testPop in lines 22–25 results in a compiler warning message (Fig. 15.13). These warnings occur because variables rawTypeStack1 and rawTypeStack2 are declared as Stacks of raw type, but methods `testPush` and `testPop` each expect a second argument that is a Stack with a specific type argument. The warnings indicate that the compiler cannot guarantee that the types manipulated by the stacks are the correct types, because we did not supply a variable declared with a type argument. Methods `testPush` (lines 31–51) and `testPop` (lines 54–74) are the same as in Fig. 15.11.

```
 1   // Fig. 15.12: RawTypeTest.java
 2   // Raw type test program.
 3
 4   public class RawTypeTest
 5   {
 6      private Double[] doubleElements = { 1.1, 2.2, 3.3, 4.4, 5.5, 6.6 };
 7      private Integer[] integerElements =
 8         { 1, 2, 3, 4, 5, 6, 7, 8, 9, 10, 11 };
 9
10      // method to test Stacks with raw types
11      public void testStacks()
12      {
13         // Stack of raw types assigned to Stack of raw types variable
14         Stack rawTypeStack1 = new Stack( 5 );
15
16         // Stack< Double > assigned to Stack of raw types variable
17         Stack rawTypeStack2 = new Stack< Double >( 5 );
18
19         // Stack of raw types assigned to Stack< Integer > variable
20         Stack< Integer > integerStack = new Stack( 10 );
21
22         testPush( "rawTypeStack1", rawTypeStack1, doubleElements );
23         testPop( "rawTypeStack1", rawTypeStack1 );
24         testPush( "rawTypeStack2", rawTypeStack2, doubleElements );
25         testPop( "rawTypeStack2", rawTypeStack2 );
26         testPush( "integerStack", integerStack, integerElements );
27         testPop( "integerStack", integerStack );
28      } // end method testStacks
29
30      // generic method pushes elements onto stack
31      public < T > void testPush( String name, Stack< T > stack,
32         T[] elements )
33      {
34         // push elements onto stack
35         try
36         {
37            System.out.printf( "\nPushing elements onto %s\n", name );
38
39            // push elements onto Stack
40            for ( T element : elements )
41            {
42               System.out.printf( "%s ", element );
43               stack.push( element ); // push element onto stack
44            } // end for
45         } // end try
```

Fig. 15.12 | Raw type test program. (Part 1 of 3.)

```
46              catch ( FullStackException fullStackException )
47              {
48                 System.out.println();
49                 fullStackException.printStackTrace();
50              } // end catch FullStackException
51           } // end method testPush
52
53           // generic method testPop pops elements from stack
54           public < T > void testPop( String name, Stack< T > stack )
55           {
56              // pop elements from stack
57              try
58              {
59                 System.out.printf( "\nPopping elements from %s\n", name );
60                 T popValue; // store element removed from stack
61
62                 // remove elements from Stack
63                 while ( true )
64                 {
65                    popValue = stack.pop(); // pop from stack
66                    System.out.printf( "%s ", popValue );
67                 } // end while
68              } // end try
69              catch( EmptyStackException emptyStackException )
70              {
71                 System.out.println();
72                 emptyStackException.printStackTrace();
73              } // end catch EmptyStackException
74           } // end method testPop
75
76           public static void main( String args[] )
77           {
78              RawTypeTest application = new RawTypeTest();
79              application.testStacks();
80           } // end main
81        } // end class RawTypeTest
```

```
Pushing elements onto rawTypeStack1
1.1 2.2 3.3 4.4 5.5 6.6
FullStackException: Stack is full, cannot push 6.6
        at Stack.push(Stack.java:30)
        at RawTypeTest.testPush(RawTypeTest.java:43)
        at RawTypeTest.testStacks(RawTypeTest.java:22)
        at RawTypeTest.main(RawTypeTest.java:79)

Popping elements from rawTypeStack1
5.5 4.4 3.3 2.2 1.1
EmptyStackException: Stack is empty, cannot pop
        at Stack.pop(Stack.java:40)
        at RawTypeTest.testPop(RawTypeTest.java:65)
        at RawTypeTest.testStacks(RawTypeTest.java:23)
        at RawTypeTest.main(RawTypeTest.java:79)
```

Fig. 15.12 | Raw type test program. (Part 2 of 3.)

```
Pushing elements onto rawTypeStack2
1.1 2.2 3.3 4.4 5.5 6.6
FullStackException: Stack is full, cannot push 6.6
        at Stack.push(Stack.java:30)
        at RawTypeTest.testPush(RawTypeTest.java:43)
        at RawTypeTest.testStacks(RawTypeTest.java:24)
        at RawTypeTest.main(RawTypeTest.java:79)

Popping elements from rawTypeStack2
5.5 4.4 3.3 2.2 1.1
EmptyStackException: Stack is empty, cannot pop
        at Stack.pop(Stack.java:40)
        at RawTypeTest.testPop(RawTypeTest.java:65)
        at RawTypeTest.testStacks(RawTypeTest.java:25)
        at RawTypeTest.main(RawTypeTest.java:79)

Pushing elements onto integerStack
1 2 3 4 5 6 7 8 9 10 11
FullStackException: Stack is full, cannot push 11
        at Stack.push(Stack.java:30)
        at RawTypeTest.testPush(RawTypeTest.java:43)
        at RawTypeTest.testStacks(RawTypeTest.java:26)
        at RawTypeTest.main(RawTypeTest.java:79)

Popping elements from integerStack
10 9 8 7 6 5 4 3 2 1
EmptyStackException: Stack is empty, cannot pop
        at Stack.pop(Stack.java:40)
        at RawTypeTest.testPop(RawTypeTest.java:65)
        at RawTypeTest.testStacks(RawTypeTest.java:27)
        at RawTypeTest.main(RawTypeTest.java:79)
```

Fig. 15.12 | Raw type test program. (Part 3 of 3.)

Figure 15.13 shows the warning messages generated by the compiler (compiled with the -Xlint:unchecked option) when the file RawTypeTest.java (Fig. 15.12) is compiled. The first warning is generated for line 20, which assigned a raw type Stack to a Stack< Integer > variable—the compiler cannot ensure that all objects in the Stack will be Integer objects. The second warning is generated for line 22. Because the second method argument is a raw type Stack variable, the compiler determines the type argument for method testPush from the Double array passed as the third argument. In this case, Double is the type argument, so the compiler expects a Stack< Double > to be passed as the second argument. The warning occurs because the compiler cannot ensure that a raw type Stack contains only Double objects. The warning at line 24 occurs for the same reason, even though the actual Stack that rawTypeStack2 references is a Stack< Double >. The compiler cannot guarantee that the variable will always refer to the same Stack object, so it must use the variable's declared type to perform all type checking. Lines 23 and 25 each generate warnings because method testPop expects as an argument a Stack for which a type argument has been specified. However, in each call to testPop, we pass a raw type Stack variable. Thus, the compiler indicates a warning because it cannot check the types used in the body of the method.

```
RawTypeTest.java:20: warning: unchecked assignment
found   : Stack
required: Stack<java.lang.Integer>
      Stack< Integer > integerStack = new Stack( 10 );
                                      ^
RawTypeTest.java:22: warning: [unchecked] unchecked method invocation:
<T>testPush(java.lang.String,Stack<T>,T[]) in RawTypeTest is applied to
(java.lang.String,Stack,java.lang.Double[])
      testPush( "rawTypeStack1", rawTypeStack1, doubleElements );
      ^
RawTypeTest.java:23: warning: [unchecked] unchecked method invocation:
<T>testPop(java.lang.String,Stack<T>) in RawTypeTest is applied to
(java.lang.String,Stack)
      testPop( "rawTypeStack1", rawTypeStack1 );
      ^
RawTypeTest.java:24: warning: [unchecked] unchecked method invocation:
<T>testPush(java.lang.String,Stack<T>,T[]) in RawTypeTest is applied to
(java.lang.String,Stack,java.lang.Double[])
      testPush( "rawTypeStack2", rawTypeStack2, doubleElements );
      ^
RawTypeTest.java:25: warning: [unchecked] unchecked method invocation:
<T>testPop(java.lang.String,Stack<T>) in RawTypeTest is applied to
(java.lang.String,Stack)
      testPop( "rawTypeStack2", rawTypeStack2 );
      ^
5 warnings
```

Fig. 15.13 | Warning messages from the compiler.

15.8 Wildcards in Methods That Accept Type Parameters

In this section, we introduce a powerful generics concept known as *wildcards*. For this purpose, we'll also introduce a new data structure from package java.util. Chapter 16, discusses the Java Collections Framework, which provides many generic data structures and algorithms that manipulate the elements of those data structures. Perhaps the simplest of these data structures is class ArrayList—a dynamically resizable, array-like data structure. As part of this discussion, you'll learn how to create an ArrayList, add elements to it and traverse those elements using an enhanced for statement.

Before we introduce wildcards, let's consider an example that helps us motivate their use. Suppose that you would like to implement a generic method sum that totals the numbers in a collection, such as an ArrayList. You would begin by inserting the numbers in the collection. As you know, generic classes can be used only with class or interface types. So the numbers would be autoboxed as objects of the type-wrapper classes. For example, any int value would be autoboxed as an Integer object, and any double value would be autoboxed as a Double object. We'd like to be able to total all the numbers in the Array-List regardless of their type. For this reason, we'll declare the ArrayList with the type argument Number, which is the superclass of both Integer and Double. In addition, method sum will receive a parameter of type ArrayList< Number > and total its elements. Figure 15.14 demonstrates totaling the elements of an ArrayList of Numbers.

```
1   // Fig. 15.14: TotalNumbers.java
2   // Summing the elements of an ArrayList.
3   import java.util.ArrayList;
4
5   public class TotalNumbers
6   {
7      public static void main( String args[] )
8      {
9         // create, initialize and output ArrayList of Numbers containing
10        // both Integers and Doubles, then display total of the elements
11        Number[] numbers = { 1, 2.4, 3, 4.1 }; // Integers and Doubles
12        ArrayList< Number > numberList = new ArrayList< Number >();
13
14        for ( Number element : numbers )
15           numberList.add( element ); // place each number in numberList
16
17        System.out.printf( "numberList contains: %s\n", numberList );
18        System.out.printf( "Total of the elements in numberList: %.1f\n",
19           sum( numberList ) );
20     } // end main
21
22     // calculate total of ArrayList elements
23     public static double sum( ArrayList< Number > list )
24     {
25        double total = 0; // initialize total
26
27        // calculate sum
28        for ( Number element : list )
29           total += element.doubleValue();
30
31        return total;
32     } // end method sum
33  } // end class TotalNumbers
```

```
numberList contains: [1, 2.4, 3, 4.1]
Total of the elements in numberList: 10.5
```

Fig. 15.14 | Totaling the numbers in an ArrayList< Number >.

Line 11 declares and initializes an array of Numbers. Because the initializers are primitive values, Java autoboxes each primitive value as an object of its corresponding wrapper type. The int values 1 and 3 are autoboxed as Integer objects, and the double values 2.4 and 4.1 are autoboxed as Double objects. Line 12 declares and creates an ArrayList object that stores Numbers and assigns it to variable numberList. Note that we do not have to specify the size of the ArrayList because it will grow automatically as we insert objects.

Lines 14–15 traverse array numbers and place each element in numberList. Method add of class ArrayList appends an element to the end of the collection. Line 17 outputs the contents of the ArrayList as a String. This statement implicitly invokes the ArrayList's toString method, which returns a string of the form "[*elements*]" in which *elements* is a comma-separated list of the elements' string representations. Lines 18–19 display the sum of the elements that is returned by the call to method sum at line 19.

Method sum (lines 23–32) receives an ArrayList of Numbers and calculates the total of the Numbers in the collection. The method uses double values to perform the calculations and returns the result as a double. Line 25 declares local variable total and initializes it to 0. Lines 28–29 use the enhanced for statement, which is designed to work with both arrays and the collections of the Collections Framework, to total the elements of the ArrayList. The for statement assigns each Number in the ArrayList to variable element, then uses method doubleValue of class Number to obtain the Number's underlying primitive value as a double value. The result is added to total. When the loop terminates, the method returns the total.

Implementing Method sum With a Wildcard Type Argument in Its Parameter

Recall that the purpose of method sum in Fig. 15.14 was to total any type of Numbers stored in an ArrayList. We created an ArrayList of Numbers that contained both Integer and Double objects. The output of Fig. 15.14 demonstrates that method sum worked properly. Given that method sum can total the elements of an ArrayList of Numbers, you might expect that the method would also work for ArrayLists that contain elements of only one numeric type, such as ArrayList< Integer >. So we modified class TotalNumbers to create an ArrayList of Integers and pass it to method sum. When we compile the program, the compiler issues the following error message:

```
sum(java.util.ArrayList<java.lang.Number>) in TotalNumbersErrors
cannot be applied to (java.util.ArrayList<java.lang.Integer>)
```

Although Number is the superclass of Integer, the compiler does not consider the parameterized type ArrayList< Number > to be a supertype of ArrayList< Integer >. If it were, then every operation we could perform on ArrayList< Number > would also work on an ArrayList< Integer >. Consider the fact that you can add a Double object to an ArrayList< Number > because a Double *is a* Number, but you cannot add a Double object to an ArrayList< Integer > because a Double *is not* an Integer. Thus, the subtype relationship does not hold.

How do we create a more flexible version of method sum that can total the elements of any ArrayList that contains elements of any subclass of Number? This is where *wildcard type arguments* are important. Wildcards enable you to specify method parameters, return values, variables or fields, etc. that act as supertypes of parameterized types. In Fig. 15.15, method sum's parameter is declared in line 50 with the type:

```
ArrayList< ? extends Number >
```

A wildcard type argument is denoted by a question mark (*?*), which by itself represents an "unknown type." In this case, the wildcard extends class Number, which means that the wildcard has an upper bound of Number. Thus, the unknown type argument must be either Number or a subclass of Number. With the parameter type shown here, method sum can receive an ArrayList argument that contains any type of Number, such as ArrayList< Integer > (line 20), ArrayList< Double > (line 33) or ArrayList< Number > (line 46).

Lines 11–20 create and initialize an ArrayList< Integer > called integerList, output its elements and total its elements by calling method sum (line 20). Lines 24–33 perform the same operations for an ArrayList< Double > called doubleList. Lines 37–46 perform the same operations for an ArrayList< Number > called numberList that contains both Integers and Doubles.

```
1   // Fig. 15.15: WildcardTest.java
2   // Wildcard test program.
3   import java.util.ArrayList;
4
5   public class WildcardTest
6   {
7      public static void main( String args[] )
8      {
9         // create, initialize and output ArrayList of Integers, then
10        // display total of the elements
11        Integer[] integers = { 1, 2, 3, 4, 5 };
12        ArrayList< Integer > integerList = new ArrayList< Integer >();
13
14        // insert elements in integerList
15        for ( Integer element : integers )
16           integerList.add( element );
17
18        System.out.printf( "integerList contains: %s\n", integerList );
19        System.out.printf( "Total of the elements in integerList: %.0f\n\n",
20           sum( integerList ) );
21
22        // create, initialize and output ArrayList of Doubles, then
23        // display total of the elements
24        Double[] doubles = { 1.1, 3.3, 5.5 };
25        ArrayList< Double > doubleList = new ArrayList< Double >();
26
27        // insert elements in doubleList
28        for ( Double element : doubles )
29           doubleList.add( element );
30
31        System.out.printf( "doubleList contains: %s\n", doubleList );
32        System.out.printf( "Total of the elements in doubleList: %.1f\n\n",
33           sum( doubleList ) );
34
35        // create, initialize and output ArrayList of Numbers containing
36        // both Integers and Doubles, then display total of the elements
37        Number[] numbers = { 1, 2.4, 3, 4.1 }; // Integers and Doubles
38        ArrayList< Number > numberList = new ArrayList< Number >();
39
40        // insert elements in numberList
41        for ( Number element : numbers )
42           numberList.add( element );
43
44        System.out.printf( "numberList contains: %s\n", numberList );
45        System.out.printf( "Total of the elements in numberList: %.1f\n",
46           sum( numberList ) );
47     } // end main
48
49     // calculate total of stack elements
50     public static double sum( ArrayList< ? extends Number > list )
51     {
52        double total = 0; // initialize total
53
```

Fig. 15.15 | Wildcard test program. (Part 1 of 2.)

```
54          // calculate sum
55          for ( Number element : list )
56              total += element.doubleValue();
57
58          return total;
59      } // end method sum
60  } // end class WildcardTest
```

```
integerList contains: [1, 2, 3, 4, 5]
Total of the elements in integerList: 15

doubleList contains: [1.1, 3.3, 5.5]
Total of the elements in doubleList: 9.9

numberList contains: [1, 2.4, 3, 4.1]
Total of the elements in numberList: 10.5
```

Fig. 15.15 | Wildcard test program. (Part 2 of 2.)

In method sum (lines 50–59), although the ArrayList argument's element types are not directly known by the method, they are known to be at least of type Number, because the wildcard was specified with the upper bound Number. For this reason line 56 is allowed, because all Number objects have a doubleValue method.

Although wildcards provide flexibility when passing parameterized types to a method, they also have some disadvantages. Because the wildcard (?) in the method's header (line 50) does not specify a type-parameter name, you cannot use it as a type name throughout the method's body (i.e., you cannot replace Number with ? in line 55). You could, however, declare method sum as follows:

> **public static** <T **extends** Number> **double** sum(ArrayList< T > list)

which allows the method to receive an ArrayList that contains elements of any Number subclass. You could then use the type parameter T throughout the method body.

If the wildcard is specified without an upper bound, then only the methods of type Object can be invoked on values of the wildcard type. Also, methods that use wildcards in their parameter's type arguments cannot be used to add elements to a collection referenced by the parameter.

Common Programming Error 15.4

Using a wildcard in a method's type parameter section or using a wildcard as an explicit type of a variable in the method body is a syntax error.

15.9 Generics and Inheritance: Notes

Generics can be used with inheritance in several ways:

- A generic class can be derived from a non-generic class. For example, the Object class is a direct or indirect superclass of every generic class.

- A generic class can be derived from another generic class. For example, generic class Stack (in package java.util) is a subclass of generic class Vector (in package java.util). We discuss these classes in Chapter 16.

- A non-generic class can be derived from a generic class. For example, non-generic class Properties (in package java.util) is a subclass of generic class Hashtable (in package java.util). We also discuss these classes in Chapter 16.

- Finally, a generic method in a subclass can override a generic method in a super-class if both methods have the same signatures.

15.10 Wrap-Up

This chapter introduced generics. You learned how to declare generic methods and classes. You learned how backward compatibility is achieved via raw types. You also learned how to use wildcards in a generic method or a generic class. In the next chapter, we demonstrate the interfaces, classes and algorithms of the Java collections framework. As you'll see, the collections presented all use the generics capabilties you learned here.

15.11 Internet and Web Resources

www.angelikalanger.com/GenericsFAQ/JavaGenericsFAQ.html
A collection of frequently asked questions about Java generics.

java.sun.com/j2se/1.5/pdf/generics-tutorial.pdf
The tutorial *Generics in the Java Programming Language* by Gilad Bracha (the specification lead for JSR-14 and a reviewer of this book) introduces generics concepts with sample code snippets.

today.java.net/pub/a/today/2003/12/02/explorations.html
today.java.net/pub/a/today/2004/01/15/wildcards.html
The articles *Explorations: Generics, Erasure, and Bridging* and *Explorations: Wildcards in the Generics Specification*, each by William Grosso, overview generics features and how to use wildcards.

16

Collections

I think this is the most extraordinary collection of talent, of human knowledge, that has ever been gathered together at the White House—with the possible exception of when Thomas Jefferson dined alone.
—John F. Kennedy

The shapes a bright container can contain!
—Theodore Roethke

Journey over all the universe in a map.
—Miguel de Cervantes

Not by age but by capacity is wisdom acquired.
—Titus Maccius Plautus

It is a riddle wrapped in a mystery inside an enigma.
—Winston Churchill

OBJECTIVES

In this chapter you'll learn:

- What collections are.

- To use class `Arrays` for array manipulations.

- To use the collections framework (prepackaged data structure) implementations.

- To use collections framework algorithms to manipulate (such as `search`, `sort` and `fill`) collections.

- To use the collections framework interfaces to program with collections polymorphically.

- To use iterators to "walk through" a collection.

- To use persistent hash tables manipulated with objects of class `Properties`.

- To use synchronization and modifiability wrappers.

Outline

16.1 Introduction

16.2 Collections Overview

16.3 Class `Arrays`

16.4 Interface `Collection` and Class `Collections`

16.5 Lists

    16.5.1 `ArrayList` and `Iterator`

    16.5.2 `LinkedList`

    16.5.3 `Vector`

16.6 Collections Algorithms

    16.6.1 Algorithm `sort`

    16.6.2 Algorithm `shuffle`

    16.6.3 Algorithms `reverse`, `fill`, `copy`, `max` and `min`

    16.6.4 Algorithm `binarySearch`

    16.6.5 Algorithms `addAll`, `frequency` and `disjoint`

16.7 Stack Class of Package `java.util`

16.8 Class `PriorityQueue` and `Interface Queue`

16.9 Sets

16.10 Maps

16.11 `Properties` Class

16.12 Synchronized Collections

16.13 Unmodifiable Collections

16.14 Abstract Implementations

16.15 Wrap-Up

16.1 Introduction

We now consider the Java *collections framework*, which contains prepackaged data structures, interfaces and algorithms for manipulating those data structures. Some examples of collections are the cards you hold in a card game, your favorite songs stored in your computer, the members of a sports team and the real-estate records in your local registry of deeds (which map book numbers and page numbers to property owners). In this chapter, we also discuss how generics (see Chapter 15) are used in the Java collections framework.

With collections, programmers use existing data structures, without concern for how they're implemented. This is a marvelous example of code reuse. You can code faster and expect excellent performance, maximizing execution speed and minimizing memory consumption. In this chapter, we discuss the collections framework interfaces that list the capabilities of each collection type, the implementation classes, the algorithms that process the collections, and the so-called *iterators* and enhanced `for` statement syntax that "walk through" collections. This chapter provides an introduction to the collections framework. For complete details, visit `java.sun.com/javase/6/docs/guide/collections`.

The Java collections framework provides ready-to-go, reusable componentry—you do not need to write your own collection classes, but you can if you wish to. The collections are standardized so that applications can share them easily without concern for the details of their implementation. The collections framework encourages further reusability. As new data structures and algorithms are developed that fit this framework, a large base of programmers will already be familiar with the interfaces and algorithms implemented by those data structures.

16.2 Collections Overview

A *collection* is a data structure—actually, an object—that can hold references to other objects. Usually, collections contain references to objects that are all of the same type. The collections framework interfaces declare the operations to be performed generically on various types of collections. Figure 16.1 lists some of the interfaces of the collections framework. Several implementations of these interfaces are provided within the framework. Programmers may also provide implementations specific to their own requirements.

The collections framework provides high-performance, high-quality implementations of common data structures and enables software reuse. These features minimize the amount of coding programmers need to do to create and manipulate collections. The classes and interfaces of the collections framework are members of package java.util. In the next section, we begin our discussion by examining the collections framework capabilities for array manipulation.

In earlier versions of Java, the classes in the collections framework stored and manipulated Object references. Thus, you could store any object in a collection. One inconvenient aspect of storing Object references occurs when retrieving them from a collection. A program normally has the need to process specific types of objects. As a result, the Object references obtained from a collection typically need to be cast to an appropriate type to allow the program to process the objects correctly.

In Java SE 5, the collections framework was enhanced with the generics capabilities we introduced in Chapter 15. This means that you can specify the exact type that will be stored in a collection rather than type Object. You also receive the benefits of compile-time type checking—the compiler ensures that you are using appropriate types with your collection and, if not, issues compile-time error messages. Also, once you specify the type stored in a collection, any reference you retrieve from the collection will have the specified type. This eliminates the need for explicit type casts that can throw ClassCastExceptions if the referenced object is not of the appropriate type. Programs that were implemented with prior Java

Interface	Description
Collection	The root interface in the collections hierarchy from which interfaces Set, Queue and List are derived.
Set	A collection that does not contain duplicates.
List	An ordered collection that can contain duplicate elements.
Map	Associates keys to values and cannot contain duplicate keys.
Queue	Typically a first-in, first-out collection that models a waiting line; other orders can be specified.

Fig. 16.1 | Some collection framework interfaces.

versions and that use collections can compile properly because the compiler automatically uses raw types when it encounters collections for which type arguments were not specified.

16.3 Class Arrays

Class **Arrays** provides `static` methods for manipulating arrays. In Chapter 7, our discussion of array manipulation was low level in the sense that we wrote the actual code to sort and search arrays. Class Arrays provides high-level methods, such as **sort** for sorting an array, `binarySearch` for searching a sorted array, **equals** for comparing arrays and **fill** for placing values into an array. These methods are overloaded for primitive-type arrays and `Object` arrays. In addition, methods sort and binarySearch are overloaded with generic versions that allow programmers to sort and search arrays containing objects of any type. Figure 16.2 demonstrates methods fill, sort, binarySearch and equals. Method main (lines 65–85) creates a UsingArrays object and invokes its methods.

```
1   // Fig. 16.2: UsingArrays.java
2   // Using Java arrays.
3   import java.util.Arrays;
4
5   public class UsingArrays
6   {
7      private int intArray[] = { 1, 2, 3, 4, 5, 6 };
8      private double doubleArray[] = { 8.4, 9.3, 0.2, 7.9, 3.4 };
9      private int filledIntArray[], intArrayCopy[];
10
11     // constructor initializes arrays
12     public UsingArrays()
13     {
14        filledIntArray = new int[ 10 ]; // create int array with 10 elements
15        intArrayCopy = new int[ intArray.length ];
16
17        Arrays.fill( filledIntArray, 7 ); // fill with 7s
18        Arrays.sort( doubleArray ); // sort doubleArray ascending
19
20        // copy array intArray into array intArrayCopy
21        System.arraycopy( intArray, 0, intArrayCopy,
22           0, intArray.length );
23     } // end UsingArrays constructor
24
25     // output values in each array
26     public void printArrays()
27     {
28        System.out.print( "doubleArray: " );
29        for ( double doubleValue : doubleArray )
30           System.out.printf( "%.1f ", doubleValue );
31
32        System.out.print( "\nintArray: " );
33        for ( int intValue : intArray )
34           System.out.printf( "%d ", intValue );
```

Fig. 16.2 | Arrays class methods. (Part 1 of 3.)

```
35
36          System.out.print( "\nfilledIntArray: " );
37          for ( int intValue : filledIntArray )
38             System.out.printf( "%d ", intValue );
39
40          System.out.print( "\nintArrayCopy: " );
41          for ( int intValue : intArrayCopy )
42             System.out.printf( "%d ", intValue );
43
44          System.out.println( "\n" );
45       } // end method printArrays
46
47       // find value in array intArray
48       public int searchForInt( int value )
49       {
50          return Arrays.binarySearch( intArray, value );
51       } // end method searchForInt
52
53       // compare array contents
54       public void printEquality()
55       {
56          boolean b = Arrays.equals( intArray, intArrayCopy );
57          System.out.printf( "intArray %s intArrayCopy\n",
58             ( b ? "==" : "!=" ) );
59
60          b = Arrays.equals( intArray, filledIntArray );
61          System.out.printf( "intArray %s filledIntArray\n",
62             ( b ? "==" : "!=" ) );
63       } // end method printEquality
64
65       public static void main( String args[] )
66       {
67          UsingArrays usingArrays = new UsingArrays();
68
69          usingArrays.printArrays();
70          usingArrays.printEquality();
71
72          int location = usingArrays.searchForInt( 5 );
73          if ( location >= 0 )
74             System.out.printf(
75                "Found 5 at element %d in intArray\n", location );
76          else
77             System.out.println( "5 not found in intArray" );
78
79          location = usingArrays.searchForInt( 8763 );
80          if ( location >= 0 )
81             System.out.printf(
82                "Found 8763 at element %d in intArray\n", location );
83          else
84             System.out.println( "8763 not found in intArray" );
85       } // end main
86    } // end class UsingArrays
```

Fig. 16.2 | Arrays class methods. (Part 2 of 3.)

```
doubleArray: 0.2 3.4 7.9 8.4 9.3
intArray: 1 2 3 4 5 6
filledIntArray: 7 7 7 7 7 7 7 7 7 7
intArrayCopy: 1 2 3 4 5 6

intArray == intArrayCopy
intArray != filledIntArray
Found 5 at element 4 in intArray
8763 not found in intArray
```

Fig. 16.2 | Arrays class methods. (Part 3 of 3.)

Line 17 calls static method fill of class Arrays to populate all 10 elements of filledIntArray with 7s. Overloaded versions of fill allow the programmer to populate a specific range of elements with the same value.

Line 18 sorts the elements of array doubleArray. The static method sort of class Arrays orders the array's elements in ascending order by default. We discuss how to sort in descending order later in the chapter. Overloaded versions of sort allow the programmer to sort a specific range of elements.

Lines 21–22 copy array intArray into array intArrayCopy. The first argument (intArray) passed to System method ***arraycopy*** is the array from which elements are to be copied. The second argument (0) is the index that specifies the starting point in the range of elements to copy from the array. This value can be any valid array index. The third argument (intArrayCopy) specifies the destination array that will store the copy. The fourth argument (0) specifies the index in the destination array where the first copied element should be stored. The last argument specifies the number of elements to copy from the array in the first argument. In this case, we copy all the elements in the array.

Line 50 calls static method binarySearch of class Arrays to perform a binary search on intArray, using value as the key. If value is found, binarySearch returns the index of the element; otherwise, binarySearch returns a negative value. The negative value returned is based on the search key's ***insertion point***—the index where the key would be inserted in the array if we were performing an insert operation. After binarySearch determines the insertion point, it changes its sign to negative and subtracts 1 to obtain the return value. For example, in Fig. 16.2, the insertion point for the value 8763 is the element with index 6 in the array. Method binarySearch changes the insertion point to –6, subtracts 1 from it and returns the value –7. Subtracting 1 from the insertion point guarantees that method binarySearch returns positive values (>= 0) if and only if the key is found. This return value is useful for inserting elements in a sorted array.

Common Programming Error 16.1

Passing an unsorted array to binarySearch is a logic error—the value returned is undefined.

Lines 56 and 60 call static method equals of class Arrays to determine whether the elements of two arrays are equivalent. If the arrays contain the same elements in the same order, the method returns true; otherwise, it returns false. The equality of each element is compared using Object method equals. Many classes override method equals to perform the comparisons in a manner specific to those classes. For example, class String declares equals to compare the individual characters in the two Strings being compared. If method equals is not overridden, the original version of method equals inherited from class Object is used.

16.4 Interface Collection and Class Collections

The **Collection** interface is the root interface in the collection hierarchy from which interfaces Set, Queue and List are derived. Interface **Set** defines a collection that does not contain duplicates. Interface **Queue** defines a collection that represents a waiting line—typically, insertions are made at the back of a queue and deletions are made from the front, though other orders can be specified. We discuss Queue and Set in Section 16.8 and Section 16.9, respectively. Interface Collection contains *bulk operations* (i.e., operations performed on an entire collection) for adding, clearing, comparing and retaining objects (or elements) in a collection. A Collection can also be converted to an array. In addition, interface Collection provides a method that returns an *Iterator* object, which allows a program to walk through the collection and remove elements from the collection during the iteration. We discuss class Iterator in Section 16.5.1. Other methods of interface Collection enable a program to determine a collection's size and whether a collection is empty.

Software Engineering Observation 16.1

Collection is used commonly as a method parameter type to allow polymorphic processing of all objects that implement interface Collection.

Software Engineering Observation 16.2

Most collection implementations provide a constructor that takes a Collection argument, thereby allowing a new collection to be constructed containing the elements of the specified collection.

Class **Collections** provides static methods that manipulate collections polymorphically. These methods implement algorithms for searching, sorting and so on. Section 16.6 discusses more about the algorithms that are available in class Collections. We also cover the *wrapper methods* of class Collections that enable you to treat a collection as a *synchronized collection* (Section 16.12) or an *unmodifiable collection* (Section 16.13). Unmodifiable collections are useful when a client of a class needs to view the elements of a collection, but should not be allowed to modify the collection by adding and removing elements. Synchronized collections are for use with a powerful capability called multithreading (discussed in Chapter 18). Multithreading enables programs to perform operations in parallel. When two or more threads of a program share a collection, there is the potential for problems to occur. As a brief analogy, consider a traffic intersection. We cannot allow all cars access to one intersection at the same time—if we did, accidents would occur. For this reason, traffic lights are provided at intersections to control access to the intersection. Similarly, we can synchronize access to a collection to ensure that only one thread manipulates the collection at a time. The synchronization wrapper methods of class Collections return synchronized versions of collections that can be shared among threads in a program.

16.5 Lists

A List (sometimes called a *sequence*) is an ordered Collection that can contain duplicate elements. Like array indices, List indices are zero based (i.e., the first element's index is zero). In addition to the methods inherited from Collection, List provides methods for manipulating elements via their indices, manipulating a specified range of elements, searching for elements and getting a *ListIterator* to access the elements.

Interface List is implemented by several classes, including classes **ArrayList**, **LinkedList** and **Vector**. Autoboxing occurs when you add primitive-type values to objects of these classes, because they store only references to objects. Class ArrayList and Vector are resizable-array implementations of List. Class LinkedList is a linked list implementation of interface List.

Class ArrayList's behavior and capabilities are similar to those of class Vector. The primary difference between Vector and ArrayList is that objects of class Vector are synchronized by default, whereas objects of class ArrayList are not. Also, class Vector is from Java 1.0, before the collections framework was added to Java. As such, Vector has several methods that are not part of interface List and are not implemented in class ArrayList, but perform identical tasks. For example, Vector methods addElement and add both append an element to a Vector, but only method add is specified in interface List and implemented by ArrayList. Unsynchronized collections provide better performance than synchronized ones. For this reason, ArrayList is typically preferred over Vector in programs that do not share a collection among threads.

Performance Tip 16.1

ArrayLists behave like Vectors without synchronization and therefore execute faster than Vectors because ArrayLists do not have the overhead of thread synchronization.

Software Engineering Observation 16.3

LinkedLists can be used to create stacks, queues, trees and deques (double-ended queues, pronounced "decks"). The collections framework provides implementations of some of these data structures.

The following three subsections demonstrate the List and Collection capabilities with several examples. Section 16.5.1 focuses on removing elements from an ArrayList with an Iterator. Section 16.5.2 focuses on ListIterator and several List- and LinkedList-specific methods. Section 16.5.3 introduces more List methods and several Vector-specific methods.

16.5.1 ArrayList and Iterator

Figure 16.3 uses an ArrayList to demonstrate several Collection interface capabilities. The program places two Color arrays in ArrayLists and uses an Iterator to remove elements in the second ArrayList collection from the first ArrayList collection.

Lines 10–13 declare and initialize two String array variables, which are declared final, so they always refer to these arrays. Recall that it is good programing practice to declare constants with keywords static and final. Lines 18–19 create ArrayList objects and assign their references to variables list and removeList, respectively. These two lists store String objects. Note that ArrayList is a generic class as of Java SE 5, so we are able to specify a type argument (String in this case) to indicate the type of the elements in each list. Both list and removeList are collections of Strings. Lines 22–23 populate list with Strings stored in array colors, and lines 26–27 populate removeList with Strings stored in array removeColors using List method **add**. Lines 32–33 output each element of list. Line 32 calls List method **size** to get the number of ArrayList elements. Line 33 uses List method **get** to retrieve individual element values. Lines 32–33 could have used the enhanced for statement. Line 36 calls method removeColors (lines 46–57), passing list and removeList as arguments. Method removeColors deletes Strings specified in removeList from the list collection. Lines 41–42 print list's elements after removeColors removes the String objects specified in removeList from the list.

```java
 1  // Fig. 16.3: CollectionTest.java
 2  // Using the Collection interface.
 3  import java.util.List;
 4  import java.util.ArrayList;
 5  import java.util.Collection;
 6  import java.util.Iterator;
 7
 8  public class CollectionTest
 9  {
10     private static final String[] colors =
11        { "MAGENTA", "RED", "WHITE", "BLUE", "CYAN" };
12     private static final String[] removeColors =
13        { "RED", "WHITE", "BLUE" };
14
15     // create ArrayList, add colors to it and manipulate it
16     public CollectionTest()
17     {
18        List< String > list = new ArrayList< String >();
19        List< String > removeList = new ArrayList< String >();
20
21        // add elements in colors array to list
22        for ( String color : colors )
23           list.add( color );
24
25        // add elements in removeColors to removeList
26        for ( String color : removeColors )
27           removeList.add( color );
28
29        System.out.println( "ArrayList: " );
30
31        // output list contents
32        for ( int count = 0; count < list.size(); count++ )
33           System.out.printf( "%s ", list.get( count ) );
34
35        // remove colors contained in removeList
36        removeColors( list, removeList );
37
38        System.out.println( "\n\nArrayList after calling removeColors: " );
39
```

Fig. 16.3 | Collection interface demonstrated via an ArrayList object. (Part 1 of 2.)

```
40          // output list contents
41          for ( String color : list )
42              System.out.printf( "%s ", color );
43      } // end CollectionTest constructor
44
45      // remove colors specified in collection2 from collection1
46      private void removeColors(
47          Collection< String > collection1, Collection< String > collection2 )
48      {
49          // get iterator
50          Iterator< String > iterator = collection1.iterator();
51
52          // loop while collection has items
53          while ( iterator.hasNext() )
54
55              if ( collection2.contains( iterator.next() ) )
56                  iterator.remove(); // remove current Color
57      } // end method removeColors
58
59      public static void main( String args[] )
60      {
61          new CollectionTest();
62      } // end main
63  } // end class CollectionTest
```

```
ArrayList:
MAGENTA RED WHITE BLUE CYAN

ArrayList after calling removeColors:
MAGENTA CYAN
```

Fig. 16.3 | Collection interface demonstrated via an ArrayList object. (Part 2 of 2.)

Method removeColors declares two Collection parameters (line 47) that allow any Collections containing strings to be passed as arguments to this method. The method accesses the elements of the first Collection (collection1) via an Iterator. Line 50 calls Collection method *iterator* to get an Iterator for the Collection. Note that interfaces Collection and Iterator are generic types. The loop-continuation condition (line 53) calls Iterator method *hasNext* to determine whether the Collection contains more elements. Method hasNext returns true if another element exists and false otherwise.

The if condition in line 55 calls Iterator method *next* to obtain a reference to the next element, then uses method *contains* of the second Collection (collection2) to determine whether collection2 contains the element returned by next. If so, line 56 calls Iterator method *remove* to remove the element from the Collection collection1.

Common Programming Error 16.2

If a collection is modified by one of its methods after an iterator is created for that collection, the iterator immediately becomes invalid—any operations performed with the iterator after this point throw ConcurrentModificationExceptions. For this reason, iterators are said to be "fail fast."

16.5.2 LinkedList

Figure 16.4 demonstrates operations on LinkedLists. The program creates two LinkedLists that contain Strings. The elements of one List are added to the other. Then all the Strings are converted to uppercase, and a range of elements is deleted.

```java
1    // Fig. 16.4: ListTest.java
2    // Using LinkLists.
3    import java.util.List;
4    import java.util.LinkedList;
5    import java.util.ListIterator;
6
7    public class ListTest
8    {
9       private static final String colors[] = { "black", "yellow",
10         "green", "blue", "violet", "silver" };
11      private static final String colors2[] = { "gold", "white",
12         "brown", "blue", "gray", "silver" };
13
14      // set up and manipulate LinkedList objects
15      public ListTest()
16      {
17         List< String > list1 = new LinkedList< String >();
18         List< String > list2 = new LinkedList< String >();
19
20         // add elements to list link
21         for ( String color : colors )
22            list1.add( color );
23
24         // add elements to list link2
25         for ( String color : colors2 )
26            list2.add( color );
27
28         list1.addAll( list2 ); // concatenate lists
29         list2 = null; // release resources
30         printList( list1 ); // print list1 elements
31
32         convertToUppercaseStrings( list1 ); // convert to uppercase string
33         printList( list1 ); // print list1 elements
34
35         System.out.print( "\nDeleting elements 4 to 6..." );
36         removeItems( list1, 4, 7 ); // remove items 4-7 from list
37         printList( list1 ); // print list1 elements
38         printReversedList( list1 ); // print list in reverse order
39      } // end ListTest constructor
40
41      // output List contents
42      public void printList( List< String > list )
43      {
44         System.out.println( "\nlist: " );
45
46         for ( String color : list )
47            System.out.printf( "%s ", color );
```

Fig. 16.4 | Lists and ListIterators. (Part 1 of 2.)

```
48
49          System.out.println();
50      } // end method printList
51
52      // locate String objects and convert to uppercase
53      private void convertToUppercaseStrings( List< String > list )
54      {
55          ListIterator< String > iterator = list.listIterator();
56
57          while ( iterator.hasNext() )
58          {
59              String color = iterator.next();  // get item
60              iterator.set( color.toUpperCase() ); // convert to uppercase
61          } // end while
62      } // end method convertToUppercaseStrings
63
64      // obtain sublist and use clear method to delete sublist items
65      private void removeItems( List< String > list, int start, int end )
66      {
67          list.subList( start, end ).clear();  // remove items
68      } // end method removeItems
69
70      // print reversed list
71      private void printReversedList( List< String > list )
72      {
73          ListIterator< String > iterator = list.listIterator( list.size() );
74
75          System.out.println( "\nReversed List:" );
76
77          // print list in reverse order
78          while ( iterator.hasPrevious() )
79              System.out.printf( "%s ", iterator.previous() );
80      } // end method printReversedList
81
82      public static void main( String args[] )
83      {
84          new ListTest();
85      } // end main
86  } // end class ListTest
```

```
list:
black yellow green blue violet silver gold white brown blue gray silver

list:
BLACK YELLOW GREEN BLUE VIOLET SILVER GOLD WHITE BROWN BLUE GRAY SILVER

Deleting elements 4 to 6...
list:
BLACK YELLOW GREEN BLUE WHITE BROWN BLUE GRAY SILVER

Reversed List:
SILVER GRAY BLUE BROWN WHITE BLUE GREEN YELLOW BLACK
```

Fig. 16.4 | Lists and ListIterators. (Part 2 of 2.)

Lines 17–18 create LinkedLists list1 and list2 of type String. Note that LinkedList is a generic class that has one type parameter for which we specify the type argument String in this example. Lines 21–26 call List method add to append elements from arrays colors and colors2 to the end of list1 and list2, respectively.

Line 28 calls List method **addAll** to append all elements of list2 to the end of list1. Line 29 sets list2 to null, so the LinkedList to which list2 referred can be garbage collected. Line 30 calls method printList (lines 42–50) to output list list1's contents. Line 32 calls method convertToUppercaseStrings (lines 53–62) to convert each String element to uppercase, then line 33 calls printList again to display the modified Strings. Line 36 calls method removeItems (lines 65–68) to remove the elements starting at index 4 up to, but not including, index 7 of the list. Line 38 calls method printReversedList (lines 71–80) to print the list in reverse order.

Method convertToUppercaseStrings (lines 53–62) changes lowercase String elements in its List argument to uppercase Strings. Line 55 calls List method **listIterator** to get a *bidirectional iterator* (i.e., an iterator that can traverse a List backward or forward) for the List. Note that ListIterator is a generic class. In this example, the ListIterator contains String objects, because method listIterator is called on a List of Strings. The while condition (line 57) calls method hasNext to determine whether the List contains another element. Line 59 gets the next String in the List. Line 60 calls String method **toUpperCase** to get an uppercase version of the String and calls List-Iterator method **set** to replace the current String to which iterator refers with the String returned by method toUpperCase. Like method toUpperCase, String method **toLowerCase** returns a lowercase version of the String.

Method removeItems (lines 65–68) removes a range of items from the list. Line 67 calls List method **subList** to obtain a portion of the List (called a *sublist*). The sublist is simply another view into the List on which subList is called. Method subList takes two arguments—the beginning and the ending index for the sublist. The ending index is not part of the range of the sublist. In this example, we pass (in line 36) 4 for the beginning index and 7 for the ending index to subList. The sublist returned is the set of elements with indices 4 through 6. Next, the program calls List method **clear** on the sublist to remove the elements of the sublist from the List. Any changes made to a sublist are also made to the original List.

Method printReversedList (lines 71–80) prints the list backward. Line 73 calls List method listIterator with the starting position as an argument (in our case, the last element in the list) to get a bidirectional iterator for the list. List method **size** returns the number of items in the List. The while condition (line 78) calls method **hasPrevious** to determine whether there are more elements while traversing the list backward. Line 79 gets the previous element from the list and outputs it to the standard output stream.

An important feature of the collections framework is the ability to manipulate the elements of one collection type (such as a set) through a different collection type (such as a list), regardless of the collection's internal implementation. The set of public methods through which collections are manipulated is called a *view*.

Class Arrays provides static method **asList** to view an array as a *List* collection (which encapsulates behavior similar to that of linked lists). A List view allows the programmer to manipulate the array as if it were a list. This is useful for adding the elements in an array to a collection (e.g., a LinkedList) and for sorting array elements. The next example demonstrates how to create a LinkedList with a List view of an array, because we cannot pass the array to a LinkedList constructor. Sorting array elements with a List view is demonstrated in Fig. 16.9. Any modifications made through the List view change the array, and any modifications made to the array change the List view. The only operation permitted on the view returned by asList is *set*, which changes the value of the view and the backing array. Any other attempts to change the view (such as adding or removing elements) result in an ***UnsupportedOperationException***.

Figure 16.5 uses method asList to view an array as a List collection and uses method ***toArray*** of a List to get an array from a LinkedList collection. The program calls method asList to create a List view of an array, which is then used for creating a LinkedList object, adds a series of strings to a LinkedList and calls method toArray to obtain an array containing references to the strings. Notice that the instantiation of LinkedList (line 13) indicates that LinkedList is a generic class that accepts one type argument—String, in this example.

```java
1   // Fig. 16.5: UsingToArray.java
2   // Using method toArray.
3   import java.util.LinkedList;
4   import java.util.Arrays;
5
6   public class UsingToArray
7   {
8      // constructor creates LinkedList, adds elements and converts to array
9      public UsingToArray()
10     {
11        String colors[] = { "black", "blue", "yellow" };
12
13        LinkedList< String > links =
14           new LinkedList< String >( Arrays.asList( colors ) );
15
16        links.addLast( "red" );      // add as last item
17        links.add( "pink" );         // add to the end
18        links.add( 3, "green" );     // add at 3rd index
19        links.addFirst( "cyan" );    // add as first item
20
21        // get LinkedList elements as an array
22        colors = links.toArray( new String[ links.size() ] );
23
24        System.out.println( "colors: " );
25
26        for ( String color : colors )
27           System.out.println( color );
28     } // end UsingToArray constructor
29
30     public static void main( String args[] )
31     {
32        new UsingToArray();
33     } // end main
34  } // end class UsingToArray
```

Fig. 16.5 | List method toArray. (Part 1 of 2.)

```
colors:
cyan
black
blue
yellow
green
red
pink
```

Fig. 16.5 | List method toArray. (Part 2 of 2.)

Lines 13–14 construct a LinkedList of Strings containing the elements of array colors and assigns the LinkedList reference to links. Note the use of Arrays method asList to return a view of the array as a List, then initialize the LinkedList with the List. Line 16 calls LinkedList method **addLast** to add "red" to the end of links. Lines 17–18 call LinkedList method **add** to add "pink" as the last element and "green" as the element at index 3 (i.e., the fourth element). Note that method addLast (line 16) is identical in function to method add (line 17). Line 19 calls LinkedList method **addFirst** to add "cyan" as the new first item in the LinkedList. The add operations are permitted because they operate on the LinkedList object, not the view returned by asList. [*Note:* When "cyan" is added as the first element, "green" becomes the fifth element in the LinkedList.]

Line 22 calls List method toArray to get a String array from links. The array is a copy of the list's elements—modifying the array's contents does not modify the list. The array passed to method toArray is of the same type that you would like method toArray to return. If the number of elements in the array is greater than or equal to the number of elements in the LinkedList, toArray copies the list's elements into its array argument and returns that array. If the LinkedList has more elements than the number of elements in the array passed to toArray, toArray allocates a new array of the same type it receives as an argument, copies the list's elements into the new array and returns the new array.

Common Programming Error 16.3

Passing an array that contains data to toArray can cause logic errors. If the number of elements in the array is smaller than the number of elements in the list on which toArray is called, a new array is allocated to store the list's elements—without preserving the array argument's elements. If the number of elements in the array is greater than the number of elements in the list, the elements of the array (starting at index zero) are overwritten with the list's elements. Array elements that are not overwritten retain their values.

16.5.3 Vector

Like ArrayList, class Vector provides the capabilities of array-like data structures that can resize themselves dynamically. Recall that class ArrayList's behavior and capabilities are similar to those of class Vector, except that ArrayLists do not provide synchronization by default. We cover class Vector here primarily because it is the superclass of class Stack, which is presented in Section 16.7.

At any time, a Vector contains a number of elements that is less than or equal to its *capacity*. The capacity is the space that has been reserved for the Vector's elements. If a

Vector requires additional capacity, it grows by a ***capacity increment*** that you specify or by a default capacity increment. If you do not specify a capacity increment or specify one that is less than or equal to zero, the system will double the size of a Vector each time additional capacity is needed.

Performance Tip 16.2
Inserting an element into a Vector whose current size is less than its capacity is a relatively fast operation.

Performance Tip 16.3
Inserting an element into a Vector that needs to grow larger to accommodate the new element is a relatively slow operation.

Performance Tip 16.4
The default capacity increment doubles the size of the Vector. This may seem a waste of storage, but it is actually an efficient way for many Vectors to grow quickly to be "about the right size." This operation is much more efficient than growing the Vector each time by only as much space as it takes to hold a single element. The disadvantage is that the Vector might occupy more space than it requires. This is a classic example of the space–time trade-off.

Performance Tip 16.5
If storage is at a premium, use Vector method trimToSize to trim a Vector's capacity to the Vector's exact size. This operation optimizes a Vector's use of storage. However, adding another element to the Vector will force the Vector to grow dynamically (again, a relatively slow operation)—trimming leaves no room for growth.

Figure 16.6 demonstrates class Vector and several of its methods. For complete information on class Vector, visit java.sun.com/javase/6/docs/api/java/util/Vector.html.

```java
 1  // Fig. 16.6: VectorTest.java
 2  // Using the Vector class.
 3  import java.util.Vector;
 4  import java.util.NoSuchElementException;
 5
 6  public class VectorTest
 7  {
 8     private static final String colors[] = { "red", "white", "blue" };
 9
10     public VectorTest()
11     {
12        Vector< String > vector = new Vector< String >();
13        printVector( vector ); // print vector
14
15        // add elements to the vector
16        for ( String color : colors )
17           vector.add( color );
18
```

Fig. 16.6 | Vector class of package java.util. (Part 1 of 3.)

```java
19          printVector( vector ); // print vector
20
21          // output the first and last elements
22          try
23          {
24             System.out.printf( "First element: %s\n", vector.firstElement());
25             System.out.printf( "Last element: %s\n", vector.lastElement() );
26          } // end try
27          // catch exception if vector is empty
28          catch ( NoSuchElementException exception )
29          {
30             exception.printStackTrace();
31          } // end catch
32
33          // does vector contain "red"?
34          if ( vector.contains( "red" ) )
35             System.out.printf( "\n\"red\" found at index %d\n\n",
36                vector.indexOf( "red" ) );
37          else
38             System.out.println( "\n\"red\" not found\n" );
39
40          vector.remove( "red" ); // remove the string "red"
41          System.out.println( "\"red\" has been removed" );
42          printVector( vector ); // print vector
43
44          // does vector contain "red" after remove operation?
45          if ( vector.contains( "red" ) )
46             System.out.printf(
47                "\"red\" found at index %d\n", vector.indexOf( "red" ) );
48          else
49             System.out.println( "\"red\" not found" );
50
51          // print the size and capacity of vector
52          System.out.printf( "\nSize: %d\nCapacity: %d\n", vector.size(),
53             vector.capacity() );
54       } // end Vector constructor
55
56       private void printVector( Vector< String > vectorToOutput )
57       {
58          if ( vectorToOutput.isEmpty() )
59             System.out.print( "vector is empty" ); // vectorToOutput is empty
60          else // iterate through the elements
61          {
62             System.out.print( "vector contains: " );
63
64             // output elements
65             for ( String element : vectorToOutput )
66                System.out.printf( "%s ", element );
67          } // end else
68
69          System.out.println( "\n" );
70       } // end method printVector
```

Fig. 16.6 | Vector class of package `java.util`. (Part 2 of 3.)

```
71
72      public static void main( String args[] )
73      {
74         new VectorTest(); // create object and call its constructor
75      } // end main
76   } // end class VectorTest
```

```
vector is empty

vector contains: red white blue

First element: red
Last element: blue

"red" found at index 0

"red" has been removed
vector contains: white blue

"red" not found

Size: 2
Capacity: 10
```

Fig. 16.6 | Vector class of package `java.util`. (Part 3 of 3.)

The application's constructor creates a Vector (line 13) of type String with an initial capacity of 10 elements and capacity increment of zero (the defaults for a Vector). Note that Vector is a generic class, which takes one argument that specifies the type of the elements stored in the Vector. A capacity increment of zero indicates that this Vector will double in size each time it needs to grow to accommodate more elements. Class Vector provides three other constructors. The constructor that takes one integer argument creates an empty Vector with the *initial capacity* specified by that argument. The constructor that takes two arguments creates a Vector with the initial capacity specified by the first argument and the *capacity increment* specified by the second argument. Each time the Vector needs to grow, it will add space for the specified number of elements in the capacity increment. The constructor that takes a Collection creates a copy of a collection's elements and stores them in the Vector.

Line 18 calls Vector method *add* to add objects (Strings in this program) to the end of the Vector. If necessary, the Vector increases its capacity to accommodate the new element. Class Vector also provides a method add that takes two arguments. This method takes an object and an integer and inserts the object at the specified index in the Vector. Method *set* will replace the element at a specified position in the Vector with a specified element. Method *insertElementAt* provides the same functionality as the method add that takes two arguments, except that the order of the parameters is reversed.

Line 25 calls Vector method *firstElement* to return a reference to the first element in the Vector. Line 26 calls Vector method *lastElement* to return a reference to the last element in the Vector. Each of these methods throws a NoSuchElementException if there are no elements in the Vector when the method is called.

Line 35 calls Vector method *contains* to determine whether the Vector contains "red". The method returns true if its argument is in the Vector—otherwise, the method returns false. Method contains uses Object method equals to determine whether the search key is equal to one of the Vector's elements. Many classes override method equals to perform the comparisons in a manner specific to those classes. For example, class String declares equals to compare the individual characters in the two Strings being compared. If method equals is not overridden, the original version of method equals inherited from class Object is used.

Common Programming Error 16.4

Without overriding method equals, *the program performs comparisons using operator* == *to determine whether two references refer to the same object in memory.*

Line 37 calls Vector method **indexOf** to determine the index of the first location in the Vector that contains the argument. The method returns –1 if the argument is not found in the Vector. An overloaded version of this method takes a second argument specifying the index in the Vector at which the search should begin.

Performance Tip 16.6

Vector *methods* contains *and* indexOf *perform linear searches of a* Vector's *contents. These searches are inefficient for large* Vectors. *If a program frequently searches for elements in a collection, consider using one of the Java Collection API's* Map *implementations (Section 16.10), which provide high-speed searching capabilities.*

Line 41 calls Vector method **remove** to remove the first occurrence of its argument from the Vector. The method returns true if it finds the element in the Vector; otherwise, the method returns false. If the element is removed, all elements after that element in the Vector shift one position toward the beginning of the Vector to fill in the position of the removed element. Class Vector also provides method **removeAllElements** to remove every element from a Vector and method **removeElementAt** to remove the element at a specified index.

Lines 53–54 use Vector methods **size** and **capacity** to determine the number of elements currently in the Vector and the number of elements that can be stored in the Vector without allocating more memory, respectively.

Line 59 calls Vector method **isEmpty** to determine whether the Vector is empty. The method returns true if there are no elements in the Vector; otherwise, the method returns false. Lines 66–67 use the enhanced for statement to print out all elements in the vector.

Among the methods introduced in Fig. 16.6, firstElement, lastElement and capacity can be used only with Vector. Other methods (e.g., add, contains, indexOf, remove, size and isEmpty) are declared by List, which means that they can be used by any class that implements List, such as Vector.

16.6 Collections Algorithms

The collections framework provides several high-performance algorithms for manipulating collection elements that are implemented as static methods of class Collections (Fig. 16.7). Algorithms sort, binarySearch, reverse, shuffle, fill and copy operate on Lists. Algorithms min, max, addAll, frequency and disjoint operate on Collections.

Software Engineering Observation 16.4

The collections framework algorithms are polymorphic. That is, each algorithm can operate on objects that implement specific interfaces, regardless of the underlying implementations.

Algorithm	Description
sort	Sorts the elements of a List.
binarySearch	Locates an object in a List.
reverse	Reverses the elements of a List.
shuffle	Randomly orders a List's elements.
fill	Sets every List element to refer to a specified object.
copy	Copies references from one List into another.
min	Returns the smallest element in a Collection.
max	Returns the largest element in a Collection.
addAll	Appends all elements in an array to a collection.
frequency	Calculates how many elements in the collection are equal to the specified element.
disjoint	Determines whether two collections have no elements in common.

Fig. 16.7 | Collections algorithms.

16.6.1 Algorithm sort

Algorithm **sort** sorts the elements of a List, which must implement the **Comparable** interface. The order is determined by the natural order of the elements' type as implemented by a compareTo method. Method compareTo is declared in interface Comparable and is sometimes called the *natural comparison method*. The sort call may specify as a second argument a **Comparator** object that determines an alternative ordering of the elements.

Sorting in Ascending Order

Figure 16.8 uses algorithm sort to order the elements of a List in ascending order (line 20). Recall that List is a generic type and accepts one type argument that specifies the list element type—line 15 declares list as a List of String. Note that lines 18 and 23 each use an implicit call to the list's toString method to output the list contents in the format shown on the second and fourth lines of the output.

```java
1  // Fig. 16.8: Sort1.java
2  // Using algorithm sort.
3  import java.util.List;
4  import java.util.Arrays;
5  import java.util.Collections;
6
7  public class Sort1
8  {
9     private static final String suits[] =
10        { "Hearts", "Diamonds", "Clubs", "Spades" };
```

Fig. 16.8 | Collections method sort. (Part 1 of 2.)

```
11
12       // display array elements
13       public void printElements()
14       {
15          List< String > list = Arrays.asList( suits ); // create List
16
17          // output list
18          System.out.printf( "Unsorted array elements:\n%s\n", list );
19
20          Collections.sort( list ); // sort ArrayList
21
22          // output list
23          System.out.printf( "Sorted array elements:\n%s\n", list );
24       } // end method printElements
25
26       public static void main( String args[] )
27       {
28          Sort1 sort1 = new Sort1();
29          sort1.printElements();
30       } // end main
31    } // end class Sort1
```

```
Unsorted array elements:
[Hearts, Diamonds, Clubs, Spades]
Sorted array elements:
[Clubs, Diamonds, Hearts, Spades]
```

Fig. 16.8 | Collections method sort. (Part 2 of 2.)

Sorting in Descending Order

Figure 16.9 sorts the same list of strings used in Fig. 16.8 in descending order. The example introduces the Comparator interface, which is used for sorting a Collection's elements in a different order. Line 21 calls Collections's method sort to order the List in descending order. The static Collections method **reverseOrder** returns a Comparator object that orders the collection's elements in reverse order.

```
1    // Fig. 16.9: Sort2.java
2    // Using a Comparator object with algorithm sort.
3    import java.util.List;
4    import java.util.Arrays;
5    import java.util.Collections;
6
7    public class Sort2
8    {
9       private static final String suits[] =
10         { "Hearts", "Diamonds", "Clubs", "Spades" };
11
12      // output List elements
13      public void printElements()
14      {
```

Fig. 16.9 | Collections method sort with a Comparator object. (Part 1 of 2.)

```
15          List< String > list = Arrays.asList( suits ); // create List
16
17          // output List elements
18          System.out.printf( "Unsorted array elements:\n%s\n", list );
19
20          // sort in descending order using a comparator
21          Collections.sort( list, Collections.reverseOrder() );
22
23          // output List elements
24          System.out.printf( "Sorted list elements:\n%s\n", list );
25       } // end method printElements
26
27       public static void main( String args[] )
28       {
29          Sort2 sort2 = new Sort2();
30          sort2.printElements();
31       } // end main
32    } // end class Sort2
```

```
Unsorted array elements:
[Hearts, Diamonds, Clubs, Spades]
Sorted list elements:
[Spades, Hearts, Diamonds, Clubs]
```

Fig. 16.9 | Collections method sort with a Comparator object. (Part 2 of 2.)

Sorting with a Comparator

Figure 16.10 creates a custom Comparator class, named TimeComparator, that implements interface Comparator to compare two Time2 objects. Class Time2, declared in Fig. 8.5, represents times with hours, minutes and seconds.

Class TimeComparator implements interface Comparator, a generic type that takes one argument (in this case Time2). Method compare (lines 7–26) performs comparisons between Time2 objects. Line 9 compares the two hours of the Time2 objects. If the hours are different (line 12), then we return this value. If this value is positive, then the first hour is greater than the second and the first time is greater than the second. If this value is negative, then the first hour is less than the second and the first time is less than the second. If this value is zero, the hours are the same and we must test the minutes (and maybe the seconds) to determine which time is greater.

```
1  // Fig. 16.10: TimeComparator.java
2  // Custom Comparator class that compares two Time2 objects.
3  import java.util.Comparator;
4
5  public class TimeComparator implements Comparator< Time2 >
6  {
7     public int compare( Time2 time1, Time2 time2 )
8     {
9        int hourCompare = time1.getHour() - time2.getHour(); // compare hour
```

Fig. 16.10 | Custom Comparator class that compares two Time2 objects.

```
10
11          // test the hour first
12          if ( hourCompare != 0 )
13             return hourCompare;
14
15          int minuteCompare =
16             time1.getMinute() - time2.getMinute(); // compare minute
17
18          // then test the minute
19          if ( minuteCompare != 0 )
20             return minuteCompare;
21
22          int secondCompare =
23             time1.getSecond() - time2.getSecond(); // compare second
24
25          return secondCompare; // return result of comparing seconds
26       } // end method compare
27    } // end class TimeComparator
```

Fig. 16.10 | Custom `Comparator` class that compares two `Time2` objects.

Figure 16.11 sorts a list using the custom Comparator class TimeComparator. Line 11 creates an ArrayList of Time2 objects. Recall that both ArrayList and List are generic types and accept a type argument that specifies the element type of the collection. Lines 13–17 create five Time2 objects and add them to this list. Line 23 calls method sort, passing it an object of our TimeComparator class (Fig. 16.10).

```
1    // Fig. 16.11: Sort3.java
2    // Sort a list using the custom Comparator class TimeComparator.
3    import java.util.List;
4    import java.util.ArrayList;
5    import java.util.Collections;
6
7    public class Sort3
8    {
9       public void printElements()
10      {
11         List< Time2 > list = new ArrayList< Time2 >(); // create List
12
13         list.add( new Time2(  6, 24, 34 ) );
14         list.add( new Time2( 18, 14, 58 ) );
15         list.add( new Time2(  6, 05, 34 ) );
16         list.add( new Time2( 12, 14, 58 ) );
17         list.add( new Time2(  6, 24, 22 ) );
18
19         // output List elements
20         System.out.printf( "Unsorted array elements:\n%s\n", list );
21
22         // sort in order using a comparator
23         Collections.sort( list, new TimeComparator() );
```

Fig. 16.11 | `Collections` method `sort` with a custom `Comparator` object. (Part 1 of 2.)

```
24
25        // output List elements
26        System.out.printf( "Sorted list elements:\n%s\n", list );
27     } // end method printElements
28
29     public static void main( String args[] )
30     {
31        Sort3 sort3 = new Sort3();
32        sort3.printElements();
33     } // end main
34  } // end class Sort3
```

```
Unsorted array elements:
[6:24:34 AM, 6:14:58 PM, 6:05:34 AM, 12:14:58 PM, 6:24:22 AM]
Sorted list elements:
[6:05:34 AM, 6:24:22 AM, 6:24:34 AM, 12:14:58 PM, 6:14:58 PM]
```

Fig. 16.11 | Collections method sort with a custom Comparator object. (Part 2 of 2.)

16.6.2 Algorithm shuffle

Algorithm *shuffle* randomly orders a List's elements. In Chapter 7, we presented a card shuffling and dealing simulation that used a loop to shuffle a deck of cards. In Fig. 16.12, we use algorithm shuffle to shuffle a deck of Card objects that might be used in a card game simulator.

Class Card (lines 8–41) represents a card in a deck of cards. Each Card has a face and a suit. Lines 10–12 declare two enum types—Face and Suit—which represent the face and the suit of the card, respectively. Method toString (lines 37–40) returns a String containing the face and suit of the Card separated by the string " of ". When an enum constant is converted to a string, the constant's identifier is used as the string representation. Normally we would use all uppercase letters for enum constants. In this example, we chose to use capital letters for only the first letter of each enum constant because we want the card to be displayed with initial capital letters for the face and the suit (e.g., "Ace of Spades").

```
1   // Fig. 16.12: DeckOfCards.java
2   // Using algorithm shuffle.
3   import java.util.List;
4   import java.util.Arrays;
5   import java.util.Collections;
6
7   // class to represent a Card in a deck of cards
8   class Card
9   {
10     public static enum Face { Ace, Deuce, Three, Four, Five, Six,
11        Seven, Eight, Nine, Ten, Jack, Queen, King };
12     public static enum Suit { Clubs, Diamonds, Hearts, Spades };
13
14     private final Face face; // face of card
15     private final Suit suit; // suit of card
```

Fig. 16.12 | Card shuffling and dealing with Collections method shuffle. (Part 1 of 3.)

```
16
17      // two-argument constructor
18      public Card( Face cardFace, Suit cardSuit )
19      {
20          face = cardFace; // initialize face of card
21          suit = cardSuit; // initialize suit of card
22      } // end two-argument Card constructor
23
24      // return face of the card
25      public Face getFace()
26      {
27          return face;
28      } // end method getFace
29
30      // return suit of Card
31      public Suit getSuit()
32      {
33          return suit;
34      } // end method getSuit
35
36      // return String representation of Card
37      public String toString()
38      {
39          return String.format( "%s of %s", face, suit );
40      } // end method toString
41  } // end class Card
42
43  // class DeckOfCards declaration
44  public class DeckOfCards
45  {
46      private List< Card > list; // declare List that will store Cards
47
48      // set up deck of Cards and shuffle
49      public DeckOfCards()
50      {
51          Card[] deck = new Card[ 52 ];
52          int count = 0; // number of cards
53
54          // populate deck with Card objects
55          for ( Card.Suit suit : Card.Suit.values() )
56          {
57              for ( Card.Face face : Card.Face.values() )
58              {
59                  deck[ count ] = new Card( face, suit );
60                  count++;
61              } // end for
62          } // end for
63
64          list = Arrays.asList( deck ); // get List
65          Collections.shuffle( list );  // shuffle deck
66      } // end DeckOfCards constructor
67
```

Fig. 16.12 | Card shuffling and dealing with Collections method shuffle. (Part 2 of 3.)

```
68        // output deck
69        public void printCards()
70        {
71           // display 52 cards in two columns
72           for ( int i = 0; i < list.size(); i++ )
73              System.out.printf( "%-20s%s", list.get( i ),
74                 ( ( i + 1 ) % 2 == 0 ) ? "\n" : "\t" );
75        } // end method printCards
76
77        public static void main( String args[] )
78        {
79           DeckOfCards cards = new DeckOfCards();
80           cards.printCards();
81        } // end main
82     } // end class DeckOfCards
```

```
King of Diamonds      Jack of Spades
Four of Diamonds      Six of Clubs
King of Hearts        Nine of Diamonds
Three of Spades       Four of Spades
Four of Hearts        Seven of Spades
Five of Diamonds      Eight of Hearts
Queen of Diamonds     Five of Hearts
Seven of Diamonds     Seven of Hearts
Nine of Hearts        Three of Clubs
Ten of Spades         Deuce of Hearts
Three of Hearts       Ace of Spades
Six of Hearts         Eight of Diamonds
Six of Diamonds       Deuce of Clubs
Ace of Clubs          Ten of Diamonds
Eight of Clubs        Queen of Hearts
Jack of Clubs         Ten of Clubs
Seven of Clubs        Queen of Spades
Five of Clubs         Six of Spades
Nine of Spades        Nine of Clubs
King of Spades        Ace of Diamonds
Ten of Hearts         Ace of Hearts
Queen of Clubs        Deuce of Spades
Three of Diamonds     King of Clubs
Four of Clubs         Jack of Diamonds
Eight of Spades       Five of Spades
Jack of Hearts        Deuce of Diamonds
```

Fig. 16.12 | Card shuffling and dealing with `Collections` method `shuffle`. (Part 3 of 3.)

Lines 55–62 populate the deck array with cards that have unique face and suit combinations. Both Face and Suit are public static enum types of class Card. To use these enum types outside of class Card, you must qualify each enum's type name with the name of the class in which it resides (i.e., Card) and a dot (.) separator. Hence, lines 55 and 57 use Card.Suit and Card.Face to declare the control variables of the for statements. Recall that method values of an enum type returns an array that contains all the constants of the enum type. Lines 55–62 use enhanced for statements to construct 52 new Cards.

The shuffling occurs in line 65, which calls static method shuffle of class Collections to shuffle the elements of the array. Method shuffle requires a List argument, so we must obtain a List view of the array before we can shuffle it. Line 64 invokes static method asList of class Arrays to get a List view of the deck array.

Method printCards (lines 69–75) displays the deck of cards in two columns. In each iteration of the loop, lines 73–74 output a card left justified in a 20-character field followed by either a newline or an empty string based on the number of cards output so far. If the number of cards is even, a newline is output; otherwise, a tab is output.

16.6.3 Algorithms reverse, fill, copy, max and min

Class Collections provides algorithms for reversing, filling and copying Lists. Algorithm *reverse* reverses the order of the elements in a List, and algorithm *fill* overwrites elements in a List with a specified value. The fill operation is useful for reinitializing a List. Algorithm *copy* takes two arguments—a destination List and a source List. Each source List element is copied to the destination List. The destination List must be at least as long as the source List; otherwise, an IndexOutOfBoundsException occurs. If the destination List is longer, the elements not overwritten are unchanged.

Each algorithm we've seen so far operates on Lists. Algorithms *min* and *max* operate on any Collection—min returns the smallest element in a Collection, and algorithm max returns the largest element in a Collection. Both algorithms can be called with a Comparator object as a second argument to perform custom comparisons of objects, such as the TimeComparator in Fig. 16.11. Figure 16.13 demonstrates the use of algorithms reverse, fill, copy, min and max. Note that the generic type List is declared to store Characters.

```java
 1   // Fig. 16.13: Algorithms1.java
 2   // Using algorithms reverse, fill, copy, min and max.
 3   import java.util.List;
 4   import java.util.Arrays;
 5   import java.util.Collections;
 6
 7   public class Algorithms1
 8   {
 9      private Character[] letters = { 'P', 'C', 'M' };
10      private Character[] lettersCopy;
11      private List< Character > list;
12      private List< Character > copyList;
13
14      // create a List and manipulate it with methods from Collections
15      public Algorithms1()
16      {
17         list = Arrays.asList( letters ); // get List
18         lettersCopy = new Character[ 3 ];
19         copyList = Arrays.asList( lettersCopy ); // list view of lettersCopy
20
21         System.out.println( "Initial list: " );
22         output( list );
23
24         Collections.reverse( list ); // reverse order
25         System.out.println( "\nAfter calling reverse: " );
26         output( list );
```

Fig. 16.13 | Collections methods reverse, fill, copy, max and min. (Part 1 of 2.)

```
27
28          Collections.copy( copyList, list ); // copy List
29          System.out.println( "\nAfter copying: " );
30          output( copyList );
31
32          Collections.fill( list, 'R' ); // fill list with Rs
33          System.out.println( "\nAfter calling fill: " );
34          output( list );
35      } // end Algorithms1 constructor
36
37      // output List information
38      private void output( List< Character > listRef )
39      {
40          System.out.print( "The list is: " );
41
42          for ( Character element : listRef )
43              System.out.printf( "%s ", element );
44
45          System.out.printf( "\nMax: %s", Collections.max( listRef ) );
46          System.out.printf( "  Min: %s\n", Collections.min( listRef ) );
47      } // end method output
48
49      public static void main( String args[] )
50      {
51          new Algorithms1();
52      } // end main
53  } // end class Algorithms1
```

```
Initial list:
The list is: P C M
Max: P  Min: C

After calling reverse:
The list is: M C P
Max: P  Min: C

After copying:
The list is: M C P
Max: P  Min: C

After calling fill:
The list is: R R R
Max: R  Min: R
```

Fig. 16.13 | Collections methods reverse, fill, copy, max and min. (Part 2 of 2.)

Line 24 calls Collections method reverse to reverse the order of list. Method reverse takes one List argument. In this case, list is a List view of array letters. Array letters now has its elements in reverse order. Line 28 copies the elements of list into copyList, using Collections method copy. Changes to copyList do not change letters, because copyList is a separate List that is not a List view for letters. Method copy requires two List arguments. Line 32 calls Collections method fill to place the string "R" in each element of list. Because list is a List view of letters, this operation changes each element in letters to "R". Method fill requires a List for the first argument and an Object for the second argument. Lines 45–46 call Collections methods max and min to find the largest and the smallest element of the collection, respectively. Recall that a List is a Collection, so lines 45–46 can pass a List to methods max and min.

16.6.4 Algorithm binarySearch

The high-speed binary search algorithm is built into the Java collections framework as a static method of class Collections. The **binarySearch** algorithm locates an object in a List (i.e., a LinkedList, a Vector or an ArrayList). If the object is found, its index is returned. If the object is not found, binarySearch returns a negative value. Algorithm binarySearch determines this negative value by first calculating the insertion point and making its sign negative. Then, binarySearch subtracts 1 from the insertion point to obtain the return value, which guarantees that method binarySearch returns positive numbers (>= 0) if and only if the object is found. If multiple elements in the list match the search key, there is no guarantee which one will be located first. Figure 16.14 uses the binarySearch algorithm to search for a series of strings in an ArrayList.

```java
1   // Fig. 16.14: BinarySearchTest.java
2   // Using algorithm binarySearch.
3   import java.util.List;
4   import java.util.Arrays;
5   import java.util.Collections;
6   import java.util.ArrayList;
7
8   public class BinarySearchTest
9   {
10      private static final String colors[] = { "red", "white",
11         "blue", "black", "yellow", "purple", "tan", "pink" };
12      private List< String > list; // ArrayList reference
13
14      // create, sort and output list
15      public BinarySearchTest()
16      {
17         list = new ArrayList< String >( Arrays.asList( colors ) );
18         Collections.sort( list ); // sort the ArrayList
19         System.out.printf( "Sorted ArrayList: %s\n", list );
20      } // end BinarySearchTest constructor
21
22      // search list for various values
23      private void search()
24      {
25         printSearchResults( colors[ 3 ] ); // first item
26         printSearchResults( colors[ 0 ] ); // middle item
27         printSearchResults( colors[ 7 ] ); // last item
28         printSearchResults( "aqua" ); // below lowest
29         printSearchResults( "gray" ); // does not exist
30         printSearchResults( "teal" ); // does not exist
31      } // end method search
32
```

Fig. 16.14 | Collections method binarySearch. (Part 1 of 2.)

```
33          // perform searches and display search result
34          private void printSearchResults( String key )
35          {
36             int result = 0;
37
38             System.out.printf( "\nSearching for: %s\n", key );
39             result = Collections.binarySearch( list, key );
40
41             if ( result >= 0 )
42                System.out.printf( "Found at index %d\n", result );
43             else
44                System.out.printf( "Not Found (%d)\n",result );
45          } // end method printSearchResults
46
47          public static void main( String args[] )
48          {
49             BinarySearchTest binarySearchTest = new BinarySearchTest();
50             binarySearchTest.search();
51          } // end main
52       } // end class BinarySearchTest
```

```
Sorted ArrayList: [black, blue, pink, purple, red, tan, white, yellow]

Searching for: black
Found at index 0

Searching for: red
Found at index 4

Searching for: pink
Found at index 2

Searching for: aqua
Not Found (-1)

Searching for: gray
Not Found (-3)

Searching for: teal
Not Found (-7)
```

Fig. 16.14 | Collections method binarySearch. (Part 2 of 2.)

Recall that both List and ArrayList are generic types (lines 12 and 17). Collections method binarySearch expects the list's elements to be sorted in ascending order, so line 18 in the constructor sorts the list with Collections method sort. If the list's elements are not sorted, the result is undefined. Line 19 outputs the sorted list. Method search (lines 23–31) is called from main to perform the searches. Each search calls method print-SearchResults (lines 34–45) to perform the search and output the results. Line 39 calls Collections method binarySearch to search list for the specified key. Method binarySearch takes a List as the first argument and an Object as the second argument. Lines 41–44 output the results of the search. An overloaded version of binarySearch takes a Comparator object as its third argument, which specifies how binarySearch should compare elements.

16.6.5 Algorithms addAll, frequency and disjoint

Class Collections also provides the algorithms ***addAll***, ***frequency*** and ***disjoint***. Algorithm addAll takes two arguments—a Collection into which to insert the new element(s) and an array that provides elements to be inserted. Algorithm frequency takes two arguments—a Collection to be searched and an Object to be searched for in the collection. Method frequency returns the number of times that the second argument appears in the collection. Algorithm disjoint takes two Collections and returns true if they have no elements in common. Figure 16.15 demonstrates the use of algorithms addAll, frequency and disjoint.

Line 19 initializes list with elements in array colors, and lines 20–22 add Strings "black", "red" and "green" to vector. Line 31 invokes method addAll to add elements in array colors to vector. Line 40 gets the frequency of String "red" in Collection vector using method frequency. Note that lines 41–42 use the new printf method to print the frequency. Line 45 invokes method disjoint to test whether Collections list and vector have elements in common.

```java
1   // Fig. 16.15: Algorithms2.java
2   // Using algorithms addAll, frequency and disjoint.
3   import java.util.List;
4   import java.util.Vector;
5   import java.util.Arrays;
6   import java.util.Collections;
7
8   public class Algorithms2
9   {
10      private String[] colors = { "red", "white", "yellow", "blue" };
11      private List< String > list;
12      private Vector< String > vector = new Vector< String >();
13
14      // create List and Vector
15      // and manipulate them with methods from Collections
16      public Algorithms2()
17      {
18         // initialize list and vector
19         list = Arrays.asList( colors );
20         vector.add( "black" );
21         vector.add( "red" );
22         vector.add( "green" );
23
24         System.out.println( "Before addAll, vector contains: " );
25
26         // display elements in vector
27         for ( String s : vector )
28            System.out.printf( "%s ", s );
29
30         // add elements in colors to list
31         Collections.addAll( vector, colors );
32
33         System.out.println( "\n\nAfter addAll, vector contains: " );
```

Fig. 16.15 | Collections method addAll, frequency and disjoint. (Part 1 of 2.)

```
34
35          // display elements in vector
36          for ( String s : vector )
37             System.out.printf( "%s ", s );
38
39          // get frequency of "red"
40          int frequency = Collections.frequency( vector, "red" );
41          System.out.printf(
42             "\n\nFrequency of red in vector: %d\n", frequency );
43
44          // check whether list and vector have elements in common
45          boolean disjoint = Collections.disjoint( list, vector );
46
47          System.out.printf( "\nlist and vector %s elements in common\n",
48             ( disjoint ? "do not have" : "have"  ) );
49       } // end Algorithms2 constructor
50
51       public static void main( String args[] )
52       {
53          new Algorithms2();
54       } // end main
55    } // end class Algorithms2
```

```
Before addAll, vector contains:
black red green

After addAll, vector contains:
black red green red white yellow blue

Frequency of red in vector: 2

list and vector have elements in common
```

Fig. 16.15 | Collections method addAll, frequency and disjoint. (Part 2 of 2.)

16.7 Stack Class of Package java.util

In this section, we investigate class **Stack** in the Java utilities package (java.util). Section 16.5.3 discussed class Vector, which implements a dynamically resizable array. Class Stack extends class Vector to implement a stack data structure. Autoboxing occurs when you add a primitive type to a Stack, because class Stack stores only references to objects. Figure 16.16 demonstrates several Stack methods. For the details of class Stack, visit java.sun.com/javase/6/docs/api/java/util/Stack.html.

Line 10 of the constructor creates an empty Stack of type Number. Class Number (in package java.lang) is the superclass of most wrapper classes (e.g., Integer, Double) for the primitive types. By creating a Stack of Number, objects of any class that extends the Number class can be pushed onto the stack. Lines 19, 21, 23 and 25 each call Stack method **push** to add objects to the top of the stack. Note the literals 12L (line 13) and 1.0F (line 15). Any integer literal that has the *suffix* **L** is a long value. An integer literal without a suffix is an int value. Similarly, any floating-point literal that has the *suffix* F is a float value. A floating-point literal without a suffix is a double value. You can learn more about numeric literals in the *Java Language Specification* at java.sun.com/docs/books/jls/second_edition/html/expressions.doc.html#224125.

```
1   // Fig. 16.16: StackTest.java
2   // Program to test java.util.Stack.
3   import java.util.Stack;
4   import java.util.EmptyStackException;
5
6   public class StackTest
7   {
8      public StackTest()
9      {
10        Stack< Number > stack = new Stack< Number >();
11
12        // create numbers to store in the stack
13        Long longNumber = 12L;
14        Integer intNumber = 34567;
15        Float floatNumber = 1.0F;
16        Double doubleNumber = 1234.5678;
17
18        // use push method
19        stack.push( longNumber ); // push a long
20        printStack( stack );
21        stack.push( intNumber ); // push an int
22        printStack( stack );
23        stack.push( floatNumber ); // push a float
24        printStack( stack );
25        stack.push( doubleNumber ); // push a double
26        printStack( stack );
27
28        // remove items from stack
29        try
30        {
31           Number removedObject = null;
32
33           // pop elements from stack
34           while ( true )
35           {
36              removedObject = stack.pop(); // use pop method
37              System.out.printf( "%s popped\n", removedObject );
38              printStack( stack );
39           } // end while
40        } // end try
41        catch ( EmptyStackException emptyStackException )
42        {
43           emptyStackException.printStackTrace();
44        } // end catch
45     } // end StackTest constructor
46
47     private void printStack( Stack< Number > stack )
48     {
49        if ( stack.isEmpty() )
50           System.out.print( "stack is empty\n\n" ); // the stack is empty
51        else // stack is not empty
52        {
53           System.out.print( "stack contains: " );
```

Fig. 16.16 | Stack class of package `java.util`. (Part 1 of 2.)

```
54
55              // iterate through the elements
56              for ( Number number : stack )
57                  System.out.printf( "%s ", number );
58
59              System.out.print( "(top) \n\n" ); // indicates top of the stack
60          } // end else
61      } // end method printStack
62
63      public static void main( String args[] )
64      {
65          new StackTest();
66      } // end main
67  } // end class StackTest
```

```
stack contains: 12 (top)

stack contains: 12 34567 (top)

stack contains: 12 34567 1.0 (top)

stack contains: 12 34567 1.0 1234.5678 (top)

1234.5678 popped
stack contains: 12 34567 1.0 (top)

1.0 popped
stack contains: 12 34567 (top)

34567 popped
stack contains: 12 (top)

12 popped
stack is empty

java.util.EmptyStackException
        at java.util.Stack.peek(Unknown Source)
        at java.util.Stack.pop(Unknown Source)
        at StackTest.<init>(StackTest.java:36)
        at StackTest.main(StackTest.java:65)
```

Fig. 16.16 | Stack class of package `java.util`. (Part 2 of 2.)

An infinite loop (lines 34–39) calls Stack method **pop** to remove the top element of the stack. The method returns a Number reference to the removed element. If there are no elements in the Stack, method pop throws an **EmptyStackException**, which terminates the loop. Class Stack also declares method **peek**. This method returns the top element of the stack without popping the element off the stack.

Line 49 calls Stack method **isEmpty** (inherited by Stack from class Vector) to determine whether the stack is empty. If it is empty, the method returns true; otherwise, the method returns false.

Method printStack (lines 47–61) uses the enhanced for statement to iterate through the elements in the stack. The current top of the stack (the last value pushed onto the stack) is the first value printed. Because class Stack extends class Vector, the entire public interface of class Vector is available to clients of class Stack.

Error-Prevention Tip 16.1

Because Stack extends Vector, all public Vector methods can be called on Stack objects, even if the methods do not represent conventional stack operations. For example, Vector method add can be used to insert an element anywhere in a stack—an operation that could "corrupt" the stack. When manipulating a Stack, only methods push and pop should be used to add elements to and remove elements from the Stack, respectively.

16.8 Class PriorityQueue and Interface Queue

In this section we investigate interface **Queue** and class **PriorityQueue** in the Java utilities package (java.util). Queue, a new collection interface introduced in Java SE 5, extends interface Collection and provides additional operations for inserting, removing and inspecting elements in a queue. PriorityQueue, one of the classes that implements the Queue interface, orders elements by their natural ordering as specified by Comparable elements' compareTo method or by a Comparator object that is supplied through the constructor.

Class PriorityQueue provides functionality that enables insertions in sorted order into the underlying data structure and deletions from the front of the underlying data structure. When adding elements to a PriorityQueue, the elements are inserted in priority order such that the highest-priority element (i.e., the largest value) will be the first element removed from the PriorityQueue.

The common PriorityQueue operations are **offer** to insert an element at the appropriate location based on priority order, **poll** to remove the highest-priority element of the priority queue (i.e., the head of the queue), **peek** to get a reference to the highest-priority element of the priority queue (without removing that element), **clear** to remove all elements in the priority queue and **size** to get the number of elements in the priority queue. Figure 16.17 demonstrates the PriorityQueue class.

```java
1   // Fig. 16.17: PriorityQueueTest.java
2   // Standard library class PriorityQueue test program.
3   import java.util.PriorityQueue;
4
5   public class PriorityQueueTest
6   {
7      public static void main( String args[] )
8      {
9         // queue of capacity 11
10        PriorityQueue< Double > queue = new PriorityQueue< Double >();
11
12        // insert elements to queue
13        queue.offer( 3.2 );
14        queue.offer( 9.8 );
15        queue.offer( 5.4 );
16
17        System.out.print( "Polling from queue: " );
18
```

Fig. 16.17 | PriorityQueue test program. (Part 1 of 2.)

```
19          // display elements in queue
20          while ( queue.size() > 0 )
21          {
22             System.out.printf( "%.1f ", queue.peek() ); // view top element
23             queue.poll(); // remove top element
24          } // end while
25       } // end main
26    } // end class PriorityQueueTest
```

```
Polling from queue: 3.2 5.4 9.8
```

Fig. 16.17 | PriorityQueue test program. (Part 2 of 2.)

Line 10 creates a PriorityQueue that stores Doubles with an initial capacity of 11 elements and orders the elements according to the object's natural ordering (the defaults for a PriorityQueue). Note that PriorityQueue is a generic class and that line 10 instantiates a PriorityQueue with a type argument Double. Class PriorityQueue provides five additional constructors. One of these takes an int and a Comparator object to create a PriorityQueue with the initial capacity specified by the int and the ordering by the Comparator. Lines 13–15 use method offer to add elements to the priority queue. Method offer throws a NullPointException if the program attempts to add a null object to the queue. The loop in lines 20–24 uses method size to determine whether the priority queue is empty (line 20). While there are more elements, line 22 uses PriorityQueue method peek to retrieve the highest-priority element in the queue for output (without actually removing the element from the queue). Line 23 removes the highest-priority element in the queue with method poll.

16.9 Sets

A *Set* is a Collection that contains unique elements (i.e., no duplicate elements). The collections framework contains several Set implementations, including *HashSet* and *TreeSet*. HashSet stores its elements in a hash table, and TreeSet stores its elements in a tree. The concept of hash tables is presented in Section 16.10. Figure 16.18 uses a HashSet to remove duplicate strings from a List. Recall that both List and Collection are generic types, so line 18 creates a List that contains String objects, and line 24 passes a Collection of Strings to method printNonDuplicates.

```
1    // Fig. 16.18: SetTest.java
2    // Using a HashSet to remove duplicates.
3    import java.util.List;
4    import java.util.Arrays;
5    import java.util.HashSet;
6    import java.util.Set;
7    import java.util.Collection;
8
9    public class SetTest
10   {
```

Fig. 16.18 | HashSet used to remove duplicate values from array of strings. (Part 1 of 2.)

```
11    private static final String colors[] = { "red", "white", "blue",
12        "green", "gray", "orange", "tan", "white", "cyan",
13        "peach", "gray", "orange" };
14
15    // create and output ArrayList
16    public SetTest()
17    {
18        List< String > list = Arrays.asList( colors );
19        System.out.printf( "ArrayList: %s\n", list );
20        printNonDuplicates( list );
21    } // end SetTest constructor
22
23    // create set from array to eliminate duplicates
24    private void printNonDuplicates( Collection< String > collection )
25    {
26        // create a HashSet
27        Set< String > set = new HashSet< String >( collection );
28
29        System.out.println( "\nNonduplicates are: " );
30
31        for ( String s : set )
32            System.out.printf( "%s ", s );
33
34        System.out.println();
35    } // end method printNonDuplicates
36
37    public static void main( String args[] )
38    {
39        new SetTest();
40    } // end main
41 } // end class SetTest
```

```
ArrayList: [red, white, blue, green, gray, orange, tan, white, cyan, peach,
gray, orange]

Nonduplicates are:
red cyan white tan gray green orange blue peach
```

Fig. 16.18 | HashSet used to remove duplicate values from array of strings. (Part 2 of 2.)

Method printNonDuplicates (lines 24–35), which is called from the constructor, takes a Collection argument. Line 27 constructs a HashSet from the Collection argument. Note that both Set and HashSet are generic types. By definition, Sets do not contain any duplicates, so when the HashSet is constructed, it removes any duplicates in the Collection. Lines 31–32 output elements in the Set.

Sorted Sets

The collections framework also includes interface **SortedSet** (which extends Set) for sets that maintain their elements in sorted order—either the elements' natural order (e.g., numbers are in ascending order) or an order specified by a Comparator. Class TreeSet implements SortedSet. The program in Fig. 16.19 places strings into a TreeSet. The strings are sorted as they are added to the TreeSet. This example also demonstrates *range-view methods*, which enable a program to view a portion of a collection.

```java
 1  // Fig. 16.19: SortedSetTest.java
 2  // Using TreeSet and SortedSet.
 3  import java.util.Arrays;
 4  import java.util.SortedSet;
 5  import java.util.TreeSet;
 6
 7  public class SortedSetTest
 8  {
 9     private static final String names[] = { "yellow", "green",
10        "black", "tan", "grey", "white", "orange", "red", "green" };
11
12     // create a sorted set with TreeSet, then manipulate it
13     public SortedSetTest()
14     {
15        // create TreeSet
16        SortedSet< String > tree =
17           new TreeSet< String >( Arrays.asList( names ) );
18
19        System.out.println( "sorted set: " );
20        printSet( tree ); // output contents of tree
21
22        // get headSet based on "orange"
23        System.out.print( "\nheadSet (\"orange\"):  " );
24        printSet( tree.headSet( "orange" ) );
25
26        // get tailSet based upon "orange"
27        System.out.print( "tailSet (\"orange\"):  " );
28        printSet( tree.tailSet( "orange" ) );
29
30        // get first and last elements
31        System.out.printf( "first: %s\n", tree.first() );
32        System.out.printf( "last : %s\n", tree.last() );
33     } // end SortedSetTest constructor
34
35     // output set
36     private void printSet( SortedSet< String > set )
37     {
38        for ( String s : set )
39           System.out.printf( "%s ",  s );
40
41        System.out.println();
42     } // end method printSet
43
44     public static void main( String args[] )
45     {
46        new SortedSetTest();
47     } // end main
48  } // end class SortedSetTest
```

Fig. 16.19 | Using SortedSets and TreeSets. (Part 1 of 2.)

```
sorted set:
black green grey orange red tan white yellow

headSet ("orange"):  black green grey
tailSet ("orange"):  orange red tan white yellow
first: black
last : yellow
```

Fig. 16.19 | Using SortedSets and TreeSets. (Part 2 of 2.)

Lines 16–17 of the constructor create a TreeSet of Strings that contains the elements of array names and assigns the SortedSet to variable tree. Both SortedSet and TreeSet are generic types. Line 20 outputs the initial set of strings using method printSet (lines 36–42), which we discuss momentarily. Line 24 calls TreeSet method **headSet** to get a subset of the TreeSet in which every element is less than "orange". The view returned from headSet is then output with printSet. If any changes are made to the subset, they will also be made to the original TreeSet, because the subset returned by headSet is a view of the TreeSet.

Line 28 calls TreeSet method **tailSet** to get a subset in which each element is greater than or equal to "orange", then outputs the result. Any changes made through the tailSet view are made to the original TreeSet. Lines 31–32 call SortedSet methods **first** and **last** to get the smallest and largest elements of the set, respectively.

Method printSet (lines 36–42) accepts a SortedSet as an argument and prints it. Lines 38–39 print each element of the SortedSet using the enhanced for statement.

16.10 Maps

Maps associate keys to values and cannot contain duplicate keys (i.e., each key can map to only one value; this is called *one-to-one mapping*). Maps differ from Sets in that Maps contain keys and values, whereas Sets contain only values. Three of the several classes that implement interface Map are **Hashtable**, **HashMap** and **TreeMap**. Hashtables and HashMaps store elements in hash tables, and TreeMaps store elements in trees. This section discusses hash tables and provides an example that uses a HashMap to store keyPvalue pairs. Interface **SortedMap** extends Map and maintains its keys in sorted order—either the elements' natural order or an order specified by a Comparator. Class TreeMap implements SortedMap.

Map Implementation with Hash Tables

Object-oriented programming languages facilitate creating new types. When a program creates objects of new or existing types, it may need to store and retrieve them efficiently. Storing and retrieving information with arrays is efficient if some aspect of your data directly matches a numerical key value and if the keys are unique and tightly packed. If you have 100 employees with nine-digit social security numbers and you want to store and retrieve employee data by using the social security number as a key, the task would require an array with one billion elements, because there are one billion unique nine-digit numbers (000,000,000–999,999,999). This is impractical for virtually all applications that use social security numbers as keys. A program that had an array that large could achieve high performance for both storing and retrieving employee records by simply using the social security number as the array index.

Numerous applications have this problem—namely, that either the keys are of the wrong type (e.g., not positive integers that correspond to array subscripts) or they are of the right type, but sparsely spread over a huge range. What is needed is a high-speed scheme for converting keys such as social security numbers, inventory part numbers and the like into unique array indices. Then, when an application needs to store something, the scheme could convert the application's key rapidly into an index, and the record could be stored at that slot in the array. Retrieval is accomplished the same way: Once the application has a key for which it wants to retrieve a data record, the application simply applies the conversion to the key—this produces the array index where the data is stored and retrieved.

The scheme we describe here is the basis of a technique called *hashing*. Why the name? When we convert a key into an array index, we literally scramble the bits, forming a kind of "mishmashed," or hashed, number. The number actually has no real significance beyond its usefulness in storing and retrieving a particular data record.

A glitch in the scheme is called a *collision*—this occurs when two different keys "hash into" the same cell (or element) in the array. We cannot store two values in the same space, so we need to find an alternative home for all values beyond the first that hash to a particular array index. There are many schemes for doing this. One is to "hash again" (i.e., to apply another hashing transformation to the key to provide a next candidate cell in the array). The hashing process is designed to distribute the values throughout the table, so the assumption is that an available cell will be found with just a few hashes.

Another scheme uses one hash to locate the first candidate cell. If that cell is occupied, successive cells are searched in order until an available cell is found. Retrieval works the same way: The key is hashed once to determine the initial location and check whether it contains the desired data. If it does, the search is finished. If it does not, successive cells are searched linearly until the desired data is found.

The most popular solution to hash-table collisions is to have each cell of the table be a hash "bucket," typically a linked list of all the key/value pairs that hash to that cell. This is the solution that Java's Hashtable and HashMap classes (from package java.util) implement. Both Hashtable and HashMap implement the Map interface. The primary differences between them are that HashMap is unsynchronized (multiple threads should not modify a HashMap concurrently), and allows null keys and null values.

A hash table's *load factor* affects the performance of hashing schemes. The load factor is the ratio of the number of occupied cells in the hash table to the total number of cells in the hash table. The closer this ratio gets to 1.0, the greater the chance of collisions.

Performance Tip 16.7

The load factor in a hash table is a classic example of a memory-space/execution-time trade-off: By increasing the load factor, we get better memory utilization, but the program runs slower, due to increased hashing collisions. By decreasing the load factor, we get better program speed, because of reduced hashing collisions, but we get poorer memory utilization, because a larger portion of the hash table remains empty.

Hash tables are complex to program. Java provides classes Hashtable and HashMap to enable programmers to use hashing without having to implement hash table mechanisms. This concept is profoundly important in our study of object-oriented programming. As discussed in earlier chapters, classes encapsulate and hide complexity (i.e., implementation details) and offer user-friendly interfaces. Properly crafting classes to exhibit such behavior is one of the most valued skills in the field of object-oriented programming. Figure 16.20 uses a HashMap to count the number of occurrences of each word in a string.

```java
 1  // Fig. 16.20: WordTypeCount.java
 2  // Program counts the number of occurrences of each word in a string
 3  import java.util.StringTokenizer;
 4  import java.util.Map;
 5  import java.util.HashMap;
 6  import java.util.Set;
 7  import java.util.TreeSet;
 8  import java.util.Scanner;
 9
10  public class WordTypeCount
11  {
12     private Map< String, Integer > map;
13     private Scanner scanner;
14
15     public WordTypeCount()
16     {
17        map = new HashMap< String, Integer >(); // create HashMap
18        scanner = new Scanner( System.in ); // create scanner
19        createMap(); // create map based on user input
20        displayMap(); // display map content
21     } // end WordTypeCount constructor
22
23     // create map from user input
24     private void createMap()
25     {
26        System.out.println( "Enter a string:" ); // prompt for user input
27        String input = scanner.nextLine();
28
29        // create StringTokenizer for input
30        StringTokenizer tokenizer = new StringTokenizer( input );
31
32        // processing input text
33        while ( tokenizer.hasMoreTokens() ) // while more input
34        {
35           String word = tokenizer.nextToken().toLowerCase(); // get word
36
37           // if the map contains the word
38           if ( map.containsKey( word ) ) // is word in map
39           {
40              int count = map.get( word ); // get current count
41              map.put( word, count + 1 );  // increment count
42           } // end if
43           else
44              map.put( word, 1 ); // add new word with a count of 1 to map
45        } // end while
46     } // end method createMap
```

Fig. 16.20 | HashMaps and Maps. (Part 1 of 2.)

```
47
48      // display map content
49      private void displayMap()
50      {
51          Set< String > keys = map.keySet(); // get keys
52
53          // sort keys
54          TreeSet< String > sortedKeys = new TreeSet< String >( keys );
55
56          System.out.println( "Map contains:\nKey\t\tValue" );
57
58          // generate output for each key in map
59          for ( String key : sortedKeys )
60              System.out.printf( "%-10s%10s\n", key, map.get( key ) );
61
62          System.out.printf(
63              "\nsize:%d\nisEmpty:%b\n", map.size(), map.isEmpty() );
64      } // end method displayMap
65
66      public static void main( String args[] )
67      {
68          new WordTypeCount();
69      } // end main
70  } // end class WordTypeCount
```

```
Enter a string:
To be or not to be: that is the question Whether 'tis nobler to suffer
Map contains:
Key                 Value
'tis                1
be                  1
be:                 1
is                  1
nobler              1
not                 1
or                  1
question            1
suffer              1
that                1
the                 1
to                  3
whether             1

size:13
isEmpty:false
```

Fig. 16.20 | HashMaps and Maps. (Part 2 of 2.)

Line 17 creates an empty HashMap with a default initial capacity (16 elements) and a default load factor (0.75)—these defaults are built into the implementation of HashMap. When the number of occupied slots in the HashMap becomes greater than the capacity times the load factor, the capacity is doubled automatically. Note that HashMap is a generic class that takes two type arguments. The first specifies the type of key (i.e., String), and the second the type of value (i.e., Integer). Recall that the type arguments passed to a generic class must be reference types, hence the second type argument is Integer, not int. Line 18 creates a Scanner that reads user input from the standard input stream. Line 19 calls method createMap (lines 24–46), which uses a map to store the number of occurrences of each word in the sentence. Line 27 invokes method nextLine of scanner to obtain the user input, and line 30 creates a *StringTokenizer* to break the input string into its component individual words. This StringTokenizer constructor takes a string argument and creates a StringTokenizer for that string and will use the white space to separate the string. The condition in the while statement in lines 33–45 uses StringTokenizer method *hasMoreTokens* to determine whether there are more tokens in the string being tokenized. If so, line 35 converts the next token to lowercase letters. The next token is obtained with a call to StringTokenizer method *nextToken* that returns a String. [*Note:* Section 25.6 discusses class StringTokenizer in detail.] Then line 38 calls Map method *containsKey* to determine whether the word is in the map (and thus has occurred previously in the string). If the Map does not contain a mapping for the word, line 44 uses Map method *put* to create a new entry in the map, with the word as the key and an Integer object containing 1 as the value. Note that autoboxing occurs when the program passes integer 1 to method put, because the map stores the number of occurrences of the word as Integer. If the word does exist in the map, line 40 uses Map method *get* to obtain the key's associated value (the count) in the map. Line 41 increments that value and uses put to replace the key's associated value in the map. Method put returns the prior value associated with the key, or null if the key was not in the map.

Method displayMap (lines 49–64) displays all the entries in the map. It uses HashMap method *keySet* (line 51) to get a set of the keys. The keys have type String in the map, so method keySet returns a generic type Set with type parameter specified to be String. Line 54 creates a TreeSet of the keys, in which the keys are sorted. The loop in lines 59–60 accesses each key and its value in the map. Line 60 displays each key and its value using format specifier %-10s to left justify each key and format specifier %10s to right justify each value. Note that the keys are displayed in ascending order. Line 63 calls Map method *size* to get the number of key–value pairs in the Map. Line 64 calls *isEmpty*, which returns a boolean indicating whether the Map is empty.

16.11 Properties Class

A *Properties* object is a persistent Hashtable that normally stores key–value pairs of strings—assuming that you use methods *setProperty* and *getProperty* to manipulate the table rather than inherited Hashtable methods put and get. By "persistent," we mean that the Properties object can be written to an output stream (possibly a file) and read back in through an input stream. A common use of Properties objects in prior versions of Java was to maintain application-configuration data or user preferences for applications. [*Note:* The *Preferences API* (package *java.util.prefs*) is meant to replace this particular use of class Properties but is beyond the scope of this book. To learn more, visit java.sun.com/javase/6/docs/technotes/guides/preferences/index.html.]

Class Properties extends class Hashtable. Figure 16.21 demonstrates several methods of class Properties.

Line 16 uses the no-argument constructor to create an empty Properties table with no default properties. Class Properties also provides an overloaded constructor that receives a reference to a Properties object containing default property values. Lines 19 and 20 each call Properties method setProperty to store a value for the specified key. If the key does not exist in the table, setProperty returns null; otherwise, it returns the previous value for that key.

Line 41 calls Properties method getProperty to locate the value associated with the specified key. If the key is not found in this Properties object, getProperty returns null. An overloaded version of this method receives a second argument that specifies the default value to return if getProperty cannot locate the key.

Line 57 calls Properties method *store* to save the contents of the Properties object to the OutputStream object specified as the first argument (in this case, FileOutputStream output). The second argument, a String, is a description of the Properties object. Class Properties also provides method *list*, which takes a PrintStream argument. This method is useful for displaying the list of properties.

Line 75 calls Properties method *load* to restore the contents of the Properties object from the InputStream specified as the first argument (in this case, a FileInput-Stream). Line 89 calls Properties method keySet to obtain a Set of the property names. Line 94 obtains the value of a property by passing a key to method getProperty.

```
1   // Fig. 16.21: PropertiesTest.java
2   // Demonstrates class Properties of the java.util package.
3   import java.io.FileOutputStream;
4   import java.io.FileInputStream;
5   import java.io.IOException;
6   import java.util.Properties;
7   import java.util.Set;
8
9   public class PropertiesTest
10  {
11     private Properties table;
12
13     // set up GUI to test Properties table
14     public PropertiesTest()
15     {
16        table = new Properties(); // create Properties table
17
18        // set properties
19        table.setProperty( "color", "blue" );
20        table.setProperty( "width", "200" );
21
22        System.out.println( "After setting properties" );
23        listProperties(); // display property values
24
25        // replace property value
26        table.setProperty( "color", "red" );
27
28        System.out.println( "After replacing properties" );
29        listProperties(); // display property values
30
31        saveProperties(); // save properties
32
```

Fig. 16.21 | Properties class of package java.util. (Part 1 of 3.)

```
33          table.clear(); // empty table
34
35          System.out.println( "After clearing properties" );
36          listProperties(); // display property values
37
38          loadProperties(); // load properties
39
40          // get value of property color
41          Object value = table.getProperty( "color" );
42
43          // check if value is in table
44          if ( value != null )
45             System.out.printf( "Property color's value is %s\n", value );
46          else
47             System.out.println( "Property color is not in table" );
48       } // end PropertiesTest constructor
49
50       // save properties to a file
51       public void saveProperties()
52       {
53          // save contents of table
54          try
55          {
56             FileOutputStream output = new FileOutputStream( "props.dat" );
57             table.store( output, "Sample Properties" ); // save properties
58             output.close();
59             System.out.println( "After saving properties" );
60             listProperties();
61          } // end try
62          catch ( IOException ioException )
63          {
64             ioException.printStackTrace();
65          } // end catch
66       } // end method saveProperties
67
68       // load properties from a file
69       public void loadProperties()
70       {
71          // load contents of table
72          try
73          {
74             FileInputStream input = new FileInputStream( "props.dat" );
75             table.load( input ); // load properties
76             input.close();
77             System.out.println( "After loading properties" );
78             listProperties(); // display property values
79          } // end try
80          catch ( IOException ioException )
81          {
82             ioException.printStackTrace();
83          } // end catch
84       } // end method loadProperties
```

Fig. 16.21 | Properties class of package java.util. (Part 2 of 3.)

```
85
86      // output property values
87      public void listProperties()
88      {
89          Set< Object > keys = table.keySet(); // get property names
90
91          // output name/value pairs
92          for ( Object key : keys )
93          {
94              System.out.printf(
95                  "%s\t%s\n", key, table.getProperty( ( String ) key ) );
96          } // end for
97
98          System.out.println();
99      } // end method listProperties
100
101     public static void main( String args[] )
102     {
103         new PropertiesTest();
104     } // end main
105 } // end class PropertiesTest
```

```
After setting properties
color    blue
width    200

After replacing properties
color    red
width    200

After saving properties
color    red
width    200

After clearing properties

After loading properties
color    red
width    200

Property color's value is red
```

Fig. 16.21 | Properties class of package java.util. (Part 3 of 3.)

16.12 Synchronized Collections

In Chapter 18, we discuss multithreading. Except for Vector and Hashtable, the collections in the collections framework are unsynchronized by default, so they can operate efficiently when multithreading is not required. Because they are unsynchronized, however, concurrent access to a Collection by multiple threads could cause indeterminate results or fatal errors. To prevent potential threading problems, synchronization wrappers are used for collections that might be accessed by multiple threads. A *wrapper* object receives method calls, adds thread synchronization (to prevent concurrent access to the collection) and delegates the calls to the wrapped collection object. The `Collections` API provides a set of `static` methods for wrapping collections as synchronized versions. Method headers for the synchronization wrappers are listed in Fig. 16.22. Details about these methods are available at java.sun.com/javase/6/docs/api/java/util/Collections.html. All these methods take a generic type and return a synchronized view of the generic type. For example, the following code creates a synchronized `List` (`list2`) that stores `String` objects:

```
List< String > list1 = new ArrayList< String >();
List< String > list2 = Collections.synchronizedList( list1 );
```

public static method headers
< T > Collection< T > synchronizedCollection(Collection< T > c)
< T > List< T > synchronizedList(List< T > aList)
< T > Set< T > synchronizedSet(Set< T > s)
< T > SortedSet< T > synchronizedSortedSet(SortedSet< T > s)
< K, V > Map< K, V > synchronizedMap(Map< K, V > m)
< K, V > SortedMap< K, V > synchronizedSortedMap(SortedMap< K, V > m)

Fig. 16.22 | Synchronization wrapper methods.

16.13 **Unmodifiable Collections**

The `Collections` API provides a set of `static` methods that create *unmodifiable wrappers* for collections. Unmodifiable wrappers throw `UnsupportedOperationExceptions` if attempts are made to modify the collection. Headers for these methods are listed in Fig. 16.23. Details about these methods are available at java.sun.com/javase/6/docs/api/java/util/Collections.html. All these methods take a generic type and return an unmodifiable view of the generic type. For example, the following code creates an unmodifiable `List` (`list2`) that stores `String` objects:

```
List< String > list1 = new ArrayList< String >();
List< String > list2 = Collections.unmodifiableList( list1 );
```

public static method headers
< T > Collection< T > unmodifiableCollection(Collection< T > c)
< T > List< T > unmodifiableList(List< T > aList)
< T > Set< T > unmodifiableSet(Set< T > s)
< T > SortedSet< T > unmodifiableSortedSet(SortedSet< T > s)
< K, V > Map< K, V > unmodifiableMap(Map< K, V > m)
< K, V > SortedMap< K, V > unmodifiableSortedMap(SortedMap< K, V > m)

Fig. 16.23 | Unmodifiable wrapper methods.

Software Engineering Observation 16.5

You can use an unmodifiable wrapper to create a collection that offers read-only access to others, while allowing read–write access to yourself. You do this simply by giving others a reference to the unmodifiable wrapper while retaining for yourself a reference to the original collection.

16.14 Abstract Implementations

The collections framework provides various abstract implementations of Collection interfaces from which the programmer can quickly "flesh out" complete customized implementations. These abstract implementations include a thin Collection implementation called an *AbstractCollection*, a thin List implementation that allows random access to its elements called an *AbstractList*, a thin Map implementation called an *AbstractMap*, a thin List implementation that allows sequential access to its elements called an *AbstractSequentialList*, a thin Set implementation called an *AbstractSet* and a thin Queue implementation called *AbstractQueue*. You can learn more about these classes at java.sun.com/javase/6/docs/api/java/util/package-summary.html.

To write a custom implementation, you can extend the abstract implementation that best meets your needs, and implement each of the class's abstract methods. Then, if your collection is to be modifiable, override any concrete methods that prevent modification.

16.15 Wrap-Up

This chapter introduced the Java collections framework. You learned how to use class Arrays to perform array manipulations. You learned the collection hierarchy and how to use the collections framework interfaces to program with collections polymorphically. You also learned several predefined algorithms for manipulating collections. In the next chapter, you will continue your study of GUI concepts, building on the techniques you learned in Chapter 11.

GUI Components: Part 2

OBJECTIVES

In this chapter you'll learn:

- To create and manipulate sliders, menus, pop-up menus and windows.

- To change the look-and-feel of a GUI, using Swing's pluggable look-and-feel.

- To create a multiple-document interface with `JDesktopPane` and `JInternalFrame`.

- To use additional layout managers.

Outline

17.1 Introduction

17.2 JSlider

17.3 Windows: Additional Notes

17.4 Using Menus with Frames

17.5 JPopupMenu

17.6 Pluggable Look-and-Feel

17.7 JDesktopPane and JInternalFrame

17.8 JTabbedPane

17.9 Layout Managers: BoxLayout and GridBagLayout

17.10 Wrap-Up

17.1 Introduction

In this chapter, we continue our study of GUIs. We discuss additional components and layout managers and lay the groundwork for building more complex GUIs.

We begin our discussion with menus that enable the user to effectively perform tasks in the program. The look-and-feel of a Swing GUI can be uniform across all platforms on which a Java program executes, or the GUI can be customized by using Swing's *pluggable look-and-feel* (*PLAF*). We provide an example that illustrates how to change between Swing's default metal look-and-feel (which looks and behaves the same across platforms), a look-and-feel that simulates *Motif* (a popular UNIX look-and-feel) and one that simulates Microsoft's Windows look-and-feel.

Many of today's applications use a multiple-document interface (MDI)—a main window (often called the parent window) containing other windows (often called child windows) to manage several open documents in parallel. For example, many e-mail programs allow you to have several e-mail windows open at the same time so that you can compose or read multiple e-mail messages. We demonstrate Swing's classes for creating multiple-document interfaces. The chapter finishes with a series of examples discussing additional layout managers for organizing graphical user interfaces.

Swing is a large and complex topic. There are many more GUI components and capabilities than can be presented here. Several more Swing GUI components are introduced in the remaining chapters of this book as they are needed.

17.2 JSlider

JSliders enable a user to select from a range of integer values. Class JSlider inherits from JComponent. Figure 17.1 shows a horizontal JSlider with *tick marks* and the *thumb* that allows a user to select a value. JSliders can be customized to display major tick marks, minor tick marks and labels for the tick marks. They also support *snap-to ticks*, which cause the thumb, when positioned between two tick marks, to snap to the closest one.

Fig. 17.1 | JSlider component with horizontal orientation.

Most Swing GUI components support user interactions through the mouse and the keyboard. For example, if a JSlider has the focus (i.e., it is the currently selected GUI component in the user interface), the left arrow key and right arrow key cause the thumb of the JSlider to decrease or increase by 1, respectively. The down arrow key and up arrow key also cause the thumb of the JSlider to decrease or increase by 1 tick, respectively. The *PgDn* (page down) *key* and *PgUp* (page up) *key* cause the thumb of the JSlider to decrease or increase by *block increments* of one-tenth of the range of values, respectively. The *Home key* moves the thumb to the minimum value of the JSlider, and the *End key* moves the thumb to the maximum value of the JSlider.

JSliders have either a horizontal orientation or a vertical orientation. For a horizontal JSlider, the minimum value is at the left end of the JSlider and the maximum is at the right end. For a vertical JSlider, the minimum value is at the bottom and the maximum is at the top. The minimum and maximum value positions on a JSlider can be reversed by invoking JSlider method *setInverted* with boolean argument true. The relative position of the thumb indicates the current value of the JSlider.

The program in Figs. 17.2–17.4 allows the user to size a circle drawn on a subclass of JPanel called OvalPanel (Fig. 17.2). The user specifies the circle's diameter with a horizontal JSlider. Class OvalPanel knows how to draw a circle on itself, using its own instance variable diameter to determine the diameter of the circle—the diameter is used as the width and height of the bounding box in which the circle is displayed. The diameter value is set when the user interacts with the JSlider. The event handler calls method setDiameter in class OvalPanel to set the diameter and calls repaint to draw the new circle. The repaint call results in a call to OvalPanel's paintComponent method.

```
1   // Fig. 17.2: OvalPanel.java
2   // A customized JPanel class.
3   import java.awt.Graphics;
4   import java.awt.Dimension;
5   import javax.swing.JPanel;
6
7   public class OvalPanel extends JPanel
8   {
9      private int diameter = 10; // default diameter of 10
10
11     // draw an oval of the specified diameter
12     public void paintComponent( Graphics g )
13     {
14        super.paintComponent( g );
15
16        g.fillOval( 10, 10, diameter, diameter ); // draw circle
17     } // end method paintComponent
18
19     // validate and set diameter, then repaint
20     public void setDiameter( int newDiameter )
21     {
22        // if diameter invalid, default to 10
23        diameter = ( newDiameter >= 0 ? newDiameter : 10 );
```

Fig. 17.2 | JPanel subclass for drawing circles of a specified diameter. (Part 1 of 2.)

```
24            repaint(); // repaint panel
25        } // end method setDiameter
26
27        // used by layout manager to determine preferred size
28        public Dimension getPreferredSize()
29        {
30            return new Dimension( 200, 200 );
31        } // end method getPreferredSize
32
33        // used by layout manager to determine minimum size
34        public Dimension getMinimumSize()
35        {
36            return getPreferredSize();
37        } // end method getMinimumSize
38    } // end class OvalPanel
```

Fig. 17.2 | JPanel subclass for drawing circles of a specified diameter. (Part 2 of 2.)

Class OvalPanel (Fig. 17.2) contains a paintComponent method (lines 12–17) that draws a filled oval (a circle in this example), a setDiameter method (lines 20–25) that changes the circle's diameter and repaints the OvalPanel, a *getPreferredSize* method (lines 28–31) that returns the preferred width and height of an OvalPanel and a *getMinimumSize* method (lines 34–37) that returns an OvalPanel's minimum width and height.

Look-and-Feel Observation 17.1

If a new GUI component has a minimum width and height (i.e., smaller dimensions would render the component ineffective on the display), override method getMinimumSize to return the minimum width and height as an instance of class Dimension.

Software Engineering Observation 17.1

For many GUI components, method getMinimumSize is implemented to return the result of a call to the component's getPreferredSize method.

Class SliderFrame (Fig. 17.3) creates the JSlider that controls the diameter of the circle. Class SliderFrame's constructor (lines 17–45) creates OvalPanel object myPanel (line 21) and sets its background color (line 22). Lines 25–26 create JSlider object diameterSlider to control the diameter of the circle drawn on the OvalPanel. The JSlider constructor takes four arguments. The first argument specifies the orientation of diameterSlider, which is HORIZONTAL (a constant in interface SwingConstants). The second and third arguments indicate the minimum and maximum integer values in the range of values for this JSlider. The last argument indicates that the initial value of the JSlider (i.e., where the thumb is displayed) should be 10.

Lines 27–28 customize the appearance of the JSlider. Method *setMajorTickSpacing* indicates that each major tick mark represents 10 values in the range of values supported by the JSlider. Method *setPaintTicks* with a true argument indicates that the tick marks should be displayed (they are not displayed by default). For other methods that are used to customize a JSlider's appearance, see the JSlider on-line documentation (java.sun.com/javase/6/docs/api/javax/swing/JSlider.html).

```
 1    // Fig. 17.3: SliderFrame.java
 2    // Using JSliders to size an oval.
 3    import java.awt.BorderLayout;
 4    import java.awt.Color;
 5    import javax.swing.JFrame;
 6    import javax.swing.JSlider;
 7    import javax.swing.SwingConstants;
 8    import javax.swing.event.ChangeListener;
 9    import javax.swing.event.ChangeEvent;
10
11    public class SliderFrame extends JFrame
12    {
13       private JSlider diameterJSlider; // slider to select diameter
14       private OvalPanel myPanel; // panel to draw circle
15
16       // no-argument constructor
17       public SliderFrame()
18       {
19          super( "Slider Demo" );
20
21          myPanel = new OvalPanel(); // create panel to draw circle
22          myPanel.setBackground( Color.YELLOW ); // set background to yellow
23
24          // set up JSlider to control diameter value
25          diameterJSlider =
26             new JSlider( SwingConstants.HORIZONTAL, 0, 200, 10 );
27          diameterJSlider.setMajorTickSpacing( 10 ); // create tick every 10
28          diameterJSlider.setPaintTicks( true ); // paint ticks on slider
29
30          // register JSlider event listener
31          diameterJSlider.addChangeListener(
32
33             new ChangeListener() // anonymous inner class
34             {
35                // handle change in slider value
36                public void stateChanged( ChangeEvent e )
37                {
38                   myPanel.setDiameter( diameterJSlider.getValue() );
39                } // end method stateChanged
40             } // end anonymous inner class
41          ); // end call to addChangeListener
42
43          add( diameterJSlider, BorderLayout.SOUTH ); // add slider to frame
44          add( myPanel, BorderLayout.CENTER ); // add panel to frame
45       } // end SliderFrame constructor
46    } // end class SliderFrame
```

Fig. 17.3 | JSlider value used to determine the diameter of a circle.

JSliders generate **ChangeEvents** (package java.swing.event) in response to user interactions. An object of a class that implements interface **ChangeListener** (package java.swing.event) and declares method **stateChanged** can respond to ChangeEvents. Lines 31–41 register a ChangeListener to handle diameterSlider's events. When

```
 1   // Fig. 17.4: SliderDemo.java
 2   // Testing SliderFrame.
 3   import javax.swing.JFrame;
 4
 5   public class SliderDemo
 6   {
 7      public static void main( String args[] )
 8      {
 9         SliderFrame sliderFrame = new SliderFrame();
10         sliderFrame.setDefaultCloseOperation( JFrame.EXIT_ON_CLOSE );
11         sliderFrame.setSize( 220, 270 ); // set frame size
12         sliderFrame.setVisible( true ); // display frame
13      } // end main
14   } // end class SliderDemo
```

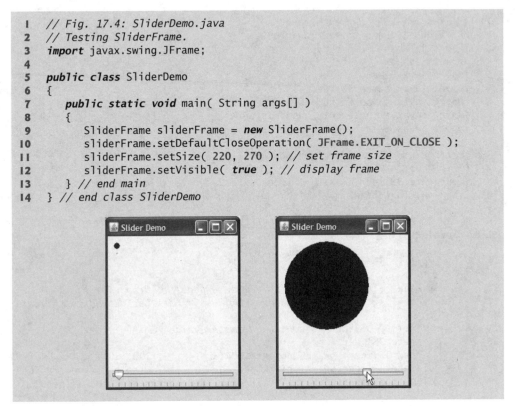

Fig. 17.4 | Test class for SliderFrame.

method stateChanged (lines 36–39) is called in response to a user interaction, line 38 calls myPanel's setDiameter method and passes the current value of the JSlider as an argument. JSlider method *getValue* returns the current thumb position.

17.3 Windows: Additional Notes

In this section, we discuss several important JFrame issues. A JFrame is a *window* with a *title bar* and a *border*. Class JFrame is a subclass of java.awt.Frame (which is a subclass of java.awt.Window). As such, JFrame is one of the few Swing GUI components that is not a lightweight GUI component. When you display a window from a Java program, the window is provided by the local platform's windowing toolkit, and therefore the window will look like every other window displayed on that platform. When a Java application executes on a Macintosh and displays a window, the window's title bar and borders will look like those of other Macintosh applications. When a Java application executes on a Microsoft Windows system and displays a window, the window's title bar and borders will look like those of other Microsoft Windows applications. And when a Java application executes on a UNIX platform and displays a window, the window's title bar and borders will look like other UNIX applications on that platform.

Class JFrame supports three operations when the user closes the window. By default, a window is hidden (i.e., removed from the screen). This can be controlled with JFrame method ***setDefaultCloseOperation***. Interface ***WindowConstants*** (package javax.swing), which class JFrame implements, declares three constants—DISPOSE_ON_CLOSE, DO_NOTHING_ON_CLOSE and HIDE_ON_CLOSE (the default)—for use with this method. Some platforms allow only a limited number of windows to be displayed on the screen. Thus, a window is a valuable resource that should be given back to the system when it is no longer needed. Class Window (an indirect superclass of JFrame) declares method ***dispose*** for this purpose. When a Window is no longer needed in an application, you should explicitly dispose of it. This can be done by calling the Window's dispose method or by calling method setDefaultCloseOperation with the argument WindowConstants.DISPOSE_ON_CLOSE. Terminating an application will return window resources to the system. Setting the default close operation to DO_NOTHING_ON_CLOSE indicates that the program will determine what to do when the user indicates that the window should be closed.

Performance Tip 17.1

A window is an expensive system resource. Return it to the system by calling its dispose method when the window is no longer needed.

By default, a window is not displayed on the screen until the program invokes the window's setVisible method (inherited from class java.awt.Component) with a true argument. A window's size should be set with a call to method setSize (inherited from class java.awt.Component). The position of a window when it appears on the screen is specified with method ***setLocation*** (inherited from class java.awt.Component).

Common Programming Error 17.1

Forgetting to call method setVisible on a window is a runtime logic error—the window is not displayed.

Common Programming Error 17.2

Forgetting to call the setSize method on a window is a runtime logic error—only the title bar appears.

When the user manipulates the window, this action generates ***window events***. Event listeners are registered for window events with Window method ***addWindowListener***. Interface ***WindowListener*** provides seven window-event-handling methods—***windowActivated*** (called when the user makes a window the active window), ***windowClosed*** (called after the window is closed), ***windowClosing*** (called when the user initiates closing of the window), ***windowDeactivated*** (called when the user makes another window the active window), ***windowDeiconified*** (called when the user restores a window from being minimized), ***windowIconified*** (called when the user minimizes a window) and ***windowOpened*** (called when a program first displays a window on the screen).

17.4 Using Menus with Frames

Menus are an integral part of GUIs. Menus allow the user to perform actions without unnecessarily cluttering a GUI with extra components. In Swing GUIs, menus can be attached only to objects of the classes that provide method ***setJMenuBar***. Two such classes are JFrame and JApplet. The classes used to declare menus are JMenuBar, JMenu, JMenuItem, JCheckBoxMenuItem and class JRadioButtonMenuItem.

Look-and-Feel Observation 17.2

Menus simplify GUIs because components can be hidden within them. These components will be visible only when the user looks for them by selecting the menu.

Class **JMenuBar** (a subclass of JComponent) contains the methods necessary to manage a *menu bar*, which is a container for menus. Class **JMenu** (a subclass of javax.swing.JMenuItem) contains the methods necessary for managing menus. Menus contain menu items and are added to menu bars or to other menus as submenus. When a menu is clicked, it expands to show its list of menu items.

Class **JMenuItem** (a subclass of javax.swing.AbstractButton) contains the methods necessary to manage *menu items*. A menu item is a GUI component inside a menu that, when selected, causes an action event. A menu item can be used to initiate an action, or it can be a *submenu* that provides more menu items from which the user can select. Submenus are useful for grouping related menu items in a menu.

Class **JCheckBoxMenuItem** (a subclass of javax.swing.JMenuItem) contains the methods necessary to manage menu items that can be toggled on or off. When a JCheckBoxMenuItem is selected, a check appears to the left of the menu item. When the JCheckBoxMenuItem is selected again, the check is removed.

Class **JRadioButtonMenuItem** (a subclass of javax.swing.JMenuItem) contains the methods necessary to manage menu items that can be toggled on or off like JCheckBoxMenuItems. When multiple JRadioButtonMenuItems are maintained as part of a ButtonGroup, only one item in the group can be selected at a given time. When a JRadioButtonMenuItem is selected, a filled circle appears to the left of the menu item. When another JRadioButtonMenuItem is selected, the filled circle of the previously selected menu item is removed.

The application in Figs. 17.5–17.6 demonstrates various menu items and how to specify special characters called *mnemonics* that can provide quick access to a menu or menu item from the keyboard. Mnemonics can be used with all subclasses of javax.swing.AbstractButton.

Class MenuFrame (Fig. 17.5) declares the GUI components and event handling for the menu items. Most of the code in this application appears in the class's constructor (lines 34–151).

```java
1   // Fig. 17.5: MenuFrame.java
2   // Demonstrating menus.
3   import java.awt.Color;
4   import java.awt.Font;
5   import java.awt.BorderLayout;
6   import java.awt.event.ActionListener;
7   import java.awt.event.ActionEvent;
8   import java.awt.event.ItemListener;
9   import java.awt.event.ItemEvent;
10  import javax.swing.JFrame;
11  import javax.swing.JRadioButtonMenuItem;
12  import javax.swing.JCheckBoxMenuItem;
13  import javax.swing.JOptionPane;
```

Fig. 17.5 | JMenus and mnemonics. (Part 1 of 5.)

```
14  import javax.swing.JLabel;
15  import javax.swing.SwingConstants;
16  import javax.swing.ButtonGroup;
17  import javax.swing.JMenu;
18  import javax.swing.JMenuItem;
19  import javax.swing.JMenuBar;
20
21  public class MenuFrame extends JFrame
22  {
23     private final Color colorValues[] =
24        { Color.BLACK, Color.BLUE, Color.RED, Color.GREEN };
25     private JRadioButtonMenuItem colorItems[]; // color menu items
26     private JRadioButtonMenuItem fonts[]; // font menu items
27     private JCheckBoxMenuItem styleItems[]; // font style menu items
28     private JLabel displayJLabel; // displays sample text
29     private ButtonGroup fontButtonGroup; // manages font menu items
30     private ButtonGroup colorButtonGroup; // manages color menu items
31     private int style; // used to create style for font
32
33     // no-argument constructor set up GUI
34     public MenuFrame()
35     {
36        super( "Using JMenus" );
37
38        JMenu fileMenu = new JMenu( "File" ); // create file menu
39        fileMenu.setMnemonic( 'F' ); // set mnemonic to F
40
41        // create About... menu item
42        JMenuItem aboutItem = new JMenuItem( "About..." );
43        aboutItem.setMnemonic( 'A' ); // set mnemonic to A
44        fileMenu.add( aboutItem ); // add about item to file menu
45        aboutItem.addActionListener(
46
47           new ActionListener() // anonymous inner class
48           {
49              // display message dialog when user selects About...
50              public void actionPerformed( ActionEvent event )
51              {
52                 JOptionPane.showMessageDialog( MenuFrame.this,
53                    "This is an example\nof using menus",
54                    "About", JOptionPane.PLAIN_MESSAGE );
55              } // end method actionPerformed
56           } // end anonymous inner class
57        ); // end call to addActionListener
58
59        JMenuItem exitItem = new JMenuItem( "Exit" ); // create exit item
60        exitItem.setMnemonic( 'x' ); // set mnemonic to x
61        fileMenu.add( exitItem ); // add exit item to file menu
62        exitItem.addActionListener(
63
64           new ActionListener() // anonymous inner class
65           {
```

Fig. 17.5 | JMenus and mnemonics. (Part 2 of 5.)

```
66          // terminate application when user clicks exitItem
67          public void actionPerformed( ActionEvent event )
68          {
69             System.exit( 0 ); // exit application
70          } // end method actionPerformed
71       } // end anonymous inner class
72    ); // end call to addActionListener
73
74    JMenuBar bar = new JMenuBar(); // create menu bar
75    setJMenuBar( bar ); // add menu bar to application
76    bar.add( fileMenu ); // add file menu to menu bar
77
78    JMenu formatMenu = new JMenu( "Format" ); // create format menu
79    formatMenu.setMnemonic( 'r' ); // set mnemonic to r
80
81    // array listing string colors
82    String colors[] = { "Black", "Blue", "Red", "Green" };
83
84    JMenu colorMenu = new JMenu( "Color" ); // create color menu
85    colorMenu.setMnemonic( 'C' ); // set mnemonic to C
86
87    // create radio button menu items for colors
88    colorItems = new JRadioButtonMenuItem[ colors.length ];
89    colorButtonGroup = new ButtonGroup(); // manages colors
90    ItemHandler itemHandler = new ItemHandler(); // handler for colors
91
92    // create color radio button menu items
93    for ( int count = 0; count < colors.length; count++ )
94    {
95       colorItems[ count ] =
96          new JRadioButtonMenuItem( colors[ count ] ); // create item
97       colorMenu.add( colorItems[ count ] ); // add item to color menu
98       colorButtonGroup.add( colorItems[ count ] ); // add to group
99       colorItems[ count ].addActionListener( itemHandler );
100   } // end for
101
102   colorItems[ 0 ].setSelected( true ); // select first Color item
103
104   formatMenu.add( colorMenu ); // add color menu to format menu
105   formatMenu.addSeparator(); // add separator in menu
106
107   // array listing font names
108   String fontNames[] = { "Serif", "Monospaced", "SansSerif" };
109   JMenu fontMenu = new JMenu( "Font" ); // create font menu
110   fontMenu.setMnemonic( 'n' ); // set mnemonic to n
111
112   // create radio button menu items for font names
113   fonts = new JRadioButtonMenuItem[ fontNames.length ];
114   fontButtonGroup = new ButtonGroup(); // manages font names
115
116   // create Font radio button menu items
117   for ( int count = 0; count < fonts.length; count++ )
118   {
```

Fig. 17.5 | JMenus and mnemonics. (Part 3 of 5.)

```
119        fonts[ count ] = new JRadioButtonMenuItem( fontNames[ count ] );
120        fontMenu.add( fonts[ count ] ); // add font to font menu
121        fontButtonGroup.add( fonts[ count ] ); // add to button group
122        fonts[ count ].addActionListener( itemHandler ); // add handler
123     } // end for
124
125     fonts[ 0 ].setSelected( true ); // select first Font menu item
126     fontMenu.addSeparator(); // add separator bar to font menu
127
128     String styleNames[] = { "Bold", "Italic" }; // names of styles
129     styleItems = new JCheckBoxMenuItem[ styleNames.length ];
130     StyleHandler styleHandler = new StyleHandler(); // style handler
131
132     // create style checkbox menu items
133     for ( int count = 0; count < styleNames.length; count++ )
134     {
135        styleItems[ count ] =
136           new JCheckBoxMenuItem( styleNames[ count ] ); // for style
137        fontMenu.add( styleItems[ count ] ); // add to font menu
138        styleItems[ count ].addItemListener( styleHandler ); // handler
139     } // end for
140
141     formatMenu.add( fontMenu ); // add Font menu to Format menu
142     bar.add( formatMenu ); // add Format menu to menu bar
143
144     // set up label to display text
145     displayJLabel = new JLabel( "Sample Text", SwingConstants.CENTER );
146     displayJLabel.setForeground( colorValues[ 0 ] );
147     displayJLabel.setFont( new Font( "Serif", Font.PLAIN, 72 ) );
148
149     getContentPane().setBackground( Color.CYAN ); // set background
150     add( displayJLabel, BorderLayout.CENTER ); // add displayJLabel
151  } // end MenuFrame constructor
152
153  // inner class to handle action events from menu items
154  private class ItemHandler implements ActionListener
155  {
156     // process color and font selections
157     public void actionPerformed( ActionEvent event )
158     {
159        // process color selection
160        for ( int count = 0; count < colorItems.length; count++ )
161        {
162           if ( colorItems[ count ].isSelected() )
163           {
164              displayJLabel.setForeground( colorValues[ count ] );
165              break;
166           } // end if
167        } // end for
168
169        // process font selection
170        for ( int count = 0; count < fonts.length; count++ )
171        {
```

Fig. 17.5 | JMenus and mnemonics. (Part 4 of 5.)

```
172              if ( event.getSource() == fonts[ count ] )
173              {
174                 displayJLabel.setFont(
175                    new Font( fonts[ count ].getText(), style, 72 ) );
176              } // end if
177           } // end for
178
179           repaint(); // redraw application
180        } // end method actionPerformed
181     } // end class ItemHandler
182
183     // inner class to handle item events from check box menu items
184     private class StyleHandler implements ItemListener
185     {
186        // process font style selections
187        public void itemStateChanged( ItemEvent e )
188        {
189           style = 0; // initialize style
190
191           // check for bold selection
192           if ( styleItems[ 0 ].isSelected() )
193              style += Font.BOLD; // add bold to style
194
195           // check for italic selection
196           if ( styleItems[ 1 ].isSelected() )
197              style += Font.ITALIC; // add italic to style
198
199           displayJLabel.setFont(
200              new Font( displayJLabel.getFont().getName(), style, 72 ) );
201           repaint(); // redraw application
202        } // end method itemStateChanged
203     } // end class StyleHandler
204  } // end class MenuFrame
```

Fig. 17.5 | JMenus and mnemonics. (Part 5 of 5.)

```
1   // Fig. 17.6: MenuTest.java
2   // Testing MenuFrame.
3   import javax.swing.JFrame;
4
5   public class MenuTest
6   {
7      public static void main( String args[] )
8      {
9         MenuFrame menuFrame = new MenuFrame(); // create MenuFrame
10        menuFrame.setDefaultCloseOperation( JFrame.EXIT_ON_CLOSE );
11        menuFrame.setSize( 500, 200 ); // set frame size
12        menuFrame.setVisible( true ); // display frame
13     } // end main
14  } // end class MenuTest
```

Fig. 17.6 | Test class for MenuFrame. (Part 1 of 2.)

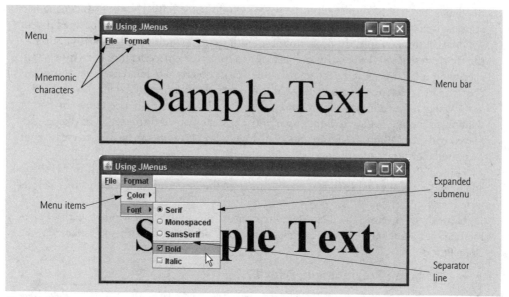

Fig. 17.6 | Test class for MenuFrame. (Part 2 of 2.)

Lines 38–76 set up the **File** menu and attach it to the menu bar. The **File** menu contains an **About...** menu item that displays a message dialog when the menu item is selected and an **Exit** menu item that can be selected to terminate the application.

Line 38 creates a JMenu and passes to the constructor the string "File" as the name of the menu. Line 39 uses JMenu method *setMnemonic* (inherited from class Abstract-Button) to indicate that F is the mnemonic for this menu. Pressing the *Alt* key and the letter *F* opens the menu, just as clicking the menu name with the mouse would. In the GUI, the mnemonic character in the menu's name is displayed with an underline. (See the screen captures in Fig. 17.6.)

Look-and-Feel Observation 17.3
Mnemonics provide quick access to menu commands and button commands through the keyboard.

Look-and-Feel Observation 17.4
Different mnemonics should be used for each button or menu item. Normally, the first letter in the label on the menu item or button is used as the mnemonic. If several buttons or menu items start with the same letter, choose the next most prominent letter in the name (e.g., x is commonly chosen for a button or menu item called Exit).

Lines 42–43 create JMenuItem aboutItem with the text "About..." and set its mnemonic to the letter A. This menu item is added to fileMenu at line 44 with JMenu method *add*. To access the **About...** menu item through the keyboard, press the *Alt* key and letter *F* to open the **File** menu, then press *A* to select the **About...** menu item. Lines 47–56 create an ActionListener to process aboutItem's action event. Lines 52–54 display a message dialog box. In most prior uses of showMessageDialog, the first argument was null. The purpose of the first argument is to specify the *parent window* that helps determine where the dialog box will be displayed. If the parent window is specified as null, the dialog box appears in the center of the screen. Otherwise, it appears centered over the specified parent window. In this example, the program specifies the parent window with MenuTest.this—the this reference of the MenuTest object. When using the this reference in an inner class, specifying this by itself refers to the inner-class object. To reference the outer-class object's this reference, qualify this with the outer-class name and a dot (.).

Dialog boxes are typically modal. A *modal dialog box* does not allow any other window in the application to be accessed until the dialog box is dismissed. The dialogs displayed with class JOptionPane are modal dialogs. Class **JDialog** can be used to create your own modal or nonmodal dialogs.

Lines 59–72 create menu item exitItem, set its mnemonic to x, add it to fileMenu and register an ActionListener that terminates the application when the user selects exitItem.

Lines 74–76 create the JMenuBar, attach it to the application window with JFrame method setJMenuBar and use JMenuBar method **add** to attach the fileMenu to the JMenuBar.

Common Programming Error 17.3

Forgetting to set the menu bar with JFrame method setJMenuBar prevents the menu bar from displaying in the JFrame.

Look-and-Feel Observation 17.5

Menus appear left to right in the order that they are added to a JMenuBar.

Lines 78–79 create menu formatMenu and set its mnemonic to r. (F is not used because that is the **File** menu's mnemonic.)

Lines 84–85 create menu colorMenu (this will be a submenu in the **Format** menu) and set its mnemonic to C. Line 88 creates JRadioButtonMenuItem array colorItems, which refers to the menu items in colorMenu. Line 89 creates ButtonGroup colorGroup, which will ensure that only one of the menu items in the **Color** submenu is selected at a time. Line 90 creates an instance of inner class ItemHandler (declared at lines 154–181) that responds to selections from the **Color** and **Font** submenus (discussed shortly). The for statement at lines 93–100 creates each JRadioButtonMenuItem in array colorItems, adds each menu item to colorMenu and to colorGroup and registers the ActionListener for each menu item.

Line 102 invokes AbstractButton method **setSelected** to select the first element in array colorItems. Line 104 adds colorMenu as a submenu of formatMenu. Line 105 invokes JMenu method **addSeparator** to add a horizontal *separator* line to the menu.

Look-and-Feel Observation 17.6

A submenu is created by adding a menu as a menu item in another menu. When the mouse is positioned over a submenu (or the submenu's mnemonic is pressed), the submenu expands to show its menu items.

Look-and-Feel Observation 17.7

Separators can be added to a menu to group menu items logically.

Look-and-Feel Observation 17.8

Any lightweight GUI component (i.e., a component that is a subclass of JComponent) can be added to a JMenu or to a JMenuBar.

Lines 108–126 create the **Font** submenu and several JRadioButtonMenuItems and select the first element of JRadioButtonMenuItem array fonts. Line 129 creates a JCheckBoxMenuItem array to represent the menu items for specifying bold and italic styles for the fonts. Line 130 creates an instance of inner class StyleHandler (declared at lines 184–203) to respond to the JCheckBoxMenuItem events. The for statement at lines 133–139 creates each JCheckBoxMenuItem, adds each menu item to fontMenu and registers the ItemListener for each menu item. Line 141 adds fontMenu as a submenu of formatMenu. Line 142 adds the formatMenu to bar (the menu bar).

Lines 145–147 create a JLabel for which the **Format** menu items control the font, font color and font style. The initial foreground color is set to the first element of array colorValues (Color.BLACK) by invoking JComponent method ***setForeground***, and the initial font is set to Serif with PLAIN style and 72-point size. Line 149 sets the background color of the window's content pane to cyan, and line 150 attaches the JLabel to the CENTER of the content pane's BorderLayout.

ItemHandler method actionPerformed (lines 157–180) uses two for statements to determine which font or color menu item generated the event and sets the font or color of the JLabel displayLabel, respectively. The if condition at line 162 uses AbstractButton method ***isSelected*** to determine the selected JRadioButtonMenuItem. The if condition at line 172 invokes the event object's getSource method to get a reference to the JRadioButtonMenuItem that generated the event. Line 175 invokes AbstractButton method getText to obtain the name of the font from the menu item.

The program calls StyleHandler method itemStateChanged (lines 187–202) if the user selects a JCheckBoxMenuItem in the fontMenu. Lines 192 and 196 determine whether either or both of the JCheckBoxMenuItems are selected and use their combined state to determine the new style of the font.

17.5 JPopupMenu

Many of today's computer applications provide so-called *context-sensitive pop-up menus*. In Swing, such menus are created with class *JPopupMenu* (a subclass of JComponent). These menus provide options that are specific to the component for which the *pop-up trigger event* was generated. On most systems, the pop-up trigger event occurs when the user presses and releases the right mouse button.

Look-and-Feel Observation 17.9

The pop-up trigger event is platform specific. On most platforms that use a mouse with multiple buttons, the pop-up trigger event occurs when the user clicks the right mouse button on a component that supports a pop-up menu.

The application in Figs. 17.7–17.8 creates a JPopupMenu that allows the user to select one of three colors and change the background color of the window. When the user clicks the right mouse button on the PopupTest window's background, a JPopupMenu containing colors appears. If the user clicks a JRadioButtonMenuItem for a color, ItemHandler method actionPerformed changes the background color of the window's content pane.

```
1   // Fig. 17.7: PopupFrame.java
2   // Demonstrating JPopupMenus.
3   import java.awt.Color;
4   import java.awt.event.MouseAdapter;
5   import java.awt.event.MouseEvent;
6   import java.awt.event.ActionListener;
7   import java.awt.event.ActionEvent;
8   import javax.swing.JFrame;
9   import javax.swing.JRadioButtonMenuItem;
10  import javax.swing.JPopupMenu;
11  import javax.swing.ButtonGroup;
12
13  public class PopupFrame extends JFrame
14  {
15     private JRadioButtonMenuItem items[]; // holds items for colors
16     private final Color colorValues[] =
17        { Color.BLUE, Color.YELLOW, Color.RED }; // colors to be used
18     private JPopupMenu popupMenu; // allows user to select color
19
20     // no-argument constructor sets up GUI
21     public PopupFrame()
22     {
23        super( "Using JPopupMenus" );
24
25        ItemHandler handler = new ItemHandler(); // handler for menu items
26        String colors[] = { "Blue", "Yellow", "Red" }; // array of colors
27
28        ButtonGroup colorGroup = new ButtonGroup(); // manages color items
29        popupMenu = new JPopupMenu(); // create pop-up menu
30        items = new JRadioButtonMenuItem[ 3 ]; // items for selecting color
31
32        // construct menu item, add to popup menu, enable event handling
33        for ( int count = 0; count < items.length; count++ )
34        {
35           items[ count ] = new JRadioButtonMenuItem( colors[ count ] );
36           popupMenu.add( items[ count ] ); // add item to pop-up menu
37           colorGroup.add( items[ count ] ); // add item to button group
38           items[ count ].addActionListener( handler ); // add handler
39        } // end for
40
41        setBackground( Color.WHITE ); // set background to white
42
43        // declare a MouseListener for the window to display pop-up menu
44        addMouseListener(
45
46           new MouseAdapter() // anonymous inner class
47           {
48              // handle mouse press event
49              public void mousePressed( MouseEvent event )
50              {
51                 checkForTriggerEvent( event ); // check for trigger
52              } // end method mousePressed
```

Fig. 17.7 | JPopupMenu for selecting colors. (Part 1 of 2.)

```
53
54        // handle mouse release event
55        public void mouseReleased( MouseEvent event )
56        {
57           checkForTriggerEvent( event ); // check for trigger
58        } // end method mouseReleased
59
60        // determine whether event should trigger popup menu
61        private void checkForTriggerEvent( MouseEvent event )
62        {
63           if ( event.isPopupTrigger() )
64              popupMenu.show(
65                 event.getComponent(), event.getX(), event.getY() );
66        } // end method checkForTriggerEvent
67        } // end anonymous inner class
68        ); // end call to addMouseListener
69     } // end PopupFrame constructor
70
71     // private inner class to handle menu item events
72     private class ItemHandler implements ActionListener
73     {
74        // process menu item selections
75        public void actionPerformed( ActionEvent event )
76        {
77           // determine which menu item was selected
78           for ( int i = 0; i < items.length; i++ )
79           {
80              if ( event.getSource() == items[ i ] )
81              {
82                 getContentPane().setBackground( colorValues[ i ] );
83                 return;
84              } // end if
85           } // end for
86        } // end method actionPerformed
87     } // end private inner class ItemHandler
88  } // end class PopupFrame
```

Fig. 17.7 | JPopupMenu for selecting colors. (Part 2 of 2.)

Line 25 of the PopupFrame constructor (lines 21–69) creates an instance of class Item-Handler (declared in lines 72–87) that will process the item events from the menu items in the pop-up menu. Line 29 creates the JPopupMenu. The for statement (lines 33–39) creates a JRadioButtonMenuItem object (line 35), adds it to popupMenu (line 36), adds it to ButtonGroup colorGroup (line 37) to maintain one selected JRadioButtonMenuItem at a time and registers its ActionListener (line 38). Line 41 sets the initial background to white by invoking method setBackground.

Lines 44–68 register a MouseListener to handle the mouse events of the application window. Methods mousePressed (lines 49–52) and mouseReleased (lines 55–58) check for the pop-up trigger event. Each method calls private utility method checkForTrigger-Event (lines 61–66) to determine whether the pop-up trigger event occurred. If it did, MouseEvent method *isPopupTrigger* returns true, and JPopupMenu method **show** displays the JPopupMenu. The first argument to method show specifies the *origin component*,

```
 1   // Fig. 17.8: PopupTest.java
 2   // Testing PopupFrame.
 3   import javax.swing.JFrame;
 4
 5   public class PopupTest
 6   {
 7      public static void main( String args[] )
 8      {
 9         PopupFrame popupFrame = new PopupFrame(); // create PopupFrame
10         popupFrame.setDefaultCloseOperation( JFrame.EXIT_ON_CLOSE );
11         popupFrame.setSize( 300, 200 ); // set frame size
12         popupFrame.setVisible( true ); // display frame
13      } // end main
14   } // end class PopupTest
```

Fig. 17.8 | Test class for `PopupFrame`.

whose position helps determine where the `JPopupMenu` will appear on the screen. The last two arguments are the *x-y* coordinates (measured from the origin component's upper-left corner) at which the `JPopupMenu` is to appear.

Look-and-Feel Observation 17.10

Displaying a `JPopupMenu` for the pop-up trigger event of multiple GUI components requires registering mouse-event handlers for each of those GUI components.

When the user selects a menu item from the pop-up menu, class `ItemHandler`'s method `actionPerformed` (lines 75–86) determines which `JRadioButtonMenuItem` the user selected and sets the background color of the window's content pane.

17.6 Pluggable Look-and-Feel

A program that uses Java's Abstract Window Toolkit GUI components (package `java.awt`) takes on the look-and-feel of the platform on which the program executes. A Java application running on a Macintosh looks like other applications running on a Macintosh. A Java application running on Microsoft Windows looks like other applications running on Microsoft Windows. A Java application running on a UNIX platform looks like other applications running on that UNIX platform. This is sometimes desirable, because it allows users of the application on each platform to use GUI components with which they are already familiar. However, it also introduces interesting portability issues.

Portability Tip 17.1

GUI components look different on different platforms and may require different amounts of space to display. This could change their layout and alignments.

Portability Tip 17.2

GUI components on different platforms have different default functionality (e.g., some platforms allow a button with the focus to be "pressed" with the space bar, and some do not).

Swing's lightweight GUI components eliminate many of these issues by providing uniform functionality across platforms and by defining a uniform cross-platform look-and-feel (known as the ***metal look-and-feel***). Swing also provides the flexibility to customize the look-and-feel to appear as a Microsoft Windows-style look-and-feel (on Window systems), a Motif-style (UNIX) look-and-feel (across all platforms) or a Macintosh look-and-feel (Mac systems).

The application in Figs. 17.9–17.10 demonstrates how to change the look-and-feel of a Swing GUI. It creates several GUI components, so you can see the change in the look-and-feel of several GUI components at the same time. The first output window shows the standard metal look-and-feel, the second shows the Motif look-and-feel, and the third shows the Windows look-and-feel.

All the GUI components and event handling in this example have been covered before, so we concentrate on the mechanism for changing the look-and-feel. Class ***UIManager*** (package `javax.swing`) contains nested class ***LookAndFeelInfo*** (a public static class) that maintains information about a look-and-feel. Line 22 declares an array of type `UIManager.LookAndFeelInfo` (note the syntax used to identify the inner class `LookAndFeelInfo`). Line 68 uses `UIManager` static method ***getInstalledLookAndFeels*** to get the array of `UIManager.LookAndFeelInfo` objects that describe each look-and-feel available on your system.

Performance Tip 17.2

Each look-and-feel is represented by a Java class. `UIManager` method `getInstalledLookAndFeels` does not load each class. Rather, it provides the names of the available look-and-feel classes so that a choice can be made (presumably once at program start-up). This reduces the overhead of having to load all the look-and-feel classes even if the program will not use some of them.

```
1   // Fig. 17.9: LookAndFeelFrame.java
2   // Changing the look and feel.
3   import java.awt.GridLayout;
4   import java.awt.BorderLayout;
5   import java.awt.event.ItemListener;
6   import java.awt.event.ItemEvent;
7   import javax.swing.JFrame;
8   import javax.swing.UIManager;
9   import javax.swing.JRadioButton;
10  import javax.swing.ButtonGroup;
11  import javax.swing.JButton;
12  import javax.swing.JLabel;
13  import javax.swing.JComboBox;
```

Fig. 17.9 | Look-and-feel of a Swing-based GUI. (Part 1 of 3.)

```
14   import javax.swing.JPanel;
15   import javax.swing.SwingConstants;
16   import javax.swing.SwingUtilities;
17
18   public class LookAndFeelFrame extends JFrame
19   {
20      // string names of look and feels
21      private final String strings[] = { "Metal", "Motif", "Windows" };
22      private UIManager.LookAndFeelInfo looks[]; // look and feels
23      private JRadioButton radio[]; // radio buttons to select look-and-feel
24      private ButtonGroup group; // group for radio buttons
25      private JButton button; // displays look of button
26      private JLabel label; // displays look of label
27      private JComboBox comboBox; // displays look of combo box
28
29      // set up GUI
30      public LookAndFeelFrame()
31      {
32         super( "Look and Feel Demo" );
33
34         JPanel northPanel = new JPanel(); // create north panel
35         northPanel.setLayout( new GridLayout( 3, 1, 0, 5 ) );
36
37         label = new JLabel( "This is a Metal look-and-feel",
38            SwingConstants.CENTER ); // create label
39         northPanel.add( label ); // add label to panel
40
41         button = new JButton( "JButton" ); // create button
42         northPanel.add( button ); // add button to panel
43
44         comboBox = new JComboBox( strings ); // create combobox
45         northPanel.add( comboBox ); // add combobox to panel
46
47         // create array for radio buttons
48         radio = new JRadioButton[ strings.length ];
49
50         JPanel southPanel = new JPanel(); // create south panel
51         southPanel.setLayout( new GridLayout( 1, radio.length ) );
52
53         group = new ButtonGroup(); // button group for looks-and-feels
54         ItemHandler handler = new ItemHandler(); // look-and-feel handler
55
56         for ( int count = 0; count < radio.length; count++ )
57         {
58            radio[ count ] = new JRadioButton( strings[ count ] );
59            radio[ count ].addItemListener( handler ); // add handler
60            group.add( radio[ count ] ); // add radio button to group
61            southPanel.add( radio[ count ] ); // add radio button to panel
62         } // end for
63
64         add( northPanel, BorderLayout.NORTH ); // add north panel
65         add( southPanel, BorderLayout.SOUTH ); // add south panel
66
```

Fig. 17.9 | Look-and-feel of a Swing-based GUI. (Part 2 of 3.)

```
67      // get installed look-and-feel information
68      looks = UIManager.getInstalledLookAndFeels();
69      radio[ 0 ].setSelected( true ); // set default selection
70   } // end LookAndFeelFrame constructor
71
72   // use UIManager to change look-and-feel of GUI
73   private void changeTheLookAndFeel( int value )
74   {
75      try // change look-and-feel
76      {
77         // set look-and-feel for this application
78         UIManager.setLookAndFeel( looks[ value ].getClassName() );
79
80         // update components in this application
81         SwingUtilities.updateComponentTreeUI( this );
82      } // end try
83      catch ( Exception exception )
84      {
85         exception.printStackTrace();
86      } // end catch
87   } // end method changeTheLookAndFeel
88
89   // private inner class to handle radio button events
90   private class ItemHandler implements ItemListener
91   {
92      // process user's look-and-feel selection
93      public void itemStateChanged( ItemEvent event )
94      {
95         for ( int count = 0; count < radio.length; count++ )
96         {
97            if ( radio[ count ].isSelected() )
98            {
99               label.setText( String.format( "This is a %s look-and-feel",
100                  strings[ count ] ) );
101               comboBox.setSelectedIndex( count ); // set combobox index
102               changeTheLookAndFeel( count ); // change look-and-feel
103            } // end if
104         } // end for
105      } // end method itemStateChanged
106   } // end private inner class ItemHandler
107 } // end class LookAndFeelFrame
```

Fig. 17.9 | Look-and-feel of a Swing-based GUI. (Part 3 of 3.)

Our utility method changeTheLookAndFeel (lines 73–87) is called by the event handler for the JRadioButtons at the bottom of the user interface. The event handler (declared in private inner class ItemHandler at lines 90–106) passes an integer representing the element in array looks that should be used to change the look-and-feel. Line 78 invokes static method **setLookAndFeel** of UIManager to change the look-and-feel. Method **get-ClassName** of class UIManager.LookAndFeelInfo determines the name of the look-and-feel class that corresponds to the UIManager.LookAndFeelInfo object. If the look-and-feel class is not already loaded, it will be loaded as part of the call to setLookAndFeel. Line 81 invokes static method **updateComponentTreeUI** of class **SwingUtilities** (package

```
1   // Fig. 17.10: LookAndFeelDemo.java
2   // Changing the look and feel.
3   import javax.swing.JFrame;
4
5   public class LookAndFeelDemo
6   {
7      public static void main( String args[] )
8      {
9         LookAndFeelFrame lookAndFeelFrame = new LookAndFeelFrame();
10        lookAndFeelFrame.setDefaultCloseOperation( JFrame.EXIT_ON_CLOSE );
11        lookAndFeelFrame.setSize( 300, 200 ); // set frame size
12        lookAndFeelFrame.setVisible( true ); // display frame
13     } // end main
14  } // end class LookAndFeelDemo
```

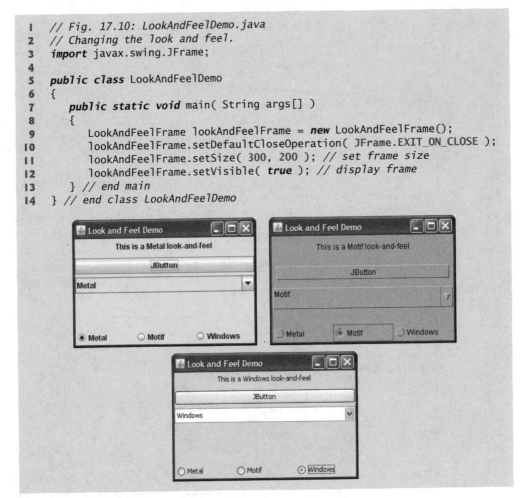

Fig. 17.10 | Test class for LookAndFeelFrame.

javax.swing) to change the look-and-feel of every GUI component attached to its argument (this instance of our application class LookAndFeelDemo) to the new look-and-feel.

17.7 JDesktopPane and JInternalFrame

Many of today's applications use a *multiple-document interface* (*MDI*)—a main window (called the *parent window*) containing other windows (called *child windows*), to manage several open *documents* that are being processed in parallel. For example, many e-mail programs allow you to have several windows open at the same time, so you can compose or read multiple e-mail messages simultaneously. Similarly, many word processors allow the user to open multiple documents in separate windows, making it possible to switch between them without having to close one to open another. The application in Figs. 17.11–17.12 demonstrates Swing's *JDesktopPane* and *JInternalFrame* classes for implementing multiple-document interfaces.

```
 1   // Fig. 17.11: DesktopFrame.java
 2   // Demonstrating JDesktopPane.
 3   import java.awt.BorderLayout;
 4   import java.awt.Dimension;
 5   import java.awt.Graphics;
 6   import java.awt.event.ActionListener;
 7   import java.awt.event.ActionEvent;
 8   import java.util.Random;
 9   import javax.swing.JFrame;
10   import javax.swing.JDesktopPane;
11   import javax.swing.JMenuBar;
12   import javax.swing.JMenu;
13   import javax.swing.JMenuItem;
14   import javax.swing.JInternalFrame;
15   import javax.swing.JPanel;
16   import javax.swing.ImageIcon;
17
18   public class DesktopFrame extends JFrame
19   {
20      private JDesktopPane theDesktop;
21
22      // set up GUI
23      public DesktopFrame()
24      {
25         super( "Using a JDesktopPane" );
26
27         JMenuBar bar = new JMenuBar(); // create menu bar
28         JMenu addMenu = new JMenu( "Add" ); // create Add menu
29         JMenuItem newFrame = new JMenuItem( "Internal Frame" );
30
31         addMenu.add( newFrame ); // add new frame item to Add menu
32         bar.add( addMenu ); // add Add menu to menu bar
33         setJMenuBar( bar ); // set menu bar for this application
34
35         theDesktop = new JDesktopPane(); // create desktop pane
36         add( theDesktop ); // add desktop pane to frame
37
38         // set up listener for newFrame menu item
39         newFrame.addActionListener(
40
41            new ActionListener() // anonymous inner class
42            {
43               // display new internal window
44               public void actionPerformed( ActionEvent event )
45               {
46                  // create internal frame
47                  JInternalFrame frame = new JInternalFrame(
48                     "Internal Frame", true, true, true, true );
49
50                  MyJPanel panel = new MyJPanel(); // create new panel
51                  frame.add( panel, BorderLayout.CENTER ); // add panel
52                  frame.pack(); // set internal frame to size of contents
```

Fig. 17.11 | Multiple-document interface. (Part 1 of 2.)

```
53
54                          theDesktop.add( frame ); // attach internal frame
55                          frame.setVisible( true ); // show internal frame
56                   } // end method actionPerformed
57               } // end anonymous inner class
58           ); // end call to addActionListener
59       } // end DesktopFrame constructor
60   } // end class DesktopFrame
61
62   // class to display an ImageIcon on a panel
63   class MyJPanel extends JPanel
64   {
65       private static Random generator = new Random();
66       private ImageIcon picture; // image to be displayed
67       private String[] images = { "yellowflowers.png", "purpleflowers.png",
68           "redflowers.png", "redflowers2.png", "lavenderflowers.png" };
69
70       // load image
71       public MyJPanel()
72       {
73           int randomNumber = generator.nextInt( 5 );
74           picture = new ImageIcon( images[ randomNumber ] ); // set icon
75       } // end MyJPanel constructor
76
77       // display imageIcon on panel
78       public void paintComponent( Graphics g )
79       {
80           super.paintComponent( g );
81           picture.paintIcon( this, g, 0, 0 ); // display icon
82       } // end method paintComponent
83
84       // return image dimensions
85       public Dimension getPreferredSize()
86       {
87           return new Dimension( picture.getIconWidth(),
88               picture.getIconHeight() );
89       } // end method getPreferredSize
90   } // end class MyJPanel
```

Fig. 17.11 | Multiple-document interface. (Part 2 of 2.)

```
1    // Fig. 17.12: DesktopTest.java
2    // Demonstrating JDesktopPane.
3    import javax.swing.JFrame;
4
5    public class DesktopTest
6    {
7        public static void main( String args[] )
8        {
9            DesktopFrame desktopFrame = new DesktopFrame();
10           desktopFrame.setDefaultCloseOperation( JFrame.EXIT_ON_CLOSE );
```

Fig. 17.12 | Test class for DeskTopFrame. (Part 1 of 2.)

```
11        desktopFrame.setSize( 600, 480 ); // set frame size
12        desktopFrame.setVisible( true ); // display frame
13    } // end main
14 } // end class DesktopTest
```

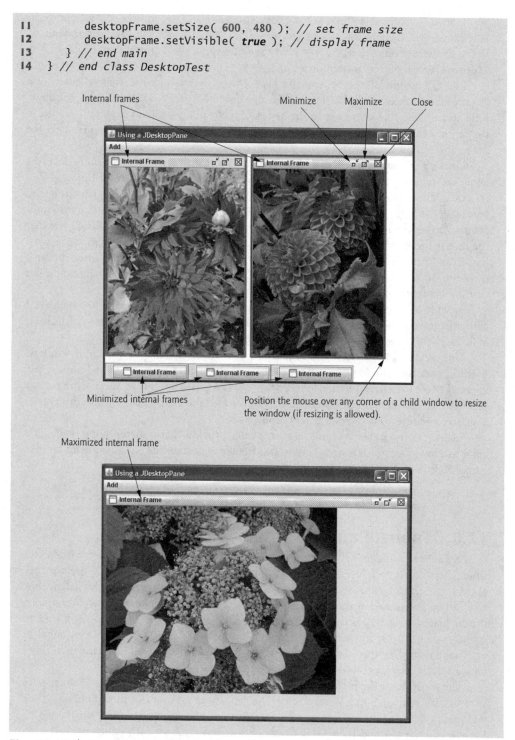

Fig. 17.12 | Test class for DeskTopFrame. (Part 2 of 2.)

Lines 27–33 create a JMenuBar, a JMenu and a JMenuItem, add the JMenuItem to the JMenu, add the JMenu to the JMenuBar and set the JMenuBar for the application window. When the user selects the JMenuItem newFrame, the application creates and displays a new JInternalFrame object containing an image.

Line 35 assigns JDesktopPane (package javax.swing) variable theDesktop a new JDesktopPane object that will be used to manage the JInternalFrame child windows. Line 36 adds the JDesktopPane to the JFrame. By default, the JDesktopPane is added to the center of the content pane's BorderLayout, so the JDesktopPane expands to fill the entire application window.

Lines 39–58 register an ActionListener to handle the event when the user selects the newFrame menu item. When the event occurs, method actionPerformed (lines 44–56) creates a JInternalFrame object in lines 47–48. The JInternalFrame constructor used here takes five arguments—a string for the title bar of the internal window, a boolean indicating whether the internal frame can be resized by the user, a boolean indicating whether the internal frame can be closed by the user, a boolean indicating whether the internal frame can be maximized by the user and a boolean indicating whether the internal frame can be minimized by the user. For each of the boolean arguments, a true value indicates that the operation should be allowed (as is the case here).

As with JFrames and JApplets, a JInternalFrame has a content pane to which GUI components can be attached. Line 50 creates an instance of our class MyJPanel (declared at lines 63–90) that is added to the JInternalFrame at line 51.

Line 52 uses JInternalFrame method *pack* to set the size of the child window. Method pack uses the preferred sizes of the components to determine the window's size. Class MyJPanel declares method *getPreferredSize* (lines 85–89) to specify the panel's preferred size for use by the pack method. Line 54 adds the JInternalFrame to the JDesktopPane, and line 55 displays the JInternalFrame.

Classes JInternalFrame and JDesktopPane provide many methods for managing child windows. See the JInternalFrame and JDesktopPane online API documentation for complete lists of these methods:

```
java.sun.com/javase/6/docs/api/javax/swing/JInternalFrame.html
java.sun.com/javase/6/docs/api/javax/swing/JDesktopPane.html
```

17.8 JTabbedPane

A *JTabbedPane* arranges GUI components into layers, of which only one is visible at a time. Users access each layer via a tab—similar to folders in a file cabinet. When the user clicks a tab, the appropriate layer is displayed. The tabs appear at the top by default but also can be positioned at the left, right or bottom of the JTabbedPane. Any component can be placed on a tab. If the component is a container, such as a panel, it can use any layout manager to lay out several components on the tab. Class JTabbedPane is a subclass of JComponent. The application in Figs. 17.13–17.14 creates one tabbed pane with three tabs. Each tab displays one of the JPanels—panel1, panel2 or panel3.

The constructor (lines 15–46) builds the GUI. Line 19 creates an empty JTabbedPane with default settings—that is, tabs across the top. If the tabs do not fit on one line, they will wrap to form additional lines of tabs. Next the constructor creates the JPanels panel1, panel2 and panel3 and their GUI components. As we set up each panel, we add it to tabbedPane, using JTabbedPane method *addTab* with four arguments. The first argument

```
1   // Fig. 17.13: JTabbedPaneFrame.java
2   // Demonstrating JTabbedPane.
3   import java.awt.BorderLayout;
4   import java.awt.Color;
5   import javax.swing.JFrame;
6   import javax.swing.JTabbedPane;
7   import javax.swing.JLabel;
8   import javax.swing.JPanel;
9   import javax.swing.JButton;
10  import javax.swing.SwingConstants;
11
12  public class JTabbedPaneFrame extends JFrame
13  {
14     // set up GUI
15     public JTabbedPaneFrame()
16     {
17        super( "JTabbedPane Demo " );
18
19        JTabbedPane tabbedPane = new JTabbedPane(); // create JTabbedPane
20
21        // set up panel1 and add it to JTabbedPane
22        JLabel label1 = new JLabel( "panel one", SwingConstants.CENTER );
23        JPanel panel1 = new JPanel(); // create first panel
24        panel1.add( label1 ); // add label to panel
25        tabbedPane.addTab( "Tab One", null, panel1, "First Panel" );
26
27        // set up panel2 and add it to JTabbedPane
28        JLabel label2 = new JLabel( "panel two", SwingConstants.CENTER );
29        JPanel panel2 = new JPanel(); // create second panel
30        panel2.setBackground( Color.YELLOW ); // set background to yellow
31        panel2.add( label2 ); // add label to panel
32        tabbedPane.addTab( "Tab Two", null, panel2, "Second Panel" );
33
34        // set up panel3 and add it to JTabbedPane
35        JLabel label3 = new JLabel( "panel three" );
36        JPanel panel3 = new JPanel(); // create third panel
37        panel3.setLayout( new BorderLayout() ); // use borderlayout
38        panel3.add( new JButton( "North" ), BorderLayout.NORTH );
39        panel3.add( new JButton( "West" ), BorderLayout.WEST );
40        panel3.add( new JButton( "East" ), BorderLayout.EAST );
41        panel3.add( new JButton( "South" ), BorderLayout.SOUTH );
42        panel3.add( label3, BorderLayout.CENTER );
43        tabbedPane.addTab( "Tab Three", null, panel3, "Third Panel" );
44
45        add( tabbedPane ); // add JTabbedPane to frame
46     } // end JTabbedPaneFrame constructor
47  } // end class JTabbedPaneFrame
```

Fig. 17.13 | JTabbedPane used to organize GUI components.

is a string that specifies the title of the tab. The second argument is an Icon reference that specifies an icon to display on the tab. If the Icon is a null reference, no image is displayed. The third argument is a Component reference that represents the GUI component to display when the user clicks the tab. The last argument is a string that specifies the tool tip

```
 1   // Fig. 17.14: JTabbedPaneDemo.java
 2   // Demonstrating JTabbedPane.
 3   import javax.swing.JFrame;
 4
 5   public class JTabbedPaneDemo
 6   {
 7      public static void main( String args[] )
 8      {
 9         JTabbedPaneFrame tabbedPaneFrame = new JTabbedPaneFrame();
10         tabbedPaneFrame.setDefaultCloseOperation( JFrame.EXIT_ON_CLOSE );
11         tabbedPaneFrame.setSize( 250, 200 ); // set frame size
12         tabbedPaneFrame.setVisible( true ); // display frame
13      } // end main
14   } // end class JTabbedPaneDemo
```

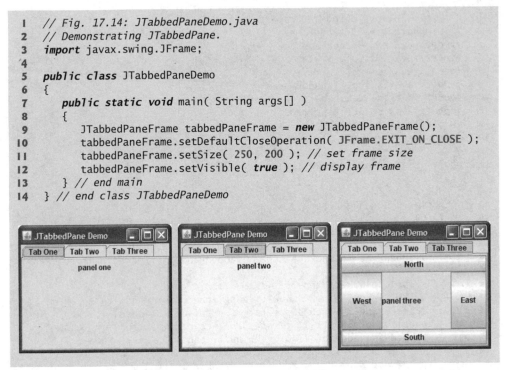

Fig. 17.14 | Test class for JTabbedPaneFrame.

for the tab. For example, line 25 adds JPanel panel1 to tabbedPane with title "Tab One" and the tool tip "First Panel". JPanels panel2 and panel3 are added to tabbedPane at lines 32 and 43. To view a tab, click it with the mouse or use the arrow keys to cycle through the tabs.

17.9 Layout Managers: BoxLayout and GridBagLayout

In Chapter 11, we introduced three layout managers—FlowLayout, BorderLayout and GridLayout. This section presents two additional layout managers (summarized in Fig. 17.15). We discuss these layout managers in the examples that follow.

Layout manager	Description
BoxLayout	A layout manager that allows GUI components to be arranged left-to-right or top-to-bottom in a container. Class Box declares a container with BoxLayout as its default layout manager and provides static methods to create a Box with a horizontal or vertical BoxLayout.
GridBagLayout	A layout manager similar to GridLayout, but unlike it in that components can vary in size and can be added in any order.

Fig. 17.15 | Additional layout managers.

BoxLayout *Layout Manager*

The BoxLayout layout manager (in package javax.swing) arranges GUI components horizontally along a container's *x*-axis or vertically along its *y*-axis. The application in Figs. 17.16–17.17 demonstrates BoxLayout and the container class Box that uses BoxLayout as its default layout manager.

```java
 1   // Fig. 17.16: BoxLayoutFrame.java
 2   // Demonstrating BoxLayout.
 3   import java.awt.Dimension;
 4   import javax.swing.JFrame;
 5   import javax.swing.Box;
 6   import javax.swing.JButton;
 7   import javax.swing.BoxLayout;
 8   import javax.swing.JPanel;
 9   import javax.swing.JTabbedPane;
10
11   public class BoxLayoutFrame extends JFrame
12   {
13      // set up GUI
14      public BoxLayoutFrame()
15      {
16         super( "Demonstrating BoxLayout" );
17
18         // create Box containers with BoxLayout
19         Box horizontal1 = Box.createHorizontalBox();
20         Box vertical1 = Box.createVerticalBox();
21         Box horizontal2 = Box.createHorizontalBox();
22         Box vertical2 = Box.createVerticalBox();
23
24         final int SIZE = 3; // number of buttons on each Box
25
26         // add buttons to Box horizontal1
27         for ( int count = 0; count < SIZE; count++ )
28            horizontal1.add( new JButton( "Button " + count ) );
29
30         // create strut and add buttons to Box vertical1
31         for ( int count = 0; count < SIZE; count++ )
32         {
33            vertical1.add( Box.createVerticalStrut( 25 ) );
34            vertical1.add( new JButton( "Button " + count ) );
35         } // end for
36
37         // create horizontal glue and add buttons to Box horizontal2
38         for ( int count = 0; count < SIZE; count++ )
39         {
40            horizontal2.add( Box.createHorizontalGlue() );
41            horizontal2.add( new JButton( "Button " + count ) );
42         } // end for
43
44         // create rigid area and add buttons to Box vertical2
45         for ( int count = 0; count < SIZE; count++ )
46         {
```

Fig. 17.16 | BoxLayout layout manager. (Part 1 of 2.)

```
47          vertical2.add( Box.createRigidArea( new Dimension( 12, 8 ) ) );
48          vertical2.add( new JButton( "Button " + count ) );
49       } // end for
50
51       // create vertical glue and add buttons to panel
52       JPanel panel = new JPanel();
53       panel.setLayout( new BoxLayout( panel, BoxLayout.Y_AXIS ) );
54
55       for ( int count = 0; count < SIZE; count++ )
56       {
57          panel.add( Box.createGlue() );
58          panel.add( new JButton( "Button " + count ) );
59       } // end for
60
61       // create a JTabbedPane
62       JTabbedPane tabs = new JTabbedPane(
63          JTabbedPane.TOP, JTabbedPane.SCROLL_TAB_LAYOUT );
64
65       // place each container on tabbed pane
66       tabs.addTab( "Horizontal Box", horizontal1 );
67       tabs.addTab( "Vertical Box with Struts", vertical1 );
68       tabs.addTab( "Horizontal Box with Glue", horizontal2 );
69       tabs.addTab( "Vertical Box with Rigid Areas", vertical2 );
70       tabs.addTab( "Vertical Box with Glue", panel );
71
72       add( tabs ); // place tabbed pane on frame
73    } // end BoxLayoutFrame constructor
74 } // end class BoxLayoutFrame
```

Fig. 17.16 | BoxLayout layout manager. (Part 2 of 2.)

Lines 19–22 create Box containers. References horizontal1 and horizontal2 are initialized with static Box method createHorizontalBox, which returns a Box container with a horizontal BoxLayout in which GUI components are arranged left-to-right. Variables vertical1 and vertical2 are initialized with static Box method *createVerticalBox*, which returns references to Box containers with a vertical BoxLayout in which GUI components are arranged top-to-bottom.

The for statement at lines 27–28 adds three JButtons to horizontal1. The for statement at lines 31–35 adds three JButtons to vertical1. Before adding each button, line 33 adds a *vertical strut* to the container with static Box method *createVerticalStrut*. A vertical strut is an invisible GUI component that has a fixed pixel height and is used to guarantee a fixed amount of space between GUI components. The int argument to method createVerticalStrut determines the height of the strut in pixels. When the container is resized, the distance between GUI components separated by struts does not change. Class Box also declares method *createHorizontalStrut* for horizontal BoxLayouts.

The for statement at lines 38–42 adds three JButtons to horizontal2. Before adding each button, line 40 adds *horizontal glue* to the container with static Box method *createHorizontalGlue*. Horizontal glue is an invisible GUI component that can be used between fixed-size GUI components to occupy additional space. Normally, extra space appears to the right of the last horizontal GUI component or below the last vertical one in

```
 1    // Fig. 17.17: BoxLayoutDemo.java
 2    // Demonstrating BoxLayout.
 3    import javax.swing.JFrame;
 4
 5    public class BoxLayoutDemo
 6    {
 7       public static void main( String args[] )
 8       {
 9          BoxLayoutFrame boxLayoutFrame = new BoxLayoutFrame();
10          boxLayoutFrame.setDefaultCloseOperation( JFrame.EXIT_ON_CLOSE );
11          boxLayoutFrame.setSize( 400, 220 ); // set frame size
12          boxLayoutFrame.setVisible( true ); // display frame
13       } // end main
14    } // end class BoxLayoutDemo
```

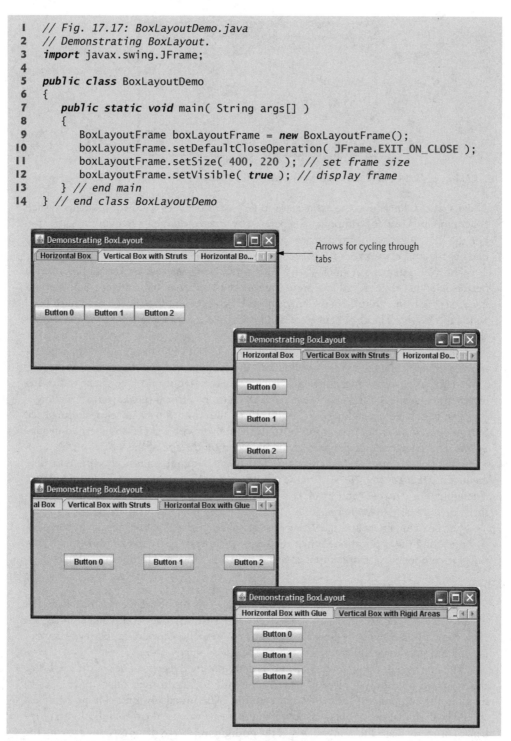

Fig. 17.17 | Test class for BoxLayoutFrame. (Part 1 of 2.)

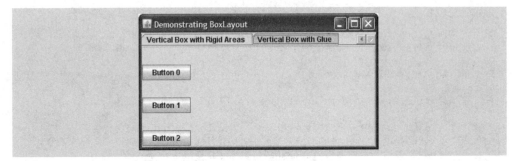

Fig. 17.17 | Test class for BoxLayoutFrame. (Part 2 of 2.)

a BoxLayout. Glue allows the extra space to be placed between GUI components. When the container is resized, components separated by glue components remain the same size, but the glue stretches or contracts to occupy the space between them. Class Box also declares method **createVerticalGlue** for vertical BoxLayouts.

The for statement at lines 45–49 adds three JButtons to vertical2. Before each button is added, line 47 adds a *rigid area* to the container with static Box method **createRigidArea**. A rigid area is an invisible GUI component that always has a fixed pixel width and height. The argument to method createRigidArea is a Dimension object that specifies the area's width and height.

Lines 52–53 create a JPanel object and set its layout to a BoxLayout in the conventional manner, using Container method setLayout. The BoxLayout constructor receives a reference to the container for which it controls the layout and a constant indicating whether the layout is horizontal (**BoxLayout.X_AXIS**) or vertical (**BoxLayout.Y_AXIS**).

The for statement at lines 55–59 adds three JButtons to panel. Before adding each button, line 57 adds a glue component to the container with static Box method **createGlue**. This component expands or contracts based on the size of the Box.

Lines 62–63 create a JTabbedPane to display the five containers in this program. The argument **JTabbedPane.TOP** sent to the constructor indicates that the tabs should appear The argument **JTabbedPane.SCROLL_TAB_LAYOUT** specifies that the tabs should scroll if there are too many to fit on one line.

The Box containers and the JPanel are attached to the JTabbedPane at lines 66–70. Try executing the application. When the window appears, resize the window to see how the glue components, strut components and rigid area affect the layout on each tab.

GridBagLayout Layout Manager

One of the most powerful predefined layout managers is **GridBagLayout** (in package java.awt). This layout is similar to GridLayout in that it arranges components in a grid. However, GridBagLayout is more flexible. The components can vary in size (i.e., they can occupy multiple rows and columns) and can be added in any order.

The first step in using GridBagLayout is determining the appearance of the GUI. For this step you need only a piece of paper. Draw the GUI and then draw a grid over it, dividing the components into rows and columns. The initial row and column numbers should be 0, so that the GridBagLayout layout manager can use the row and column numbers to properly place the components in the grid. Figure 17.18 demonstrates drawing the lines for the rows and columns over a GUI.

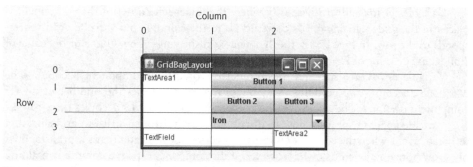

Fig. 17.18 | Designing a GUI that will use GridBagLayout.

A *GridBagConstraints* object describes how a component is placed in a Grid-BagLayout. Several GridBagConstraints fields are summarized in Fig. 17.19.

GridBagConstraints field *anchor* specifies the relative position of the component in an area that it does not fill. The variable anchor is assigned one of the following GridBag-Constraints constants: *NORTH, NORTHEAST, EAST, SOUTHEAST, SOUTH, SOUTHWEST, WEST, NORTHWEST* or *CENTER*. The default value is CENTER.

GridBagConstraints field fill defines how the component grows if the area in which it can be displayed is larger than the component. The variable fill is assigned one of the following GridBagConstraints constants: *NONE, VERTICAL, HORIZONTAL* or *BOTH*. The default value is NONE, which indicates that the component will not grow in either direction. VERTICAL indicates that it will grow vertically. HORIZONTAL indicates that it will grow horizontally. BOTH indicates that it will grow in both directions.

GridBagConstraints field	Description
anchor	Specifies the relative position (NORTH, NORTHEAST, EAST, SOUTHEAST, SOUTH, SOUTHWEST, WEST, NORTHWEST, CENTER) of the component in an area that it does not fill.
fill	Resizes the component in specified direction (NONE, HORIZONTAL, VERTICAL, BOTH) when the display area is larger than the component.
gridx	The column in which the component will be placed.
gridy	The row in which the component will be placed.
gridwidth	The number of columns the component occupies.
gridheight	The number of rows the component occupies.
weightx	The amount of extra space to allocate horizontally. The grid slot can become wider when extra space is available.
weighty	The amount of extra space to allocate vertically. The grid slot can become taller when extra space is available.

Fig. 17.19 | GridBagConstraints fields.

Variables *gridx* and *gridy* specify where the upper-left corner of the component is placed in the grid. Variable gridx corresponds to the column, and variable gridy corresponds to the row. In Fig. 17.18, the JComboBox (displaying "Iron") has a gridx value of 1 and a gridy value of 2.

Variable *gridwidth* specifies the number of columns a component occupies. The JComboBox occupies two columns. Variable *gridheight* specifies the number of rows a component occupies. The JTextArea on the left side of Fig. 17.18 occupies three rows.

Variable *weightx* specifies how to distribute extra horizontal space to grid slots in a GridBagLayout when the container is resized. A zero value indicates that the grid slot does not grow horizontally on its own. However, if the component spans a column containing a component with nonzero weightx value, the component with zero weightx value will grow horizontally in the same proportion as the other component(s) in the same column. This is because each component must be maintained in the same row and column in which it was originally placed.

Variable *weighty* specifies how to distribute extra vertical space to grid slots in a GridBagLayout when the container is resized. A zero value indicates that the grid slot does not grow vertically on its own. However, if the component spans a row containing a component with nonzero weighty value, the component with zero weighty value grows vertically in the same proportion as the other component(s) in the same row.

In Fig. 17.18, the effects of weighty and weightx cannot easily be seen until the container is resized and additional space becomes available. Components with larger weight values occupy more of the additional space than those with smaller weight values.

Components should be given nonzero positive weight values—otherwise they will "huddle" together in the middle of the container. Figure 17.20 shows the GUI of Fig. 17.18 with all weights set to zero.

The application in Figs. 17.21–17.22 uses the GridBagLayout layout manager to arrange the components of the GUI in Fig. 17.18. The application does nothing except demonstrate how to use GridBagLayout.

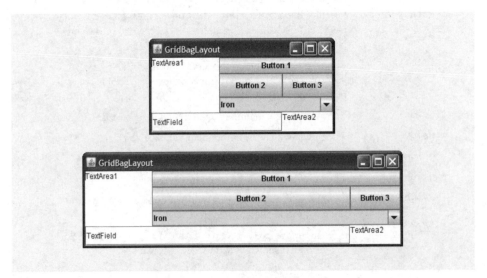

Fig. 17.20 | GridBagLayout with the weights set to zero.

```java
 1   // Fig. 17.21: GridBagFrame.java
 2   // Demonstrating GridBagLayout.
 3   import java.awt.GridBagLayout;
 4   import java.awt.GridBagConstraints;
 5   import java.awt.Component;
 6   import javax.swing.JFrame;
 7   import javax.swing.JTextArea;
 8   import javax.swing.JTextField;
 9   import javax.swing.JButton;
10   import javax.swing.JComboBox;
11
12   public class GridBagFrame extends JFrame
13   {
14      private GridBagLayout layout; // layout of this frame
15      private GridBagConstraints constraints; // constraints of this layout
16
17      // set up GUI
18      public GridBagFrame()
19      {
20         super( "GridBagLayout" );
21         layout = new GridBagLayout();
22         setLayout( layout ); // set frame layout
23         constraints = new GridBagConstraints(); // instantiate constraints
24
25         // create GUI components
26         JTextArea textArea1 = new JTextArea( "TextArea1", 5, 10 );
27         JTextArea textArea2 = new JTextArea( "TextArea2", 2, 2 );
28
29         String names[] = { "Iron", "Steel", "Brass" };
30         JComboBox comboBox = new JComboBox( names );
31
32         JTextField textField = new JTextField( "TextField" );
33         JButton button1 = new JButton( "Button 1" );
34         JButton button2 = new JButton( "Button 2" );
35         JButton button3 = new JButton( "Button 3" );
36
37         // weightx and weighty for textArea1 are both 0: the default
38         // anchor for all components is CENTER: the default
39         constraints.fill = GridBagConstraints.BOTH;
40         addComponent( textArea1, 0, 0, 1, 3 );
41
42         // weightx and weighty for button1 are both 0: the default
43         constraints.fill = GridBagConstraints.HORIZONTAL;
44         addComponent( button1, 0, 1, 2, 1 );
45
46         // weightx and weighty for comboBox are both 0: the default
47         // fill is HORIZONTAL
48         addComponent( comboBox, 2, 1, 2, 1 );
49
50         // button2
51         constraints.weightx = 1000;  // can grow wider
52         constraints.weighty = 1;     // can grow taller
```

Fig. 17.21 | GridBagLayout layout manager. (Part 1 of 2.)

```
53        constraints.fill = GridBagConstraints.BOTH;
54        addComponent( button2, 1, 1, 1, 1 );
55
56        // fill is BOTH for button3
57        constraints.weightx = 0;
58        constraints.weighty = 0;
59        addComponent( button3, 1, 2, 1, 1 );
60
61        // weightx and weighty for textField are both 0, fill is BOTH
62        addComponent( textField, 3, 0, 2, 1 );
63
64        // weightx and weighty for textArea2 are both 0, fill is BOTH
65        addComponent( textArea2, 3, 2, 1, 1 );
66     } // end GridBagFrame constructor
67
68     // method to set constraints on
69     private void addComponent( Component component,
70        int row, int column, int width, int height )
71     {
72        constraints.gridx = column; // set gridx
73        constraints.gridy = row; // set gridy
74        constraints.gridwidth = width; // set gridwidth
75        constraints.gridheight = height; // set gridheight
76        layout.setConstraints( component, constraints ); // set constraints
77        add( component ); // add component
78     } // end method addComponent
79  } // end class GridBagFrame
```

Fig. 17.21 | GridBagLayout layout manager. (Part 2 of 2.)

The GUI consists of three JButtons, two JTextAreas, a JComboBox and a JTextField. The layout manager for the content pane is GridBagLayout. Lines 21–22 create the Grid-BagLayout object and set the layout manager for the JFrame to layout. Line 23 creates the GridBagConstraints object used to determine the location and size of each component in the grid. Lines 26–35 create each GUI component that will be added to the content pane.

Lines 39–40 configure JTextArea textArea1 and add it to the content pane. The values for weightx and weighty values are not specified in constraints, so each has the value zero by default. Thus, the JTextArea will not resize itself even if space is available. However, it spans multiple rows, so the vertical size is subject to the weighty values of JButtons button2 and button3. When either button is resized vertically based on its weighty value, the JTextArea is also resized.

Line 39 sets variable fill in constraints to GridBagConstraints.BOTH, causing the JTextArea to always fill its entire allocated area in the grid. An anchor value is not specified in constraints, so the default CENTER is used. We do not use variable anchor in this application, so all the components will use the default. Line 40 calls our utility method addComponent (declared at lines 69–78). The JTextArea object, the row, the column, the number of columns to span and the number of rows to span are passed as arguments.

JButton button1 is the next component added (lines 43–44). By default, the weightx and weighty values are still zero. The fill variable is set to HORIZONTAL—the component will always fill its area in the horizontal direction. The vertical direction is not filled. The

```
 1    // Fig. 17.22: GridBagDemo.java
 2    // Demonstrating GridBagLayout.
 3    import javax.swing.JFrame;
 4
 5    public class GridBagDemo
 6    {
 7       public static void main( String args[] )
 8       {
 9          GridBagFrame gridBagFrame = new GridBagFrame();
10          gridBagFrame.setDefaultCloseOperation( JFrame.EXIT_ON_CLOSE );
11          gridBagFrame.setSize( 300, 150 ); // set frame size
12          gridBagFrame.setVisible( true ); // display frame
13       } // end main
14    } // end class GridBagDemo
```

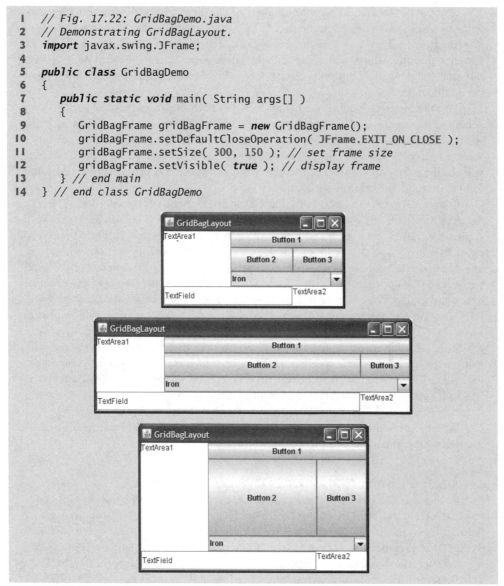

Fig. 17.22 | Test class for GridBagFrame.

weighty value is zero, so the button will become taller only if another component in the same row has a nonzero weighty value. JButton button1 is located at row 0, column 1. One row and two columns are occupied.

JComboBox comboBox is the next component added (line 48). By default, the weightx and weighty values are zero, and the fill variable is set to HORIZONTAL. The JComboBox button will grow only in the horizontal direction. Note that the weightx, weighty and fill variables retain the values set in constraints until they are changed. The JComboBox button is placed at row 2, column 1. One row and two columns are occupied.

JButton button2 is the next component added (lines 51–54). It is given a weightx value of 1000 and a weighty value of 1. The area occupied by the button is capable of growing in the vertical and horizontal directions. The fill variable is set to BOTH, which specifies that the button will always fill the entire area. When the window is resized, button2 will grow. The button is placed at row 1, column 1. One row and one column are occupied.

JButton button3 is added next (lines 57–59). Both the weightx value and weighty value are set to zero, and the value of fill is BOTH. JButton button3 will grow if the window is resized—it is affected by the weight values of button2. Note that the weightx value for button2 is much larger than that for button3. When resizing occurs, button2 will occupy a larger percentage of the new space. The button is placed at row 1, column 2. One row and one column are occupied.

Both the JTextField textField (line 62) and JTextArea textArea2 (line 65) have a weightx value of 0 and a weighty value of 0. The value of fill is BOTH. The JTextField is placed at row 3, column 0, and the JTextArea at row 3, column 2. The JTextField occupies one row and two columns, the JTextArea one row and one column.

Method addComponent's parameters are a Component reference component and integers row, column, width and height. Lines 72–73 set the GridBagConstraints variables gridx and gridy. The gridx variable is assigned the column in which the Component will be placed, and the gridy value is assigned the row in which the Component will be placed. Lines 74–75 set the GridBagConstraints variables gridwidth and gridheight. The gridwidth variable specifies the number of columns the Component will span in the grid, and the gridheight variable specifies the number of rows the Component will span in the grid. Line 76 sets the GridBagConstraints for a component in the GridBagLayout. Method **setConstraints** of class GridBagLayout takes a Component argument and a GridBagConstraints argument. Line 77 adds the component to the JFrame.

When you execute this application, try resizing the window to see how the constraints for each GUI component affect its position and size in the window.

GridBagConstraints *Constants* RELATIVE *and* REMAINDER

Instead of gridx and gridy, a variation of GridBagLayout uses GridBagConstraints constants **RELATIVE** and **REMAINDER**. RELATIVE specifies that the next-to-last component in a particular row should be placed to the right of the previous component in the row. REMAINDER specifies that a component is the last component in a row. Any component that is not the second-to-last or last component on a row must specify values for GridbagConstraints variables gridwidth and gridheight. The application in Figs. 17.23–17.24 arranges components in GridBagLayout, using these constants.

Lines 21–22 create a GridBagLayout and use it to set the JFrame's layout manager. The components that are placed in GridBagLayout are created in lines 27–38—they are a JComboBox, a JTextField, a JList and five JButtons.

The JTextField is added first (lines 41–45). The weightx and weighty values are set to 1. The fill variable is set to BOTH. Line 44 specifies that the JTextField is the last component on the line. The JTextField is added to the content pane with a call to our utility method addComponent (declared at lines 79–83). Method addComponent takes a Component argument and uses GridBagLayout method setConstraints to set the constraints for the Component. Method add attaches the component to the content pane.

```java
 1   // Fig. 17.23: GridBagFrame2.java
 2   // Demonstrating GridBagLayout constants.
 3   import java.awt.GridBagLayout;
 4   import java.awt.GridBagConstraints;
 5   import java.awt.Component;
 6   import javax.swing.JFrame;
 7   import javax.swing.JComboBox;
 8   import javax.swing.JTextField;
 9   import javax.swing.JList;
10   import javax.swing.JButton;
11
12   public class GridBagFrame2 extends JFrame
13   {
14      private GridBagLayout layout; // layout of this frame
15      private GridBagConstraints constraints; // constraints of this layout
16
17      // set up GUI
18      public GridBagFrame2()
19      {
20         super( "GridBagLayout" );
21         layout = new GridBagLayout();
22         setLayout( layout ); // set frame layout
23         constraints = new GridBagConstraints(); // instantiate constraints
24
25         // create GUI components
26         String metals[] = { "Copper", "Aluminum", "Silver" };
27         JComboBox comboBox = new JComboBox( metals );
28
29         JTextField textField = new JTextField( "TextField" );
30
31         String fonts[] = { "Serif", "Monospaced" };T
32         JList list = new JList( fonts );
33
34         String names[] = { "zero", "one", "two", "three", "four" };
35         JButton buttons[] = new JButton[ names.length ];
36
37         for ( int count = 0; count < buttons.length; count++ )
38            buttons[ count ] = new JButton( names[ count ] );
39
40         // define GUI component constraints for textField
41         constraints.weightx = 1;
42         constraints.weighty = 1;
43         constraints.fill = GridBagConstraints.BOTH;
44         constraints.gridwidth = GridBagConstraints.REMAINDER;
45         addComponent( textField );
46
47         // buttons[0] -- weightx and weighty are 1: fill is BOTH
48         constraints.gridwidth = 1;
49         addComponent( buttons[ 0 ] );
50
51         // buttons[1] -- weightx and weighty are 1: fill is BOTH
52         constraints.gridwidth = GridBagConstraints.RELATIVE;
53         addComponent( buttons[ 1 ] );
```

Fig. 17.23 | GridBagConstraints constants RELATIVE and REMAINDER. (Part 1 of 2.)

```
54
55          // buttons[2] -- weightx and weighty are 1: fill is BOTH
56          constraints.gridwidth = GridBagConstraints.REMAINDER;
57          addComponent( buttons[ 2 ] );
58
59          // comboBox -- weightx is 1: fill is BOTH
60          constraints.weighty = 0;
61          constraints.gridwidth = GridBagConstraints.REMAINDER;
62          addComponent( comboBox );
63
64          // buttons[3] -- weightx is 1: fill is BOTH
65          constraints.weighty = 1;
66          constraints.gridwidth = GridBagConstraints.REMAINDER;
67          addComponent( buttons[ 3 ] );
68
69          // buttons[4] -- weightx and weighty are 1: fill is BOTH
70          constraints.gridwidth = GridBagConstraints.RELATIVE;
71          addComponent( buttons[ 4 ] );
72
73          // list -- weightx and weighty are 1: fill is BOTH
74          constraints.gridwidth = GridBagConstraints.REMAINDER;
75          addComponent( list );
76       } // end GridBagFrame2 constructor
77
78       // add a component to the container
79       private void addComponent( Component component )
80       {
81          layout.setConstraints( component, constraints );
82          add( component ); // add component
83       } // end method addComponent
84    } // end class GridBagFrame2
```

Fig. 17.23 | GridBagConstraints constants RELATIVE and REMAINDER. (Part 2 of 2.)

JButton buttons[0] (lines 48–49) has weightx and weighty values of 1. The fill variable is BOTH. Because buttons[0] is not one of the last two components on the row, it is given a gridwidth of 1 and so will occupy one column. The JButton is added to the content pane with a call to utility method addComponent.

JButton buttons[1] (lines 52–53) has weightx and weighty values of 1. The fill variable is BOTH. Line 52 specifies that the JButton is to be placed relative to the previous component. The Button is added to the JFrame with a call to addComponent.

JButton buttons[2] (lines 56–57) has weightx and weighty values of 1. The fill variable is BOTH. This JButton is the last component on the line, so REMAINDER is used. The JButton is added to the content pane with a call to addComponent.

The JComboBox (lines 60–62) has a weightx of 1 and a weighty of 0. The JComboBox will not grow in the vertical direction. The JComboBox is the only component on the line, so REMAINDER is used. The JComboBox is added to the content pane with a call to addComponent.

JButton buttons[3] (lines 65–67) has weightx and weighty values of 1. The fill variable is BOTH. This JButton is the only component on the line, so REMAINDER is used. The JButton is added to the content pane with a call to addComponent.

```
 1   // Fig. 17.24: GridBagDemo2.java
 2   // Demonstrating GridBagLayout constants.
 3   import javax.swing.JFrame;
 4
 5   public class GridBagDemo2
 6   {
 7      public static void main( String args[] )
 8      {
 9         GridBagFrame2 gridBagFrame = new GridBagFrame2();
10         gridBagFrame.setDefaultCloseOperation( JFrame.EXIT_ON_CLOSE );
11         gridBagFrame.setSize( 300, 200 ); // set frame size
12         gridBagFrame.setVisible( true ); // display frame
13      } // end main
14   } // end class GridBagDemo2
```

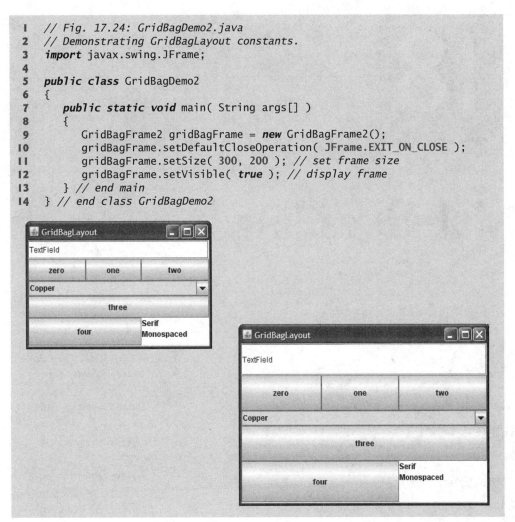

Fig. 17.24 | Test class for GridBagDemo2.

JButton buttons[4] (lines 70–71) has weightx and weighty values of 1. The fill variable is BOTH. This JButton is the next-to-last component on the line, so RELATIVE is used. The JButton is added to the content pane with a call to addComponent.

The JList (lines 74–75) has weightx and weighty values of 1. The fill variable is BOTH. The JList is added to the content pane with a call to addComponent.

17.10 Wrap-Up

This chapter completes our introduction to GUI. In this chapter, you learned about more advanced GUI topics, such as menus, sliders, pop-up menus and the multiple-document interface. All these components can be added to existing applications to make them easier to use and understand. In the next chapter, you'll learn about multithreading, a powerful capability that allows applications to use threads to perform multiple tasks at once.

18

Multithreading

OBJECTIVES

In this chapter you'll learn:

- What threads are and why they are useful.
- How threads enable you to manage concurrent activities.
- The life cycle of a thread.
- Thread priorities and scheduling.
- To create and execute `Runnable`s.
- Thread synchronization.
- What producer/consumer relationships are and how they are implemented with multithreading.
- To enable multiple threads to update Swing GUI components in a thread-safe manner.
- About interfaces `Callable` and `Future`, which you can use with threading to execute tasks that return results.

The most general definition of beauty…Multeity in Unity.
—Samuel Taylor Coleridge

Do not block the way of inquiry.
—Charles Sanders Peirce

A person with one watch knows what time it is; a person with two watches is never sure.
—Proverb

Learn to labor and to wait.
—Henry Wadsworth Longfellow

The world is moving so fast these days that the man who says it can't be done is generally interrupted by someone doing it.
—Elbert Hubbard

Outline

18.1 Introduction

18.2 Thread States: Life Cycle of a Thread

18.3 Thread Priorities and Thread Scheduling

18.4 Creating and Executing Threads

    18.4.1 `Runnable`s and the `Thread` Class

    18.4.2 Thread Management with the `Executor` Framework

18.5 Thread Synchronization

    18.5.1 Unsynchronized Data Sharing

    18.5.2 Synchronized Data Sharing—Making Operations Atomic

18.6 Producer/Consumer Relationship without Synchronization

18.7 Producer/Consumer Relationship: `ArrayBlockingQueue`

18.8 Producer/Consumer Relationship with Synchronization

18.9 Producer/Consumer Relationship: Bounded Buffers

18.10 Producer/Consumer Relationship: The `Lock` and `Condition` Interfaces

18.11 Multithreading with GUI

    18.11.1 Performing Computations in a Worker Thread

    18.11.2 Processing Intermediate Results with `SwingWorker`

18.12 Other Classes and Interfaces in `java.util.concurrent`

18.13 Wrap-Up

18.1 Introduction

It would be nice if we could focus our attention on performing only one action at a time and performing it well, but that is usually difficult to do. The human body performs a great variety of operations *in parallel*—or, as we'll say throughout this chapter, *concurrently*. Respiration, blood circulation, digestion, thinking and walking, for example, can occur concurrently. All the senses—sight, touch, smell, taste and hearing—can be employed at once. Computers, too, can perform operations concurrently. It is common for personal computers to compile a program, send a file to a printer and receive electronic mail messages over a network concurrently. Only computers that have multiple processors can truly execute multiple instructions concurrently. Operating systems on single-processor computers create the illusion of concurrent execution by rapidly switching between activities, but on such computers only a single instruction can execute at once.

Most programming languages do not enable you to specify concurrent activities. Rather, the languages provide sequential control statements which enable you to specify that only one action at a time should be performed, with execution proceeding to the next action after the previous one has finished. Historically, concurrency has been implemented with operating system primitives available only to experienced systems programmers.

The Ada programming language, developed by the United States Department of Defense, made concurrency primitives widely available to defense contractors building military command-and-control systems. However, Ada has not been widely used in academia and industry.

Java makes concurrency available to you through the language and APIs. You specify that an application contains separate ***threads of execution***, where each thread has its own method-call stack and program counter, allowing it to execute concurrently with other threads while sharing application-wide resources such as memory with these other threads. This capability, called ***multithreading***, is not available in the core C and C++ languages, which influenced the design of Java.

Performance Tip 18.1

A problem with single-threaded applications that can lead to poor responsiveness is that lengthy activities must complete before others can begin. In a multithreaded application, threads can be distributed across multiple processors (if available) so that multiple tasks execute concurrently and the application can operate more efficiently. Multithreading can also increase performance on single-processor systems that simulate concurrency—when one thread cannot proceed (because, for example, it is waiting for the result of an I/O operation), another can use the processor.

Unlike languages that do not have built-in multithreading capabilities (such as C and C++) and must therefore make nonportable calls to operating system multithreading primitives, Java includes multithreading primitives as part of the language itself and as part of its libraries. This facilitates manipulating threads in a portable manner across platforms.

We'll discuss many applications of ***concurrent programming***. For example, when downloading a large file (e.g., an image, an audio clip or a video clip) over the Internet, the user may not want to wait until the entire clip downloads before starting the playback. To solve this problem, we can put multiple threads to work—one to download the clip, and another to play it. These activities proceed concurrently. To avoid choppy playback, we ***synchronize*** (coordinate the actions of) the threads so that the player thread doesn't begin until there is a sufficient amount of the clip in memory to keep the player thread busy.

The Java Virtual Machine (JVM) uses threads as well. In addition to creating threads to run a program, the JVM also may create threads for performing housekeeping tasks such as garbage collection.

Writing multithreaded programs can be tricky. Although the human mind can perform functions concurrently, people find it difficult to jump between parallel trains of thought. To see why multithreaded programs can be difficult to write and understand, try the following experiment: Open three books to page 1, and try reading the books concurrently. Read a few words from the first book, then a few from the second, then a few from the third, then loop back and read the next few words from the first book, and so on. After this experiment, you'll appreciate many of the challenges of multithreading—switching between the books, reading briefly, remembering your place in each book, moving the book you're reading closer so that you can see it and pushing the books you are not reading aside—and, amid all this chaos, trying to comprehend the content of the books!

Programming concurrent applications is a difficult and error-prone undertaking. If you find that you must use synchronization in a program, you should follow some simple guidelines. First, *use existing classes from the Java API* (such as the ArrayBlockingQueue class we discuss in Section 18.7, Producer/Consumer Relationship: ArrayBlockingQueue) *that manage synchronization for you*. The classes in the Java API are written by experts, have been fully tested and debugged, operate efficiently and help you avoid common traps and pitfalls. Second, if you find that you need more custom functionality than that provided in the Java APIs, you should use the synchronized keyword and Object methods wait, notify and notifyAll (discussed in Section 18.5 and Section 18.8). Finally, if you need even more complex capabilities, then you should use the Lock and Condition interfaces that are introduced in Section 18.10.

The Lock and Condition interfaces should be used only by advanced programmers who are familiar with the common traps and pitfalls of concurrent programming. We explain these topics in this chapter for several reasons—they provide a solid basis for understanding how concurrent applications synchronize access to shared memory; the concepts are important to understand, even if an application does not use these tools explicitly; and by showing you the complexity involved in using these low-level features, we hope to impress upon you the importance of using prepackaged concurrency capabilities whenever possible.

18.2 Thread States: Life Cycle of a Thread

At any time, a thread is said to be in one of several *thread states*—illustrated in the UML state diagram in Fig. 18.1. Several of the terms in the diagram are defined in later sections.

A new thread begins its life cycle in the *new* state. It remains in this state until the program starts the thread, which places it in the *runnable* state. A thread in the *runnable* state is considered to be executing its task.

Sometimes a *runnable* thread transitions to the *waiting* state while it waits for another thread to perform a task. A *waiting* thread transitions back to the *runnable* state only when another thread notifies the waiting thread to continue executing.

A *runnable* thread can enter the *timed waiting* state for a specified interval of time. It transitions back to the *runnable* state when that time interval expires or when the event it is waiting for occurs. *Timed waiting* and *waiting* threads cannot use a processor, even if one is available. A *runnable* thread can transition to the *timed waiting* state if it provides an optional wait interval when it is waiting for another thread to perform a task. Such a thread returns to the *runnable* state when it is notified by another thread or when the timed

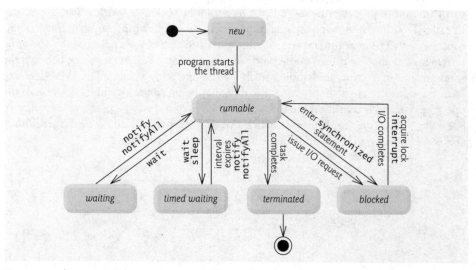

Fig. 18.1 | Thread life-cycle UML state diagram.

interval expires—whichever comes first. Another way to place a thread in the *timed waiting* state is to put a *runnable* thread to sleep. A **sleeping thread** remains in the *timed waiting* state for a designated period of time (called a **sleep interval**), after which it returns to the *runnable* state. Threads sleep when they momentarily do not have work to perform. For example, a word processor may contain a thread that periodically backs up (i.e., writes a copy of) the current document to disk for recovery purposes. If the thread did not sleep between successive backups, it would require a loop in which it continually tested whether it should write a copy of the document to disk. This loop would consume processor time without performing productive work, thus reducing system performance. In this case, it is more efficient for the thread to specify a sleep interval (equal to the period between successive backups) and enter the *timed waiting* state. This thread is returned to the *runnable* state when its sleep interval expires, at which point it writes a copy of the document to disk and reenters the *timed waiting* state.

A *runnable* thread transitions to the **blocked** state when it attempts to perform a task that cannot be completed immediately and it must temporarily wait until that task completes. For example, when a thread issues an input/output request, the operating system blocks the thread from executing until that I/O request completes—at that point, the *blocked* thread transitions to the *runnable* state, so it can resume execution. A *blocked* thread cannot use a processor, even if one is available.

A *runnable* thread enters the **terminated** state (sometimes called the **dead** state) when it successfully completes its task or otherwise terminates (perhaps due to an error). In the UML state diagram of Fig. 18.1, the *terminated* state is followed by the UML final state (the bull's-eye symbol) to indicate the end of the state transitions.

At the operating system level, Java's *runnable* state typically encompasses two separate states (Fig. 18.2). The operating system hides these states from the Java Virtual Machine (JVM), which sees only the *runnable* state. When a thread first transitions to the *runnable* state from the *new* state, the thread is in the **ready** state. A *ready* thread enters the **running** state (i.e., begins executing) when the operating system assigns the thread to a processor—also known as **dispatching the thread**. In most operating systems, each thread is given a small amount of processor time—called a **quantum** or **timeslice**—with which to perform its task. (Deciding how large the quantum should be is a key topic in operating systems courses.) When its quantum expires, the thread returns to the *ready* state and the operating system assigns another thread to the processor (see Section 18.3). Transitions between the *ready* and *running* states are handled solely by the operating system. The JVM does not "see" the transitions—it simply views the thread as being *runnable* and leaves it up to the operating system to transition the thread between *ready* and *running*. The process that an operating system uses to determine which thread to dispatch is called **thread scheduling** and is dependent on thread priorities (discussed in the next section).

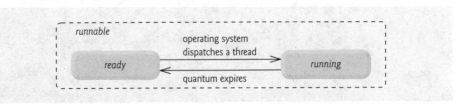

Fig. 18.2 | Operating system's internal view of Java's *runnable* state.

18.3 Thread Priorities and Thread Scheduling

Every Java thread has a *thread priority* that helps the operating system determine the order in which threads are scheduled. Java priorities range between MIN_PRIORITY (a constant of 1) and MAX_PRIORITY (a constant of 10). By default, every thread is given priority NORM_PRIORITY (a constant of 5). Each new thread inherits the priority of the thread that created it. Informally, higher-priority threads are more important to a program and should be allocated processor time before lower-priority threads. However, thread priorities cannot guarantee the order in which threads execute.

[*Note:* The constants (MAX_PRIORITY, MIN_PRIORITY and NORM_PRIORITY) are declared in the Thread class. It is recommended that you do not explicitly create and use Thread objects to implement concurrency, but rather use the Executor interface (which is described in Section 18.4.2). The Thread class contains some useful static methods, which we discuss later in the chapter.]

Most operating systems support timeslicing, which enables threads of equal priority to share a processor. Without timeslicing, each thread in a set of equal-priority threads runs to completion (unless it leaves the *runnable* state and enters the *waiting* or *timed waiting* state, or gets interrupted by a higher-priority thread) before other threads of equal priority get a chance to execute. With timeslicing, even if a thread has not finished executing when its quantum expires, the processor is taken away from the thread and given to the next thread of equal priority, if one is available.

An operating system's *thread scheduler* determines which thread runs next. One simple thread scheduler implementation keeps the highest-priority thread *running* at all times and, if there is more than one highest-priority thread, ensures that all such threads execute for a quantum each in *round-robin* fashion. Figure 18.3 illustrates a *multilevel priority queue* for threads. In the figure, assuming a single-processor computer, threads A and B each execute for a quantum in round-robin fashion until both threads complete execution. This means that A gets a quantum of time to run. Then B gets a quantum. Then A gets another quantum. Then B gets another quantum. This continues until one thread completes. The processor then devotes all its power to the thread that remains (unless another priority 10 thread becomes ready). Next, thread C runs to completion (assuming that no higher-priority threads arrive). Threads D, E and F each execute for a quantum in round-robin fashion until they all complete execution (again assuming that no higher-priority threads arrive). This process continues until all threads run to completion.

When a higher-priority thread enters the *ready* state, the operating system generally preempts the currently *running* thread (an operation known as *preemptive scheduling*). Depending on the operating system, higher-priority threads could postpone—possibly indefinitely—the execution of lower-priority threads. Such *indefinite postponement* is sometimes referred to more colorfully as *starvation*.

Java provides higher-level concurrency utilities to hide some of this complexity and make multithreaded programs less error prone. Thread priorities are used behind the scenes to interact with the operating system, but most programmers who use Java multithreading will not be concerned with setting and adjusting thread priorities.

 Portability Tip 18.1

Thread scheduling is platform dependent—the behavior of a multithreaded program could vary across different Java implementations.

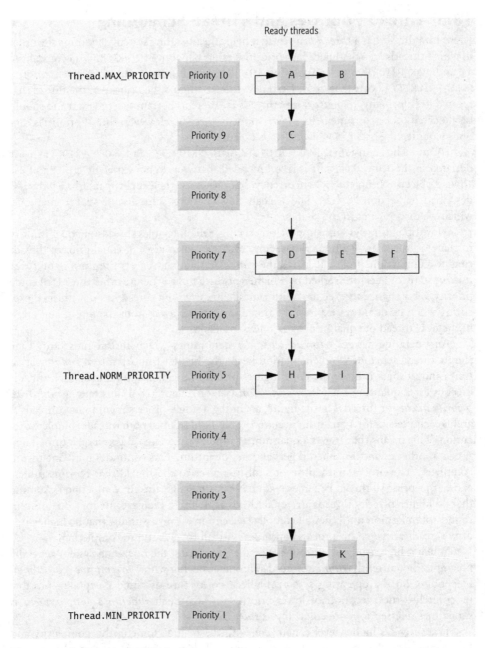

Fig. 18.3 | Thread-priority scheduling.

Portability Tip 18.2

When designing multithreaded programs consider the threading capabilities of all the platforms on which the programs will execute. Using priorities other than the default will make your programs' behavior platform specific. If portability is your goal, don't adjust thread priorities.

18.4 Creating and Executing Threads

The preferred means of creating multithreaded Java applications is by implementing the Runnable interface (of package java.lang). A Runnable object represents a "task" that can execute concurrently with other tasks. The Runnable interface declares a single method, run, which contains the code that defines the task that a Runnable object should perform. When a thread executing a Runnable is created and started, the thread calls the Runnable object's run method, which executes in the new thread.

18.4.1 Runnables and the Thread Class

Class PrintTask (Fig. 18.4) implements Runnable (line 5), so that multiple PrintTasks can execute concurrently. Variable sleepTime (line 7) stores a random integer value from 0 to 5 seconds created in the PrintTask constructor (line 16). Each thread running a PrintTask sleeps for the amount of time specified by sleepTime, then outputs its task's name and a message indicating that it's done sleeping.

```java
1   // Fig. 18.4: PrintTask.java
2   // PrintTask class sleeps for a random time from 0 to 5 seconds
3   import java.util.Random;
4
5   public class PrintTask implements Runnable
6   {
7      private final int sleepTime; // random sleep time for thread
8      private final String taskName; // name of task
9      private final static Random generator = new Random();
10
11     public PrintTask( String name )
12     {
13        taskName = name; // set task name
14
15        // pick random sleep time between 0 and 5 seconds
16        sleepTime = generator.nextInt( 5000 ); // milliseconds
17     } // end PrintTask constructor
18
19     // method run contains the code that a thread will execute
20     public void run()
21     {
22        try // put thread to sleep for sleepTime amount of time
23        {
24           System.out.printf( "%s going to sleep for %d milliseconds.\n",
25              taskName, sleepTime );
26           Thread.sleep( sleepTime ); // put thread to sleep
27        } // end try
28        catch ( InterruptedException exception )
29        {
30           System.out.printf( "%s %s\n", taskName,
31              "terminated prematurely due to interruption" );
32        } // end catch
33
```

Fig. 18.4 | PrintTask class sleeps for a random time from 0 to 5 seconds. (Part 1 of 2.)

```
34          // print task name
35          System.out.printf( "%s done sleeping\n", taskName );
36      } // end method run
37  } // end class PrintTask
```

Fig. 18.4 | PrintTask class sleeps for a random time from 0 to 5 seconds. (Part 2 of 2.)

A PrintTask executes when a thread calls the PrintTask's run method. Lines 24–25 display a message indicating the name of the currently executing task and that the task is going to sleep for sleepTime milliseconds. Line 26 invokes static method sleep of class Thread to place the thread in the *timed waiting* state for the specified amount of time. At this point, the thread loses the processor, and the system allows another thread to execute. When the thread awakens, it reenters the *runnable* state. When the PrintTask is assigned to a processor again, line 35 outputs a message indicating that the task is done sleeping, then method run terminates. Note that the catch at lines 28–32 is required because method sleep might throw a (checked) ***InterruptedException*** if the sleeping thread's ***interrupt*** method is called.

Figure 18.5 creates Thread objects to execute PrintTasks. Lines 12–14 create three threads, each of which specifies a new PrintTask to execute. Lines 19–21 call Thread method start on each of the threads—each call invokes the corresponding Runnable's run method to execute the task. Line 23 outputs a message indicating that all of the threads' tasks have been started and that the main method is finished executing.

```
1   // Fig. 18.5: ThreadCreator.java
2   // Creating and starting three threads to execute Runnables.
3   import java.lang.Thread;
4
5   public class ThreadCreator
6   {
7      public static void main( String[] args )
8      {
9         System.out.println( "Creating threads" );
10
11         // create each thread with a new targeted runnable
12         Thread thread1 = new Thread( new PrintTask( "task1" ) );
13         Thread thread2 = new Thread( new PrintTask( "task2" ) );
14         Thread thread3 = new Thread( new PrintTask( "task3" ) );
15
16         System.out.println( "Threads created, starting tasks." );
17
18         // start threads and place in runnable state
19         thread1.start(); // invokes task1's run method
20         thread2.start(); // invokes task2's run method
21         thread3.start(); // invokes task3's run method
22
23         System.out.println( "Tasks started, main ends.\n" );
24      } // end main
25   } // end class RunnableTester
```

Fig. 18.5 | Creating and starting three threads to execute Runnables. (Part 1 of 2.)

```
Creating threads
Threads created, starting tasks
Tasks started, main ends

task3 going to sleep for 491 milliseconds
task2 going to sleep for 71 milliseconds
task1 going to sleep for 3549 milliseconds
task2 done sleeping
task3 done sleeping
task1 done sleeping
```

```
Creating threads
Threads created, starting tasks
task1 going to sleep for 4666 milliseconds
task2 going to sleep for 48 milliseconds
task3 going to sleep for 3924 milliseconds
Tasks started, main ends

thread2 done sleeping
thread3 done sleeping
thread1 done sleeping
```

Fig. 18.5 | Creating and starting three threads to execute Runnables. (Part 2 of 2.)

The code in method main executes in the ***main thread***, a thread created by the JVM. The code in the run method of PrintTask (lines 20–36 of Fig. 18.4) executes in the threads created in lines 12–14 of Fig. 18.5. When method main terminates, the program itself continues running because there are still threads that are alive (i.e., any of the three threads we created that have not yet reached the *terminated* state). The program will not terminate until its last thread completes execution, at which point the JVM will also terminate.

The sample outputs for this program show each task's name and sleep time as the thread goes to sleep. The thread with the shortest sleep time normally awakens first, indicates that it's done sleeping and terminates. In Section 18.9, we discuss multithreading issues that could prevent the thread with the shortest sleep time from awakening first. In the first output, the main thread terminates before any of the other threads output their names and sleep times. This shows that the main thread runs to completion before any of the other threads get a chance to run. In the second output, all of the threads output their names and sleep times before the main thread terminates. This shows that the operating system allowed other threads to execute before the main thread terminated. This is an example of the round-robin scheduling we discussed in Section 18.3. Also notice that in the first example output, task3 goes to sleep first and task1 goes to sleep last, even though we started task1's thread first. This illustrates the fact that we cannot predict the order in which threads will be scheduled, even if we know the order in which they were created and started. Finally, in each of the outputs, notice that the order in which the threads indicate that they are done sleeping matches the smallest to largest sleep times of the three threads. Although this is the reasonable and intuitive order for these threads to finish their tasks, the threads are not guaranteed to finish in this order.

18.4.2 Thread Management with the Executor Framework

Though it is possible to create threads explicitly as in Figure 18.5, it is recommended that you use the Executor interface to manage the execution of Runnable objects for you. An *Executor* object typically creates and manages a group of threads called a *thread pool* to execute Runnables. Using an Executor has many advantages over creating threads yourself. Executors can reuse existing threads to eliminate the overhead of creating a new thread for each task and can improve performance by optimizing the number of threads to ensure that the processor stays busy, without creating so many threads that the application runs out of resources.

The Executor interface declares a single method named *execute* which accepts a Runnable as an argument. The Executor assigns every Runnable passed to its execute method to one of the available threads in the thread pool. If there are no available threads, the Executor creates a new thread or waits for a thread to become available and assigns that thread the Runnable that was passed to method execute.

Interface *ExecutorService* (of package java.util.concurrent) is an interface that extends Executor and declares a number of other methods for managing the life cycle of an Executor. An object that implements the ExecutorService interface can be created using static methods declared in class Executors (of package java.util.concurrent). We use interface ExecutorService and a method of class *Executors* in the next application, which executes three tasks.

Figure 18.6 uses an ExecutorService object to manage threads that execute Print-Tasks. Method main (lines 8–29) creates and names three PrintTask objects (lines 11–13). Line 18 uses Executors method *newCachedThreadPool* to obtain an ExecutorService that creates new threads as they are needed by the application. These threads are used by threadExecutor to execute the Runnables.

```
1   // Fig. 18.6: TaskExecutor.java
2   // Using an ExecutorService to execute Runnables.
3   import java.util.concurrent.Executors;
4   import java.util.concurrent.ExecutorService;
5
6   public class TaskExecutor
7   {
8      public static void main( String[] args )
9      {
10        // create and name each runnable
11        PrintTask task1 = new PrintTask( "task1" );
12        PrintTask task2 = new PrintTask( "task2" );
13        PrintTask task3 = new PrintTask( "task3" );
14
15        System.out.println( "Starting Executor" );
16
17        // create ExecutorService to manage threads
18        ExecutorService threadExecutor = Executors.newCachedThreadPool();
19
20        // start threads and place in runnable state
21        threadExecutor.execute( task1 ); // start task1
```

Fig. 18.6 | Using an ExecutorService to execute Runnables. (Part 1 of 2.)

```
22          threadExecutor.execute( task2 ); // start task2
23          threadExecutor.execute( task3 ); // start task3
24
25          // shut down worker threads when their tasks complete
26          threadExecutor.shutdown();
27
28          System.out.println( "Tasks started, main ends.\n" );
29       } // end main
30    } // end class TaskExecutor
```

```
Starting Executor
Tasks started, main ends

task1 going to sleep for 4806 milliseconds
task2 going to sleep for 2513 milliseconds
task3 going to sleep for 1132 milliseconds
thread3 done sleeping
thread2 done sleeping
thread1 done sleeping
```

```
Starting Executor
task1 going to sleep for 1342 milliseconds
task2 going to sleep for 277 milliseconds
task3 going to sleep for 2737 milliseconds
Tasks started, main ends

task2 done sleeping
task1 done sleeping
task3 done sleeping
```

Fig. 18.6 | Using an ExecutorService to execute Runnables. (Part 2 of 2.)

Lines 21–23 each invoke the ExecutorService's execute method. This method executes the Runnable passed to it as an argument (in this case a PrintTask) some time in the future. The specified task may execute in one of the threads in the ExecutorService's thread pool, in a new thread created to execute it, or in the thread that called the execute method; the ExecutorService manages these details. Method execute returns immediately from each invocation—the program does not wait for each PrintTask to finish. Line 26 calls ExecutorService method **shutdown**, which notifies the ExecutorService to stop accepting new tasks, but continues executing tasks that have already been submitted. Once all of the previously submitted Runnables have completed, the threadExecutor terminates. Line 28 outputs a message indicating that the tasks were started and the main thread is finishing its execution. The sample outputs for this program are similar to those of the previous program and again demonstrate the nondeterminism of thread scheduling.

18.5 Thread Synchronization

When multiple threads share an object and that object is modified by one or more of the threads, indeterminate results may occur (as we'll see in the examples) unless access to the shared object is managed properly. If one thread is in the process of updating a shared object and another thread also tries to update it, it is unclear which thread's update takes effect. When this happens, the program's behavior cannot be trusted—sometimes the program will produce the correct results, and sometimes it won't. In either case, there will be no indication that the shared object was manipulated incorrectly.

The problem can be solved by giving only one thread at a time *exclusive access* to code that manipulates the shared object. During that time, other threads desiring to manipulate the object are kept waiting. When the thread with exclusive access to the object finishes manipulating it, one of the threads that was waiting is allowed to proceed. This process, called *thread synchronization*, coordinates access to shared data by multiple concurrent threads. By synchronizing threads in this manner, you can ensure that each thread accessing a shared object excludes all other threads from doing so simultaneously—this is called *mutual exclusion*.

A common way to perform synchronization is to use Java's built-in *monitors*. Every object has a monitor and a *monitor lock* (or *intrinsic lock*). The monitor ensures that its object's monitor lock is held by a maximum of only one thread at any time. Monitors and monitor locks can thus be used to enforce mutual exclusion. If an operation requires the executing thread to hold a lock while the operation is performed, a thread must acquire the lock before proceeding with the operation. Other threads attempting to perform an operation that requires the same lock will be *blocked* until the first thread releases the lock, at which point the *blocked* threads may attempt to acquire the lock and proceed with the operation.

To specify that a thread must hold a monitor lock to execute a block of code, the code should be placed in a *synchronized statement*. Such code is said to be *guarded* by the monitor lock; a thread must *acquire the lock* to execute the synchronized statements. The monitor allows only one thread at a time to execute statements within synchronized blocks that lock on the same object, as only one thread at a time can hold the monitor lock. The synchronized statements are declared using the *synchronized keyword*:

```
synchronized ( object )
{
    statements
} // end synchronized statement
```

where *object* is the object whose monitor lock will be acquired; *object* is normally this if it is the object in which the synchronized statement appears. If several synchronized statements are trying to execute on an object at the same time, only one of them may be active on the object—all the other threads attempting to enter a synchronized statement on the same object are placed in the *blocked* state.

When a synchronized statement finishes executing, the object's monitor lock is released and the operating system can allow one of the *blocked* threads attempting to enter a synchronized statement to acquire the lock to proceed. Java also allows *synchronized methods*. Such a method is equivalent to a synchronized statement enclosing the entire body of a method and using this as the object whose monitor lock will be acquired. You can specify a method as synchronized by placing the synchronized keyword before the method's return type in the method declaration.

18.5.1 Unsynchronized Data Sharing

We now present an example to illustrate the dangers of sharing an object across threads without proper synchronization. In this example, two Runnables maintain references to a single integer array. Each Runnable writes five values to the array, then terminates. This may seem harmless, but it can result in errors if the array is manipulated without synchronization.

Class SimpleArray

An object of class SimpleArray (Fig. 18.7) will be shared across multiple threads. Simple-Array will enable those threads to place int values into array (declared at line 7). Line 8 initializes variable writeIndex, which will be used to determine the array element that should be written to next. The constructor (lines 12–15) creates an integer array of the desired size.

```java
1   // Fig. 18.7: SimpleArray.java
2   // Class that manages an integer array to be shared by multiple threads.
3   import java.util.Random;
4
5   public class SimpleArray // CAUTION: NOT THREAD SAFE!
6   {
7      private final int array[]; // the shared integer array
8      private int writeIndex = 0; // index of next element to be written
9      private final static Random generator = new Random();
10
11     // construct a SimpleArray of a given size
12     public SimpleArray( int size )
13     {
14        array = new int[ size ];
15     } // end constructor
16
17     // add a value to the shared array
18     public void add( int value )
19     {
20        int position = writeIndex; // store the write index
21
22        try
23        {
24           // put thread to sleep for 0-499 milliseconds
25           Thread.sleep( generator.nextInt( 500 ) );
26        } // end try
27        catch ( InterruptedException ex )
28        {
29           ex.printStackTrace();
30        } // end catch
31
32        // put value in the appropriate element
33        array[ position ] = value;
34        System.out.printf( "%s wrote %2d to element %d.\n",
35           Thread.currentThread().getName(), value, position );
36
37        ++writeIndex; // increment index of element to be written next
38        System.out.printf( "Next write index: %d\n", writeIndex );
39     } // end method add
40
```

Fig. 18.7 | Class that manages an integer array to be shared by multiple threads. (Part 1 of 2.)

```
41        // used for outputting the contents of the shared integer array
42        public String toString()
43        {
44            String arrayString = "\nContents of SimpleArray:\n";
45
46            for ( int i = 0; i < array.length; i++ )
47                arrayString += array[ i ] + " ";
48
49            return arrayString;
50        } // end method toString
51    } // end class SimpleArray
```

Fig. 18.7 | Class that manages an integer array to be shared by multiple threads. (Part 2 of 2.)

Method add (lines 18–39) allows new values to be inserted at the end of the array. Line 20 stores the current writeIndex value. Line 25 puts the thread that invokes add to sleep for a random interval from 0 to 499 milliseconds. This is done to make the problems associated with unsynchronized access to shared data more obvious. After the thread is done sleeping, line 33 inserts the value passed to add into the array at the element specified by position. Lines 34–35 output a message indicating the executing thread's name, the value that was inserted in the array and where it was inserted. Line 37 increments writeIndex so that the next call to add will insert a value in the array's next element. Lines 42–50 override method toString to create a String representation of the array's contents.

Class ArrayWriter

Class ArrayWriter (Fig. 18.8) implements the interface Runnable to define a task for inserting values in a SimpleArray object. The constructor (lines 10–14) takes two arguments—an integer value, which is the first value this task will insert in the SimpleArray object, and a reference to the SimpleArray object. Line 20 invokes method add on the SimpleArray object. The task completes after three consecutive integers beginning with startValue are added to the SimpleArray object.

```
1    // Fig. 18.8: ArrayWriter.java
2    // Adds integers to an array shared with other Runnables
3    import java.lang.Runnable;
4
5    public class ArrayWriter implements Runnable
6    {
7        private final SimpleArray sharedSimpleArray;
8        private final int startValue;
9
10       public ArrayWriter( int value, SimpleArray array )
11       {
12           startValue = value;
13           sharedSimpleArray = array;
14       } // end constructor
15
```

Fig. 18.8 | Adds integers to an array shared with other Runnables. (Part 1 of 2.)

```
16        public void run()
17        {
18           for ( int i = startValue; i < startValue + 3; i++ )
19           {
20              sharedSimpleArray.add( i ); // add an element to the shared array
21           } // end for
22        } // end method run
23     } // end class ArrayWriter
```

Fig. 18.8 | Adds integers to an array shared with other Runnables. (Part 2 of 2.)

Class *SharedArrayTest*

Class SharedArrayTest executes two ArrayWriter tasks that add values to a single SimpleArray object. Line 12 constructs a six-element SimpleArray object. Lines 15–16 create two new ArrayWriter tasks, one that places the values 1–3 in the SimpleArray object, and one that places the values 11–13. Lines 19–21 create an ExecutorService and execute the two ArrayWriters. Line 23 invokes the ExecutorService's shutDown method to prevent additional tasks from starting and to enable the application to terminate when the currently executing tasks complete execution.

```
 1     // Fig 18.9: SharedArrayTest.java
 2     // Executes two Runnables to add elements to a shared SimpleArray.
 3     import java.util.concurrent.Executors;
 4     import java.util.concurrent.ExecutorService;
 5     import java.util.concurrent.TimeUnit;
 6
 7     public class SharedArrayTest
 8     {
 9        public static void main( String[] arg )
10        {
11           // construct the shared object
12           SimpleArray sharedSimpleArray = new SimpleArray( 6 );
13
14           // create two tasks to write to the shared SimpleArray
15           ArrayWriter writer1 = new ArrayWriter( 1, sharedSimpleArray );
16           ArrayWriter writer2 = new ArrayWriter( 11, sharedSimpleArray );
17
18           // execute the tasks with an ExecutorService
19           ExecutorService executor = Executors.newCachedThreadPool();
20           executor.execute( writer1 );
21           executor.execute( writer2 );
22
23           executor.shutdown();
24
25           try
26           {
27              // wait 1 minute for both writers to finish executing
28              boolean tasksEnded = executor.awaitTermination(
29                 1, TimeUnit.MINUTES );
30
```

Fig. 18.9 | Executes two Runnables to insert values in a shared array. (Part 1 of 2.)

```
31              if ( tasksEnded )
32                  System.out.println( sharedSimpleArray ); // print contents
33              else
34                  System.out.println(
35                      "Timed out while waiting for tasks to finish." );
36          } // end try
37          catch ( InterruptedException ex )
38          {
39              System.out.println(
40                  "Interrupted while wait for tasks to finish." );
41          } // end catch
42      } // end main
43  } // end class SharedArrayTest
```

```
pool-1-thread-1 wrote  1 to element 0.
Next write index: 1
pool-1-thread-1 wrote  2 to element 1.
Next write index: 2
pool-1-thread-1 wrote  3 to element 2.
Next write index: 3
pool-1-thread-2 wrote 11 to element 0.
Next write index: 4
pool-1-thread-2 wrote 12 to element 4.
Next write index: 5
pool-1-thread-2 wrote 13 to element 5.
Next write index: 6

Contents of SimpleArray:
11 2 3 0 12 13
```

First pool-1-thread-1 wrote the value 1 to element 0. Later pool-1-thread-2 wrote the value 11 to element 0, thus overwriting the previously stored value.

Fig. 18.9 | Executes two Runnables to insert values in a shared array. (Part 2 of 2.)

Recall that ExecutorService method shutdown returns immediately. Thus any code that appears after the call to ExecutorService method shutdown in line 23 will continue executing as long as the main thread is still assigned to a processor. We'd like to output the SimpleArray object to show you the results *after* the threads complete their tasks. So, we need the program to wait for the threads to complete before main outputs the SimpleArray object's contents. Interface ExecutorService provides the *awaitTermination* method for this purpose. This method returns control to its caller either when all tasks executing in the ExecutorService complete or when the specified timeout elapses. If all tasks are completed before awaitTermination times out, this method returns true; otherwise it returns false. The two arguments to awaitTermination represent a timeout value and a unit of measure specified with a constant from class TimeUnit (in this case, TimeUnit.MINUTES). In this example, if both tasks complete before awaitTermination times out, line 32 displays the SimpleArray object's contents. Otherwise, lines 34–35 print a message indicating that the tasks did not finish executing before awaitTermination timed out.

The output in Fig. 18.9 demonstrates the problems (highlighted in the output) that can be caused by failure to synchronize access to shared data. The value 1 was written to element 0, then overwritten later by the value 11. Also, when writeIndex was incremented to 3, nothing was written to that element, as indicated by the 0 in that element of the printed array.

Recall that we have added calls to Thread method sleep between operations on the shared data to emphasize the unpredictability of thread scheduling and increase the likelihood of producing erroneous output. It is important to note that even if these operations were allowed to proceed at their normal pace, you could still see errors in the program's output. However, modern processors can handle the simple operations of the Simple-Array method add so quickly that you might not see the errors caused by the two threads executing this method concurrently, even if you tested the program dozens of times. One of the challenges of multithreaded programming is spotting the errors—they may occur so infrequently that a broken program does not produce incorrect results during testing, creating the illusion that the program is correct.

18.5.2 Synchronized Data Sharing—Making Operations Atomic

The output errors of Fig. 18.9 can be attributed to the fact that the shared object, Simple-Array, is not ***thread safe***—SimpleArray is susceptible to errors if it is accessed concurrently by multiple threads. The problem lies in method add, which stores the value of writeIndex, places a new value in that element, then increments writeIndex. Such a method would present no problem in a single-threaded program. However, if one thread obtains the value of writeIndex, there is no guarantee that another thread cannot come along and increment writeIndex before the first thread has had a chance to place a value in the array. If this happens, the first thread will be writing to the array based on a ***stale value*** of writeIndex—a value that is no longer valid. Another possibility is that one thread might obtain the value of writeIndex after another thread adds an element to the array but before writeIndex is incremented. In this case, too, the first thread would write to the array based on an invalid value for writeIndex.

SimpleArray is not thread safe because it allows any number of threads to read and modify shared data concurrently, which can cause errors. To make SimpleArray thread safe, we must ensure that no two threads can access it at the same time. We also must ensure that while one thread is in the process of storing writeIndex, adding a value to the array, and incrementing writeIndex, no other thread may read or change the value of writeIndex or modify the contents of the array at any point during these three operations. In other words, we want these three operations—storing writeIndex, writing to the array, incrementing writeIndex—to be an ***atomic operation***, which cannot be divided into smaller suboperations. While no processor can carry out all three stages of the add method in a single clock cycle to make the operation truly atomic, we can simulate atomicity by ensuring that only one thread carries out the three operations at a time. Any other threads that need to perform the operation must wait until the first thread has finished the add operation in its entirety.

Atomicity can be achieved using the synchronized keyword. By placing our three suboperations in a synchronized statement or synchronized method, only one thread at a time will be allowed to acquire the lock and perform the operations. When that thread has completed all of the operations in the synchronized block and releases the lock, another thread may acquire the lock and begin executing the operations. This ensures that a thread executing the operations will see the actual values of the shared data and that these values will not change unexpectedly in the middle of the operations as a result of another thread's modifying them.

Software Engineering Observation 18.1

Place all accesses to mutable data that may be shared by multiple threads inside synchronized statements or synchronized methods that synchronize on the same lock. When performing multiple operations on shared data, hold the lock for the entirety of the operation to ensure that the operation is effectively atomic.

Figure 18.10 displays class SimpleArray with the proper synchronization. Notice that it's identical to the SimpleArray class of Fig. 18.7, except that add is now a synchronized method (line 19). So, only one thread at a time can execute this method. We reuse classes ArrayWriter (Fig. 18.8) and SharedArrayTest (Fig. 18.9) from the previous example.

```
1   // Fig. 18.10: SimpleArray.java
2   // Class that manages an integer array to be shared by multiple threads.
3   import java.util.Random;
4
5   public class SimpleArray
6   {
7      private final int array[]; // the shared integer array
8      private int writeIndex = 0; // index of next element to be written
9      private final static Random generator = new Random();
10
11      // construct a SimpleArray of a given size
12      public SimpleArray( int size )
13      {
14         array = new int[ size ];
15      } // end constructor
16
17      // add a value to the shared array
18      public synchronized void add( int value )
19      {
20         int position = writeIndex; // store the write index
21
22         try
23         {
24            // put thread to sleep for 0-499 milliseconds
25            Thread.sleep( generator.nextInt( 500 ) );
26         } // end try
27         catch ( InterruptedException ex )
28         {
29            ex.printStackTrace();
30         } // end catch
31
32         // put value in the appropriate element
33         array[ position ] = value;
34         System.out.printf( "%s wrote %2d to element %d.\n",
35            Thread.currentThread().getName(), value, position );
36
37         ++writeIndex; // increment index of element to be written next
38         System.out.printf( "Next write index: %d\n", writeIndex );
39      } // end method add
```

Fig. 18.10 | Class that manages an integer array to be shared by multiple threads with synchronization. (Part 1 of 2.)

```
40
41      // used for outputting the contents of the shared integer array
42      public String toString()
43      {
44         String arrayString = "\nContents of SimpleArray:\n";
45
46         for ( int i = 0; i < array.length; i++ )
47            arrayString += array[ i ] + " ";
48
49         return arrayString;
50      } // end method toString
51   } // end class SimpleArray
```

```
pool-1-thread-1 wrote  1 to element 0.
Next write index: 1
pool-1-thread-2 wrote 11 to element 1.
Next write index: 2
pool-1-thread-2 wrote 12 to element 2.
Next write index: 3
pool-1-thread-2 wrote 13 to element 3.
Next write index: 4
pool-1-thread-1 wrote  2 to element 4.
Next write index: 5
pool-1-thread-1 wrote  3 to element 5.
Next write index: 6

Contents of SimpleArray:
1 11 12 13 2 3
```

Fig. 18.10 | Class that manages an integer array to be shared by multiple threads with synchronization. (Part 2 of 2.)

Line 18 declares method as synchronized, making all of the operations in this method behave as a single, atomic operation. Line 20 performs the first suboperation—storing the value of writeIndex. Line 33 defines the second suboperation, writing an element to the element at the index position. Line 37 increments writeIndex. When the method finishes executing at line 39, the executing thread releases the SimpleArray lock, making it possible for another thread to begin executing the add method.

In the synchronized add method, we print messages to the console indicating the progress of threads as they execute this method, in addition to performing the actual operations required to insert a value in the array. We do this so that the messages will be printed in the correct order, allowing you to see whether the method is properly synchronized by comparing these outputs with those of the previous, unsynchronized example. We continue to output messages from synchronized blocks in later examples for demonstration purposes; typically, however, I/O *should not* be performed in synchronized blocks, because it's important to minimize the amount of time that an object is "locked."

Performance Tip 18.2

Keep the duration of synchronized statements as short as possible while maintaining the needed synchronization. This minimizes the wait time for blocked threads. Avoid performing I/O, lengthy calculations and operations that do not require synchronization with a lock held.

Another note on thread safety: We have said that it is necessary to synchronize access to all data that may be shared across multiple threads. Actually, this synchronization is necessary only for *mutable data*, or data that may change in its lifetime. If the shared data will not change in a multithreaded program, then it is not possible for a thread to see old or incorrect values as a result of another thread's manipulating that data.

When you share immutable data across threads, declare the corresponding data fields final to indicate that variables' values will not change after they are initialized. This prevents accidental modification of the shared data later in a program, which could compromise thread safety. Labeling object references as final indicates that the reference will not change, but it does not guarantee that the object itself is immutable—this depends entirely on the properties of the object. However, it is still good practice to mark references that will not change as final, as doing so forces the object's constructor to be atomic—the object will be fully constructed with all its fields initialized before it is accessed by the program.

Good Programming Practice 18.1

Always declare data fields that you do not expect to change as final. Primitive variables that are declared as final can safely be shared across threads. An object reference that is declared as final ensures that the object it refers to will be fully constructed and initialized before it is used by the program and prevents the reference from pointing to another object.

18.6 Producer/Consumer Relationship without Synchronization

In a *producer/consumer relationship*, the *producer* portion of an application generates data and stores it in a shared object, and the *consumer* portion of an application reads data from the shared object. The producer/consumer relationship separates the task of identifying work to be done from the tasks involved in actually carrying out the work. One example of a common producer/consumer relationship is *print spooling*. Although a printer might not be available when you want to print from an application (i.e., the producer), you can still "complete" the print task, as the data is temporarily placed on disk until the printer becomes available. Similarly, when the printer (i.e., a consumer) is available, it doesn't have to wait until a current user wants to print. The spooled print jobs can be printed as soon as the printer becomes available. Another example of the producer/consumer relationship is an application that copies data onto CDs by placing data in a fixed-size buffer, which is emptied as the CD-RW drive "burns" the data onto the CD.

In a multithreaded producer/consumer relationship, a *producer thread* generates data and places it in a shared object called a *buffer*. A *consumer thread* reads data from the buffer. This relationship requires synchronization to ensure that values are produced and consumed properly. All operations on mutable data that is shared by multiple threads (e.g., the data in the buffer) must be guarded with a lock to prevent corruption, as discussed in Section 18.5. Operations on the buffer data shared by a producer and consumer thread are also *state dependent*—the operations should proceed only if the buffer is in the correct state. If the buffer is in a not-full state, the producer may produce; if the buffer is in a not-empty state, the consumer may consume. All operations that access the buffer must use synchronization to ensure that data is written to the buffer or read from the buffer only if the buffer is in the proper state. If the producer attempting to put the next data into the buffer determines that it is full, the producer thread should wait until there is space to write a new value. If a consumer thread finds the buffer empty or finds that the previous data has already been read, the consumer must also wait for new data to become available.

Consider how logic errors can arise if we do not synchronize access among multiple threads manipulating shared data. Our next example (Fig. 18.11–Fig. 18.15) implements a producer/consumer relationship without the proper synchronization. A producer thread writes the numbers 1 through 10 into a shared buffer—a single memory location shared between two threads (a single int variable called buffer in line 6 of Fig. 18.14 in this example). The consumer thread reads this data from the shared buffer and displays the data. The program's output shows the values that the producer writes (produces) into the shared buffer and the values that the consumer reads (consumes) from the shared buffer.

Each value the producer thread writes to the shared buffer must be consumed exactly once by the consumer thread. However, the threads in this example erroneously are not synchronized. Therefore, data can be lost or garbled if the producer places new data into the shared buffer before the consumer reads the previous data. Also, data can be incorrectly duplicated if the consumer consumes data again before the producer produces the next value. To show these possibilities, the consumer thread in the following example keeps a total of all the values it reads. The producer thread produces values from 1 through 10. If the consumer reads each value produced once and only once, the total will be 55. However, if you execute this program several times, you'll see that the total is not always 55 (as shown in the outputs in Fig. 18.10). To emphasize the point, the producer and consumer threads in the example each sleep for random intervals of up to three seconds between performing their tasks. Thus, we do not know when the producer thread will attempt to write a new value, or when the consumer thread will attempt to read a value.

The program consists of interface Buffer (Fig. 18.11) and four classes—Producer (Fig. 18.12), Consumer (Fig. 18.13), UnsynchronizedBuffer (Fig. 18.14) and SharedBufferTest (Fig. 18.15). Interface Buffer declares methods set (line 6) and get (line 9) that a Buffer must implement to enable the Producer thread to place a value in the Buffer and the Consumer thread to retrieve a value from the Buffer, respectively. Some programmers prefer to call these methods put and take, respectively. In subsequent examples, methods set and get will call methods that throw InterruptedExceptions. We declare each method with a throws clause here so that we don't have to modify this interface for the later examples Figure 18.14 shows the implementation of this interface.

Class Producer (Fig. 18.12) implements the Runnable interface, allowing it to be executed as a task in a separate thread. The constructor (lines 11–14) initializes the Buffer reference sharedLocation with an object created in main (line 14 of Fig. 18.15) and

```
1   // Fig. 18.11: Buffer.java
2   // Buffer interface specifies methods called by Producer and Consumer.
3   public interface Buffer
4   {
5      // place int value into Buffer
6      public void set( int value ) throws InterruptedException;
7
8      // return int value from Buffer
9      public int get() throws InterruptedException;
10  } // end interface Buffer
```

Fig. 18.11 | Buffer interface specifies methods called by Producer and Consumer.

passed to the constructor in the parameter shared. As we'll see, this is an Unsynchronized-Buffer object that implements the interface Buffer without synchronizing access to the shared object. The Producer thread in this program executes the tasks specified in the method run (lines 17–39). Each iteration of the loop (lines 21–35) invokes Thread method sleep (line 25) to place the Producer thread into the *timed waiting* state for a random time interval between 0 and 3 seconds. When the thread awakens, line 26 passes the value of control variable count to the Buffer object's set method to set the shared buffer's value. Line 27 keeps a total of all the values produced so far and line 28 outputs that value. When the loop completes, lines 37–38 display a message indicating that the Producer has finished producing data and is terminating. Next, method run terminates, which indicates that the Producer completed its task. It is important to note that any method called from a Runnable's run method (e.g., Buffer method set) executes as part of that task's thread of execution. This fact becomes important in Section 18.7 when we add synchronization to the producer/consumer relationship.

```java
1   // Fig. 18.12: Producer.java
2   // Producer with a run method that inserts the values 1 to 10 in buffer.
3   import java.util.Random;
4
5   public class Producer implements Runnable
6   {
7      private final static Random generator = new Random();
8      private final Buffer sharedLocation; // reference to shared object
9
10     // constructor
11     public Producer( Buffer shared )
12     {
13        sharedLocation = shared;
14     } // end Producer constructor
15
16     // store values from 1 to 10 in sharedLocation
17     public void run()
18     {
19        int sum = 0;
20
21        for ( int count = 1; count <= 10; count++ )
22        {
23           try // sleep 0 to 3 seconds, then place value in Buffer
24           {
25              Thread.sleep( generator.nextInt( 3000 ) ); // random sleep
26              sharedLocation.set( count ); // set value in buffer
27              sum += count; // increment sum of values
28              System.out.printf( "\t%2d\n", sum );
29           } // end try
30           // if lines 25 or 26 get interrupted, print stack trace
31           catch ( InterruptedException exception )
32           {
33              exception.printStackTrace();
34           } // end catch
35        } // end for
```

Fig. 18.12 | Producer with a run method that inserts the values 1 to 10 in buffer. (Part 1 of 2.)

```
36
37              System.out.println(
38                  "Producer done producing\nTerminating Producer" );
39          } // end method run
40      } // end class Producer
```

Fig. 18.12 | Producer with a run method that inserts the values 1 to 10 in buffer. (Part 2 of 2.)

Class Consumer (Fig. 18.13) also implements interface Runnable, allowing the Consumer to execute concurrently with the Producer. The constructor (lines 11–14) initializes Buffer reference sharedLocation with an object that implements the Buffer interface created in main (Fig. 18.15) and passed to the constructor as the parameter shared. As we'll see, this is the same UnsynchronizedBuffer object that is used to initialize the Producer object—thus, the two threads share the same object. The Consumer thread in this program performs the tasks specified in method run (lines 17–39). The loop at lines 21–35 iterates 10 times. Each iteration invokes Thread method sleep (line 26) to put the Consumer thread into the *timed waiting* state for up to 3 seconds. Next, line 27 uses the Buffer's get method to retrieve the value in the shared buffer, then adds the value to variable sum. Line 28 displays the total of all the values consumed so far. When the loop completes, lines 37–38 display a line indicating the sum of the consumed values. Then method run terminates, which indicates that the Consumer completed its task. Once both threads enter the *terminated* state, the program ends.

```
 1   // Fig. 18.13: Consumer.java
 2   // Consumer with a run method that loops, reading 10 values from buffer.
 3   import java.util.Random;
 4
 5   public class Consumer implements Runnable
 6   {
 7      private final static Random generator = new Random();
 8      private final Buffer sharedLocation; // reference to shared object
 9
10      // constructor
11      public Consumer( Buffer shared )
12      {
13         sharedLocation = shared;
14      } // end Consumer constructor
15
16      // read sharedLocation's value 10 times and sum the values
17      public void run()
18      {
19         int sum = 0;
20
21         for ( int count = 1; count <= 10; count++ )
22         {
23            // sleep 0 to 3 seconds, read value from buffer and add to sum
24            try
25            {
26               Thread.sleep( generator.nextInt( 3000 ) );
```

Fig. 18.13 | Consumer with a run method that loops, reading 10 values from buffer. (Part 1 of 2.)

```
27                    sum += sharedLocation.get();
28                    System.out.printf( "\t\t\t%2d\n", sum );
29                 } // end try
30                 // if lines 26 or 27 get interrupted, print stack trace
31                 catch ( InterruptedException exception )
32                 {
33                    exception.printStackTrace();
34                 } // end catch
35              } // end for
36
37              System.out.printf( "\n%s %d\n%s\n",
38                 "Consumer read values totaling", sum, "Terminating Consumer" );
39           } // end method run
40        } // end class Consumer
```

Fig. 18.13 | Consumer with a run method that loops, reading 10 values from buffer. (Part 2 of 2.)

[*Note:* We call method sleep in method run of the Producer and Consumer classes to emphasize the fact that in multithreaded applications, it is unpredictable when each thread will perform its task and for how long it will perform the task when it has a processor. Normally, these thread scheduling issues are the job of the computer's operating system, beyond the control of the Java developer. In this program, our thread's tasks are quite simple—the Producer writes the values 1 to 10 to the buffer, and the Consumer reads 10 values from the buffer and adds each value to variable sum. Without the sleep method call, and if the Producer executes first, given today's phenomenally fast processors, the Producer would likely complete its task before the Consumer got a chance to execute. If the Consumer executed first, it would likely consume garbage data ten times, then terminate before the Producer could produce the first real value.]

Class UnsynchronizedBuffer (Fig. 18.14) implements interface Buffer (line 4). An object of this class is shared between the Producer and the Consumer. Line 6 declares instance variable buffer and initializes it with the value –1. This value is used to demonstrate the case in which the Consumer attempts to consume a value before the Producer ever places a value in buffer. Methods set (lines 9–13) and get (lines 16–20) do not synchronize access to the field buffer. Method set simply assigns its argument to buffer (line 12), and method get simply returns the value of buffer (line 19).

```
1     // Fig. Fig. 18.14: UnsynchronizedBuffer.java
2     // UnsynchronizedBuffer maintains the shared integer that is accessed by
3     // a producer thread and a consumer thread via methods set and get.
4     public class UnsynchronizedBuffer implements Buffer
5     {
6        private int buffer = -1; // shared by producer and consumer threads
7
8        // place value into buffer
9        public void set( int value ) throws InterruptedException
10       {
11          System.out.printf( "Producer writes\t%2d", value );
```

Fig. 18.14 | UnsynchronizedBuffer maintains the shared integer that is accessed by a producer thread and a consumer thread via methods set and get. (Part 1 of 2.)

```
12          buffer = value;
13      } // end method set
14
15      // return value from buffer
16      public int get() throws InterruptedException
17      {
18          System.out.printf( "Consumer reads\t%2d", buffer );
19          return buffer;
20      } // end method get
21  } // end class UnsynchronizedBuffer
```

Fig. 18.14 | UnsynchronizedBuffer maintains the shared integer that is accessed by a producer thread and a consumer thread via methods set and get. (Part 2 of 2.)

Class SharedBufferTest contains method main (lines 9–25). Line 11 creates an ExecutorService to execute the Producer and Consumer Runnables. Line 14 creates an UnsynchronizedBuffer object and assigns it to Buffer variable sharedLocation. This object stores the data that the Producer and Consumer threads will share. Lines 23–24 create and execute the Producer and Consumer. Note that the Producer and Consumer constructors are each passed the same Buffer object (sharedLocation), so each object is initialized with a reference to the same Buffer. These lines also implicitly launch the threads and call each Runnable's run method. Finally, line 26 calls method shutdown so that the application can terminate when the threads executing the Producer and Consumer complete their tasks. When main terminates (line 27), the main thread of execution enters the *terminated* state. Recall from the overview of this example that we would like the Producer to execute first and every value produced by the Producer to be consumed exactly once by the Consumer. However, when we study the first output of Fig. 18.15, we see that the Producer writes the values 1, 2 and 3 before the Consumer reads its first value (3). Therefore, the values 1 and 2 are lost. Later, the values 5, 6 and 9 are lost, while 7 and 8 are read twice and 10 is read four times. So the first output produces an incorrect total of 77, instead of the correct total of 55. In the second output, the Consumer reads the value -1 before the Producer ever writes a value. The Consumer reads the value 1 five times before the Producer writes the value 2. Meanwhile, the values 5, 7, 8, 9 and 10 are all lost—the last four because the Consumer terminates before the Producer. An incorrect consumer total of 19 is displayed. (Lines in the output where the Producer or Consumer has acted out of order are highlighted.) This example clearly demonstrates that access to a shared object by concurrent threads must be controlled carefully or a program may produce incorrect results.

To solve the problems of lost and duplicated data, Section 18.7 presents an example in which we use an ArrayBlockingQueue (from package java.util.concurrent) to synchronize access to the shared object, guaranteeing that each and every value will be processed once and only once.

```
1  // Fig. 18.15: SharedBufferTest.java
2  // Application with two threads manipulating an unsynchronized buffer.
3  import java.util.concurrent.ExecutorService;
4  import java.util.concurrent.Executors;
```

Fig. 18.15 | Application with two threads manipulating an unsynchronized buffer. (Part 1 of 3.)

```
5
6    public class SharedBufferTest
7    {
8       public static void main( String[] args )
9       {
10          // create new thread pool with two threads
11          ExecutorService application = Executors.newCachedThreadPool();
12
13          // create UnsynchronizedBuffer to store ints
14          Buffer sharedLocation = new UnsynchronizedBuffer();
15
16          System.out.println(
17             "Action\t\tValue\tSum of Produced\tSum of Consumed" );
18          System.out.println(
19             "------\t\t-----\t---------------\t---------------\n" );
20
21          // execute the Producer and Consumer, giving each of them access
22          // to sharedLocation
23          application.execute( new Producer( sharedLocation ) );
24          application.execute( new Consumer( sharedLocation ) );
25
26          application.shutdown(); // terminate application when tasks complete
27       } // end main
28    } // end class SharedBufferTest
```

```
Action              Value   Sum of Produced Sum of Consumed
------              -----   --------------- ---------------

Producer writes  1       1
Producer writes  2       3                            ----- 1 is lost
Producer writes  3       6                            ----- 2 is lost
Consumer reads   3                       3
Producer writes  4      10
Consumer reads   4                       7
Producer writes  5      15
Producer writes  6      21                           ----- 5 is lost
Producer writes  7      28                           ----- 6 is lost
Consumer reads   7                      14
Consumer reads   7                      21            ----- 7 read again
Producer writes  8      36
Consumer reads   8                      29
Consumer reads   8                      37            ----- 8 read again
Producer writes  9      45
Producer writes 10      55                           ----- 9 is lost

Producer done producing
Terminating Producer
Consumer reads  10                      47
Consumer reads  10                      57            ----- 10 read again
Consumer reads  10                      67            ----- 10 read again
Consumer reads  10                      77            ----- 10 read again

Consumer read values totaling 77
Terminating Consumer
```

Fig. 18.15 | Application with two threads manipulating an unsynchronized buffer. (Part 2 of 3.)

```
Action          Value  Sum of Produced  Sum of Consumed
------          -----  ---------------  ---------------

Consumer reads  -1                      -1   ──── reads -1 bad data
Producer writes 1      1
Consumer reads  1                       0
Consumer reads  1                       1    ──── I read again
Consumer reads  1                       2    ──── I read again
Consumer reads  1                       3    ──── I read again
Consumer reads  1                       4    ──── I read again
Producer writes 2      3
Consumer reads  2                       6
Producer writes 3      6
Consumer reads  3                       9
Producer writes 4      10
Consumer reads  4                       13
Producer writes 5      15
Producer writes 6      21                     ──── 5 is lost
Consumer reads  6                       19

Consumer read values totaling 19
Terminating Consumer
Producer writes 7      28                     ──── 7 never read
Producer writes 8      36                     ──── 8 never read
Producer writes 9      45                     ──── 9 never read
Producer writes 10     55                     ──── 10 never read

Producer done producing
Terminating Producer
```

Fig. 18.15 | Application with two threads manipulating an unsynchronized buffer. (Part 3 of 3.)

18.7 Producer/Consumer Relationship: `ArrayBlockingQueue`

One way to synchronize producer and consumer threads is to use classes from Java's concurrency package that encapsulate the synchronization for you. Java includes the class *`ArrayBlockingQueue`* (from package `java.util.concurrent`)—a fully implemented, thread-safe buffer class that implements interface *`BlockingQueue`*. This interface extends the `Queue` interface discussed in Chapter 16 and declares methods *`put`* and *`take`*, the blocking equivalents of `Queue` methods `offer` and `poll`, respectively. Method `put` places an element at the end of the `BlockingQueue`, waiting if the queue is full. Method `take` removes an element from the head of the `BlockingQueue`, waiting if the queue is empty. These methods make class `ArrayBlockingQueue` a good choice for implementing a shared buffer. Because method `put` blocks until there is room in the buffer to write data, and method `take` blocks until there is new data to read, the producer must produce a value first, the consumer correctly consumes only after the producer writes a value and the producer correctly produces the next value (after the first) only after the consumer reads the previous (or first) value. `ArrayBlockingQueue` stores the shared data in an array. The array's size is specified as an argument to the `ArrayBlockingQueue` constructor. Once created, an `ArrayBlocking-Queue` is fixed in size and will not expand to accommodate extra elements.

The program in Fig. 18.16 and Fig. 18.17 demonstrates a `Producer` and a `Consumer` accessing an `ArrayBlockingQueue`. Class `BlockingBuffer` (Fig. 18.16) uses an `Array-`

BlockingQueue object that stores an Integer (line 7). Line 11 creates the ArrayBlocking-Queue and passes 1 to the constructor so that the object holds a single value, as we did with the UnsynchronizedBuffer of Fig. 18.14. Note that lines 7 and 11 use generics, which we discussed in Chapters 15–16. We discuss multiple-element buffers in Section 18.9. Because our BlockingBuffer class uses the thread-safe ArrayBlockingQueue class to manage access to the shared buffer, BlockingBuffer is itself thread safe, even though we have not implemented the synchronization ourselves.

BlockingBuffer implements interface Buffer (Fig. 18.11) and use classes Producer (Fig. 18.12 modified to remove line 28) and Consumer (Fig. 18.13 modified to remove line 28) from the example in Section 18.6. This approach demonstrates that the threads accessing the shared object are unaware that their buffer accesses are now synchronized. The synchronization is handled entirely in the set and get methods of BlockingBuffer by calling the synchronized ArrayBlockingQueue methods put and take, respectively. Thus, the Producer and Consumer Runnables are properly synchronized simply by calling the shared object's set and get methods.

```java
1   // Fig. 18.16: BlockingBuffer.java
2   // Creates a synchronized buffer using an ArrayBlockingQueue.
3   import java.util.concurrent.ArrayBlockingQueue;
4
5   public class BlockingBuffer implements Buffer
6   {
7      private final ArrayBlockingQueue<Integer> buffer; // shared buffer
8
9      public BlockingBuffer()
10     {
11        buffer = new ArrayBlockingQueue<Integer>( 1 );
12     } // end BlockingBuffer constructor
13
14     // place value into buffer
15     public void set( int value ) throws InterruptedException
16     {
17        buffer.put( value ); // place value in buffer
18        System.out.printf( "%s%2d\t%s%d\n", "Producer writes ", value,
19           "Buffer cells occupied: ", buffer.size() );
20     } // end method set
21
22     // return value from buffer
23     public int get() throws InterruptedException
24     {
25        int readValue = 0; // initialize value read from buffer
26
27        readValue = buffer.take(); // remove value from buffer
28        System.out.printf( "%s %2d\t%s%d\n", "Consumer reads ",
29           readValue, "Buffer cells occupied: ", buffer.size() );
30
31        return readValue;
32     } // end method get
33  } // end class BlockingBuffer
```

Fig. 18.16 | Creates a synchronized buffer using an ArrayBlockingQueue.

Line 17 in method set (lines 15–20) calls the `ArrayBlockingQueue` object's put method. This method call blocks if necessary until there is room in the buffer to place the value. Method get (lines 23–32) calls the `ArrayBlockingQueue` object's take method (line 27). This method call blocks if necessary until there is an element in the buffer to remove. Lines 18–19 and 28–29 use the `ArrayBlockingQueue` object's *size* method to display the total number of elements currently in the `ArrayBlockingQueue`.

Class `BlockingBufferTest` (Fig. 18.17) contains the main method that launches the application. Line 11 creates an `ExecutorService`, and line 14 creates a `BlockingBuffer` object and assigns its reference to the `Buffer` variable `sharedLocation`. Lines 16–17 execute the `Producer` and `Consumer` Runnables. Line 19 calls method shutdown to end the application when the threads finish executing the `Producer` and `Consumer` tasks.

Note that while methods put and take of `ArrayBlockingQueue` are properly synchronized, `BlockingBuffer` methods set and get (Fig. 18.16) are not declared to be synchronized. Thus, the statements performed in method set—the put operation (line 19) and the output (lines 20–21)—are not atomic; nor are the statements in method get—the take operation (line 36) and the output (lines 37–38). So there is no guarantee that each output will occur immediately after the corresponding put or take operation, and the outputs may appear out of order. Even they do, the `ArrayBlockingQueue` object is properly synchronizing access to the data, as evidenced by the fact that the sum of values read by the consumer is always correct.

```java
1    // Fig. 18.17: BlockingBufferTest.java
2    // Two threads manipulating a blocking buffer.
3    import java.util.concurrent.ExecutorService;
4    import java.util.concurrent.Executors;
5
6    public class BlockingBufferTest
7    {
8       public static void main( String[] args )
9       {
10          // create new thread pool with two threads
11          ExecutorService application = Executors.newCachedThreadPool();
12
13          // create BlockingBuffer to store ints
14          Buffer sharedLocation = new BlockingBuffer();
15
16          application.execute( new Producer( sharedLocation ) );
17          application.execute( new Consumer( sharedLocation ) );
18
19          application.shutdown();
20       } // end main
21    } // end class BlockingBufferTest
```

```
Producer writes  1      Buffer cells occupied: 1
Consumer reads   1      Buffer cells occupied: 0
Producer writes  2      Buffer cells occupied: 1
Consumer reads   2      Buffer cells occupied: 0
```

Fig. 18.17 | Two threads manipulating a blocking buffer. (Part 1 of 2.)

```
Producer writes   3    Buffer cells occupied: 1
Consumer reads    3    Buffer cells occupied: 0
Producer writes   4    Buffer cells occupied: 1
Consumer reads    4    Buffer cells occupied: 0
Producer writes   5    Buffer cells occupied: 1
Consumer reads    5    Buffer cells occupied: 0
Producer writes   6    Buffer cells occupied: 1
Consumer reads    6    Buffer cells occupied: 0
Producer writes   7    Buffer cells occupied: 1
Consumer reads    7    Buffer cells occupied: 0
Producer writes   8    Buffer cells occupied: 1
Consumer reads    8    Buffer cells occupied: 0
Producer writes   9    Buffer cells occupied: 1
Consumer reads    9    Buffer cells occupied: 0
Producer writes  10    Buffer cells occupied: 1

Producer done producing
Terminating Producer
Consumer reads   10    Buffer cells occupied: 0

Consumer read values totaling 55
Terminating Consumer
```

Fig. 18.17 | Two threads manipulating a blocking buffer. (Part 2 of 2.)

18.8 Producer/Consumer Relationship with Synchronization

The previous example showed how multiple threads can share a single-element buffer in a thread-safe manner by using the ArrayBlockingQueue class that encapsulates the synchronization necessary to protect the shared data. For educational purposes, we now explain how you can implement a shared buffer yourself using the synchronized keyword. Using an ArrayBlockingQueue will result in more maintainable and better performing code.

The first step in synchronizing access to the buffer is to implement methods get and set as synchronized methods. This requires that a thread obtain the monitor lock on the Buffer object before attempting to access the buffer data, but it does not solve the state-dependence problem associated with producer/consumer relationships. We must ensure that threads proceed with an operation only if the buffer is in the proper state. We need a way to allow our threads to wait, depending on whether certain conditions are true. In the case of placing a new item in the buffer, the condition that allows the operation to proceed is that the buffer is not full. In the case of fetching an item from the buffer, the condition that allows the operation to proceed is that the buffer is not empty. If the condition in question is true, the operation may proceed; if it is false, the thread must wait until it becomes true. When a thread is waiting on a condition, it is removed from contention for the processor, placed in the object's wait queue and the lock it holds is released.

Methods wait, notify and notifyAll

Methods wait, notify and notifyAll, which are declared in class Object and inherited by all other classes, can be used with conditions to make threads wait when they cannot perform their tasks. If a thread obtains the monitor lock on an object, then determines that it cannot continue with its task on that object until some condition is satisfied, the thread can call Object method *wait*; this releases the monitor lock on the object, and the thread waits in the *waiting* state while the other threads try to enter the object's synchronized statement(s) or method(s). When a thread executing a synchronized statement (or method) completes or satisfies the condition on which another thread may be waiting, it can call Object method *notify* to allow a waiting thread to transition to the *runnable* state again. At this point, the thread that was transitioned from the *wait* state to the *runnable* state can attempt to reacquire the monitor lock on the object. Even if the thread is able to reacquire the monitor lock, it still might not be able to perform its task at this time—in which case the thread will reenter the *waiting* state and implicitly release the monitor lock. If a thread calls *notifyAll*, then all the threads waiting for the monitor lock become eligible to reacquire the lock (that is, they all transition to the *runnable* state). Remember that only one thread at a time can obtain the monitor lock on the object—other threads that attempt to acquire the same monitor lock will be *blocked* until the monitor lock becomes available again (i.e., until no other thread is executing in a synchronized statement on that object).

Common Programming Error 18.1

*It is an error if a thread issues a wait, a notify or a notifyAll on an object without having acquired a lock for it. This causes an **IllegalMonitorStateException**.*

Error-Prevention Tip 18.1

It is a good practice to use notifyAll to notify waiting threads to become runnable. Doing so avoids the possibility that your program would forget about waiting threads, which would otherwise starve.

The application in Fig. 18.18 and Fig. 18.19 demonstrates a Producer and a Consumer accessing a shared buffer with synchronization. In this case, the Producer always produces a value first, the Consumer correctly consumes only after the Producer produces a value and the Producer correctly produces the next value only after the Consumer consumes the previous (or first) value. We reuse interface Buffer and classes Producer and Consumer from the example in Section 18.6. The synchronization is handled in the set and get methods of class SynchronizedBuffer (Fig. 18.18), which implements interface Buffer (line 4). Thus, the Producer's and Consumer's run methods simply call the shared object's synchronized set and get methods.

```
1   // Fig. 18.18: SynchronizedBuffer.java
2   // Synchronizing access to shared data using Object
3   // methods wait and notify.
4   public class SynchronizedBuffer implements Buffer
5   {
6      private int buffer = -1; // shared by producer and consumer threads
7      private boolean occupied = false; // whether the buffer is occupied
8
9      // place value into buffer
10     public synchronized void set( int value )
11     {
```

Fig. 18.18 | Synchronizing access to shared data using Object methods wait and notify. (Part 1 of 2.)

```
12          // while there are no empty locations, place thread in waiting state
13          while ( occupied )
14          {
15             // output thread information and buffer information, then wait
16             System.out.println( "Producer tries to write." );
17             displayState( "Buffer full. Producer waits." );
18             wait();
19          } // end while
20
21          buffer = value; // set new buffer value
22
23          // indicate producer cannot store another value
24          // until consumer retrieves current buffer value
25          occupied = true;
26
27          displayState( "Producer writes " + buffer );
28
29          notifyAll(); // tell waiting thread(s) to enter runnable state
30       } // end method set; releases lock on SynchronizedBuffer
31
32       // return value from buffer
33       public synchronized int get()
34       {
35          // while no data to read, place thread in waiting state
36          while ( !occupied )
37          {
38             // output thread information and buffer information, then wait
39             System.out.println( "Consumer tries to read." );
40             displayState( "Buffer empty. Consumer waits." );
41             wait();
42          } // end while
43
44          // indicate that producer can store another value
45          // because consumer just retrieved buffer value
46          occupied = false;
47
48          displayState( "Consumer reads " + buffer );
49
50          notifyAll(); // tell waiting thread(s) to enter runnable state
51
52          return buffer;
53       } // end method get; releases lock on SynchronizedBuffer
54
55       // display current operation and buffer state
56       public void displayState( String operation )
57       {
58          System.out.printf( "%-40s%d\t\t%b\n\n", operation, buffer,
59             occupied );
60       } // end method displayState
61    } // end class SynchronizedBuffer
```

Fig. 18.18 | Synchronizing access to shared data using Object methods wait and notify. (Part 2 of 2.)

Fields and Methods of Class SynchronizedBuffer

Class SynchronizedBuffer contains two fields—buffer (line 6) and occupied (line 7). Method set (lines 10–30) and method get (lines 33–53) are declared as synchronized— only one thread can call either of these methods at a time on a particular Synchronized-Buffer object. Field occupied is used to determine whether it is the Producer's or the Consumer's turn to perform a task. This field is used in conditional expressions in both the set and get methods. If occupied is false, then buffer is empty, so the Consumer cannot read the value of buffer, but the Producer can place a value into buffer. If occupied is true, the Consumer can read a value from buffer, but the Producer cannot place a value into buffer.

Method set and the Producer Thread

When the Producer thread's run method invokes synchronized method set, the thread implicitly attempts to acquire the SynchronizedBuffer object's monitor lock. If the monitor lock is available, the Producer thread implicitly acquires the lock. Then the loop at lines 13–19 first determines whether occupied is true. If so, buffer is full, so line 16 outputs a message indicating that the Producer thread is trying to write a value, and line 17 invokes method displayState (lines 56–60) to output another message indicating that buffer is full and that the Producer thread is waiting until there is space. Line 18 invokes method wait (inherited from Object by SynchronizedBuffer) to place the thread that called method set (i.e., the Producer thread) in the *waiting* state for the SynchronizedBuffer object. The call to wait causes the calling thread to implicitly release the lock on the SynchronizedBuffer object. This is important because the thread cannot currently perform its task and because other threads (in this case, the Consumer) should be allowed to access the object to allow the condition (occupied) to change. Now another thread can attempt to acquire the SynchronizedBuffer object's lock and invoke the object's set or get method.

The Producer thread remains in the *waiting* state until another thread notifies the Producer that it may proceed—at which point the Producer returns to the *runnable* state and attempts to implicitly reacquire the lock on the SynchronizedBuffer object. If the lock is available, the Producer thread reacquires the lock, and method set continues executing with the next statement after the wait call. Because wait is called in a loop, the loop-continuation condition is tested again to determine whether the thread can proceed. If not, then wait is invoked again—otherwise, method set continues with the next statement after the loop.

Line 21 in method set assigns the value to the buffer. Line 25 sets occupied to true to indicate that the buffer now contains a value (i.e., a consumer can read the value, but a Producer cannot yet put another value there). Line 27 invokes method displayState to output a message indicating that the Producer is writing a new value into the buffer. Line 29 invokes method notifyAll (inherited from Object). If any threads are waiting on the SynchronizedBuffer object's monitor lock, those threads enter the *runnable* state and can now attempt to reacquire the lock. Method notifyAll returns immediately, and method set then returns to the calling method (i.e., the Producer's run method). When method set returns, it implicitly releases the monitor lock on the SynchronizedBuffer object.

Method get and the Consumer Thread

Methods get and set are implemented similarly. When the Consumer thread's run method invokes synchronized method get, the thread attempts to acquire the monitor lock on the SynchronizedBuffer object. If the lock is available, the Consumer thread acquires it. Then the while loop at lines 36–42 determines whether occupied is false. If so, the buffer is empty, so line 39 outputs a message indicating that the Consumer thread is trying to read a value, and line 40 invokes method displayState to output a message indicating that the buffer is empty and that the Consumer thread is waiting. Line 41 invokes method wait to place the thread that called method get (i.e., the Consumer) in the *waiting* state for the SynchronizedBuffer object. Again, the call to wait causes the calling thread to implicitly release the lock on the SynchronizedBuffer object, so another thread can attempt to acquire the SynchronizedBuffer object's lock and invoke the object's set or get method. If the lock on the SynchronizedBuffer is not available (e.g., if the Producer has not yet returned from method set), the Consumer is blocked until the lock becomes available.

The Consumer thread remains in the *waiting* state until it is notified by another thread that it may proceed—at which point the Consumer thread returns to the *runnable* state and attempts to implicitly reacquire the lock on the SynchronizedBuffer object. If the lock is available, the Consumer reacquires the lock, and method get continues executing with the next statement after wait. Because wait is called in a loop, the loop-continuation condition is tested again to determine whether the thread can proceed with its execution. If not, wait is invoked again—otherwise, method get continues with the next statement after the loop. Line 46 sets occupied to false to indicate that buffer is now empty (i.e., a Consumer cannot read the value, but a Producer can place another value in buffer), line 48 calls method displayState to indicate that the consumer is reading and line 50 invokes method notifyAll. If any threads are in the *waiting* state for the lock on this SynchronizedBuffer object, they enter the *runnable* state and can now attempt to reacquire the lock. Method notifyAll returns immediately, then method get returns the value of buffer to its caller. When method get returns, the lock on the SynchronizedBuffer object is implicitly released.

Error-Prevention Tip 18.2

Always invoke method wait in a loop that tests the condition the task is waiting on. It is possible that a thread will reenter the runnable *state (via a timed wait or another thread calling notify-All) before the condition is satisfied. Testing the condition again ensures that the thread will not erroneously execute if it was notified early.*

Testing Class SynchronizedBuffer

Class SharedBufferTest2 (Fig. 18.19) is similar to class SharedBufferTest (Fig. 18.15). SharedBufferTest2 contains method main (lines 8–24), which launches the application. Line 11 creates an ExecutorService to run the Producer and Consumer tasks. Line 14 creates a SynchronizedBuffer object and assigns its reference to Buffer variable shared-Location. This object stores the data that will be shared between the Producer and

```
1   // Fig. 18.19: SharedBufferTest2.java
2   // Two threads manipulating a synchronized buffer.
3   import java.util.concurrent.ExecutorService;
4   import java.util.concurrent.Executors;
5
```

Fig. 18.19 | Two threads manipulating a synchronized buffer. (Part 1 of 3.)

```
6   public class SharedBufferTest2
7   {
8      public static void main( String[] args )
9      {
10        // create a newCachedThreadPool
11        ExecutorService application = Executors.newCachedThreadPool();
12
13        // create SynchronizedBuffer to store ints
14        Buffer sharedLocation = new SynchronizedBuffer();
15
16        System.out.printf( "%-40s%s\t\t%s\n%-40s%s\n\n", "Operation",
17           "Buffer", "Occupied", "---------", "------\t\t--------" );
18
19        // execute the Producer and Consumer tasks
20        application.execute( new Producer( sharedLocation ) );
21        application.execute( new Consumer( sharedLocation ) );
22
23        application.shutdown();
24     } // end main
25  } // end class SharedBufferTest2
```

Operation	Buffer	Occupied
---------	------	--------
Consumer tries to read. Buffer empty. Consumer waits.	-1	false
Producer writes 1	1	true
Consumer reads 1	1	false
Consumer tries to read. Buffer empty. Consumer waits.	1	false
Producer writes 2	2	true
Consumer reads 2	2	false
Producer writes 3	3	true
Consumer reads 3	3	false
Producer writes 4	4	true
Producer tries to write. Buffer full. Producer waits.	4	true
Consumer reads 4	4	false
Producer writes 5	5	true
Consumer reads 5	5	false
Producer writes 6	6	true
Producer tries to write. Buffer full. Producer waits.	6	true

Fig. 18.19 | Two threads manipulating a synchronized buffer. (Part 2 of 3.)

Consumer reads 6	6	false
Producer writes 7	7	true
Producer tries to write. Buffer full. Producer waits.	7	true
Consumer reads 7	7	false
Producer writes 8	8	true
Consumer reads 8	8	false
Consumer tries to read. Buffer empty. Consumer waits.	8	false
Producer writes 9	9	true
Consumer reads 9	9	false
Consumer tries to read. Buffer empty. Consumer waits.	9	false
Producer writes 10	10	true
Consumer reads 10	10	false
Producer done producing Terminating Producer		
Consumer read values totaling 55 Terminating Consumer		

Fig. 18.19 | Two threads manipulating a synchronized buffer. (Part 3 of 3.)

Consumer. Lines 16–17 display the column heads for the output. Lines 20–21 execute a Producer and a Consumer. Finally, line 23 calls method shutdown to end the application when the Producer and Consumer complete their tasks. When method main ends (line 24), the main thread of execution terminates.

Study the outputs in Fig. 18.19. Observe that every integer produced is consumed exactly once—no values are lost, and no values are consumed more than once. The synchronization ensures that the Producer produces a value only when the buffer is empty and the Consumer consumes only when the buffer is full. The Producer always goes first, the Consumer waits if the Producer has not produced since the Consumer last consumed, and the Producer waits if the Consumer has not yet consumed the value that the Producer most recently produced. Execute this program several times to confirm that every integer produced is consumed exactly once. In the sample output, note the highlighted lines indicating when the Producer and Consumer must wait to perform their respective tasks.

18.9 Producer/Consumer Relationship: Bounded Buffers

The program in Section 18.8 uses thread synchronization to guarantee that two threads manipulate data in a shared buffer correctly. However, the application may not perform optimally. If the two threads operate at different speeds, one of the threads will spend more (or most) of its time waiting. For example, in the program in Section 18.8 we shared a single integer variable between the two threads. If the Producer thread produces values faster than the Consumer can consume them, then the Producer thread waits for the Consumer, because there are no other locations in the buffer in which to place the next value. Similarly, if the Consumer consumes values faster than the Producer produces them, the Consumer waits until the Producer places the next value in the shared buffer. Even when we have threads that operate at the same relative speeds, those threads may occasionally become "out of sync" over a period of time, causing one of them to wait for the other. We cannot make assumptions about the relative speeds of concurrent threads—interactions that occur with the operating system, the network, the user and other components can cause the threads to operate at different speeds. When this happens, threads wait. When threads wait excessively, programs become less efficient, interactive programs become less responsive and applications suffer longer delays.

Bounded Buffers

To minimize the amount of waiting time for threads that share resources and operate at the same average speeds, we can implement a *bounded buffer* that provides a fixed number of buffer cells into which the Producer can place values, and from which the Consumer can retrieve those values. (In fact, we have already done this with the ArrayBlockingQueue class in Section 18.7.) If the Producer temporarily produces values faster than the Consumer can consume them, the Producer can write additional values into the extra buffer space (if any are available). This capability enables the Producer to perform its task even though the Consumer is not ready to retrieve the current value being produced. Similarly, if the Consumer consumes faster than the Producer produces new values, the Consumer can read additional values (if there are any) from the buffer. This enables the Consumer to keep busy even though the Producer is not ready to produce additional values.

Note that even a bounded buffer is inappropriate if the Producer and the Consumer operate consistently at different speeds. If the Consumer always executes faster than the Producer, then a buffer containing one location is enough. Additional locations would simply waste memory. If the Producer always executes faster, only a buffer with an "infinite" number of locations would be able to absorb the extra production. However, if the Producer and Consumer execute at about the same average speed, a bounded buffer helps to smooth the effects of any occasional speeding up or slowing down in either thread's execution.

The key to using a bounded buffer with a Producer and Consumer that operate at about the same speed is to provide the buffer with enough locations to handle the anticipated "extra" production. If, over a period of time, we determine that the Producer often produces as many as three more values than the Consumer can consume, we can provide a buffer of at least three cells to handle the extra production. Making the buffer too small would cause threads to wait longer; making the buffer too large would waste memory.

Performance Tip 18.3

Even when using a bounded buffer, it is possible that a producer thread could fill the buffer, which would force the producer to wait until a consumer consumed a value to free an element in the buffer. Similarly, if the buffer is empty at any given time, a consumer thread must wait until the producer produces another value. The key to using a bounded buffer is to optimize the buffer size to minimize the amount of thread wait time, while not wasting space.

Bounded Buffers Using ArrayBlockingQueue

The simplest way to implement a bounded buffer is to use an ArrayBlockingQueue for the buffer so that all of the synchronization details are handled for you. This can be done by reusing the example from Section 18.7 and simply passing the desired size for the bounded buffer into the ArrayBlockingQueue constructor. Rather than repeat our previous Array-BlockingQueue example with a different size, we instead present an example that illustrates how you can build a bounded buffer yourself. Again, note that using an ArrayBlocking-Queue will result in more maintainable and better performing code.

Implementing Your Own Bounded Buffer as a Circular Buffer

The program in Fig. 18.20 and Fig. 18.21 demonstrates a Producer and a Consumer accessing a bounded buffer with synchronization. We implement the bounded buffer in class CircularBuffer (Fig. 18.20) as a *circular buffer* that uses a shared array of three elements. A circular buffer writes into and reads from the array elements in order, beginning at the

```java
 1   // Fig. 18.20: CircularBuffer.java
 2   // Synchronizing access to a shared three-element bounded buffer.
 3   public class CircularBuffer implements Buffer
 4   {
 5      private final int[] buffer = { -1, -1, -1 }; // shared buffer
 6
 7      private int occupiedCells = 0; // count number of buffers used
 8      private int writeIndex = 0; // index of next element to write to
 9      private int readIndex = 0; // index of next element to read
10
11      // place value into buffer
12      public synchronized void set( int value ) throws InterruptedException
13      {
14         // output thread information and buffer information, then wait;
15         // while no empty locations, place thread in blocked state
16         while ( occupiedCells == buffer.length )
17         {
18            System.out.printf( "Buffer is full. Producer waits.\n" );
19            wait(); // wait until a buffer cell is free
20         } // end while
21
22         buffer[ writeIndex ] = value; // set new buffer value
23
24         // update circular write index
25         writeIndex = ( writeIndex + 1 ) % buffer.length;
26
27         ++occupiedCells; // one more buffer cell is full
28         displayState( "Producer writes " + value );
29         notifyAll(); // notify threads waiting to read from buffer
30      } // end method set
31
32      // return value from buffer
33      public synchronized int get() throws InterruptedException
34      {
```

Fig. 18.20 | Synchronizing access to a shared three-element bounded buffer. (Part 1 of 2.)

```
35      // wait until buffer has data, then read value;
36      // while no data to read, place thread in waiting state
37      while ( occupiedCells == 0 )
38      {
39         System.out.printf( "Buffer is empty. Consumer waits.\n" );
40         wait(); // wait until a buffer cell is filled
41      } // end while
42
43      int readValue = buffer[ readIndex ]; // read value from buffer
44
45      // update circular read index
46      readIndex = ( readIndex + 1 ) % buffer.length;
47
48      --occupiedCells; // one fewer buffer cells are occupied
49      displayState( "Consumer reads " + readValue );
50      notifyAll(); // notify threads waiting to write to buffer
51
52      return readValue;
53   } // end method get
54
55   // display current operation and buffer state
56   public void displayState( String operation )
57   {
58      // output operation and number of occupied buffer cells
59      System.out.printf( "%s%s%d)\n%s", operation,
60         " (buffer cells occupied: ", occupiedCells, "buffer cells:  " );
61
62      for ( int value : buffer )
63         System.out.printf( " %2d  ", value ); // output values in buffer
64
65      System.out.print( "\n                " );
66
67      for ( int i = 0; i < buffer.length; i++ )
68         System.out.print( "---- " );
69
70      System.out.print( "\n                " );
71
72      for ( int i = 0; i < buffer.length; i++ )
73      {
74         if ( i == writeIndex && i == readIndex )
75            System.out.print( " WR" ); // both write and read index
76         else if ( i == writeIndex )
77            System.out.print( " W  " ); // just write index
78         else if ( i == readIndex )
79            System.out.print( "  R  " ); // just read index
80         else
81            System.out.print( "     " ); // neither index
82      } // end for
83
84      System.out.println( "\n" );
85   } // end method displayState
86 } // end class CircularBuffer
```

Fig. 18.20 | Synchronizing access to a shared three-element bounded buffer. (Part 2 of 2.)

first cell and moving toward the last. When a Producer or Consumer reaches the last element, it returns to the first and begins writing or reading, respectively, from there. In this version of the producer/consumer relationship, the Consumer consumes a value only when the array is not empty and the Producer produces a value only when the array is not full. The statements that created and started the thread objects in the main method of class SharedBufferTest2 (Fig. 18.19) now appear in class CircularBufferTest (Fig. 18.21).

Line 5 initializes array buffer as a three-element integer array that represents the circular buffer. Variable occupiedCells (line 7) counts the number of elements in buffer that contain data to be read. When occupiedBuffers is 0, there is no data in the circular buffer and the Consumer must wait—when occupiedCells is 3 (the size of the circular buffer), the circular buffer is full and the Producer must wait. Variable writeIndex (line 8) indicates the next location in which a value can be placed by a Producer. Variable read-Index (line 9) indicates the position from which the next value can be read by a Consumer.

CircularBuffer method set (lines 12–30) performs the same tasks as in Fig. 18.18, with a few modifications. The loop at lines 16–20 determines whether the Producer must wait (i.e., all buffers are full). If so, line 18 indicates that the Producer is waiting to perform its task. Then line 19 invokes method wait, causing the Producer thread to release the CircularBuffer's lock and wait until there is space for a new value to be written into the buffer. When execution continues at line 22 after the while loop, the value written by the Producer is placed in the circular buffer at location writeIndex. Then line 25 updates writeIndex for the next call to CircularBuffer method set. This line is the key to the "circularity" of the buffer. When writeIndex is incremented past the end of the buffer, the line sets it to 0. Line 27 increments occupiedCells, because there is now one more value in the buffer that the Consumer can read. Next, line 28 invokes method displayState (lines 56–85) to update the output with the value produced, the number of occupied buffers, the contents of the buffers and the current writeIndex and readIndex. Line 29 invokes method notifyAll to transition *waiting* threads to the runnable state, so that a waiting Consumer thread (if there is one) can now try again to read a value from the buffer.

CircularBuffer method get (lines 33–53) also performs the same tasks as it did in Fig. 18.18, with a few minor modifications. The loop at lines 37–41 determines whether the Consumer must wait (i.e., all buffer cells are empty). If the Consumer must wait, line 39 updates the output to indicate that the Consumer is waiting to perform its task. Then line 40 invokes method wait, causing the current thread to release the lock on the Circular-Buffer and wait until data is available to read. When execution eventually continues at line 43 after a notifyAll call from the Producer, readValue is assigned the value at location readIndex in the circular buffer. Then line 46 updates readIndex for the next call to CircularBuffer method get. This line and line 25 implement the "circularity" of the buffer. Line 48 decrements occupiedCells, because there is now one more position in the buffer in which the Producer thread can place a value. Line 49 invokes method display-State to update the output with the consumed value, the number of occupied buffers, the contents of the buffers and the current writeIndex and readIndex. Line 50 invokes method notifyAll to allow any Producer threads waiting to write into the Circular-Buffer object to attempt to write again. Then line 52 returns the consumed value to the caller.

Method displayState (lines 56–85) outputs the state of the application. Lines 62–63 output the current values of the buffer cells. Line 63 uses method printf with a "%2d" format specifier to print the contents of each buffer with a leading space if it is a single digit. Lines 70–82 output the current writeIndex and readIndex with the letters W and R, respectively.

Testing Class *CircularBuffer*

Class CircularBufferTest (Fig. 18.21) contains the main method that launches the application. Line 11 creates the ExecutorService, and line 14 creates a CircularBuffer object and assigns its reference to CircularBuffer variable sharedLocation. Line 17 invokes the CircularBuffer's displayState method to show the initial state of the buffer. Lines 20–21 execute the Producer and Consumer tasks. Line 23 calls method shutdown to end the application when the threads complete the Producer and Consumer tasks.

Each time the Producer writes a value or the Consumer reads a value, the program outputs a message indicating the action performed (a read or a write), the contents of buffer, and the location of writeIndex and readIndex. In the output of Fig. 18.21, the Producer first writes the value 1. The buffer then contains the value 1 in the first cell and the value –1 (the default value that we use for output purposes) in the other two cells. The write index is updated to the second cell, while the read index stays at the first cell. Next, the Consumer reads 1. The buffer contains the same values, but the read index has been updated to the second cell. The Consumer then tries to read again, but the buffer is empty and the Consumer is forced to wait. Note that only once in this execution of the program was it necessary for either thread to wait.

```java
1   // Fig. 18.21: CircularBufferTest.java
2   // Producer and Consumer threads manipulating a circular buffer.
3   import java.util.concurrent.ExecutorService;
4   import java.util.concurrent.Executors;
5
6   public class CircularBufferTest
7   {
8      public static void main( String[] args )
9      {
10        // create new thread pool with two threads
11        ExecutorService application = Executors.newCachedThreadPool();
12
13        // create CircularBuffer to store ints
14        CircularBuffer sharedLocation = new CircularBuffer();
15
16        // display the initial state of the CircularBuffer
17        sharedLocation.displayState( "Initial State" );
18
19        // execute the Producer and Consumer tasks
20        application.execute( new Producer( sharedLocation ) );
21        application.execute( new Consumer( sharedLocation ) );
22
23        application.shutdown();
24     } // end main
25   } // end class CircularBufferTest
```

Fig. 18.21 | Producer and Consumer threads manipulating a circular buffer. (Part 1 of 3.)

```
Initial State (buffer cells occupied: 0)
buffer cells:    -1    -1    -1
                ---- ---- ----
                 WR

Producer writes 1 (buffer cells occupied: 1)
buffer cells:     1    -1    -1
                ---- ---- ----
                 R    W

Consumer reads 1 (buffer cells occupied: 0)
buffer cells:     1    -1    -1
                ---- ---- ----
                      WR

Buffer is empty. Consumer waits.
Producer writes 2 (buffer cells occupied: 1)
buffer cells:     1     2    -1
                ---- ---- ----
                      R    W

Consumer reads 2 (buffer cells occupied: 0)
buffer cells:     1     2    -1
                ---- ---- ----
                           WR

Producer writes 3 (buffer cells occupied: 1)
buffer cells:     1     2     3
                ---- ---- ----
                 W          R

Consumer reads 3 (buffer cells occupied: 0)
buffer cells:     1     2     3
                ---- ---- ----
                 WR

Producer writes 4 (buffer cells occupied: 1)
buffer cells:     4     2     3
                ---- ---- ----
                 R    W

Producer writes 5 (buffer cells occupied: 2)
buffer cells:     4     5     3
                ---- ---- ----
                 R          W

Consumer reads 4 (buffer cells occupied: 1)
buffer cells:     4     5     3
                ---- ---- ----
                      R    W

Producer writes 6 (buffer cells occupied: 2)
buffer cells:     4     5     6
                ---- ---- ----
                 W    R
```

Fig. 18.21 | Producer and Consumer threads manipulating a circular buffer. (Part 2 of 3.)

```
Producer writes 7 (buffer cells occupied: 3)
buffer cells:    7    5    6
                ---- ---- ----
                       WR

Consumer reads 5 (buffer cells occupied: 2)
buffer cells:    7    5    6
                ---- ---- ----
                  W    R

Producer writes 8 (buffer cells occupied: 3)
buffer cells:    7    8    6
                ---- ---- ----
                       WR

Consumer reads 6 (buffer cells occupied: 2)
buffer cells:    7    8    6
                ---- ---- ----
                  R         W

Consumer reads 7 (buffer cells occupied: 1)
buffer cells:    7    8    6
                ---- ---- ----
                  R    W

Producer writes 9 (buffer cells occupied: 2)
buffer cells:    7    8    9
                ---- ---- ----
                  W    R

Consumer reads 8 (buffer cells occupied: 1)
buffer cells:    7    8    9
                ---- ---- ----
                  W         R

Consumer reads 9 (buffer cells occupied: 0)
buffer cells:    7    8    9
                ---- ---- ----
                  WR

Producer writes 10 (buffer cells occupied: 1)
buffer cells:   10    8    9
                ---- ---- ----
                  R    W


Producer done producing
Terminating Producer
Consumer reads 10 (buffer cells occupied: 0)
buffer cells:   10    8    9
                ---- ---- ----
                  WR


Consumer read values totaling: 55
Terminating Consumer
```

Fig. 18.21 | Producer and Consumer threads manipulating a circular buffer. (Part 3 of 3.)

18.10 Producer/Consumer Relationship: The Lock and Condition Interfaces

Though the synchronized keyword provides for most basic thread synchronization needs, Java provides other tools to assist in developing concurrent programs. In this section, we discuss the Lock and Condition interfaces, which were introduced in Java SE 5. These interfaces give programmers more precise control over thread synchronization, but are more complicated to use.

Interface Lock and Class ReentrantLock

Any object can contain a reference to an object that implements the Lock interface (of package java.util.concurrent.locks). A thread calls the Lock's lock method to acquire the lock. Once a Lock has been obtained by one thread, the Lock object will not allow another thread to obtain the Lock until the first thread releases the Lock (by calling the Lock's *unlock* method). If several threads are trying to call method lock on the same Lock object at the same time, only one of these threads can obtain the lock—all the others are placed in the *waiting* state for that lock. When a thread calls method unlock, the lock on the object is released and a waiting thread attempting to lock the object proceeds.

Class **ReentrantLock** (of package java.util.concurrent.locks) is a basic implementation of the Lock interface. The constructor for a ReentrantLock takes a boolean argument that specifies whether the lock has a *fairness policy*. If the argument is true, the ReentrantLock's fairness policy is "the longest-waiting thread will acquire the lock when it is available." Such a fairness policy guarantees that indefinite postponement (also called starvation) cannot occur. If the fairness policy argument is set to false, there is no guarantee as to which waiting thread will acquire the lock when it is available.

 Software Engineering Observation 18.2

Using a ReentrantLock with a fairness policy avoids indefinite postponement.

 Performance Tip 18.4

Using a ReentrantLock with a fairness policy can decrease program performance significantly.

Condition Objects and Interface Condition

If a thread that owns a Lock determines that it cannot continue with its task until some condition is satisfied, the thread can wait on a *condition object*. Using Lock objects allows you to explicitly declare the condition objects on which a thread may need to wait. For example, in the producer/consumer relationship, producers can wait on one object and consumers can wait on another. This is not possible when using the synchronized keywords and an object's built-in monitor lock. Condition objects are associated with a specific Lock and are created by calling a Lock's **newCondition** method, which returns an object that implements the **Condition** interface (of package java.util.concurrent.locks). To wait on a condition object, the thread can call the Condition's **await** method. This immediately releases the associated Lock and places the thread in the *waiting* state for that Condition. Other threads can then try to obtain the Lock. When a *runnable* thread completes a task and determines that the *waiting* thread can now continue, the *runnable* thread can call Condition method **signal** to allow a thread in that Condition's *waiting* state to return to the *runnable* state. At this point, the thread that transitioned from the *waiting* state to the *runnable* state can attempt to reacquire the Lock. Even if it is able to reacquire the Lock, the thread still might not be able to perform its task at this time—in which case the thread can call the Condition's await method to release the Lock and reenter the *waiting* state. If multiple threads are in a Condition's *waiting* state when signal is called, the default implementation of Condition signals the longest-waiting thread to transition to the *runnable* state. If a thread calls Condition method *signalAll*, then all the threads waiting for that condition transition to the *runnable* state and become eligible to reacquire the Lock. Only one of those threads can obtain the Lock on the object—the others will wait until the Lock becomes available again. If the Lock has a fairness policy, the longest-waiting thread acquires the Lock. When a thread is finished with a shared object, it must call method unlock to release the Lock.

Common Programming Error 18.2

Deadlock occurs when a waiting thread (let us call this thread1) cannot proceed because it is waiting (either directly or indirectly) for another thread (let us call this thread2) to proceed, while simultaneously thread2 cannot proceed because it is waiting (either directly or indirectly) for thread1 to proceed. The two threads are waiting for each other, so the actions that would enable each thread to continue execution can never occur.

Error-Prevention Tip 18.3

When multiple threads manipulate a shared object using locks, ensure that if one thread calls method await to enter the waiting *state for a condition object, a separate thread eventually will call Condition method signal to transition the thread waiting on the condition object back to the* runnable *state. If multiple threads may be waiting on the condition object, a separate thread can call Condition method signalAll as a safeguard to ensure that all the waiting threads have another opportunity to perform their tasks. If this is not done, starvation might occur.*

Common Programming Error 18.3

An IllegalMonitorStateException occurs if a thread issues an await, a signal, or a signalAll on a condition object without having acquired the lock for that condition object.

Lock and Condition vs. the synchronized Keyword

In some applications, using Lock and Condition objects may be preferable to using the synchronized keyword. Locks allow you to interrupt waiting threads or to specify a timeout for waiting to acquire a lock, which is not possible using the synchronized keyword. Also, a Lock is not constrained to be acquired and released in the same block of code, which is the case with the synchronized keyword. Condition objects allow you to specify multiple condition objects on which threads may wait. Thus, it is possible indicate to waiting threads that a specific condition object is now true by calling signal or signallAll on that Condition object. With the synchronized keyword, there is no way to explicitly state the condition on which threads are waiting, and thus there is no way to notify threads waiting on one condition that they may proceed without also signaling threads waiting on any other conditions. There are other possible advantages to using Lock and Condition objects, but note that generally it is best to use the synchronized keyword unless your application requires advanced synchronization capabilities. Using interfaces Lock and Condition is error prone—unlock is not guaranteed to be called, whereas the monitor in a synchronized statement will always be released when the statement completes execution.

Using Locks and Conditions to Implement Synchronization

To illustrate how to use the Lock and Condition interfaces, we now implement the producer/consumer relationship using Lock and Condition objects to coordinate access to a shared single-element buffer (Fig. 18.22 and Fig. 18.23). In this case, each produced value is correctly consumed exactly once.

Class SynchronizedBuffer (Fig. 18.22) contains five fields. Line 11 creates a new object of type ReentrantLock and assigns its reference to Lock variable accessLock. The ReentrantLock is created without the fairness policy because at any time only a single Producer or Consumer will be waiting to acquire the Lock in this example. Lines 14–15 create two Conditions using Lock method newCondition. Condition canWrite contains a queue for a Producer thread waiting while the buffer is full (i.e., there is data in the buffer that the Consumer has not read yet). If the buffer is full, the Producer calls method await on this Condition. When the Consumer reads data from a full buffer, it calls method signal on this Condition. Condition canRead contains a queue for a Consumer thread waiting while the buffer is empty (i.e., there is no data in the buffer for the Consumer to read). If the buffer is empty, the Consumer calls method await on this Condition. When the Producer writes to the empty buffer, it calls method signal on this Condition. The int variable buffer (line 17) holds the shared data. The boolean variable occupied (line 18) keeps track of whether the buffer currently holds data (that the Consumer should read).

```java
 1   // Fig. 18.22: SynchronizedBuffer.java
 2   // Synchronizing access to a shared integer using the Lock and Condition
 3   // interfaces
 4   import java.util.concurrent.locks.Lock;
 5   import java.util.concurrent.locks.ReentrantLock;
 6   import java.util.concurrent.locks.Condition;
 7
 8   public class SynchronizedBuffer implements Buffer
 9   {
10      // Lock to control synchronization with this buffer
11      private final Lock accessLock = new ReentrantLock();
12
13      // conditions to control reading and writing
14      private final Condition canWrite = accessLock.newCondition();
15      private final Condition canRead = accessLock.newCondition();
16
17      private int buffer = -1; // shared by producer and consumer threads
18      private boolean occupied = false; // whether buffer is occupied
19
20      // place int value into buffer
21      public void set( int value ) throws InterruptedException
22      {
23         accessLock.lock(); // lock this object
24
25         // output thread information and buffer information, then wait
26         try
27         {
```

Fig. 18.22 | Synchronizing access to a shared integer using the Lock and Condition interfaces. (Part 1 of 3.)

```
28          // while buffer is not empty, place thread in waiting state
29          while ( occupied )
30          {
31             System.out.println( "Producer tries to write." );
32             displayState( "Buffer full. Producer waits." );
33             canWrite.await(); // wait until buffer is empty
34          } // end while
35
36          buffer = value; // set new buffer value
37
38          // indicate producer cannot store another value
39          // until consumer retrieves current buffer value
40          occupied = true;
41
42          displayState( "Producer writes " + buffer );
43
44          // signal thread waiting to read from buffer
45          canRead.signal();
46       } // end try
47       finally
48       {
49          accessLock.unlock(); // unlock this object
50       } // end finally
51    } // end method set
52
53    // return value from buffer
54    public int get() throws InterruptedException
55    {
56       int readValue = 0; // initialize value read from buffer
57       accessLock.lock(); // lock this object
58
59       // output thread information and buffer information, then wait
60       try
61       {
62          // while no data to read, place thread in waiting state
63          while ( !occupied )
64          {
65             System.out.println( "Consumer tries to read." );
66             displayState( "Buffer empty. Consumer waits." );
67             canRead.await(); // wait until buffer is full
68          } // end while
69
70          // indicate that producer can store another value
71          // because consumer just retrieved buffer value
72          occupied = false;
73
74          readValue = buffer; // retrieve value from buffer
75          displayState( "Consumer reads " + readValue );
76
77          // signal thread waiting for buffer to be empty
78          canWrite.signal();
79       } // end try
```

Fig. 18.22 | Synchronizing access to a shared integer using the Lock and Condition interfaces. (Part 2 of 3.)

```
80          finally
81          {
82              accessLock.unlock(); // unlock this object
83          } // end finally
84
85          return readValue;
86      } // end method get
87
88      // display current operation and buffer state
89      public void displayState( String operation )
90      {
91          System.out.printf( "%-40s%d\t\t%b\n\n", operation, buffer,
92              occupied );
93      } // end method displayState
94  } // end class SynchronizedBuffer
```

Fig. 18.22 | Synchronizing access to a shared integer using the Lock and Condition interfaces. (Part 3 of 3.)

Line 23 in method set calls method lock on the SynchronizedBuffer's accessLock. If the lock is available (i.e., no other thread has acquired this lock), method lock returns immediately (this thread now owns the lock) and the thread continues. If the lock is unavailable (i.e., it is held by another thread), this method waits until the lock is released by the other thread. After the lock is acquired, the try block in lines 26–46 executes. Line 29 tests occupied to determine whether buffer is full. If it is, lines 31–32 display a message indicating that the thread will wait. Line 33 calls Condition method await on the canWrite condition object, which temporarily releases the SynchronizedBuffer's Lock and waits for a signal from the Consumer that buffer is available for writing. When buffer is available, the method proceeds, writing to buffer (line 36), setting occupied to true (line 40) and displaying a message indicating that the producer wrote a value (line 42). Line 45 calls Condition method signal on condition object canRead to notify the waiting Consumer (if there is one) that the buffer has new data to be read. Line 49 calls method unlock from a finally block to release the lock and allow the Consumer to proceed.

Error-Prevention Tip 18.4

Place calls to Lock method unlock in a finally block. If an exception is thrown, unlock must still be called or deadlock could occur.

Line 57 of method get (lines 54–86) calls method lock to acquire the Lock. This method waits until the Lock is available. Once the Lock is acquired, line 63 tests whether occupied is false, indicating that the buffer is empty. If the buffer is empty, line 67 calls method await on condition object canRead. Recall that method signal is called on variable canRead in the set method (line 45). When the Condition object is signaled, the get method continues. Line 72 sets occupied to false, line 74 stores the value of buffer in readValue and line 75 outputs the readValue. Then line 78 signals the condition object canWrite. This will awaken the Producer if it is indeed waiting for the buffer to be emptied. Line 82 calls method unlock from a finally block to release the lock, and line 85 returns readValue to the calling method.

Common Programming Error 18.4

Forgetting to signal a waiting thread is a logic error. The thread will remain in the waiting state, which will prevent the thread from proceeding. Such waiting can lead to indefinite postponement or deadlock.

Class SharedBufferTest2 (Fig. 18.23) is identical to that of Fig. 18.19. Study the outputs in Fig. 18.23. Observe that every integer produced is consumed exactly once—no values are lost, and no values are consumed more than once. The Lock and Condition objects ensure that the Producer and Consumer cannot perform their tasks unless it is their turn. The Producer must go first, the Consumer must wait if the Producer has not produced since the Consumer last consumed and the Producer must wait if the Consumer has not yet consumed the value that the Producer most recently produced. Execute this program several times to confirm that every integer produced is consumed exactly once. In the sample output, note the highlighted lines indicating when the Producer and Consumer must wait to perform their respective tasks.

```java
1   // Fig. 18.23: SharedBufferTest2.java
2   // Two threads manipulating a synchronized buffer.
3   import java.util.concurrent.ExecutorService;
4   import java.util.concurrent.Executors;
5
6   public class SharedBufferTest2
7   {
8      public static void main( String[] args )
9      {
10        // create new thread pool with two threads
11        ExecutorService application = Executors.newCachedThreadPool();
12
13        // create SynchronizedBuffer to store ints
14        Buffer sharedLocation = new SynchronizedBuffer();
15
16        System.out.printf( "%-40s%s\t\t%s\n%-40s%s\n\n", "Operation",
17           "Buffer", "Occupied", "---------", "------\t\t--------" );
18
19        // execute the Producer and Consumer tasks
20        application.execute( new Producer( sharedLocation ) );
21        application.execute( new Consumer( sharedLocation ) );
22
23        application.shutdown();
24     } // end main
25  } // end class SharedBufferTest2
```

Operation	Buffer	Occupied
---------	------	--------
Producer writes 1	1	true
Producer tries to write. Buffer full. Producer waits.	1	true

Fig. 18.23 | Two threads manipulating a synchronized buffer. (Part 1 of 2.)

Consumer reads 1	1	false
Producer writes 2	2	true
Producer tries to write. Buffer full. Producer waits.	2	true
Consumer reads 2	2	false
Producer writes 3	3	true
Consumer reads 3	3	false
Producer writes 4	4	true
Consumer reads 4	4	false
Consumer tries to read. Buffer empty. Consumer waits.	4	false
Producer writes 5	5	true
Consumer reads 5	5	false
Consumer tries to read. Buffer empty. Consumer waits.	5	false
Producer writes 6	6	true
Consumer reads 6	6	false
Producer writes 7	7	true
Consumer reads 7	7	false
Producer writes 8	8	true
Consumer reads 8	8	false
Producer writes 9	9	true
Consumer reads 9	9	false
Producer writes 10	10	true
Producer done producing Terminating Producer Consumer reads 10	10	false
Consumer read values totaling 55 Terminating Consumer		

Fig. 18.23 | Two threads manipulating a synchronized buffer. (Part 2 of 2.)

18.11 Multithreading with GUI

Swing applications present a unique set of challenges for multithreaded programming. All Swing applications have a single thread, called the *event dispatch thread*, to handle interactions with the application's GUI components. Typical interactions include updating GUI components or processing user actions such as mouse clicks. All tasks that require interaction with an application's GUI are placed in an event queue and are executed sequentially by the event dispatch thread.

Swing GUI components are not thread safe—they cannot be manipulated by multiple threads without the risk of incorrect results. Unlike the other examples presented in this chapter, thread safety in GUI applications is achieved not by synchronizing thread actions, but by ensuring that Swing components are accessed from only a single thread—the event dispatch thread. This technique is called *thread confinement*. Allowing just one thread to access non-thread-safe objects eliminates the possibility of corruption due to multiple threads accessing these objects concurrently.

Usually it is sufficient to perform simple calculations on the event dispatch thread in sequence with GUI component manipulations. If an application must perform a lengthy computation in response to a user interface interaction, the event dispatch thread cannot attend to other tasks in the event queue while the thread is tied up in that computation. This causes the GUI components to become unresponsive. It is preferable to handle a long-running computation in a separate thread, freeing the event dispatch thread to continue managing other GUI interactions. Of course, to update the GUI based on the computation's results, you must update the GUI from the event dispatch thread, rather than from the worker thread that performed the computation.

Class *SwingWorker*

Java SE 6 provides class *SwingWorker* (in package `javax.swing`) to perform long-running computations in a worker thread and to update Swing components from the event dispatch thread based on the computations' results. SwingWorker implements the `Runnable` interface, meaning that a SwingWorker object can be scheduled to execute in a separate thread. The SwingWorker class provides several methods to simplify performing computations in a worker thread and making the results available for display in a GUI. Some common SwingWorker methods are described in Fig. 18.24.

Method	Description
doInBackground	Defines a long computation and is called in a worker thread.
done	Executes on the event dispatch thread when doInBackground returns.
execute	Schedules the SwingWorker object to be executed in a worker thread.
get	Waits for the computation to complete, then returns the result of the computation (i.e., the return value of doInBackground).
publish	Sends intermediate results from the doInBackground method to the process method for processing on the event dispatch thread.
process	Receives intermediate results from the publish method and processes these results on the event dispatch thread.
setProgress	Sets the progress property to notify any property change listeners on the event dispatch thread of progress bar updates.

Fig. 18.24 | Commonly used SwingWorker methods.

18.11.1 Performing Computations in a Worker Thread

In the next example, a GUI provides components for a user to enter a number n and get the nth Fibonacci number, which we calculate using the recursive algorithm discussed in Section 6.16. Since the recursive algorithm is time consuming for large values, we use a SwingWorker object to perform the calculation in a worker thread. The GUI also provides a separate set of components that get the next Fibonacci number in the sequence with each click of a button, beginning with fibonacci(1). This set of components performs its short computation directly in the event dispatch thread.

Class BackgroundCalculator (Fig. 18.25) performs the recursive Fibonacci calculation in a worker thread. This class extends SwingWorker (line 8), overriding the methods doInBackground and done. Method doInBackground (lines 21–25) computes the nth Fibonacci number in a worker thread and returns the result. Method done (lines 28–44) displays the result in a JLabel.

```java
 1   // Fig. 18.25: BackgroundCalculator.java
 2   // SwingWorker subclass for calculating Fibonacci numbers
 3   // in a background thread.
 4   import javax.swing.SwingWorker;
 5   import javax.swing.JLabel;
 6   import java.util.concurrent.ExecutionException;
 7
 8   public class BackgroundCalculator extends SwingWorker< String, Object >
 9   {
10      private final int n; // Fibonacci number to calculate
11      private final JLabel resultJLabel; // JLabel to display the result
12
13      // constructor
14      public BackgroundCalculator( int number, JLabel label )
15      {
16         n = number;
17         resultJLabel = label;
18      } // end BackgroundCalculator constructor
19
20      // long-running code to be run in a worker thread
21      public String doInBackground()
22      {
23         long nthFib = fibonacci( n );
24         return String.valueOf( nthFib );
25      } // end method doInBackground
26
27      // code to run on the event dispatch thread when doInBackground returns
28      protected void done()
29      {
30         try
31         {
32            // get the result of doInBackground and display it
33            resultJLabel.setText( get() );
34         } // end try
```

Fig. 18.25 | SwingWorker subclass for calculating Fibonacci numbers in a background thread. (Part 1 of 2.)

```
35          catch ( InterruptedException ex )
36          {
37             resultJLabel.setText( "Interrupted while waiting for results." );
38          } // end catch
39          catch ( ExecutionException ex )
40          {
41             resultJLabel.setText(
42                "Error encountered while performing calculation." );
43          } // end catch
44       } // end method done
45
46       // recursive method fibonacci; calculates nth Fibonacci number
47       public long fibonacci( long number )
48       {
49          if ( number == 0 || number == 1 )
50             return number;
51          else
52             return fibonacci( number - 1 ) + fibonacci( number - 2 );
53       } // end method fibonacci
54    } // end class BackgroundCalculator
```

Fig. 18.25 | SwingWorker subclass for calculating Fibonacci numbers in a background thread. (Part 2 of 2.)

Note that SwingWorker is a generic class. In line 8, the first type parameter is String and the second is Object. The first type parameter indicates the type returned by the doIn-Background method; the second indicates the type that is passed between the publish and process methods to handle intermediate results. Since we do not use publish and process in this example, we simply use Object as the second type parameter. We discuss publish and process in Section 18.11.2.

A BackgroundCalculator object can be instantiated from a class that controls a GUI. A BackgroundCalculator maintains instance variables for an integer that represents the Fibonacci number to be calculated and a JLabel that displays the results of the calculation (lines 10–11). The BackgroundCalculator constructor (lines 14–18) initializes these instance variables with the arguments that are passed to the constructor.

Software Engineering Observation 18.3

Any GUI components that will be manipulated by SwingWorker methods, such as components that will be updated from methods process or done, should be passed to the SwingWorker subclass's constructor and stored in the subclass object. This gives these methods access to the GUI components they will manipulate.

When method execute is called on a BackgroundCalculator object, the object is scheduled for execution in a worker thread. Method doInBackground is called from the worker thread and invokes the fibonacci method (lines 47–53), passing instance variable n as an argument (line 23). Method fibonacci uses recursion to compute the Fibonacci of n. When fibonacci returns, method doInBackground returns the result.

After doInBackground returns, method done is called from the event dispatch thread. This method attempts to set the result JLabel to the return value of doInBackground by calling method get to retrieve this return value (line 33). Method get waits for the result to be ready if necessary, but since we call it from method done, the computation will be complete before get is called. Lines 35–38 catch `InterruptedException` if the current thread is interrupted while waiting for get to return. Lines 39–43 catch `ExecutionException`, which is thrown if an exception occurs during the computation.

Class `FibonacciNumbers` (Fig. 18.26) displays a window containing two sets of GUI components—one set to compute a Fibonacci number in a worker thread and another to get the next Fibonacci number in response to the user's clicking a `JButton`. The constructor (lines 38–109) places these components in separate titled `JPanel`s. Lines 46–47 and 78–79 add two `JLabel`s, a `JTextField` and a `JButton` to the `workerJPanel` to allow the user to enter an integer whose Fibonacci number will be calculated by the `BackgroundWorker`. Lines 84–85 and 103 add two `JLabel`s and a `JButton` to the event dispatch thread panel to allow the user to get the next Fibonacci number in the sequence. Instance variables n1 and n2 contain the previous two Fibonacci numbers in the sequence and are initialized to 0 and 1, respectively (lines 29–30). Instance variable count stores the most recently computed sequence number and is initialized to 1 (line 31). The two `JLabel`s display count and n2 initially, so that the user will see the text Fibonacci of 1: 1 in the eventThreadJPanel when the GUI starts.

```
 1   // Fig. 18.26: FibonacciNumbers.java
 2   // Using SwingWorker to perform a long calculation with
 3   // intermediate results displayed in a GUI.
 4   import java.awt.GridLayout;
 5   import java.awt.event.ActionEvent;
 6   import java.awt.event.ActionListener;
 7   import javax.swing.JButton;
 8   import javax.swing.JFrame;
 9   import javax.swing.JPanel;
10   import javax.swing.JLabel;
11   import javax.swing.JTextField;
12   import javax.swing.border.TitledBorder;
13   import javax.swing.border.LineBorder;
14   import java.awt.Color;
15   import java.util.concurrent.ExecutionException;
16
17   public class FibonacciNumbers extends JFrame
18   {
19      // components for calculating the Fibonacci of a user-entered number
20      private final JPanel workerJPanel =
21         new JPanel( new GridLayout( 2, 2, 5, 5 ) );
22      private final JTextField numberJTextField = new JTextField();
23      private final JButton goJButton = new JButton( "Go" );
24      private final JLabel fibonacciJLabel = new JLabel();
25
26      // components and variables for getting the next Fibonacci number
27      private final JPanel eventThreadJPanel =
28         new JPanel( new GridLayout( 2, 2, 5, 5 ) );
29      private int n1 = 0; // initialize with first Fibonacci number
```

Fig. 18.26 | Using `SwingWorker` to perform a long calculation with intermediate results displayed in a GUI. (Part 1 of 4.)

```
30        private int n2 = 1; // initialize with second Fibonacci number
31        private int count = 1;
32        private final JLabel nJLabel = new JLabel( "Fibonacci of 1: " );
33        private final JLabel nFibonacciJLabel =
34           new JLabel( String.valueOf( n2 ) );
35        private final JButton nextNumberJButton = new JButton( "Next Number" );
36
37        // constructor
38        public FibonacciNumbers()
39        {
40           super( "Fibonacci Numbers" );
41           setLayout( new GridLayout( 2, 1, 10, 10 ) );
42
43           // add GUI components to the SwingWorker panel
44           workerJPanel.setBorder( new TitledBorder(
45              new LineBorder( Color.BLACK ), "With SwingWorker" ) );
46           workerJPanel.add( new JLabel( "Get Fibonacci of:" ) );
47           workerJPanel.add( numberJTextField );
48           goJButton.addActionListener(
49              new ActionListener()
50              {
51                 public void actionPerformed( ActionEvent event )
52                 {
53                    int n;
54
55                    try
56                    {
57                       // retrieve user's input as an integer
58                       n = Integer.parseInt( numberJTextField.getText() );
59                    } // end try
60                    catch( NumberFormatException ex )
61                    {
62                       // display an error message if the user did not
63                       // enter an integer
64                       fibonacciJLabel.setText( "Enter an integer." );
65                       return;
66                    } // end catch
67
68                    // indicate that the calculation has begun
69                    fibonacciJLabel.setText( "Calculating..." );
70
71                    // create a task to perform calculation in background
72                    BackgroundCalculator task =
73                       new BackgroundCalculator( n, fibonacciJLabel );
74                    task.execute(); // execute the task
75                 } // end method actionPerformed
76              } // end anonymous inner class
77           ); // end call to addActionListener
78           workerJPanel.add( goJButton );
79           workerJPanel.add( fibonacciJLabel );
80
```

Fig. 18.26 | Using SwingWorker to perform a long calculation with intermediate results displayed in a GUI. (Part 2 of 4.)

```
81        // add GUI components to the event-dispatching thread panel
82        eventThreadJPanel.setBorder( new TitledBorder(
83           new LineBorder( Color.BLACK ), "Without SwingWorker" ) );
84        eventThreadJPanel.add( nJLabel );
85        eventThreadJPanel.add( nFibonacciJLabel );
86        nextNumberJButton.addActionListener(
87           new ActionListener()
88           {
89              public void actionPerformed( ActionEvent event )
90              {
91                 // calculate the Fibonacci number after n2
92                 int temp = n1 + n2;
93                 n1 = n2;
94                 n2 = temp;
95                 ++count;
96
97                 // display the next Fibonacci number
98                 nJLabel.setText( "Fibonacci of " + count + ": " );
99                 nFibonacciJLabel.setText( String.valueOf( n2 ) );
100             } // end method actionPerformed
101          } // end anonymous inner class
102       ); // end call to addActionListener
103       eventThreadJPanel.add( nextNumberJButton );
104
105    add( workerJPanel );
106    add( eventThreadJPanel );
107    setSize( 275, 200 );
108    setVisible( true );
109 } // end constructor
110
111    // main method begins program execution
112    public static void main( String[] args )
113    {
114       FibonacciNumbers application = new FibonacciNumbers();
115       application.setDefaultCloseOperation( EXIT_ON_CLOSE );
116    } // end main
117 } // end class FibonacciNumbers
```

Fig. 18.26 | Using SwingWorker to perform a long calculation with intermediate results displayed in a GUI. (Part 3 of 4.)

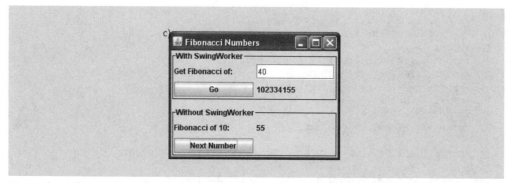

Fig. 18.26 | Using SwingWorker to perform a long calculation with intermediate results displayed in a GUI. (Part 4 of 4.)

Lines 48–77 register the event handler for the goJButton. If the user clicks this JButton, line 58 gets the value entered in the numberJTextField and attempts to parse it as an integer. Lines 72–73 create a new BackgroundCalculator object, passing in the user-entered value and the fibonacciJLabel that is used to display the calculation's results. Line 74 calls method execute on the BackgroundCalculator, scheduling it for execution in a separate worker thread. Method execute does not wait for the BackgroundCalculator to finish executing. It returns immediately, allowing the GUI to continue processing other events while the computation is performed.

If the user clicks the nextNumberJButton in the eventThreadJPanel, the event handler registered in lines 86–102 executes. The previous two Fibonacci numbers stored in n1 and n2 are added together and count is incremented to determine the next number in the sequence (lines 92–95). Then lines 98–99 update the GUI to display the next number. The code to perform these calculations is written directly in method actionPerformed, so these calculations are performed on the event dispatch thread. Handling such short computations in the event dispatch thread does not cause the GUI to become unresponsive, like the recursive algorithm for calculating the Fibonacci of a large number. Because the longer Fibonacci computation is performed in a separate worker thread using the Swing-Worker, it is possible to get the next Fibonacci number while the recursive computation is still in progress.

18.11.2 Processing Intermediate Results with SwingWorker

We have presented an example that uses the SwingWorker class to execute a long process in a background thread and update the GUI when the process is finished. We now present an example of updating the GUI with intermediate results before the long process completes. Figure 18.27 presents class PrimeCalculator, which extends SwingWorker to compute the first *n* primes in a worker thread. In addition to the doInBackground and done methods used in the previous example, this class uses SwingWorker methods publish, process and setProgress. In this example, method publish sends prime numbers to method process as they are found, method process displays these primes in a GUI component and method setProgress updates the progress property. We later show how to use this property to update a JProgressBar.

```
1    // Fig. 18.27: PrimeCalculator.java
2    // Calculates the first n primes, displaying them as they are found.
3    import javax.swing.JTextArea;
4    import javax.swing.JLabel;
5    import javax.swing.JButton;
6    import javax.swing.SwingWorker;
7    import java.util.Random;
8    import java.util.List;
9    import java.util.concurrent.ExecutionException;
10
11   public class PrimeCalculator extends SwingWorker< Integer, Integer >
12   {
13      private final Random generator = new Random();
14      private final JTextArea intermediateJTextArea; // displays found primes
15      private final JButton getPrimesJButton;
16      private final JButton cancelJButton;
17      private final JLabel statusJLabel; // displays status of calculation
18      private final boolean primes[]; // boolean array for finding primes
19      private boolean stopped = false; // flag indicating cancelation
20
21      // constructor
22      public PrimeCalculator( int max, JTextArea intermediate, JLabel status,
23         JButton getPrimes, JButton cancel )
24      {
25         intermediateJTextArea = intermediate;
26         statusJLabel = status;
27         getPrimesJButton = getPrimes;
28         cancelJButton = cancel;
29         primes = new boolean[ max ];
30
31         // initialize all primes array values to true
32         for ( int i = 0; i < max; i ++ )
33            primes[ i ] = true;
34      } // end constructor
35
36      // finds all primes up to max using the Sieve of Eratosthenes
37      public Integer doInBackground()
38      {
39         int count = 0; // the number of primes found
40
41         // starting at the third value, cycle through the array and put
42         // false as the value of any greater number that is a multiple
43         for ( int i = 2; i < primes.length; i++ )
44         {
45            if ( stopped ) // if calculation has been canceled
46               return count;
47            else
48            {
49               setProgress( 100 * ( i + 1 ) / primes.length );
50
51               try
52               {
```

Fig. 18.27 | Calculates the first *n* primes, displaying them as they are found. (Part 1 of 3.)

```
53                    Thread.currentThread().sleep( generator.nextInt( 5 ) );
54                 } // end try
55                 catch ( InterruptedException ex )
56                 {
57                    statusJLabel.setText( "Worker thread interrupted" );
58                    return count;
59                 } // end catch
60
61                 if ( primes[ i ] ) // i is prime
62                 {
63                    publish( i ); // make i available for display in prime list
64                    ++count;
65
66                    for ( int j = i + i; j < primes.length; j += i )
67                       primes[ j ] = false; // i is not prime
68                 } // end if
69              } // end else
70           } // end for
71
72           return count;
73        } // end method doInBackground
74
75        // displays published values in primes list
76        protected void process( List< Integer > publishedVals )
77        {
78           for ( int i = 0; i < publishedVals.size(); i++ )
79              intermediateJTextArea.append( publishedVals.get( i ) + "\n" );
80        } // end method process
81
82        // code to execute when doInBackground completes
83        protected void done()
84        {
85           getPrimesJButton.setEnabled( true ); // enable Get Primes button
86           cancelJButton.setEnabled( false ); // disable Cancel button
87
88           int numPrimes;
89
90           try
91           {
92              numPrimes = get(); // retrieve doInBackground return value
93           } // end try
94           catch ( InterruptedException ex )
95           {
96              statusJLabel.setText( "Interrupted while waiting for results." );
97              return;
98           } // end catch
99           catch ( ExecutionException ex )
100          {
101             statusJLabel.setText( "Error performing computation." );
102             return;
103          } // end catch
104
```

Fig. 18.27 | Calculates the first *n* primes, displaying them as they are found. (Part 2 of 3.)

```
105          statusJLabel.setText( "Found " + numPrimes + " primes." );
106      } // end method done
107
108      // sets flag to stop looking for primes
109      public void stopCalculation()
110      {
111          stopped = true;
112      } // end method stopCalculation
113  } // end class PrimeCalculator
```

Fig. 18.27 | Calculates the first *n* primes, displaying them as they are found. (Part 3 of 3.)

Class `PrimeCalculator` extends `SwingWorker` (line 11), with the first type parameter indicating the return type of method `doInBackground` and the second indicating the type of intermediate results passed between methods `publish` and `process`. In this case, both type parameters are `Integers`. The constructor (lines 22–34) takes as arguments an integer that indicates the upper limit of the prime numbers to locate, a `JTextArea` used to display primes in the GUI, one `JButton` for initiating a calculation and one for canceling it, and a `JLabel` used to display the status of the calculation.

Lines 32–33 initialize the elements of the `boolean` array primes to true. `PrimeCalculator` uses this array and the *Sieve of Eratosthenes* algorithm to find all primes less than max. The Sieve of Eratosthenes takes a list of natural numbers of any length and, beginning with the first prime number, filters out all multiples of that prime. It then moves to the next prime, which will be the next number that is not yet filtered out, and eliminates all of its multiples. It continues until the end of the list is reached and all non-primes have been filtered out. Algorithmically, we begin with element 2 of the `boolean` array and set the cells corresponding to all values that are multiples of 2 to `false` to indicate that they are divisible by 2 and thus not prime. We then move to the next array element, check whether it is `true`, and if so set all of its multiples to `false` to indicate that they are divisible by the current index. When the whole array has been traversed in this way, all indices that contain `true` are prime, as they have no divisors.

In method `doInBackground` (lines 37–73), the control variable i for the loop (lines 43–70) controls the current index for implementing the Sieve of Eratosthenes. Line 45 tests the `stopped` boolean flag, which indicates whether the user has clicked the **Cancel** button. If `stopped` is `true`, the method returns the number of primes found so far (line 46) without finishing the computation.

If the calculation is not canceled, line 49 calls method `setProgress` to update the progress property with the percentage of the array that has been traversed so far. Line 53 puts the currently executing thread to sleep for up to 4 milliseconds. We discuss the reason for this shortly. Line 61 tests whether the element of array primes at the current index is `true` (and thus prime). If so, line 63 passes the index to method `publish` so that it can be displayed as an intermediate result in the GUI and line 64 increments the number of primes found. Lines 66–67 set all multiples of the current index to `false` to indicate that they are not prime. When the entire `boolean` array has been traversed, the number of primes found is returned at line 72.

Lines 76–80 declare method `process`, which executes in the event dispatch thread and receives its argument `publishedVals` from method `publish`. The passing of values between publish in the worker thread and process in the event dispatch thread is asynchronous; process is not necessarily invoked for every call to publish. All Integers published since the last call to process are received as a List by method process. Lines 78–79 iterate through this list and display the published values in a JTextArea. Because the computation in method doInBackground progresses quickly, publishing values often, updates to the JTextArea can pile up on the event dispatch thread, causing the GUI to become sluggish. In fact, when searching for a large enough number of primes, the event dispatch thread may receive so many requests in quick succession to update the JTextArea that the thread will run out of memory in its event queue. This is why we put the worker thread to sleep for a few milliseconds between each potential call to publish. The calculation is slowed just enough to allow the event dispatch thread to keep up with requests to update the JTextArea with new primes, enabling the GUI to update smoothly and remain responsive.

Lines 83–106 define method done. When the calculation is finished or canceled, method done enables the **Get Primes** button and disables the **Cancel** button (lines 85–86). Line 92 gets the return value—the number of primes found—from method doInBackground. Lines 94–103 catch the exceptions thrown by method get and display an appropriate error message in the statusJLabel. If no exceptions occur, line 105 sets the statusJLabel to indicate the number of primes found.

Lines 109–112 define public method stopCalculation, which is invoked when the **Cancel** button is clicked. This method sets the flag stopped at line 111 so that doInBackground will return without finishing its calculation the next time it tests this flag. Though SwingWorker provides a method cancel, this method simply calls Thread method interrupt on the worker thread. Using the boolean flag instead of cancel allows us to stop the calculation cleanly, return a value from doInBackground and ensure that method done is called even though the calculation did not run to completion, without the risk of throwing an InterruptedException associated with interrupting the worker thread.

Class FindPrimes (Fig. 18.28) displays a JTextField that allows the user to enter a number, a JButton to begin finding all primes less than that number and a JTextArea to display the primes. A JButton allows the user to cancel the calculation, and a JProgressBar indicates the calculation's progress. The FindPrimes constructor (lines 32–125) initializes these components and displays them in a JFrame using BorderLayout.

Lines 42–94 register the event handler for the getPrimesJButton. When the user clicks this JButton, lines 47–49 reset the JProgressBar and clear the displayPrimes-JTextArea and the statusJLabel. Lines 53–63 parse the value in the JTextField and display an error message if the value is not an integer. Lines 66–68 construct a new PrimeCalculator object, passing as arguments the integer the user entered, the display-PrimesJTextArea for displaying the primes, the statusJLabel and the two JButtons.

Lines 71–85 register a PropertyChangeListener for the new PrimeCalculator object using an anonymous inner class. **PropertyChangeListener** is an interface from package java.beans that defines a single method, propertyChange. Every time method setProgress is invoked on a PrimeCalculator, the PrimeCalculator generates a PropertyChangeEvent to indicate that the progress property has changed. Method propertyChange listens for these events. Line 78 tests whether a given PropertyChangeEvent indicates a change to the progress property. If so, line 80 gets the new value of the property and line 81 updates the JProgressBar with the new progress property value. The **Get Primes**

JButton is disabled (line 88) so that only one calculation that updates the GUI can execute at a time, and the **Cancel** JButton is enabled (line 89) to allow the user to stop the computation before it completes. Line 91 executes the PrimesCalculator to begin finding primes. If the user clicks the cancelJButton, the event handler registered at lines 107–115 calls PrimeCalculator method stopCalculation (line 112) and the calculation returns early.

```java
1    // Fig 18.28: FindPrimes.java
2    // Using a SwingWorker to display prime numbers and update a JProgressBar
3    // while the prime numbers are being calculated.
4    import javax.swing.JFrame;
5    import javax.swing.JTextField;
6    import javax.swing.JTextArea;
7    import javax.swing.JButton;
8    import javax.swing.JProgressBar;
9    import javax.swing.JLabel;
10   import javax.swing.JPanel;
11   import javax.swing.JScrollPane;
12   import javax.swing.ScrollPaneConstants;
13   import java.awt.BorderLayout;
14   import java.awt.GridLayout;
15   import java.awt.event.ActionListener;
16   import java.awt.event.ActionEvent;
17   import java.util.concurrent.ExecutionException;
18   import java.beans.PropertyChangeListener;
19   import java.beans.PropertyChangeEvent;
20
21   public class FindPrimes extends JFrame
22   {
23      private final JTextField highestPrimeJTextField = new JTextField();
24      private final JButton getPrimesJButton = new JButton( "Get Primes" );
25      private final JTextArea displayPrimesJTextArea = new JTextArea();
26      private final JButton cancelJButton = new JButton( "Cancel" );
27      private final JProgressBar progressJProgressBar = new JProgressBar();
28      private final JLabel statusJLabel = new JLabel();
29      private PrimeCalculator calculator;
30
31      // constructor
32      public FindPrimes()
33      {
34         super( "Finding Primes with SwingWorker" );
35         setLayout( new BorderLayout() );
36
37         // initialize panel to get a number from the user
38         JPanel northJPanel = new JPanel();
39         northJPanel.add( new JLabel( "Find primes less than: " ) );
40         highestPrimeJTextField.setColumns( 5 );
41         northJPanel.add( highestPrimeJTextField );
42         getPrimesJButton.addActionListener(
43            new ActionListener()
44            {
```

Fig. 18.28 | Using a SwingWorker to display prime numbers and update a JProgressBar while the prime numbers are being calculated. (Part 1 of 4.)

```
45              public void actionPerformed( ActionEvent e )
46              {
47                  progressJProgressBar.setValue( 0 ); // reset JProgressBar
48                  displayPrimesJTextArea.setText( "" ); // clear JTextArea
49                  statusJLabel.setText( "" ); // clear JLabel
50
51                  int number;
52
53                  try
54                  {
55                      // get user input
56                      number = Integer.parseInt(
57                          highestPrimeJTextField.getText() );
58                  } // end try
59                  catch ( NumberFormatException ex )
60                  {
61                      statusJLabel.setText( "Enter an integer." );
62                      return;
63                  } // end catch
64
65                  // construct a new PrimeCalculator object
66                  calculator = new PrimeCalculator( number,
67                      displayPrimesJTextArea, statusJLabel, getPrimesJButton,
68                      cancelJButton );
69
70                  // listen for progress bar property changes
71                  calculator.addPropertyChangeListener(
72                      new PropertyChangeListener()
73                      {
74                          public void propertyChange( PropertyChangeEvent e )
75                          {
76                              // if the changed property is progress,
77                              // update the progress bar
78                              if ( e.getPropertyName().equals( "progress" ) )
79                              {
80                                  int newValue = ( Integer ) e.getNewValue();
81                                  progressJProgressBar.setValue( newValue );
82                              } // end if
83                          } // end method propertyChange
84                      } // end anonymous inner class
85                  ); // end call to addPropertyChangeListener
86
87                  // disable Get Primes button and enable Cancel button
88                  getPrimesJButton.setEnabled( false );
89                  cancelJButton.setEnabled( true );
90
91                  calculator.execute(); // execute the PrimeCalculator object
92              } // end method ActionPerformed
93          } // end anonymous inner class
94      ); // end call to addActionListener
95      northJPanel.add( getPrimesJButton );
```

Fig. 18.28 | Using a SwingWorker to display prime numbers and update a JProgressBar while the prime numbers are being calculated. (Part 2 of 4.)

```
96
97          // add a scrollable JList to display results of calculation
98          displayPrimesJTextArea.setEditable( false );
99          add( new JScrollPane( displayPrimesJTextArea,
100            ScrollPaneConstants.VERTICAL_SCROLLBAR_ALWAYS,
101            ScrollPaneConstants.HORIZONTAL_SCROLLBAR_NEVER ) );
102
103         // initialize a panel to display cancelJButton,
104         // progressJProgressBar, and statusJLabel
105         JPanel southJPanel = new JPanel( new GridLayout( 1, 3, 10, 10 ) );
106         cancelJButton.setEnabled( false );
107         cancelJButton.addActionListener(
108            new ActionListener()
109            {
110               public void actionPerformed( ActionEvent e )
111               {
112                  calculator.stopCalculation(); // cancel the calculation
113               } // end method ActionPerformed
114            } // end anonymous inner class
115         ); // end call to addActionListener
116         southJPanel.add( cancelJButton );
117         progressJProgressBar.setStringPainted( true );
118         southJPanel.add( progressJProgressBar );
119         southJPanel.add( statusJLabel );
120
121         add( northJPanel, BorderLayout.NORTH );
122         add( southJPanel, BorderLayout.SOUTH );
123         setSize( 350, 300 );
124         setVisible( true );
125      } // end constructor
126
127      // main method begins program execution
128      public static void main( String[] args )
129      {
130         FindPrimes application = new FindPrimes();
131         application.setDefaultCloseOperation( EXIT_ON_CLOSE );
132      } // end main
133   } // end class FindPrimes
```

Fig. 18.28 | Using a SwingWorker to display prime numbers and update a JProgressBar while the prime numbers are being calculated. (Part 3 of 4.)

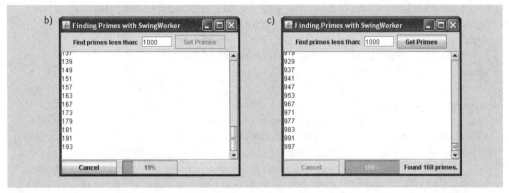

Fig. 18.28 | Using a `SwingWorker` to display prime numbers and update a `JProgressBar` while the prime numbers are being calculated. (Part 4 of 4.)

18.12 Other Classes and Interfaces in `java.util.concurrent`

Interface `Runnable` provides only the most basic functionality for multithreaded programming. In fact, this interface has several limitations. Suppose a `Runnable` encounters a problem and tries to throw a checked exception. The run method is not declared to throw any exceptions, so the problem must be handled within the `Runnable`—the exception cannot be passed to the calling thread. Now suppose a `Runnable` is performing a long calculation and the application wants to retrieve the result of that calculation. The run method cannot return a value, so the application must use shared data to pass the value back to the calling thread. This also involves the overhead of synchronizing access to the data. The developers of the concurrency APIs introduced in Java SE 5 recognized these limitations and created a new interface to fix them. The ***Callable*** interface (of package `java.util.concurrent`) declares a single method named ***call***. This interface is designed to be similar to the Runnable interface—allowing an action to be performed concurrently in a separate thread—but the `call` method allows the thread to return a value or to throw a checked exception.

An application that creates a `Callable` likely wants to run the `Callable` concurrently with other `Runnables` and `Callables`. The `ExecutorService` interface provides method ***submit***, which will execute a `Callable` passed in as its argument. The submit method returns an object of type ***Future*** (of package `java.util.concurrent`), which is an interface that represents the executing `Callable`. The `Future` interface declares method ***get*** to return the result of the `Callable` and provides other methods to manage a `Callable`'s execution.

18.13 Wrap-Up

In this chapter, you learned that concurrency has historically been implemented with operating system primitives available only to experienced systems programmers, but that Java makes concurrency available to you through the language and APIs. You also learned that the JVM itself creates threads to run a program, and that it also may create threads to perform housekeeping tasks such as garbage collection.

We discussed the life cycle of a thread and the states that a thread may occupy during its lifetime. We also discussed Java's thread priorities, which help the system schedule threads for execution. You learned that you should avoid manipulating Java thread priorities directly and you learned about problems associated with thread priorities, such as indefinite postponement (sometimes called starvation).

Next, we presented the interface Runnable, which is used to specify a task that can execute concurrently with other tasks. This interface's run method is invoked by the thread executing the task. We showed how to execute a Runnable object by associating it with an object of class Thread. Then we showed how to use the Executor interface to manage the execution of Runnable objects via thread pools, which can reuse existing threads to eliminate the overhead of creating a new thread for each task and can improve performance by optimizing the number of threads to ensure that the processor stays busy.

You learned that when multiple threads share an object and one or more of them modify that object, indeterminate results may occur unless access to the shared object is managed properly. We showed you how to solve this problem via thread synchronization, which coordinates access to shared data by multiple concurrent threads. You learned several techniques for performing synchronization—first with the built-in class ArrayBlockingQueue (which handles all the synchronization details for you), then with Java's built-in monitors and the synchronized keyword, and finally with interfaces Lock and Condition.

We discussed the fact that Swing GUIs are not thread safe, so all interactions with and modifications to the GUI must be performed in the event dispatch thread. We also discussed the problems associated with performing long-running calculations in the event dispatch thread. Then we showed how you can use Java SE 6's SwingWorker class to perform long-running calculations in worker threads. You learned how to display the results of a SwingWorker in a GUI when the calculation completed and how to display intermediate results while the calculation was still in process.

Finally, we discussed the Callable and Future interfaces, which enable you to execute tasks that return results and to obtain those results, respectively. We use the multithreading techniques introduced here again in Chapter 19, Networking, to help build multithreaded servers that can interact with multiple clients concurrently.

Networking

OBJECTIVES

In this chapter you'll learn:

- To understand Java networking with URLs, sockets and datagrams.

- To implement Java networking applications by using sockets and datagrams.

- To understand how to implement Java clients and servers that communicate with one another.

- To understand how to implement network-based collaborative applications.

- To construct a multithreaded server.

Outline

19.1 Introduction
19.2 Manipulating URLs
19.3 Reading a File on a Web Server
19.4 Establishing a Simple Server Using Stream Sockets
19.5 Establishing a Simple Client Using Stream Sockets
19.6 Client/Server Interaction with Stream Socket Connections
19.7 Connectionless Client/Server Interaction with Datagrams
19.8 Client/Server Tic-Tac-Toe Using a Multithreaded Server
19.9 Security and the Network
19.10 [Web Bonus] Case Study: DeitelMessenger Server and Client
19.11 Wrap-Up

19.1 Introduction

There is much excitement about the Internet and the World Wide Web. The Internet ties the information world together. The World Wide Web makes the Internet easy to use and gives it the flair and sizzle of multimedia. Organizations see the Internet and the web as crucial to their information-systems strategies. Java provides a number of built-in networking capabilities that make it easy to develop Internet-based and web-based applications. Java can enable programs to search the world for information and to collaborate with programs running on other computers internationally, nationally or just within an organization. Java can enable applets and applications to communicate with one another (subject to security constraints).

Java's fundamental networking capabilities are declared by classes and interfaces of package **java.net**, through which Java offers **stream-based communications** that enable applications to view networking as streams of data. The classes and interfaces of package java.net also offer **packet-based communications** for transmitting individual **packets** of information—commonly used to transmit audio and video over the Internet. In this chapter, we show how to create and manipulate sockets and how to communicate with packets and streams of data.

Our discussion of networking focuses on both sides of the **client/server relationship**. The **client** requests that some action be performed, and the **server** performs the action and responds to the client. A common implementation of the request-response model is between web browsers and web servers. When a user selects a website to browse through a browser (the client application), a request is sent to the appropriate web server (the server application). The server normally responds to the client by sending an appropriate HTML web page.

We introduce Java's **socket-based communications**, which enable applications to view networking as if it were file I/O—a program can read from a **socket** or write to a socket as simply as reading from a file or writing to a file. The socket is simply a software construct that represents one endpoint of a connection. We show how to create and manipulate stream sockets and datagram sockets.

With ***stream sockets***, a process establishes a ***connection*** to another process. While the connection is in place, data flows between the processes in continuous ***streams***. Stream sockets are said to provide a ***connection-oriented service***. The protocol used for transmission is the popular ***TCP*** (***Transmission Control Protocol***).

With ***datagram sockets***, individual ***packets*** of information are transmitted. This is not appropriate for everyday programmers, because the protocol used—***UDP***, the ***User Datagram Protocol***—is a ***connectionless service***, and thus does not guarantee that packets arrive in any particular order. With UDP, packets can even be lost or duplicated. Significant extra programming is required on your part to deal with these problems (if you choose to do so). UDP is most appropriate for network applications that do not require the error checking and reliability of TCP. Stream sockets and the TCP protocol will be more desirable for the vast majority of Java programmers.

Performance Tip 19.1

Connectionless services generally offer greater performance but less reliability than connection-oriented services.

Portability Tip 19.1

TCP, UDP and related protocols enable a great variety of heterogeneous computer systems (i.e., computer systems with different processors and different operating systems) to intercommunicate.

We also introduce a case study in which we implement a client/server chat application similar to the instant-messaging services popular on the web today. This case study is provided as a web bonus at www.deitel.com/books/javafp/. The application incorporates many networking techniques introduced in this chapter. It also introduces ***multicasting***, in which a server can publish information and clients can subscribe to that information. Each time the server publishes more information, all subscribers receive it. Throughout the examples of this chapter, we'll see that many of the networking details are handled by the Java APIs.

19.2 Manipulating URLs

The Internet offers many protocols. The ***Hypertext Transfer Protocol*** (***HTTP***), which forms the basis of the World Wide Web, uses ***URIs*** (***Uniform Resource Identifiers***) to identify data on the Internet. URIs that specify the locations of documents are called ***URLs*** (***Uniform Resource Locators***). Common URLs refer to files or directories and can reference objects that perform complex tasks, such as database lookups and Internet searches. If you know the HTTP URL of a publicly available HTML document anywhere on the web, you can access it through HTTP.

Java makes it easy to manipulate URLs. When you use a URL that refers to the exact location of a resource (e.g., a web page) as an argument to the ***showDocument*** method of interface **AppletContext**, the browser in which the applet is executing will display that resource. The applet in Figs. 19.1–19.2 demonstrates simple networking capabilities. It enables the user to select a web page from a JList and causes the browser to display the corresponding page. In this example, the networking is performed by the browser.

```
 1   <html>
 2   <title>Site Selector</title>
 3   <body>
 4      <applet code = "SiteSelector.class" width = "300" height = "75">
 5         <param name = "title0" value = "Java Home Page">
 6         <param name = "location0" value = "http://java.sun.com/">
 7         <param name = "title1" value = "Deitel">
 8         <param name = "location1" value = "http://www.deitel.com/">
 9         <param name = "title2" value = "JGuru">
10         <param name = "location2" value = "http://www.jGuru.com/">
11         <param name = "title3" value = "JavaWorld">
12         <param name = "location3" value = "http://www.javaworld.com/">
13      </applet>
14   </body>
15   </html>
```

Fig. 19.1 | HTML document to load SiteSelector applet.

```
 1   // Fig. 19.2: SiteSelector.java
 2   // This program loads a document from a URL.
 3   import java.net.MalformedURLException;
 4   import java.net.URL;
 5   import java.util.HashMap;
 6   import java.util.ArrayList;
 7   import java.awt.BorderLayout;
 8   import java.applet.AppletContext;
 9   import javax.swing.JApplet;
10   import javax.swing.JLabel;
11   import javax.swing.JList;
12   import javax.swing.JScrollPane;
13   import javax.swing.event.ListSelectionEvent;
14   import javax.swing.event.ListSelectionListener;
15
16   public class SiteSelector extends JApplet
17   {
18      private HashMap< Object, URL > sites; // site names and URLs
19      private ArrayList< String > siteNames; // site names
20      private JList siteChooser; // list of sites to choose from
21
22      // read HTML parameters and set up GUI
23      public void init()
24      {
25         sites = new HashMap< Object, URL >(); // create HashMap
26         siteNames = new ArrayList< String >(); // create ArrayList
27
28         // obtain parameters from HTML document
29         getSitesFromHTMLParameters();
30
31         // create GUI components and layout interface
32         add( new JLabel( "Choose a site to browse" ), BorderLayout.NORTH );
33
```

Fig. 19.2 | Loading a document from a URL into a browser. (Part 1 of 3.)

```
34          siteChooser = new JList( siteNames.toArray() ); // populate JList
35          siteChooser.addListSelectionListener(
36            new ListSelectionListener() // anonymous inner class
37            {
38                // go to site user selected
39                public void valueChanged( ListSelectionEvent event )
40                {
41                    // get selected site name
42                    Object object = siteChooser.getSelectedValue();
43
44                    // use site name to locate corresponding URL
45                    URL newDocument = sites.get( object );
46
47                    // get applet container
48                    AppletContext browser = getAppletContext();
49
50                    // tell applet container to change pages
51                    browser.showDocument( newDocument );
52                } // end method valueChanged
53            } // end anonymous inner class
54          ); // end call to addListSelectionListener
55
56          add( new JScrollPane( siteChooser ), BorderLayout.CENTER );
57      } // end method init
58
59      // obtain parameters from HTML document
60      private void getSitesFromHTMLParameters()
61      {
62          String title; // site title
63          String location; // location of site
64          URL url; // URL of location
65          int counter = 0; // count number of sites
66
67          title = getParameter( "title" + counter ); // get first site title
68
69          // loop until no more parameters in HTML document
70          while ( title != null )
71          {
72              // obtain site location
73              location = getParameter( "location" + counter );
74
75              try // place title/URL in HashMap and title in ArrayList
76              {
77                  url = new URL( location ); // convert location to URL
78                  sites.put( title, url ); // put title/URL in HashMap
79                  siteNames.add( title ); // put title in ArrayList
80              } // end try
81              catch ( MalformedURLException urlException )
82              {
83                  urlException.printStackTrace();
84              } // end catch
85
```

Fig. 19.2 | Loading a document from a URL into a browser. (Part 2 of 3.)

```
86              counter++;
87              title = getParameter( "title" + counter ); // get next site title
88          } // end while
89      } // end method getSitesFromHTMLParameters
90  } // end class SiteSelector
```

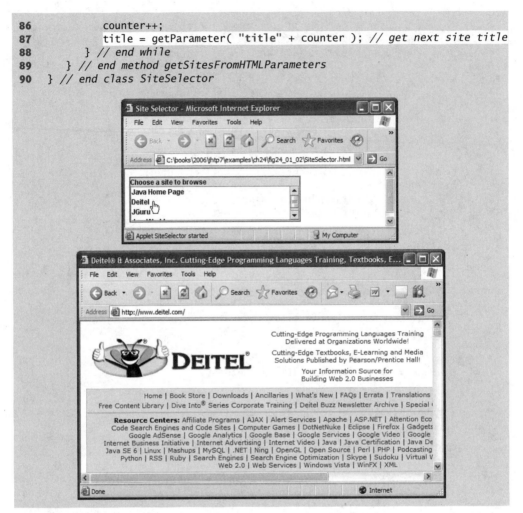

Fig. 19.2 | Loading a document from a URL into a browser. (Part 3 of 3.)

This applet takes advantage of *applet parameters* specified in the HTML document that invokes the applet. When browsing the World Wide Web, you'll often come across applets that are in the public domain—you can use them free of charge on your own web pages (normally in exchange for crediting the applet's creator). Many applets can be customized via parameters supplied from the HTML file that invokes the applet. For example, Fig. 19.1 contains the HTML that invokes the applet SiteSelector in Fig. 19.2.

The HTML document contains eight parameters specified with the *param tag*—these lines must appear between the starting and ending applet tags. The applet can read these values and use them to customize itself. Any number of param tags can appear between the starting and ending applet tags. Each parameter has a *name* and a *value*. Applet method *getParameter* retrieves the value associated with a specific parameter name and returns it as a string. The argument passed to getParameter is a string containing the name of the parameter in the param element. In this example, parameters represent the title and location of each website the user can select. Parameters specified for this applet are named title#, where the value of # starts at 0 and increments by 1 for each new title. Each title should have a corresponding location parameter of the form location#, where the value of # starts at 0 and increments by 1 for each new location. The statement

```
String title = getParameter( "title0" );
```

gets the value associated with parameter "title0" and assigns it to reference title. If there is no param tag containing the specified parameter, getParameter returns null.

The applet (Fig. 19.2) obtains from the HTML document (Fig. 19.1) the choices that will be displayed in the applet's JList. Class SiteSelector uses a HashMap (package java.util) to store the website names and URLs. In this example, the *key* is the string in the JList that represents the website name, and the *value* is a URL object that stores the location of the website to display in the browser.

Class SiteSelector also contains an ArrayList (package java.util) in which the site names are placed so that they can be used to initialize the JList (one version of the JList constructor receives an array of Objects which is returned by ArrayList's toArray method). An ArrayList is a dynamically resizable array of references. Class ArrayList provides method add to add a new element to the end of the ArrayList. (We provide discussions of classes ArrayList and HashMap in Chapter 16.)

Lines 25–26 in the applet's init method (lines 23–57) create a HashMap object and an ArrayList object. Line 29 calls our utility method getSitesFromHTMLParameters (declared at lines 60–89) to obtain the HTML parameters from the HTML document that invoked the applet.

Method getSitesFromHTMLParameters uses Applet method getParameter (line 67) to obtain a website title. If the title is not null, the loop in lines 70–88 begins executing. Line 73 uses Applet method getParameter to obtain the website location. Line 77 uses the location as the value of a new URL object. The URL constructor determines whether its argument represents a valid URL. If not, the URL constructor throws a *Malformed-URLException*. Note that the URL constructor must be called in a try block. If the URL constructor generates a MalformedURLException, the call to printStackTrace (line 83) causes the program to output a stack trace to the Java console. On Windows machines, the Java console can be viewed by right clicking the Java icon in the notification area of the taskbar. Then the program attempts to obtain the next website title. The program does not add the site for the invalid URL to the HashMap, so the title will not be displayed in the JList.

For a proper URL, line 78 places the title and URL into the HashMap, and line 79 adds the title to the ArrayList. Line 87 gets the next title from the HTML document. When the call to getParameter at line 87 returns null, the loop terminates.

When method getSitesFromHTMLParameters returns to init, lines 32–56 construct the applet's GUI. Line 32 adds the JLabel "Choose a site to browse" to the NORTH of the JFrame's BorderLayout. Line 34 creates JList siteChooser to allow the user to select a web page to view. Lines 35–54 register a ListSelectionListener to handle the siteChooser's events. Line 56 adds siteChooser to the CENTER of the BorderLayout.

When the user selects one of the websites listed in siteChooser, the program calls method valueChanged (lines 39–52). Line 42 obtains the selected site name from the

JList. Line 45 passes the selected site name (the *key*) to HashMap method get, which locates and returns a reference to the corresponding URL object (the *value*) that is assigned to reference newDocument.

Line 48 uses Applet method ***getAppletContext*** to get a reference to an AppletContext object that represents the applet container. Line 51 uses the AppletContext reference browser to invoke method showDocument, which receives a URL object as an argument and passes it to the AppletContext (i.e., the browser). The browser displays in the current browser window the World Wide Web resource associated with that URL. In this example, all the resources are HTML documents.

For programmers familiar with *HTML frames*, there is a second version of Applet-Context method showDocument that enables an applet to specify the so-called *target frame* in which to display the web resource. This second version takes two arguments—a URL object specifying the resource to display and a string representing the target frame. There are some special target frames that can be used as the second argument. The target frame **_blank** results in a new web browser window to display the content from the specified URL. The target frame **_self** specifies that the content from the specified URL should be displayed in the same frame as the applet (the applet's HTML page is replaced in this case). The target frame **_top** specifies that the browser should remove the current frames in the browser window, then display the content from the specified URL in the current window. [*Note:* If you are interested in learning more about HTML, please visit our Resource Centers on extensible hypertext markup language (XHTML; www.deitel.com/xhtml/) and the web page formatting capability called Cascading Style Sheets (CSS; www.deitel.com/css21/).]

Error-Prevention Tip 19.1

The applet in Fig. 19.2 must be run from a web browser, such as Mozilla or Microsoft Internet Explorer, to see the results of displaying another web page. The appletviewer is capable only of executing applets—it ignores all other HTML tags. If the websites in the program contained Java applets, only those applets would appear in the appletviewer when the user selected a website. Each applet would execute in a separate appletviewer window.

19.3 Reading a File on a Web Server

Our next example once again hides the networking details from us. The application in Fig. 19.3 uses Swing GUI component **JEditorPane** (from package javax.swing) to display the contents of a file on a web server. The user enters a URL in the JTextField at the top of the window, and the application displays the corresponding document (if it exists) in the JEditorPane. Class JEditorPane is able to render both plain text and HTML-formatted text, as illustrated in the two screen captures (Fig. 19.4), so this application acts as a simple web browser. The application also demonstrates how to process ***HyperlinkEvents*** when the user clicks a hyperlink in the HTML document. The techniques shown in this example can also be used in applets. However, an applet is allowed to read files only on the server from which it was downloaded.

The application class ReadServerFile contains JTextField enterField, in which the user enters the URL of the file to read and JEditorPane contentsArea to display the contents of the file. When the user presses the *Enter* key in enterField, the application calls method actionPerformed (lines 31–34). Line 33 uses ActionEvent method getActionCommand to get the string the user input in the JTextField and passes the string to utility method getThePage (lines 61–74).

```
1   // Fig. 19.3: ReadServerFile.java
2   // Use a JEditorPane to display the contents of a file on a web server.
3   import java.awt.BorderLayout;
4   import java.awt.event.ActionEvent;
5   import java.awt.event.ActionListener;
6   import java.io.IOException;
7   import javax.swing.JEditorPane;
8   import javax.swing.JFrame;
9   import javax.swing.JOptionPane;
10  import javax.swing.JScrollPane;
11  import javax.swing.JTextField;
12  import javax.swing.event.HyperlinkEvent;
13  import javax.swing.event.HyperlinkListener;
14
15  public class ReadServerFile extends JFrame
16  {
17     private JTextField enterField; // JTextField to enter site name
18     private JEditorPane contentsArea; // to display website
19
20     // set up GUI
21     public ReadServerFile()
22     {
23        super( "Simple Web Browser" );
24
25        // create enterField and register its listener
26        enterField = new JTextField( "Enter file URL here" );
27        enterField.addActionListener(
28           new ActionListener()
29           {
30              // get document specified by user
31              public void actionPerformed( ActionEvent event )
32              {
33                 getThePage( event.getActionCommand() );
34              } // end method actionPerformed
35           } // end inner class
36        ); // end call to addActionListener
37
38        add( enterField, BorderLayout.NORTH );
39
40        contentsArea = new JEditorPane(); // create contentsArea
41        contentsArea.setEditable( false );
42        contentsArea.addHyperlinkListener(
43           new HyperlinkListener()
44           {
45              // if user clicked hyperlink, go to specified page
46              public void hyperlinkUpdate( HyperlinkEvent event )
47              {
48                 if ( event.getEventType() ==
49                    HyperlinkEvent.EventType.ACTIVATED )
```

Fig. 19.3 | Reading a file by opening a connection through a URL. (Part 1 of 2.)

```
50                      getThePage( event.getURL().toString() );
51               } // end method hyperlinkUpdate
52            } // end inner class
53         ); // end call to addHyperlinkListener
54
55         add( new JScrollPane( contentsArea ), BorderLayout.CENTER );
56         setSize( 400, 300 ); // set size of window
57         setVisible( true ); // show window
58      } // end ReadServerFile constructor
59
60      // load document
61      private void getThePage( String location )
62      {
63         try // load document and display location
64         {
65            contentsArea.setPage( location ); // set the page
66            enterField.setText( location ); // set the text
67         } // end try
68         catch ( IOException ioException )
69         {
70            JOptionPane.showMessageDialog( this,
71               "Error retrieving specified URL", "Bad URL",
72               JOptionPane.ERROR_MESSAGE );
73         } // end catch
74      } // end method getThePage
75   } // end class ReadServerFile
```

Fig. 19.3 | Reading a file by opening a connection through a URL. (Part 2 of 2.)

Line 65 invokes JEditorPane method *setPage* to download the document specified by location and display it in the JEditorPane. If there is an error downloading the document, method setPage throws an IOException. Also, if an invalid URL is specified, a MalformedURLException (a subclass of IOException) occurs. If the document loads successfully, line 66 displays the current location in enterField.

Typically, an HTML document contains *hyperlinks*—text, images or GUI components which, when clicked, provide quick access to another document on the web. If a JEditorPane contains an HTML document and the user clicks a hyperlink, the JEditor-

```
1    // Fig. 19.4: ReadServerFileTest.java
2    // Create and start a ReadServerFile.
3    import javax.swing.JFrame;
4
5    public class ReadServerFileTest
6    {
7       public static void main( String args[] )
8       {
9          ReadServerFile application = new ReadServerFile();
10         application.setDefaultCloseOperation( JFrame.EXIT_ON_CLOSE );
11      } // end main
12   } // end class ReadServerFileTest
```

Fig. 19.4 | Test class for ReadServerFile. (Part 1 of 2.)

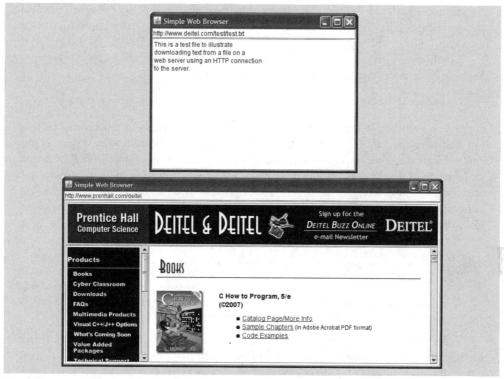

Fig. 19.4 | Test class for `ReadServerFile`. (Part 2 of 2.)

Pane generates a ***HyperlinkEvent*** (package `javax.swing.event`) and notifies all registered ***HyperlinkListeners*** (package `javax.swing.event`) of that event. Lines 42–53 register a `HyperlinkListener` to handle `HyperlinkEvents`. When a `HyperlinkEvent` occurs, the program calls method ***hyperlinkUpdate*** (lines 46–51). Lines 48–49 use `HyperlinkEvent` method ***getEventType*** to determine the type of the `HyperlinkEvent`. Class `HyperlinkEvent` contains a `public` nested class called ***EventType*** that declares three `static` `EventType` objects, which represent the hyperlink event types. ***ACTIVATED*** indicates that the user clicked a hyperlink to change web pages, ***ENTERED*** indicates that the user moved the mouse over a hyperlink and ***EXITED*** indicates that the user moved the mouse away from a hyperlink. If a hyperlink was `ACTIVATED`, line 50 uses `HyperlinkEvent` method ***getURL*** to obtain the URL represented by the hyperlink. Method `toString` converts the returned URL to a string that can be passed to utility method `getThePage`.

Look-and-Feel Observation 19.1

A `JEditorPane` generates `HyperlinkEvents` only if it is uneditable.

19.4 Establishing a Simple Server Using Stream Sockets

The two examples discussed so far use high-level Java networking capabilities to communicate between applications. In the examples, it was not your responsibility to establish the connection between a client and a server. The first program relied on the web browser to communicate with a web server. The second program relied on a JEditorPane to perform the connection. This section begins our discussion of creating your own applications that can communicate with one another.

Establishing a simple server in Java requires five steps. *Step 1* is to create a **Server-Socket** object. A call to the ServerSocket constructor, such as

```
ServerSocket server = new ServerSocket( portNumber, queueLength );
```

registers an available TCP *port number* and specifies the maximum number of clients that can wait to connect to the server (i.e., the *queue length*). The port number is used by clients to locate the server application on the server computer. This is often called the *handshake point*. If the queue is full, the server refuses client connections. The constructor establishes the port where the server waits for connections from clients—a process known as *binding the server to the port*. Each client will ask to connect to the server on this *port*. Only one application at a time can be bound to a specific port on the server.

Software Engineering Observation 19.1

Port numbers can be between 0 and 65,535. Most operating systems reserve port numbers below 1024 for system services (e.g., e-mail and World Wide Web servers). Generally, these ports should not be specified as connection ports in user programs. In fact, some operating systems require special access privileges to bind to port numbers below 1024.

Programs manage each client connection with a **Socket** object. In *Step 2*, the server listens indefinitely (or *blocks*) for an attempt by a client to connect. To listen for a client connection, the program calls ServerSocket method **accept**, as in

```
Socket connection = server.accept();
```

which returns a Socket when a connection with a client is established. The Socket allows the server to interact with the client. The interactions with the client actually occur at a different server port from the handshake point. This allows the port specified in *Step 1* to be used again in a multithreaded server to accept another client connection. We demonstrate this concept in Section 19.8.

Step 3 is to get the OutputStream and InputStream objects that enable the server to communicate with the client by sending and receiving bytes. The server sends information to the client via an OutputStream and receives information from the client via an InputStream. The server invokes method **getOutputStream** on the Socket to get a reference to the Socket's OutputStream and invokes method **getInputStream** on the Socket to get a reference to the Socket's InputStream.

The stream objects can be used to send or receive individual bytes or sequences of bytes with the OutputStream's method write and the InputStream's method read, respectively. Often it is useful to send or receive values of primitive types (e.g., int and double) or Serializable objects (e.g., Strings or other serializable types) rather than sending bytes. In this case, we can use the techniques discussed in Chapter 14 to wrap other stream types (e.g., ObjectOutputStream and ObjectInputStream) around the OutputStream and InputStream associated with the Socket. For example,

```
ObjectInputStream input =
   new ObjectInputStream( connection.getInputStream() );
```

```
ObjectOutputStream output =
   new ObjectOutputStream( connection.getOutputStream() );
```

The beauty of establishing these relationships is that whatever the server writes to the ObjectOutputStream is sent via the OutputStream and is available at the client's InputStream, and whatever the client writes to its OutputStream (with a corresponding ObjectOutputStream) is available via the server's InputStream. The transmission of the data over the network is seamless and is handled completely by Java.

Step 4 is the *processing* phase, in which the server and the client communicate via the OutputStream and InputStream objects. In *Step 5*, when the transmission is complete, the server closes the connection by invoking the **close** method on the streams and on the Socket.

Software Engineering Observation 19.2

With sockets, network I/O appears to Java programs to be similar to sequential file I/O. Sockets hide much of the complexity of network programming from the programmer.

Software Engineering Observation 19.3

With Java's multithreading, we can create multithreaded servers that can manage many simultaneous connections with many clients. This multithreaded-server architecture is precisely what popular network servers use.

Software Engineering Observation 19.4

A multithreaded server can take the Socket returned by each call to accept and create a new thread that manages network I/O across that Socket. Alternatively, a multithreaded server can maintain a pool of threads (a set of already existing threads) ready to manage network I/O across the new Sockets as they are created. See Chapter 18 for more information on multithreading.

Performance Tip 19.2

In high-performance systems in which memory is abundant, a multithreaded server can be implemented to create a pool of threads that can be assigned quickly to handle network I/O across each new Socket as it is created. Thus, when the server receives a connection, it need not incur the overhead of thread creation. When the connection is closed, the thread is returned to the pool for reuse.

19.5 Establishing a Simple Client Using Stream Sockets

Establishing a simple client in Java requires four steps. In *Step 1*, we create a Socket to connect to the server. The Socket constructor establishes the connection to the server. For example, the statement

```
Socket connection = new Socket( serverAddress, port );
```

uses the Socket constructor with two arguments—the server's address (*serverAddress*) and the *port* number. If the connection attempt is successful, this statement returns a Socket. A connection attempt that fails throws an instance of a subclass of IOException, so many programs simply catch IOException. An **UnknownHostException** occurs specifically when the system is unable to resolve the server address specified in the call to the Socket constructor to a corresponding IP address.

In *Step 2*, the client uses Socket methods getInputStream and getOutputStream to obtain references to the Socket's InputStream and OutputStream. As we mentioned in the preceding section, we can use the techniques of Chapter 14 to wrap other stream types around the InputStream and OutputStream associated with the Socket. If the server is sending information in the form of actual types, the client should receive the information in the same format. Thus, if the server sends values with an ObjectOutputStream, the client should read those values with an ObjectInputStream.

Step 3 is the processing phase in which the client and the server communicate via the InputStream and OutputStream objects. In *Step 4*, the client closes the connection when the transmission is complete by invoking the close method on the streams and on the Socket. The client must determine when the server is finished sending information so that it can call close to close the Socket connection. For example, the InputStream method read returns the value –1 when it detects end-of-stream (also called EOF—end-of-file). If an ObjectInputStream is used to read information from the server, an EOFException occurs when the client attempts to read a value from a stream on which end-of-stream is detected.

19.6 Client/Server Interaction with Stream Socket Connections

Figures 19.5 and 19.7 use stream sockets to demonstrate a simple *client/server chat application*. The server waits for a client connection attempt. When a client connects to the server, the server application sends the client a String object (recall that Strings are Serializable objects) indicating that the connection was successful. Then the client displays the message. The client and server applications each provide textfields that allow the user to type a message and send it to the other application. When the client or the server sends the string "TERMINATE", the connection terminates. Then the server waits for the next client to connect. The declaration of class Server appears in Fig. 19.5. The declaration of class Client appears in Fig. 19.7. The screen captures showing the execution between the client and the server are shown as part of Fig. 19.7.

Server Class
Server's constructor (lines 30–55) creates the server's GUI, which contains a JTextField and a JTextArea. Server displays its output in the JTextArea. When the main method (lines 7–12 of Fig. 19.6) executes, it creates a Server object, specifies the window's default close operation and calls method runServer (declared at lines 58–87).

Method runServer sets up the server to receive a connection and processes one connection at a time. Line 62 creates a ServerSocket called server to wait for connections. The ServerSocket listens for a connection from a client at port 12345. The second argument to the constructor is the number of connections that can wait in a queue to connect to the server (100 in this example). If the queue is full when a client attempts to connect, the server refuses the connection.

Common Programming Error 19.1

Specifying a port that is already in use or specifying an invalid port number when creating a ServerSocket results in a BindException.

```
1    // Fig. 19.5: Server.java
2    // Set up a server that will receive a connection from a client, send
3    // a string to the client, and close the connection.
4    import java.io.EOFException;
5    import java.io.IOException;
6    import java.io.ObjectInputStream;
7    import java.io.ObjectOutputStream;
8    import java.net.ServerSocket;
9    import java.net.Socket;
10   import java.awt.BorderLayout;
11   import java.awt.event.ActionEvent;
12   import java.awt.event.ActionListener;
13   import javax.swing.JFrame;
14   import javax.swing.JScrollPane;
15   import javax.swing.JTextArea;
16   import javax.swing.JTextField;
17   import javax.swing.SwingUtilities;
18
19   public class Server extends JFrame
20   {
21      private JTextField enterField; // inputs message from user
22      private JTextArea displayArea; // display information to user
23      private ObjectOutputStream output; // output stream to client
24      private ObjectInputStream input; // input stream from client
25      private ServerSocket server; // server socket
26      private Socket connection; // connection to client
27      private int counter = 1; // counter of number of connections
28
29      // set up GUI
30      public Server()
31      {
32         super( "Server" );
33
34         enterField = new JTextField(); // create enterField
35         enterField.setEditable( false );
36         enterField.addActionListener(
37            new ActionListener()
38            {
39               // send message to client
40               public void actionPerformed( ActionEvent event )
41               {
42                  sendData( event.getActionCommand() );
43                  enterField.setText( "" );
44               } // end method actionPerformed
45.           } // end anonymous inner class
46         ); // end call to addActionListener
47
48         add( enterField, BorderLayout.NORTH );
49
50         displayArea = new JTextArea(); // create displayArea
51         add( new JScrollPane( displayArea ), BorderLayout.CENTER );
52
```

Fig. 19.5 | Server portion of a client/server stream-socket connection. (Part 1 of 4.)

```
53          setSize( 300, 150 ); // set size of window
54          setVisible( true ); // show window
55       } // end Server constructor
56
57       // set up and run server
58       public void runServer()
59       {
60          try // set up server to receive connections; process connections
61          {
62             server = new ServerSocket( 12345, 100 ); // create ServerSocket
63
64             while ( true )
65             {
66                try
67                {
68                   waitForConnection(); // wait for a connection
69                   getStreams(); // get input & output streams
70                   processConnection(); // process connection
71                } // end try
72                catch ( EOFException eofException )
73                {
74                   displayMessage( "\nServer terminated connection" );
75                } // end catch
76                finally
77                {
78                   closeConnection(); // close connection
79                   counter++;
80                } // end finally
81             } // end while
82          } // end try
83          catch ( IOException ioException )
84          {
85             ioException.printStackTrace();
86          } // end catch
87       } // end method runServer
88
89       // wait for connection to arrive, then display connection info
90       private void waitForConnection() throws IOException
91       {
92          displayMessage( "Waiting for connection\n" );
93          connection = server.accept(); // allow server to accept connection
94          displayMessage( "Connection " + counter + " received from: " +
95             connection.getInetAddress().getHostName() );
96       } // end method waitForConnection
97
98       // get streams to send and receive data
99       private void getStreams() throws IOException
100      {
101         // set up output stream for objects
102         output = new ObjectOutputStream( connection.getOutputStream() );
103         output.flush(); // flush output buffer to send header information
104
```

Fig. 19.5 | Server portion of a client/server stream-socket connection. (Part 2 of 4.)

```
105         // set up input stream for objects
106         input = new ObjectInputStream( connection.getInputStream() );
107
108         displayMessage( "\nGot I/O streams\n" );
109      } // end method getStreams
110
111      // process connection with client
112      private void processConnection() throws IOException
113      {
114         String message = "Connection successful";
115         sendData( message ); // send connection successful message
116
117         // enable enterField so server user can send messages
118         setTextFieldEditable( true );
119
120         do // process messages sent from client
121         {
122            try // read message and display it
123            {
124               message = ( String ) input.readObject(); // read new message
125               displayMessage( "\n" + message ); // display message
126            } // end try
127            catch ( ClassNotFoundException classNotFoundException )
128            {
129               displayMessage( "\nUnknown object type received" );
130            } // end catch
131
132         } while ( !message.equals( "CLIENT>>> TERMINATE" ) );
133      } // end method processConnection
134
135      // close streams and socket
136      private void closeConnection()
137      {
138         displayMessage( "\nTerminating connection\n" );
139         setTextFieldEditable( false ); // disable enterField
140
141         try
142         {
143            output.close(); // close output stream
144            input.close(); // close input stream
145            connection.close(); // close socket
146         } // end try
147         catch ( IOException ioException )
148         {
149            ioException.printStackTrace();
150         } // end catch
151      } // end method closeConnection
152
153      // send message to client
154      private void sendData( String message )
155      {
156         try // send object to client
157         {
```

Fig. 19.5 | Server portion of a client/server stream-socket connection. (Part 3 of 4.)

```
158                output.writeObject( "SERVER>>> " + message );
159                output.flush(); // flush output to client
160                displayMessage( "\nSERVER>>> " + message );
161            } // end try
162            catch ( IOException ioException )
163            {
164                displayArea.append( "\nError writing object" );
165            } // end catch
166        } // end method sendData
167
168        // manipulates displayArea in the event-dispatch thread
169        private void displayMessage( final String messageToDisplay )
170        {
171            SwingUtilities.invokeLater(
172                new Runnable()
173                {
174                    public void run() // updates displayArea
175                    {
176                        displayArea.append( messageToDisplay ); // append message
177                    } // end method run
178                } // end anonymous inner class
179            ); // end call to SwingUtilities.invokeLater
180        } // end method displayMessage
181
182        // manipulates enterField in the event-dispatch thread
183        private void setTextFieldEditable( final boolean editable )
184        {
185            SwingUtilities.invokeLater(
186                new Runnable()
187                {
188                    public void run() // sets enterField's editability
189                    {
190                        enterField.setEditable( editable );
191                    } // end method run
192                } // end inner class
193            ); // end call to SwingUtilities.invokeLater
194        } // end method setTextFieldEditable
195    } // end class Server
```

Fig. 19.5 | Server portion of a client/server stream-socket connection. (Part 4 of 4.)

```
1    // Fig. 19.6: ServerTest.java
2    // Test the Server application.
3    import javax.swing.JFrame;
4
5    public class ServerTest
6    {
7        public static void main( String args[] )
8        {
9            Server application = new Server(); // create server
10            application.setDefaultCloseOperation( JFrame.EXIT_ON_CLOSE );
```

Fig. 19.6 | Test class for Server. (Part 1 of 2.)

```
11        application.runServer(); // run server application
12      } // end main
13  } // end class ServerTest
```

Fig. 19.6 | Test class for Server. (Part 2 of 2.)

Line 68 calls method waitForConnection (declared at lines 90–96) to wait for a client connection. After the connection is established, line 69 calls method getStreams (declared at lines 99–109) to obtain references to the streams for the connection. Line 70 calls method processConnection (declared at lines 112–133) to send the initial connection message to the client and to process all messages received from the client. The finally block (lines 76–80) terminates the client connection by calling method closeConnection (lines 136–151) even if an exception occurs. Method displayMessage (lines 169–180) is called from these methods to use the event dispatch thread to display messages in the application's JTextArea.

Method waitForConnection (lines 90–96) uses ServerSocket method accept (line 93) to wait for a connection from a client. When a connection occurs, the resulting Socket is assigned to connection. Method accept blocks until a connection is received (i.e., the thread in which accept is called stops executing until a client connects). Lines 94–95 output the host name of the computer that made the connection. Socket method *getInetAddress* returns an *InetAddress* (package java.net) containing information about the client computer. InetAddress method *getHostName* returns the host name of the client computer. For example, there is a special IP address (127.0.0.1) and host name (localhost) that is useful for testing networking applications on your local computer (this is also known as the *loopback address*). If getHostName is called on an InetAddress containing 127.0.0.1, the corresponding host name returned by the method would be localhost.

Method getStreams (lines 99–109) obtains the Socket's streams and uses them to initialize an ObjectOutputStream (line 102) and an ObjectInputStream (line 106), respectively. Note the call to ObjectOutputStream method *flush* at line 103. This statement causes the ObjectOutputStream on the server to send a *stream header* to the corresponding client's ObjectInputStream. The stream header contains such information as the version of object serialization being used to send objects. This information is required by the ObjectInputStream so that it can prepare to receive those objects correctly.

Software Engineering Observation 19.5

When using an ObjectOutputStream and ObjectInputStream to send and receive data over a network connection, always create the ObjectOutputStream first and flush the stream so that the client's ObjectInputStream can prepare to receive the data. This is required only for networking applications that communicate using ObjectOutputStream and ObjectInputStream.

Performance Tip 19.3

A computer's input and output components are typically much slower than its memory. Output buffers typically are used to increase the efficiency of an application by sending larger amounts of data fewer times, thus reducing the number of times an application accesses the computer's input and output components.

Line 114 of method processConnection (lines 112–133) calls method sendData to send "SERVER>>> Connection successful" as a string to the client. The loop at lines 120–132 executes until the server receives the message "CLIENT>>> TERMINATE". Line 124 uses ObjectInputStream method readObject to read a String from the client. Line 125 invokes method displayMessage to append the message to the JTextArea.

When the transmission is complete, method processConnection returns, and the program calls method closeConnection (lines 136–151) to close the streams associated with the Socket and close the Socket. Then the server waits for the next connection attempt from a client by continuing with line 68 at the beginning of the while loop.

When the user of the server application enters a string in the text field and presses the *Enter* key, the program calls method actionPerformed (lines 40–44), which reads the string from the text field and calls utility method sendData (lines 154–166) to send the string to the client. Method sendData writes the object, flushes the output buffer and appends the same string to the textarea in the server window. It is not necessary to invoke displayMessage to modify the textarea here, because method sendData is called from an event handler—thus, sendData executes as part of the event-dispatch thread.

Note that Server receives a connection, processes it, closes it and waits for the next connection. A more likely scenario would be a Server that receives a connection, sets it up to be processed as a separate thread of execution, then immediately waits for new connections. The separate threads that process existing connections can continue to execute while the Server concentrates on new connection requests. This makes the server more efficient, because multiple client requests can be processed concurrently. We demonstrate a multithreaded server in Section 19.8.

Client Class

Like class Server, class Client's (Fig. 19.7) constructor (lines 29–56) creates the GUI of the application (a JTextField and a JTextArea). Client displays its output in the textarea. When method main (lines 7–19 of Fig. 19.8) executes, it creates an instance of class Client, specifies the window's default close operation and calls method runClient (declared at lines 59–79). In this example, you can execute the client from any computer on the Internet and specify the IP address or host name of the server computer as a command-line argument to the program. For example, the command

```
java Client 192.168.1.15
```

attempts to connect to the Server on the computer with IP address 192.168.1.15.

```
1   // Fig. 19.7: Client.java
2   // Client that reads and displays information sent from a Server.
3   import java.io.EOFException;
4   import java.io.IOException;
5   import java.io.ObjectInputStream;
6   import java.io.ObjectOutputStream;
7   import java.net.InetAddress;
8   import java.net.Socket;
9   import java.awt.BorderLayout;
10  import java.awt.event.ActionEvent;
```

Fig. 19.7 | Client portion of a stream-socket connection between client and server. (Part 1 of 5.)

```java
11   import java.awt.event.ActionListener;
12   import javax.swing.JFrame;
13   import javax.swing.JScrollPane;
14   import javax.swing.JTextArea;
15   import javax.swing.JTextField;
16   import javax.swing.SwingUtilities;
17
18   public class Client extends JFrame
19   {
20      private JTextField enterField; // enters information from user
21      private JTextArea displayArea; // display information to user
22      private ObjectOutputStream output; // output stream to server
23      private ObjectInputStream input; // input stream from server
24      private String message = ""; // message from server
25      private String chatServer; // host server for this application
26      private Socket client; // socket to communicate with server
27
28      // initialize chatServer and set up GUI
29      public Client( String host )
30      {
31         super( "Client" );
32
33         chatServer = host; // set server to which this client connects
34
35         enterField = new JTextField(); // create enterField
36         enterField.setEditable( false );
37         enterField.addActionListener(
38            new ActionListener()
39            {
40               // send message to server
41               public void actionPerformed( ActionEvent event )
42               {
43                  sendData( event.getActionCommand() );
44                  enterField.setText( "" );
45               } // end method actionPerformed
46            } // end anonymous inner class
47         ); // end call to addActionListener
48
49         add( enterField, BorderLayout.NORTH );
50
51         displayArea = new JTextArea(); // create displayArea
52         add( new JScrollPane( displayArea ), BorderLayout.CENTER );
53
54         setSize( 300, 150 ); // set size of window
55         setVisible( true ); // show window
56      } // end Client constructor
57
58      // connect to server and process messages from server
59      public void runClient()
60      {
61         try // connect to server, get streams, process connection
62         {
63            connectToServer(); // create a Socket to make connection
```

Fig. 19.7 | Client portion of a stream-socket connection between client and server. (Part 2 of 5.)

```
64          getStreams(); // get the input and output streams
65          processConnection(); // process connection
66       } // end try
67       catch ( EOFException eofException )
68       {
69          displayMessage( "\nClient terminated connection" );
70       } // end catch
71       catch ( IOException ioException )
72       {
73          ioException.printStackTrace();
74       } // end catch
75       finally
76       {
77          closeConnection(); // close connection
78       } // end finally
79    } // end method runClient
80
81    // connect to server
82    private void connectToServer() throws IOException
83    {
84       displayMessage( "Attempting connection\n" );
85
86       // create Socket to make connection to server
87       client = new Socket( InetAddress.getByName( chatServer ), 12345 );
88
89       // display connection information
90       displayMessage( "Connected to: " +
91          client.getInetAddress().getHostName() );
92    } // end method connectToServer
93
94    // get streams to send and receive data
95    private void getStreams() throws IOException
96    {
97       // set up output stream for objects
98       output = new ObjectOutputStream( client.getOutputStream() );
99       output.flush(); // flush output buffer to send header information
100
101      // set up input stream for objects
102      input = new ObjectInputStream( client.getInputStream() );
103
104      displayMessage( "\nGot I/O streams\n" );
105   } // end method getStreams
106
107   // process connection with server
108   private void processConnection() throws IOException
109   {
110      // enable enterField so client user can send messages
111      setTextFieldEditable( true );
112
113      do // process messages sent from server
114      {
115         try // read message and display it
116         {
```

Fig. 19.7 | Client portion of a stream-socket connection between client and server. (Part 3 of 5.)

```
117              message = ( String ) input.readObject(); // read new message
118              displayMessage( "\n" + message ); // display message
119           } // end try
120           catch ( ClassNotFoundException classNotFoundException )
121           {
122              displayMessage( "\nUnknown object type received" );
123           } // end catch
124
125        } while ( !message.equals( "SERVER>>> TERMINATE" ) );
126     } // end method processConnection
127
128     // close streams and socket
129     private void closeConnection()
130     {
131        displayMessage( "\nClosing connection" );
132        setTextFieldEditable( false ); // disable enterField
133
134        try
135        {
136           output.close(); // close output stream
137           input.close(); // close input stream    1
138           client.close(); // close socket
139        } // end try
140        catch ( IOException ioException )
141        {
142           ioException.printStackTrace();
143        } // end catch
144     } // end method closeConnection
145
146     // send message to server
147     private void sendData( String message )
148     {
149        try // send object to server
150        {
151           output.writeObject( "CLIENT>>> " + message );
152           output.flush(); // flush data to output
153           displayMessage( "\nCLIENT>>> " + message );
154        } // end try
155        catch ( IOException ioException )
156        {
157           displayArea.append( "\nError writing object" );
158        } // end catch
159     } // end method sendData
160
161     // manipulates displayArea in the event-dispatch thread
162     private void displayMessage( final String messageToDisplay )
163     {
164        SwingUtilities.invokeLater(
165           new Runnable()
166           {
167              public void run() // updates displayArea
168              {
```

Fig. 19.7 | Client portion of a stream-socket connection between client and server. (Part 4 of 5.)

```
169                    displayArea.append( messageToDisplay );
170                  } // end method run
171                } // end anonymous inner class
172            ); // end call to SwingUtilities.invokeLater
173        } // end method displayMessage
174
175        // manipulates enterField in the event-dispatch thread
176        private void setTextFieldEditable( final boolean editable )
177        {
178            SwingUtilities.invokeLater(
179               new Runnable()
180               {
181                  public void run() // sets enterField's editability
182                  {
183                     enterField.setEditable( editable );
184                  } // end method run
185               } // end anonymous inner class
186            ); // end call to SwingUtilities.invokeLater
187        } // end method setTextFieldEditable
188    } // end class Client
```

Fig. 19.7 | Client portion of a stream-socket connection between client and server. (Part 5 of 5.)

Client method runClient (lines 59–79) sets up the connection to the server, processes messages received from the server and closes the connection when communication is complete. Line 63 calls method connectToServer (declared at lines 82–92) to perform the connection. After connecting, line 64 calls method getStreams (declared at lines 95–105) to obtain references to the Socket's stream objects. Then line 65 calls method processConnection (declared at lines 108–126) to receive and display messages sent from the server. The finally block (lines 75–78) calls closeConnection (lines 129–144) to close the streams and the Socket even if an exception has occurred. Method displayMessage (lines 162–173) is called from these methods to use the event-dispatch thread to display messages in the application's textarea.

Method connectToServer (lines 82–92) creates a Socket called client (line 87) to establish a connection. The method passes two arguments to the Socket constructor—the IP address of the server computer and the port number (12345) where the server application is awaiting client connections. In the first argument, InetAddress static method **getByName** returns an InetAddress object containing the IP address specified as a command-line argument to the application (or 127.0.0.1 if no command-line arguments are specified). Method getByName can receive a string containing either the actual IP address or the host name of the server. The first argument also could have been written other ways. For the localhost address 127.0.0.1, the first argument could be specified with either of the following expressions:

```
InetAddress.getByName( "localhost" )
InetAddress.getLocalHost()
```

Also, there are versions of the Socket constructor that receive a string for the IP address or host name. The first argument could have been specified as "127.0.0.1" or "localhost". We chose to demonstrate the client/server relationship by connecting between applica-

```
 I    // Fig. 19.8: ClientTest.java
 2    // Test the Client class.
 3    import javax.swing.JFrame;
 4
 5    public class ClientTest
 6    {
 7       public static void main( String args[] )
 8       {
 9          Client application; // declare client application
10
11          // if no command line args
12          if ( args.length == 0 )
13             application = new Client( "127.0.0.1" ); // connect to localhost
14          else
15             application = new Client( args[ 0 ] ); // use args to connect
16
17          application.setDefaultCloseOperation( JFrame.EXIT_ON_CLOSE );
18          application.runClient(); // run client application
19       } // end main
20    } // end class ClientTest
```

Server

```
Waiting for connection
Connection 1 received from: localhost
Got I/O streams

SERVER>>> Connection successful
CLIENT>>> Hello server person!
SERVER>>> Hi back to you, client person!
CLIENT>>> TERMINATE
Terminating connection
Waiting for connection
```

Client

```
Attempting connection
Connected to: localhost
Got I/O streams

SERVER>>> Connection successful
CLIENT>>> Hello server person!
SERVER>>> Hi back to you, client person!
CLIENT>>> TERMINATE
Client terminated connection
Closing connection
```

Fig. 19.8 | Class that tests the `Client`.

tions executing on the same computer (`localhost`). Normally, this first argument would be the IP address of another computer. The `InetAddress` object for another computer can be obtained by specifying the computer's IP address or host name as the argument to `InetAddress` method `getByName`. The `Socket` constructor's second argument is the server port number. This must match the port number at which the server is waiting for connections (called the handshake point). Once the connection is made, lines 90–91 display a message in the text area indicating the name of the server computer to which the client has connected.

The `Client` uses an `ObjectOutputStream` to send data to the server and an `Object-InputStream` to receive data from the server. Method `getStreams` (lines 95–105) creates the `ObjectOutputStream` and `ObjectInputStream` objects that use the streams associated with the client socket.

Method `processConnection` (lines 108–126) contains a loop that executes until the client receives the message `"SERVER>>> TERMINATE"`. Line 117 reads a `String` object from the server. Line 118 invokes `displayMessage` to append the message to the textarea.

When the transmission is complete, method `closeConnection` (lines 129–144) closes the streams and the `Socket`.

When the user of the client application enters a string in the text field and presses the *Enter* key, the program calls method `actionPerformed` (lines 41–45) to read the string and invoke utility method `sendData` (147–159) to send the string to the server. Method `send-Data` writes the object, flushes the output buffer and appends the same string to the `JText-Area` in the client window. Once again, it is not necessary to invoke utility method `displayMessage` to modify the textarea here, because method `sendData` is called from an event handler.

19.7 Connectionless Client/Server Interaction with Datagrams

We have been discussing connection-oriented, streams-based transmission. Now we consider *connectionless transmission with datagrams*.

Connection-oriented transmission is like the telephone system in which you dial and are given a connection to the telephone of the person with whom you wish to communicate. The connection is maintained for the duration of the call, even when you are not talking.

Connectionless transmission with datagrams is more like the way the postal service carries mail. If a large message will not fit in one envelope, you break it into separate message pieces that you place in separate, sequentially numbered envelopes. Each letter is then mailed at the same time. The letters could arrive in order, out of order or not at all (though rare, it does happen). The person at the receiving end reassembles the message pieces into sequential order before attempting to make sense of the message. If your message is small enough to fit in one envelope, you need not worry about the "out-of-sequence" problem, but it is still possible that your message might not arrive. One difference between datagrams and postal mail is that duplicates of datagrams can arrive at the receiving computer.

Figures 19.9–19.12 use datagrams to send packets of information via the User Datagram Protocol (UDP) between a client application and a server application. In the `Client` application (Fig. 19.11), the user types a message into a text field and presses *Enter*. The program converts the message into a byte array and places it in a datagram packet that is sent to the server. The `Server` (Fig. 19.9) receives the packet and displays the information in it, then *echoes* the packet back to the client. Upon receiving the packet, the client displays the information it contains.

Server Class

Class `Server` (Fig. 19.9) declares two **DatagramPackets** that the server uses to send and receive information and one **DatagramSocket** that sends and receives the packets. The Server constructor (lines 19–37) creates the graphical user interface in which the packets of information will be displayed. Line 30 creates the `DatagramSocket` in a `try` block. Line 30 uses the `DatagramSocket` constructor that takes an integer port number argument (5000 in this example) to bind the server to a port where it can receive packets from clients. `Clients` sending packets to this `Server` specify the same port number in the packets they send. A **SocketException** is thrown if the `DatagramSocket` constructor fails to bind the `DatagramSocket` to the specified port.

Common Programming Error 19.2

Specifying a port that is already in use or specifying an invalid port number when creating a DatagramSocket results in a SocketException.

```java
1   // Fig. 19.9: Server.java
2   // Server that receives and sends packets from/to a client.
3   import java.io.IOException;
4   import java.net.DatagramPacket;
5   import java.net.DatagramSocket;
6   import java.net.SocketException;
7   import java.awt.BorderLayout;
8   import javax.swing.JFrame;
9   import javax.swing.JScrollPane;
10  import javax.swing.JTextArea;
11  import javax.swing.SwingUtilities;
12
13  public class Server extends JFrame
14  {
15     private JTextArea displayArea; // displays packets received
16     private DatagramSocket socket; // socket to connect to client
17
18     // set up GUI and DatagramSocket
19     public Server()
20     {
21        super( "Server" );
22
23        displayArea = new JTextArea(); // create displayArea
24        add( new JScrollPane( displayArea ), BorderLayout.CENTER );
25        setSize( 400, 300 ); // set size of window
26        setVisible( true ); // show window
27
28        try // create DatagramSocket for sending and receiving packets
29        {
30           socket = new DatagramSocket( 5000 );
31        } // end try
32        catch ( SocketException socketException )
33        {
34           socketException.printStackTrace();
35           System.exit( 1 );
36        } // end catch
37     } // end Server constructor
38
39     // wait for packets to arrive, display data and echo packet to client
40     public void waitForPackets()
41     {
42        while ( true )
43        {
44           try // receive packet, display contents, return copy to client
45           {
46              byte data[] = new byte[ 100 ]; // set up packet
47              DatagramPacket receivePacket =
48                 new DatagramPacket( data, data.length );
49
50              socket.receive( receivePacket ); // wait to receive packet
51
```

Fig. 19.9 | Server side of connectionless client/server computing with datagrams. (Part 1 of 2.)

```
52              // display information from received packet
53              displayMessage( "\nPacket received:" +
54
55                 "\nFrom host: " + receivePacket.getAddress() +
56                 "\nHost port: " + receivePacket.getPort() +
57                 "\nLength: " + receivePacket.getLength() +
58                 "\nContaining:\n\t" + new String( receivePacket.getData(),
59                    0, receivePacket.getLength() ) );
60
61              sendPacketToClient( receivePacket ); // send packet to client
62           } // end try
63           catch ( IOException ioException )
64           {
65              displayMessage( ioException.toString() + "\n" );
66              ioException.printStackTrace();
67           } // end catch
68        } // end while
69     } // end method waitForPackets
70
71     // echo packet to client
72     private void sendPacketToClient( DatagramPacket receivePacket )
73        throws IOException
74     {
75        displayMessage( "\n\nEcho data to client..." );
76
77        // create packet to send
78        DatagramPacket sendPacket = new DatagramPacket(
79           receivePacket.getData(), receivePacket.getLength(),
80           receivePacket.getAddress(), receivePacket.getPort() );
81
82        socket.send( sendPacket ); // send packet to client
83        displayMessage( "Packet sent\n" );
84     } // end method sendPacketToClient
85
86     // manipulates displayArea in the event-dispatch thread
87     private void displayMessage( final String messageToDisplay )
88     {
89        SwingUtilities.invokeLater(
90           new Runnable()
91           {
92              public void run() // updates displayArea
93              {
94                 displayArea.append( messageToDisplay ); // display message
95              } // end method run
96           } // end anonymous inner class
97        ); // end call to SwingUtilities.invokeLater
98     } // end method displayMessage
99  } // end class Server
```

Fig. 19.9 | Server side of connectionless client/server computing with datagrams. (Part 2 of 2.)

Server method waitForPackets (lines 40–68) uses an infinite loop to wait for packets to arrive at the Server. Lines 47–48 create a DatagramPacket in which a received packet of information can be stored. The DatagramPacket constructor for this purpose

```
 1    // Fig. 19.10: ServerTest.java
 2    // Tests the Server class.
 3    import javax.swing.JFrame;
 4
 5    public class ServerTest
 6    {
 7       public static void main( String args[] )
 8       {
 9          Server application = new Server(); // create server
10          application.setDefaultCloseOperation( JFrame.EXIT_ON_CLOSE );
11          application.waitForPackets(); // run server application
12       } // end main
13    } // end class ServerTest
```

Server window after packet
of data is received from Client

```
Server                          _ □ ✕

Packet received:
From host: /192.168.1.60
Host port: 1229
Length: 20
Containing:
              first message packet

Echo data to client...Packet sent
```

Fig. 19.10 | Class that tests the Server.

receives two arguments—a byte array in which the data will be stored and the length of the array. Line 50 uses DatagramSocket method *receive* to wait for a packet to arrive at the Server. Method receive blocks until a packet arrives, then stores the packet in its DatagramPacket argument. The method throws an IOException if an error occurs while receiving a packet.

When a packet arrives, lines 53–58 call method displayMessage (declared at lines 86–97) to append the packet's contents to the textarea. DatagramPacket method *getAddress* (line 54) returns an InetAddress object containing the host name of the computer from which the packet was sent. Method *getPort* (line 55) returns an integer specifying the port number through which the host computer sent the packet. Method *getLength* (line 56) returns an integer representing the number of bytes of data sent. Method *getData* (line 57) returns a byte array containing the data. Lines 57–58 initialize a String object using a three-argument constructor that takes a byte array, the offset and the length. This String is then appended to the text to display.

After displaying a packet, line 60 calls method sendPacketToClient (declared at lines 71–83) to create a new packet and send it to the client. Lines 77–79 create a DatagramPacket and pass four arguments to its constructor. The first argument specifies the byte array to send. The second argument specifies the number of bytes to send. The third argument specifies the client computer's Internet address, to which the packet will be sent. The fourth argument specifies the port where the client is waiting to receive packets. Line 81 sends the packet over the network. Method *send* of DatagramSocket throws an IOException if an error occurs while sending a packet.

Client Class

Class Client (Fig. 19.11) works similarly to class Server, except that the Client sends packets only when the user types a message in a text field and presses the *Enter* key. When this occurs, the program calls method actionPerformed (lines 32–57), which converts the string the user entered into a byte array (line 41). Lines 44–45 create a DatagramPacket and initialize it with the byte array, the length of the string that was entered by the user, the IP address to which the packet is to be sent (InetAddress.getLocalHost() in this example) and the port number at which the Server is waiting for packets (5000 in this example). Line 47 sends the packet. Note that the client in this example must know that the server is receiving packets at port 5000—otherwise, the server will not receive the packets.

```java
1   // Fig. 19.11: Client.java
2   // Client that sends and receives packets to/from a server.
3   import java.io.IOException;
4   import java.net.DatagramPacket;
5   import java.net.DatagramSocket;
6   import java.net.InetAddress;
7   import java.net.SocketException;
8   import java.awt.BorderLayout;
9   import java.awt.event.ActionEvent;
10  import java.awt.event.ActionListener;
11  import javax.swing.JFrame;
12  import javax.swing.JScrollPane;
13  import javax.swing.JTextArea;
14  import javax.swing.JTextField;
15  import javax.swing.SwingUtilities;
16
17  public class Client extends JFrame
18  {
19     private JTextField enterField; // for entering messages
20     private JTextArea displayArea; // for displaying messages
21     private DatagramSocket socket; // socket to connect to server
22
23     // set up GUI and DatagramSocket
24     public Client()
25     {
26        super( "Client" );
27
28        enterField = new JTextField( "Type message here" );
29        enterField.addActionListener(
30           new ActionListener()
31           {
32              public void actionPerformed( ActionEvent event )
33              {
34                 try // create and send packet
35                 {
```

Fig. 19.11 | Client side of connectionless client/server computing with datagrams. (Part 1 of 3.)

```
36                   // get message from textfield
37                   String message = event.getActionCommand();
38                   displayArea.append( "\nSending packet containing: " +
39                      message + "\n" );
40
41                   byte data[] = message.getBytes(); // convert to bytes
42
43                   // create sendPacket
44                   DatagramPacket sendPacket = new DatagramPacket( data,
45                      data.length, InetAddress.getLocalHost(), 5000 );
46
47                   socket.send( sendPacket ); // send packet
48                   displayArea.append( "Packet sent\n" );
49                   displayArea.setCaretPosition(
50                      displayArea.getText().length() );
51               } // end try
52               catch ( IOException ioException )
53               {
54                   displayMessage( ioException.toString() + "\n" );
55                   ioException.printStackTrace();
56               } // end catch
57            } // end actionPerformed
58         } // end inner class
59      ); // end call to addActionListener
60
61      add( enterField, BorderLayout.NORTH );
62
63      displayArea = new JTextArea();
64      add( new JScrollPane( displayArea ), BorderLayout.CENTER );
65
66      setSize( 400, 300 ); // set window size
67      setVisible( true ); // show window
68
69      try // create DatagramSocket for sending and receiving packets
70      {
71         socket = new DatagramSocket();
72      } // end try
73      catch ( SocketException socketException )
74      {
75         socketException.printStackTrace();
76         System.exit( 1 );
77      } // end catch
78   } // end Client constructor
79
80   // wait for packets to arrive from Server, display packet contents
81   public void waitForPackets()
82   {
83      while ( true )
84      {
85         try // receive packet and display contents
86         {
87            byte data[] = new byte[ 100 ]; // set up packet
```

Fig. 19.11 | Client side of connectionless client/server computing with datagrams. (Part 2 of 3.)

```
 88                    DatagramPacket receivePacket = new DatagramPacket(
 89                       data, data.length );
 90
 91                    socket.receive( receivePacket ); // wait for packet
 92
 93                    // display packet contents
 94                    displayMessage( "\nPacket received:" +
 95                       "\nFrom host: " + receivePacket.getAddress() +
 96                       "\nHost port: " + receivePacket.getPort() +
 97                       "\nLength: " + receivePacket.getLength() +
 98                       "\nContaining:\n\t" + new String( receivePacket.getData(),
 99                          0, receivePacket.getLength() ) ) );
100                 } // end try
101                 catch ( IOException exception )
102                 {
103                    displayMessage( exception.toString() + "\n" );
104                    exception.printStackTrace();
105                 } // end catch
106              } // end while
107           } // end method waitForPackets
108
109           // manipulates displayArea in the event-dispatch thread
110           private void displayMessage( final String messageToDisplay )
111           {
112              SwingUtilities.invokeLater(
113                 new Runnable()
114                 {
115                    public void run() // updates displayArea
116                    {
117                       displayArea.append( messageToDisplay );
118                    } // end method run
119                 } // end inner class
120              ); // end call to SwingUtilities.invokeLater
121           } // end method displayMessage
122        } // end class Client
```

Fig. 19.11 | Client side of connectionless client/server computing with datagrams. (Part 3 of 3.)

Note that the DatagramSocket constructor call (line 71) in this application does not specify any arguments. This no-argument constructor allows the computer to select the next available port number for the DatagramSocket. The client does not need a specific port number, because the server receives the client's port number as part of each DatagramPacket sent by the client. Thus, the server can send packets back to the same computer and port number from which it receives a packet of information.

Client method waitForPackets (lines 81–107) uses an infinite loop to wait for packets from the server. Line 91 blocks until a packet arrives. This does not prevent the user from sending a packet, because the GUI events are handled in the event-dispatch thread. It only prevents the while loop from continuing until a packet arrives at the Client. When a packet arrives, line 91 stores it in receivePacket, and lines 94–99 call method displayMessage (declared at lines 110–121) to display the packet's contents in the textarea.

```
 1    // Fig. 19.12: ClientTest.java
 2    // Tests the Client class.
 3    import javax.swing.JFrame;
 4
 5    public class ClientTest
 6    {
 7       public static void main( String args[] )
 8       {
 9          Client application = new Client(); // create client
10          application.setDefaultCloseOperation( JFrame.EXIT_ON_CLOSE );
11          application.waitForPackets(); // run client application
12       } // end main
13    } // end class ClientTest
```

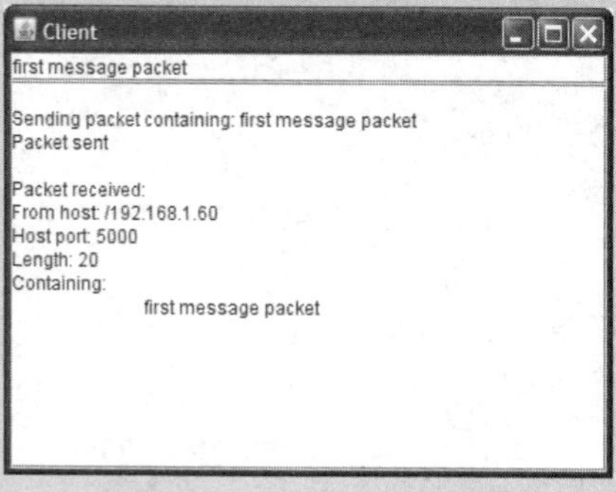

Client window after sending
packet to Server and receiving packet back
from Server

Fig. 19.12 | Class that tests the Client.

19.8 Client/Server Tic-Tac-Toe Using a Multithreaded Server

In this section, we present the popular game Tic-Tac-Toe implemented by using client/server techniques with stream sockets. The program consists of a TicTacToeServer application (Figs. 19.13–19.14) that allows two TicTacToeClient applications (Figs. 19.15–19.16) to connect to the server and play Tic-Tac-Toe. Sample outputs are shown in Fig. 19.17.

TicTacToeServer Class

As the TicTacToeServer receives each client connection, it creates an instance of inner-class Player (lines 182–301 of Fig. 19.13) to process the client in a separate thread. These threads enable the clients to play the game independently. The first client to connect to the server is player X and the second is player O. Player X moves first. The server maintains the board information so it can determine whether a player's move is valid or invalid.

We begin with a discussion of the server side of the Tic-Tac-Toe game. When the TicTacToeServer application executes, the main method (lines 7–12 of Fig. 19.14) creates a TicTacToeServer object called application. The constructor (lines 34–69 of Fig. 19.13) attempts to set up a ServerSocket. If successful, the program displays the server window, then main invokes the TicTacToeServer method execute (lines 72–100). Method execute loops twice, blocking at line 79 each time while waiting for a client connection. When a client connects, line 79 creates a new Player object to manage the connection as a separate thread, and line 80 executes the Player in the runGame thread pool.

```
1   // Fig. 19.13: TicTacToeServer.java
2   // This class maintains a game of Tic-Tac-Toe for two clients.
3   import java.awt.BorderLayout;
4   import java.net.ServerSocket;
5   import java.net.Socket;
6   import java.io.IOException;
7   import java.util.Formatter;
8   import java.util.Scanner;
9   import java.util.concurrent.ExecutorService;
10  import java.util.concurrent.Executors;
11  import java.util.concurrent.locks.Lock;
12  import java.util.concurrent.locks.ReentrantLock;
13  import java.util.concurrent.locks.Condition;
14  import javax.swing.JFrame;
15  import javax.swing.JTextArea;
16  import javax.swing.SwingUtilities;
17
18  public class TicTacToeServer extends JFrame
19  {
20     private String[] board = new String[ 9 ]; // tic-tac-toe board
21     private JTextArea outputArea; // for outputting moves
22     private Player[] players; // array of Players
23     private ServerSocket server; // server socket to connect with clients
24     private int currentPlayer; // keeps track of player with current move
25     private final static int PLAYER_X = 0; // constant for first player
26     private final static int PLAYER_O = 1; // constant for second player
27     private final static String[] MARKS = { "X", "O" }; // array of marks
28     private ExecutorService runGame; // will run players
29     private Lock gameLock; // to lock game for synchronization
30     private Condition otherPlayerConnected; // to wait for other player
31     private Condition otherPlayerTurn; // to wait for other player's turn
32
33     // set up tic-tac-toe server and GUI that displays messages
34     public TicTacToeServer()
35     {
36        super( "Tic-Tac-Toe Server" ); // set title of window
37
38        // create ExecutorService with a thread for each player
39        runGame = Executors.newFixedThreadPool( 2 );
40        gameLock = new ReentrantLock(); // create lock for game
41
42        // condition variable for both players being connected
43        otherPlayerConnected = gameLock.newCondition();
44
45        // condition variable for the other player's turn
46        otherPlayerTurn = gameLock.newCondition();
47
48        for ( int i = 0; i < 9; i++ )
49           board[ i ] = new String( "" ); // create tic-tac-toe board
50        players = new Player[ 2 ]; // create array of players
51        currentPlayer = PLAYER_X; // set current player to first player
52
```

Fig. 19.13 | Server side of the client/server Tic-Tac-Toe program. (Part 1 of 6.)

```
53          try
54          {
55              server = new ServerSocket( 12345, 2 ); // set up ServerSocket
56          } // end try
57          catch ( IOException ioException )
58          {
59              ioException.printStackTrace();
60              System.exit( 1 );
61          } // end catch
62
63          outputArea = new JTextArea(); // create JTextArea for output
64          add( outputArea, BorderLayout.CENTER );
65          outputArea.setText( "Server awaiting connections\n" );
66
67          setSize( 300, 300 ); // set size of window
68          setVisible( true ); // show window
69       } // end TicTacToeServer constructor
70
71       // wait for two connections so game can be played
72       public void execute()
73       {
74          // wait for each client to connect
75          for ( int i = 0; i < players.length; i++ )
76          {
77              try // wait for connection, create Player, start runnable
78              {
79                  players[ i ] = new Player( server.accept(), i );
80                  runGame.execute( players[ i ] ); // execute player runnable
81              } // end try
82              catch ( IOException ioException )
83              {
84                  ioException.printStackTrace();
85                  System.exit( 1 );
86              } // end catch
87          } // end for
88
89          gameLock.lock(); // lock game to signal player X's thread
90
91          try
92          {
93              players[ PLAYER_X ].setSuspended( false ); // resume player X
94              otherPlayerConnected.signal(); // wake up player X's thread
95          } // end try
96          finally
97          {
98              gameLock.unlock(); // unlock game after signalling player X
99          } // end finally
100      } // end method execute
101
102      // display message in outputArea
103      private void displayMessage( final String messageToDisplay )
104      {
```

Fig. 19.13 | Server side of the client/server Tic-Tac-Toe program. (Part 2 of 6.)

```
105        // display message from event-dispatch thread of execution
106        SwingUtilities.invokeLater(
107          new Runnable()
108          {
109            public void run() // updates outputArea
110            {
111              outputArea.append( messageToDisplay ); // add message
112            } // end  method run
113          } // end inner class
114        ); // end call to SwingUtilities.invokeLater
115      } // end method displayMessage
116
117      // determine if move is valid
118      public boolean validateAndMove( int location, int player )
119      {
120        // while not current player, must wait for turn
121        while ( player != currentPlayer )
122        {
123          gameLock.lock(); // lock game to wait for other player to go
124
125          try
126          {
127            otherPlayerTurn.await(); // wait for player's turn
128          } // end try
129          catch ( InterruptedException exception )
130          {
131            exception.printStackTrace();
132          } // end catch
133          finally
134          {
135            gameLock.unlock(); // unlock game after waiting
136          } // end finally
137        } // end while
138
139        // if location not occupied, make move
140        if ( !isOccupied( location ) )
141        {
142          board[ location ] = MARKS[ currentPlayer ]; // set move on board
143          currentPlayer = ( currentPlayer + 1 ) % 2; // change player
144
145          // let new current player know that move occurred
146          players[ currentPlayer ].otherPlayerMoved( location );
147
148          gameLock.lock(); // lock game to signal other player to go
149
150          try
151          {
152            otherPlayerTurn.signal(); // signal other player to continue
153          } // end try
154          finally
155          {
156            gameLock.unlock(); // unlock game after signaling
157          } // end finally
```

Fig. 19.13 | Server side of the client/server Tic-Tac-Toe program. (Part 3 of 6.)

```
158
159            return true; // notify player that move was valid
160         } // end if
161      else // move was not valid
162         return false; // notify player that move was invalid
163   } // end method validateAndMove
164
165   // determine whether location is occupied
166   public boolean isOccupied( int location )
167   {
168      if ( board[ location ].equals( MARKS[ PLAYER_X ] ) ||
169         board [ location ].equals( MARKS[ PLAYER_O ] ) )
170         return true; // location is occupied
171      else
172         return false; // location is not occupied
173   } // end method isOccupied
174
175   // place code in this method to determine whether game over
176   public boolean isGameOver()
177   {
178      return false; // this is left as an exercise
179   } // end method isGameOver
180
181   // private inner class Player manages each Player as a runnable
182   private class Player implements Runnable
183   {
184      private Socket connection; // connection to client
185      private Scanner input; // input from client
186      private Formatter output; // output to client
187      private int playerNumber; // tracks which player this is
188      private String mark; // mark for this player
189      private boolean suspended = true; // whether thread is suspended
190
191      // set up Player thread
192      public Player( Socket socket, int number )
193      {
194         playerNumber = number; // store this player's number
195         mark = MARKS[ playerNumber ]; // specify player's mark
196         connection = socket; // store socket for client
197
198         try // obtain streams from Socket
199         {
200            input = new Scanner( connection.getInputStream() );
201            output = new Formatter( connection.getOutputStream() );
202         } // end try
203         catch ( IOException ioException )
204         {
205            ioException.printStackTrace();
206            System.exit( 1 );
207         } // end catch
208      } // end Player constructor
209
```

Fig. 19.13 | Server side of the client/server Tic-Tac-Toe program. (Part 4 of 6.)

```
210       // send message that other player moved
211       public void otherPlayerMoved( int location )
212       {
213           output.format( "Opponent moved\n" );
214           output.format( "%d\n", location ); // send location of move
215           output.flush(); // flush output
216       } // end method otherPlayerMoved
217
218       // control thread's execution
219       public void run()
220       {
221           // send client its mark (X or O), process messages from client
222           try
223           {
224               displayMessage( "Player " + mark + " connected\n" );
225               output.format( "%s\n", mark ); // send player's mark
226               output.flush(); // flush output
227
228               // if player X, wait for another player to arrive
229               if ( playerNumber == PLAYER_X )
230               {
231                   output.format( "%s\n%s", "Player X connected",
232                       "Waiting for another player\n" );
233                   output.flush(); // flush output
234
235                   gameLock.lock(); // lock game to  wait for second player
236
237                   try
238                   {
239                       while( suspended )
240                       {
241                           otherPlayerConnected.await(); // wait for player O
242                       } // end while
243                   } // end try
244                   catch ( InterruptedException exception )
245                   {
246                       exception.printStackTrace();
247                   } // end catch
248                   finally
249                   {
250                       gameLock.unlock(); // unlock game after second player
251                   } // end finally
252
253                   // send message that other player connected
254                   output.format( "Other player connected. Your move.\n" );
255                   output.flush(); // flush output
256               } // end if
257               else
258               {
259                   output.format( "Player O connected, please wait\n" );
260                   output.flush(); // flush output
261               } // end else
262
```

Fig. 19.13 | Server side of the client/server Tic-Tac-Toe program. (Part 5 of 6.)

```
263                // while game not over
264                while ( !isGameOver() )
265                {
266                    int location = 0; // initialize move location
267
268                    if ( input.hasNext() )
269                        location = input.nextInt(); // get move location
270
271                    // check for valid move
272                    if ( validateAndMove( location, playerNumber ) )
273                    {
274                        displayMessage( "\nlocation: " + location );
275                        output.format( "Valid move.\n" ); // notify client
276                        output.flush(); // flush output
277                    } // end if
278                    else // move was invalid
279                    {
280                        output.format( "Invalid move, try again\n" );
281                        output.flush(); // flush output
282                    } // end else
283                } // end while
284            } // end try
285            finally
286            {
287                try
288                {
289                    connection.close(); // close connection to client
290                } // end try
291                catch ( IOException ioException )
292                {
293                    ioException.printStackTrace();
294                    System.exit( 1 );
295                } // end catch
296            } // end finally
297        } // end method run
298
299        // set whether or not thread is suspended
300        public void setSuspended( boolean status )
301        {
302            suspended = status; // set value of suspended
303        } // end method setSuspended
304    } // end class Player
305 } // end class TicTacToeServer
```

Fig. 19.13 | Server side of the client/server Tic-Tac-Toe program. (Part 6 of 6.)

```
1  // Fig. 19.14: TicTacToeServerTest.java
2  // Tests the TicTacToeServer.
3  import javax.swing.JFrame;
4
5  public class TicTacToeServerTest
6  {
```

Fig. 19.14 | Class that tests the Tic-Tac-Toe server. (Part 1 of 2.)

```
7        public static void main( String args[] )
8        {
9           TicTacToeServer application = new TicTacToeServer();
10          application.setDefaultCloseOperation( JFrame.EXIT_ON_CLOSE );
11          application.execute();
12       } // end main
13    } // end class TicTacToeServerTest
```

Fig. 19.14 | Class that tests the Tic-Tac-Toe server. (Part 2 of 2.)

When the TicTacToeServer creates a Player, the Player constructor (lines 192–208) receives the Socket object representing the connection to the client and gets the associated input and output streams. Line 201 creates a Formatter (see Chapter 24) by wrapping it around the output stream of the socket. The Player's run method (lines 219–297) controls the information that is sent to and received from the client. First, it passes to the client the character that the client will place on the board when a move is made (line 225). Line 226 calls Formatter method *flush* to force this output to the client. Line 241 suspends player X's thread as it starts executing, because player X can move only after player O connects.

After player O connects, the game can be played, and the run method begins executing its while statement (lines 264–283). Each iteration of this loop reads an integer (line 269) representing the location where the client wants to place a mark, and line 272 invokes the TicTacToeServer method validateAndMove (declared at lines 118–163) to check the move. If the move is valid, line 275 sends a message to the client to this effect. If not, line 280 sends a message indicating that the move was invalid. The program maintains board locations as numbers from 0 to 8 (0 through 2 for the first row, 3 through 5 for the second row and 6 through 8 for the third row).

Method validateAndMove (lines 118–163 in class TicTacToeServer) allows only one player at a time to move, thereby preventing them from modifying the state information of the game simultaneously. If the Player attempting to validate a move is not the current player (i.e., the one allowed to make a move), it is placed in a *wait* state until its turn to move. If the position for the move being validated is already occupied on the board, validMove returns false. Otherwise, the server places a mark for the player in its local representation of the board (line 142), notifies the other Player object (line 146) that a move has been made (so that the client can be sent a message), invokes method signal (line 152) so that the waiting Player (if there is one) can validate a move and returns true (line 159) to indicate that the move is valid.

TicTacToeClient Class

Each TicTacToeClient application (Fig. 19.15) maintains its own GUI version of the Tic-Tac-Toe board on which it displays the state of the game. The clients can place a mark only in an empty square on the board. Inner class Square (lines 205–262 of Fig. 19.15) implements each of the nine squares on the board. When a TicTacToeClient begins execution, it creates a JTextArea in which messages from the server and a representation of the board using nine Square objects are displayed. The startClient method (lines 80–100) opens a connection to the server and gets the associated input and output streams from the Socket object. Lines 85–86 make a connection to the server. Class TicTacToeClient implements interface Runnable so that a separate thread can read messages from the server. This approach enables the user to interact with the board (in the event dispatch thread) while waiting for messages from the server. After establishing the connection to the server, line 99 executes the client with the worker ExecutorService. The run method (lines 103–124) controls the separate thread of execution. The method first reads the mark character (X or O) from the server (line 105), then loops continuously (lines 121–125) and reads messages from the server (line 124). Each message is passed to the processMessage method (lines 129–156) for processing.

If the message received is "Valid move.", lines 134–135 display the message "Valid move, please wait." and call method setMark (lines 173–184) to set the client's mark in the current square (the one in which the user clicked), using SwingUtilities method invokeLater to ensure that the GUI updates occur in the event dispatch thread. If the message received is "Invalid move, try again.", line 139 displays the message so that the user can click a different square. If the message received is "Opponent moved.", line 145 reads an integer from the server indicating where the opponent moved, and lines 149–150 place a mark in that square of the board (again using SwingUtilities method invokeLater to ensure that the GUI updates occur in the event dispatch thread). If any other message is received, line 155 simply displays the message. Figure 19.17 shows sample screen captures of two applications interacting via the TicTacToeServer.

```
1   // Fig. 19.15: TicTacToeClient.java
2   // Client that let a user play Tic-Tac-Toe with another across a network.
3   import java.awt.BorderLayout;
4   import java.awt.Dimension;
5   import java.awt.Graphics;
6   import java.awt.GridLayout;
7   import java.awt.event.MouseAdapter;
8   import java.awt.event.MouseEvent;
9   import java.net.Socket;
10  import java.net.InetAddress;
11  import java.io.IOException;
12  import javax.swing.JFrame;
13  import javax.swing.JPanel;
```

Fig. 19.15 | Client side of the client/server Tic-Tac-Toe program. (Part 1 of 6.)

```
14   import javax.swing.JScrollPane;
15   import javax.swing.JTextArea;
16   import javax.swing.JTextField;
17   import javax.swing.SwingUtilities;
18   import java.util.Formatter;
19   import java.util.Scanner;
20   import java.util.concurrent.Executors;
21   import java.util.concurrent.ExecutorService;
22
23   public class TicTacToeClient extends JFrame implements Runnable
24   {
25      private JTextField idField; // textfield to display player's mark
26      private JTextArea displayArea; // JTextArea to display output
27      private JPanel boardPanel; // panel for tic-tac-toe board
28      private JPanel panel2; // panel to hold board
29      private Square board[][]; // tic-tac-toe board
30      private Square currentSquare; // current square
31      private Socket connection; // connection to server
32      private Scanner input; // input from server
33      private Formatter output; // output to server
34      private String ticTacToeHost; // host name for server
35      private String myMark; // this client's mark
36      private boolean myTurn; // determines which client's turn it is
37      private final String X_MARK = "X"; // mark for first client
38      private final String O_MARK = "O"; // mark for second client
39
40      // set up user-interface and board
41      public TicTacToeClient( String host )
42      {
43         ticTacToeHost = host; // set name of server
44         displayArea = new JTextArea( 4, 30 ); // set up JTextArea
45         displayArea.setEditable( false );
46         add( new JScrollPane( displayArea ), BorderLayout.SOUTH );
47
48         boardPanel = new JPanel(); // set up panel for squares in board
49         boardPanel.setLayout( new GridLayout( 3, 3, 0, 0 ) );
50
51         board = new Square[ 3 ][ 3 ]; // create board
52
53         // loop over the rows in the board
54         for ( int row = 0; row < board.length; row++ )
55         {
56            // loop over the columns in the board
57            for ( int column = 0; column < board[ row ].length; column++ )
58            {
59               // create square
60               board[ row ][ column ] = new Square( ' ', row * 3 + column );
61               boardPanel.add( board[ row ][ column ] ); // add square
62            } // end inner for
63         } // end outer for
64
65         idField = new JTextField(); // set up textfield
66         idField.setEditable( false );
```

Fig. 19.15 | Client side of the client/server Tic-Tac-Toe program. (Part 2 of 6.)

```
67          add( idField, BorderLayout.NORTH );
68
69          panel2 = new JPanel(); // set up panel to contain boardPanel
70          panel2.add( boardPanel, BorderLayout.CENTER ); // add board panel
71          add( panel2, BorderLayout.CENTER ); // add container panel
72
73          setSize( 300, 225 ); // set size of window
74          setVisible( true ); // show window
75
76          startClient();
77     } // end TicTacToeClient constructor
78
79     // start the client thread
80     public void startClient()
81     {
82          try // connect to server, get streams and start outputThread
83          {
84              // make connection to server
85              connection = new Socket(
86                  InetAddress.getByName( ticTacToeHost ), 12345 );
87
88              // get streams for input and output
89              input = new Scanner( connection.getInputStream() );
90              output = new Formatter( connection.getOutputStream() );
91          } // end try
92          catch ( IOException ioException )
93          {
94              ioException.printStackTrace();
95          } // end catch
96
97          // create and start worker thread for this client
98          ExecutorService worker = Executors.newFixedThreadPool( 1 );
99          worker.execute( this ); // execute client
100     } // end method startClient
101
102     // control thread that allows continuous update of displayArea
103     public void run()
104     {
105          myMark = input.nextLine(); // get player's mark (X or O)
106
107          SwingUtilities.invokeLater(
108              new Runnable()
109              {
110                  public void run()
111                  {
112                      // display player's mark
113                      idField.setText( "You are player \"" + myMark + "\"" );
114                  } // end method run
115              } // end anonymous inner class
116          ); // end call to SwingUtilities.invokeLater
117
118          myTurn = ( myMark.equals( X_MARK ) ); // determine if client's turn
119
```

Fig. 19.15 | Client side of the client/server Tic-Tac-Toe program. (Part 3 of 6.)

```
120        // receive messages sent to client and output them
121        while ( true )
122        {
123           if ( input.hasNextLine() )
124              processMessage( input.nextLine() );
125        } // end while
126     } // end method run
127
128     // process messages received by client
129     private void processMessage( String message )
130     {
131        // valid move occurred
132        if ( message.equals( "Valid move." ) )
133        {
134           displayMessage( "Valid move, please wait.\n" );
135           setMark( currentSquare, myMark ); // set mark in square
136        } // end if
137        else if ( message.equals( "Invalid move, try again" ) )
138        {
139           displayMessage( message + "\n" ); // display invalid move
140           myTurn = true; // still this client's turn
141        } // end else if
142        else if ( message.equals( "Opponent moved" ) )
143        {
144           int location = input.nextInt(); // get move location
145           input.nextLine(); // skip newline after int location
146           int row = location / 3; // calculate row
147           int column = location % 3; // calculate column
148
149           setMark( board[ row ][ column ],
150              ( myMark.equals( X_MARK ) ? O_MARK : X_MARK ) ); // mark move
151           displayMessage( "Opponent moved. Your turn.\n" );
152           myTurn = true; // now this client's turn
153        } // end else if
154        else
155           displayMessage( message + "\n" ); // display the message
156     } // end method processMessage
157
158     // manipulate outputArea in event-dispatch thread
159     private void displayMessage( final String messageToDisplay )
160     {
161        SwingUtilities.invokeLater(
162           new Runnable()
163           {
164              public void run()
165              {
166                 displayArea.append( messageToDisplay ); // updates output
167              } // end method run
168           } // end inner class
169        ); // end call to SwingUtilities.invokeLater
170     } // end method displayMessage
171
```

Fig. 19.15 | Client side of the client/server Tic-Tac-Toe program. (Part 4 of 6.)

```
172    // utility method to set mark on board in event-dispatch thread
173    private void setMark( final Square squareToMark, final String mark )
174    {
175       SwingUtilities.invokeLater(
176          new Runnable()
177          {
178             public void run()
179             {
180                squareToMark.setMark( mark ); // set mark in square
181             } // end method run
182          } // end anonymous inner class
183       ); // end call to SwingUtilities.invokeLater
184    } // end method setMark
185
186    // send message to server indicating clicked square
187    public void sendClickedSquare( int location )
188    {
189       // if it is my turn
190       if ( myTurn )
191       {
192          output.format( "%d\n", location ); // send location to server
193          output.flush();
194          myTurn = false; // not my turn anymore
195       } // end if
196    } // end method sendClickedSquare
197
198    // set current Square
199    public void setCurrentSquare( Square square )
200    {
201       currentSquare = square; // set current square to argument
202    } // end method setCurrentSquare
203
204    // private inner class for the squares on the board
205    private class Square extends JPanel
206    {
207       private String mark; // mark to be drawn in this square
208       private int location; // location of square
209
210       public Square( String squareMark, int squareLocation )
211       {
212          mark = squareMark; // set mark for this square
213          location = squareLocation; // set location of this square
214
215          addMouseListener(
216             new MouseAdapter()
217             {
218                public void mouseReleased( MouseEvent e )
219                {
220                   setCurrentSquare( Square.this ); // set current square
221
222                   // send location of this square
223                   sendClickedSquare( getSquareLocation() );
```

Fig. 19.15 | Client side of the client/server Tic-Tac-Toe program. (Part 5 of 6.)

```
224              } // end method mouseReleased
225            } // end anonymous inner class
226          ); // end call to addMouseListener
227       } // end Square constructor
228
229       // return preferred size of Square
230       public Dimension getPreferredSize()
231       {
232          return new Dimension( 30, 30 ); // return preferred size
233       } // end method getPreferredSize
234
235       // return minimum size of Square
236       public Dimension getMinimumSize()
237       {
238          return getPreferredSize(); // return preferred size
239       } // end method getMinimumSize
240
241       // set mark for Square
242       public void setMark( String newMark )
243       {
244          mark = newMark; // set mark of square
245          repaint(); // repaint square
246       } // end method setMark
247
248       // return Square location
249       public int getSquareLocation()
250       {
251          return location; // return location of square
252       } // end method getSquareLocation
253
254       // draw Square
255       public void paintComponent( Graphics g )
256       {
257          super.paintComponent( g );
258
259          g.drawRect( 0, 0, 29, 29 ); // draw square
260          g.drawString( mark, 11, 20 ); // draw mark
261       } // end method paintComponent
262    } // end inner-class Square
263 } // end class TicTacToeClient
```

Fig. 19.15 | Client side of the client/server Tic-Tac-Toe program. (Part 6 of 6.)

```
1  // Fig. 19.16: TicTacToeClientTest.java
2  // Tests the TicTacToeClient class.
3  import javax.swing.JFrame;
4
5  public class TicTacToeClientTest
6  {
7     public static void main( String args[] )
8     {
```

Fig. 19.16 | Test class for the Tic-Tac-Toe client. (Part 1 of 2.)

```
 9          TicTacToeClient application; // declare client application
10
11          // if no command line args
12          if ( args.length == 0 )
13             application = new TicTacToeClient( "127.0.0.1" ); // localhost
14          else
15             application = new TicTacToeClient( args[ 0 ] ); // use args
16
17          application.setDefaultCloseOperation( JFrame.EXIT_ON_CLOSE );
18       } // end main
19    } // end class TicTacToeClientTest
```

Fig. 19.16 | Test class for the Tic-Tac-Toe client. (Part 2 of 2.)

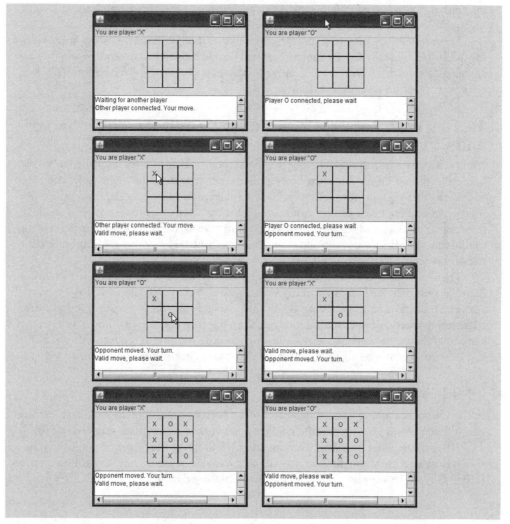

Fig. 19.17 | Sample outputs from the client/server Tic-Tac-Toe program.

19.9 Security and the Network

As much as we look forward to writing a great variety of powerful network-based applications, our efforts may be limited because of security concerns. Many web browsers, such as Mozilla and Microsoft Internet Explorer, by default prohibit Java applets from doing file processing on the machines on which they execute. Think about it. A Java applet is designed to be sent to your browser via an HTML document that could be downloaded from any web server in the world. Often you'll know very little about the sources of Java applets that will execute on your system. To allow these applets free rein with your files could be disastrous.

A more subtle situation occurs with limiting the machines to which executing applets can make network connections. To build truly collaborative applications, we would ideally like to have our applets communicate with machines almost anywhere. The Java security manager in a web browser often restricts an applet so that it can communicate only with the machine from which it was originally downloaded.

These restrictions may seem too strict. However, the Java Security API now provides capabilities for digitally signed applets that will enable browsers to determine whether an applet is downloaded from a *trusted source*. A trusted applet can be given additional access to the computer on which it is executing.

19.10 [Web Bonus] Case Study: DeitelMessenger Server and Client

[*Note:* This case study is available at www.deitel.com/books/javafp/.] Chat rooms have become common on the Internet. They provide a central location where users can chat with each other via short text messages. Each participant can see all messages that the other users post, and each user can post messages. This case study integrates many of the Java networking, multithreading and Swing GUI features you have learned thus far to build an online chat system. We also introduce *multicasting*, which enables an application to send DatagramPackets to groups of clients.

The DeitelMessenger case study is a significant application that uses many intermediate Java features, such as networking with Sockets, DatagramPackets and MulticastSockets, multithreading and Swing GUI. The case study also demonstrates good software engineering practices by separating interface from implementation, enabling developers to support different network protocols and provide different user interfaces. After reading this case study, you'll be able to build more significant networking applications.

19.11 Wrap-Up

In this chapter, you have learned the basics of network programming in Java. You learned two different methods of sending data over a network: streams-based networking using TCP/IP and datagrams-based networking using UDP. In the next chapter, you'll learn basic database concepts, how to interact with data in a database using SQL and how to use JDBC to allow Java applications to manipulate database data.

Accessing Databases with JDBC

It is a capital mistake to theorize before one has data.
—Arthur Conan Doyle

Now go, write it before them in a table, and note it in a book, that it may be for the time to come for ever and ever.
—The Holy Bible, Isaiah 30:8

Get your facts first, and then you can distort them as much as you please.
—Mark Twain

I like two kinds of men: domestic and foreign.
—Mae West

OBJECTIVES

In this chapter you'll learn:

- Relational database concepts.

- To use Structured Query Language (SQL) to retrieve data from and manipulate data in a database.

- To use the JDBC™ API of package `java.sql` to access databases.

- To use the RowSet interface from package `javax.sql` to manipulate databases.

- To use JDBC 4.0's automatic JDBC driver discovery.

- To use PreparedStatements to create precompiled SQL statements with parameters.

- How transaction processing makes database applications more robust.

Outline

20.1 Introduction

20.2 Relational Databases

20.3 Relational Database Overview: The **books** Database

20.4 SQL

    20.4.1 Basic **SELECT** Query

    20.4.2 **WHERE** Clause

    20.4.3 **ORDER BY** Clause

    20.4.4 Merging Data from Multiple Tables: **INNER JOIN**

    20.4.5 **INSERT** Statement

    20.4.6 **UPDATE** Statement

    20.4.7 **DELETE** Statement

20.5 Instructions for Installing MySQL and MySQL Connector/J

20.6 Instructions for Setting Up a MySQL User Account

20.7 Creating Database **books** in MySQL

20.8 Manipulating Databases with JDBC

    20.8.1 Connecting to and Querying a Database

    20.8.2 Querying the **books** Database

20.9 RowSet Interface

20.10 Java DB/Apache Derby

20.11 **PreparedStatement**s

20.12 Stored Procedures

20.13 Transaction Processing

20.14 Wrap-Up

20.15 Web Resources

20.1 Introduction

A *database* is an organized collection of data. There are many different strategies for organizing data to facilitate easy access and manipulation. A *database management system* (*DBMS*) provides mechanisms for storing, organizing, retrieving and modifying data for many users. Database management systems allow for the access and storage of data without concern for the internal representation of data.

Today's most popular database systems are relational databases, where the data is stored without consideration of its physical structure (Section 20.2). A language called *SQL*—pronounced "sequel," or as its individual letters—is the international standard language used almost universally with relational databases to perform *queries* (i.e., to request information that satisfies given criteria) and to manipulate data. [*Note:* As you learn about SQL, you'll see some authors writing "a SQL statement" (which assumes the pronunciation "sequel") and others writing "an SQL statement" (which assumes that the individual letters are pronounced). In this book we pronounce SQL as "sequel."]

Some popular *relational database management systems* (*RDBMSs*) are Microsoft SQL Server, Oracle, Sybase, IBM DB2, Informix, PostgreSQL and MySQL. The JDK now comes with a pure-Java RDBMS called Java DB—Sun's version of Apache Derby. In this chapter, we present examples using MySQL and Java DB.

Java programs communicate with databases and manipulate their data using the *JDBC™ API*. A *JDBC driver* enables Java applications to connect to a database in a particular DBMS and allows you to manipulate that database using the JDBC API.

Software Engineering Observation 20.1

Using the JDBC API enables developers to change the underlying DBMS without modifying the Java code that accesses the database.

Most popular database management systems now provide JDBC drivers. There are also many third-party JDBC drivers available. In this chapter, we introduce JDBC and use it to manipulate MySQL and Java DB databases. The techniques demonstrated here can also be used to manipulate other databases that have JDBC drivers. Check your DBMS's documentation to determine whether your DBMS comes with a JDBC driver. If not, third-party vendors provide JDBC drivers for many DBMSs.

For more information on JDBC, visit

```
java.sun.com/javase/technologies/database/index.jsp
```

This site contains JDBC information including the JDBC specification, FAQs, a learning resource center and software downloads to search for JDBC drivers for your DBMS,

```
developers.sun.com/product/jdbc/drivers/
```

This site provides a search engine to help you locate drivers appropriate for your DBMS.

20.2 Relational Databases

A *relational database* is a logical representation of data that allows the data to be accessed without consideration of its physical structure. A relational database stores data in *tables*. Figure 20.1 illustrates a sample table that might be used in a personnel system. The table name is Employee, and its primary purpose is to store the attributes of an employee. Tables are composed of *rows*, and rows are composed of *columns* in which values are stored. This table consists of six rows. The Number column of each row in this table is the table's *primary key*—a column (or group of columns) in a table with a unique value that cannot be duplicated in other rows. This guarantees that each row can be identified by its primary key. Good examples of primary key columns are a social security number, an employee ID number and a part number in an inventory system, as values in each of these columns are guaranteed to be unique. The rows in Fig. 20.1 are displayed in order by primary key. In this case, the rows are listed in increasing order, but we could also use decreasing order.

Rows in tables are not guaranteed to be stored in any particular order. As we'll demonstrate in an upcoming example, programs can specify ordering criteria when requesting data from a database.

Each column represents a different data attribute. Rows are normally unique (by primary key) within a table, but particular column values may be duplicated between rows. For example, three different rows in the Employee table's Department column contain number 413.

	Number	Name	Department	Salary	Location
	23603	Jones	413	1100	New Jersey
	24568	Kerwin	413	2000	New Jersey
Row	34589	Larson	642	1800	Los Angeles
	35761	Myers	611	1400	Orlando
	47132	Neumann	413	9000	New Jersey
	78321	Stephens	611	8500	Orlando
	Primary key		Column		

Fig. 20.1 | Employee table sample data.

Different users of a database are often interested in different data and different relationships among the data. Most users require only subsets of the rows and columns. To obtain these subsets, we use queries to specify which data to select from a table. You use SQL to define complex queries that select data from a table. For example, you might select data from the Employee table to create a result that shows where each department is located, and present the data sorted in increasing order by department number. This result is shown in Fig. 20.2. SQL queries are discussed in Section 20.4.

Department	Location
413	New Jersey
611	Orlando
642	Los Angeles

Fig. 20.2 | Result of selecting distinct Department and Location data from table Employee.

20.3 Relational Database Overview: The books Database

We now overview relational databases in the context of a sample books database we created for this chapter. Before we discuss SQL, we overview the tables of the books database. We use this database to introduce various database concepts, including how to use SQL to obtain information from the database and to manipulate the data. We provide a script to create the database. You can find the script in the examples directory for this chapter. Section 20.5 explains how to use this script.

The database consists of three tables: authors, authorISBN and titles. The authors table (described in Fig. 20.3) consists of three columns that maintain each author's unique ID number, first name and last name. Figure 20.4 contains sample data from the authors table of the books database.

The authorISBN table (described in Fig. 20.5) consists of two columns that maintain each ISBN and the corresponding author's ID number. This table associates authors with their books. Both columns are foreign keys that represent the relationship between the

Column	Description
authorID	Author's ID number in the database. In the books database, this integer column is defined as *autoincremented*—for each row inserted in this table, the authorID value is increased by 1 automatically to ensure that each row has a unique authorID. This column represents the table's primary key.
firstName	Author's first name (a string).
lastName	Author's last name (a string).

Fig. 20.3 | authors table from the books database.

authorID	firstName	lastName
1	Harvey	Deitel
2	Paul	Deitel
3	Andrew	Goldberg
4	David	Choffnes

Fig. 20.4 | Sample data from the authors table.

Column	Description
authorID	The author's ID number, a foreign key to the authors table.
isbn	The ISBN for a book, a foreign key to the titles table.

Fig. 20.5 | authorISBN table from the books database.

tables authors and titles—one row in table authors may be associated with many rows in table titles, and vice versa. Figure 20.6 contains sample data from the authorISBN table of the books database. [*Note:* To save space, we have split the contents of this table into two columns, each containing the authorID and isbn columns.] The authorID column is a *foreign key*—a column in this table that matches the primary key column in another table (i.e., authorID in the authors table). Foreign keys are specified when creating a table. The foreign key helps maintain the *Rule of Referential Integrity:* Every foreign-key value must appear as another table's primary-key value. This enables the DBMS to determine whether the authorID value for a particular book is valid. Foreign keys also allow related data in multiple tables to be selected from those tables for analytic purposes—this is known as *joining* the data.

authorID	isbn	authorID	isbn
1	0131869000	2	0131450913
2	0131869000	1	0131828274
1	0131483986	2	0131828274
2	0131483986	3	0131450913
1	0131450913	4	0131828274

Fig. 20.6 | Sample data from the `authorISBN` table of `books`.

The `titles` table described in Fig. 20.7 consists of four columns that stand for the ISBN, the title, the edition number and the copyright year. The table is in Fig. 20.8.

There is a one-to-many relationship between a primary key and a corresponding foreign key (e.g., one publisher can publish many books). A foreign key can appear many times in its own table, but can appear only once (as the primary key) in another table. Figure 20.9 is an *entity-relationship* (*ER*) *diagram* for the books database. This diagram shows the database tables and the relationships among them. The first compartment in each box contains the table's name. The names in italic are primary keys. A table's primary

Column	Description
isbn	ISBN of the book (a string). The table's primary key. ISBN is an abbreviation for "International Standard Book Number"—a numbering scheme that publishers use to give every book a unique identification number.
title	Title of the book (a string).
editionNumber	Edition number of the book (an integer).
copyright	Copyright year of the book (a string).

Fig. 20.7 | `titles` table from the `books` database.

isbn	title	editionNumber	copyright
0131869000	Visual Basic How to Program	3	2006
0131525239	Visual C# How to Program	2	2006
0132222205	Java How to Program	7	2007
0131857576	C++ How to Program	5	2005
0132404168	C How to Program	5	2007
0131450913	Internet & World Wide Web How to Program	3	2004

Fig. 20.8 | Sample data from the `titles` table of the `books` database .

Fig. 20.9 | Table relationships in the books database.

key uniquely identifies each row in the table. Every row must have a primary-key value, and that value must be unique in the table. This is known as the ***Rule of Entity Integrity***.

Common Programming Error 20.1

Not providing a value for every column in a primary key breaks the Rule of Entity Integrity and causes the DBMS to report an error.

Common Programming Error 20.2

Providing the same value for the primary key in multiple rows causes the DBMS to report an error.

The lines connecting the tables (Fig. 20.9) represent the relationships between the tables. Consider the line between the authorISBN and authors tables. On the authors end of the line, there is a 1, and on the authorISBN end, there is an infinity symbol (∞), indicating a ***one-to-many relationship*** in which every author in the authors table can have an arbitrary number of books in the authorISBN table. Note that the relationship line links the authorID column in the table authors (i.e., its primary key) to the authorID column in table authorISBN (i.e., its foreign key). The authorID column in the authorISBN table is a foreign key.

Common Programming Error 20.3

Providing a foreign-key value that does not appear as a primary-key value in another table breaks the Rule of Referential Integrity and causes the DBMS to report an error.

The line between the titles and authorISBN tables illustrates another one-to-many relationship; a title can be written by any number of authors. In fact, the sole purpose of the authorISBN table is to provide a many-to-many relationship between the authors and titles tables—an author can write any number of books and a book can have any number of authors.

20.4 SQL

We now provide an overview of SQL in the context of our books database. You'll be able to use the SQL discussed here in the examples later in the chapter and in examples in Chapters 21–23.

The next several subsections discuss the SQL keywords listed in Fig. 20.10 in the context of SQL queries and statements. Other SQL keywords are beyond this text's scope. To learn other keywords, refer to the SQL reference guide supplied by the vendor of the RDBMS you are using. [*Note:* For more information on SQL, refer to the web resources in Section 20.15.]

SQL keyword	Description
SELECT	Retrieves data from one or more tables.
FROM	Tables involved in the query. Required in every SELECT.
WHERE	Criteria for selection that determine the rows to be retrieved, deleted or updated. Optional in a SQL query or a SQL statement.
GROUP BY	Criteria for grouping rows. Optional in a SELECT query.
ORDER BY	Criteria for ordering rows. Optional in a SELECT query.
INNER JOIN	Merge rows from multiple tables.
INSERT	Insert rows into a specified table.
UPDATE	Update rows in a specified table.
DELETE	Delete rows from a specified table.

Fig. 20.10 | SQL query keywords.

20.4.1 Basic SELECT Query

Let us consider several SQL queries that extract information from database books. A SQL query "selects" rows and columns from one or more tables in a database. Such selections are performed by queries with the SELECT keyword. The basic form of a SELECT query is

> *SELECT * FROM* tableName

in which the *asterisk (*)* indicates that all columns from the *tableName* table should be retrieved. For example, to retrieve all the data in the authors table, use

> *SELECT * FROM* authors

Most programs do not require all the data in a table. To retrieve only specific columns from a table, replace the asterisk (*) with a comma-separated list of the column names. For example, to retrieve only the columns authorID and lastName for all rows in the authors table, use the query

> *SELECT* authorID, lastName *FROM* authors

This query returns the data listed in Fig. 20.11.

authorID	lastName
1	Deitel
2	Deitel
3	Goldberg
4	Choffnes

Fig. 20.11 | Sample authorID and lastName data from the authors table.

Software Engineering Observation 20.2

For most queries, the asterisk (*) should not be used to specify column names. In general, you process results by knowing in advance the order of the columns in the result—for example, selecting authorID *and* lastName *from table* authors *ensures that the columns will appear in the result with* authorID *as the first column and* lastName *as the second column. Programs typically process result columns by specifying the column number in the result (starting from number 1 for the first column). Selecting columns by name also avoids returning unneeded columns and protects against changes in the actual order of the columns in the table(s).*

Common Programming Error 20.4

If you assume that the columns are always returned in the same order from a query that uses the asterisk (*), the program may process the results incorrectly. If the column order in the table(s) changes or if additional columns are added at a later time, the order of the columns in the result would change accordingly.

20.4.2 WHERE Clause

In most cases, it is necessary to locate rows in a database that satisfy certain *selection criteria*. Only rows that satisfy the selection criteria (formally called *predicates*) are selected. SQL uses the optional WHERE *clause* in a query to specify the selection criteria for the query. The basic form of a query with selection criteria is

> *SELECT columnName1* , *columnName2* , ... *FROM tableName WHERE criteria*

For example, to select the title, editionNumber and copyright columns from table titles for which the copyright date is greater than 2005, use the query

```
SELECT title, editionNumber, copyright
    FROM titles
    WHERE copyright > '2005'
```

Figure 20.12 shows the result of the preceding query. The WHERE clause criteria can contain the operators <, >, <=, >=, =, <> and LIKE. Operator *LIKE* is used for *pattern matching* with wildcard characters *percent (%)* and *underscore (_)*. Pattern matching allows SQL to search for strings that match a given pattern.

A pattern that contains a percent character (%) searches for strings that have zero or more characters at the percent character's position in the pattern. For example, the next query locates the rows of all the authors whose last name starts with the letter D:

```
SELECT authorID, firstName, lastName
    FROM authors
    WHERE lastName LIKE 'D%'
```

This query selects the two rows shown in Fig. 20.13—two of the four authors have a last name starting with the letter D (followed by zero or more characters). The % in the WHERE clause's LIKE pattern indicates that any number of characters can appear after the letter D in the lastName. Note that the pattern string is surrounded by single-quote characters.

Portability Tip 20.1

See the documentation for your database system to determine whether SQL is case sensitive on your system and to determine the syntax for SQL keywords (i.e., should they be all uppercase letters, all lowercase letters or some combination of the two?).

title	editionNumber	copyright
Visual C# How to Program	2	2006
Visual Basic 2005 How to Program	3	2006
Java How to Program	7	2007
C How to Program	5	2007

Fig. 20.12 | Sampling of titles with copyrights after 2005 from table `titles`.

authorID	firstName	lastName
1	Harvey	Deitel
2	Paul	Deitel

Fig. 20.13 | Authors whose last name starts with D from the `authors` table.

Portability Tip 20.2

Read your database system's documentation carefully to determine whether your system supports the LIKE *operator. The SQL we discuss is supported by most RDBMSs, but it is always a good idea to check the features of SQL that are supported by your RDBMS.*

An underscore (_) in the pattern string indicates a single wildcard character at that position in the pattern. For example, the following query locates the rows of all the authors whose last names start with any character (specified by _), followed by the letter o, followed by any number of additional characters (specified by %):

```
SELECT authorID, firstName, lastName
   FROM authors
   WHERE lastName LIKE '_o%'
```

The preceding query produces the row shown in Fig. 20.14, because only one author in our database has a last name that contains the letter o as its second letter.

authorID	firstName	lastName
3	Andrew	Goldberg

Fig. 20.14 | The only author from the `authors` table whose last name contains o as the second letter.

20.4.3 ORDER BY Clause

The rows in the result of a query can be sorted into ascending or descending order by using the optional ORDER BY *clause*. The basic form of a query with an ORDER BY clause is

```
SELECT columnName1, columnName2, ... FROM tableName ORDER BY column ASC
SELECT columnName1, columnName2, ... FROM tableName ORDER BY column DESC
```

where ASC specifies ascending order (lowest to highest), DESC specifies descending order (highest to lowest) and *column* specifies the column on which the sort is based. For example, to obtain the list of authors in ascending order by last name (Fig. 20.15), use the query

```
SELECT authorID, firstName, lastName
    FROM authors
    ORDER BY lastName ASC
```

Note that the default sorting order is ascending, so ASC is optional. To obtain the same list of authors in descending order by last name (Fig. 20.16), use the query

```
SELECT authorID, firstName, lastName
    FROM authors
    ORDER BY lastName DESC
```

Multiple columns can be used for sorting with an ORDER BY clause of the form

```
ORDER BY column1 sortingOrder, column2 sortingOrder, ...
```

where *sortingOrder* is either ASC or DESC. Note that the *sortingOrder* does not have to be identical for each column. The query

```
SELECT authorID, firstName, lastName
    FROM authors
    ORDER BY lastName, firstName
```

sorts all the rows in ascending order by last name, then by first name. If any rows have the same last name value, they are returned sorted by first name (Fig. 20.17).

authorID	firstName	lastName
4	David	Choffnes
1	Harvey	Deitel
2	Paul	Deitel
3	Andrew	Goldberg

Fig. 20.15 | Sample data from table authors in ascending order by lastName.

authorID	firstName	lastName
3	Andrew	Goldberg
1	Harvey	Deitel
2	Paul	Deitel
4	David	Choffnes

Fig. 20.16 | Sample data from table authors in descending order by lastName.

authorID	firstName	lastName
4	David	Choffnes
1	Harvey	Deitel
2	Paul	Deitel
4	Andrew	Goldberg

Fig. 20.17 | Sample data from `authors` in ascending order by `lastName` and `firstName`.

The WHERE and ORDER BY clauses can be combined in one query, as in

```
SELECT isbn, title, editionNumber, copyright
    FROM titles
    WHERE title LIKE '%How to Program'
    ORDER BY title ASC
```

which returns the `isbn`, `title`, `editionNumber` and `copyright` of each book in the `titles` table that has a `title` ending with "How to Program" and sorts them in ascending order by `title`. A portion of the query results are shown in Fig. 20.18.

isbn	title	edition -Number	copy- right
0132404168	C How to Program	5	2007
0131857576	C++ How to Program	5	2005
0131450913	Internet and World Wide Web How to Program	3	2004
0132222205	Java How to Program	7	2007
0131869000	Visual Basic 2005 How to Program	3	2006
013152539	Visual C# How to Program	2	2006

Fig. 20.18 | Sampling of books from table `titles` whose titles end with How to Program in ascending order by `title`.

20.4.4 Merging Data from Multiple Tables: INNER JOIN

Database designers often split related data into separate tables to ensure that a database does not store data redundantly. For example, the books database has tables authors and titles. We use an authorISBN table to store the relationship data between authors and their corresponding titles. If we did not separate this information into individual tables, we would need to include author information with each entry in the titles table. This would result in the database storing duplicate author information for authors who wrote multiple books. Often, it is necessary to merge data from multiple tables into a single result. Referred to as joining the tables, this is specified by an INNER JOIN operator in the query. An INNER JOIN merges rows from two tables by matching values in columns that are common to the tables. The basic form of an INNER JOIN is:

```
SELECT columnName1, columnName2, ...
FROM table1
INNER JOIN table2
    ON table1.columnName = table2.columnName
```

The **ON *clause*** of the INNER JOIN specifies the columns from each table that are compared to determine which rows are merged. For example, the following query produces a list of authors accompanied by the ISBNs for books written by each author:

```
SELECT firstName, lastName, isbn
FROM authors
INNER JOIN authorISBN
    ON authors.authorID = authorISBN.authorID
ORDER BY lastName, firstName
```

The query merges the firstName and lastName columns from table authors with the isbn column from table authorISBN, sorting the result in ascending order by lastName and firstName. Note the use of the syntax *tableName.columnName* in the ON clause. This syntax, called a ***qualified name***, specifies the columns from each table that should be compared to join the tables. The "*tableName*." syntax is required if the columns have the same name in both tables. The same syntax can be used in any query to distinguish columns in different tables that have the same name. In some systems, table names qualified with the database name can be used to perform cross-database queries. As always, the query can contain an ORDER BY clause. Figure 20.19 depicts a portion of the results of the preceding query, ordered by lastName and firstName. [*Note:* To save space, we split the result of the query into two columns, each containing the firstName, lastName and isbn columns.]

Software Engineering Observation 20.3

If a SQL statement includes columns with the same name from multiple tables, the statement must precede those column names with their table names and a dot (e.g., authors.authorID).

firstName	lastName	isbn	firstName	lastName	isbn
David	Choffnes	0131828274	Paul	Deitel	0131525239
Harvey	Deitel	0131525239	Paul	Deitel	0132404168
Harvey	Deitel	0132404168	Paul	Deitel	0131869000
Harvey	Deitel	0131869000	Paul	Deitel	0132222205
Harvey	Deitel	0132222205	Paul	Deitel	0131450913
Harvey	Deitel	0131450913	Paul	Deitel	0131525239
Harvey	Deitel	0131525239	Paul	Deitel	0131857576
Harvey	Deitel	0131857576	Paul	Deitel	0131828274
Harvey	Deitel	0131828274	Andrew	Goldberg	0131450913

Fig. 20.19 | Sampling of authors and ISBNs for the books they have written in ascending order by lastName and firstName.

Common Programming Error 20.5

Failure to qualify names for columns that have the same name in two or more tables is an error.

20.4.5 INSERT Statement

The INSERT statement inserts a row into a table. The basic form of this statement is

> **INSERT INTO** *tableName* (*columnName1*, *columnName2*, … , *columnNameN*)
>   **VALUES** (*value1*, *value2*, … , *valueN*)

where *tableName* is the table in which to insert the row. The *tableName* is followed by a comma-separated list of column names in parentheses (this list is not required if the INSERT operation specifies a value for every column of the table in the correct order). The list of column names is followed by the SQL keyword VALUES and a comma-separated list of values in parentheses. The values specified here must match the columns specified after the table name in both order and type (e.g., if *columnName1* is supposed to be the firstName column, then *value1* should be a string in single quotes representing the first name). Always explicitly list the columns when inserting rows. If the table's column order changes or a new column is added, using only VALUES may cause an error. The INSERT statement

> **INSERT INTO** authors (firstName, lastName)
>   **VALUES** ('Sue', 'Smith')

inserts a row into the authors table. The statement indicates that values are provided for the firstName and lastName columns. The corresponding values are 'Sue' and 'Smith'. We do not specify an authorID in this example because authorID is an autoincremented column in the authors table. For every row added to this table, MySQL assigns a unique authorID value that is the next value in the autoincremented sequence (i.e., 1, 2, 3 and so on). In this case, Sue Smith would be assigned authorID number 5. Figure 20.20 shows the authors table after the INSERT operation. [*Note:* Not every database management system supports autoincremented columns. Check the documentation for your DBMS for alternatives to autoincremented columns.]

Common Programming Error 20.6

It is normally an error to specify a value for an autoincrement column.

authorID	firstName	lastName
1	Harvey	Deitel
2	Paul	Deitel
3	Andrew	Goldberg
4	David	Choffnes
5	Sue	Smith

Fig. 20.20 | Sample data from table Authors after an INSERT operation.

Common Programming Error 20.7

SQL uses the single-quote (') character as a delimiter for strings. To specify a string containing a single quote (e.g., O'Malley) in a SQL statement, the string must have two single quotes in the position where the single-quote character appears in the string (e.g., `'O''Malley'`). The first of the two single-quote characters acts as an escape character for the second. Not escaping single-quote characters in a string that is part of a SQL statement is a SQL syntax error.

20.4.6 UPDATE Statement

An UPDATE statement modifies data in a table. The basic form of the UPDATE statement is

> **UPDATE** *tableName*
>   **SET** *columnName1 = value1*, *columnName2 = value2*, ..., *columnNameN = valueN*
>   **WHERE** *criteria*

where *tableName* is the table to update. The *tableName* is followed by keyword SET and a comma-separated list of column name/value pairs in the format *columnName = value*. The optional WHERE clause provides criteria that determine which rows to update. Though not required, the WHERE clause is typically used, unless a change is to be made to every row. The UPDATE statement

> **UPDATE** authors
>   **SET** lastName = 'Jones'
>   **WHERE** lastName = 'Smith' **AND** firstName = 'Sue'

updates a row in the authors table. The statement indicates that lastName will be assigned the value Jones for the row in which lastName is equal to Smith and firstName is equal to Sue. [*Note:* If there are multiple rows with the first name "Sue" and the last name "Smith," this statement will modify all such rows to have the last name "Jones."] If we know the authorID in advance of the UPDATE operation (possibly because we searched for it previously), the WHERE clause can be simplified as follows:

> **WHERE** AuthorID = 5

Figure 20.21 shows the authors table after the UPDATE operation has taken place.

authorID	firstName	lastName
1	Harvey	Deitel
2	Paul	Deitel
3	Andrew	Goldberg
4	David	Choffnes
5	Sue	Jones

Fig. 20.21 | Sample data from table authors after an UPDATE operation.

20.4.7 DELETE Statement

A SQL DELETE statement removes rows from a table. The basic form of a DELETE is

> **DELETE FROM** *tableName* **WHERE** *criteria*

where *tableName* is the table from which to delete. The optional WHERE clause specifies the criteria used to determine which rows to delete. If this clause is omitted, all the table's rows are deleted. The DELETE statement

```
DELETE FROM authors
    WHERE lastName = 'Jones' AND firstName = 'Sue'
```

deletes the row for Sue Jones in the authors table. If we know the authorID in advance of the DELETE operation, the WHERE clause can be simplified as follows:

```
WHERE authorID = 5
```

Figure 20.22 shows the authors table after the DELETE operation has taken place.

authorID	firstName	lastName
1	Harvey	Deitel
2	Paul	Deitel
3	Andrew	Goldberg
4	David	Choffnes

Fig. 20.22 | Sample data from table authors after a DELETE operation.

20.5 Instructions for Installing MySQL and MySQL Connector/J

MySQL 5.0 Community Edition is an open-source database management system that executes on many platforms, including Windows, Solaris, Linux, and Macintosh. Complete information about MySQL is available from www.mysql.com. The examples in Section 20.8 and Section 20.9 manipulate MySQL databases.

Installing MySQL
To install MySQL Community Edition:

1. To learn about the installation requirements for your platform, visit the site dev.mysql.com/doc/refman/5.0/en/installing-cs.html.

2. Visit dev.mysql.com/downloads/mysql/5.0.html and download the installer for your platform. For the MySQL examples in this chapter, you need only the Windows Essentials package on Microsoft Windows, or the Standard package on most other platforms. [*Note:* For these instructions, we assume you are running Microsoft Windows. Complete installation instructions for other platforms are available at dev.mysql.com/doc/refman/5.0/en/installing.html.]

3. Double click mysql-essential-5.0.67-win32.msi to start the installer. [*Note:* This name may differ based on the current version of MySQL 5.0.] Click **Next >**.

4. Choose **Typical** for the **Setup Type** and click **Next >**. Then click **Install**.

When the installation completes, click **Next >** twice, then **Finish** to begin configuring the serrver. To configure the server:

1. Click **Next >** then select **Standard Configuration** and click **Next >** again.

2. You have the option of installing MySQL as a Windows service, which enables the MySQL server to begin executing automatically each time your system starts. For our examples, this is unnecessary, so uncheck **Install as a Windows Service**, then check **Include Bin Directory in Windows PATH**. This will enable you to use the MySQL commands in the Windows Command Prompt.

3. Click **Next >** then click **Execute** to perform the server configuration.

4. Click **Finish** to close the wizard.

Installing MySQL Connector/J

To use MySQL with JDBC, you also need to install *MySQL Connector/J* (the J stands for Java)—a JDBC driver that allows programs to use JDBC to interact with MySQL. MySQL Connector/J can be downloaded from

```
dev.mysql.com/downloads/connector/j/5.1.html
```

The documentation for Connector/J is located at `dev.mysql.com/doc/connector/j/en/connector-j.html`. At the time of this writing, the current generally available release of MySQL Connector/J is 5.1.7. To install MySQL Connector/J:

1. Download `mysql-connector-java-5.1.7.tar.gz`.

2. Open `mysql-connector-java-5.1.7.tar.gz` with a file extractor, such as WinZip (`www.winzip.com`). Extract its contents to the `C:\` drive. This will create a directory named `mysql-connector-java-5.1.7`. This folder's `docs` subdirectory contains the documentation for MySQL Connector/J (`connector-j.pdf`). You can also view it online at `dev.mysql.com/doc/connector/j/en/connector-j.html`.

20.6 Instructions for Setting Up a MySQL User Account

For the MySQL examples to execute correctly, you need to set up a user account that allows users to create, delete and modify a database. After MySQL is installed, follow the steps below to set up a user account (these steps assume MySQL is installed in its default installation directory):

1. Open a Command Prompt and start the database server by executing the command `mysqld-nt.exe`. Note that this command has no output—it simply starts the MySQL server. Do not close this window—doing so terminates the server.

2. Next, you'll start the MySQL monitor so you can set up a user account, open another Command Prompt and execute the command

```
mysql -h localhost -u root
```

The `-h` option indicates the host (i.e., computer) on which the MySQL server is running—in this case your local computer (`localhost`). The `-u` option indicates the user account that will be used to log in to the server—`root` is the default user account that is created during installation to allow you to configure the server. Once you've logged in, you'll see a `mysql>` prompt at which you can type commands to interact with the MySQL server.

3. At the `mysql>` prompt, type

   ```
   USE mysql;
   ```

   to select the built-in database named `mysql`, which stores server information, such as user accounts and their privileges for interacting with the server. Note that each command must end with a semicolon. To confirm the command, MySQL issues the message "Database changed."

4. Next, you'll add the `javafp` user account to the `mysql` built-in database. The `mysql` database contains a table called `user` with columns that represent the user's name, password and various privileges. To create the `javafp` user account with the password `javafp`, execute the following commands from the `mysql>` prompt:

   ```
   create user 'javafp'@'localhost' identified by 'javafp';
   grant select, insert, update, delete, create, drop, references,
       execute on *.* to 'javafp'@'localhost';
   ```

   This creates the `javafp` user with the privileges needed to create the databases used in this chapter and manipulate those databases.

5. Type the command

   ```
   exit;
   ```

   to terminate the MySQL monitor.

20.7 Creating Database books in MySQL

For each MySQL database we discuss in this book, we provide a SQL script in a file with the `.sql` extension that sets up the database and its tables. You can execute these scripts in the MySQL monitor. In the examples directory for this chapter, you'll find the SQL script `books.sql` to create the `books` database. For the following steps, we assume that the MySQL server (`mysqld-nt.exe`) is still running. To execute the `books.sql` script:

1. Open a Command Prompt and use the `cd` command to change directories to the location that contains the `books.sql` script.

2. Start the MySQL monitor by typing

   ```
   mysql -h localhost -u javafp -p
   ```

   The `-p` option prompts you for the password for the `javafp` user account. When prompted, enter the password `javafp`.

3. Execute the script by typing

   ```
   source books.sql;
   ```

   This creates a new directory named `books` in the server's data directory—located on Windows at `C:\Program Files\MySQL\MySQL Server 5.0\data` by default. This new directory contains the `books` database.

4. Type the command

   ```
   exit;
   ```

   to terminate the MySQL monitor. You are now ready to proceed to the first JDBC example.

20.8 Manipulating Databases with JDBC

In this section, we present two examples. The first example introduces how to connect to a database and query the database. The second example demonstrates how to display the result of the query in a JTable.

20.8.1 Connecting to and Querying a Database

The example of Fig. 20.23 performs a simple query on the books database that retrieves the entire authors table and displays the data. The program illustrates connecting to the database, querying the database and processing the result. The following discussion presents the key JDBC aspects of the program. [*Note:* Sections 20.5—20.7 demonstrate how to start the MySQL server, configure a user account and create the books database. These steps *must* be performed before executing the program of Fig. 20.23.]

```java
 1   // Fig. 20.23: DisplayAuthors.java
 2   // Displaying the contents of the authors table.
 3   import java.sql.Connection;
 4   import java.sql.Statement;
 5   import java.sql.DriverManager;
 6   import java.sql.ResultSet;
 7   import java.sql.ResultSetMetaData;
 8   import java.sql.SQLException;
 9
10   public class DisplayAuthors
11   {
12      // database URL
13      static final String DATABASE_URL = "jdbc:mysql://localhost/books";
14
15      // launch the application
16      public static void main( String args[] )
17      {
18         Connection connection = null; // manages connection
19         Statement statement = null; // query statement
20         ResultSet resultSet = null; // manages results
21
22         // connect to database books and query database
23         try
24         {
25            // establish connection to database
26            connection = DriverManager.getConnection(
27               DATABASE_URL, "javafp", "javafp" );
28
29            // create Statement for querying database
30            statement = connection.createStatement();
31
32            // query database
33            resultSet = statement.executeQuery(
34               "SELECT authorID, firstName, lastName FROM authors" );
35
36            // process query results
37            ResultSetMetaData metaData = resultSet.getMetaData();
```

Fig. 20.23 | Displaying the contents of the authors table. (Part 1 of 2.)

```
38            int numberOfColumns = metaData.getColumnCount();
39            System.out.println( "Authors Table of Books Database:\n" );
40
41            for ( int i = 1; i <= numberOfColumns; i++ )
42               System.out.printf( "%-8s\t", metaData.getColumnName( i ) );
43            System.out.println();
44
45            while ( resultSet.next() )
46            {
47               for ( int i = 1; i <= numberOfColumns; i++ )
48                  System.out.printf( "%-8s\t", resultSet.getObject( i ) );
49               System.out.println();
50            } // end while
51         } // end try
52         catch ( SQLException sqlException )
53         {
54            sqlException.printStackTrace();
55         } // end catch
56         finally // ensure resultSet, statement and connection are closed
57         {
58            try
59            {
60               resultSet.close();
61               statement.close();
62               connection.close();
63            } // end try
64            catch ( Exception exception )
65            {
66               exception.printStackTrace();
67            } // end catch
68         } // end finally
69      } // end main
70   } // end class DisplayAuthors
```

```
Authors Table of Books Database:

authorID        firstName       lastName
1               Harvey          Deitel
2               Paul            Deitel
3               Andrew          Goldberg
4               David           Choffnes
```

Fig. 20.23 | Displaying the contents of the authors table. (Part 2 of 2.)

Lines 3–8 import the JDBC interfaces and classes from package java.sql used in this program. Line 13 declares a string constant for the database URL. This identifies the name of the database to connect to, as well as information about the protocol used by the JDBC driver (discussed shortly). Method main (lines 16–69) connects to the books database, queries the database, displays the result of the query and closes the database connection.

In past versions of Java, programs were required to load an appropriate database driver before connecting to a database. JDBC 4.0, part of Java SE 6, supports *automatic driver discovery*—you are no longer required to load the database driver in advance. To ensure that the program can locate the database driver class, you must include the class's location in the program's classpath when you execute the program. For MySQL, you include the file `mysql-connector-java-5.1.7-bin.jar` (in the `C:\mysql-connector-java-5.1.7` directory) in your program's classpath, as in:

```
java -classpath
    .;c:\mysql-connector-java-5.1.7\mysql-connector-java-5.1.7-bin.jar
    DisplayAuthors
```

In the `-classpath` option of the preceding command, notice the period (.) at the beginning of the classpath information. If this period is missing, the JVM will not look for classes in the current directory and thus will not find the `DisplayAuthors` class file. You may also copy the `mysql-connector-java-5.1.7-bin.jar` file to your JDK's `\jre\lib\ext` folder. After doing so, you can run the application simply using the command

```
java DisplayAuthors
```

Software Engineering Observation 20.4

Most major database vendors provide their own JDBC database drivers, and many third-party vendors provide JDBC drivers as well. For more information on JDBC drivers, visit the Sun Microsystems JDBC website, `servlet.java.sun.com/products/jdbc/drivers`.

Lines 26–27 of Fig. 20.23 create a `Connection` object (package `java.sql`) referenced by `connection`. An object that implements interface `Connection` manages the connection between the Java program and the database. `Connection` objects enable programs to create SQL statements that manipulate databases. The program initializes `connection` with the result of a call to static method `getConnection` of class `DriverManager` (package `java.sql`), which attempts to connect to the database specified by its URL. Method `getConnection` takes three arguments—a `String` that specifies the database URL, a `String` that specifies the username and a `String` that specifies the password. The username and password are set in Section 20.6. If you used a different username and password, you need to replace the username (second argument) and password (third argument) passed to method `getConnection` in line 27. The URL locates the database (possibly on a network or in the local file system of the computer). The URL `jdbc:mysql://localhost/books` specifies the protocol for communication (`jdbc`), the *subprotocol* for communication (`mysql`) and the location of the database (`//localhost/books`, where `localhost` is the host running the MySQL server and `books` is the database name). The subprotocol `mysql` indicates that the program uses a MySQL-specific subprotocol to connect to the MySQL database. If the `DriverManager` cannot connect to the database, method `getConnection` throws a `SQLException` (package `java.sql`). Figure 20.24 lists the JDBC driver names and database URL formats of several popular RDBMSs.

RDBMS	Database URL format
MySQL	`jdbc:mysql://`*hostname*:*portNumber*/*databaseName*
ORACLE	`jdbc:oracle:thin:@`*hostname*:*portNumber*:*databaseName*

Fig. 20.24 | Popular JDBC database URL formats. (Part 1 of 2.)

RDBMS	Database URL format
DB2	`jdbc:db2:`*hostname*`:`*portNumber*`/`*databaseName*
Java DB/Apache Derby	`jdbc:derby:`*dataBaseName* (embedded) `jdbc:derby://`*hostname*`:`*portNumber*`/`*databaseName* (network)
Microsoft SQL Server	`jdbc:sqlserver://`*hostname*`:`*portNumber*`;databaseName=`*dataBaseName*
Sybase	`jdbc:sybase:Tds:`*hostname*`:`*portNumber*`/`*databaseName*

Fig. 20.24 | Popular JDBC database URL formats. (Part 2 of 2.)

Software Engineering Observation 20.5

Most database management systems require the user to log in before accessing the database contents. `DriverManager` method `getConnection` is overloaded with versions that enable the program to supply the user name and password to gain access.

Line 30 invokes `Connection` method `createStatement` to obtain an object that implements interface `Statement` (package `java.sql`). The program uses the `Statement` object to submit SQL to the database.

Lines 33–34 use the `Statement` object's `executeQuery` method to submit a query that selects all the author information from table `authors`. This method returns an object that implements interface `ResultSet` and contains the query results. The `ResultSet` methods enable the program to manipulate the query result.

Lines 37–50 process the `ResultSet`. Line 37 obtains the metadata for the `ResultSet` as a `ResultSetMetaData` (package `java.sql`) object. The *metadata* describes the `ResultSet`'s contents. Programs can use metadata programmatically to obtain information about the `ResultSet`'s column names and types. Line 38 uses `ResultSetMetaData` method `getColumnCount` to retrieve the number of columns in the `ResultSet`. Lines 41–42 display the column names.

Software Engineering Observation 20.6

Metadata enables programs to process `ResultSet` contents dynamically when detailed information about the `ResultSet` is not known in advance.

Lines 45–50 display the data in each `ResultSet` row. First, the program positions the `ResultSet` cursor (which points to the row being processed) to the first row in the `ResultSet` with method `next` (line 45). Method `next` returns `boolean` value `true` if it is able to position to the next row; otherwise, the method returns `false`.

Common Programming Error 20.8

Initially, a `ResultSet` cursor is positioned before the first row. A `SQLException` occurs if you attempt to access a `ResultSet`'s contents before positioning the `ResultSet` cursor to the first row with method `next`.

If there are rows in the `ResultSet`, line 48 extracts the contents of one column in the current row. When processing a `ResultSet`, it is possible to extract each column of the `ResultSet` as a specific Java type. In fact, `ResultSetMetaData` method `getColumnType` returns a constant integer from class Types (package java.sql) indicating the type of a specified column. Programs can use these values in a switch statement to invoke ResultSet methods that return the column values as appropriate Java types. If the type of a column is Types.INTEGER, ResultSet method getInt returns the column value as an int. ResultSet *get* methods typically receive as an argument either a column number (as an int) or a column name (as a String) indicating which column's value to obtain. Visit

java.sun.com/javase/6/docs/technotes/guides/jdbc/getstart/
    GettingStartedTOC.fm.html

for detailed mappings of SQL data types to Java types and to determine the appropriate ResultSet method to call for each SQL data type.

Performance Tip 20.1

If a query specifies the exact columns to select from the database, the ResultSet contains the columns in the specified order. In this case, using the column number to obtain the column's value is more efficient than using the column name. The column number provides direct access to the specified column. Using the column name requires a search of the column names to locate the appropriate column.

For simplicity, this example treats each value as an Object. The program retrieves each column value with ResultSet method getObject (line 48) and prints the String representation of the Object. Note that, unlike array indices, which start at 0, ResultSet column numbers start at 1. The finally block (lines 56–68) closes the ResultSet (line 60), the Statement (line 61) and the database Connection (line 62). [*Note:* Lines 60–62 will throw NullPointerExceptions if the ResultSet, Statement or Connection objects were not created properly. In production code, you should check the variables that refer to these objects to see if they are null before you call close.]

Common Programming Error 20.9

Specifying column number 0 when obtaining values from a ResultSet causes a SQLException.

Common Programming Error 20.10

A SQLException occurs if you attempt to manipulate a ResultSet after closing the Statement that created it. The ResultSet is discarded when the corresponding Statement is closed.

Software Engineering Observation 20.7

Each Statement object can open only one ResultSet object at a time. When a Statement returns a new ResultSet, the Statement closes the prior ResultSet. To use multiple ResultSets in parallel, separate Statement objects must return the ResultSets.

20.8.2 Querying the books Database

The next example (Fig. 20.25 and Fig. 20.28) allows the user to enter any query into the program. The example displays the result of a query in a JTable, using a TableModel object to provide the ResultSet data to the JTable. A JTable is a swing GUI component that can be bound to a database to display the results of a query. Class ResultSetTableModel (Fig. 20.25) performs the connection to the database via a TableModel and maintains the ResultSet. Class DisplayQueryResults (Fig. 20.28) creates the GUI and specifies an instance of class ResultSetTableModel to provide data for the JTable.

ResultSetTableModel Class

Class ResultSetTableModel (Fig. 20.25) extends class AbstractTableModel (package javax.swing.table), which implements interface TableModel. Class ResultSetTable-Model overrides TableModel methods getColumnClass, getColumnCount, getColumn-Name, getRowCount and getValueAt. The default implementations of TableModel methods isCellEditable and setValueAt (provided by AbstractTableModel) are not overridden, because this example does not support editing the JTable cells. The default implementations of TableModel methods addTableModelListener and removeTable-ModelListener (provided by AbstractTableModel) are not overridden, because the implementations of these methods in AbstractTableModel properly add and remove event listeners.

```
 1    // Fig. 20.25: ResultSetTableModel.java
 2    // A TableModel that supplies ResultSet data to a JTable.
 3    import java.sql.Connection;
 4    import java.sql.Statement;
 5    import java.sql.DriverManager;
 6    import java.sql.ResultSet;
 7    import java.sql.ResultSetMetaData;
 8    import java.sql.SQLException;
 9    import javax.swing.table.AbstractTableModel;
10
11    // ResultSet rows and columns are counted from 1 and JTable
12    // rows and columns are counted from 0. When processing
13    // ResultSet rows or columns for use in a JTable, it is
14    // necessary to add 1 to the row or column number to manipulate
15    // the appropriate ResultSet column (i.e., JTable column 0 is
16    // ResultSet column 1 and JTable row 0 is ResultSet row 1).
17    public class ResultSetTableModel extends AbstractTableModel
18    {
19       private Connection connection;
20       private Statement statement;
21       private ResultSet resultSet;
22       private ResultSetMetaData metaData;
23       private int numberOfRows;
24
25       // keep track of database connection status
26       private boolean connectedToDatabase = false;
27
28       // constructor initializes resultSet and obtains its meta data object;
29       // determines number of rows
30       public ResultSetTableModel( String url, String username,
31          String password, String query ) throws SQLException
32       {
33          // connect to database
34          connection = DriverManager.getConnection( url, username, password );
35
36          // create Statement to query database
37          statement = connection.createStatement(
38             ResultSet.TYPE_SCROLL_INSENSITIVE,
39             ResultSet.CONCUR_READ_ONLY );
```

Fig. 20.25 | A TableModel that supplies ResultSet data to a JTable. (Part 1 of 4.)

```
40
41          // update database connection status
42          connectedToDatabase = true;
43
44          // set query and execute it
45          setQuery( query );
46      } // end constructor ResultSetTableModel
47
48      // get class that represents column type
49      public Class getColumnClass( int column ) throws IllegalStateException
50      {
51          // ensure database connection is available
52          if ( !connectedToDatabase )
53             throw new IllegalStateException( "Not Connected to Database" );
54
55          // determine Java class of column
56          try
57          {
58             String className = metaData.getColumnClassName( column + 1 );
59
60             // return Class object that represents className
61             return Class.forName( className );
62          } // end try
63          catch ( Exception exception )
64          {
65             exception.printStackTrace();
66          } // end catch
67
68          return Object.class; // if problems occur above, assume type Object
69      } // end method getColumnClass
70
71      // get number of columns in ResultSet
72      public int getColumnCount() throws IllegalStateException
73      {
74          // ensure database connection is available
75          if ( !connectedToDatabase )
76             throw new IllegalStateException( "Not Connected to Database" );
77
78          // determine number of columns
79          try
80          {
81             return metaData.getColumnCount();
82          } // end try
83          catch ( SQLException sqlException )
84          {
85             sqlException.printStackTrace();
86          } // end catch
87
88          return 0; // if problems occur above, return 0 for number of columns
89      } // end method getColumnCount
90
```

Fig. 20.25 | A TableModel that supplies ResultSet data to a JTable. (Part 2 of 4.)

```
91      // get name of a particular column in ResultSet
92      public String getColumnName( int column ) throws IllegalStateException
93      {
94          // ensure database connection is available
95          if ( !connectedToDatabase )
96              throw new IllegalStateException( "Not Connected to Database" );
97
98          // determine column name
99          try
100         {
101             return metaData.getColumnName( column + 1 );
102         } // end try
103         catch ( SQLException sqlException )
104         {
105             sqlException.printStackTrace();
106         } // end catch
107
108         return ""; // if problems, return empty string for column name
109     } // end method getColumnName
110
111     // return number of rows in ResultSet
112     public int getRowCount() throws IllegalStateException
113     {
114         // ensure database connection is available
115         if ( !connectedToDatabase )
116             throw new IllegalStateException( "Not Connected to Database" );
117
118         return numberOfRows;
119     } // end method getRowCount
120
121     // obtain value in particular row and column
122     public Object getValueAt( int row, int column )
123         throws IllegalStateException
124     {
125         // ensure database connection is available
126         if ( !connectedToDatabase )
127             throw new IllegalStateException( "Not Connected to Database" );
128
129         // obtain a value at specified ResultSet row and column
130         try
131         {
132             resultSet.absolute( row + 1 );
133             return resultSet.getObject( column + 1 );
134         } // end try
135         catch ( SQLException sqlException )
136         {
137             sqlException.printStackTrace();
138         } // end catch
139
140         return ""; // if problems, return empty string object
141     } // end method getValueAt
142
```

Fig. 20.25 | A TableModel that supplies ResultSet data to a JTable. (Part 3 of 4.)

```
143        // set new database query string
144        public void setQuery( String query )
145            throws SQLException, IllegalStateException
146        {
147            // ensure database connection is available
148            if ( !connectedToDatabase )
149                throw new IllegalStateException( "Not Connected to Database" );
150
151            // specify query and execute it
152            resultSet = statement.executeQuery( query );
153
154            // obtain meta data for ResultSet
155            metaData = resultSet.getMetaData();
156
157            // determine number of rows in ResultSet
158            resultSet.last(); // move to last row
159            numberOfRows = resultSet.getRow(); // get row number
160
161            // notify JTable that model has changed
162            fireTableStructureChanged();
163        } // end method setQuery
164
165        // close Statement and Connection
166        public void disconnectFromDatabase()
167        {
168            if ( connectedToDatabase )
169            {
170                // close Statement and Connection
171                try
172                {
173                    resultSet.close();
174                    statement.close();
175                    connection.close();
176                } // end try
177                catch ( SQLException sqlException )
178                {
179                    sqlException.printStackTrace();
180                } // end catch
181                finally // update database connection status
182                {
183                    connectedToDatabase = false;
184                } // end finally
185            } // end if
186        } // end method disconnectFromDatabase
187    }  // end class ResultSetTableModel
```

Fig. 20.25 | A `TableModel` that supplies `ResultSet` data to a `JTable`. (Part 4 of 4.)

The `ResultSetTableModel` constructor (lines 30–46) accepts four `String` arguments—the URL of the database, the username, the password and the default query to perform. The constructor throws any exceptions that occur in its body back to the application that created the `ResultSetTableModel` object, so that the application can determine how to handle the exception (e.g., report an error and terminate the application).

Line 34 establishes a connection to the database. Lines 37–39 invoke Connection method createStatement to create a Statement object. This example uses a version of method createStatement that takes two arguments—the result set type and the result set concurrency. The *result set type* (Fig. 20.26) specifies whether the ResultSet's cursor is able to scroll in both directions or forward only and whether the ResultSet is sensitive to changes. ResultSets that are sensitive to changes reflect those changes immediately after they are made with methods of interface ResultSet. If a ResultSet is insensitive to changes, the query that produced the ResultSet must be executed again to reflect any changes made. The *result set concurrency* (Fig. 20.27) specifies whether the ResultSet can be updated with ResultSet's update methods. This example uses a ResultSet that is scrollable, insensitive to changes and read only. Line 45 invokes our method setQuery (lines 144–163) to perform the default query.

ResultSet static type constant	Description
TYPE_FORWARD_ONLY	Specifies that a ResultSet's cursor can move only in the forward direction (i.e., from the first to the last row in the ResultSet).
TYPE_SCROLL_INSENSITIVE	Specifies that a ResultSet's cursor can scroll in either direction and that the changes made to the ResultSet during ResultSet processing are not reflected in the ResultSet unless the program queries the database again.
TYPE_SCROLL_SENSITIVE	Specifies that a ResultSet's cursor can scroll in either direction and that the changes made to the ResultSet during ResultSet processing are reflected immediately in the ResultSet.

Fig. 20.26 | ResultSet constants for specifying ResultSet type.

ResultSet static concurrency constant	Description
CONCUR_READ_ONLY	Specifies that a ResultSet cannot be updated (i.e., changes to the ResultSet contents cannot be reflected in the database with ResultSet's update methods).
CONCUR_UPDATABLE	Specifies that a ResultSet can be updated (i.e., changes to the ResultSet contents can be reflected in the database with ResultSet's update methods).

Fig. 20.27 | ResultSet constants for specifying result properties.

Portability Tip 20.3

Some JDBC drivers do not support scrollable ResultSets. In such cases, the driver typically returns a ResultSet in which the cursor can move only forward. For more information, see your database driver documentation.

Portability Tip 20.4

Some JDBC drivers do not support updatable ResultSets. In such cases, the driver typically returns a read-only ResultSet. For more information, see your database driver documentation.

Common Programming Error 20.11

Attempting to update a ResultSet when the database driver does not support updatable ResultSets causes SQLFeatureNotSupportedExceptions.

Common Programming Error 20.12

Attempting to move the cursor backward through a ResultSet when the database driver does not support backward scrolling causes a SQLException.

Method getColumnClass (lines 49–69) returns a Class object that represents the superclass of all objects in a particular column. The JTable uses this information to configure the default cell renderer and cell editor for that column in the JTable. Line 58 uses ResultSetMetaData method getColumnClassName to obtain the fully qualified class name for the specified column. Line 51 loads the class and returns the corresponding Class object. If an exception occurs, the catch in lines 63–66 prints a stack trace and line 68 returns Object.class—the Class instance that represents class Object—as the default type. [*Note:* Line 58 uses the argument column + 1. Like arrays, JTable row and column numbers are counted from 0. However, ResultSet row and column numbers are counted from 1. Thus, when processing ResultSet rows or columns for use in a JTable, it is necessary to add 1 to the row or column number to manipulate the appropriate ResultSet row or column.]

Method getColumnCount (lines 72–89) returns the number of columns in the model's underlying ResultSet. Line 81 uses ResultSetMetaData method getColumnCount to obtain the number of columns in the ResultSet. If an exception occurs, the catch in lines 83–86 prints a stack trace and line 88 returns 0 as the default number of columns.

Method getColumnName (lines 92–109) returns the name of the column in the model's underlying ResultSet. Line 101 uses ResultSetMetaData method getColumnName to obtain the column name from the ResultSet. If an exception occurs, the catch in lines 103–106 prints a stack trace and line 108 returns the empty string as the default column name.

Method getRowCount (lines 112–119) returns the number of rows in the model's underlying ResultSet. When method setQuery (lines 144–163) performs a query, it stores the number of rows in variable numberOfRows.

Method getValueAt (lines 122–141) returns the Object in a particular row and column of the model's underlying ResultSet. Line 132 uses ResultSet method absolute to position the ResultSet cursor at a specific row. Line 133 uses ResultSet method getObject to obtain the Object in a specific column of the current row. If an exception occurs, the catch in lines 135–138 prints a stack trace and line 140 returns an empty string as the default value.

Method setQuery (lines 144–163) executes the query it receives as an argument to obtain a new ResultSet (line 152). Line 155 gets the ResultSetMetaData for the new ResultSet. Line 158 uses ResultSet method last to position the ResultSet cursor at the last row in the ResultSet. [*Note:* This can be slow if the table contains many rows.] Line 159 uses ResultSet method getRow to obtain the row number for the current row in the

ResultSet. Line 162 invokes method fireTableStructureChanged (inherited from class AbstractTableModel) to notify any JTable using this ResultSetTableModel object as its model that the structure of the model has changed. This causes the JTable to repopulate its rows and columns with the new ResultSet data. Method setQuery throws any exceptions that occur in its body back to the application that invoked setQuery.

Method disconnectFromDatabase (lines 166–186) implements an appropriate termination method for class ResultSetTableModel. A class designer should provide a public method that clients of the class must invoke explicitly to free resources that an object has used. In this case, method disconnectFromDatabase closes the ResultSet, Statement and Connection (lines 173–175), which are considered limited resources. Clients of the ResultSetTableModel class should always invoke this method when the instance of this class is no longer needed. Before releasing resources, line 168 verifies whether the connection is already terminated. If not, the method proceeds. Note that the other methods in class ResultSetTableModel each throw an IllegalStateException if connectedToDatabase is false. Method disconnectFromDatabase sets connectedTo-Database to false (line 183) to ensure that clients do not use an instance of ResultSet-TableModel after that instance has already been terminated. IllegalStateException is an exception from the Java libraries that is appropriate for indicating this error condition.

DisplayQueryResults Class

Class DisplayQueryResults (Fig. 20.28) implements the application's GUI and interacts with the ResultSetTableModel via a JTable object. This application also demonstrates the JTable sorting and filtering capabilities introduced in Java SE 6.

```
1   // Fig. 20.28: DisplayQueryResults.java
2   // Display the contents of the Authors table in the books database.
3   import java.awt.BorderLayout;
4   import java.awt.event.ActionListener;
5   import java.awt.event.ActionEvent;
6   import java.awt.event.WindowAdapter;
7   import java.awt.event.WindowEvent;
8   import java.sql.SQLException;
9   import java.util.regex.PatternSyntaxException;
10  import javax.swing.JFrame;
11  import javax.swing.JTextArea;
12  import javax.swing.JScrollPane;
13  import javax.swing.ScrollPaneConstants;
14  import javax.swing.JTable;
15  import javax.swing.JOptionPane;
16  import javax.swing.JButton;
17  import javax.swing.Box;
18  import javax.swing.JLabel;
19  import javax.swing.JTextField;
20  import javax.swing.RowFilter;
21  import javax.swing.table.TableRowSorter;
22  import javax.swing.table.TableModel;
23
```

Fig. 20.28 | Displays contents of the database books. (Part 1 of 5.)

```
24   public class DisplayQueryResults extends JFrame
25   {
26      // database URL, username and password
27      static final String DATABASE_URL = "jdbc:mysql://localhost/books";
28      static final String USERNAME = "javafp";
29      static final String PASSWORD = "javafp";
30
31      // default query retrieves all data from authors table
32      static final String DEFAULT_QUERY = "SELECT * FROM authors";
33
34      private ResultSetTableModel tableModel;
35      private JTextArea queryArea;
36
37      // create ResultSetTableModel and GUI
38      public DisplayQueryResults()
39      {
40         super( "Displaying Query Results" );
41
42         // create ResultSetTableModel and display database table
43         try
44         {
45            // create TableModel for results of query SELECT * FROM authors
46            tableModel = new ResultSetTableModel( DATABASE_URL,
47               USERNAME, PASSWORD, DEFAULT_QUERY );
48
49            // set up JTextArea in which user types queries
50            queryArea = new JTextArea( DEFAULT_QUERY, 3, 100 );
51            queryArea.setWrapStyleWord( true );
52            queryArea.setLineWrap( true );
53
54            JScrollPane scrollPane = new JScrollPane( queryArea,
55               ScrollPaneConstants.VERTICAL_SCROLLBAR_AS_NEEDED,
56               ScrollPaneConstants.HORIZONTAL_SCROLLBAR_NEVER );
57
58            // set up JButton for submitting queries
59            JButton submitButton = new JButton( "Submit Query" );
60
61            // create Box to manage placement of queryArea and
62            // submitButton in GUI
63            Box boxNorth = Box.createHorizontalBox();
64            boxNorth.add( scrollPane );
65            boxNorth.add( submitButton );
66
67            // create JTable delegate for tableModel
68            JTable resultTable = new JTable( tableModel );
69
70            JLabel filterLabel = new JLabel( "Filter:" );
71            final JTextField filterText = new JTextField();
72            JButton filterButton = new JButton( "Apply Filter" );
73            Box boxSouth = boxNorth.createHorizontalBox();
74
75            boxSouth.add( filterLabel );
76            boxSouth.add( filterText );
```

Fig. 20.28 | Displays contents of the database books. (Part 2 of 5.)

```
77              boxSouth.add( filterButton );
78
79              // place GUI components on content pane
80              add( boxNorth, BorderLayout.NORTH );
81              add( new JScrollPane( resultTable ), BorderLayout.CENTER );
82              add( boxSouth, BorderLayout.SOUTH );
83
84              // create event listener for submitButton
85              submitButton.addActionListener(
86
87                  new ActionListener()
88                  {
89                      // pass query to table model
90                      public void actionPerformed( ActionEvent event )
91                      {
92                          // perform a new query
93                          try
94                          {
95                              tableModel.setQuery( queryArea.getText() );
96                          } // end try
97                          catch ( SQLException sqlException )
98                          {
99                              JOptionPane.showMessageDialog( null,
100                                 sqlException.getMessage(), "Database error",
101                                 JOptionPane.ERROR_MESSAGE );
102
103                             // try to recover from invalid user query
104                             // by executing default query
105                             try
106                             {
107                                 tableModel.setQuery( DEFAULT_QUERY );
108                                 queryArea.setText( DEFAULT_QUERY );
109                             } // end try
110                             catch ( SQLException sqlException2 )
111                             {
112                                 JOptionPane.showMessageDialog( null,
113                                     sqlException2.getMessage(), "Database error",
114                                     JOptionPane.ERROR_MESSAGE );
115
116                                 // ensure database connection is closed
117                                 tableModel.disconnectFromDatabase();
118
119                                 System.exit( 1 ); // terminate application
120                             } // end inner catch
121                         } // end outer catch
122                     } // end actionPerformed
123                 } // end ActionListener inner class
124             ); // end call to addActionListener
125
126             final TableRowSorter< TableModel > sorter =
127                 new TableRowSorter< TableModel >( tableModel );
128             resultTable.setRowSorter( sorter );
```

Fig. 20.28 | Displays contents of the database books. (Part 3 of 5.)

```
129          setSize( 500, 250 ); // set window size
130          setVisible( true ); // display window
131
132          // create listener for filterButton
133          filterButton.addActionListener(
134             new ActionListener()
135             {
136                // pass filter text to listener
137                public void actionPerformed( ActionEvent e )
138                {
139                   String text = filterText.getText();
140
141                   if ( text.length() == 0 )
142                      sorter.setRowFilter( null );
143                   else
144                   {
145                      try
146                      {
147                         sorter.setRowFilter(
148                            RowFilter.regexFilter( text ) );
149                      } // end try
150                      catch ( PatternSyntaxException pse )
151                      {
152                         JOptionPane.showMessageDialog( null,
153                            "Bad regex pattern", "Bad regex pattern",
154                            JOptionPane.ERROR_MESSAGE );
155                      } // end catch
156                   } // end else
157                } // end method actionPerfomed
158             } // end annonymous inner class
159          ); // end call to addActionLister
160       } // end try
161       catch ( SQLException sqlException )
162       {
163          JOptionPane.showMessageDialog( null, sqlException.getMessage(),
164             "Database error", JOptionPane.ERROR_MESSAGE );
165
166          // ensure database connection is closed
167          tableModel.disconnectFromDatabase();
168
169          System.exit( 1 ); // terminate application
170       } // end catch
171
172       // dispose of window when user quits application (this overrides
173       // the default of HIDE_ON_CLOSE)
174       setDefaultCloseOperation( DISPOSE_ON_CLOSE );
175
176       // ensure database connection is closed when user quits application
177       addWindowListener(
178
179          new WindowAdapter()
180          {
```

Fig. 20.28 | Displays contents of the database books. (Part 4 of 5.)

```
181            // disconnect from database and exit when window has closed
182            public void windowClosed( WindowEvent event )
183            {
184               tableModel.disconnectFromDatabase();
185               System.exit( 0 );
186            } // end method windowClosed
187         } // end WindowAdapter inner class
188      ); // end call to addWindowListener
189   } // end DisplayQueryResults constructor
190
191   // execute application
192   public static void main( String args[] )
193   {
194      new DisplayQueryResults();
195   } // end main
196 } // end class DisplayQueryResults
```

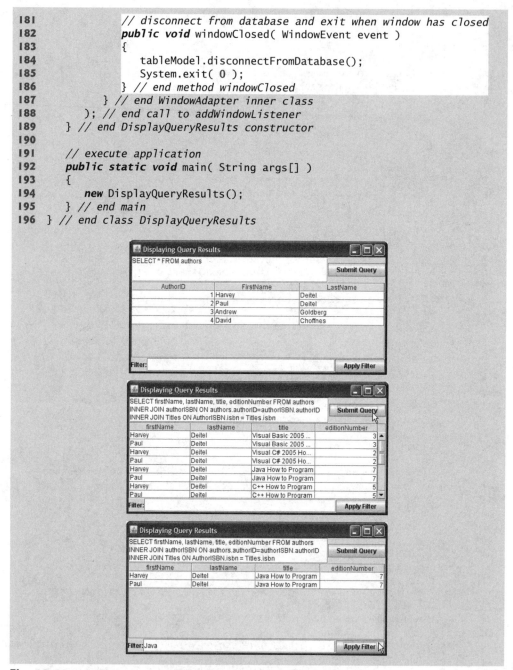

Fig. 20.28 | Displays contents of the database books. (Part 5 of 5.)

Lines 27–29 and 32 declare the URL, username, password and default query that are passed to the `ResultSetTableModel` constructor to make the initial connection to the database and perform the default query. The `DisplayQueryResults` constructor (lines 38–

189) creates a ResultSetTableModel object and the GUI for the application. Line 68 creates the JTable object and passes a ResultSetTableModel object to the JTable constructor, which then registers the JTable as a listener for TableModelEvents generated by the ResultSetTableModel.

Lines 85–124 register an event handler for the submitButton that the user clicks to submit a query to the database. When the user clicks the button, method actionPerformed (lines 90–122) invokes method setQuery from the class ResultSetTableModel to execute the new query. If the user's query fails (e.g., because of a syntax error in the user's input), lines 107–108 execute the default query. If the default query also fails, there could be a more serious error, so line 117 ensures that the database connection is closed and line 119 exits the program. The screen captures in Fig. 20.28 show the results of two queries. The first screen capture shows the default query that retrieves all the data from table authors of database books. The second screen capture shows a query that selects each author's first name and last name from the authors table and combines that information with the title and edition number from the titles table. Try entering your own queries in the text area and clicking the **Submit Query** button to execute the query.

As of Java SE 6, JTables now allow users to sort rows by the data in a specific column. Lines 126–127 use the *TableRowSorter* class (from package *javax.swing.table*) to create an object that uses our ResultSetTableModel to sort rows in the JTable that displays query results. When the user clicks the title of a particular JTable column, the TableRowSorter interacts with the underlying TableModel to reorder the rows based on the data in that column. Line 128 uses JTable method *setRowSorter* to specify the TableRowSorter for resultTable.

JTables can now show subsets of the data from the underlying TableModel. This is known as filtering the data. Lines 133–159 register an event handler for the filterButton that the user clicks to filter the data. In method actionPerformed (lines 137–157), line 139 obtains the filter text. If the user did not specify filter text, line 142 uses JTable method *setRowFilter* to remove any prior filter by setting the filter to null. Otherwise, lines 147–148, use setRowFilter to specify a *RowFilter* (from package javax.swing) based on the user's input. Class RowFilter provides several methods for creating filters. The static method *regexFilter* receives a String containing a regular expression pattern as its argument and an optional set of indices that specify which columns to filter. If no indices are specified, then all the columns are searched. In this example, the regular expression pattern is the text the user typed. Once the filter is set, the data displayed in the JTable is updated based on the filtered TableModel.

20.9 RowSet Interface

In the previous examples, you learned how to query a database by explicitly establishing a Connection to the database, preparing a Statement for querying the database and executing the query. In this section, we demonstrate the RowSet interface, which configures the database connection and prepares query statements automatically. The interface RowSet provides several *set* methods that allow you to specify the properties needed to establish a connection (such as the database URL, user name and password of the database) and create a Statement (such as a query). RowSet also provides several *get* methods that return these properties.

There are two types of RowSet objects—connected and disconnected. A *connected* **RowSet** object connects to the database once and remains connected until the application terminates. A *disconnected* RowSet object connects to the database, executes a query to retrieve the data from the database and then closes the connection. A program may change the data in a disconnected RowSet while it is disconnected. Modified data can be updated in the database after a disconnected RowSet reestablishes the connection with the database.

Package *javax.sql.rowset* contains two subinterfaces of RowSet—JdbcRowSet and CachedRowSet. *JdbcRowSet*, a connected RowSet, acts as a wrapper around a ResultSet object, and allows you to scroll through and update the rows in the ResultSet. Recall that by default, a ResultSet object is non-scrollable and read only—you must explicitly set the result set type constant to TYPE_SCROLL_INSENSITIVE and set the result set concurrency constant to CONCUR_UPDATABLE to make a ResultSet object scrollable and updatable. A JdbcRowSet object is scrollable and updatable by default. *CachedRowSet*, a disconnected RowSet, caches the data of a ResultSet in memory and disconnects from the database. Like JdbcRowSet, a CachedRowSet object is scrollable and updatable by default. A Cached-RowSet object is also serializable, so it can be passed between Java applications through a network, such as the Internet. However, CachedRowSet has a limitation—the amount of data that can be stored in memory is limited. Package javax.sql.rowset contains three other subinterfaces of RowSet. For details of these interfaces, visit java.sun.com/javase/6/docs/technotes/guides/jdbc/getstart/rowsetImpl.html.

Portability Tip 20.5

A RowSet can provide scrolling capability for drivers that do not support scrollable ResultSets.

Figure 20.29 reimplements the example of Fig. 20.23 using a RowSet. Rather than establish the connection and create a Statement explicitly, Fig. 20.29 uses a JdbcRowSet object to create a Connection and a Statement automatically.

```java
1   // Fig. 20.29: JdbcRowSetTest.java
2   // Displaying the contents of the authors table using JdbcRowSet.
3   import java.sql.ResultSetMetaData;
4   import java.sql.SQLException;
5   import javax.sql.rowset.JdbcRowSet;
6   import com.sun.rowset.JdbcRowSetImpl; // Sun's JdbcRowSet implementation
7
8   public class JdbcRowSetTest
9   {
10      // JDBC driver name and database URL
11      static final String DATABASE_URL = "jdbc:mysql://localhost/books";
12      static final String USERNAME = "javafp";
13      static final String PASSWORD = "javafp";
14
15      // constructor connects to database, queries database, processes
16      // results and displays results in window
17      public JdbcRowSetTest()
18      {
```

Fig. 20.29 | Displaying the authors table using JdbcRowSet. (Part I of 2.)

```
19        // connect to database books and query database
20        try
21        {
22            // specify properties of JdbcRowSet
23            JdbcRowSet rowSet = new JdbcRowSetImpl();
24            rowSet.setUrl( DATABASE_URL ); // set database URL
25            rowSet.setUsername( USERNAME ); // set username
26            rowSet.setPassword( PASSWORD ); // set password
27            rowSet.setCommand( "SELECT * FROM authors" ); // set query
28            rowSet.execute(); // execute query
29
30            // process query results
31            ResultSetMetaData metaData = rowSet.getMetaData();
32            int numberOfColumns = metaData.getColumnCount();
33            System.out.println( "Authors Table of Books Database:\n" );
34
35            // display rowset header
36            for ( int i = 1; i <= numberOfColumns; i++ )
37                System.out.printf( "%-8s\t", metaData.getColumnName( i ) );
38            System.out.println();
39
40            // display each row
41            while ( rowSet.next() )
42            {
43                for ( int i = 1; i <= numberOfColumns; i++ )
44                    System.out.printf( "%-8s\t", rowSet.getObject( i ) );
45                System.out.println();
46            } // end while
47
48            // close the underlying ResultSet, Statement and Connection
49            rowSet.close();
50        } // end try
51        catch ( SQLException sqlException )
52        {
53            sqlException.printStackTrace();
54            System.exit( 1 );
55        } // end catch
56    } // end DisplayAuthors constructor
57
58    // launch the application
59    public static void main( String args[] )
60    {
61        JdbcRowSetTest application = new JdbcRowSetTest();
62    } // end main
63 } // end class JdbcRowSetTest
```

```
Authors Table of Books Database:

authorID        firstName        lastName
1               Harvey           Deitel
2               Paul             Deitel
3               Andrew           Goldberg
4               David            Choffnes
```

Fig. 20.29 | Displaying the authors table using JdbcRowSet. (Part 2 of 2.)

The package **com.sun.rowset** provides Sun's reference implementations of the interfaces in package javax.sql.rowset. Line 23 uses Sun's reference implementation of the JdbcRowSet interface—**JdbcRowSetImpl**—to create a JdbcRowSet object. We used class JdbcRowSetImpl here to demonstrate the capability of the JdbcRowSet interface. Other databases may provide their own RowSet implementations.

Lines 24–26 set the RowSet properties that are used by the DriverManager to establish a connection to the database. Line 24 invokes JdbcRowSet method **setUrl** to specify the database URL. Line 25 invokes JdbcRowSet method **setUsername** to specify the username. Line 26 invokes JdbcRowSet method **setPassword** to specify the password. Line 27 invokes JdbcRowSet method **setCommand** to specify the SQL query that will be used to populate the RowSet. Line 28 invokes JdbcRowSet method **execute** to execute the SQL query. Method execute performs four actions—it establishes a Connection to the database, prepares the query Statement, executes the query and stores the ResultSet returned by query. The Connection, Statement and ResultSet are encapsulated in the JdbcRowSet object.

The remaining code is almost identical to Fig. 20.23, except that line 31 obtains a ResultSetMetaData object from the JdbcRowSet, line 41 uses the JdbcRowSet's next method to get the next row of the result and line 44 uses the JdbcRowSet's getObject method to obtain a column's value. Line 49 invokes JdbcRowSet method **close**, which closes the RowSet's encapsulated ResultSet, Statement and Connection. In a Cached-RowSet, invoking close also releases the memory held by that RowSet. Note that the output of this application is the same as that of Fig. 20.23.

20.10 Java DB/Apache Derby

As of JDK 6, Sun Microsystems now bundles the open-source, pure Java database *Java DB* (the Sun branded version of Apache Derby) with the JDK. In Section 20.11, we use Java DB to demonstrate so-called PreparedStatements. Before you can execute the application in the next section, you must set up the AddressBook database in Java DB. Section 20.11 uses the embedded version of Java DB. There is also a network version that executes similarly to the MySQL DBMS introduced earlier in the chapter. For the purpose of the following steps, we assume you are running Microsoft Windows with Java installed in its default location.

1. Java DB comes with several batch files to configure and run it. Before executing these batch files from a command prompt, you must set the environment variable JAVA_HOME to refer to the JDK's C:\Program Files\Java\jdk1.6.0 installation directory.

2. Open the batch file setEmbeddedCP.bat (located in C:\Program Files\Sun\JavaDB\bin) in a text editor such as Notepad. Locate the line

   ```
   @rem set DERBY_INSTALL=
   ```

   and change it to

   ```
   @set DERBY_INSTALL=C:\Program Files\Sun\JavaDB
   ```

   Save your changes and close this file.

3. Open a Command Prompt and change directories to C:\Program Files\Sun\ JavaDB\bin. Then, type setEmbeddedCP.bat and press *Enter* to set the environment variables required by Java DB.

4. An embedded Java DB database must reside in the same location as the application that manipulates the database. For this reason, change to the directory that contains the code for Figs. 20.30–20.32. This directory contains a SQL script address.sql that builds the AddressBook database.

5. Execute the command

```
"C:\Program Files\Sun\JavaDB\bin\ij"
```

to start the command-line tool for interacting with Java DB. The double quotes are necessary because the path contains a space. This will display the ij> prompt.

6. At the ij> prompt type

```
connect 'jdbc:derby:AddressBook;create=true;user=javafp;
    password=javafp';
```

to create the AddressBook database in the current directory. This command also creates the user javafp with the password javafp for accessing the database.

7. To create the database table and insert sample data in the database type

```
run 'address.sql';
```

8. To terminate the Java DB command-line tool, type

```
exit;
```

You are now ready to execute the AddressBook application in Section 20.12.

20.11 PreparedStatements

Interface *PreparedStatement* enables you to create compiled SQL statements that execute more efficiently than Statement objects. PreparedStatements also can specify parameters, making them more flexible than Statements. Programs can execute the same query repeatedly with different parameter values. For example, in the books database, you might want to locate all book titles for an author with a specific last name and first name, and you might want to execute that query for several authors. With a PreparedStatement, that query is defined as follows:

```
PreparedStatement authorBooks = connection.prepareStatement(
    "SELECT lastName, firstName, title " +
    "FROM authors INNER JOIN authorISBN " +
        "ON authors.authorID=authorISBN.authorID " +
    "INNER JOIN titles " +
        "ON authorISBN.isbn=titles.isbn " +
    "WHERE lastName = ? AND firstName = ?" );
```

The two question marks (?) in the the preceding SQL statement's last line are placeholders for values that will be passed as part of the query to the database. Before executing a PreparedStatement, the program must specify the parameter values by using the Prepared-Statement interface's *set* methods.

For the preceding query, both parameters are strings that can be set with Prepared-Statement method ***setString*** as follows:

```
authorBooks.setString( 1, "Deitel" );
authorBooks.setString( 2, "Paul" );
```

Method setString's first argument represents the number of the parameter being set and the second argument is that parameter's value. Parameter numbers are counted from 1, starting with the first question mark (?). When the program executes the preceding PreparedStatement with the parameter values shown here, the SQL statement passed to the database is

```
SELECT lastName, firstName, title
FROM authors INNER JOIN authorISBN
   ON authors.authorID=authorISBN.authorID
INNER JOIN titles
   ON authorISBN.isbn=titles.isbn
WHERE lastName = 'Deitel' AND firstName = 'Paul'
```

Method setString automatically escapes String parameter values as necessary. For example, if the last name is O'Brien, the statement

```
authorBooks.setString( 1, "O'Brien" );
```

escapes the ' character in O'Brien by replacing it with two single-quote characters.

Performance Tip 20.2

PreparedStatements are more efficient than Statements when executing SQL statements multiple times and with different parameter values.

Error-Prevention Tip 20.1

Use PreparedStatements with parameters for queries that receive String values as arguments to ensure that the Strings are quoted properly in the SQL statement.

Interface PreparedStatement provides *set* methods for each supported SQL type. It is important to use the *set* method that is appropriate for the parameter's SQL type in the database—SQLExceptions occur when a program attempts to convert a parameter value to an incorrect type. For a complete list of interface PreparedStatement's *set* methods, see java.sun.com/javase/6/docs/api/java/sql/PreparedStatement.html.

Address Book Application that Uses PreparedStatements

We now present an address book application that enables you to browse existing entries, add new entries and search for entries with a specific last name. Our AddressBook Java DB database contains an Addresses table with the columns addressID, firstName, lastName, email and phoneNumber. The column addressID is a so-called identity column. This is the SQL standard way to represent an autoincremented column. The SQL script we provide for this database uses the SQL ***IDENTITY*** keyword to mark the addressID column as an identity column. For more information on using the IDENTITY keyword and creating databases, see the Java DB Developer's Guide at developers.sun.com/docs/javadb/10.4.2.0/devguide/derbydev.pdf.

Our address book application consists of three classes—Person (Fig. 20.30), Person-Queries (Fig. 20.31) and AddressBookDisplay (Fig. 20.32). Class Person is a simple class that represents one person in the address book. The class contains fields for the address ID, first name, last name, email address and phone number, as well as *set* and *get* methods for manipulating these fields.

```java
1   // Fig. 20.30: Person.java
2   // Person class that represents an entry in an address book.
3   public class Person
4   {
5      private int addressID;
6      private String firstName;
7      private String lastName;
8      private String email;
9      private String phoneNumber;
10
11     // no-argument constructor
12     public Person()
13     {
14     } // end no-argument Person constructor
15
16     // constructor
17     public Person( int id, String first, String last,
18        String emailAddress, String phone )
19     {
20        setAddressID( id );
21        setFirstName( first );
22        setLastName( last );
23        setEmail( emailAddress );
24        setPhoneNumber( phone );
25     } // end five-argument Person constructor
26
27     // sets the addressID
28     public void setAddressID( int id )
29     {
30        addressID = id;
31     } // end method setAddressID
32
33     // returns the addressID
34     public int getAddressID()
35     {
36        return addressID;
37     } // end method getAddressID
38
39     // sets the firstName
40     public void setFirstName( String first )
41     {
42        firstName = first;
43     } // end method setFirstName
44
```

Fig. 20.30 | Person class that represents an entry in an AddressBook. (Part 1 of 2.)

```
45      // returns the first name
46      public String getFirstName()
47      {
48         return firstName;
49      } // end method getFirstName
50
51      // sets the lastName
52      public void setLastName( String last )
53      {
54         lastName = last;
55      } // end method setLastName
56
57      // returns the first name
58      public String getLastName()
59      {
60         return lastName;
61      } // end method getLastName
62
63      // sets the email address
64      public void setEmail( String emailAddress )
65      {
66         email = emailAddress;
67      } // end method setEmail
68
69      // returns the email address
70      public String getEmail()
71      {
72         return email;
73      } // end method getEmail
74
75      // sets the phone number
76      public void setPhoneNumber( String phone )
77      {
78         phoneNumber = phone;
79      } // end method setPhoneNumber
80
81      // returns the email address
82      public String getPhoneNumber()
83      {
84         return phoneNumber;
85      } // end method getPhoneNumber
86   } // end class Person
```

Fig. 20.30 | Person class that represents an entry in an AddressBook. (Part 2 of 2.)

Class PersonQueries

Class PersonQueries (Fig. 20.31) manages the address book application's database connection and creates the PreparedStatements that the application uses to interact with the database. Lines 18–20 declare three PreparedStatement variables. The constructor (lines 23–49) connects to the database at lines 27–28.

Lines 31–32 invoke Connection method *prepareStatement* to create the Prepared-Statement named selectAllPeople that selects all the rows in the Addresses table. Lines 35–36 create the PreparedStatement named selectPeopleByLastName with a parameter.

This statement selects all the rows in the Addresses table that match a particular last name. Notice the ? character that is used to specify the last name parameter. Lines 39–42 create the PreparedStatement named insertNewPerson with four parameters that represent the first name, last name, email address and phone number for a new entry. Again, notice the ? characters used to represent these parameters.

```java
1   // Fig. 20.31: PersonQueries.java
2   // PreparedStatements used by the Address Book application
3   import java.sql.Connection;
4   import java.sql.DriverManager;
5   import java.sql.PreparedStatement;
6   import java.sql.ResultSet;
7   import java.sql.SQLException;
8   import java.util.List;
9   import java.util.ArrayList;
10
11  public class PersonQueries
12  {
13     private static final String URL = "jdbc:derby:AddressBook";
14     private static final String USERNAME = "javafp";
15     private static final String PASSWORD = "javafp";
16
17     private Connection connection = null; // manages connection
18     private PreparedStatement selectAllPeople = null;
19     private PreparedStatement selectPeopleByLastName = null;
20     private PreparedStatement insertNewPerson = null;
21
22     // constructor
23     public PersonQueries()
24     {
25        try
26        {
27           connection =
28              DriverManager.getConnection( URL, USERNAME, PASSWORD );
29
30           // create query that selects all entries in the AddressBook
31           selectAllPeople =
32              connection.prepareStatement( "SELECT * FROM Addresses" );
33
34           // create query that selects entries with a specific last name
35           selectPeopleByLastName = connection.prepareStatement(
36              "SELECT * FROM Addresses WHERE LastName = ?" );
37
38           // create insert that adds a new entry into the database
39           insertNewPerson = connection.prepareStatement(
40              "INSERT INTO Addresses " +
41              "( FirstName, LastName, Email, PhoneNumber ) " +
42              "VALUES ( ?, ?, ?, ? )" );
43        } // end try
44        catch ( SQLException sqlException )
45        {
46           sqlException.printStackTrace();
```

Fig. 20.31 | An interface that stores all the queries to be used by AddressBook. (Part 1 of 4.)

```
47              System.exit( 1 );
48          } // end catch
49      } // end PersonQueries constructor
50
51      // select all of the addresses in the database
52      public List< Person > getAllPeople()
53      {
54          List< Person > results = null;
55          ResultSet resultSet = null;
56
57          try
58          {
59              // executeQuery returns ResultSet containing matching entries
60              resultSet = selectAllPeople.executeQuery();
61              results = new ArrayList< Person >();
62
63              while ( resultSet.next() )
64              {
65                  results.add( new Person(
66                      resultSet.getInt( "addressID" ),
67                      resultSet.getString( "firstName" ),
68                      resultSet.getString( "lastName" ),
69                      resultSet.getString( "email" ),
70                      resultSet.getString( "phoneNumber" ) ) );
71              } // end while
72          } // end try
73          catch ( SQLException sqlException )
74          {
75              sqlException.printStackTrace();
76          } // end catch
77          finally
78          {
79              try
80              {
81                  resultSet.close();
82              } // end try
83              catch ( SQLException sqlException )
84              {
85                  sqlException.printStackTrace();
86                  close();
87              } // end catch
88          } // end finally
89
90          return results;
91      } // end method getAllPeople
92
93      // select person by last name
94      public List< Person > getPeopleByLastName( String name )
95      {
96          List< Person > results = null;
97          ResultSet resultSet = null;
98
```

Fig. 20.31 | An interface that stores all the queries to be used by AddressBook. (Part 2 of 4.)

```
 99        try
100        {
101           selectPeopleByLastName.setString( 1, name ); // specify last name
102
103           // executeQuery returns ResultSet containing matching entries
104           resultSet = selectPeopleByLastName.executeQuery();
105
106           results = new ArrayList< Person >();
107
108           while ( resultSet.next() )
109           {
110              results.add( new Person(
111                 resultSet.getInt( "addressID" ),
112                 resultSet.getString( "firstName" ),
113                 resultSet.getString( "lastName" ),
114                 resultSet.getString( "email" ),
115                 resultSet.getString( "phoneNumber" ) ) );
116           } // end while
117        } // end try
118        catch ( SQLException sqlException )
119        {
120           sqlException.printStackTrace();
121        } // end catch
122        finally
123        {
124           try
125           {
126              resultSet.close();
127           } // end try
128           catch ( SQLException sqlException )
129           {
130              sqlException.printStackTrace();
131              close();
132           } // end catch
133        } // end finally
134
135        return results;
136     } // end method getPeopleByName
137
138     // add an entry
139     public int addPerson(
140        String fname, String lname, String email, String num )
141     {
142        int result = 0;
143
144        // set parameters, then execute insertNewPerson
145        try
146        {
147           insertNewPerson.setString( 1, fname );
148           insertNewPerson.setString( 2, lname );
149           insertNewPerson.setString( 3, email );
150           insertNewPerson.setString( 4, num );
151
```

Fig. 20.31 | An interface that stores all the queries to be used by `AddressBook`. (Part 3 of 4.)

```
152                // insert the new entry; returns # of rows updated
153                result = insertNewPerson.executeUpdate();
154          } // end try
155          catch ( SQLException sqlException )
156          {
157                sqlException.printStackTrace();
158                close();
159          } // end catch
160
161          return result;
162    } // end method addPerson
163
164    // close the database connection
165    public void close()
166    {
167          try
168          {
169                connection.close();
170          } // end try
171          catch ( SQLException sqlException )
172          {
173                sqlException.printStackTrace();
174          } // end catch
175    } // end method close
176 } // end interface PersonQueries
```

Fig. 20.31 | An interface that stores all the queries to be used by AddressBook. (Part 4 of 4.)

Method getAllPeople (lines 52–91) executes PreparedStatement selectAllPeople (line 60) by calling method *executeQuery*, which returns a ResultSet containing the rows that match the query (in this case, all the rows in the Addresses table). Lines 61–71 place the query results in an ArrayList of Person objects, which is returned to the caller at line 90. Method getPeopleByLastName (lines 94–136) uses PreparedStatement method *setString* to set the parameter to selectPeopleByLastName. Then, line 105 executes the query and lines 106–116 place the query results in an ArrayList of Person objects. Line 135 returns the ArrayList to the caller.

Method addPerson (lines 139–162) uses PreparedStatement method setString (lines 147–150) to set the parameters for the insertNewPerson PreparedStatement. Line 153 uses PreparedStatement method *executeUpdate* to insert the new record. This method returns an integer indicating the number of rows that were updated (or inserted) in the database. Method close (lines 165–175) simply closes the database connection.

Class AddressBookDisplay

The AddressBookDisplay (Fig. 20.32) application uses an object of class PersonQueries to interact with the database. Line 59 creates the PersonQueries object used throughout class AddressBookDisplay. When the user presses the **Browse All Entries** JButton, the browseButtonActionPerformed handler (lines 309–335) is called. Line 313 calls the method getAllPeople on the PersonQueries object to obtain all the entries in the database. The user can then scroll through the entries using the **Previous** and **Next** JButtons. When the user presses the **Find** JButton, the queryButtonActionPerformed handler (lines

265–287) is called. Lines 267–268 call method getPeopleByLastName on the PersonQue-ries object to obtain the entries in the database that match the specified last name. If there are several such entries, the user can then scroll through them using the **Previous** and **Next** JButtons.

```
 1   // Fig. 20.32: AddressBookDisplay.java
 2   // A simple address book
 3   import java.awt.event.ActionEvent;
 4   import java.awt.event.ActionListener;
 5   import java.awt.event.WindowAdapter;
 6   import java.awt.event.WindowEvent;
 7   import java.awt.FlowLayout;
 8   import java.awt.GridLayout;
 9   import java.util.List;
10   import javax.swing.JButton;
11   import javax.swing.Box;
12   import javax.swing.JFrame;
13   import javax.swing.JLabel;
14   import javax.swing.JPanel;
15   import javax.swing.JTextField;
16   import javax.swing.WindowConstants;
17   import javax.swing.BoxLayout;
18   import javax.swing.BorderFactory;
19   import javax.swing.JOptionPane;
20
21   public class AddressBookDisplay extends JFrame
22   {
23      private Person currentEntry;
24      private PersonQueries personQueries;
25      private List< Person > results;
26      private int numberOfEntries = 0;
27      private int currentEntryIndex;
28
29      private JButton browseButton;
30      private JLabel emailLabel;
31      private JTextField emailTextField;
32      private JLabel firstNameLabel;
33      private JTextField firstNameTextField;
34      private JLabel idLabel;
35      private JTextField idTextField;
36      private JTextField indexTextField;
37      private JLabel lastNameLabel;
38      private JTextField lastNameTextField;
39      private JTextField maxTextField;
40      private JButton nextButton;
41      private JLabel ofLabel;
42      private JLabel phoneLabel;
43      private JTextField phoneTextField;
44      private JButton previousButton;
45      private JButton queryButton;
46      private JLabel queryLabel;
47      private JPanel queryPanel;
```

Fig. 20.32 | A simple address book. (Part 1 of 8.)

```
48      private JPanel navigatePanel;
49      private JPanel displayPanel;
50      private JTextField queryTextField;
51      private JButton insertButton;
52
53      // no-argument constructor
54      public AddressBookDisplay()
55      {
56         super( "Address Book" );
57
58         // establish database connection and set up PreparedStatements
59         personQueries = new PersonQueries();
60
61         // create GUI
62         navigatePanel = new JPanel();
63         previousButton = new JButton();
64         indexTextField = new JTextField( 2 );
65         ofLabel = new JLabel();
66         maxTextField = new JTextField( 2 );
67         nextButton = new JButton();
68         displayPanel = new JPanel();
69         idLabel = new JLabel();
70         idTextField = new JTextField( 10 );
71         firstNameLabel = new JLabel();
72         firstNameTextField = new JTextField( 10 );
73         lastNameLabel = new JLabel();
74         lastNameTextField = new JTextField( 10 );
75         emailLabel = new JLabel();
76         emailTextField = new JTextField( 10 );
77         phoneLabel = new JLabel();
78         phoneTextField = new JTextField( 10 );
79         queryPanel = new JPanel();
80         queryLabel = new JLabel();
81         queryTextField = new JTextField( 10 );
82         queryButton = new JButton();
83         browseButton = new JButton();
84         insertButton = new JButton();
85
86         setLayout( new FlowLayout( FlowLayout.CENTER, 10, 10 ) );
87         setSize( 400, 300 );
88         setResizable( false );
89
90         navigatePanel.setLayout(
91            new BoxLayout( navigatePanel, BoxLayout.X_AXIS ) );
92
93         previousButton.setText( "Previous" );
94         previousButton.setEnabled( false );
95         previousButton.addActionListener(
96            new ActionListener()
97            {
98               public void actionPerformed( ActionEvent evt )
99               {
```

Fig. 20.32 | A simple address book. (Part 2 of 8.)

```
100                     previousButtonActionPerformed( evt );
101                 } // end method actionPerformed
102             } // end anonymous inner class
103         ); // end call to addActionListener
104
105         navigatePanel.add( previousButton );
106         navigatePanel.add( Box.createHorizontalStrut( 10 ) );
107
108         indexTextField.setHorizontalAlignment(
109             JTextField.CENTER );
110         indexTextField.addActionListener(
111             new ActionListener()
112             {
113                 public void actionPerformed( ActionEvent evt )
114                 {
115                     indexTextFieldActionPerformed( evt );
116                 } // end method actionPerformed
117             } // end anonymous inner class
118         ); // end call to addActionListener
119
120         navigatePanel.add( indexTextField );
121         navigatePanel.add( Box.createHorizontalStrut( 10 ) );
122
123         ofLabel.setText( "of" );
124         navigatePanel.add( ofLabel );
125         navigatePanel.add( Box.createHorizontalStrut( 10 ) );
126
127         maxTextField.setHorizontalAlignment(
128             JTextField.CENTER );
129         maxTextField.setEditable( false );
130         navigatePanel.add( maxTextField );
131         navigatePanel.add( Box.createHorizontalStrut( 10 ) );
132
133         nextButton.setText( "Next" );
134         nextButton.setEnabled( false );
135         nextButton.addActionListener(
136             new ActionListener()
137             {
138                 public void actionPerformed( ActionEvent evt )
139                 {
140                     nextButtonActionPerformed( evt );
141                 } // end method actionPerformed
142             } // end anonymous inner class
143         ); // end call to addActionListener
144
145         navigatePanel.add( nextButton );
146         add( navigatePanel );
147
148         displayPanel.setLayout( new GridLayout( 5, 2, 4, 4 ) );
149
150         idLabel.setText( "Address ID:" );
151         displayPanel.add( idLabel );
```

Fig. 20.32 | A simple address book. (Part 3 of 8.)

```
152
153        idTextField.setEditable( false );
154        displayPanel.add( idTextField );
155
156        firstNameLabel.setText( "First Name:" );
157        displayPanel.add( firstNameLabel );
158        displayPanel.add( firstNameTextField );
159
160        lastNameLabel.setText( "Last Name:" );
161        displayPanel.add( lastNameLabel );
162        displayPanel.add( lastNameTextField );
163
164        emailLabel.setText( "Email:" );
165        displayPanel.add( emailLabel );
166        displayPanel.add( emailTextField );
167
168        phoneLabel.setText( "Phone Number:" );
169        displayPanel.add( phoneLabel );
170        displayPanel.add( phoneTextField );
171        add( displayPanel );
172
173        queryPanel.setLayout(
174           new BoxLayout( queryPanel, BoxLayout.X_AXIS) );
175
176        queryPanel.setBorder( BorderFactory.createTitledBorder(
177           "Find an entry by last name" ) );
178        queryLabel.setText( "Last Name:" );
179        queryPanel.add( Box.createHorizontalStrut( 5 ) );
180        queryPanel.add( queryLabel );
181        queryPanel.add( Box.createHorizontalStrut( 10 ) );
182        queryPanel.add( queryTextField );
183        queryPanel.add( Box.createHorizontalStrut( 10 ) );
184
185        queryButton.setText( "Find" );
186        queryButton.addActionListener(
187           new ActionListener()
188           {
189              public void actionPerformed( ActionEvent evt )
190              {
191                 queryButtonActionPerformed( evt );
192              } // end method actionPerformed
193           } // end anonymous inner class
194        ); // end call to addActionListener
195
196        queryPanel.add( queryButton );
197        queryPanel.add( Box.createHorizontalStrut( 5 ) );
198        add( queryPanel );
199
200        browseButton.setText( "Browse All Entries" );
201        browseButton.addActionListener(
202           new ActionListener()
203           {
```

Fig. 20.32 | A simple address book. (Part 4 of 8.)

```
204              public void actionPerformed( ActionEvent evt )
205              {
206                  browseButtonActionPerformed( evt );
207              } // end method actionPerformed
208          } // end anonymous inner class
209      ); // end call to addActionListener
210
211      add( browseButton );
212
213      insertButton.setText( "Insert New Entry" );
214      insertButton.addActionListener(
215          new ActionListener()
216          {
217              public void actionPerformed( ActionEvent evt )
218              {
219                  insertButtonActionPerformed( evt );
220              } // end method actionPerformed
221          } // end anonymous inner class
222      ); // end call to addActionListener
223
224      add( insertButton );
225
226      addWindowListener(
227          new WindowAdapter()
228          {
229              public void windowClosing( WindowEvent evt )
230              {
231                  personQueries.close(); // close database connection
232                  System.exit( 0 );
233              } // end method windowClosing
234          } // end anonymous inner class
235      ); // end call to addWindowListener
236
237      setVisible( true );
238  } // end no-argument constructor
239
240  // handles call when previousButton is clicked
241  private void previousButtonActionPerformed( ActionEvent evt )
242  {
243      currentEntryIndex--;
244
245      if ( currentEntryIndex < 0 )
246          currentEntryIndex = numberOfEntries - 1;
247
248      indexTextField.setText( "" + ( currentEntryIndex + 1 ) );
249      indexTextFieldActionPerformed( evt );
250  } // end method previousButtonActionPerformed
251
252  // handles call when nextButton is clicked
253  private void nextButtonActionPerformed( ActionEvent evt )
254  {
255      currentEntryIndex++;
```

Fig. 20.32 | A simple address book. (Part 5 of 8.)

```
256
257         if ( currentEntryIndex >= numberOfEntries )
258            currentEntryIndex = 0;
259
260         indexTextField.setText( "" + ( currentEntryIndex + 1 ) );
261         indexTextFieldActionPerformed( evt );
262      } // end method nextButtonActionPerformed
263
264      // handles call when queryButton is clicked
265      private void queryButtonActionPerformed( ActionEvent evt )
266      {
267         results =
268            personQueries.getPeopleByLastName( queryTextField.getText() );
269         numberOfEntries = results.size();
270
271         if ( numberOfEntries != 0 )
272         {
273            currentEntryIndex = 0;
274            currentEntry = results.get( currentEntryIndex );
275            idTextField.setText( "" + currentEntry.getAddressID() );
276            firstNameTextField.setText( currentEntry.getFirstName() );
277            lastNameTextField.setText( currentEntry.getLastName() );
278            emailTextField.setText( currentEntry.getEmail() );
279            phoneTextField.setText( currentEntry.getPhoneNumber() );
280            maxTextField.setText( "" + numberOfEntries );
281            indexTextField.setText( "" + ( currentEntryIndex + 1 ) );
282            nextButton.setEnabled( true );
283            previousButton.setEnabled( true );
284         } // end if
285         else
286            browseButtonActionPerformed( evt );
287      } // end method queryButtonActionPerformed
288
289      // handles call when a new value is entered in indextTextField
290      private void indexTextFieldActionPerformed( ActionEvent evt )
291      {
292         currentEntryIndex =
293            ( Integer.parseInt( indexTextField.getText() ) - 1 );
294
295         if ( numberOfEntries != 0 && currentEntryIndex < numberOfEntries )
296         {
297            currentEntry = results.get( currentEntryIndex );
298            idTextField.setText("" + currentEntry.getAddressID() );
299            firstNameTextField.setText( currentEntry.getFirstName() );
300            lastNameTextField.setText( currentEntry.getLastName() );
301            emailTextField.setText( currentEntry.getEmail() );
302            phoneTextField.setText( currentEntry.getPhoneNumber() );
303            maxTextField.setText( "" + numberOfEntries );
304            indexTextField.setText( "" + ( currentEntryIndex + 1 ) );
305         } // end if
306      } // end method indexTextFieldActionPerformed
307
```

Fig. 20.32 | A simple address book. (Part 6 of 8.)

```
308        // handles call when browseButton is clicked
309        private void browseButtonActionPerformed( ActionEvent evt )
310        {
311           try
312           {
313              results = personQueries.getAllPeople();
314              numberOfEntries = results.size();
315
316              if ( numberOfEntries != 0 )
317              {
318                 currentEntryIndex = 0;
319                 currentEntry = results.get( currentEntryIndex );
320                 idTextField.setText( "" + currentEntry.getAddressID() );
321                 firstNameTextField.setText( currentEntry.getFirstName() );
322                 lastNameTextField.setText( currentEntry.getLastName() );
323                 emailTextField.setText( currentEntry.getEmail() );
324                 phoneTextField.setText( currentEntry.getPhoneNumber() );
325                 maxTextField.setText( "" + numberOfEntries );
326                 indexTextField.setText( "" + ( currentEntryIndex + 1 ) );
327                 nextButton.setEnabled( true );
328                 previousButton.setEnabled( true );
329              } // end if
330           } // end try
331           catch ( Exception e )
332           {
333              e.printStackTrace();
334           } // end catch
335        } // end method browseButtonActionPerformed
336
337        // handles call when insertButton is clicked
338        private void insertButtonActionPerformed( ActionEvent evt )
339        {
340           int result = personQueries.addPerson( firstNameTextField.getText(),
341              lastNameTextField.getText(), emailTextField.getText(),
342              phoneTextField.getText() );
343
344           if ( result == 1 )
345              JOptionPane.showMessageDialog( this, "Person added!",
346                 "Person added", JOptionPane.PLAIN_MESSAGE );
347           else
348              JOptionPane.showMessageDialog( this, "Person not added!",
349                 "Error", JOptionPane.PLAIN_MESSAGE );
350
351           browseButtonActionPerformed( evt );
352        } // end method insertButtonActionPerformed
353
354        // main method
355        public static void main( String args[] )
356        {
357           new AddressBookDisplay();
358        } // end method main
359  } // end class AddressBookDisplay
```

Fig. 20.32 | A simple address book. (Part 7 of 8.)

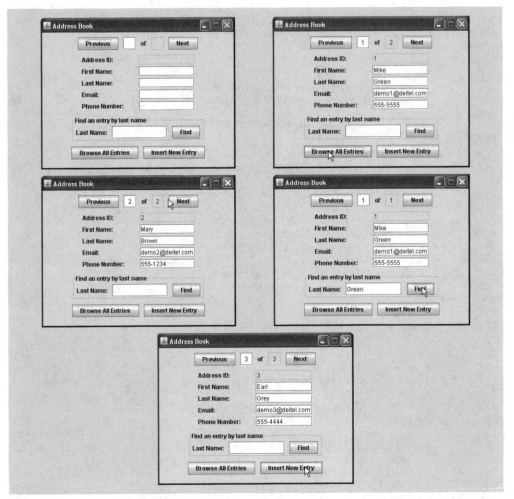

Fig. 20.32 | A simple address book. (Part 8 of 8.)

To add a new entry into the AddressBook database, the user can enter the first name, last name, email and phone number (the AddressID will autoincrement) in the JText-Fields and press the **Insert New Entry** JButton. When the user presses **Insert New Entry**, the insertButtonActionPerformed handler (lines 338–352) is called. Lines 340–342 call the method addPerson on the PersonQueries object to add a new entry to the database.

The user can then view different entries by pressing the **Previous** JButton or **Next** JButton, which results in calls to methods previousButtonActionPerformed (lines 241–250) or nextButtonActionPerformed (lines 253–262), respectively. Alternatively, the user can enter a number in the indexTextField and press *Enter* to view a particular entry.

20.12 Stored Procedures

Many database management systems can store individual SQL statements or sets of SQL statements in a database, so that programs accessing that database can invoke them. Such named collections of SQL statements are called *stored procedures*. JDBC enables programs to invoke stored procedures using objects that implement the interface **CallableStatement**. CallableStatements can receive arguments specified with the methods inherited from interface PreparedStatement. In addition, CallableStatements can specify *output parameters* in which a stored procedure can place return values. Interface CallableStatement includes methods to specify which parameters in a stored procedure are output parameters. The interface also includes methods to obtain the values of output parameters returned from a stored procedure.

Portability Tip 20.6

Although the syntax for creating stored procedures differs across database management systems, the interface CallableStatement provides a uniform interface for specifying input and output parameters for stored procedures and for invoking stored procedures.

Portability Tip 20.7

According to the Java API documentation for interface CallableStatement, for maximum portability between database systems, programs should process the update counts or ResultSets returned from a CallableStatement before obtaining the values of any output parameters.

20.13 Transaction Processing

Many database applications require guarantees that a series of database insertions, updates and deletions executes properly before the applications continue processing the next database operation. For example, when you transfer money electronically between bank accounts, several factors determine if the transaction is successful. You begin by specifying the source account and the amount you wish to transfer from that account to a destination account. Next, you specify the destination account. The bank checks the source account to determine if there are sufficient funds in the account to complete the transfer. If so, the bank withdraws the specified amount from the source account and, if all goes well, deposits the money into the destination account to complete the transfer. What happens if the transfer fails after the bank withdraws the money from the source account? In a proper banking system, the bank redeposits the money in the source account. How would you feel if the money was subtracted from your source account and the bank *did not* deposit the money in the destination account?

Transaction processing enables a program that interacts with a database to treat a database operation (or set of operations) as a single operation. Such an operation also is known as an *atomic operation* or a *transaction*. At the end of a transaction, a decision can be made either to *commit the transaction* or *roll back the transaction*. Committing the transaction finalizes the database operation(s); all insertions, updates and deletions performed as part of the transaction cannot be reversed without performing a new database operation. Rolling back the transaction leaves the database in its state prior to the database operation. This is useful when a portion of a transaction fails to complete properly. In our bank-account-transfer discussion, the transaction would be rolled back if the deposit could not be made into the destination account.

Java provides transaction processing via methods of interface Connection. Method **setAutoCommit** specifies whether each SQL statement commits after it completes (a true argument) or if several SQL statements should be grouped as a transaction (a false argument). If the argument to setAutoCommit is false, the program must follow the last SQL statement in the transaction with a call to Connection method *commit* (to commit the changes to the database) or Connection method *rollback* (to return the database to its state prior to the transaction). Interface Connection also provides method *getAutoCommit* to determine the autocommit state for the Connection.

20.14 Wrap-Up

In this chapter, you learned basic database concepts, how to interact with data in a database using SQL and how to use JDBC to allow Java applications to manipulate MySQL and Java DB databases. You learned about the SQL commands SELECT, INSERT, UPDATE and DELETE, as well as clauses such as WHERE, ORDER BY and INNER JOIN. You learned the explicit steps for obtaining a Connection to the database, creating a Statement to interact with the database's data, executing the statement and processing the results. Then you used a RowSet to simplify the process of connecting to a database and creating statements. You used PreparedStatements to create precompiled SQL statements. You also learned how to create and configure databases in both MySQL and Java DB. We also provided overviews of CallableStatements and transaction processing. In the next chapter, you'll learn about web application development with JavaServer Faces.

20.15 Web Resources

java.sun.com/javase/technologies/database/index.jsp
Sun Microsystems, Inc.'s Java SE database technologies home page.

java.sun.com/docs/books/tutorial/jdbc/index.html
The Java Tutorial's JDBC track.

developers.sun.com/product/jdbc/drivers
Sun Microsystems search engine for locating JDBC drivers.

www.sql.org
This SQL portal provides links to many resources, including SQL syntax, tips, tutorials, books, magazines, discussion groups, companies with SQL services, SQL consultants and free software.

www.datadirect.com/developer/jdbc/topics/perfoptjdbc/index.ssp
White paper that discusses designing a good JDBC application.

java.sun.com/javase/6/docs/technotes/guides/jdbc/index.html
Sun Microsystems JDBC API documentation.

www.jguru.com/faq/JDBC
The JGuru JDBC FAQs.

www.mysql.com
This site is the MySQL database home page. You can download the latest versions of MySQL and MySQL Connector/J and access their online documentation.

dev.mysql.com/doc/refman/5.0/en/index.html
MySQL reference manual.

java.sun.com/javase/6/docs/technotes/guides/jdbc/getstart/rowsetImpl.html
Overviews the RowSet interface and its subinterfaces. This site also discusses the reference implementations of these interfaces from Sun and their usage.

java.sun.com/developer/Books/JDBCTutorial/chapter5.html
Chapter 5 (RowSet Tutorial) of the book *The JDBC 2.0 API Tutorial and Reference, Second Edition*.

JavaServer Faces™ Web Applications

OBJECTIVES

In this chapter you'll learn:

- Web application development using Java Technologies and Netbeans.

- To create JavaServer Pages with JavaServer Faces components.

- To create web applications consisting of multiple pages.

- To validate user input on a web page.

- To maintain user-specific state information throughout a web application with session tracking and cookies.

Outline

21.1 Introduction
21.2 Simple HTTP Transactions
21.3 Multitier Application Architecture
21.4 Java Web Technologies
    21.4.1 Servlets
    21.4.2 JavaServer Pages
    21.4.3 JavaServer Faces
    21.4.4 Web Technologies in Netbeans
21.5 Creating and Running a Simple Application in Netbeans
    21.5.1 Examining a JSP Document
    21.5.2 Examining a Page Bean File
    21.5.3 Event-Processing Life Cycle
    21.5.4 Building a Web Application in Netbeans
21.6 JSF Components
    21.6.1 Text and Graphics Components
    21.6.2 Validation Using Validator Components and Custom Validators
21.7 Session Tracking
    21.7.1 Cookies
    21.7.2 Session Tracking with Session Beans
21.8 Wrap-Up

21.1 Introduction

In this chapter, we introduce web application development in Java. Web-based applications create content for web browser clients. This content includes Extensible HyperText Markup Language (XHTML), client-side scripting, images and binary data. If you are not familiar with XHTML, visit our XHTML Resource Center at www.deitel.com/XHTML/ for introductions, tutorials and other resources that will help you learn XHTML. For a complete list of our Resource Centers, visit www.deitel.com/ResourceCenters.html.

This chapter begins with an overview of multitier application architecture and Java's web technologies for implementing multitier applications. We then present several web application examples. The first example introduces you to Java web development. In the second example, we build a web application that simply shows the look-and-feel of several web application GUI components. Next, we show how to use validation components and custom validation methods to ensure that user input is valid before it is submitted for processing on the server. The chapter finishes with two examples of maintaining user-specific information in a web application. Chapter 22 continues our discussion of Java web application development with more advanced concepts.

Throughout this chapter and Chapter 22, we use the *Netbeans 6.1* IDE and the *GlassFish v2 UR2* open source application server. To implement the examples presented in this chapter, you must install these software products. Netbeans is available from

    www.netbeans.org/downloads/index.html

Download and execute the "Web and Java EE" or the "All" version of the installer. Both versions will install the Netbeans IDE and the GlassFish server. Once you've installed Netbeans, run it. Then, use the **Help** menu's **Check for Updates** option to make sure you have the most up-to-date components.

Much of the code that we present in this chapter is generated by the Netbeans IDE. We've reformatted this code and deleted the Javadoc comments that the IDE generates to match our coding conventions used throughout this book and to save space. We sometimes show only a portion of the code. In such cases, we provide comments indicating where code was removed, and all line numbers match the complete example source code.

21.2 Simple HTTP Transactions

Let's consider what occurs behind the scenes when a user requests a web page in a browser. In its simplest form, a web page is nothing more than an XHTML document that describes to a web browser how to display and format the document's information. XHTML documents normally contain hyperlinks that link to different pages or to other parts of the same page. When the user clicks a hyperlink, the requested web page loads into the user's web browser. Similarly, the user can type the address of a page into the browser's address field.

URIs

The HTTP protocol allows clients and servers to interact and exchange information in a uniform and reliable manner. HTTP uses URIs (Uniform Resource Identifiers) to identify data on the Internet. URIs that specify document locations are called URLs (Uniform Resource Locators). Common URLs refer to files, directories or objects that perform complex tasks, such as database lookups and Internet searches. If you know the URL of a publicly available resource or file anywhere on the web, you can access it through HTTP.

Parts of a URL

A URL contains information that directs a browser to the resource that the user wishes to access. Computers that run *web-server* software make such resources available. Let's examine the components of the URL

```
http://www.deitel.com/books/downloads.html
```

The `http://` indicates that the resource is to be obtained using the HTTP protocol. The middle portion, `www.deitel.com`, is the server's fully qualified *hostname*—the name of the server on which the resource resides. The computer that houses and maintains resources is usually is referred to as the *host*. The hostname `www.deitel.com` is translated into an *IP address*—a unique numerical value that identifies the server, much as a telephone number uniquely defines a particular phone line. This translation is performed by a ***domain-name system (DNS) server***—a computer that maintains a database of host-names and their corresponding IP addresses—and the process is called a ***DNS lookup***. To test web applications, you'll often use your computer as the host. This host is referred to using the reserved domain name `localhost`, which translates to the IP address `127.0.0.1`. (See `en.wikipedia.org/wiki/IP_address` for more information on IP addresses.)

The remainder of the URL (i.e., `/books/downloads.html`) specifies both the name of the requested resource (the XHTML document `downloads.html`) and its path, or location (`/books`), on the web server. The path could specify the location of an actual directory on the web server's file system. For security reasons, however, the path normally specifies the location of a ***virtual directory***. The server translates the virtual directory into a real location on the server (or on another computer on the server's network), thus hiding the true location of the resource. Some resources are created dynamically using other information stored on the server computer, such as a database. The hostname in the URL for such a resource specifies the correct server; the path and resource information identify the resource with which to interact to respond to the client's request.

Making a Request and Receiving a Response

When given a URL, a web browser performs an HTTP transaction to retrieve and display the web page at that address. Figure 21.1 illustrates the transaction, showing the interaction between the web browser (the client) and the web server application (the server).

In Fig. 21.1, the web browser sends an HTTP request to the server. The request (in its simplest form) is

```
GET /books/downloads.html HTTP/1.1
```

The word *GET* is an *HTTP method* indicating that the client wishes to obtain a resource from the server. The remainder of the request provides the path name of the resource (e.g., an XHTML document) and the protocol's name and version number (HTTP/1.1). The client's request also contains some required and optional headers, such as Host (which identifies the target computer) or User-Agent (which identifies the browser type and version).

Any server that understands HTTP (version 1.1) can translate this request and respond appropriately. Figure 21.2 depicts the server responding to a request. The server first responds by sending a line of text that indicates the HTTP version, followed by a numeric code and a phrase describing the status of the transaction. For example,

```
HTTP/1.1 200 OK
```

indicates success, whereas

```
HTTP/1.1 404 Not found
```

informs the client that the web server could not locate the requested resource. On a successful request, the server appends the requested document to the HTTP response. A complete list of numeric codes indicating the status of an HTTP transaction can be found at www.w3.org/Protocols/rfc2616/rfc2616-sec10.html.

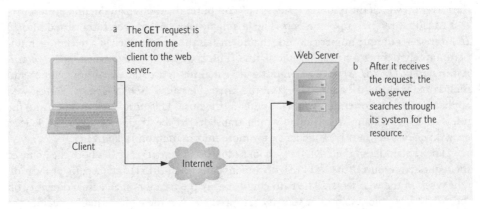

a   The GET request is sent from the client to the web server.

Web Server

b   After it receives the request, the web server searches through its system for the resource.

Client

Internet

Fig. 21.1 | Client interacting with web server. *Step 1:* The GET request.

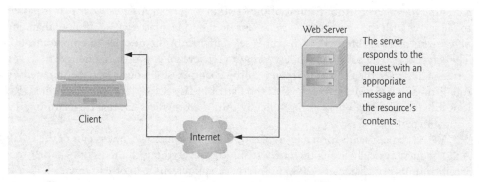

Fig. 21.2 | Client interacting with web server. *Step 2:* The HTTP response.

HTTP Headers

The server then sends one or more *HTTP headers*, which provide additional information about the data that will be sent. In this case, the server is sending an XHTML text document, so one HTTP header for this example would read:

```
Content-type: text/html
```

The information provided in this header specifies the *Multipurpose Internet Mail Extensions (MIME)* type of the content that the server is transmitting to the browser. MIME is an Internet standard that specifies data formats so that programs can interpret data correctly. For example, the MIME type text/plain indicates that the sent information is text that can be displayed directly, without any interpretation of the content as XHTML markup. Similarly, the MIME type image/jpeg indicates that the content is a JPEG image. When the browser receives this MIME type, it attempts to display the image. For a list of available MIME types, visit www.w3schools.com/media/media_mimeref.asp.

The header or set of headers is followed by a blank line, which indicates to the client browser that the server is finished sending HTTP headers. The server then sends the contents of the requested XHTML document (downloads.html). The client-side browser parses the XHTML markup it receives and *renders* (or displays) the results. The server normally keeps the connection open to process other requests from the client.

HTTP GET and POST Requests

The two most common *HTTP request types* (also known as *request methods*) are GET and POST. A GET request typically asks for a specific resource on a server. Common uses of GET requests are to retrieve an XHTML document or an image or to fetch search results based on a user-submitted search term. A POST request typically posts (or sends) data to a server. Common uses of POST requests are to send form data or documents to a server.

An HTTP request often posts data to a *server-side form handler* that processes the data. For example, when a user performs a search or participates in a web-based survey, the web server receives the information specified in the XHTML form as part of the request. GET requests and POST requests can both be used to send form data to a web server, yet each request type sends the information differently.

A GET request sends information to the server in the URL, e.g., www.google.com/search?q=deitel. In this case, search is the name of Google's server-side form handler, q is the name of a variable in Google's search form and deitel is the search term. A ? separates the *query string* from the rest of the URL in a request. A *name/value* pair is passed to the server with the *name* and the *value* separated by an equals sign (=). If more than one *name/value* pair is submitted, each pair is separated from the next by an ampersand (&). The server uses data passed in a query string to retrieve an appropriate resource from the server. The server then sends a *response* to the client. A GET request may be initiated by submitting an XHTML form whose method attribute is set to "get", by typing the URL (possibly containing a query string) directly into the browser's address bar or through a normal hyperlink.

A POST request sends form data as part of the HTTP message, not as part of the URL. A GET request typically limits the query string (i.e., everything to the right of the ?) to a specific number of characters (2083 in Internet Explorer; more in other browsers), so it is often necessary to send large pieces of information using the POST method. The POST method is also sometimes preferred because it hides the submitted data from the user by embedding it in an HTTP message. If a form submits hidden input values along with user-submitted data, the POST method might generate a URL like www.searchengine.com/search. The form data still reaches the server for processing, but the user does not see the exact information sent.

> **Software Engineering Observation 21.1**
>
> *The data sent in a POST request is not part of the URL, and the user can't see the data by default. However, there are tools available that expose this data, so you should not assume that the data is secure just because a POST request is used.*

Client-Side Caching

Browsers often *cache* (save on disk) web pages for quick reloading. If there are no changes between the version stored in the cache and the current version on the web, this speeds up your browsing experience. An HTTP response can indicate the length of time for which the content remains "fresh." If this amount of time has not been reached, the browser can avoid another request to the server. Otherwise, the browser requests the document from the server. Thus, the browser minimizes the amount of data that must be downloaded for you to view a web page. Browsers typically do not cache the server's response to a POST request, because the next POST might not return the same result. For example, in a survey, many users could visit the same web page and answer a question. The survey results could then be displayed for the user. Each new answer changes the overall results of the survey.

When you use a web-based search engine, the browser normally supplies the information you specify in an XHTML form to the search engine with a GET request. The search engine performs the search, then returns the results to you as a web page. Such pages are sometimes cached by the browser in case you perform the same search again.

21.3 Multitier Application Architecture

Web-based applications are *multitier applications* (sometimes referred to as *n-tier applications*). Multitier applications divide functionality into separate *tiers* (i.e., logical groupings of functionality). Although tiers can be located on the same computer, the tiers of web-based applications typically reside on separate computers. Figure 21.3 presents the basic structure of a three-tier web-based application.

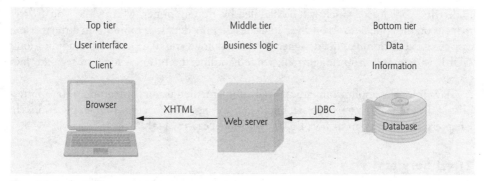

Fig. 21.3 | Three-tier architecture.

The *information tier* (also called the *data tier* or the *bottom tier*) maintains data pertaining to the application. This tier typically stores data in a relational database management system (RDBMS). We discussed RDBMSs in Chapter 20. For example, a retail store might have a database for storing product information, such as descriptions, prices and quantities in stock. The same database also might contain customer information, such as user names, billing addresses and credit card numbers. This tier can contain multiple databases, which together comprise the data needed for our application.

The *middle tier* implements *business logic*, *controller logic* and *presentation logic* to control interactions between the application's clients and the application's data. The middle tier acts as an intermediary between data in the information tier and the application's clients. The middle-tier controller logic processes client requests (such as requests to view a product catalog) and retrieves data from the database. The middle-tier presentation logic then processes data from the information tier and presents the content to the client. Web applications typically present data to clients as XHTML documents.

Business logic in the middle tier enforces *business rules* and ensures that data is reliable before the server application updates the database or presents the data to users. Business rules dictate how clients can and cannot access application data, and how applications process data. For example, a business rule in the middle tier of a retail store's web-based application might ensure that all product quantities remain positive. A client request to set a negative quantity in the bottom tier's product-information database would be rejected by the middle tier's business logic.

The *client tier*, or *top tier*, is the application's user interface, which gathers input and displays output. Users interact directly with the application through the user interface (typically viewed in a web browser), keyboard and mouse. In response to user actions (e.g., clicking a hyperlink), the client tier interacts with the middle tier to make requests and to retrieve data from the information tier. The client tier then displays the data retrieved from the middle tier to the user. The client tier never directly interacts with the information tier.

21.4 Java Web Technologies

Java web technologies continually evolve to provide developers with higher levels of abstraction and greater separation of the application's tiers. This separation makes web applications more maintainable and extensible. It also allows for an effective division of labor. A graphic designer can build the application's user interface without concern for the underlying page logic, which will be handled by a programmer. Meanwhile, you are free to focus on the application's business logic, leaving the details of building an attractive and easy-to-use application to the designer. Netbeans allows you to develop a web application's GUI in a drag-and-drop design tool, while handling the business logic in separate Java classes.

Java multitier applications are typically implemented using the features of Java Enterprise Edition (Java EE). The technologies we use to develop web applications in Chapters 21–22 are part of Java EE 5 (java.sun.com/javaee).

21.4.1 Servlets

Servlets are the lowest-level view of web development technologies in Java that we'll discuss in this chapter. They use the HTTP request/response model of communication between client and server.

Servlets extend a server's functionality by allowing it to generate dynamic content. For instance, servlets can dynamically generate custom XHTML documents, help provide secure access to a website, interact with databases on behalf of a client and maintain unique session information for each client. A web server component called the *servlet container* executes and interacts with servlets. Packages *javax.servlet* and *javax.servlet.http* provide the classes and interfaces to define servlets. The servlet container receives HTTP requests from a client and directs each request to the appropriate servlet. The servlet processes the request and returns an appropriate response to the client—usually in the form of an XHTML or XML (Extensible Markup Language) document to display in the browser. XML is a language used to exchange structured data on the web.

Architecturally, all servlets must implement the *Servlet* interface of package javax.servlet, which ensures that each servlet can execute in the framework provided by the servlet container. Interface Servlet declares methods used by the servlet container to manage the servlet's life cycle. A servlet's life cycle begins when the servlet container loads it into memory—usually in response to the first request for the servlet. Before the servlet can handle that request, the container invokes the servlet's init method, which is called only once during a servlet's life cycle to initialize the servlet. After init completes execution, the servlet is ready to respond to its first request. All requests are handled by a servlet's *service method,* which is the key method in defining a servlet's functionality. The service method receives the request, processes it and sends a response to the client. During a servlet's life cycle, service is called once per request. Each new request is typically handled in a separate thread of execution (managed by the servlet container), so each servlet must be thread safe. When the servlet container terminates the servlet (e.g. when the servlet container needs more memory or when it is shut down), the servlet's destroy method is called to release any resources held by the servlet.

21.4.2 JavaServer Pages

JavaServer Pages (*JSP*) technology is an extension of servlet technology. Each JSP is translated by the JSP container into a servlet. Unlike servlets, JSPs help you separate presentation from content. JavaServer Pages enable web application programmers to create dynamic content by reusing predefined components and by interacting with components using server-side scripting. JSP programmers can use special software components called

JavaBeans and custom tag libraries that encapsulate complex, dynamic functionality. A *JavaBean* is a reusable component that follows certain conventions for class design and that can be manipulated visually in a builder tool such as Netbeans or Eclipse. JavaBeans classes that allow reading and writing of instance variables must provide appropriate *get* and *set* methods—together, these define properties of JavaBeans classes. The complete set of class design conventions is discussed in the JavaBeans specification (java.sun.com/javase/technologies/desktop/javabeans/glasgow/index.html).

Custom Tag Libraries
Custom tag libraries are a powerful feature of JSP that allows Java developers to hide code for database access and other complex operations in *custom tags*. To use such capabilities, you simply add the custom tags to the page. This simplicity enables web-page designers who are not familiar with Java to enhance web pages with powerful dynamic content and dynamic processing capabilities. The JSP classes and interfaces are located in the packages javax.servlet.jsp and javax.servlet.jsp.tagext.

JSP Components
There are four key components to JSPs—directives, actions, scripting elements and tag libraries. *Directives* are messages to the *JSP container*—the web server component that executes JSPs. Directives enable you to specify page settings, to include content from other resources and to specify custom tag libraries for use in JSPs. *Actions* encapsulate functionality in predefined tags that programmers can embed in JSPs. Actions often are performed based on the information sent to the server as part of a particular client request. They also can create Java objects for use in JSPs. *Scripting elements* enable you to insert Java code that interacts with components in a JSP (and possibly other web application components) to perform request processing. *Tag libraries* are part of the *tag extension mechanism* that enables programmers to create custom tags. Such tags enable web-page designers to manipulate JSP content without prior Java knowledge. The *JavaServer Pages Standard Tag Library* (*JSTL*) provides the functionality for many common web application tasks, such as iterating over a collection of objects and executing SQL statements.

Static Content
JSPs can contain other static content. For example, JSPs normally include XHTML or XML markup. Such markup is known as *fixed-template data* or *fixed-template text*. Any literal text or XHTML markup in a JSP is translated to a String literal in the servlet representation of the JSP.

Processing a JSP Request
When a JSP-enabled server receives the first request for a JSP, the JSP container translates the JSP into a servlet that handles the current request and future requests to the JSP. JSPs thus rely on the same request/response mechanism as servlets to process requests from and send responses to clients.

Performance Tip 21.1
Some JSP containers translate JSPs into servlets at the JSP's deployment time (i.e., when the application is placed on a web server). This eliminates the translation overhead for the first client that requests each JSP, as the JSP will be translated before it is ever requested by a client.

21.4.3 JavaServer Faces

JavaServer Faces (JSF)—supported by Java Enterprise Edition 5 (Java EE 5) compliant servers, like GlassFish v2 UR2—is a web application framework that simplifies the design of an application's user interface and further separates a web application's presentation from its business logic. A *framework* provides libraries and sometimes software tools to help you organize and build your applications. Though the JSF framework can use many technologies to define the pages in web applications, this chapter focuses on JSF applications that use JavaServer Pages. JSF provides a set of user interface components, or *JSF components*, that simplify web-page design. These components are similar to the Swing components used to build GUI applications. JSF provides two JSP custom tag libraries for adding these components to a JSP page. JSF also includes APIs for handling component events (such as processing component state changes and validating user input), navigating between web application pages and more. You design the look-and-feel of a page with JSF by adding elements to a JSP document and manipulating their attributes. You define the page's behavior separately in related Java source-code files.

Though the standard JSF components are sufficient for most basic web applications, you can also write custom component libraries. Additional component libraries are available through the *Java BluePrints* project—which shows best practices for developing Java applications. Many other vendors provide JSF component libraries. For example, Oracle provides almost 100 components in its ADF Faces library. [*Note:* There are many other popular web application frameworks, including Spring, Struts and Hibernate—each of which is also supported in Netbeans. We've chosen to demonstrate only JavaServer Faces.]

21.4.4 Web Technologies in Netbeans

Netbeans web applications that use the JavaServer Faces framework consist of one or more JSP web pages. These JSP files have the filename extension `.jsp` and contain the web pages' GUI elements. The JSPs can also contain JavaScript to add functionality to the page. JSPs can be customized in Netbeans by adding JSF components, including labels, text fields, images, buttons and other GUI components. The IDE allows you to design pages visually by dragging and dropping these components onto a page; you can also customize a web page by editing the `.jsp` file manually.

Every JSP file created in Netbeans represents a web page and has a corresponding JavaBean class called the *page bean*. A JavaBean class must have a default (or no-argument) constructor, and *get* and *set* methods for all of the bean's properties (i.e., instance variables). The page bean defines properties for each of the page's elements that you wish to interact with programmatically. The page bean also contains event handlers and page life-cycle methods for managing tasks such as page initialization and rendering, and other supporting code for the web application.

Every Netbeans JSF web application defines three more JavaBeans. The **RequestBean** object is maintained in *request scope*—it exists only for an HTTP request's duration. A **SessionBean** object has *session scope*—it exists throughout a user's browsing session or until the session times out. There is a unique SessionBean object for each user. Finally, the **ApplicationBean** object has *application scope*—it is shared by all instances of an application and exists as long as the application remains deployed on a web server. This object is used for applicationwide data storage or processing; only one instance exists for the application, regardless of the number of open sessions.

21.5 Creating and Running a Simple Application in Netbeans

Our first example displays the web server's time of day in a browser window. When run, this program displays the text "Current Time on the Web Server", followed by the web server's time. The application contains a single web page and, as mentioned previously, consists of two related files—a JSP document (Fig. 21.4) and a supporting page bean file (Fig. 21.6). The application also has the three scoped data beans for request, session and application scopes that are not used in this example. We first discuss the markup in the JSP document, the application output and the code in the page bean file, then we provide step-by-step instructions for creating this web application. [*Note:* The markup in Fig. 21.4 and other JSP file listings in this chapter is the same as the markup that appears in Netbeans, but we've reformatted these listings for presentation purposes.]

```
1   <?xml version="1.0" encoding="UTF-8"?>
2
3   <!-- Fig. 21.4 Time.jsp -->
4   <!-- JSP document generated by Netbeans that displays -->
5   <!-- the current time on the web server -->
6   <jsp:root version="2.1" xmlns:f="http://java.sun.com/jsf/core"
7      xmlns:h="http://java.sun.com/jsf/html"
8      xmlns:jsp="http://java.sun.com/JSP/Page"
9      xmlns:webuijsf="http://www.sun.com/webui/webuijsf">
10     <jsp:directive.page contentType="text/html;charset=UTF-8"
11        pageEncoding="UTF-8"/>
12     <f:view>
13        <webuijsf:page id="page1">
14           <webuijsf:html id="html1">
15              <webuijsf:head id="head1" title="Web Time: A Simple Example">
16                 <webuijsf:link id="link1" url="/resources/stylesheet.css"/>
17                 <webuijsf:meta content="60" httpEquiv="refresh"/>
18              </webuijsf:head>
19              <webuijsf:body id="body1" style="-rave-layout: grid">
20                 <webuijsf:form id="form1">
21                    <webuijsf:staticText id="timeHeader"
22                       style="font-size: 18px; left: 24px; top: 24px;
23                          position: absolute"
24                       text="Current time on the web server:"/>
25                    <webuijsf:staticText binding="#{Time.clockText}"
26                       id="clockText" style="background-color: black;
27                          color: yellow; font-size: 18px; left: 24px;
28                          top: 48px; position: absolute"/>
29                 </webuijsf:form>
30              </webuijsf:body>
31           </webuijsf:html>
32        </webuijsf:page>
33     </f:view>
34  </jsp:root>
```

Fig. 21.4 | JSP document generated by Netbeans that displays the current time on the web server. (Part 1 of 2.)

Fig. 21.4 | JSP document generated by Netbeans that displays the current time on the web server. (Part 2 of 2.)

Netbeans generates most of the markup shown in Fig. 21.4 when you set the web page's title, drag two **Static Text** components onto the page and set the properties of the **Static Text** components. ***Static Text*** components display text that cannot be edited by the user. We show these steps shortly.

21.5.1 Examining a JSP Document

The JSP documents in this and the following examples are generated almost entirely by Netbeans, which provides a visual editor that allows you to build a page's GUI by dragging and dropping components onto a design area. The IDE generates a JSP file in response to your interactions. Line 1 of Fig. 21.4 is the XML declaration, indicating the fact that the JSP is expressed in XML syntax and the version of XML that is used. Lines 3–5 are comments that we added to the JSP to indicate its figure number, filename and purpose.

Line 6 begins the JSP's root element. All JSPs must have this ***jsp:root*** element, which has a `version` attribute to indicate the JSP version being used (line 6) and one or more `xmlns` attributes (lines 6–9). Each ***xmlns attribute*** specifies a prefix and a URL for a tag library, allowing the page to use elements from that library. For example, line 8 allows the page to use the standard JSP elements, but each element's tag must be preceded by the `jsp` prefix. All JSPs generated by Netbeans include the tag libraries specified in lines 6–9 (the JSF core components library, the JSF HTML components library, the JSP standard components library and the JSF user interface components library).

Lines 10–11 are the ***jsp:directive.page*** element. Its `contentType` attribute specifies the MIME type (`text/html`) and the character set (`UTF-8`) the page uses. The `pageEncoding` attribute specifies the character encoding used by the page source. These attributes help the client (typically a web browser) determine how to render the content.

All pages containing JSF components are represented in a ***component tree*** (similar to the one shown in Fig. 21.5) with the root JSF element ***f:view***, which is of type ***UIViewRoot***. This component tree structure is represented in a JSP by nesting all JSF component tags inside the `f:view` element (lines 12–33 in this example).

Lines 13–18 begin the JSP's definition with the ***webuijsf:page***, ***webuijsf:html*** and ***webuijsf::head*** elements, all from the `webuijsf` (JSF user interface components) tag library. The `webuijsf:head` element (lines 15–18) has a `title` attribute that specifies the page's title. This element also contains a ***webuijsf:link*** element (line 16) that specifies the CSS stylesheet used by the page, and a ***webuijsf:meta*** element (line 17) that causes the page to refresh every 60 seconds. The ***webuijsf:body*** element (lines 19–30) contains

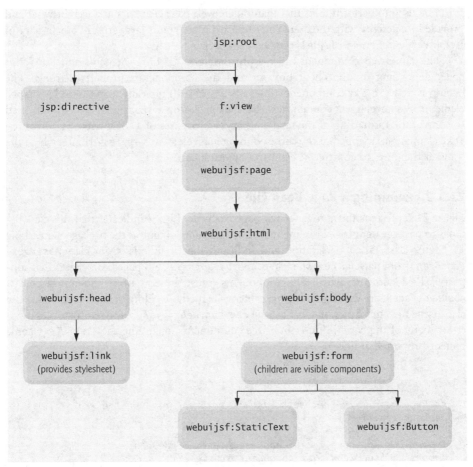

Fig. 21.5 | Sample JSF component tree within a JSP document.

a *webuijsf:form* element (lines 20–29), which contains two *webuijsf:staticText* components (lines 21–24 and 25–28) that display the page's text. The timeHeader component (lines 21–24) has a text attribute (line 24) that specifies the text to display (i.e., "Current time on the web server"). The clockText component (lines 25–28) does not specify a text attribute because this component's text will be set programmatically.

The webuijsf:staticText element at lines 25–28 has the attribute binding = "#{Time.clockText}" (line 25). This attribute uses *JSF Expression Language* notation (i.e., #{Time.clockText}) to reference the clockText property in the Time class that represents the page bean (you'll see this class in Fig. 21.6). You can bind an attribute of a JSP element to the value of a property in any of the web application's JavaBeans. For instance, the text attribute of a webuijsf:staticText component can be bound to an int property in the application's SessionBean (as you'll see in Section 21.7.2).

All the JSP's elements are mapped by the application server to a combination of XHTML elements and JavaScript code that enables the browser to render the page. JavaScript is a scripting language that is interpreted in all of today's popular web browsers.

It can be used to perform tasks that manipulate web-page elements in a web browser and provide interactivity with the user. You can learn more about JavaScript in our JavaScript Resource Center at www.deitel.com/JavaScript/.

The same web component can map to different XHTML elements and JavaScript code, depending on the client browser and the component's property settings. The webuijsf:staticText components (lines 21–24, 25–28) typically map to XHTML *span* elements. A span element contains text that is displayed on a web page and is typically used to control the formatting of the text. The style attributes of a JSP's webuijsf:static-Text element are mapped to the corresponding span element's style attribute, which the browser then uses to control the element's appearance.

21.5.2 Examining a Page Bean File

Figure 21.6 presents the autogenerated page bean file. Line 3 indicates that this class belongs to package webtime. This line specifies the project's name as the package name. Line 11 begins class Time's declaration and indicates that it inherits from class **Abstract-PageBean** (from package **com.sun.rave.web.ui.appbase**). All page bean classes that support JSP documents with JSF components must inherit from the abstract class AbstractPageBean, which provides page life-cycle methods. Note that the IDE makes the class name match the page name. Package **com.sun.webui.jsf.component** provides classes for many of the basic JSF user interface components, including the StaticText component (imported at line 6).

```
1   // Fig. 21.6: Time.java
2   // Page bean file that sets clockText to the time on the web server
3   package webtime;
4
5   import com.sun.rave.web.ui.appbase.AbstractPageBean;
6   import com.sun.webui.jsf.component.StaticText;
7   import javax.faces.FacesException;
8   import java.text.DateFormat;
9   import java.util.Date;
10
11  public class Time extends AbstractPageBean
12  {
13     private void _init() throws Exception
14     {
15     } // end method _init
16
17     private StaticText clockText = new StaticText();
18
19     public StaticText getClockText()
20     {
21        return clockText;
22     } // end method getClockText
23
24     public void setClockText( StaticText st )
25     {
```

Fig. 21.6 | Page bean file that sets clockText to the time on the web server. (Part 1 of 3.)

```
26          this.clockText = st;
27       } // end method setClockText
28
29       public Time()
30       {
31       } // end constructor
32
33       @Override
34       public void init()
35       {
36          super.init();
37
38          try
39          {
40             _init();
41          } // end try
42          catch ( Exception e )
43          {
44             log( "Page1 Initialization Failure" , e );
45             throw e instanceof FacesException ? ( FacesException ) e :
46                new FacesException( e );
47          } // end catch
48       } // end method init
49
50       // method called when a postback occurs
51       @Override
52       public void preprocess()
53       {
54       } // end method preprocess
55
56       // method called before the page is rendered
57       @Override
58       public void prerender()
59       {
60          clockText.setValue( DateFormat.getTimeInstance(
61             DateFormat.LONG ).format( new Date() ) );
62       } // end method prerender
63
64       // method called after rendering completes, if init was called
65       @Override
66       public void destroy()
67       {
68       } // end method
69
70       // returns a reference to the session bean
71       protected SessionBean1 getSessionBean1()
72       {
73          return ( SessionBean1 ) getBean( "SessionBean1" );
74       } // end method
75
76       // returns a reference to the request bean
77       protected RequestBean1 getRequestBean1()
78       {
```

Fig. 21.6 | Page bean file that sets clockText to the time on the web server. (Part 2 of 3.)

```
79        return ( RequestBean1 ) getBean( "RequestBean1" );
80     } // end method
81
82     // returns a reference to the application bean
83     protected ApplicationBean1 getApplicationBean1()
84     {
85        return ( ApplicationBean1 ) getBean( "ApplicationBean1" );
86     } // end method
87  } // end class Time
```

Fig. 21.6 | Page bean file that sets `clockText` to the time on the web server. (Part 3 of 3.)

This page bean file defines a variable (line 17) for programmatically interacting with the `clockText` element of the JSP document of Fig. 21.4. The IDE also autogenerates *get* and *set* methods (lines 19–27) for this variable, as you'll see in Section 21.5.4, *Step 9*. The `clockText` variable is of type `StaticText`.

The only logic required in this page is to set the `clockText` component's text to the current time on the server. We do this in the `prerender` method (lines 58–62). The meaning of this and other page bean methods is discussed in Section 21.5.3. Lines 60–61 fetch and format the time on the server and set the value of `clockText` to that time.

21.5.3 Event-Processing Life Cycle

Several methods in the page bean tie into the JSF *event-processing life cycle's* four major stages—initialization, preprocessing, prerendering and destruction. Each corresponds to a method in the page bean class—`init`, `preprocess`, `prerender` and `destroy`, respectively. Netbeans creates these overridden methods, so you can customize them to handle life-cycle processing tasks, such as rendering an element on a page only if a user clicks a button.

The *init method* (Fig. 21.6, lines 34–48) is called by the JSP container the first time the page is requested and on postbacks. A *postback* occurs when form data is submitted, and the page and its contents are sent to the server to be processed. Method `init` invokes its superclass version (line 36) then tries to call the method `_init` (declared in lines 13–15). The `_init` method is also automatically generated and handles component initialization tasks (if there are any), such as setting the options for a group of radio buttons.

The *preprocess method* (lines 52–54) is called after `init`, but only if the page is processing a postback. The *prerender method* (lines 58–62) is called just before a page is rendered (i.e., displayed) by the browser. This method should be used to set component properties; properties that are set sooner (such as in method `init`) may be overwritten before the page is actually rendered by the browser. For this reason, we set the value of `clockText` in the `prerender` method.

Finally, the *destroy method* (lines 66–68) is called after the page has been rendered, but only if the `init` method was called. This method handles tasks such as freeing resources used to render the page.

21.5.4 Building a Web Application in Netbeans

Now that we have presented the JSP file, the page bean file and the resulting XHTML web page sent to the web browser, we discuss the steps to create this application. To build the `WebTime` application, perform the following steps in Netbeans:

Step 1: Creating the Web Application Project

Select **File > New Project...** to display the **New Project** dialog. In this dialog, select **Web** in the **Categories** pane, **Web Application** in the **Projects** pane and click **Next >**. Change the project name to WebTime. In the **Project Location** field, specify where you'd like to store the project. These settings will create a WebTime directory to store the project's files in the parent directory you specified. Keep the other default settings and click **Next >**. Keep the default options for **Server and Settings** and click **Next >**. Select **Visual Web JavaServer Faces** as the framework to use in this web application, then click **Finish** to create the web application project.

Step 2: Examining the Visual Editor Window of the New Project

The next several figures describe important Netbeans features, beginning with the *visual editor* window (Fig. 21.7). Netbeans creates a single web page named Page1 for each new project. This page is open by default in the visual editor in **Design** *mode* when the project first loads. As you drag and drop new components onto the page, **Design** mode allows you to see how the browser will render your page. The JSP file for this page, named Page1.jsp, can be viewed by clicking the **JSP** button at the top of the visual editor or by right clicking anywhere in the visual editor and selecting **Edit JSP Source**. As mentioned previously, each web page is supported by a page bean file. Netbeans creates a file named Page1.java when a new project is created. To open it, click the **Java** button at the top of the visual editor or right click anywhere in the visual editor and select **Edit Java Source**.

The **Preview in Browser** button at the top of the visual editor window allows you to view your pages in a browser without having to build and run the application. The **Refresh** button redraws the page in the visual editor. The **Show Virtual Forms** button allows you to see which form elements participate in virtual forms (discussed in Chapter 22). The **Target Browser Size** drop-down list lets you specify the optimal browser resolution for viewing the page and lets you see what the page will look like in different screen resolutions.

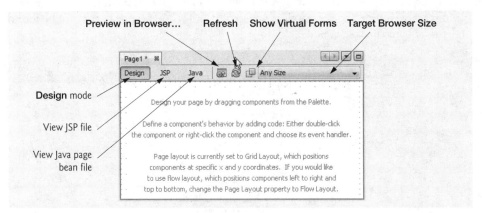

Fig. 21.7 | Visual editor window in **Design** mode.

Step 3: Examining the Palette in Netbeans

Figure 21.8 shows the *Palette* displayed in the IDE when the project loads. Part (a) displays the **Woodstock Basic** list of web components, and part (b) displays the **Woodstock Layout** components. Woodstock is a set of user interface components for JavaServer Faces applications. You can learn more about these components at `woodstock.dev.java.net`. We discuss specific components in Fig. 21.8 as they are used throughout the chapter.

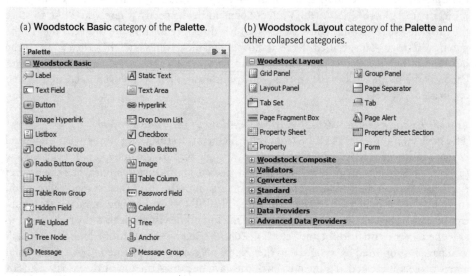

Fig. 21.8 | Palette in Netbeans.

Step 4: Examining the Projects Window

Figure 21.9 displays the **Projects** window, which appears in the upper-left corner of the IDE. This window displays the hierarchy of all files included in the project. The JSP files for each page are listed under the **Web Pages** node. This node also includes the **resources** folder, which contains the CSS stylesheet for the project and any other files the pages may need to display properly, such as image files. The Java source code, including the page bean file for each web page and the application, session and request scope beans, can be found under the **Source Packages** node.

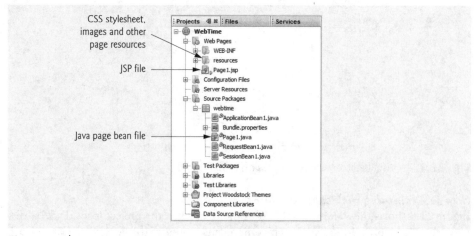

Fig. 21.9 | **Projects** window for the WebTime project.

Step 5: Examining the JSP and Java Files in the IDE

Figure 21.10 displays `Page1.jsp`—the JSP document generated by Netbeans for `Page1`. [*Note:* We reformatted the code to match our coding conventions.] Click the **JSP** button at the top of the visual editor to view this file. When this file is first created, it contains elements for setting up the page, including linking to the page's style sheet and declaring the JSF libraries that will be used. By default, Netbeans does not show line numbers in the source-code editor. To view the line numbers, select **View > Show Line Numbers.**

Figure 21.11 displays part of `Page1.java`—the page bean file generated by Netbeans for `Page1`. Click the **Java** button at the top of the visual editor to open the page bean file. This file contains a Java class with the same name as the page (i.e., `Page1`), which extends the `AbstractPageBean` class. As previously mentioned, `AbstractPageBean` has several methods that manage the page's life cycle. Four of these methods—`init`, `preprocess`, `prerender` and `destroy`—are overridden by `Page1.java`. Other than method `init`, these methods are initially empty. They serve as placeholders for you to customize the behavior of your web application.

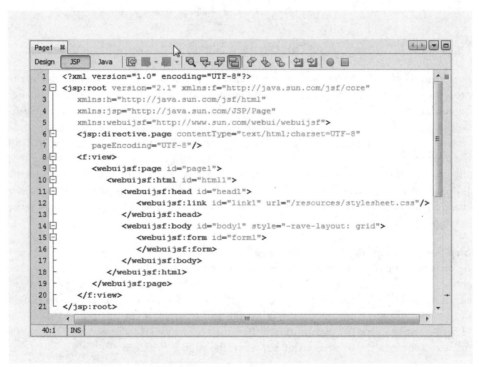

Fig. 21.10 | JSP document generated for Page1 by Netbeans.

Step 6: Renaming the JSP and Java Files

Typically, you'll want to rename the JSP and Java files, so that their names are relevant to your application. Right click `Page1.jsp` in the **Projects** window and select **Refactor > Rename...** to display the **Rename Page1** dialog. Enter the new name, `Time`, and check the **Apply Rename on Comments** checkbox. To make the changes immediately, click the **Refactor** button. If you wish to preview the changes before they're applied, click the **Preview**

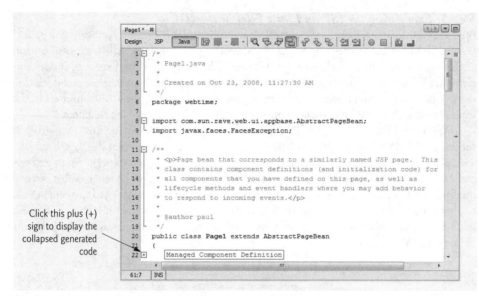

Click this plus (+) sign to display the collapsed generated code

Fig. 21.11 | Page bean file for `Page1.jsp` generated by Netbeans.

button to display the **Refactoring** window at the bottom of the IDE. *Refactoring* is the process of modifying source code to improve its readability and reusability without changing its behavior—for example, by renaming methods or variables, or breaking long methods into shorter ones. Netbeans has built-in refactoring tools that automate some refactoring tasks. Using these tools to rename the project files updates the name of the JSP file to `Time.jsp` and its corresponding page bean file to `Time.java`. The refactoring tool also changes the class name in the page bean file and all of the attribute bindings in the JSP document to reflect the new class name. If you choose to preview the refactoring changes, none of the changes will be made until you click the **Do Refactoring** button in the **Refactoring** window.

Step 7: Changing the Title of the Page
Before designing the content of the web page, we give it the title `"Web Time: A Simple Example"`. By default, the page does not have a title when it is generated by the IDE. To add a title, open the JSP file in **Design** mode. In the **Properties** window, enter the new title next to the **Title** property and press *Enter*. View the JSP to see that the attribute `title="Web Time: A Simple Example"` was automatically added to the `webuijsf:head` tag. The page's title will appear in the browser's title bar when the page is rendered.

Step 8: Designing the Page
Designing a web page is simple in Netbeans. To add components to the page in **Design** mode, drag and drop them from the **Palette** onto the page. Each component is an object that has properties, methods and events. You can set these properties and events visually using the **Properties** window or programmatically in the page bean file.

The IDE generates the JSP tags for the components you drag and drop using a grid layout, as specified in the `webuijsf:body` tag. The components are rendered using *absolute positioning*—they appear exactly where they are dropped on the page. As you add components, the `style` attribute in each component's JSP element will include the number of pixels from the top and left margins of the page at which the component is positioned.

This example uses two **Static Text** components. To add the first one, drag and drop it from the **Palette**'s **Woodstock Basic** components list to the page. Edit the component's text by typing `"Current time on the web server:"` directly into the component. The text can also be edited by changing the component's `text` property in the **Properties** window. Netbeans is a WYSIWYG (What You See Is What You Get) editor—when you make a change to a page in **Design** mode, the IDE creates the markup (visible in **JSP** mode) necessary to achieve the desired visual effects seen in **Design** mode. After adding the text to the web page, switch to **JSP** mode. You should see that the IDE nested a `webuijsf:staticText` element (with the `text` attribute that contains the text you just entered) in the `webuijsf:form` element inside the `webuijsf:body` element. The **Static Text** component is bound to the object `staticText1` in the page bean file. Back in **Design** mode, click the **Static Text** component to select it. In the **Properties** window, click the ellipsis button (⊞) next to the `style` property to open a dialog box to edit the text's style. Select 18 px for the font size and click **OK**. Again in the **Properties** window, change the `id` property to `time-Header`. Setting the `id` property also changes the name of the component's corresponding variable name in the page bean and updates its `binding` attribute in the JSP accordingly. The IDE should now appear as in Fig. 21.12. You can view the JSP file to see that `font-size: 18 px` has been added to the `style` attribute and the `id` attribute has been changed to `timeHeader` in the component's tag.

Drop a second **Static Text** component onto the page and set its `id` to `clockText`. Edit its `style` property so that the font size is 18 px, the text color is `yellow`, and the background color is `black`. Do not edit the component's text, as this will be set programmatically in the page bean file. The component will display with the text *Static Text* in the IDE, but will not display any text at runtime unless the text is set programmatically. Figure 21.13 shows the IDE after the second component is added.

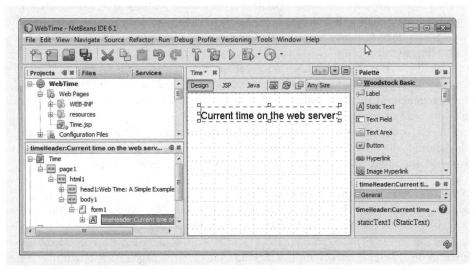

Fig. 21.12 | `Time.jsp` after inserting the first **Static Text** component.

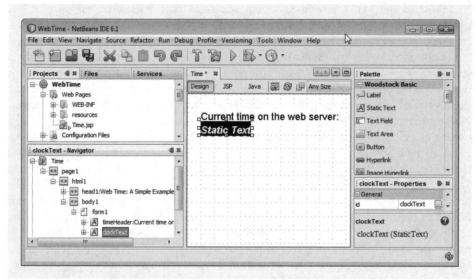

Fig. 21.13 | `Time.jsp` after adding the second `StaticText` component.

Step 9: Adding Page Logic

After designing the user interface, you can modify the page bean file to set the text of the `clockText` element. To interact with a JSF component programmatically, you must first right click the control in **Design** mode and select **Add Binding Attribute**. In the page bean file, this creates a variable that you can use to interact with the component as well as *set* and *get* methods for accessing the component.

In this example, we add a statement to method `prerender` (lines 58–62 of Fig. 21.6). Recall that we use method `prerender` to ensure that `clockText` will be updated each time the page is refreshed. Lines 60–61 of Fig. 21.6 programmatically set the text of `clockText` to the current time on the server. For this statement to work, you'll also need the two `imports` shown in lines 8–9 of Fig. 21.6. The IDE can insert these `import` statements for you. Simply right click in the code editor window and select **Fix Imports** from the pop-up menu that appears

We'd like this page to refresh once per minute to display an up-to-date time. To accomplish this, add `<webuijsf:meta content = "60" httpEquiv = "refresh" />` to the JSP document, as the last element nested in the `webuijsf:head` element. This element tells the browser to reload the page automatically every 60 seconds. You can also add this tag by dragging a **Meta** component from the **Advanced** section of the **Palette** to your page, then setting the component's `content` attribute to 60 and its `httpEquiv` attribute to `refresh`. If you do this, the **Meta** component will show up in the **Outline** window.

Step 10: Examining the Navigator Window

Figure 21.14 displays the Netbeans ***Navigator*** *window*. We expanded the **Time** node, which represents the page bean file and shows the contents of the component tree. The request, session and application scope beans are collapsed, as we have not added any properties to these beans in this example. Clicking an item in the page's component tree selects the item in the visual editor.

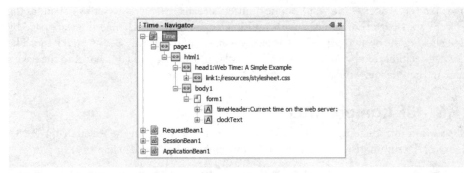

Fig. 21.14 | **Outline** window in Netbeans.

Step 11: Running the Application

After creating the web page, you can view it several ways. First, you can select **Run > Build Project**, and after the build completes, select **Run > Run Project**, to run the application in a browser window. You can also run a project that has already been built by pressing the **Run Project** icon (▷) in the toolbar at the top of the IDE or by pressing *F6*. Note that if changes are made to a project, the project must be rebuilt before they'll be reflected when the application is viewed in a browser. Because this application was built on the local file system, the URL displayed in the address bar of the browser when the application is run will be http://localhost:8080/WebTime/ (Fig. 21.6), where 8080 is the port number on which the test server—GlassFish v2 UR2—runs by default.

Alternatively, you can press *Ctrl + F5* to build the application, then run it in debug mode—the Netbeans built-in debugger can help you troubleshoot applications. If you press *F6*, the program executes without debugging enabled.

Error-Prevention Tip 21.1

If you have trouble building your project due to errors in the Netbeans-generated XML files used for building, try cleaning the project and building again. You can do this by selecting **Run > Clean and Build Project** *or by pressing* Shift + F11.

Error-Prevention Tip 21.2

If you attempt to clean and rebuild your project and receive an error message indicating that one or more files could not be deleted, stop the GlassFish server, then attempt the clean and rebuild process again. To stop the server, click the **Services** *tab in Netbeans, expand the* **Servers** *node, right click* **GlassFish v2** *and select* **Stop**. *Once the server has stopped running, select* **Run > Clean and Build Project** *or press* Shift + F11 *to clean and rebuild the project.*

Finally, you can run your built application by opening a browser window and typing the web page's URL in the **Address** field. Since your application resides on the local file system, you must first start the GlassFish application server. If you have previously run the application using one of the methods above, the server will already be started. Otherwise, you can start the server from the IDE by opening the **Services** tab (located in the same panel as the **Projects**), expanding the **Servers** node, right clicking **GlassFish v2** and selecting **Start**. Then you can type the URL (including the port number for the application server, 8080) in the browser to execute the application. For this example it is not necessary to type the entire URL, http://localhost:8080/WebTime/faces/Time.jsp. The path to the file

`Time.jsp` (i.e., `faces/Time.jsp`) can be omitted, because this file was set by default as the project's start page. For projects with multiple pages, you can change the start page by right clicking the desired page in the **Projects** window and selecting **Set As Start Page**. The start page is indicated by an icon with a green play button symbol (🔲) next to the page's name in the **Projects** window.

21.6 JSF Components

This section introduces some of the JSF components featured in the **Palette** (Fig. 21.8). Figure 21.15 summarizes some of the JSF components used in the chapter examples.

JSF component	Description
Label	Displays text that can be associated with an input element.
Static Text	Displays text that the user cannot edit.
Text Field	Gathers user input and displays text.
Button	Triggers an event when clicked.
Hyperlink	Displays a hyperlink.
Drop Down List	Displays a drop-down list of choices.
Radio Button Group	Groups radio buttons.
Image	Displays images (e.g., GIF and JPG).

Fig. 21.15 | Commonly used JSF components.

21.6.1 Text and Graphics Components

Figure 21.16 displays a simple form for gathering user input. This example uses most of the components in Fig. 21.15. All the code in Fig. 21.16 was generated by Netbeans in response to actions performed in **Design** mode. To create this application from scratch, review the steps in Section 21.5.4. This example does not perform a task when the user clicks **Register**. Later, we demonstrate how to add functionality to many of these components.

```
1   <?xml version="1.0" encoding="UTF-8"?>
2
3   <!-- Fig.21.16: WebComponents.jsp -->
4   <!-- Registration form that demonstrates JSF components -->
5   <jsp:root version="2.1" xmlns:f="http://java.sun.com/jsf/core"
6     xmlns:h="http://java.sun.com/jsf/html"
7     xmlns:jsp="http://java.sun.com/JSP/Page"
8     xmlns:webuijsf="http://www.sun.com/webui/webuijsf">
9     <jsp:directive.page contentType="text/html;charset=UTF-8"
10        pageEncoding="UTF-8"/>
11    <f:view>
12      <webuijsf:page id="page1">
13        <webuijsf:html id="html1">
```

Fig. 21.16 | Registration form that demonstrates JSF components. (Part 1 of 3.)

```
14            <webuijsf:head id="head1">
15               <webuijsf:link id="link1" url="/resources/stylesheet.css"/>
16            </webuijsf:head>
17            <webuijsf:body id="body1" style="-rave-layout: grid">
18               <webuijsf:form id="form1">
19                  <webuijsf:staticText id="headerText"
20                     style="font-size: 18px; left: 24px; top: 24px;
21                        position: absolute"
22                     text="This is a sample registration form"/>
23                  <webuijsf:staticText id="instructionText"
24                     style="font-style: italic; left: 24px; top: 48px;
25                        position: absolute"
26                     text="Please fill in all fields and click Register"/>
27                  <webuijsf:image id="userImage" style="left: 24px;
28                     top: 72px; position: absolute"
29                     url="/resources/user.png"/>
30                  <h:panelGrid columns="4" id="gridPanel"
31                     style="height: 96px; left: 24px; top: 96px;
32                        position: absolute" width="456">
33                     <webuijsf:image id="firstNameImage"
34                        url="/resources/fname.png"/>
35                     <webuijsf:textField id="firstNameTextField"/>
36                     <webuijsf:image id="lastNameImage"
37                        url="/resources/lname.png"/>
38                     <webuijsf:textField id="lastNameTextField"/>
39                     <webuijsf:image id="emailImage"
40                        url="/resources/email.png"/>
41                     <webuijsf:textField id="emailTextField"/>
42                     <webuijsf:image id="phoneImage"
43                        url="/resources/phone.png"/>
44                     <webuijsf:textField id="phoneTextField"/>
45                  </h:panelGrid>
46                  <webuijsf:image id="publicationsImage"
47                     style="position: absolute; left: 24px; top: 216px"
48                     url="/resources/publications.png"/>
49                  <webuijsf:staticText id="publicationText"
50                     style="left: 216px; top: 216px; position: absolute"
51                     text="Which book would you like information about?"/>
52                  <webuijsf:dropDown id="booksDropDown" items=
53                     "#{WebComponents.booksDropDownDefaultOptions.
54                        options}"
55                     style="position: absolute; left: 24px; top: 240px"/>
56                  <webuijsf:hyperlink id="deitelHyperlink"
57                     style="position: absolute; left: 24px; top: 264px"
58                     text="Click here to learn more about our books"
59                     url="http://www.deitel.com"/>
60                  <webuijsf:image id="osImage" style="left: 24px;
61                     top: 312px; position: absolute"
62                     url="/resources/os.png"/>
63                  <webuijsf:radioButtonGroup id="osRadioButtonGroup"
64                     items="#{WebComponents.
65                        osRadioButtonGroupDefaultOptions.options}"
66                     style="left: 24px; top: 336px; position: absolute"/>
```

Fig. 21.16 | Registration form that demonstrates JSF components. (Part 2 of 3.)

```
67                         <webuijsf:button id="registerButton" style="left: 359px;
68                             top: 456px; position: absolute; width: 96px"
69                             text="Register"/>
70                     </webuijsf:form>
71                 </webuijsf:body>
72             </webuijsf:html>
73         </webuijsf:page>
74     </f:view>
75 </jsp:root>
```

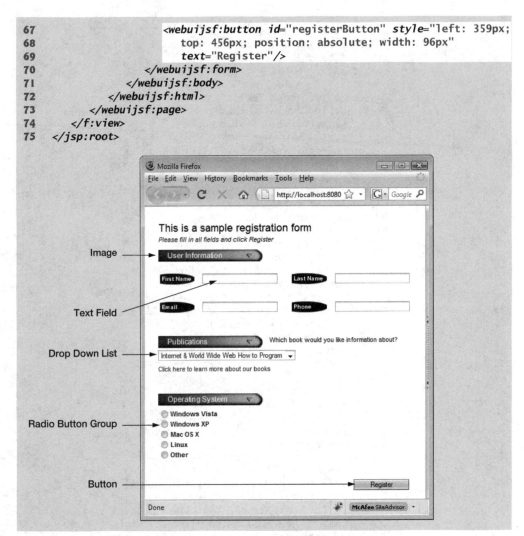

Fig. 21.16 | Registration form that demonstrates JSF components. (Part 3 of 3.)

Recall that Netbeans uses absolute positioning by default, so components are rendered wherever they were dropped in the visual editor. In this example, in addition to absolute positioning, we use a ***Grid Panel*** component (lines 30–45) from the **Palette**'s **Woodstock Layout** component group. The h: prefix indicates that it can be found in the JSF HTML tag library. This component—an object of class HtmlPanelGrid in package javax.faces.component.html—controls the positioning of the components it contains. The **Grid Panel** component allows the designer to specify the number of columns the grid should contain. Components may then be dropped inside the panel, and they will automatically be repositioned into evenly spaced columns in the order in which they are dropped. When the number of components exceeds the number of columns, the panel moves the additional components to a new row. The **Grid Panel** behaves like an XHTML table and is in fact rendered as an XHTML table in the browser. In this example, we use the **Grid Panel** to control the positions of the **Image** and **Text Field** components in the user information section of the page.

Adding a Formatting Component to a Web Page
To create the layout for the **User Information** section of the form shown in Fig. 21.16, drag a **Grid Panel** component onto the page. In the **Properties** window, change the component's id to gridPanel and set the component's columns property to 4. The component also has properties to control the cell padding, cell spacing and other elements of the component's appearance. In this case, accept the defaults for these properties. Now you can simply drag the **Images** and **Text Fields** for user information into the **Grid Panel**. The **Grid Panel** will manage their spacing and their organization into rows and columns.

Examining Web Components on a Sample Registration Form
Here we focus on the new user interface elements in the example. Lines 27–29 of Fig. 21.16 define an ***Image***, an object of class ImageComponent which inserts an image into a web page. The images in this example are located in the ch21\images directory. Images to be displayed on a web page must be placed in the project's resources folder. To add images to the project, drop an **Image** component onto the page and click the ellipsis button (▦) next to the url property in the **Properties** window. This opens a dialog in which you can select the image to display. Since no images have been added to the resources folder yet, click the **Add File** button, locate the image ch21\images directory and click the **Add File** button to copy the file you selected into the project's resources folder in the Web Pages folder. Now you can select the image and click **OK** to insert it into the page.

Lines 30–45 contain an h:panelGrid element representing the **Grid Panel** component. Within this element, there are eight **Image** and ***Text Field*** components. **Text Fields** allow you to obtain text input from the user. For example, line 35 defines a **Text Field** control used to obtain the first name. You can label a **Text Field** by setting its label property, which places text directly above the **Text Field**. Alternatively, you can label a **Text Field** by dragging and dropping a **Label** component onto the page, which allows you to customize the **Label**'s position and style. In this example, we're using images to indicate the purpose of each **Text Field**.

The order in which **Text Fields** are dragged to the page is the order in which their JSP elements are added to the JSP document. By default, when a user presses the *Tab* key to navigate between input fields, the focus shifts from component to component in the order the JSP elements occur in the JSP document. To specify the navigation order, you can drag components onto the page in the appropriate order, or you can set each input field's tabIndex property in the **Properties** window to explicitly set the tab order. A component with a tab index of 1 will be the first in the tab sequence.

Lines 52–55 define a ***Drop Down List***. When a user clicks the drop-down list, it expands and displays a list from which the user can make a selection. This component is an object of class DropDown and is bound to the object booksDropDownDefaultOptions, a SingleSelectOptionsList object that manages the list of options. This object can be configured automatically by right clicking the drop-down list in **Design** mode and selecting **Configure Default Options...**, which opens the **Options Customizer** dialog box so you can add options to the list. Each option consists of a display String that the user will see in the browser and a value String that is returned when you programmatically retrieve the user's selection from the drop-down list. Netbeans constructs the SingleSelectOptionsList object in the page bean file based on the display-value pairs entered in the **Options Customizer** dialog box. To view the code that constructs the object, close the dialog box by clicking **OK**, open the page bean file, and expand the **Managed Component Definition** node that follows the class definition's opening curly brace. The object is constructed in the _init method, which is called by method init the first time the page loads.

The **Hyperlink** component (lines 56–59) of class Hyperlink adds a hyperlink to a web page. The url property of this component specifies the resource (http://www.deitel.com in this case) that is requested when a user clicks the hyperlink. By default, **Hyperlink** components cause pages to open in the same browser window, but you can set the component's target property to change this behavior.

Lines 63–66 define a **Radio Button Group** component of class RadioButtonGroup, which provides a series of radio buttons from which the user can select only one. Like a **Drop Down List**, a **Radio Button Group** is bound to a SingleSelectOptionList object. The options can be edited by right clicking the component and selecting **Configure Default Options....** Also like the drop-down list, the SingleSelectOptionsList is automatically generated by the IDE and placed in the _init method of the page bean class.

Lines 67–69 define a **Button** component of class Button that triggers an action when clicked. A **Button** component typically maps to an input XHTML element with attribute type set to submit. As stated earlier, clicking the **Register** button in this example does not do anything.

21.6.2 Validation Using Validator Components and Custom Validators

Validating user input is an important step in collecting information from users. Form *validation* helps prevent processing errors due to incomplete or improperly formatted user input. For example, you may perform validation to ensure that all required fields contain data or that a zip-code field has the correct number of digits. Netbeans provides three validator components. A **Length Validator** determines whether a field contains an acceptable number of characters. **Double Range Validator**s and **Long Range Validator**s determine whether numeric input falls within acceptable ranges. Package *javax.faces.validators* contains the classes for these validators. Netbeans also allows custom validation with validator methods in the page bean file. The following example demonstrates validation using both a validator component and custom validation.

Validating Form Data in a Web Application

The example in this section prompts the user to enter a name, e-mail address and phone number. After the user enters any data, but before the data is sent to the web server, validation ensures that the user entered a value in each field, that the entered name does not exceed 30 characters, and that the e-mail address and phone-number values are in an acceptable format. If the client does not have JavaScript enabled, then the validation is performed on the server. In this example, (555) 123-4567, 555-123-4567 and 123-4567 are all considered valid phone numbers. Once the data is submitted, the web server responds by displaying an appropriate message and a **Grid Panel** component repeating the submitted information. Note that a real business application would typically store the submitted data in a database or in a file on the server. We simply send the data back to the page to demonstrate that the server received the data.

Building the Web Page

[*Note:* To create this application from scratch, review the steps in Section 21.5.4.] This web application introduces the **Label** and **Message** JSF components from the **Woodstock Basic** section of the **Palette**. Each of the page's three text fields should have its own label and message. *Label* components describe other components and can be associated with user input fields by setting their for property. *Message* components display error messages when validation fails. This page requires three **Text Field**s, three **Label**s and three **Message**s, as well as a submit **Button**. To associate the **Label** components and **Message** components with their corresponding **Text Field** components, hold the *Ctrl* and *Shift* keys, then drag the label or message to the appropriate **Text Field**. In the **Properties** window, notice that each **Label** and **Message** component's for property is set to the appropriate **Text Field**.

You should also add a **Static Text** component to display a validation success message at the bottom of the page. Set the text to "Thank you for your submission.
We received the following information:" and change the component's id to resultText. In the **Properties** window, unset the component's rendered and escaped properties. The *rendered* property controls whether the component will be displayed the first time the page loads. Setting *escape* to false (i.e., unchecked) enables the browser to recognize the <br/> tag so it can start a new line of text rather than display the characters "<br/>" in the web page.

Look-and-Feel Observation 21.1

When you set a component's rendered *property to* false *(unchecked), the component no longer appears in the visual editor. To select such a control so you can manipulate its properties, use the* **Navigator** *window in* **Design** *mode (as shown in Fig. 21.12).*

Add a **Grid Panel** component below the resultText component. The panel should have two columns, one for displaying **Static Text** components that label the user's validated data (named nameText, emailText and phoneText, respectively), and one for displaying **Static Text** components that display that data (named nameValueText, emailValueText and phoneValueText, respectively). The panel's rendered property should be set to false so that it is not initially displayed.

Adding Binding Attributes for Programmatically Interacting with Components

Recall that for each control you plan to interact with programmatically, you must right click the control in **Design** mode and select **Add Binding Attribute** to add a property for the control to the page bean file. In this example, you should do this for each of the **Text Field** components (so you can obtain their values), for the resultText **Static Text** component (so you can display it), for the **Grid Panel** component (so you can display it) and for the **Static Text** components nameValueText, emailValueText and phoneValueText in the **Grid Panel** (so you can set their text).

Reviewing the JSP Document

The JSP file for this page is displayed in Fig. 21.17. Lines 31–35, 42–46 and 54–58 define webuijsf:textFields for retrieving the user's name, e-mail address and phone number, respectively. Lines 28–30, 39–41 and 51–53 define webuijsf:labels for each of these text fields. Lines 36–38, 47–50 and 59–62 define the text fields' *webuijsf:message* elements.

Lines 63–66 define a **Submit** webuijsf:button. Lines 67–71 create a webuijsf:static-Text named resultText that displays text when the user successfully submits the form, and lines 72–91 define a webuijsf:panelGrid that contains components for displaying the validated user input in the browser.

```
1    <?xml version="1.0" encoding="UTF-8"?>
2
3    <!-- Fig. 21.17 Validation.jsp -->
4    <!-- JSP that demonstrates validation of user input. -->
5    <jsp:root version="2.1" xmlns:f="http://java.sun.com/jsf/core"
6       xmlns:h="http://java.sun.com/jsf/html"
7       xmlns:jsp="http://java.sun.com/JSP/Page"
8       xmlns:webuijsf="http://www.sun.com/webui/webuijsf">
9       <jsp:directive.page contentType="text/html;charset=UTF-8"
10          pageEncoding="UTF-8"/>
11      <f:view>
12         <webuijsf:page id="page1">
13            <webuijsf:html id="html1">
14               <webuijsf:head id="head1">
15                  <webuijsf:link id="link1" url="/resources/stylesheet.css"/>
16               </webuijsf:head>
17               <webuijsf:body id="body1" style="-rave-layout: grid">
18                  <webuijsf:form id="form1">
19                     <webuijsf:staticText id="headerText"
20                        style="font-size: 18px; left: 24px; top: 24px;
21                           position: absolute"
22                        text="Please fill out the following form:"/>
23                     <webuijsf:staticText id="instructionText"
24                        style="font-style: italic; left: 24px; top: 48px;
25                           position: absolute"
26                        text="All fields are required and must contain
27                           valid information."/>
28                     <webuijsf:label for="nameTextField" id="nameLabel"
29                        style="left: 24px; top: 72px; position: absolute"
30                        text="Name:"/>
31                     <webuijsf:textField binding="#{Page1.nameTextField}"
32                        columns="30" id="nameTextField" required="true"
33                        style="position: absolute; left: 96px; top: 72px"
34                        validatorExpression=
35                           "#{Page1.nameLengthValidator.validate}"/>
36                     <webuijsf:message for="nameTextField" id="nameMessage"
37                        showDetail="false" showSummary="true"
38                        style="left: 312px; top: 72px; position: absolute"/>
39                     <webuijsf:label for="emailTextField" id="emailLabel"
40                        style="left: 24px; top: 96px; position: absolute"
41                        text="E-Mail:"/>
42                     <webuijsf:textField binding="#{Page1.emailTextField}"
43                        columns="30" id="emailTextField" required="true"
44                        style="left: 96px; top: 96px; position: absolute"
45                        validatorExpression=
46                           "#{Page1.emailTextField.validate}"/>
```

Fig. 21.17 | JSP that demonstrates validation of user input. (Part 1 of 4.)

```
47          <webuijsf:message for="emailTextField"
48              id="emailMessage" showDetail="false"
49              showSummary="true"
50              style="left: 312px; top: 96px; position: absolute"
51          <webuijsf:label for="phoneTextField" id="phoneLabel"
52              style="left: 24px; top: 120px; position: absolute"
53              text="Phone:"/>
54          <webuijsf:textField binding="#{Page1.phoneTextField}"
55              columns="30" id="phoneTextField" required="true"
56              style="left: 96px; top: 120px; position: absolute"
57              validatorExpression=
58                  "#{Page1.phoneTextField_validate}"/>
59          <webuijsf:message for="phoneTextField"
60              id="phoneMessage" showDetail="false"
61              showSummary="true" style="left: 312px; top: 120px;
62                  position: absolute"/>
63          <webuijsf:button actionExpression=
64              "#{Page1.submitButton_action}" id="submitButton"
65              style="position: absolute; left: 24px; top: 144px"
66              text="Submit"/>
67          <webuijsf:staticText binding="#{Page1.resultText}"
68              escape="false" id="resultText" rendered="false"
69              style="left: 24px; top: 168px; position: absolute"
70              text="Thank you for your submission.&lt;br/&gt;We
71                  received the following information:"/>
72          <h:panelGrid binding="#{Page1.gridPanel}"
73              columns="2" id="gridPanel" rendered="false"
74              style="border-width: 1px; border-style: solid;
75                  background-color: #ffff99; height: 96px;
76                  left: 24px; top: 216px; position: absolute"
77              width="264">
78              <webuijsf:staticText id="nameText" text="Name:"/>
79              <webuijsf:staticText
80                  binding="#{Page1.nameValueText}"
81                  id="nameValueText"/>
82              <webuijsf:staticText id="emailText"
83                  text="E-Mail:"/>
84              <webuijsf:staticText
85                  binding="#{Page1.emailValueText}"
86                  id="emailValueText"/>
87              <webuijsf:staticText id="phoneText" text="Phone:"/>
88              <webuijsf:staticText
89                  binding="#{Page1.phoneValueText}"
90                  id="phoneValueText"/>
91          </h:panelGrid>
92      </webuijsf:form>
93      </webuijsf:body>
94      </webuijsf:html>
95      </webuijsf:page>
96  </f:view>
97  </jsp:root>
```

Fig. 21.17 | JSP that demonstrates validation of user input. (Part 2 of 4.)

(a) Submitting the form before entering any information.

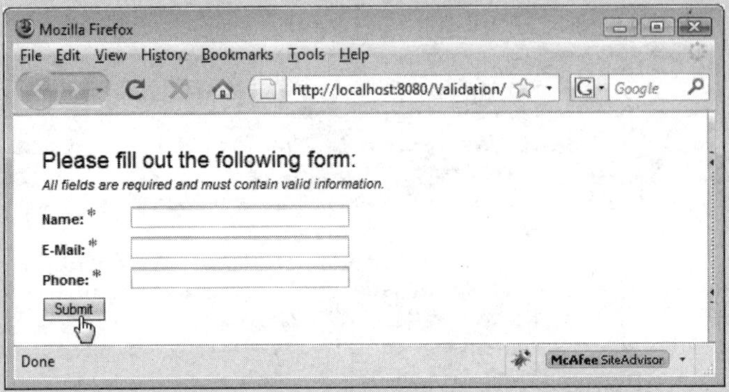

(b) Error messages displayed after submitting the empty form.

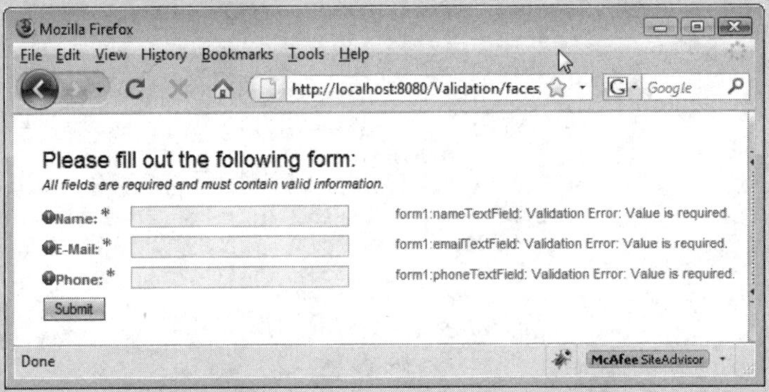

(c) Error messages displayed after submitting invalid information.

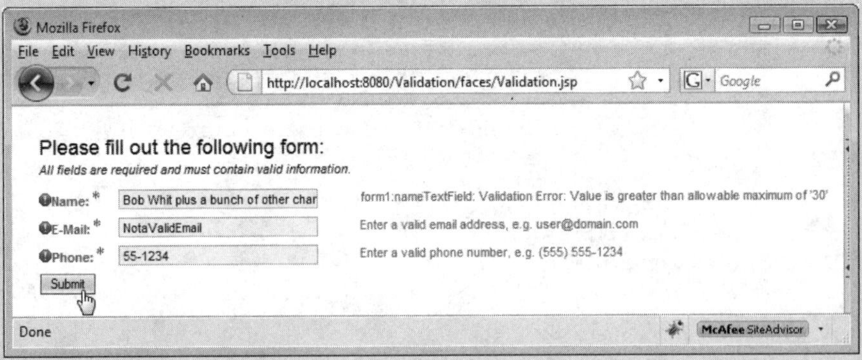

Fig. 21.17 | JSP that demonstrates validation of user input. (Part 3 of 4.)

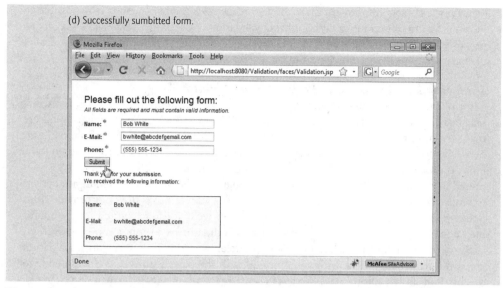

Fig. 21.17 | JSP that demonstrates validation of user input. (Part 4 of 4.)

Setting the Required *Property of an Input Component*

Ensuring that the user has made a selection or entered some text in a required input element is a basic type of validation. This is accomplished by checking the ***required*** box in the element's **Properties** window. If you add a validator component or custom validator method to an input field, the field's required property must be set to true (checked) for validation to occur. Each of the three input webuijsf:textFields in this example has its required property set to true. Also note in the visual editor that the label for a required field is automatically marked by a red asterisk. If a user submits this form with empty text fields, the default error message for a required field will be displayed in the empty field's associated webuijsf:message component. To customize the error message, you must provide a custom validator.

Using the LengthValidator *Component*

In this example, we use the **Length Validator** component (found in the **Validators** section of the **Palette**) to ensure that the length of the user's name does not exceed 30 characters. This might be useful to ensure that a value will fit in a particular database field.

To add a **Length Validator** to a component, simply drag the validator from the **Palette** and drop it onto the field to validate. A **lengthValidator1** node will appear in the **Outline** window. To edit the validation component's properties, click this node and set the maximum and minimum properties to the desired number of characters in the **Properties** window. Here, we set only the maximum property to 30. We also changed the component's id to nameLengthValidator. Notice that the nameTextField's validatorExpression property has been bound to the nameLengthValidator's validate method in the page bean file (lines 34–35). Remember that most client-side validation can be circumvented, so important validation should always be performed on the server.

This validator allows users to type as much text in the field as they wish, and if they exceed the limit, the default length validation error message will be displayed in the field's webuijsf:message component after the user clicks the **Submit** button. It is possible to limit the length of user input without using validation. By setting a **Text Field**'s maxLength property, the **Text Field**'s cursor will not advance beyond the maximum allowable number of characters, so the user cannot submit data that exceeds the length limit.

Using Regular Expressions to Perform Custom Validation

Some of the most common validation tasks involve validating user input. For instance, it may be necessary to check user-entered e-mail addresses and telephone numbers to ensure that they conform to the standard formatting for valid e-mail addresses and phone numbers. Matching user input against a regular expression is an effective way to ensure that the input is properly formatted. This is frequently done on the client side before data is submitted to the server so the user is notified immediately if they supply invalid input. Servers typically revalidate the data as well for security purposes. Netbeans does not provide components for validation using regular expressions, so we'll add our own custom validator methods to the page bean file. To add a custom validator to an input component, right click the component and select **Edit Event Handler > validate**. This creates a validation method for the component with an empty body in the page bean file. We'll add code to this method shortly. Note that both emailTextField and phoneTextField's validator-Expression attributes are bound to their respective custom validation methods in the page bean file (lines 45–46 and 57–58).

Examining the Page Bean File for a Form That Receives User Input

Figure 21.18 contains the page bean file for the JSP file in Fig. 21.17. Line 21 sets the maximum length for the nameLengthValidator, which is a property of this page bean. Recall that the name text field was bound to this property in the JSP document. Methods emailTextField_validate (lines 189–200) and phoneTextField_validate (lines 204–216) are the custom validator methods that verify the user-entered e-mail address and phone number, respectively. The submitButton_action method (lines 219–230) echoes the data back to the user if validation succeeds. The validator methods are called before the event handler, so if validation fails, submitButton_action will not be called and the user input will not be echoed.

```
1   // Fig. 21.18: Validation.java
2   // Validating user input.
3   package validation;
4
5   import com.sun.rave.web.ui.appbase.AbstractPageBean;
6   import com.sun.webui.jsf.component.StaticText;
7   import com.sun.webui.jsf.component.TextField;
8   import javax.faces.FacesException;
9   import javax.faces.application.FacesMessage;
10  import javax.faces.component.UIComponent;
11  import javax.faces.component.html.HtmlPanelGrid;
12  import javax.faces.context.FacesContext;
13  import javax.faces.validator.LengthValidator;
14  import javax.faces.validator.ValidatorException;
15
```

Fig. 21.18 | Page bean for validating user input and redisplaying that input if valid. (Part 1 of 3.)

```
16   public class Validation extends AbstractPageBean
17   {
18      // Managed Component Definition
19      private void _init() throws Exception
20      {
21         nameLengthValidator.setMaximum( 30 );
22      } // end method _init
23
24      // To save space, we omitted the code in lines 24-186. The complete
25      // source code is provided with this chapter's examples.
26
187      // validates entered e-mail address against the regular expression
188      // that represents the form of a valid e-mail address
189      public void emailTextField_validate( FacesContext context,
190         UIComponent component, Object value )
191      {
192         String email = String.valueOf( value );
193
194         // if entered e-mail address is not in a valid format
195         if ( !email.matches(
196            "\\w+([-+.']\\w+)*@\\w+([-.]\\w+)*\\.\\w+([-.]\\w+)*" ) ) {
197            throw new ValidatorException( new FacesMessage(
198               "Enter a valid e-mail address, e.g. user@domain.com" ) )
199         } // end if
200      } // end method emailTextField_validate
201
202      // validates entered phone number against the regular expression
203      // that represents the form of a valid phone number
204      public void phoneTextField_validate( FacesContext context,
205         UIComponent component, Object value )
206      {
207         String phone = String.valueOf( value );
208
209         // if entered phone number is not in a valid format
210         if ( !phone.matches(
211            "((\\(\\d{3}\\) ?)|(\\d{3}-))?\\d{3}-\\d{4}" ) )
212         {
213            throw new ValidatorException( new FacesMessage(
214               "Enter a valid phone number, e.g. (555) 555-1234" ) );
215         } // end if
216      } // end method phoneTextField_validate
217
218      // displays the values the user entered and submitted
219      public String submitButton_action()
220      {
221         String name = String.valueOf( nameTextField.getValue() );
222         String email = String.valueOf( emailTextField.getValue() );
223         String phone = String.valueOf( phoneTextField.getValue() );
224         nameValueText.setValue( name );
225         emailValueText.setValue( email );
226         phoneValueText.setValue( phone );
227         gridPanel.setRendered( true );
```

Fig. 21.18 | Page bean for validating user input and redisplaying that input if valid. (Part 2 of 3.)

```
228          resultText.setRendered( true );
229          return null;
230       } // end method submitButton_action
231    } // end class Validation
```

Fig. 21.18 | Page bean for validating user input and redisplaying that input if valid. (Part 3 of 3.)

The two custom validator methods in this page bean file validate a text field's contents against a regular expression using the String method match, which takes a regular expression as an argument and returns true if the String conforms to the specified format.

For the emailTextField_validate method, we use the validation expression

$$\text{\textbackslash w+([-+.']\textbackslash w+)*@\textbackslash w+([-.]\textbackslash w+)*\textbackslash.\textbackslash w+([-.]\textbackslash w+)*}$$

Note that each backslash in the regular expression String (line 196) must be escaped with another backslash (as in \\), because the backslash character normally represents the beginning of an escape sequence in Java. This regular expression indicates that an e-mail address is valid if the part before the @ symbol contains one or more word characters (i.e., alphanumeric characters or underscores), followed by zero or more Strings comprised of a hyphen, plus sign, period or apostrophe and additional word characters. After the @ symbol, a valid e-mail address must contain one or more groups of word characters potentially separated by hyphens or periods, followed by a required period and another group of one or more word characters potentially separated by hyphens or periods. For example, the e-mail addresses bob's-personal.email@white.email.com, bob-white@my-email.com and bob.white@email.com are all valid. If the user enters text in emailTextField that does not have the correct format and attempts to submit the form, lines 197–198 throw a ValidatorException. The Message component catches this exception and displays the message in red.

The regular expression in phoneTextField_validate ensures that the phoneTextBox contains a valid phone number before the form is submitted. The user input is matched against the regular expression

$$\text{((\textbackslash(\textbackslash d\{3\}\textbackslash) ?)|(\textbackslash d\{3\}-))?\textbackslash d\{3\}-\textbackslash d\{4\}}$$

(Again, each backslash is escaped in the regular expression String in line 211.) This expression indicates that a phone number can contain a three-digit area code either in parentheses and followed by an optional space or without parentheses and followed by a required hyphen. After an optional area code, a phone number must contain three digits, a hyphen and another four digits. For example, (555) 123-4567, 555-123-4567 and 123-4567 are all valid phone numbers. If a user enters an invalid phone number, lines 213–214 throw a ValidatorException The Message component catches this exception and displays the error message in red.

If all six validators are successful (i.e., each TextField contains data, the name is less than 30 characters and the e-mail address and phone number are valid), clicking the **Submit** button sends the form's data to the server. As shown in Fig. 21.17(d), the submitButton_action method displays the submitted data in a gridPanel (lines 221–227) and displays the resultsText **Static Text** component (line 228).

21.7 Session Tracking

In the early days of the Internet, e-businesses could not provide the kind of customized service typically experienced in "brick-and-mortar" stores. To address this problem, e-businesses began to establish mechanisms by which they could personalize users' browsing experiences, tailoring content to individual users while enabling them to bypass irrelevant information. Businesses achieve this level of service by tracking each customer's movement through their websites and combining the collected data with information provided by the consumer, including billing information, personal preferences, interests and hobbies.

Personalization

Personalization makes it possible for e-businesses to communicate effectively with their customers and also improves the user's ability to locate desired products and services. Companies that provide content of particular interest to users can establish relationships with customers and build on those relationships over time. Furthermore, by targeting consumers with personal offers, recommendations, advertisements, promotions and services, e-businesses create customer loyalty. Websites can use sophisticated technology to allow visitors to customize home pages to suit their individual needs and preferences. Similarly, online shopping sites often store personal information for customers, tailoring notifications and special offers to their interests. Such services encourage customers to visit sites and make purchases more frequently.

Privacy

A trade-off exists, however, between personalized e-business service and protection of privacy. Some consumers embrace the idea of tailored content, but others fear the possible adverse consequences if the info they provide to e-businesses is released or collected by tracking technologies. Consumers and privacy advocates ask: What if the e-business to which we give personal data sells or gives that information to another organization without our knowledge? What if we do not want our actions on the Internet—a supposedly anonymous medium—to be tracked and recorded by unknown parties? What if unauthorized parties gain access to sensitive private data, such as credit card numbers or medical history? All of these are questions that must be debated and addressed by programmers, consumers, e-businesses and lawmakers alike.

Recognizing Clients

To provide personalized services to consumers, e-businesses must be able to recognize clients when they request information from a site. As we have discussed, the request/response system on which the web operates is facilitated by HTTP. Unfortunately, HTTP is a stateless protocol—it does not support persistent connections that would enable web servers to maintain state information regarding particular clients. So, web servers cannot determine whether a request comes from a particular client or whether a series of requests comes from one or several clients. To circumvent this problem, sites can provide mechanisms to identify individual clients. A session represents a unique client on a website. If the client leaves a site and then returns later, the client will still be recognized as the same user. To help the server distinguish among clients, each client must identify itself to the server.

Tracking individual clients, known as *session tracking*, can be achieved in a number of ways in JSPs. One popular technique uses cookies (Section 21.7.1); another uses the SessionBean object (Section 21.7.2). Additional session-tracking techniques include using input form elements of type "hidden" and URL rewriting. With "hidden" form elements, a Web Form can write session-tracking data into a form in the web page that it returns to the client in response to a prior request. When the user submits the form in the new web page, all the form data, including the "hidden" fields, is sent to the form handler on the web server. With URL rewriting, the web server embeds session-tracking information directly in the URLs of hyperlinks that the user clicks to send subsequent requests to the web server.

21.7.1 Cookies

Cookies provide web developers with a tool for personalizing web pages. A cookie is a piece of data typically stored in a text file on the user's computer. A cookie maintains information about the client during and between browser sessions. The first time a user visits the website, the user's computer might receive a cookie; this cookie is then reactivated each time the user revisits that site. The aim is to create an anonymous record containing data that is used to personalize the user's future visits to the site. For example, cookies in a shopping application might store unique identifiers for users. When a user adds items to an online shopping cart or performs another task resulting in a request to the web server, the server receives a cookie from the client containing the user's unique identifier. The server then uses the unique identifier to locate the shopping cart and perform any necessary processing.

In addition to identifying users, cookies also can indicate clients' shopping preferences. When a web server receives a request from a client, the server can examine the cookie(s) it sent to the client during previous communications, identify the client's preferences and immediately display products of interest to the client.

Every HTTP-based interaction between a client and a server includes a header containing information either about the request (when the communication is from the client to the server) or about the response (when the communication is from the server to the client). When a page receives a request, the header includes information such as the request type (e.g., GET or POST) and any cookies that have been sent previously from the server to be stored on the client machine. When the server formulates its response, the header information contains any cookies the server wants to store on the client computer and other information, such as the MIME type of the response.

The *expiration date* of a cookie determines how long the cookie remains on the client's computer. If you do not set an expiration date for a cookie, the web browser maintains the cookie for the duration of the browsing session. Otherwise, the web browser maintains the cookie until the expiration date occurs. When the browser requests a resource from a web server, cookies previously sent to the client by that web server are returned to the web server as part of the request formulated by the browser. Cookies are deleted when they *expire*.

Portability Tip 21.1

Clients may disable cookies in their web browsers for more privacy. When such clients use web applications that depend on cookies to maintain state information, the applications will not execute correctly.

Using Cookies to Provide Book Recommendations

The next web application shows how to use cookies. The example contains two pages. In the Options.jsp page (Figs. 21.19 and 21.21), users select a favorite programming language from a group of radio buttons and submit the form to the web server for processing. The web server responds by creating a cookie that stores the selected language and the ISBN number for a recommended book on that topic. The server then renders different components in the browser that allow the user either to view the options and select another favorite programming language or to view the Recommendations.jsp page in our application (Figs. 21.22–21.23), which lists recommended books pertaining to the programming language(s) that the user selected. Because we'll be programmatically hiding and showing the components in the Options.jsp file, each component in the page requires a binding attribute. When the user clicks the hyperlink to view the recommended books, the cookies previously stored on the client are sent to the server, read by the application and used to form the recommended books list.

The Options.jsp file in Fig. 21.19 contains a **Radio Button Group** (lines 24–28) with the options **Java**, **C++**, **Visual Basic 2008**, **Visual C# 2008** and **Internet & Web**. Recall that you can set the display and value Strings of radio buttons by right clicking the **Radio Button Group** and selecting **Configure Default Options....** The code for these options is shown in lines 22–34 of Fig. 21.21. The user selects a programming language by clicking a radio button, then pressing **Submit** to send the selection to the server. This makes an HTTP POST request to the web application on the server, which obtains the user's selection, creates a cookie containing the selection and adds it to the HTTP response header that is sent to the client as part of the response. The browser then stores the cookie on the client computer.

```
 1   <?xml version="1.0" encoding="UTF-8"?>
 2
 3   <!-- Fig. 21.19: Options.jsp -->
 4   <!-- JSP file that allows the user to select a programming language -->
 5   <jsp:root version="2.1" xmlns:f="http://java.sun.com/jsf/core"
 6      xmlns:h="http://java.sun.com/jsf/html"
 7      xmlns:jsp="http://java.sun.com/JSP/Page"
 8      xmlns:webuijsf="http://www.sun.com/webui/webuijsf">
 9      <jsp:directive.page contentType="text/html;charset=UTF-8"
10         pageEncoding="UTF-8"/>
11      <f:view>
12         <webuijsf:page id="page1">
13            <webuijsf:html id="html1">
14               <webuijsf:head id="head1">
15                  <webuijsf:link id="link1" url="/resources/stylesheet.css"/>
16               </webuijsf:head>
17               <webuijsf:body id="body1" style="-rave-layout: grid">
18                  <webuijsf:form id="form1">
19                     <webuijsf:staticText
20                        binding="#{Options.instructionText}"
21                        id="instructionText" style="font-size: 18px;
22                           left: 24px; top: 24px; position: absolute"
23                        text="Select a programming language:"/>
```

Fig. 21.19 | JSP file that allows the user to select a programming language. (Part 1 of 3.)

```
24              <webuijsf:radioButtonGroup
25                  binding="#{Options.languageRadioButtonGroup}"
26                  id="languageRadioButtonGroup" items="#{Options.
27                      languageRadioButtonGroupDefaultOptions.options}"
28                  style="left: 24px; top: 48px; position: absolute"/>
29              <webuijsf:button
30                  actionExpression="#{Options.submitButton_action}"
31                  binding="#{Options.submitButton}" id="submitButton"
32                  style="left: 23px; top: 168px; position: absolute"
33                  text="Submit"/>
34              <webuijsf:staticText binding="#{Options.responseText}"
35                  id="responseText" rendered="false"
36                  style="font-size: 18px; left: 24px; top: 24px;
37                      position: absolute"/>
38              <webuijsf:hyperlink
39                  actionExpression="#{Options.languagesLink_action}"
40                  binding="#{Options.languagesLink}" id="languagesLink"
41                  rendered="false" style="left: 24px; top: 72px;
42                      position: absolute"
43                  text="Click here to choose another language."/>
44              <webuijsf:hyperlink
45                  binding="#{Options.recommendationsLink}"
46                  id="recommendationsLink" rendered="false"
47                  style="left: 24px; top: 96px; position: absolute"
48                  text="Click here to get book recommendations."
49                  url="/faces/Recommendations.jsp"/>
50          </webuijsf:form>
51        </webuijsf:body>
52      </webuijsf:html>
53    </webuijsf:page>
54  </f:view>
55 </jsp:root>
```

(a) User selects a programming language and clicks **Submit** to rerequest `Options.jsp`.

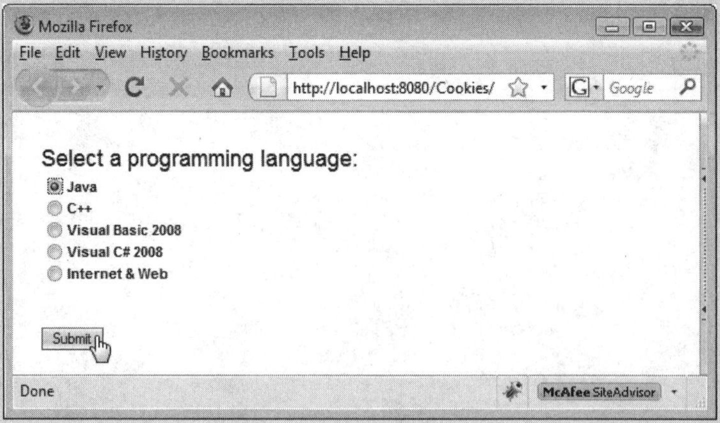

Fig. 21.19 | JSP file that allows the user to select a programming language. (Part 2 of 3.)

(b) `Options.jsp` displays a welcome message and provides links allowing the user to select another language or view book recommendations. User chooses to select another language, which rerequests `Options.jsp`.

(c) User selects a programming language and clicks **Submit** to rerequest `Options.jsp`.

(d) `Options.jsp` displays a welcome message and provides links allowing the user to select another language or view book recommendations. User chooses to view book recommendations.

Fig. 21.19 | JSP file that allows the user to select a programming language. (Part 3 of 3.)

When the user clicks **Submit**, the `webuijsf:staticText`, `webuijsf:radioButton-Group` and `webuijsf:button` elements used to select a language are hidden, and a `webuijsf:staticText` and two `webuijsf:hyperlink` elements are displayed. One `webuijsf:staticText` and both `webuijsf:hyperlinks` initially have their rendered properties set to `false` (lines 35, 41, and 46). This indicates that these components are not visible when the page loads, as we want the user's first view of the page to include only the components for selecting a programming language and submitting the selection.

The first hyperlink (lines 38–43) requests this page, and the second (lines 44–49) requests `Recommendations.jsp`. The `url` property is not set for the first link; we discuss this momentarily. The second link's `url` property is set to `/faces/Recommendations.jsp`. Recall that earlier in the chapter, we set a `url` property to a remote website (`http://www.deitel.com`). To set this property to a page within the current application, you can click the ellipsis button (▣) next to the `url` property in the **Properties** window to open a dialog containing a list of the application's pages, then select an existing page as the link's destination.

Adding and Linking to a New Web Page
To set the `url` property to a destination page (i.e., `Recommendations.jsp`) in the current application, the destination page must already exist. To create `Recommendations.jsp`, right click the **Web Pages** node in the **Projects** window and select **New > Visual Web JSF Page...** from the menu that appears. In the **New Visual Web JSF Page** dialog, change the name of the page to `Recommendations` and click **Finish** to create the files `Recommendations.jsp` and `Recommendations.java`. (We discuss the contents of these files shortly.) You can now select `Recommendations.jsp` as the `url` value for `recommendationsLink`. You can see the `url`'s value in line 49.

Hiding and Showing Elements of a Page and Rerequesting the Page
When the user clicks the `languagesLink`, we'd like to rerequest `Options.jsp` and display the list of options so the user can make another choice. Rather than setting the `languagesLink`'s `url` property, we'll add an action handler for this component to the page bean. You can do this by right clicking `languagesLink` in the **Navigator** window (while in **Design** mode) and selecting **Edit action Event Handler**. The action handler will enable us to show and hide components of the page without redirecting the user to another page. Specifying a destination `url` would override the component's action handler and redirect the user to the specified page. So it is important that we do not set the `url` property in this case, because we want to hide some elements of the page and show others. Since we use the `languagesLink` to reload the current page, we simply return `null` from its action handler, which causes `Options.jsp` to reload.

Adding an Action Handler to a Hyperlink and Redirecting to Another Page
If you need to add an action handler to a hyperlink that should also direct the user to another page, you must add a rule to the **Page Navigation** file (Fig. 21.20). [*Note:* This is not required for the current example.] To edit this file, right click anywhere in the visual designer and select **Page Navigation**. Click the plus (⊞) icon for `Options.jsp` in the navigation designer to display its components that might cause the page to request another page. Locate the link whose navigation rule you would like to set (e.g., `recommendationsLink`) and drag it to the destination page (e.g., `Recommendations.jsp`). Now the link can direct

the user to a new page (Recommendations.jsp) and you can also place code in the **Hyper-link** component's action handler that will execute when the user clicks the link. Editing the **Page Navigation** file is also useful when you would like action elements that cannot specify a url property, such as buttons, to direct users to another page.

Fig. 21.20 | Editing the **Page Navigation** file.

Page Bean File for Options.jsp

Figure 21.21 contains the code that writes a cookie to the client machine when the user selects a programming language. The file also determines which components appear on the page, displaying either the components for choosing a language or the hyperlinks for navigating through the application, depending on the user's actions.

```
1   // Fig. 21.21: Options.java
2   // Page bean that stores user's language selection
3   // as a cookie on the client.
4   package cookies;
5
6   import com.sun.rave.web.ui.appbase.AbstractPageBean;
7   import com.sun.webui.jsf.component.Button;
8   import com.sun.webui.jsf.component.Hyperlink;
9   import com.sun.webui.jsf.component.RadioButtonGroup;
10  import com.sun.webui.jsf.component.StaticText;
11  import com.sun.webui.jsf.model.SingleSelectOptionsList;
12  import java.util.HashMap;
13  import javax.faces.FacesException;
14  import javax.servlet.http.Cookie;
15  import javax.servlet.http.HttpServletResponse;
16
17  public class Options extends AbstractPageBean
18  {
19     // Managed Component Definition
20     private void _init() throws Exception
21     {
22        languageRadioButtonGroupDefaultOptions.setOptions(
23           new com.sun.webui.jsf.model.Option[]
24           {
25              new com.sun.webui.jsf.model.Option( "Java", "Java" ),
26              new com.sun.webui.jsf.model.Option( "C++", "C++" ),
27              new com.sun.webui.jsf.model.Option( "Visual-Basic-2008",
```

Fig. 21.21 | Page bean that stores the user's language selection in a client cookie. (Part 1 of 3.)

```
28              "Visual Basic 2008" ),
29          new com.sun.webui.jsf.model.Option( "Visual-C#-2008",
30              "Visual C# 2008" ),
31          new com.sun.webui.jsf.model.Option( "Internet-&-Web",
32              "Internet & Web" )
33       } // end array initializer
34    ); // end call to setOptions
35 } // end method _init
36
37 private SingleSelectOptionsList languageRadioButtonGroupDefaultOptions =
38    new SingleSelectOptionsList();
39
40 // To save space, we omitted the code in lines 40-121. The complete
41 // source code is provided with this chapter's examples.
42
122 private HashMap<String, String> books = new HashMap<String, String>();
123
124 // Construct a new page bean instance and initialize the properties
125 // that map languages to ISBN numbers of recommended books.
126 public Options()
127 {
128    // initialize HashMap object of values to be stored as cookies.
129    books.put( "Java", "0132222205" );
130    books.put( "C++", "0136152503" );
131    books.put( "Visual-Basic-2008", "013605305X" );
132    books.put( "Visual-C#-2008", "013605322X" );
133    books.put( "Internet-&-Web", "0131752421" );
134 } // end Options constructor
135
136 // To save space, we omitted the code in lines 136-185. The complete
137 // source code is provided with this chapter's examples.
138
186 // Action handler for the Submit button. Checks whether a language
187 // was selected and, if so, creates a cookie for that language and
188 // sets the responseText to indicate the chosen language.
189 public String submitButton_action()
190 {
191    String message = "Welcome to Cookies! You ";
192
193    // if the user made a selection
194    if ( languageRadioButtonGroup.getSelected() != null )
195    {
196       String language =
197          languageRadioButtonGroup.getSelected().toString();
198       message += "selected " + language.replace( '-', ' ' ) + ".";
199
200       // get ISBN number of book for the given language
201       String ISBN = books.get( language );
202
203       // create cookie using language-ISBN name-value pair
204       Cookie cookie = new Cookie( language, ISBN );
205
```

Fig. 21.21 | Page bean that stores the user's language selection in a client cookie. (Part 2 of 3.)

```
206            // add cookie to response header to place it on user's machine
207            HttpServletResponse response =
208               ( HttpServletResponse ) getExternalContext().getResponse();
209            response.addCookie( cookie );
210         } // end if
211         else
212         {
213            message += "did not select a language.";
214         } // end else
215
216         responseText.setValue( message );
217         languageRadioButtonGroup.setRendered( false ); // hide
218         instructionText.setRendered( false ); // hide
219         submitButton.setRendered( false ); // hide
220         responseText.setRendered( true ); // show
221         languagesLink.setRendered( true ); // show
222         recommendationsLink.setRendered( true ); // show
223         return null; // reloads the page
224      } // end method submitButton_action
225
226      // redisplay the components for selecting a language
227      public String languagesLink_action()
228      {
229         responseText.setRendered( false ); // hide
230         languagesLink.setRendered( false ); // hide
231         recommendationsLink.setRendered( false ); // hide
232         languageRadioButtonGroup.setRendered( true ); // show
233         instructionText.setRendered( true ); // show
234         submitButton.setRendered( true ); // show
235         return null; // reloads the page
236      } // end method languagesLink_action
237   } // end class Options
```

Fig. 21.21 | Page bean that stores the user's language selection in a client cookie. (Part 3 of 3.)

As mentioned previously, the _init method handles component initialization. Since this page contains a RadioButtonGroup object that requires initialization, method _init (lines 20–35) constructs an array of Option objects to be displayed by the buttons.

Lines 129–133 in the constructor initialize a HashMap object (defined at line 122)—a data structure that stores key/value pairs. In this case, the keys and values are Strings. The application uses the key to store and retrieve the associated value in the HashMap object. In this example, the keys contain the programming language names, and the values contain the ISBN numbers for the recommended books. Class HashMap provides method put, which takes as arguments a key and a value. A value that is added via method put is placed in the HashMap at a location determined by the key. The value for a specific HashMap entry can be determined by invoking the method get on the HashMap object with that value's key as an argument.

Note that Netbeans can automatically import any missing packages your Java file needs. For example, after adding the HashMap object to Options.java, you can right click in the Java editor window and select **Fix Imports** to import java.util.HashMap. This option can also remove unused import declarations.

Clicking **Submit** invokes the event handler `submitButton_action` (lines 189–224), which displays a message indicating the selected language in the `responseText` element and adds a new cookie to the response. If a language was selected (line 194), the selected item is retrieved (line 197). Line 198 adds the selected language to the `message` string.

Line 201 retrieves the ISBN for the selected language from the books `HashMap` object. Then line 204 creates a new `Cookie` object (in package `javax.servlet.http`), using the selected language as the cookie's name and a corresponding ISBN as the cookie's value. This cookie is added to the HTTP response header in lines 207–209. An object of class `HttpServletResponse` (from package `javax.servlet.http`) represents the response. This object can be accessed by invoking the inherited method `getExternalContext` on the page bean, then invoking `getResponse` on the resulting object. If a language was not selected, line 213 sets the results message to indicate that no selection was made. [*Note:* Cookie names cannot contain whitespace. For this reason, we hyphenated the multiword names that represent the cookie names (i.e., the programming language names in this example) in lines 27, 28, 31 and 131–133. We use `String` method `replace` to replace the hyphens with spaces when we display the language name in the book recommendations page.]

Lines 216–222 control the appearance of the page after the user clicks **Submit**. Line 216 sets the `responseText` to display the `String msg`. Since the user has just submitted a language selection, the components used to collect the selection are hidden (lines 217–219), and `responseText` and the links used to navigate the application are displayed (lines 220–222). The action handler returns `null` at line 223, which reloads `Options.jsp`.

Lines 227–236 contain the `languagesLink`'s event handler. When the user clicks this link, `responseText` and the two links are hidden (lines 229–231), and the components that allow the user to select a language are redisplayed (lines 232–234). The method returns `null` at line 235, causing `Options.jsp` to reload.

Displaying Book Recommendations Based on Cookie Values

After clicking **Submit**, the user may request a book recommendation. The book recommendations hyperlink forwards the user to `Recommendations.jsp` (Fig. 21.22) to display recommendations based on the user's language selections.

`Recommendations.jsp` contains a **Label** (lines 19–22), a **Text Area** (lines 23–26) and a **Hyperlink** (lines 27–30). The **Label** displays the text `Recommendations` at the top of the page. A *Text Area* component can display multiple lines of text. The **Text Area** in this example displays the recommendations created by the `Recommendations.java` page bean (Fig. 21.23), or the text `"No Recommendations. Please select a language."` The **Hyperlink** allows the user to return to `Options.jsp` (specified by the link's `url`) to select additional languages.

```
 1   <?xml version="1.0" encoding="UTF-8"?>
 2
 3   <!-- Fig. 21.22 Recommendations.jsp -->
 4   <!-- Displays book recommendations using cookies -->
 5   <jsp:root version="2.1" xmlns:f="http://java.sun.com/jsf/core"
 6       xmlns:h="http://java.sun.com/jsf/html"
 7       xmlns:jsp="http://java.sun.com/JSP/Page"
 8       xmlns:webuijsf="http://www.sun.com/webui/webuijsf">
```

Fig. 21.22 | JSP file that displays book recommendations based on cookies. (Part 1 of 2.)

```
 9    <jsp:directive.page contentType="text/html;charset=UTF-8"
10       pageEncoding="UTF-8"/>
11    <f:view>
12       <webuijsf:page id="page1">
13          <webuijsf:html id="html1">
14             <webuijsf:head id="head1">
15                <webuijsf:link id="link1" url="/resources/stylesheet.css"/>
16             </webuijsf:head>
17             <webuijsf:body id="body1" style="-rave-layout: grid">
18                <webuijsf:form id="form1">
19                   <webuijsf:label for="recommendationsTextArea"
20                      id="recommendationsLabel" style="font-size: 14px;
21                         left: 24px; top: 24px; position: absolute"
22                      text="Recommendations"/>
23                   <webuijsf:textArea
24                      binding="#{Recommendations.recommendationsTextArea}"
25                      columns="60" id="recommendationsTextArea" rows="6"
26                      style="left: 24px; top: 48px; position: absolute"/>
27                   <webuijsf:hyperlink id="optionsLink"
28                      style="left: 24px; top: 168px; position: absolute"
29                      text="Click here to choose another language."
30                      url="/faces/Options.jsp"/>
31                </webuijsf:form>
32             </webuijsf:body>
33          </webuijsf:html>
34       </webuijsf:page>
35    </f:view>
36 </jsp:root>
```

Fig. 21.22 | JSP file that displays book recommendations based on cookies. (Part 2 of 2.)

Page Bean That Creates Book Recommendations from Cookies

In Recommendations.java (Fig. 21.23), method prerender (lines 65–96) retrieves the cookies from the client, using the request object's getCookies method (lines 68–70). An object of class HttpServletRequest (from package javax.servlet.http) represents the request. This object can be obtained by invoking method getExternalContext on the page bean, then invoking getRequest on the resulting object. The call to getCookies returns an array of the cookies previously written to the client. Cookies can be read by an application only if they were created by a server in the domain in which the application is

```
1   // Fig. 21.23: Recommendations.java
2   // Displays book recommendations based on cookies that
3   // contain the user's selected programming languages.
4   package cookies;
5
6   import com.sun.rave.web.ui.appbase.AbstractPageBean;
7   import com.sun.webui.jsf.component.TextArea;
8   import javax.faces.FacesException;
9   import javax.servlet.http.Cookie;
10  import javax.servlet.http.HttpServletRequest;
11
12  public class Recommendations extends AbstractPageBean
13  {
14     // To save space, we omitted the code in lines 14-62. The complete
15     // source code is provided with this chapter's examples.
16
63     // process and display user's selections
64     @Override
65     public void prerender()
66     {
67        // retrieve cookies
68        HttpServletRequest request =
69           ( HttpServletRequest ) getExternalContext().getRequest();
70        Cookie[] cookies = request.getCookies();
71
72        // if there are cookies, store the corresponding
73        // books and ISBN numbers in a String
74        String recommendations = "";
75
76        if ( cookies.length > 1 )
77        {
78           for ( int i = 0; i < cookies.length - 1; i++ )
79           {
80              String language = cookies[ i ].getName().replace( '-', ' ' );
81
82              // ignore cookie created when user returns to
83              // Options.jsp from Recommendations.jsp
84              if ( !language.equals( "/Recommendations.jsp" ) )
85                 recommendations += language + " How to Program.  ISBN#: " +
86                    cookies[ i ].getValue() + "\n";
87           } // end for
88        } // end if
89        else
90        {
91           recommendations =
92              "No recommendations. Please select a language.";
93        } // end else
94
95        recommendationsTextArea.setText( recommendations );
96     } // end method prerender
97
```

Fig. 21.23 | Page bean that displays book recommendations based on cookies storing user's selected languages. (Part 1 of 2.)

```
98        // To save space, we omitted the code in lines 98-116. The complete
99        // source code is provided with this chapter's examples.
100    } // end class Recommendations
```

Fig. 21.23 | Page bean that displays book recommendations based on cookies storing user's selected languages. (Part 2 of 2.)

running—for security reasons, a web server cannot access cookies created by servers in other domains. For example, a cookie created by a web server in the deitel.com domain cannot be read by a web server in any other domain.

Line 76 determines whether at least one cookie exists. Lines 78–87 add the information in the cookie(s) to the string recommendations, provided that the cookie's name is not "/Recommendations.jsp"—a cookie by this name is added when the user returns from Recommendations.jsp to Options.jsp. The loop retrieves the name and value of each cookie, using the control variable to determine the current value in the cookie array. If no language was selected, lines 91–92 assign recommendations a message instructing the user to select a language. Line 95 sets recommendationsTextArea to display the resulting recommendations string. We summarize commonly used Cookie methods in Fig. 21.24.

Method	Description
getDomain	Returns a String containing the cookie's domain (i.e., the domain from which the cookie was written). This determines which web servers can receive the cookie. By default, cookies are sent to the web server that originally sent the cookie to the client. Changing the Domain property causes the cookie to be returned to a web server other than the one that originally wrote it.
getMaxAge	Returns an int indicating how many seconds the cookie will persist on the browser. This is –1 by default, meaning the cookie will persist until the browser is shut down.
getName	Returns a String containing the cookie's name.
getPath	Returns a String containing the path to a directory on the server to which the cookie applies. Cookies can be "targeted" to specific directories on the web server. By default, a cookie is returned only to applications operating in the same directory as the application that sent the cookie or a subdirectory of that directory. Changing the Path property causes the cookie to be returned to a directory other than the one from which it was originally written.
getSecure	Returns a bool value indicating whether the cookie should be transmitted through a secure protocol. The value true causes a secure protocol to be used.
getValue	Returns a String containing the cookie's value.

Fig. 21.24 | javax.servlet.http.Cookie methods.

21.7.2 Session Tracking with Session Beans

You can also perform session tracking with the subclass of ***AbstractSessionBean*** that is provided in each web application you create with Netbeans. By default, the subclass is named SessionBean1. When a user requests a page in the web application, a SessionBean1 object is created on the server. Properties of this object can be accessed throughout a browser session by invoking the method getSessionBean1 on the page bean. To demonstrate session-tracking techniques using the SessionBean1, we modified the page bean files in Figs. 21.21 and 21.23 so that they use the SessionBean1 object to store the user's language selections. We begin with the updated Options.jsp file (Fig. 21.25). Figure 21.27 presents the SessionBean1.java file, and Fig. 21.28 presents the modified page bean file for Options.jsp.

The Options.jsp file in Fig. 21.25 is similar to the one from the cookies example (Fig. 21.19). Lines 38–47 define two webuijsf:staticText elements that were not present in the cookies example. The first element displays the text "Number of selections so far:". The second element's text attribute is bound to property numberOfSelections in the SessionBean1 object (line 47). We discuss how to bind the text attribute to a session bean property momentarily.

```xml
1   <?xml version="1.0" encoding="UTF-8"?>
2
3   <!-- Fig. 21.25 Options.jsp -->
4   <!-- JSP file that allows the user to select a programming language -->
5   <jsp:root version="2.1" xmlns:f="http://java.sun.com/jsf/core"
6      xmlns:h="http://java.sun.com/jsf/html"
7      xmlns:jsp="http://java.sun.com/JSP/Page"
8      xmlns:webuijsf="http://www.sun.com/webui/webuijsf">
9      <jsp:directive.page contentType="text/html;charset=UTF-8"
10        pageEncoding="UTF-8"/>
11     <f:view>
12        <webuijsf:page id="page1">
13           <webuijsf:html id="html1">
14              <webuijsf:head id="head1">
15                 <webuijsf:link id="link1" url="/resources/stylesheet.css"/>
16              </webuijsf:head>
17              <webuijsf:body id="body1" style="-rave-layout: grid">
18                 <webuijsf:form id="form1">
19                    <webuijsf:staticText
20                       binding="#{Options.instructionText}"
21                       id="instructionText" style="font-size: 18px;
22                          left: 24px; top: 24px; position: absolute"
23                       text="Select a programming language:"/>
24                    <webuijsf:radioButtonGroup
25                       binding="#{Options.languageRadioButtonGroup}"
26                       id="languageRadioButtonGroup" items="#{Options.
27                          languageRadioButtonGroupDefaultOptions.options}"
28                       style="left: 24px; top: 48px; position: absolute"/>
29                    <webuijsf:button
30                       actionExpression="#{Options.submitButton_action}"
31                       binding="#{Options.submitButton}" id="submitButton"
32                       style="left: 23px; top: 168px; position: absolute"
33                       text="Submit"/>
```

Fig. 21.25 | JSP file that allows the user to select a programming language. (Part 1 of 3.)

```
34              <webuijsf:staticText binding="#{Options.responseText}"
35                  id="responseText" rendered="false"
36                  style="font-size: 18px; left: 24px; top: 24px;
37                      position: absolute"/>
38              <webuijsf:staticText
39                  binding="#{Options.selectionsText}"
40                  id="selectionsText" rendered="false"
41                  style="left: 24px; top: 72px; position: absolute"
42                  text="Number of selections so far:"/>
43              <webuijsf:staticText
44                  binding="#{Options.selectionsValueText}"
45                  id="selectionsValueText" rendered="false"
46                  style="left: 168px; top: 72px; position: absolute"
47                  text="#{SessionBean1.numberOfSelections}"/>
48              <webuijsf:hyperlink
49                  actionExpression="#{Options.languagesLink_action}"
50                  binding="#{Options.languagesLink}" id="languagesLink"
51                  rendered="false" style="left: 24px; top: 96px;
52                      position: absolute"
53                  text="Click here to choose another language."/>
54              <webuijsf:hyperlink
55                  binding="#{Options.recommendationsLink}"
56                  id="recommendationsLink" rendered="false"
57                  style="left: 24px; top: 120px; position: absolute"
58                  text="Click here to get book recommendations."
59                  url="/faces/Recommendations.jsp"/>
60          </webuijsf:form>
61        </webuijsf:body>
62      </webuijsf:html>
63    </webuijsf:page>
64  </f:view>
65 </jsp:root>
```

(a) User selects a programming language and clicks **Submit** to rerequest Options.jsp.

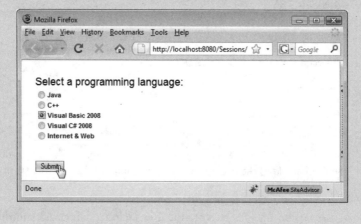

Fig. 21.25 | JSP file that allows the user to select a programming language. (Part 2 of 3.)

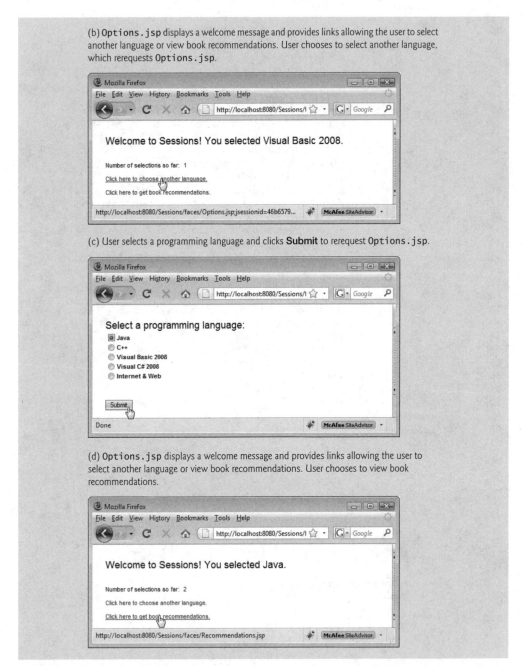

(b) Options.jsp displays a welcome message and provides links allowing the user to select another language or view book recommendations. User chooses to select another language, which rerequests Options.jsp.

(c) User selects a programming language and clicks **Submit** to rerequest Options.jsp.

(d) Options.jsp displays a welcome message and provides links allowing the user to select another language or view book recommendations. User chooses to view book recommendations.

Fig. 21.25 | JSP file that allows the user to select a programming language. (Part 3 of 3.)

Adding Properties to the SessionBean

This example uses session tracking to store the user's selected languages and the number of selections the user makes. To store session information, we add properties to the SessionBean1 class.

Begin by double clicking the SessionBean1 node in the **Navigator** window to open SessionBean1.java in the editor. Declare a numberOfSelections instance variable of type int to store the number of selections the user makes. Next, right click the variable in the editor and select **Refactor > Encapsulate Fields…**. In the dialog that appears, keep the default options and click the **Refactor** button. This creates *get* and *set* methods for instance variable numberOfSelections at the bottom of the source-code file. Together, the instance variable and its *get* and *set* methods represent the bean's numberOfSelections property.

As you'll see, we manipulate property numberOfSelections in the page bean file to keep track of the number of languages the user selects. You can see in Fig. 21.25(b) and (d) that we display this value in the page each time the user makes another selection. To display the value in the selectionsValueText element, change to **Design** mode, right click the element in the **Navigator** window or the visual editor and select **Bind to Data…**. In the **Bind to Data** dialog (Fig. 21.26), click the **Bind to an Object** tab, select property numberOfSelections in the SessionBean1 node and click **OK**. The selectionsValueText element is now bound to the value of SessionBean1's numberOfSelections property. When the property's value changes, the text in the page changes accordingly—you need not programmatically set the text in the page bean file.

Now that we've added a property to class SessionBean1 to store the number of selections, let's add another property to store the selections themselves. We'd like to store selections as key/value pairs of the selected language and the ISBN number of a related book, similar to the way selections were stored using cookies. To do this, add a HashMap instance variable named selections to class SessionBean1, then refactor the code to create the *get* and *set* methods as you did for numberOfSelections. The two properties we added are shown in the SessionBean1.java file (Fig. 21.27).

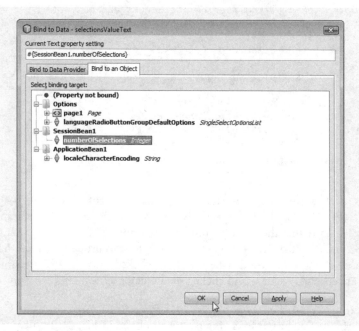

Fig. 21.26 | **Bind to Data** dialog.

```
 1    // Fig. 21.27: SessionBean1.java
 2    // SessionBean file for storing language selections.
 3    package sessions;
 4
 5    import com.sun.rave.web.ui.appbase.AbstractSessionBean;
 6    import java.util.HashMap;
 7    import javax.faces.FacesException;
 8
 9    public class SessionBean1 extends AbstractSessionBean
10    {
11       private int numberOfSelections; // stores number of languages selected
12
13       // stores HashMap containing user's selections
14       private HashMap<String, String> selections =
15          new HashMap<String, String>();
16
17       // To save space, we omitted the code in lines 17-69. The complete
18       // source code is provided with this chapter's examples.
19
70       public int getNumberOfSelections()
71       {
72          return numberOfSelections;
73       } // end method getNumberOfSelections
74
75       public void setNumberOfSelections( int numberOfSelections )
76       {
77          this.numberOfSelections = numberOfSelections;
78       } // end method setNumberOfSelections
79
80       public HashMap<String, String> getSelectedLanguages()
81       {
82          return selections;
83       } // end method getSelectedLanguages
84
85       public void setSelectedLanguages( HashMap<String, String> selections )
86       {
87          this.selections = selections;
88       } // end method setSelectedLanguages
89    } // end class SessionBean1
```

Fig. 21.27 | SessionBean file for storing language selections.

Line 11 declares the numberOfSelections instance variable, and lines 70–73 and 75–78 define its *get* and *set* methods, respectively, to complete the numberOfSelections property. Lines 14–15 define the HashMap object selections that will store user selections. Lines 80–83 and 85–88 are the *get* and *set* methods for this property. Recall that the IDE generated the *get* and *set* methods when we right clicked each instance variable, selected **Refactor > Encapsulate Fields...** and clicked the **Refactor** button.

Manipulating Session Bean Properties in a Page Bean File
The page bean file for the Options.jsp page is displayed in Fig. 21.28. Because much of this example is identical to the preceding one, we discuss only the new features. Since we

are not using cookies in this example, we don't need to hyphenate the programming language names that were previously used as cookie names (lines 24, 26, 28 and 151–153).

```
1   // Fig. 21.8: Options.java
2   // Page bean that stores user's language selection in a SessionBean.
3   package sessions;
4
5   import com.sun.rave.web.ui.appbase.AbstractPageBean;
6   import com.sun.webui.jsf.component.Button;
7   import com.sun.webui.jsf.component.Hyperlink;
8   import com.sun.webui.jsf.component.RadioButtonGroup;
9   import com.sun.webui.jsf.component.StaticText;
10  import com.sun.webui.jsf.model.SingleSelectOptionsList;
11  import java.util.HashMap;
12  import javax.faces.FacesException;
13
14  public class Options extends AbstractPageBean
15  {
16     // Managed Component Definition"
17     private void _init() throws Exception
18     {
19        languageRadioButtonGroupDefaultOptions.setOptions(
20           new com.sun.webui.jsf.model.Option[]
21           {
22              new com.sun.webui.jsf.model.Option( "Java", "Java" ),
23              new com.sun.webui.jsf.model.Option( "C++", "C++" ),
24              new com.sun.webui.jsf.model.Option( "Visual Basic 2008",
25                 "Visual Basic 2008" ),
26              new com.sun.webui.jsf.model.Option( "Visual C# 2008",
27                 "Visual C# 2008" ),
28              new com.sun.webui.jsf.model.Option( "Internet & Web",
29                 "Internet & Web" )
30           } // end array initializer
31        ); // end call to setOptions
32     } // end method _init
33
34     private SingleSelectOptionsList languageRadioButtonGroupDefaultOptions =
35        new SingleSelectOptionsList();
36
37     // To save space, we omitted the code in lines 36-139. The complete
38     // source code is provided with this chapter's examples.
39
142    private HashMap<String, String> books = new HashMap<String, String>();
143
144    // Construct a new page bean instance and initialize the properties
145    // that map languages to ISBN numbers of recommended books.
146    public Options()
147    {
148       // initialize HashMap object of values to be stored as cookies.
149       books.put( "Java", "0132222205" );
150       books.put( "C++", "0136152503" );
151       books.put( "Visual Basic 2008", "013605305X" );
```

Fig. 21.28 | Page bean that stores language selections in a SessionBean property. (Part 1 of 3.)

```
152        books.put( "Visual C# 2008", "013605322X" );
153        books.put( "Internet & Web", "0131752421" );
154     } // end Options constructor
155
156     // To save space, we omitted the code in lines 156-205. The complete
157     // source code is provided with this chapter's examples.
158
206     // Action handler for the Submit button. Checks whether a language
207     // was selected and, if so, creates a cookie for that language and
208     // sets the responseText to indicate the chosen language.
209     public String submitButton_action()
210     {
211        String message = "Welcome to Sessions! You ";
212
213        // if the user made a selection
214        if ( languageRadioButtonGroup.getSelected() != null )
215        {
216           String language =
217              languageRadioButtonGroup.getSelected().toString();
218           message += "selected " + language + ".";
219
220           // get ISBN number of book for the given language
221           String ISBN = books.get( language );
222
223           // add the selection to the SessionBean's Properties object
224           HashMap<String, String> selections =
225              getSessionBean1().getSelectedLanguages();
226           String result = selections.put( language, ISBN );
227
228           // increment numSelections in the SessionBean and update
229           // selectedLanguages if user has not made this selection before
230           if ( result == null )
231           {
232              int selected = getSessionBean1().getNumberOfSelections();
233              getSessionBean1().setNumberOfSelections( ++selected );
234           } // end if
235        } // end if
236        else
237        {
238           message += "did not select a language.";
239        } // end else
240
241        responseText.setValue( message );
242        languageRadioButtonGroup.setRendered( false ); // hide
243        instructionText.setRendered( false ); // hide
244        submitButton.setRendered( false ); // hide
245        responseText.setRendered( true ); // show
246        selectionsText.setRendered( true ); // show
247        selectionsValueText.setRendered( true ); // show
248        languagesLink.setRendered( true ); // show
249        recommendationsLink.setRendered( true ); // show
250        return null; // reloads the page
251     } // end method submitButton_action
```

Fig. 21.28 | Page bean that stores language selections in a `SessionBean` property. (Part 2 of 3.)

```
252
253      // redisplay the components for selecting a language
254      public String languagesLink_action()
255      {
256         responseText.setRendered( false ); // hide
257         selectionsText.setRendered( false ); // hide
258         selectionsValueText.setRendered( false ); // hide
259         languagesLink.setRendered( false ); // hide
260         recommendationsLink.setRendered( false ); // hide
261         languageRadioButtonGroup.setRendered( true ); // show
262         instructionText.setRendered( true ); // show
263         submitButton.setRendered( true ); // show
264         return null; // reloads the page
265      } // end method languagesLink_action
266   } // end class Options
```

Fig. 21.28 | Page bean that stores language selections in a `SessionBean` property. (Part 3 of 3.)

The `submitButton`'s action handler (lines 209–251) stores the user's selections in `SessionBean1` and increments the number of selections made, if necessary. Lines 224–225 retrieve from `SessionBean1` the `HashMap` object that contains the user's selections. Line 226 adds the current selection to the `HashMap`. Method `put` returns the value previously associated with the new key, or `null` if this key was not already stored in the `HashMap` object. If adding the new property returns `null`, then the user has made a new selection. In this case, lines 232–233 increment `SessionBean1`'s `numberOfSelections` property. Lines 242–249 and the `languaguesLink` action handler (lines 254–265) control the components that are displayed, just as in the cookies examples.

Software Engineering Observation 21.2

A benefit of using session bean properties (rather than cookies) is that they can store any type of object (not just `Strings`) as attribute values. This provides you with increased flexibility and power in maintaining client-state information.

Displaying Recommendations Based on Session Values

As in the cookies example, this application provides a link to `Recommendations.jsp`, which displays a list of book recommendations based on the user's language selections. Since this JSP is identical to the version in Fig. 21.22, we show only the sample output of this page in Fig. 21.29.

Page Bean That Creates Book Recommendations from a SessionBean Property

Figure 21.30 presents the page bean for `Recommendations.jsp`. Again, much of it is similar to the page bean used in the cookies example. We discuss only the new features. Lines 67–68 retrieve the `HashMap` object containing the user's selections from the session bean, and line 69 retrieves the number of selections made. If any selections were made, lines 78–82 append book recommendations to the string `recommendations`. Line 78 uses the `HashMap`'s `keySet` method to obtain a `Set` of the keys in the `HashMap`, and line 81 uses each key to obtain the ISBN of the corresponding book.

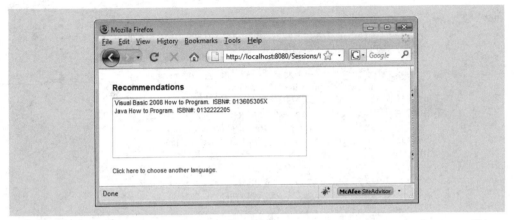

Fig. 21.29 | JSP file that displays book recommendations based on language selections stored in session scope.

```java
 1   // Fig. 21.30: Recommendations.java
 2   // Displays book recommendations based on a HashMap property in the
 3   // session bean that contains the user's selected programming languages.
 4   package sessions;
 5
 6   import com.sun.rave.web.ui.appbase.AbstractPageBean;
 7   import com.sun.webui.jsf.component.TextArea;
 8   import java.util.HashMap;
 9   import javax.faces.FacesException;
10
11   public class Recommendations extends AbstractPageBean
12   {
13      // To save space, we omitted the code in lines 13-61. The complete
14      // source code is provided with this chapter's examples.
15
62      // process and display user's selections
63      @Override
64      public void prerender()
65      {
66         // retrieve user's selections and number of selections made
67         HashMap<String, String> languages =
68            getSessionBean1().getSelectedLanguages();
69         int numberSelected = getSessionBean1().getNumberOfSelections();
70
71         // if there are selections, store the corresponding
72         // books and ISBN numbers in a String
73         String recommendations = "";
74
75         // if at least one selection was made
76         if ( numberSelected > 0 )
77         {
78            for ( String language : languages.keySet() )
79            {
```

Fig. 21.30 | Displays book recommendations based on a `SessionBean` property. (Part 1 of 2.)

```
80                    recommendations += language + " How to Program.  ISBN#: " +
81                       languages.get( language ) + "\n";
82                } // end for
83             } // end if
84             else
85             {
86                recommendations =
87                   "No recommendations. Please select a language.";
88             } // end else
89
90             recommendationsTextArea.setText( recommendations );
91          } // end method prerender
92
93          // To save space, we omitted the code in lines 93-112. The complete
94          // source code is provided with this chapter's examples.
112       } // end class Recommendations
```

Fig. 21.30 | Displays book recommendations based on a `SessionBean` property. (Part 2 of 2.)

21.8 Wrap-Up

In this chapter, we introduced web application development using JavaServer Pages and JavaServer Faces in Netbeans. We began by discussing the simple HTTP transactions that take place when you request and receive a web page through a web browser. We then discussed the three tiers (i.e., the client or top tier, the business logic or middle tier and the information or bottom tier) that comprise most web applications.

You learned the role of JSP files and page bean files, and the relationship between them. You learned how to use Netbeans to visually build web applications using Netbeans's drag-and-drop capabilities, then you compiled and executed them.

We demonstrated several common JSF components used for displaying text and images on web pages. We also discussed validation components and custom validator methods, which allow you to ensure that user input satisfies the requirements of your application.

We discussed the benefits of maintaining user information across multiple pages of a website. We then demonstrated how you can include such functionality in a web application using either cookies or properties of the session bean class that is included in each web application.

In Chapter 22, we continue our discussion of Java web application development with more advanced concepts. You'll learn how to access a database from a JSF web application, how to use AJAX-enabled JSF components and how to use virtual forms. AJAX helps web-based applications provide the interactivity and responsiveness that users typically expect of desktop applications.

22

Ajax-Enabled JavaServer™ Faces Web Applications

OBJECTIVES

In this chapter you'll learn:

- To use data providers to access databases from web applications built in Netbeans.
- The basic principles and advantages of Ajax technology.
- To use Ajax-enabled JSF components in a Netbeans web application project.
- To configure virtual forms that enable subsets of a form's input components to be submitted to the server.

Whatever is in any way beautiful hath its source of beauty in itself, and is complete in itself; praise forms no part of it.
—Marcus Aurelius Antoninus

There is something in a face, An air, and a peculiar grace, Which boldest painters cannot trace.
—William Somerville

Cato said the best way to keep good acts in memory was to refresh them with new.
—Francis Bacon

I never forget a face, but in your case I'll make an exception.
—Groucho Marx

Painting is only a bridge linking the painter's mind with that of the viewer.
—Eugéne Delacroix

Outline

22.1 Introduction

22.2 Accessing Databases in Web Applications

    22.2.1 Building a Web Application That Displays Data from a Database

    22.2.2 Modifying the Page Bean File for the **AddressBook** Application

22.3 Ajax-Enabled JSF Components

22.4 Creating an Autocomplete **Text Field** and Using Virtual Forms

    22.4.1 Configuring Virtual Forms

    22.4.2 JSP File with Virtual Forms and an Autocomplete **Text Field**

    22.4.3 Providing Suggestions for an Autocomplete **Text Field**

    22.4.4 Displaying the Contact's Information

22.5 Wrap-Up

22.1 Introduction

This chapter continues our discussion of web application development with several advanced concepts. We discuss accessing, updating and searching databases in a web application, adding virtual forms to web pages to enable subsets of a form's input components to be submitted to the server, and using Ajax-enabled component libraries to improve application performance and component responsiveness.

We present a single address book application developed in three stages to illustrate these concepts. The application is backed by a Java DB database for storing the contact names and their addresses.

The address book application presents a form that allows the user to enter a new name and address to store in the address book, and it displays the contents of the address book in table format. It also provides a search form that allows the user to search for a contact and, if found, display the contact's address. The first version of this application demonstrates how to add contacts to the database and how to display the list of contacts in a JSF **Table** component. In the second version, we add an Ajax-enabled Autocomplete **Text Field** component and enable it to suggest a list of contact names as the user types. When the user selects a contact, the contact's information is displayed.

This chapter's examples, like those in Chapter 21, were developed in Netbeans. Some of the Woodstock components that come with Netbeans, such as the **Text Field** component, are Ajax enabled. These components use the Dojo Toolkit on the client side in the web browser. Dojo is a cross-browser, cross-platform JavaScript library for creating rich client-side user interfaces and performing Ajax interactions with web servers. For more information on this toolkit, see our Dojo Resource Center at www.deitel.com/dojo/.

22.2 Accessing Databases in Web Applications

Many web applications access databases to store and retrieve persistent data. In this section, we build a web application that uses a Java DB database to store contacts in the address book and display contacts from the address book on a web page.

The web page enables the user to enter new contacts in a form. This form consists of **Text Field** components for the contact's first name, last name, street address, city, state and zip code. The form also has a **Submit** button to send the data to the server and a **Clear** button to reset the form's fields. The application stores the address book information in a database named AddressBook, which has a single table named Addresses. (We provide this database in the examples directory for this chapter. You can download the examples from www.deitel.com/books/javafp/). This example also introduces the **Table** JSF component, which displays the addresses from the database in tabular format.

22.2.1 Building a Web Application That Displays Data from a Database

We now explain how to build the AddressBook application's GUI and set up a data binding that allows the **Table** component to display information from the database. We present the generated JSP file later in the section, and we discuss the related page bean file in Section 22.2.2. To build the AddressBook application, perform the following steps:

Step 1: Creating the Project
In Netbeans, create a new **Web Application** project named AddressBook. Be sure to select **Visual Web JavaServer Faces** as the framework, as you did in Chapter 21. Rename the JSP and page bean files from Page1 to AddressBook using the refactoring tools.

Step 2: Creating the Form for User Input
In **Design** mode, create the form shown in Fig. 22.1. Add a **Static Text** component containing "Add a contact to the address book:". Use the component's style property to set the font size to 18px. Add six pairs of **Label** and **Text Field** components to the page. Rename the **Text Field**s firstNameTextField, lastNameTextField, streetTextField, cityTextField, stateTextField and zipTextField. Set each **Text Field**'s required property to true (checked) by selecting the **Text Field**, then clicking the required property's checkbox. Associate each **Label** with its corresponding **Text Field** by holding the *Ctrl* and *Shift* keys, then dragging the label to the appropriate **Text Field**. Add a binding attribute to the page bean for each **Text Field** (right click the component and select **Add Binding Attribute**). Finally, add **Submit** and **Clear** buttons. Set the **Submit** button's *primary* property to true (checked) to make it more prominent on the page than the **Clear** button and to allow the user to submit a new contact by pressing *Enter* rather than by clicking the button. Set the **Clear** button's *reset* property to true (checked) to prevent validation when the user clicks the button—since we're clearing the fields, we don't need to ensure that they

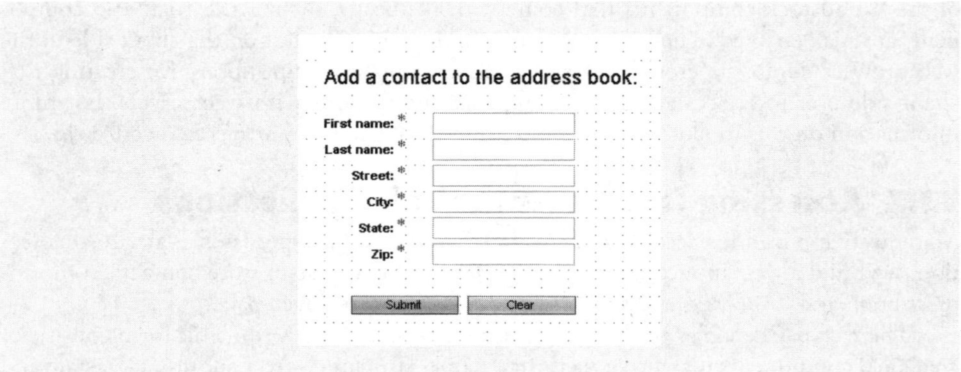

Add a contact to the address book:

First name: *
Last name: *
Street: *
City: *
State: *
Zip: *

Submit   Clear

Fig. 22.1 | AddressBook application form for adding a contact.

contain information. We discuss the **Submit** button's action handler when we present the page bean file. The **Clear** button does not need an action-handler method—setting reset to true automatically configures the button to reset all of the page's input fields.

Step 3: Adding a Table Component to the Page

Drag a **Table** component from the **Basic** section of the **Palette** to the page and place it just below the two **Button** components. Name it addressesTable. The **Table** component formats and displays data from database tables. In the **Properties** window, change the **Table's** title property to Contacts. We show how to configure the **Table** to interact with the AddressBook database shortly.

Step 4: Creating a Java DB Database

This example uses a database called AddressBook to store the address information. To create this database, perform the following steps:

1. In the Netbeans **Services** tab (to the right of the **Projects** and **Files** tabs), expand the **Databases** node, then right click **Java DB** and select **Create Database....**

2. Enter the name of the database to create (AddressBook), a username (test) and a password (test).

3. If you wish to change the location where the database is stored on your system, click the **Properties...** button and specify the new location.

4. Click **OK** to create the database.

In the **Services** tab, the preceding steps create a new entry in the **Databases** node showing the URL of the database (jdbc:derby://localhost:1527/AddressBook). The new Java DB database resides on the local machine and accepts connections on port 1527.

Step 5: Adding a Table and Data to the AddressBook Database

You can use the **Services** tab to create tables and to execute SQL statements that populate the database with data:

1. In the **Services** tab and expand the **Databases** node.

2. Netbeans must be connected to the database to execute SQL statements. If Netbeans is already connected to the database, the icon ▥ is displayed next to the database's URL (jdbc:derby://localhost:1527/AddressBook). In this case, proceed to *Step 3*. If Netbeans is not connected to the database, the icon ▨ appears next to the database's URL. In this case, right click the icon and select **Connect....** Once connected, the icon changes to ▥.

3. Expand the node for the AddressBook database, right click the **Tables** node and select **Execute Command...** to open a **SQL Command** editor in Netbeans. We provided the file AddressBook.sql in this chapter's examples folder. Open that file in a text editor, copy the SQL statements and paste them into the **SQL Command** editor in Netbeans. Then, highlight all the SQL commands, right click inside the **SQL Command** editor and select **Run Selection**. This will create the Addresses table with the sample data shown in Fig. 22.2. You may need to refresh (right click it and select **Refresh**) and expand the **Tables** node to see the new table. You can view the data in the table by expanding the **Tables** node, right clicking **ADDRESSES** and selecting **View Data....**

FirstName	LastName	Street	City	State	Zip
Bob	Green	5 Bay St.	San Francisco	CA	94133
Liz	White	100 5th Ave.	New York	NY	10011
Mike	Brown	3600 Delmar Blvd.	St. Louis	MO	63108
Mary	Green	300 Massachusetts Ave.	Boston	MA	02115
John	Gray	500 South St.	Philadelphia	PA	19147
Meg	Gold	1200 Stout St.	Denver	CO	80204
James	Blue	1000 Harbor Ave.	Seattle	WA	98116
Sue	Black	1000 Michigan Ave.	Chicago	IL	60605

Fig. 22.2 | Addresses table data.

Step 6: Binding the Table Component to the Addresses Table of the AddressBook Database

Now that we've configured the **AddressBook** database and created the Addresses table, let's configure the **Table** component to display the AddressBook data. Drag the database table from the **Services** tab and drop it on the **Table** component to create the binding.

To select specific columns to display, right click the **Table** component and select **Bind to Data** to display the **Bind to Data** dialog containing the list of the columns in the Addresses database table (Fig. 22.3). The items under the **Selected** heading will be displayed in the **Table**. To remove a column, select it and click the < button. We'd like to display all the columns in this example, so you should simply click **OK** to exit the dialog.

By default, the **Table** uses the database table's column names in all uppercase letters as headings. To change these headings, select a column and edit its headerText property in the **Properties** window. To select a column, click the column's name in the **Design** mode. We also changed the id property of each column to make the variable names in the code more readable. In **Design** mode, your **Table**'s column heads should appear as in Fig. 22.4. If any of the column heads wrap to two lines, you can increase the width of the table.

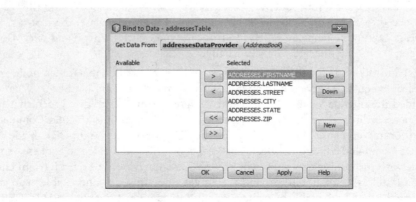

Fig. 22.3 | Dialog for binding to the Addresses table.

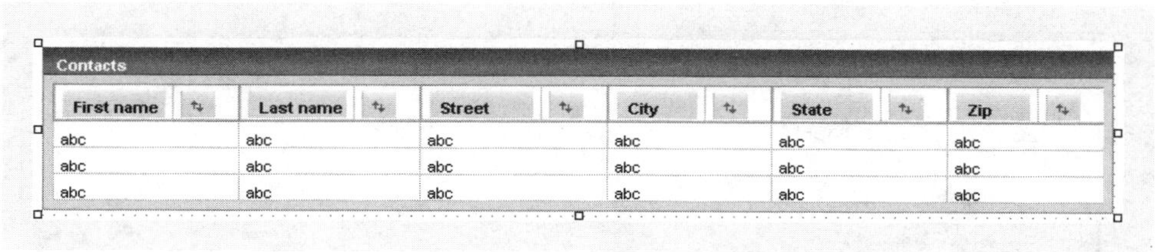

Fig. 22.4 | `Table` component after binding it to a database table and editing its column names for display purposes.

An address book might contain many contacts, so we'd like to display only a few at a time. Setting the table's *paginationControls* property to `true` (checked) in the **Properties** window configures this **Table** for automatic pagination. This adds buttons to the bottom of the **Table** for moving forward and backward between groups of contacts. You may use the **Table Layout** dialog's **Options** tab to select the number of rows to display at a time. To view this tab, right click the **Table**'s header, select **Table Layout...**, then click the **Options** tab. For this example, we set the **Page Size** property to 5. Click the **OK** button to apply the changes.

Next, set the `addressesTable`'s *internalVirtualForm* property to `true` (checked). Virtual forms allow subsets of a form's input components to be submitted to the server. Setting this property prevents the pagination control buttons on the **Table** from submitting the **Text Field**s on the form every time the user wishes to view the next group of contacts. Virtual forms are discussed in Section 22.4.1.

Binding the **Table** component to a data provider added the object `addressesData-Provider` (an instance of class `CachedRowSetDataProvider`) to the **AddressBook** node in the **Navigator** window. A *CachedRowSetDataProvider* provides a scrollable RowSet that can be bound to a **Table** component to display the RowSet's data. This data provider is a wrapper for a `CachedRowSet` object. If you click the **addressesDataProvider** node in the **Navigator** window, you can see in the **Properties** window that its `CachedRowSet` property is set to `addressesRowSet`, a session bean property that implements interface `Cached-RowSet`.

Step 7: Modifying addressesRowSet's SQL Statement
The `CachedRowSet` object wrapped by our `addressesDataProvider` is configured by default to execute a SQL query that selects all the data in the `Addresses` table of the `AddressBook` database. You can edit this SQL query. To do so, ensure that you are in **Design** mode for the page bean, then expand the `SessionBean1` node in the **Navigator** window and double click the `addressesRowSet` element to open the query editor window (Fig. 22.5). We'd like to edit the SQL statement so that records with duplicate last names are sorted by last name, then by first name. To do this, click the **Sort Type** column next to the **LASTNAME** row and select **Ascending**. Then, repeat this for the **FIRSTNAME** row. Notice that the expression

> ***ORDER BY*** `TEST.ADDRESSES.LASTNAME` ***ASC***, `TEST.ADDRESSES.FIRSTNAME` ***ASC***

was added to the end of the SQL statement at the bottom of the editor. Save your application (**File > Save All**), then close the query editor tab.

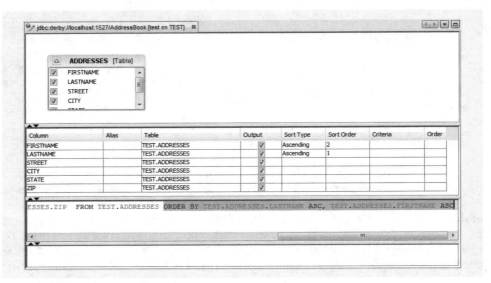

Fig. 22.5 | Editing addressesRowSet's SQL statement.

Step 8: Adding Validation

It is important to validate the form data on this page to ensure that the data can be successfully inserted into the AddressBook database. All of the database's columns are of type varchar (except the ID column) and have length restrictions. For this reason, you should either add a **Length Validator** to each **Text Field** component or set each **Text Field** component's maxLength property. We chose to do the latter. The first name, last name, street, city, state and zip code **Text Field** components may not exceed 30, 30, 150, 30, 2 and 5 characters, respectively.

Finally, drag a **Message Group** component onto your page to the right of the **Text Fields**. This component displays system messages. We use it to display an error message when an attempt to add a contact to the database fails. Set the **Message Group**'s show-GlobalOnly property to true (checked) to prevent component-level validation error messages from being displayed here.

Reviewing the JSP Document for a Web Page That Interacts with a Database

The JSP file for the application is shown in Fig. 22.6. This file contains a large amount of generated markup for components you learned in Chapter 21. We discuss the markup for only the components that are new in this example.

Lines 18–72 contain the JSF components for the form that gathers user input. Lines 73–120 define the **Table** element (webuijsf:table) that displays address information from the database. **Table**s may have multiple groups of rows displaying different data. This **Table** has a single webuijsf:tableRowGroup with a start tag in lines 79–81. The row group's sourceData attribute is bound to our addressesDataProvider in the page bean and given the variable name currentRow. The row group also defines the **Table**'s columns. Each webuijsf:tableColumn element (e.g., lines 82–88) contains a webuijsf:static-Text element with its text attribute bound to a column in the data provider currentRow. These webuijsf:staticText elements enable the **Table** to display each row's data.

```
 1  <?xml version="1.0" encoding="UTF-8"?>
 2  <!-- Fig. 22.6: AddressBook.jsp -->
 3  <!-- AddressBook JSP with an add form and a Table JSF component. -->
 4  <jsp:root version="2.1" xmlns:f="http://java.sun.com/jsf/core"
 5     xmlns:h="http://java.sun.com/jsf/html"
 6     xmlns:jsp="http://java.sun.com/JSP/Page"
 7     xmlns:webuijsf="http://www.sun.com/webui/webuijsf">
 8     <jsp:directive.page contentType="text/html;charset=UTF-8"
 9        pageEncoding="UTF-8"/>
10     <f:view>
11        <webuijsf:page id="page1">
12           <webuijsf:html id="html1">
13              <webuijsf:head id="head1">
14                 <webuijsf:link id="link1" url="/resources/stylesheet.css"/>
15              </webuijsf:head>
16              <webuijsf:body id="body1" style="-rave-layout: grid">
17                 <webuijsf:form id="form1">
18                    <webuijsf:staticText id="instructionText"
19                       style="font-size: 18px; left: 24px; top: 24px;
20                          position: absolute"
21                       text="Add a contact to the address book:"/>
22                    <webuijsf:label for="firstNameTextField"
23                       id="firstNameLabel" style="left: 24px; top: 72px;
24                          position: absolute" text="First name:"/>
25                    <webuijsf:textField
26                       binding="#{AddressBook.firstNameTextField}"
27                       id="firstNameTextField" maxLength="30"
28                       required="true" style="left: 120px; top: 72px;
29                          position: absolute"/>
30                    <webuijsf:label for="lastNameTextField"
31                       id="lastNameLabel" style="left: 25px; top: 96px;
32                          position: absolute" text="Last name:"/>
33                    <webuijsf:textField
34                       binding="#{AddressBook.lastNameTextField}"
35                       id="lastNameTextField" maxLength="30" required="true"
36                       style="left: 120px; top: 96px; position: absolute"/>
37                    <webuijsf:label for="streetTextField" id="streetLabel"
38                       style="left: 49px; top: 120px; position: absolute"
39                       text="Street:"/>
40                    <webuijsf:textField
41                       binding="#{AddressBook.streetTextField}"
42                       id="streetTextField" maxLength="150" required="true"
43                       style="left: 120px; top: 120px; position: absolute"/>
44                    <webuijsf:label for="cityTextField" id="cityLabel"
45                       style="left: 62px; top: 144px; position: absolute"
46                       text="City:"/>
47                    <webuijsf:textField
48                       binding="#{AddressBook.cityTextField}"
49                       id="cityTextField" maxLength="30" required="true"
50                       style="left: 120px; top: 144px; position: absolute"/>
51                    <webuijsf:label for="stateTextField" id="stateLabel"
52                       style="left: 55px; top: 168px; position: absolute"
53                       text="State:"/>
```

Fig. 22.6 | AddressBook JSP with an add form and a **Table** JSF component (Part 1 of 4.)

```
54    <webuijsf:textField
55        binding="#{AddressBook.stateTextField}"
56        id="stateTextField" maxLength="2" required="true"
57        style="left: 120px; top: 168px; position: absolute"/>
58    <webuijsf:label for="zipTextField" id="zipLabel"
59        style="left: 66px; top: 192px; position: absolute"
60        text="Zip:"/>
61    <webuijsf:textField
62        binding="#{AddressBook.zipTextField}"
63        id="zipTextField" maxLength="5" required="true"
64        style="left: 120px; top: 192px; position: absolute"/>
65    <webuijsf:button
66        actionExpression="#{AddressBook.submitButton_action}"
67        id="submitButton" primary="true" style="left: 47px;
68            top: 240px; position: absolute; width: 95px"
69        text="Submit"/>
70    <webuijsf:button id="clearButton" reset="true"
71        style="left: 150px; top: 240px; position: absolute;
72            width: 96px" text="Clear"/>
73    <webuijsf:table augmentTitle="false"
74        binding="#{AddressBook.addressesTable}"
75        id="addressesTable" paginateButton="true"
76        paginationControls="true" style="left: 24px;
77            top: 288px; position: absolute"
78        title="Contacts" width="744">
79        <webuijsf:tableRowGroup id="tableRowGroup1" rows="5"
80            sourceData="#{AddressBook.addressesDataProvider}"
81            sourceVar="currentRow">
82            <webuijsf:tableColumn headerText="First name"
83                id="firstNameColumn"
84                sort="ADDRESSES.FIRSTNAME">
85                <webuijsf:staticText id="staticText1"
86                    text="#{currentRow.value[
87                        'ADDRESSES.FIRSTNAME']}"/>
88            </webuijsf:tableColumn>
89            <webuijsf:tableColumn headerText="Last name"
90                id="lastNameColumn" sort="ADDRESSES.LASTNAME">
91                <webuijsf:staticText id="staticText2"
92                    text="#{currentRow.value[
93                        'ADDRESSES.LASTNAME']}"/>
94            </webuijsf:tableColumn>
95            <webuijsf:tableColumn headerText="Street"
96                id="streetColumn" sort="ADDRESSES.STREET">
97                <webuijsf:staticText id="staticText3"
98                    text="#{currentRow.value[
99                        'ADDRESSES.STREET']}"/>
100           </webuijsf:tableColumn>
101           <webuijsf:tableColumn headerText="City"
102               id="cityColumn" sort="ADDRESSES.CITY">
103               <webuijsf:staticText id="staticText4"
104                   text="#{currentRow.value[
105                       'ADDRESSES.CITY']}"/>
106           </webuijsf:tableColumn>
```

Fig. 22.6 | AddressBook JSP with an add form and a **Table** JSF component (Part 2 of 4.)

```
107                                <webuijsf:tableColumn headerText="State"
108                                   id="stateColumn" sort="ADDRESSES.STATE">
109                                   <webuijsf:staticText id="staticText5"
110                                      text="#{currentRow.value[
111                                         'ADDRESSES.STATE']}"/>
112                                </webuijsf:tableColumn>
113                                <webuijsf:tableColumn headerText="zip"
114                                   id="zipColumn" sort="ADDRESSES.ZIP">
115                                   <webuijsf:staticText id="staticText6"
116                                      text="#{currentRow.value[
117                                         'ADDRESSES.ZIP']}"/>
118                                </webuijsf:tableColumn>
119                             </webuijsf:tableRowGroup>
120                          </webuijsf:table>
121                          <webuijsf:messageGroup id="messageGroup1"
122                             showGlobalOnly="true"
123                             style="left: 264px; top: 72px; position: absolute"/>
124                       </webuijsf:form>
125                    </webuijsf:body>
126                 </webuijsf:html>
127              </webuijsf:page>
128          </f:view>
129      </jsp:root>
```

(a) Adding a new contact to the database.

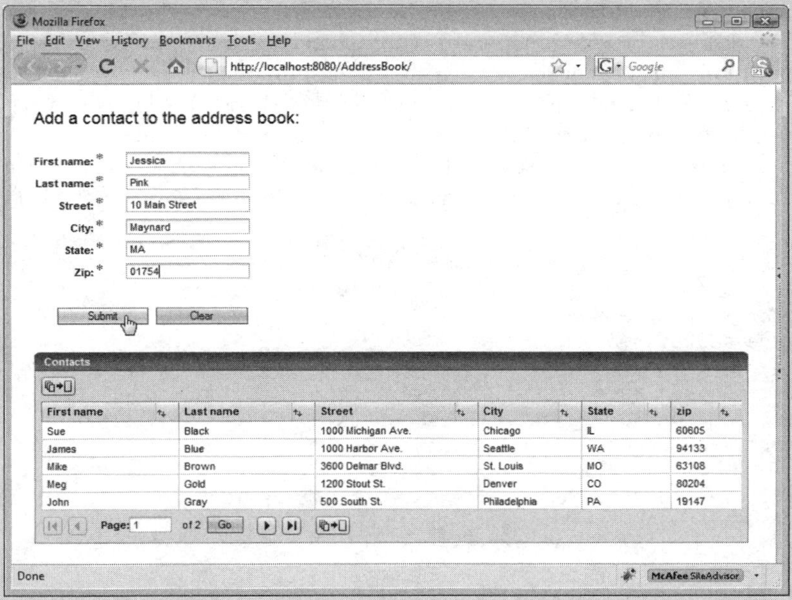

Fig. 22.6 | AddressBook JSP with an add form and a **Table** JSF component (Part 3 of 4.)

(b) Page 2 of the **Table** showing the new database entry.

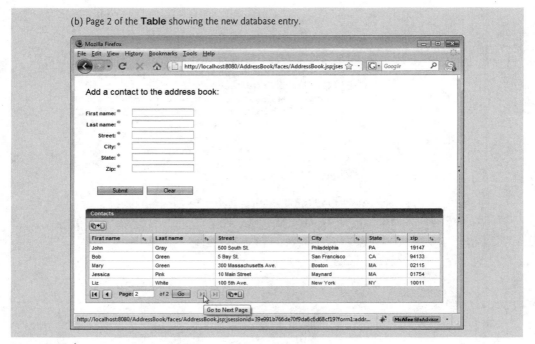

Fig. 22.6 | AddressBook JSP with an add form and a **Table** JSF component (Part 4 of 4.)

Session Bean for the AddressBook Application

Figure 22.7 displays the SessionBean1.java file generated by Netbeans for the Address-Book application. The CachedRowSet that the **Table** component's data provider uses to access the AddressBook database is a property of this class (lines 31–41). The _init method (lines 13–29) configures addressesRowSet to interact with the AddressBook database). Lines 15–16 connect the row set to the database. Lines 17–27 set addressesRowSet's SQL command to the query configured in Fig. 22.5. Line 28 sets the RowSet's table name.

```java
 1    // Fig. 22.7: SessionBean1.java
 2    // Session bean initializes the data source for the
 3    // AddressBook database.
 4    package addressbook;
 5
 6    import com.sun.rave.web.ui.appbase.AbstractSessionBean;
 7    import com.sun.sql.rowset.CachedRowSetXImpl;
 8    import javax.faces.FacesException;
 9
10    public class SessionBean1 extends AbstractSessionBean
11    {
12        // Managed Component Definition
13        private void _init() throws Exception
14        {
```

Fig. 22.7 | Session bean initializes the data source for the AddressBook database. (Part 1 of 2.)

```
15        addressesRowSet.setDataSourceName(
16           "java:comp/env/jdbc/TEST_ApacheDerby" );
17        addressesRowSet.setCommand(
18           "SELECT ALL " +
19              "TEST.ADDRESSES.FIRSTNAME, " +
20              "TEST.ADDRESSES.LASTNAME, " +
21              "TEST.ADDRESSES.STREET, " +
22              "TEST.ADDRESSES.CITY, " +
23              "TEST.ADDRESSES.STATE, " +
24              "TEST.ADDRESSES.ZIP " +
25              "FROM TEST.ADDRESSES " +
26           "ORDER BY TEST.ADDRESSES.LASTNAME ASC, " +
27              "TEST.ADDRESSES.FIRSTNAME ASC" );
28        addressesRowSet.setTableName( "ADDRESSES" );
29     } // end method _init
30
31     private CachedRowSetXImpl addressesRowSet = new CachedRowSetXImpl();
32
33     public CachedRowSetXImpl getAddressesRowSet()
34     {
35        return addressesRowSet;
36     } // end method getAddressesRowSet
37
38     public void setAddressesRowSet( CachedRowSetXImpl crsxi )
39     {
40        this.addressesRowSet = crsxi;
41     } // end method setAddressesRowSet
42
43     // To save space, we omitted the code in lines 42-88. The complete
44     // source code is provided with this chapter's examples.
45  } // end class SessionBean1
```

Fig. 22.7 | Session bean initializes the data source for the AddressBook database. (Part 2 of 2.)

22.2.2 Modifying the Page Bean File for the AddressBook Application

After building the web page and configuring the components used in this example, double click the **Submit** button to create its action event handler in the page bean file. The code to insert a contact into the database is placed in this method. The page bean with the completed event handler is shown in Fig. 22.8 below.

```
1   // Fig. 22.8: AddressBook.java
2   // Page bean for adding a contact to the address book.
3   package addressbook;
4
5   import com.sun.data.provider.RowKey;
6   import com.sun.data.provider.impl.CachedRowSetDataProvider;
7   import com.sun.rave.web.ui.appbase.AbstractPageBean;
8   import com.sun.webui.jsf.component.Table;
9   import com.sun.webui.jsf.component.TextField;
```

Fig. 22.8 | Page bean for adding a contact to the address book. (Part 1 of 3.)

```
10   import javax.faces.FacesException;
11
12   public class AddressBook extends AbstractPageBean
13   {
14      // Managed Component Definition
15      private void _init() throws Exception
16      {
17         addressesTable.setInternalVirtualForm( true );
18         addressesDataProvider.setCachedRowSet(
19            ( javax.sql.rowset.CachedRowSet ) getValue(
20               "#{SessionBean1.addressesRowSet}" ) );
21      } // end method _init
22
23      private Table addressesTable = new Table();
24
25      public Table getAddressesTable()
26      {
27         return addressesTable;
28      } // end method getAddressesTable
29
30      public void setAddressesTable( Table t )
31      {
32         this.addressesTable = t;
33      } // end method setAddressesTable
34
35      private CachedRowSetDataProvider addressesDataProvider =
36         new CachedRowSetDataProvider();
37
38      public CachedRowSetDataProvider getAddressesDataProvider()
39      {
40         return addressesDataProvider;
41      } // end method getAddressesDataProvider
42
43      public void setAddressesDataProvider( CachedRowSetDataProvider crsdp )
44      {
45         this.addressesDataProvider = crsdp;
46      } // end method setAddressesDataProvider
47
48      // To save space, we omitted the code in lines 48-149. The complete
49      // source code is provided with this chapter's examples.
50
150     @Override
151     public void prerender()
152     {
153        addressesDataProvider.refresh();
154     } // end method prerender
155
156     @Override
157     public void destroy()
158     {
159        addressesDataProvider.close();
160     } // end method destroy
```

Fig. 22.8 | Page bean for adding a contact to the address book. (Part 2 of 3.)

```
161
162      // To save space, we omitted the code in lines 162-176. The complete
163      // source code is provided with this chapter's examples.
164
177      // action handler that adds a contact to the AddressBook
178      // database when the user clicks submit
179      public String submitButton_action()
180      {
181          // check whether a row can be appended
182          if ( addressesDataProvider.canAppendRow() )
183          {
184              try
185              {
186                  // append new row and move cursor to that row
187                  RowKey rk = addressesDataProvider.appendRow();
188                  addressesDataProvider.setCursorRow( rk );
189
190                  // set values for the new row's columns
191                  addressesDataProvider.setValue( "ADDRESSES.FIRSTNAME",
192                      firstNameTextField.getValue() );
193                  addressesDataProvider.setValue( "ADDRESSES.LASTNAME",
194                      lastNameTextField.getValue() );
195                  addressesDataProvider.setValue( "ADDRESSES.STREET",
196                      streetTextField.getValue() );
197                  addressesDataProvider.setValue( "ADDRESSES.CITY",
198                      cityTextField.getValue() );
199                  addressesDataProvider.setValue( "ADDRESSES.STATE",
200                      stateTextField.getValue() );
201                  addressesDataProvider.setValue( "ADDRESSES.ZIP",
202                      zipTextField.getValue() );
203
204                  // commit the changes to the database
205                  addressesDataProvider.commitChanges();
206
207                  // reset text fields
208                  firstNameTextField.setValue( "" );
209                  lastNameTextField.setValue( "" );
210                  streetTextField.setValue( "" );
211                  cityTextField.setValue( "" );
212                  stateTextField.setValue( "" );
213                  zipTextField.setValue( "" );
214              } // end try
215              catch ( Exception ex )
216              {
217                  error( "The address book was not updated. " +
218                      ex.getMessage() );
219              } // end catch
220          } // end if
221
222          return null;
223      } // end method submitButton_action
224  } // end class AddressBook
```

Fig. 22.8 | Page bean for adding a contact to the address book. (Part 3 of 3.)

Line 17 in method `_init` sets the **Table** component's `internalVirtualForm` property to `true`. This prevents the pagination control buttons on the **Table** from submitting the form's **Text Field**s every time the user wishes to view the next group of contacts. Lines 18–20 set the `addressesDataProvider`'s `CachedRowSet` so the table rows can be populated with the contents of the database.

Lines 179–223 contain the event-handling code for the **Submit** button. Line 182 determines whether a new row can be appended to the data provider. If so, we append a new row (line 187). Every row in a `CachedRowSetDataProvider` has its own key; method ***appendRow*** returns the key for the new row. Line 188 sets the data provider's cursor to the new row, so that any changes we make to the data provider affect that row. Lines 191–202 set each of the row's columns to the values the user entered in the corresponding **Text Field**s. Line 205 stores the new contact by calling method ***commitChanges*** of class `Cached-RowSetDataProvider` to insert the new row into the **AddressBook** database.

Lines 208–213 clear the form's **Text Field**s. If these lines are omitted, the fields will retain their current values after the database is updated and the page reloads. Also, the **Clear** button will not work properly if the **Text Field**s are not cleared. Rather than emptying the **Text Field**s, it resets them to the values they held the last time the form was submitted.

Lines 215–219 catch any exceptions that might occur while updating the **Address-Book** database. If an exception occurs, lines 217–218 display a message in the page's **Mes-sageGroup** component indicating that the database was not updated and showing the exception's error message.

In method `prerender`, we added line 153 which calls `CachedRowSetDataProvider` method ***refresh*** to reexecute the wrapped `CachedRowSet`'s SQL statement and re-sort the **Table**'s rows so that the new row is displayed in the proper order. If you do not call `refresh`, the new address is displayed at the end of the **Table** (since we appended the new row to the end of the data provider). The IDE automatically generated code to free resources used by the data provider (line 159) in the `destroy` method. Run the application to test its functionality.

22.3 Ajax-Enabled JSF Components

The term *Ajax*—short for *Asynchronous JavaScript and XML*—was coined by Jesse James Garrett of Adaptive Path, Inc. in February 2005 to describe a range of technologies for developing highly responsive, dynamic web applications. Ajax applications include Google Maps, Yahoo's FlickR and many more. Ajax separates the user interaction portion of an application from its server interaction, enabling both to proceed asynchronously in parallel. This enables Ajax web-based applications to perform at speeds approaching those of desktop applications, reducing or even eliminating the performance advantage that desktop applications have traditionally had over web-based applications. This has huge ramifications for the desktop applications industry—the applications platform of choice is starting to shift from the desktop to the web. Many people believe that the web—especially in the context of abundant open-source software, inexpensive computers and exploding Internet bandwidth—will create the next major growth phase for Internet companies.

Ajax makes asynchronous calls to the server to exchange small amounts of data with each call. Where normally the entire page would be submitted and reloaded with every user interaction on a web page, Ajax allows only the necessary portions of the page to reload, saving time and resources.

Ajax applications typically make use of client-side scripting technologies such as JavaScript to interact with page elements. They use the browser's ***XMLHttpRequestObject*** to perform the asynchronous exchanges with the web server that make Ajax applications so responsive. This object can be used by most scripting languages to pass XML data from the client to the server and to process XML data sent from the server back to the client.

Using Ajax technologies in web applications can dramatically improve performance, but programming in Ajax is complex and error prone. It requires page designers to know both scripting and markup languages. *Ajax libraries*—such as the Dojo Toolkit used by JSF—make it possible to reap Ajax's benefits without the labor of writing "raw" Ajax. These libraries provide Ajax-enabled page elements that can be included in web pages simply by adding library-defined tags to the page's markup. We limit our discussion of building Ajax applications to using the JSF Woodstock components in Netbeans.

Traditional Web Applications

Figure 22.9 presents the typical interactions between the client and the server in a traditional web application, such as one that uses a user registration form. First, the user fills in the form's fields, then submits the form (Fig. 22.9, *Step 1*). The browser generates a request to the server, which receives the request and processes it (*Step 2*). The server generates and sends a response containing the exact page that the browser will render (*Step 3*), which causes the browser to load the new page (*Step 4*) and temporarily makes the browser window blank. Note that the client *waits* for the server to respond and *reloads the entire page* with the data from the response (*Step 4*). While such a *synchronous request* is being processed on the server, the user cannot interact with the client web page. Frequent long periods of waiting, due perhaps to Internet congestion, have led some users to refer to the World Wide Web as the "World Wide Wait." If the user interacts with and submits another form, the process begins again (*Steps 5–8*).

This model was originally designed for a web of hypertext documents—what some people call the "brochure web." As the web evolved into a full-scale applications platform,

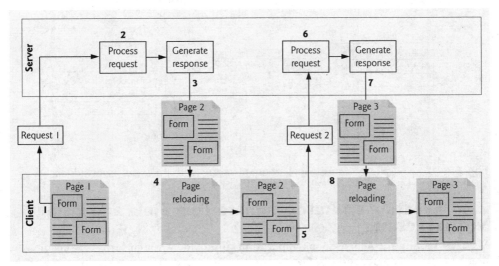

Fig. 22.9 | Classic web application reloading the page for every user interaction.

the model shown in Fig. 22.9 yielded "choppy" application performance. Every full-page refresh required users to reestablish their understanding of the full-page contents. Users began to demand a model that would yield the responsive feel of desktop applications.

Ajax Web Applications

Ajax applications add a layer between the client and the server to manage communication between the two (Fig. 22.10). When the user interacts with the page, the client creates an XMLHttpRequest object to manage a request (*Step 1*). The XMLHttpRequest object sends the request to the server (*Step 2*) and awaits the response. The requests are **asynchronous**, so the user can continue interacting with the application on the client side while the server processes the earlier request concurrently. Other user interactions could result in additional requests to the server (*Steps 3* and *4*). Once the server responds to the original request (*Step 5*), the XMLHttpRequest object that issued the request calls a client-side function to process the data returned by the server. This function—known as a **callback function**— uses **partial page updates** (*Step 6*) to display the data in the existing web page *without reloading the entire page*. At the same time, the server may be responding to the second request (*Step 7*) and the client side may be starting to do another partial page update (*Step 8*). The callback function updates only a designated part of the page. Such partial page updates help make web applications more responsive, making them feel more like desktop applications. The web application does not load a new page while the user interacts with it.

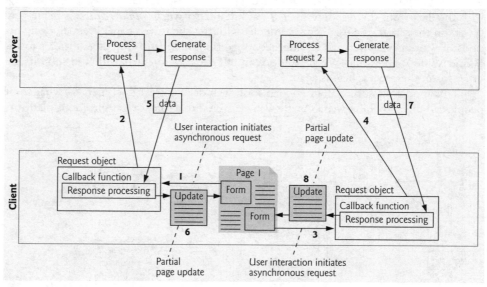

Fig. 22.10 | Ajax-enabled web application interacting with the server asynchronously.

22.4 Creating an Autocomplete Text Field and Using Virtual Forms

We now modify the AddressBook application to provide a search form that enables the user to locate a contact and display the contact's information. We take advantage of the

Text Field component's built-in Ajax capabilities to provide autocomplete functionality—the **Text Field** provides a list of suggestions as the user types. It obtains the suggestions from a data source, such as a database or web service. Eventually, the updated application will allow users to search the address book by last name. If the user selects a contact, the application will display the contact's information in a **Text Area** component.

Adding Search Components to the AddressBook.jsp Page

Using the AddressBook application from Section 22.2, drop a **Static Text** component named searchText below addressesTable. Change its text to "Search the address book by last name:" and change its font size to 18px. Now drag a **Text Field** component to the page and name it lastNameSearchTextField. Set this field's required and autoComplete properties to true. Add a **Label** named nameSearchLabel containing the text "Last name:" to the left of the **Text Field** and associate it with the **Text Field**. Finally, add a button called searchButton with the text Find to the right of the **Text Field**.

22.4.1 Configuring Virtual Forms

Virtual forms are used when you would like a button to submit a subset of the page's input fields to the server. Recall that we previously enabled the **Table**'s internal virtual forms so that clicking the pagination buttons would not submit the data in the **Text Field**s used to add a contact to the AddressBook database. Virtual forms are particularly useful for displaying multiple forms on the same page. They allow you to specify a *submitter* component and one or more *participant* components for a form. When the virtual form's submitter component is clicked, only the values of its participant components will be submitted to the server. We use virtual forms in our AddressBook application to separate the form for adding a contact from the form for searching the database.

To add virtual forms to the page, right click the **Submit** button on the upper form and select **Configure Virtual Forms...** to display the **Configure Virtual Forms** dialog. Click **New** to add a virtual form, then click in the **Name** column and change the new form's name to addForm. Double click the cell under the **Submit** column and change the option to **Yes** to indicate that this button should be used to submit the addForm virtual form. Click **OK** to exit the dialog. Next, hold the *Ctrl* key and click each of the **Text Field**s used to enter a contact's information in the upper form. Right click one of the selected **Text Field**s and choose **Configure Virtual Forms...**. Double click the cell under the addForm's **Participate** column to change the option to **Yes**, indicating that the values in these **Text Field**s should be submitted to the server when the form is submitted. Click **OK** to exit.

Repeat the process described above to create a second virtual form named searchForm for the lower form. The **Find Button** should submit the searchForm, and lastNameSearchTextField should participate in the searchForm. Figure 22.11 shows the **Configure Virtual Forms** dialog after both virtual forms have been added.

Next, return to **Design** mode and click the **Show Virtual Forms** button (🖳) at the top of the Visual Designer panel to display a legend of the virtual forms on the page. Your virtual forms should be configured as in Fig. 22.12. The **Text Field**s outlined in blue participate in the virtual form addForm. Those outlined in green participate in the virtual form searchForm. The components outlined with a dashed line submit their respective forms. A color key is provided at the bottom right of the **Design** area so that you know which components belong to each virtual form.

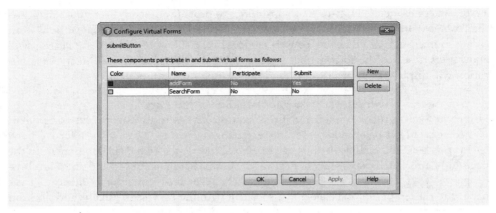

Fig. 22.11 | **Configure Virtual Forms** dialog.

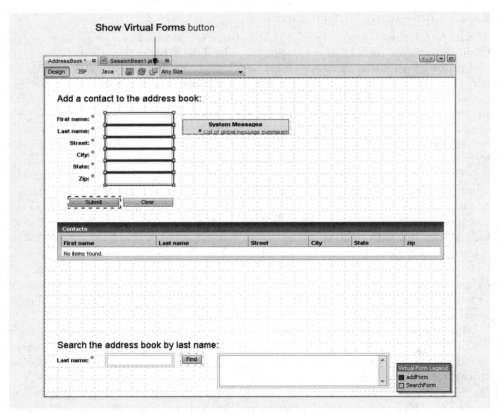

Fig. 22.12 | Virtual forms legend.

22.4.2 JSP File with Virtual Forms and an Autocomplete Text Field

Figure 22.13 presents the JSP file generated by Netbeans for this stage of the AddressBook application. We focus only on the new features of this JSP.

Lines 17–22 configure the virtual forms for this page. Lines 137–141 define the **Text Field** component with the autocomplete functionality. Notice that the **Text Field**'s *auto-Complete* attribute is set to "true", which enables the component to submit Ajax requests to the server. The **Text Field**'s *autoCompleteExpression* attribute is bound to the method that will be called (SessionBean1.getOptions) to provide the list of options the **Text Field** component should suggest. We discuss how to implement this method in Section 22.4.3.

```
 1  <?xml version="1.0" encoding="UTF-8"?>
 2  <!-- Fig. 22.13: AddressBook.jsp -->
 3  <!-- AddressBook JSP with an add form and a Table JSF component. -->
 4  <jsp:root version="2.1" xmlns:f="http://java.sun.com/jsf/core"
 5    xmlns:h="http://java.sun.com/jsf/html"
 6    xmlns:jsp="http://java.sun.com/JSP/Page"
 7    xmlns:webuijsf="http://www.sun.com/webui/webuijsf">
 8  <jsp:directive.page contentType="text/html;charset=UTF-8"
 9    pageEncoding="UTF-8"/>
10  <f:view>
11      <webuijsf:page id="page1">
12          <webuijsf:html id="html1">
13              <webuijsf:head id="head1" webuiJsfx="true">
14                  <webuijsf:link id="link1" url="/resources/stylesheet.css"/>
15              </webuijsf:head>
16              <webuijsf:body id="body1" style="-rave-layout: grid">
17                  <webuijsf:form id="form1" virtualFormsConfig=
18                      "addForm | firstNameTextField lastNameTextField
19                      streetTextField cityTextField stateTextField
20                      zipTextField | submitButton ,
21                      SearchForm | lastNameSearchTextField searchTextArea |
22                      searchButton">
23                      <webuijsf:staticText id="instructionText"
24                          style="font-size: 18px; left: 24px; top: 24px;
25                              position: absolute"
26                          text="Add a contact to the address book:"/>
27                      <webuijsf:label for="firstNameTextField"
28                          id="firstNameLabel" style="left: 24px; top: 72px;
29                              position: absolute" text="First name:"/>
30                      <webuijsf:textField
31                          binding="#{AddressBook.firstNameTextField}"
32                          id="firstNameTextField" maxLength="30"
33                          required="true" style="left: 120px; top: 72px;
34                              position: absolute"/>
35                      <webuijsf:label for="lastNameTextField"
36                          id="lastNameLabel" style="left: 25px; top: 96px;
37                              position: absolute" text="Last name:"/>
38                      <webuijsf:textField
39                          binding="#{AddressBook.lastNameTextField}"
40                          id="lastNameTextField" maxLength="30" required="true"
41                          style="left: 120px; top: 96px; position: absolute"/>
42                      <webuijsf:label for="streetTextField" id="streetLabel"
43                          style="left: 49px; top: 120px; position: absolute"
44                          text="Street:"/>
```

Fig. 22.13 | AddressBook JSP with an **AutoComplete Text Field** component. (Part 1 of 4.)

```
45                              <webuijsf:textField
46                                  binding="#{AddressBook.streetTextField}"
47                                  id="streetTextField" maxLength="150" required="true"
48                                  style="left: 120px; top: 120px; position: absolute"/>
49                              <webuijsf:label for="cityTextField" id="cityLabel"
50                                  style="left: 62px; top: 144px; position: absolute"
51                                  text="City:"/>
52                              <webuijsf:textField
53                                  binding="#{AddressBook.cityTextField}"
54                                  id="cityTextField" maxLength="30" required="true"
55                                  style="left: 120px; top: 144px; position: absolute"/>
56                              <webuijsf:label for="stateTextField" id="stateLabel"
57                                  style="left: 55px; top: 168px; position: absolute"
58                                  text="State:"/>
59                              <webuijsf:textField
60                                  binding="#{AddressBook.stateTextField}"
61                                  id="stateTextField" maxLength="2" required="true"
62                                  style="left: 120px; top: 168px; position: absolute"/>
63                              <webuijsf:label for="zipTextField" id="zipLabel"
64                                  style="left: 66px; top: 192px; position: absolute"
65                                  text="Zip:"/>
66                              <webuijsf:textField
67                                  binding="#{AddressBook.zipTextField}"
68                                  id="zipTextField" maxLength="5" required="true"
69                                  style="left: 120px; top: 192px; position: absolute"/>
70                              <webuijsf:button
71                                  actionExpression="#{AddressBook.submitButton_action}"
72                                  id="submitButton" primary="true" style="left: 47px;
73                                      top: 240px; position: absolute; width: 95px"
74                                  text="Submit"/>
75                              <webuijsf:button id="clearButton" reset="true"
76                                  style="left: 150px; top: 240px; position: absolute;
77                                  width: 96px" text="Clear"/>
78                              <webuijsf:table augmentTitle="false"
79                                  binding="#{AddressBook.addressesTable}"
80                                  id="addressesTable" paginateButton="true"
81                                  paginationControls="true" style="left: 24px;
82                                      top: 288px; position: absolute"
83                                  title="Contacts" width="744">
84                                  <webuijsf:tableRowGroup id="tableRowGroup1" rows="5"
85                                      sourceData="#{AddressBook.addressesDataProvider}"
86                                      sourceVar="currentRow">
87                                      <webuijsf:tableColumn headerText="First name"
88                                          id="firstNameColumn"
89                                          sort="ADDRESSES.FIRSTNAME">
90                                          <webuijsf:staticText id="staticText1"
91                                              text="#{currentRow.value[
92                                                  'ADDRESSES.FIRSTNAME']}"/>
93                                      </webuijsf:tableColumn>
94                                      <webuijsf:tableColumn headerText="Last name"
95                                          id="lastNameColumn" sort="ADDRESSES.LASTNAME">
96                                          <webuijsf:staticText id="staticText2"
```

Fig. 22.13 | AddressBook JSP with an **AutoComplete Text Field** component. (Part 2 of 4.)

```
 97                                text="#{currentRow.value[
 98                                  'ADDRESSES.LASTNAME']}"/>
 99                       </webuijsf:tableColumn>
100                       <webuijsf:tableColumn headerText="Street"
101                          id="streetColumn" sort="ADDRESSES.STREET">
102                          <webuijsf:staticText id="staticText3"
103                             text="#{currentRow.value[
104                               'ADDRESSES.STREET']}"/>
105                       </webuijsf:tableColumn>
106                       <webuijsf:tableColumn headerText="City"
107                          id="cityColumn" sort="ADDRESSES.CITY">
108                          <webuijsf:staticText id="staticText4"
109                            text="#{currentRow.value[
110                               'ADDRESSES.CITY']}"/>
111                       </webuijsf:tableColumn>
112                       <webuijsf:tableColumn headerText="State"
113                          id="stateColumn" sort="ADDRESSES.STATE">
114                          <webuijsf:staticText id="staticText5"
115                            text="#{currentRow.value[
116                               'ADDRESSES.STATE']}"/>
117                       </webuijsf:tableColumn>
118                       <webuijsf:tableColumn headerText="zip"
119                          id="zipColumn" sort="ADDRESSES.ZIP">
120                          <webuijsf:staticText id="staticText6"
121                             text="#{currentRow.value[
122                               'ADDRESSES.ZIP']}"/>
123                       </webuijsf:tableColumn>
124                    </webuijsf:tableRowGroup>
125                 </webuijsf:table>
126                 <webuijsf:messageGroup id="messageGroup1"
127                    showGlobalOnly="true"
128                    style="left: 264px; top: 72px; position: absolute"/>
129                 <webuijsf:staticText id="searchText"
130                    style="font-size: 18px; left: 24px; top: 516px;
131                       position: absolute"
132                    text="Search the address book by last name:"/>
133                 <webuijsf:label for="lastNameSearchTextField"
134                    id="lastNameSearchLabel"
135                    style="left: 24px; top: 552px; position: absolute"
136                    text="Last name:"/>
137                 <webuijsf:textField autoComplete="true"
138                    autoCompleteExpression="#{SessionBean1.getOptions}"
139                    binding="#{AddressBook.lastNameSearchTextField}"
140                    id="lastNameSearchTextField" required="true"
141                    style="left: 120px; top: 552px; position: absolute"/>
142                 <webuijsf:button
143                    actionExpression="#{AddressBook.searchButton_action}"
144                    id="searchButton" style="left: 263px; top: 552px;
145                       position: absolute; width: 38px" text="Find"/>
146                 <webuijsf:textArea
147                    binding="#{AddressBook.searchTextArea}" columns="50"
148                    id="searchTextArea" rows="4" style="left: 336px;
149                       top: 552px; position: absolute; z-index: 500"/>
```

Fig. 22.13 | AddressBook JSP with an **AutoComplete Text Field** component. (Part 3 of 4.)

```
150                      </webuijsf:form>
151                    </webuijsf:body>
152                  </webuijsf:html>
153                </webuijsf:page>
154            </f:view>
155  </jsp:root>
```

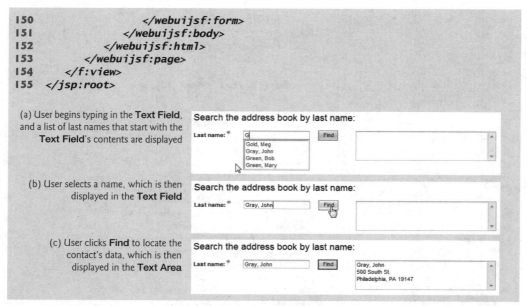

(a) User begins typing in the **Text Field**, and a list of last names that start with the **Text Field**'s contents are displayed

(b) User selects a name, which is then displayed in the **Text Field**

(c) User clicks **Find** to locate the contact's data, which is then displayed in the **Text Area**

Fig. 22.13 | AddressBook JSP with an **AutoComplete Text Field** component. (Part 4 of 4.)

22.4.3 Providing Suggestions for an Autocomplete Text Field

Figure 22.14 displays the application's session bean file. It includes the **getOptions** method, which provides the suggestions for the autocomplete **Text Field**. Much of the code in this file is identical to Fig. 22.7, so we discuss only the new features here.

```
 1   // Fig. 22.14: SessionBean1.java
 2   // Session bean initializes the data source for the AddressBook
 3   // database and provides Options for the autocomplete capability.
 4   package addressbook;
 5
 6   import com.sun.data.provider.impl.CachedRowSetDataProvider;
 7   import com.sun.rave.web.ui.appbase.AbstractSessionBean;
 8   import com.sun.sql.rowset.CachedRowSetXImpl;
 9   import com.sun.webui.jsf.model.AutoComplete;
10   import javax.faces.FacesException;
11   import com.sun.webui.jsf.model.Option;
12   import java.util.ArrayList;
13
14   public class SessionBean1 extends AbstractSessionBean
15       implements AutoComplete
16   {
17       // To save space, we omitted the code in lines 17-94. The complete
18       // source code is provided with this chapter's examples.
19
```

Fig. 22.14 | Session bean initializes the data source for the AddressBook database and provides Options for the autocomplete capability. (Part 1 of 3.)

```
95      // search for last names that match the specified filter string
96      public Option[] getOptions( String filter )
97      {
98          // create ArrayList to store matching names as Options
99          ArrayList< Option > list = new ArrayList< Option >();
100
101         // get AddressBook page bean's addressesDataProvider
102         AddressBook addressBook = (AddressBook) getBean( "AddressBook" );
103         CachedRowSetDataProvider addressesDataProvider =
104            addressBook.getAddressesDataProvider();
105
106         try
107         {
108            // move to first row in database
109            boolean hasNext = addressesDataProvider.cursorFirst();
110
111            // while there are records
112            while ( hasNext )
113            {
114               // get a name from the database
115               String name =
116                  (String) addressesDataProvider.getValue(
117                  "ADDRESSES.LASTNAME" ) + ", " +
118                  (String) addressesDataProvider.getValue(
119                  "ADDRESSES.FIRSTNAME" );
120
121               // if the name in the database starts with the prefix,
122               // add it to the list of suggestions
123               if ( name.toLowerCase().startsWith( filter.toLowerCase() ) )
124               {
125                  list.add( new Option( name, name ) );
126               } // end if
127               else
128               {
129                  // terminate the loop if the filter prefix is
130                  // alphabetically less than the remaining names
131                  if ( filter.compareTo( name ) < 0 )
132                  {
133                     break;
134                  } // end if
135               } // end else
136
137               // move cursor to next row of database
138               hasNext = addressesDataProvider.cursorNext();
139            } // end while
140         } // end try
141         catch ( Exception ex )
142         {
143            list.add( new Option( "Exception",
144               "Exception getting matching names." ) );
145         } // end catch
```

Fig. 22.14 | Session bean initializes the data source for the AddressBook database and provides Options for the autocomplete capability. (Part 2 of 3.)

```
146
147        return list.toArray( new Option[ list.size() ] ); // return Options
148    } // end method getOptions
149 } // end class SessionBean1
```

Fig. 22.14 | Session bean initializes the data source for the AddressBook database and provides Options for the autocomplete capability. (Part 3 of 3.)

Method getOptions (lines 96–148) is invoked after every keystroke in the autocomplete **Text Field** to update the list of suggestions based on what the user typed. The class in which you define getOptions must implement the interface AutoComplete (package com.sun.webui.jsf.model), which declares a getOptions method that receives a string (filter) containing the text the user has entered and returns an array of Options (package com.sun.webui.jsf.model) to be displayed by an autocomplete **Text Field**. The method iterates through the addressesDataProvider, retrieves the name from each row, checks whether the name begins with the letters typed so far and, if so, adds the name to list (an ArrayList of Options created at line 99). Lines 102–104 get the AddressBook bean and use it to obtain the addressesDataProvider. Line 109 sets the cursor to the first row in the data provider. Line 112 determines whether there are more rows in the data provider. If so, lines 115–119 retrieve the last and first names from the current row and create a String in the format *last name, first name*. Line 123 compares the lowercase versions of name and filter to determine whether the name starts with the characters in filter (i.e, the characters typed so far). If so, the name is a match and line 125 adds it to list.

Recall that the data provider wraps a CachedRowSet object that contains a SQL query which returns the rows in the database sorted by last name, then first name. This allows us to stop iterating through the data provider once we reach a row whose name comes alphabetically after the text entered by the user—names in the rows beyond this will all be alphabetically greater and thus are not potential matches. If the name does not match the text entered so far, line 131 tests whether the current name is alphabetically greater than the filter. If so, line 133 terminates the loop.

Performance Tip 22.1

*When using database columns to provide suggestions in an autocomplete **Text Field**, sorting the columns eliminates the need to check every row in the database for potential matches. This significantly improves autocomplete performance when dealing with a large database.*

If the name is neither a match nor alphabetically greater than filter, line 138 moves the cursor to the next row in the data provider. While there are more rows, the loop checks whether the name in the next row matches the filter and should be added to list.

Lines 141–145 catch any exceptions generated while searching the database. Lines 143–144 add text to the suggestion box indicating the error to the user.

Once the loop terminates, line 147 converts the ArrayList of Options to an array of Options and returns the array. The data in the array is sent to the client web browser as the response to the initial Ajax request, then used to display a drop-down list of the matching database entries. This is handled by the Dojo JavaScript code that JSF outputs to render the **Text Field** component on the client. The user can click one of the displayed entries to select it, then press the **Find** button to display the selected contact's information. We discuss the **Find** button's event handler next.

22.4.4 Displaying the Contact's Information

Figure 22.15 displays the page bean file for the JSP in Fig. 22.13. The event-handling method searchButton_action displays the selected contact's information. Much of the code in this file is identical to Fig. 22.8, so we show only the new features here.

```java
 1    // Fig. 22.15: AddressBook.java
 2    // Page bean for adding a contact to the address book
 3    // and displaying a contact's information
 4    package addressbook;
 5
 6    import com.sun.data.provider.RowKey;
 7    import com.sun.data.provider.impl.CachedRowSetDataProvider;
 8    import com.sun.rave.web.ui.appbase.AbstractPageBean;
 9    import com.sun.webui.jsf.component.Table;
10    import com.sun.webui.jsf.component.TextArea;
11    import com.sun.webui.jsf.component.TextField;
12    import com.sun.webui.jsf.model.DefaultOptionsList;
13    import javax.faces.FacesException;
14
15    public class AddressBook extends AbstractPageBean
16    {
17       // To save space, we omitted the code in lines 17-122. The complete
18       // source code is provided with this chapter's examples.
19
123      private TextField lastNameSearchTextField = new TextField();
124
125      public TextField getLastNameSearchTextField()
126      {
127         return lastNameSearchTextField;
128      }
129
130      public void setLastNameSearchTextField( TextField tf )
131      {
132         this.lastNameSearchTextField = tf;
133      }
134
135      private TextArea searchTextArea = new TextArea();
136
137      public TextArea getSearchTextArea()
138      {
139         return searchTextArea;
140      }
141
142      public void setSearchTextArea( TextArea ta )
143      {
144         this.searchTextArea = ta;
145      }
146
147      // To save space, we omitted the code in lines 147-251. The complete
148      // source code is provided with this chapter's examples.
149
```

Fig. 22.15 | Page bean that suggests names in the AutoComplete Text Field. (Part 1 of 2.)

```
252        // locate and display the selected contact's information
253        public String searchButton_action()
254        {
255           // get selected name and split into tokens
256           String name = lastNameSearchTextField.getText().toString();
257           String[] names = name.split( ", " );
258
259           // locate the RowKey for the row in database containing this nam
260           RowKey row = addressesDataProvider.findFirst(
261              new String[] { "ADDRESSES.LASTNAME", "ADDRESSES.FIRSTNAME" },
262              new String[] { names[0], names[1] } );
263
264           // move to the row in the database
265           addressesDataProvider.setCursorRow( row );
266
267           // obtain contact information
268           String result = name + "\n" +
269              addressesDataProvider.getValue( "ADDRESSES.STREET" ) + "\n" +
270              addressesDataProvider.getValue( "ADDRESSES.CITY" ) + ", " +
271              addressesDataProvider.getValue( "ADDRESSES.STATE" ) + " " +
272              addressesDataProvider.getValue( "ADDRESSES.ZIP" ) + "\n";
273
274           searchTextArea.setText( result ); // display the contact information
275           return null;
276        } // end method searchButton_action
277     } // end class AddressBook
```

Fig. 22.15 | Page bean that suggests names in the **AutoComplete Text Field**. (Part 2 of 2.)

Lines 253–276 define method searchButton_action. Line 256 obtains the text from the lastNameSearchTextField, then line 257 parses the name into a last name and a first name. Lines 260–262 use the addressDataProvider's findFirst method to find the first entry in the database with the specified last name and first name. This method returns a RowKey that uniquely identifies that row in the database table. Line 265 moves the cursor to that row. Lines 268–272 obtain the remaining data for the contact and build a result string, which is then displayed in the **Text Area** (line 274).

22.5 Wrap-Up

In this chapter, we presented a case study on building a web application that interacts with a database and provides rich user interaction using an Ajax-enabled JSF component. We first built an AddressBook application that allowed a user to add and browse contacts. You learned how to insert user input into a Java DB database and how to display the contents of a database on a web page using a **Table** JSF component. You also learned that some of the Woodstock JSF components are Ajax enabled. We extended the AddressBook application to include an autocomplete **Text Field** component. We showed how to use a database to display suggestions as the user types in the **Text Field**. You also learned how to use virtual forms to submit subsets of a form's input components to the server for processing.

In Chapter 23, you'll learn how to create and consume Java web services. You'll use Netbeans to create web services and consume them from desktop and web applications.

JAX-WS Web Services

OBJECTIVES

In this chapter you will learn:

- What a web service is.

- How to publish and consume web services in Netbeans.

- The elements that comprise services, such as service descriptions and classes that implement web services.

- How to create client desktop and web applications that invoke web service methods.

- The important part that XML and the Simple Object Access Protocol (SOAP) play in enabling web services.

- How to use session tracking in web services to maintain client-state information.

- How to connect to databases from web services.

- How to pass objects of user-defined types to and return them from a web service.

Outline

23.1 Introduction
23.2 Java Web Services Basics
23.3 Creating, Publishing, Testing and Describing a Web Service
    23.3.1 Creating a Web Application Project and Adding a Web Service Class in Netbeans
    23.3.2 Defining the `HugeInteger` Web Service in Netbeans
    23.3.3 Publishing the `HugeInteger` Web Service from Netbeans
    23.3.4 Testing the `HugeInteger` Web Service with GlassFish Application Server's `Tester` Web Page
    23.3.5 Describing a Web Service with the Web Service Description Language (WSDL)
23.4 Consuming a Web Service
    23.4.1 Creating a Client in Netbeans to Consume the `HugeInteger` Web Service
    23.4.2 Consuming the `HugeInteger` Web Service
23.5 SOAP
23.6 Session Tracking in Web Services
    23.6.1 Creating a `Blackjack` Web Service
    23.6.2 Consuming the `Blackjack` Web Service
23.7 Consuming a Database-Driven Web Service from a Web Application
    23.7.1 Creating the `Reservation` Database
    23.7.2 Creating a Web Application to Interact with the `Reservation` Web Service
23.8 Passing an Object of a User-Defined Type to a Web Service
23.9 Wrap-Up

23.1 Introduction

This chapter introduces web services, which promote software portability and reusability in applications that operate over the Internet. A *web service* is a software component stored on one computer that can be accessed via method calls by an application (or other software component) on another computer over a network. Web services communicate using such technologies as XML and HTTP. Several Java APIs facilitate web services. In this chapter, we use the JAX-WS Java APIs, which are based on the *Simple Object Access Protocol (SOAP)*—an XML-based protocol that allows web services and clients to communicate, even if the client and the web service are written in different languages. There are other web services technologies, such as Representational State Transfer (REST), which we do not cover in this chapter. REST is a network architecture that uses the web's traditional request/response mechanisms such as GET and POST requests. In Java, the JAX-RS APIs are used to implement REST-based web services. For information on SOAP-based and REST-based web services, visit our Web Services Resource Centers:

    www.deitel.com/WebServices/
    www.deitel.com/RESTWebServices/

These Resource Centers include information on designing and implementing web services in many languages, and information about web services offered by companies such as Google, Amazon and eBay. You'll also find many additional tools for publishing and consuming web services. For more information about REST-based Java web services, check out the Jersey project:

```
jersey.dev.java.net/
```

To learn more the basics of XML, see the following tutorials:

```
www.deitel.com/articles/xml_tutorials/20060401/XMLBasics/
www.deitel.com/articles/xml_tutorials/20060401/XMLStructuringData/
```

and visit our XML Resource Center:

```
www.deitel.com/XML/
```

Business-to-Business Transactions

Web services have important implications for *business-to-business* (*B2B*) *transactions*. They enable businesses to conduct transactions via standardized, widely available web services rather than relying on proprietary applications. Web services and SOAP are platform and language independent, so companies can collaborate via web services without worrying about the compatibility of their hardware, software and communications technologies. Companies such as Amazon, Google, eBay, PayPal and many others are using web services to their advantage by making their server-side applications available to partners via web services.

By purchasing web services and using extensive free web services that are relevant to their businesses, companies can spend less time developing new applications and can create innovative new applications. E-businesses can use web services to provide their customers with enhanced shopping experiences. Consider an online music store. The store's website links to information about various CDs, enabling users to purchase the CDs, to learn about the artists, to find more titles by those artists, to find other artists' music they may enjoy, and more. Another company that sells concert tickets provides a web service that displays upcoming concert dates for various artists and allows users to buy tickets. By consuming the concert-ticket web service on its site, the online music store can provide an additional service to its customers, increase its site traffic and perhaps earn a commission on concert-ticket sales. The company that sells concert tickets also benefits from the business relationship by selling more tickets and possibly by receiving revenue from the online music store for the use of the web service.

Any Java programmer with a knowledge of web services can write applications that "consume" web services. The resulting applications would call web service methods of objects running on servers that could be thousands of miles away.

Netbeans

Netbeans is one of the many tools that enable programmers to "publish" and/or "consume" web services. We demonstrate how to use Netbeans to implement web services using the JAX-WS APIs and how to invoke them from client applications. For each example, we provide the web service's code, then present a client application that uses the web service. Our first examples build web services and client applications in Netbeans. Then we demonstrate web services that use more sophisticated features, such as manipulating databases with JDBC and manipulating class objects. For information on downloading and installing the Netbeans and the GlassFish v2 UR2 server, see Section 21.1.

23.2 Java Web Services Basics

A web service normally resides on a *server*. The application (i.e., the client) that accesses the web service sends a method call over a network to the remote machine, which processes the call and returns a response over the network to the application. This kind of distributed computing is beneficial in many applications. For example, a client application without direct access to a database on a remote server might be able to retrieve the data via a web service. Similarly, an application lacking the processing power to perform specific computations could use a web service to take advantage of another system's superior resources.

In Java, a web service is implemented as a class. In previous chapters, all the pieces of an application resided on one machine. The class that represents the web service resides on a server—it's not part of the client application.

Making a web service available to receive client requests is known as *publishing a web service*; using a web service from a client application is known as *consuming a web service*. An application that consumes a web service consists of two parts—an object of a *service endpoint interface (SEI)* class (sometimes called a *proxy class*) for interacting with the web service and a client application that consumes the web service by invoking methods on the object of the service endpoint interface. The client code invokes methods on the service endpoint interface object, which handles the details of passing method arguments to and receiving return values from the web service on the client's behalf. This communication can occur over a local network, over the Internet or even with a web service on the same computer. The web service performs the corresponding task and returns the results to the service endpoint interface object, which then returns the results to the client code. Figure 23.1 depicts the interactions among the client code, the SEI object and the web service. As you'll soon see, Netbeans creates these service endpoint interface classes for you.

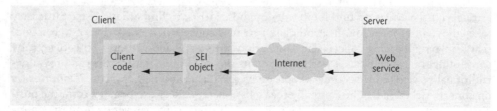

Fig. 23.1 | Interaction between a web service client and a web service.

Requests to and responses from web services created with *JAX-WS* (one of many different web service frameworks) are typically transmitted via SOAP. Any client capable of generating and processing SOAP messages can interact with a web service, regardless of the language in which the web service is written. We discuss SOAP in Section 23.5.

23.3 Creating, Publishing, Testing and Describing a Web Service

The following subsections demonstrate how to create, publish and test a HugeInteger web service that performs calculations with positive integers up to 100 digits long (maintained as arrays of digits). Such integers are much larger than Java's integral primitive types can represent (though the Java API does provide class BigInteger for arbitrary precision integers). The HugeInteger web service provides methods that take two "huge integers" (represented as Strings) and determine their sum, their difference, which is larger, which is smaller, or whether the two numbers are equal. These methods will be services available to other applications via the web—hence the term web services.

23.3.1 Creating a Web Application Project and Adding a Web Service Class in Netbeans

When you create a web service in Netbeans, you focus on the web service's logic and let the IDE handle the web service's infrastructure. To create a web service in Netbeans, you first create a **Web Application** project. Netbeans uses this project type for web services that are invoked by other applications.

Creating a Web Application Project in Netbeans
To create a web application, perform the following steps:

1. Select **File > New Project** to open the **New Web Application** dialog.

2. Select **Java Web** from the dialog's **Categories** list, then select **Web Application** from the **Projects** list. Click **Next >**.

3. Specify the name of your project (HugeInteger) in the **Project Name** field and specify where you'd like to store the project in the **Project Location** field. You can click the **Browse** button to select the location. Click **Next >**.

4. Select **GlassFish v2** from the **Server** drop-down list and **Java EE 5** from the **Java EE Version** drop-down list.

5. Click **Finish** to dismiss the **New Web Application** dialog.

This creates a web application that will run in a web browser, similar to the projects used in Chapters 21 and 22.

Adding a Web Service Class to a Web Application Project
Perform the following steps to add a web service class to the project:

1. In the **Projects** tab in Netbeans, right click the **HugeInteger** project's node and select **New > Web Service...** to open the **New Web Service** dialog.

2. Specify HugeInteger in the **Web Service Name** field.

3. Specify com.deitel.java.hugeinteger in the **Package** field.

4. Click **Finish** to dismiss the **New Web Service** dialog.

The IDE generates a sample web service class with the name you specified in *Step 2*. You can find this class in the **Projects** tab under the project's **Web Services** node. In this class, you'll define the methods that your web service makes available to client applications. When you eventually build your application, the IDE will generate other supporting files (which we'll discuss shortly) for your web service.

23.3.2 Defining the HugeInteger Web Service in Netbeans

Figure 23.2 contains the HugeInteger web service's code. You can implement this code yourself in the HugeInteger.java file created in Section 23.3.1, or you can simply replace the code in HugeInteger.java with a copy of our code from this example's folder. You can find this file in the project's `src\java\com\deitel\java\hugeinteger` folder. The book's examples can be downloaded from www.deitel.com/books/javafp/.

```java
1   // Fig. 23.2: HugeInteger.java
2   // HugeInteger web service that performs operations on large integers.
3   package com.deitel.java.hugeinteger;
4
5   import javax.jws.WebService; // program uses the annotation @WebService
6   import javax.jws.WebMethod; // program uses the annotation @WebMethod
7   import javax.jws.WebParam; // program uses the annotation @WebParam
8
9   @WebService( // annotates the class as a web service
10     name = "HugeInteger", // sets service endpoint interface name
11     serviceName = "HugeIntegerService" ) // sets the service name
12  public class HugeInteger
13  {
14     private final static int MAXIMUM = 100; // maximum number of digits
15     public int[] number = new int[ MAXIMUM ]; // stores the huge integer
16
17     // returns a String representation of a HugeInteger
18     public String toString()
19     {
20        String value = "";
21
22        // convert HugeInteger to a String
23        for ( int digit : number )
24           value = digit + value; // places next digit at beginning of value
25
26        // locate position of first nonzero digit
27        int length = value.length();
28        int position = -1;
29
30        for ( int i = 0; i < length; i++ )
31        {
32           if ( value.charAt( i ) != '0' )
33           {
34              position = i; // first nonzero digit
35              break;
36           }
37        } // end for
38
39        return ( position != -1 ? value.substring( position ) : "0" );
40     } // end method toString
41
42     // creates a HugeInteger from a String
43     public static HugeInteger parseHugeInteger( String s )
44     {
45        HugeInteger temp = new HugeInteger();
46        int size = s.length();
47
48        for ( int i = 0; i < size; i++ )
49           temp.number[ i ] = s.charAt( size - i - 1 ) - '0';
```

Fig. 23.2 | HugeInteger web service that performs operations on large integers. (Part 1 of 3.)

```
50
51        return temp;
52     } // end method parseHugeInteger
53
54     // WebMethod that adds huge integers represented by String arguments
55     @WebMethod( operationName = "add" )
56     public String add( @WebParam( name = "first" ) String first,
57        @WebParam( name = "second" ) String second )
58     {
59        int carry = 0; // the value to be carried
60        HugeInteger operand1 = HugeInteger.parseHugeInteger( first );
61        HugeInteger operand2 = HugeInteger.parseHugeInteger( second );
62        HugeInteger result = new HugeInteger(); // stores addition result
63
64        // perform addition on each digit
65        for ( int i = 0; i < MAXIMUM; i++ )
66        {
67           // add corresponding digits in each number and the carried value;
68           // store result in the corresponding column of HugeInteger result
69           result.number[ i ] =
70              ( operand1.number[ i ] + operand2.number[ i ] + carry ) % 10;
71
72           // set carry for next column
73           carry =
74              ( operand1.number[ i ] + operand2.number[ i ] + carry ) / 10;
75        } // end for
76
77        return result.toString();
78     } // end WebMethod add
79
80     // WebMethod that subtracts integers represented by String arguments
81     @WebMethod( operationName = "subtract" )
82     public String subtract( @WebParam( name = "first" ) String first,
83        @WebParam( name = "second" ) String second )
84     {
85        HugeInteger operand1 = HugeInteger.parseHugeInteger( first );
86        HugeInteger operand2 = HugeInteger.parseHugeInteger( second );
87        HugeInteger result = new HugeInteger(); // stores difference
88
89        // subtract bottom digit from top digit
90        for ( int i = 0; i < MAXIMUM; i++ )
91        {
92           // if the digit in operand1 is smaller than the corresponding
93           // digit in operand2, borrow from the next digit
94           if ( operand1:number[ i ] < operand2.number[ i ] )
95              operand1.borrow( i );
96
97           // subtract digits
98           result.number[ i ] = operand1.number[ i ] - operand2.number[ i ];
99        } // end for
100
101        return result.toString();
102     } // end WebMethod subtract
```

Fig. 23.2 | HugeInteger web service that performs operations on large integers. (Part 2 of 3.)

```
103
104      // borrow 1 from next digit
105      private void borrow( int place )
106      {
107          if ( place >= MAXIMUM )
108              throw new IndexOutOfBoundsException();
109          else if ( number[ place + 1 ] == 0 ) // if next digit is zero
110              borrow( place + 1 ); // borrow from next digit
111
112          number[ place ] += 10; // add 10 to the borrowing digit
113          --number[ place + 1 ]; // subtract one from the digit to the left
114      } // end method borrow
115
116      // WebMethod that returns true if first integer is greater than second
117      @WebMethod( operationName = "bigger" )
118      public boolean bigger( @WebParam( name = "first" ) String first,
119          @WebParam( name = "second" ) String second )
120      {
121          try // try subtracting first from second
122          {
123              String difference = subtract( first, second );
124              return !difference.matches( "^[0]+$" );
125          } // end try
126          catch ( IndexOutOfBoundsException e ) // first is less than second
127          {
128              return false;
129          } // end catch
130      } // end WebMethod bigger
131
132      // WebMethod that returns true if the first integer is less than second
133      @WebMethod( operationName = "smaller" )
134      public boolean smaller( @WebParam( name = "first" ) String first,
135          @WebParam( name = "second" ) String second )
136      {
137          return bigger( second, first );
138      } // end WebMethod smaller
139
140      // WebMethod that returns true if the first integer equals the second
141      @WebMethod( operationName = "equals" )
142      public boolean equals( @WebParam( name = "first" ) String first,
143          @WebParam( name = "second" ) String second )
144      {
145          return !( bigger( first, second ) || smaller( first, second ) );
146      } // end WebMethod equals
147  } // end class HugeInteger
```

Fig. 23.2 | `HugeInteger` web service that performs operations on large integers. (Part 3 of 3.)

Lines 5–7 import the annotations used in this example. By default, each new web service class created with the JAX-WS APIs is a *POJO (plain old Java object)*, meaning that—unlike prior web services APIs—you do not need to extend a class or implement an interface to create a web service. When you deploy a web application containing a class that uses the @WebService annotation, the server (GlassFish in our case) recognizes that the class implements a web service and creates all the *server-side artifacts* that support the web service—that is, the framework that allows the web service to wait for client requests and respond to those requests once the service is deployed on an application server. Popular application servers that support Java web services include GlassFish (glassfish.dev.java.net), Apache Tomcat (tomcat.apache.org), BEA Weblogic Server (www.bea.com) and JBoss Application Server (www.jboss.org/products/jbossas). We use GlassFish in this chapter.

Lines 9–11 contain a @WebService annotation (imported at line 5) with properties name and serviceName. The *@WebService annotation* indicates that class HugeInteger implements a web service. The annotation is followed by a set of parentheses containing optional annotation attributes. The annotation's *name attribute* (line 10) specifies the name of the service endpoint interface class that will be generated for the client. The annotation's *serviceName attribute* (line 11) specifies the service name, which is also the name of the class that the client uses to obtain a service endpoint interface object. If the serviceName attribute is not specified, the web service's name is assumed to be the java class name followed by the word Service. Netbeans places the @WebService annotation at the beginning of each new web service class you create. You can then add the name and serviceName properties in the parentheses following the annotation.

Line 14 declares the constant MAXIMUM that specifies the maximum number of digits for a HugeInteger (i.e., 100 in this example). Line 15 creates the array that stores the digits in a huge integer. Lines 18–40 declare method toString, which returns a String representation of a HugeInteger without any leading 0s. Lines 43–52 declare static method parseHugeInteger, which converts a String into a HugeInteger. The web service's methods add, subtract, bigger, smaller and equals use parseHugeInteger to convert their String arguments to HugeIntegers for processing.

HugeInteger methods add, subtract, bigger, smaller and equals are tagged with the *@WebMethod annotation* (lines 55, 81, 117, 133 and 141) to indicate that they can be called remotely. Any methods that are not tagged with @WebMethod are not accessible to clients that consume the web service. Such methods are typically utility methods within the web service class. Note that the @WebMethod annotations each use the *operationName* attribute to specify the method name that is exposed to the web service's client. If the operationName is not specified, it is set to the actual Java method's name.

Common Programming Error 23.1

Failing to expose a method as a web method by declaring it with the @WebMethod annotation prevents clients of the web service from accessing the method. There is one exception—if none of the class's methods are declared with the @WebMethod annotation, then all the public methods of the class will be exposed as web methods.

Common Programming Error 23.2

Methods with the @WebMethod annotation cannot be static. An object of the web service class must exist for a client to access the service's web methods.

Each web method in class HugeInteger specifies parameters that are annotated with the *@WebParam annotation* (e.g., lines 56–57 of method add). The optional @WebParam attribute *name* indicates the parameter name that is exposed to the web service's clients.

Lines 55–78 and 81–102 declare `HugeInteger` web methods `add` and `subtract`. We assume for simplicity that `add` does not result in overflow (i.e., the result will be 100 digits or fewer) and that `subtract`'s first argument will always be larger than the second. The `subtract` method calls method `borrow` (lines 105–114) when it is necessary to borrow 1 from the next digit to the left in the first argument—that is, when a particular digit in the left operand is smaller than the corresponding digit in the right operand. Method `borrow` adds 10 to the appropriate digit and subtracts 1 from the next digit to the left. This utility method is not intended to be called remotely, so it is not tagged with `@WebMethod`.

Lines 117–130 declare `HugeInteger` web method `bigger`. Line 123 invokes method `subtract` to calculate the difference between the numbers. If the first number is less than the second, this results in an exception. In this case, `bigger` returns `false`. If `subtract` does not throw an exception, then line 124 returns the result of the expression

```
!difference.matches( "^[0]+$" )
```

This expression calls `String` method `matches` to determine whether the `String` difference matches the regular expression `"^[0]+$"`, which determines whether the `String` consists only of one or more 0s. The symbols ^ and $ indicate that `matches` should return `true` only if the entire `String` difference matches the regular expression. We then use the logical negation operator (!) to return the opposite `boolean` value. Thus, if the numbers are equal (i.e., their difference is 0), the preceding expression returns `false`—the first number is not greater than the second. Otherwise, the expression returns `true`.

Lines 133–146 declare methods `smaller` and `equals`. Method `smaller` returns the result of invoking method `bigger` (line 137) with the arguments reversed—if `first` is less than `second`, then `second` is greater than `first`. Method `equals` invokes methods `bigger` and `smaller` (line 145). If either `bigger` or `smaller` returns `true`, line 145 returns `false`, because the numbers are not equal. If both methods return `false`, the numbers are equal and line 145 returns `true`.

23.3.3 Publishing the HugeInteger Web Service from Netbeans

Now that we've created the `HugeInteger` web service class, we'll use Netbeans to build and publish (i.e., deploy) the web service so that clients can consume its services. Netbeans handles all the details of building and deploying a web service for you. This includes creating the framework required to support the web service. Right click the project name (`HugeInteger`) in the Netbeans **Projects** tab to display the popup menu shown in Fig. 23.3. To determine if there are any compilation errors in your project, select the **Build** option. When the project compiles successfully, you can select **Deploy** to deploy the project to the server you selected when you set up the web application in Section 23.3.1. If the code in the project has changed since the last build, selecting **Deploy** also builds the project. Selecting **Run** executes the web application. If the web application was not previously built or deployed, this option performs these tasks first. Note that both the **Deploy** and **Run** options also start the application server (in our case GlassFish) if it is not already running. To ensure that all source-code files in a project are recompiled during the next build operation, you can use the **Clean** or **Clean and Build** options. If you have not already done so, select **Deploy** now. [*Note:* You can also publish a web service using a standard Java SE 6 application. For more information, see the article `today.java.net/pub/a/today/2007/07/03/jax-ws-web-services-without-ee-containers.html`.]

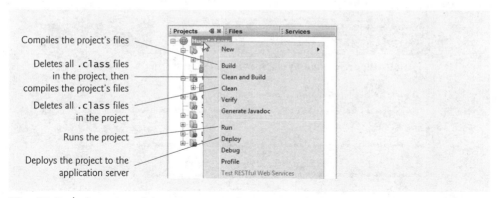

Compiles the project's files

Deletes all .class files in the project, then compiles the project's files

Deletes all .class files in the project

Runs the project

Deploys the project to the application server

Fig. 23.3 | A portion of the popup menu that appears when you right click a project name in the Netbeans **Projects** tab.

23.3.4 Testing the HugeInteger Web Service with GlassFish Application Server's Tester Web Page

The next step is to test the HugeInteger web service. We previously selected the GlassFish application server to execute this web application. This server can dynamically create a web page for testing a web service's methods from a web browser. To enable this capability:

1. Right click the project name (HugeInteger) in the Netbeans **Projects** tab and select **Properties** from the popup menu to display the **Project Properties** dialog.

2. Click **Run** under **Categories** to display the options for running the project.

3. In the **Relative URL** field, type /HugeIntegerService?Tester.

4. Click **OK** to dismiss the **Project Properties** dialog.

The **Relative URL** field specifies what should happen when the web application executes. If this field is empty, then the web application's default JSP displays when you run the project. When you specify /HugeIntegerService?Tester in this field, then run the project, the GlassFish application server builds the Tester web page and loads it into your web browser. Figure 23.4 shows the Tester web page for the HugeInteger web service.

You can also display the Tester web page by expanding the project's **Web Services** folder in the **Projects** window, right clicking the **HugeInteger** node in that folder and selecting **Test Web Service**.

Once you've deployed the web service, you can also type the URL

```
http://localhost:8080/HugeInteger/HugeIntegerService?Tester
```

in your web browser to view the Tester web page. Note that HugeIntegerService is the name (specified in line 11 of Fig. 23.2) that clients, including the Tester web page, use to access the web service.

To test HugeInteger's web methods, type two positive integers into the text fields to the right of a particular method's button, then click the button to invoke the web method and see the result. Figure 23.5 shows the results of invoking HugeInteger's add method with the values 99999999999999999 and 1. Note that the number 99999999999999999 is larger than primitive type long can represent.

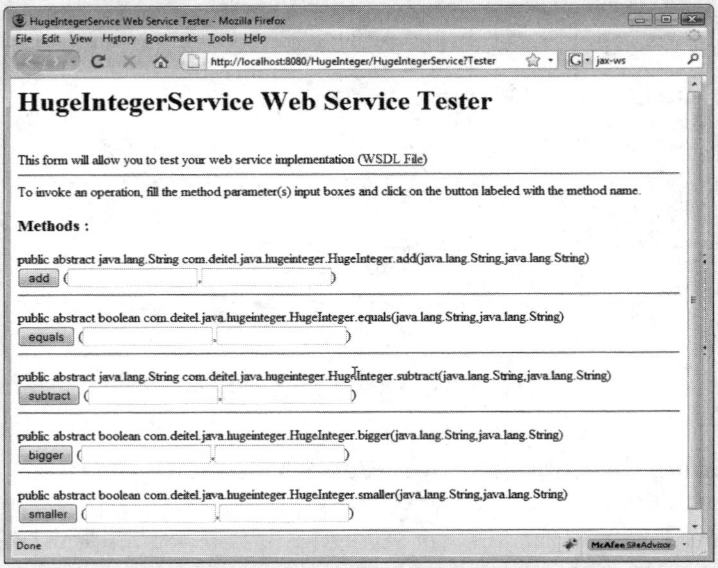

Fig. 23.4 | Tester web page created by GlassFish for the HugeInteger web service.

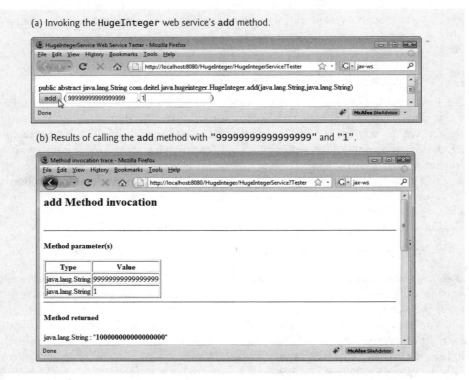

(a) Invoking the HugeInteger web service's add method.

(b) Results of calling the add method with "99999999999999999" and "1".

Fig. 23.5 | Testing HugeInteger's add method.

Note that you can access the web service only when the application server is running. If Netbeans launches the application server for you, it will automatically shut it down when you close Netbeans. To keep the application server up and running, you can launch it independently of Netbeans before you deploy or run web applications in Netbeans. See the GlassFish Quick Start Guide at `glassfish.dev.java.net/downloads/quickstart/index.html` for information on starting and stopping the server manually.

Testing the HugeInteger Web Service from Another Computer

If your computer is connected to a network and allows HTTP requests, then you can test the web service from another computer on the network by typing the following URL (where *host* is the hostname or IP address of the computer on which the web service is deployed) into a browser on another computer:

```
http://host:8080/HugeInteger/HugeIntegerService?Tester
```

Note to Windows XP and Windows Vista Users

For security reasons, computers running Windows XP or Windows Vista do not allow HTTP requests from other computers by default. To allow other computers to connect to your computer using HTTP, perform the following steps on Windows XP:

1. Select **Start > Control Panel** to open your system's **Control Panel** window, then double click **Windows Firewall** to view the **Windows Firewall** settings dialog.

2. In the **Windows Firewall** dialog, click the **Exceptions** tab, then click **Add Port...** and add port 8080 with the name GlassFish.

3. Click **OK** to dismiss the **Windows Firewall** settings dialog.

To allow other computers to connect to your Windows Vista computer using HTTP, perform the following steps:

1. Open the **Control Panel**, switch to **Classic View** and double click **Windows Firewall** to open the **Windows Firewall** dialog.

2. In the **Windows Firewall** dialog click the **Change Settings...** link.

3. In the **Windows Firewall** dialog, click the **Exceptions** tab, then click **Add Port...** and add port 8080 with the name GlassFish.

4. Click **OK** to dismiss the **Windows Firewall** settings dialog.

You may also be asked to unblock `java.exe` the first time you run the GlassFish server.

23.3.5 Describing a Web Service with the Web Service Description Language (WSDL)

Once you implement a web service and deploy it on an application server, a client application can consume the web service. To do so, however, the client must know where to find the web service and must be provided with a description of how to interact with it—that is, what methods are available, what parameters they expect and what each method returns. For this, JAX-WS uses the *Web Service Description Language (WSDL)*—a standard XML vocabulary for describing web services in a platform-independent manner.

You do not need to understand WSDL to take advantage of it—the GlassFish application server generates a web service's WSDL dynamically for you, and client tools can parse the WSDL to help create the client-side service endpoint interface class that a client uses to access the web service. Since the WSDL is created dynamically, clients always receive a deployed web service's most up-to-date description. To view the WSDL for the HugeInteger web service (Fig. 23.6), enter the following URL in your browser:

```
http://localhost:8080/HugeInteger/HugeIntegerService?WSDL
```

or click the **WSDL File** link in the Tester web page (shown in Fig. 23.4).

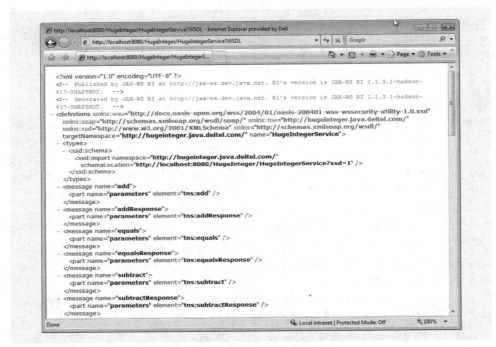

Fig. 23.6 | A portion of the .wsdl file for the HugeInteger web service.

Accessing the HugeInteger Web Service's WSDL from Another Computer

Eventually, you'll want clients on other computers to use your web service. Such clients need access to the web service's WSDL, which they would access with the following URL:

```
http://host:8080/HugeInteger/HugeIntegerService?WSDL
```

where *host* is the hostname or IP address of the computer on which the web service is deployed. As we discussed in Section 23.3.4, this will work only if your computer allows HTTP connections from other computers—as is the case for publicly accessible web and application servers.

23.4 Consuming a Web Service

Now that we've defined and deployed our web service, we can consume it from a client application. A web service client can be any type of application or even another web service. You enable a client application to consume a web service by *adding a web service reference* to the application. This process defines the service endpoint interface class that allows the client to access the web service.

23.4.1 Creating a Client in Netbeans to Consume the HugeInteger Web Service

In this section, you'll use Netbeans to create a client Java desktop GUI application, then you'll add a web service reference to the project so the client can access the web service. When you add the web service reference, the IDE creates and compiles the *client-side artifacts*—the framework of Java code that supports the client-side service endpoint interface class. The client then calls methods on an object of the service endpoint interface class, which uses the rest of the artifacts to interact with the web service.

Creating a Desktop Application Project in Netbeans
Before performing the steps in this section, ensure that the HugeInteger web service has been deployed and that the GlassFish application server is running (see Section 23.3.3). Perform the following steps to create a client Java desktop application in Netbeans:

1. Select **File > New Project...** to open the **New Project** dialog.

2. Select **Java** from the **Categories** list and **Java Application** from the **Projects** list, then click **Next >**.

3. Specify the name UsingHugeInteger in the **Project Name** field and uncheck the **Create Main Class** checkbox. Later, you'll add a subclass of JFrame that contains a main method.

4. Click **Finish** to create the project.

Adding a Web Service Reference to an Application
Next, you'll add a web service reference to your application so that it can interact with the HugeInteger web service. To add a web service reference, perform the following steps.

1. Right click the project name (UsingHugeInteger) in the Netbeans **Projects** tab and select **New > Web Service Client...** from the popup menu to display the **New Web Service Client** dialog (Fig. 23.7).

2. In the **WSDL URL** field, specify the URL http://localhost:8080/HugeInteger/ HugeIntegerService?WSDL (Fig. 23.7). This URL tells the IDE where to find the web service's WSDL description. [*Note:* If the GlassFish application server is located on a different computer, replace localhost with the hostname or IP address of that computer.] The IDE uses this WSDL description to generate the client-side artifacts that compose and support the service endpoint interface. Note that the **New Web Service Client** dialog enables you to search for web services in several locations. Many companies simply distribute the exact WSDL URLs for their web services, which you can place in the **WSDL URL** field.

3. Click **Finish** to create the web service reference and dismiss the **New Web Service Client** dialog.

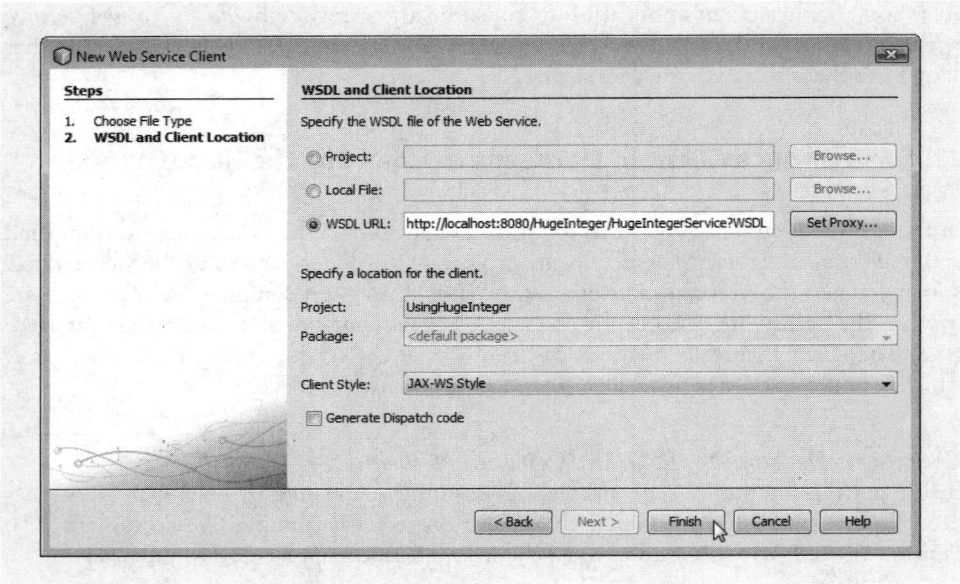

Fig. 23.7 | **New Web Service Client** dialog.

In the Netbeans **Projects** tab, the UsingHugeInteger project now contains a **Web Service References** folder with the HugeInteger web service's service endpoint interface (Fig. 23.8). Note that the service endpoint interface's name is listed as HugeIntegerService, as we specified in line 11 of Fig. 23.2.

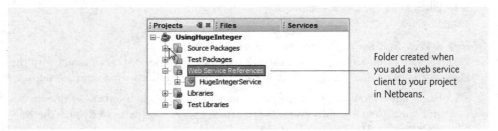

Fig. 23.8 | Netbeans **Project** tab after adding a web service reference to the project.

When you specify the web service you want to consume, Netbeans accesses the web service's WSDL information and copies it into a file in your project (named HugeInteger-Service.wsdl in this example). You can view this file by double clicking the HugeIntegerService node in the project's **Web Service References** folder or from the **Files** tab by expanding the nodes in the UsingHugeInteger project's xml-resources folder (Fig. 23.9). If the web service changes, the client-side artifacts and the client's copy of the WSDL file can be regenerated by right clicking the HugeIntegerService node shown in Fig. 23.8 and selecting **Refresh Client**.

You can view the IDE-generated client-side artifacts by selecting the Netbeans **Files** tab and expanding the UsingHugeInteger project's **build** folder as shown in Fig. 23.10.

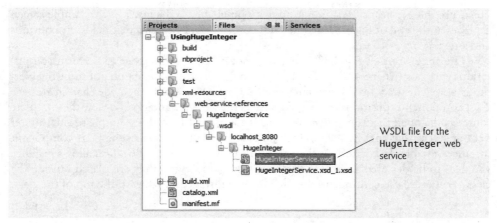

Fig. 23.9 | Locating the `HugeIntegerService.wsdl` file in the Netbeans **Files** tab.

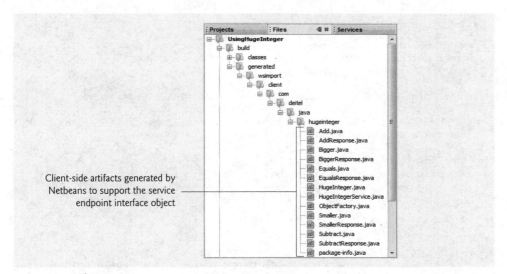

Fig. 23.10 | Viewing the `HugeInteger` web service's client-side artifacts generated by Netbeans.

23.4.2 Consuming the HugeInteger Web Service

For this example, we use a GUI application to interact with the `HugeInteger` web service. To build the client application's GUI, you must first add a subclass of `JFrame` to the project. To do so, perform the following steps:

1. Right click the project name in the Netbeans **Project** tab and select **New > JFrame Form...** to display the **New JFrame Form** dialog.

2. Specify `UsingHugeIntegerJFrame` in the **Class Name** field.

3. Specify `com.deitel.java.hugeintegerclient` in the **Package** field.

4. Click **Finish** to close the **New JFrame Form** dialog.

Next, use the Netbeans GUI design tools to build the GUI shown in the sample screen captures at the end of Fig. 23.11. The GUI consists of a label, two text fields, five buttons and a text area.

The application in Fig. 23.11 uses the HugeInteger web service to perform computations with positive integers up to 100 digits long. To save space, we do not show the Netbeans autogenerated initComponents method, which contains the code that creates the GUI components, positions them and registers their event handlers. To view the complete source code, open the UsingHugeIntegerJFrame.java file in this example's folder under src\java\com\deitel\java\hugeintegerclient. Netbeans places the GUI component instance-variable declarations at the end of the class (lines 317–326). Java allows instance variables to be declared anywhere in a class's body as long as they are placed outside the class's methods. We continue to declare our own instance variables at the top of the class.

```
 1    // Fig. 23.11: UsingHugeIntegerJFrame.java
 2    // Client desktop application for the HugeInteger web service.
 3    package com.deitel.java.hugeintegerclient;
 4
 5    import com.deitel.java.hugeinteger.HugeInteger;
 6    import com.deitel.java.hugeinteger.HugeIntegerService;
 7    import javax.swing.JOptionPane;
 8
 9    public class UsingHugeIntegerJFrame extends javax.swing.JFrame
10    {
11       // references the service endpoint interface object (i.e., the proxy)
12       private HugeInteger hugeIntegerProxy;
13
14       // no-argument constructor
15       public UsingHugeIntegerJFrame()
16       {
17          initComponents();
18
19          try
20          {
21             // create the objects for accessing the HugeInteger web service
22             HugeIntegerService hugeIntegerService = new HugeIntegerService();
23             hugeIntegerProxy = hugeIntegerService.getHugeIntegerPort();
24          } // end try
25          catch ( Exception exception )
26          {
27             exception.printStackTrace();
28             System.exit( 1 );
29          } // end catch
30       } // end UsingHugeIntegerJFrame constructor
31
32       // The initComponents method is autogenerated by Netbeans and is called
33       // from the constructor to initialize the GUI. This method is not shown
34       // here to save space. Open UsingHugeIntegerJFrame.java in this
35       // example's folder to view the complete generated code.
36
```

Fig. 23.11 | Client desktop application for the HugeInteger web service. (Part 1 of 6.)

```
145    // invokes HugeInteger web service's add method to add HugeIntegers
146    private void addJButtonActionPerformed(
147       java.awt.event.ActionEvent evt )
148    {
149       String firstNumber = firstJTextField.getText();
150       String secondNumber = secondJTextField.getText();
151
152       if ( isValid( firstNumber ) && isValid( secondNumber ) )
153       {
154          try
155          {
156             resultsJTextArea.setText(
157                hugeIntegerProxy.add( firstNumber, secondNumber ) );
158          } // end try
159          catch ( Exception e )
160          {
161             JOptionPane.showMessageDialog( this, e.toString(),
162                "Add method failed", JOptionPane.ERROR_MESSAGE );
163             e.printStackTrace();
164          } // end catch
165       } // end if
166    }
167
168    // invokes HugeInteger web service's subtract method to subtract the
169    // second HugeInteger from the first
170    private void subtractJButtonActionPerformed(
171       java.awt.event.ActionEvent evt )
172    {
173       String firstNumber = firstJTextField.getText();
174       String secondNumber = secondJTextField.getText();
175
176       if ( isValid( firstNumber ) && isValid( secondNumber ) )
177       {
178          try
179          {
180             resultsJTextArea.setText(
181                hugeIntegerProxy.subtract( firstNumber, secondNumber ) );
182          } // end try
183          catch ( Exception e )
184          {
185             JOptionPane.showMessageDialog( this, e.toString(),
186                "Subtract method failed", JOptionPane.ERROR_MESSAGE );
187             e.printStackTrace();
188          } // end catch
189       } // end if
190    }
191
192    // invokes HugeInteger web service's bigger method to determine whether
193    // the first HugeInteger is greater than the second
194    private void greaterThanJButtonActionPerformed(
195       java.awt.event.ActionEvent evt )
196    {
197       String firstNumber = firstJTextField.getText();
```

Fig. 23.11 | Client desktop application for the HugeInteger web service. (Part 2 of 6.)

```
198            String secondNumber = secondJTextField.getText();
199
200            if ( isValid( firstNumber ) && isValid( secondNumber ) )
201            {
202               try
203               {
204                  boolean result =
205                     hugeIntegerProxy.bigger( firstNumber, secondNumber );
206                  resultsJTextArea.setText( String.format( "%s %s %s %s",
207                     firstNumber, ( result ? "is" : "is not" ), "greater than",
208                     secondNumber ) );
209               } // end try
210               catch ( Exception e )
211               {
212                  JOptionPane.showMessageDialog( this, e.toString(),
213                     "Bigger method failed", JOptionPane.ERROR_MESSAGE );
214                  e.printStackTrace();
215               } // end catch
216            } // end if
217         }
218
219         // invokes HugeInteger web service's smaller method to determine
220         // whether the first HugeInteger is less than the second
221         private void lessThanJButtonActionPerformed(
222            java.awt.event.ActionEvent evt )
223         {
224            String firstNumber = firstJTextField.getText();
225            String secondNumber = secondJTextField.getText();
226
227            if ( isValid( firstNumber ) && isValid( secondNumber ) )
228            {
229               try
230               {
231                  boolean result =
232                     hugeIntegerProxy.smaller( firstNumber, secondNumber );
233                  resultsJTextArea.setText( String.format( "%s %s %s %s",
234                     firstNumber, ( result ? "is" : "is not" ), "less than",
235                     secondNumber ) );
236               } // end try
237               catch ( Exception e )
238               {
239                  JOptionPane.showMessageDialog( this, e.toString(),
240                     "Smaller method failed", JOptionPane.ERROR_MESSAGE );
241                  e.printStackTrace();
242               } // end catch
243            } // end if
244         }
245
246         // invokes HugeInteger web service's equals method to determine whether
247         // the first HugeInteger is equal to the second
248         private void equalsJButtonActionPerformed(
249            java.awt.event.ActionEvent evt )
250         {
```

Fig. 23.11 | Client desktop application for the HugeInteger web service. (Part 3 of 6.)

```
251         String firstNumber = firstJTextField.getText();
252         String secondNumber = secondJTextField.getText();
253
254         if ( isValid( firstNumber ) && isValid( secondNumber ) )
255         {
256            try
257            {
258               boolean result =
259                  hugeIntegerProxy.equals( firstNumber, secondNumber );
260               resultsJTextArea.setText( String.format( "%s %s %s %s",
261                  firstNumber, ( result ? "is" : "is not" ), "equal to",
262                  secondNumber ) );
263            } // end try
264            catch ( Exception e )
265            {
266               JOptionPane.showMessageDialog( this, e.toString(),
267                  "Equals method failed", JOptionPane.ERROR_MESSAGE );
268               e.printStackTrace();
269            } // end catch
270         } // end if
271      }
272
273      // checks the size of a String to ensure that it is not too big
274      // to be used as a HugeInteger; ensure only digits in String
275      private boolean isValid( String number )
276      {
277         // check String's length
278         if ( number.length() > 100 )
279         {
280            JOptionPane.showMessageDialog( this,
281               "HugeIntegers must be <= 100 digits.",
282               "HugeInteger Overflow", JOptionPane.ERROR_MESSAGE );
283            return false;
284         } // end if
285
286         // look for nondigit characters in String
287         for ( char c : number.toCharArray() )
288         {
289            if ( !Character.isDigit( c ) )
290            {
291               JOptionPane.showMessageDialog( this,
292                  "There are nondigits in the String",
293                  "HugeInteger Contains Nondigit Characters",
294                  JOptionPane.ERROR_MESSAGE );
295               return false;
296            } // end if
297         } // end for
298
299         return true; // number can be used as a HugeInteger
300      } // end method validate
301
```

Fig. 23.11 | Client desktop application for the HugeInteger web service. (Part 4 of 6.)

```
302        // main method begins execution
303        public static void main( String args[] )
304        {
305           java.awt.EventQueue.invokeLater(
306              new Runnable()
307              {
308                 public void run()
309                 {
310                    new UsingHugeIntegerJFrame().setVisible( true );
311                 } // end method run
312              } // end anonymous inner class
313           ); // end call to java.awt.EventQueue.invokeLater
314        } // end main
315
316        // Variables declaration - do not modify
317        private javax.swing.JButton addJButton;
318        private javax.swing.JLabel directionsJLabel;
319        private javax.swing.JButton equalsJButton;
320        private javax.swing.JTextField firstJTextField;
321        private javax.swing.JButton greaterThanJButton;
322        private javax.swing.JButton lessThanJButton;
323        private javax.swing.JScrollPane resultsJScrollPane;
324        private javax.swing.JTextArea resultsJTextArea;
325        private javax.swing.JTextField secondJTextField;
326        private javax.swing.JButton subtractJButton;
327        // End of variables declaration
328     } // end class UsingHugeIntegerJFrame
```

Fig. 23.11 | Client desktop application for the HugeInteger web service. (Part 5 of 6.)

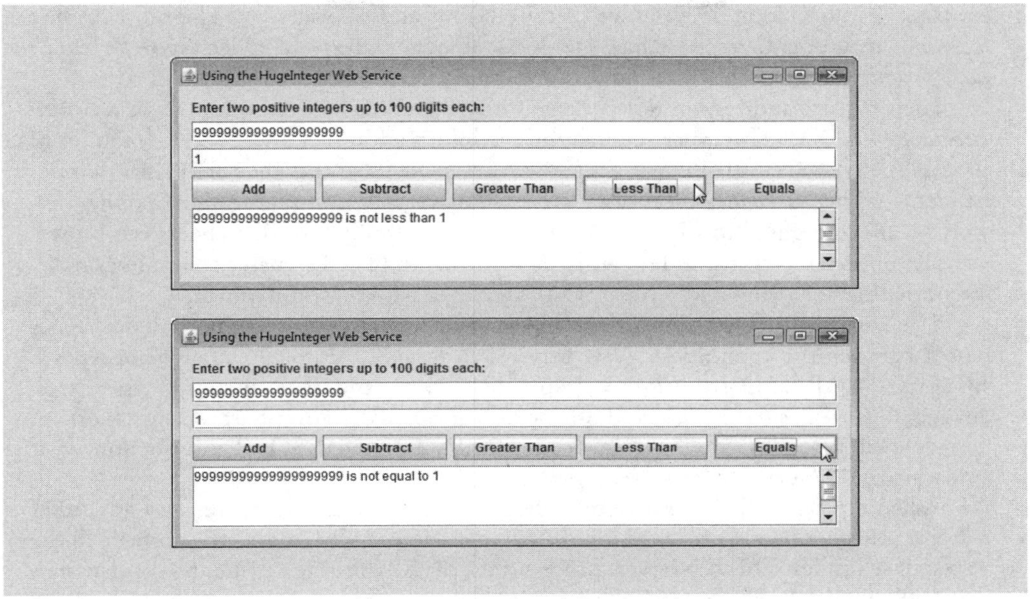

Fig. 23.11 | Client desktop application for the `HugeInteger` web service. (Part 6 of 6.)

Lines 5–6 import the classes `HugeInteger` and `HugeIntegerService` that enable the client application to interact with the web service. Notice that we do not have `import` declarations for most of the GUI components used in this example. When you create a GUI in Netbeans, it uses fully qualified class names (such as `javax.swing.JFrame` in line 9), so `import` declarations are unnecessary.

Line 12 declares a variable of type `HugeInteger` that will refer to the service endpoint interface object. Line 22 in the constructor creates an object of type `HugeIntegerService`. Line 23 uses this object's `getHugeIntegerPort` method to obtain the `HugeInteger` service endpoint interface object that the application uses to invoke the web service's methods.

Lines 156–157, 180–181, 204–205, 231–232 and 258–259 in the various `JButton` event handlers invoke the `HugeInteger` web service's web methods. Note that each call is made on the local service endpoint interface object that is referenced by `hugeInte-gerProxy`. This object then communicates with the web service on the client's behalf.

The user enters two integers, each up to 100 digits long. Clicking a `JButton` causes the application to invoke a web method to perform the corresponding task and return the result. Our client application cannot process 100-digit numbers directly. Instead it passes `String` representations of these numbers to the web service's web methods, which perform tasks for the client. The client application then uses the return value of each operation to display an appropriate message. [*Note:* For simplicity in this example, we assume that the first number in a subtraction operation is larger than the second.]

23.5 SOAP

SOAP (Simple Object Access Protocol) is a platform-independent protocol that uses XML to facilitate remote procedure calls, typically over HTTP. SOAP is one common protocol for passing information between web service clients and web services. The protocol that transmits request-and-response messages is also known as the web service's *wire format* or *wire protocol*, because it defines how information is sent "along the wire."

Each request and response is packaged in a *SOAP message* (also known as a *SOAP envelope*)—an XML "wrapper" containing the information that a web service requires to process the message. SOAP messages are written in XML so that they are platform independent. Many *firewalls*—security barriers that restrict communication among networks—are configured to allow HTTP traffic to pass through so that clients can browse websites on web servers behind firewalls. Thus, XML and HTTP enable computers on different platforms to send and receive SOAP messages with few limitations.

The wire format used to transmit requests and responses must support all data types passed between the applications. Web services also use SOAP for the many data types it supports. SOAP supports primitive types (e.g., int) and their wrapper types (e.g., Integer), as well as Date, Time and others. SOAP can also transmit arrays and objects of user-defined types (as you'll see in Section 23.8). For more SOAP information, visit www.w3.org/TR/soap/.

When a program invokes a web method, the request, the arguments and any other relevant information are packaged in a SOAP message and sent to the server on which the web service resides. The web service processes the SOAP message's contents (contained in a SOAP envelope), which specify the method that the client wishes to invoke and the method's arguments. This process of interpreting a SOAP message's contents is known as *parsing a SOAP message*. After the web service receives and parses a request, the proper method is called with any specified arguments, and the response is sent back to the client in another SOAP message. The client-side service endpoint interface parses the response, which contains the result of the method call, and returns the result to the client application.

Figure 23.5 used the HugeInteger web service's Tester web page to show the result of invoking HugeInteger's add method with the values 99999999999999999 and 1. The Tester web page also shows the SOAP request and response messages (which were not previously shown). Figure 23.12 shows the SOAP messages in the Tester web page from Fig. 23.5 after the calculation. In the request message from Fig. 23.12, the text

```
<ns2:add xmlns:ns2="http://hugeinteger.java.deitel.com/">
    <first>99999999999999999</first>
    <second>1</second>
</ns2:add>
```

specifies the method to call (add), the method's arguments (first and second) and the arguments' values (99999999999999999 and 1). Similarly, the text

```
<ns2:addResponse xmlns:ns2="http://hugeinteger.java.deitel.com/">
    <return>100000000000000000</return>
</ns2:addResponse>
```

from the response message in Fig. 23.12 specifies the return value of method add. As with the WSDL for a web service, the SOAP messages are generated for you automatically, so you don't need to understand the details of SOAP or XML to take advantage of it when publishing and consuming web services.

Fig. 23.12 | SOAP messages for the `HugeInteger` web service's `add` method as shown by the GlassFish application server's `Tester` web page.

23.6 Session Tracking in Web Services

Section 21.7 described the advantages of using session tracking to maintain client-state information so you can personalize the users' browsing experiences. Now we'll incorporate session tracking into a web service. Suppose a client application needs to call several methods from the same web service, possibly several times each. In such a case, it can be beneficial for the web service to maintain state information for the client, thus eliminating the need for client information to be passed between the client and the web service multiple times. For example, a web service that provides local restaurant reviews could store the client user's street address during the initial request, then use it to return personalized, localized results in subsequent requests. Storing session information also enables a web service to distinguish between clients.

23.6.1 Creating a `Blackjack` Web Service

Our next example is a web service that assists you in developing a blackjack card game. The `Blackjack` web service (Fig. 23.13) provides web methods to shuffle a deck of cards, deal a card from the deck and evaluate a hand of cards. After presenting the web service, we use it to serve as the dealer for a game of blackjack (Fig. 23.14). The `Blackjack` web service uses an `HttpSession` object to maintain a unique deck of cards for each client application. Several clients can use the service at the same time, but web method calls made by a specific client use only the deck of cards stored in that client's session. Our example uses the following blackjack rules:

Two cards each are dealt to the dealer and the player. The player's cards are dealt face up. Only the first of the dealer's cards is dealt face up. Each card has a value. A card numbered 2 through 10 is worth its face value. Jacks, queens and kings each count as 10. Aces can count as 1 or 11—whichever value is more beneficial to the player (as we'll soon see). If the sum of the player's two initial cards is 21 (i.e., the player was dealt a card valued at 10 and an ace, which counts as 11 in this situation), the player has "blackjack" and immediately wins the game—if the dealer does not also have blackjack (which would result in a "push"—i.e., a tie). Otherwise, the player can begin taking additional cards one at a time. These cards are dealt face up, and the player decides when to stop taking cards. If the player "busts" (i.e., the sum of the player's cards exceeds 21), the game is over, and the player loses. When the player is satisfied with the current set of cards, the player "stands" (i.e., stops taking cards), and the dealer's hidden card is revealed. If the dealer's total is 16 or less, the dealer must take another card; otherwise, the dealer must stand. The dealer must continue taking cards until the sum of the dealer's cards is greater than or equal to 17. If the dealer exceeds 21, the player wins. Otherwise, the hand with the higher point total wins. If the dealer and the player have the same point total, the game is a "push," and no one wins. Note that the value of an ace for a dealer depends on the dealer's other card(s) and the casino's house rules. A dealer typically must hit for totals of 16 or less and must stand for totals of 17 or more. However, for a "soft 17"—a hand with a total of 17 with one ace counted as 11—some casinos require the dealer to hit and some require the dealer to stand (we require the dealer to stand). Such a hand is known as a "soft 17" because taking another card cannot bust the hand.

The web service (Fig. 23.13) stores each card as a String consisting of a number, 1–13, representing the card's face (ace through king, respectively), followed by a space and a digit, 0–3, representing the card's suit (hearts, diamonds, clubs or spades, respectively). For example, the jack of clubs is represented as "11 2" and the two of hearts as "2 0". To create and deploy this web service, follow the steps that we presented in Sections 23.3.2–23.3.3 for the HugeInteger service.

```
1   // Fig. 23.13: Blackjack.java
2   // Blackjack web service that deals cards and evaluates hands
3   package com.deitel.java.blackjack;
4
5   import java.util.ArrayList;
6   import java.util.Random;
7   import javax.annotation.Resource;
8   import javax.jws.WebMethod;
9   import javax.jws.WebParam;
10  import javax.jws.WebService;
11  import javax.servlet.http.HttpServletRequest;
12  import javax.servlet.http.HttpSession;
13  import javax.xml.ws.WebServiceContext;
14  import javax.xml.ws.handler.MessageContext;
15
16  @WebService( name = "Blackjack", serviceName = "BlackjackService" )
17  public class Blackjack
18  {
```

Fig. 23.13 | Blackjack web service that deals cards and evaluates hands. (Part 1 of 3.)

```
19    // use @Resource to create a WebServiceContext for session tracking
20    private @Resource WebServiceContext webServiceContext;
21    private MessageContext messageContext; // used in session tracking
22    private HttpSession session; // stores attributes of the session
23
24    // deal one card
25    @WebMethod( operationName = "dealCard" )
26    public String dealCard()
27    {
28       String card = "";
29
30       ArrayList< String > deck =
31          ( ArrayList< String > ) session.getAttribute( "deck" );
32
33       card = deck.get( 0 ); // get top card of deck
34       deck.remove( 0 ); // remove top card of deck
35
36       return card;
37    } // end WebMethod dealCard
38
39    // shuffle the deck
40    @WebMethod( operationName = "shuffle" )
41    public void shuffle()
42    {
43       // obtain the HttpSession object to store deck for current client
44       messageContext = webServiceContext.getMessageContext();
45       session = ( ( HttpServletRequest ) messageContext.get(
46          MessageContext.SERVLET_REQUEST ) ).getSession();
47
48       // populate deck of cards
49       ArrayList< String > deck = new ArrayList< String >();
50
51       for ( int face = 1; face <= 13; face++ ) // loop through faces
52          for ( int suit = 0; suit <= 3; suit++ ) // loop through suits
53             deck.add( face + " " + suit ); // add each card to deck
54
55       String tempCard; // holds card temporarily during swapping
56       Random randomObject = new Random(); // generates random numbers
57       int index; // index of randomly selected card
58
59       for ( int i = 0; i < deck.size(); i++ ) // shuffle
60       {
61          index = randomObject.nextInt( deck.size() - 1 );
62
63          // swap card at position i with randomly selected card
64          tempCard = deck.get( i );
65          deck.set( i, deck.get( index ) );
66          deck.set( index, tempCard );
67       } // end for
68
69       // add this deck to user's session
70       session.setAttribute( "deck", deck );
71    } // end WebMethod shuffle
```

Fig. 23.13 | Blackjack web service that deals cards and evaluates hands. (Part 2 of 3.)

```
72
73       // determine a hand's value
74       @WebMethod( operationName = "getHandValue" )
75       public int getHandValue( @WebParam( name = "hand" ) String hand )
76       {
77          // split hand into cards
78          String[] cards = hand.split( "\t" );
79          int total = 0; // total value of cards in hand
80          int face; // face of current card
81          int aceCount = 0; // number of aces in hand
82
83          for ( int i = 0; i < cards.length; i++ )
84          {
85             // parse string and get first int in String
86             face = Integer.parseInt(
87                cards[ i ].substring( 0, cards[ i ].indexOf( " " ) ) );
88
89             switch ( face )
90             {
91                case 1: // if ace, increment aceCount
92                   ++aceCount;
93                   break;
94                case 11: // jack
95                case 12: // queen
96                case 13: // king
97                   total += 10;
98                   break;
99                default: // otherwise, add face
100                  total += face;
101                  break;
102            } // end switch
103         } // end for
104
105         // calculate optimal use of aces
106         if ( aceCount > 0 )
107         {
108            // if possible, count one ace as 11
109            if ( total + 11 + aceCount - 1 <= 21 )
110               total += 11 + aceCount - 1;
111            else // otherwise, count all aces as 1
112               total += aceCount;
113         } // end if
114
115         return total;
116      } // end WebMethod getHandValue
117   } // end class Blackjack
```

Fig. 23.13 | Blackjack web service that deals cards and evaluates hands. (Part 3 of 3.)

Session Tracking in Web Services

A client of the Blackjack web service first calls method shuffle (lines 40–71) to shuffle the deck of cards and place the deck into an HttpSession object that is specific to that client. To use session tracking in a web service, you must include code for the resources that maintain the session-state information. In the past, you had to write the sometimes tedious code to create these resources. JAX-WS, however, handles this for you via the *@Resource annotation*. This annotation enables tools like Netbeans to "inject" support objects into your class, thus allowing you to focus on your business logic rather than the support code. The server is responsible for initializing the support objects. The concept of using annotations to add code that supports your classes is known as *dependency injection*. Annotations such as @WebService, @WebMethod and @WebParam also perform dependency injection.

Line 20 injects a WebServiceContext object into your class. A *WebServiceContext* object enables a web service to access and maintain information such as session state for a specific request. As you look through the code in Fig. 23.13, you'll notice that we never explicitly create the WebServiceContext object—that code is injected into the class by the @Resource annotation. Line 21 declares a variable of interface type *MessageContext* that the web service will use to obtain an HttpSession object for the current client. Line 22 declares the HttpSession variable that the web service will use to manipulate the session-state information.

Line 44 in method shuffle uses the WebServiceContext object that was injected in line 20 to obtain a MessageContext object. Lines 45–46 then use the MessageContext object's get method to obtain the HttpSession object for the current client. Method get receives a constant indicating what to get from the MessageContext. In this case, the constant MessageContext.SERVLET_REQUEST indicates that we'd like to get the HttpServlet-Request object for the current client. We then call the HttpServletRequest method *getSession* to obtain the HttpSession object.

Lines 49–70 generate an ArrayList representing a deck of cards, shuffle the deck and store the deck in the client's session object. Lines 51–53 generate Strings in the form "*face suit*" to represent each possible card in the deck. Lines 59–67 shuffle the deck by swapping each card with another card selected at random. Line 70 uses HttpSession method *setAttribute* to insert the ArrayList in the session object to maintain the deck between method calls from a particular client.

Lines 25–37 define method dealCard as a web method. Lines 30–31 use the session object to obtain the "deck" session attribute that was stored in line 70 of method shuffle. Method *getAttribute* takes as a parameter a String that identifies the Object to obtain from the session state. The HttpSession can store many Objects, provided that each has a unique identifier. Note that method shuffle must be called before method dealCard is called the first time for a client—otherwise, an exception occurs at line 33, because get-Attribute returns null at lines 30–31. After obtaining the user's deck, dealCard gets the top card from the deck (line 33), removes it from the deck (line 34) and returns the card's value as a String (line 36). Without using session tracking, the deck of cards would need to be passed back and forth with each method call. Session tracking makes the dealCard method easy to call (it requires no arguments) and eliminates the overhead of sending the deck over the network multiple times.

Method getHandValue (lines 74–116) determines the total value of the cards in a hand by trying to attain the highest score possible without going over 21. Recall that an ace can be counted as either 1 or 11, and all face cards count as 10. This method does not use the session object, because the deck of cards is not used in this method.

As you'll soon see, the client application maintains a hand of cards as a String in which each card is separated by a tab character. Line 78 tokenizes the hand of cards (represented by hand) into individual cards by calling String method split and passing to it a String containing the delimiter characters (in this case, just a tab). Method split uses the delimiter characters to separate tokens in the String. Lines 83–103 count the value of each card. Lines 86–87 retrieve the first integer—the face—and use that value in the switch statement (lines 89–102). If the card is an ace, the method increments variable aceCount. We discuss how this variable is used shortly. If the card is an 11, 12 or 13 (jack, queen or king), the method adds 10 to the total value of the hand (line 97). If the card is anything else, the method increases the total by that value (line 100).

Because an ace can have either of two values, additional logic is required to process aces. Lines 106–113 of method getHandValue process the aces after all the other cards. If a hand contains several aces, only one ace can be counted as 11. The condition in line 109 determines whether counting one ace as 11 and the rest as 1 will result in a total that does not exceed 21. If this is possible, line 110 adjusts the total accordingly. Otherwise, line 112 adjusts the total, counting each ace as 1.

Method getHandValue maximizes the value of the current cards without exceeding 21. Imagine, for example, that the dealer has a 7 and receives an ace. The new total could be either 8 or 18. However, getHandValue always maximizes the value of the cards without going over 21, so the new total is 18.

23.6.2 Consuming the Blackjack Web Service

The blackjack application in Fig. 23.14 keeps track of the player's and dealer's cards, and the web service tracks the cards that have been dealt. The constructor (lines 34–83) sets up the GUI (line 36), changes the window's background color (line 40) and creates the Blackjack web service's service endpoint interface object (lines 46–47). In the GUI, each player has 11 JLabels—the maximum number of cards that can be dealt without automatically exceeding 21 (i.e., four aces, four twos and three threes). These JLabels are placed in an ArrayList of JLabels (lines 59–82), so we can index the ArrayList during the game to determine the JLabel that will display a particular card image.

```
1   // Fig. 23.14: BlackjackGameJFrame.java
2   // Blackjack game that uses the Blackjack Web Service.
3   package com.deitel.java.blackjackclient;
4
5   import com.deitel.java.blackjack.Blackjack;
6   import com.deitel.java.blackjack.BlackjackService;
7   import java.awt.Color;
8   import java.util.ArrayList;
9   import javax.swing.ImageIcon;
10  import javax.swing.JLabel;
11  import javax.swing.JOptionPane;
12  import javax.xml.ws.BindingProvider;
13
14  public class BlackjackGameJFrame extends javax.swing.JFrame
15  {
16     private String playerCards;
17     private String dealerCards;
18     private ArrayList<JLabel> cardboxes; // list of card image JLabels
```

Fig. 23.14 | Blackjack game that uses the Blackjack web service. (Part 1 of 11.)

```
19    private int currentPlayerCard; // player's current card number
20    private int currentDealerCard; // blackjackProxy's current card number
21    private BlackjackService blackjackService; // used to obtain proxy
22    private Blackjack blackjackProxy; // used to access the web service
23
24    // enumeration of game states
25    private enum GameStatus
26    {
27       PUSH, // game ends in a tie
28       LOSE, // player loses
29       WIN, // player wins
30       BLACKJACK // player has blackjack
31    } // end enum GameStatus
32
33    // no-argument constructor
34    public BlackjackGameJFrame()
35    {
36       initComponents();
37
38       // due to a bug in Netbeans, we must change the JFrame's background
39       // color here rather than in the designer
40       getContentPane().setBackground( new Color( 0, 180, 0 ) );
41
42       // initialize the blackjack proxy
43       try
44       {
45          // create the objects for accessing the Blackjack web service
46          blackjackService = new BlackjackService();
47          blackjackProxy = blackjackService.getBlackjackPort();
48
49          // enable session tracking
50          ( (BindingProvider) blackjackProxy ).getRequestContext().put(
51             BindingProvider.SESSION_MAINTAIN_PROPERTY, true );
52       } // end try
53       catch ( Exception e )
54       {
55          e.printStackTrace();
56       } // end catch
57
58       // add JLabels to cardBoxes ArrayList for programmatic manipulation
59       cardboxes = new ArrayList<JLabel>();
60
61       cardboxes.add( dealerCard1JLabel );
62       cardboxes.add( dealerCard2JLabel );
63       cardboxes.add( dealerCard3JLabel );
64       cardboxes.add( dealerCard4JLabel );
65       cardboxes.add( dealerCard5JLabel );
66       cardboxes.add( dealerCard6JLabel );
67       cardboxes.add( dealerCard7JLabel );
68       cardboxes.add( dealerCard8JLabel );
69       cardboxes.add( dealerCard9JLabel );
70       cardboxes.add( dealerCard10JLabel );
71       cardboxes.add( dealerCard11JLabel );
```

Fig. 23.14 | Blackjack game that uses the Blackjack web service. (Part 2 of 11.)

```
72          cardboxes.add( playerCard1JLabel );
73          cardboxes.add( playerCard2JLabel );
74          cardboxes.add( playerCard3JLabel );
75          cardboxes.add( playerCard4JLabel );
76          cardboxes.add( playerCard5JLabel );
77          cardboxes.add( playerCard6JLabel );
78          cardboxes.add( playerCard7JLabel );
79          cardboxes.add( playerCard8JLabel );
80          cardboxes.add( playerCard9JLabel );
81          cardboxes.add( playerCard10JLabel );
82          cardboxes.add( playerCard11JLabel );
83      } // end constructor
84
85      // play the dealer's hand
86      private void dealerPlay()
87      {
88          try
89          {
90              // while the value of the dealers's hand is below 17
91              // the dealer must continue to take cards
92              String[] cards = dealerCards.split( "\t" );
93
94              // display dealer's cards
95              for ( int i = 0; i < cards.length; i++ )
96              {
97                  displayCard( i, cards[i] );
98              }
99
100             while ( blackjackProxy.getHandValue( dealerCards ) < 17 )
101             {
102                 String newCard = blackjackProxy.dealCard(); // deal new card
103                 dealerCards += "\t" + newCard; // deal new card
104                 displayCard( currentDealerCard, newCard );
105                 ++currentDealerCard;
106                 JOptionPane.showMessageDialog( this, "Dealer takes a card",
107                     "Dealer's turn", JOptionPane.PLAIN_MESSAGE );
108             } // end while
109
110             int dealersTotal = blackjackProxy.getHandValue( dealerCards );
111             int playersTotal = blackjackProxy.getHandValue( playerCards );
112
113             // if dealer busted, player wins
114             if ( dealersTotal > 21 )
115             {
116                 gameOver( GameStatus.WIN );
117                 return;
118             } // end if
119
120             // if dealer and player are below 21
121             // higher score wins, equal scores is a push
122             if ( dealersTotal > playersTotal )
123             {
```

Fig. 23.14 | Blackjack game that uses the Blackjack web service. (Part 3 of 11.)

```
124             gameOver( GameStatus.LOSE );
125          }
126          else if ( dealersTotal < playersTotal )
127          {
128             gameOver( GameStatus.WIN );
129          }
130          else
131          {
132             gameOver( GameStatus.PUSH );
133          }
134       } // end try
135       catch ( Exception e )
136       {
137          e.printStackTrace();
138       } // end catch
139    } // end method dealerPlay
140
141    // displays the card represented by cardValue in specified JLabel
142    private void displayCard( int card, String cardValue )
143    {
144       try
145       {
146          // retrieve correct JLabel from cardBoxes
147          JLabel displayLabel = cardboxes.get( card );
148
149          // if string representing card is empty, display back of card
150          if ( cardValue.equals( "" ) )
151          {
152             displayLabel.setIcon( new ImageIcon( getClass().getResource(
153                "/com/deitel/java/blackjackclient/" +
154                "blackjack_images/cardback.png" ) ) );
155             return;
156          } // end if
157
158          // retrieve the face value of the card
159          String face = cardValue.substring( 0, cardValue.indexOf( " " ) );
160
161          // retrieve the suit of the card
162          String suit =
163             cardValue.substring( cardValue.indexOf( " " ) + 1 );
164
165          char suitLetter; // suit letter used to form image file
166
167          switch ( Integer.parseInt( suit ) )
168          {
169             case 0: // hearts
170                suitLetter = 'h';
171                break;
172             case 1: // diamonds
173                suitLetter = 'd';
174                break;
```

Fig. 23.14 | Blackjack game that uses the Blackjack web service. (Part 4 of 11.)

```
175             case 2: // clubs
176                suitLetter = 'c';
177                break;
178             default: // spades
179                suitLetter = 's';
180                break;
181          } // end switch
182
183          // set image for displayLabel
184          displayLabel.setIcon( new ImageIcon( getClass().getResource(
185             "/com/deitel/java/blackjackclient/blackjack_images/" +
186             face + suitLetter + ".png" ) ) );
187       } // end try
188       catch ( Exception e )
189       {
190          e.printStackTrace();
191       } // end catch
192    } // end method displayCard
193
194    // displays all player cards and shows appropriate message
195    private void gameOver( GameStatus winner )
196    {
197       String[] cards = dealerCards.split( "\t" );
198
199       // display blackjackProxy's cards
200       for ( int i = 0; i < cards.length; i++ )
201       {
202          displayCard( i, cards[i] );
203       }
204
205       // display appropriate status image
206       if ( winner == GameStatus.WIN )
207       {
208          statusJLabel.setText( "You win!" );
209       }
210       else if ( winner == GameStatus.LOSE )
211       {
212          statusJLabel.setText( "You lose." );
213       }
214       else if ( winner == GameStatus.PUSH )
215       {
216          statusJLabel.setText( "It's a push." );
217       }
218       else // blackjack
219       {
220          statusJLabel.setText( "Blackjack!" );
221       }
222
223       // display final scores
224       int dealersTotal = blackjackProxy.getHandValue( dealerCards );
225       int playersTotal = blackjackProxy.getHandValue( playerCards );
226       dealerTotalJLabel.setText( "Dealer: " + dealersTotal );
227       playerTotalJLabel.setText( "Player: " + playersTotal );
```

Fig. 23.14 | Blackjack game that uses the Blackjack web service. (Part 5 of 11.)

```
228
229        // reset for new game
230        standJButton.setEnabled( false );
231        hitJButton.setEnabled( false );
232        dealJButton.setEnabled( true );
233    } // end method gameOver
234
235    // The initComponents method is autogenerated by Netbeans and is called
236    // from the constructor to initialize the GUI. This method is not shown
237    // here to save space. Open BlackjackGameJFrame.java in this
238    // example's folder to view the complete generated code (lines 235-541)
239
542    // handles dealJButton click
543    private void dealJButtonActionPerformed(
544        java.awt.event.ActionEvent evt )
545    {
546        String card; // stores a card temporarily until it's added to a hand
547
548        // clear card images
549        for ( int i = 0; i < cardboxes.size(); i++ )
550        {
551            cardboxes.get( i ).setIcon( null );
552        }
553
554        statusJLabel.setText( "" );
555        dealerTotalJLabel.setText( "" );
556        playerTotalJLabel.setText( "" );
557
558        // create a new, shuffled deck on remote machine
559        blackjackProxy.shuffle();
560
561        // deal two cards to player
562        playerCards = blackjackProxy.dealCard(); // add first card to hand
563        displayCard( 11, playerCards ); // display first card
564        card = blackjackProxy.dealCard(); // deal second card
565        displayCard( 12, card ); // display second card
566        playerCards += "\t" + card; // add second card to hand
567
568        // deal two cards to blackjackProxy, but only show first
569        dealerCards = blackjackProxy.dealCard(); // add first card to hand
570        displayCard( 0, dealerCards ); // display first card
571        card = blackjackProxy.dealCard(); // deal second card
572        displayCard( 1, "" ); // display back of card
573        dealerCards += "\t" + card; // add second card to hand
574
575        standJButton.setEnabled( true );
576        hitJButton.setEnabled( true );
577        dealJButton.setEnabled( false );
578
579        // determine the value of the two hands
580        int dealersTotal = blackjackProxy.getHandValue( dealerCards );
581        int playersTotal = blackjackProxy.getHandValue( playerCards );
582
```

Fig. 23.14 | Blackjack game that uses the Blackjack web service. (Part 6 of 11.)

```
583        // if hands both equal 21, it is a push
584        if ( playersTotal == dealersTotal && playersTotal == 21 )
585        {
586           gameOver( GameStatus.PUSH );
587        }
588        else if ( dealersTotal == 21 ) // blackjackProxy has blackjack
589        {
590           gameOver( GameStatus.LOSE );
591        }
592        else if ( playersTotal == 21 ) // blackjack
593        {
594           gameOver( GameStatus.BLACKJACK );
595        }
596
597        // next card for blackjackProxy has index 2
598        currentDealerCard = 2;
599
600        // next card for player has index 13
601        currentPlayerCard = 13;
602     } // end method dealJButtonActionPerformed
603
604     // handles standJButton click
605     private void hitJButtonActionPerformed(
606        java.awt.event.ActionEvent evt )
607     {
608        // get player another card
609        String card = blackjackProxy.dealCard(); // deal new card
610        playerCards += "\t" + card; // add card to hand
611
612        // update GUI to display new card
613        displayCard( currentPlayerCard, card );
614        ++currentPlayerCard;
615
616        // determine new value of player's hand
617        int total = blackjackProxy.getHandValue( playerCards );
618
619        if ( total > 21 ) // player busts
620        {
621           gameOver( GameStatus.LOSE );
622        }
623        else if ( total == 21 ) // player cannot take any more cards
624        {
625           hitJButton.setEnabled( false );
626           dealerPlay();
627        } // end if
628     } // end method hitJButtonActionPerformed
629
630     // handles standJButton click
631     private void standJButtonActionPerformed(
632        java.awt.event.ActionEvent evt )
633     {
634        standJButton.setEnabled( false );
```

Fig. 23.14 | Blackjack game that uses the Blackjack web service. (Part 7 of 11.)

```
635        hitJButton.setEnabled( false );
636        dealJButton.setEnabled( true );
637        dealerPlay();
638     } // end method standJButtonActionPerformed
639
640     // begins application execution
641     public static void main( String args[] )
642     {
643        java.awt.EventQueue.invokeLater(
644           new Runnable()
645           {
646              public void run()
647              {
648                 new BlackjackGameJFrame().setVisible( true );
649              }
650           }
651        ); // end call to java.awt.EventQueue.invokeLater
652     } // end main
653
654     // Variables declaration - do not modify
655     private javax.swing.JButton dealJButton;
656     private javax.swing.JLabel dealerCard10JLabel;
657     private javax.swing.JLabel dealerCard11JLabel;
658     private javax.swing.JLabel dealerCard1JLabel;
659     private javax.swing.JLabel dealerCard2JLabel;
660     private javax.swing.JLabel dealerCard3JLabel;
661     private javax.swing.JLabel dealerCard4JLabel;
662     private javax.swing.JLabel dealerCard5JLabel;
663     private javax.swing.JLabel dealerCard6JLabel;
664     private javax.swing.JLabel dealerCard7JLabel;
665     private javax.swing.JLabel dealerCard8JLabel;
666     private javax.swing.JLabel dealerCard9JLabel;
667     private javax.swing.JLabel dealerJLabel;
668     private javax.swing.JLabel dealerTotalJLabel;
669     private javax.swing.JButton hitJButton;
670     private javax.swing.JLabel playerCard10JLabel;
671     private javax.swing.JLabel playerCard11JLabel;
672     private javax.swing.JLabel playerCard1JLabel;
673     private javax.swing.JLabel playerCard2JLabel;
674     private javax.swing.JLabel playerCard3JLabel;
675     private javax.swing.JLabel playerCard4JLabel;
676     private javax.swing.JLabel playerCard5JLabel;
677     private javax.swing.JLabel playerCard6JLabel;
678     private javax.swing.JLabel playerCard7JLabel;
679     private javax.swing.JLabel playerCard8JLabel;
680     private javax.swing.JLabel playerCard9JLabel;
681     private javax.swing.JLabel playerJLabel;
682     private javax.swing.JLabel playerTotalJLabel;
683     private javax.swing.JButton standJButton;
684     private javax.swing.JLabel statusJLabel;
685     // End of variables declaration
686  } // end class BlackjackGameJFrame
```

Fig. 23.14 | Blackjack game that uses the Blackjack web service. (Part 8 of 11.)

a) Dealer and player hands after the user clicks the **Deal** JButton.

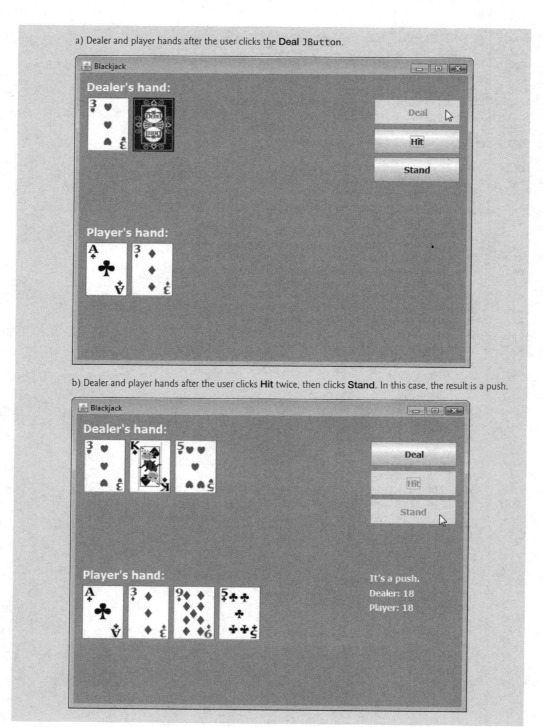

b) Dealer and player hands after the user clicks **Hit** twice, then clicks **Stand**. In this case, the result is a push.

Fig. 23.14 | Blackjack game that uses the Blackjack web service. (Part 9 of 11.)

c) Dealer and player hands after the user clicks **Stand** based on the initial hand. In this case, the player wins.

d) Dealer and player hands after the user is dealt blackjack.

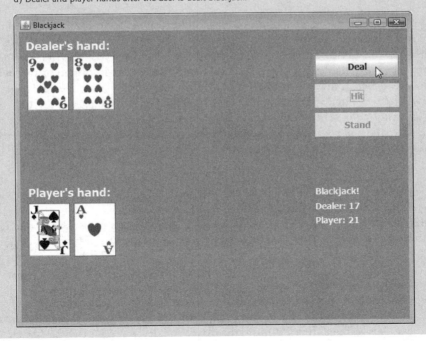

Fig. 23.14 | Blackjack game that uses the Blackjack web service. (Part 10 of 11.)

e) Dealer and player hands after the dealer is dealt blackjack.

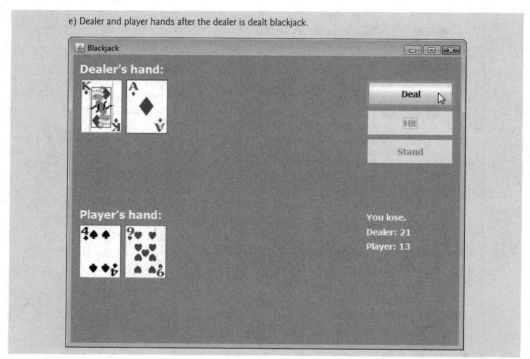

Fig. 23.14 | Blackjack game that uses the Blackjack web service. (Part 11 of 11.)

With JAX-WS, the client application must indicate whether it wants to allow the web service to maintain session information. Lines 50–51 in the constructor perform this task. We first cast the service endpoint interface object to interface type BindingProvider. A **BindingProvider** enables the client to manipulate the request information that will be sent to the server. This information is stored in an object that implements interface **RequestContext**. The BindingProvider and RequestContext are part of the framework that is created by the IDE when you add a web service client to the application. Next, we invoke the BindingProvider's **getRequestContext** *method* to obtain the RequestContext object. Then we call the RequestContext's **put** *method* to set the property

    BindingProvider.SESSION_MAINTAIN_PROPERTY

to true. This enables the client side of the session-tracking mechanism, so that the web service knows which client is invoking the service's web methods.

Method gameOver (lines 195–233) displays all the dealer's cards, shows the appropriate message in statusJLabel and displays the final point totals of both the dealer and the player. Method gameOver receives as an argument a member of the GameStatus enumeration (defined in lines 25–31). The enumeration represents whether the player tied, lost or won the game; its four members are PUSH, LOSE, WIN and BLACKJACK.

When the player clicks the **Deal** JButton, method dealJButtonActionPerformed (lines 543–602) clears all of the JLabels that display cards or game status information. Next, the deck is shuffled (line 559), and the player and dealer receive two cards each (lines 562–573). Lines 580–581 then total each hand. If the player and the dealer both obtain scores of 21, the program calls method gameOver, passing GameStatus.PUSH (line 586). If only the dealer has 21, the program passes GameStatus.LOSE to method gameOver (line 590). If only the player has 21 after the first two cards are dealt, the program passes GameStatus.BLACKJACK to method gameOver (line 594).

If dealJButtonActionPerformed does not call gameOver, the player can take more cards by clicking the **Hit** JButton, which calls hitJButtonActionPerformed in lines 605–628. Each time a player clicks **Hit**, the program deals the player one more card (line 609) and displays it in the GUI (line 613). If the player exceeds 21, the game is over and the player loses (line 621). If the player has exactly 21, the player is not allowed to take any more cards (line 625), and method dealerPlay is called (line 626).

Method dealerPlay (lines 86–139) displays the dealer's cards, then deals cards to the dealer until the dealer's hand has a value of 17 or more (lines 110–108). If the dealer exceeds 21, the player wins (line 116); otherwise, the values of the hands are compared, and gameOver is called with the appropriate argument (lines 122–133).

Clicking the **Stand** JButton indicates that a player does not want to be dealt another card. Method standJButtonActionPerformed (lines 631–638) disables the **Hit** and **Stand** buttons, enables the **Deal** button, then calls method dealerPlay.

Method displayCard (lines 142–192) updates the GUI to display a newly dealt card. The method takes as arguments an integer index for the JLabel in the ArrayList that must have its image set and a String representing the card. An empty String indicates that we wish to display the card face down. If method displayCard receives a String that's not empty, the program extracts the face and suit from the String and uses this information to display the correct image. The switch statement (lines 167–181) converts the number representing the suit to an integer and assigns the appropriate character to variable suitLetter (h for hearts, d for diamonds, c for clubs and s for spades). The character in suitLetter is used to complete the image's filename (lines 184–186). *You must add the folder blackjack_images to your project so that lines 152–154 and 184–186 can access the images properly.* To do so, copy the folder blackjack_images from this chapter's examples folder and paste it into the project's src\com\deitel\java\blackjackclient folder.

In this example, you learned how to set up a web service to support session handling so that you could keep track of each client's session state. You also learned how to indicate from a desktop client application that it wishes to take part in session tracking. You'll now learn how to access a database from a web service and how to consume a web service from a client web application.

23.7 Consuming a Database-Driven Web Service from a Web Application

Our prior examples accessed web services from desktop applications created in Netbeans. However, we can just as easily use them in web applications created with Netbeans. In fact, because web-based businesses are becoming increasingly prevalent, it is common for web applications to consume web services. In this section, we present an airline reservation web service that receives information regarding the type of seat a customer wishes to reserve and makes a reservation if such a seat is available. Later in the section, we present a web application that allows a customer to specify a reservation request, then uses the airline reservation web service to attempt to execute the request.

23.7.1 Creating the Reservation Database

In this example, our web service uses a Reservation database containing a single table named Seats to locate a seat matching a client's request. To build the Reservation database, review the steps presented in Section 22.2.1 for building the AddressBook database. This chapter's examples directory contains the Seats.sql SQL script to build the seats table and populate it with sample data. The sample data is shown in Fig. 23.15.

number	location	class	taken
1	Aisle	Economy	0
2	Aisle	Economy	0
3	Aisle	First	0
4	Middle	Economy	0
5	Middle	Economy	0
6	Middle	First	0
7	Window	Economy	0
8	Window	Economy	0
9	Window	First	0
10	Window	First	0

Fig. 23.15 | Data from the seats table.

Creating the Reservation Web Service

You can now create a web service that uses the Reservation database (Fig. 23.16). The airline reservation web service has a single web method—reserve (lines 26–78)—which searches the Seats table to locate a seat matching a user's request. The method takes two arguments—a String representing the desired seat type (i.e., "Window", "Middle" or "Aisle") and a String representing the desired class type (i.e., "Economy" or "First"). If it finds an appropriate seat, method reserve updates the database to make the reservation and returns true; otherwise, no reservation is made, and the method returns false. Note that the statements at lines 34–39 and lines 44–48 that query and update the database use objects of JDBC types ResultSet and PreparedStatement.

Software Engineering Observation 23.1

Using PreparedStatements to create SQL statements is highly recommended to secure against so-called SQL injection attacks in which executable code is inserted SQL code. The site www.owasp.org/index.php/Preventing_SQL_Injection_in_Java provides a summary of SQL injection attacks and ways to mitigate against them.

```
1   // Fig. 23.16: Reservation.java
2   // Airline reservation web service.
3   package com.deitel.java.reservation;
4
```

Fig. 23.16 | Airline reservation web service. (Part 1 of 3.)

```
 5    import java.sql.Connection;
 6    import java.sql.DriverManager;
 7    import java.sql.PreparedStatement;
 8    import java.sql.ResultSet;
 9    import java.sql.SQLException;
10    import javax.jws.WebMethod;
11    import javax.jws.WebParam;
12    import javax.jws.WebService;
13
14    @WebService( name = "Reservation", serviceName = "ReservationService" )
15    public class Reservation
16    {
17       private static final String DATABASE_URL =
18          "jdbc:derby://localhost:1527/Reservation";
19       private static final String USERNAME = "test";
20       private static final String PASSWORD = "test";
21       private Connection connection;
22       private PreparedStatement lookupSeat;
23       private PreparedStatement reserveSeat;
24
25       // a WebMethod that can reserve a seat
26       @WebMethod( operationName = "reserve" )
27       public boolean reserve( @WebParam( name = "seatType" ) String seatType,
28          @WebParam( name = "classType" ) String classType )
29       {
30          try
31          {
32             connection = DriverManager.getConnection(
33                DATABASE_URL, USERNAME, PASSWORD );
34             lookupSeat = connection.prepareStatement(
35                "SELECT \"number\" FROM \"seats\" WHERE (\"taken\" = 0) " +
36                "AND (\"location\" = ?) AND (\"class\" = ?)" );
37             lookupSeat.setString( 1, seatType );
38             lookupSeat.setString( 2, classType );
39             ResultSet resultSet = lookupSeat.executeQuery();
40
41             // if requested seat is available, reserve it
42             if ( resultSet.next() )
43             {
44                int seat = resultSet.getInt( 1 );
45                reserveSeat = connection.prepareStatement(
46                   "UPDATE \"seats\" SET \"taken\"=1 WHERE \"number\"=?" );
47                reserveSeat.setInt( 1, seat );
48                reserveSeat.executeUpdate();
49                return true;
50             } // end if
51
52             return false;
53          } // end try
54          catch ( SQLException e )
55          {
56             e.printStackTrace();
```

Fig. 23.16 | Airline reservation web service. (Part 2 of 3.)

```
57              return false;
58          } // end catch
59          catch ( Exception e )
60          {
61              e.printStackTrace();
62              return false;
63          } // end catch
64          finally
65          {
66              try
67              {
68                  lookupSeat.close();
69                  reserveSeat.close();
70                  connection.close();
71              } // end try
72              catch ( Exception e )
73              {
74                  e.printStackTrace();
75                  return false;
76              } // end catch
77          } // end finally
78      } // end WebMethod reserve
79  } // end class Reservation
```

Fig. 23.16 | Airline reservation web service. (Part 3 of 3.)

Our database contains four columns—the seat number (i.e., 1–10), the seat type (i.e., Window, Middle or Aisle), the class type (i.e., Economy or First) and a column containing either 1 (true) or 0 (false) to indicate whether the seat is taken. Lines 34–39 retrieve the seat numbers of any available seats matching the requested seat and class type. This statement fills the resultSet with the results of the query

```
SELECT "number"
FROM "seats"
WHERE ("taken" = 0) AND ("type" = type) AND ("class" = class)
```

The parameters *type* and *class* in the query are replaced with values of method reserve's seatType and classType parameters. When you use the Netbeans tools to create a database table and its columns, the Netbeans tools automatically place the table and column names in double quotes. For this reason, you must place the table and column names in double quotes in the SQL statements that interact with the Reservation database.

If resultSet is not empty (i.e., at least one seat is available that matches the selected criteria), the condition in line 42 is true and the web service reserves the first matching seat number. Recall that ResultSet method next returns true if a nonempty row exists, and positions the cursor on that row. We obtain the seat number (line 44) by accessing resultSet's first column (i.e., resultSet.getInt(1)—the first column in the row). Then lines 45–48 configure a PreparedStatement and execute the SQL:

```
UPDATE "seats"
SET "taken" = 1
WHERE ("number" = number)
```

which marks the seat as taken in the database. The parameter *number* is replaced with the value of `seat`. Method `reserve` returns `true` (line 49) to indicate that the reservation was successful. If there are no matching seats, or if an exception occurred, method `reserve` returns `false` (lines 52, 57, 62 and 75) to indicate that no seats matched the user's request.

23.7.2 Creating a Web Application to Interact with the Reservation Web Service

This section presents a `ReservationClient` web application that consumes the `Reservation` web service. The application allows users to select seats based on class (`"Economy"` or `"First"`) and location (`"Aisle"`, `"Middle"` or `"Window"`), then submit their requests to the airline reservation web service. If the database request is not successful, the application instructs the user to modify the request and try again. The application presented here was built using the techniques presented in Chapters 21–22. We assume that you've already read those chapters, and thus know how to build a web application's GUI, create event handlers and add properties to a web application's session bean (Section 21.7.2).

Reserve.jsp

`Reserve.jsp` (Fig. 23.17) defines two `DropDownLists` and a `Button`. The `seatTypeDropDown` (lines 23–28) displays all the seat types from which users can select. The `classTypeDropDownList` (lines 29–35) provides choices for the class type. When the user makes a selection from each of these, corresponding event handlers store the selected values in the session bean. We added `seatType` and `classType` properties to the session bean for this purpose. Users click the `reserveButton` (lines 36–40) to submit requests after making selections from the `DropDownLists`. The page also defines three `Labels`—`instructionLabel` (lines 18–22) to display instructions, `successLabel` (lines 41–44) to indicate a successful reservation and `errorLabel` (lines 45–49) to display a message if there are no seats that match the user's selection. The page bean file (Fig. 23.18) contains the event handlers for `seatTypeDropDown`, `classTypeDropDown` and `reserveButton`.

```
 1   <?xml version="1.0" encoding="UTF-8"?>
 2   <!-- Fig. 23.17 Reserve.jsp -->
 3   <!-- JSP that allows a user to select a seat -->
 4   <jsp:root version="2.1" xmlns:f="http://java.sun.com/jsf/core"
 5      xmlns:h="http://java.sun.com/jsf/html"
 6      xmlns:jsp="http://java.sun.com/JSP/Page"
 7      xmlns:webuijsf="http://www.sun.com/webui/webuijsf">
 8      <jsp:directive.page contentType="text/html;charset=UTF-8"
 9         pageEncoding="UTF-8"/>
10      <f:view>
11         <webuijsf:page id="page1">
12            <webuijsf:html id="html1">
13               <webuijsf:head id="head1">
14                  <webuijsf:link id="link1" url="/resources/stylesheet.css"/>
15               </webuijsf:head>
16               <webuijsf:body id="body1" style="-rave-layout: grid">
17                  <webuijsf:form id="form1">
```

Fig. 23.17 | JSP that allows a user to select a seat. (Part 1 of 3.)

```
18          <webuijsf:label binding="#{Reserve.instructionLabel}"
19             id="instructionLabel"
20             style="left: 24px; top: 24px; position: absolute"
21             text="Please select the seat type and class to
22                reserve:"/>
23          <webuijsf:dropDown binding="#{Reserve.seatTypeDropDown}"
24             id="seatTypeDropDown" items="#{Reserve.
25                seatTypeDropDownDefaultOptions.options}"
26             style="left: 24px; top: 48px; position: absolute"
27             valueChangeListenerExpression=
28                "#{Reserve.seatTypeDropDown_processValueChange}"/>
29          <webuijsf:dropDown
30             binding="#{Reserve.classTypeDropDown}"
31             id="classTypeDropDown" items="#{Reserve.
32                classTypeDropDownDefaultOptions.options}"
33             style="left: 96px; top: 48px; position: absolute"
34             valueChangeListenerExpression="#{Reserve.
35                classTypeDropDown_processValueChange}"/>
36          <webuijsf:button
37             actionExpression="#{Reserve.reserveButton_action}"
38             binding="#{Reserve.reserveButton}" id="reserveButton"
39             style="left: 191px; top: 48px; position: absolute"
40             text="Reserve"/>
41          <webuijsf:label binding="#{Reserve.successLabel}"
42             id="successLabel" rendered="false" style="left: 24px;
43                top: 24px; position: absolute"
44             text="Your reservation has been made. Thank you!"/>
45          <webuijsf:label binding="#{Reserve.errorLabel}"
46             id="errorLabel" rendered="false" style="color: red;
47                left: 24px; top: 96px; position: absolute"
48             text="This type of seat is not available. Please
49                modify your request and try again."/>
50       </webuijsf:form>
51    </webuijsf:body>
52    </webuijsf:html>
53    </webuijsf:page>
54 </f:view>
55 </jsp:root>
```

a) Selecting a seat:

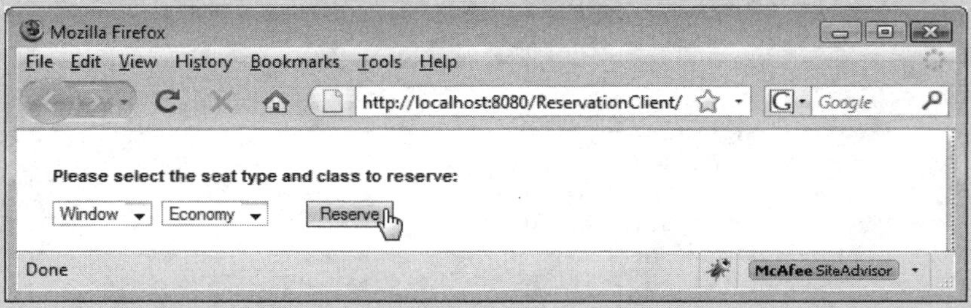

Fig. 23.17 | JSP that allows a user to select a seat. (Part 2 of 3.)

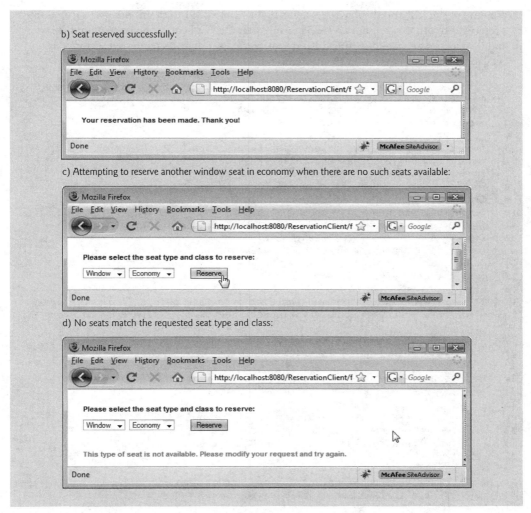

Fig. 23.17 | JSP that allows a user to select a seat. (Part 3 of 3.)

Reserve.java

Figure 23.18 contains the page bean code that provides the logic for Reserve.jsp. As discussed in Section 21.5.2, the class that represents the page's bean extends AbstractPage-Bean. When the user selects a value in one of the DropDownLists, the corresponding event handler—seatTypeDropDown_processValueChange (lines 199–204) or classTypeDrop-Down_processValueChange (lines 207–212)—is called to set the session properties seat-Type and classType, which we added to the web application's session bean. The values of these properties are used as the arguments in the call to the web service's reserve method. When the user clicks **Reserve** in the JSP, the event handler reserveButton_action (lines 215–248) executes. Lines 219–221 use the service endpoint interface object (created in lines 40–41) to invoke the web service's reserve method, passing the selected seat type and class type as arguments. If reserve returns true, lines 225–230 hide the GUI components in the JSP and display the successLabel (line 229) to thank the user for making a reservation; otherwise, lines 234–239 ensure that the GUI components remain displayed and display the errorLabel (line 239) to notify the user that the requested seat type is not available and instruct the user to try again.

```java
 1   // Fig. 23.18: Reserve.java
 2   // Page bean for seat reservation client.
 3   package reservationclient;
 4
 5   import com.deitel.java.reservation.Reservation;
 6   import com.deitel.java.reservation.ReservationService;
 7   import com.sun.rave.web.ui.appbase.AbstractPageBean;
 8   import com.sun.webui.jsf.component.Button;
 9   import com.sun.webui.jsf.component.DropDown;
10   import com.sun.webui.jsf.component.Label;
11   import com.sun.webui.jsf.model.SingleSelectOptionsList;
12   import javax.faces.FacesException;
13   import javax.faces.event.ValueChangeEvent;
14
15   public class Reserve extends AbstractPageBean
16   {
17      // references the service endpoint interface object (i.e., the proxy)
18      private Reservation reservationServiceProxy; // reference to proxy
19
20      // Managed Component Definition
21      private void _init() throws Exception
22      {
23         seatTypeDropDownDefaultOptions.setOptions(
24            new com.sun.webui.jsf.model.Option[]
25            {
26               new com.sun.webui.jsf.model.Option( "Aisle", "Aisle" ),
27               new com.sun.webui.jsf.model.Option( "Middle", "Middle" ),
28               new com.sun.webui.jsf.model.Option( "Window", "Window" )
29            }
30         );
31         classTypeDropDownDefaultOptions.setOptions(
32            new com.sun.webui.jsf.model.Option[]
33            {
34               new com.sun.webui.jsf.model.Option( "Economy", "Economy" ),
35               new com.sun.webui.jsf.model.Option( "First", "First" )
36            }
37         );
38
39         // get service endpoint interface
40         ReservationService reservationService = new ReservationService();
41         reservationServiceProxy = reservationService.getReservationPort();
42      } // end method _init
43
44      // Lines 44-197 of the autogenerated code have been removed to save
45      // space. The complete code is available in this example's folder.
46
```

Fig. 23.18 | Page bean for seat reservation client. (Part 1 of 2.)

```
198    // store selected seat type in session bean
199    public void seatTypeDropDown_processValueChange(
200       ValueChangeEvent event )
201    {
202       getSessionBean1().setSeatType(
203          ( String ) seatTypeDropDown.getSelected() );
204    } // end method seatTypeDropDown_processValueChange
205
206    // store selected class in session bean
207    public void classTypeDropDown_processValueChange(
208       ValueChangeEvent event )
209    {
210       getSessionBean1().setClassType(
211          ( String ) classTypeDropDown.getSelected() );
212    } // end method classTypeDropDown_processValueChange
213
214    // invoke the web service when the user clicks Reserve button
215    public String reserveButton_action()
216    {
217       try
218       {
219          boolean reserved = reservationServiceProxy.reserve(
220             getSessionBean1().getSeatType(),
221             getSessionBean1().getClassType() );
222
223          if ( reserved ) // display successLabel; hide all others
224          {
225             instructionLabel.setRendered( false );
226             seatTypeDropDown.setRendered( false );
227             classTypeDropDown.setRendered( false );
228             reserveButton.setRendered( false );
229             successLabel.setRendered( true );
230             errorLabel.setRendered( false );
231          } // end if
232          else // display all but successLabel
233          {
234             instructionLabel.setRendered( true );
235             seatTypeDropDown.setRendered( true );
236             classTypeDropDown.setRendered( true );
237             reserveButton.setRendered( true );
238             successLabel.setRendered( false );
239             errorLabel.setRendered( true );
240          } // end else
241       } // end try
242       catch ( Exception e )
243       {
244          e.printStackTrace();
245       } // end catch
246
247       return null;
248    } // end method reserveButton_action
249 } // end class Reserve
```

Fig. 23.18 | Page bean for seat reservation client. (Part 2 of 2.)

23.8 Passing an Object of a User-Defined Type to a Web Service

The web methods we've demonstrated so far each receive and return only primitive values or Strings. Web services also can receive and return objects of user-defined types—known as *custom types*. This section presents an EquationGenerator web service that generates random arithmetic questions of type Equation. The client is a math-tutoring desktop application in which the user selects the type of mathematical question to attempt (addition, subtraction or multiplication) and the skill level of the user—level 1 uses one-digit numbers in each question, level 2 uses two-digit numbers and level 3 uses three-digit numbers. The client passes this information to the web service, which then generates an Equation consisting of random numbers with the proper number of digits. The client application receives the Equation, displays the sample question to the user in a Java application, allows the user to provide an answer and checks the answer to determine whether it is correct.

Serialization of User-Defined Types

We mentioned earlier that all types passed to and from SOAP web services must be supported by SOAP. How, then, can SOAP support a type that is not even created yet? Custom types that are sent to or from a web service are serialized into XML format. This process is referred to as *XML serialization*. The process of serializing objects to XML and deserializing objects from XML is handled for you automatically.

Requirements for User-Defined Types Used with Web Methods

A class that is used to specify parameter or return types in web methods must meet several requirements:

1. It must provide a public default or no-argument constructor. When a web service or web service consumer receives an XML serialized object, the JAX-WS framework must be able to call this constructor when deserializing the object (i.e., converting it from XML back to a Java object).

2. Instance variables that should be serialized in XML format must have public *set* and *get* methods to access the private instance variables (recommended), or the instance variables must be declared public (not recommended).

3. Non-public instance variables that should be serialized must provide both *set* and *get* methods (even if they have empty bodies); otherwise, they're not serialized.

Any instance variable that is not serialized simply receives its default value (or the value provided by the no-argument constructor) when an object of the class is deserialized.

Common Programming Error 23.3

A runtime error occurs if an attempt is made to deserialize an object of a class that does not have a default or no-argument constructor.

Defining Class Equation

Figure 23.19 defines class Equation. Lines 18–31 define a constructor that takes three arguments—two ints representing the left and right operands and a String that represents the arithmetic operation to perform. The constructor sets the leftOperand, rightOperand and operationType instance variables, then calculates the appropriate result. The no-argument constructor (lines 13–16) calls the three-argument constructor (lines 18–31) and passes default values. We do not use the no-argument constructor explicitly, but the XML serialization mechanism uses it when objects of this class are deserialized. Because we provide a constructor with parameters, we must explicitly define the no-argument constructor in this class so that objects of the class can be passed to or returned from web methods.

```java
1   // Fig. 23.19: Equation.java
2   // Class Equation that contains information about an equation
3   package com.deitel.java.equationgenerator;
4
5   public class Equation
6   {
7      private int leftOperand;
8      private int rightOperand;
9      private int resultValue;
10     private String operationType;
11
12     // required no-argument constructor
13     public Equation()
14     {
15        this( 0, 0, "+" );
16     } // end no-argument constructor
17
18     public Equation( int leftValue, int rightValue, String type )
19     {
20        leftOperand = leftValue;
21        rightOperand = rightValue;
22        operationType = type;
23
24        //determine resultValue
25        if ( operationType.equals( "+" ) ) // addition
26           resultValue = leftOperand + rightOperand;
27        else if ( operationType.equals( "-" ) ) // subtraction
28           resultValue = leftOperand - rightOperand;
29        else // multiplication
30           resultValue = leftOperand * rightOperand;
31     } // end three-argument constructor
32
33     // method that overrides Object.toString()
34     public String toString()
35     {
36        return leftOperand + " " + operationType + " " +
37           rightOperand + " = " + resultValue;
38     } // end method toString
39
40     // returns the left-hand side of the equation as a String
41     public String getLeftHandSide()
42     {
43        return leftOperand + " " + operationType + " " + rightOperand;
44     } // end method getLeftHandSide
45
```

Fig. 23.19 | Class `Equation` that stores information about an equation. (Part 1 of 3.)

```
46      // returns the right-hand side of the equation as a String
47      public String getRightHandSide()
48      {
49         return "" + resultValue;
50      } // end method getRightHandSide
51
52      // gets the leftOperand
53      public int getLeftOperand()
54      {
55         return leftOperand;
56      } // end method getLeftOperand
57
58      // gets the rightOperand
59      public int getRightOperand()
60      {
61         return rightOperand;
62      } // end method getRightOperand
63
64      // gets the resultValue
65      public int getReturnValue()
66      {
67         return resultValue;
68      } // end method getResultValue
69
70      // gets the operationType
71      public String getOperationType()
72      {
73         return operationType;
74      } // end method getOperationType
75
76      // required setter
77      public void setLeftHandSide( String value )
78      {
79         // empty body
80      } // end setLeftHandSide
81
82      // required setter
83      public void setRightHandSide( String value )
84      {
85         // empty body
86      } // end setRightHandSide
87
88      // required setter
89      public void setLeftOperand( int value )
90      {
91         // empty body
92      } // end method setLeftOperand
93
94      // required setter
95      public void setRightOperand( int value )
96      {
97         // empty body
98      } // end method setRightOperand
```

Fig. 23.19 | Class Equation that stores information about an equation. (Part 2 of 3.)

```
99
100     // required setter
101     public void setReturnValue( int value )
102     {
103         // empty body
104     } // end method setResultOperand
105
106     // required setter
107     public void setOperationType( String value )
108     {
109         // empty body
110     } // end method setOperationType
111 } // end class Equation
```

Fig. 23.19 | Class `Equation` that stores information about an equation. (Part 3 of 3.)

Class `Equation` defines methods `getLeftHandSide` and `setLeftHandSide` (lines 41–44 and 77–80); `getRightHandSide` and `setRightHandSide` (lines 47–50 and 83–86); `getLeftOperand` and `setLeftOperand` (lines 53–56 and 89–92); `getRightOperand` and `setRightOperand` (lines 59–62 and 95–98); `getReturnValue` and `setReturnValue` (lines 65–68 and 101–104); and `getOperationType` and `setOperationType` (lines 71–74 and 107–110). The client of the web service does not need to modify the values of the instance variables. However, recall that a property can be serialized only if it has both a *get* and a *set* accessor, or if it is `public`. So we provided *set* methods with empty bodies for each of the class's instance variables. Method `getLeftHandSide` (lines 41–44) returns a `String` representing everything to the left of the equals (=) sign in the equation, and `getRightHandSide` (lines 47–50) returns a `String` representing everything to the right of the equals (=) sign. Method `getLeftOperand` (lines 53–56) returns the integer to the left of the operator, and `getRightOperand` (lines 59–62) returns the integer to the right of the operator. Method `getResultValue` (lines 65–68) returns the solution to the equation, and `getOperationType` (lines 71–74) returns the operator in the equation. The client in this example does not use the `rightHandSide` property, but we included it so future clients can use it.

Creating the *EquationGenerator* Web Service
Figure 23.20 presents the `EquationGenerator` web service, which creates random, customized `Equations`. This web service contains only method `generateEquation` (lines 18–31), which takes two parameters—the mathematical operation (one of "+", "-" or "*") and an `int` representing the difficulty level (1–3).

```
1   // Fig. 23.20: Generator.java
2   // Web service that generates random equations
3   package com.deitel.java.equationgenerator;
4
5   import java.util.Random;
6   import javax.jws.WebMethod;
7   import javax.jws.WebParam;
8   import javax.jws.WebService;
9
```

Fig. 23.20 | Web service that generates random equations. (Part 1 of 2.)

```
10   @WebService( name = "EquationGenerator",
11      serviceName = "EquationGeneratorService" )
12   public class EquationGenerator
13   {
14      private int minimum;
15      private int maximum;
16
17      // generates a math equation and returns it as an Equation object
18      @WebMethod( operationName = "generateEquation" )
19      public Equation generateEquation(
20         @WebParam( name = "operation" ) String operation,
21         @WebParam( name = "difficulty" ) int difficulty )
22      {
23         minimum = ( int ) Math.pow( 10, difficulty - 1 );
24         maximum = ( int ) Math.pow( 10, difficulty );
25
26         Random randomObject = new Random();
27
28         return new Equation(
29            randomObject.nextInt( maximum - minimum ) + minimum,
30            randomObject.nextInt( maximum - minimum ) + minimum, operation );
31      } // end method generateEquation
32   } // end class EquationGenerator
```

Fig. 23.20 | Web service that generates random equations. (Part 2 of 2.)

Testing the EquationGenerator Web Service

Figure 23.21 shows the result of testing the EquationGenerator service with the Tester web page. In part (*b*), note that the web method's return value is XML encoded. However, this example differs from previous ones in that the XML specifies the values for all the data of the returned XML serialized object. The service endpoint interface class receives this return value and deserializes it into an object of class Equation, then passes it to the client.

(a) Using the EquationGenerator web service's Tester web page to generate an Equation.

Fig. 23.21 | Testing a web method that returns an XML serialized Equation object. (Part 1 of 2.)

(b) Result of generating an `Equation`.

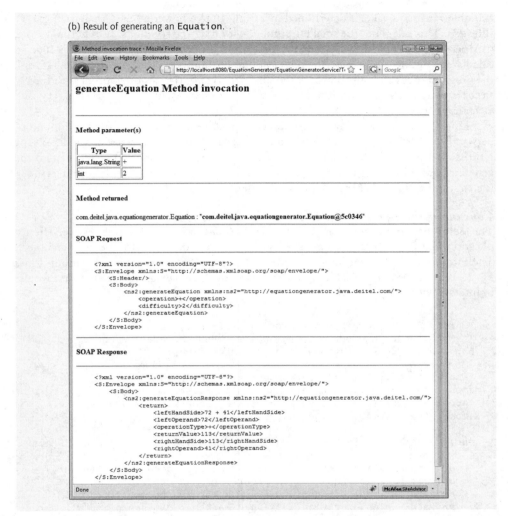

Fig. 23.21 | Testing a web method that returns an XML serialized `Equation` object. (Part 2 of 2.)

Note that an `Equation` object is *not* being passed between the web service and the client. Rather, the information in the object is being sent as XML-encoded data. Clients created using Java will take the information and create a new `Equation` object. Clients created on other platforms, however, may use the information differently. Readers creating clients on other platforms should check the web services documentation for the specific platform they are using, to see how their clients may process custom types.

Details of the EquationGenerator Web Service

Let's examine web method `generateEquation` more closely. Lines 23–24 of Fig. 23.20 define the upper and lower bounds of the random numbers that the method uses to generate an `Equation`. To set these limits, the program first calls `static` Math method pow.

Variable minimum's value is determined by raising 10 to a power one less than difficulty (line 23). This calculates the smallest number with difficulty digits. If difficulty is 1, minimum is 1; if difficulty is 2, minimum is 10; and if difficulty is 3, minimum is 100. To calculate the value of maximum (the upper bound for numbers used to form an Equation), the program raises 10 to the power of the specified difficulty argument (line 24). If difficulty is 1, maximum is 10; if difficulty is 2, maximum is 100; and if difficulty is 3, maximum is 1000.

Lines 28–30 create and return a new Equation object consisting of two random numbers and the String operation received by generateEquation. Random method nextInt returns an int that is less than the specified upper bound. Method generateEquation generates operand values that are greater than or equal to minimum but less than maximum (i.e., a number with difficulty number of digits).

Consuming the EquationGenerator Web Service

The **Math Tutor** application (Fig. 23.22) uses the EquationGenerator web service. The application calls the web service's generateEquation method to create an Equation object. The tutor then displays the left-hand side of the Equation and waits for user input. Lines 12–13 declare instance variables of types EquationGenerator and Equation that we use to interact with the web service.

```java
1   // Fig. 23.22: EquationGeneratorClientJFrame.java
2   // Math tutoring program using web services to generate equations.
3   package com.deitel.java.equationgeneratorclient;
4
5   import com.deitel.java.equationgenerator.Equation;
6   import com.deitel.java.equationgenerator.EquationGenerator;
7   import com.deitel.java.equationgenerator.EquationGeneratorService;
8   import javax.swing.JOptionPane;
9
10  public class EquationGeneratorClientJFrame extends javax.swing.JFrame
11  {
12     private EquationGenerator proxy; // used to access the web service
13     private Equation equation; // represents an equation
14     private int answer; // the user's answer to the question
15     private String operation = "+"; // mathematical operation +, - or *
16     private int difficulty = 1; // 1, 2 or 3 digits in each number
17
18     // constructor creates new form EquationGeneratorClientJFrame
19     public EquationGeneratorClientJFrame()
20     {
21        initComponents();
22
23        try
24        {
25           // get service endpoint interface
26           EquationGeneratorService service =
27              new EquationGeneratorService();
28           proxy = service.getEquationGeneratorPort();
29        } // end try
```

Fig. 23.22 | Math tutoring application. (Part 1 of 4.)

```
30          catch ( Exception ex )
31          {
32              ex.printStackTrace();
33              System.exit( 1 );
34          } // end catch
35      } // end constructor
36
37      // The initComponents method is autogenerated by Netbeans and is called
38      // from the constructor to initialize the GUI. This method is not shown
39      // here to save space. Open EquationGeneratorClientJFrame.java in this
40      // example's folder to view the complete generated code (lines 37-154).
41
155     // obtains the mathematical operation selected by the user
156     private void operationJComboBoxItemStateChanged(
157         java.awt.event.ItemEvent evt )
158     {
159         String item = ( String ) operationJComboBox.getSelectedItem();
160
161         if ( item.equals( "Addition" ) )
162             operation = "+"; // user selected addition
163         else if ( item.equals( "Subtraction" ) )
164             operation = "-"; // user selected subtraction
165         else
166             operation = "*"; // user selected multiplication
167     } // end method operationJComboBoxItemStateChanged
168
169     // obtains the difficulty level selected by the user
170     private void levelJComboBoxItemStateChanged(
171         java.awt.event.ItemEvent evt )
172     {
173         // indices start at 0, so add 1 to get the difficulty level
174         difficulty = levelJComboBox.getSelectedIndex() + 1;
175     } // end method levelJComboBoxItemStateChanged
176
177     // generates a new Equation based on user's selections
178     private void generateJButtonActionPerformed(
179         java.awt.event.ActionEvent evt )
180     {
181         try
182         {
183             equation = proxy.generateEquation( operation, difficulty );
184             answer = equation.getReturnValue();
185             equationJLabel.setText( equation.getLeftHandSide() + " =" );
186             checkAnswerJButton.setEnabled( true );
187         } // end try
188         catch ( Exception e )
189         {
190             e.printStackTrace();
191         } // end catch
192     } // end method generateJButtonActionPerformed
193
```

Fig. 23.22 | Math tutoring application. (Part 2 of 4.)

```
194     // checks the user's answer
195     private void checkAnswerJButtonActionPerformed(
196        java.awt.event.ActionEvent evt )
197     {
198        if ( answerJTextField.getText().equals( "" ) )
199        {
200           JOptionPane.showMessageDialog(
201              this, "Please enter your answer." );
202        } // end if
203
204        int userAnswer = Integer.parseInt( answerJTextField.getText() );
205
206        if ( userAnswer == answer )
207        {
208           equationJLabel.setText( "" );
209           answerJTextField.setText( "" );
210           checkAnswerJButton.setEnabled( false );
211           JOptionPane.showMessageDialog( this, "Correct! Good Job!",
212              "Correct", JOptionPane.PLAIN_MESSAGE );
213        } // end if
214        else
215        {
216           JOptionPane.showMessageDialog( this, "Incorrect. Try again.",
217              "Incorrect", JOptionPane.PLAIN_MESSAGE );
218        } // end else
219     } // end method checkAnswerJButtonActionPerformed
220
221     public static void main(String args[])
222     {
223        java.awt.EventQueue.invokeLater(
224           new Runnable()
225           {
226              public void run()
227              {
228                 new EquationGeneratorClientJFrame().setVisible( true );
229              } // end method Run
230           } // end new Runnable
231        ); // end call to java.awt.EventQueue.invokeLater
232     } // end main
233
234     // Variables declaration - do not modify
235     private javax.swing.JLabel answerJLabel;
236     private javax.swing.JTextField answerJTextField;
237     private javax.swing.JButton checkAnswerJButton;
238     private javax.swing.JLabel equationJLabel;
239     private javax.swing.JButton generateJButton;
240     private javax.swing.JComboBox levelJComboBox;
241     private javax.swing.JLabel levelJLabel;
242     private javax.swing.JComboBox operationJComboBox;
243     private javax.swing.JLabel operationJLabel;
244     private javax.swing.JLabel questionJLabel;
245     // End of variables declaration
246  } // end class EquationGeneratorClientJFrame
```

Fig. 23.22 | Math tutoring application. (Part 3 of 4.)

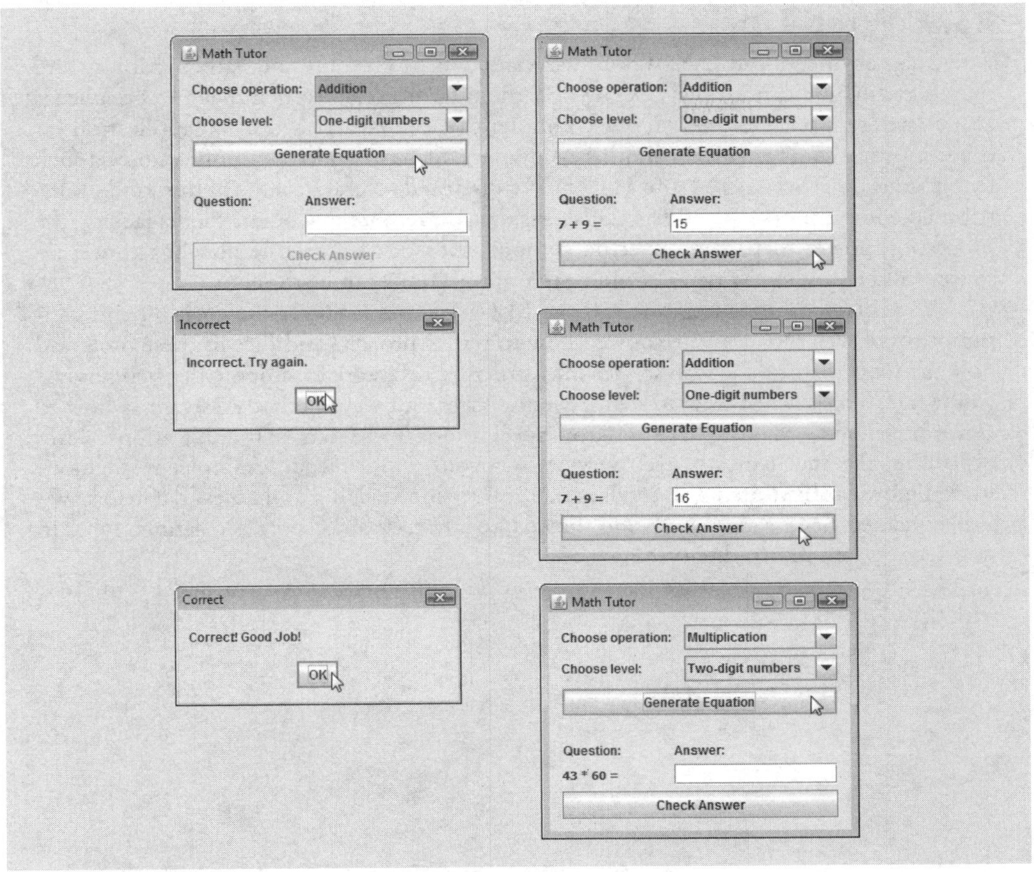

Fig. 23.22 | Math tutoring application. (Part 4 of 4.)

After displaying an equation, the application waits for the user to enter an answer. The default setting for the difficulty level is **One-digit numbers**, but the user can change this by choosing a level from the **Choose level** JComboBox. Clicking any of the levels invokes levelJComboBoxItemStateChanged (lines 170–175), which sets the variable difficulty to the level selected by the user. Although the default setting for the question type is **Addition**, the user also can change this by selecting an operation from the **Choose operation** JComboBox. Doing so invokes operationJComboBoxItemStateChanged (lines 156–167), which sets the String operation to the appropriate mathematical symbol.

When the user clicks the **Generate Equation** JButton, method generateButton-ActionPerformed (lines 178–192) invokes the EquationGenerator web service's generateEquation (line 183) method, which returns an Equation object. After receiving the Equation object from the web service, the handler obtains the Equation's correct answer (line 184) and lefthand side, then displays the left-hand side in equationJLabel (line 185) and enables the checkAnswerJButton so that the user can submit an answer. When the user clicks the **Check Answer** JButton, method checkAnswerJButtonActionPerformed (lines 195–219) determines whether the user provided the correct answer.

23.9 Wrap-Up

This chapter introduced JAX-WS web services, which promote software portability and reusability in applications that operate over the Internet. You learned that a web service is a software component stored on one computer that can be accessed by an application (or other software component) on another computer over a network, communicating via such technologies as XML, SOAP and HTTP. We discussed several benefits of this kind of distributed computing—e.g., clients can access data on remote machines, clients lacking the processing power to perform specific computations can leverage remote machines' resources and entirely new types of innovative applications can be developed.

We explained how Netbeans and the JAX-WS APIs facilitate the creation and consumption of web services. We showed how to set up projects and files in these tools and how the tools manage the web service infrastructure necessary to support the web services you create. You learned how to define web services and web methods, as well as how to consume them both from Java desktop applications and from web applications. After explaining the mechanics of web services with our HugeInteger example, we demonstrated more sophisticated web services that use session tracking and access databases. We also explained XML serialization and showed how to pass objects of user-defined types to web services and return them from web services.

The next chapter discusses formatting output with method System.out.printf and with class Formatter.

24

Formatted Output

All the news that's fit to print.
—Adolph S. Ochs

What mad pursuit? What struggle to escape?
—John Keats

Remove not the landmark on the boundary of the fields.
—Amenehope

OBJECTIVES

In this chapter you'll learn:

- To understand input and output streams.
- To use `printf` formatting.
- To print with field widths and precisions.
- To use formatting flags in the `printf` format string.
- To print with an argument index.
- To output literals and escape sequences.
- To format output with class `Formatter`.

Outline

24.1 Introduction
24.2 Streams
24.3 Formatting Output with `printf`
24.4 Printing Integers
24.5 Printing Floating-Point Numbers
24.6 Printing Strings and Characters
24.7 Printing Dates and Times
24.8 Other Conversion Characters
24.9 Printing with Field Widths and Precisions
24.10 Using Flags in the `printf` Format String
24.11 Printing with Argument Indices
24.12 Printing Literals and Escape Sequences
24.13 Formatting Output with Class `Formatter`
24.14 Wrap-Up

24.1 Introduction

An important part of the solution to any problem is the presentation of the results. In this chapter, we discuss the formatting features of method *printf* and class Formatter (package java.util). Method printf formats and outputs data to the standard output stream—System.out. Class *Formatter* formats and outputs data to a specified destination, such as a string or a file output stream.

Many features of printf were discussed earlier in the text. This chapter summarizes those features and introduces others, such as displaying date and time data in various formats, reordering output based on the index of the argument and displaying numbers and strings with various flags.

24.2 Streams

Input and output are usually performed with streams, which are sequences of bytes. In input operations, the bytes flow from a device (e.g., a keyboard, a disk drive, a network connection) to main memory. In output operations, bytes flow from main memory to a device (e.g., a display screen, a printer, a disk drive, a network connection).

When program execution begins, three streams are connected to the program automatically. Normally, the standard input stream is connected to the keyboard, and the standard output stream is connected to the screen. A third stream, the *standard error stream* (System.err), is typically connected to the screen and is used to output error messages so they can be viewed immediately—even when the standard output stream is writing into a file. Operating systems typically allow these streams to be redirected to other devices. Streams are discussed in detail in Chapter 14, Files and Streams, and Chapter 19, Networking.

24.3 Formatting Output with `printf`

Precise output formatting is accomplished with printf. [*Note:* Java SE 5 borrowed this feature from the C programming language.] Method printf can perform the following formatting capabilities, each of which is discussed in this chapter:

1. Rounding floating-point values to an indicated number of decimal places.
2. Aligning a column of numbers with decimal points appearing one above the other.
3. Right justification and left justification of outputs.
4. Inserting literal characters at precise locations in a line of output.
5. Representing floating-point numbers in exponential format.
6. Representing integers in octal and hexadecimal format.
7. Displaying all types of data with fixed-size field widths and precisions.
8. Displaying dates and times in various formats.

Every call to printf supplies as the first argument a *format string* that describes the output format. The format string may consist of *fixed text* and *format specifiers*. Fixed text is output by printf just as it would be output by System.out methods print or println. Each format specifier is a placeholder for a value and specifies the type of data to output. Format specifiers also may include optional formatting information.

In the simplest form, each format specifier begins with a percent sign (%) and is followed by a *conversion character* that represents the data type of the value to output. For example, the format specifier %s is a placeholder for a string, and the format specifier %d is a placeholder for an int value. The optional formatting information is specified between the percent sign and the conversion character. The optional formatting information includes an argument index, flags, field width and precision. We define each of these and show examples of them throughout this chapter.

24.4 Printing Integers

An integer is a whole number, such as 776, 0 or –52, that contains no decimal point. Integer values are displayed in one of several formats. Figure 24.1 describes the *integral conversion characters*.

Conversion character	Description
d	Display a decimal (base 10) integer.
o	Display an octal (base 8) integer.
x or X	Display a hexadecimal (base 16) integer. X causes the digits 0–9 and the letters A–F to be displayed and x causes the digits 0–9 and a–f to be displayed.

Fig. 24.1 | Integer conversion characters.

Figure 24.2 prints an integer using each of the integral conversions. In lines 9–10, note that the plus sign is not displayed by default, but the minus sign is. Later in this chapter (Fig. 24.14) we'll see how to force plus signs to print.

The printf method has the form

```
printf( format-string, argument-list );
```

```
1   // Fig. 24.2: IntegerConversionTest.java
2   // Using the integral conversion characters.
3
4   public class IntegerConversionTest
5   {
6      public static void main( String args[] )
7      {
8         System.out.printf( "%d\n", 26 );
9         System.out.printf( "%d\n", +26 );
10        System.out.printf( "%d\n", -26 );
11        System.out.printf( "%o\n", 26 );
12        System.out.printf( "%x\n", 26 );
13        System.out.printf( "%X\n", 26 );
14     } // end main
15  } // end class IntegerConversionTest
```

```
26
26
-26
32
1a
1A
```

Fig. 24.2 | Using integer conversion characters.

where *format-string* describes the output format, and *argument-list* contains the values that correspond to each format specifier in *format-string*. There can be many format specifiers in one format string.

Each format string in lines 8–10 specifies that printf should output a decimal integer (%d) followed by a newline character. At the format specifier's position, printf substitutes the value of the first argument after the format string. If the format string contained multiple format specifiers, at each subsequent format specifier's position, printf would substitute the value of the next argument in the argument list. The %o format specifier in line 11 outputs the integer in octal format. The %x format specifier in line 12 outputs the integer in hexadecimal format. The %X format specifier in line 13 outputs the integer in hexadecimal format with capital letters.

24.5 Printing Floating-Point Numbers

A floating-point value contains a decimal point, as in 33.5, 0.0 or -657.983. Floating-point values are displayed in one of several formats. Figure 24.3 describes the floating-point conversions. The **conversion characters e** and **E** display floating-point values in **computerized scientific notation** (also called **exponential notation**). Exponential notation is the computer equivalent of the scientific notation used in mathematics. For example, the value 150.4582 is represented in scientific notation in mathematics as

$$1.504582 \times 10^2$$

and is represented in exponential notation as

1.504582e+02

in Java. This notation indicates that 1.504582 is multiplied by 10 raised to the second power (e+02). The e stands for "exponent."

Conversion character	Description
e or E	Display a floating-point value in exponential notation. When E is used, the output is displayed in uppercase letters.
f	Display a floating-point value in decimal format.
g or G	Display a floating-point value in either the floating-point format f or the exponential format e based on the magnitude of the value. If the magnitude is less than 10^{-3}, or greater than or equal to 10^7, the floating-point value is printed with e (or E). Otherwise, the value is printed in format f. When conversion character G is used, the output is displayed in uppercase letters.
a or A	Display a floating-point number in hexadecimal format. When A is used, the output is displayed in uppercase letters.

Fig. 24.3 | Floating-point conversion characters.

Values printed with the conversion characters e, E and f are output with six digits of precision to the right of the decimal point by default (e.g., 1.045921)—other precisions must be specified explicitly. For values printed with the conversion character g, the precision represents the total number of digits displayed, excluding the exponent. The default is six digits (e.g., 12345678.9 is displayed as 1.23457e+07). ***Conversion character f*** always prints at least one digit to the left of the decimal point. Conversion characters e and E print lowercase e and uppercase E preceding the exponent and always print exactly one digit to the left of the decimal point. Rounding occurs if the value being formatted has more significant digits than the precision.

Conversion character g (or *G*) prints in either e (E) or f format, depending on the floating-point value. For example, the values 0.0000875, 87500000.0, 8.75, 87.50 and 875.0 are printed as 8.750000e-05, 8.750000e+07, 8.750000, 87.500000 and 875.000000 with the conversion character g. The value 0.0000875 uses e notation because the magnitude is less than 10-3. The value 87500000.0 uses e notation because the magnitude is greater than 107. Figure 24.4 demonstrates each of the floating-point conversion characters.

```java
// Fig. 24.4: FloatingNumberTest.java
// Using floating-point conversion characters.

public class FloatingNumberTest
{
   public static void main( String args[] )
   {
      System.out.printf( "%e\n", 12345678.9 );
      System.out.printf( "%e\n", +12345678.9 );
```

Fig. 24.4 | Using floating-point conversion characters. (Part 1 of 2.)

```
10          System.out.printf( "%e\n", -12345678.9 );
11          System.out.printf( "%E\n", 12345678.9 );
12          System.out.printf( "%f\n", 12345678.9 );
13          System.out.printf( "%g\n", 12345678.9 );
14          System.out.printf( "%G\n", 12345678.9 );
15       } // end main
16    } // end class FloatingNumberTest
```

```
1.234568e+07
1.234568e+07
-1.234568e+07
1.234568E+07
12345678.900000
1.23457e+07
1.23457E+07
```

Fig. 24.4 | Using floating-point conversion characters. (Part 2 of 2.)

24.6 Printing Strings and Characters

The c and s conversion characters are used to print individual characters and strings, respectively. Conversion character s can also print objects with the results of implicit calls to method toString. *Conversion characters c and C require a char argument. Conversion characters s and S can take a String or any Object (this includes all subclasses of Object)* as an argument. When an object is passed to the conversion character s, the program implicitly uses the object's toString method to obtain the String representation of the object. When conversion characters C and S are used, the output is displayed in uppercase letters. The program shown in Fig. 24.5 displays characters, strings and objects with conversion characters c and s. Note that autoboxing occurs at line 10 when an int constant is assigned to an Integer object. Line 15 associates an Integer object argument to the conversion character s, which implicitly invokes the toString method to get the integer value. Note that you can also output an Integer object using the %d format specifier. In this case, the int value in the Integer object will be unboxed and output.

```
1    // Fig. 24.5: CharStringConversion.java
2    // Using character and string conversion characters.
3
4    public class CharStringConversion
5    {
6       public static void main( String args[] )
7       {
8          char character = 'A';  // initialize char
9          String string = "This is also a string";  // String object
10         Integer integer = 1234;  // initialize integer (autoboxing)
11
12         System.out.printf( "%c\n", character );
13         System.out.printf( "%s\n", "This is a string" );
14         System.out.printf( "%s\n", string );
```

Fig. 24.5 | Using character and string conversion characters. (Part 1 of 2.)

```
15        System.out.printf( "%S\n", string );
16        System.out.printf( "%s\n", integer ); // implicit call to toString
17    } // end main
18 } // end class CharStringConversion
```

```
A
This is a string
This is also a string
THIS IS ALSO A STRING
1234
```

Fig. 24.5 | Using character and string conversion characters. (Part 2 of 2.)

Common Programming Error 24.1

Using %c to print a string causes an IllegalFormatConversionException—a string cannot be converted to a character.

24.7 Printing Dates and Times

With the *conversion character **t** or **T***, we can print dates and times in various formats. Conversion character t or T is always followed by a *conversion suffix character* that specifies the date and/or time format. When conversion character T is used, the output is displayed in uppercase letters. Figure 24.6 lists the common conversion suffix characters for formatting *date and time compositions* that display both the date and the time. Figure 24.7 lists the common conversion suffix characters for formatting dates. Figure 24.8 lists the common conversion suffix characters for formatting times. To view the complete list of conversion suffix characters, visit the website java.sun.com/javase/6/docs/api/java/util/Formatter.html.

Conversion suffix character	Description
c	Display date and time formatted as day month date hour:minute:second time-zone year with three characters for day and month, two digits for date, hour, minute and second and four digits for year—for example, Wed Mar 03 16:30:25 GMT-05:00 2004. The 24-hour clock is used. In this example, GMT-05:00 is the time zone.
F	Display date formatted as year-month-date with four digits for the year and two digits each for the month and the date (e.g., 2004-05-04).
D	Display date formatted as month/day/year with two digits each for the month, day and year (e.g., 03/03/04).

Fig. 24.6 | Date and time composition conversion suffix characters. (Part 1 of 2.)

Conversion suffix character	Description
r	Display time formatted as hour:minute:second AM|PM with two digits each for the hour, minute and second (e.g., 04:30:25 PM). The 12-hour clock is used.
R	Display time formatted as hour:minute with two digits each for the hour and minute (e.g., 16:30). The 24-hour clock is used.
T	Display time formatted as hour:minute:second with two digits for the hour, minute and second (e.g., 16:30:25). The 24-hour clock is used.

Fig. 24.6 | Date and time composition conversion suffix characters. (Part 2 of 2.)

Conversion suffix character	Description
A	Display full name of the day of the week (e.g., Wednesday).
a	Display the three-character short name of the day of the week (e.g., Wed).
B	Display full name of the month (e.g., March).
b	Display the three-character short name of the month (e.g., Mar).
d	Display the day of the month with two digits, padding with leading zeros as necessary (e.g., 03).
m	Display the month with two digits, padding with leading zeros as necessary (e.g., 07).
e	Display the day of month without leading zeros (e.g., 3).
Y	Display the year with four digits (e.g., 2004).
y	Display the last two digits of the year with leading zeros as necessary (e.g., 04).
j	Display the day of the year with three digits, padding with leading zeros as necessary (e.g., 016).

Fig. 24.7 | Date formatting conversion suffix characters.

Conversion suffix character	Description
H	Display hour in 24-hour clock with a leading zero as necessary (e.g., 16).
I	Display hour in 12-hour clock with a leading zero as necessary (e.g., 04).

Fig. 24.8 | Time formatting conversion suffix characters. (Part 1 of 2.)

Conversion suffix character	Description
k	Display hour in 24-hour clock without leading zeros (e.g., 16).
l	Display hour in 12-hour clock without leading zeros (e.g., 4).
M	Display minute with a leading zero as necessary (e.g., 06).
S	Display second with a leading zero as necessary (e.g., 05).
Z	Display the abbreviation for the time zone (e.g., GMT-05:00, stands for Eastern Standard Time, which is 5 hours behind Greenwich Mean Time).
p	Display morning or afternoon marker in lowercase (e.g., pm).
P	Display morning or afternoon marker in uppercase (e.g., PM).

Fig. 24.8 | Time formatting conversion suffix characters. (Part 2 of 2.)

Figure 24.9 uses the conversion character t with the conversion suffix characters to display dates and times in various formats. Conversion character t requires the corresponding argument to be of type long, Long, *Calendar* or *Date* (both in package java.util)—objects of each of these classes can represent dates and times. Class Calendar is the preferred class for this purpose because some constructors and methods in class Date are replaced by those in class Calendar. Line 10 invokes static method *getInstance* of Calendar to obtain a calendar with the current date and time. Lines 13–17, 20–22 and 25–26 use this Calendar object in printf statements as the value to be formatted with conversion character t. Note that lines 20–22 and 25–26 use the optional *argument index* ("1$") to indicate that all format specifiers in the format string use the first argument after the format string in the argument list. You'll learn more about argument indices in Section 24.11. Using the argument index eliminates the need to repeatedly list the same argument.

```java
1   // Fig. 24.9: DateTimeTest.java
2   // Formatting dates and times with conversion character t and T.
3   import java.util.Calendar;
4
5   public class DateTimeTest
6   {
7      public static void main( String args[] )
8      {
9         // get current date and time
10        Calendar dateTime = Calendar.getInstance();
11
12        // printing with conversion characters for date/time compositions
13        System.out.printf( "%tc\n", dateTime );
14        System.out.printf( "%tF\n", dateTime );
15        System.out.printf( "%tD\n", dateTime );
16        System.out.printf( "%tr\n", dateTime );
```

Fig. 24.9 | Formatting dates and times with conversion character t. (Part 1 of 2.)

```
17          System.out.printf( "%tT\n", dateTime );
18
19          // printing with conversion characters for date
20          System.out.printf( "%1$tA, %1$tB %1$td, %1$tY\n", dateTime );
21          System.out.printf( "%1$TA, %1$TB %1$Td, %1$TY\n", dateTime );
22          System.out.printf( "%1$ta, %1$tb %1$te, %1$ty\n", dateTime );
23
24          // printing with conversion characters for time
25          System.out.printf( "%1$tH:%1$tM:%1$tS\n", dateTime );
26          System.out.printf( "%1$tZ %1$tI:%1$tM:%1$tS %tP", dateTime );
27    } // end main
28  } // end class DateTimeTest
```

```
Thu Nov 30 18:23:10 EST 2006
2006-11-30
11/30/06
06:23:10 PM
18:23:10
Thursday, November 30, 2006
THURSDAY, NOVEMBER 30, 2006
Thu, Nov 30, 06
18:23:10
EST 06:23:10 PM
```

Fig. 24.9 | Formatting dates and times with conversion character t. (Part 2 of 2.)

24.8 Other Conversion Characters

The remaining conversion characters are *b*, *B*, *h*, *H*, *%* and *n*. These are described in Fig. 24.10.

Conversion character	Description
b or B	Print "true" or "false" for the value of a boolean or Boolean. These conversion characters can also format the value of any reference. If the reference is non-null, "true" is output; otherwise, "false" is output. When conversion character B is used, the output is displayed in uppercase letters.
h or H	Print the string representation of an object's hash-code value in hexadecimal format. If the corresponding argument is null, "null" is printed. When conversion character H is used, the output is displayed in uppercase letters.
%	Print the percent character.
n	Print the platform-specific line separator (e.g., \r\n on Windows or \n on UNIX/LINUX).

Fig. 24.10 | Other conversion specifiers.

Lines 9–10 of Fig. 24.11 use %b to print the value of boolean values false and true. Line 11 associates a String to %b, which returns true because it is not null. Line 12 associates a null object to %B, which displays FALSE because test is null. Lines 13–14 use %h to print the string representations of the hash-code values for strings "hello" and "Hello". These values could be used to store or locate the strings in a Hashtable or HashMap (both discussed in Chapter 16, Collections). Note that the hash-code values for these two strings differ because one string starts with a lowercase letter and the other with an uppercase letter. Line 15 uses %H to print null in uppercase letters. The last two printf statements (lines 16–17) use %% to print the % character in a string and %n to print a plat-form-specific line separator.

Common Programming Error 24.2

Trying to print a literal percent character using % rather than %% in the format string might cause a difficult-to-detect logic error. When % appears in a format string, it must be followed by a con-version character in the string. The single percent could accidentally be followed by a legitimate conversion character, thus causing a logic error.

```
1   // Fig. 24.11: OtherConversion.java
2   // Using the b, B, h, H, % and n conversion characters.
3
4   public class OtherConversion
5   {
6      public static void main( String args[] )
7      {
8         Object test = null;
9         System.out.printf( "%b\n", false );
10        System.out.printf( "%b\n", true );
11        System.out.printf( "%b\n", "Test" );
12        System.out.printf( "%B\n", test );
13        System.out.printf( "Hashcode of \"hello\" is %h\n", "hello" );
14        System.out.printf( "Hashcode of \"Hello\" is %h\n", "Hello" );
15        System.out.printf( "Hashcode of null is %H\n", test );
16        System.out.printf( "Printing a %% in a format string\n" );
17        System.out.printf( "Printing a new line %nnext line starts here" );
18     } // end main
19  } // end class OtherConversion
```

```
false
true
true
FALSE
Hashcode of "hello" is 5e918d2
Hashcode of "Hello" is 42628b2
Hashcode of null is NULL
Printing a % in a format string
Printing a new line
next line starts here
```

Fig. 24.11 | Using the b, B, h, H, % and n conversion characters.

24.9 Printing with Field Widths and Precisions

The exact size of a field in which data is printed is specified by a *field width*. If the field width is larger than the data being printed, the data will be right justified within that field by default. (We demonstrate left justification in Section 24.10.) The programmer inserts an integer representing the field width between the percent sign (%) and the conversion character (e.g., %4d) in the format specifier. Figure 24.12 prints two groups of five numbers each, right justifying those numbers that contain fewer digits than the field width. Note that the field width is increased to print values wider than the field and that the minus sign for a negative value uses one character position in the field. Also, if no field width is specified, the data prints in exactly as many positions as it needs. Field widths can be used with all format specifiers except the line separator (%n).

Common Programming Error 24.3

Not providing a sufficiently large field width to handle a value to be printed can offset other data being printed and produce confusing outputs. Know your data!

```java
1   // Fig. 24.12: FieldWidthTest.java
2   // Right justifying integers in fields.
3
4   public class FieldWidthTest
5   {
6      public static void main( String args[] )
7      {
8         System.out.printf( "%4d\n", 1 );
9         System.out.printf( "%4d\n", 12 );
10        System.out.printf( "%4d\n", 123 );
11        System.out.printf( "%4d\n", 1234 );
12        System.out.printf( "%4d\n\n", 12345 ); // data too large
13
14        System.out.printf( "%4d\n", -1 );
15        System.out.printf( "%4d\n", -12 );
16        System.out.printf( "%4d\n", -123 );
17        System.out.printf( "%4d\n", -1234 ); // data too large
18        System.out.printf( "%4d\n", -12345 ); // data too large
19     } // end main
20  } // end class RightJustifyTest
```

```
   1
  12
 123
1234
12345

  -1
 -12
-123
-1234
-12345
```

Fig. 24.12 | Right justifying integers in fields.

Method `printf` also provides the ability to specify the precision with which data is printed. Precision has different meanings for different types. When used with floating-point conversion characters e and f, the precision is the number of digits that appear after the decimal point. When used with conversion character g, the precision is the maximum number of significant digits to be printed. When used with conversion character s, the precision is the maximum number of characters to be written from the string. To use precision, place between the percent sign and the conversion specifier a decimal point (.) followed by an integer representing the precision. Figure 24.13 demonstrates the use of precision in format strings. Note that when a floating-point value is printed with a precision smaller than the original number of decimal places in the value, the value is rounded. Also note that the format specifier %.3g indicates that the total number of digits used to display the floating-point value is 3. Because the value has three digits to the left of the decimal point, the value is rounded to the ones position.

The field width and the precision can be combined by placing the field width, followed by a decimal point, followed by a precision between the percent sign and the conversion character, as in the statement

```
printf( "%9.3f", 123.456789 );
```

which displays 123.457 with three digits to the right of the decimal point right justified in a nine-digit field—this number will be preceded in its field by two blanks.

```
1   // Fig. 24.13: PrecisionTest.java
2   // Using precision for floating-point numbers and strings.
3   public class PrecisionTest
4   {
5      public static void main( String args[] )
6      {
7         double f = 123.94536;
8         String s = "Happy Birthday";
9
10        System.out.printf( "Using precision for floating-point numbers\n" );
11        System.out.printf( "\t%.3f\n\t%.3e\n\t%.3g\n\n", f, f, f );
12
13        System.out.printf( "Using precision for strings\n" );
14        System.out.printf( "\t%.11s\n", s );
15     } // end main
16  } // end class PrecisionTest
```

```
Using precision for floating-point numbers
        123.945
        1.239e+02
        124

Using precision for strings
        Happy Birth
```

Fig. 24.13 | Using precision for floating-point numbers and strings.

24.10 Using Flags in the `printf` Format String

Various flags may be used with method `printf` to supplement its output formatting capabilities. Seven flags are available for use in format strings (Fig. 24.14).

To use a flag in a format string, place the flag immediately to the right of the percent sign. Several flags may be used in the same format specifier. Figure 24.15 demonstrates right justification and left justification of a string, an integer, a character and a floating-point number. Note that line 9 serves as a counting mechanism for the screen output.

Flag	Description
– (minus sign)	Left justify the output within the specified field.
+ (plus sign)	Display a plus sign preceding positive values and a minus sign preceding negative values.
space	Print a space before a positive value not printed with the + flag.
#	Prefix 0 to the output value when used with the octal conversion character o. Prefix 0x to the output value when used with the hexadecimal conversion character x.
0 (zero)	Pad a field with leading zeros.
, (comma)	Use the locale-specific thousands separator (i.e., ',' for U.S. locale) to display decimal and floating-point numbers.
(	Enclose negative numbers in parentheses.

Fig. 24.14 | Format string flags.

```java
1   // Fig. 24.15: MinusFlagTest.java
2   // Right justifying and left justifying values.
3
4   public class MinusFlagTest
5   {
6      public static void main( String args[] )
7      {
8         System.out.println( "Columns:" );
9         System.out.println( "0123456789012345678901234567890123456789\n" );
10        System.out.printf( "%10s%10d%10c%10f\n\n", "hello", 7, 'a', 1.23 );
11        System.out.printf(
12           "%-10s%-10d%-10c%-10f\n", "hello", 7, 'a', 1.23 );
13     } // end main
14  } // end class MinusFlagTest
```

```
Columns:
0123456789012345678901234567890123456789

     hello         7         a  1.230000

hello     7         a         1.230000
```

Fig. 24.15 | Right justifying and left justifying values.

Figure 24.16 prints a positive number and a negative number, each with and without the +*flag*. Note that the minus sign is displayed in both cases, but the plus sign is displayed only when the + flag is used.

```
 1    // Fig. 24.16: PlusFlagTest.java
 2    // Printing numbers with and without the + flag.
 3
 4    public class PlusFlagTest
 5    {
 6       public static void main( String args[] )
 7       {
 8          System.out.printf( "%d\t%d\n", 786, -786 );
 9          System.out.printf( "%+d\t%+d\n", 786, -786 );
10       } // end main
11    } // end class PlusFlagTest
```

```
786        -786
+786       -786
```

Fig. 24.16 | Printing numbers with and without the + flag.

Figure 24.17 prefixes a space to the positive number with the *space flag*. This is useful for aligning positive and negative numbers with the same number of digits. Note that the value -547 is not preceded by a space in the output because of its minus sign. Figure 24.18 uses the *# flag* to prefix 0 to the octal value and *0x* to the hexadecimal value.

```
 1    // Fig. 24.17: SpaceFlagTest.java
 2    // Printing a space before non-negative values.
 3
 4    public class SpaceFlagTest
 5    {
 6       public static void main( String args[] )
 7       {
 8          System.out.printf( "% d\n% d\n", 547, -547 );
 9       } // end main
10    } // end class SpaceFlagTest
```

```
 547
-547
```

Fig. 24.17 | Using the space flag to print a space before nonnegative values.

```
 1    // Fig. 24.18: PoundFlagTest.java
 2    // Using the # flag with conversion characters o and x.
 3
 4    public class PoundFlagTest
 5    {
 6       public static void main( String args[] )
 7       {
 8          int c = 31;        // initialize c
 9
10          System.out.printf( "%#o\n", c );
```

Fig. 24.18 | Using the # flag with conversion characters o and x. (Part 1 of 2.)

```
11          System.out.printf( "%#x\n", c );
12      } // end main
13  } // end class PoundFlagTest
```

```
037
0x1f
```

Fig. 24.18 | Using the # flag with conversion characters o and x. (Part 2 of 2.)

Figure 24.19 combines the + flag, the *0 flag* and the space flag to print 452 in a field of width 9 with a + sign and leading zeros, next prints 452 in a field of width 9 using only the 0 flag, then prints 452 in a field of width 9 using only the space flag.

```
1   // Fig. 24.19: ZeroFlagTest.java
2   // Printing with the 0 (zero) flag fills in leading zeros.
3
4   public class ZeroFlagTest
5   {
6       public static void main( String args[] )
7       {
8           System.out.printf( "%+09d\n", 452 );
9           System.out.printf( "%09d\n", 452 );
10          System.out.printf( "% 9d\n", 452 );
11      } // end main
12  } // end class ZeroFlagTest
```

```
+00000452
000000452
      452
```

Fig. 24.19 | Printing with the 0 (zero) flag fills in leading zeros.

Figure 24.20 uses the comma (,) flag to display a decimal and a floating-point number with the thousands separator. Figure 24.21 encloses negative numbers in parentheses using the (flag. Note that the value 50 is not enclosed in parentheses in the output because it is a positive number.

```
1   // Fig. 24.20: CommaFlagTest.java
2   // Using the comma (,) flag to display numbers with thousands separator.
3
4   public class CommaFlagTest
5   {
6       public static void main( String args[] )
7       {
8           System.out.printf( "%,d\n", 58625 );
9           System.out.printf( "%,.2f", 58625.21 );
```

Fig. 24.20 | Using the comma (,) flag to display numbers with the thousands separator. (Part 1 of 2.)

```
10              System.out.printf( "%,.2f", 12345678.9 );
11      } // end main
12  } // end class CommaFlagTest
```

```
58,625
58,625.21
12,345,678.90
```

Fig. 24.20 | Using the comma (,) flag to display numbers with the thousands separator. (Part 2 of 2.)

```
1   // Fig. 24.21: ParenthesesFlagTest.java
2   // Using the ( flag to place parentheses around negative numbers.
3
4   public class ParenthesesFlagTest
5   {
6      public static void main( String args[] )
7      {
8         System.out.printf( "%(d\n", 50 );
9         System.out.printf( "%(d\n", -50 );
10        System.out.printf( "%(.1e\n", -50.0 );
11     } // end main
12  } // end class ParenthesesFlagTest
```

```
50
(50)
(5.0e+01)
```

Fig. 24.21 | Using the (flag to place parentheses around negative numbers.

24.11 Printing with Argument Indices

An *argument index* is an optional integer followed by a $ sign that indicates the argument's position in the argument list. For example, lines 20–21 and 24–25 in Fig. 24.9 use argument index "1$" to indicate that all format specifiers use the first argument in the argument list. Argument indices enable programmers to reorder the output so that the arguments in the argument list are not necessarily in the order of their corresponding format specifiers. Argument indices also help avoid duplicating arguments. Figure 24.22 demonstrates how to print arguments in the argument list in reverse order using the argument index.

```
1   // Fig. 24.22: ArgumentIndexTest
2   // Reordering output with argument indices.
3
4   public class ArgumentIndexTest
5   {
6      public static void main( String args[] )
7      {
```

Fig. 24.22 | Reordering output with argument indices. (Part 1 of 2.)

```
 8          System.out.printf(
 9              "Parameter list without reordering: %s %s %s %s\n",
10              "first", "second", "third", "fourth" );
11          System.out.printf(
12              "Parameter list after reordering: %4$s %3$s %2$s %1$s\n",
13              "first", "second", "third", "fourth" );
14      } // end main
15  } // end class ArgumentIndexTest
```

```
Parameter list without reordering: first second third fourth
Parameter list after reordering: fourth third second first
```

Fig. 24.22 | Reordering output with argument indices. (Part 2 of 2.)

24.12 Printing Literals and Escape Sequences

Most literal characters to be printed in a printf statement can simply be included in the format string. However, there are several "problem" characters, such as the quotation mark (") that delimits the format string itself. Various control characters, such as newline and tab, must be represented by escape sequences. An escape sequence is represented by a backslash (\), followed by an escape character. Figure 24.23 lists the escape sequences and the actions they cause.

Common Programming Error 24.4

Attempting to print as literal data in a printf statement a double quote or backslash character without preceding that character with a backslash to form a proper escape sequence might result in a syntax error.

Escape sequence	Description
\' (single quote)	Output the single quote (') character.
\" (double quote)	Output the double quote (") character.
\\ (backslash)	Output the backslash (\) character.
\b (backspace)	Move the cursor back one position on the current line.
\f (new page or form feed)	Move the cursor to the start of the next logical page.
\n (newline)	Move the cursor to the beginning of the next line.
\r (carriage return)	Move the cursor to the beginning of the current line.
\t (horizontal tab)	Move the cursor to the next horizontal tab position.

Fig. 24.23 | Escape sequences.

24.13 Formatting Output with Class Formatter

So far, we have discussed displaying formatted output to the standard output stream. What should we do if we want to send formatted outputs to other output streams or devices, such as a JTextArea or a file? The solution relies on class Formatter (in package java.util), which provides the same formatting capabilities as printf. Formatter is a utility class that enables programmers to output formatted data to a specified destination, such as a file on disk. By default, a Formatter creates a string in memory. Figure 24.24 demonstrates how to use a Formatter to build a formatted string, which is then displayed in a message dialog.

```java
1   // Fig. Fig. 24.24: FormatterTest.java
2   // Format string with class Formatter.
3   import java.util.Formatter;
4   import javax.swing.JOptionPane;
5
6   public class FormatterTest
7   {
8      public static void main( String args[] )
9      {
10        // create Formatter and format output
11        Formatter formatter = new Formatter();
12        formatter.format( "%d = %#o = %#X", 10, 10, 10 );
13
14        // display output in JOptionPane
15        JOptionPane.showMessageDialog( null, formatter.toString() );
16     } // end main
17  } // end class FormatterTest
```

```
Message                    [X]

  (i)   10 = 012 = 0XA

              OK
```

Fig. 24.24 | Formatting output with class Formatter.

Line 11 creates a Formatter object using the default constructor, so this object will build a string in memory. Other constructors are provided to allow you to specify the destination to which the formatted data should be output. For details, see java.sun.com/javase/6/docs/api/java/util/Formatter.html.

Line 12 invokes method **format** to format the output. Like printf, method format takes a format string and an argument list. The difference is that printf sends the formatted output directly to the standard output stream, while format sends the formatted output to the destination specified by its constructor (a string in memory in this program). Line 15 invokes the Formatter's toString method to get the formatted data as a string, which is then displayed in a message dialog.

Note that class String also provides a static convenience method named format that enables you to create a string in memory without the need to first create a Formatter object. Lines 11–12 and line 15 in Fig. 24.24 could have been replaced by

```java
String s = String.format( "%d = %#o = %#^x", 10, 10, 10 );
JOptionPane.showMessageDialog( null, s );
```

24.14 Wrap-Up

This chapter summarized how to display formatted output with various format characters and flags. We displayed decimal numbers using format characters d, o, x and X. We displayed floating-point numbers using format characters e, E, f, g and G. We displayed date and time in various format using format characters t and T and their conversion suffix characters. You learned how to display output with field widths and precisions. We introduced the flags +, -, space, #, 0, comma and (that are used together with the format characters to produce output. We also demonstrated how to format output with class Formatter. In the next chapter, we discuss the String class's methods for manipulating strings. We also introduce regular expressions and demonstrate how to validate user input with regular expressions.

25

Strings, Characters and Regular Expressions

The chief defect of Henry King
Was chewing little bits of string.
—Hilaire Belloc

Vigorous writing is concise.
A sentence should contain no
unnecessary words, a
paragraph no unnecessary
sentences.
—William Strunk, Jr.

I have made this letter longer
than usual, because I lack
the time to make it short.
—Blaise Pascal

OBJECTIVES

In this chapter you'll learn:

- To create and manipulate immutable character string objects of class `String`.

- To create and manipulates mutable character string objects of class `StringBuilder`.

- To create and manipulate objects of class `Character`.

- To use a `StringTokenizer` object to break a `String` object into tokens.

- To use regular expressions to validate `String` data entered into an application.

Outline

25.1 Introduction
25.2 Fundamentals of Characters and Strings
25.3 Class `String`
  25.3.1 `String` Constructors
  25.3.2 `String` Methods `length`, `charAt` and `getChars`
  25.3.3 Comparing Strings
  25.3.4 Locating Characters and Substrings in Strings
  25.3.5 Extracting Substrings from Strings
  25.3.6 Concatenating Strings
  25.3.7 Miscellaneous `String` Methods
  25.3.8 `String` Method `valueOf`
25.4 Class `StringBuilder`
  25.4.1 `StringBuilder` Constructors
  25.4.2 `StringBuilder` Methods `length`, `capacity`, `setLength` and
    `ensureCapacity`
  25.4.3 `StringBuilder` Methods `charAt`, `setCharAt`, `getChars` and `reverse`
  25.4.4 `StringBuilder` `append` Methods
  25.4.5 `StringBuilder` Insertion and Deletion Methods
25.5 Class `Character`
25.6 Class `StringTokenizer`
25.7 Regular Expressions, Class `Pattern` and Class `Matcher`
25.8 Wrap-Up

25.1 Introduction

This chapter introduces Java's string- and character-processing capabilities. The techniques discussed here are appropriate for validating program input, displaying information to users and other text-based manipulations. They are also appropriate for developing text editors, word processors, page-layout software, computerized typesetting systems and other kinds of text-processing software. We have already presented several string-processing capabilities in earlier chapters. This chapter discusses in detail the capabilities of class `String`, class `StringBuilder` and class `Character` from the java.lang package and class `StringTokenizer` from the java.util package. These classes provide the foundation for string and character manipulation in Java.

The chapter also discusses regular expressions that provide applications with the capability to validate input. The functionality is located in the `String` class along with classes `Matcher` and `Pattern` located in the java.util.regex package.

25.2 Fundamentals of Characters and Strings

Characters are the fundamental building blocks of Java source programs. Every program is composed of a sequence of characters that—when grouped together meaningfully—are interpreted by the computer as a series of instructions used to accomplish a task. A program may contain *character literals*. A character literal is an integer value represented as a character in single quotes. For example, 'z' represents the integer value of z, and '\n' represents the integer value of newline. The value of a character literal is the integer value of the character in the *Unicode character set*. Appendix B presents the integer equivalents of the characters in the ASCII character set, which is a subset of Unicode. For detailed information on Unicode, visit www.unicode.org.

Recall from Section 2.2 that a string is a sequence of characters treated as a single unit. A string may include letters, digits and various *special characters,* such as +, -, *, / and $. A string is an object of class String. *String literals* (stored in memory as String objects) are written as a sequence of characters in double quotation marks, as in:

```
"John Q. Doe"              (a name)
"9999 Main Street"         (a street address)
"Waltham, Massachusetts"   (a city and state)
"(201) 555-1212"           (a telephone number)
```

A string may be assigned to a String reference. The declaration

```
String color = "blue";
```

initializes String variable color to refer to a String object that contains the string "blue".

Performance Tip 25.1

Java treats all string literals with the same contents as a single String object that has many references to it. This conserves memory.

25.3 Class String

Class String is used to represent strings in Java. The next several subsections cover many of class String's capabilities.

25.3.1 String Constructors

Class String provides constructors for initializing String objects in a variety of ways. Four of the constructors are demonstrated in the main method of Fig. 25.1.

```
 1   // Fig. 25.1: StringConstructors.java
 2   // String class constructors.
 3
 4   public class StringConstructors
 5   {
 6      public static void main( String args[] )
 7      {
 8         char charArray[] = { 'b', 'i', 'r', 't', 'h', ' ', 'd', 'a', 'y' };
 9         String s = new String( "hello" );
10
11         // use String constructors
12         String s1 = new String();
13         String s2 = new String( s );
14         String s3 = new String( charArray );
15         String s4 = new String( charArray, 6, 3 );
```

Fig. 25.1 | String class constructors. (Part 1 of 2.)

```
16
17          System.out.printf(
18            "s1 = %s\ns2 = %s\ns3 = %s\ns4 = %s\n",
19            s1, s2, s3, s4 ); // display strings
20      } // end main
21  } // end class StringConstructors
```

```
s1 =
s2 = hello
s3 = birth day
s4 = day
```

Fig. 25.1 | String class constructors. (Part 2 of 2.)

Line 12 instantiates a new String object using class String's no-argument constructor and assigns its reference to s1. The new String object contains no characters (the *empty string*) and has a length of 0.

Line 13 instantiates a new String object using class String's constructor that takes a String as an argument and assigns its reference to s2. The new String contains the same sequence of characters as the one that is passed as an argument to the constructor.

Software Engineering Observation 25.1

*It is not necessary to copy an existing String object. String objects are **immutable**—their character contents cannot be changed after they are created, because class String does not provide any methods that allow the contents of a String object to be modified.*

Line 14 instantiates a new String object and assigns its reference to s3 using class String's constructor that takes a char array as an argument. The new String object contains a copy of the characters in the array.

Line 15 instantiates a new String object and assigns its reference to s4 using class String's constructor that takes a char array and two integers as arguments. The second argument specifies the starting position (the offset) from which characters in the array are accessed. Remember that the first character is at position 0. The third argument specifies the number of characters (the count) to access in the array. The new String object contains a string formed from the accessed characters. If the offset or the count specified as an argument results in accessing an element outside the bounds of the character array, a StringIndexOutOfBoundsException is thrown.

Common Programming Error 25.1

Attempting to access a character that is outside the bounds of a string results in a StringIndexOutOfBoundsException.

25.3.2 String Methods length, charAt and getChars

String methods *length*, charAt and *getChars* return the length of a string, obtain the character at a specific location in a string and retrieve a set of characters from a string as a char array, respectively. The application in Fig. 25.2 demonstrates each of these methods.

Line 15 uses String method length to determine the number of characters in string s1. Like arrays, strings know their own length. However, unlike arrays, you cannot access a String's length via a length field—instead you must call the String's length method.

```
1   // Fig. 25.2: StringMiscellaneous.java
2   // This application demonstrates the length, charAt and getChars
3   // methods of the String class.
4
5   public class StringMiscellaneous
6   {
7      public static void main( String args[] )
8      {
9         String s1 = "hello there";
10        char charArray[] = new char[ 5 ];
11
12        System.out.printf( "s1: %s", s1 );
13
14        // test length method
15        System.out.printf( "\nLength of s1: %d", s1.length() );
16
17        // loop through characters in s1 with charAt and display reversed
18        System.out.print( "\nThe string reversed is: " );
19
20        for ( int count = s1.length() - 1; count >= 0; count-- )
21           System.out.printf( "%s ", s1.charAt( count ) );
22
23        // copy characters from string into charArray
24        s1.getChars( 0, 5, charArray, 0 );
25        System.out.print( "\nThe character array is: " );
26
27        for ( char character : charArray )
28           System.out.print( character );
29
30        System.out.println();
31     } // end main
32  } // end class StringMiscellaneous
```

```
s1: hello there
Length of s1: 11
The string reversed is: e r e h t   o l l e h
The character array is: hello
```

Fig. 25.2 | String class character-manipulation methods.

Lines 20–21 print the characters of the string s1 in reverse order (and separated by spaces). String method charAt (line 21) returns the character at a specific position in the string. Method charAt receives an integer argument that is used as the index and returns the character at that position. Like arrays, the first element of a string is at position 0.

Line 24 uses String method getChars to copy the characters of a string into a character array. The first argument is the starting index in the string from which characters are to be copied. The second argument is the index that is one past the last character to be copied from the string. The third argument is the character array into which the characters are to be copied. The last argument is the starting index where the copied characters are placed in the target character array. Next, line 28 prints the char array contents one character at a time.

25.3.3 Comparing Strings

Chapter 7 discussed sorting and searching arrays. Frequently, the information being sorted or searched consists of strings that must be compared to place them into the proper order or to determine whether a string appears in an array (or other collection). Class String provides several methods for comparing strings.

To understand what it means for one string to be greater than or less than another, consider the process of alphabetizing a series of last names. You would, no doubt, place "Jones" before "Smith" because the first letter of "Jones" comes before the first letter of "Smith" in the alphabet. But the alphabet is more than just a list of 26 letters—it is an ordered set of characters. Each letter occurs in a specific position within the set. Z is more than just a letter of the alphabet—it is specifically the twenty-sixth letter of the alphabet.

How does the computer know that one letter comes before another? All characters are represented in the computer as numeric codes (see Appendix B). When the computer compares strings, it actually compares the numeric codes of the characters in the strings.

Figure 25.3 demonstrates String methods equals, equalsIgnoreCase, compareTo and *regionMatches* and using the equality operator == to compare String objects.

```
 1   // Fig. 25.3: StringCompare.java
 2   // String methods equals, equalsIgnoreCase, compareTo and regionMatches.
 3
 4   public class StringCompare
 5   {
 6      public static void main( String args[] )
 7      {
 8         String s1 = new String( "hello" ); // s1 is a copy of "hello"
 9         String s2 = "goodbye";
10         String s3 = "Happy Birthday";
11         String s4 = "happy birthday";
12
13         System.out.printf(
14            "s1 = %s\ns2 = %s\ns3 = %s\ns4 = %s\n\n", s1, s2, s3, s4 );
15
16         // test for equality
17         if ( s1.equals( "hello" ) )   // true
18            System.out.println( "s1 equals \"hello\"" );
19         else
20            System.out.println( "s1 does not equal \"hello\"" );
21
22         // test for equality with ==
23         if ( s1 == "hello" )   // false; they are not the same object
24            System.out.println( "s1 is the same object as \"hello\"" );
25         else
26            System.out.println( "s1 is not the same object as \"hello\"" );
27
28         // test for equality (ignore case)
29         if ( s3.equalsIgnoreCase( s4 ) )   // true
30            System.out.printf( "%s equals %s with case ignored\n", s3, s4 );
31         else
32            System.out.println( "s3 does not equal s4" );
```

Fig. 25.3 | String comparisons. (Part 1 of 2.)

```
33
34            // test compareTo
35            System.out.printf(
36                "\ns1.compareTo( s2 ) is %d", s1.compareTo( s2 ) );
37            System.out.printf(
38                "\ns2.compareTo( s1 ) is %d", s2.compareTo( s1 ) );
39            System.out.printf(
40                "\ns1.compareTo( s1 ) is %d", s1.compareTo( s1 ) );
41            System.out.printf(
42                "\ns3.compareTo( s4 ) is %d", s3.compareTo( s4 ) );
43            System.out.printf(
44                "\ns4.compareTo( s3 ) is %d\n\n", s4.compareTo( s3 ) );
45
46            // test regionMatches (case sensitive)
47            if ( s3.regionMatches( 0, s4, 0, 5 ) )
48                System.out.println( "First 5 characters of s3 and s4 match" );
49            else
50                System.out.println(
51                    "First 5 characters of s3 and s4 do not match" );
52
53            // test regionMatches (ignore case)
54            if ( s3.regionMatches( true, 0, s4, 0, 5 ) )
55                System.out.println( "First 5 characters of s3 and s4 match" );
56            else
57                System.out.println(
58                    "First 5 characters of s3 and s4 do not match" );
59        } // end main
60    } // end class StringCompare
```

```
s1 = hello
s2 = goodbye
s3 = Happy Birthday
s4 = happy birthday

s1 equals "hello"
s1 is not the same object as "hello"
Happy Birthday equals happy birthday with case ignored

s1.compareTo( s2 ) is 1
s2.compareTo( s1 ) is -1
s1.compareTo( s1 ) is 0
s3.compareTo( s4 ) is -32
s4.compareTo( s3 ) is 32

First 5 characters of s3 and s4 do not match
First 5 characters of s3 and s4 match
```

Fig. 25.3 | String comparisons. (Part 2 of 2.)

The condition at line 17 uses method equals to compare string s1 and the string literal "hello" for equality. Method equals (a method of class Object overridden in String) tests any two objects for equality—the strings contained in the two objects are identical. The method returns true if the contents of the objects are equal, and false otherwise. The preceding condition is true because string s1 was initialized with the string literal "hello". Method equals uses a *lexicographical comparison*—it compares the integer Unicode values (see www.unicode.com, for more information) that represent each character in each string. Thus, if the string "hello" is compared with the string "HELLO", the result is false, because the integer representation of a lowercase letter is different from that of the corresponding uppercase letter.

The condition at line 23 uses the equality operator == to compare string s1 for equality with the string literal "hello". Operator == has different functionality when it is used to compare references than when it is used to compare values of primitive types. When primitive-type values are compared with ==, the result is true if both values are identical. When references are compared with ==, the result is true if both references refer to the same object in memory. To compare the actual contents (or state information) of objects for equality, a method must be invoked. In the case of Strings, that method is equals. The preceding condition evaluates to false at line 23 because the reference s1 was initialized with the statement

    s1 = *new* String("hello");

which creates a new String object with a copy of string literal "hello" and assigns the new object to variable s1. If s1 had been initialized with the statement

    s1 = "hello";

which directly assigns the string literal "hello" to variable s1, the condition would be true. Remember that Java treats all string literal objects with the same contents as one String object to which there can be many references. Thus, lines 8, 17 and 23 all refer to the same String object "hello" in memory.

Common Programming Error 25.2

Comparing references with == can lead to logic errors, because == compares the references to determine whether they refer to the same object, not whether two objects have the same contents. When two identical (but separate) objects are compared with ==, the result will be false. When comparing objects to determine whether they have the same contents, use method equals.

If you are sorting Strings, you may compare them for equality with method equalsIgnoreCase, which ignores whether the letters in each string are uppercase or lowercase when performing the comparison. Thus, the string "hello" and the string "HELLO" compare as equal. Line 29 uses String method equalsIgnoreCase to compare string s3—Happy Birthday—for equality with string s4—happy birthday. The result of this comparison is true because the comparison ignores case sensitivity.

Lines 35–44 use method compareTo to compare strings. Method compareTo is declared in the Comparable interface and implemented in the String class. Line 36 compares string s1 to string s2. Method compareTo returns 0 if the strings are equal, a negative number if the string that invokes compareTo is less than the string that is passed as an argument and a positive number if the string that invokes compareTo is greater than the string that is passed as an argument. Method compareTo uses a lexicographical comparison—it compares the numeric values of corresponding characters in each string. (For more information on the exact value returned by the compareTo method, see java.sun.com/javase/6/docs/api/java/lang/String.html.)

The condition at line 47 uses String method regionMatches to compare portions of two strings for equality. The first argument is the starting index in the string that invokes the method. The second argument is a comparison string. The third argument is the starting index in the comparison string. The last argument is the number of characters to compare between the two strings. The method returns true only if the specified number of characters are lexicographically equal.

Finally, the condition at line 54 uses a five-argument version of String method regionMatches to compare portions of two strings for equality. When the first argument is true, the method ignores the case of the characters being compared. The remaining arguments are identical to those described for the four-argument regionMatches method.

Figure 25.4 demonstrates String methods **startsWith** and **endsWith**. Method main creates array strings containing the strings "started", "starting", "ended" and "ending". The rest of main consists of three for statements that test the elements of the array to determine whether they start with or end with a particular set of characters.

```java
1   // Fig. 25.4: StringStartEnd.java
2   // String methods startsWith and endsWith.
3
4   public class StringStartEnd
5   {
6      public static void main( String args[] )
7      {
8         String strings[] = { "started", "starting", "ended", "ending" };
9
10        // test method startsWith
11        for ( String string : strings )
12        {
13           if ( string.startsWith( "st" ) )
14              System.out.printf( "\"%s\" starts with \"st\"\n", string );
15        } // end for
16
17        System.out.println();
18
19        // test method startsWith starting from position 2 of string
20        for ( String string : strings )
21        {
22           if ( string.startsWith( "art", 2 ) )
23              System.out.printf(
24                 "\"%s\" starts with \"art\" at position 2\n", string );
25        } // end for
26
27        System.out.println();
28
29        // test method endsWith
30        for ( String string : strings )
31        {
32           if ( string.endsWith( "ed" ) )
33              System.out.printf( "\"%s\" ends with \"ed\"\n", string );
34        } // end for
35     } // end main
36  } // end class StringStartEnd
```

Fig. 25.4 | String class startsWith and endsWith methods. (Part 1 of 2.)

```
"started" starts with "st"
"starting" starts with "st"

"started" starts with "art" at position 2
"starting" starts with "art" at position 2

"started" ends with "ed"
"ended" ends with "ed"
```

Fig. 25.4 | String class startsWith and endsWith methods. (Part 2 of 2.)

Lines 11–15 use the version of method startsWith that takes a String argument. The condition in the if statement (line 13) determines whether each String in the array starts with the characters "st". If so, the method returns true and the application prints that String. Otherwise, the method returns false and nothing happens.

Lines 20–25 use the startsWith method that takes a String and an integer as arguments. The integer specifies the index at which the comparison should begin in the string. The condition in the if statement (line 22) determines whether each String in the array has the characters "art" beginning with the third character in each string. If so, the method returns true and the application prints the String.

The third for statement (lines 30–34) uses method endsWith, which takes a String argument. The condition at line 32 determines whether each String in the array ends with the characters "ed". If so, the method returns true and the application prints the String.

25.3.4 Locating Characters and Substrings in Strings

Often it is useful to search for a character or set of characters in a string. For example, if you are creating your own word processor, you might want to provide a capability for searching through documents. Figure 25.5 demonstrates the many versions of String methods *indexOf* and *lastIndexOf* that search for a specified character or substring in a string. All the searches in this example are performed on the string letters (initialized with "abcdefghijklmabcdefghijklm") in method main. Lines 11–16 use method indexOf to locate the first occurrence of a character in a string. If method indexOf finds the character, it returns the character's index in the string—otherwise, indexOf returns –1. There are two versions of indexOf that search for characters in a string. The expression in line 12 uses the version of method indexOf that takes an integer representation of the character to find. The expression at line 14 uses another version of method indexOf, which takes two integer arguments—the character and the starting index at which the search of the string should begin.

```
1   // Fig. 25.5: StringIndexMethods.java
2   // String searching methods indexOf and lastIndexOf.
3
4   public class StringIndexMethods
5   {
6      public static void main( String args[] )
7      {
8         String letters = "abcdefghijklmabcdefghijklm";
```

Fig. 25.5 | String class searching methods. (Part 1 of 2.)

```
 9
10          // test indexOf to locate a character in a string
11          System.out.printf(
12             "'c' is located at index %d\n", letters.indexOf( 'c' ) );
13          System.out.printf(
14             "'a' is located at index %d\n", letters.indexOf( 'a', 1 ) );
15          System.out.printf(
16             "'$' is located at index %d\n\n", letters.indexOf( '$' ) );
17
18          // test lastIndexOf to find a character in a string
19          System.out.printf( "Last 'c' is located at index %d\n",
20             letters.lastIndexOf( 'c' ) );
21          System.out.printf( "Last 'a' is located at index %d\n",
22             letters.lastIndexOf( 'a', 25 ) );
23          System.out.printf( "Last '$' is located at index %d\n\n",
24             letters.lastIndexOf( '$' ) );
25
26          // test indexOf to locate a substring in a string
27          System.out.printf( "\"def\" is located at index %d\n",
28             letters.indexOf( "def" ) );
29          System.out.printf( "\"def\" is located at index %d\n",
30             letters.indexOf( "def", 7 ) );
31          System.out.printf( "\"hello\" is located at index %d\n\n",
32             letters.indexOf( "hello" ) );
33
34          // test lastIndexOf to find a substring in a string
35          System.out.printf( "Last \"def\" is located at index %d\n",
36             letters.lastIndexOf( "def" ) );
37          System.out.printf( "Last \"def\" is located at index %d\n",
38             letters.lastIndexOf( "def", 25 ) );
39          System.out.printf( "Last \"hello\" is located at index %d\n",
40             letters.lastIndexOf( "hello" ) );
41       } // end main
42    } // end class StringIndexMethods
```

```
'c' is located at index 2
'a' is located at index 13
'$' is located at index -1

Last 'c' is located at index 15
Last 'a' is located at index 13
Last '$' is located at index -1

"def" is located at index 3
"def" is located at index 16
"hello" is located at index -1

Last "def" is located at index 16
Last "def" is located at index 16
Last "hello" is located at index -1
```

Fig. 25.5 | String class searching methods. (Part 2 of 2.)

The statements at lines 19–24 use method lastIndexOf to locate the last occurrence of a character in a string. Method lastIndexOf performs the search from the end of the string toward the beginning. If method lastIndexOf finds the character, it returns the index of the character in the string—otherwise, lastIndexOf returns –1. There are two versions of lastIndexOf that search for characters in a string. The expression at line 20 uses the version that takes the integer representation of the character. The expression at line 22 uses the version that takes two integer arguments—the integer representation of the character and the index from which to begin searching backward.

Lines 27–40 demonstrate versions of methods indexOf and lastIndexOf that each take a String as the first argument. These versions perform identically to those described earlier except that they search for sequences of characters (or substrings) that are specified by their String arguments. If the substring is found, these methods return the index in the string of the first character in the substring.

25.3.5 Extracting Substrings from Strings

Class String provides two substring methods to enable a new String object to be created by copying part of an existing String object. Each method returns a new String object. Both methods are demonstrated in Fig. 25.6.

The expression letters.substring(20) at line 12 uses the substring method that takes one integer argument. The argument specifies the starting index in the original string letters from which characters are to be copied. The substring returned contains a copy of the characters from the starting index to the end of the string. Specifying an index outside the bounds of the string causes a *StringIndexOutOfBoundsException*.

The expression letters.substring(3, 6) at line 15 uses the substring method that takes two integer arguments. The first argument specifies the starting index from which characters are copied in the original string. The second argument specifies the index one beyond the last character to be copied (i.e., copy up to, but not including, that index in the string). The substring returned contains a copy of the specified characters from the

```
1    // Fig. 25.6: SubString.java
2    // String class substring methods.
3
4    public class SubString
5    {
6       public static void main( String args[] )
7       {
8          String letters = "abcdefghijklmabcdefghijklm";
9
10         // test substring methods
11         System.out.printf( "Substring from index 20 to end is \"%s\"\n",
12            letters.substring( 20 ) );
13         System.out.printf( "%s \"%s\"\n",
14            "Substring from index 3 up to, but not including 6 is",
15            letters.substring( 3, 6 ) );
16      } // end main
17   } // end class SubString
```

```
Substring from index 20 to end is "hijklm"
Substring from index 3 up to, but not including 6 is "def"
```

Fig. 25.6 | String class substring methods.

original string. Specifying an index outside the bounds of the string causes a StringIndexOutOfBoundsException.

25.3.6 Concatenating Strings

String method *concat* (Fig. 25.7) concatenates two String objects and returns a new String object containing the characters from both original strings. The expression s1.concat(s2) at line 13 forms a string by appending the characters in string s2 to the characters in string s1. The original Strings to which s1 and s2 refer are not modified.

```java
1   // Fig. 25.7: StringConcatenation.java
2   // String concat method.
3
4   public class StringConcatenation
5   {
6       public static void main( String args[] )
7       {
8           String s1 = new String( "Happy " );
9           String s2 = new String( "Birthday" );
10
11          System.out.printf( "s1 = %s\ns2 = %s\n\n",s1, s2 );
12          System.out.printf(
13              "Result of s1.concat( s2 ) = %s\n", s1.concat( s2 ) );
14          System.out.printf( "s1 after concatenation = %s\n", s1 );
15      } // end main
16  } // end class StringConcatenation
```

```
s1 = Happy
s2 = Birthday

Result of s1.concat( s2 ) = Happy Birthday
s1 after concatenation = Happy
```

Fig. 25.7 | String method concat.

25.3.7 Miscellaneous String Methods

Class String provides several methods that return modified copies of strings or that return character arrays. These methods are demonstrated in the application in Fig. 25.8.

```java
1   // Fig. 25.8: StringMiscellaneous2.java
2   // String methods replace, toLowerCase, toUpperCase, trim and toCharArray.
3
4   public class StringMiscellaneous2
5   {
6       public static void main( String args[] )
7       {
8           String s1 = new String( "hello" );
9           String s2 = new String( "GOODBYE" );
```

Fig. 25.8 | String methods replace, toLowerCase, toUpperCase, trim and toCharArray. (Part I of 2.)

```
10          String s3 = new String( "   spaces   " );
11
12          System.out.printf( "s1 = %s\ns2 = %s\ns3 = %s\n\n", s1, s2, s3 );
13
14          // test method replace
15          System.out.printf(
16             "Replace 'l' with 'L' in s1: %s\n\n", s1.replace( 'l', 'L' ) );
17
18          // test toLowerCase and toUpperCase
19          System.out.printf( "s1.toUpperCase() = %s\n", s1.toUpperCase() );
20          System.out.printf( "s2.toLowerCase() = %s\n\n", s2.toLowerCase() );
21
22          // test trim method
23          System.out.printf( "s3 after trim = \"%s\"\n\n", s3.trim() );
24
25          // test toCharArray method
26          char charArray[] = s1.toCharArray();
27          System.out.print( "s1 as a character array = " );
28
29          for ( char character : charArray )
30             System.out.print( character );
31
32          System.out.println();
33       } // end main
34    } // end class StringMiscellaneous2
```

```
s1 = hello
s2 = GOODBYE
s3 =    spaces

Replace 'l' with 'L' in s1: heLLo

s1.toUpperCase() = HELLO
s2.toLowerCase() = goodbye

s3 after trim = "spaces"

s1 as a character array = hello
```

Fig. 25.8 | String methods replace, toLowerCase, toUpperCase, trim and toCharArray. (Part 2 of 2.)

Line 16 uses String method replace to return a new String object in which every occurrence in string s1 of character 'l' (lowercase el) is replaced with character 'L'. Method replace leaves the original string unchanged. If there are no occurrences of the first argument in the string, method replace returns the original string.

Line 19 uses String method toUpperCase to generate a new String with uppercase letters where corresponding lowercase letters exist in s1. The method returns a new String object containing the converted string and leaves the original string unchanged. If there are no characters to convert, method toUpperCase returns the original string.

Line 20 uses String method toLowerCase to return a new String object with lowercase letters where corresponding uppercase letters exist in s2. The original string remains unchanged. If there are no characters in the original string to convert, toLowerCase returns the original string.

Line 23 uses String method **_trim_** to generate a new String object that removes all white-space characters that appear at the beginning or end of the string on which trim operates. The method returns a new String object containing the string without leading or trailing white space. The original string remains unchanged.

Line 26 uses String method **_toCharArray_** to create a new character array containing a copy of the characters in string s1. Lines 29–30 output each char in the array.

25.3.8 String Method valueOf

As we've seen, every object in Java has a toString method that enables a program to obtain the object's string representation. Unfortunately, this technique cannot be used with primitive types because they do not have methods. Class String provides static methods that take an argument of any type and convert the argument to a String object. Figure 25.9 demonstrates the String class **_valueOf_** methods.

The expression String.valueOf(charArray) at line 18 uses the character array charArray to create a new String object. The expression String.valueOf(charArray, 3, 3) at line 20 uses a portion of the character array charArray to create a new String object.

```java
1   // Fig. 25.9: StringValueOf.java
2   // String valueOf methods.
3
4   public class StringValueOf
5   {
6      public static void main( String args[] )
7      {
8         char charArray[] = { 'a', 'b', 'c', 'd', 'e', 'f' };
9         boolean booleanValue = true;
10        char characterValue = 'Z';
11        int integerValue = 7;
12        long longValue = 10000000000L; // L suffix indicates long
13        float floatValue = 2.5f; // f indicates that 2.5 is a float
14        double doubleValue = 33.333; // no suffix, double is default
15        Object objectRef = "hello"; // assign string to an Object reference
16
17        System.out.printf(
18           "char array = %s\n", String.valueOf( charArray ) );
19        System.out.printf( "part of char array = %s\n",
20           String.valueOf( charArray, 3, 3 ) );
21        System.out.printf(
22           "boolean = %s\n", String.valueOf( booleanValue ) );
23        System.out.printf(
24           "char = %s\n", String.valueOf( characterValue ) );
25        System.out.printf( "int = %s\n", String.valueOf( integerValue ) );
26        System.out.printf( "long = %s\n", String.valueOf( longValue ) );
27        System.out.printf( "float = %s\n", String.valueOf( floatValue ) );
28        System.out.printf(
29           "double = %s\n", String.valueOf( doubleValue ) );
30        System.out.printf( "Object = %s", String.valueOf( objectRef ) );
31     } // end main
32  } // end class StringValueOf
```

Fig. 25.9 | String class valueOf methods. (Part 1 of 2.)

```
char array = abcdef
part of char array = def
boolean = true
char = Z
int = 7
long = 10000000000
float = 2.5
double = 33.333
Object = hello
```

Fig. 25.9 | String class valueOf methods. (Part 2 of 2.)

The second argument specifies the starting index from which the characters are used. The third argument specifies the number of characters to be used.

There are seven other versions of method valueOf, which take arguments of type boolean, char, int, long, float, double and Object, respectively. These are demonstrated in lines 21–25. Note that the version of valueOf that takes an Object as an argument can do so because all Objects can be converted to Strings with method toString.

[*Note:* Lines 12–13 use literal values 10000000000L and 2.5f as the initial values of long variable longValue and float variable floatValue, respectively. By default, Java treats integer literals as type int and floating-point literals as type double. Appending the letter L to the literal 10000000000 and appending letter f to the literal 2.5 indicates to the compiler that 10000000000 should be treated as a long and that 2.5 should be treated as a float. An uppercase L or lowercase l can be used to denote a variable of type long and an uppercase F or lowercase f can be used to denote a variable of type float.]

25.4 Class StringBuilder

Once a String object is created, its contents can never change. We now discuss the features of class **StringBuilder** for creating and manipulating dynamic string information—that is, modifiable strings. Every StringBuilder is capable of storing a number of characters specified by its capacity. If the capacity of a StringBuilder is exceeded, the capacity is automatically expanded to accommodate the additional characters. Class StringBuilder is also used to implement operators + and += for String concatenation.

Performance Tip 25.2

Java can perform certain optimizations involving String objects (such as sharing one String object among multiple references) because it knows these objects will not change. Strings (not StringBuilders) should be used if the data will not change.

Performance Tip 25.3

In programs that frequently perform string concatenation, or other string modifications, it is often more efficient to implement the modifications with class StringBuilder.

Software Engineering Observation 25.2

*StringBuilders are not thread safe. If multiple threads require access to the same dynamic string information, use class **StringBuffer** in your code. Classes StringBuilder and StringBuffer are identical, but class StringBuffer is thread safe.*

25.4.1 StringBuilder Constructors

Class StringBuilder provides four constructors. We demonstrate three of these in Fig. 25.10. Line 8 uses the no-argument StringBuilder constructor to create a StringBuilder with no characters in it and an initial capacity of 16 characters (the default for a StringBuilder). Line 9 uses the StringBuilder constructor that takes an integer argument to create a StringBuilder with no characters in it and the initial capacity specified by the integer argument (i.e., 10). Line 10 uses the StringBuilder constructor that takes a String argument (in this case, a string literal) to create a StringBuilder containing the characters in the String argument. The initial capacity is the number of characters in the String argument plus 16.

Lines 12–14 use the method toString of class StringBuilder to output the StringBuilders with the printf method. In Section 25.4.4, we discuss how Java uses StringBuilder objects to implement the + and += operators for string concatenation.

```
1    // Fig. 25.10: StringBuilderConstructors.java
2    // StringBuilder constructors.
3
4    public class StringBuilderConstructors
5    {
6       public static void main( String args[] )
7       {
8          StringBuilder buffer1 = new StringBuilder();
9          StringBuilder buffer2 = new StringBuilder( 10 );
10         StringBuilder buffer3 = new StringBuilder( "hello" );
11
12         System.out.printf( "buffer1 = \"%s\"\n", buffer1.toString() );
13         System.out.printf( "buffer2 = \"%s\"\n", buffer2.toString() );
14         System.out.printf( "buffer3 = \"%s\"\n", buffer3.toString() );
15      } // end main
16   } // end class StringBuilderConstructors
```

```
buffer1 = ""
buffer2 = ""
buffer3 = "hello"
```

Fig. 25.10 | StringBuilder class constructors.

25.4.2 StringBuilder Methods length, capacity, setLength and ensureCapacity

StringBuilder methods *length* and *capacity* return the number of characters currently in a StringBuilder and the number of characters that can be stored in a StringBuilder without allocating more memory, respectively. Method *ensureCapacity* guarantees that a StringBuilder has at least the specified capacity. Method setLength increases or decreases the length of a StringBuilder. Figure 25.11 demonstrates these methods.

The application contains one StringBuilder called buffer. Line 8 uses the StringBuilder constructor that takes a String argument to initialize the StringBuilder with "Hello, how are you?". Lines 10–11 print the contents, length and capacity of the StringBuilder. Note in the output window that the capacity of the StringBuilder is

```
 1   // Fig. 25.11: StringBuilderCapLen.java
 2   // StringBuilder length, setLength, capacity and ensureCapacity methods.
 3
 4   public class StringBuilderCapLen
 5   {
 6      public static void main( String args[] )
 7      {
 8         StringBuilder buffer = new StringBuilder( "Hello, how are you?" );
 9
10         System.out.printf( "buffer = %s\nlength = %d\ncapacity = %d\n\n",
11            buffer.toString(), buffer.length(), buffer.capacity() );
12
13         buffer.ensureCapacity( 75 );
14         System.out.printf( "New capacity = %d\n\n", buffer.capacity() );
15
16         buffer.setLength( 10 );
17         System.out.printf( "New length = %d\nbuffer = %s\n",
18            buffer.length(), buffer.toString() );
19      } // end main
20   } // end class StringBuilderCapLen
```

```
buffer = Hello, how are you?
length = 19
capacity = 35

New capacity = 75

New length = 10
buffer = Hello, how
```

Fig. 25.11 | StringBuilder methods length and capacity.

initially 35. Recall that the StringBuilder constructor that takes a String argument initializes the capacity to the length of the string passed as an argument plus 16.

Line 13 uses method ensureCapacity to expand the capacity of the StringBuilder to a minimum of 75 characters. Actually, if the original capacity is less than the argument, the method ensures a capacity that is the greater of the number specified as an argument and twice the original capacity plus 2. The StringBuilder's current capacity remains unchanged if it is more than the specified capacity.

> **Performance Tip 25.4**
>
> *Dynamically increasing the capacity of a StringBuilder can take a relatively long time. Executing a large number of these operations can degrade the performance of an application. If a StringBuilder is going to increase greatly in size, possibly multiple times, setting its capacity high at the beginning will increase performance.*

Line 16 uses method setLength to set the StringBuilder's length to 10. If the specified length is less than the StringBuilder's current number of characters, the buffer is truncated to the specified length (i.e., the remaining characters in the StringBuilder are discarded). If the specified length is greater than the StringBuilder's current number of characters, null characters (characters with the numeric representation 0) are appended until the total number of characters in the StringBuilder is equal to the specified length.

25.4.3 StringBuilder Methods charAt, setCharAt, getChars and reverse

StringBuilder methods *charAt*, *setCharAt*, *getChars* and *reverse* manipulate the characters in a StringBuilder. Each of these methods is demonstrated in Fig. 25.12.

Method charAt (line 12) takes an integer argument and returns the character in the StringBuilder at that index. Method getChars (line 15) copies characters from a StringBuilder into the character array passed as an argument. This method takes four arguments—the starting index from which characters should be copied in the String-Builder, the index one past the last character to be copied from the StringBuilder, the character array into which the characters are to be copied and the starting location in the character array where the first character should be placed. Method setCharAt (lines 21 and 22) takes an integer and a character argument and sets the character at the specified

```
1   // Fig. 25.12: StringBuilderChars.java
2   // StringBuilder methods charAt, setCharAt, getChars and reverse.
3
4   public class StringBuilderChars
5   {
6      public static void main( String args[] )
7      {
8         StringBuilder buffer = new StringBuilder( "hello there" );
9
10        System.out.printf( "buffer = %s\n", buffer.toString() );
11        System.out.printf( "Character at 0: %s\nCharacter at 4: %s\n\n",
12           buffer.charAt( 0 ), buffer.charAt( 4 ) );
13
14        char charArray[] = new char[ buffer.length() ];
15        buffer.getChars( 0, buffer.length(), charArray, 0 );
16        System.out.print( "The characters are: " );
17
18        for ( char character : charArray )
19           System.out.print( character );
20
21        buffer.setCharAt( 0, 'H' );
22        buffer.setCharAt( 6, 'T' );
23        System.out.printf( "\n\nbuffer = %s", buffer.toString() );
24
25        buffer.reverse();
26        System.out.printf( "\n\nbuffer = %s\n", buffer.toString() );
27     } // end main
28  } // end class StringBuilderChars
```

```
buffer = hello there
Character at 0: h
Character at 4: o

The characters are: hello there

buffer = Hello There

buffer = erehT olleH
```

Fig. 25.12 | StringBuilder class character-manipulation methods.

position in the `StringBuilder` to the character argument. Method `reverse` (line 25) reverses the contents of the `StringBuilder`.

Common Programming Error 25.3

Attempting to access a character that is outside the bounds of a `StringBuilder` *(i.e., with an index less than 0 or greater than or equal to the* `StringBuilder`'s *length) results in a* `StringIndexOutOfBoundsException`.

25.4.4 StringBuilder append Methods

Class `StringBuilder` provides overloaded **append** methods (demonstrated in Fig. 25.13) to allow values of various types to be appended to the end of a `StringBuilder`. Versions are provided for each of the primitive types and for character arrays, `String`s, `Object`s, `StringBuilder`s and `CharSequence`s. (Remember that method `toString` produces a string representation of any `Object`.) Each of the methods takes its argument, converts it to a string and appends it to the `StringBuilder`.

```java
1   // Fig. 25.13: StringBuilderAppend.java
2   // StringBuilder append methods.
3
4   public class StringBuilderAppend
5   {
6      public static void main( String args[] )
7      {
8         Object objectRef = "hello";
9         String string = "goodbye";
10        char charArray[] = { 'a', 'b', 'c', 'd', 'e', 'f' };
11        boolean booleanValue = true;
12        char characterValue = 'Z';
13        int integerValue = 7;
14        long longValue = 10000000000L;
15        float floatValue = 2.5f; // f suffix indicates 2.5 is a float
16        double doubleValue = 33.333;
17
18        StringBuilder lastBuffer = new StringBuilder( "last buffer" );
19        StringBuilder buffer = new StringBuilder();
20
21        buffer.append( objectRef );
22        buffer.append( "\n" ); // each of these contains new line
23        buffer.append( string );
24        buffer.append( "\n" );
25        buffer.append( charArray );
26        buffer.append( "\n" );
27        buffer.append( charArray, 0, 3 );
28        buffer.append( "\n" );
29        buffer.append( booleanValue );
30        buffer.append( "\n" );
31        buffer.append( characterValue );
32        buffer.append( "\n" );
33        buffer.append( integerValue );
34        buffer.append( "\n" );
```

Fig. 25.13 | `StringBuilder` class append methods. (Part 1 of 2.)

```
35          buffer.append( longValue );
36          buffer.append( "\n" );
37          buffer.append( floatValue );
38          buffer.append( "\n" );
39          buffer.append( doubleValue );
40          buffer.append( "\n" );
41          buffer.append( lastBuffer );
42
43          System.out.printf( "buffer contains %s\n", buffer.toString() );
44     } // end main
45  } // end StringBuilderAppend
```

```
buffer contains hello
goodbye
abcdef
abc
true
Z
7
10000000000
2.5
33.333
last buffer
```

Fig. 25.13 | StringBuilder class append methods. (Part 2 of 2.)

Actually, the compiler uses StringBuilder and the append methods to implement the + and += operators for String concatenation. For example, assuming the declarations

```
String string1 = "hello";
String string2 = "BC";
int value = 22;
```

the statement

```
String s = string1 + string2 + value;
```

concatenates "hello", "BC" and 22. The concatenation is performed as follows:

```
new StringBuilder().append( "hello" ).append( "BC" ).append(
   22 ).toString();
```

First, Java creates an empty StringBuilder, then appends to it the string "hello", the string "BC" and the integer 22. Next, StringBuilder's method toString converts the StringBuilder to a String object to be assigned to String s. The statement

```
s += "!";
```

is performed as follows:

```
s = new StringBuilder().append( s ).append( "!" ).toString();
```

First, Java creates an empty StringBuilder, then it appends to the StringBuilder the current contents of s followed by "!". Next, StringBuilder's method toString converts the StringBuilder to a string representation, and the result is assigned to s.

25.4.5 StringBuilder Insertion and Deletion Methods

Class StringBuilder provides overloaded *insert* methods to allow values of various types to be inserted at any position in a StringBuilder. Versions are provided for each of the primitive types and for character arrays, Strings, Objects and CharSequences. Each method takes its second argument, converts it to a string and inserts it immediately preceding the index specified by the first argument. The first argument must be greater than or equal to 0 and less than the length of the StringBuilder—otherwise, a StringIndexOutOfBoundsException occurs. Class StringBuilder also provides methods *delete* and *deleteCharAt* for deleting characters at any position in a StringBuilder. Method delete takes two arguments—the starting index and the index one past the end of the characters to delete. All characters beginning at the starting index up to but not including the ending index are deleted. Method deleteCharAt takes one argument—the index of the character to delete. Invalid indices cause both methods to throw a StringIndexOutOfBoundsException. Methods insert, delete and deleteCharAt are demonstrated in Fig. 25.14.

```java
 1   // Fig. 25.14: StringBuilderInsert.java
 2   // StringBuilder methods insert, delete and deleteCharAt.
 3
 4   public class StringBuilderInsert
 5   {
 6      public static void main( String args[] )
 7      {
 8         Object objectRef = "hello";
 9         String string = "goodbye";
10         char charArray[] = { 'a', 'b', 'c', 'd', 'e', 'f' };
11         boolean booleanValue = true;
12         char characterValue = 'K';
13         int integerValue = 7;
14         long longValue = 10000000;
15         float floatValue = 2.5f; // f suffix indicates that 2.5 is a float
16         double doubleValue = 33.333;
17
18         StringBuilder buffer = new StringBuilder();
19
20         buffer.insert( 0, objectRef );
21         buffer.insert( 0, "  " ); // each of these contains two spaces
22         buffer.insert( 0, string );
23         buffer.insert( 0, "  " );
24         buffer.insert( 0, charArray );
25         buffer.insert( 0, "  " );
26         buffer.insert( 0, charArray, 3, 3 );
27         buffer.insert( 0, "  " );
28         buffer.insert( 0, booleanValue );
29         buffer.insert( 0, "  " );
30         buffer.insert( 0, characterValue );
31         buffer.insert( 0, "  " );
32         buffer.insert( 0, integerValue );
33         buffer.insert( 0, "  " );
34         buffer.insert( 0, longValue );
```

Fig. 25.14 | StringBuilder methods insert and delete. (Part 1 of 2.)

```
35          buffer.insert( 0, "   " );
36          buffer.insert( 0, floatValue );
37          buffer.insert( 0, "   " );
38          buffer.insert( 0, doubleValue );
39
40          System.out.printf(
41             "buffer after inserts:\n%s\n\n", buffer.toString() );
42
43          buffer.deleteCharAt( 10 ); // delete 5 in 2.5
44          buffer.delete( 2, 6 ); // delete .333 in 33.333
45
46          System.out.printf(
47             "buffer after deletes:\n%s\n", buffer.toString() );
48      } // end main
49 } // end class StringBuilderInsert
```

```
buffer after inserts:
33.333  2.5  10000000  7  K  true  def  abcdef  goodbye  hello

buffer after deletes:
33  2.  10000000  7  K  true  def  abcdef  goodbye  hello
```

Fig. 25.14 | StringBuilder methods insert and delete. (Part 2 of 2.)

25.5 Class Character

Java provides eight type-wrapper classes—Boolean, Character, Double, Float, Byte, Short, Integer and Long—that enable primitive-type values to be treated as objects. In this section, we present class Character—the type-wrapper class for primitive type char.

Most Character methods are static methods designed for convenience in processing individual char values. These methods take at least a character argument and perform either a test or a manipulation of the character. Class Character also contains a constructor that receives a char argument to initialize a Character object. Most of the methods of class Character are presented in the next three examples. For more information on class Character (and all the type-wrapper classes), see the java.lang package in the Java API documentation.

Figure 25.15 demonstrates some static methods that test characters to determine whether they are a specific character type and the static methods that perform case conversions on characters. You can enter any character and apply the methods to the character.

Line 15 uses Character method *isDefined* to determine whether character c is defined in the Unicode character set. If so, the method returns true, and otherwise, it returns false. Line 16 uses Character method *isDigit* to determine whether character c is a defined Unicode digit. If so, the method returns true, and otherwise, it returns false.

Line 18 uses Character method *isJavaIdentifierStart* to determine whether c is a character that can be the first character of an identifier in Java—that is, a letter, an underscore (_) or a dollar sign ($). If so, the method returns true, and otherwise, it returns false. Line 20 uses Character method *isJavaIdentifierPart* to determine whether character c is a character that can be used in an identifier in Java—that is, a digit, a letter, an underscore (_) or a dollar sign ($). If so, the method returns true, and otherwise, false.

Line 21 uses Character method *isLetter* to determine whether character c is a letter. If so, the method returns true, and otherwise, false. Line 23 uses Character method *isLetterOrDigit* to determine whether character c is a letter or a digit. If so, the method returns true, and otherwise, false.

```
1    // Fig. 25.15: StaticCharMethods.java
2    // Static Character testing methods and case conversion methods.
3    import java.util.Scanner;
4
5    public class StaticCharMethods
6    {
7       public static void main( String args[] )
8       {
9          Scanner scanner = new Scanner( System.in ); // create scanner
10         System.out.println( "Enter a character and press Enter" );
11         String input = scanner.next();
12         char c = input.charAt( 0 ); // get input character
13
14         // display character info
15         System.out.printf( "is defined: %b\n", Character.isDefined( c ) );
16         System.out.printf( "is digit: %b\n", Character.isDigit( c ) );
17         System.out.printf( "is first character in a Java identifier: %b\n",
18            Character.isJavaIdentifierStart( c ) );
19         System.out.printf( "is part of a Java identifier: %b\n",
20            Character.isJavaIdentifierPart( c ) );
21         System.out.printf( "is letter: %b\n", Character.isLetter( c ) );
22         System.out.printf(
23            "is letter or digit: %b\n", Character.isLetterOrDigit( c ) );
24         System.out.printf(
25            "is lower case: %b\n", Character.isLowerCase( c ) );
26         System.out.printf(
27            "is upper case: %b\n", Character.isUpperCase( c ) );
28         System.out.printf(
29            "to upper case: %s\n", Character.toUpperCase( c ) );
30         System.out.printf(
31            "to lower case: %s\n", Character.toLowerCase( c ) );
32      } // end main
33   } // end class StaticCharMethods
```

```
Enter a character and press Enter
A
is defined: true
is digit: false
is first character in a Java identifier: true
is part of a Java identifier: true
is letter: true
is letter or digit: true
is lower case: false
is upper case: true
to upper case: A
to lower case: a
```

Fig. 25.15 | Character class static methods for testing characters and converting character case. (Part 1 of 2.)

```
Enter a character and press Enter
8
is defined: true
is digit: true
is first character in a Java identifier: false
is part of a Java identifier: true
is letter: false
is letter or digit: true
is lower case: false
is upper case: false
to upper case: 8
to lower case: 8
```

```
Enter a character and press Enter
$
is defined: true
is digit: false
is first character in a Java identifier: true
is part of a Java identifier: true
is letter: false
is letter or digit: false
is lower case: false
is upper case: false
to upper case: $
to lower case: $
```

Fig. 25.15 | Character class static methods for testing characters and converting character case. (Part 2 of 2.)

Line 25 uses Character method *isLowerCase* to determine whether character c is a lowercase letter. If so, the method returns true, and otherwise, false. Line 27 uses Character method *isUpperCase* to determine whether character c is an uppercase letter. If so, the method returns true, and otherwise, false.

Line 29 uses Character method *toUpperCase* to convert the character c to its uppercase equivalent. The method returns the converted character if the character has an uppercase equivalent, and otherwise, the method returns its original argument. Line 31 uses Character method *toLowerCase* to convert the character c to its lowercase equivalent. The method returns the converted character if the character has a lowercase equivalent, and otherwise, the method returns its original argument.

Figure 25.16 demonstrates static Character methods *digit* and *forDigit*, which convert characters to digits and digits to characters, respectively, in different number systems. Common number systems include decimal (base 10), octal (base 8), hexadecimal (base 16) and binary (base 2). The base of a number is also known as its *radix*.

Line 28 uses method forDigit to convert the integer digit into a character in the number system specified by the integer radix (the base of the number). For example, the decimal integer 13 in base 16 (the radix) has the character value 'd'. Lowercase and uppercase letters represent the same value in number systems. Line 35 uses method digit to convert the character c into an integer in the number system specified by the integer radix (the base of the number). For example, the character 'A' is the base 16 (the radix) representation of the base 10 value 10. The radix must be between 2 and 36, inclusive.

Figure 25.17 demonstrates the constructor and several non-static methods of class Character—***charValue***, toString and equals. Lines 8–9 instantiate two Character

```
 1   // Fig. 25.16: StaticCharMethods2.java
 2   // Static Character conversion methods.
 3   import java.util.Scanner;
 4
 5   public class StaticCharMethods2
 6   {
 7      // create StaticCharMethods2 object execute application
 8      public static void main( String args[] )
 9      {
10         Scanner scanner = new Scanner( System.in );
11
12         // get radix
13         System.out.println( "Please enter a radix:" );
14         int radix = scanner.nextInt();
15
16         // get user choice
17         System.out.printf( "Please choose one:\n1 -- %s\n2 -- %s\n",
18            "Convert digit to character", "Convert character to digit" );
19         int choice = scanner.nextInt();
20
21         // process request
22         switch ( choice )
23         {
24            case 1: // convert digit to character
25               System.out.println( "Enter a digit:" );
26               int digit = scanner.nextInt();
27               System.out.printf( "Convert digit to character: %s\n",
28                  Character.forDigit( digit, radix ) );
29               break;
30
31            case 2: // convert character to digit
32               System.out.println( "Enter a character:" );
33               char character = scanner.next().charAt( 0 );
34               System.out.printf( "Convert character to digit: %s\n",
35                  Character.digit( character, radix ) );
36               break;
37         } // end switch
38      } // end main
39   } // end class StaticCharMethods2
```

```
Please enter a radix:
16
Please choose one:
1 -- Convert digit to character
2 -- Convert character to digit
2
Enter a character:
A
Convert character to digit: 10
```

Fig. 25.16 | Character class static conversion methods. (Part 1 of 2.)

```
Please enter a radix:
16
Please choose one:
1 -- Convert digit to character
2 -- Convert character to digit
1
Enter a digit:
13
Convert digit to character: d
```

Fig. 25.16 | Character class static conversion methods. (Part 2 of 2.)

objects by autoboxing the character constants 'A' and 'a', respectively. Line 12 uses Character method charValue to return the char value stored in Character object c1. Line 12 returns a string representation of Character object c2 using method toString. The condition in the if...else statement at lines 14–17 uses method equals to determine whether the object c1 has the same contents as the object c2 (i.e., the characters inside each object are equal).

```
 1    // Fig. 25.17: OtherCharMethods.java
 2    // Non-static Character methods.
 3
 4    public class OtherCharMethods
 5    {
 6       public static void main( String args[] )
 7       {
 8          Character c1 = 'A';
 9          Character c2 = 'a';
10
11          System.out.printf(
12             "c1 = %s\nc2 = %s\n\n", c1.charValue(), c2.toString() );
13
14          if ( c1.equals( c2 ) )
15             System.out.println( "c1 and c2 are equal\n" );
16          else
17             System.out.println( "c1 and c2 are not equal\n" );
18       } // end main
19    } // end class OtherCharMethods
```

```
c1 = A
c2 = a

c1 and c2 are not equal
```

Fig. 25.17 | Character class non-static methods.

25.6 Class StringTokenizer

When you read a sentence, your mind breaks the sentence into *tokens*—individual words and punctuation marks, each of which conveys meaning to you. Compilers also perform tokenization. They break up statements into individual pieces like keywords, identifiers, operators and other programming-language elements. We now study Java's StringTokenizer class (from package java.util), which breaks a string into its component tokens. Tokens are separated from one another by *delimiters*, typically white-space characters such as space, tab, newline and carriage return. Other characters can also be used as delimiters to separate tokens. The application in Fig. 25.18 demonstrates class StringTokenizer.

When the user presses the *Enter* key, the input sentence is stored in variable sentence. Line 17 creates a StringTokenizer for sentence. This StringTokenizer constructor takes a string argument and creates a StringTokenizer for it, and will use the default delimiter string " \t\n\r\f" consisting of a space, a tab, a carriage return and a newline for tokenization. There are two other constructors for class StringTokenizer. In the version that takes two String arguments, the second String is the delimiter string. In the version that takes three arguments, the second String is the delimiter string and the third argument (a boolean) determines whether the delimiters are also returned as tokens (only if the argument is true). This is useful if you need to know what the delimiters are.

```java
1    // Fig. 25.18: TokenTest.java
2    // StringTokenizer class.
3    import java.util.Scanner;
4    import java.util.StringTokenizer;
5
6    public class TokenTest
7    {
8       // execute application
9       public static void main( String args[] )
10      {
11         // get sentence
12         Scanner scanner = new Scanner( System.in );
13         System.out.println( "Enter a sentence and press Enter" );
14         String sentence = scanner.nextLine();
15
16         // process user sentence
17         StringTokenizer tokens = new StringTokenizer( sentence );
18         System.out.printf( "Number of elements: %d\nThe tokens are:\n",
19            tokens.countTokens() );
20
21         while ( tokens.hasMoreTokens() )
22            System.out.println( tokens.nextToken() );
23      } // end main
24   } // end class TokenTest
```

```
Enter a sentence and press Enter
This is a sentence with seven tokens
Number of elements: 7
The tokens are:
This
is
a
sentence
with
seven
tokens
```

Fig. 25.18 | StringTokenizer object used to tokenize strings.

Line 19 uses `StringTokenizer` method `countTokens` to determine the number of tokens in the string to be tokenized. The condition at line 21 uses `StringTokenizer` method ***hasMoreTokens*** to determine whether there are more tokens in the string being tokenized. If so, line 22 prints the next token in the `String`. The next token is obtained with a call to `StringTokenizer` method ***nextToken***, which returns a `String`. The token is output using `println`, so subsequent tokens appear on separate lines.

If you would like to change the delimiter string while tokenizing a string, you may do so by specifying a new delimiter string in a `nextToken` call as follows:

```
tokens.nextToken( newDelimiterString );
```

This feature is not demonstrated in Fig. 25.18.

25.7 Regular Expressions, Class `Pattern` and Class `Matcher`

Regular expressions are sequences of characters and symbols that define a set of strings. They are useful for validating input and ensuring that data is in a particular format. For example, a ZIP code must consist of five digits, and a last name must contain only letters, spaces, apostrophes and hyphens. One application of regular expressions is to facilitate the construction of a compiler. Often, a large and complex regular expression is used to validate the syntax of a program. If the program code does not match the regular expression, the compiler knows that there is a syntax error within the code.

Class `String` provides several methods for performing regular-expression operations, the simplest of which is the matching operation. `String` method ***matches*** receives a string that specifies the regular expression and matches the contents of the `String` object on which it is called to the regular expression. The method returns a `boolean` indicating whether the match succeeded.

A regular expression consists of literal characters and special symbols. Figure 25.19 specifies some ***predefined character classes*** that can be used with regular expressions. A character class is an escape sequence that represents a group of characters. A digit is any numeric character. A ***word character*** is any letter (uppercase or lowercase), any digit or the underscore character. A whitespace character is a space, a tab, a carriage return, a newline or a form feed. Each character class matches a single character in the string we are attempting to match with the regular expression.

Regular expressions are not limited to these predefined character classes. The expressions employ various operators and other forms of notation to match complex patterns. We examine several of these techniques in the application in Figs. 25.20 and 25.21 which

Character	Matches	Character	Matches
\d	any digit	\D	any nondigit
\w	any word character	\W	any nonword character
\s	any white-space character	\S	any nonwhite-space

Fig. 25.19 | Predefined character classes.

validates user input via regular expressions. [*Note:* This application is not designed to match all possible valid user input.]

Figure 25.20 validates user input. Line 9 validates the first name. To match a set of characters that does not have a predefined character class, use square brackets, []. For example, the pattern "[aeiou]" matches a single character that is a vowel. Character ranges are represented by placing a dash (-) between two characters. In the example, "[A-Z]" matches a single uppercase letter. If the first character in the brackets is "^", the expression accepts any character other than those indicated. However, it is important to note that "[^Z]" is not the same as "[A-Y]", which matches uppercase letters A–Y—"[^Z]" matches any character other than capital Z, including lowercase letters and non-letters such as the newline character. Ranges in character classes are determined by the letters' integer values. In this example, "[A-Za-z]" matches all uppercase and lowercase letters. The range "[A-z]" matches all letters and also matches those characters (such as % and 6) with an integer value between uppercase Z and lowercase a (for more information on integer values of characters see Appendix B, ASCII Character Set). Like predefined character classes, character classes delimited by square brackets match a single character in the search object.

```java
1   // Fig. 25.20: ValidateInput.java
2   // Validate user information using regular expressions.
3
4   public class ValidateInput
5   {
6      // validate first name
7      public static boolean validateFirstName( String firstName )
8      {
9         return firstName.matches( "[A-Z][a-zA-Z]*" );
10     } // end method validateFirstName
11
12     // validate last name
13     public static boolean validateLastName( String lastName )
14     {
15        return lastName.matches( "[a-zA-z]+([ '-][a-zA-Z]+)*" );
16     } // end method validateLastName
17
18     // validate address
19     public static boolean validateAddress( String address )
20     {
21        return address.matches(
22           "\\d+\\s+([a-zA-Z]+|[a-zA-Z]+\\s[a-zA-Z]+)" );
23     } // end method validateAddress
24
25     // validate city
26     public static boolean validateCity( String city )
27     {
28        return city.matches( "([a-zA-Z]+|[a-zA-Z]+\\s[a-zA-Z]+)" );
29     } // end method validateCity
30
31     // validate state
32     public static boolean validateState( String state )
33     {
```

Fig. 25.20 | Validating user information using regular expressions. (Part 1 of 2.)

```
34              return state.matches( "([a-zA-Z]+|[a-zA-Z]+\\s[a-zA-Z]+)" ) ;
35          } // end method validateState
36
37          // validate zip
38          public static boolean validateZip( String zip )
39          {
40              return zip.matches( "\\d{5}" );
41          } // end method validateZip
42
43          // validate phone
44          public static boolean validatePhone( String phone )
45          {
46              return phone.matches( "[1-9]\\d{2}-[1-9]\\d{2}-\\d{4}" );
47          } // end method validatePhone
48      } // end class ValidateInput
```

Fig. 25.20 | Validating user information using regular expressions. (Part 2 of 2.)

```
1   // Fig. 25.21: Validate.java
2   // Validate user information using regular expressions.
3   import java.util.Scanner;
4
5   public class Validate
6   {
7       public static void main( String[] args )
8       {
9           // get user input
10          Scanner scanner = new Scanner( System.in );
11          System.out.println( "Please enter first name:" );
12          String firstName = scanner.nextLine();
13          System.out.println( "Please enter last name:" );
14          String lastName = scanner.nextLine();
15          System.out.println( "Please enter address:" );
16          String address = scanner.nextLine();
17          System.out.println( "Please enter city:" );
18          String city = scanner.nextLine();
19          System.out.println( "Please enter state:" );
20          String state = scanner.nextLine();
21          System.out.println( "Please enter zip:" );
22          String zip = scanner.nextLine();
23          System.out.println( "Please enter phone:" );
24          String phone = scanner.nextLine();
25
26          // validate user input and display error message
27          System.out.println( "\nValidate Result:" );
28
29          if ( !ValidateInput.validateFirstName( firstName ) )
30              System.out.println( "Invalid first name" );
31          else if ( !ValidateInput.validateLastName( lastName ) )
32              System.out.println( "Invalid last name" );
33          else if ( !ValidateInput.validateAddress( address ) )
34              System.out.println( "Invalid address" );
```

Fig. 25.21 | Inputs and validates data from user using the ValidateInput class. (Part 1 of 2.)

```
35          else if ( !ValidateInput.validateCity( city ) )
36              System.out.println( "Invalid city" );
37          else if ( !ValidateInput.validateState( state ) )
38              System.out.println( "Invalid state" );
39          else if ( !ValidateInput.validateZip( zip ) )
40              System.out.println( "Invalid zip code" );
41          else if ( !ValidateInput.validatePhone( phone ) )
42              System.out.println( "Invalid phone number" );
43          else
44              System.out.println( "Valid input.  Thank you." );
45      } // end main
46  } // end class Validate
```

```
Please enter first name:
Jane
Please enter last name:
Doe
Please enter address:
123 Some Street
Please enter city:
Some City
Please enter state:
SS
Please enter zip:
123
Please enter phone:
123-456-7890

Validate Result:
Invalid zip code
```

```
Please enter first name:
Jane
Please enter last name:
Doe
Please enter address:
123 Some Street
Please enter city:
Some City
Please enter state:
SS
Please enter zip:
12345
Please enter phone:
123-456-7890

Validate Result:
Valid input.  Thank you.
```

Fig. 25.21 | Inputs and validates data from user using the `ValidateInput` class. (Part 2 of 2.)

In line 9, the asterisk after the second character class indicates that any number of letters can be matched. In general, when the regular-expression operator "*" appears in a regular expression, the application attempts to match zero or more occurrences of the subexpression immediately preceding the "*". Operator "+" attempts to match one or more occurrences of the subexpression immediately preceding "+". So both "A*" and "A+" will match "AAA", but only "A*" will match an empty string.

If method `validateFirstName` returns `true` (line 29), the application attempts to validate the last name (line 31) by calling `validateLastName` (lines 13–16 of Fig. 25.20). The regular expression to validate the last name matches any number of letters split by spaces, apostrophes or hyphens.

Line 33 validates the address by calling method `validateAddress` (lines 19–23 of Fig. 25.20). The first character class matches any digit one or more times (\\d+). Note that two \ characters are used, because \ normally starts an escape sequences in a string. So \\d in a Java string represents the regular expression pattern \d. Then we match one or more white-space characters (\\s+). The character "|" allows a match of the expression to its left or to its right. For example, "Hi (John|Jane)" matches both "Hi John" and "Hi Jane". The parentheses are used to group parts of the regular expression. In this example, the left side of | matches a single word, and the right side matches two words separated by any amount of white space. So the address must contain a number followed by one or two words. Therefore, "10 Broadway" and "10 Main Street" are both valid addresses in this example. The city (lines 26–29 of Fig. 25.20) and state (lines 32–35 of Fig. 25.20) methods also match any word of at least one character or, alternatively, any two words of at least one character if the words are separated by a single space. This means both `Waltham` and `West Newton` would match.

Quantifiers

The asterisk (*) and plus (+) are formally called *quantifiers*. Figure 25.22 lists all the quantifiers. We have already discussed how the asterisk (*) and plus (+) quantifiers work. All quantifiers affect only the subexpression immediately preceding the quantifier. Quantifier question mark (?) matches zero or one occurrences of the expression that it quantifies. A set of braces containing one number ({n}) matches exactly n occurrences of the expression it quantifies. We demonstrate this quantifier to validate the zip code in Fig. 25.20 at line 40. Including a comma after the number enclosed in braces matches at least n occurrences of the quantified expression. The set of braces containing two numbers ({n, m}), matches between n and m occurrences of the expression that it qualifies. Quantifiers may be applied to patterns enclosed in parentheses to create more complex regular expressions.

Quantifier	Matches
*	Matches zero or more occurrences of the pattern.
+	Matches one or more occurrences of the pattern.
?	Matches zero or one occurrences of the pattern.
{n}	Matches exactly n occurrences.
{$n,$}	Matches at least n occurrences.
{n, m}	Matches between n and m (inclusive) occurrences.

Fig. 25.22 | Quantifiers used in regular expressions.

All of the quantifiers are *greedy*. This means that they will match as many occurrences as they can as long as the match is still successful. However, if any of these quantifiers is followed by a question mark (?), the quantifier becomes *reluctant* (sometimes called *lazy*). It then will match as few occurrences as possible as long as the match is still successful.

The zip code (line 40 in Fig. 25.20) matches a digit five times. This regular expression uses the digit character class and a quantifier with the digit 5 between braces. The phone number (line 46 in Fig. 25.20) matches three digits (the first one cannot be zero) followed by a dash followed by three more digits (again the first one cannot be zero) followed by four more digits.

String Method `matches` checks whether an entire string conforms to a regular expression. For example, we want to accept "Smith" as a last name, but not "9@Smith#". If only a substring matches the regular expression, method `matches` returns `false`.

Replacing Substrings and Splitting Strings

Sometimes it is useful to replace parts of a string or to split a string into pieces. For this purpose, class `String` provides methods *replaceAll*, *replaceFirst* and *split*. These methods are demonstrated in Fig. 25.23.

Method `replaceAll` replaces text in a string with new text (the second argument) wherever the original string matches a regular expression (the first argument). Line 14 replaces every instance of "*" in `firstString` with "^". Note that the regular expression ("*") precedes character * with two backslashes. Normally, * is a quantifier indicating that a regular expression should match any number of occurrences of a preceding pattern. However, in line 14, we want to find all occurrences of the literal character *—to do this, we must escape character * with character \. Escaping a special regular-expression character with \ instructs the matching engine to find the actual character. Since the expression is stored in a Java string and \ is a special character in Java strings, we must include an additional \. So the Java string "*" represents the regular-expression pattern * which matches a single * character in the search string. In line 19, every match for the regular expression "stars" in `firstString` is replaced with "carets".

```java
 1   // Fig. 25.23: RegexSubstitution.java
 2   // Using methods replaceFirst, replaceAll and split.
 3
 4   public class RegexSubstitution
 5   {
 6      public static void main( String args[] )
 7      {
 8         String firstString = "This sentence ends in 5 stars *****";
 9         String secondString = "1, 2, 3, 4, 5, 6, 7, 8";
10
11         System.out.printf( "Original String 1: %s\n", firstString );
12
13         // replace '*' with '^'
14         firstString = firstString.replaceAll( "\\*", "^" );
15
16         System.out.printf( "^ substituted for *: %s\n", firstString );
17
```

Fig. 25.23 | Methods `replaceFirst`, `replaceAll` and `split`. (Part 1 of 2.)

```
18          // replace 'stars' with 'carets'
19          firstString = firstString.replaceAll( "stars", "carets" );
20
21          System.out.printf(
22              "\"carets\" substituted for \"stars\": %s\n", firstString );
23
24          // replace words with 'word'
25          System.out.printf( "Every word replaced by \"word\": %s\n\n",
26              firstString.replaceAll( "\\w+", "word" ) );
27
28          System.out.printf( "Original String 2: %s\n", secondString );
29
30          // replace first three digits with 'digit'
31          for ( int i = 0; i < 3; i++ )
32              secondString = secondString.replaceFirst( "\\d", "digit" );
33
34          System.out.printf(
35              "First 3 digits replaced by \"digit\" : %s\n", secondString );
36          String output = "String split at commas: [";
37
38          String[] results = secondString.split( ",\\s*" ); // split on commas
39
40          for ( String string : results )
41              output += "\"" + string + "\", "; // output results
42
43          // remove the extra comma and add a bracket
44          output = output.substring( 0, output.length() - 2 ) + "]";
45          System.out.println( output );
46      } // end main
47  } // end class RegexSubstitution
```

```
Original String 1: This sentence ends in 5 stars *****
^ substituted for *: This sentence ends in 5 stars ^^^^^
"carets" substituted for "stars": This sentence ends in 5 carets ^^^^^
Every word replaced by "word": word word word word word word ^^^^^

Original String 2: 1, 2, 3, 4, 5, 6, 7, 8
First 3 digits replaced by "digit" : digit, digit, digit, 4, 5, 6, 7, 8
String split at commas: ["digit", "digit", "digit", "4", "5", "6", "7", "8"]
```

Fig. 25.23 | Methods `replaceFirst`, `replaceAll` and `split`. (Part 2 of 2.)

Method `replaceFirst` (line 32) replaces the first occurrence of a pattern match. Java Strings are immutable, therefore method `replaceFirst` returns a new string in which the appropriate characters have been replaced. This line takes the original string and replaces it with the string returned by `replaceFirst`. By iterating three times we replace the first three instances of a digit (\d) in `secondString` with the text "digit".

Method `split` divides a string into several substrings. The original string is broken in any location that matches a specified regular expression. Method `split` returns an array of strings containing the substrings between matches for the regular expression. In line 38, we use method `split` to tokenize a string of comma-separated integers. The argument is the regular expression that locates the delimiter. In this case, we use the regular expression ",\\s*" to separate the substrings wherever a comma occurs. By matching any white-space characters, we eliminate extra spaces from the resulting substrings. Note that the commas and white-space characters are not returned as part of the substrings. Again, note that the Java string ",\\s*" represents the regular expression ,\s*.

Classes *Pattern* and Matcher

In addition to the regular-expression capabilities of class String, Java provides other classes in package java.util.regex that help developers manipulate regular expressions. Class *Pattern* represents a regular expression. Class *Matcher* contains both a regular-expression pattern and a CharSequence in which to search for the pattern.

CharSequence is an interface that allows read access to a sequence of characters. The interface requires that the methods charAt, length, subSequence and toString be declared. Both String and StringBuilder implement interface CharSequence, so an instance of either of these classes can be used with class Matcher.

Common Programming Error 25.4

A regular expression can be tested against an object of any class that implements interface CharSequence, but the regular expression must be a String. Attempting to create a regular expression as a StringBuilder is an error.

If a regular expression will be used only once, static Pattern method *matches* can be used. This method takes a string that specifies the regular expression and a CharSequence on which to perform the match. This method returns a boolean indicating whether the search object (the second argument) matches the regular expression.

If a regular expression will be used more than once, it is more efficient to use static Pattern method *compile* to create a specific Pattern object for that regular expression. This method receives a string representing the pattern and returns a new Pattern object, which can then be used to call method *matcher*. This method receives a CharSequence to search and returns a Matcher object.

Matcher provides method *matches*, which performs the same task as Pattern method matches, but receives no arguments—the search pattern and search object are encapsulated in the Matcher object. Class Matcher provides other methods, including *find*, *lookingAt*, *replaceFirst* and *replaceAll*.

Figure 25.24 presents a simple example that employs regular expressions. This program matches birthdays against a regular expression. The expression matches only birthdays that do not occur in April and that belong to people whose names begin with "J".

Lines 11–12 create a Pattern by invoking static Pattern method compile. The dot character "." in the regular expression (line 12) matches any single character except a newline character.

Line 20 creates the Matcher object for the compiled regular expression and the matching sequence (string1). Lines 22–23 use a while loop to iterate through the string. Line 22 uses Matcher method find to attempt to match a piece of the search object to the search pattern. Each call to this method starts at the point where the last call ended, so multiple matches can be found. Matcher method lookingAt performs the same way, except that it always starts from the beginning of the search object and will always find the first match if there is one.

```
 1   // Fig. 25.24: RegexMatches.java
 2   // Demonstrating Classes Pattern and Matcher.
 3   import java.util.regex.Matcher;
 4   import java.util.regex.Pattern;
 5
 6   public class RegexMatches
 7   {
 8      public static void main( String args[] )
 9      {
10         // create regular expression
11         Pattern expression =
12            Pattern.compile( "J.*\\d[0-35-9]-\\d\\d-\\d\\d" );
13
14         String string1 = "Jane's Birthday is 05-12-75\n" +
15            "Dave's Birthday is 11-04-68\n" +
16            "John's Birthday is 04-28-73\n" +
17            "Joe's Birthday is 12-17-77";
18
19         // match regular expression to string and print matches
20         Matcher matcher = expression.matcher( string1 );
21
22         while ( matcher.find() )
23            System.out.println( matcher.group() );
24      } // end main
25   } // end class RegexMatches
```

```
Jane's Birthday is 05-12-75
Joe's Birthday is 12-17-77
```

Fig. 25.24 | Regular expressions checking birthdays.

Common Programming Error 25.5

Method matches (from class String, Pattern *or* Matcher*) will return* true *only if the entire search object matches the regular expression. Methods* find *and* lookingAt *(from class* Matcher*) will return* true *if a portion of the search object matches the regular expression.*

Line 23 uses Matcher method *group*, which returns the string from the search object that matches the search pattern. The string that is returned is the one that was last matched by a call to find or lookingAt. The output in Fig. 25.24 shows the two matches that were found in string1.

25.8 Wrap-Up

In this chapter, you learned about more String methods for selecting portions of Strings and manipulating Strings. You also learned about the Character class and some of the methods it declares to handle chars. The chapter also discussed the capabilities of the StringBuilder class for creating Strings. The end of the chapter discussed regular expressions, which provide a powerful capability to search and match portions of Strings that fit a particular pattern.

Operator Precedence Chart

A.1 Operator Precedence

Operators are shown in decreasing order of precedence from top to bottom (Fig. A.1).

Operator	Description	Associativity
++ --	unary postfix increment unary postfix decrement	right to left
++ -- + - ! ~ (*type*)	unary prefix increment unary prefix decrement unary plus unary minus unary logical negation unary bitwise complement unary cast	right to left
* / %	multiplication division remainder	left to right
+ -	addition or string concatenation subtraction	left to right
<< >> >>>	left shift signed right shift unsigned right shift	left to right

Fig. A.1 | Operator precedence chart. (Part 1 of 2.)

Operator	Description	Associativity

`<`
`<=`
`>`
`>=`
`instanceof`
	less than
	less than or equal to
	greater than
	greater than or equal to
	type comparison
		left to right

`==` `!=`	is equal to is not equal to	left to right
`&`	bitwise AND boolean logical AND	left to right
`^`	bitwise exclusive OR boolean logical exclusive OR	left to right
`|`	bitwise inclusive OR boolean logical inclusive OR	left to right
`&&`	conditional AND	left to right
`||`	conditional OR	left to right
`?:`	conditional	right to left

`=`
`+=`
`-=`
`*=`
`/=`
`%=`
`&=`
`^=`
`|=`
`<<=`
`>>=`
`>>>=`
	assignment
	addition assignment
	subtraction assignment
	multiplication assignment
	division assignment
	remainder assignment
	bitwise AND assignment
	bitwise exclusive OR assignment
	bitwise inclusive OR assignment
	bitwise left shift assignment
	bitwise signed-right-shift assignment
	bitwise unsigned-right-shift assignment
		right to left

Fig. A.1 | Operator precedence chart. (Part 2 of 2.)

ASCII Character Set

	0	1	2	3	4	5	6	7	8	9
0	nul	soh	stx	etx	eot	enq	ack	bel	bs	ht
1	nl	vt	ff	cr	so	si	dle	dc1	dc2	dc3
2	dc4	nak	syn	etb	can	em	sub	esc	fs	gs
3	rs	us	sp	!	"	#	$	%	&	'
4	(	)	*	+	,	-	.	/	0	1
5	2	3	4	5	6	7	8	9	:	;
6	<	=	>	?	@	A	B	C	D	E
7	F	G	H	I	J	K	L	M	N	O
8	P	Q	R	S	T	U	V	W	X	Y
9	Z	[	\	]	^	_	'	a	b	c
10	d	e	f	g	h	i	j	k	l	m
11	n	o	p	q	r	s	t	u	v	w
12	x	y	z	{			}	~	del		

Fig. B.1 | ASCII character set.

The digits at the left of the table are the left digits of the decimal equivalent (0–127) of the character code, and the digits at the top of the table are the right digits of the character code. For example, the character code for "F" is 70, and the character code for "&" is 38.

Most users of this book are interested in the ASCII character set used to represent English characters on many computers. The ASCII character set is a subset of the Unicode character set used by Java to represent characters from most of the world's languages. For more information on the Unicode character set, see www.unicode.org.

Keywords and Reserved Words

Java Keywords				
abstract	assert	boolean	break	byte
case	catch	char	class	continue
default	do	double	else	enum
extends	final	finally	float	for
if	implements	import	instanceof	int
interface	long	native	new	package
private	protected	public	return	short
static	strictfp	super	switch	synchronized
this	throw	throws	transient	try
void	volatile	while		
Keywords that are not currently used				
const	goto			

Fig. C.1 | Java keywords.

Java also contains the reserved words `true` and `false`, which are `boolean` literals, and `null`, which is the literal that represents a reference to nothing. Like keywords, these reserved words cannot be used as identifiers.

Primitive Types

Type	Size in bits	Values	Standard
boolean		true or false	
[*Note:* A boolean's representation is specific to the Java Virtual Machine on each platform.]			
char	16	'\u0000' to '\uFFFF' (0 to 65535)	(ISO Unicode character set)
byte	8	-128 to $+127$ (-2^7 to $2^7 - 1$)	
short	16	$-32{,}768$ to $+32{,}767$ (-2^{15} to $2^{15} - 1$)	
int	32	$-2{,}147{,}483{,}648$ to $+2{,}147{,}483{,}647$ (-2^{31} to $2^{31} - 1$)	
long	64	$-9{,}223{,}372{,}036{,}854{,}775{,}808$ to $+9{,}223{,}372{,}036{,}854{,}775{,}807$ (-2^{63} to $2^{63} - 1$)	
float	32	*Negative range:* $-3.4028234663852886E+38$ to $-1.40129846432481707e-45$ *Positive range:* $1.40129846432481707e-45$ to $3.4028234663852886E+38$	(IEEE 754 floating point)
double	64	*Negative range:* $-1.7976931348623157E+308$ to $-4.94065645841246544e-324$ *Positive range:* $4.94065645841246544e-324$ to $1.7976931348623157E+308$	(IEEE 754 floating point)

Fig. D.1 | Java primitive types.

For more information on IEEE 754 visit grouper.ieee.org/groups/754/. For more information on Unicode, see www.unicode.org.

E

GroupLayout

E.1 Introduction

Java SE 6 includes a powerful new layout manager called *GroupLayout*, which is the default layout manager in the Netbeans 5.5 IDE (www.netbeans.org). In this appendix, we overview GroupLayout, then demonstrate how to use the Netbeans 5.5 IDE's *Matisse GUI designer* to create a GUI using GroupLayout to position the components. Netbeans generates the GroupLayout code for you automatically. Though you can write Group-Layout code by hand, in most cases you'll use a GUI design tool like the one provided by Netbeans to take advantage of GroupLayout's power. For more details on GroupLayout, see the list of web resources at the end of this appendix.

E.2 GroupLayout Basics

Chapters 11 and 17 presented several layout managers that provide basic GUI layout capabilities. We also discussed how to combine layout managers and multiple containers to create more complex layouts. Most layout managers do not give you precise control over the positioning of components. In Chapter 17, we discussed the GridBagLayout, which provides more precise control over the position and size of your GUI components. It allows you to specify the horizontal and vertical position of each component, the number of rows and columns each component occupies in the grid, and how components grow and shrink as the size of the container changes. This is all specified at once with a GridBagCon-straints object. Class GroupLayout is the next step in layout management. GroupLayout is more flexible, because you can specify the horizontal and vertical layouts of your components independently.

Sequential and Parallel Arrangements

Components are arranged either sequentially or in parallel. The three JButtons in Fig. E.1 are arranged with *sequential horizontal orientation*—they appear left to right in sequence. Vertically, the components are arranged in parallel, so, in a sense, they "occupy the same vertical space." Components can also be arranged sequentially in the vertical

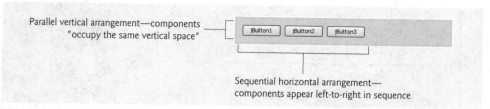

Fig. E.1 | JButtons arranged sequentially for their horizontal orientation and in parallel for their vertical orientation.

direction and in parallel in the horizontal direction, as you'll see in Section E.3. To prevent overlapping components, components with parallel vertical orientation are normally arranged with sequential horizontal orientation (and vice versa).

Groups and Alignment

To create more complex user interfaces, GroupLayout allows you to create *groups* that contain sequential or parallel elements. Within a group you can have GUI components, other groups and gaps. Placing a group within another group is similar to building a GUI using nested containers, such as a JPanel that contains other JPanels, which in turn contain GUI components.

When you create a group, you can specify the *alignment* of the group's elements. Class GroupLayout contains four constants for this purpose—LEADING, TRAILING, CENTER and BASELINE. The constant BASELINE applies only to vertical orientations. In horizontal orientation, the constants LEADING, TRAILING and CENTER represent left justified, right justified and centered, respectively. In vertical orientation, LEADING, TRAILING and CENTER align the components at their tops, bottoms or vertical centers, respectively. Aligning components with BASELINE indicates they should be aligned using the baseline of the font for the components' text. For more information about font baselines, see Section 12.4.

Spacing

GroupLayout by default uses the recommended GUI design guidelines of the underlying platform for spacing between components. The **addGap** method of GroupLayout nested classes **GroupLayout.Group**, **GroupLayout.SequentialGroup** and **GroupLayout.ParallelGroup** allows you to control the spacing between components.

Sizing Components

By default, GroupLayout uses each component's getMinimumSize, getMaximumSize and getPreferredSize methods to help determine the component's size. You can override the default settings.

E.3 Building a ColorChooser

We now present a ColorChooser application to demonstrate the GroupLayout layout manager. The application consists of three JSlider objects, each representing the values from 0 to 255 for specifying the red, green and blue values of a color. The selected values for each JSlider will be used to display a filled rectangle of the specified color. We build the application using Netbeans 5.5. For an more detailed introduction to developing GUI applications in the NetBeans IDE, see www.netbeans.org/kb/trails/matisse.html.

Create a New Project

Begin by opening a new NetBeans project. Select **File > New Project...**. In the **New Project** dialog, choose **General** from the **Categories** list and **Java Application** from the **Projects** list then click **Next >**. Specify ColorChooser as the project name and uncheck the **Create Main Class** checkbox. You can also specify the location of your project in the **Project Location** field. Click **Finish** to create the project.

Add a New Subclass of JFrame to the Project

In the IDE's **Projects** tab just below the **File** menu and toolbar (Fig. E.2), expand the **Source Packages** node. Right-click the **<default package>** node that appears and select **New > JFrame Form**. In the **New JPanel Form** dialog, specify ColorChooser as the class name and click **Finish**. This subclass of JFrame will display the application's GUI components. The Netbeans window should now appear similar to Fig. E.3 with the ColorChooser class shown in **Design** view. The **Source** and **Design** buttons at the top of the ColorChooser.java window allow you to switch between editing the source code and designing the GUI.

    Design view shows only the ColorChooser's client area (i.e., the area that will appear inside the window's borders). To build a GUI visually, you can drag GUI components from the **Palette** window onto the client area. You can configure the properties of each component by selecting it, then modifying the property values that appear in the **Properties** window (Fig. E.3). When you select a component, the **Properties** window displays three buttons—**Properties**, **Events** and **Code** (see Fig. E.4)—that enable you to configure various aspects of the component.

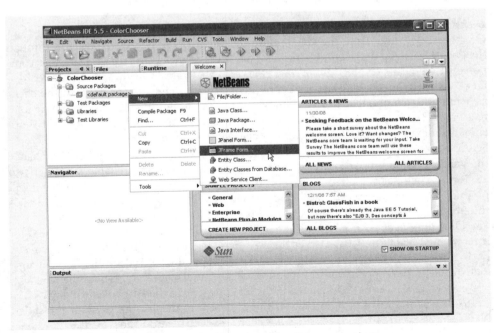

Fig. E.2 | Adding a new **JFrame Form** to the ColorChooser project.

Projects tab   ColorChooser.java shown in **Design** view   client area   **Palette** window

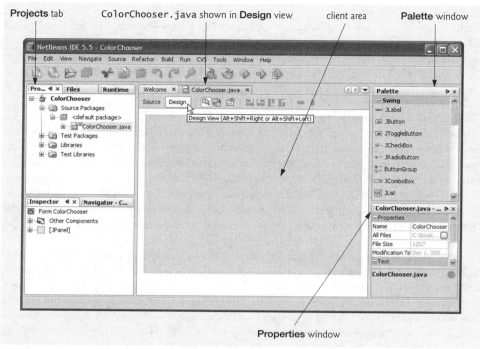

Fig. E.3 | Class ColorChooser shown in the Netbeans **Design** view.

Build the GUI

Drag three JSliders from the **Palette** onto the JFrame (you may need to scroll through the **Palette**). As you drag components near the edges of the client area or near other components, Netbeans displays *guide lines* (Fig. E.4) that show you the recommended distances and alignments between the component you are dragging, the edges of the client area and other components. As you follow the steps to build the GUI, use the guide lines to arrange the components into three rows and three columns as in Fig. E.5. Use the **Properties** window to rename the JSliders to redJSlider, greenJSlider and blueJSlider. Select the first JSlider, then click the **Code** button in the **Properties** window and change the **Variable Name** property to redSlider. Repeat this process to rename the other two JSliders. Then, select each JSlider and change its maximum property to 255 so that it will produce values in the range 0–255, and change its value property to 0 so the JSlider's thumb will initially be at the left of the JSlider.

Drag three JLabels from the **Palette** to the JFrame to label each JSlider with the color it represents. Name the JLabels redJLabel, greenJLabel and blueJLabel, respectively. Each JLabel should be placed to the left of the corresponding JSlider (Fig. E.5). Change each JLabel's **text** property either by double clicking the JLabel and typing the new text, or by selecting the JLabel and changing the **text** property in the **Properties** window.

Add a JTextField next to each of the JSliders to display the value of the slider. Name the JTextFields redJTextField, greenJTextField and blueJTextField, respectively. Change each JTextField's **text** property to 0 using the same techniques as you did for the JLabels. Change each JTextField's **columns** property to 4.

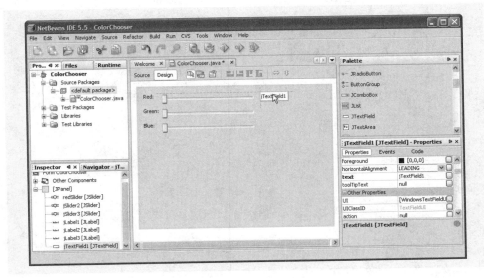

Fig. E.4 | Positioning the first JTextField.

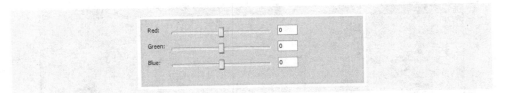

Fig. E.5 | Layout of the JLabels, JSliders and JTextFields.

Double click the border of the client area to display the **Set Form Designer Size** dialog and change the first number (which represents the width) to 410, then click **OK**. This makes the client area wide enough to accommodate the JPanel you'll add next. Finally, add a JPanel named colorJPanel to the right of this group of components. Use the guide lines as shown in Fig. E.6 to place the JPanel. Change this JPanel's background color to display the selected color. Finally, drag the bottom border of the client area toward the top of the **Design** area until you see the snap-to line that shows the recommended height of the client area (based on the components in the client area) as shown in Fig. E.7.

Editing the Source Code and Adding Event Handlers

The IDE automatically generated the GUI code, including methods for initializing components and aligning them using the GroupLayout layout manager. We must add the desired functionality to the components' event handlers. To add an event handler for a component, right click it and position the mouse over the **Events** option in the pop-up menu. You can then select the category of event you wish to handle and the specific event within that category. For example, to add the JSlider event handlers for this example, right click each JSlider and select **Events > Change > stateChanged**. When you do this, Netbeans adds a ChangeListener to the JSlider and switches from **Design** view to **Source** view where you can place code in the event handler. Use the **Design** button to return to **Design**

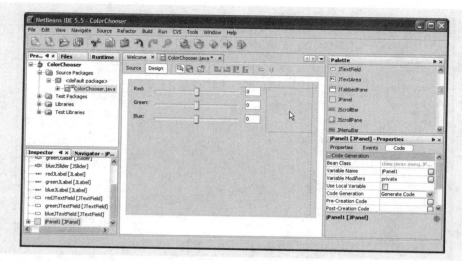

Fig. E.6 | Positioning the JPanel.

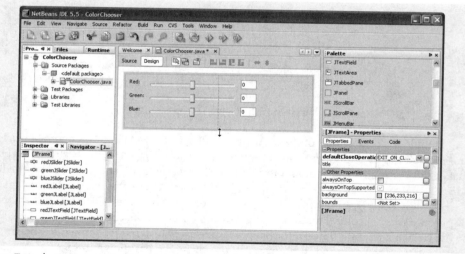

Fig. E.7 | Setting the height of the client area.

view and repeat the preceding steps to add the event handlers for the other two JSliders. To complete the event handlers, first add the method in Fig. E.8. In each JSlider event handler set the corresponding JTextField to the new value of the JSlider, then call method changeColor. Finally, in the constructor after the call to initComponents, add the line

```
colorJPanel.setBackground( java.awt.Color.BLACK );
```

Figure E.9 shows the completed ColorChooser class exactly as it is generated in Netbeans "in the raw." More and more software development is done with tools that generate complex code like this, saving you the time and effort of doing it yourself.

```
1    // changes the colorJPanel's background color based on the current
2    // values of the JSliders
3    public void changeColor()
4    {
5       colorJPanel.setBackground( new java.awt.Color(
6          redJSlider.getValue(), greenJSlider.getValue(),
7          blueJSlider.getValue() ) );
8    } // end method changeColor
```

Fig. E.8 | Method that changes the colorJPanel's background color based on the values of the three JSliders.

```
1    /*
2     * ColorChooser.java
3     *
4     * Created on December 2, 2006, 9:25 AM
5     */
6
7    /**
8     *
9     * @author  paul
10    */
11   public class ColorChooser extends javax.swing.JFrame
12   {
13
14      /** Creates new form ColorChooser */
15      public ColorChooser()
16      {
17         initComponents();
18         colorJPanel.setBackground( java.awt.Color.BLACK );
19      }
20
21      // changes the colorJPanel's background color based on the current
22      // values of the JSliders
23      public void changeColor()
24      {
25         colorJPanel.setBackground( new java.awt.Color(
26            redJSlider.getValue(), greenJSlider.getValue(),
27            blueJSlider.getValue() ) );
28      } // end method changeColor
29
30      /** This method is called from within the constructor to
31       * initialize the form.
32       * WARNING: Do NOT modify this code. The content of this method is
33       * always regenerated by the Form Editor.
34       */
35      // <editor-fold defaultstate="collapsed" desc=" Generated Cod
36      private void initComponents()
37      {
38         redJSlider = new javax.swing.JSlider();
39         greenJSlider = new javax.swing.JSlider();
```

Fig. E.9 | ColorChooser class that uses GroupLayout for its GUI layout. (Part 1 of 6.)

```
40          blueJSlider = new javax.swing.JSlider();
41          redJLabel = new javax.swing.JLabel();
42          greenJLabel = new javax.swing.JLabel();
43          blueJLabel = new javax.swing.JLabel();
44          redJTextField = new javax.swing.JTextField();
45          greenJTextField = new javax.swing.JTextField();
46          blueJTextField = new javax.swing.JTextField();
47          colorJPanel = new javax.swing.JPanel();
48
49          setDefaultCloseOperation(javax.swing.WindowConstants.EXIT_ON_CLOSE);
50          redJSlider.setMaximum(255);
51          redJSlider.setValue(0);
52          redJSlider.addChangeListener(new javax.swing.event.ChangeListener()
53          {
54             public void stateChanged(javax.swing.event.ChangeEvent evt)
55             {
56                redJSliderStateChanged(evt);
57             }
58          });
59
60          greenJSlider.setMaximum(255);
61          greenJSlider.setValue(0);
62          greenJSlider.addChangeListener(
new javax.swing.event.ChangeListener()
63          {
64             public void stateChanged(javax.swing.event.ChangeEvent evt)
65             {
66                greenJSliderStateChanged(evt);
67             }
68          });
69
70          blueJSlider.setMaximum(255);
71          blueJSlider.setValue(0);
72          blueJSlider.addChangeListener(new javax.swing.event.ChangeListener()
73          {
74             public void stateChanged(javax.swing.event.ChangeEvent evt)
75             {
76                blueJSliderStateChanged(evt);
77             }
78          });
79
80          redJLabel.setText("Red:");
81
82          greenJLabel.setText("Green:");
83
84          blueJLabel.setText("Blue:");
85
86          redJTextField.setColumns(4);
87          redJTextField.setText("0");
88
89          greenJTextField.setColumns(4);
90          greenJTextField.setText("0");
91
```

Fig. E.9 | ColorChooser class that uses GroupLayout for its GUI layout. (Part 2 of 6.)

```
92          blueJTextField.setColumns(4);
93          blueJTextField.setText("0");
94
95          javax.swing.GroupLayout colorJPanelLayout =
new javax.swing.GroupLayout(colorJPanel);
96          colorJPanel.setLayout(colorJPanelLayout);
97          colorJPanelLayout.setHorizontalGroup(
98             colorJPanelLayout.createParallelGroup(
javax.swing.GroupLayout.Alignment.LEADING)
99             .addGap(0, 100, Short.MAX_VALUE)
100         );
101         colorJPanelLayout.setVerticalGroup(
102            colorJPanelLayout.createParallelGroup(
javax.swing.GroupLayout.Alignment.LEADING)
103            .addGap(0, 100, Short.MAX_VALUE)
104         );
105
106         javax.swing.GroupLayout layout = new
javax.swing.GroupLayout(getContentPane());
107         getContentPane().setLayout(layout);
108         layout.setHorizontalGroup(
109            layout.createParallelGroup(
javax.swing.GroupLayout.Alignment.LEADING)
110            .addGroup(layout.createSequentialGroup()
111               .addContainerGap()
112               .addGroup(layout.createParallelGroup(
javax.swing.GroupLayout.Alignment.LEADING)
113                  .addComponent(greenJLabel)
114                  .addComponent(blueJLabel)
115                  .addComponent(redJLabel))
116               .addPreferredGap(
javax.swing.LayoutStyle.ComponentPlacement.RELATED)
117                  .addGroup(layout.createParallelGroup(
javax.swing.GroupLayout.Alignment.LEADING)
118                     .addGroup(layout.createSequentialGroup()
119                        .addComponent(blueJSlider,
javax.swing.GroupLayout.PREFERRED_SIZE, javax.swing.GroupLayout.DEFAULT_SIZE,
javax.swing.GroupLayout.PREFERRED_SIZE)
120                        .addPreferredGap(
javax.swing.LayoutStyle.ComponentPlacement.RELATED)
121                        .addComponent(blueJTextField,
javax.swing.GroupLayout.PREFERRED_SIZE, javax.swing.GroupLayout.DEFAULT_SIZE,
javax.swing.GroupLayout.PREFERRED_SIZE))
122                     .addGroup(layout.createSequentialGroup()
123                        .addComponent(greenJSlider,
javax.swing.GroupLayout.PREFERRED_SIZE, javax.swing.GroupLayout.DEFAULT_SIZE,
javax.swing.GroupLayout.PREFERRED_SIZE)
124
.addPreferredGap(javax.swing.LayoutStyle.ComponentPlacement.RELATED)
125                        .addComponent(greenJTextField,
javax.swing.GroupLayout.PREFERRED_SIZE, javax.swing.GroupLayout.DEFAULT_SIZE,
javax.swing.GroupLayout.PREFERRED_SIZE))
126                     .addGroup(layout.createSequentialGroup()
```

Fig. E.9 | ColorChooser class that uses GroupLayout for its GUI layout. (Part 3 of 6.)

```
127                         .addComponent(redJSlider,
javax.swing.GroupLayout.PREFERRED_SIZE, javax.swing.GroupLayout.DEFAULT_SIZE,
javax.swing.GroupLayout.PREFERRED_SIZE)
128
.addPreferredGap(javax.swing.LayoutStyle.ComponentPlacement.RELATED)
129                         .addComponent(redJTextField,
javax.swing.GroupLayout.PREFERRED_SIZE, javax.swing.GroupLayout.DEFAULT_SIZE,
javax.swing.GroupLayout.PREFERRED_SIZE)))
130                 .addPreferredGap(
javax.swing.LayoutStyle.ComponentPlacement.RELATED, 9, Short.MAX_VALUE)
131                 .addComponent(colorJPanel,
javax.swing.GroupLayout.PREFERRED_SIZE, javax.swing.GroupLayout.DEFAULT_SIZE,
javax.swing.GroupLayout.PREFERRED_SIZE)
132                 .addContainerGap())
133         );
134     layout.setVerticalGroup(
135         layout.createParallelGroup(
javax.swing.GroupLayout.Alignment.LEADING)
136             .addGroup(layout.createSequentialGroup()
137             .addContainerGap()
138             .addGroup(layout.createParallelGroup(
javax.swing.GroupLayout.Alignment.LEADING)
139                 .addComponent(colorJPanel,
javax.swing.GroupLayout.PREFERRED_SIZE, javax.swing.GroupLayout.DEFAULT_SIZE,
javax.swing.GroupLayout.PREFERRED_SIZE)
140                     .addGroup(layout.createSequentialGroup()
141                     .addGroup(layout.createParallelGroup(
javax.swing.GroupLayout.Alignment.LEADING)
142                         .addComponent(redJSlider,
javax.swing.GroupLayout.PREFERRED_SIZE, javax.swing.GroupLayout.DEFAULT_SIZE,
javax.swing.GroupLayout.PREFERRED_SIZE)
143                         .addComponent(redJTextField,
javax.swing.GroupLayout.PREFERRED_SIZE, javax.swing.GroupLayout.DEFAULT_SIZE,
javax.swing.GroupLayout.PREFERRED_SIZE)
144                         .addComponent(redJLabel))
145                     .addPreferredGap(
javax.swing.LayoutStyle.ComponentPlacement.RELATED)
146                     .addGroup(layout.createParallelGroup(
javax.swing.GroupLayout.Alignment.LEADING)
147                         .addGroup(layout.createSequentialGroup()
148                         .addGroup(layout.createParallelGroup(
javax.swing.GroupLayout.Alignment.LEADING)
149                             .addComponent(greenJLabel)
150                             .addComponent(greenJSlider,
javax.swing.GroupLayout.PREFERRED_SIZE, javax.swing.GroupLayout.DEFAULT_SIZE,
javax.swing.GroupLayout.PREFERRED_SIZE))
151                         .addPreferredGap(
javax.swing.LayoutStyle.ComponentPlacement.RELATED)
152                         .addGroup(
layout.createParallelGroup(javax.swing.GroupLayout.Alignment.LEADING)
153                             .addComponent(blueJLabel)
154                             .addGroup(layout.createParallelGroup(
javax.swing.GroupLayout.Alignment.TRAILING)
```

Fig. E.9 | ColorChooser class that uses GroupLayout for its GUI layout. (Part 4 of 6.)

```
155                                    .addComponent(blueJTextField,
javax.swing.GroupLayout.PREFERRED_SIZE, javax.swing.GroupLayout.DEFAULT_SIZE,
javax.swing.GroupLayout.PREFERRED_SIZE)
156                                    .addComponent(blueJSlider,
javax.swing.GroupLayout.PREFERRED_SIZE, javax.swing.GroupLayout.DEFAULT_SIZE,
javax.swing.GroupLayout.PREFERRED_SIZE))))
157                                 .addComponent(greenJTextField,
javax.swing.GroupLayout.PREFERRED_SIZE, javax.swing.GroupLayout.DEFAULT_SIZE,
javax.swing.GroupLayout.PREFERRED_SIZE))))
158                    .addContainerGap(javax.swing.GroupLayout.DEFAULT_SIZE,
Short.MAX_VALUE))
159          );
160          pack();
161     }// </editor-fold>
162
163     private void blueJSliderStateChanged(javax.swing.event.ChangeEvent evt)
164     {
165        blueJTextField.setText( "" + blueJSlider.getValue() );
166        changeColor();
167     }
168
169     private void greenJSliderStateChanged(
javax.swing.event.ChangeEvent evt)
170     {
171        greenJTextField.setText( "" + greenJSlider.getValue() );
172        changeColor();
173     }
174
175     private void redJSliderStateChanged(
javax.swing.event.ChangeEvent evt)
176     {
177        redJTextField.setText( "" + redJSlider.getValue() );
178        changeColor();
179     }
180
181     /**
182      * @param args the command line arguments
183      */
184     public static void main(String args[])
185     {
186        java.awt.EventQueue.invokeLater(new Runnable()
187        {
188           public void run()
189           {
190              new ColorChooser().setVisible(true);
191           }
192        });
193     }
194
195     // Variables declaration - do not modify
196     private javax.swing.JLabel blueJLabel;
197     private javax.swing.JSlider blueJSlider;
198     private javax.swing.JTextField blueJTextField;
```

Fig. E.9 | ColorChooser class that uses GroupLayout for its GUI layout. (Part 5 of 6.)

```
199      private javax.swing.JPanel colorJPanel;
200      private javax.swing.JLabel greenJLabel;
201      private javax.swing.JSlider greenJSlider;
202      private javax.swing.JTextField greenJTextField;
203      private javax.swing.JLabel redJLabel;
204      private javax.swing.JSlider redJSlider;
205      private javax.swing.JTextField redJTextField;
206      // End of variables declaration
207
208   }
```

Fig. E.9 | ColorChooser class that uses GroupLayout for its GUI layout. (Part 6 of 6.)

Method initComponents (lines 36–161) was entirely generated by Netbeans based on your interactions with the GUI designer. This method contains the code that creates and formats the GUI. Lines 38–93 construct and initialize the GUI components. Lines 95–161 specify the layout of those components using GroupLayout. Lines 108–133 specify the horizontal group and lines 134–159 specify the vertical group.

We manually added the statement that changes the colorJPanel's background color in line 18 and the changeColor method in lines 23–28. When the user moves the thumb on one of the JSliders, the JSlider's event handler sets the text in its corresponding JTextField to the JSlider's new value (lines 165, 171 and 177), then calls method changeColor (lines 166, 172 and 178) to update the colorJPanel's background color. Method changeColor gets the current value of each JSlider (lines 26–27) and uses these values as the arguments to the Color constructor to create a new Color.

E.4 GroupLayout Web Resources

weblogs.java.net/blog/tpavek/archive/2006/02/getting_to_know_1.html
Part 1 of Tomas Pavek's GroupLayout blog post overviews GroupLayout theory.

weblogs.java.net/blog/tpavek/archive/2006/03/getting_to_know.html
Part 2 of Tomas Pavek's GroupLayout blog post presents a complete GUI implemented with Group-Layout.

java.sun.com/javase/6/docs/api/javax/swing/GroupLayout.html
API documentation for class GroupLayout.

F

Java Desktop Integration Components (JDIC)

F.1 Introduction

The *Java Desktop Integration Components (JDIC)* are part of an open-source project aimed at allowing better integration between Java applications and the platforms on which they execute. Some JDIC features include:

- interacting with the underlying platform to launch native applications (such as web browsers and email clients)
- displaying a splash screen when an application begins execution to indicate to the user that the application is loading
- creating icons in the system tray (also called the taskbar status area or notification area) to provide access to Java applications running in the background
- registering file-type associations, so that files of specified types will automatically open in corresponding Java applications
- creating installer packages, and more.

The JDIC homepage (jdic.dev.java.net/) includes an introduction to JDIC, downloads, documentation, FAQs, demos, articles, blogs, announcements, incubator projects, a developer's page, forums, mailing lists, and more. Java SE 6 now includes some of the features mentioned above. We discuss several of these features here.

F.2 Splash Screens

Java application users often perceive a performance problem, because nothing appears on the screen when you first launch an application. One way to show a user that your program is loading is to display a *splash screen*—a borderless window that appears temporarily while an application loads. Java SE 6 provides the new command-line option *-splash* for the java command to accomplish this task. This option enables you to specify a PNG, GIF or JPG image that should display when your application begins loading. To demonstrate this new option, we created a program (Fig. F.1) that sleeps for 5 seconds (so you can view the splash screen) then displays a message at the command line. The directory for this example includes a PNG format image to use as the splash screen. To display the splash screen when this application loads, use the command

```
java -splash:DeitelBug.png SplashDemo
```

```java
1   // Fig. F.1: SplashDemo.java
2   // Splash screen demonstration.
3   public class SplashDemo
4   {
5      public static void main( String[] args )
6      {
7         try
8         {
9            Thread.sleep( 5000 );
10        } // end try
11        catch ( InterruptedException e )
12        {
13           e.printStackTrace();
14        } // end catch
15
16        System.out.println(
17           "This was the splash screen demo." );
18     } // end method main
19  } // end class SplashDemo
```

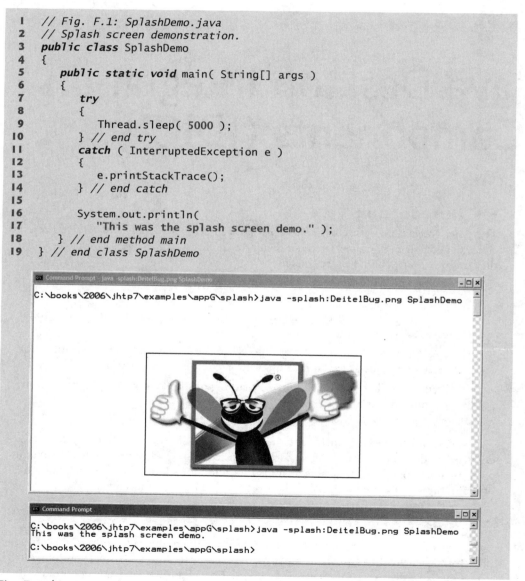

Fig. F.1 | Spash screen displayed with the -splash option to the java command.

Once you've initiated the splash screen display, you can interact with it programmatically via the *SplashScreen* class of the java.awt package. You might do this to add some dynamic content to the splash screen. For more information on working with splash screens, see the following sites:

```
java.sun.com/developer/technicalArticles/J2SE/Desktop/javase6/
    splashscreen/
java.sun.com/javase/6/docs/api/java/awt/SplashScreen.html
```

F.3 Desktop Class

Java SE 6's new *Desktop* class enables you to specify a file or URI that you'd like to open using the underlying platform's appropriate application. For example, if Firefox is your computer's default browser, you can use the Desktop class's browse method to open a web site in Firefox. In addition, you can open an email composition window in your system's default email client, open a file in its associated application and print a file using the associated application's print command. Figure F.2 demonstrates the first three of these capabilities.

The event handler at lines 22–52 obtains the index number of the task the user selects in the tasksJComboBox (line 25) and the String that represents the file or URI to process (line 26). Line 28 uses Desktop static method *isDesktopSupported* to determine whether class Desktop's features are supported on the platform on which this application runs. If they are, line 32 uses Desktop static method *getDesktop*, to obtain a Desktop object. If the user selected the option to open the default browser, line 37 creates a new URI object using the String input as the site to display in the browser, then passes the URI object to Desktop method *browse* which invokes the system's default browser and passes the URI to the browser for display. If the user selects the option to open a file in its associated program, line 40 creates a new File object using the String input as the file to open, then passes the File object to Desktop method *open* which passes the file to the appropriate application to open the file. Finally, if the user selects the option to compose an email, line 43 creates a new URI object using the String input as the email address to which the email will be sent, then passes the URI object to Desktop method *mail* which invokes the system's default email client and passes the URI to the email client as the email recipient. You can learn more about class Desktop at

```
java.sun.com/javase/6/docs/api/java/awt/Desktop.html
```

```
1   // Fig. F.2: DesktopDemo.java
2   // Use Desktop to launch default browser, open a file in its associated
3   // application and compose an email in the default email client.
4   import java.awt.Desktop;
5   import java.io.File;
6   import java.io.IOException;
7   import java.net.URI;
8
```

Fig. F.2 | Use Desktop to launch the default browser, open a file in its associated application and compose an email in the default email client. (Part 1 of 3.)

```java
 9  public class DesktopDemo extends javax.swing.JFrame
10  {
11      // constructor
12      public DesktopDemo()
13      {
14          initComponents();
15      } // end DesktopDemo constructor
16
17      // To save space, lines 20-84 of the Netbeans autogenerated GUI code
18      // are not shown here. The complete code for this example is located in
19      // the file DesktopDemo.java in this example's directory.
20
21      // determine selected task and perform the task
22      private void doTaskJButtonActionPerformed(
23          java.awt.event.ActionEvent evt)
24      {
25          int index = tasksJComboBox.getSelectedIndex();
26          String input = inputJTextField.getText();
27
28          if ( Desktop.isDesktopSupported() )
29          {
30              try
31              {
32                  Desktop desktop = Desktop.getDesktop();
33
34                  switch ( index )
35                  {
36                      case 0: // open browser
37                          desktop.browse( new URI( input ) );
38                          break;
39                      case 1: // open file
40                          desktop.open( new File( input ) );
41                          break;
42                      case 2: // open email composition window
43                          desktop.mail( new URI( input ) );
44                          break;
45                  } // end switch
46              } // end try
47              catch ( Exception e )
48              {
49                  e.printStackTrace();
50              } // end catch
51          } // end if
52      } // end method doTaskJButtonActionPerformed
53
54      public static void main(String args[])
55      {
56          java.awt.EventQueue.invokeLater(
57              new Runnable()
58              {
```

Fig. F.2 | Use `Desktop` to launch the default browser, open a file in its associated application and compose an email in the default email client. (Part 2 of 3.)

```
59              public void run()
60              {
61                  new DesktopDemo().setVisible(true);
62              }
63          }
64      );
65  } // end method main
66
67  // Variables declaration - do not modify
68  private javax.swing.JButton doTaskJButton;
69  private javax.swing.JLabel inputJLabel;
70  private javax.swing.JTextField inputJTextField;
71  private javax.swing.JLabel instructionLabel;
72  private javax.swing.JComboBox tasksJComboBox;
73  // End of variables declaration
74  }
```

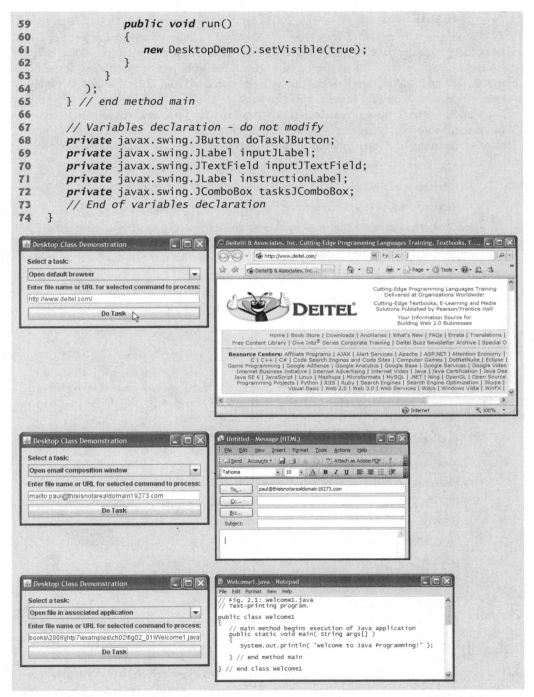

Fig. F.2 | Use Desktop to launch the default browser, open a file in its associated application and compose an email in the default email client. (Part 3 of 3.)

F.4 Tray Icons

Tray icons generally appear in your system's system tray, taskbar status area or notification area. They typically provide quick access to applications that are executing in the background on your system. When you position the mouse over one of these icons, a tooltip appears indicating what application the icon represents. If you click the icon, a popup menu appears with options for that application.

Classes SystemTray and TrayIcon (both from package java.awt) enable you to create and manage your own tray icons in a platform independent manner. Class **SystemTray** provides access to the underlying platform's system tray—the class consists of three methods:

- static method **getDefaultSystemTray** returns the system tray
- method **addTrayIcon** adds a new TrayIcon to the system tray
- method **removeTrayIcon** removes an icon from the system tray

Class **TrayIcon** consists of several methods allowing users to specify an icon, a tooltip and a pop-up menu for the icon. In addition, tray icons support ActionListeners, MouseListeners and MouseMotionListeners. You can learn more about classes System-Tray and TrayIcon at

> java.sun.com/javase/6/docs/api/java/awt/SystemTray.html
> java.sun.com/javase/6/docs/api/java/awt/TrayIcon.html

F.5 JDIC Incubator Projects

The JDIC Incubator Projects are developed, maintained and owned by members of the Java community. These projects are associated with, but not distributed with, JDIC. The Incubator Projects may eventually become part of the JDIC project once they have been fully developed and meet certain criteria. For more information about the Incubator Projects and to learn how you can setup an Incubator Project, visit

> jdic.dev.java.net/#incubator

Current Incubator Projects include:

- FileUtil—A file utility API that extends the java.io.File class.
- Floating Dock Top-level Window—A Java API for developing a floating dock toplevel window.
- Icon Service—Returns a Java icon object from a native icon specification.
- Misc API —Hosts simple (one method, one class type of) APIs.
- Music Player Control API—Java API that controls native music players.
- SaverBeans Screensaver SDK—Java screensaver development kit.
- SystemInfo—Checks the system information.

F.6 JDIC Demos

The JDIC site includes demos for FileExplorer, the browser package, the TrayIcon package, the Floating Dock class and the Wallpaper API (jdic.dev.java.net/#demos). The source code for these demos is included in the JDIC download (jdic.dev.java.net/servlets/ ProjectDocumentList). For more demos, check out some of the incubator projects.

Using the Java API Documentation

G.1 Introduction

The Java class library contains thousands of predefined classes and interfaces that programmers can use to write their own applications. These classes are grouped into packages based on their functionality. For example, the classes and interfaces used for file processing are grouped into the java.io package, and the classes and interfaces for networking applications are grouped into the java.net package. The *Java API documentation* lists the public and protected members of each class and the public members of each interface in the Java class library. The documentation overviews all the classes and interfaces, summarizes their members (i.e., the fields, constructors and methods of classes, and the fields and methods of interfaces) and provides detailed descriptions of each member. Most Java programmers rely on this documentation when writing programs. Normally, programmers would search the API to find the following:

1. The package that contains a particular class or interface.

2. Relationships between a particular class or interface and other classes and interfaces.

3. Class or interface constants—normally declared as public static final fields.

4. Constructors to determine how an object of the class can be initialized.

5. The methods of a class to determine whether they are static or non-static, the number and types of the arguments you need to pass, the return types and any exceptions that might be thrown from the method.

In addition, programmers often rely on the documentation to discover classes and interfaces that they have not used before. For this reason, we demonstrate the documentation with classes you know and classes you may not have studied yet. We show how to use the documentation to locate the information you need to use a class or interface effectively.

G.2 Navigating the Java API

The Java API documentation can be downloaded to your local hard disk or viewed online. To download the Java API documentation, go to `java.sun.com/javase/6/download.jsp` and locate the **DOWNLOAD** link in the **Java SE 6 Documentation** section. You'll be asked to accept a license agreement. To do this, click **Accept**, then click **Continue**. Click the **Java(TM) SE Development Kit Documentation 6** link to begin the download. After downloading the file, you can use a ZIP file-extraction program, such as WinZip (`www.winzip.com`), to extract the files. If you are using Windows, extract the contents to your JDK's installation directory. (See the *Before You Begin* section of this book for information on installing Java.) To view the API documentation on your local hard disk in Microsoft Windows, open `C:\Program Files\Java\jdk1.6.0\docs\api\index.html` page in your browser. To view the API documentation on line, go to `java.sun.com/javase/6/docs/api/index.html` (Fig. G.1).

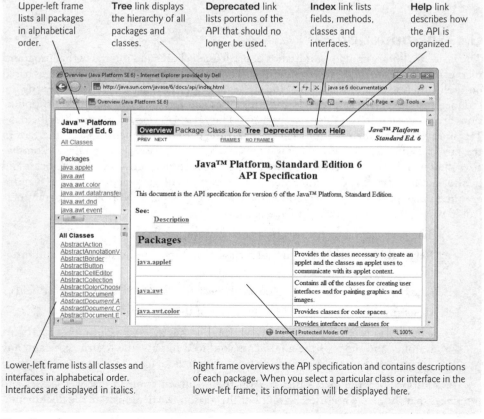

Fig. G.1 | Java API overview.

Frames in the API Documentation's `index.html` *Page*

The API documentation is divided into three frames (see Fig. G.1). The upper-left frame lists all of the Java API's packages in alphabetical order. The lower-left frame initially lists the Java API's classes and interfaces in alphabetical order. Interface names are displayed in italic. When you click a specific package in the upper-left frame, the lower-left frame lists the classes and interfaces of the selected package. The right frame initially provides a brief description of each package of the Java API specification—read this overview to become familiar wth the general capabilities of the Java APIs. If you select a class or interface in the lower-left frame, the right frame displays information about that class or interface.

Important Links in the `index.html` *Page*

At the top of the right frame (Fig. G.1), there are four links—***Tree***, ***Deprecated***, ***Index*** and ***Help***. The **Tree** link displays the hierarchy of all packages, classes and interfaces in a tree structure. The **Deprecated** link displays interfaces, classes, exceptions, fields, constructors and methods that should no longer be used. The **Index** link displays classes, interfaces, fields, constructors and methods in alphabetical order. The **Help** link describes how the API documentation is organized. You should probably begin by reading the **Help** page.

Viewing the **Index** *Page*

If you do not know the name of the class you are looking for, but you do know the name of a method or field, you can use the documentation's index to locate the class. The **Index** link is located near the upper-right corner of the right frame. The index page (Fig. G.2) displays fields, constructors, methods, interfaces and classes in alphabetical order. For example, if you are looking for `Scanner` method `hasNextInt`, but do not know the class

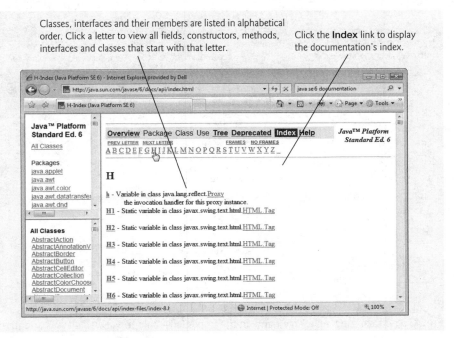

Fig. G.2 | Viewing the **Index** page.

name, you can click the **H** link to go to the alphabetical listing of all items in the Java API that begin with "h". Scroll to method `hasNextInt` (Fig. G.3). Once there, each method named `hasNextInt` is listed with the package name and class to which the method belongs. From there, you can click the class name to view the class's complete details, or you can click the method name to view the method's details.

Viewing a Specific Package

When you click the package name in the upper-left frame, all classes and interfaces from that package are displayed in the lower-left frame and are divided into five subsections—**Interfaces, Classes, Enums, Exceptions** and **Errors**—each listed alphabetically. For example, the contents of package `javax.swing` are displayed in the lower-left frame (Fig. G.4)

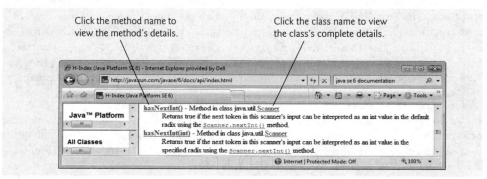

Fig. G.3 | Scroll to method `hasNextInt`.

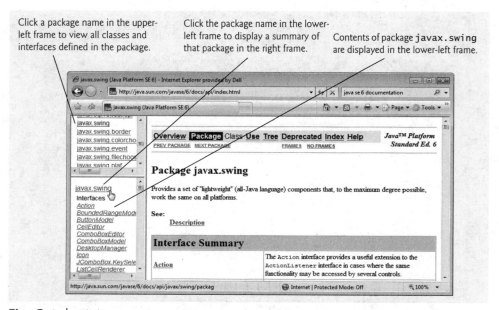

Fig. G.4 | Clicking a package name in the upper-left frame to view all classes and interfaces declared in this package.

when you click `javax.swing` in the upper-left frame. You can click the package name in the lower-left frame to get an overview of the package. If you think that a package contains several classes that could be useful in your application, the package overview can be especially helpful.

Viewing the Details of a Class

When you click a class name or interface name in the lower-left frame, the right frame displays the details of that class or interface. First you'll see the class's package name followed by a hierarchy that shows the class's relationship to other classes. You'll also see a list of the interfaces implemented by the class and the class's known subclasses. Figure G.5 shows the beginning of the documentation page for class `JButton` from the `javax.swing` package. The page first shows the package name in which the class appears. This is followed by the

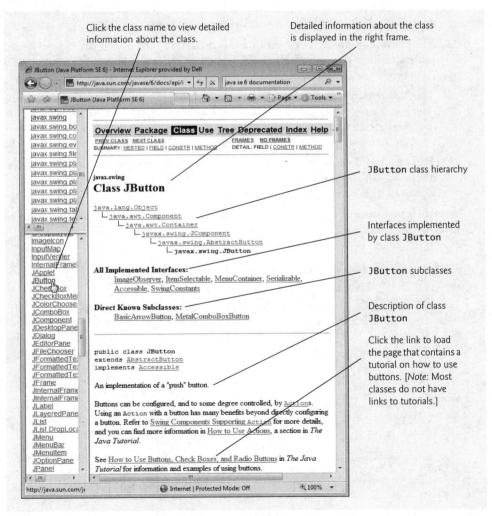

Fig. G.5 | Clicking a class name to view detailed information about the class.

class hierarchy that leads to class JButton, the interfaces class JButton implements and the subclasses of class JButton. The bottom of the right frame shows the beginning of class JButton's description. Note that when you look at the documentation for an interface, the right frame does not display a hierarchy for that interface. Instead, the right frame lists the interface's superinterfaces, known subinterfaces and known implementing classes.

Summary Sections in a Class's Documentation Page

Other parts of each API page are listed below. Each part is presented only if the class contains or inherits the items specified. Class members shown in the summary sections are public unless they are explicitly marked as protected. A class's private members are not shown in the documentation, because they cannot be used directly in your programs.

1. The **Nested Class Summary** section summarizes the class's public and protected nested classes—i.e., classes that are defined inside the class. Unless explicitly specified, these classes are public and non-static.

2. The **Field Summary** section summarizes the class's public and protected fields. Unless explicitly specified, these fields are public and non-static. Figure G.6 shows the Field Summary section of class Color.

3. The **Constructor Summary** section summarizes the class's constructors. Constructors are not inherited, so this section appears in the documentation for a class only if the class declares one or more constructors. Figure G.7 shows the Constructor Summary section of class JButton.

4. The **Method Summary** section summarizes the class's public and protected methods. Unless explicitly specified, these methods are public and non-static. Figure G.8 shows the Method Summary section of class BufferedInputStream.

Note that the summary sections typically provide only a one-sentence description of a class member. Additional details are presented in the detail sections discussed next.

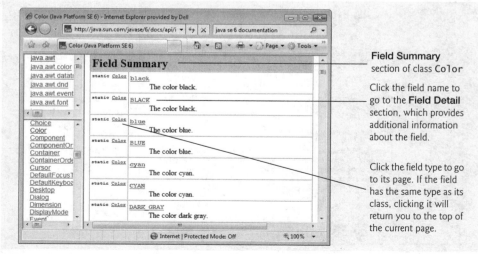

Fig. G.6 | Field Summary section of class Color.

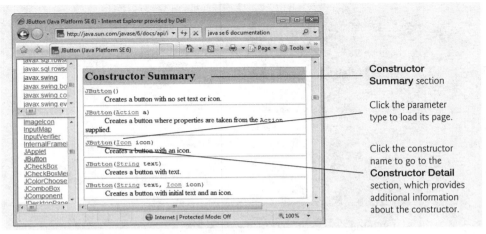

Fig. G.7 | **Constructor Summary** section of class `JButton`.

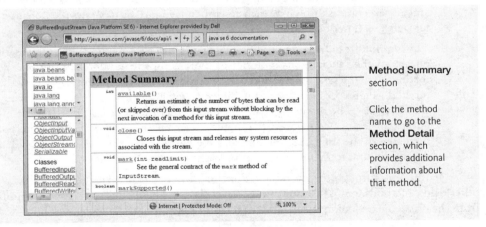

Fig. G.8 | **Method Summary** section of class `BufferedInputStream`.

Detail Sections in a Class's Documentation Page

After the summary sections are detail sections that normally provide more discussion of particular class members. There is not a detail section for nested classes. When you click the link in the **Nested Class Summary** for a particular nested class, a documentation page describing that nested class is displayed. The detail sections are described below.

1. The ***Field Detail*** section provides the declaration of each field. It also discusses each field, including the field's modifiers and meaning. Figure G.9 shows the **Field Detail** section of class `Color`.

2. The ***Constructor Detail*** section provides the first line of each constructor's declaration and discusses the constructors. The discussion includes the modifiers of

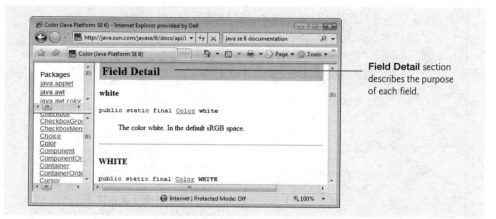

Fig. G.9 | **Field Detail** section of class `Color`.

each constructor, a description of each constructor, each constructor's parameters and any exceptions thrown by each constructor. Figure G.10 shows the **Constructor Detail** section of class `JButton`.

3. The ***Method Detail*** section provides the first line of each method. The discussion of each method includes its modifiers, a more complete method description, the method's parameters, the method's return type and any exceptions thrown by the method. Figure G.11 shows the **Method Detail** section of class `BufferedInputStream`. The method details show you other methods that might be of interest (labeled as **See Also**). If the method overrides a method of the superclass, the name of the superclass method and the name of the superclass are provided so you can link to the method or superclass for more information.

As you look through the documentation, you'll notice that there are often links to other fields, methods, nested-classes and top-level classes. These links enable you to jump from the class you are looking at to another relevant portion of the documentation.

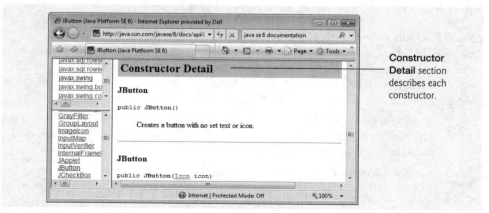

Fig. G.10 | **Constructor Detail** section of class `JButton`.

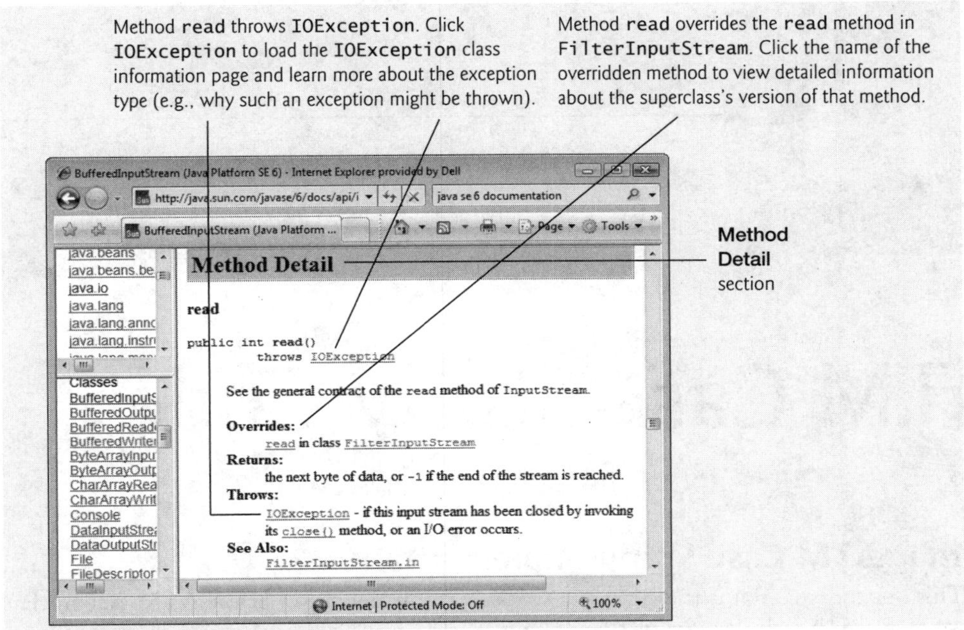
Method read throws IOException. Click IOException to load the IOException class information page and learn more about the exception type (e.g., why such an exception might be thrown).
Method read overrides the read method in FilterInputStream. Click the name of the overridden method to view detailed information about the superclass's version of that method.
Method Detail section
BufferedInputStream (Java Platform SE 6) - Internet Explorer provided by Dell
Method Detail
read
public int read()
throws IOException
See the general contract of the read method of InputStream.
Overrides:
read in class FilterInputStream
Returns:
the next byte of data, or -1 if the end of the stream is reached.
Throws:
IOException - if this input stream has been closed by invoking its close() method, or an I/O error occurs.
See Also:
FilterInputStream.in
Internet | Protected Mode: Off

Fig. G.11 | **Method Detail** section of class `BufferedInputStream`.

ATM Case Study Code

H.1 ATM Case Study Implementation

This appendix contains the complete working implementation of the ATM system that we designed in the Software Engineering Case Study sections found at the ends of Chapters 3–8 and 10. The implementation comprises 670 lines of Java code. We consider the classes in the order in which we identified them in Section 3.9:

- ATM
- Screen
- Keypad
- CashDispenser
- DepositSlot
- Account
- BankDatabase
- Transaction
- BalanceInquiry
- Withdrawal
- Deposit

We apply the guidelines discussed in Section 8.18 and Section 10.8 to code these classes based on how we modeled them in the UML class diagrams of Figs. 10.19 and 10.20. To develop the bodies of class methods, we refer to the activity diagrams presented in Section 5.9 and the communication and sequence diagrams presented in Section 7.13. Note that our ATM design does not specify all the program logic and may not specify all the attributes and operations required to complete the ATM implementation. This is a normal part of the object-oriented design process. As we implement the system, we complete the program logic and add attributes and behaviors as necessary to construct the ATM system specified by the requirements document in Section 2.8.

We conclude the discussion by presenting a Java application (ATMCaseStudy) that starts the ATM and puts the other classes in the system in use. Recall that we are developing a first version of the ATM system that runs on a personal computer and uses the computer's keyboard and monitor to approximate the ATM's keypad and screen. We also only simulate the actions of the ATM's cash dispenser and deposit slot. We attempt to implement the system, however, so that real hardware versions of these devices could be integrated without significant changes in the code.

H.2 Class ATM

Class ATM (Fig. H.1) represents the ATM as a whole. Lines 6–12 implement the class's attributes. We determine all but one of these attributes from the UML class diagrams of Figs. 10.19 and 10.20. Note that we implement the UML Boolean attribute user-Authenticated in Fig. 10.20 as a boolean attribute in Java (line 6). Line 7 declares an attribute not found in our UML design—an int attribute currentAccountNumber that keeps track of the account number of the current authenticated user. We'll soon see how the class uses this attribute. Lines 8–12 declare reference-type attributes corresponding to the ATM class's associations modeled in the class diagram of Fig. 10.19. These attributes allow the ATM to access its parts (i.e., its Screen, Keypad, CashDispenser and DepositSlot) and interact with the bank's account information database (i.e., a BankDatabase object).

```java
 1   // ATM.java
 2   // Represents an automated teller machine
 3
 4   public class ATM
 5   {
 6      private boolean userAuthenticated; // whether user is authenticated
 7      private int currentAccountNumber; // current user's account number
 8      private Screen screen; // ATM's screen
 9      private Keypad keypad; // ATM's keypad
10      private CashDispenser cashDispenser; // ATM's cash dispenser
11      private DepositSlot depositSlot; // ATM's deposit slot
12      private BankDatabase bankDatabase; // account information database
13
14      // constants corresponding to main menu options
15      private static final int BALANCE_INQUIRY = 1;
16      private static final int WITHDRAWAL = 2;
17      private static final int DEPOSIT = 3;
18      private static final int EXIT = 4;
19
20      // no-argument ATM constructor initializes instance variables
21      public ATM()
22      {
23         userAuthenticated = false; // user is not authenticated to start
24         currentAccountNumber = 0; // no current account number to start
25         screen = new Screen(); // create screen
```

Fig. H.1 | Class ATM represents the ATM. (Part 1 of 4.)

```
26          keypad = new Keypad(); // create keypad
27          cashDispenser = new CashDispenser(); // create cash dispenser
28          depositSlot = new DepositSlot(); // create deposit slot
29          bankDatabase = new BankDatabase(); // create acct info database
30      } // end no-argument ATM constructor
31
32      // start ATM
33      public void run()
34      {
35          // welcome and authenticate user; perform transactions
36          while ( true )
37          {
38              // loop while user is not yet authenticated
39              while ( !userAuthenticated )
40              {
41                  screen.displayMessageLine( "\nWelcome!" );
42                  authenticateUser(); // authenticate user
43              } // end while
44
45              performTransactions(); // user is now authenticated
46              userAuthenticated = false; // reset before next ATM session
47              currentAccountNumber = 0; // reset before next ATM session
48              screen.displayMessageLine( "\nThank you! Goodbye!" );
49          } // end while
50      } // end method run
51
52      // attempts to authenticate user against database
53      private void authenticateUser()
54      {
55          screen.displayMessage( "\nPlease enter your account number: " );
56          int accountNumber = keypad.getInput(); // input account number
57          screen.displayMessage( "\nEnter your PIN: " ); // prompt for PIN
58          int pin = keypad.getInput(); // input PIN
59
60          // set userAuthenticated to boolean value returned by database
61          userAuthenticated =
62              bankDatabase.authenticateUser( accountNumber, pin );
63
64          // check whether authentication succeeded
65          if ( userAuthenticated )
66          {
67              currentAccountNumber = accountNumber; // save user's account #
68          } // end if
69          else
70              screen.displayMessageLine(
71                  "Invalid account number or PIN. Please try again." );
72      } // end method authenticateUser
73
74      // display the main menu and perform transactions
75      private void performTransactions()
76      {
77          // local variable to store transaction currently being processed
78          Transaction currentTransaction = null;
```

Fig. H.1 | Class ATM represents the ATM. (Part 2 of 4.)

```
79
80        boolean userExited = false; // user has not chosen to exit
81
82        // loop while user has not chosen option to exit system
83        while ( !userExited )
84        {
85           // show main menu and get user selection
86           int mainMenuSelection = displayMainMenu();
87
88           // decide how to proceed based on user's menu selection
89           switch ( mainMenuSelection )
90           {
91              // user chose to perform one of three transaction types
92              case BALANCE_INQUIRY:
93              case WITHDRAWAL:
94              case DEPOSIT:
95
96                 // initialize as new object of chosen type
97                 currentTransaction =
98                    createTransaction( mainMenuSelection );
99
100                currentTransaction.execute(); // execute transaction
101                break;
102             case EXIT: // user chose to terminate session
103                screen.displayMessageLine( "\nExiting the system..." );
104                userExited = true; // this ATM session should end
105                break;
106             default: // user did not enter an integer from 1-4
107                screen.displayMessageLine(
108                   "\nYou did not enter a valid selection. Try again." );
109                break;
110          } // end switch
111       } // end while
112    } // end method performTransactions
113
114    // display the main menu and return an input selection
115    private int displayMainMenu()
116    {
117       screen.displayMessageLine( "\nMain menu:" );
118       screen.displayMessageLine( "1 - View my balance" );
119       screen.displayMessageLine( "2 - Withdraw cash" );
120       screen.displayMessageLine( "3 - Deposit funds" );
121       screen.displayMessageLine( "4 - Exit\n" );
122       screen.displayMessage( "Enter a choice: " );
123       return keypad.getInput(); // return user's selection
124    } // end method displayMainMenu
125
126    // return object of specified Transaction subclass
127    private Transaction createTransaction( int type )
128    {
129       Transaction temp = null; // temporary Transaction variable
130
```

Fig. H.1 | Class ATM represents the ATM. (Part 3 of 4.)

```
131        // determine which type of Transaction to create
132        switch ( type )
133        {
134           case BALANCE_INQUIRY: // create new BalanceInquiry transaction
135              temp = new BalanceInquiry(
136                 currentAccountNumber, screen, bankDatabase );
137              break;
138           case WITHDRAWAL: // create new Withdrawal transaction
139              temp = new Withdrawal( currentAccountNumber, screen,
140                 bankDatabase, keypad, cashDispenser );
141              break;
142           case DEPOSIT: // create new Deposit transaction
143              temp = new Deposit( currentAccountNumber, screen,
144                 bankDatabase, keypad, depositSlot );
145              break;
146        } // end switch
147
148        return temp; // return the newly created object
149     } // end method createTransaction
150  } // end class ATM
```

Fig. H.1 | Class ATM represents the ATM. (Part 4 of 4.)

Lines 15–18 declare integer constants that correspond to the four options in the ATM's main menu (i.e., balance inquiry, withdrawal, deposit and exit). Lines 21–30 declare class ATM's constructor, which initializes the class's attributes. When an ATM object is first created, no user is authenticated, so line 23 initializes userAuthenticated to false. Likewise, line 24 initializes currentAccountNumber to 0 because there is no current user yet. Lines 25–28 instantiate new objects to represent the parts of the ATM. Recall that class ATM has composition relationships with classes Screen, Keypad, CashDispenser and DepositSlot, so class ATM is responsible for their creation. Line 29 creates a new BankDatabase. [*Note:* If this were a real ATM system, the ATM class would receive a reference to an existing database object created by the bank. However, in this implementation we are only simulating the bank's database, so class ATM creates the BankDatabase object with which it interacts.]

The class diagram of Fig. 10.20 does not list any operations for class ATM. We now implement one operation (i.e., public method) in class ATM that allows an external client of the class (i.e., class ATMCaseStudy) to tell the ATM to run. ATM method run (lines 33–50) uses an infinite loop (lines 36–49) to repeatedly welcome a user, attempt to authenticate the user and, if authentication succeeds, allow the user to perform transactions. After an authenticated user performs the desired transactions and chooses to exit, the ATM resets itself, displays a goodbye message to the user and restarts the process. We use an infinite loop here to simulate the fact that an ATM appears to run continuously until the bank turns it off (an action beyond the user's control). An ATM user has the option to exit the system, but does not have the ability to turn off the ATM completely.

Inside method run's infinite loop, lines 39–43 cause the ATM to repeatedly welcome and attempt to authenticate the user as long as the user has not been authenticated (i.e., !userAuthenticated is true). Line 41 invokes method displayMessageLine of the ATM's screen to display a welcome message. Like Screen method displayMessage designed in the case study, method displayMessageLine (declared in lines 13–16 of Fig. H.2) displays a message to the user, but this method also outputs a newline after displaying the message. We have added this method during implementation to give class Screen's clients more control over the placement of displayed messages. Line 42 invokes class ATM's private utility method authenticateUser (declared in lines 53–72) to attempt to authenticate the user.

We refer to the requirements document to determine the steps necessary to authenticate the user before allowing transactions to occur. Line 55 of method authenticateUser invokes method displayMessage of the ATM's screen to prompt the user to enter an account number. Line 56 invokes method getInput of the ATM's keypad to obtain the user's input, then stores the integer value entered by the user in a local variable accountNumber. Method authenticateUser next prompts the user to enter a PIN (line 57), and stores the PIN input by the user in a local variable pin (line 58). Next, lines 61–62 attempt to authenticate the user by passing the accountNumber and pin entered by the user to the bankDatabase's authenticateUser method. Class ATM sets its userAuthenticated attribute to the boolean value returned by this method—userAuthenticated becomes true if authentication succeeds (i.e., accountNumber and pin match those of an existing Account in bankDatabase) and remains false otherwise. If userAuthenticated is true, line 67 saves the account number entered by the user (i.e., accountNumber) in the ATM attribute currentAccountNumber. The other methods of class ATM use this variable whenever an ATM session requires access to the user's account number. If userAuthenticated is false, lines 70–71 use the screen's displayMessageLine method to indicate that an invalid account number and/or PIN was entered and the user must try again. Note that we set currentAccountNumber only after authenticating the user's account number and the associated PIN—if the database could not authenticate the user, currentAccountNumber remains 0.

After method run attempts to authenticate the user (line 42), if userAuthenticated is still false, the while loop in lines 39–43 executes again. If userAuthenticated is now true, the loop terminates and control continues with line 45, which calls class ATM's utility method performTransactions.

Method performTransactions (lines 75–112) carries out an ATM session for an authenticated user. Line 78 declares a local Transaction variable to which we assign a BalanceInquiry, Withdrawal or Deposit object representing the ATM transaction currently being processed. Note that we use a Transaction variable here to allow us to take advantage of polymorphism. Also note that we name this variable after the role name included in the class diagram of Fig. 3.18—currentTransaction. Line 80 declares another local variable—a boolean called userExited that keeps track of whether the user has chosen to exit. This variable controls a while loop (lines 83–111) that allows the user to execute an unlimited number of transactions before choosing to exit. Within this loop, line 86 displays the main menu and obtains the user's menu selection by calling an ATM utility method displayMainMenu (declared in lines 115–124). This method displays the main menu by invoking methods of the ATM's screen and returns a menu selection obtained from the user through the ATM's keypad. Line 86 stores the user's selection returned by displayMainMenu in local variable mainMenuSelection.

After obtaining a main menu selection, method performTransactions uses a switch statement (lines 89–110) to respond to the selection appropriately. If mainMenuSelection is equal to any of the three integer constants representing transaction types (i.e., if the user chose to perform a transaction), lines 97–98 call utility method createTransaction (declared in lines 127–149) to return a newly instantiated object of the type that corresponds to the selected transaction. Variable currentTransaction is assigned the reference returned by createTransaction, then line 100 invokes method execute of this transaction to execute it. We'll discuss Transaction method execute and the three Transaction subclasses shortly. Note that we assign the Transaction variable currentTransaction an object of one of the three Transaction subclasses so that we can execute transactions polymorphically. For example, if the user chooses to perform a balance inquiry, mainMenuSelection equals BALANCE_INQUIRY, leading createTransaction to return a BalanceInquiry object. Thus, currentTransaction refers to a BalanceInquiry and invoking currentTransaction.execute() results in BalanceInquiry's version of execute being called.

Method createTransaction (lines 127–149) uses a switch statement (lines 132–146) to instantiate a new Transaction subclass object of the type indicated by the parameter type. Recall that method performTransactions passes mainMenuSelection to this method only when mainMenuSelection contains a value corresponding to one of the three transaction types. Therefore type equals either BALANCE_INQUIRY, WITHDRAWAL or DEPOSIT. Each case in the switch statement instantiates a new object by calling the appropriate Transaction subclass constructor. Note that each constructor has a unique parameter list, based on the specific data required to initialize the subclass object. A BalanceInquiry requires only the account number of the current user and references to the ATM's screen and the bankDatabase. In addition to these parameters, a Withdrawal requires references to the ATM's keypad and cashDispenser, and a Deposit requires references to the ATM's keypad and depositSlot. We discuss the transaction classes in more detail in Sections H.9–H.12.

After executing a transaction (line 100 in performTransactions), userExited remains false and the while loop in lines 83–111 repeats, returning the user to the main menu. However, if a user does not perform a transaction and instead selects the main menu option to exit, line 104 sets userExited to true causing the condition of the while loop (!userExited) to become false. This while is the final statement of method performTransactions, so control returns to the calling method run. If the user enters an invalid main menu selection (i.e., not an integer from 1–4), lines 107–108 display an appropriate error message, userExited remains false and the user returns to the main menu to try again.

When performTransactions returns control to method run, the user has chosen to exit the system, so lines 46–47 reset the ATM's attributes userAuthenticated and currentAccountNumber to prepare for the next ATM user. Line 48 displays a goodbye message before the ATM starts over and welcomes the next user.

H.3 Class Screen

Class Screen (Fig. H.2) represents the screen of the ATM and encapsulates all aspects of displaying output to the user. Class Screen approximates a real ATM's screen with a computer monitor and outputs text messages using standard console output methods System.out.print, System.out.println and System.out.printf. In this case study, we designed class Screen to have one operation—displayMessage. For greater flexibility in displaying messages to the Screen, we now declare three Screen methods—displayMessage, displayMessageLine and displayDollarAmount.

```
 1    // Screen.java
 2    // Represents the screen of the ATM
 3
 4    public class Screen
 5    {
 6       // display a message without a carriage return
 7       public void displayMessage( String message )
 8       {
 9          System.out.print( message );
10       } // end method displayMessage
11
12       // display a message with a carriage return
13       public void displayMessageLine( String message )
14       {
15          System.out.println( message );
16       } // end method displayMessageLine
17
18       // displays a dollar amount
19       public void displayDollarAmount( double amount )
20       {
21          System.out.printf( "$%,.2f", amount );
22       } // end method displayDollarAmount
23    } // end class Screen
```

Fig. H.2 | Class Screen represents the screen of the ATM.

Method displayMessage (lines 7–10) takes a String as an argument and prints it to the console using System.out.print. The cursor stays on the same line, making this method appropriate for displaying prompts to the user. Method displayMessageLine (lines 13–16) does the same using System.out.println, which outputs a newline to move the cursor to the next line. Finally, method displayDollarAmount (lines 19–22) outputs a properly formatted dollar amount (e.g., $1,234.56). Line 21 uses method System.out.printf to output a double value formatted with commas to increase readability and two decimal places. See Chapter 24, Formatted Output, for more information about formatting output with printf.

H.4 Class Keypad

Class Keypad (Fig. H.3) represents the keypad of the ATM and is responsible for receiving all user input. Recall that we are simulating this hardware, so we use the computer's keyboard to approximate the keypad. We use class Scanner to obtain console input from the user. A computer keyboard contains many keys not found on the ATM's keypad. However, we assume that the user presses only the keys on the computer keyboard that also appear on the keypad—the keys numbered 0–9 and the *Enter* key.

Line 3 of class Keypad imports class Scanner for use in class Keypad. Line 7 declares Scanner variable input as an instance variable. Line 12 in the constructor creates a new Scanner object that reads input from the standard input stream (System.in) and assigns the object's reference to variable input. Method getInput (declared in lines 16–19) invokes Scanner method nextInt (line 18) to return the next integer input by the user. [*Note:* Method nextInt can throw an InputMismatchException if the user enters non-integer

```
1    // Keypad.java
2    // Represents the keypad of the ATM
3    import java.util.Scanner; // program uses Scanner to obtain user input
4
5    public class Keypad
6    {
7       private Scanner input; // reads data from the command line
8
9       // no-argument constructor initializes the Scanner
10      public Keypad()
11      {
12         input = new Scanner( System.in );
13      } // end no-argument Keypad constructor
14
15      // return an integer value entered by user
16      public int getInput()
17      {
18         return input.nextInt(); // we assume that user enters an integer
19      } // end method getInput
20   } // end class Keypad
```

Fig. H.3 | Class Keypad represents the ATM's keypad.

input. Because the real ATM's keypad permits only integer input, we assume that no exception will occur and do not attempt to fix this problem. See Chapter 13, Exception Handling, for information on catching exceptions.] Recall that nextInt obtains all the input used by the ATM. Keypad's getInput method simply returns the integer input by the user. If a client of class Keypad requires input that satisfies some particular criteria (i.e., a number corresponding to a valid menu option), the client must perform the appropriate error checking.

H.5 Class CashDispenser

Class CashDispenser (Fig. H.4) represents the cash dispenser of the ATM. Line 7 declares constant INITIAL_COUNT, which indicates the initial count of bills in the cash dispenser when the ATM starts (i.e., 500). Line 8 implements attribute count (modeled in Fig. 10.20), which keeps track of the number of bills remaining in the CashDispenser at any time. The constructor (lines 11–14) sets count to the initial count. Class CashDispenser has two public methods—dispenseCash (lines 17–21) and isSufficient-CashAvailable (lines 24–32). The class trusts that a client (i.e., Withdrawal) calls dispenseCash only after establishing that sufficient cash is available by calling isSufficientCashAvailable. Thus, dispenseCash simply simulates dispensing the requested amount without checking whether sufficient cash is available.

Method isSufficientCashAvailable (lines 24–32) has a parameter amount that specifies the amount of cash in question. Line 26 calculates the number of $20 bills required to dispense the specified amount. The ATM allows the user to choose only withdrawal amounts that are multiples of $20, so we divide amount by 20 to obtain the number of billsRequired. Lines 28–31 return true if the CashDispenser's count is greater than or equal to billsRequired (i.e., enough bills are available) and false otherwise (i.e., not

```
 1    // CashDispenser.java
 2    // Represents the cash dispenser of the ATM
 3
 4    public class CashDispenser
 5    {
 6       // the default initial number of bills in the cash dispenser
 7       private final static int INITIAL_COUNT = 500;
 8       private int count; // number of $20 bills remaining
 9
10       // no-argument CashDispenser constructor initializes count to default
11       public CashDispenser()
12       {
13          count = INITIAL_COUNT; // set count attribute to default
14       } // end CashDispenser constructor
15
16       // simulates dispensing of specified amount of cash
17       public void dispenseCash( int amount )
18       {
19          int billsRequired = amount / 20; // number of $20 bills required
20          count -= billsRequired; // update the count of bills
21       } // end method dispenseCash
22
23       // indicates whether cash dispenser can dispense desired amount
24       public boolean isSufficientCashAvailable( int amount )
25       {
26          int billsRequired = amount / 20; // number of $20 bills required
27
28          if ( count >= billsRequired  )
29             return true; // enough bills available
30          else
31             return false; // not enough bills available
32       } // end method isSufficientCashAvailable
33    } // end class CashDispenser
```

Fig. H.4 | Class CashDispenser represents the ATM's cash dispenser.

enough bills). For example, if a user wishes to withdraw $80 (i.e., billsRequired is 4), but only three bills remain (i.e., count is 3), the method returns false.

Method dispenseCash (lines 17–21) simulates cash dispensing. If our system were hooked up to a real hardware cash dispenser, this method would interact with the device to physically dispense cash. Our simulated version of the method simply decreases the count of bills remaining by the number required to dispense the specified amount (line 20). Note that it is the responsibility of the client of the class (i.e., Withdrawal) to inform the user that cash has been dispensed—CashDispenser cannot interact directly with Screen.

H.6 Class DepositSlot

Class DepositSlot (Fig. H.5) represents the deposit slot of the ATM. Like the version of class CashDispenser presented here, this version of class DepositSlot merely simulates the functionality of a real hardware deposit slot. DepositSlot has no attributes and only one method—isEnvelopeReceived (lines 8–11)—that indicates whether a deposit envelope was received.

```
1   // DepositSlot.java
2   // Represents the deposit slot of the ATM
3
4   public class DepositSlot
5   {
6      // indicates whether envelope was received (always returns true,
7      // because this is only a software simulation of a real deposit slot)
8      public boolean isEnvelopeReceived()
9      {
10         return true; // deposit envelope was received
11      } // end method isEnvelopeReceived
12   } // end class DepositSlot
```

Fig. H.5 | Class DepositSlot represents the ATM's deposit slot.

Recall from the requirements document that the ATM allows the user up to two minutes to insert an envelope. The current version of method isEnvelopeReceived simply returns true immediately (line 10), because this is only a software simulation, and we assume that the user has inserted an envelope within the required time frame. If an actual hardware deposit slot were connected to our system, method isEnvelopeReceived might be implemented to wait for a maximum of two minutes to receive a signal from the hardware deposit slot indicating that the user has indeed inserted a deposit envelope. If isEnvelopeReceived were to receive such a signal within two minutes, the method would return true. If two minutes elapsed and the method still had not received a signal, then the method would return false.

H.7 Class Account

Class Account (Fig. H.6) represents a bank account. Each Account has four attributes (modeled in Fig. 10.20)—accountNumber, pin, availableBalance and totalBalance. Lines 6–9 implement these attributes as private fields. Variable availableBalance represents the amount of funds available for withdrawal. Variable totalBalance represents the amount of funds available, plus the amount of deposited funds still pending confirmation or clearance.

Class Account has a constructor (lines 12–19) that takes an account number, the PIN established for the account, the initial available balance and the initial total balance as arguments. Lines 15–18 assign these values to the class's attributes (i.e., fields).

Method validatePIN (lines 22–28) determines whether a user-specified PIN (i.e., parameter userPIN) matches the PIN associated with the account (i.e., attribute pin). Recall that we modeled this method's parameter userPIN in the UML class diagram of Fig. 6.28. If the two PINs match, the method returns true (line 25); otherwise, it returns false (line 27).

Methods getAvailableBalance (lines 31–34) and getTotalBalance (lines 37–40) are *get* methods that return the values of double attributes availableBalance and totalBalance, respectively.

Method credit (lines 43–46) adds an amount of money (i.e., parameter amount) to an Account as part of a deposit transaction. Note that this method adds the amount only to attribute totalBalance (line 45). The money credited to an account during a deposit

```java
1   // Account.java
2   // Represents a bank account
3
4   public class Account
5   {
6      private int accountNumber; // account number
7      private int pin; // PIN for authentication
8      private double availableBalance; // funds available for withdrawal
9      private double totalBalance; // funds available + pending deposits
10
11     // Account constructor initializes attributes
12     public Account( int theAccountNumber, int thePIN,
13        double theAvailableBalance, double theTotalBalance )
14     {
15        accountNumber = theAccountNumber;
16        pin = thePIN;
17        availableBalance = theAvailableBalance;
18        totalBalance = theTotalBalance;
19     } // end Account constructor
20
21     // determines whether a user-specified PIN matches PIN in Account
22     public boolean validatePIN( int userPIN )
23     {
24        if ( userPIN == pin )
25           return true;
26        else
27           return false;
28     } // end method validatePIN
29
30     // returns available balance
31     public double getAvailableBalance()
32     {
33        return availableBalance;
34     } // end getAvailableBalance
35
36     // returns the total balance
37     public double getTotalBalance()
38     {
39        return totalBalance;
40     } // end method getTotalBalance
41
42     // credits an amount to the account
43     public void credit( double amount )
44     {
45        totalBalance += amount; // add to total balance
46     } // end method credit
47
48     // debits an amount from the account
49     public void debit( double amount )
50     {
51        availableBalance -= amount; // subtract from available balance
52        totalBalance -= amount; // subtract from total balance
53     } // end method debit
```

Fig. H.6 | Class Account represents a bank account. (Part 1 of 2.)

```
54
55      // returns account number
56      public int getAccountNumber()
57      {
58          return accountNumber;
59      } // end method getAccountNumber
60  } // end class Account
```

Fig. H.6 | Class `Account` represents a bank account. (Part 2 of 2.)

does not become available immediately, so we modify only the total balance. We assume that the bank updates the available balance appropriately at a later time. Our implementation of class `Account` includes only methods required for carrying out ATM transactions. Therefore, we omit the methods that some other bank system would invoke to add to attribute `availableBalance` (to confirm a deposit) or subtract from attribute `totalBalance` (to reject a deposit).

Method `debit` (lines 49–53) subtracts an amount of money (i.e., parameter `amount`) from an `Account` as part of a withdrawal transaction. This method subtracts the amount from both attribute `availableBalance` (line 51) and attribute `totalBalance` (line 52), because a withdrawal affects both measures of an account balance.

Method `getAccountNumber` (lines 56–59) provides access to an `Account`'s account-Number. We include this method in our implementation so that a client of the class (i.e., `BankDatabase`) can identify a particular `Account`. For example, `BankDatabase` contains many `Account` objects, and it can invoke this method on each of its `Account` objects to locate the one with a specific account number.

H.8 Class BankDatabase

Class `BankDatabase` (Fig. H.7) models the bank's database with which the ATM interacts to access and modify a user's account information. We determine one reference-type attribute for class `BankDatabase` based on its composition relationship with class `Account`. Recall from Fig. 10.19 that a `BankDatabase` is composed of zero or more objects of class `Account`. Line 6 implements attribute `accounts`—an array of `Account` objects—to implement this composition relationship. Class `BankDatabase` has a no-argument constructor (lines 9–14) that initializes `accounts` to contain a set of new `Account` objects. For the sake of testing the system, we declare `accounts` to hold just two array elements (line 11), which we instantiate as new `Account` objects with test data (lines 12–13). Note that the `Account` constructor has four parameters—the account number, the PIN assigned to the account, the initial available balance and the initial total balance.

Recall that class `BankDatabase` serves as an intermediary between class `ATM` and the actual `Account` objects that contain a user's account information. Thus, the methods of class `BankDatabase` do nothing more than invoke the corresponding methods of the `Account` object belonging to the current ATM user.

We include `private` utility method `getAccount` (lines 17–28) to allow the BankDatabase to obtain a reference to a particular `Account` within array `accounts`. To locate the user's `Account`, the `BankDatabase` compares the value returned by method `getAccountNumber` for each element of `accounts` to a specified account number until it finds a match. Lines 20–25 traverse the accounts array. If the account number of currentAccount equals the value of parameter accountNumber, the method immediately returns the currentAccount. If no account has the given account number, then line 27 returns null.

```java
1   // BankDatabase.java
2   // Represents the bank account information database
3
4   public class BankDatabase
5   {
6      private Account accounts[]; // array of Accounts
7
8      // no-argument BankDatabase constructor initializes accounts
9      public BankDatabase()
10     {
11        accounts = new Account[ 2 ]; // just 2 accounts for testing
12        accounts[ 0 ] = new Account( 12345, 54321, 1000.0, 1200.0 );
13        accounts[ 1 ] = new Account( 98765, 56789, 200.0, 200.0 );
14     } // end no-argument BankDatabase constructor
15
16     // retrieve Account object containing specified account number
17     private Account getAccount( int accountNumber )
18     {
19        // loop through accounts searching for matching account number
20        for ( Account currentAccount : accounts )
21        {
22           // return current account if match found
23           if ( currentAccount.getAccountNumber() == accountNumber )
24              return currentAccount;
25        } // end for
26
27        return null; // if no matching account was found, return null
28     } // end method getAccount
29
30     // determine whether user-specified account number and PIN match
31     // those of an account in the database
32     public boolean authenticateUser( int userAccountNumber, int userPIN )
33     {
34        // attempt to retrieve the account with the account number
35        Account userAccount = getAccount( userAccountNumber );
36
37        // if account exists, return result of Account method validatePIN
38        if ( userAccount != null )
39           return userAccount.validatePIN( userPIN );
40        else
41           return false; // account number not found, so return false
42     } // end method authenticateUser
43
44     // return available balance of Account with specified account number
45     public double getAvailableBalance( int userAccountNumber )
46     {
47        return getAccount( userAccountNumber ).getAvailableBalance();
48     } // end method getAvailableBalance
```

Fig. H.7 | Class BankDatabase represents the bank's account information database. (Part 1 of 2.)

```
49
50      // return total balance of Account with specified account number
51      public double getTotalBalance( int userAccountNumber )
52      {
53         return getAccount( userAccountNumber ).getTotalBalance();
54      } // end method getTotalBalance
55
56      // credit an amount to Account with specified account number
57      public void credit( int userAccountNumber, double amount )
58      {
59         getAccount( userAccountNumber ).credit( amount );
60      } // end method credit
61
62      // debit an amount from of Account with specified account number
63      public void debit( int userAccountNumber, double amount )
64      {
65         getAccount( userAccountNumber ).debit( amount );
66      } // end method debit
67   } // end class BankDatabase
```

Fig. H.7 | Class BankDatabase represents the bank's account information database. (Part 2 of 2.)

Method authenticateUser (lines 32–42) proves or disproves the identity of an ATM user. This method takes a user-specified account number and user-specified PIN as arguments and indicates whether they match the account number and PIN of an Account in the database. Line 35 calls method getAccount, which returns either an Account with userAccountNumber as its account number or null to indicate that userAccountNumber is invalid. If getAccount returns an Account object, line 39 returns the boolean value returned by that object's validatePIN method. Note that BankDatabase's authenticate-User method does not perform the PIN comparison itself—rather, it forwards userPIN to the Account object's validatePIN method to do so. The value returned by Account method validatePIN indicates whether the user-specified PIN matches the PIN of the user's Account, so method authenticateUser simply returns this value to the client of the class (i.e., ATM).

BankDatabase trusts the ATM to invoke method authenticateUser and receive a return value of true before allowing the user to perform transactions. BankDatabase also trusts that each Transaction object created by the ATM contains the valid account number of the current authenticated user and that this is the account number passed to the remaining BankDatabase methods as argument userAccountNumber. Methods getAvailableBalance (lines 45–48), getTotalBalance (lines 51–54), credit (lines 57–60) and debit (lines 63–66) therefore simply retrieve the user's Account object with utility method getAccount, then invoke the appropriate Account method on that object. We know that the calls to getAccount within these methods will never return null, because userAccountNumber must refer to an existing Account. Note that getAvailableBalance and getTotalBalance return the values returned by the corresponding Account methods. Also note that credit and debit simply redirect parameter amount to the Account methods they invoke.

```
1    // Transaction.java
2    // Abstract superclass Transaction represents an ATM transaction
3
4    public abstract class Transaction
5    {
6       private int accountNumber; // indicates account involved
7       private Screen screen; // ATM's screen
8       private BankDatabase bankDatabase; // account info database
9
10      // Transaction constructor invoked by subclasses using super()
11      public Transaction( int userAccountNumber, Screen atmScreen,
12         BankDatabase atmBankDatabase )
13      {
14         accountNumber = userAccountNumber;
15         screen = atmScreen;
16         bankDatabase = atmBankDatabase;
17      } // end Transaction constructor
18
19      // return account number
20      public int getAccountNumber()
21      {
22         return accountNumber;
23      } // end method getAccountNumber
24
25      // return reference to screen
26      public Screen getScreen()
27      {
28         return screen;
29      } // end method getScreen
30
31      // return reference to bank database
32      public BankDatabase getBankDatabase()
33      {
34         return bankDatabase;
35      } // end method getBankDatabase
36
37      // perform the transaction (overridden by each subclass)
38      abstract public void execute();
39   } // end class Transaction
```

Fig. H.8 | Abstract superclass Transaction represents an ATM transaction.

H.9 Class Transaction

Class Transaction (Fig. H.8) is an abstract superclass that represents the notion of an ATM transaction. It contains the common features of subclasses BalanceInquiry, Withdrawal and Deposit. This class expands upon the "skeleton" code first developed in Section 10.8. Line 4 declares this class to be abstract. Lines 6–8 declare the class's private attributes. Recall from the class diagram of Fig. 10.20 that class Transaction contains an attribute accountNumber (line 6) that indicates the account involved in the Transaction. We derive attributes screen (line 7) and bankDatabase (line 8) from class Transaction's associations modeled in Fig. 10.19—all transactions require access to the ATM's screen and the bank's database.

Class `Transaction` has a constructor (lines 11–17) that takes the current user's account number and references to the ATM's screen and the bank's database as arguments. Because `Transaction` is an abstract class, this constructor will never be called directly to instantiate `Transaction` objects. Instead, the constructors of the `Transaction` subclasses will use `super` to invoke this constructor.

Class `Transaction` has three `public` *get* methods—`getAccountNumber` (lines 20–23), `getScreen` (lines 26–29) and `getBankDatabase` (lines 32–35). `Transaction` subclasses inherit these methods from `Transaction` and use them to gain access to class `Transaction`'s `private` attributes.

Class `Transaction` also declares an `abstract` method `execute` (line 38). It does not make sense to provide an implementation for this method, because a generic transaction cannot be executed. Thus, we declare this method to be `abstract` and force each `Transaction` subclass to provide its own concrete implementation that executes that particular type of transaction.

H.10 Class `BalanceInquiry`

Class `BalanceInquiry` (Fig. H.9) extends `Transaction` and represents a balance inquiry ATM transaction. `BalanceInquiry` does not have any attributes of its own, but it inherits `Transaction` attributes `accountNumber`, `screen` and `bankDatabase`, which are accessible through `Transaction`'s `public` *get* methods. The `BalanceInquiry` constructor takes arguments corresponding to these attributes and simply forwards them to `Transaction`'s constructor using `super` (line 10).

Class `BalanceInquiry` overrides `Transaction`'s abstract method `execute` to provide a concrete implementation (lines 14–35) that performs the steps involved in a balance inquiry. Lines 17–18 get references to the bank database and the ATM's screen by invoking methods inherited from superclass `Transaction`. Lines 21–22 retrieve the available balance of the account involved by invoking method `getAvailableBalance` of `bankDatabase`. Note that line 22 uses inherited method `getAccountNumber` to get the account number of the current user, which it then passes to `getAvailableBalance`. Lines 25–26 retrieve the total balance of the current user's account. Lines 29–34 display the balance information on the ATM's screen. Recall that `displayDollarAmount` takes a `double` argument and outputs it to the screen formatted as a dollar amount. For example, if a user's `availableBalance` is `1000.5`, line 31 outputs `$1,000.50`. Note that line 34 inserts a blank line of output to separate the balance information from subsequent output (i.e., the main menu repeated by class `ATM` after executing the `BalanceInquiry`).

H.11 Class `Withdrawal`

Class `Withdrawal` (Fig. H.10) extends `Transaction` and represents a withdrawal ATM transaction. This class expands upon the "skeleton" code for this class developed in Fig. 10.22. Recall from the class diagram of Fig. 10.19 that class `Withdrawal` has one attribute, `amount`, which line 6 implements as an `int` field. Figure 10.19 models associations between class `Withdrawal` and classes `Keypad` and `CashDispenser`, for which lines 7–8 implement reference-type attributes `keypad` and `cashDispenser`, respectively. Line 11 declares a constant corresponding to the cancel menu option. We'll soon discuss how the class uses this constant.

```
 1   // BalanceInquiry.java
 2   // Represents a balance inquiry ATM transaction
 3
 4   public class BalanceInquiry extends Transaction
 5   {
 6      // BalanceInquiry constructor
 7      public BalanceInquiry( int userAccountNumber, Screen atmScreen,
 8         BankDatabase atmBankDatabase )
 9      {
10         super( userAccountNumber, atmScreen, atmBankDatabase );
11      } // end BalanceInquiry constructor
12
13      // performs the transaction
14      public void execute()
15      {
16         // get references to bank database and screen
17         BankDatabase bankDatabase = getBankDatabase();
18         Screen screen = getScreen();
19
20         // get the available balance for the account involved
21         double availableBalance =
22            bankDatabase.getAvailableBalance( getAccountNumber() );
23
24         // get the total balance for the account involved
25         double totalBalance =
26            bankDatabase.getTotalBalance( getAccountNumber() );
27
28         // display the balance information on the screen
29         screen.displayMessageLine( "\nBalance Information:" );
30         screen.displayMessage( " - Available balance: " );
31         screen.displayDollarAmount( availableBalance );
32         screen.displayMessage( "\n - Total balance:      " );
33         screen.displayDollarAmount( totalBalance );
34         screen.displayMessageLine( "" );
35      } // end method execute
36   } // end class BalanceInquiry
```

Fig. H.9 | Class `BalanceInquiry` represents a balance inquiry ATM transaction.

Class `Withdrawal`'s constructor (lines 14–24) has five parameters. It uses `super` to pass parameters `userAccountNumber`, `atmScreen` and `atmBankDatabase` to superclass `Transaction`'s constructor to set the attributes that `Withdrawal` inherits from `Transaction`. The constructor also takes references `atmKeypad` and `atmCashDispenser` as parameters and assigns them to reference-type attributes `keypad` and `cashDispenser`.

Class `Withdrawal` overrides `Transaction`'s abstract method execute with a concrete implementation (lines 27–84) that performs the steps involved in a withdrawal. Line 29 declares and initializes a local `boolean` variable `cashDispensed`. This variable indicates whether cash has been dispensed (i.e., whether the transaction has completed successfully) and is initially `false`. Line 30 declares local `double` variable `availableBalance`, which will store the user's available balance during a withdrawal transaction. Lines 33–34 get references to the bank database and the ATM's screen by invoking methods inherited from superclass `Transaction`.

Lines 37–82 contain a do...while statement that executes its body until cash is dispensed (i.e., until cashDispensed becomes true) or until the user chooses to cancel (in which case, the loop terminates). We use this loop to continuously return the user to the start of the transaction if an error occurs (i.e., the requested withdrawal amount is greater than the user's available balance or greater than the amount of cash in the cash dispenser). Line 40 displays a menu of withdrawal amounts and obtains a user selection by calling private utility method displayMenuOfAmounts (declared in lines 88–132). This method displays the menu of amounts and returns either an int withdrawal amount or an int constant CANCELED to indicate that the user has chosen to cancel the transaction.

```java
1   // Withdrawal.java
2   // Represents a withdrawal ATM transaction
3
4   public class Withdrawal extends Transaction
5   {
6      private int amount; // amount to withdraw
7      private Keypad keypad; // reference to keypad
8      private CashDispenser cashDispenser; // reference to cash dispenser
9
10     // constant corresponding to menu option to cancel
11     private final static int CANCELED = 6;
12
13     // Withdrawal constructor
14     public Withdrawal( int userAccountNumber, Screen atmScreen,
15        BankDatabase atmBankDatabase, Keypad atmKeypad,
16        CashDispenser atmCashDispenser )
17     {
18        // initialize superclass variables
19        super( userAccountNumber, atmScreen, atmBankDatabase );
20
21        // initialize references to keypad and cash dispenser
22        keypad = atmKeypad;
23        cashDispenser = atmCashDispenser;
24     } // end Withdrawal constructor
25
26     // perform transaction
27     public void execute()
28     {
29        boolean cashDispensed = false; // cash was not dispensed yet
30        double availableBalance; // amount available for withdrawal
31
32        // get references to bank database and screen
33        BankDatabase bankDatabase = getBankDatabase();
34        Screen screen = getScreen();
35
36        // loop until cash is dispensed or the user cancels
37        do
38        {
39           // obtain a chosen withdrawal amount from the user
40           amount = displayMenuOfAmounts();
41
```

Fig. H.10 | Class Withdrawal represents a withdrawal ATM transaction. (Part 1 of 3.)

```
42          // check whether user chose a withdrawal amount or canceled
43          if ( amount != CANCELED )
44          {
45              // get available balance of account involved
46              availableBalance =
47                  bankDatabase.getAvailableBalance( getAccountNumber() );
48
49              // check whether the user has enough money in the account
50              if ( amount <= availableBalance )
51              {
52                  // check whether the cash dispenser has enough money
53                  if ( cashDispenser.isSufficientCashAvailable( amount ) )
54                  {
55                      // update the account involved to reflect the withdrawal
56                      bankDatabase.debit( getAccountNumber(), amount );
57
58                      cashDispenser.dispenseCash( amount ); // dispense cash
59                      cashDispensed = true; // cash was dispensed
60
61                      // instruct user to take cash
62                      screen.displayMessageLine( "\nYour cash has been" +
63                          " dispensed. Please take your cash now." );
64                  } // end if
65                  else // cash dispenser does not have enough cash
66                      screen.displayMessageLine(
67                          "\nInsufficient cash available in the ATM." +
68                          "\n\nPlease choose a smaller amount." );
69              } // end if
70              else // not enough money available in user's account
71              {
72                  screen.displayMessageLine(
73                      "\nInsufficient funds in your account." +
74                      "\n\nPlease choose a smaller amount." );
75              } // end else
76          } // end if
77          else // user chose cancel menu option
78          {
79              screen.displayMessageLine( "\nCanceling transaction..." );
80              return; // return to main menu because user canceled
81          } // end else
82      } while ( !cashDispensed );
83
84  } // end method execute
85
86  // display a menu of withdrawal amounts and the option to cancel;
87  // return the chosen amount or 0 if the user chooses to cancel
88  private int displayMenuOfAmounts()
89  {
90      int userChoice = 0; // local variable to store return value
91
92      Screen screen = getScreen(); // get screen reference
93
```

Fig. H.10 | Class Withdrawal represents a withdrawal ATM transaction. (Part 2 of 3.)

```
 94          // array of amounts to correspond to menu numbers
 95          int amounts[] = { 0, 20, 40, 60, 100, 200 };
 96
 97          // loop while no valid choice has been made
 98          while ( userChoice == 0 )
 99          {
100             // display the menu
101             screen.displayMessageLine( "\nWithdrawal Menu:" );
102             screen.displayMessageLine( "1 - $20" );
103             screen.displayMessageLine( "2 - $40" );
104             screen.displayMessageLine( "3 - $60" );
105             screen.displayMessageLine( "4 - $100" );
106             screen.displayMessageLine( "5 - $200" );
107             screen.displayMessageLine( "6 - Cancel transaction" );
108             screen.displayMessage( "\nChoose a withdrawal amount: " );
109
110             int input = keypad.getInput(); // get user input through keypad
111
112             // determine how to proceed based on the input value
113             switch ( input )
114             {
115                case 1: // if the user chose a withdrawal amount
116                case 2: // (i.e., chose option 1, 2, 3, 4 or 5), return the
117                case 3: // corresponding amount from amounts array
118                case 4:
119                case 5:
120                   userChoice = amounts[ input ]; // save user's choice
121                   break;
122                case CANCELED: // the user chose to cancel
123                   userChoice = CANCELED; // save user's choice
124                   break;
125                default: // the user did not enter a value from 1-6
126                   screen.displayMessageLine(
127                      "\nInvalid selection. Try again." );
128             } // end switch
129          } // end while
130
131          return userChoice; // return withdrawal amount or CANCELED
132       } // end method displayMenuOfAmounts
133    } // end class Withdrawal
```

Fig. H.10 | Class Withdrawal represents a withdrawal ATM transaction. (Part 3 of 3.)

Method displayMenuOfAmounts (lines 88–132) first declares local variable user-Choice (initially 0) to store the value that the method will return (line 90). Line 92 gets a reference to the screen by calling method getScreen inherited from superclass Transaction. Line 95 declares an integer array of withdrawal amounts that correspond to the amounts displayed in the withdrawal menu. We ignore the first element in the array (index 0) because the menu has no option 0. The while statement at lines 98–129 repeats until userChoice takes on a value other than 0. We'll see shortly that this occurs when the user makes a valid selection from the menu. Lines 101–108 display the withdrawal menu on the screen and prompt the user to enter a choice. Line 110 obtains integer input through the keypad. The switch statement at lines 113–128 determines how to proceed based on the user's input. If the user selects a number between 1 and 5, line 120 sets userChoice to the value of the element in amounts at index input. For example, if the user enters 3 to withdraw $60, line 120 sets userChoice to the value of amounts[3] (i.e., 60). Line 120 terminates the switch. Variable userChoice no longer equals 0, so the while at lines 98–129 terminates and line 131 returns userChoice. If the user selects the cancel menu option, lines 123–124 execute, setting userChoice to CANCELED and causing the method to return this value. If the user does not enter a valid menu selection, lines 126–127 display an error message and the user is returned to the withdrawal menu.

The if statement at line 43 in method execute determines whether the user has selected a withdrawal amount or chosen to cancel. If the user cancels, lines 79–80 execute and display an appropriate message to the user before returning control to the calling method (i.e., ATM method performTransactions). If the user has chosen a withdrawal amount, lines 46–47 retrieve the available balance of the current user's Account and store it in variable availableBalance. Next, the if statement at line 50 determines whether the selected amount is less than or equal to the user's available balance. If it is not, lines 72–74 display an appropriate error message. Control then continues to the end of the do...while, and the loop repeats because cashDispensed is still false. If the user's balance is high enough, the if statement at line 53 determines whether the cash dispenser has enough money to satisfy the withdrawal request by invoking the cashDispenser's isSufficientCashAvailable method. If this method returns false, lines 66–68 display an appropriate error message and the do...while repeats. If sufficient cash is available, then the requirements for the withdrawal are satisfied, and line 56 debits amount from the user's account in the database. Lines 58–59 then instruct the cash dispenser to dispense the cash to the user and set cashDispensed to true. Finally, lines 62–63 display a message to the user that cash has been dispensed. Because cashDispensed is now true, control continues after the do...while. No additional statements appear below the loop, so the method returns control to class ATM.

H.12 Class Deposit

Class Deposit (Fig. H.11) extends Transaction and represents a deposit ATM transaction. Recall from the class diagram of Fig. 10.20 that class Deposit has one attribute amount, which line 6 implements as an int field. Lines 7–8 create reference-type attributes keypad and depositSlot that implement the associations between class Deposit and classes Keypad and DepositSlot modeled in Fig. 10.19. Line 9 declares a constant CANCELED that corresponds to the value a user enters to cancel. We'll soon discuss how the class uses this constant.

Like class Withdrawal, class Deposit contains a constructor (lines 12–22) that passes three parameters to superclass Transaction's constructor using super. The constructor also has parameters atmKeypad and atmDepositSlot, which it assigns to corresponding attributes (lines 20–21).

Method execute (lines 25–65) overrides abstract method execute in superclass Transaction with a concrete implementation that performs the steps required in a deposit transaction. Lines 27–28 get references to the database and the screen. Line 30 prompts the user to enter a deposit amount by invoking private utility method promptForDepositAmount (declared in lines 68–84) and sets attribute amount to the value

```java
 1   // Deposit.java
 2   // Represents a deposit ATM transaction
 3
 4   public class Deposit extends Transaction
 5   {
 6      private double amount; // amount to deposit
 7      private Keypad keypad; // reference to keypad
 8      private DepositSlot depositSlot; // reference to deposit slot
 9      private final static int CANCELED = 0; // constant for cancel option
10
11      // Deposit constructor
12      public Deposit( int userAccountNumber, Screen atmScreen,
13         BankDatabase atmBankDatabase, Keypad atmKeypad,
14         DepositSlot atmDepositSlot )
15      {
16         // initialize superclass variables
17         super( userAccountNumber, atmScreen, atmBankDatabase );
18
19         // initialize references to keypad and deposit slot
20         keypad = atmKeypad;
21         depositSlot = atmDepositSlot;
22      } // end Deposit constructor
23
24      // perform transaction
25      public void execute()
26      {
27         BankDatabase bankDatabase = getBankDatabase(); // get reference
28         Screen screen = getScreen(); // get reference
29
30         amount = promptForDepositAmount(); // get deposit amount from user
31
32         // check whether user entered a deposit amount or canceled
33         if ( amount != CANCELED )
34         {
35            // request deposit envelope containing specified amount
36            screen.displayMessage(
37               "\nPlease insert a deposit envelope containing " );
38            screen.displayDollarAmount( amount );
39            screen.displayMessageLine( "." );
40
41            // receive deposit envelope
42            boolean envelopeReceived = depositSlot.isEnvelopeReceived();
43
44            // check whether deposit envelope was received
45            if ( envelopeReceived )
46            {
47               screen.displayMessageLine( "\nYour envelope has been " +
48                  "received.\nNOTE: The money just deposited will not " +
49                  "be available until we verify the amount of any " +
50                  "enclosed cash and your checks clear." );
51
```

Fig. H.11 | Class Deposit represents a deposit ATM transaction. (Part 1 of 2.)

```
52              // credit account to reflect the deposit
53              bankDatabase.credit( getAccountNumber(), amount );
54          } // end if
55          else // deposit envelope not received
56          {
57              screen.displayMessageLine( "\nYou did not insert an " +
58                  "envelope, so the ATM has canceled your transaction." );
59          } // end else
60      } // end if
61      else // user canceled instead of entering amount
62      {
63          screen.displayMessageLine( "\nCanceling transaction..." );
64      } // end else
65  } // end method execute
66
67  // prompt user to enter a deposit amount in cents
68  private double promptForDepositAmount()
69  {
70      Screen screen = getScreen(); // get reference to screen
71
72      // display the prompt
73      screen.displayMessage( "\nPlease enter a deposit amount in " +
74          "CENTS (or 0 to cancel): " );
75      int input = keypad.getInput(); // receive input of deposit amount
76
77      // check whether the user canceled or entered a valid amount
78      if ( input == CANCELED )
79          return CANCELED;
80      else
81      {
82          return ( double ) input / 100; // return dollar amount
83      } // end else
84  } // end method promptForDepositAmount
85 } // end class Deposit
```

Fig. H.11 | Class Deposit represents a deposit ATM transaction. (Part 2 of 2.)

returned. Method promptForDepositAmount asks the user to enter a deposit amount as an integer number of cents (because the ATM's keypad does not contain a decimal point; this is consistent with many real ATMs) and returns the double value representing the dollar amount to be deposited.

Line 70 in method promptForDepositAmount gets a reference to the ATM's screen. Lines 73–74 display a message on the screen asking the user to input a deposit amount as a number of cents or "0" to cancel the transaction. Line 75 receives the user's input from the keypad. The if statement at lines 78–83 determines whether the user has entered a real deposit amount or chosen to cancel. If the user chooses to cancel, line 79 returns the constant CANCELED. Otherwise, line 82 returns the deposit amount after converting from the number of cents to a dollar amount by casting input to a double, then dividing by 100. For example, if the user enters 125 as the number of cents, line 82 returns 125.0 divided by 100, or 1.25—125 cents is $1.25.

The if statement at lines 33–64 in method execute determines whether the user has chosen to cancel the transaction instead of entering a deposit amount. If the user cancels, line 63 displays an appropriate message, and the method returns. If the user enters a deposit amount, lines 36–39 instruct the user to insert a deposit envelope with the correct amount. Recall that Screen method displayDollarAmount outputs a double formatted as a dollar amount.

Line 42 sets a local boolean variable to the value returned by depositSlot's isEnvelopeReceived method, indicating whether a deposit envelope has been received. Recall that we coded method isEnvelopeReceived (lines 8–11 of Fig. H.5) to always return true, because we are simulating the functionality of the deposit slot and assume that the user always inserts an envelope. However, we code method execute of class Deposit to test for the possibility that the user does not insert an envelope—good software engineering demands that programs account for all possible return values. Thus, class Deposit is prepared for future versions of isEnvelopeReceived that could return false. Lines 47–53 execute if the deposit slot receives an envelope. Lines 47–50 display an appropriate message to the user. Line 53 then credits the deposit amount to the user's account in the database. Lines 57–58 will execute if the deposit slot does not receive a deposit envelope. In this case, we display a message to the user stating that the ATM has canceled the transaction. The method then returns without modifying the user's account.

H.13 Class ATMCaseStudy

Class ATMCaseStudy (Fig. H.12) is a simple class that allows us to start, or "turn on," the ATM and test the implementation of our ATM system model. Class ATMCaseStudy's main method (lines 7–11) does nothing more than instantiate a new ATM object named theATM (line 9) and invoke its run method (line 10) to start the ATM.

```
1   // ATMCaseStudy.java
2   // Driver program for the ATM case study
3
4   public class ATMCaseStudy
5   {
6      // main method creates and runs the ATM
7      public static void main( String[] args )
8      {
9         ATM theATM = new ATM();
10        theATM.run();
11     } // end main
12  } // end class ATMCaseStudy
```

Fig. H.12 | ATMCaseStudy.java starts the ATM.

H.14 Wrap-Up

Congratulations on completing the entire software engineering ATM case study! We hope you found this experience to be valuable and that it reinforced many of the concepts that you learned in Chapters 1–10. We would sincerely appreciate your comments, criticisms and suggestions. You can reach us at deitel@deitel.com. We'll respond promptly.

UML 2: Additional Diagram Types

I.1 Introduction

If you read the optional Software Engineering Case Study sections in Chapters 2–8 and 10, you should now have a comfortable grasp on the UML diagram types that we use to model our ATM system. The UML 2 provides a total of 13 diagram types. The end of Section 2.8 summarizes the six diagram types that we use in the case study. This appendix lists and briefly defines the seven remaining diagram types.

I.2 Additional Diagram Types

The following are the seven diagram types that we have chosen not to use in our Software Engineering Case Study.

- *Object diagrams* model a "snapshot" of the system by modeling a system's objects and their relationships at a specific point in time. Each object represents an instance of a class from a class diagram, and there may be several objects created from one class. For our ATM system, an object diagram could show several distinct Account objects side by side, illustrating that they are all part of the bank's account database.

- *Component diagrams* model the *artifacts* and *components*—resources (which include source files)—that make up the system.

- *Deployment diagrams* model the runtime requirements of the system (such as the computer or computers on which the system will reside), memory requirements for the system, or other devices the system requires during execution.

- *Package diagrams* model the hierarchical structure of *packages* (which are groups of classes) in the system at compile-time and the relationships that exist between the packages.

- *Composite structure diagrams* model the internal structure of a complex object at runtime. Composite structure diagrams are new in UML 2 and allow system designers to hierarchically decompose a complex object into smaller parts. Composite structure diagrams are beyond the scope of our case study. Composite structure diagrams are more appropriate for larger industrial applications, which exhibit complex groupings of objects at execution time.

- *Interaction overview diagrams*, which are new in UML 2, provide a summary of control flow in the system by combining elements of several types of behavioral diagrams (e.g., activity diagrams, sequence diagrams).

- *Timing diagrams*, also new in UML 2, model the timing constraints imposed on stage changes and interactions between objects in a system.

If you are interested in learning more about these diagrams and advanced UML topics, please visit www.uml.org and the Web resources listed at the ends of Section 1.9 and Section 2.8.

Using the Debugger

OBJECTIVES

In this appendix you'll learn:

- To set breakpoints to debug applications.
- To use the `run` command to run an application through the debugger.
- To use the `stop` command to set a breakpoint.
- To use the `cont` command to continue execution.
- To use the `print` command to evaluate expressions.
- To use the `set` command to change variable values during program execution.
- To use the `step`, `step up` and `next` commands to control execution.
- To use the `watch` command to see how a field is modified during program execution.
- To use the `clear` command to list breakpoints or remove a breakpoint.

Outline

J.1 Introduction

J.2 Breakpoints and the `run`, `stop`, `cont` and `print` Commands

J.3 The `print` and `set` Commands

J.4 Controlling Execution Using the `step`, `step up` and `next` Commands

J.5 The `watch` Command

J.6 The `clear` Command

J.7 Wrap-Up

J.1 Introduction

In Chapter 2, you learned that there are two types of errors—syntax errors and logic errors—and you learned how to eliminate syntax errors from your code. Logic errors do not prevent the application from compiling successfully, but they do cause an application to produce erroneous results when it runs. The JDK 5.0 includes software called a *debugger* that allows you to monitor the execution of your applications so you can locate and remove logic errors. The debugger will be one of your most important application development tools. Many IDEs provide their own debuggers similar to the one included in the JDK or provide a graphical user interface to the JDK's debugger.

This appendix demonstrates key features of the JDK's debugger using command-line applications that receive no input from the user. The same debugger features discussed here can be used to debug applications that take user input, but debugging such applications requires a slightly more complex setup. To focus on the debugger features, we have opted to demonstrate the debugger with simple command-line applications involving no user input. You can also find more information on the Java debugger at `java.sun.com/javase/6/docs/tooldocs/windows/jdb.html`.

J.2 Breakpoints and the `run`, `stop`, `cont` and `print` Commands

We begin our study of the debugger by investigating *breakpoints*, which are markers that can be set at any executable line of code. When application execution reaches a breakpoint, execution pauses, allowing you to examine the values of variables to help determine whether logic errors exist. For example, you can examine the value of a variable that stores the result of a calculation to determine whether the calculation was performed correctly. Note that setting a breakpoint at a line of code that is not executable (such as a comment) causes the debugger to display an error message.

To illustrate the features of the debugger, we use application `AccountTest` (Fig. J.1), which creates and manipulates an object of class `Account` (Fig. 3.13). Execution of `AccountTest` begins in `main` (lines 7–24). Line 9 creates an `Account` object with an initial balance of $50.00. Recall that `Account`'s constructor accepts one argument, which specifies the `Account`'s initial `balance`. Lines 12–13 output the initial account balance using `Account` method `getBalance`. Line 15 declares and initializes a local variable `depositAmount`. Lines 17–19 then print `depositAmount` and add it to the `Account`'s `balance` using its `credit` method. Finally, lines 22–23 display the new `balance`. [*Note:* The Appendix J examples directory contains a copy of `Account.java` identical to the one in Fig. 3.13.]

In the following steps, you'll use breakpoints and various debugger commands to examine the value of the variable depositAmount declared in AccountTest (Fig. J.1).

1. *Opening the* Command Prompt *window and changing directories.* Open the Command Prompt window by selecting **Start > Programs > Accessories > Command Prompt**. Change to the directory containing the appendix's examples by typing cd C:\examples\debugger [*Note:* If your examples are in a different directory, use that directory here.]

2. *Compiling the application for debugging.* The Java debugger works only with .class files that were compiled with the **-g** compiler option, which generates information that is used by the debugger to help you debug your applications. Compile the application with the -g command-line option by typing javac -g AccountTest.java Account.java. This command compiles both AccountTest.java and Account.java. The command java -g *.java compiles all of the working directory's .java files for debugging.

```java
1    // Fig. N.1: AccountTest.java
2    // Create and manipulate an Account object.
3
4    public class AccountTest
5    {
6       // main method begins execution
7       public static void main( String args[] )
8       {
9          Account account = new Account( 50.00 ); // create Account object
10
11         // display initial balance of Account object
12         System.out.printf( "initial account balance: $%.2f\n",
13            account.getBalance() );
14
15         double depositAmount = 25.0; // deposit amount
16
17         System.out.printf( "\nadding %.2f to account balance\n\n",
18            depositAmount );
19         account.credit( depositAmount ); // add to account balance
20
21         // display new balance
22         System.out.printf( "new account balance: $%.2f\n",
23            account.getBalance() );
24      } // end main
25
26   } // end class AccountTest
```

```
initial account balance: $50.00

adding 25.00 to account balance

new account balance: $75.00
```

Fig. J.1 | AccountTest class creates and manipulates an Account object.

3. *Starting the debugger.* In the **Command Prompt**, type *jdb* (Fig. J.2). This command will start the Java debugger and enable you to use its features.

4. *Running an application in the debugger.* Run the AccountTest application through the debugger by typing *run* AccountTest (Fig. J.3). If you do not set any breakpoints before running your application in the debugger, the application will run just as it would using the java command.

5. *Restarting the debugger.* To make proper use of the debugger, you must set at least one breakpoint before running the application. Restart the debugger by typing jdb.

6. *Inserting breakpoints in Java.* You set a breakpoint at a specific line of code in your application. The line numbers used in these steps are from the source code in Fig. J.1. Set a breakpoint at line 12 in the source code by typing stop at AccountTest:12 (Fig. J.4). The *stop command* inserts a breakpoint at the line number specified after the command. You can set as many breakpoints as necessary. Set another breakpoint at line 19 by typing stop at AccountTest:19 (Fig. J.4). When the application runs, it suspends execution at any line that contains a breakpoint. The application is said to be in *break mode* when the debugger pauses the application's execution. Breakpoints can be set even after the debugging process has begun. Note that the debugger command stop in, followed by a class name, a period and a method name (e.g., stop in Account.credit) instructs the debugger to set a breakpoint at the first executable statement in the specified method. The debugger pauses execution when program control enters the method.

```
Command Prompt - jdb                                              _□×
C:\>cd C:\examples\debugger

C:\examples\debugger>javac -g AccountTest.java Account.java

C:\examples\debugger>jdb
Initializing jdb ...
> _
```

Fig. J.2 | Starting the Java debugger.

```
Command Prompt                                                    _□×
C:\examples\debugger>jdb
Initializing jdb ...
> run AccountTest
run   AccountTest
Set uncaught java.lang.Throwable
Set deferred uncaught java.lang.Throwable
>
VM Started: initial account balance: $50.00

adding 25.00 to account balance

new account balance: $75.00

The application exited
```

Fig. J.3 | Running the AccountTest application through the debugger.

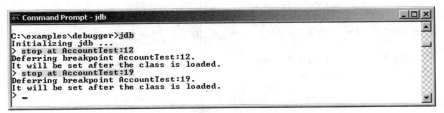

Fig. J.4 | Setting breakpoints at lines 12 and 19.

7. *Running the application and beginning the debugging process.* Type run AccountTest to execute your application and begin the debugging process (Fig. J.5). Note that the debugger prints text indicating that breakpoints were set at lines 12 and 19. The debugger calls each breakpoint a "deferred breakpoint" because each was set before the application began running in the debugger. The application pauses when execution reaches the breakpoint on line 12. At this point, the debugger notifies you that a breakpoint has been reached and it displays the source code at that line (12). That line of code is the next statement that will execute.

8. *Using the **cont** command to resume execution.* Type cont. The **cont** *command* causes the application to continue running until the next breakpoint is reached (line 19), at which point the debugger notifies you (Fig. J.6). Note that Account-Test's normal output appears between messages from the debugger.

9. *Examining a variable's value.* Type print depositAmount to display the current value stored in the depositAmount variable (Fig. J.7). The **print** *command* allows you to peek inside the computer at the value of one of your variables. This command will help you find and eliminate logic errors in your code. Note that the value displayed is 25.0—the value assigned to depositAmount in line 15 of Fig. J.1.

10. *Continuing application execution.* Type cont to continue the application's execution. There are no more breakpoints, so the application is no longer in break mode. The application continues executing and eventually terminates (Fig. J.8). The debugger will stop when the application ends.

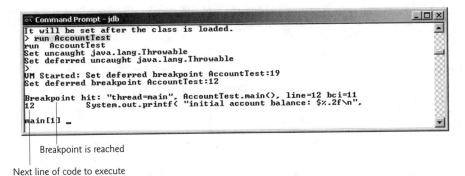

Fig. J.5 | Restarting the AccountTest application.

Another breakpoint is reached

```
⌨ Command Prompt - jdb                                              _□×
main[1] cont
initial account balance: $> 50.00

adding 25.00 to account balance

Breakpoint hit: "thread=main", AccountTest.main(), line=19 bci=58
19              account.credit( depositAmount ); // add to account balance

main[1] _
```

Fig. J.6 | Execution reaches the second breakpoint.

```
⌨ Command Prompt - jdb                                              _□×
main[1] print depositAmount
 depositAmount = 25.0
main[1] _
```

Fig. J.7 | Examining the value of variable depositAmount.

```
⌨ Command Prompt                                                    _□×
 depositAmount = 25.0
main[1] cont
new account balance: $75.00
>
The application exited

C:\examples\debugger>_
```

Fig. J.8 | Continuing application execution and exiting the debugger.

In this section, you learned how to enable the debugger and set breakpoints so that you can examine variables with the print command while an application is running. You also learned how to use the cont command to continue execution after a breakpoint is reached.

J.3 The print and set Commands

In the preceding section, you learned how to use the debugger's print command to examine the value of a variable during program execution. In this section, you'll learn how to use the print command to examine the value of more complex expressions. You'll also learn the **set command**, which allows the programmer to assign new values to variables.

For this section, we assume that you have followed *Step 1* and *Step 2* in Section J.2 to open the **Command Prompt** window, change to the directory containing this appendix's examples (e.g., C:\examples\debugger) and compile the AccountTest application (and class Account) for debugging.

1. *Starting debugging.* In the **Command Prompt**, type jdb to start the Java debugger.

2. *Inserting a breakpoint.* Set a breakpoint at line 19 in the source code by typing stop at AccountTest:19.

3. *Running the application and reaching a breakpoint.* Type run AccountTest to begin the debugging process (Fig. J.9). This will cause AccountTest's main to execute until the breakpoint at line 19 is reached. This suspends application execution and switches the application into break mode. At this point, the statements in lines 9–13 created an Account object and printed the initial balance of the Ac-

count obtained by calling its getBalance method. The statement in line 15 (Fig. J.1) declared and initialized local variable depositAmount to 25.0. The statement in line 19 is the next statement that will execute.

4. *Evaluating arithmetic and boolean expressions.* Recall from Section J.2 that once the application has entered break mode, you can explore the values of the application's variables using the debugger's print command. You can also use the print command to evaluate arithmetic and boolean expressions. In the **Command Prompt** window, type print depositAmount - 2.0. Note that the print command returns the value 23.0 (Fig. J.10). However, this command does not actually change the value of depositAmount. In the **Command Prompt** window, type print depositAmount == 23.0. Expressions containing the == symbol are treated as boolean expressions. The value returned is false (Fig. J.10) because deposit-Amount does not currently contain the value 23.0—depositAmount is still 25.0.

5. *Modifying values.* The debugger allows you to change the values of variables during the application's execution. This can be valuable for experimenting with different values and for locating logic errors in applications. You can use the debugger's set command to change the value of a variable. Type set deposit-Amount = 75.0. The debugger changes the value of depositAmount and displays its new value (Fig. J.11).

```
C:\examples\debugger>jdb
Initializing jdb ...
> stop at AccountTest:19
Deferring breakpoint AccountTest:19.
It will be set after the class is loaded.
> run AccountTest
run  AccountTest
Set uncaught java.lang.Throwable
Set deferred uncaught java.lang.Throwable
>
VM Started: Set deferred breakpoint AccountTest:19
initial account balance: $50.00

adding 25.00 to account balance

Breakpoint hit: "thread=main", AccountTest.main(), line=19 bci=58
19            account.credit( depositAmount ); // add to account balance

main[1] _
```

Fig. J.9 | Application execution suspended when debugger reaches the breakpoint at line 19.

```
main[1] print depositAmount - 2.0
 depositAmount - 2.0 = 23.0
main[1] print depositAmount == 23.0
 depositAmount == 23.0 = false
main[1] _
```

Fig. J.10 | Examining the values of an arithmetic and boolean expression.

```
 depositAmount == 23.0 = false
main[1] set depositAmount = 75.0
 depositAmount = 75.0 = 75.0
main[1] _
```

Fig. J.11 | Modifying values.

6. *Viewing the application result.* Type cont to continue application execution. Line 19 of AccountTest (Fig. J.1) executes, passing depositAmount to Account method credit. Method main then displays the new balance. Note that the result is $125.00 (Fig. J.12). This shows that the preceding step changed the value of depositAmount from its initial value (25.0) to 75.0.

In this section, you learned how to use the debugger's print command to evaluate arithmetic and boolean expressions. You also learned how to use the set command to modify the value of a variable during your application's execution.

J.4 Controlling Execution Using the step, step up and next Commands

Sometimes you'll need to execute an application line by line to find and fix errors. Walking through a portion of your application this way can help you verify that a method's code executes correctly. In this section, you'll learn how to use the debugger for this task. The commands you learn in this section allow you to execute a method line by line, execute all the statements of a method at once or execute only the remaining statements of a method (if you have already executed some statements within the method).

Once again, we assume you are working in the directory containing this appendix's examples and have compiled for debugging with the -g compiler option.

1. *Starting the debugger.* Start the debugger by typing jdb.

2. *Setting a breakpoint.* Type stop at AccountTest:19 to set a breakpoint at line 19.

3. *Running the application.* Run the application by typing run AccountTest. After the application displays its two output messages, the debugger indicates that the breakpoint has been reached and displays the code at line 19 (Fig. J.13). The debugger and application then pause and wait for the next command to be entered.

4. *Using the step command.* The **step command** executes the next statement in the application. If the next statement to execute is a method call, control transfers to the called method. The step command enables you to enter a method and study the individual statements of that method. For instance, you can use the print and set commands to view and modify the variables within the method. You'll now use the step command to enter the credit method of class Account (Fig. 3.13) by typing step (Fig. J.14). The debugger indicates that the step has been completed and displays the next executable statement—in this case, line 21 of class Account (Fig. 3.13).

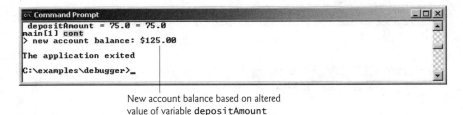

New account balance based on altered
value of variable depositAmount

Fig. J.12 | Output displayed after the debugging process.

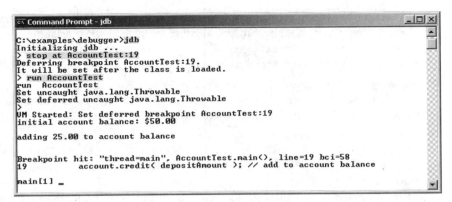

Fig. J.13 | Reaching the breakpoint in the AccountTest application.

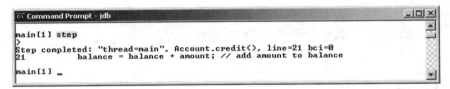

Fig. J.14 | Stepping into the credit method.

5. *Using the **step up** command.* After you have stepped into the credit method, type ***step up***. This command executes the remaining statements in the method and returns control to the place where the method was called. The credit method contains only one statement to add the method's parameter amount to instance variable balance. The step up command executes this statement, then pauses before line 22 in AccountTest. Thus, the next action to occur will be to print the new account balance (Fig. J.15). In lengthy methods, you may want to look at a few key lines of code, then continue debugging the caller's code. The step up command is useful for situations in which you do not want to continue stepping through the entire method line by line.

6. *Using the **cont** command to continue execution.* Enter the cont command (Fig. J.16) to continue execution. The statement at lines 22–23 executes, displaying the new balance, then the application and the debugger terminate.

7. *Restarting the debugger.* Restart the debugger by typing jdb.

8. *Setting a breakpoint.* Breakpoints persist only until the end of the debugging session in which they are set—once the debugger exits, all breakpoints are removed.

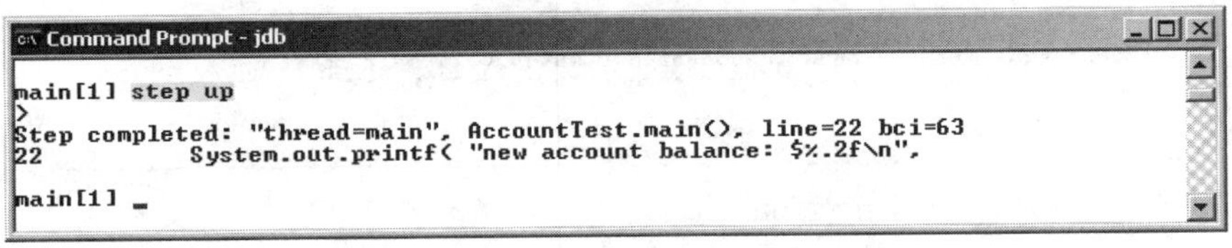

```
Command Prompt - jdb                                        _ □ ×
main[1] step up
>
Step completed: "thread=main", AccountTest.main(), line=22 bci=63
22            System.out.printf( "new account balance: $%.2f\n",
main[1] _
```

Fig. J.15 | Stepping out of a method.

(In Section J.6, you'll learn how to manually clear a breakpoint before the end of the debugging session.) Thus, the breakpoint set for line 19 in *Step 2* no longer exists upon restarting the debugger in *Step 7*. To reset the breakpoint at line 19, once again type stop at AccountTest:19.

9. *Running the application.* Type run AccountTest to run the application. As in *Step 3*, AccountTest runs until the breakpoint at line 19 is reached, then the debugger pauses and waits for the next command (Fig. J.17).

10. *Using the next command.* Type **next**. This command behaves like the step command, except when the next statement to execute contains a method call. In that case, the called method executes in its entirety and the application advances to the next executable line after the method call (Fig. J.18). Recall from *Step 4* that the step command would enter the called method. In this example, the next command causes Account method credit to execute, then the debugger pauses at line 22 in AccountTest.

Fig. J.16 | Continuing execution of the AccountTest application.

Fig. J.17 | Reaching the breakpoint in the AccountTest application.

Fig. J.18 | Stepping over a method call.

11. *Using the exit command.* Use the *exit command* to end the debugging session (Fig. J.19). This command causes the AccountTest application to immediately terminate rather than execute the remaining statements in main. Note that when debugging some types of applications (e.g., GUI applications), the application continues to execute even after the debugging session ends.

In this section, you learned how to use the debugger's step and step up commands to debug methods called during your application's execution. You saw how the next command can be used to step over a method call. You also learned that the exit command ends a debugging session.

J.5 The watch Command

In this section, we present the *watch command*, which tells the debugger to watch a field. When that field is about to change, the debugger will notify you. In this section, you'll learn how to use the watch command to see how the Account object's field balance is modified during the execution of the AccountTest application.

As in the preceding two sections, we assume that you have followed *Step 1* and *Step 2* in Section J.2 to open the **Command Prompt**, change to the correct examples directory and compile classes AccountTest and Account for debugging (i.e., with the -g compiler option).

1. *Starting the debugger.* Start the debugger by typing jdb.

2. *Watching a class's field.* Set a watch on Account's balance field by typing watch Account.balance (Fig. J.20). You can set a watch on any field during execution of the debugger. Whenever the value in a field is about to change, the debugger enters break mode and notifies you that the value will change. Watches can be placed only on fields, not on local variables.

3. *Running the application.* Run the application with the command run Account-Test. The debugger will now notify you that field balance's value will change (Fig. J.21). When the application begins, an instance of Account is created with an initial balance of $50.00 and a reference to the Account object is assigned to the local variable account (line 9, Fig. J.1). Recall from Fig. 3.13 that when the

```
main[1] exit

C:\examples\debugger>_
```

Fig. J.19 | Exiting the debugger.

```
C:\examples\debugger>jdb
Initializing jdb ...
> watch Account.balance
Deferring watch modification of Account.balance.
It will be set after the class is loaded.
> _
```

Fig. J.20 | Setting a watch on Account's balance field.

```
Command Prompt - jdb                                          _ □ ×
It will be set after the class is loaded.
> run AccountTest
run  AccountTest
Set uncaught java.lang.Throwable
Set deferred uncaught java.lang.Throwable
>
VM Started: Set deferred watch modification of Account.balance

Field (Account.balance) is 0.0, will be 50.0: "thread=main", Account.<init>(), 1
ine=15 bci=12
15              balance = initialBalance;

main[1] _
```

Fig. J.21 | `AccountTest` application stops when `account` is created and its `balance` field will be modified.

constructor for this object runs, if parameter `initialBalance` is greater than 0.0, instance variable `balance` is assigned the value of parameter `initialBalance`. The debugger notifies you that the value of `balance` will be set to 50.0.

4. *Adding money to the account.* Type cont to continue executing the application. The application executes normally before reaching the code on line 19 of Fig. J.1 that calls `Account` method `credit` to raise the `Account` object's `balance` by a specified amount. The debugger notifies you that instance variable `balance` will change (Fig. J.22). Note that although line 19 of class `AccountTest` calls method `credit`, it is line 21 in `Account`'s method `credit` that actually changes the value of `balance`.

5. *Continuing execution.* Type cont—the application will finish executing because the application does not attempt any additional changes to `balance` (Fig. J.23).

6. *Restarting the debugger and resetting the watch on the variable.* Type jdb to restart the debugger. Once again, set a watch on the `Account` instance variable `balance` by typing the watch `Account.balance`, then type run `AccountTest` to run the application (Fig. J.24).

```
Command Prompt - jdb                                          _ □ ×
main[1] cont
> initial account balance: $50.00

adding 25.00 to account balance

Field (Account.balance) is 50.0, will be 75.0: "thread=main", Account.credit(),
line=21 bci=7
21              balance = balance + amount; // add amount to balance

main[1] _
```

Fig. J.22 | Changing the value of `balance` by calling `Account` method `credit`.

```
Command Prompt                                                _ □ ×
main[1] cont
new account balance: $75.00
>
The application exited

C:\examples\debugger>_
```

Fig. J.23 | Continuing execution of `AccountTest`.

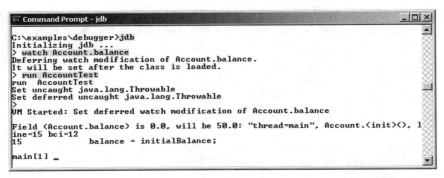

Fig. J.24 | Restarting the debugger and resetting the watch on the variable balance.

7. *Removing the watch on the field.* Suppose you want to watch a field for only part of a program's execution. You can remove the debugger's watch on variable balance by typing *unwatch* Account.balance (Fig. J.25). Type cont—the application will finish executing without reentering break mode.

8. *Closing the Command Prompt window.* Close the **Command Prompt** window by clicking its close button.

In this section, you learned how to use the watch command to enable the debugger to notify you of changes to the value of a field throughout the life of an application. You also learned how to use the unwatch command to remove a watch on a field before the end of the application.

J.6 The clear Command

In the preceding section, you learned to use the unwatch command to remove a watch on a field. The debugger also provides the clear command to remove a breakpoint from an application. You'll often need to debug applications containing repetitive actions, such as a loop. You may want to examine the values of variables during several, but possibly not all, of the loop's iterations. If you set a breakpoint in the body of a loop, the debugger will pause before each execution of the line containing a breakpoint. After determining that the loop is working properly, you may want to remove the breakpoint and allow the remaining iterations to proceed normally. In this section, we use the compound interest application in Fig. 5.6 to demonstrate how the debugger behaves when you set a breakpoint in the body of a for statement and how to remove a breakpoint in the middle of a debugging session.

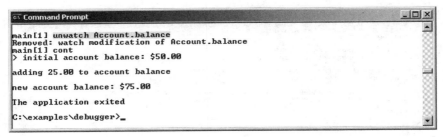

Fig. J.25 | Removing the watch on variable balance.

1. *Opening the* **Command Prompt** *window, changing directories and compiling the application for debugging.* Open the **Command Prompt** window, then change to the directory containing this appendix's examples. For your convenience, we have provided a copy of the `Interest.java` file in this directory. Compile the application for debugging by typing `javac -g Interest.java`.

2. *Starting the debugger and setting breakpoints.* Start the debugger by typing `jdb`. Set breakpoints at lines 13 and 22 of class `Interest` by typing `stop at Interest:13`, then `stop at Interest:22` (Fig. J.26).

3. *Running the application.* Run the application by typing `run Interest`. The application executes until reaching the breakpoint at line 13 (Fig. J.27).

4. *Continuing execution.* Type `cont` to continue—the application executes line 13, printing the column headings `"Year"` and `"Amount on deposit"`. Note that line 13 appears before the `for` statement at lines 16–23 in `Interest` (Fig. 5.6) and thus executes only once. Execution continues past line 13 until the breakpoint at line 22 is reached during the first iteration of the `for` statement (Fig. J.28).

5. *Examining variable values.* Type `print year` to examine the current value of variable `year` (i.e., the `for`'s control variable). Print the value of variable `amount` too (Fig. J.29).

6. *Continuing execution.* Type `cont` to continue execution. Line 22 executes and prints the current values of `year` and `amount`. After the `for` enters its second iteration, the debugger notifies you that the breakpoint at line 22 has been reached a second time. Note that the debugger pauses each time a line where a breakpoint has been set is about to execute—when the breakpoint appears in a loop, the debugger pauses during each iteration. Print the values of variables `year` and `amount` again to see how the values have changed since the first iteration of the `for` (Fig. J.30).

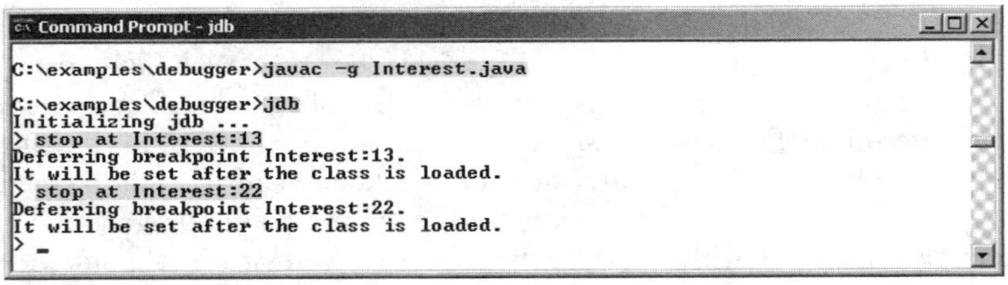

Fig. J.26 | Setting breakpoints in the `Interest` application.

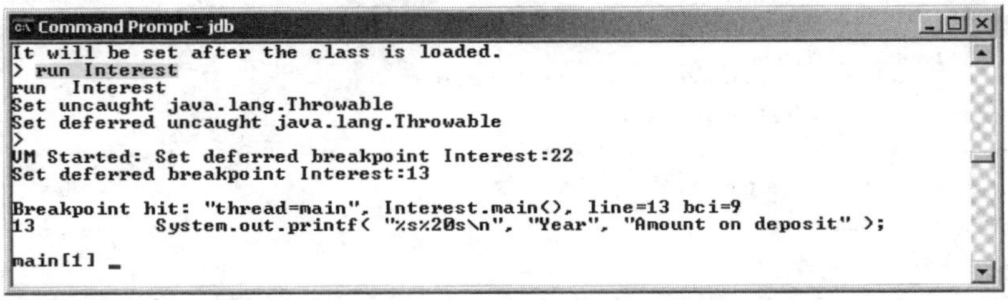

Fig. J.27 | Reaching the breakpoint at line 13 in the `Interest` application.

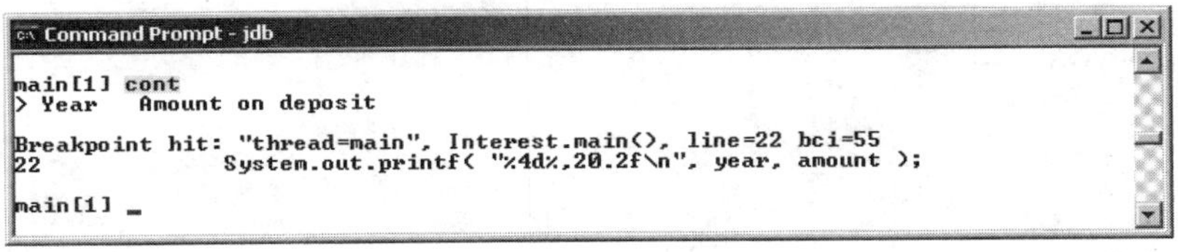

Fig. J.28 | Reaching the breakpoint at line 22 in the Interest application.

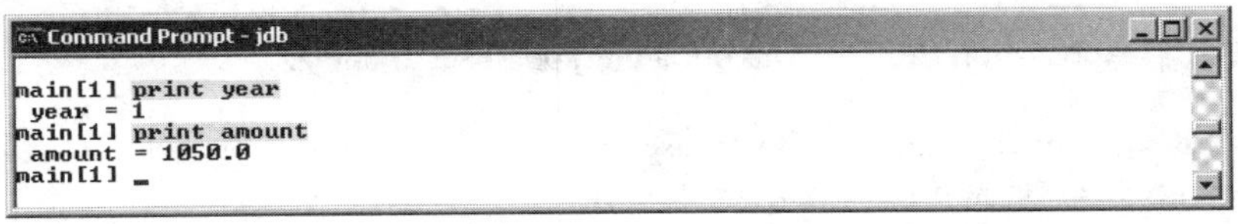

Fig. J.29 | Printing year and amount during the first iteration of Interest's for.

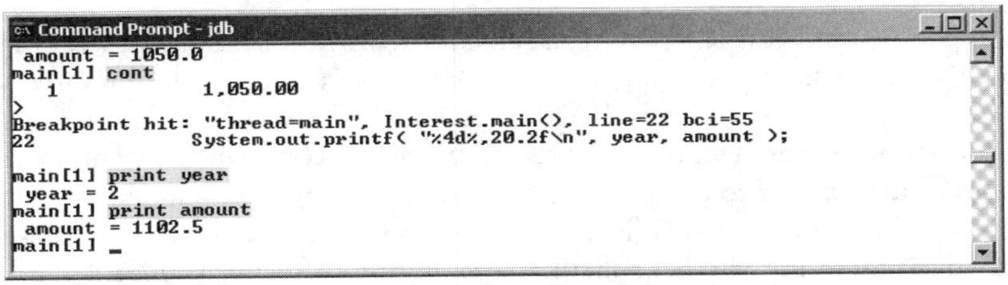

Fig. J.30 | Printing year and amount during the second iteration of Interest's for.

7. *Removing a breakpoint.* You can display a list of all of the breakpoints in the application by typing *clear* (Fig. J.31). Suppose you are satisfied that the Interest application's for statement is working properly, so you want to remove the breakpoint at line 22 and allow the remaining iterations of the loop to proceed normally. You can remove the breakpoint at line 22 by typing clear Interest:22. Now type clear to list the remaining breakpoints in the application. The debugger should indicate that only the breakpoint at line 13 remains (Fig. J.31). Note that this breakpoint has already been reached and thus will no longer affect execution.

8. *Continuing execution after removing a breakpoint.* Type cont to continue execution. Recall that execution last paused before the printf statement in line 22. If the breakpoint at line 22 was removed successfully, continuing the application will produce the correct output for the current and remaining iterations of the for statement without the application halting (Fig. J.32).

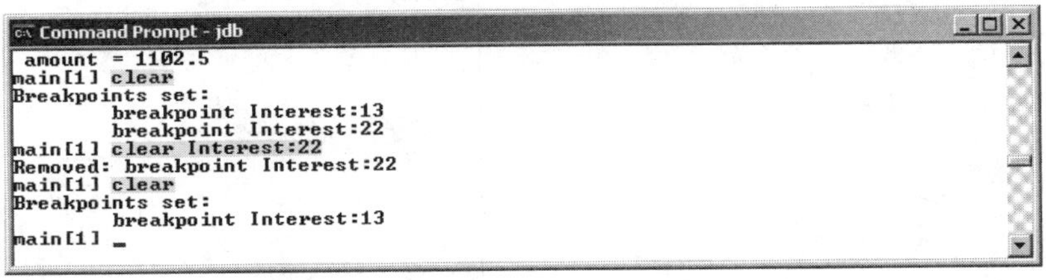

Fig. J.31 | Removing the breakpoint at line 22.

```
Command Prompt                                                    _|□|x|
        breakpoint Interest:13
main[1] cont
   2          1,102.50
   3          1,157.63
   4          1,215.51
   5          1,276.28
   6          1,340.10
   7          1,407.10
   8          1,477.46
   9          1,551.33
  10          1,628.89
>
The application exited

C:\examples\debugger>_
```

Fig. J.32 | Application executes without a breakpoint set at line 22.

In this section, you learned how to use the clear command to list all the breakpoints set for an application and remove a breakpoint.

J.7 Wrap-Up

In this appendix, you learned how to insert and remove breakpoints in the debugger. Breakpoints allow you to pause application execution so you can examine variable values with the debugger's print command. This capability will help you locate and fix logic errors in your applications. You saw how to use the print command to examine the value of an expression and how to use the set command to change the value of a variable. You also learned debugger commands (including the step, step up and next commands) that can be used to determine whether a method is executing correctly. You learned how to use the watch command to keep track of a field throughout the life of an application. Finally, you learned how to use the clear command to list all the breakpoints set for an application or remove individual breakpoints to continue execution without breakpoints.

Index

[*Note:* Page references for defining occurrences of terms appear in ***bold italic***.]

Symbols

∧, boolean logical exclusive OR 142, 144
   truth table 144
_ SQL wildcard character 799, 800
, (comma) formatting flag **129**
--, predecrement/postdecrement **109**, 110
-, subtraction 38, 39
!, logical NOT 142, **144**
   truth table 145
!=, not equals 40
? (wildcard type argument) 583
?:, ternary conditional operator **92**, 112
. dot separator 59
, flag **1006**
(flag **1006**
{, left brace 26
}, right brace 26
* SQL wildcard character 798
* wildcard in a file name 60
*, multiplication 38, 39
/, division 38, 39
/* */ traditional comment 24
/** */ Java documentation comment 24
//, end-of-line comment 24
\, escape character 31
\', single-quote-character escape sequence 1010
\", double-quote escape sequence 31, 1010
\\, backslash-character escape sequence 1010
\b, escape sequence 1010
\f, form-feed escape sequence 1010
\n, newline escape sequence 31, 1010
\r, carriage-return escape sequence 31, 1010
\t, horizontal tab escape sequence 31, 1010
&, boolean logical AND 142, **144**
&&, conditional AND 142, 143
   truth table 142
flag **1006**, 1007
% conversion character **1002**
% SQL wildcard character 799
%, remainder 38, 39

%% format specifier 1003
%b format specifier **145**
%c format specifier 999
%d format specifier 37, **995**, 996
%f format specifier 75
%o octal format specifier 996
%s format specifier 32, 995
- flag **1006**
+ flag **1006**
- (minus sign) formatting flag 129
+, addition 38, 39
+, string concatenation 1028
++, preincrement/postincrement **109**
+=, addition assignment operator **109**, 136
+=, string concatenation assignment operator 1029
<, less than 40
<=, less than or equal 40
=, assignment operator 36
== to determine whether two references refer to the same object 334
==, is equal to 40
>, greater than 40
>= greater than or equal to 40
|, boolean logical inclusive OR 142, **144**
||, conditional OR 142, 143
   truth table 143

Numerics

0 flag **212**
0 format flag 254
0x (hexadecimal prefix) **1007**
127.0.0.1 (localhost IP address) 849
127.0.0.1 (localhost) 761

A

abbreviating assignment expressions 109
abnormally terminate a program 215
abs method of Math 157
absolute method of Result-Set 819
absolute path 521, 525
absolute positioning **866**
absolute value 157

abstract class 338, 343, 344, 362
abstract data type (ADT) 253, **283**, 285
abstract implementation 634
abstract keyword 343
abstract method 343, 345, 347, 378, 401, 1053
abstract superclass 343, 378
Abstract Window Toolkit (AWT) 387, 652
Abstract Window Toolkit (AWT) package 166
Abstract Window Toolkit Event package 166
AbstractButton class 404, 407, 642, 647
   addItemListener method **410**
   isSelected method 649
   setMnemonic method 647
   setRolloverIcon method 406
   setSelected method 648
AbstractCollection class 634
AbstractList class 634
AbstractMap class 634
AbstractPageBean class 860, 865, 979
AbstractQueue class 634
AbstractSequentialList class 634
AbstractSessionBean class 895
AbstractSet class 634
AbstractTableModel class 814, 820
   fireTableStructureChanged method 820
accept method of class ServerSocket 754, 761
access modifier 58, 66, 291
   private 66, 302
   protected 256, 276, **302**
   public 58, 302
access shared data 701
accessor method 266
Account class (ATM case study) 50, 80, 83, 114, 115, 195, 244, 245, 247, 248, 249

Account class with an instance variable of type double 74
AccountRecord class for serializable objects 542
AccountRecord maintains information for one account 526
acquire the lock **688**
action 91, 96, 283, **855**
action expression in the UML 89, 92, 149
action key 434
action of an object 148
action oriented 14
action state in the UML 89, 149
action state symbol 89
action/decision model of programming 92
ActionEvent class 398, 399, 403, 451
   getActionCommand method 399, 407
ActionListener class 398
ActionListener interface 403
   actionPerformed method 399, 401, 445, 451
actionPerformed method of ActionListener 399, 401, 445, 451
ACTIVATED constant of nested class EventType 753
activation in a UML sequence diagram 247
activation record 163, 193
activity diagram 89, 89, 92, 125
   do...while statement 131
   for statement 126
   if statement 91
   if...else statement 92
   in the UML 51, 96, 148, 149, 150, 152
   sequence statement 89
   switch statement 139
   while statement 96
activity in the UML 51, 89, 148, 151
actor in use case in the UML 49
actual type arguments 561
acyclic gradient **482**
Ada programming language 677

adapter class 427
Adapter Classes used to implement event handlers 431
add a web service reference to an application in Netbeans 947
add an event handler in Netbeans 1059
Add Binding Attribute 868, 908
add method
  ButtonGroup 413
  JFrame 392
  LinkedList 601
  List 595
  Vector 604
add method of ArrayList 582
add method of class ArrayList 749
add method of class JMenu 647
add method of class JMenuBar 648
addActionListener method of JTextField 398
addAll method
  Collections 606, 617
  List 599
addFirst method of LinkedList 601
addGap method of class GroupLayout.Group 1056
addGap method of class GroupLayout.ParallelGroup 1056
addGap method of class GroupLayout.SequentialGroup 1056
adding a web service reference to a project in Netbeans 947
addItemListener method of AbstractButton 410
addition 38, 39
addition compound assignment operator, += 109
addition program that displays the sum of two numbers 33
addKeyListener method of Component 437
addLast method of LinkedList 601
addListSelectionListener method of JList 419
addMouseListener method of Component 427
addMouseMotionListener method of Component 427
addPoint method of class Polygon 477, 479
addSeparator method of class JMenu 648
addTab method of class JTabbedPane 660
addTableModelListener method of TableModel 814
addTrayIcon method of class SystemTray 1072

addWindowListener method of class Window 641
ADF Faces 856
ADT (abstract data type) 283
aggregation in the UML 82
Agile Software Development 18
agile software development xxiii
Ajax 18, 922
Ajax (Asynchronous JavaScript and XML) 920
Ajax-enabled component libraries 907
Ajax-enabled JSF components xxiii
AJAX-enabled web applications xxiii
Ajax libraries 921
Ajax web application 922
algebraic notation 38
algorithm 92, 190, 605
algorithm in Java Collections Framework 605
aligning components in GroupLayout 1056
aligning decimal points in output 995
alphabetizing 1018
analysis stage of the software life cycle 48
analyzing a project's requirements 15
anchor field of class GridBagConstraints 667
AND 805, 806
angle brackets (< and >) 561
Annotations
  @Resource 961
  @WebMethod 941
  @WebParam 941
  @WebService 941
  dependency injection 961
annotations xxiii
anonymous inner class 416, 417, 433
Apache Derby xxii, 828
Apache Software Foundation 19
Apache Tomcat 941
API 155
API (application programming interface) 34, 155
API Documentation (java.sun.com/javase/6/docs/) 5
API documentation (java.sun.com/javase/6/docs/api/) 165, 167
API links
  Deprecated 1075
  Help 1075
  Index 1075
  Tree 1075
append method of class StringBuilder 1032
appendRow method of class CachedRowSetDataProvider 920

applet 748
Applet class
  getAppletContext method 750
  getParameter method 748
Applet Package 165
applet parameter 748
AppletContext interface 745
  showDocument method 745, 750
applets in the public domain 748
application 23, 25, 58
  command-line arguments 158
application programming interface (API) 5, 155
application scope 856
application server 848
Application servers
  Apache Tomcat 941
  BEA Weblogic Server 941
  GlassFish 941
  JBoss Application Server 941
ApplicationBean 856
arc 474
arc angle 474
arc width and arc height for rounded rectangles 473
Arc2D class 454
  CHORD constant 484
  OPEN constant 484
  PIE constant 484
Arc2D.Double class 480
archive files 288
Arcs displayed with drawArc and fillArc 475
args parameter 240
argument index 995, 1001, 1009
argument list 996
argument promotion 164
argument to a method 27, 61
arithmetic compound assignment operators 109
arithmetic operators 37
arithmetic overflow 283, 497
ArithmeticException class 491, 497
array 203, 516, 749
  length field 204
  pass an array element to a method 221
  pass an array to a method 221
array-access expression 204
array-creation expression 205
array initializer 207
  nested 230
array initializer for multidimensional array 229
array of one-dimensional arrays 229, 230
ArrayBlockingQueue class 701, 703, 714
  size method 705

arraycopy method of System 592
array-creation expression in the context of generics 568
ArrayIndexOutOfBoundsException 479
ArrayIndexOutOfBoundsException class 215, 488
ArrayList class 250, 581, 594, 615, 749, 962
  add method 582, 749
  toString method 582
Arrays class 590
  asList method 599, 600
  binarySearch method 590
  equals method 590
  fill method 590
  sort method 590
Arrays class methods 590
arrow 89
arrow key 434
arrowhead in a UML sequence diagram 247
ascending order 592
  ASC in SQL 800, 801, 802
ascent 467
ASCII (American Standard Code for Information Interchange) character set 139, 517
ASCII character set Appendix 1052
asList method of Arrays 599, 600
assert statement 513, 1053
assertion 512
Assigning superclass and subclass references to superclass and subclass variables 341
assignment operator, = 36, 37, 42
assignment operators 109
associate
  left to right 112
  right to left 105, 112
association (in the UML) 80, 82, 294
  name 81
association in the UML 15
associativity of operators 39, 43, 112
  right to left 39
asterisk (*) SQL wildcard character 798
asynchronous call 246
asynchronous event 497
Asynchronous JavaScript and XML (Ajax) 920
asynchronous request 922
ATM (automated teller machine) case study 44, 48
ATM class (ATM case study) 80, 81, 82, 114, 116, 148, 195, 243, 244, 245, 246, 247, 292
ATM system 49, 50, 78, 79, 113, 147, 194, 291

atomic operation **693**, 845
attribute 291, 294
  compartment in a class diagram 115
  declaration in the UML 116, 117
  in the UML 60, 80, 84, 113, 114, **116**, 147, 151
  name in the UML 116
  type in the UML **116**
attribute in the UML 14, 377
attribute of a class 4
`authorISBN` table of books database 794, 795
`authors` table of books database 794, 795
auto commit state 846
autobox an `int` 565
autoboxing 565
`autoComplete` attribute of a **Text Field** 925
`AutoComplete` interface 930
  `getOptions` method 928, 930
`autoComplete` property of a JSF **Text Field** component 923
auto-complete text field 923
auto-complete **Text Field** component 923
`autoCompleteExpression` attribute of a **Text Field** 925
autoincremented 795, 804
automated teller machine (ATM) 44, 48
  user interface 44
automated teller machine (ATM) case study xxii
automatic driver discovery **810**
automatic driver discovery (JDBC 4) xxii
automatic garbage collection 500
automatic scrolling 419
average 97, 99
`await` method of interface `Condition` 720, 724
`awaitTermination` method of interface `ExecutorService` 692
AWT (Abstract Window Toolkit) 387
  components 387
`AWTEvent` class 400

B

B conversion character **1002**
b conversion character **1002**
B programming language 3
B2B (business-to-business) transactions 935
background color 461, 463
backslash (\) 30, 1010

`BalanceInquiry` class (ATM case study) 80, 83, 114, 115, 116, 149, 194, 195, 243, 244, 245, 246, 247, 293, 373, 374, 375
`BankDatabase` class (ATM case study) 80, 83, 114, 195, 243, 244, 245, 246, 247, 248, 249, 292, 294
bar chart 210, 211
Bar chart printing program 211
bar of asterisks 210, 211
base case **184**, 188, 190
base class **299**
base of a number 1037
`BASELINE` alignment constant in `GroupLayout` 1056
baseline of the font 465
`BasePlusCommissionEmployee` class derived from `CommissionEmployee` 354
`BasePlusCommissionEmployee` class represents an employee that receives a base salary in addition to a commission 309
`BasePlusCommissionEmployee3` inherits protected instance variables from `CommissionEmployee2` 319
`BasePlusCommissionEmployee4` class that extends `CommissionEmployee3`, which provides only private instance variables 325
`BasicStroke` class 454, 483
  `CAP_ROUND` constant 484
  `JOIN_ROUND` constant 484
batch file 528
BCPL programming language 3
BEA Weblogic Server **941**
behavior 14, 194
behavior of a class 4
behavior of the system 148, 151, 245
behaviors in the UML 14
Bell Laboratories 4
bidirectional iterator **599**
bidirectional navigability in the UML 293
`BigDecimal` class 130, 187
`BigInteger` class 187, 936
binary arithmetic operators 105
binary digit (bit) 517
binary file 519
binary operator 36, 38, 144
binary search algorithm 615
`binarySearch` method of `Arrays` 590
  of `Collections` 606, 615, 616
`BindException` class 756
binding a JSF **Table** to a database table 910
binding attribute 868, 885

binding the server to the port 754, 768
`BindingProvider` interface 972
  `getRequestContext` method 972
bit (binary digit) **517**
blackjack 957
blank line 25
`_blank` target frame 750
block 94, 103, 160, 754, 771
block increment of a `JSlider` 637
block until connection received 761
blocked state **680**, 688
`BlockingQueue` interface 703
  `put` method 703, 705
  `take` method 703, 705
blogosphere 18
blogs 18
body
  of a class declaration 26
  of a loop 96
  of a method 26
  of an `if` statement 39
Bohm, C. 88
`BOLD` constant of class `Font` 464, 465
Booch, Grady 15, 16
book-title capitalization 385, 404
books database 794
  table relationships 797
`boolean`
  promotions 164
`Boolean` attribute in the UML 114
`boolean` expression 92, 1115
boolean logical AND, & 142, 144
boolean logical exclusive OR, ^ 142, 144
  truth table 144
boolean logical inclusive OR, | 144
`boolean` primitive type 92, 1053, 1054, 1115
border of a `JFrame` 640
`BorderLayout` class 426, 437, 438, 442, 451
  `CENTER` constant 426, 442, 444
  `EAST` constant 426, 442
  `NORTH` constant 426, 442
  `SOUTH` constant 426, 442
  `WEST` constant 426, 442
`BOTH` constant of class `GridBagConstraints` 667
bottom tier 853
bounded buffer 713
bounding rectangle 472, 474, 637

`Box` class 451, 662, 664
  `createGlue` method 666
  `createHorizontalBox` method 451, 664
  `createHorizontalGlue` method 664
  `createHorizontalStrut` method 664
  `createRigidArea` method 666
  `createVerticalBox` method 664
  `createVerticalGlue` method 666
  `createVerticalStrut` method 664
  `X_AXIS` constant 666
  `Y_AXIS` constant 666
boxing 565
`BoxLayout` class 451, 662, 663
`BoxLayout` layout manager 663
braces ({ and }) 94, 95, 103, 123, 132
braces not required 136
braces, { } 207
braille screen reader 388
branch in the UML 149
break 1053
break mode 1112
break statement 136, 139, 140
breakpoint 1110
  inserting 1112, 1114
  listing 1123
  removing 1123
bricks-and-mortar store 883
brightness 463
brittle software 321
`browse` method of class `Desktop` 1069
browser package demo 1072
browsing 748
buffer 550, 696, 697
`BufferedImage` class 483
  `createGraphics` method 483
  `TYPE_INT_RGB` constant 483
`BufferedInputStream` class 551
`BufferedOutputStream` class 550
  `flush` method 551
`BufferedReader` class 551
`BufferedWriter` class 551
Build option in Netbeans 942
building-block approach to creating programs 5, 15
built-in type 35
bulk operation 593
business-critical computing 495
business logic 853
business rule 853
business-to-business (B2B) transactions 935
button 382

Button JSF component 870, 874
   primary property **908**
   reset property **908**
button label 404
ButtonGroup class 410, 642, 651
   add method 413
byte 517
byte-based stream 519
byte keyword 1054
byte primitive type 132, 517, 1053
   promotions 164
ByteArrayInputStream class 551
ByteArrayOutputStream class 551
bytecode 7, 28
bytecode verifier 8

C

C++ programming language 4
cache 852
CachedRowSet 916
CachedRowSet interface **826**, 911
   close method 828
CachedRowSet-DataPro-vider class
   commitChanges method 920
CachedRowSetDataProvid-er class 911, 920
   appendRow method 920
   refresh method 920
Calculating values to be placed into elements of an array 208
calculations 53, 89
Calendar class 1001
   getInstance method 1001
call-by-reference 223
call-by-value 223
call method of interface Callable 741
Callable interface 741
   call method 741
CallableStatement inter-face 845
callback function **922**
calling method (caller) 58, 66
CANCEL_OPTION constant of JFileChooser 555
canRead method of File 521
canWrite method of File 521
CAP_ROUND constant of class BasicStroke 484
capacity increment of a Vector 601, 602, 604
capacity method
   of class StringBuilder 1029
   of Vector 605
capacity of a StringBuilder 1028

Caps Lock key 435
card games 215
Card Shuffling and Dealing 218
card shuffling and dealing with Collections meth-od shuffle 610
carriage return 31
case keyword **136**, 1053
case sensitive 25
case sensitivity of Java com-mands 10
case studies xxii
CashDispenser class (ATM case study) 80, 81, 82, 114, 115, 195, 249
casino 167, 173
cast
   downcast **340**
cast operator 104, 165
catch an exception 492
catch block **494**, 497, 501, 504, 507
catch clause **494**, 1053
catch keyword 494
catch-or-declare requirement 499
catch superclass exception type 500
cd to change directories 28
ceil method of Math 157
CENTER alignment constant in GroupLayout 1056
CENTER constant of Border-Layout 426, 442, 444
CENTER constant of class GridBagConstraints 667
CENTER constant of FlowLay-out 442
center mouse button click 430
centered 439
chained exception 509
ChangeEvent class 639
ChangeListener interface 639
   stateChanged method 639
changing look-and-feel of a Swing-based GUI 655
chapter dependency chart xxiv
char
   array 1016
   primitive type **35**, 132
   promotions 164
char keyword 1053, 1054
character 166, 517
   constant **139**
   literal **1014**
   set 517
character-based stream **519**
Character class 1014, 1035
   charValue method **1038**
   digit method **1037**
   forDigit method **1037**
   isDefined method **1035**
   isDigit method **1035**

Character class (cont.)
   isJavaIdentifier-Part method **1035**
   isJavaIdentifier-Start method **1035**
   isLetter method **1036**
   isLetterOrDigit meth-od **1036**
   isLowerCase method **1037**
   isUpperCase method **1037**
   non-static methods **1039**
   static conversion meth-ods **1038**
   static methods for test-ing characters and con-verting character case **1036**
   toLowerCase method **1037**
   toUpperCase method **1037**
CharArrayReader class 551
CharArrayWriter class 551
charAt method
   of class String 1016
   of class StringBuilder 1031
CharSequence interface 1048
charValue method of class Character 1038
checkbox 404, 410
checkbox label 408
checked exception **498**
Checking with assert that a value is within range 513
child window 636, **656**, 660
Choosing colors with JColor-Chooser 462
CHORD constant of class Arc2D 484
circular buffer 714
clarity 2
class 4, 14, 116, 155, 194, 198, 291
   class keyword 58
   constructor 59, 70, 294
   data hiding 66
   declaration 25
   declare a method 57
   default constructor 70
   field 65
   file 28
   get method 260
   instance variable 56, 65, 157
   instantiating an object 57
   name 25, 287, 294
   set method 260
   user defined 25
class 517
class average 96
class-average problem 97, 101
class cannot extend a final class 360

Class class 334, 359, 392, 819
   getName method 335, 359
   getResource method 392
Class declaration with one method 57
Class declaration with one meth-od that has a parameter 61
class diagram
   for the ATM system model 83, 85
   in the UML 50, 80, 82, 113, 115, 195, 291, 294
class diagram in the UML 375, 376, 377
.class file 7, 8, 28
   separate one for every class 259
class hierarchy 299, 344
class instance creation expres-sion 59, 72
class keyword 25, 58, 1053
class library 130, 282, 300, 333
class loader 8, 288, 392
class method **156**
class name
   fully qualified 64
Class that manages an integer array to be shared by multi-ple threads 689
Class that manages an integer array to be shared by multi-ple threads with synchroni-zation 694
class variable 157, 274
classwide information 274
ClassCastException class 488, 566
Classes
   AbstractButton 404, 407, 642, 647
   AbstractCollection 634
   AbstractList 634
   AbstractMap 634
   AbstractPageBean 860, 979
   AbstractQueue 634
   AbstractSequential-List 634
   AbstractSessionBean 895
   AbstractSet 634
   AbstractTableModel 814, 820
   ActionEvent 398, 399, 403, 451
   ActionListener 398
   Arc2D 454
   Arc2D.Double 480
   ArithmeticException 491
   ArrayBlockingQueue 701, 703, 714
   ArrayIndexOutOf-BoundsException 488

Classes (cont.)

ArrayList 250, 581, 594, 615, 749
Arrays 590
AWTEvent 400
BasicStroke 454, 483
BigDecimal 130, 187
BigInteger 187, 936
BindException 756
BorderLayout 426, 437, 438, 442, 451
Box 451, 662, 664
BoxLayout 451, 662, 663
BufferedImage 483
BufferedInputStream 551
BufferedOutput-Stream 550
BufferedReader 551
BufferedWriter 551
ButtonGroup 410, 642, 651
ByteArrayInput-Stream 551
ByteArrayOutput-Stream 551
CachedRowSetDataProvider 911, 920
Calendar 1001
ChangeEvent 639
Character 1014, 1032, 1035
CharArrayReader 551
CharArrayWriter 551
Class 334, 359, 392, 819
ClassCastException 488, 566
Collections 563, 593
Color 454
Component 388, 422, 457, 641, 672
ComponentAdapter 427
ComponentListener 439
Container 388, 419, 438, 447
ContainerAdapter 427
Cookie 892
DatagramPacket 768, 790
DatagramSocket 768
DataInputStream 550
DataOutputStream 550
Date 1001
Desktop 1069
Dimension 638
Double 581
DriverManager 811
Ellipse2D 454
Ellipse2D.Double 480
Ellipse2D.Float 480
EmptyStackException 620
EnumSet class 273
Error 498
EventListenerList 401
Exception 498

Classes (cont.)

ExecutionException 730
Executors 686
File 520
FileInputStream 520
FileOutputStream 520
FileReader 520, 552
FileWriter 520
FilterInputStream 550
FilterOutputStream 550
FlowLayout 391, 438
FocusAdapter 427
Font 408, 454, 465
FontMetrics 454, 467
Formatter 520, 994
Frame 640
GeneralPath 454, 484
GradientPaint 454, 482
Graphics 433, 434, 454, 478
Graphics2D 454, 479, 483
GridBagConstraints 667, 672
GridBagLayout 662, 666, 668, 672
GridLayout 438, 445
GroupLayout 1055
GroupLayout.Group 1056
GroupLayout.ParallelGroup 1056
GroupLayout.SequentialGroup 1056
HashMap 625, 749, 891, 892, 899, 900
HashSet 622
Hashtable 625
HttpServletRequest 893
HttpServletResponse 892
HyperlinkEvent 750, 753
IllegalMonitorState-Exception 707, 721
ImageIcon 392
InetAddress 761, 766, 771, 772
InputEvent 423, 430, 434
InputMismatchExcep-tion 491
InputStream 550, 754, 755, 756
InputStreamReader 552
Integer 385, 581
InterruptedExcep-tion 684
ItemEvent 410, 413
JApplet 641
JButton 386, 404, 407, 445
JCheckBox 386, 407

Classes (cont.)

JCheckBoxMenuItem 641, 642, 649
JColorChooser 461, 462
JComboBox 386, 414, 668
JComponent 388, 389, 391, 401, 414, 417, 431, 447, 454
JdbcRowSetImpl 828
JDesktopPane 656
JDialog 648
JEditorPane 750
JFileChooser 552
JFrame 640
JInternalFrame 656, 660
JLabel 386, 389
JList 386, 417
JMenu 641, 642, 649, 660
JMenuBar 641, 642, 648, 660
JMenuItem 641, 642, 660
JOptionPane 383
JPanel 386, 430, 431, 438, 447, 637
JPasswordField 394, 399
JPopupMenu 649, 651
JProgressBar 737
JRadioButton 407, 410, 413
JRadioButtonMenuIt-em 641, 642, 649, 651
JScrollPane 419, 422, 451, 451
JSlider 636, 637, 638, 1056
JTabbedPane 660, 666
JTable 813
JTextArea 449, 451, 668, 672
JTextComponent 394, 397, 449, 451
JTextField 386, 394, 398, 401, 449
JToggleButton 407
KeyAdapter 427
KeyEvent 403, 434
Line2D 454, 484
Line2D.Double 480
LinearGradientPaint 482
LineNumberReader 551
LinkedList 594
ListSelectionEvent 417
ListSelectionModel 419
MalformedURLExcep-tion 749
Matcher 1014, 1048
Math 156
MouseAdapter 427, 428
MouseEvent 403, 423, 651
MouseMotionAdapter 427, 431
MouseWheelEvent 423

Classes (cont.)

NullPointerExcep-tion 488
Number 581
Object 273
ObjectInputStream 520, 754, 756, 761
ObjectOutputStream 520
OutputStream 550, 754, 755, 756
OutputStreamWriter 552
Pattern 1014, 1048
PipedInputStream 550
PipedOutputStream 550
PipedReader 552
PipedWriter 552
Point 433
Polygon 454, 476
PrintStream 550
PrintWriter 552
PriorityQueue 621
Properties 629, 899
RadialGradientPaint 482
Random 166, 167
Reader 551
Rectangle2D 454
Rectangle2D.Double 480
ReentrantLock 720, 722
RoundRectangle2D 454
RoundRectangle2D.Double 480, 483
RoundRectangle2D.Dou-ble 483
RowFilter 825
RuntimeException 499, 506
Scanner 35, 62
ServerSocket 754, 756, 775
Socket 754, 767, 782, 783
SocketException 768
SplashScreen 1069
SQLException 811
SQLFeatureNotSup-portedException 819
Stack 618
StackTraceElement 509
String 1014
StringBuffer 1028
StringBuilder 1014, 1028
StringIndexOutOf-BoundsException 1024, 1032
StringReader 552
StringTokenizer 629, 1014, 1040
StringWriter 552
SwingUtilities 655
SwingWorker 727
SystemColor 482

Classes (cont.)
SystemTray 1072
TableModelEvent 825
TableRowSorter 825
TexturePaint 454, 482, 483
Thread 681, 684
Throwable 498, 506
TrayIcon 1072
TreeMap 625
TreeSet 622
Types 813
UIManager 653
UIViewRoot 858
UnknownHostException 755
UnsupportedOperationException 600
ValidatorException 882
Vector 594, 601
Window 640, 641
WindowAdapter 427
Writer 551
classified listings 17
ClassName.this 648
classpath 288, 811
-classpath command line argument to javac 289
-classpath command-line argument 527
CLASSPATH environment variable 29, 289
-classpath option 811
Clean and Build option in Netbeans 942
Clean option in Netbeans 942
clear debugger command 1123
clear method
of List 599
of PriorityQueue 621
clearRect method of class Graphics 470
click a button 394, 404
click count 428
click the mouse 407
click the scroll arrows 416
client 744
client code 340
client connection 754
Client desktop application for the HugeInteger web service 950
Client interacting with server and web server. Step 1 The GET request 850
Client interacting with server and web server. Step 2 The HTTP response 851
client of a class 14, 194, 245, 283
client of an object 68
Client portion of a stream-socket connection between a client and a server 762
client-server relationship 744
client-side artifacts 947

Client side of connectionless client/server computing with datagrams 772
Client side of the client/server Tic-Tac-Toe program 783
client tier 853
client/server chat 756
clone method of Object 334
Cloneable interface 334
cloning objects
deep copy 334
shallow copy 334
close a window 389, 394
close method
of CachedRowSet 828
of Formatter 531
of JdbcRowSet 828
of ObjectOutputStream 547
close method of class Socket 755
closed polygons 476
closePath method of class GeneralPath 486
code reuse 299, 588
Code Search Engines and Code Sites xxviii
coin tossing 168
collaboration 243, 246
collaboration diagram in the UML 51, 245
collaboration in the UML 242
collaborative applications 790
collection 589
collection hierarchy 593
collection implementation 632
Collection interface 589, 593, 596, 605
contains method 596
demonstrated via an ArrayList object 595
iterator method 596
collections
synchronized collection 593
unmodifiable collection 593
Collections class 563, 593
addAll method 606, 617
binarySearch method 606, 615, 616
copy method 606, 613
disjoint method 606, 617
fill method 606, 613
frequency method 606, 617
max method 606, 613
min method 606, 613
reverse method 606, 613
reverseOrder method 607
shuffle method 606, 610, 612
sort method 606
wrapper methods 593
collections framework 588

Collections method addAll, frequency and disjoint 617
Collections method binarySearch 615
Collections method sort 606
Collections method sort with a Comparator object 607
Collections methods addAll, frequency and disjoint 617
Collections methods reverse, fill, copy, max and min 613
collision in a hashtable 626
color 454
Color changed for drawing 459
color chooser dialog 463
Color class 454
getBlue method 458, 460
getColor method 458
getGreen method 458, 460
getRed method 458, 460
setColor method 458
Color constant 457, 460
color manipulation 456
color swatches 463
column 229, 793, 793, 794
column number in a result set 799
columns of a two-dimensional array 229
com.sun.rave.web.ui.appbase package 860
com.sun.rowset package 828
com.sun.webui.jsf.component package 860
com.sun.webui.jsf.model package 930
combo box 382, 413
comma (,) 127
comma (,) formatting flag 129
comma in an argument list 32
comma-separated list 127
of parameters 160
of arguments 32, 35
command-and-control software system 677
command button 404
command line 27
command-line argument 158, 240, 242
Command Prompt 7, 27
command window 27, 30
comment 24, 35
end-of-line (single-line), // 24, 27, 35
Javadoc 24, 849
multiple line 24
single line 24, 27, 35
commercial applications 516

CommissionEmployee class derived from Employee 352
CommissionEmployee class represents an employee paid a percentage of gross sales 304
CommissionEmployee class test program 307
CommissionEmployee2 with protected instance variables 316
CommissionEmployee3 class uses methods to manipulate its private instance variables 322
CommissionEmployee4's constructor outputs text 328
commit a transaction 845
commit method of interface Connection 846
commitChanges method of class CachedRowSet-DataProvider 920
Common Programming Errors overview xxvii
Commonly used JSF components 870
communication diagram in the UML 51, 245, 246
Comparable interface 372, 563, 606, 1020
compareTo method 606
Comparable<T> interface
compareTo method 563
Comparator interface 606
Comparator object 607, 613, 623, 625
in sort 607
compareTo method
of class String 1018, 1020
of Comparable 606
compareTo method of Comparable<T> 563
compareTo method of interface Comparable 372
comparing String objects 1018
comparison operator 372
compilation error 24
compile 28
compile a program 7
compile method of class Pattern 1048
compile-time error 24
compiler error 24
compiler options
-d 286
compile-time type safety 557
compiling an application with multiple Classes 60
complex curve 484
complexity theory 190
component 4, 166, 422

Component class 388, 422, 456, 457, 463, 641, 672
    addKeyListener method 437
    addMouseListener method 427
    addMouseMotionListener method 427
    getMaximumSize method 1056
    getMinimumSize method 638, 1056
    getPreferredSize method 638, 1056
    repaint method 434
    setBackground method 463
    setFont method 408
    setLocation method 641
    setSize method 641
    setVisible method 445, 641
component in the UML 15
component of an array 203
component tree 858
ComponentAdapter class 427
ComponentListener interface 427, 439
composition 81, 82, 85, 267, 300, 301
    in the UML 81
Composition demonstration 270
Compound 127
compound assignment operators 109, 111
compound interest 127
    calculations with for 128
computerized scientific notation 996
Computing the sum of the elements of an array 210
concat method of class String 1025
concatenate strings 277
concatenation 161, 1028
concrete class 343
concrete subclass 347
CONCUR_READ_ONLY constant 818
CONCUR_UPDATABLE constant 818
concurrency 677
concurrent access to a Collection by multiple threads 632
concurrent operations 677
concurrent programming 678
concurrent threads 701
condition 39, 131
Condition interface 720, 722
    await method 720, 724
    signal method 720
    signalAll method 721
condition object 720
conditional AND, && 142, 143, 144
    truth table 142

conditional expression 92, 254
conditional operator, ?: 92, 112
conditional OR, || 142, 143
    truth table 143
Configure Virtual Forms... 923
confusing the equality operator == with the assignment operator = 42
connect to a database 809
connect to server 754, 755
connected lines 476
connected RowSet 826
connection 745, 755, 766, 768, 775, 783
connection between client and server terminates 756
connection between Java program and database 811
Connection interface 811, 813, 818, 845
    commit method 846
    createStatement method 812, 818
    getAutoCommit method 846
    prepareStatement method 832
    rollBack method 846
    setAutoCommit method 845
connection-oriented service 745
connection-oriented, streams-based transmission 768
connection port 754
connectionless service 745, 768
connectionless transmission 768, 769
consistent state 254, 260
constant 279
constant (declare in an interface) 371, 373
constant integral expression 132, 138
constant variable 139, 209, 279
    declare 209
    must be initialized 209
constructor 59, 70, 294
    call another constructor of the same class using this 262
    naming 71
    no argument 262
    overloaded 259
    parameter list 71
constructor call order 331
Constructor Detail section in API 1079
Constructor Summary section in API 1078
constructors cannot specify a return type 72
consume memory 193
consumed 399
consumer 696
consumer electronic device 4

consumer thread 696
consuming a web service 936, 945
cont debugger command 1113
Container class 388, 419, 438, 447
    setLayout method 391, 441, 444, 447, 666
    validate method 447
container class 267
container for menus 642
ContainerAdapter class 427
ContainerListener interface 427
contains method
    of Collection 596
    of Vector 604
containsKey method of Map 629
content pane 419, 649
    setBackground method 419
context-sensitive popup menu 649
continue 1053
continue statement 139, 140
    terminating a single iteration of a for statement 141
control statement 88, 90, 91, 120, 192
    nesting 90
    stacking 90
Control Statements enhanced for 219
control variable 120, 121, 122, 124
controller logic 853
controlling expression of a switch 136
controls 383
converge on a base case 184
conversion character 995
    % 1002
    A 997
    a 997
    B 1002
    b 1002
    C 998
    c 998
    d 995
    E 996, 997
    e 996, 997
    f 997
    G 997
    g 997
    H 1002
    h 1002
    n 1002
    o 995
    S 998
    s 998
    T 999
    t 999
    X 995
    x 995

conversion suffix character 999
    A 1000
    a 1000
    B 1000
    b 1000
    c 999
    D 999
    d 1000
    e 1000
    F 999
    H 1000
    I 1000
    j 1000
    k 1000
    l 1001
    M 1001
    m 1000
    P 1001
    p 1001
    R 1000
    r 1000
    S 1001
    T 1000
    Y 1000
    y 1000
    Z 1001
convert
    an integral value to a floating-point value 165
cookie 884, 885, 893, 895
    deletion 884
    domain 895
    expiration 884
    expiration date 884
    header 884
Cookie class 892
    getDomain method 895
    getMaxAge method 895
    getName method 895
    getPath method 895
    getSecure method 895
    getValue method 895
Cookies array 893
coordinate system 454, 456
coordinates (0, 0) 454
copy method of Collections 606, 613
copying objects
    deep copy 334
    shallow copy 334
Copying selected text from one text area to another 449
core package 28
cos method of Math 157
cosine 157
counter-controlled repetition 97, 103, 106, 120, 121, 122, 192
    with the for repetition statement 122
    with the while repetition statement 121
Craigslist 17
craps (casino game) 167, 173
create a desktop application in Netbeans 947
create a package 284
create a reusable class 284
create a Socket 755

create a web application in Netbeans 937
create an object of a class 59
create new classes from existing
class declarations 304
createGlue method of class
Box 666
createGraphics method of
class BufferedImage 483
createHorizontalBox
method of Box 451
createHorizontalBox
method of class Box 664
createHorizontalGlue
method of class Box 664
createHorizontalStrut
method of class Box 664
createRigidArea method of
class Box 666
createStatement method of
Connection 812, 818
createVerticalBox meth-
od of class Box 664
createVerticalGlue meth-
od of class Box 666
createVerticalStrut
method of class Box 664
Creating a GradeBook object
and passing a String to its
displayMessage method
62
creating a Java DB database in
Netbeans 909
Creating a sequential text file
528
Creating an object of Grade-
Book and calling its dis-
playMessage method 59
creating and initializing an array 206
Creating and manipulating a
GradeBook object 68
Credit inquiry program 536
cross-platform GUI development 386
CSS (Cascading Style Sheets)
stylesheet 858, 864
<Ctrl>-d 135
Ctrl key 420, 437
Ctrl key 135
<Ctrl>-z 135
cursor 27, 30
curve 484
Custom Comparator class that
compares two Time2 ob-
jects 608
custom drawing area 431
custom tag libraries 855
custom tags 855
custom type 982
customized subclass of JPanel
431
cyclic gradient 482

D

-d compiler option 286
dangling-else problem 93
dashed lines 480

data abstraction 283
data hiding 66
data hierarchy 517, 518
data in support of actions 283
data integrity 266
data provider 911
data representation 283
data structure 203, 267
data tier 853
database 519, 792, 797
table 793
database-driven multitier web
address book xxiii
database management system
(DBMS) 519, 792
datagram packet 745, 768
datagram socket 745, 768
DatagramPacket class 768,
790
getAddress method 771
getData method 771
getLength method 771
getPort method 771
DatagramSocket class 768
receive method 771
send method 772
DataInput interface 550
DataInputStream class 550
DataOutput interface 550
writeBoolean method
550
writeByte method 550
writeBytes method 550
writeChar method 550
writeChars method 550
writeDouble method
550
writeFloat method 550
writeInt method 550
writeLong method 550
writeShort method 550
writeUTF method 550
DataOutputStream class 550
date 166
date and time compositions
999
Date class 1001
declaration 268
date formatting 995
DB2 792
dead state 680
deadlock 721, 725
dealing 215
debugger 1110
break mode 1112
breakpoint 1110
clear command 1123
cont command 1113
defined 1110, 1110
exit command 1119
-g compiler option 1111
inserting breakpoints 1112
jdb command 1112
logic error 1110
next command 1118
print command 1113,
1115

debugger (cont.)
run command 1112, 1114
set command 1114, 1115
step command 1116
step up command 1117
stop command 1112,
1114
suspending program exe-
cution 1114
unwatch command 1119,
1121
watch command 1119
decimal digit 517
decimal integer 995
decimal integer formatting 37
decision 39, 91
decision in the UML 149
decision symbol in the UML 91
declaration 34
class 25, 26
import 34, 36
method 26
declare a constant variable 209
declare a method of a class 57
declare constants with Interfaces 371
decrement of a control variable
120
decrement operator, -- 109,
110
dedicated drawing area 430
deep copy 334
default capacity increment 602
default case 170
default case in a switch
136, 138
default constructor 70, 265,
306
of an anonymous inner
class 417
default exception handler 507
default initial value 67
default keyword 1053
default layout of the content
pane 451
default package 64
default upper bound (Object)
of a type parameter 569
default value 67, 113
define a custom drawing area
431
degree 474
Deitel® Buzz Online newsletter
20
Deitel® Buzz Online newsletter
20
deitel@deitel.com 3
del.icio.us 17
delegation event model 401
delete method of class
StringBuilder 1034
DELETE SQL statement 798,
805, 806
deleteCharAt method of
class String 1034
delimiter for tokens 1040
delimiter string 1040
dependency chart (chapters)
xxiv

dependency injection 961
dependent condition 143
Deploy option in Netbeans
942
deploying a web service 942
Deposit class (ATM case
study) 80, 83, 114, 194,
195, 244, 245, 250, 293,
373, 374, 375
DepositSlot class (ATM case
study) 80, 81, 82, 114, 195,
245, 293
Deprecated link in API 1075
dequeue operation of queue
284
derived class 299
descending order 592
descending sort (DESC) 800,
801
descent 467
descriptive words and phrases
113, 115
deserialized object 541
Design mode in Java Studio
Creator 2 908
Design mode in Netbeans
863, 867
design patterns xxiii, 19
design process 15, 44, 50, 195,
200
design specification 50
Design view in Netbeans 1057
Desktop class 1069
browse method 1069
getDesktop method
1069
isDesktopSupported
method 1069
mail method 1069
open method 1069
destroy method (JavaServer
Faces) 862, 865, 920
dialog box 383, 647
Dialog font 465
DialogInput font 465
diamond in the UML 89
dice game 173
Die-rolling program using arrays instead of switch 212
digit 35, 1037, 1041
digit method of class Character 1037
digitally signed applets 790
Dimension class 638
direct superclass 299, 301
directive 855
DIRECTORIES_ONLY constant
of JFileChooser 555
directory 520, 522
directory name 521
directory separator 288
disconnected RowSet 826
disjoint method of Collections 606, 617
disk 516
disk I/O completion 497
dismiss a dialog 385

dispatch
    a thread **680**
    an event **403**
display a line of text 27
display monitor 454
display output 53
Displaying multiple lines with method `Sys-tem.out.printf` 32
Displaying the `authors` table from the books database 809
Displaying the `authors` table using `JdbcRowSet` 826
`DisplayQueryResults` for querying database books 820
`dispose` method of class `Win-dow` 641
`DISPOSE_ON_CLOSE` constant of interface `WindowCon-stants` 641
distance between values (ran-dom numbers) 172
divide-and-conquer approach 155, 184
divide by zero 8, 491
division 38, 39
division by zero is undefined 284
DNS (domain name system) server 849
DNS lookup 849
do...while repetition state-ment 90, 130, 131, 1053
document 636, **656**
Dojo Toolkit 907, 930
dollar signs ($) 25
domain name system (DNS) server 849
dot (.) separator 59, 129, 156, 274, 480
dotted line in the UML **90**
(double) cast **104**
`Double` class 581
double-precision floating-point number 73
`double` primitive type 35, 73, 101, 1053, 1054
    promotions 164
double quotes, " 27, 30, 31
Double Range Validator JSF component 874
double-selection statement 90
`doubleValue` method of `Num-ber` 583
downcast 358
downcasting 340
drag the scroll box 416
dragging the mouse to high-light 451
`draw` method of class `Graphics2D` **483**
draw shapes 454
`draw3DRect` method of class `Graphics` 470, 473
`drawArc` method of class `Graphics` 474
drawing color 458

Drawing lines, rectangles and ovals 471
drawing on the screen 456
`drawLine` method of class `Graphics` 470
`drawOval` method of class `Graphics` 471, 473
`drawPolygon` method of class `Graphics` 476, 477, 478
`drawPolyline` method of class `Graphics` 476, 478
`drawRect` method of class `Graphics` 470, 483
`drawRoundRect` method of class `Graphics` 472
`drawString` method of class `Graphics` 460
`DriverManager` class **811**
    `getConnection` method **811**
drop-down list 386, **413**
Drop Down List JSF compo-nent 870, 873
dummy value **100**
duplicate key 625
duplicate of datagram 768
dynamic binding 358
dynamic content 4
dynamically resizable array 618, 749

E

EAST constant of `BorderLay-out` 426, 442
EAST constant of class `Grid-BagConstraints` 667
echo character of `JPassword-Field` 394
echoes a packet back to the cli-ent 768
Eclipse Foundation 19
edit a program 7
Edit menu 382
editor 7
element of an array 203, 204
element of chance 167
elided UML diagram 80
eliminate resource leaks 501
`Ellipse2D` class 454
`Ellipse2D.Double` class 480
`Ellipse2D.Float` class 480
ellipsis (. . .) in a method pa-rameter list 239
`else` 92
`else` keyword 1053
emacs 7
email 754
`Employee` abstract superclass 348
`Employee` class hierarchy test program 355
`Employee` class that imple-ments `Payable` 366
`Employee` class with references to other objects 269
employee identification num-ber 517

empty statement (a semicolon, ;) 43, 95, 132
empty string 399, **1016**
`EmptyStackException` class 570, **620**
`EmptyStackException` class declaration 570
`en.wikipedia.org/wiki/IP_address` 849
encapsulation 14, 360
enclosing `try` block 506
end cap **483**
End key 434
"end of data entry" 100
end-of-file (EOF) 756
    indicator **135**
    marker 519
end-of-line (single-line) com-ment, // 24, 27, 35
end-of-stream 756
`EndOfFileException` 549
`endsWith` method of class `String` **1021**
enhanced `for` statement 219
enqueue operation of queue 284
`ensureCapacity` method of class `StringBuilder` **1029**
Enter (or *Return*) key 401
`ENTERED` constant of nested class `EventType` 753
entity-relationship diagram 796
`enum` 176
    constant 270
    constructor 270
    declaration 270
    `EnumSet` class 273
    keyword 176
    `values` method 272
`enum` keyword 1053
enumeration 176
enumeration constant 176
`EnumSet` class 273
    `java.sun.com/javase/6/docs/api/java/util/EnumSet.html` 273
    `range` method 273
environment variable
    CLASSPATH 29
    PATH 28
EOF (end-of-file) 756
equal likelihood 169
Equality and relational opera-tors 40
equality operator == to com-pare `String` objects 1018
equality operators 39
`equals` method of `Arrays` 590
`equals` method of class `String` 1018, 1020
`equals` method of `Object` 334
`equalsIgnoreCase` method of class `String` 1018, 1020
erasure 562, 563, 565

`Error` class 498
Error-Prevention Tips overview xxvii
error-processing code 489
escape character 30, 805
`escape` property of a **Static Text** component 875
escape sequence 31, 35, 525, 1010
    newline, \n 31, 35
event 148, 373, 394, 457
event classes 400
event dispatch thread 726
event driven 394
event-driven process 457
event handler 373, 394
event handling 394, 397, 401
    event source 399
event ID 403
event listener 372, 373, 401, 428
    adapter class 427
    interface 397, 399, 401, 403, 422, 427
event object 401
event processing life cycle 862
event processing lifecycle 860, 865
    `destroy` method 862, 865, 920
    `init` method 862, 865
    `preprocess` method 862, 865
    `prerender` method 862
event processingcycle
    `prerender` method 865
event registration 398
event source 399, 401
`EventListenerList` class 401
`EventObject` class
    `getSource` method 399, 410
`EventType` nested class
    ACTIVATED constant 753
    ENTERED constant 753
    EXITED constant 753
`EventType` nested class of `Hy-perlinkEvent` 753
exception 214, 488
`Exception` class 498
exception handler 494
exception handling 488
Exception-handling example with divide-by-zero 492
exception parameter 494
exceptions
    `ArrayIndexOutOf-BoundsException` 215
execute 28
`execute` method of `JdbcRowSet` 828
`execute` method of the `Exec-utor` interface 686, 687
`executeQuery` method of in-terface `PreparedState-ment` 836

executeQuery method of Statement 812

executeUpdate method of interface PreparedStatement 836

executing an application 9

ExecutionException class 730

Executor interface 686
execute method 686, 687

Executors class 686
newCachedThreadPool method 686

ExecutorService interface 686, 741
awaitTermination-method 692
shutdown method 687
submit method 741

exists method of File 521

exit debugger command 1119

exit method of class System 501

exit method of System 528

exit point
of a control statement 90

EXITED constant of nested class EventType 753

exiting a for statement 140

exp method of Math 157

expanded submenu 647

expiration date of a cookie 884

explicit conversion 104

exponential format 995

exponential method 157

exponential notation 996

exponentiation operator 129

expression 37

extend a class 299

extending a class 365

extends keyword 304, 313, 1053

extensibility 340

Extensible HyperText Markup Language (XHTML) 849

Extensible Hypertext Markup Language (XHTML) 848

extensible language 16, 59, 284

Extensible Markup Language (XML) 854

extensions mechanism (extending Java with additional class libraries) 288

external event 422

extreme programming xxiii, 18

F

f:view element 858

FaceBook 17

factorial 184

Factorial calculations with a recursive method 186

factorial method 185

fairness policy of a lock 720

false 1053

false keyword 39, 91, 92

fault tolerant 36

fault-tolerant program 488

fibonacci method 189

Fibonacci numbers generated with a recursive method 188

Fibonacci series 187, 190

Fibonacci series defined recursively 187

field 14, 65, 517
default initial value 67

Field Detail section in API 1079

field of a class 178, 518

Field Summary section in API 1078

field width 128, 995, 1003

FIFO (first-in, first-out) 284

file 518

File class 520
canRead method 521
canWrite method 521
exists method 521
File methods 521
getAbsolutePath method 522
getName method 522
getParent method 522
getPath method 522
isAbsolute method 521
isDirectory method 521
isFile method 521, 522
lastModified method 522
length method 522
list method 522
used to obtain file and directory information 523

File methods 521

file name 26

Filename extension .jsp 856

file processing 520, 790

File.pathSeparator 525

FileExplorer demo 1072

FileInputStream class 520, 541, 543, 547, 550, 630

FileNotFoundException class 528

FileOutputStream class 520, 541, 543, 550, 630

FileReader class 520, 552

FILES_AND_DIRECTORIES constant of JFileChooser 555

FILES_ONLY constant of JFileChooser 555

FileUtil incubator project 1072

FileWriter class 520, 552

fill method
of Arrays 592
of Collections 606, 613

fill method of Arrays 590

fill method of class Graphics2D 483, 486

fill pattern 483

fill texture 483

fill with color 454

fill3DRect method of class Graphics 470, 473

fillArc method of class Graphics 474

filled-in shape 483

filled rectangle 458

filled three-dimensional rectangle 470

fillOval method of class Graphics 471, 473

fillOval method of Graphics 434

fillPolygon method of class Graphics 477, 478

fillRect method of class Graphics 458, 470, 483

fillRoundRect method of class Graphics 472

filter 550

filter stream 550

FilterInputStream class 550

FilterOutputStream class 550

final
keyword 139, 157, 279
local variable 416
variable initialized with a constructor argument 280, 281
variable must be initialized 281

final class 360

final Classes and methods java.sun.com/docs/books/tutorial/java/IandI/final.html 360

final keyword 209, 360, 696, 1053

final state in the UML 89, 149

final value 121

final variable 209

finalize method 273, 273, 276
of Object 334

finally block 494, 500, 506, 724

finally clause 500, 501, 1053

finally keyword 494

find method of class Matcher 1048

fireTableStructureChanged method of AbstractTableModel 820

firewall 956

first-in, first-out (FIFO) data structure 284

first method of SortedSet 625

firstElement method of Vector 604

five-pointed star 484

fixed text 37
in a format string 32

fixed text in a format string 995

fixed-template data 855

fixed-template text 855

flag value 100

flags 995, 1005

Flickr 17

float
literal suffix F 618

float primitive type 35, 73, 1053, 1054
promotions 164

Floating Dock demo 1072

Floating Dock Toplevel Window incubator project 1072

floating-point constant 128

floating-point literal 74

floating-point number 73, 100, 101, 103, 618, 997
division 104
double precision 73
double primitive type 73
float primitive type 73
single precision 73

floating-point conversion specifiers 1004

floating-point literal
double by default 74

floor method of Math 157

flow of control 96, 103

flow of control in the if…else statement 92

FlowLayout allows components to flow over multiple lines 439

FlowLayout class 391, 438
CENTER constant 442
LEFT constant 442
RIGHT constant 442
setAlignment method 442

flush method
of BufferedOutputStream 551

flush method of class Formatter 782

flush method of class ObjectOutputStream 761

focus 394

focus for a GUI application 637, 653

FocusAdapter class 427

FocusListener interface 427

font
manipulation 456
name 465
size 465
style 465

Font class 408, 454, 465
BOLD constant 464, 465
getFamily method 464, 467
getName method 464, 465

Font class (cont.)
getSize method 464, 465
getStyle method 464, 467
isBold method 464, 467
isItalic method 464, 467
isPlain method 464, 467
ITALIC constant 464, 465
PLAIN constant 464, 465
font information 454
font manipulation 456
font metrics 467
ascent 469
descent 469
height 469
leading 469
font style 407
FontMetrics class 454, 467
getAscent method 468
getDescent method 468
getFontMetrics method 467
getHeight method 468
getLeading method 468
for property of a JSF input field 875
for repetition statement 90, 122, 125, 126, 127, 129, 1053
activity diagram 126
example 125
header 123
for statement
enhanced 219
forDigit method of class Character 1037
foreign key 795, 797
formal parameter 160
formal type parameter 561
format method
of Formatter 531
of String 254
format method of Formatter 1011
format method of String 1011
format specifier 32, 995
%.2f for floating-point numbers with precision 105
%b for boolean values 145
%d 37
%f 75
%s 32
format specifiers
%% 1003
%B 1003
%b 1002
%c 998
%d 995, 996
%E 998
%e 997
%f 75, 998
%G 998
%g 998
%H 1003

format specifiers (cont.)
%h 1003
%n 1003
%o 996
%S 999
%s 995, 998
%X 996
%x 996
format string 32, 995, 1005
formatted output 1002
, (comma) formatting flag 129
%f format specifier 75
– (minus sign) formatting flag 129
0 flag 212, 254
aligning decimal points in output 995
boolean values 145
comma (,) formatting flag 129
conversion character 995
date and time compositions 999
date and time conversion suffix characters 999
dates 995
exponential format 995
field width 128, 995
floating-point numbers 75
inserting literal characters 995
integers in hexadecimal format 995
integers in octal format 995
left justification 995
left justify 129
minus sign (–) formatting flag 129
precision 75, 995
right justification 128, 995
rounding 995
times 995
Formatter class 520, 528, 994, 1011
close method 531
flush method 782
format method 531, 1011
toString method 1011
FormatterClosedException 531
formatting
display formatted data 32
Formatting date and time with conversion character t 1001
Formatting output with class Formatter 1011
fragile software 321
Frame class 640
framework 856
frequency method of Collections 606, 617
FROM SQL clause 798
FullStackException class declaration 569
fully qualified class name 64, 165, 287

function 14
function key 434
Future interface 741
get method 741

G

-g command line option to javac 1111
game playing 167
Game programming xxviii
game programming 19
garbage collection 678
garbage collector 273, 276, 497, 500
gc method of System 278
general class average problem 100
general path 484
generalities 339
generalization in the UML 374
GeneralPath class 454, 484
closePath method 486
lineTo method 486
moveTo method 486
generic class 567
Generic class Stack declaration 567
Generic class Stack test program 570
generic Classes 557
generic collections xxiii
generic interface 563
generic method 557, 560, 566
Generic method maximum after erasure is performed by the compiler 565
Generic method maximum with an upper bound on its type parameter 564
Generic method printArray after erasure is performed by the compiler 563
generics xxiii, 557, 589
? (wildcard type argument) 583
actual type arguments 561
angle brackets (< and >) 561
bound parameter 563
default upper bound (Object) of a type parameter 569
erasure 562
formal type parameter 561
method 560
parameterized class 567
parameterized type 567
scope of a type parameter 569
type parameter 561
type parameter section 561
type variable 561
upper bound of a type parameter 563, 565
upper bound of a wildcard 583
wildcard type argument 583

generics (cont.)
wildcard without an upper bound 585
wildcards 581, 583
get a value 68
GET HTTP request 850
get method
of List 595
of Map 629
get method 68, 260, 266
get method of interface Future 741
get method of interface MessageContext 961
get request 852
getAbsolutePath method of File 522
getActionCommand method of ActionEvent 399, 407
getAddress method of class DatagramPacket 771
getAppletContext method of class Applet 750
getAscent method of class FontMetrics 468
getAttribute method of interface HttpSession 961
getAutoCommit method of interface Connection 846
getBlue method of class Color 458, 460
getByName method of class InetAddress 766
getChars method
of class String 1016
of class StringBuilder 1031
getClass method of Object 334, 359, 392
getClassName method of class StackTraceElement 509
getClassName method of class UIManager.LookAndFeelInfo 655
getClickCount method of MouseEvent 430
getColor method of class Color 458
getColor method of class Graphics 458
getColumnClass method of TableModel 814, 819
getColumnClassName method of ResultSetMetaData 819
getColumnCount method of ResultSetMetaData 812, 819
getColumnCount method of TableModel 814, 819
getColumnName method of ResultSetMetaData 819
getColumnName method of TableModel 814, 819
getColumnType method of ResultSetMetaData 812
getConnection method of DriverManager 811

getContentPane method of JFrame 419
getData method of class DatagramPacket 771
getDefaultSystemTray method of class SystemTray 1072
getDescent method of class FontMetrics 468
getDesktop method of class Desktop 1069
getEventType method of class HyperlinkEvent 753
getFamily method of class Font 464, 467
getFileName method of class StackTraceElement 509
getFont method of class Graphics 465, 465
getFontMetrics method of class FontMetrics 467
getFontMetrics method of class Graphics 468
getGreen method of class Color 458, 460
getHeight method of class FontMetrics 468
getHostName method of class InetAddress 761
getIcon method of JLabel 393
getInetAddress method of class Socket 761
getInputStream method of class Socket 754, 756
getInstalledLookAndFeels method of class UIManager 653
getInstance method of Calendar 1001
getInt method of ResultSet 813
getKeyChar method of KeyEvent 437
getKeyCode method of KeyEvent 437
getKeyModifiersText method of KeyEvent 437
getKeyText method of KeyEvent 437
getLeading method of class FontMetrics 468
getLength method of class DatagramPacket 771
getLineNumber method of class StackTraceElement 509
getLocalHost method of class InetAddress 766, 772
getMaximumSize method of class Component 1056
getMessage method of class Throwable 506
getMethodName method of class StackTraceElement 509

getMinimumSize method of class Component 638, 1056
getModifiers method of InputEvent 437
getName method of 335
getName method of Class 359
getName method of class Font 464, 465
getName method of File 522
getObject method of ResultSet 813, 819
getOptions method of AutoComplete interface 928, 930
getOutputStream method of class Socket 754
getParameter method of class Applet 748
getParent method of File 522
getPassword method of JPasswordField 399
getPath method of File 522
getPoint method of MouseEvent 434
getPort method of class DatagramPacket 771
getPreferredSize method of class Component 638, 1056
getPreferredSize method of class JComponent 660
getProperty method of Properties 629
getRed method of class Color 458, 460
getRequestContext method of interface BindingProvider 972
getResource method of 392
getRow method of ResultSet 819
getRowCount method of TableModel 814, 819
getSelected Index method of JList 419
getSelectedFile method of JFileChooser 555
getSelectedIndex method of JComboBox 417
getSelectedText method of JTextComponent 451
getSelectedValues method of JList 422
getSession method of interface HttpSession 961
getSize method of class Font 464, 465
getSource method of EventObject 399, 410
getStackTrace method of class Throwable 506
getStateChange method of ItemEvent 417
getStyle method of class Font 464, 467
getText method of class JTextComponent 649

getText method of JLabel 393
gettingreal.37signals.com/toc.php 19
getURL method of class HyperlinkEvent 753
getValue method of class JSlider 640
getValueAt method of TableModel 814, 819
getX method of MouseEvent 427
getY method of MouseEvent 427
.gif 392
GIF (Graphics Interchange Format) 392
glass pane 419
GlassFish 941
GlassFish application server Tester web page 943
GlassFish v2 UR2 application server 848, 856, 869
golden mean 187
golden ratio 187
Good Programming Practices overview xxvi
Google 17
Google Maps 18
Gosling, James 4
goto elimination 88
goto statement 88
GradeBook class that contains a courseName instance variable and methods to set and get its value 65
GradeBook class using a two-dimensional array to store grades 233
GradeBook class using an array to store test grades 224
GradeBook class with a constructor to initialize the course name 71
GradeBook constructor used to specify the course name at the time each GradeBook object is created 72
gradient 482
GradientPaint class 454, 482
graph information 211
graphical modeling language (UML) xxiv
Graphical User Interface (GUI) 373
graphical user interface (GUI) 166, 372, 382
design tool 438
graphics 431
Graphics class 433, 434, 454, 456, 478
clearRect method 470
draw3DRect method 470, 473
Graphics class (cont.)
drawArc method 474
drawLine method 470

drawOval method 471, 473
drawPolygon method 476, 477, 478
drawPolyline method 476, 478
drawRect method 470, 483
drawRoundRect method 472
drawString method 460
fill3DRect method 470, 473
fillArc method 474
fillOval method 434, 471, 473
fillPolygon method 477, 478
fillRect method 458, 470, 483
fillRoundRect method 472
getColor method 458
getFont method 465, 465
getFontMetrics method 468
setColor method 483
setFont method 465
graphics context 456
graphics in a platform-independent manner 456
Graphics Interchange Format (GIF) 392
Graphics method setFont changes the drawing font 465
Graphics2D class 454, 479, 483, 486
draw method 483
fill method 483, 486
rotate method 486
setPaint method 482
setStroke method 483
translate method 486
greedy quantifier 1046
grid 445
grid for GridBagLayout layout manager 666
Grid Panel JSF component 872
GridBagConstraints class 667, 672
anchor field 667
BOTH constant 667
CENTER constant 667
EAST constant 667
gridheight field 668
gridwidth field 668
gridx field 668
gridy field 668
HORIZONTAL constant 667
instance variables 667
NONE constant 667
NORTH constant 667
NORTHEAST constant 667
GridBagConstraints class (cont.)
NORTHWEST constant 667

RELATIVE constant 672
REMAINDER constant 672
SOUTH constant 667
SOUTHEAST constant 667
SOUTHWEST constant 667
VERTICAL constant 667
weightx field 668
weighty field 668
WEST constant 667
GridBagConstraints constants RELATIVE and RE-MAINDER 673
GridBagLayout class 662, 666, 668, 672
    setConstraints method 672
GridBagLayout layout manager 669
gridheight field of class GridBagConstraints 668
GridLayout class 438, 445
GridLayout containing six buttons 445
gridwidth field of class GridBagConstraints 668
gridx field of class GridBag-Constraints 668
gridy field of class GridBag-Constraints 668
GROUP BY 798
group method of class Match-er 1049
grouper.ieee.org/groups/754/ 1054
GroupLayout 1055
    default layout manager in Netbeans 1055
GroupLayout class 1055
    BASELINE alignment constant 1056
    CENTER alignment constant 1056
    groups 1056
    LEADING aligning components 1056
    LEADING alignment constant 1056
    parallel layout of GUI components 1055
    recommended GUI design guidelines 1056
    sequential horizontal orientation 1055
    sequential layout of GUI components 1055
    spacing between components 1056
    TRAILING alignment constant 1056
GroupLayout.Group class 1056
    addGap method 1056
GroupLayout.Parallel-Group class 1056
    addGap method 1056
GroupLayout.Sequential-Group class 1056

addGap method 1056
groups in GroupLayout 1056
guard condition in the UML 91, 92, 149
guarding code with a lock 688
GUI (Graphical User Interface) 372, 373
    component 382, 383
    design tool 438
guide lines (Netbeans) 1058, 1059

H

H conversion character 1002
h conversion character 1002
handle an exception 492
handshake point 754, 767
has-a relationship 82, 267, 300
hash bucket 626
hash table 622, 626
hashCode method of Object 335
hashing 626
HashMap class 625, 749, 891, 892, 899, 900
    get method 891
    keySet method 629, 903
    put method 891
HashMaps and Maps 627
HashSet class 622
HashSet used to remove duplicate values from an array of strings 622
Hashtable class 625, 626
hash-table collisions 626
hasMoreTokens method of class StringTokenizer 1041
hasMoreTokens method of StringTokenizer 629
hasNext method
    of class Scanner 136
    of Iterator 596, 599
    of Scanner 531
hasPrevious method of Lis-tIterator 599
header 123
headSet method of TreeSet 625
heavyweight components 387
height 467
height of a rectangle in pixels 459
Help link in API 1075
helper method 138
hexadecimal integer 995
hidden
    element 884
    field 884
"hidden" fields 178
hidden form element 884
hide a dialog 385
hide implementation details 256, 283, 284
Home key 434
HORIZONTAL constant of class GridBagConstraints 667
horizontal coordinate 454

horizontal gap space 444
horizontal glue 664
horizontal JSlider component 636
horizontal scrollbar policy 452
horizontal tab 31
HORIZONTAL_SCROLLBAR_ALWAYS constant of JScrollPane 451
HORIZONTAL_SCROLLBAR_AS_NEEDED constant of JScrollPane 451
HORIZONTAL_SCROLLBAR_NEVER constant of JScrollPane 452
host 849
host name 766
hostname 849
hot spots in bytecode 8
HourlyEmployee class derived from Employee 351
HTML document 748
HTML document to load Si-teSelector applet 746
HTML frame 750
HTTP (HyperText Transfer Protocol) 745
HTTP (Hypertext Transfer Protocol) 883
    being used with firewalls 956
    header 851
    method 850
    request type 851
    stateless protocol 883
    transaction 850
HttpServletRequest class 893
HttpServletResponse class 892
HttpSession 961
HttpSession interface
    getAttribute method 961
    getSession method 961
    setAttribute method 961
hue 463
HugeInteger web service that performs operations on large integers 938
hybrid language 4
hyperlink 750, 752
Hyperlink JSF component 870, 874
HyperlinkEvent class 750
    EventType nested class 753
    getEventType method 753
    getURL method 753
HyperlinkListener interface 753
    hyperlinkUpdate method 753
hyperlinkUpdate method of interface HyperlinkLis-tener 753

HyperText Transfer Protocol (HTTP) 745, 851
Hypertext Transfer Protocol (HTTP) 883

I

I/O performance enhancement 550
icon 385
Icon interface 392
Icon Service incubator project 1072
IDE 7
identifier 25, 35
identity column 830
IDENTITY keyword (SQL) 830
IDEs
    Netbeans 935
IEEE 754 floating point 1054
if single-selection statement 39, 42, 90, 91, 132, 1053
    activity diagram 91
if...else double-selection statement 90, 91, 92, 103, 132
    activity diagram 92
ignoring element zero 214
IllegalMonitorStateEx-ception class 707, 721
IllegalStateException 535
Image JSF component 870, 873
ImageIcon class 392
immutable 276, 1016
immutable String object 1016
implement an interface 338, 362, 369
implement multiple Interfaces 365
implementation-dependent code 256
implementation inheritance 346
implementation of a function 347
implementation phase 378
implementation process 195, 291
implements 1053
implements keyword 362, 366
implicit conversion 104
import declaration 34, 36, 64, 165, 286, 1053
increment 127
    a control variable 121
    expression 140
    of a for statement 125
increment and decrement operators 110
increment of a control variable 120
increment operator, ++ 109
indefinite postponement 681, 725
indefinite repetition 101

indentation 26, 92, 93

independent software vendor 5

independent software vendor (ISV) 333

index (subscript) 203

Index link in API 1075

index of a JComboBox 416

index zero 204

indexOf method of class String 1022

indexOf method of Vector 605

IndexOutOfBoundsException class 613

indirect recursion 184

indirect recursive call 184

indirect superclass 299, 301

InetAddress class 761, 766, 771, 772

 getByName method 766

 getHostName method 761

 getLocalHost method 766, 772

infinite loop 96, 104, 124, 125, 770, 774

infinite recursion 187, 192, 194

infinity symbol 797

information hiding 14, 283, 360

information tier 853

inheritance 14, 299, 304, 373, 374, 376, 377, 378

 Examples 300

 extends keyword 304, 313

 hierarchy 301

 hierarchy for university CommunityMembers 301

 implementation vs. interface inheritance 346

 multiple 299

 single 299

inheritance hierarchy 344

_init method 862, 891

init method 862, 865

initComponents autogenerated method in Netbeans 1066

initial capacity of a Vector 604

initial state in the UML 89, 148, 149

initial value of an attribute 116

initial value of control variable 120

initialize a variable in a declaration 35

initializer list 207

Initializing an array using command-line arguments 241

Initializing the elements of an array to zero 207

Initializing the elements of an array with an array initializer 208

Initializing two-dimensional arrays 231

initializing two-dimensional arrays in declarations 231

initiate an action 642

inlining method calls 360

inner class 398, 410, 433, 648

 anonymous 416

 can access the members of its top-level class 407

 object of 410

 relationship between an inner class and its top-level class 410

INNER JOIN SQL clause 798, 802

innermost square brackets 214

input 884

input data from the keyboard 53

Input data from user and validates it using the ValidateInput class 1043

input dialog 383

input/output 520

input/output package 166

input/output operations 89

InputEvent class 423, 430, 434

 getModifiers method 437

 isAltDown method 430, 437

 isControlDown method 437

 isMetaDown method 430, 437

 isShiftDown method 437

InputMismatchException class 491, 494

InputStream class 541, 550, 630, 754, 755, 756

InputStreamReader class 552

Inputting and outputting floating-point numbers with Account objects 76

insert an item into a container object 267

insert method of class StringBuilder 1034

INSERT SQL statement 798, 804

insertElementAt method of Vector 604

inserting literal characters in the output 995

insertion point 592, 615

installation instructions (JDK) java.sun.com/javase/ 6/webnotes/install/index.html 5

instance (non-static) method 278

instance of a class 66

instance variable 56, 65, 66, 74, 157

instanceof operator 358, 1053

instantiate 14

instantiating an object of a class 57

int keyword 1054

int primitive type 35, 101, 109, 132, 1053

 promotions 164

integer 33

 division 100

 mathematics 283

 quotient 38

 value 35

integer array 207

Integer class 242

Integer class 385, 581

 parseInt method 242, 385

integer conversion characters 995

integer division 38

integers

 suffix L 618

integral expression 138

integrated development environment 7

intelligent consumer electronic device 4

interaction between a web service client and a web service 936

interaction diagram in the UML 245

interactions among objects 242, 246, 283

interest rate 127

interface 14, 338, 362, 370, 812

 Runnable 372

 Serializable 372

 SwingConstants 373

 tagging interface 542

interface declaration 361

interface inheritance 346

interface keyword 361, 370, 1053

Interfaces 361

 ActionListener 403

 AppletContext 745

 BlockingQueue 703

 CachedRowSet 826, 911

 Callable 741

 CallableStatement 845

 ChangeListener 639

 CharSequence 1048

 Cloneable 334

Interfaces (cont.)

 Collection 589, 593, 605

 Comparable 372, 563, 606, 1020

 Comparator 606

 ComponentListener 427

 Condition 720, 722

 Connection 811, 813, 818

 ContainerListener 427

 DataInput 550

 DataOutput 550

 Executor 686

 ExecutorService 686, 741

 FocusListener 427

 Future 741

 HyperlinkListener 753

 Icon 392

 ItemListener 410, 649

 Iterator 593

 JdbcRowSet 826

 KeyListener 403, 427, 434, 437

 LayoutManager 438, 442

 LayoutManager2 442

 List 589, 599

 ListIterator 594

 ListSelectionListener 419, 749

 Lock 720

 Map 589, 625

 MessageContext 961

 MouseInputListener 422, 427

 MouseListener 403, 422, 427, 651

 MouseMotionListener 403, 422, 427

 MouseWheelListener 423

 ObjectInput 541

 ObjectOutput 541

 PreparedStatement 845

 PropertyChangeListener 737

 Queue 589, 593, 621, 703

 RequestContext 972

 ResultSet 812

 ResultSetMetaData 812

 RowSet 825

 Runnable 683, 783

 Serializable 541

 Servlet 854

 Set 589, 593, 622

 SortedMap 625

 SortedSet 623

 Statement 813

 SwingConstants 392, 638

 TableModel 813

Interfaces (cont.)
WebServiceContext 961
WindowConstants **641**
WindowListener 427, **641**
internal data representation 284
internal frame closable 660
internal frame maximizable 660
internal frame minimizable 660
internal frame resizable 660
internalVirtualForms property of a **Table** 911
internationalization 166
Internet 3, 745
Internet address 771
Internet Business Initiative 17
Internet domain name in reverse order 286
Internet telephony 17
interrupt method of class Thread **684**
InterruptedException class **684**
intrinsic lock **688**
Invoice class that implements Payable 364
invoke a method 70
IOException 546
IP address **849**
IP address of the server 766
is-a relationship 300, 339
isAbsolute method of File 521
isActionKey method of KeyEvent 437
isAltDown method of InputEvent 430, 437
isBold method of class Font 464, 467
isControlDown method of InputEvent 437
isDefined method of class Character 1035
isDesktopSupported method of class Desktop 1069
isDigit method of class Character 1035
isDirectory method of File 521
isEmpty method of Map 629
isEmpty method of Stack 620
isEmpty method of Vector 605
isFile method of File 521, 522
isItalic method of class Font 464, 467
isJavaIdentifierPart method of class Character 1035
isJavaIdentifierStart method of class Character 1035
isLetter method of class Character 1036
isLetterOrDigit method of class Character 1036

isLowerCase method of class Character 1037
isMetaDown method of InputEvent 430, 437
isMetaDown method of MouseEvent 430
isPlain method of class Font 464, 467
isPopupTrigger method of class MouseEvent **651**
isSelected method of class AbstractButton **649**
isSelected method of JCheckBox 410
isShiftDown method of InputEvent 437
isUpperCase method of class Character 1037
ITALIC constant of class Font 464, 465
ItemEvent class 410, 413
getStateChange method 417
ItemListener interface 410, 649
itemStateChanged method 410, 649
itemStateChanged method of interface ItemListener 410, 649
iterating (looping) 99
iteration 192
of a loop 120, 140
Iterative factorial solution 192
iterative model 48
iteratively 185
iterator 345, 588
iterator class 345
Iterator interface 593
hasNext method 596
next method 596
remove method 596
iterator method of Collection 596

J

Jacobson, Ivar 15, 16
Jacopini, G. 88
JApplet class 641
java 8
Java 2 2
Java 2D (java.sun.com/products/java-media/2D/index.html) 479
Java 2D API 454, 479
Java 2D shapes 480
Java Abstract Window Toolkit (AWT) package 166
Java Abstract Window Toolkit Event package 166
Java Abstract Window Toolkit Package (AWT) 166
Java API 155, 372

Java API documentation 9, 37, 1073
download from java.sun.com 282
java.sun.com/javase/6/docs/api/ 282
Java API Documentation (java.sun.com/javase/6/docs/) 5
Java API Interfaces 372
Java Applet Package 165
Java Application Programming Interface (Java API) 34, 155, 165
Java applications programming interface (API) 5
Java Assessment and Certification xxviii
Java BluePrints **856**
Java class libraries 5
Java class library 34, **155**
Java Collections Framework 557
java command 9, 23
-splash option 1067
Java compiler 7
Java DB xxii, 793, 828, 907
Java DB Developer's Guide developers.sun.com/docs/javadb/10.4.2.0/devguide/derbydev.pdf 830
Java debugger 1110
Java Design Patterns xxviii
Java Desktop Integration Components (JDIC) xxiii
Java development environment 6
Java Development Kit (JDK) 2
Java download (java.sun.com/javase/downloads/index.jsp) 2
Java EE 5 xxviii, 856
Java EE 5 (java.sun.com/javaee) 854
Java Enterprise Edition (Java EE) 3, 854
Java Enterprise Edition 5 856
.java extension 7
.java file name extension 25, 57
Java fonts
Dialog 465
DialogInput 465
Monospaced 465
SansSerif 465
Serif 465
Java Foundation Classes (JFC) 386
Java HotSpot compiler 8
Java Input/Output Package 166
java interpreter 28
Java Keywords 1053
Java Language Package 166
Java Micro Edition (Java ME) 3
Java Networking Package **166**

Java Resource Centers at www.deitel.com/ResourceCenters.html 28
Java SE 6 xxviii
Java SE 6 API documentation (java.sun.com/javase/6/docs/api/) 165, 167
Java SE 6 package overview (java.sun.com/javase/6/docs/api/overview-summary.html) 167
Java SE Development Kit (JDK) 24
Java SE Development Kit 6.0 (JDK 6.0) 28
Java Security API 790
Java Standard Edition 6 ("Mustang") xxii
Java Standard Edition 6 (Java SE 6) 2
Java Studio Creator 2
binding a JSF **Table** to a database table 910
Java Swing Event Package 167
Java Swing GUI Components Package 166
Java Text Package 166
Java Utilities Package 166
Java Virtual Machine (JVM) 7, 9, 23
java.applet package 165
java.awt package 166, 387, 456, 457, 476, 479, 652
java.awt.color package 479
java.awt.event package 166, 167, 400, 402, 427, 437
java.awt.font package 479
java.awt.geom package 479, 480
java.awt.image package 479
java.awt.image.renderable package 479
java.awt.print package 479
java.beans package 737
java.io package 166, **520**
java.lang package 36, 156, 166, 278, 304, 333, 683, 1014
imported in every Java program 36
java.net package 166, 744
java.sql package 810, 812
java.sun.com 167
java.sun.com/docs/books/tutorial/java/IandI/final.html 360
java.sun.com/j2se/1.5.0/docs/api/java/util/Vector.html 602
java.sun.com/j2se/1.5.0/docs/api/javax/swing/JOptionPane.html 385

java.sun.com/j2se/5.0/ docs/api/java/awt/ Component.html 388, 389, 520, 521

java.sun.com/j2se/5.0/ docs/api/java/util/ Stack.html 618

java.sun.com/j2se/5.0/ docs/guide/collec- tions 588

java.sun.com/javase/6/ docs/api/ 37, 282

java.sun.com/javase/6/ docs/api/index.html 9

java.sun.com/javase/6/ docs/api/java/util/ Formatter.html 999, 1011

java.sun.com/javase/6/ docs/api/java/util/ Scanner.html 274

java.sun.com/javase/6/ docs/technotes/ guides/jdbc/get- start/GettingStart- edTOC.fm.html 813

java.sun.com/javase/6/ download.jsp 9

java.sun.com/javase/ downloads/index.jsp 37

java.sun.com/products/ java-media/2D/in- dex.html 479

java.sun.com/products/ java-media/2D/in- dex.html (Java 2D) 479

java.text package 166

java.util package 34, 166, 167, 581, 589, 618, 1001, 1014, 1040
Calendar class **1001**
Date class **1001**

java.util.concurrent package 686, 703, 741

java.util.concur- rent.locks package 720

java.util.prefs package **629**

java.util.regex package 1014

Java's view of a file of *n* bytes 519

Java2D API 479

Java2D general paths 484

Java2D shapes 480

JavaBean 855, 856, 859

javac compiler 7, 28

Javadoc comment 24, 849

javadoc Tool Home Page at java.sun.com/j2se/ javadoc 24

javadoc utility program 24

JavaScript 856

JavaServer Faces (JSF) xxii, 856
Button component 870, 874
components 856

JavaServer Faces (JSF) (cont.)
Drop Down List compo- nent 870, 873
Grid Panel component 872
Hyperlink component 870, 874
Image component 870, 873
Label component 870, 875
Message component 875
Message Group com- ponent 912
Meta component 868
Radio Button Group component 870, 874
Static Text component 858, 860, 870
Table component 908, 910
Text Area component 892
Text Field component 870, 873

JavaServer Pages (JSP) 854, 856
action 855
directive 855
root element 858
scripting element 855
XML declaration 858
xmlns attributes 858

JavaServer Pages Standard Tag Library (JSTL) 855

javax.faces.validators package 874

javax.servlet package 854

javax.servlet.http pack- age 854, 892, 893

javax.servlet.jsp package 855

javax.serv- let.jsp.tagext package 855

javax.sql.rowset package 826

javax.swing package 166, 167, 383, 386, 392, 401, 404, 451, 461, 641, 653, 660

javax.swing.event package 167, 401, 419, 427, 639

javax.swing.table package 814, 825

JAX-WS 936

JBoss Application Server 941

JButton class 386, 404, 407, 445

JCheckBox buttons and item events 408

JCheckBox class 386, 407
isSelected method 410

JCheckBoxMenuItem class 641, 642, 649

JColorChooser 462

JColorChooser class 461, 463

showDialog method 462

JColorChooser dialog 461

JComboBox class 386, 414, 668
getSelectedIndex method 417
setMaximumRowCount method 416

JComboBox that displays a list of image names 414

JComponent class 388, 389, 391, 401, 414, 417, 431, 447, 454
getPreferredSize method 660
listenerList field 401
paintComponent meth- od 431, 454, 637, 638
repaint method 457
setForeground method 649
setOpaque method 431, 434
setToolTipText meth- od 391

jdb command 1112

JDBC
API 793, 809, 845
driver 793, 811

JDBC 4 xxii

JDBC driver type 811

JDBC drivers
developers.sun.com/ product/jdbc/ drivers/ 793

JDBC information
java.sun.com/javase/ technologies/da- tabase/index.jsp 793

JDBC website 811

jdbc:db2j:books 811

jdbc:mysql://localhost/ books 811

JdbcRowSet interface 826
close method 828
execute method 828
setCommand method 828
setPassword method 828
setUrl method 828
setUsername method 828

JdbcRowSetImpl class 828

JDesktopPane class 656

JDialog class 648

JDIC (Java Desktop Integra- tion Components)
addTrayIcon method of class SystemTray 1072
browse method of class Desktop 1069
browser package demo 1072
Demos 1072
Desktop class **1069**
FileExplorer demo 1072

JDIC (cont.)
FileUtil incubator project 1072
Floating Dock demo 1072
Floating Dock Toplevel Window incubator project 1072
getDefaultSystem- Tray method of class SystemTray 1072
getDesktop method of class Desktop 1069
Icon Service incubator project 1072
Incubator Projects 1072
isDesktopSupported method of class Desk- top 1069
java command –splash option 1067
mail method of class Desktop 1069
Music Player Control API incubator project 1072
open method of class Desktop 1069
removeTrayIcon meth- od of class System- Tray 1072
SaverBeans Screensaver SDK incubator project 1072
–splash command-line option to the java command 1067
splash screen 1067
SplashScreen class **1069**
SystemInfo incubator proj- ect 1072
SystemTray class **1072**
Tray icons 1072
TrayIcon class **1072**
TrayIcon package demo 1072
Wallpaper API demo 1072

JDK 6.0 (Java SE Development Kit 6.0) 28

JDK installation instructions
java.sun.com/javase/ 6/webnotes/in- stall/index.html 5

JEditorPane class 750
setPage method 752

Jesse James Garrett 920

JFC (Java Foundation Classes) 386

JFileChooser class 552
CANCEL_OPTION constant 555
FILES_AND_DIRECTORIE S constant 555
FILES_ONLY constant 555
getSelectedFile meth- od 555
setFileSelection- Mode method 554
showOpenDialog meth- od 555

JFileChooser dialog 552

JFrame class 640
  add method 392
  EXIT_ON_CLOSE 393
  getContentPane method 419
  setDefaultCloseOperation method 393, 641
  setJMenuBar method 641, 648
  setSize method 393
  setVisible method 393
JFrame.EXIT_ON_CLOSE 393
JInternalFrame class 656, 660
JIT compiler 8
JLabel class 386, 389
  getIcon method 393
  getText method 393
  setHorizontalAlignment method 392
  setHorizontalTextPosition method 393
  setIcon method 392, 393
  setText method 393
  setVerticalAlignment method 392
  setVerticalTextPosition method 393
JLabels with text and icons 389
JList class 386, 417
  addListSelectionListener method 419
  getSelected Index method 419
  getSelectedValues method 422
  setFixedCellHeight method 422
  setFixedCellWidth method 422
  setListData method 422
  setSelectionMode method 419
  setVisibleRowCount method 419
JList that allows multiple selections 420
JList that displays a list of colors 417
JMenu class 641, 642, 649, 660
  add method 647
  addSeparator method 648
JMenuBar class 641, 642, 648, 660
  add method 648
JMenuItem class 641, 642, 660
JMenus and mnemonics 642
JOIN_ROUND constant of class BasicStroke 484
joining database tables 795, 802
Joint Photographic Experts Group (JPEG) 392

JOptionPane class 383, 384
  constants for message dialogs 386
  PLAIN_MESSAGE constant 385
  showInputDialog method 384
  showMessageDialog method 385
JOptionPane constants for message dialogs
  JOptionPane.ERROR_MESSAGE 386
  JOption-Pane.INFORMATION_MESSAGE 386
  JOption-Pane.PLAIN_MESSAGE 386
  JOption-Pane.QUESTION_MESSAGE 386
  JOptionPane.WARNING_MESSAGE 386
JPanel class 386, 430, 431, 438, 447, 637
JPanel subclass for drawing circles of a specified diameter 637
JPanel with five JButtons in a GridLayout attached to the SOUTH region of a BorderLayout 447
JPasswordField class 394, 399
  getPassword method 399
.jpeg 392
JPEG (Joint Photographic Experts Group) 392
.jpg 392
JPopupMenu class 649, 651
  show method 651
JPopupMenu for selecting colors 650
JProgressBar class 737
JRadioButton class 407, 410, 413
JRadioButtonMenuItem class 641, 642, 649, 651
JRadioButtons and ButtonGroups 411
JScrollPane class 419, 422, 451, 451
  HORIZONTAL_SCROLLBAR_ALWAYS constant 451
  HORIZONTAL_SCROLLBAR_AS_NEEDED constant 451
  HORIZONTAL_SCROLLBAR_NEVER constant 452
  setHorizontalScrollBarPolicy method 451
  VERTICAL_SCROLLBAR_ALWAYS constant 451
  VERTICAL_SCROLLBAR_AS_NEEDED constant 451
  VERTICAL_SCROLLBAR_NEVER constant 452

JScrollPane scrollbar policies 451
JSF
  for property of an input field 875
JSF (JavaServer Faces) 856
JSF components 856, 860
JSF elements
  webjsfui:staticText 912
  webuijsf:table 912
  webuijsf:tableColumn 912
  webuijsf:tableRowGroup 912
JSF Expression Language 859
JSlider class 636, 637, 1056
  block increment 637
  getValue method 640
  major tick marks 636
  minor tick marks 636
  setInverted method 637
  setMajorTickSpacing method 638
  setPaintTicks method 638
  setVerticalScrollBarPolicy method 451
  snap-to ticks 636
  thumb 636
  tick marks 636
JSlider value used to determine the diameter of a circle 639
JSP (JavaServer Pages) 854
JSP container 855
.jsp filename extension 856
jsp:directive.page element 858
jsp:root element 858
JSTL (JavaServer Pages Standard Tag Library) 855
JTabbedPane class 660, 666
  addTab method 660
  SCROLL_TAB_LAYOUT constant 666
  TOP constant 666
JTabbedPane used to organize GUI components 661
JTable class 813
  RowFilter 825
  setRowFilter method 825
  setRowSorter method 825
  TableRowSorter 825
JTable sorting and filtering xxiii
JTextArea class 449, 451, 668, 670
  setLineWrap method 451
JTextComponent class 394, 397, 449, 451
  getSelectedText method 451
  getText method 649
  setEditable method 397

  setText method 451
JTextField class 386, 394, 398, 401, 449
  addActionListener method 398
JTextFields and JPasswordFields 394
JToggleButton class 407
just-in-time compilation 8
just-in-time (JIT) compiler 8

K

key constant 437, 437
key event 403, 434
Key event handling 435
key/value pair 626, 891, 899
KeyAdapter class 427
keyboard 33, 383
KeyEvent class 403, 434
  getKeyChar method 437
  getKeyCode method 437
  getKeyModifiersText method 437
  getKeyText method 437
  isActionKey method 437
KeyListener interface 403, 427, 434
  keyPressed method 434, 437
  keyReleased method 434
  keyTyped method 434
Keypad class (ATM case study) 50, 80, 81, 82, 195, 243, 244, 245, 247, 293, 296
keyPressed method of KeyListener 434, 437
keyReleased method of KeyListener 434
keySet method of class HashMap 903
keySet method of HashMap 629
keySet method of Properties 630
keyTyped method of KeyListener 434
keyword 25, 90
Keywords
  abstract 343
  boolean 92, 1115
  case 136
  catch 494
  char 35
  class 25, 58
  default 136
  do 90
  else 90
  enum 176
  extends 304, 313
  false 92, 1053
  final 139, 157, 209, 696
  finally 494
  float 35
  for 90
  if 39, 42, 90
  implements 362
  import 34

Keywords (cont.)
    instanceof 358
    interface 361
    new 59, 205, 206
    null 70, 205, 1053
    private 66, 266
    public 25, 57, 58, 66
    reserved but not used by
        Java 1053
    return 65, 163
    static 129
    super 303, 327
    switch 90
    synchronized 678, **688**
    table of Keywords and re-
        served words 1053
    this 257, 278
    throw 504
    true 92, 1053
    try 494
    void 26, 58
    while 90
Koenig, Andrew 488

L

label 382, **389**
label in a switch 136
Label JSF component 870,
    875
labels for tick marks 636
LAMP 19
language package 166
last-in, first-out (LIFO) order
    573
last method of ResultSet
    819
last method of SortedSet
    625
lastElement method of Vec-
    tor 604
last-in, first-out (LIFO) 163
lastIndexOf method of class
    String 1022
last-in-first-out (LIFO) 283
lastModified method of
    File 522
late binding 358
layout manager 391, 426, 438,
    447, 1055
    BorderLayout 426
    FlowLayout 391
layoutContainer method of
    LayoutManager 442
LayoutManager interface
    438, 442
    layoutContainer meth-
        od 442
LayoutManager2 interface
    442
lazy quantifier **1046**
leading 467
LEADING alignment constant
    in GroupLayout 1056
left brace, { 26, 34
LEFT constant of FlowLayout
    442
left justification 995
left justified 92, 392, 439

left justify output **129**
left justifying strings in a field
    1006
left-mouse-button click 430
Left, center and right mouse-
    button clicks 428
length field of an array 204
length method of class
    String 1016
length method of class
    StringBuilder 1029
length method of File 522
Length Validator 912
Length Validator JSF com-
    ponent 874, 879
letter 517
lexicographical comparison
    1019, 1020
library classes 5
life-cycle methods 862
life cycle of a thread 679, 680
life-cycle methods 860, 865
    destroy 862, 865
    init 862, 865
    preprocess 862, 865
    prerender 862, 865
lifeline of an object in a UML
    sequence diagram 247
LIFO (last-in, first-out) 163,
    283
LIFO (last-in, first-out) order
    573
lightweight GUI component
    387, 640, 649
LIKE SQL clause 799, 800,
    802
line 454, 470, 478
line join 483
line wrapping 451
Line2D class 454, 484
Line2D.Double class 480
LinearGradientPaint class
    482
LineNumberReader class 551
lineTo method of class Gen-
    eralPath 486
linked list 267, 599
LinkedList class 594, 615
    add method 601
    addFirst method 601
    addLast method 601
Linux 7, 19, 27, 528
list 416
List interface 589, 593, 599,
    606, 607, 613
    add method 595
    addAll method 599
    clear method 599
    get method 595
    listIterator method
        599
    size method 595, 599
    subList method 599
    toArray method 600
list method of File 522, 525
list method of Properties
    630
List method toArray 600
listen for events 399

listenerList field of JCom-
    ponent 401
ListIterator interface 594
    hasPrevious method
        599
    set method 599
listIterator method of
    List 599
Lists and ListIterators
    597
ListSelectionEvent class
    417
ListSelectionListener
    interface 419, 749
    valueChanged method
        419
ListSelectionModel class
    419
    MULTIPLE_INTERVAL_
        SELECTION constant
        419
    MULTIPLE_INTERVAL_SE
        LECTION constant 420,
        422
    SINGLE_INTERVAL_ SE-
        LECTION constant 419
    SINGLE_INTERVAL_SELE
        CTION constant 420,
        422
    SINGLE_SELECTION con-
        stant 419
literals
    floating point 74
live-code approach xxvi, 2
load factor **626**
load method of Properties
    630
loading a document from a
    URL into a browser 746
local variable 64, 98, 178, 180,
    259
locale 166
localhost 849
localhost (127.0.0.1) ad-
    dress 761
localization **388**
lock an object 709, 710
Lock interface 720
    lock method 720, 724
    newCondition method
        720, 722
    unlock method 720, 724
lock method of interface Lock
    720, 724
log method of Math 157
logarithm 157
logic error 36, 123, 385, 1110
logical complement operator, !
    144
logical input operations 551
logical negation, ! 144, 145
logical negation, or logical
    NOT (!) operator truth ta-
    ble 145
logical operators 142, 144, 145
logical output operations 551
long
    literal suffix L 618
long keyword 1053, 1054
long promotions 164

Long Range Validator JSF
    component 874
look-and-feel 387, 388, 438,
    652
Look-and-Feel Observations
    overview xxvii
Look-and-feel of a Swing-based
    GUI 653
look-and-feel of an application
    387
LookAndFeelInfo nested
    class of class UIManager
    653
lookingAt method of class
    Matcher 1048
loop 96
    body 130
    continuation condition 90
    counter 120
    infinite 96, 104
loop-continuation condition
    120, 121, 122, 124, 125,
    126, 130, 131, 140, 215
loopback address 761
lowercase letter 25, 517
lowered rectangle 473

M

m-by-*n* array 229
Mac OS X 7, 27, 528
Macintosh 456
Macintosh look-and-feel 653
magnetic tape 516
mail method of class Desktop
    1069
main method 26, 27, 34, 59
main thread 685
major tick marks of JSlider
    636
make your point (game of
    craps) 173
making decisions 53
MalformedURLException
    class 749
many-to-many relationship
    797
many-to-one relationship in the
    UML 83
Map interface 589, 625
    containsKey method
        629
    get method 629
    isEmpty method 629
    put method 629
    size method 629
mappings of SQL types to Java
    types 813
mark an object for garbage col-
    lection 273, 275, 278
mashups 18
Matcher class 1014, **1048**
    find method 1048
    group method 1049
    lookingAt method 1048
    matches method 1048

Matcher class (cont.)
    replaceAll method
        1048
    replaceFirst method
        1048
matcher method of class Pat-
    tern 1048
matches method of class
    Matcher 1048
matches method of class Pat-
    tern 1048
matches method of class
    String 1041
matching catch block 494
Math class 156, 987
    abs method 157
    ceil method 157
    cos method 157
    E constant **156**
    exp method 157
    floor method 157
    log method 157
    max method 157
    min method 157
    PI constant **156**
    pow method 129, 130,
        156, 157
    random method 167, 168
    sqrt method 156, 157,
        164
    tan method 157
Matisse GUI designer (Net-
    beans) **1055**
max algorithm 613
max method of Collections
    606, **613**
max method of Math 157
maximize a window 389, 659
maximized internal frame 659
maximum method 158
MDI (Multiple Document In-
    terface) 636, **656**
memory buffer 551
memory consumption 588
memory leak 273, 500
memory-space/execution-time
    trade-off 626
memory utilization 626
menu 382, 383, 449, 641, 642
menu bar 382, 383, 642, 648
menu item 642, 647
merge in the UML 150
Merge records from Tables 802
merge symbol in the UML 96
message 14, 70
message (send to an object) 56
message dialog 383, 385
    types 385
Message Group JSF compo-
    nent **912**
message in the UML 242, 245,
    246, 247
Message JSF component 875
message passing in the UML
    247
MessageContext interface
    961
    get method 961
Meta component (JSF) 868

Meta key 430
metadata 812
metal look-and-feel 636, **653**
method 4, **14**, **26**, 291
    declaration 26
    local variable 64
    parameter 61, 63
    parameter list 63
    return type 66
    signature 182
    static 129
method call 56, 160
method-call stack 163
Method calls made within the
    call fibonacci(3) 191
Method calls on the program
    execution stack 191
method declaration 160
Method Detail section in API
    1080
method header 58
method overloading 180
method parameter list 239
Method Summary section in
    API **1078**
methods implicitly final 360
Methods replaceFirst, re-
    placeAll and split 1046
Microsoft Internet Explorer
    790
Microsoft SQL Server 792
Microsoft Windows 135, 456,
    640, 652
Microsoft Windows-style look-
    and-feel 653
middle mouse button 430
middle tier 853
MIME (Multipurpose Internet
    Mail Extensions) **851**, 884
min algorithm 613
min method of Collections
    606, **613**
min method of Math 157
minimize a window 389, 641,
    659
minimize internal frame 659
minor tick marks of JSlider
    636
minus sign (–) formatting flag
    129
minus sign (–) indicating pri-
    vate visibility in the UML
    291
mission-critical computing 495
mnemonic 388, 642, 647, 648
modal dialog 463
modal dialog box 648
model of a software system 81,
    117, 375
modifier key 437
modularizing a program with
    methods 155
modules in Java 155
monetary calculations 130
monitor 688
monitor lock 688
Monospaced Java font 465
Motif look-and-feel 636

Motif-style (UNIX) look-and-
    feel 636, 653
mouse 383
mouse-button click 430
mouse click 428
mouse event 403, 422
mouse event handling 423
mouse events 651
mouse wheel 423
MouseAdapter class 427, 428
mouseClicked method of
    MouseListener 422, 428
mouseDragged method of
    MouseMotionListener
    423, 431
mouseEntered method of
    MouseListener 423
MouseEvent class 403, 423,
    651
    getClickCount method
        430
    getPoint method 434
    getX method 427
    getY method 427
    isAltDown method 430
    isMetaDown method 430
    isPopupTrigger meth-
        od 651
mouseExited method of
    MouseListener 423
MouseInputListener inter-
    face 422, 427
MouseListener interface
    403, 422, 427, 651
    mouseClicked method
        422, 428
    mouseEntered method
        423
    mouseExited method
        423
    mousePressed method
        422, 651
    mouseReleased method
        423, 651
MouseMotionAdapter class
    427, 431
MouseMotionListener in-
    terface 403, 422, 427
    mouseDragged method
        423, 431
    mouseMoved method 423,
        431
mouseMoved method of
    MouseMotionListener
    423, 431
mousePressed method of in-
    terface MouseListener
    651
mousePressed method of
    MouseListener 422
mouseReleased method of
    interface MouseListener
    651
mouseReleased method of
    MouseListener 423

MouseWheelListener inter-
    face 423
    mouseWheelMoved meth-
        od 423
mouseWheelMoved method of
    MouseWheelListener
    423
moveTo method of class Gen-
    eralPath 486
Mozilla 790
Mozilla Foundation 19
MS-DOS prompt 27, 7
multi-button mouse 430
multicast 745, 790
multidimensional array 229,
    230
multilevel priority queue **681**
multiple class declarations
    in one source-code file 259
multiple document interface
    (MDI) 636, **656**, 657
multiple inheritance 299
multiple-line comment 24
multiple-selection list 417,
    419, 420, 422
multiple-selection statement 90
MULTIPLE_INTERVAL_ SE-
    LECTION constant of List-
    SelectionModel 419,
    420, 422
multiplication, * 37, 39
multiplicative operators: *, /
    and % 105
multiplicity 80, 81
Multipurpose Internet Mail
    Extensions (MIME) 851,
    884
multithreaded user interfaces
    xxiii
multithreading 593, **678**
multitier application 852
Music Player Control API incu-
    bator project 1072
mutable data 696
mutator method 266
mutual exclusion **688**
mutually exclusive options 410
MySpace 17
MySQL xxii, **19**, 792
MySQL 5.0 Comminity Edi-
    tion 806
MySQL Connector/J 807
MySQL database 808
mysqld-nt.exe 807

N

n conversion character 1002
n-tier application 852
name attribute of @WebSer-
    vice annotation 941
name collision 287
name conflict 287
name of a param 748
named constant 209
native keyword 1053
natural comparison method
    606
natural logarithm 157

navigability arrow in the UML 292

Navigator window **868**

negative arc angles 474

negative degree 474

nested array initializer 230

nested class 398, 653

  relationship between an inner class and its top-level class 410

Nested Class Summary section in API **1078**

nested control statements **106**, 170

  Examination-results problem 106

nested for statement 211, 231, 232, 233, 236

nested if...else selection statement 93, 94

nested message in the UML 247

nested parentheses 38

nesting 92

NetBeans xxiii

Netbeans **848**

  add a web service reference to an application 947

  creating a Java DB database 909

  Services tab 910

  Show Line Numbers 865

  visual editor **863**

NetBeans 5.5 IDE 1056

  add an event handler 1059

  create a new project 1057

  Design view 1057

  GroupLayout **1055**

  guide lines **1058**, 1059

  Palette window 1057, 1058

  Properties window 1057, 1058

  snap-to alignment grid 1059

Netbeans 5.5 IDE 1055, 1056

  Design view 1057

  initComponents auto-generated method 1066

  Source view 1057

Netbeans IDE **935**

  create a desktop application **947**

  create a web application 937

  New JFrame Form dialog 949

  New Web Application dialog 937

  New Web Service Client dialog 947

  New Web Service dialog 937

  Project Properties dialog 943

  Web Application project **937**

Netbeans Matisse GUI designer **1055**

network message arrival 497

networking 516

networking package 166

New JFrame Form dialog 949

new keyword 59, 205, 206, 1053

new Scanner(System.in) expression 35

new state 679

New Web Application dialog 937

New Web Service Client dialog 947

New Web Service dialog 937

newCachedThreadPool method of class Executors 686

newCondition method of interface Lock 720, 722

newline character 30

newline escape sequence, \n 31, 35, 1015

next method

  of Iterator 596

  of ResultSet 812

  of Scanner 62

nextDouble method of class Scanner 77

nextInt method of class Random 988

nextInt method of Random 168, 169

nextLine method of class Scanner 61

nextLine method of Scanner 629

nextToken method of class StringTokenizer **1041**

nextToken method of StringTokenizer 629

no-argument constructor 262, 264, 265

non-primitive type 69

non-static class member 278

NONE constant of class GridBagConstraints 667

NORTH constant of BorderLayout 426, 442

NORTH constant of class GridBagConstraints 667

NORTHEAST constant of class GridBagConstraints 667

NORTHWEST constant of class GridBagConstraints 667

NoSuchElementException 531, 535

note in the UML 89

Notepad 7

notify method of class Object 707

notify method of Object 335

notifyAll method of class Object 707, 709, 710

notifyAll method of Object 335

noun phrase in requirements document 78, 79, 113

null 1053

null keyword 67, 70, 113, 205, 385

NullPointerException class 488

Num Lock key 434

Number class 581

  doubleValue method 583

number systems 1037

O

object 2

object (or instance) 13, 14, 245

Object class 273, 299, 304, 549

  clone method 334

  equals method 334

  finalize method 334

  getClass method 334, 359, 392

  hashCode method 335

  notify method 335, 707

  notifyAll method 335, 707, 709, 710

  toString method 307, 335

  wait method 335, 707

Object Management Group (OMG) 16

object of a derived class 340

object of a derived class is instantiated 327

object orientation 13

object-oriented analysis and design (OOAD) 15

object-oriented design (OOD) 14, 44, 50, 78, 113, 117, 194, 291

object-oriented design using the UML xxiv

object-oriented language 14

object-oriented programming (OOP) 2, 4, 14, 15, 44, 252, 299

object serialization 541, 761

ObjectInput interface 541

  readObject method 541

ObjectInputStream class 520, 541, 542, 547, 754, 756, 761

object-oriented analysis and design (OOAD) 15

ObjectOutput interface 541

  writeObject method 541

ObjectOutputStream class 520, 541, 542, 630

  close method 547

  flush method 761

octal integer 995

off-by-one error 123

offer method of Priority-Queue 621

OMG (Object Management Group) 16

ON clause 803

one-to-many relationship 797

one-to-one mapping **625**

one-, two- or three-button mouse 430

one-to-many relationship in the UML 83

one-to-one relationship in the UML 83

OOAD (object-oriented analysis and design) 15

OOD (object-oriented design) xxiv, 14, 44, 50, 78, 113, 117, 194

OOP (object-oriented programming) 14, 15, 44, 252, 299

opaque Swing GUI components 431

open a file 519

OPEN constant of class Arc2D 484

open method of class Desktop 1069

open source software xxiii, 19

operand 36, 104

operation compartment in a class diagram 195

operation in the UML 14, 60, 80, 194, 198, 294, 295, 377

operation parameter in the UML 63, 195, 198

operationName attribute of the @WebMethod annotation **941**

operations of an abstract data type 283

operator precedence 39, 189

  operator precedence chart 105

  Operator Precedence Chart Appendix 1050

  rules 39

Operators

  ^, boolean logical exclusive OR 142, **144**

  --, predecrement/postdecrement 109

  --, prefix decrement/postfix decrement 110

  !, logical NOT 142, **144**

  ?:, ternary conditional operator 92, 112

  &, boolean logical AND 142, **144**

  &&, conditional AND 142, 143

  ++, prefix increment/postfix increment 110

  ++, preincrement/postincrement 109

  +=, addition assignment operator 109, 136

Operators (cont.)
= 36, 37, 42
|, boolean logical inclusive OR 142, 144
||, conditional OR 142, 143
arithmetic 37
binary 36, 38
boolean logical AND, & 142, 144
boolean logical exclusive OR, ^ 142, 144
boolean logical inclusive OR, | 144
cast 104
compound assignment 109, 111
conditional AND, && 142, 143, 144
conditional operator, ?: 92, 112
conditional OR, || 142, 143, 144
decrement operator, -- 109, 110
increment and decrement 110
increment, ++ 109
logical complement, ! 144
logical negation, ! 144
logical operators 142, 144, 145
multiplication, * 37
multiplicative: *, / and % 105
postfix decrement 109
postfix increment 109
prefix decrement 109
prefix increment 109
remainder, % 37, 38, 39
subtraction, - 39
optical disk 516
optional package 288
Oracle Corporation 792
order 88
ORDER BY SQL clause 798, 800, 801, 802
ordering of records 798
origin component 651
out-of-bounds array index 214, 497
output 27, 31
output cursor 27, 30
output parameter for a CallableStatement 845
OutputStream class 541, 550, 754, 755, 756
OutputStreamWriter class 552
outside the bounds of an array 214
oval 470, 473
oval bounded by a rectangle 473
oval filled with gradually changing colors 482
overflow 497
overload a method 180, 181
overloaded constructors 259

Overloaded constructors used to initialize Time2 objects 264
overloaded method 558
overloaded method declarations 181
    with identical parameter lists cause compilation errors 183
overloading generic methods 566
override a superclass method 302, 307

P

pack method of class Window 660
package 34, 165, 284, 1108
package access 290
Package-access members of a class are accessible by other Classes in the same package 290
package access members of a class 290
package-access methods 290
package declaration 285
package directory names 287
package directory structure 285
package keyword 1053
package name 64, 286
package overview (java.sun.com/javase/6/docs/api/overview-summary.html) 167
Packages 155
    com.sun.rave.web.ui.appbase 860
    com.sun.webui.jsf.component 860
    com.sun.webui.jsf.model 930
    default package 64
    java.applet 165
    java.awt 166, 387, 457, 479, 652
    java.awt.color 479
    java.awt.event 166, 167, 400, 402, 427, 437
    java.awt.font 479
    java.awt.geom 479, 480
    java.awt.image 479
    java.awt.image.renderable 479
    java.awt.print 479
    java.beans 737
    java.io 166, 520
    java.lang 36, 156, 166, 304, 333, 683, 1014
    java.net 166, 744
    java.sql 810, 812
    java.text 166
    java.util 34, 166, 167, 581, 1014, 1040
    java.util.concurrent 686, 703, 741

Packages (cont.)
    java.util.concurrent.locks 720
    java.util.prefs 629
    java.util.regex 1014
    javax.faces.validators 874
    javax.servlet 854
    javax.servlet.http 854, 892, 893
    javax.servlet.jsp 855
    javax.servlet.jsp.tagext 855
    javax.sql.rowset 826
    javax.swing 166, 167, 383, 386, 392, 404, 451, 461, 641, 653, 660
    javax.swing.event 167, 401, 419, 427, 639
    javax.swing.table 814, 825
    of the Java API 165
packet 744, 768
packet-based communications 744
page bean 856
Page Down key 434
page layout software 1014
page name 64, 286
Page Up key 434
paginationControls property of a Table 911
Paint object 482
paintComponent method of class JComponent 454, 637, 638
paintComponent method of JComponent 431
Palette 863, 866, 870
panel 447
parallel layout of GUI components 1055
parallel operations 677
param tag 748
parameter 61, 63
    formal 160
parameter in the UML 63, 195, 198
parameter list 63, 71
parameterized class 567
parameterized type 567
parent directory 522
parent window 636, 656
parent window for a dialog box 647
parent window specified as null 648
parentheses 26, 38
    nested 38
parseInt method of Integer 242, 385
parsing a SOAP message 956
partial page update 922
participant in a virtual form 923
pass an array element to a method 221

pass an array to a method 221
pass-by-reference 223
pass-by-value 221, 223
Passing a generic type Stack to a generic method 574
Passing arrays and individual array elements to methods 221
passing options to a program 240
password 394
PATH environment variable xxxii, 28
path information 521
path to a resource 849
pathSeparator static field of File 525
pattern 480
Pattern class 1014, 1048
    compile method 1048
    matcher method 1048
    matches method 1048
pattern matching 799
pattern of 1s and 0s 517
Payable interface declaration 363
Payable interface hierarchy UML class diagram 363
Payable interface test program processing Invoices and Employees polymorphically 370
payroll file 518, 519
peek method of PriorityQueue 621
peek method of Stack 620
percent (%) SQL wildcard character 799
perform a calculation 53
perform a task 58
perform an action 27
Performance Tips overview xxvii
performing operations concurrently 677
persistent data 516
persistent Hashtable 629
persistent information 883
personalization 883
photo sharing 17
PHP 19
physical input operation 551
physical output operation 551
PIE constant of class Arc2D 484
pie-shaped arc 483
pipe 550
PipedInputStream class 550
PipedOutputStream class 550
PipedReader class 552
PipedWriter class 552
pixel ("picture element") 454
PLAF (pluggable look-and-feel) 636
PLAIN constant of class Font 464, 465
PLAIN_MESSAGE 385
platform dependency 681

pluggable look-and-feel (PLAF) **636**

pluggable look-and-feel package **388**

plus sign (+) indicating public visibility in the UML 291

.png 392

PNG (Portable Network Graphics) 392

point 465

Point class **433**

POJO (Plain Old Java Object) **940**

poll analysis program 213

poll method of Priority-Queue **621**

polygon 476, 478

Polygon class 454, 476
    addPoint method 477, 479

Polygons displayed with draw-Polygon and fillPolygon 477

polyline 476

polylines 476

polymorphic processing of collections 593

polymorphic processing of related exceptions 500

polymorphic programming 345

polymorphic screen manager 339

polymorphically process Invoices and Employees 370

polymorphism 139, 335, 337, 338, 339

pool of threads 755

pop method of Stack 620

popped 163

popup trigger event **649**, 651

port 754

port number 754, 755, 766, 768, 774

portability 8, 456

Portability Tips overview xxvii

portable 7

portable GUI 166

Portable Network Graphics (PNG) 392

position number 203

positive and negative arc angles 474

positive degrees 474

postback **862**

postcondition **512**

postdecrement **110**

postfix decrement operator **109**

postfix increment operator **109**, 124

PostgreSQL 792

postincrement **110**, 112

Pow method of class Math (Java) 987

pow method of Math 129, 130, 156, 157

power (exponent) 157

power of 2 larger than 100 95

precedence 39, 43, 112, 189
    arithmetic operators 39
    chart 39

precedence chart 105

Precedence Chart Appendix 1050

precision 995, 997
    format of a floating-point number 105

precision of a floating-point value 73

precision of a formatted floating-point number 75

precondition **512**

predecrement **110**

predefined character class **1041**

predicate **799**

predicate method 267

preemptive scheduling **681**

Preferences API **629**

prefix decrement operator **109**

prefix increment operator **109**

preincrement **110**, 111

Preincrementing and postincrementing 111

prepackaged data structures 588

PreparedStatement interface **829**, 830, 832, 833, **845**
    API documentation (java.sun.com/javase/6/docs/api/java/sql/PreparedStatement.html) 830
    executeQuery method 836
    executeUpdate method 836
    setString method 830, 836

prepareStatement method of interface Connection 832

preprocess method 862, 865

prerender method 862, 865

presentation logic 853

primary key 793, 797

primary property of a JSF **Button 908**

primitive type 69, 112, 164, 203
    passed by value 223
    promotions 164

primitive types 35
    boolean 1115
    byte 132
    char 35, 132
    double 73, 101
    float 35, 73
    int 35, 101, 109, 132
    names are Keywords 35
    short 132

principal in an interest calculation 127

principle of least privilege **279**

print a line of text 27

print debugger command 1113

print method of System.out 29, 30

print on multiple lines 29, 30

print spooling **696**

printArray generic method 561

printArray method in which actual type names are replaced by convention with the generic name E 560

printf method of System.out 994

Printing a line of text with multiple statements 29

Printing array elements using generic method printArray 560

Printing array elements using overloaded methods 558

Printing multiple lines of text with a single statement 31

Printing positive and negative numbers with and without the + flag 1007

println method of System.out 27, 30

printStackTrace method of class Throwable 506

PrintStream class 550, 630

PrintWriter class **531**, 552

priority of a thread **681**

priority scheduling 682

PriorityQueue class **621**
    clear method 621
    offer method 621
    peek method 621
    poll method 621
    size method 621

PriorityQueue test program 621

privacy protection 883

private
    access modifier 257
    data 266
    field 266
    keyword 266

private access modifier 66, 302

private keyword 291, 1053

Private members of Time1 are not accessible 257

private static
    class member 274

private superclass members cannot be accessed in subclass 314

probability 168

procedural programming language 14

producer **696**

producer thread **696**

producer/consumer relationship **696**, 716

program-development process 283

program execution stack 163

program in the general 337

program in the specific 337

programmer-declared method maximum that has three double parameters 159

programmer-defined class 25

Programming Projects xxviii

Project Properties dialog 943

Projects window 864

promotion **104**
    of arguments **164**
    rules 104, **164**

promotions for primitive types 164

prompt 36

Properties class 629, 899
    getProperty method 629
    keySet method 630
    list method 630
    load method 630
    setProperty method 629
    store method 630

Properties class of package java.util 630

Properties window 866

property of a JavaBean class 855

propertyChange method of interface Property-ChangeListener 737

PropertyChangeListener interface 737
    propertyChange method 737

proprietary class 333

protected
    access modifier 256, 276

protected access modifier 302, 1053

protected superclass members inherited into subclass BasePlusCommission-Employee3 320

protocol for communication (jdbc) 811

proxy class for a web service **936**

pseudorandom number 168, 172

public
    access modifier 57, 58, 66, 302
    class 25
    interface 253
    keyword 25, 66, 291, 294, 295
    member of a subclass 302
    method 254, 256
    method encapsulated in an object 256
    service 253
    static class members 274
    static method 274

public abstract method 361

public final static data 361

public keyword 1053

publishing a web service **936**, 942
pure Java components **386**
push method of Stack **618**
pushed 163
put method of interface BlockingQueue **703**, 705
put method of interface RequestContext 972
put method of Map **629**

Q

qualified name **803**
quantifiers used in regular expressions **1045**
quantum **680**
query 792, 794
query a database 809
query method **266**
query string **852**
QUESTION_MESSAGE 386
queue 267, 284, 593
Queue interface 589, 593, **621**, 703
queue length 754
queue to the server 756

R

RadialGradientPaint class 482
radians 157
radio button **404**, **410**
radio button group **410**
Radio Button Group JSF component 870, 874
radix **1037**
raised rectangle 473
Random class 166, 167, 988
    java.sun.com/javase/6/docs/api/java/util/Random.html 168
    nextInt method **168**, 169
    setSeed method 172
random method of Math 167, 168
random numbers 172
    difference between values 172
    element of chance **167**
    generation 215
    processing 166
    pseudorandom number **168**
    scaling **168**
    scaling factor **168**, 171, 172
    seed **168**
    seed value 172
    shift a range **168**
    shifting value **168**, 171, 172
range method of EnumSet 273
range-view methods 624

rapid application development (RAD) **282**
rapid prototyping xxiii
rapid web applications development xxiii
ratio of successive Fibonacci numbers 187
Rational Software Corporation 16, 50
Rational Unified Process™ 50
raw type **577**
Raw type test program 578
RDBMS (relational database management system) 853
read-only file 547
read-only text 389
read-only variable **209**
Reader class 551
Reading a file by opening a connection through a URL 751
reading a file on a web server 750
readObject method of ObjectInput 541
readObject method of ObjectInputStream 549
ready state 680
real number 35, 101
realization in the UML 363
receive a connection 756
receive data from a server 767
receive method of class DatagramSocket 771
reclaim memory 278
recognizing clients 883
recommended GUI design guidelines used by GroupLayout 1056
record 517, 525
record key **518**
recover from an error 215
rectangle 454, 458, 470
Rectangle2D class 454
Rectangle2D.Double class 480
recursion
    overhead 193
    recursion step **184**, 189, 190
    recursive call **184**, 188, 190
    recursive evaluation 185
    Recursive evaluation of 5! 185
    recursive factorial method 185
    recursive method **183**
    recursively generating Fibonacci numbers 190
redirect a stream 520
redundant parentheses 38
ReentrantLock class 720, 722
refactoring xxiii, 19, 866
refer to an object 70
reference 70
reference type 69, 203, 290
refresh method of class CachedRowSetDataProvider 920

regexFilter method 825
regexFilter method of class RowFilter 825
regionMatches method of class String **1018**
register a port 754
register an ActionListener 648
registered listener 402
registering the event handler 397
regular expression 880, **1041**
    ^ 1042
    ? 1045
    . 1048
    {n} 1045
    * 1044
    \D 1041
    \d 1041
    \S 1041
    \s 1041
    \W 1041
    \w 1041
    + 1045
    | 1045
Regular expressions checking birthdays 1049
reinventing the wheel 5, 34
relational database 792, **793**
relational database management system (RDBMS) 792, 853
relational database table 793
relational operators **39**
relationship between an inner class and its top-level class 410
RELATIVE constant of class GridBagConstraints 672
relative path 521
release a lock 709, 710
release a resource 501
reload an entire web page 921
reluctant quantifier **1046**
remainder 38
REMAINDER constant of class GridBagConstraints 672
remainder operator, % 37, 39
remove duplicate String 622
remove method 620
remove method of Iterator 596
remove method of Vector 605
removeAllElements method of Vector 605
removeElementAt method of Vector 605
removeTableModelListener method of TableModel 814
removeTrayIcon method of class SystemTray 1072
rendered property of a JSF component 875
rendering XHTML in a web browser 851

Reordering output with argument index 1009
repaint method of class JComponent 457
repaint method of Component 434
repetition 90
    counter controlled 103, 106
    sentinel controlled 100, 101, 103
repetition statement 90, **95**, 192
    do...while 90, 130, 131, 131
    do/while 90
    for 90, 126
    while 90, 95, 96, 99, 103, 121
repetition structure **89**
repetition terminates 95
replaceAll method
    of class Matcher **1048**
    of class String **1046**
replaceFirst method
    of class Matcher **1048**
    of class String **1046**
Representational State Transfer (REST) 934
representing integers in hexadecimal format 995
representing integers in octal format 995
request method 851
request scope **856**
RequestBean **856**
RequestContext interface 972
    put method 972
required property **879**
requirements 15, 48
requirements document 13, 44, 48, 49
requirements gathering 48
reserved word 90
    false **91**
    null 67, 70, 113, 385
    true **91**
reserved words 1053
reset property of a JSF **Button** 908
resizable array 749
    implementation of a List 594
resolution 454
@Resource annotation **961**
resource leak 273, **500**
responses to a survey 213
REST (Representational State Transfer) 934
result 799
result set concurrency **818**
result set type **818**

ResultSet interface 812, 818, 819
  absolute method 819
  column name 813
  column number 813
  CONCUR_READ_ONLY constant 818
  CONCUR_UPDATABLE constant 818
  concurrency constant 818
  getInt method 813
  getObject method 813, 819
  getRow method 819
  last method 819
  next method 812
  TYPE_FORWARD_ONLY constant 818
  TYPE_SCROLL_INSENSIT IVE constant 818
  TYPE_SCROLL_SENSITIV E constant 818
ResultSetMetaData interface 812, 819
  getColumnClassName method 819
  getColumnCount method 812, 819
  getColumnName method 819
  getColumnType method 812
ResultSetTableModel enables a JTable to display the contents of a ResultSet 814
resumption model of exception handling 495
rethrow an exception 504
return keyword 163, 1053
return message in the UML 247
return statement 184
return type in the UML 195, 200
return type of a method 66
reusability 567
reusable software components 4, 165, 300
reuse 15, 34
reverse 613
reverse method of class StringBuilder 1031
reverse method of Collections 606, 613
reverseOrder method of Collections 607
RGB value 457, 463
Richards, Martin 3
right aligned 439
right brace, } 26, 34, 98, 103
RIGHT constant of FlowLayout 442
right justification 995, 1003
right justify output 128
right justifying integers 1004
Right justifying integers in a field 1004
rigid area of class Box 666

Ritchie, Dennis 4
robust 36
robust application 488, 495
role in the UML 81
role name in the UML 81
roll back a transaction 845
rollback method of interface Connection 846
Rolling a six-sided die 6000 times 170
rolling two dice 173
rollover Icon 406
root directory 521
root element 858
rotate method of class Graphics2D 486
round a floating-point number for display purposes 105
round-robin scheduling 681
rounded rectangle 471, 483
rounded rectangle (for representing a state in a UML state diagram) 148
rounding 995
rounding a number 38, 100, 129, 157
RoundRectangle2D class 454
RoundRectangle2D.Double class 480, 483
row 793, 797, 798, 799, 800, 804
RowFilter class 825
rows of a two-dimensional array 229
rows to be retrieved 798
RowSet getting started guide java.sun.com/javase/ 6/docs/technotes/ guides/jdbc/get- start/rowsetIm- pl.html 826
RowSet interface 825
RSS feeds 18
Ruby on Rails 19
Rule of Entity Integrity 797
Rule of Referential Integrity 795
rule of thumb (heuristic) 141
rules of operator precedence 39, 189
Rumbaugh, James 15, 16
run debugger command 1112
run method of interface Runnable 683, 782
Run option in Netbeans 942
runtime logic error 385
Runnable interface 372, 683, 783
  run method 683, 782
runnable state 679
running an application 9
running state 680
runtime logic error 36
RuntimeException class 499, 506

S

SAAS (Software as a Service) 19

SalariedEmployee class derived from Employee 349
SalariedEmployee class that implements interface Payable method getPaymentAmount 368
Salesforce 17
SansSerif Java font 465
saturation 463
SaverBeans Screensaver SDK incubator project 1072
savings account 127
scalar 221
scaling (random numbers) 168
scaling factor (random numbers) 168, 171, 172
Scanner class 34, 35
  hasNext method 136
  java.sun.com/javase/ 6/docs/api/java/ util/Scanner.html 274
  next method 62
  nextDouble method 77
  nextLine method 61, 629
scheduling threads 681
scientific notation 996
scope 124
Scope class demonstrating scopes of a field and local variables 178
scope of a declaration 177
scope of a type parameter 569
scope of a variable 124
Screen class (ATM case study) 80, 82, 195, 243, 244, 245, 247, 249, 293
screen cursor 31
screen-manager program 339
scripting element 855
scroll 415, 419
scroll arrow 416
scroll box 416
Scroll Lock key 435
SCROLL_TAB_LAYOUT constant of class JTabbedPane 666
scrollbar 419, 451
scrollbar of a JComboBox 416
scrollbar policies 451
search engine 852
Second Life 17
secondary storage devices 516
sector 474
secure protocol 895
security 8
SecurityException 528
seed value (random numbers) 168, 172
SEI (service endpoint interface) 936
SELECT SQL keyword 798, 799, 800, 801, 802
selected 410
selected text in a JTextArea 451
selecting an item from a menu 394
selecting data from a table 794

selection 90
selection criteria 799
selection mode 419
selection statement 90
  if 90, 91, 132
  if...else 90, 91, 92, 103, 132
  switch 90, 132, 138
selection structure 88
self-documenting code 36
_self target frame 750
Semantic Web 18
semicolon (;) 27, 35, 42
send data to a server 767
send message 70
send method of class DatagramSocket 772
sentence-style capitalization 385
sentinel-controlled repetition 100, 101, 103, 101, 103
sentinel value 100, 103
separator character 525
separator line in a menu 647, 648
sequence 90, 594
sequence diagram in the UML 51, 245
sequence of messages in the UML 246
sequence structure 88
sequence-structure activity diagram 89
SequenceInputStream class 551
sequential-access file 517, 519, 525, 755
sequential execution 88
Sequential file created using ObjectOutputStream 544
Sequential file read using an ObjectInputStream 547
Sequential file reading using a Scanner 532
sequential horizontal orientation in GroupLayout 1055
sequential layout of GUI components 1055
Serializable interface 372, 541
serialized object 541
Serif Java font 465
server 744, 936
server port number 767
Server portion of a client/server stream-socket connection 757
server response 852
server-side artifacts 941
server-side form handler 851
server side of connectionless client/server computing with datagrams 769
Server side of the client/server Tic-Tac-Toe program 776
server waits for connections from clients 754
server's Internet address 755

server-side form handler 851
ServerSocket class 754, 756, 775
   accept method 754, 761
service endpoint interface (SEI) 936
serviceName attribute of @WebService annotation 941
services oriented architecture (SOA) xxiii
Services tab in Netbeans 910
servlet 854
servlet container 854
Servlet interface 854
   destroy method 854
   init method 854
   service method 854
session 883
session scope 856
session tracking 884
   in web services 957
SessionBean 856
set a value 68
set debugger command 1114
Set interface 589, 593, 622, 623, 625
set method 68, 260
set method of ListIterator 599
set method of Vector 604
set of constants
   as an interface 372
Set of recursive calls for fibonacci(3) 189
SET SQL clause 805
set up event handling 397
setAlignment method of FlowLayout 442
setAttribute method of interface HttpSession 961
setAutoCommit method of interface Connection 845
setBackground method of class Component 463
setBackground method of Component 419
setCharAt method of class StringBuilder 1031
setColor method of class Graphics 458, 483
setCommand method of Jdb-cRowSet interface 828
setConstraints method of class GridBagLayout 672
setDefaultCloseOperation method of class JFrame 641
setDefaultCloseOperation method of JFrame 393
setEditable method of JTextComponent 397
setErr method of System 520
setFileSelectionMode method of JFileChooser 554

setFixedCellHeight method of JList 422
setFixedCellWidth method of JList 422
setFont method of class Graphics 465
setFont method of Component 408
setForeground method of class JComponent 649
setHorizontalAlignment method of JLabel 392
setHorizontalScrollBar-Policy method of JScrollPane 451
setHorizontalTextPosition method of JLabel 393
setIcon method of JLabel 392, 393
setIn method of System 520
setInverted method of class JSlider 637
setJMenuBar method of class JFrame 641, 648
setLayout method of class Container 666
setLayout method of Container 391, 441, 444, 447
setLineWrap method of JTextArea 451
setListData method of JList 422
setLocation method of class Component 641
setLookAndFeel method of class UIManager 655
setMajorTickSpacing method of class JSlider . 638
setMaximumRowCount method of JComboBox 416
setMnemonic method of class AbstractButton 647
setOpaque method of JComponent 431, 434
setOut method of System 520
setPage method of class JEditorPane 752
setPaint method of class Graphics2D 482
setPaintTicks method of class JSlider 638
setPassword method of Jdb-cRowSet interface 828
setProperty method of Properties 629
setRolloverIcon method of AbstractButton 406
setRowFilter method of class JTable 825
setRowSorter method of class JTable 825
setSeed method of class Random 172
setSelected method of class AbstractButton 648

setSelectionMode method of JList 419
setSize method of class Component 641
setSize method of JFrame 393
setString method of interface PreparedStatement 830, 836
setStroke method of class Graphics2D 483
setText method of JLabel 393
setText method of JTextComponent 451
Setting the PATH environment variable xxxii
setToolTipText method of JComponent 391
setUrl method of JdbcRow-Set interface 828
setUsername method of Jdb-cRowSet interface 828
setVerticalAlignment method of JLabel 392
setVerticalScrollBar-Policy method of JSlider 451
setVerticalTextPosition method of JLabel 393
setVisible method of class Component 641
setVisible method of Component 445
setVisible method of JFrame 393
setVisibleRowCount method of JList 419
shadow a field 178
shallow copy 334
shape 480
Shape class hierarchy 301, 302
Shape object 483
shared buffer 697
shell 27
shell prompt in UNIX 7
shell script 528
Shift 437
shift (random numbers) 168
shifted and scaled random integers 169
shifting value 168
shifting value (random numbers) 171, 172
short-circuit evaluation 143
short keyword 1053, 1054
short primitive type 132
short promotions 164
shortcut key 642
Show Line Numbers 865
show method of class JPopupMenu 651
showDialog method of class JColorChooser 462
showDocument method of class AppletContext 745, 750
showInputDialog method of JOptionPane 384

showMessageDialog method of JOptionPane 385
showOpenDialog method of JFileChooser 555
shuffle algorithm 610
shuffle method of Collections 606, 610, 612
shutdown method of class ExecutorService 687
side effect 144
Sieve of Eratosthenes 736
signal method of interface Condition 720, 724
signal value 100
signalAll method of interface Condition 721
signature 183
signature of a method 182
simple condition 141
simple name 287
Simple Object Access Protocol (SOAP) 934
simulate a middle-mouse-button click on a one- or two-button mouse 430
simulate a right-mouse-button click on a one-button mouse 430
simulation 167
sin method of Math 157
sine 157
single-entry/single-exit control statements 90
single inheritance 299
single-line (end-of-line) comment 24, 27, 35
single-precision floating-point number 73
single-quote character 799
single quotes 1015
single-selection statement 90
single-selection list 417
single static import 278
single-type-import declaration 288
SINGLE_INTERVAL_ SELECTION constant of ListSelectionModel 419, 420, 422
SINGLE_SELECTION constant of ListSelectionModel 419
single-selection statement if 91
SingleSelectOptionsList class 873
SingleSelectOptionsList object 874
size method
   of List 595, 599
   of Map 629
   of PriorityQueue 621
   of Vector 605
size method of class Array-BlockingQueue 705
Skype 17
sleep interval 680
sleep method of class Thread 684, 698, 699, 700

sleeping thread **680**
small circles in the UML **89**
small diamond symbol (for representing a decision in a UML activity diagram) 149
snap-to ticks for `JSlider` 636
SOA (services oriented architecture) xxiii
SOAP 936
  envelope **956**
  message **956**
  parsing a SOAP message 956
  SOAP request for the `HugeInteger` web service 957
  www.w3.org/TR/soap/ 956
SOAP (Simple Object Access Protocol) **934**
social bookmarking 17
social networking 17
socket 744
socket-based communication 744
`Socket` class 754, 767, 782, 783
  `close` method 755
  `getInetAddress` method 761
  `getInputStream` method 754, 756
  `getOutputStream` method 754
`SocketException` class 768
Software as a Service (SAAS) **19**
software asset 15
software engineering 266
Software Engineering Case Study xxiv
Software Engineering Observations overview xxvii
software life cycle 48
software reuse 5, 155, 283, 284, 299, 557
solid circle (for representing an initial state in a UML diagram) in the UML **148**, 149
solid circle enclosed in an open circle (for representing the end of a UML activity diagram) 149
solid circle in the UML **89**
solid circle surrounded by a hollow circle in the UML 89
solid diamonds (representing composition) in the UML 81
sort 590, 592
`sort` method of `Arrays` 590
`sort` method of `Collections` 606
sorted order 623, 625
`SortedMap` interface **625**
`SortedSet` interface 623, 625
  `first` method **625**
  `last` method 625
sorting

descending order 607
  with a `Comparator` 608
source code 333
Source view in Netbeans 1057
SOUTH constant of `Border-Layout` 426, 442
SOUTH constant of class `Grid-BagConstraints` 667
SOUTHEAST constant of class `GridBagConstraints` 667
SOUTHWEST constant of class `GridBagConstraints` 667
space flag 1006, 1007
spacing between components in `GroupLayout` 1056
span element 860
special character 35, 1015
special symbol 517
specialization 299
specialization in the UML 374
specifics 339
spiral 187
`-splash` command-line option to the java command 1067
splash screen 1067
`SplashScreen` class 1069
split a statement over multiple lines 32
`split` method of class `String` 1046
SQL 792, 794, 797, 798, 804
  DELETE statement 798, 805
  FROM clause 798
  GROUP BY 798
  IDENTITY keyword **830**
  INNER JOIN clause 798, 802
  INSERT statement 798, 804
  LIKE clause 799, 800
  ON clause 803
  ORDER BY clause 798, **800**, 802
  SELECT query 798, 799, 800, 801, 802
  SET clause 805
  UPDATE statement 798
  VALUES clause 804
  WHERE clause 799
`.sql` 808
SQL (Structured Query Language) 829
SQL keyword 797
SQL script 808
SQL statement 844, 845
`SQLException` class 811, 813, 830
`SQLFeatureNotSupported-Exception` class 819
`sqrt` method of `Math` 156, 157, 164
square brackets, [ ] 204, 214
square root 157
stack 163, 267, 283, 567

method call stack 163
  program execution stack 163
  stack overflow 164
`Stack` class 620
  `isEmpty` method **620**
  of package `java.util` 618, 619
  `peek` method 620
  `pop` method 620
  `push` method 618
stack frame 163
`Stack` generic class 567
  `Stack< Double >` 576
  `Stack< Integer >` 576
stack trace 491
stack unwinding 505
stacking control statements 92
`StackTraceElement` class 509
  `getClassName` method 509
  `getFileName` method 509
  `getLineNumber` method 509
  `getMethodName` method 509
stale value 693
standard error stream 503, 994
standard error stream (`System.err`) 520, 550
standard input stream (`System.in`) 35, 519
standard output stream 503, 994
standard output stream (`System.out`) 27, 519, 550
standard reusable component 300
standard time format 255
"standardized, interchangeable parts" 15
start page 870
starting angle 474
`startsWith` method of class `String` 1021
starvation 681
state 50
state button 407
state dependent 696
state diagram for the ATM object 148
state diagram in the UML 148
state in the UML 50, 149
state machine diagram in the UML 50, 148
state of an object 113, 147, 148
`stateChanged` method of interface `ChangeListener` 639
stateless protocol 883
`Statement` 812
statement 27, 58
`Statement` interface 812, 813, 829
  `executeQuery` method 812
Statements

break 136, 139, 140
`continue` 139
control statement 88, 90, 91
control-statement nesting 90
control-statement stacking 90
`do...while` 90, 130, 131
double selection 90
empty 43, 95
empty statement 95
`for` 90, 122, 125, 126, 127, 129
`if` 39, 90, 91, 132
`if...else` 90, 91, 92, 103, 132
multiple selection 90
nested 106
nested `if...else` 93, 94
repetition 89, 90, 95
`return` 163
selection 88, 90
single selection 90
`switch` 90, 132, 138
`switch` multiple-selection statement 170
`while` 90, 95, 96, 99, 103, 121
`static`
  class member 274
  class member demonstration 276
  class variable 274
  field (class variable) 274
  method 59, 129
static binding 360
`static` class variable used maintain a count of the number of `Employee` objects in memory 275
`static` import 278, 371
  of `Math` methods 279
  on demand 278
`static` keyword 1053
`static` method cannot access non-`static` class members 278
Static Text JSF component 858, 860, 870
`step` debugger command 1116
`step up` debugger command 1117
`stop` debugger command 1112
`store` method of `Properties` 630
stored procedure 845
straight-line form 38
stream 503, 994
stream header 761
stream of bytes 519
stream processing 516
stream socket 745, 756, 775
stream-based communications 744
streams 745
streams-based transmission 768
`strictfp` keyword 1053

string 27, 166
  of characters 27
String array 205
String class 1014
  charAt method 1016, 1031
  compareTo method 1018, 1020
  concat method 1025
  deleteCharAt method 1034
  endsWith method 1021
  equals method 1018, 1020
  equalsIgnoreCase method 1018, 1020
  format method 254, 1011
  getChars method 1016
  indexOf method 1022
  lastIndexOf method 1022
  length method 1016
  matches method 1041
  regionMatches method 1018
  replaceAll method 1046
  replaceFirst method 1046
  split method 1046
  startsWith method 1021
  substring method 1024
  toCharArray method 1027
  toLowerCase 599
  toUpperCase 599
  valueOf method 1027
String class character-manipulation methods 1017
String class constructors 1015
String class searching methods 1022
String class startsWith and endsWith methods 1021
String class substring methods 1024
String class valueOf methods 1027
String comparisons 1018
string concatenation 161, 277
string literal 1015
String method concat 1025
String methods replace, toLowerCase, toUpperCase, trim and toCharArray 1025
StringBuffer class 1028
StringBuilder class 1014, 1028
  append method 1032
  capacity method 1029
  charAt method 1031
  constructors 1029
  delete method 1034
  ensureCapacity method 1029
  getChars method 1031

insert method 1034
length method 1029
reverse method 1031
setCharAt method 1031
trim method 1027
StringBuilder class append methods 1032
StringBuilder class character-manipulation methods 1031
StringBuilder class constructors 1029
StringBuilder method length and capacity 1030
StringBuilder methods insert and delete 1034
StringIndexOutOfBoundsException class 1024, 1032
StringReader class 552
StringTokenizer class 629, 1014, 1040
  hasMoreTokens method 629, 1041
  nextToken method 629, 1041
StringTokenizer object used to tokenize strings 1040
StringWriter class 552
Stroke object 483
strongly typed languages 112
Stroustrup, Bjarne 4, 488
structure of a system 117, 148
structured programming 88, 141
Structured Query Language (SQL) 792, 794, 797
style sheet 858, 864
subclass 299, 374
sublist 599
subList method of List 599
submenu 642
submit method of class ExecutorService 741
submitter in a virtual form 923
subprotocol for communication 811
subscript (index) 203
substring method of String 1024
subtraction 38
  operator, - 39
suffix F 618
suffix F for float literals 618
suffix L for long literals 618
sum the elements of an array 210
Summing integers with the for repetition statement 127
Sun Java System Application Server 937
super keyword 303, 327, 1053
  call superclass constructor 315
superclass 299, 374
  constructor 306

constructor call syntax 315
default constructor 306
direct 299, 301
indirect 299, 301
method overridden in a subclass 326
Superclass private instance variables are accessible to a subclass via public or protected methods inherited by the subclass 326
survey 214
sweep 474
sweep counterclockwise 474
Swing Event Package 167
Swing GUI components 386
Swing GUI components package 166
SwingConstants interface 373, 392, 638
SwingUtilities class 655
  updateComponentTreeUI method 655
SwingWorker 727
  cancel method 737
  doInBackground method 727, 729
  done method 727, 729
  execute method 727
  get method 727
  process method 727, 736
  publish method 727, 736
  setProgress method 727, 736
switch logic 139
switch multiple-selection statement 90, 132, 138, 170, 1053
  activity diagram with break statements 139
  case label 136
  controlling expression 136
  default case 136, 138, 170
  testing multiple input values 132
Sybase 792
synchronization 688, 707
synchronization wrapper 632
synchronize 678
synchronize access to a collection 593
synchronized
  keyword 633, 688
  method 688
  statement 688
synchronized collection 593
synchronized keyword 678, 1053
synchronous call 245
synchronous error 497
synchronous request 921
syntax 24
syntax error 24, 27, 28
system 50
system behavior 50
System class
  arraycopy 592

exit method 501, 528
setErr method 520
setIn method 520
setOut 520
system requirements 48
system service 754
system structure 50
System.err (standard error stream) 520, 550, 994
System.err stream 502
System.in (standard input stream) 519
System.out
  print method 29, 30
  println method 27, 30
System.out (standard output stream) 27, 519, 550
System.out.print method 29, 30
System.out.printf method 32
System.out.println method 27, 30
SystemColor class 482
SystemInfo incubator project 1072
SystemTray class 1072
  addTrayIcon method 1072
  getDefaultSystemTray method 1072
  removeTrayIcon method 1072

T

tab 1010
tab character, \t 25, 31
tab stops 31
table 229, 793
Table component (JSF) 910
  internalVirtualForms property 911
  paginationControls property 911
table element 229
Table JSF component 908
table of values 229
TableModel interface 813, 814
  addTableModelListener 814

`TableModel` interface (cont.)
  `getColumnClass` method 814, 819
  `getColumnCount` method 814, 819
  `getColumnName` method 814, 819
  `getRowCount` method 814
  `getValueAt` method 814
  `removeTableModelListener` 814
`TableModelEvent` class 825
`TableRowSorter` class 825
tabular format 207
tag extension mechanism 855
tag library 855, 858
tagging an interface 542
tagging interface 363, 542
`tailSet` method of `TreeSet` 625
take method of class `BlockingQueue` 703, 705
tan method of `Math` 157
tangent 157
target frame 750
  `_blank` 750
  `_self` 750
  `_top` 750
TCP (Transmission Control Protocol) 745
Technorati 18
telephone system 768
temporary 104
Terminal application (Max OS X) 7
terminal window 27
terminate an application 647
terminate successfully 528
terminated state **680**
termination housekeeping 273, 334
termination model of exception handling 495
termination test 192
ternary operator 92
test a web service 943
testing a web service from another computer 945
Testing the `factorial` method 186
Testing the `fibonacci` method 188
Testing the iterative factorial solution 193
Text Area JSF component 892
text editor 1014
Text Field
  `autoComplete` attribute 925
  `autoCompleteExpression` attribute 925
Text Field component auto-complete 923
Text Field JSF component 870, 873
text file **519**
Text Package 166

Text-printing program 23
`TexturePaint` class 454, 482, 483
thick lines 480
`this`
  keyword 257, 278
  reference 257
  to call another constructor of the same class 262
  used implicitly and explicitly to refer to members of an object 258
`this` keyword 1053
Thompson, Ken 3
thread 495
  life cycle 679, 680
  of execution 678
  priority scheduling 682
  scheduling 680, 700
  state 679
  synchronization 632, **688**
`Thread` class 681, 684
  `interrupt` method **684**
  `sleep` method **684**
thread confinement 727
thread-life-cycle statechart diagram 679, 680
thread pool **686**
thread priority **681**
thread safe 693, 727
thread scheduler **681**
thread states
  blocked 680, **688**
  dead 680
  new 679
  ready 680
  runnable 679
  running 680
  terminated 680
  timed waiting 679
  waiting 679
`Thread.MAX_PRIORITY` 681
`Thread.MIN_PRIORITY` 681
`Thread.NORM_PRIORITY` 681
three-button mouse 430
three-dimensional rectangle 470
throw an exception 490, 491, 494
throw keyword 504, 1053
throw point 491
throw statement **504**
`Throwable` class 498, 506
  `getMessage` method **506**
  `getStackTrace` method 506
  `printStackTrace` method **506**
`Throwable` class hierarchy 498
`Throwable` methods `getMessage`, `getStackTrace` and `printStackTrace` 507
throws clause 496
throws keyword 1053
thumb of `JSlider` 636, 638
thumb position of `JSlider` 640
Tic-Tac-Toe 775
tick marks on `JSlider` 636

tier in a multitier application 852
time formatting 995
`Time1` abstract data type implementation as a class 285
`Time1` class declaration maintains the time in 24-hour format 253
`Time1` object used in a program 287
`Time1` object used in an application 255
`Time2` class with overloaded constructors 260
timed waiting state 679
timeslice **680**
timeslicing 681
title bar 382, 389, **640**
title bar of a window 385
title bar of internal window 660
`titles` table of books database 794, 796
`toArray` method of `List` 600, 601
`toCharArray` method of class `String` 1027
toggle buttons 404
token 166
token of a `String` 1039
tokenization 1039
`toLowerCase` method of class `Character` 1037
`toLowerCase` of `String` 599
tool tips 388, 392, 393
top 620
`TOP` constant of class `JTabbedPane` 666
top-level class 398
`_top` target frame 750
top tier 853
`toString` method of `ArrayList` 582, 606
`toString` method of `Formatter` 1011
`toString` method of `Object` 307, 335
Totaling the numbers in an `ArrayList<Number>` 582
`toUpperCase` method of class `Character` 1037
`toUpperCase` of `String` 599
track mouse events 424
tracking customers 883
traditional comment 24
traditional web application 921
`TRAILING` alignment constant in `GroupLayout` 1056
trailing white-space characters 1027
`Transaction` class (ATM case study) 374, 375, 376, 378, 380
transaction processing 845
transfer of control 88
`transient` keyword 543, 1053
transition arrow 91, 92, 96
transition arrow in the UML 89, 96

transition between states in the UML 148, 150
transition in the UML 89
`translate` method of class `Graphics2D` 486
transparency of a JComponent 431
transparent Swing GUI components 431
traverse an array **231**
Tray icons 1072
`TrayIcon` class **1072**
`TrayIcon` package demo 1072
tree 622
Tree link in API **1075**
`TreeMap` class 625
`TreeSet` class 622, 623, 625
  `headSet` method **625**
  `tailSet` method **625**
trigger an event 386
trigonometric cosine 157
trigonometric sine 157
trigonometric tangent 157
trim method of class `StringBuilder` 1027
`trimToSize` method of `Vector` 602
true 39, 91, 92, 1053
truncate 38
truncate fractional part of a calculation 100
truncated **528**
trusted source 790
truth table **142**
truth tables
  for operator ^ 144
  for operator ! 145
  for operator && 142
  for operator || 143
try block 494, 507
try block terminates 495
try keyword 494, 1053
try statement **496**
24-hour clock format 253
two-dimensional array **229**, 231
two-dimensional array with three rows and four columns 230
two-dimensional graphics 479
two-dimensional shapes 454
type 35
type argument 570
type-import-on-demand declaration 288
type parameter 561, 567, 577
  scope 569
  section **561**, 567
type variable **561**
type-wrapper class 563, 1035
  implements `Comparable` 563
`TYPE_FORWARD_ONLY` constant **818**
`TYPE_INT_RGB` constant of class `BufferedImage` 483
`TYPE_SCROLL_INSENSITIVE` constant **818**

TYPE_SCROLL_SENSITIVE constant 818
Types class 813
typesetting system 1014
typing in a text field 394

U

UDP (User Datagram Protocol) 745, 768
ui:staticText JSF element 912
ui:table JSF element 912
UIManager class 653
   getInstalledLookAndFeels method 653
   LookAndFeelInfo nested class 653
   setLookAndFeel method 655
UIManager.LookAndFeelInfo class
   getClassName method 655
UIViewRoot class 858
UML
   activity diagram 89, 89, 92, 96, 125, 131
   aggregation 82
   arrow 89
   association 15, 80
   attribute 14
   behavior 14
   class diagram 60
   component 15
   diamond 91
   dotted line 90
   elided diagram 80
   final state 89
   guard condition 91
   many-to-one relationship 83
   merge symbol 96
   multiplicity 80
   note 89
   one-to-many relationship 83
   one-to-one relationship 83
   operation 14
   role name 81
   solid circle 89
   solid circle surrounded by a hollow circle 89
   solid diamond representing composition 81
UML (Unified Modeling Language) 13, 15, 44, 50, 80, 89, 115, 117, 374
   diagram 50
UML Activity Diagram
   small diamond symbol (for representing a decision) in the UML 149
   solid circle (for representing an initial state) in the UML 149

UML Activity Diagram (cont.)
   solid circle enclosed in an open circle (for representing the end of an activity) in the UML 149
UML Class Diagram 80
   attribute compartment 115
   operation compartment 195
UML Partners 16
UML Sequence Diagram
   activation 247
   arrowhead 247
   lifeline 247
UML State Diagram
   rounded rectangle (for representing a state) in the UML 148
   solid circle (for representing an initial state) in the UML 148
UML Use Case Diagram
   actor 49
   use case 49
unary cast operator 104
unary operator 104, 144
uncaught exception 495
unchecked exceptions 498
uncovering a component 457
underlying data structure 621
underscore (_) SQL wildcard character 799, 800
uneditable JTextArea 449
uneditable text or icons 386
Unicode character set 113, 139, 517, 1015, 1020, 1035, 1054
Unicode value of the character typed 437
Unified Modeling Language (UML) xxii, 13, 15, 44, 50, 80, 89, 115, 117, 374
Uniform Resource Identifier (URI) 522, 745, 849
Uniform Resource Locator (URL) 522, 745, 849
universal-time format 253, 254, 255
UNIX 7, 27, 528, 652
Unix 135
UnknownHostException class 755
unlock method of interface Lock 720, 724
unmodifiable collection 593
unmodifiable wrapper 633
unspecified number of arguments 239
UnsupportedOperationException 633
UnsupportedOperationException class 600
unwatch debugger command 1121
unwinding the method-call stack 505
UPDATE SQL statement 798, 805

updateComponentTreeUI method of class SwingUtilities 655
upper bound 564
   of a type parameter 565
   of a wildcard 583
upper-left corner of a GUI component 454
upper-left x-coordinate 458
upper-left y-coordinate 458
uppercase letter 25, 35
URI (Uniform Resource Identifier) 522, 745, 849
URL (Uniform Resource Locator) 522, 745, 749, 849
   rewriting 884
use case diagram in the UML 49, 50
use case in the UML 48
use case modeling 48
User Datagram Protocol (UDP) 745, 768
user-defined class 25
user interface 853
Using floating-point conversion characters 997
Using integer conversion characters 996
Using SortedSets and TreeSets 624
Using the , flag to display number with thousands separator 1008
Using the (flag to place parentheses around negative numbers 1009
Using the # flag with conversion characters o and x 1007
Using the 0 (zero) flag 1008
Using the character and string conversion characters 998
Using the enhanced for statement to total integers in an array 220
Using the space flag to print a space before non-negative values 1007
Using variable-length argument lists 239
Utilities Package 166
utility method 138

V

valid identifier 35
validate method of Container 447
Validating user information using regular expressions 1042
validation 874
ValidatorException class 882
Validators
   Double Range 874
   Length 874, 879
   Long Range 874
validity checking 266
value of a param 748

valueChanged method of ListSelectionListener 419
valueOf method of class String 1027
VALUES 804
values method of an enum 272
VALUES SQL clause 804
varargs (variable-length argument lists) 239
variable 33, 34
   name 35
   non-primitive type 69
   reference type 69
variable declaration statement 34
variable is not modifiable 279
variable-length argument list 239
variable scope 124
Vector class 250, 594, 601, 602
   add method 604
   capacity method 605
   contains method 604
   firstElement method 604
   indexOf method 605
   insertElementAt method 604
   isEmpty method 605
   lastElement method 604
   remove method 605
   removeAllElements method 605
   removeElementAt method 605
   set method 604
   size method 605
   trimToSize method 602
Vector class of package java.util 602
verb phrase in requirements document 194
VERTICAL constant of class GridBagConstraints 667
vertical coordinate 454
vertical gap space 444
vertical scrolling 451
vertical strut 664
VERTICAL_SCROLLBAR_ALWAYS constant of JScrollPane 451
VERTICAL_SCROLLBAR_AS_NEEDED constant of JScrollPane 451
VERTICAL_SCROLLBAR_NEVER constant of JScrollPane 452
vi 7
video game 168
video sharing 17
View 382
view 599
virtual directory 849
virtual forms 911, 923

participant **923**
submitter **923**
virtual key code **437**
virtual machine (VM) **7**
virtual world **17**
visibility in the UML **291**
visibility marker in the UML **291**
visual editor **858**
visual editor (Netbeans) **863**
visual feedback **407**
`void` keyword **26, 58, 1053**
`volatile` keyword **1053**

W

wait for a new connection **756**
`wait` method of class `Object` **707**
`wait` method of `Object` **335**
waiting line **593**
waiting state **679**
waiting thread **709**
Wallpaper API demo **1072**
`watch` debugger command **1119, 1119**
waterfall model **48**
Web 2.0 xxiii, **17**
Web 3.0 **18**
web application
    Ajax **922**
    traditional **921**
web application development **848**
web application framework **856**
Web Application project **937**
Web browser **382**
web browser **750**
web server **754, 849**
web service **934**
    implemented as a class **936**
    publishing a web service **942**
Web Service Description Language (WSDL) **945**
web service reference **947**
web services **18**
    `@Resource` annotation **961**
    `@WebMethod` annotation **941**
    `@WebParam` annotation **941**
    `@WebService` annotation **941**
    adding a web service reference to an application **947**
    Build option in Netbeans **942**
    Clean and Build option in Netbeans 942
    Clean option in Netbeans 942
    Client desktop application for the `HugeInteger` web service **950**

web services (cont.)
    client-side artifacts **947**
    consuming a web service **936, 945**
    Deploy option in Net-beans 942
    deploying a web service 942
    GlassFish application server's **Tester** web page 943
    JAX-WS **936**
    `MessageContext` inter-face **961**
    `name` attribute of `@Web-Service` annotation **941**
    parsing a SOAP message **956**
    POJO (Plain Old Java Ob-ject) **940**
    proxy class **936**
    publishing a web service **936**
    `RequestContext` inter-face **972**
    REST **934**
    Run option in Netbeans 942
    server-side artifacts **941**
    `serviceName` attribute of `@WebService` annota-tion **941**
    SOAP **936**
    SOAP envelope **956**
    SOAP message **956**
    test a web service 943
    testing a web service from another computer 945
    user-defined types **982**
    Web Service Description Language (WSDL) **945**
    web service reference **947**
    `WebServiceContext` in-terface **961**
    wire format **956**
    wire protocol **956**
    www.w3.org/TR/soap/ **956**
`@WebMethod` annotation **941**
    `operationName` attri-bute **941**
`@WebParam` annotation **941**
    `name` element **941**
`@WebService` annotation **941**
    `name` attribute **941**
    `serviceName` attribute **941**
`WebServiceContext` inter-face **961**
Websites
    developers.sun.com/ product/jdbc/ drivers/ 793
    en.wikipedia.org/ wiki/IP_address 849
    grouper.ieee.org/ groups/754/ 1054

Websites (cont.)
    java.sun.com 167
    java.sun.com/j2se/ 1.5.0/docs/api/ javax/swing/JOp-tionPane.html 385
    java.sun.com/j2se/ 5.0/docs/api/ java/awt/Compo-nent.html 388, 389, 520, 521
    java.sun.com/j2se/ 5.0/docs/api/ java/util/ Stack.html 618
    java.sun.com/j2se/ 5.0/docs/api/ java/util/Vec-tor.html 602
    java.sun.com/j2se/ 5.0/docs/guide/ collections 588
    java.sun.com/javase/ 6/docs/api/ 37, 282
    java.sun.com/javase/ 6/docs/api/java/ util/Format-ter.html 999, 1011
    java.sun.com/javase/ 6/docs/api/java/ util/Scanner.html 274
    java.sun.com/javase/ 6/docs/api/over-view-summary.html 167
    java.sun.com/javase/ 6/docs/technotes/ guides/jdbc/get-start/Getting-StartedTOC.fm.htm l 813
    java.sun.com/javase/ 6/docs/technotes/ guides/jdbc/get-start/rowsetIm-pl.html 826
    java.sun.com/javase/ downloads/in-dex.jsp 37
    java.sun.com/javase/ technologies/da-tabase/index.jsp 793
    java.sun.com/prod-ucts/java-media/ 2D/index.html 479
    javadoc Tool Home Page at java.sun.com/ javase/6/docs/ technotes/guides/ javadoc/index.ht-ml 24
    www.bluej.org 7
    www.codegear.com 7

Websites (cont.)
    www.deitel.com/Re-sourceCenters.ht-ml 3
    www.eclipse.org 7
    www.jcreator.com 7
    www.jedit.org 7
    www.jgrasp.org 7
    www.mysql.com/prod-ucts/mysql/ 806
    www.netbeans.org 7
    www.omg.org 16
    www.uml.org 16, 82, 90
    www.w3.org/Proto-cols/rfc2616/ rfc2616-sec10.ht-ml 850
    webuijsf:body element **858**
    webuijsf:form element **859**
    webuijsf:head element **858**
    webuijsf:html element **858**
    webuijsf:link element **858**
    webuijsf:message element **875**
    webuijsf:meta element **858**
    webuijsf:page element **858**
    webuijsf:staticText ele-ment **859**
    webuijsf:tableColumn JSF element **912**
    webuijsf:tableRowGroup JSF element **912**
    `weightx` field of class `Grid-BagConstraints` **668**
    `weighty` field of class `Grid-BagConstraints` **668**
    `WEST` constant of `BorderLay-out` **426, 442**
    `WEST` constant of class `Grid-BagConstraints` **667**
    `WHERE` SQL clause **798, 799, 799, 800, 802, 805, 806**
    `while` repetition statement **90, 95, 96, 99, 103, 121, 1053**
        activity diagram in the UML 96
    white space **25, 27, 43**
        characters **25, 1027, 1041**
    whitespace character **1040**
    whole/part relationship **81**
    widgets **383**
    width **470**
    width of a rectangle in pixels **459**
    Wikipedia 17
    Wildcard test program 584
    wildcards **581, 583**
        type argument **583**
        upper bound **583**
    window **640**
    `Window` class **640, 641**
        `addWindowListener` method **641**
        `dispose` method **641**
        `pack` method **660**
    window event-handling meth-ods **427**
    window events **641**
    window gadgets **383**

windowActivated method of interface WindowListener 641

WindowAdapter class 427

windowClosed method of interface WindowListener 641

windowClosing method of interface WindowListener 641

WindowConstants interface 641

   DISPOSE_ON_CLOSE constant 641

windowDeactivated method of interface WindowListener 641

windowDeiconified method of interface WindowListener 641

windowIconified method of interface WindowListener 641

windowing system 387

WindowListener interface 427, 641

   windowActivated method 641

   windowClosed method 641

   windowClosing method 641

   windowDeactivated method 641

   windowDeiconified method 641

   windowIconified method 641

   windowOpened method 641

windowOpened method of interface WindowListener 641

Windows 5, 135, 528

Windows look-and-feel 636, 653

Windows Notepad 7

Windows Vista 945

Windows XP

   allow web requests 945

   HTTP access from other computers on the network 945

wire format 956

wire protocol 956

Withdrawal class (ATM case study) 80, 81, 83, 114, 149, 151, 194, 195, 243, 244, 245, 247, 248, 249, 294, 295, 373, 374, 375, 376, 378

word character 1041

word processor 1014, 1022

workflow 89

workflow of an object in the UML 148

"World Wide Wait" 921

World Wide Web (WWW) 3, 4, 748

wrap stream types 754, 756

wrapper methods of the Collections class 593

wrapper object (collections) 632

wrapping stream objects 541, 547

wrapping text in a JTextArea 451

writeable 521

writeBoolean method of DataOutput 550

writeByte method of DataOutput 550

writeBytes method of DataOutput 550

writeChar method of DataOutput 550

writeChars method

of DataOutput 550

writeDouble method of DataOutput 550

writeFloat method of DataOutput 550

writeInt method of DataOutput 550

writeLong method of DataOutput 550

writeObject method of ObjectOutput 541 of ObjectOutputStream 547

Writer class 551

writeShort method of DataOutput 550

writeUTF method of DataOutput 550

WSDL (Web Service Description Language) 945

www 18

www.agilealliance.org 18

www.agilemanifesto.org 18

www.bluej.org 7

www.codegear.com 7

www.craigslist.org 18

www.deitel.com 2

www.deitel.com/books/javafp/ 2

www.deitel.com/newsletter/subscribe.html 3, 17

www.deitel.com/resourcecenters.html 17

www.eclipse.org 7

www.housingmaps.com 18

www.jcreator.com 7

www.jedit.org 7

www.jgrasp.org 7

www.mysql.com 806

www.netbeans.org 7

www.omg.org 16

www.uml.org 82, 90

WYSIWYG (What You See Is What You Get) editor 867

X

x-coordinate 454, 478

X_AXIS constant of class Box 666

x-axis 454

XHTML (Extensible HyperText Markup Language) 849

XHTML (Extensible Hypertext Markup Language) 848

   span element 860

XML 854

XML declaration 858

XML serialization 982

XMLHttpRequestObject 921

xmlns attributes 858

XP (Extreme Programming) 18

y

y-coordinate 454, 478

Y_AXIS constant of class Box 666

y-axis 454

YouTube 17

z

0 (zero) flag 1006, 1008

zeroth element 204

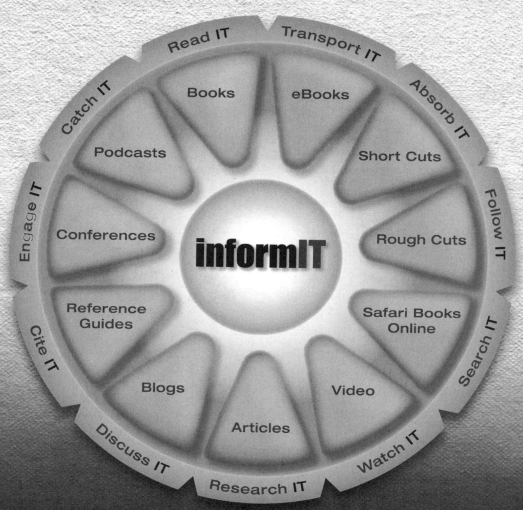

FREE Online
Edition

Your purchase of **Java™ for Programmers** includes access to a free online edition for 45 days through the Safari Books Online subscription service. Nearly every Prentice Hall book is available online through Safari Books Online, along with more than 5,000 other technical books and videos from publishers such as Addison-Wesley Professional, Cisco Press, Exam Cram, IBM Press, O'Reilly, Que, and Sams.

SAFARI BOOKS ONLINE allows you to search for a specific answer, cut and paste code, download chapters, and stay current with emerging technologies.

Activate your FREE Online Edition at www.informit.com/safarifree

> **STEP 1:** Enter the coupon code: URSQZAI.

> **STEP 2:** New Safari users, complete the brief registration form. Safari subscribers, just log in.

If you have difficulty registering on Safari or accessing the online edition, please e-mail customer-service@safaribooksonline.com